Italoamericana

Edited by Francesco Durante

ꙮ Italoamericana

The Literature of the
Great Migration, 1880–1943

General Editor of the American Edition
ROBERT VISCUSI

Translations Editor
ANTHONY JULIAN TAMBURRI

Bibliographic Editor
JAMES J. PERICONI

Fordham University Press | *New York* | *2014*

Library of Congress Control Number: 2014931287

Printed in the United States of America

16 15 14   5 4 3 2 1

First edition

Contents

PART III. On Stage (and Off)

PART IV. Anarchists, Socialists, Fascists, and Antifascists

PART V. Integrated Apocalyptics

Preface

This volume is dedicated to the period of the Great Emigration of the nineteenth and twentieth centuries, and therefore to the experience of the Little Italies, the Italian ghettoes of America that were its first and most glaring outcome. This volume follows upon my exploration, begun four years ago, of the first literary traces left by the Italians in the United States[1] and completes what might be considered its most important—and probably its least known—phase. Indeed, this period includes the main body of the literary works springing directly from America's Little Italies. Literary people in Italy systematically ignored—if not openly condemned—this production, calling it anachronistic, amateurish, and unbearably "wild." But these works represent the site where the emigrants' native culture was contaminated by American culture, even if at a generally popular or only partially cultured level. The result is an unforeseeably new universe. These works also represent a moment of passage or, to put it in a better way, the necessary link between the experience of the fathers who came to America armed only with their cultural baggage from home, and that of their children who, merely a generation or two later, would recount their moving saga directly in English.

The period examined here goes from 1880, the conventional date of the beginning of the transoceanic Great Emigration, to that traumatic and definitive divide, World War II. During the 1940s, the experience of the first immigrant generation came to a close precisely because of the political alignments imposed by the war. By then this generation's writers had given their best. Their contribution is the

1. Francesco Durante, *Italoamericana: storia della letteratura degli italiani negli Stati Uniti* (Milan: Mondadori, 2001).

subject of the present work. Admittedly, it is true that even after the end of World War II, the country's Little Italies continued to exist a few decades more and to support a rather substantial publishing activity in Italian. But from the point of view of the present work, such activity—particularly its more explicitly literary expressions—appears as so many already-consumed fossils: that is, a sort of residual arcadia made for the most part of an overflowing of dilettantish poetry tending to celebrate itself within a circle of pathetic coteries and academies located on the American side of the ocean. Not only were these coteries totally separated from the beating heart of Italian and/or American culture, but neither were they any longer legitimated by the actual social condition of Italian Americans. Moreover, it is quite true that especially in the 1950s there were new migratory waves from Italy to the United States. They, too, produced some literature, albeit a much lesser amount with respect to the earlier period. Anyhow, nothing that revealed that trait of novelty or originality that had distinguished the emigration of the nineteenth and twentieth centuries. In the best cases, such as that of Joseph Tusiani (born in 1924), the prevailing "ethnic" connotation of the Great Emigration has by now dissolved into a totally other dimension. Tusiani, "poet in four languages" (Italian, Latin, English, and the Gargano dialect), could in no way be confused with one of the writers of the old Little Italies, and even less with one of the dilettante poets of the new Italian American "underbrush." On the contrary, he has himself denounced the latter's relentless belatedness.

There has been an inability to distinguish between different phases of the immigrant story. Thus, we see a tendency to include in the same indistinct panorama of blunt mediocrity and of wishful thinking literary works that do not belong there, work that instead, represent a much more historically and artistically varied landscape. This careless confusion led Italian culture, for a long time following very authoritative opinions, such as those of Giuseppe Prezzolini and Emilio Cecchi between the 1940s and 1950s, to ignore the complexity and diversity of the Italian American spirit. So paltry did the literature of our emigrants appear that entire ranks of worthy scholars deemed it much more useful and "correct"—not to say interesting—to direct their attention to other, contiguous strands of research, like the African American and Jewish American ones. This picture of basic ignorance was due to the almost total absence of historical-critical studies and works of reference, as well as the extremely difficult and laborious process of finding the texts. One could truly say that until the 1980s nobody read them, either in Italy or in America. In fact, those few who did browse through these texts limited themselves to citing a few of them by hearsay and, in the process, repeated uncritically the few, inessential bits of information recorded by others. Usually, their interest in this literature was an offshoot of doing research in other fields. Primarily social-historical research, one is tempted to say, was the only kind that one encountered when it came to emigration studies.

Today things have changed considerably. Scholarly research has advanced in surprising ways over the last twenty years. Generally speaking, it has followed a path aimed at reevaluating first of all the work of the first generation of Italian American writers in English, from John Fante to Mario Puzo. Reading these works has led scholars to study the cultural, if not specifically literary, background from which those works drew their life-blood. In the United States, renewed interest in these writers coincided with the opportunities given to scholars—they themselves of Italian American origin—to look back on their family roots with greater detachment and a more sophisticated critical approach. In Italy, on the other hand, this critical revival seems to have been triggered by the realization that our country had by now changed from one historically marked by emigration to one of immigration. This circumstance is undoubtedly "external," but it probably contributed considerably to a growing need for a deeper understanding of the newcomers—and also encouraged us to identify with them, but now without shame. In short, we were able to recall a time "when we were the Albanians," as the subtitle of a recent bestseller by Gian Antonio Stella has it.

The present volume, as we shall see, gathers together a large number of authors and covers almost all literary genres: from poetry and theater to memoirs, fiction, and a wide variety of social and political commentary. This is enough for me to say that the world of Italian America between the nineteenth and twentieth centuries is indeed one of extraordinary wealth and complexity, enough, perhaps to make this anthology more than justified. And yet I am perfectly aware that it is "provisional," a sort of permanent workshop constantly open to new research and further discoveries. It fills dizzying gaps of knowledge with respect to most of the authors under consideration—their unknown biographies and at times their even more unknown publication records. It also proposes a historical ordering of the major currents in which the Italian American literary experience sought to organize itself. In short, the book looks forward to other scholarly research that will go even deeper into the libraries and archives that I have visited (some seventy of them between Italy and the United States). And—why not?—perhaps a new author or title will be miraculously discovered. There are still thousands of attics to pick through and perhaps in a few of them a surviving copy of some lost novel by Bernardino Ciambelli or the typescript of some play by Riccardo Cordiferro or an unfindable volume of some lost Italian American newspaper awaits us in silence. And these hopes might be channeled into an attempt to create an institute which is still scandalously lacking in Italy: a real and true Museum and/or Archive of Emigration capable of reviving once and for all the epic of millions and millions of our expatriate fellow countrymen. No matter how short our memory, this undoubtedly remains the most significant fact of our entire history.

If this volume will help to consolidate a new sensibility in this field, it will mean that it has reached the most important goal its author set for himself.

NAPLES, FEBRUARY 2005

Postscript

In the earlier volume of *Italoamericana* I thanked many persons whose help was precious to me. For the sake of brevity, I will not mention them here again, but I should thank every one of them all the same. To this list I would like to add the names of Veronica Park, whose exquisite kindness I widely took advantage of in the rich Biblioteca di Magistero in Florence; and of Generoso Picone, who allowed me to read the extremely rare *I drammi dell'emigrazione* by Bernardino Ciambelli. I am also indebted to Patrizia Asproni for being a perfect host. I must also thank Angelo Agrippa, Mirella Armiero, and Natascia Festa for having helped me critically reread my manuscript.

To my father, Domenico Durante, who did not live to see this volume in print, but who was the happiest man in the world when he had the earlier one in his hands, I owe everything that a man can owe to the person who made him a man.

Acknowledgments

The American edition of *Italoamericana* has had many friends and many translators.

Generous donors have made this edition possible: Laura Baudo Sillerman, Anthony and Margo Viscusi, James Periconi, Robert and Nancy Viscusi, Anthony and Maria Tamburri, John and Jean Nonna, William Tonielli and Lisa A. Mansourian, Mr. and Mrs. Joseph R. Perella, John Leopoldo Fiorilla, Thomas DePietro, The National Italian American Foundation, Judith Rosenthal, Lucio A. Noto, Irene and Joseph Neglia, Mary E. Caponegro, William Arnone, Stephen Boatti, B. Amore, Santina Spadaro, Fred Gardaphe, Frederick P. Schaffer, Bernice Riccio, Robert Oppedisano, Carl J. Morelli, Richard L. Mattiaccio Esq., Mrs. Lucille Maffia, Marcella Luiso, Josephine G. Hendin, Daniel M. Healy, Tom Ferraro, Hon. David S. Ferriero, Louise Del Juidice, Harriet Cooper, Mary Jo Bona, Victor A. Basile, Lisa M. Vaia, Peter Carravetta, Carol and Charles Rampino, and Anonymous (2) and several anonymous donors.

Rather than assign this work to a single translator, or even a small team, we decided to assure it some tonal variety that would be the moral, if not the precise philological, equivalent of the original text. Italian American writing in English has become a mature vineyard, and we had many competent translators of poetry, prose, and dramatic text from whom we could choose.

Franca and Bill Boelhower translated the long introductions to the five parts of the book. The headnotes to the selections were all translated by Irene Mitchell Musillo. The footnotes were translated by Steven Belluscio. Translators of prose included George De Stefano, Gil Fagiani, Paolo Giordano, Mark Pietralunga, Martha King, and Giulia Prestia. Translators of poetry included Luigi Bonaffini,

Michael Palma, Maria Enrico, Peter Carravetta, Emanuel di Pasquale, Chiara Mazzucchelli, Peter Covino, Pasquale Verdicchio, and Robert Viscusi. Translators of plays included Laura Ruberto, Martha King and Emelise Aleandri. Richard Mattiaccio, in turn, helped us with the Neapolitan dialect, wherever it occurred, whether in texts or in paratextual matter; Chiara Mazzucchelli did the same with Sicilian expressions. The American editors and most of the translators have been members of the Italian American Writers Association or of the Italian American Studies Association. These groups have fostered the discursive community that has made Italian American writing a professional concern.

Coordinating the work of so many translators has often been too much for the editors, but we have been ably assisted by two excellent people. At the Calandra Institute, Rosaria Musco organized the initial correspondence and set up our arrangements with translators during the first two years. Suklima Roy at Brooklyn College became the de facto project coordinator during these last two years. Without her patience, calm, hard work, and unfailing intelligence, this ship might have run aground many times over.

As this American edition is the product of a true collaboration of many people involved, from the fundraisers and subsequent contributors to the numerous translators/scholars mentioned above, it is, at the same time, the beneficiary of other scholarly and creative works we have consulted along the way. That said, we wish also to include in our heartfelt gratitude and appreciation the many scholars whose work has also assisted us in making this edition useful to readers of English. The list would be interminable, and so we list those people whose pages, in this regard, we actually turned at one point or another during the past four years: Emelise Aleandri, Rose Basile Green, Mary Jo Bona, Philip V. Cannistraro, Donna Gabaccia, Fred Gardaphe, Josephine Gattuso Hendin, Matthew Frye Jacobson, Martino Marazzi, Sebastiano Martelli, Jerry Meyer, James Periconi, Nunzio Pernicone, John Paul Russo, Joseph Sciorra, and Rudolph Vecoli.

In the years that have elapsed since the publication of this work in Italy, several important texts have come to light, several new works have been published. The distinguished collector and bibliographer James J. Periconi graciously undertook the task of bringing the (already very full) bibliography up to date with the state of the field. We are grateful to him and to all who have made this a truly communal contribution.

Robert Viscusi
Anthony Julian Tamburri

Introduction to the American Edition

༄ *Robert Viscusi*

If you do not remember who assassinated the king of Italy or who carved the great stone figure of Abraham Lincoln in Washington, there is no need to feel bad. You are not alone. Even Italian Americans do not always know the names of these Italian immigrants—*italoamericani*—who did notable things. Such deeds belong to a period that lies in darkness. The dawn of legible memory for the English-speaking people who now call themselves Italian Americans mostly begins around the time they abandoned the Italian language as their primary means of verbal expression. Though the communities of *italoamericani* that began to proliferate and grow in the United States after 1880 were to become large, even massive, much of what they did, as well as almost all of what they said or wrote, has disappeared from view, along with the knowledge of the many Italian languages ("dialects") they used. They were a huge population. Many millions arrived between 1880 and 1924, when immigration was shut down. Many returned to Italy. But at least five million remained. They swelled the U.S. population, which in 1880 was a little over 50 million; by 1924, it was 114 million. Italians alone accounted for more than 8 percent of that increase. New York City was the second most populous Italian city in the world, after Naples, itself the second largest city in Europe. All these immigrants spoke some variety of Italian when they arrived, and most went on doing so for the rest of their lives. They read and wrote newspaper articles, poetry, plays, novels, essays, histories, and all in Italian. They supported a vast production in every branch of literature. If you can name five of their writers, consider yourself an expert.

What happened? How did all this come to be forgotten? This is a chapter in imperialist history.

The Colony

Nowadays, when we speak of *italoamericani,* those who came from Italy during this period, we speak of their world as an immigrant culture. This was not how *italoamericani* thought of it during the years before the Second World War. They had learned to look at the world through Italian eyes. Italy saw itself as an expanding empire, and Italian America saw itself as a *colony,* one of Italy's many colonies. It was a particular sort of colony, to be sure: not a discrete territorial entity but instead a series of encampments of Italian labor and entrepôts for Italian goods, urban ghettos and work camps in the countryside, linked among themselves and to the homeland by ties of language, history, politics, religion, culture, family, and, above all, material interest. During this entire period, the Kingdom of Italy expressed the glories of bourgeois culture by carrying the banner of national/imperial ambition for Italians throughout the world, a performance that rose to its dizziest heights during the 1930s and led to Italy's catastrophic military alliance with Germany and Japan on September 27, 1940. After Italy declared war on the United States on December 11, 1941, the ties that had joined Italian Americans to Italy and to one another began to unravel, and the nature of the colonial complex began to change rapidly. In the long string of diplomatic misadventures that blot the pages of Italian history, there is nothing to equal this one for blind folly. Some of the results are familiar. Italy, a rising industrial nation, was flattened by the Americans and the English. After the war ended, Italy became, and remains to this day, an American protectorate, where U.S. Air Force F-16s patrol the skies daily and the American embassy in Rome houses a detachment of four hundred U.S. Marines. Other results are less familiar. Mussolini's declaration was not only a folly but also a betrayal, profound and unforgivable, of the *italoamericani.* The dictator had cultivated them for nearly two decades. Support for his Fascist dream was widespread in the colonia.[1] He had seduced the Italians in America. Now he abandoned them to their fate. The day after he declared war, the American government announced that all Italian immigrants who had not yet taken citizenship (at least 700,000) had to register as enemy aliens. Some even ended in concentration camps. In the Italian neighborhoods, signs went up: "Don't speak the enemy's language. Speak American."[2]

1. See Philip V. Cannistraro, *Blackshirts in Little Italy: Italian Americans and Fascism 1921–29,* VIA Folios 17 (West Lafayette, Ind.: Bordighera, 1999).
2. Lawrence Di Stasi, ed., "How World War II Iced Italian American Culture," in *La Storia Segreta: A Secret History of Italian American Evacuation and Internment During World War II* (Berkeley: Heyday Books, 2001), 307.

No wonder, then, that entire generations of Italian Americans have never learned how to read the pages of their own literary history. Most Italian Americans, by 1941, felt entirely committed to the country where their children had been born. Mussolini had expected many of them to come to Italy and fight by the side of the Fascists, just as many *italoamericani* had returned to Italy during the First World War to fight and die in the struggle with Austria. No such exodus occurred this time. Younger Italian Americans already had been speaking English for at least a generation, thanks to public schools and libraries. By now, even their immigrant parents and grandparents, though many of them had been proud of Mussolini's achievements in Italy, had grown effectively more attached to their own achievements in the United States, and they no longer cared to go back. Instead, they worried about speaking Italian in public, or even at home; many, perhaps most, of them closed off the future of the language by no longer teaching it to their own children and grandchildren. Their colonial literature entered a period where it would become mostly incomprehensible to Italian Americans.

This book is an anthology of writings by Italians in the United States, works published during the years 1880 to 1943. It presents, translated into idiomatic modern English, the writings of many of the leading novelists, poets, journalists, memoirists, and essayists of the great period of Italian colonial writing in the United States. Not only does it present these writers in English, but it also presents them through the eyes of an accomplished Italian writer, editor, and scholar who has read them with enthusiasm and an extraordinary taste for what they have to offer. Francesco Durante, editorial director of the *Corriere del Mezzogiorno* in Naples and author of many books, translator of American novelists from John Fante to Bret Easton Ellis, allows Americans to see Italoamerica as an Italian sees it. And not just any Italian, but one with habits of mind and action that uniquely equip him to interpret these texts for American readers—a journalist, a literary scholar, an Americanist.

An Italian Eye

Durante understands the historical situation of the immigrants. He is Italian enough that he does not share the immigrants' defensiveness about their identity. More than once, he reprints pieces that display racist themes that moved many immigrants, or accounts of systematic exploitation of women, or early and continuing evidence of Italian criminal activity. Indeed, Durante allows us to read this history without the burden of the usual abject narrative that creeps into accounts of Italian migration to the United States, especially when Italian Americans write those accounts. All Americans, not only Italian Americans, come to this history with a lot of baggage: Ellis Island, exploitation, racism, sexism, war, prejudice, and social dysfunction of every kind, from insanity to organized crime. Durante knows all this, shows all this, has a genuine sympathy with the distress and displacement of the immigrants, but he doesn't carry it as a weight of his own. This gives his picture a surprising clarity and emotional balance. Italian Americans in particular have had the habit of weighting their histories with resentment—or, as Giuseppe Prezzolini memorably called it, touchiness[3]—an irritability arising from memories of exclusion in Italy and more memories of exclusion in the United States. Justifiable as such feelings may seem, they do cloud the retrospect with strong feelings and strong words. Durante is admirably free of this defect. He is also, perhaps even more admirably, free of another hypersensitive response: the impatience and shame that bourgeois Italians like himself often display when dealing with Italian immigrants to the United States. What, then, *does* Italoamerica look like when seen through the eyes of this particularly well-informed and open-minded Italian?

For one thing, it is a land of newspapers. Hundreds, all over the United States. Dailies in the largest cities, weeklies and monthlies elsewhere. Durante, himself a journalist of the first rank, is well equipped to appreciate newspapers as cultural protagonists. In a colony, they have especially large roles to play. The political scientist Benedict Anderson has said that newspapers are the workshop where a nationalist consciousness is built. Newspapers allow for the creation of what Anderson calls an "imagined community."[4] The imagined community where the *italoamericani* lived was very much Italy—not just national Italy, either, but a transnational Italy that was something new. An event in Buenos Aires might have resonances in Washington, Toronto, London, and Milan. All these places belonged to the migration circuit.[5] Many of our writers had visited all these cities in their travels. Wherever they were living in the United States, from San Francisco to Boston, many immigrants saw things with a global eye that they would have been far less likely to develop had they remained nestled in the towns and cities where they had been born—places where they would have expected to die, joining their ancestors who had entered and left the world, often as not, in the same bedrooms, if not always in precisely the same beds. In thus acquiring a certain transnational sensibility, they became, paradoxically, more Italian than they could have become in Italy. There,

3. Giuseppe Prezzolini, "Perché gli italoamericani sono permalosi," in *I trapiantati* (Milan: Longanesi, 1963), 449–457.
4. Benedict Anderson, *Imagined Communities: Reflections on the Origin and Spread of Nationalism* (London: Verso, 1991).
5. See Donna Gabaccia, *Italy's Many Diasporas* (New York: Routledge, 2000).

these immigrants had spoken local languages, and their knowledge had been mostly local knowledge. The trip across the ocean had changed the shape of their physical and mental habitations. They were now in touch with many diverse ideas of who they were. They also began to speak a much more variegated language. The Italoamerican newspapers were generally not written in dialect, but in Italian. It was not always very idiomatic national Italian, though it was still closer to the national language than to anything else. Reading the stories and poems these newspapers also published, one can see that the immigrants were living in an intense contact zone, where not only national Italian and English were spoken, but also many Italic languages, from Ladin to Palermitano. In this zone, *italoamericani* often came to speak mixtures of Italian languages rarely heard before or since.

Italian speech and newspapers lost their hold on Italians after World War II, when the young no longer spoke Italian and their elders made less noise and spectacle about it than they had customarily done in the years before the war. Durante's anthology gives us access to the newspapers that *italoamericani* perused for three generations. Here we read how they thought and argued about national and international politics—democratic, fascist, socialist, anarchist. Here we read the poems and novels and plays that reflected their concerns as a transplanted people. Durante understands the day-by-day quality of historical process. His introductions to the sections and his headnotes to the selections in this anthology usher us into the world of the *italoamericani* in its historical, economic, and interpersonal intricacies in a way that few if any American or Italian American scholars have been able to match or even to imagine. The texture of a bygone world is the first thing to disappear. Durante's ability to bring this texture back to life is itself an excellent reason to read this book.

A Literature

Durante conveys the energy not just of the moment but also of a thriving colonial literature. Its energy emerges from continuous interaction with other cultures and other languages. Durante presents, early in this volume, Ferdinando Fontana's story "Shine? . . . Shine!," which dramatizes a fact about American life that startled the immigrants: the *italoamericani* find themselves in the company of African Americans who are often their social superiors. This new relationship runs counter to the unconscious but deeply held prejudices of the *italoamericani*, and their writers make the most of the internal conflicts that result. The story revolves around their sudden awareness of a fresh otherness, something that transfixes their attention, a colonial moment familiar in accounts of Europeans' experiences on other continents. The coordinates have shifted. Not far behind Fontana,

Durante gives us Gino Carlo Speranza, who makes a blunt equivalence between the situations of blacks and of Italian immigrants when he adapts as a title the notorious question posed by the leading African American intellectual W. E. B. Du Bois, "How Does It Feel to Be a Problem?" This upheaval of expectations is a frequent experience. In this literature the would-be colonizing Italian often finds himself startled when he falls to the rank of the colonized "dago." Colonial conflicts challenge not only the ethnic beliefs of the *italoamericani* but their moral categories as well. They encounter an incomprehensible bind after the introduction of prohibition in 1918. Wine is a staple element in their diet, as well as in the Catholic liturgy. It is easy for *italoamericani* to see this new restriction as an act of massive hypocrisy. Al Capone, the most notorious Italian gangster of the 1920s, presents himself turning one set of Puritan ideals against another, defending his bootlegging in the moral tone of an American bureaucrat: "Public Service Is My Motto."

Migration produces a system of broken links and vivid contrasts in the colony. Italoamerican literature brings us close to the interior experience of immigrants, finding in the general disarray many unexpected excitements to exploit. It thrives, for example, on tales of sexual irregularities that flourish when spouses and lovers are separated by distance and inadvertence. Narratives of bartered daughters, white slavery, runaway brides, and avenging husbands take place in the shadows of ships along the edges of Manhattan piers or in the overcrowded tenements of Five Points. Then there is the druglike effect that migration produces in simple people from simple places suddenly exposed to the radiant allure of American wealth. Love stories blossom in the Italian language, but, improbably enough, on snowy sidewalks seen against backdrops of Vanderbilt mansions. American life, with its glittering promises, raises levels of temptation and anxiety to sometimes unbearable heights.

Do these colonial writings in fact constitute a literature? At the minimum, they constitute the origins of a literature. They speak words in a context where new meanings are continually springing into life. Thus we find a heavy traffic in linguistic interference, for example, in Riccardo Cordiferro's poem "Il 'Polisso Italo-Americano'": "*sanamagogna*" for "son of a gun," "*tiffe e loffere*" for "thieves and loafers," "*Blakenda*" for "Black Hand," and so on. These anglicisms bring into the Italian language the linguistic upheaval of the New York street. It is as if Italians were snaking through an alley crowded with people from all the countries of Europe and the Americas, and we can hear worlds colliding in the chaos of words. Indeed, the promiscuous heterogeneity of life in these overpopulated places gives to this literature, for all its focus on intensely inhabited towns in the old world and urban villages in the new, a cosmopolitan texture. It applies and adapts to new situations a wide range of literary intelligence. In the fiction of Bernardino Ciambelli, for example, a narrative of sexual abuse and immigrant helplessness does not receive the journalist pathos and sociological objectivization that one finds, say, in the accounts of Jacob Riis; instead, Ciambelli employs the rhetorical and poetic machinery, the historical and operatic narrative rituals, that endow the characters and their destinies with subjective intensity and dramatic dignity. Their names alone are suggestive: in the selection here entitled "The Victim," we meet Vittoria Ruiz, the designated sacrifice; Napoleone Ghirendini, the white slaver; and Rinaldo Ruiz, the roué. These migrants are not just the playthings of fate, but they also struggle to make their destinies, even against overwhelming forces. It makes perfect sense that both Durante and his colleague Martino Marazzi call Ciambelli the "Homer of the migration."

Perhaps the strongest argument that these works have a collective identity as a literature comes from their specific attention to the nature of the Italian colony in America, a place like no other. To see this colony in action calls for a little imagining, or else a lot of old photographs. At the outset, one can imagine streets all mud giving way to cobbles, sidewalks mostly wood giving way to slate. In offices and saloons, plenty of spittoons. Outside, a rattle of carriages and four-in-hands and hackney cabs, broughams and buckboards and horse-drawn omnibuses mingling with the chug and thunder of steam locomotives, sometimes drawing freight into town, sometimes screaming along the elevated rails above newly cobbled streets. The background often showed the transitional disarray of townscapes in a Western, a not entirely adventitious similarity. This was a period of rapid change, when new things and new people were appearing every day, and yesterday's ways and themes were rapidly acquiring the golden aura of the glorious past. During the 1880s and 1890s, when Buffalo Bill Cody was shaping the eternal myth of the Old West, Carlo Barsotti, the founding editor of *Il Progresso Italo-Americano*, was inventing the Italian *colonia* in the pages of his daily paper, and he was constructing the eternal altar of Italian New York, with a marble and granite column monumentalizing Cristoforo Colombo just at the point where Broadway meets Central Park. Colombo was even older than the Old West. *Italoamericani* during this period continually evoked the notion, almost the hallucination, of their privilege—that they were settling a wild country, and that they were doing so by right, as descendants of this "first European."

The pictures belong to a familiar cinematic vocabulary. There were swells in high collars and diamond stickpins, sitting at the dais at club dinners. Outside, there was shooting in the streets. It was easy to find women whose virtue was under continuous challenge. There was a steady river of hardworking people wearing soiled aprons; there were men in rumpled suits giving speeches to strikers. There were labor contractors, con men, outright thieves, white slavers. The poor, unimaginably destitute, lived under the harsh Darwinian laws of the labor market.

All of this background is described in many works by Italian travelers—Dario Papa, Ferdinando Fontana, Camillo Cianfarra. Cianfarra creates a character, a colonial intellectual named Savini, who guides the Italian visitor in New York. In a memorable passage, he explains the immigrants' destiny. They leave Italy, he says, with the firm intention "to return to their homeland where they will again embrace the wife, pay off the mortgage, and resume the primitive life." It does not work out that way:

> With this mirage before them, they have said goodbye to their wives and children. They have seen the last peaks of their mountains disappear from the horizon. They have faced the dangers of the sea, the horrors of the unknown. And they are here [in New York], within reach of those who will drag them off to the sulfur mines of South Carolina, where one works in water up to the knees, or to plow the fields of Alabama where there are laws that can still force a worker to labor against his will. And from mining centers in Pennsylvania, from the desolate places of Arizona, from the pampas of New Mexico, from the rocks of Colorado, from all the furthest points of the U.S., their savings flow here, to these banks, in order to be saved without interest or to be transmitted at whatever rate the banker finds agreeable.

> And often one of these banks suddenly closes its doors, and from all over the American Union comes a single scream, a harrowing scream, however impotent, that tells you of the nameless deprivations, of the thousand tricks by which a dollar was taken by the rapacious hand of a contractor and "bosso," in order for it then to disappear into the pockets of a monster that spends it in some remote part of the globe.

America's challenge was not only Darwinian, but it was also revolutionary. This was a country with egalitarian ideals in race and gender and politics. Italy was mostly innocent of such ideals. The Italians had a hard time accepting the American context—its democratic innovations, its stunning hypocrisies. Capone was not the last gangster to challenge the moral smugness of the Americans. His descendants, real and imagined, down to Joe Colombo and Vito Corleone, belong to the myth of Italian Americans as gunslingers like Jesse James and Billy the Kid.

Their violence, their opposition to the forces of law, sometimes seems to be a form of political resistance, other times just a collateral effect of the expansionist violence that was the real engine of the Wild West.

If that famous theme presented the myth of capitalist triumph as it appeared in the lands of the New World, the anarchist and socialist movements were the armies of resistance to this closing of the frontier and enclosure of the continent.

Intellectuals, Including the Man Who Shot the King of Italy

The Wild West included, alongside its familiar mining camps and cowboys, small Italian newspapers and determined Italian strikers. Politics were often radical in out-of-the-way places. For example, Paterson, New Jersey, was the center of anarchist activity in the United States, activity so determined that it made a permanent mark in Italy. When, in 1898, Umberto I of Italy awarded the rank of Great Cross Cavalier of the Military Order of Savoy to General Bava Beccaris as a reward for shooting down and killing as many as four hundred demonstrators (the reported numbers vary) during a bread strike in Milan, the response among leftists was universal in the Italian world. Gaetano Bresci, an immigrant silk worker in Paterson and a follower of Errico Malatesta, traveled to Italy. After the Royal Regatta at Monza on July 29, Bresci approached the royal carriage and killed the king with two shots to the head.

A large section of this volume, Part IV, is devoted to the extreme political groups that flourished in this period—"anarchists, socialists, fascists." It is clear when reading the writings of political activists that, whether they were nationalists or internationalists, their thinking grew out of the issues that consumed the thinking of intellectuals in Italy throughout this long period. Even when socialists and communists and labor organizers were deeply involved in labor issues in American mines and factories, they were still mindful of conditions in Italy, of deep structural injustices in Italian society, of bitter and fruitless struggles for survival there. Many had been radicalized before they arrived in the United States, and conditions there affirmed what they had already come to believe; others were embittered for the first time by their monumental disappointment with the America they found.

The temper of this political discourse is so filled with rage and confusion that it calls for some historical perspective. Italy, whether in the peninsula or in the colonies, was massively engaged in the struggle to become a full-fledged European country, one whose economic and military institutions could stand comparison with those of England and France and Austria. The struggle had begun after the fall of Napoleon (1814) and gathered force during the Risorgimento (1821–1861).

After the successful political unification of Italy in 1861 began the real work of nationalizing a country that had itself for centuries been a collection of imperial provinces and disconnected kingdoms. Old rivalries, new wounds, and the sheer weight of the task led to ceaseless turmoil. A great distance separated the Risorgimento's ambitions from its achievements. Many Italians lived in a miasma of disappointment and resentment. These feelings, this political temper, followed them to the New World.

When *italoamericani* wrote about Italy, some expressed admiration and longing for the feathered helmets and the crested arches, and there was a brisk trade in songs of hopeless longing for the mothers and sweethearts left behind. But in the newspapers, as well as in the novels that generally appeared first as newspaper serials, one also met a bracing realism about life in Italy, and about the life being lived deep inside the veins and arteries of the Italian labor empire, where so many of the immigrants found themselves, lured in by promises of riches, kept in by contractors who stole their wages and by company towns where the cost of food and rent always outpaced the wages, so that the factories and mines became effectively debtors' prisons. The women were constantly in danger. Often they were the victims of bosses. They worked long hours in bad conditions. Even more often, they were simply the victims of men, brutal lovers and husbands, adventurers and pimps. It is remarkable, reading the narratives in this anthology, how much bitterness one encounters, how often and how readily these immigrants connected Italy with a hard life.

The anarchists and socialists saw these feelings as perfectly just responses to a world whose inequities they understood theoretically, practically, and dramatically. The leaders of these movements lived aloud. They spoke their minds. They acted on their convictions. They traveled ceaselessly, marching in protests, speaking for strikers, starting newspapers. They practiced free love. Men like Carlo Tresca and women like Virgilia D'Andrea mounted unflinching and unbending opposition to the imperialist wars and industrialist exploitation that were naturalized facts of life for the mass of Americans and Europeans in their time. From his desk in the office of his journal *Il Martello*, Tresca took on all the *prominenti* of the Italian colony, from Carlo Barsotti to Generoso Pope, never hesitating to call them indelible names and to match them threat for threat. He would show up at the Casa Italiana of Columbia University, where the Italian department was controlled by Fascist supporters, and break up their meetings, sometimes shouting, other times using his fists. Tresca was effective enough as a gadfly that Mussolini was always trying to extinguish him, finally exerting all his influence to see that the anarchist editor was shot down in the winter of 1943, on the sidewalk of

Sixteenth Street and Fifth Avenue in New York City, right outside the offices of *Il Martello*.

The Fascists, too, did not hide their feelings. They wrote startling poems on the glories of the Duce, sometimes affecting Latin epigrams and often accepting the notion of an identity between this leader and the military *imperatori* of ancient Rome. Rosa Zagnoni Marinoni, a regular contributor to the pro-Fascist journal *Il Carroccio*, published there an English-language poem entitled "To Mussolini, the Immortal," which opens with these stirring lines:

> There is the lure of the jungle in your eyes.
> Eagle wings have swept your pensive brow.
> You have the untamed majesty of lions
> Who scorn to follow, but unconscious reign.

These troublesome sentiments suggest the emotional appeal that Fascism had for many Italians and Italian Americans. The sense of eternal humiliation that drove the Risorgimento and that arose again after the Treaty of Versailles gave point to the Fascist saying that lies behind this poem: "*Meglio un giorno da leone che cento da pecora*" (Better one day as a lion than a hundred as a sheep). Fascist dreams of glory depended more on such emotional appeals than upon any appeal to reason. While millions of Italian Americans were susceptible to these allures, most of their radical activists were not. The anarchists and socialists were not often united, but in their opposition to Fascism, they were as one. All these groups, whatever their orientation, shared a dramatic style of politics, a taste for violent rhetoric and for loud parades and disturbances.

A Futurist Theater

Political activists mostly haunted the offices of the dozens of newspapers and printing houses they used in their struggle. Another entire wing of *scrittori italo-americani* spent a good deal of their time in cafes, where they met and wrote, where they acted and sang their portraits of *la vita coloniale*.

A large section of this volume is devoted to the colonial theater. The theme is enormous. It touches the Italian opera, a vast subject in itself; it touches the most successful of all the literary journals published in Italian in the United States, *La Follia di New York*, where one found a great deal of satire and parody and, above all, the theatrical caricatures produced by Enrico Caruso. Italoamerican theater included the heroic puppet plays of the *pupi siciliani*, where Rinaldo and Orlando crossed swords with the paladins of Saladin; the theater included melodramas of honor and revenge complete with moustachioed villains and outraged husbands brandishing pistols; it included police-blotter thrillers with murderers, plotters, panders and, especially, heroic detectives. There were divas and songwriters, one of whom was the grandfather of the filmmaker Francis Ford Coppola. This suggestive fact implies that immigrant cafes and theaters were the incubators of the great achievements of Italian American cinema and theater in the past forty years. Nothing, except perhaps the *prosciutti* and *provoloni* hanging over the counters in the Italian grocery stores, gives a sharper taste of the vivacity that characterized the Italian confrontation with the New World.

In Durante's account, this brio was above all Neapolitan. The lively and even chaotic revues of Neapolitan theater, its *macchiette*, became the prototypes for a new form, the *macchietta coloniale*. "The *macchietta* is a typical product of Neapolitan theater," Durante writes. "It was a 'total' show including singing, reciting, pantomime, and quick costume changes. Not by chance was it well liked by the futurists." The *macchietta* was, at its heart, an impersonation. The actor incarnated a comic type. He would sing, recite poetry, improvise a monologue. It was a loose form, and anything could happen. It was well suited to the drama of colonial life, where everyday events often included startling novelties like the telephone or the florid pretenses of local politicians. The *macchietisti* improvised powerful comedy and pathos on such themes. The colonial vaudevilles touch a lot of themes we do not hear much about anymore. *Macchietisti* were especially hard on the *prominenti*, the colonial big shots who draped themselves with sashes and medals on holidays and marched in parades—generals and admirals on holidays, but undertakers and butchers the rest of the time.

The *macchietisti* make it clear that Futurism, as a practical response to social changes, was an aesthetic program that, without the benefit of a label, had flourished in the colonies for decades, long before Filippo Tommaso Marinetti coined its bourgeois Italian form in 1909, in his manifestoes condemning the old and elevating the new, praising speed, violence, youth, and destruction. The Futurist theater of colonial life did not need to evoke these qualities as if they were essences or demons, because these were the very weather of days and nights in New York. Protagonists, not ideals.

Italoamericana itself owes a lot to the *macchietta coloniale*. This anthology is not an encyclopedia of life in the *colonia*, though the introductory essays and headnotes provide a panoramic array of biographical, historical, political, and literary information. It is rather a series of rapid takes—stories, poems, editorials, manifestos, brief plays, chapters of novels—that give the reader the sense of an entire world. Fast cuts of a long-ago future, originating everywhere in the United

States from Boston to California, from New Orleans to Minnesota. Durante's work belongs to that genre of modernist anthology that was pioneered in Italy by Elio Vittorini with his *Americana* in 1941, a book that aimed to introduce Italian readers to the whole range of American fiction. It did not quite accomplish that, but it succeeded in bringing genuine American experiments in free speech into the classical studios of Rome and Venice. Americanists like Vittorini and Pavese owed something to the Futurists, but even more to their own hatred of Fascism. America became for these literary intellectuals a new version of what it had been to the immigrants: the future, not as designed by bourgeois theorists and artists in Milan and Paris, but rather the future as it was being lived by ordinary people, many of them Italians, escaping from the oldness of old Europe and crossing the ocean to land in a laboratory of new expressions and new freedoms. This is a place where speed and violence are not Futurist slogans but simply the music of daily life. Francesco Durante belongs to this tradition of Americanists.

Americans, Including the Man Who Carved the Statue of Abraham Lincoln

Getulio Piccirilli was one of a family of seven sculptors who came to New York from Massa Carrara. They lived and worked on East 142nd Street in the Bronx, and they carved the marble for brand-name American sculptors who worked in clay: John Quincy Adams Ward, Augustus Saint-Gaudens, Daniel Chester French. French made a maquette in clay of the statue of Abraham Lincoln, and then commissioned Getulio Piccirilli, who both carved, and supervised the carving of, the twenty-eight blocks of Georgia marble that make up the statue that looks out over the Capitol Mall.[6] The Piccirilli signature, like invisible ink under a heat lamp, has only now begun to attract attention. Likewise, Francesco Durante's enterprise endows many signatures with a new legibility.

Durante has contributed not only to Italian American literature, but to the Americanist strain in Italian literature as well. Readers of Italian letters will remember the story of a thirty-year-old Sicilian who has lived in northern Italy and has not seen his mother in fifteen years. Now he is returning to visit her in the small mountain town where he was born. On the boat train to Messina, he eats some bread and cheese. The other passengers have nothing to eat except oranges. A small Sicilian man, watching this northerner eating, takes out a small orange and consumes it rapidly.

---

6. Josef Vincent Lombardo, *Attilio Picirilli, The Life of an American Sculptor* (New York: Pitman, 1944), 292.

"A Sicilian never eats in the morning," he said suddenly. "Are you an American?" he added.

He spoke with desperation, yet gently. . . . He spoke the last three words excitedly, in a strident tense voice, as if it were somehow essential to the peace of his soul to know if I were American.

I observed this, and said: "Yes, I am American. For the last fifteen years."[7]

This is the voice of the narrator in Elio Vittorini's *Conversazione in Sicilia*, a novel published and censored in 1941. In that same year, Vittorini published the anthology that opened American literature to Italian readers, *Americana*. It was also censored, though both books were republished the following year.

Why did Vittorini's narrator call himself an American? Vittorini, too, had left Sicily at fifteen and moved as far north as he could get. He had begun adult life as a supporter of Fascism when it was hard to distinguish from Socialism, but by the mid-1930s, he was turning to Communism and at the same time to Americanism as well. What did America mean to Vittorini and to the many writers, among them Cesare Pavese and Italo Calvino, who followed similar paths? America was a reminder that there was a place where the poor might eat and the silent might speak. A great novelty of *Americana* is Vittorini's notion that Italian literature has something important to learn from American writing. Vittorini's *Conversazione in Sicilia* visibly exploits the clean lines of Ernest Hemingway's prose, a stylistic choice that amounted to an act of political resistance in an age of overblown Fascist rhetoric, allowing Vittorini to represent the brutal poverty of Sicily under the Fascists with a prose that was just as economical as the diet of the Sicilians, who often ate but once a day, and poorly—often nothing but the small oranges grown on their own trees.

Durante's *Italoamericana* takes a similarly radical stance, positing that Italians of the 2000s have something important to learn from the writings of *italoamericani* in the age of migration. In this respect, his work keeps company with Martino Marazzi's *Misteri di Little Italy* (2001) and Gian Antonio Stella's *L'orda: Quando gli albanesi eravamo noi* (2002) (*The Horde: When the Albanians Were Us*). For these writers, Italy's emigrant past is a large and unexplored, even suppressed, fund of experience and expression, very much to be considered now that Italy has become a place where people go to settle, rather than a place they leave. In short, the writ-

---

7. Elio Vittorini, *In Sicily*, trans. Wilfrid David (New York: New Directions, 1949); first published as *Conversazione in Sicilia* (Milano: Bompiani, 1941), 24–25.

ings of Italian immigrants in 1905 New York suddenly had important things to say to Milan in 2005.

Masses of strangers speaking strange languages to strange gods strike fear along the comfortable streets of home. Many Italians find it hard to see past that fear. But emigrant Italians inspired similar reactions in New Orleans and New Bedford a century ago. Today it is Bengalis and Somalis who produce these feelings in Mestre and Ostia. Durante's anthology is an introduction to the underworld of feeling that lives among these unwelcome foreigners. At the close of this anthology, Durante gives us Edward Corsi, a great immigrant success story, who came to America in 1907 at the age of ten, became a lawyer when he grew up, and was appointed Commissioner of Immigration at Ellis Island in 1931. In his English-language memoir of life as an official of Ellis Island, Corsi describes the experience of an immigrant named Nathan Cohen, whom the immigration bureaucrats did not know how to handle. Cohen had come to the United States from Russia by way of Argentina and Brazil. While in America, he had started a business that later failed; his wife then ran off with another man, and Cohen lost his mind. Brazil would not take him back, nor would Argentina. After almost a decade of shuttling this man back and forth among nations that refused to admit him, it was finally discovered that Cohen had once joined the Knights of Pythias in Jacksonville, Florida, and that organization accordingly now assumed his care, placing him in a home for the insane in Green Farms, Connecticut, where he later died. The persistent turbulence of his lostness is a central element in his story as Corsi tells it. This turbulence, in one or another of its many forms, has never failed to assault immigrants when they first step ashore on Ellis Island in New York Bay or on Lampedusa in the Mediterranean, halfway between Sicily and Africa.

In *Son of Italy*, Pascal D'Angelo describes his boyhood as a shepherd in Abruzzo in terms that would have made sense to Theocritus or Vergil. His entry into American life features the capital universe of labor gangs building the mechanical utopia of elevated trains and chain-drive motor transports. The whole arrangement deeply unsettled the sensibilities of a young Italian male who had grown up in the company of sheep and goats on mountainsides. The central figures of such narratives are Futurist subjects. They feel themselves the sites of abrupt shifts, swift updrafts, sudden falls.

Their destiny has become a universal possibility. This is the subtext of *Italoamericana*: the whole anthology recalls a century of displacement and universal loss, and it serves to remind Italians, whether in Denver or in Turin, of who they once were and who they might yet again be.

This new effect continues to grow. It has been pouring into Italy now for thirty or forty years, changing the complexions of classrooms in the Veneto and raising continual challenges along that country's many borders—Malta in the Mediterranean between Spain and Italy, Lecce on the Adriatic opposite Montenegro, Varese in the foothills of the Swiss Alps.

In the Italian American corner of the future, the literature of the Italian migration has suffered two cruel blows of chance. Many of its works first appeared in newspapers that are now yellowing and crumbling in attics and libraries. Even works that were published in more durable forms have fallen into darkness. Most Italians are not interested in reading these texts, and most Italian Americans are not capable of doing so. *Italoamericana*, in this American edition, opens these works to all who can read English, and we firmly hope that those readers will want more, that they will seek to read further texts of Arturo Giovannitti and Emanuel Carnevali; that they will want to see translated more of Riccardo Cordiferro, more of Severina Magni, all of Bernardino Ciambelli. Earlier, I said that if you can name "five of their writers," consider yourself an expert. So here you are already an expert. And that is just for starters. In Durante's anthology, many voices long silenced will be heard and will again have names. In this edition, many Americans, Italian or not, will know their names, and for the first time.

Italoamericana

PART I

Chronicle of the Great Exodus

Introduction

Around 1880 the Italian immigration to North America—which up to that point had grown at a relatively modest, if constant, rate[1]—sharply increased. A human flood, mostly from the south of Italy but also from the north-central region (most typically, Lucchesia), started inundating the United States. Villages and small towns from the rural districts of the Apennines, Abruzzo, Calabria, and Sicily gradually emptied out. The numbers are impressive: about 5 million Italians had departed in the course of roughly forty years, until in the early 1920s the United States promulgated more restrictive immigration laws. From the beginning the rate had been high. A statistical survey of the decade 1876–1887 made by the University of Genoa supplies an astonishing picture. In this decade from the Lucanian territory of Lagonegro—the homeland of renowned musicians from Viggiano and Corleto—26,917 people, or a quarter of the total population (an average of 2,243.08 persons per year) emigrated; from the district of Sala Consilina, Salerno, 22,241 people—a little less than one-third of the total (1,853.42 per year); from the territory of Potenza, Basilicata, 27,992 people, or one-fifth of the total (2,332.67 per year).[2] In 1896, for the first time, "the three migratory flows from Austria-Hungary, Italy, and Russia outstripped the volume of arrivals from the United Kingdom, Germany, and Scandinavia."[3]

1. For this kind of "prologue" to the mass immigration, with particular reference to southern Italy, and for those more interested in immigration to the United States, see especially the first chapters of De Clementi 1999 as well as the same author's contribution ("*La grande migrazione*") in Bevilacqua, De Clementi, and Franzina 2001.

2. Del Vecchio 1892.

3. Schlesinger 1980, 100.

The historical investigation of this phenomenon, its causes, and its effects on people's lives in Italy has produced a very rich bibliography, which the reader may consult for further information. This present introduction will not repeat a well-known story that has been fully updated and expounded in works such as Emilio Franzina's *Gli italiani al nuovo mondo* (1994) and the important *Storia dell'emigrazione italiana* (2001), edited by Franzina, Piero Bevilacqua, and Andreina De Clementi. Instead, it will deal with the Italian American literary corpus and its major writers thematically. But before beginning, I will provide the reader with material that, even if not strictly "literary," will hopefully sum up some of the most important aspects linked to this protracted period of mass emigration. Let me repeat, this material is Italian American, namely, produced in the United States or directly connected with the migratory experience itself. This choice implies the exclusion of a significant—and sometimes astonishing—number of documents written by travelers, scholars, polemicists, and literati who confronted this experience from a strictly Italian perspective. An exception has been made in the case of Ferdinandino Fontana's harsh testimonial because this author worked as a journalist in New York, for however short a time.

This opening selection covers a forty-year span, ranging from the early 1880s to the early 1920s. During this period there were several attempts by the American authorities to restrict immigration, such as the cautious introduction of various literacy tests that legislators attempted to toughen as early as 1880. (In 1893, President Cleveland vetoed the harshest of these tests.) They were followed by other measures in the late 1910s: for example, the Espionage Act of 1917 aimed at blocking the influx of dangerous revolutionaries who were subsequently expelled from the country. The crucial phase of restriction initiatives began in March 1919, when the Republican nativist Albert Johnson was appointed chair of the House Committee on Immigration. He enthusiastically sponsored the antiradical movement during the "months of hysteria" of late 1919–early 1920 and advocated a drastic revision of the 1921 measures, which allotted immigration quotas to the various nationalities based on the 1910 census. Due to this revision of the law, arrivals to the United States were severely reduced. Each group was allowed 2 percent of the quota assigned it according to the census of 1890, when the ratio between the old and the new immigration was still largely in favor of the former. In this way the Italian quota dropped from 42,000 to 4,000 persons; the Polish quota from 31,000 to 6,000; the Greek from 3,000 to 100; and so on. The debate over the Johnson Bill was propped up by a huge tide of opinion, which ranged from the Ku Klux Klan to Samuel Gompers's American Federation of Labor. It was extensive and exhaustive and settled for a temporary solution that accepted various amendments to the original text. President Coolidge signed the bill into law in May 1924.[4]

The texts presented in this section are chronologically ordered so as to offer a diachronic view of the phenomenon of immigration and to highlight its most conspicuous aspects, like the exploitation of the so-called unskilled workers who represented the great mass of the Italian labor force. Rejected by Gompers's syndicalist representatives, they ended up being sucked into the famous *padrone* system, the iniquitous manpower brokerage network which in those years represented one of the most substantial sources of capital accumulation for an enterprising class of nouveaux riches. However, these notorious colonial *prominenti* (the local business and political elite) were able to fulfill an essential function of intraethnic binding, as several thoroughly Americanized authors recognized at the beginning of the century. The passage here included from Rocco Corresca's exceptional autobiographical narrative recounts a harsh experience of marginality and testifies to the complex and multifaceted theme of work.

This section also deals with another important theme: the American reaction to the new and hardly welcomed immigration from Southern and Eastern Europe (Italians, Greeks, Slavs, Jews, and so on). From the start these immigrants heavily disturbed and aroused suspicion in the Anglo-Saxon population, owing especially to the shameless exhibition of their miserable condition—an exhibition that also impressed visiting Italian travelers. As Giuseppe Sormani, who traveled to the United States in the late 1880s, wrote, with an alarming tendency to generalize: "It is painful to admit—but these pages are not meant to flatter any *amor proprio*— that, while in the other colonies the neighborhood slums represent the exception, they are the rule among the Italians." In this same observer's view, the immigrants could be subdivided into a number of significant categories, all rather disturbing. For example, "those whom laziness has thrown unto the road to perdition and have therefore an account to square with the law," or "those who have tried every possible way to get by without toiling and were not able to reach their goal; the slothful who act as (itinerant) lovers of the musical or singing art, and finally—the most numerous—the have-nots who are attracted to the mirage of a possible change of condition."[5]

This is the point of view of a journalist from Milan interested primarily in the emblems of American modernity. No wonder then that on several occasions at-

---

4. For all of this subject matter, it remains essential to consult the classic Higham 1971, in particular the last chapter, "Closing the Gates."

5. The cited passages are treated in Sormani 1888, 19.

tempts were made to restrict immigration legally and, in particular, to discipline it by de facto excluding the unwelcome elements (among them the Italians) as thoroughly as possible. Furthermore, serious manifestations of racism against Italians occurred in many parts of the country, culminating in frequent, terrible outbursts of violence. The most sensational of them took place in New Orleans in 1891. Eleven Sicilians, members of a thriving community that held a veritable monopoly over the fruit and vegetable markets, had been charged with the killing of the city's vice sheriff, a man named Hennessy. On the verge of being acquitted—some fully, others for lack of evidence—they were removed by force from the jail where they were still detained. They were then lynched by an enraged crowd, incited and protected by an ad hoc committee. This was the most serious episode of lynching in American history.[6] Curiously, this and other equally grave incidents—like the other major lynching of five Italians in Tallulah, Alabama, in 1899—received remarkably little attention in the literature of the period. The more so if we consider that this literature was thoroughly seduced by the pathetic almost ad nauseam.[7] There was a louder echo of such events in the newspapers. The excerpt included here was written by Luigi Roversi and is an example of a polemical exchange that, it must be said, was rather sedate and dignified.

Anti-Italian prejudice was based on the radical difference between the new intimidating aliens and the dominant Anglo-Saxon model. Soon such prejudice embraced the idea that a potential criminal was hiding behind every Italian immigrant. In a *Life* cartoon of 1911, the abominable "Wop" was still portrayed with

6. For the history of this episode and the political consequences it provoked—from the withdrawal of the Italian ambassador in Washington to requests for compensation to the widespread fear that the Italian navy intended to strike the American coasts, which were not yet protected by an adequate means of defense—see Gambino 1978 and Rimanelli-Postman 1992. On the theme of the lynching of Italians in the United States, examined case by case, see Salvetti 2003.

7. Exemplary of the coldness with which jurist Augusto Pierantoni took up this question is a ponderous essay appearing in two installments. In "Italia Coloniale" (1904), he preoccupies himself by way of preliminaries with finding a legal foundation for lynching as a rudimentary form of popular justice before ultimately denying such conditions in the New Orleans episode, asserting that "on the contrary, it had the character of the violation of the individual rights written in the federal and state constitutions. . . . In the embryonic life of the colony, lynching is the justice or the defense of the honest against delinquency; in constituted societies, it is an atrocious, barbarous deed that assumes the nature of conjoined offenses. The murder, the violence against the prison guards, the usurpation of sovereign power, and the massacre are the qualifications of the tragedy of 14 March. To have called it a 'lynching' was a deplorable abuse of words" (Pierantoni 1904, 447). Analogous opinions were expressed by the same author elsewhere in the American press (see Pierantoni 1903).

negroid features and polishing an American's shoes. The cartoon was accompanied by the following quatrain:

A pound of spaghett' and a red-a bandan'
A stilet' and a corduroy suit;
Add garlic wat make for him stronga da mus'
And a talent for black-a da boot![8]

Such words as "Wop," "Macaroni," "Guinea," and "Dago" suggest that the range of derogatory epithets aimed at the Italians was quite broad. "Wop" in particular was derived from the Neapolitan *guappo.* "Guinea" and "Dago" have more uncertain etymons: the latter term could be generically extended to the entire mass of "Latinos." For this reason it has been taken as a corruption for the Spanish "Diego," which was also the name of Christopher Columbus's son. Eugenio Camillo Branchi, however, has suggested a more imaginative and particularly significant origin:

It is thought to be the Italian pronunciation of the English phrase "They go!" In this way, the officials at Ellis Island indicated the departure of the thousands and thousands of Italians who arrived every week—real human herds in all their misery and filth. In itself the epithet is not offensive, but as is always the case, it is the tune that makes the music.[9]

The belief became widespread that it was Italians who brought to America the dark menace of the mafia and the camorra. This was also due to the popular opinion that the Italian newcomers were wild, rowdy, hot-tempered, and easily driven to commit crimes of passion. These beliefs persisted despite the facts: Italian American newspapers pointed out that the rate of criminality among Italians in America was actually lower and less alarming than that of other groups, especially the

8. La Gumina 1973.

9. Branchi 1927, 113n. It is well known that nicknames of this sort were given to all immigrants: the Irish, for example, were "micks" and "paddies," the Chinese "chinks," the Jews "kikes," and so on. According to the optimistic vision of Lord, Trenor, and Barrows 1905, 227, the extreme variety of immigration was a guarantee against the rooting of as strong a prejudice as that experienced by one group: "While there are many races of immigrants in America, they may be greeted with prejudice, but it cannot be as bitterly shown and cannot continue as long as it would if there were only two elements concerned." On anti-Italian prejudice in America, see also the lively reconstruction of Stella 2002.

Irish. The people's obsession with the "Mano Nera" or Black Hand was given full attention in the American newspapers and soon in the cinema as well, but with an inverse effect. At a time when the Italian rackets were not yet organized but thrived on episodic and disconnected adventures, many criminals (for example, racketeers and extortionists) took advantage of the opportunity to sign their anonymous threats with the terrifying symbol of the "Black Hand." This intriguing theme no doubt inspired the Italian colony's collective imagination and was indeed treated in several novels and theatrical productions. But the smartest members of the community clearly believed that it was all just a pretense. For example, in his play *Il martire del dovere ovvero Giuseppe Petrosino* (see Part II) the novelist Bernardino Ciambelli has a certain Don Raffaele, the head of a prostitution ring, remark:

> Listen here. What we could do is kidnap a beautiful girl and put her up in our boarding-school. Then we could write a threatening letter to her parents stating this: Unless you send us $1,000 or $2,000, you will not see your daughter again. Her parents will think that it's the Black Hand and not us. A husband wants to abandon his wife and write a nice letter full of threats, and he can tell his wife, "I have to run away or else they'll bump me off." A banker is not able to return his clients' money and wants to justify his flight; he spreads it around that he is being threatened by the Black Hand and he's forced to close down his business. A shopkeeper wants to go bankrupt and when they ask him to account for the money, he says, "I had to give it to the Black Hand." Do you understand now what this terrible syndicate, which frightens so many people and makes the police work so hard, is all about?

On the other hand, the qualitative leap occurred exactly when Giuseppe Petrosino, head of the New York Italian police squad, was murdered. The year was 1909, and the death of the Italian American detective in Palermo, Sicily, disclosed for the first time the existence of a transatlantic criminal connection. In this way, broad sectors of American public opinion were confirmed in their belief that the Italian government was lax or even quite willing to let disreputable people emigrate to America. But this is still small stuff in comparison with what would happen in the 1920s when Prohibition coincided with the drying-up of the traditional source of profit deriving from the importation and management of new labor, thanks to the drastic imposition of the immigration quota law. Possibly, the effects of this new situation led to a diversification of energies that were then invested in organized delinquency.[10] And with the passing of time mythical figures such as Al Capone and Lucky Luciano rivaled other famous "imported" gangsters such as Dutch Schulz (Arthur Simon Flegenheimer), the son of German Jews, and the Polish Jew Meyer Lansky (Maier Suchowljansky).

The rise of an Italian American underworld was favored by extremely harsh socioeconomic conditions aggravated by the added burden of ethnic prejudice. All in all, the Italians at some point would have had to learn to "defend" themselves. That is to say, they would have to find within their own community the strength to oppose the injustices to which they were exposed. Even today, Italian Americans are still sensitive to their being associated with the underworld. One could argue that their struggle to combat negative stereotypes dates back to the 1870s: stereotypes are slightly toned down by America's current obsession with the politically correct but are still sensationally fertile in the field of popular entertainment. Suffice it to mention two recent television productions, both of them created by Italian Americans: the series *The Sopranos* and the reality show *Growing Up Gotti*, whose protagonist is Victoria, the daughter of the famous "godfather." Indeed, Italian Americans blame the American milieu for much of the birth and growth of the Italian rackets.[11] Not by chance, in the mid-1920s the Italian American scholar John Horace Mariano invited his readers to make a leap forward and overcome an old ungrounded prejudice:

> Let us dismiss from our minds once and for all time, then, the erroneous idea that our Italian immigrants are inherently criminal and fill our jails. . . . It is not our Italian immigrants who present a problem but it is their children. . . . For while the Italian immigrant is not found in proportion to his numbers in our disciplinary institutions, his children are met there in overwhelming numbers.[12]

Obviously, this kind of observation works from the notion of an America that forces its immigrants to become criminal almost in self-defense. In any case, not they but their children born and raised in America present the real problem. We

10. On this theme, see, among others, the acute observations of Dore 1964.

11. Very significant, and to the point, is Schiavo 1962, in which the author, for a long time the leading authority on the history of Italian American immigration to the United States, reveals his insights on the Mafia problem, tackling the issue with historical precision. He does not neglect, for example, to stress "how Mussolini smashed the Mafia and the Allies tried to revive it" and also mentions "America's heritage of violence and corruption."

12. Mariano 1925, 127.

have here another aspect of a thesis of justification, not without some validity, which also surfaces in the form of a passionate plea in the excerpt from Gino Carlo Speranza. A second-generation Italian American, he was one of the most respected scholars of the problem of the new immigrant in the early 1920s.

On the other hand, it would be a remarkable omission to forget the influence of the mafia on the American imagination, particularly in the realm of cinema. This influence precedes the Warner Brothers' memorable trilogy: Mervyn LeRoy's *Little Caesar* (1930), with Edward G. Robinson and Douglas Fairbanks Jr.; William Wellman's *The Public Enemy* (1931), with James Cagney; and Howard Hawks's *Scarface* (1932), with Paul Muni. The last of these movies is clearly based on the life of Al Capone, who was in the news at the time. Certainly the most famous Italian American gangster, Al Capone—his attitude, his language, and his "style"—represents the wicked archetype of Italian American culture. In the course of Italian American literary history, novels such as Mario Puzo's *The Godfather* (1969) will thoroughly—and frequently—rework this inevitable theme, using that same attitude, language, and style as an oblique and disturbing source of "authorship." For this reason this section includes a short but significant interview with Al Capone: a "character" and "phenomenon" that was capable of capturing America's attention far more than any other personage coming out of the Little Italies of the early 1890s.

These ethnic enclaves gradually sprang up in practically every city in America, especially in the big cities of the East but also in cities such as Chicago and San Francisco. By the second decade of the twentieth century, New York was already the most densely populated "Italian" city after Naples. Such cities were in a certain sense extraterritorial spaces where the newly arrived immigrants found the world they had left behind almost fully recreated in the New World. They might have lived their entire lives speaking their own dialects, reading Italian newspapers, attending Italian shows, and eating Italian food without ever coming into contact with American reality, not even in their workplaces, since they were recruited by Italian bosses and assigned to Italian work crews. (This is what the great mass of first-generation Italian Americans actually did.) The labor unions and the anarchist and socialist political organizations—such as the IWW (International Workers of the World)—were prominent among those who tried to alter such conditions, but with little success. There was a strong need to provide Italian workers with a sense of class consciousness that would deter them from working for cheap wages, thereby inflaming those who had already been a part of the work force for a long time. This consciousness could only be achieved outside the reassuring womb of the colony, with its rites of ranting and stale *italianità*. Such rites were actually presided over by those members of the social and cultural elite who often owned the newspapers and of course had every interest in maintaining the status quo. See here the welcome address of one of the most famous among them, Carlo Barsotti, who printed it in the first number of *Il Progresso Italo-Americano*. In 1893, the tragic events of Aigues Mortes represented another terrible outburst of anti-Italian violence that occurred in France and ended with the slaughter of dozens of workers from Piemonte, Italy. Consequently, as the *Progresso* testified, the community leaders—the local business and political elite—were ready to "justify the behavior of these wretched people, who, unaware of the harm they are doing and the risk they are running, are willing to replace those who cling to the extreme resource of the strike in order to avoid being knocked off in the struggle for life."[13]

The problem of Americanization, however, started to be felt also outside the political-syndicalist perspective. After the first phase of the Great Immigration, the immigrants began to settle down in substantial numbers. This phase affected the so-called birds of passage: those who stayed in the New World for limited periods of time and returned home almost every year; or those who underwent indescribable sacrifices for a relatively short length of time, with the idea of eventually returning to Italy and living comfortably there for the rest of their life. Very likely, they were also heading for bitter disappointment. It now became necessary to obtain citizenship in order to convince oneself that he or she was American and to resolve the cultural and practical contradictions that life suspended between two worlds entailed.[14] This important theme conceals specific consequences such as military service, a problem that emerged dramatically for Italian immigrants with the outbreak of World War I. And it also led to typical generational ruptures between the parents from Italy and their children who were either born or grew up in America.

Already at the beginning of the century, Bonaventura Piscopo, the parish priest of the Church of the Most Precious Blood, was able to report to Senner, the Com-

---

13. This was expressed by Protasio Neri of Hallowell, Maine, in a long letter published in the New York paper *Cristoforo Colombo* on September 21, 1893. It is worth remembering that this newspaper leaned left and was particularly militant and polemical on social issues. In 1894, for example, it led a bitter campaign against the abuses of the *padrone* system.

14. An example is the experience of a young Comasco destined to become a great coin collector, Solone Ambrosoli, who in the pathetic verses of *Partendo da New York* (*Leaving New York*, 187), bids farewell to one reality: the "fatal America, / Land of dreams and sorrow" that failed to fulfill the poet's wishes: "And I too hoped the rosy / American hope, / Irresistible charm / to the great human crowd, / And I too experienced the hardships, / the hunger and the torment, / And I will never forget them."

missioner of Immigration of the Port of New York, that "all the Italian priests during Mass, at Sunday school, and in the confessional, are obliged to use English if they have any hope of being understood by the second generation."[15]

An excerpt from *Gli americani nella vita moderna osservati da un italiano* (The Americans in Modern Life as Observed by an Italian) by Alberto Pecorini, an atypical figure of a "colonial" polemicist, deals specifically with the difficult relationship between fathers and children. As we shall see, the theme of Americanization will indeed be viewed with suspicion by the cleverest of the nationalist journalists of the colony, Agostino De Biasi (see Part IV). And through him, Americanization will also be viewed skeptically by Italian American fascists, leading Italian consulate officers to adopt an ambiguous stance. This issue was perhaps the one that most intensely preoccupied the immigrants. The problem might be viewed differently according to the historical moment and the generational factor, the already-mentioned dissimilarities between Italian fathers and their American children. Italian identity always asserts itself when Americanization, more or less forced, is contested. This is borne out in the lucid observations of an important intellectual like Alberto Tarchiani, who is represented here by an article, written in the fateful year of 1915, that belongs to his little-known Italian American "prehistory." On the other hand, the theme of Americanization will be revived through repeated appeals to moderation addressed to the American authorities.

In 1919, for example, when confronted with the Wilson solution for the Fiume question, the Protestant minister Henry Charles Sartorio remarked that the Italians of America were right to feel betrayed, to the point of considering appeals to naturalization as no longer appropriate. According to Sartorio, the Italian American immigrant

is still strongly patriotic with respect to his country of origin and has not yet learned to appreciate and love America. He feels that the decisions taken by the head of this nation have done an injustice to the land he loves and he strongly resents it. So many people are surprised that President Wilson, in the course of the debate on European affairs, has taken a position that is bound to exasperate millions of American inhabitants of Italian, Polish, and other origins. If the matter had been given more attention, they might have been ready to transform themselves into loyal American citizens.

And, in any case:

15. Cited in Lord, Trenor, and Barrows 1905, 242.

Americanization must be a slow, psychological process. In no way can it be forced. Every time a new center for Americanization has been opened in an Italian quarter, there has been the same reaction that occurs when a Catholic mission is opened in a Protestant quarter with the aim to convert the heretics, or vice versa. As a result, everybody is on his guard.[16]

In 1925 the Johnson Bill sealed the fate of the "historical" immigration to the United States. The Italian American intellectual Matteo Teresi still tried passionately to defeat the restrictions applied to Italian immigration. He upheld the reasons for Americanization as the purchase "of new, diverse, and characteristic values: the engrafting of the Italic offshoot onto the great trunk of American life." He argued that "the best school of Americanism is economic justice, the honest working of free institutions, and friendly respect for the races gathered here so as to enrich with new elements the life of this still young and rapidly developing nation." Finally, he launched an accusation: those who declare that the Italians are "unassimilable" want the American "elders"—that is to say, those already settled here generations ago—to maintain "political dominance" over the newcomers, deemed "bothersome competitors."[17]

The famous and tragic affair of the anarchists Sacco and Vanzetti, a real milestone in Italian American history, can in some way contribute to this picture. It is, in fact, coincident to this important trial that America began nationwide to reflect on the theme of multiethnicity, against a judiciary malfeasance clearly rooted in ethnic prejudice. The Sacco and Vanzetti case split the history of Italian Americans in two. After that trial it would never be the same again.

16. Sartorio 1919. Presumed a descendant of Emanuele Sartorio, a Sicilian exile who taught at a Mazzinian folk school in New York, Enrico (or Henry Charles) Sartorio was a very active Protestant pastor in Boston. An instructor at Harvard, he wrote numerous articles in newspapers and journals, as well as the books *Social and Religious Life of Italians in America* (Boston, 1918) and *Americani d'oggigiorno* (Americans Today; Bologna, 1920), the latter noteworthy because it painted a more thorough picture of America than that found in sensationalistic Italian travel books. On Enrico Sartorio, see also Martellone 1975, and Massara 1976, 117–118.

17. Teresi 1925, from the preface and the chapter titled "Discussioni utili" ("Useful Discussions," 217–240) from the book *Con la patria nel cuore* (With My Country in My Heart), a collection of articles on highly diverse topics (there is even an article called "In Defense of Prostitution: Contributed to the Campaign against Venereal Disease") published in several Italian American newspapers. Born 1875 in Alia (Palermo), Teresi came to the United States in 1907. Having earned a law degree, he became a bank associate in Rochester, New York. Among his writings, the pamphlet *L'ultima menzogna religiosa–La Democrazia Cristiana* (The Latest Religious Lie–Christian Democracy, 1910), *Il sogno di un emigrato* (Dream of an Immigrant, 1932), and *Canto dei figli d'Italia* (Song for the Children of Italy) for music are of interest. See Schiavo 1966–67.

The travel literature of the late 1800s and early 1900s abounds in descriptions of Little Italy. First and foremost, obviously, is the historical Mulberry Bend in lower Manhattan, close to the mythical, dangerous Five Points also made famous by Martin Scorsese's movie *Gangs of New York*. In effect, many American journalists and writers used this area as the site for their investigations.[18] When American muckraking journalism was in vogue, for example, Jacob Riis (himself an adoptive American of Danish origins) published his enlightening report in which he disclosed to his readers *How the Other Half Lives*. This book (1890) is now considered a classic of the genre. There were also those who did not limit themselves to studying the situation in America and sought to trace the entire immigrant trajectory, from their place of departure to their point of arrival. Thus, Broughton Brandenburg, the author of the sensational book *Imported Americans* (1903), tells "the story of the experience of an American in disguise and his wife" who in this way had been able to "study at close range the problem of immigration" on the ships, in Sicily, and in Naples. This book matches Francis Edward Clark's *Our Italian Fellow Citizens in Their Old Homes and Their New* (1919), where he acknowledges "a native politeness about the unspoiled Italian, however poor he may be, that is very charming." At the same time, he spotted some stigmata of irreconcilable difference, like "the habit of promiscuous spitting everywhere, and on all occasions," directly connected with (indeed, induced by) "the filth of Italy."[19] Neither should one forget the richly documented *The Italian Emigration of Our Times,* also published in 1919, by the Harvard sociologist Robert E. Foerster, or the older study *The Italian in America* by Eliot Lord, John D. Trenor, and Samuel J. Barrows (1905). This volume was part of a series devoted to each migratory wave and, as the authors explained, it was prompted by America's urgent need to solve the immigrant problem by making the newcomers conform to its standards.

To these friendly voices one must add those of the large number of Protestant missionaries who worked in the Italian colonies, like Anna C. Ruddy, author of the important *The Heart of the Stranger: A Story of Little Italy* (1908) or William Edwards Davenport, a peculiar poet, benefactor, and author since the 1890s of the enthusiastic, Whitmanian, and almost mystic *The Beggar-Man of Brooklyn Heights and Other Chants from the Italian Settlement*. However, alongside the goodwill of the many who tried to understand, there was a whole literature that expressed a popular stance in favor of an immediate restriction of immigration—a story that more than a century later is now being repeated, and this time in Italy.

18. The most complete survey of Italian testimonials on the subject is offered by Massara 1976.
19. Clark 1919, 97, 109.

The spectacle of Little Italy, picturesque and blood curdling at the same time, is presented here from the New York perspective of Ferdinando Fontana and from the Bostonian perspective of Gaetano Conte, a Protestant minister in the famous Italian quarter of the North End. Those fabled streets—in New York, Boston, and many other cities—and those same people will be the main protagonists of the "colonial" literature, which will be discussed more fully in the course of this book.

Translated by Franca and Bill Boelhower

To the Readers

∾ *Carlo Barsotti*

Bagni di San Giuliano (today, San Giuliano Terme, Lucca), Italy, January 4, 1850–Coytesville, New Jersey, March 30, 1927

Carlo Barsotti was the torment and delight of a host of polemical editors, who accused him of every kind of nefariousness, among other things, of having made money managing suspicious small hotels and of having cheated the trustees of Little Italy, resulting in the bankruptcy (1897) of their bank. Yet, despite troubled private affairs and passionate colonial[1] diatribes, Carlo Barsotti (whose name will recur often in this book) was the founder of the daily *Il Progresso Italo-Americano*, which among the Italian American newspapers in New York was the most long-lived and widely circulated. In 1928, the newspaper passed to Generoso Pope, who made it the pillar of support for Fascism until 1942. By 1980, it had completed a century of life, in an unbroken editorial succession composed of Piero Pirri Ardizzone (*Giornale di Siciliaii*); of Carlo Caracciolo (*Espresso*); of the *Società Pubblicità Editoriale;* and of the vice president of the Chase Manhattan Bank, Dominick Scaglione. It ceased publication in 1988. *Il Progresso Italo-Americano* therefore followed the whole trajectory of the great Italian emigration to the United States. Published here is the editorial of December 13 with which Barsotti announced the birth of the newspaper, in that prophetic year of 1880, which historically and chronologically signaled the formidable beginning of the great Italian exodus.

1. Throughout this volume, Durante uses the noun *colony* and its inflections to describe the Italian American communities in the United States.

ESSENTIAL BIBLIOGRAPHY

DAB; DBI.

࿄

Establishing a daily newspaper in New York, in a language that is unknown to the vast majority of the population that boasts the most advanced and influential journalism in the entire world is a bold undertaking and fraught with difficulty.

Throughout the United States, where thousands of Italians are scattered, a daily newspaper written in our beautiful language does not exist. We have a few weeklies and biweeklies; one, perhaps, considered becoming a daily but has not succeeded until now.

There have been several attempts, including a recent one, and due to the large and numerous obstacles, they became fewer.

In these efforts, in trials undertaken by others, we became convinced that an Italian daily newspaper, in an appropriate size, with ample space for the most diverse content, when done with conscience, attention, and love, is something useful, necessary, and that surely must survive.

Therefore, convinced that the Italians of New York and the United States enthusiastically desire a newspaper in their own language which will excite and disseminate that culture and can better educate our character and foster our prosperity, today we found *Il Progresso Italo-Americano*. Having seriously provided for the required work to be done with care and diligence, accurately reporting on our dear homeland far away, and closely following the daily events of this adoptive land that hosts us, we believe, and this will be our most cherished reward, that *Il Progresso Italo-Americano*, in its scope, content, and elegance in print will not blush when compared with the periodicals of other sister colonies.

We have entrusted the editorial office to a young man[2] who is serious, practical, culturally well-rounded, and who over the last four years has completed his exams in journalism and Italian literature with honors, and who finding himself for some time in New York studied—on behalf of the premier newspapers in Rome and Naples—the conditions of Italians in the United States and the moral and physical state of this supreme and flourishing republic.

Every newspaper receives its sentence and its sanction from the way in which it is received by the public. Given this first assay, we maintain the firm belief that Italians will remember our work with fondness.

2. Adolfo Rossi.

We have founded a printing plant exclusively for the newspaper, which we will support through considerable effort and sacrifice, not for profit but to respond to a need our compatriots deeply feel.

So then if Italians, having read this first issue, believe that *Il Progresso Italo-Americano* serves to raise the national prestige and to refute the defamation with which detractors have tried to degrade our name, they will feel a duty to lend prompt and effective support which is essential to assure a beautiful, long, and happy life for *Il Progresso Italo-Americano*.

What if unfortunately this does not happen; who will be to blame?

It is best not to think about it. With the confidence that comes from purity of intentions and certainty that the road to travel will traverse friendly territory, we courageously approach the task without boring readers with plans delivered in bombastic language; facts, not idle chatter, are required, *res non verba*.[3]

Il Progresso Italo-Americano places itself among the noble ranks of the free press, independent of any party, which features *The Herald* at the top, and the debate will be held first and foremost by gentlemen, because when debate is a chivalrous battle of ideas, it becomes a true victory.

Onwards!

3. Deeds, not words.

Shine? . . . Shine?

༄ *Ferdinando Fontana*

Milan, Italy, January 1, 1850–Lugano, Switzerland, May 10, 1919

The testimony of Ferdinando Fontana, who in 1881–82, with his colleague Dario Papa, made a journey through the United States from New York to San Francisco, offers firsthand documentation of the epoch of the great Italian emigration. Above all, it strongly presents the way the phenomenon of America was perceived in Italy. Still permeated with the spirit of the Risorgimento and therefore with nationalistic pride, the Italians viewed America with a mixture of surprise, frustration, and disdain, though in their country the great social questions had also come to the fore. In respect to these, however, Fontana was very sensitive. Born poor, interrupting his studies to dedicate himself to more humble trades before finding solid work in the theater and in newspapers, he stayed close to social circles (actually, "Il Socialismo" is the name of one of his most notable small poems), to the extent that, involved in the insurrection in Milan in 1898, he had to flee to Switzerland.

Fontana is an outstanding figure in the events of the second Milanese antibourgeois artistic movement *scapigliatura*. He was a poet; a librettist of operettas and operas (even of Puccini's early operas *Le Villi* [The fairies], 1883, and *Edgar,* 1889); a dramatist in literary Italian and Milanese dialect; and a journalist and travel writer. In this last category, he produced such books as *Un briciolo di mezzaluna* (A Fragment of the Crescent); *Montecarlo; Tra gli Arabi* (Among the Arabs); *New-York* (1884, jointly with Dario Papa); and a collection of *Viaggi* (Travels) in two volumes, published in Milan in 1893.

Prominently portrayed in *New-York* is the spectacle of the degradation and misery of Italian immigrants, from the Battery to the streets of the city. The mockery, the prejudices, and the hostility they underwent are other themes Fontana faces with vehemence: "Understandably, a part of the fault derives from the mother-land, which left that mass of peasants brutalized, while the other part derives from America, which let the proprietors of those hovels earn formidable incomes, keeping the factories in the condition of primitive caves" (Prezzolini). A further element, very much in evidence here: educated travelers like Fontana were carriers of Risorgimento ideology. They had inflated notions of Italy's social and cultural heritage, notions that made it very difficult for them to look directly at the actual work Italian immigrants were able to do in the United States. There is also space, however, for hope, according to Fontana, for encouraging the spirit of adaptation and enterprise, through which many have achieved enviable results. During his visit to New York, Fontana became friends with Adolfo Rossi and Carlo Barsotti, described in the book, as well as a contributor to the *Progresso Italo-Americano.*

ESSENTIAL BIBLIOGRAPHY

DBI; Prezzolini 1963, 417–423.

൶

New-York, January 23, 1882

In my last letter I wrote to you: "New-York has given me not a few disappointments; I'm doing OK and I shine shoes at my place . . . for some reasons that would be too long to enumerate."

Now in your dear letter, which I got today, you ask me insistently about those reasons. You write, "I well know that the shoeshine men in New-York are all or almost all Italians, and so I can guess those reasons; but it also seems that you overstate out of delicacy (or considerateness), not wanting to imagine before you, in an act so humble as shining shoes, any of our compatriots. After all, there are Italian shoeshines in Italy, too, and as far as I know when you were over there, didn't you use to shine shoes with your esteemed hands?"

And you argue well. . . . But what do you want me to tell you? I witnessed a scene here so repellent that, since my first days here and from then on, I was not ever able to overcome that "exaggerated delicacy" for which you reproach me.

That scene gave me a lot to think about. It was a duet that reawakened in me an entire symphony of pity and bitterness. I cannot resist the temptation to repeat it to you in minute detail.

There were two men at a street corner, one kneeling at the feet of the other. The one standing belonged to one of the races less fit for noble and great concepts, more insensitive, in fact, to any growth in civil progress; he belonged to that race that, for a long time was considered even unworthy of the adjective "human," and therefore despised and sold under the name of a type of wood, and kept enslaved by the right of incontestable supremacy on the part of those stronger.

To raise that race, to free it from its abject condition—in which it lived in these countries, in which it still lives elsewhere—it took and it takes special and very powerful interests, leaps of sublime pity stirred in the breast of its very bosses by the sight of its agonies; it took rivers of blood, and enormous sacrifices of welfare and of money.

But not even today can that race say that it is really redeemed in the United States. Politically it is, civilly, no. One must admit that it showed so little will power in taking the trouble for its own rehabilitation; it revealed itself so tepid in the desire to profit from its political liberty, won at such a high price, to put itself on equal footing with its liberators on the path of civilization and human dignity; through deeds it proclaimed itself so inept and apathetic to flattery and to the more living of the arts and sciences, that, even now, its most ardent defenders (and we are such) cannot hope for its complete redemption from the slow work of centuries.

For the time being, content to let them vote and sit on the benches of the assemblies, the "Yankees" refuse to offer individuals of that race access into their own homes, or rather they admit them only as domestic servants. The more liberal Yankees, faced with the bitterest reproaches, would endure the great pain of sitting at a hotel's table d'hôte, at which, among the fellow diners, sat a person of that race; but the more liberal of the Yankees, having once achieved that great act of rebellion against the prejudices of their own compatriots, once seated at the table, would rather cut out their tongues than say a word to that person.

That race does not ignore the scorn in which it is held, but rather has put up with it for a long time and with almost no resistance. A blend of childishness and fierceness, it manages by laughing, showing two big rows of those legendary milk-white teeth, in the midst of the scorn that surrounds it. Rather than taste that disparagement, with that apathy that distinguishes it, it closes in on itself and now is almost glad about the scorn it has suffered, exactly because that scorn offers the better opportunity to make a life completely apart from it. It enjoys its own segregation and sees with a clear eye the disparagement that strengthens it, stoic in poverty and grossly noisy if a few dollars are jingling in its pockets.

You have already understood that the man who was standing was a black person.

The man who was kneeling at his feet belonged to the most elect race of humanity; or rather, he belonged to the flower of the flower of this elect race. Its forefathers had dominated the world a good three times, so much so that it could call itself three times sacred and meritorious among men. Its brothers, still today—despite centuries and centuries of martyrs, of aggression, of suspect attacks on their vitality, of internal discord (instigated and rekindled by the most passionate nature, by the pitiless misfortune that embitters the best and at times makes them mad, and by tyrants, who turned those discords to their infamous advantage); in spite of bitterness without end, in short, the siblings of that kneeling man, today still, I say, in a few years of freedom, showed that they had taken such steps on the path of modern civilization as to arouse the envy of their neighbors.

Memories of having conquered the ancient world with the valor of its armies, the Middle Ages with the lure of religion, recent times with the sweet fragrance of the arts and the brilliance of the sciences, the siblings of that man kneeling at the feet of a black person had inspired in modern peoples, with the reconquest of 1859, the political idea of nationalities that Germany thereafter pursued; and, when that idea had been affirmed on battlefields, the siblings of that man now kneeling at the feet of a black man, were forced to assert it now, in making peace.

In the veins of that man—kneeling at the feet of an individual representative of the barbarous indifference to every inducement of civilization—coursed blood more noble, purer, more generous and precious than any other human being can boast. Perhaps one of his ancestors had subjugated a province of Gaul or Spain; perhaps one had worn the cardinal's purple robes, perhaps one had modeled statues or painted pictures now admired in museums by thousands of people who have come to see them from the most remote parts of the earth, as if drawn by an irresistible urge. Perhaps an ancestor of that man now kneeling shamefully before a black man, had dissolved, with his warm melodies, the ice of crudity in the hearts of the Thracians and the Germans, perhaps that same man would have known, through an instinct almost traditional, how to judge the beauty of a rhythm or a work of art better than any rich Yankee.

Well then, this man, this representative of the flower of the human race, of blood historically called noble, this Italian (you already understood that's who

I meant) was shining the shoes of that representative of race that until recently had been enslaved, and still scorned, ever resistant to any civilized refinement, inferior—perhaps!

And that fellow, this representative of the lowest race, this black man— triumphantly blissful, was firmly, even despotically, placing his huge right foot on the shoeshine's box. With his broad chest thrust forward, his whole being assuming a pose of excessive haughtiness and dressed in fake high style, his boisterous mouth in a broad grin that showed off to the eyes of passersby two close-packed rows of milk-white teeth pressing on a fat Havana cigar, that black man was there, his neck taut, his pitch-black face in the air, triumphant, blowing stinking puffs of smoke, twirling a cane made of a rare wood orna- mented with gold, his right hand covered by a yellow glove, of a paradoxical yellow!

And it seemed that that black man cried out from every pore to that "noble Latin blood" that was bent down before him:

"Grandson of Julius Caesar and Marco Polo; cousin of the blessed Angelico; seed of Dante Alighieri; kin of Raphael, Domenichino and Michelangelo; descendant of Giordano Bruno; brother of Garibaldi and Cavour; polish, polish well, my shoe leather! My shoes, me John, the black man, who loves best about the white man's civilization—its alcoholic drinks! Me, who boasts among my ancestors (and not very distant ones) the flower of cannibals! Me, blood brother of the Zulus! Me, who, when I was still a child, they used to whip me until I was bloody and brand me with a red-hot iron, so that I would have dared to prefer suicide or revolt, even at the cost of death, to such shame! Me, lover of tattooing, which, according to a certain Humboldt, is the emblem of an uncouth nature. Polish! Polish! Shine! Shine!

"Down, at my feet! In the filth and the mud! Shamed in the sight of every- one! You also are scorned, most noble Latin blood, just like me (that I don't give a damn about, however); indeed, at this moment, even more than me! Polish! Polish! And that breath of your mouth, with which they say your forefathers warmed and planted in barbarous breasts the germs of civilization, you use it now in order to blow on the leather of my boots, unsurpassable method for making them rival the sparkle of the black diamond! Ah, you boast of belonging to a people that, in every age, has lavished splendors of every kind on the entire world? Well, today lavish splendors on my shoes! It will not be precisely the same thing, but at least you will be able to say that you've kept your traditions. "Ah, did your kin gloriously handle swords and pastorals, and paint-brushes, and chisels, and lutes, and instruments of science and commerce? Ah, the hands of your siblings, still living, were they gloriously bloodstained from smashing chains and building barricades and reconstructing a new civilization? Well, we will see if you also can earn yourself immortal fame equal to theirs, sublimely wielding the brush or mixing the colors—divine art—of the American patina!"

Ah, from that day, when in the streets of New York those numerous compatriots of mine assail me almost every twenty steps I take with the characteristic cry, "Shine? Shine?" ("*Splendori? Splendori?*" from antonomastic force of habit, or better, "*Lucidare? Lucidare?*") I run away saddened. It seems to me that I would join the Negroes in disdaining them, if I let them shine my shoes; that I would add another insult and putdown to the many that are hurled at them, and that, as their brother in nationality, I must refrain from doing so out of genuine, and not exaggerated delicacy.

And that's why I shine shoes with my own dear hands, without feeling bad about it. I dare say, indeed, that this somewhat gymnastic exercise I do when I've just gotten out of bed in the morning is good for my health. Even more: I would recommend it to these health-minded types who, having just woken up, take up weight lifting, exercise bicycles, or parallel bars, all methods evidently much more expensive than mine.

And, while I shine my shoes in the morning, how many fond memories fill my daydreams! Memories of boarding school, when, in thirty minutes, you had to jump out of bed, wash up, get dressed, clean up completely, to make the bed and to retrieve some apple or some sweets you've been given by your mother and hidden under the pillows with all the care and secretiveness of a political prisoner, who hides the escape tools that he made with patience and tenacity.

But for now I will keep these memories for myself, and you will believe me.

Your most affectionate friend,
F. Fontana

Translated by George De Stefano

For Humanity

∾ *Luigi Roversi*

Bologna, Italy, December 8, 1859–New York, New York, 1927

Luigi Roversi, who took a degree in law in Italy, was a lawyer and doctor of letters. He was a correspondent of the *Gazzetta* of Turin, of *L'Italia del Popolo* (The Italy of the People), and of *Il Risorgimento* (The Awakening); he also wrote literary pieces for *La Patria* (The Fatherland) of Bologna, submitting short stories and poems to the press. Through maternal descent, he was the nephew of Paolo Bovi Campeggi, an associate of Garibaldi's in New York.

Roversi emigrated to America and became subeditor of *Il Progresso Italo-Americano* and of *L'Araldo Italiano* (The Italian Herald). He was a correspondent from New York of various newspapers, among which, *Il Resto del Carlino* (The Change from a Carlino) and the *Illustrazione Italiana* (Italian Illustration); he was also the political and literary editor of *La Follia di New York* (The New York Madness) and editor of the *Stella d'Italia* (Star of Italy). Married to the Englishwoman Clara Nobbs, he enjoyed notable prestige among the first colonial journalists. In 1906, he was assigned the supervision of the section on the Italians in the United States at the Exposition of Milan, and in 1922 he was nominated Knight of the Crown. Between the end of the nineteenth century and the first years of the new century, he was the secretary and assistant to General Luigi Palma di Cesnola, director of the Metropolitan Museum of Art. In 1898, he published a biographical profile of the general, *Luigi Palma di Cesnola and the Metropolitan Museum of Art*, and in 1901, *Ricordi canavesani* (Memories from Canavese), on Cesnola's voyage to Italy (Cesnola was born in Rivaroli Canavese, near Turin). He also published *Church and State in Italy* (1880) and *Essays on Italian Art* (1883).

26

Roversi was a lecturer for the Board of Education of New York on themes of civic education, literature, and art; a literary and drama critic; and a teacher at the people's university, promoted in New York by the Socialist Party. With his brother Domenico, he had been a pioneer of socialism in Emilia Romagna until the last years of the 1870s, in the circle of Camillo Prampolini, Giacomo Maffei, and others.

The text published here reproduces his speech at the mass meeting of protest promoted by the colonial press after the lynching of eleven Italians in New Orleans.

ESSENTIAL BIBLIOGRAPHY

De Gubernatis 1880, 83; Gerbi 1962; Leonard 1907 (article); Roversi 1898, 1901.

ᔓ

Ladies and Gentlemen, Fellow Countrymen,

Although around me sounds and reverberates a loud, powerful, and sublime note of *italianità*; although, around me, the tricolor flag at half mast speaks of the fatherland in mourning, and therefore, of our heart in mourning; although at the invitation of the Italian press, the colony is reunited and comes together in diverse and opposing factions with admirable unanimity and moving harmony, whose lessons shouldn't be lost, I want to forget I am Italian!

I want to forget that an Italian, Christopher Columbus, was the prophet and discoverer of this land, the first and unique source of wealth, peace, liberty, and salvation. Above all, I want to forget our bitterest enemies and most tenacious opponents. I want to forget those legions of thousands upon thousands of Italian workers who, covered with sweat and often with blood, created the economic glory of North America, in the immense railroad network, the ostentatious Roman-style bridges, the canals, quarries, irrigation systems, wherever, in short, there was a need for arms of iron and shoulders of steel and not workers weakened by whiskey or depraved by vice.

I want to forget that Italians were among those who resolved the question of Alabama. Count Federico Sclopis[1]—supreme judge—helped America evade the horrors and disasters of war with England. Yes, to be more impartial, I want to forget everything, I want to forget all this, in order to not remember

---

1. Federico Sclopis di Salerano (1798–1878) was sent by Victor Emmanuel II to Geneva in 1871, where he was appointed president of the tribunal in the United States and was against Great Britain in the case of damages against USS *Alabama* during the Civil War.

that around you—men—I'm speaking as a man—in name and from the point of view of humanity.

And, as a man, I censure and condemn the authorities of New Orleans who, having kept in jail even those acquitted, under the hypocritical excuse of protecting them from vigilantes, handed them over to murderers like a flock of sheep to the slaughter. I censure and condemn the savage crowd responsible for the material crime, and the instigators, who still freely and calmly roam the streets of New Orleans. The latter are the more guilty and reprehensible. I censure and condemn the desecrators of dead bodies, who dragged them bloody against paving stones, hanged them on trees and lampposts, and made them obscene targets for shootings without the police intervening to stop these craven, vile acts.

I censure and condemn that part of the American press that calls the murdered murderers, rejoicing in the slaughter, as well as in the sanctimonious sermon. The inevitable correction of the law's deficiency only adds mockery to the crime, and denies the survivors' families the right to any compensation and from the Italian government any sort of reparation.

No, it is impossible to imagine a more profound moral perversion than that which the authorities and the press of New Orleans gave to us and to its citizenry. It's impossible! One could say that America's much-praised civilization is a colossal hypocrisy. One could say it is composed of a gang of ex-slave holders who, keeping one hand on the constitution, sarcastically clasp in the other the slave's whip. It is a menagerie of wild ferocious beasts who return to their savage state. It is a festering sore that oozes through the bandages and spreads out disgustingly in view of everyone.

One could say the law is a joke, public order mere nonsense, its social protection a trap. One could say the horrors of Russia are transplanted here, along with something that makes it worse. That while in Russia the torturer and executioner are but one person, the Czar, in America—or at least New Orleans—the executioners number in the thousands and thousands: lawyers, journalists, merchants, the so-called "*prominenti*," the rich bourgeoisie, well fed or on their way to becoming so.

No, it is impossible; and there are those who tremble at hearing the word *anarchist* and who, after the Haymarket Massacre in Chicago, seriously proposed to expel and incarcerate as many foreigners as possible in America who professed socialist ideas and aspirations!

Now what anarchy is worse than the one that rules in New Orleans? What greater danger and more shameful disgrace to the community and to public order than that in New Orleans, where a part of the citizenry is made up of hangmen in general, and another part made up of passive, cowardly spectators? In truth I tell you that if the order of a conservative republic ought to be like the one that permitted and sanctioned the deeds of March 14, 1891, to that Republican order is preferable Anarchy with its dynamite or Autocracy with its permanent gallows. At least neither of these is hypocrisy, and one can see it for what it is.

And what are we to say of the moral pressures, to which the jurors who absolved the Sicilians must now submit? The sanctity of the oath doesn't protect them, nor does their common background, nor is their verdict a pure matter of conscience between them and God. Nothing of the sort. The Band of Brigands terrorizes New Orleans and has as a boss a murderous ex-judge. He torments them in a million ways, submits them to an odious inquisition. He would, if he could, bring back the rack and rope torture to coerce a false confession.

It is of no use, and in fact this morning, a dispatch from New Orleans announces that the foreman Seligman has declared that if he and his colleagues absolved the defendants, it was because the testimony of their accusers was insufficient, because there wasn't proof of guilt, because they considered them innocent, and that if he had to judge them again he would judge them as he already judged them the first time. Honor be to him, who in the middle of all that muck, all that bloody mess, in that swarm of scared and trembling rabbits, rises straight and upright like an ancient knight, defending his cause to the death, come what may.

Honor be to him; yet alas, in front of this foreigner who proclaims the innocence of the Italians, there is an Italian (as the same dispatch says) who approves of the massacre. Oh from our womb, should there really arise Judases, at this moment? Or should the hand of misfortune really burden us, when union, solidarity, and the need to forget are more than ever necessary? . . . Also this seems impossible; but at times the impossible is true, especially at times of agonizing trials, such as we are now subjected to.

But it doesn't matter: faith sustains us, tempers the curses on our lips, stops the feelings of disdain. There is faith that the illustrious representatives of Italian government in Washington and in Rome, as they were vigilant guardians of national honor in the first hour of catastrophe, will remain firm, resolute, and unyielding in their demand for reparations. Should they not do it, they would be traitors and would force the betrayed to disown the fatherland that these colonies—at a distance of 4,000 miles!—love with more intensity and fervor than do their brothers across the ocean, pleased by its sun and sea, by its fascination, and by its poetry as of a living God! . . .

The fatherland! As Poland's sons in exile carried within themselves, almost a relic, a piece of their land, every Italian—coming to America—brought not a material symbol of Italy, but her sacred thought, her august image as mother and queen, the memory of her Calvaries and of her Easters, all of Italy!

And it is for this that here, taking leave of you and thanking you for indulging me with your attention, I want to return to being and feeling Italian. And as an Italian—as the least of the least—who in your language battles from the press gallery in this country of voluntary exile—I applaud the seriousness and dignity that you protest tonight in the name of Italy and your steadfast avowal that—from tonight on, in the name of Italy, in the name of our 11 slaughtered brothers from New Orleans, in the name of a blood bath that has reddened the white hair of old parents, wives, and orphans, in the name of the 11 ghosts that demand and impose on you to avenge and pacify— harmony and peace may stay with us forever!

Translated by Gil Fagiani

The Biography of a Bootblack

ᕫ *Rocco Corresca*

Between 1902 and 1906, the weekly *The Independent*, directed by Hamilton Holt, published seventy-five autobiographies of ordinary people, mostly immigrants and anonymous workers in the most modest ranks—miners, cooks, washerwomen, drivers, and so forth. The issue of December 4, 1902, published "The Biography of a Bootblack," signed by one R. Corresca, The text reveals that the name was purely conventional. No further data of identification are available, aside from those furnished by the text.

A brief introductory note clarified that autobiographical information was presented to the reader. It reads:

> The story of Rocco Corresca is presented almost as he told it to a representative of *The Independent*. There are changes of language and some suppressions, but no change of meaning has been made. The ideas and statements of fact are all his, and, astonishing as it may seem to Americans, much of the experience is typical of thousands of Italians who come to this country penniless and make their fortunes, though beginning as low down in the scale as the narrator. Rocco is known to many people as "Joe." He claims that he has always been known as Rocco but that the name Corresca was given him when he went aboard the ship that brought him here. It was entered on the books. He has since kept it for official purposes and proposes to be known by it in the future. —Editor.

ESSENTIAL BIBLIOGRAPHY

Basile Green 1974, 34, 53; Stein-Taft 1971.

☙

When I was a very small boy I lived in Italy in a large house with many other small boys, who were all dressed alike and were taken care of by nuns. It was a good place, situated on the side of the mountain, where grapes and melons and oranges and plums were growing. The nuns taught us our letters and how to pray and say the catechism, and we worked in the fields during the middle of the day. We always had enough to eat and good beds to sleep in at night, and sometimes there were feast days, when we marched about wearing flowers.

Those were good times and they lasted till I was nearly eight years of age. Then an old man came and said he was my grandfather. He showed some papers and cried over me and said that the money had come at last and now he could take me to his beautiful home. He seemed very glad to see me, and after they looked at his papers he took me away and we went to the big city—Naples. He kept talking about his beautiful house, but when we got there it was a dark cellar that he lived in and I did not like it at all. Very rich people were on the first floor. They had carriages and servants and music and plenty of good things to eat, but we were down below in the cellar and had nothing. There were four other boys in the cellar and the old man said they were all my brothers. All were larger than I and they beat me at first till one day Francisco said that they should not beat me any more, and then Paulo, who was the largest of all, fought him till Francisco drew a knife and gave him a cut. Then Paulo, too, got a knife and said that he would kill Francisco, but the old man knocked them both down with a stick and took their knives away and gave them beatings.

Each morning we boys all went out to beg and we begged all day near the churches and at night near the theatres, running to the carriages and opening the doors and then getting in the way of the people so that they had to give us money or walk over us. The old man often watched us, and at night he took all the money, except when we could hide something.

We played tricks on the people, for when we saw some coming that we thought were rich I began to cry and covered my face and stood on one foot, and the others gathered around me and said, "Don't cry! Don't cry!"

Then the ladies would stop and ask, "What is he crying about? What is the matter, little boy?"

Francisco or Paulo would answer, "He is very sad because his mother is dead and they have laid her in the grave."

Then the ladies would give me money, and the others would take most of it from me.

The old man told us to follow the Americans and the English people, as they were all rich, and if we annoyed them enough they would give us plenty of money. He taught us that if a young man was walking with a young woman he would always give us silver because he would be ashamed to let the young woman see him give us less. There was also a great church where sick people were cured by the saints, and when they came out they were so glad that they gave us money.

Begging was not bad in the summertime because we went all over the streets and there was plenty to see, and if we got much money we could spend some buying things to eat. The old man knew we did that. He used to feel us and smell us to see if we had eaten anything, and he often beat us for eating when we had not eaten.

Early in the morning we had breakfast of black bread rubbed over with garlic or with a herring to give it a flavor. The old man would eat the garlic or the herring himself, but he would rub our bread with it, which he said was as good. He told us that boys should not be greedy and that it was good to fast and that all the saints had fasted. He had a figure of a saint in one corner of the cellar and prayed night and morning that the saint would help him to get money. He made us pray, too, for he said that it was good luck to be religious.

We used to sleep on the floor, but often we could not sleep much because men came in very late at night and played cards with the old man. He sold them wine from a barrel that stood on one end of the table that was there, and if they drank much he won their money. One night he won so much that he was glad and promised the saint some candles for his altar in the church. But that was to get more money. Two nights after that the same men who had lost the money came back and said that they wanted to play again. They were very friendly and laughing, but they won all the money and the old man said they were cheating. So they beat him and went away. When he got up again he took a stick and knocked down the saint's figure and said that he would give no more candles.

I was with the old man for three years. I don't believe that he was my grandfather, though he must have known something about me because he had those papers.

It was very hard in the wintertime for we had no shoes and we shivered a great deal. The old man said that we were no good, that we were ruining him, that we did not bring in enough money. He told me that I was fat and that people would not give money to fat beggars. He beat me, too, because I didn't like to steal, as I had heard it was wrong.

"Ah!" said he, "that is what they taught you at that place, is it? To disobey your grandfather that fought with Garibaldi! That is a fine religion!"

The others all stole as well as begged, but I didn't like it and Francisco didn't like it either.

Then the old man said to me, "If you don't want to be a thief you can be a cripple. That is an easy life, and they make a great deal of money."

I was frightened then, and that night I heard him talking to one of the men that came to see him. He asked how much he would charge to make me a good cripple like those that crawl about the church. They had a dispute, but at last they agreed and the man said that I should be made so that people would shudder and give me plenty of money.

I was much frightened, but I did not make a sound and in the morning I went out to beg with Francisco. I said to him, "I am going to run away. I don't believe 'Tony is my grandfather. I don't believe that he fought for Garibaldi, and I don't want to be a cripple, no matter how much money the people may give."

"Where will you go?" Francisco asked me.

"I don't know," I said, "somewhere." He thought awhile and then he said, "I will go, too."

So we ran away out of the city and begged from the country people as we went along. We came to a village down by the sea and a long way from Naples and there we found some fishermen and they took us aboard their boat. We were with them five years, and though it was a very hard life we liked it well because there was always plenty to eat. Fish do not keep long and those that we did not sell we ate.

The chief fisherman, whose name was Ciguciano, had a daughter, Teresa, who was very beautiful, and though she was two years younger than I, she could cook and keep house quite well. She was a kind, good girl and he was a good man. When we told him about the old man who told us he was our grandfather, the fisherman said he was an old rascal who should be in prison for life. Teresa cried much when she heard that he was going to make me a cripple. Ciguciano said that all the old man had taught us was wrong—that it was bad to beg, to steal and to tell lies. He called in the priest, and the priest said the same thing and was very angry at the old man in Naples; he taught us to read and write in the evenings. He also taught us our duties to the church and said that the saints were good and would only help men to do good things, and that it was a wonder that lightning from heaven had not struck the old man dead when he knocked down the saint's figure.

We grew large and strong with the fisherman, and he told us that we were getting too big for him, that he could not afford to pay us the money that we were worth. He was a fine, honest man—one in a thousand.

Now and then I had heard things about America—that it was a far off country where everybody was rich and that Italians went there and made plenty of money, so that they could return to Italy and live in pleasure ever after. One day I met a young man who pulled out a handful of gold and told me he had made that in America in a few days.

I said I should like to go there, and he told me that if I went he would take care of me and see that I was safe. I told Francisco and he wanted to go, too. So we said good-bye to our good friends. Teresa cried and kissed us both, and the priest came and shook our hands and told us to be good men, and that no matter where we went God and his saints were always near us and that if we lived well we should all meet again in heaven. We cried, too, for it was our home, that place. Ciguciano gave us money and slapped us on the back and said that we should be great. But he felt bad, too, at seeing us go away after all that time.

The young man took us to a big ship and got us work away down where the fires are. We had to carry coal to the place where it could be thrown on the fires. Francisco and I were very sick from the great heat at first and lay on the coal for a long time, but they threw water on us and made us get up. We could not stand on our feet well, for everything was going around and we had no strength. We said that we wished we had stayed in Italy no matter how much gold there was in America. We could not eat for three days and could not do much work. Then we got better, and sometimes we went up above and looked about. There was no land anywhere, and we were much surprised. How could the people tell where to go when there was no land to steer by?

We were so long on the water that we began to think we should never get to America or that, perhaps, there was not any such place, but at last we saw land and came up to New York.

We were glad to get over without giving money, but I have heard since that we should have been paid for our work among the coal and that the young man who had sent us got money for it. We were all landed on an island and the bosses there said that Francisco and I must go back because we had not enough money, but a man named Bartolo came up and told them that we were brothers and he was our uncle and would take care of us. He brought two other men who swore that they knew us in Italy and that Bartolo was our uncle. I had never seen any of them before, but even then Bartolo might be my uncle, so I did not say anything. The bosses of the island let us go out with Bartolo after he had made the oath.

We came to Brooklyn to a wooden house on Adams Street that was full of Italians from Naples. Bartolo had a room on the third floor and there were fifteen men in the room, all boarding with Bartolo. He did the cooking on a stove in the middle of the room and there were beds all around the sides, one bed above another. It was very hot in the room, but we were soon asleep, for we were very tired.

The next morning, early, Bartolo told us to go out and pick rags and get bottles. He gave us bags and hooks and showed us the ash barrels. On the streets where the fine houses are, the people are very careless and put out good things, like mattresses and umbrellas, clothes, hats and boots. We brought all these to Bartolo and he made them new again and sold them on the sidewalk; but mostly we brought rags and bones. The rags we had to wash in the back yard and then we hung them to dry on lines under the ceiling in our room. The bones we kept under the beds till Bartolo could find a man to buy them.

Most of the men in our room worked at digging the sewer. Bartolo got them the work and they paid him about one quarter of their wages. Then he charged them for board and he bought the clothes for them, too. So they got little money after all.

Bartolo was always saying that the rent of the room was so high that he could not make anything, but he was really making plenty. He was what they call a padrone and is now a very rich man. The men that were living with him had just come to the country and could not speak English. They had all been sent by the young man we met in Italy. Bartolo told us all that we must work for him, and that if we did not the police would come and put us in prison.

He gave us very little money, and our clothes were some of those that were found on the street. Still we had enough to eat and we had meat quite often, which we never had in Italy. Bartolo got it from the butcher—the meat that he could not sell to the other people—but it was quite good meat. Bartolo cooked it in the pan while we all sat on our beds in the evening. Then he cut it into small bits and passed the pan around, saying, "See what I do for you, and yet you are not glad. I am too kind a man, that is why I am so poor."

We were with Bartolo nearly a year, but some of our countrymen who had been in the place a long time said that Bartolo had no right to us and we could get work for a dollar and a half a day, which, when you make it lire (reckoned in the Italian currency) is very much. So we went away one day to Newark and got work on the street. Bartolo came after us and made a great noise, but the boss said that if he did not go away soon the police would have him. Then he went, saying that there was no justice in this country.

We paid a man five dollars each for getting us the work and we were with that boss for six months. He was Irish, but a good man and he gave us our money every Saturday night. We lived much better than with Bartolo, and when the work was done we each had nearly $200 saved. Plenty of the men spoke English and they taught us, and we taught them to read and write. That was at night, for we had a lamp in our room, and there were only five other men who lived in that room with us.

We got up at half-past five o'clock every morning and made coffee on the stove and had a breakfast of bread and cheese, onions, garlic, and red herrings. We went to work at seven o'clock and in the middle of the day we had soup and bread in a place where we got it for two cents a plate. In the evenings we had a good dinner with meat of some kind and potatoes. We got from the butcher the meat that other people would not buy because they said it was old, but they don't know what is good. We paid four or five cents a pound for it and it was the best, though I have heard of people paying sixteen cents a pound.

When the Newark boss told us that there was no more work, Francisco and I talked about what we would do, and we went back to Brooklyn to a saloon near Hamilton Ferry, where we got a job cleaning it out and slept in a little room upstairs. There was a bootblack named Michael on the corner, and when I had time I helped him and learned the business. Francisco cooked the lunch in the saloon and he, too, worked for the bootblack and we were soon able to give the best shine.

Then we thought we would go into business and we got a basement on Hamilton Avenue, near the Ferry, and put four chairs in it. We paid $75 for the chairs and all the other things. We had tables and looking glasses there and curtains. We took the papers that had pictures in them and made the place high toned. Outside we had a big sign that said:

THE BEST SHINE FOR TEN CENTS

Men that did not want to pay ten cents could get a good shine for five cents, but it was not an oil shine. We had two boys helping us and paid each of them fifty cents a day. The rent of the place was $20 a month, so the expenses were very great, but we made money from the beginning. We slept in the basement, but got our meals in the saloon till we could put a stove in our place, and then Francisco cooked for us all. That would not do, though, because some of our customers said that they did not like to smell garlic and onions and red herrings. I thought that was strange, but we had to do what the customers said. So we got the woman who lived upstairs to give us our meals and paid her $1.50 a week each. She gave the boys soup in the middle of the day—five cents for two plates.

We remembered the priest, the friend of Ciguciano, and what he had said to us about religion, and as soon as we came to the country we began to go to the Italian church. The priest we found here was a good man, but he asked the people for money for the church. The Italians did not like to give because they said it looked like buying religion. The priest says it is different here from Italy because all the churches there are what they call endowed, while here all they have is what the people give. Of course Francisco and I understand that, but the Italians who cannot read and write shake their hands and say that it is wrong for a priest to want money.

We had said that when we saved $1,000 each we would go back to Italy and buy a farm, but now that the time is coming we are so busy and making so much money that we think we will stay. We have opened another parlor near South Ferry, in New York. We have to pay $30 a month rent, but the business is very good. The boys in this place charge sixty cents a day because there is so much work.

At first we did not know much of this country, but by and by we learned. There are here plenty of Protestants who are heretics, but they have a religion, too. Many of the finest churches are Protestant, but they have no saints and no altars, which seems strange.

These people are without a king such as ours in Italy. It is what they call a Republic, as Garibaldi wanted, and every year in the fall the people vote. They wanted us to vote last fall, but we did not. A man came and said that he would get us made Americans for fifty cents and then we could get two dollars for our votes. I talked to some of our people, and they told me that we should have to put a paper in a box telling who we wanted to govern us.

I went with five men to the court, and when they asked me how long I had been in the country I told them two years. Afterward my countrymen said I was a fool and would never learn politics. "You should have said you were five years here and then we would swear to it," was what they told me.

There are two kinds of people that vote here, Republicans and Democrats. I went to a Republican meeting and the man said that the Republicans want a Republic and the Democrats are against it. He said that Democrats are for a king whose name is Bryan and who is an Irishman. There are some good Irishmen, but many of them insult Italians. They call us Dagoes. So I will be a Republican.

I like this country now, and I don't see why we should have a king. Garibaldi didn't want a king, and he was the greatest man that ever lived.

Francisco and I are to be Americans in three years. The court gave us papers and said we must wait and we must be able to read some things and tell who the ruler of the country is.

There are plenty of rich Italians here, men who a few years ago had nothing and now have so much money that they could not count all their dollars in a week. The richest ones go away from the other Italians and live with the Americans.

We have joined a club and have much pleasure in the evenings. The club has rooms down in Sackett Street and we meet many people and are learning new things all the time. We were very ignorant when we came here, but now we have learned much.

On Sundays we get a horse and carriage from the grocer and go down to Coney Island. We go to the theatres often, and other evenings we go to the houses of our friends and play cards.

I am nineteen years of age now and have $700 saved. Francisco is twenty-one and has about $900. We shall open some more parlors soon. I know an Italian who was a bootblack ten years ago and now bosses bootblacks all over the city, who has so much money that if it was turned into gold it would weigh more than himself.

Francisco and I have a room to ourselves now and some people call us "swells." Ciguciano said that we should be great men. Francisco bought a gold watch with a gold chain as thick as his thumb. He is a very handsome fellow, and I think he likes a young lady that he met at a picnic out at Ridgewood.

I often think of Ciguciano and Teresa. He is a good man, one in a thousand, and she was very beautiful. May be I shall write to them about coming to this country.

BROOKLYN, N.Y.

(Originally in English)

Little Italy

∾ *Gaetano Conte*

Sessa Aurunca (Caserta), Italy, April 10, 1859–Florence, Italy, August 26, 1917

Gaetano Conte was sent to school in Naples by his father, and in that city Gaetano came to know the Dutch count and missionary Oswald Papengouth. He converted to Protestantism. Because of this, his father Luigi put him out of the house, and Gaetano managed to earn a living working as a *precettore* (tutor). In 1882, he entered the Opera Metodista Episcopale, which was directed at that time by the American Leroy M. Vernon. The first place he was sent was the little town of Venosa in Basilicata, then to Naples (where he came in contact with Freemasonry), and then to Palermo, Rome, and Foggia. In 1893, he went to the United States and became pastor of the Italian Methodist Episcopal Church in Boston. He founded a workers' association named for George Washington, as well as a bilingual magazine. He returned to Italy in 1903 and was sent first to Palermo, then to Venice. In 1911, thanks to strong disagreements, he resigned from the Episcopal Church. He moved to Florence, where he tried to introduce Unitarian doctrine to Italy, also publishing a collection of booklets on this theme. He founded the Associazione Italiana dei Liberi Credenti (Italian Association of Free Believers) and the journal *La riforma italiana* (The Italian Reformation).

Dieci anni in America (Ten Years in America) is the title of a book in which Conte published his memories of a long pastorship among the Italians of the North End, the Little Italy of Boston. In 1893, he departed from Genoa with his five children "to educate them in a pure and Christian environment, and then, upon becoming adults, he would take them back to Italy, full of good will and trained for the struggle for the common good" (Conte 1903). His book represents one of the first attempts to systematically organize the Italian American problem—eliminating verbose and vain schemes of patriotism and centering upon the concrete reality of problems—and he generally does not dwell on polemics. With an attitude typical of many Evangelical journalists, Conte, who in Boston had the opportunity to frequent intellectual circles at a high level, sought to understand the reasons behind those Americans most hostile to the immigration. "Often in Italy," he writes, "we judge America harshly, because it does not welcome our emigrants, and it creates societies to impede the immigration. We are right; we presume the impossible! Men love the things that conform to their dispositions. Now what conformity of ideas, of sentiments, of traditions, of habits ever exists between our emigrant and the American people?" (Conte 1903).

ESSENTIAL BIBLIOGRAPHY

Conte 1903, 1906; Hartley 2011; Martellone 1975.

૰

[Little Italy.] That's what the Americans call the Italian quarter located to the North of the city, near the port.

This is the area where the memorable early days of the War of Independence unfolded, and also where, a good deal later, not a few notorious events occurred. Coming here to live, we inherited the bad reputation of the latter times, and the comparison between the glorious past and the poor present of this quarter certainly is not to our advantage.

The most notable monuments of historical interest are situated at the borders of our colony. From one side the Old North Church, from whose bell tower Paul Revere, with two lanterns, alerted the patriotic farmers of the nearby countryside that the English troops were advancing by sea, and from where they prepared the resistance. Next to it is the Copps Hill Cemetery, whence the English field batteries advanced on the insurgents at Bunker Hill. Here is the port famous for the "Boston Tea Party," here the celebrated Faneuil Hall, known as the cradle of liberty, here the little square where the first blood was spilled for Independence, and here the house of Paul Revere, now inhabited by poor Southern Italian farmers.

In this part of the city lived Adams, Hancock, Revere, Otis, and with them generations of heroes, who are more and more idealized in the popular mind, given both the distance from those times and the comparison with today's poor inhabitants.

Our emigrants live in wretched and unhealthy homes, in which the lack of room and light combine with the most sickening filth: three or four to a bed; six to eight to a room. Only one of them has a family, the others stay as boarders, paying from 7 to 10 lire a month for the right to a place to sleep and wash. This agglomeration of people in such places is clearly harmful to health and morale. In all these hovels there is only a single lavatory, in the cellar or in the middle of narrow and dark stairways, from which in both cases, stench and germs spread like a bugle blast into the already unhealthy apartments. Then the rooms, being generally made of wood, host thousands of insects of many colors and shapes, such that sometimes only an axe or fire can get rid of them. To that, if one adds the lack of bathing facilities and the habit of failing to use them, the absence of a woman's touch, the type of work the emigrants do, the poverty and the consequent humiliation, one has an eloquent and disturbing picture of the life of our peasants here.

In 1895 a special commission established by the City Council reported that the living conditions in the North End constitute a "real threat to the public health."

The Twentieth Century Club, comprising individuals interested in economic and social issues, in 1897 undertook a study of the problem of living conditions of the poor, and in the following year published a report which, in speaking about our quarter, found "the homes to be dangerous to the lives of their inhabitants because they lacked repairs, running water, and drains, light and ventilation."

Prof. F. W. Chandler, a city architect, describes them thus: "Ceilings and walls broken down and dirty, dark cellars full of stagnant water, broken water pipes, rooms dark and crammed, cellars used as bedrooms, dark and narrow stairways, dark and humid lavatories, many for a long time, from cold or other reasons, rendered unsuitable, inadequate for the number of inhabitants and located where they shouldn't be; apartments lacking light and ventilation, houses in such ruin to be of constant threat to the lives of the tenants."

One of our women, a domestic servant, in fact, lived in a room only a little more than four meters square. In it there was the conjugal bed and the stove, and on the ground the pallet of her brother-in-law and a friend of his.

Now this state of affairs, awful to everyone, seems quite monstrous to the Americans, who rightfully give so much importance to their homes.

In fact Arnold Toynbee says in this regard that "It is not possible to exaggerate the importance of family life. What is freedom worth without it? What is public education worth without it? No nation can ensure its greatness if it is not founded on healthy family life. And it is not possible to have a healthy family in such an environment."

Regarding these hovels, Dr. E. R. L. Gould, in an article that appeared in one of the most authoritative newspapers, added that "The family reveals the character of society, and where the domestic influences beneficial to health, happiness, and virtue cannot thrive, one must inevitably be prepared for deleterious social consequences. Intelligent people can modify the effects of a bad room, but the poor, weak-willed and heedless, endure all the effects."

In such houses, among such influences, live our emigrants, and their children are exposed there to every type of corruption.

Nor should one think that such dwellings come cheaply. They, according to the 1891 census, yield a 15 percent profit to their owners, which forces the generally poor tenants to cluster together, to squeeze together, I would say almost lie on top of each other.

In that same census it was verified that in two districts, occupied by Italians, there were 154 families that each occupied a single room and 459 that had an average of two persons per room. But these figures are well below the actual ones, since the census was taken during the daytime and it is the common practice of our emigrants to fill up empty spaces of the room in the evening, spreading mattresses on the floor at a late hour, when one presumes that the police will not make inspections.

And from 1891 on, the conditions have not at all improved, since on one hand the Board of Health has ordered the renovation of some thirty houses but on the other hand the number of old ones keeps dwindling, whether because of the growth in factories and shops or because of the arrival of new emigrants, so that the problem today has become more difficult than ever.

In 1895, in the sixth and eighth districts, where our people live, there was an overall total of 50,990 persons, and only five years later there were 59,363 inhabitants, of which 25,000 were Italians.

City statistics from 1891 to 1901 show that the population increased from 457,772 to 573,579, i.e., by 25.3 percent, while the number of dwellings grew only from 53,429 to 65,600, i.e. 22.8 percent.

But this increase has little to do with the North End, where the absolute lack of space (the area being almost entirely surrounded by the sea) makes the construction of new buildings impossible, while the population grows in inverse proportion, given the well-known fact that the poor have a greater number of children.

The Boston *Herald*, in a December 28 news article, reported that, in a house in Clinton inhabited by Italians, health department agents had found 85 males and five females sleeping in twenty-one rooms that had been divided into six apartments. Men, women, and children were all mixed together, without regard to sex or family. Not a window or a door was left ajar to refresh the air during the night.

And the police said that the conditions were worse during the previous summer, when a greater number of workers was employed to build a water tank nearby.

It is no wonder that in such a field death harvests a greater number of victims. In fact, while in the entire city the average annual death rate is 1 out of every 48 inhabitants, in our quarter it's one out of every 41, which if not excessive is certainly not too little. And the proposition stands out more clearly when one regards the statistics by district.[1]

Certainly the law does not permit such a state of affairs, and therefore those who are animated by a humanitarian spirit often have been roused, and still are roused, but till now with little success. The capitalists have found that that it is not profitable to build new houses at the costly terms now demanded by law as long as the old ones are still standing which, costing little, would create for them an untenable competition.

The Health Department, often reminded about the fulfillment of its duty, has taken refuge behind the shortcomings of the current laws. But public opinion, at this point strongly hostile to the present state of things, will force its hand to one and to the others, and the North End will be "ripped up" like its worthy Neapolitan emulator.

But when, by force of law and the commitment of the most willing, new workers' housing rises in more healthy locations, will the Italian immigrants be willing to leave the current neighborhood, which with its churches, banks, stores, so resembles their native villages? And those who were forced here by need or by municipal regulations, with the change of location would they change their habits and have a home, a house, a family? I little believe it. In New York our immigrants have gone from the lower part of the city, from "downtown" to "uptown," but they brought uptown the very habits of Mulberry Street.

As long as emigration is temporary and our peasant miserly, he will prefer to adapt as best he can and to save as much as possible. Certain reforms must come more from inside than from outside. Our émigrés will seek out better comforts and conditions only when, in stable housing, and dominated by the environment and prompted by their school-educated children, they feel more strongly the prodding of personal dignity, morally and financially uplifted by the needs of life more than by the rule of law.

But is all of Little Italy populated by peasants like these? Certainly not. Looking at the city one notices at a glance the crowding together of the various migrations

---

1. In 1900 the median of mortality was 1 per 39 inhabitants in District 6 (North End), 1 per 42 in District 5, 1 per 80 inhabitants in District 25, 1 per 72 inhabitants in District 24, 1 per 71 inhabitants in District 23, 1 per 69 inhabitants in District 20 (Annual Report of the Registry, Department of Boston, 1891). Here one must note that the longer numbers indicate the better neighborhoods, and vice versa.

that have lived in it, so that the oldest, to the degree they do venture out, move to the city's east side, while the new and poorer throng the North and the West. Thus among the citizenry one distinguishes the various layers of a civilization more or less densely American, depending on the greater or lesser age of the various generations of immigrants. One can say as much of any colony, in which the average observer sees the gradual infiltration of new ideas and customs into the old milieu.

Among our peasants, those who have lived here several years stand above the newly arrived by dint of experience and independence. The former already claim to speak English, having been able, for lack of anything better, to substitute Italian words for English ones having the same sound. Thus, instead of Everett, he will say: "via diretta" [straight road], and instead of Hanover Street, "la nuova stretta" [the new street]. One time, during the last presidential election, a good fellow asked what I thought about Michelino. I looked at him dumbfounded, racking my brain to recall if there had been some boy by that name, sick or ne'er-do-well, whom I perhaps forgotten to help out, but it was in vain. "How is it," he said, "that you do not know Michelino? Who are the papers and the public always talking about today if not him?" And, after a bit I finally understood that he meant to say McKinley!

And from this fellow on, there's an ascending scale of more civilized persons. There is the peddler and the retail fruit vendor (at one time a very lucrative monopoly for us that now is passing to the Greeks), and the artisan who knows nothing of art, because of the practice common here in the small firms of parceling out a job through use of machines, so that no one person by himself makes an entire object. So it goes for the manufacture of shoes, cheap jewelry, sweets, textiles, clothing and furniture: to get a piece of bread, our workers are forced to labor in these factories, where they find badly paid work.

There follows a better class of real workers who find employment in the custom tailor shops, or among the casters of statues and artistic ornaments, among mosaic workers, etc. And above them is a real phalanx of barbers, who in general don't give a bad image of themselves. In Italy many of them were more than barbers, and here they were forced to take up such work, generally considered servile. They constitute a good element, and through their continuous contact with the public, they are, of our people, the most Americanized. Through their work, the existing prejudice today against this type of labor little by little will be dispelled.

An American speaker of uncommon talent once was talking about immigration and, during his speech, with a smile that seemed to say "I've hit on something good," noted that the Italians were the *cleanest* people in the country. The audience received his statement with evident signs of incredulity and he then set out to prove his proposition. "Who in fact is it," he asked, "who shines our shoes?

Who digs our sewers? Who shaves our beards? Who clears our streets of rags and paper garbage? Who sharpens and cleans our knives? They all are Italians, unable to bear seeing humanity in filth."

But if, instead of being of ungenerous spirit, he had bothered to examine the facts better, he would have seen that often the bread, the fruits, the cakes, the clothes, the silks that he buys, music that he hears, the statues he admires in the museum, all this comes from the same people that he bitterly mocks. However, in his defense, one must acknowledge that few of our merchants, with the exception of the fruit vendors, do business with Americans, which does not take into account those who have changed their last names to English ones so that they won't be recognized as Italians. Most of our merchants instead sell Italian products at retail, which isn't much, unless to a business selling pasta and potatoes they add a banking office. There are however importers, generally Genoans, who establish respectable commercial firms.

Among those who have made their way outside our colony with great success, some make plaster reproductions of objets d'art and several are wine dealers or innkeepers; these latter ones, however, more than with Americans, strictly speaking, work with people of other nationalities who have been settled here for a while, to whom drunkenness and groups of tipsy hotel guests are of little concern. Among ours, four such institutions predominated on this decade's vice market: one of them failed because of excessive luxury, two were closed because of too much obvious immorality, and another has stayed in business through the protection of corrupt police.

But the ascending scale does not end here, and rises further to a solid nucleus of doctors, several lawyers, a few pharmacists and several clergymen, Catholics and Protestants, a city councilman and a member of the state legislature.

Nor is it much different in the Italian world of New York, where, in Manhattan alone, there are 2300 shoemakers, 1300 food vendors, 1500 tailors, 3000 barbershops, 500 butchers and bakers, 200 tobacconists and 600 fruit sellers.

Today, people like this, gathered in Boston's Italian quarter, with its three Catholic churches, recently also provided with schools, with approximately forty mutual aid societies, two musical bands, more than thirty so-called banks, constitute an Italian town of 25,000 inhabitants, all to itself, as if embedded in the great city, and therefore called "Little Italy." Many of the houses in our quarter are becoming the properties of Italians, and those that they already own are worth $2,325,800, according to the 1900 census.

Some of them were acquired with much sweat, when business was going well, especially the fruit and citrus trades. Others, alas, recall the suffering and the tears of the poor peasants, taken advantage of by greedy vampires; others still resound with the idiotic laughter of drunken wretches and of the corrupt kisses of fallen women, others finally are the fruit of unheard of sacrifices of so much that is necessary to life, sacrifices made to the mere desire to accumulate cash. It is well that one at this point knows that whoever comes to this country can find bread and work, but fortune and riches no more—unless he prostitutes himself by trafficking in vice, or condemns himself to a miserable and abject life.

And here it is the place to speak of another shameful source of income to which not a few of our people condemn themselves, through the lust for money.

In the great markets of Boston, unfortunately places too close to the Italian quarter, those shopkeepers have the habit of depositing in some barrels, placed outside the door, the trash from their stores, waiting for the garbage trucks to come by and take away this often filthy and stinking stuff.

Today, whoever passes through those places in the early morning encounters a depressing and sickening scene. A number of women, Italian children and workers, still not having risen above the poverty level, go there to scrounge some vegetables or meat. And while one of our women passes with her treasure, glad to have resolved for yet another day the problem of her appetite, others nearby express the various feelings that the unpleasant scene arouses in them.

Here's the Irishman who, drunk and stinking from constantly chewing tobacco, smiles sarcastically and insults the poor wretched woman: Filthy Italian! There's the American who stops a moment, about to rebuke the poor woman, but then shrugs his shoulders, looks at his watch, and rushes away, and mutters, Italians! None of my concern. And there's the respectable Italian, the merchant, who has gotten rich here. He watches the scene, it pains him in his heart, but if at that moment someone asks him: Are you Italian? No, sir, he answers, and keeps going.

We recall an anecdote reported to us by an eyewitness. A poor woman reaches for a peach, when she sees in bottom of a barrel something useful. She bends down to reach it when a miserable coward grabs her by the feet and pushes her down headfirst. The scene attracts the attention and arouses the cruel hilarity of passersby. Street urchins throw big snowballs at the poor woman, while she, through the struggle to free herself, exposes her nakedness. Finally the barrel falls over and she manages to free herself.

But from this one must not infer that there is excessive poverty among our people here, as we will say more broadly later. We cannot form any idea of the collective life of our colony without spending some time studying the two other important manifestations of the character of our life: the press and the associations.

"Here in the United States there are a couple (only a couple) of Italian dailies, which, with unfurled sails, successfully negotiate the breakers of colonial journalism. There's also a couple (only a couple) of weeklies that are holding up well; there is also a monthly magazine (only one) that does well and does not defy logic or syntax. Other publications more or less Italian have been clinging to existence for some time, and the public puts up with them out of habit, as one does with flies when one can't chase them away. (This parenthesis is intended to let our readers know that we're not concerned with these still-living papers. We're talking about the many weekly, daily, or monthly publications, which, year after year, go from baptism to tomb, and on to resurrection, to then once again die out.)

"We collect these ephemeral ones that are born and die with an almost mathematical frequency, in the bosom of our larger and smaller colonies in the American Republic.

"During this year of grace that is reaching its sunset, some fifty new newspapers, all "dedicated to the interests of workers of our nationality in America," unexpectedly appeared, all bearing the by-now traditional slogan 'the only Italian newspaper of this state or this city.' "

Among the most salient or most significant names in their philology we have noticed "Eureka" (meaning, "I have found it") then "The Ass," "The Butterfly," "The Frog," that have been taken from the three popular newspaper of the same names that have had great success in Italy, followed by "The Eagle," "The Hippogriff," "The Lion," and another animal that I don't remember, perhaps "The Pig," then those of certain tools that lend themselves well to punishing men and donkeys, like "The Riding Crop," "The Lash," "The Curry-Comb," "The Whip," "The Vises," then those of stars and asteroids and meteors, like: "The Star," "The Comet," "The Planet," "The Earth," "The Lightning," "The Lightning Bolt," "The Thunder," then many, many names that cannot be categorized, because they come from all over the dictionary, in no particular order: "The Boot," "The Mask," "The Scimitar," "The Sabre Stroke," "The Bottle" and then "Satan," "Charon," "Cerberus," "Pluto," "Lucifer" and so forth. It's not right for us, nor useful for our readers' knowledge, to know under which auspices such waste-paper creatures rise up and come to life only to then die out for lack of nourishment.

We can assert, however, that since, in ninety out of every 100 cases, such enigmas of the press are the product of marital secrets between some university professors "unemployed and fresh from the mountains of Italy, and some big shot," of ample girth, who feels the irresistible need to release into the air a burden of self-laudatory adjectives that the writer blends into his line as he writes. Most of the time the marriage ends like this: the big shot, after a few issues of the new publication created with his money, gets accustomed to the laudatory adjectives and feels hurt in the pocketbook when he has to squeeze yet more funds out of it, so to put an end to it, he kicks out the professor. He who received the kicks tries to underhand-edly scrounge some more money from the big shot, flees from his kicks, goes to a nearby city, starts another paper, and unloads a sewer of insults against his first patron—the one who kicked him out.

Et sic transit gloria mundi.

And so it goes as far as the number, the name and the origin of such weeklies, but what can one say about their substance? Not being able to live by their own virtue, one must add, they live entirely on gossip and worse, the so-called "paid ads" being the sole source of income beyond the few subscriptions gotten out of worthless people, who in that way buy for a dollar false compliments, or to persons who fear the appearance of "official notices" that would not redound to their glory. It certainly would be our good fortune if these papers, disseminators of fratricidal hatreds, would disappear once and for all.

From New York however, come three good daily newspapers, which, although lacking a defined political and social program, are good news sources, and besides keeping up the use of the language, they connect the colonies to each other and all of them to the motherland. The trade unions are all about mutual aid, some Catholic, others liberal: some flourishing, other stunted: some civilian, others military. They are gatherings of people, interested in mutual aid, but lacking a cause and a defining character. What pushes some to found associations is the ambition to be called President: others join them out of a mad desire to dress up like Italian military officers. With the same indifference they celebrate the 20th of September and the arrival of Monsignor Satolli, getting dressed for a funeral as for a picnic in the countryside.

In 1895 a parade was being held to commemorate the 20th of September. At a certain point some dissidents from a military society, accompanied by an usher, stopped the marching column and seized the association's banners. Right away a brawl erupted. To seize the flag by hand is an act of supreme treachery! Out come the swords, the general on horseback cries out ferociously, and one defends with one's life the honored emblem! And our good countrymen cry out, gesticulate, make noise, and after an hour of shameful din are surrounded by the police and led to prison, dressed as generals and colonels. It is painful to say it, but it's true. To the shame of the Italian colony and the fatherland, while the good and serious citizens keep to themselves, some, lacking education and seriousness, expect, in the name of equality, to leave behind their miserable poverty by putting it on display.

To watch them, predominant in the workers' associations, one would have to say that the distinctive characters of "Little Italy" are the internal struggles characteristic of the breed, the noisy verbosity of the ignorant, the facile enthusiasm for any worthwhile undertaking, so easily extinguished at the first sign of difficulties. One must say that fortunately such maladjusted meddlers are but a relative minority in comparison to the serious persons, to the large numbers of peace-loving peasants, strangers to these things, from which they flee. And where there is less of this element, in the associations, the group and its capital are greater. Only two or three mutual aid societies, as a matter of fact, can be said to be truly serious and worthy of consideration. In the past few years, however, a new element has come to better regulate this aspect of the colony's social life.

Two secret societies, the Foresters of America and the Knights of Pythias, have welcomed Italians and founded Italian courts or lodges. The importance of such a development is inestimable.

Such orders are governed by American supreme councils, under whose jurisdiction and vigilance the lodges must operate. An assigned delegate observes the work of the individual courts and acts as an arbitrator of the clashes that not infrequently break out. In my opinion, this is the first and most important step by the Americans towards the education of Italian workers.

The fact that the societies are secret strikes their fancy, and leads many to join: then interest keeps them there, as the courts have excellent revenue and are a first-rate social fund.

The duty, then, to debate according to parliamentary rules and to call one's adversary "brother," responds to one of the greatest needs of our workers, whose nature is poorly contained by the bonds of logic and good manners. But it is time now to leave "Little Italy" and to consider our emigrants from the economic, political, and moral point of view, as they were revealed to me in this decade.

Translated by George De Stefano

How It Feels to Represent a Problem

∾ *Gino Carlo Speranza*

Bridgeport, Connecticut, 1872–New York, 1927

Gino Carlo Speranza, was the son of Carlo Leonardo, who emigrated to America with his wife in 1868 and became a professor at Yale and Columbia. After the age of twelve, Speranza spent nine years in his parents' birthplace, Verona, and then returned to America in 1895, where he completed his studies and undertook a legal career. From 1897, he was the legal advisor to the Italian Consulate in New York and a member of the Emigration Commission of the State of New York. As corresponding secretary of the Society for the Protection of Italian Immigrants, Speranza learned that native Americans, for all their concern to impress on the foreigner the importance of assimilation, very often provided very poor examples of what it is to be an American. The subtitle of this article by Speranza was "A Consideration of Certain Causes Which Prevent or Retard Assimilation." In 1906, on an assignment for the Italian government, he produced a study on the conditions of the emigrant workers in West Virginia, published in *Bolletino dell'emigrazione*. In 1915, after the outbreak of World War I, he went to Italy as a correspondent for the *New York Evening Post* and *Outlook*; in 1917, after the United States entered the war, he served as a volunteer at the American embassy to Rome, where he remained until 1919.

His intensive correspondence with newspapers and reviews, writing articles on immigration, dates from the first years of the twentieth century. In 1914, he wrote several stories for the *Atlantic Monthly*. He published a book, *Race or Nation* (1927), that was destined to provoke controversy in that it takes the position of the most radically conservative theory of assimilation that was being tested, departing from the much more mild and humanitarian positions in Catholic newspapers at the beginning of the century. In a political-social climate profoundly marked by drastic restrictive measures in respect to immigration, Speranza, in *Race or Nation,* expressed strong doubts about the real possibilities of a rapprochement between Anglo-Saxons and Latins. He arrived at the conclusion that it was necessary to safeguard the WASP foundation of the nation and suggested further restrictions upon the immigration flux—a policy of dismantling the old "colonial" world: the abolition of the sectarian character of religious instruction; and aside from the issue of naturalization (for which he proposed a ten-year residency, instead of the prescribed five, to obtain citizenship), the abandonment of every loyalty bearing upon the country of origin in case of conflict with American interests. In 1941, edited by his wife Florence Colgate and introduced by Arthur Livingston, *The Diary of Gino Speranza* was published, in two volumes. A diary of his Italian sojourn between 1915 and 1919, it is interesting as much for the richness of its observations of a political-diplomatic character in the war period as for its singular example of a "voyage in Italy," following itineraries that were not the traditional ones.

ESSENTIAL BIBLIOGRAPHY

Peragallo 1949, 202–208.

☙

The American nation seems to like to do some of its thinking aloud. Possibly this is true of other nations, but with this difference, that in the case of the American, the thinking aloud is not suppressed even when it deals with what may be termed the "country's guests." Older nations, perhaps because they lack the daring self-sufficiency of the young, prefer, in similar cases, to think in a whisper. All countries have problems to grapple with, economic, political, or social; but with America even the labor problem is popularly discussed as if its solution depended on that of the immigration problem.

Now, considering the large percentage of foreign-born in the population of the United States, it is a strange fact how few Americans ever consider how very unpleasant, to say the least, it must be to the foreigners living in their midst to be constantly looked upon either as a national problem or a national peril. And this trying situation is further strained by the tone in which the discussion is carried on, as if it applied to utter strangers miles and miles away, instead of to a large number of resident fellow citizens. Perhaps this attitude may be explained by the fact that to the vast majority of Americans "foreigner" is synonymous with the popular conception of the immigrant as a poor, ignorant, and uncouth stranger, seeking for better luck in a new land. But poverty and ignorance and uncouthness, even if they exist as general characteristics of our immigrants, do not necessarily exclude intelligence and sensitiveness. Too often, let it be said, does the American of common schooling interpret differences from his own standards and habits of life, as necessarily signs of inferiority. Foreignness of features or of apparel is for him often the denial of brotherhood. Often, again, the fine brow and aquiline nose of the Latin will seem to the American to betoken a criminal type rather than the impress of a splendid racial struggle.

Then there is another large class of "plain Americans" who justify a trying discussion of the stranger within the gates by the self-satisfying plea that the foreigner should be so glad to be in the "land of the free" that he cannot mind hearing a few "unpleasant truths" about himself.

This is not an attempt to show that the tide of immigration does not carry with it an ebb of squalor and ignorance and undesirable elements. It is rather an endeavor to look at the problem, as it were, *from the inside.* For if America's salvation from this foreign invasion lies in her capacity to assimilate such foreign elements, the first step in the process must be a thorough knowledge of the element that should be absorbed.

Many imagine that the record and strength of the American democracy suffice of themselves to make the foreigner love the new land and engender in him a desire to serve it; that, in other words, assimilation is the natural tendency. Assimilation, however, is a dual process of forces interacting one upon the other. Economically, this country can act like a magnet in drawing the foreigner to these shores, but you cannot rely on its magnetic force to make the foreigner *an American.* To bring about assimilation the larger mass should not remain passive. It must attract, *actively attract*, the smaller foreign body.

It is with this in mind that I say that if my countrymen here keep apart, if they herd in great and menacing city colonies, if they do not learn your language, if they know little about your country, the fault is as much yours as theirs. And if you wish to reach us you will have to batter down some of the walls you have yourselves built up to keep us from you. What I wish to examine, then, is how and what Americans are contributing to the process of the assimilation of my countrymen who have come here to live among them.

I have before me a pamphlet which a well-known American society prints for distribution among arriving immigrants. On the title page is the motto: *A Welcome to Immigrants and Some Good Advice.* The pamphlet starts out by telling the arriving stranger that this publication is presented to him "by an American patriotic society, whose duty is to teach American principles"—a statement that must somewhat bewilder foreigners. Then it proceeds to advise him. In America, it tells him, "You need not be rich to be happy and respected." "In other countries," it proceeds, "the people belong to the government. They are called subjects. They are under the power of some emperor, king, duke, or other ruler," which permits the belief that the patriotic author of this pamphlet is conversant mostly with medieval history. There are some surprising explanations of the Constitution, showing as wide a knowledge of American constitutional history as of that of modern Europe—but space forbids their quotation. "If the common people of other countries had faith in each other, there would be no czars, kaisers, and kings ruling them under the pretext of divine right." This is certainly a gem of historical exposition.

Then, in order to make the stranger feel comfortable, it tells him, "You must be honest and honorable, clean in your person, and decent in your talk." Which, of course, the benighted foreigner reads as a new decalogue. With characteristic modesty, the author reserves for the last praise of his country: "Ours," he says, "is the strongest government in the world, because it is the people's government." Then he loses all self-restraint in a patriotic enthusiasm. "We have more good land in cultivation than in all Europe. We have more coal, and oil, and iron, and copper, than can be found in all the countries of Europe. We can raise enough foodstuffs to feed all the rest of the world. We have more railroads and navigable rivers than can be found in the rest of the civilized world. We have more free schools than the rest of the world. . . . So great is the extent (of our country), so varied its resources, that its people are not dependent on the rest of the world for what they absolutely need. Can there be any better proof that this is the best country in the world? Yes, here is one better proof. Our laws are better and more justly carried out."

Of course, criticism by the stranger within your gates seems ungracious; but whenever it is attempted, it is suppressed by this common question: "If you don't like it, why don't you go back?" The answer is never given, but it exists. For the majority of us, this is our home and we have worked very hard for everything we have earned or won. And if we find matter for criticism, it is because nothing is perfect; and if we institute comparisons, it is because, having lived in two lands, we have more of the wherewithal for comparisons than those who have lived in only one country.

Then there is the American press. How is it aiding our assimilation? It would not be difficult to name those few newspapers in the United States that give space either as news or editorially, to nonsensational events or problems with which Europe is grappling. As regards Italy, there is such a dearth of information of vital importance that little, if anything, is known by the average American, of the economic or political progress of that country. Columns on Mussolini, half-page headlines on the Mafia, but never a word on the wonderful industrial development in northern Italy, never a notice of the financial policies that have brought Italian finances to a successful state!

What is the American press doing to help assimilate this "menacing" element in the Republic?

"Why is it," was asked of a prominent American journalist, "that you print news about Italians which you would not of other nationalities?"

"Well, it is this way," was the answer, "if we published them about the Irish or the Germans, we should be buried with letters of protest; the Italians do not seem to object."

It would be nearer the truth to say that they have learned the uselessness of objecting unless they can back up the objection by a "solid Italian vote."

One result of the unfriendliness of the popular American press is that it drives Italians to support a rather unwholesome Italian colonial press. Why should they read American papers that chronicle only the misdeeds of their compatriots? Better support a local press that, however poor and ofttimes dishonest, keeps up the courage of these expatriates by telling them what young Italy is bravely doing at home and abroad. But this colonial press widens the cleavage between the nations, puts new obstacles in the way of assimilation, and keeps up racial differences.

To feel that we are considered a problem is not calculated to make us sympathize with your efforts in our behalf, and those very efforts are, as a direct result, very likely to be misdirected. My countrymen in America, ignorant though many of them are, and little in touch with Americans, nevertheless feel keenly that they are looked upon by the masses as a problem. It is, in part, because of that feeling that they fail to take an interest in American life or to easily mix with the natives. And though it may seem far-fetched, I believe that the feeling that they are unwelcome begets in them a distrust of those defenses to life, liberty, and property which the new country is presumed to put at their disposal. They have no excess of confidence in your courts and it is not surprising, however lamentable, that the more hotheaded sometimes take the law into their own hands. You cannot expect the foreigner of the humbler class to judge beyond his experience—and his experience of American justice may be comprised in what he learns in some of the minor tribunals controlled by politicians, and in what he has heard of the unpunished lynchings of his countrymen in some parts of the new land. What appeal can the doctrine of state supremacy and federal noninterference make to him? Imagine what you would think of Italian justice if the American sailors in Venice, in resisting arrest by the constituted authorities, had been strung up to a telegraph pole by an infuriated Venetian mob, and the government at Rome had said, with the utmost courtesy: "We are very sorry and greatly deplore it, but we can't interfere with the autonomy of the province of Venetia!"

I am aware that the question is often asked: If these people are sensitive about being discussed as a problem and a menace, why do they come here? It is a question asked every day in the guise of an argument, a final and crushing argument. But is it really an argument? Is it not rather a question susceptible of a very clear and responsive answer? They come because this is a new country and there is a great deal of room here, and because you invite them. If you really did not want them, you could keep them out, as you have done with the Chinese. . . .

It is true that, as a nationality, Italians have not forced recognition; though numerically strong, there is no such "Italian vote" as to interest politicians. They have founded no important institutions; they have no strong and well-administered societies as have the Germans and the Irish. They have no representative press, and well-organized movements among them for their own good are rare. Those who believe in assimilation may be thankful for all these things; for it could be held that it is harder to assimilate bodies or colonies well organized as foreign elements, than individuals held together in imperfect cohesion.

Yet the Italian in America as an individual is making good progress. In New York City, the individual holdings of Italians in savings banks is over $15 million; they have some 4,000 real estate holdings of the clear value of $20 million. About 10,000 stores in the city are owned by Italians at an estimated value of $7 million, and to this must be added about $7.5 million invested in wholesale business. The estimated material value of the property of the Italian colony in New York is over $60 million, a value much below that of the Italian colonies of St. Louis, San Francisco, Boston, and Chicago, but, a fair showing for the great "dumping ground" of America.

But the sympathetic observer will find the most remarkable progress on what may be called the spiritual side of the Italians among us. It is estimated that there are more than 50,000 Italian children in the public schools of New York City and adjacent cities where Italians are settled. Many an Italian laborer sends his son to Italy to "finish his education" and when he cannot afford this luxury of doubtful value, he gets him one of the *maestri* of Little Italy to perfect him in his native language. In higher education, you will find Italians winning honors in several of our colleges, universities, and professional schools. I know of one Italian who saves money barbering during the summer and on Sundays, to pay his way through Columbia University. I know of another who went through one of our best universities on money voluntarily advanced by a generous and farseeing professor. The money was repaid with interest and the boy is making a mark in the field of mathematics. I know of a third, the winner of a university scholarship, who paid his way by assisting in editing an Italian paper during spare hours; a fourth, who won the fellowship for the American School at Rome, and thus an American institution sent an Italian to perfect his special scholarship in Italy.

New York City now counts 115 Italian registered physicians, 63 pharmacists, 4 dentists, 21 lawyers, 15 public school teachers, 9 architects, 4 manufacturers of technical instruments, and 7 mechanical engineers. There are two Italian steamship lines with biweekly sailings, sixteen daily and weekly papers, and several private schools. Italians support several churches, one modest but very efficient hospital, one well-organized savings bank, and a chamber of commerce. They have presented three monuments to the municipality, one, the statue of Columbus, a valuable work of art. They are raising funds to build a school in Verdi's honor, under the auspices of the Children's Aid Society, and are planning to organize a trust company.

I have given the statistics for New York City because the Italian colony on Manhattan is less flourishing than those in other large American cities. So that what is hopeful for New York is even more promising in Philadelphia, St. Louis, and Boston. . . .

There is one more question that an Italian, speaking for his countrymen here, may urge upon Americans who are interested in the problem of assimilation. It is this: that you should make my countrymen love your country by making them see what is truly good and noble in it. Too many of them, far too many, know of America only what they learn from the corrupt politician, the boss, the *banchiere*, and the ofttimes rough policeman. I have been in certain labor camps in the South where my countrymen were forced to work under the surveillance of armed guards. I have spoken to some who had been bound to a mule and whipped to work like slaves. I have met others who bore the marks of brutal abuse committed by cruel bosses with the consent of their superiors. What conception of American liberty can these foreigners have?

This, then, is the duty upon those who represent what is good and enduring in Americanism—to teach these foreigners the truth about America. Remember these foreigners are essentially men and women like yourselves, whatever the superficial differences may be. This is the simple fact far too often forgotten—if not actually denied. And this must be the excuse if you discuss these people as a menace, pitching your discussion as if we were beyond hearing, and beneath feeling, and sometimes even as if beyond redemption.

Make us feel that America has good friends, intelligent, clear-sighted friends; friends that will not exploit us; friends that will not be interested merely because of what Italy did in the past for all civilization, but friends that will extend to us the sympathy which is due from one man to another. You will thereby make us not merely fellow voters, but will prepare us for the supreme test of real assimilation—the wish to consider the adopted country as a new and dear fatherland.

FROM *THE SURVEY*, MAY 7, 1904

The Children of Emigrants

❧ *Alberto Pecorini*

1881–1957

Alberto Pecorini was a journalist, one "of those misfits: adventurers, people of talent—now exploited, now blackmailers, eccentric and excited, now subversive, now nationalists, sometimes anarchists, sometimes semi-scholars, other times bankrupt; always ready to fight with the pen and perhaps with punches in defense of their ideals and of their persons, and attack the ideals and persons of others, in a tone rising many octaves above the level of their financial means and of the circulation of their periodicals" (Prezzolini). In New York, at the beginning of the twentieth century, Pecorini directed the newspaper *Il Cittadino* (The Citizen), which, after being sold to the businessman Joseph Personeni, was directed by Alberto Tarchiani from 1907 to 1917. In Italy, Pecorini, who had converted to Protestantism, belonged to the Montclair (New Jersey) Italian Evangelical Missionary Society. He wrote *Gli americani nella vita moderna osservati da un italiano* (The Americans in Modern Life, Observed by an Italian), issued by the publisher Treves in 1909. Prezzolini's judgment of the book was very favorable, especially in relation to the part regarding the Italian Americans, with whom the author manifests very little satisfaction, bringing out in particular the problem of the instruction of children. Later on, he published an interesting bilingual book, *La storia dell'America/The Story of America*, prepared for the Massachusetts Society of the Colonial Dames (Boston: Marshall Jones, 1920). Mrs. Barrett Wendell remarked in the "Introduction" that this book was designed to be "of real use to the community." Pecorini, whose *Grammatica Enciclopedica* (Encyclopedic Grammar, 1911) circulated in America in 1935, died in Argentina.

ESSENTIAL BIBLIOGRAPHY

Prezzolini 1963, 237–242.

∾

One of the most important aspects of Italian immigration in the United States is that it has become increasingly permanent in nature. Children of Italian parents attend public and parochial American schools throughout the United States, and are estimated at one hundred and fifty thousand, of which fifty thousand are in the City of New York alone.

The concentration of these immigrants in major cities is a direct result of their poverty and ignorance. How could one suggest that poor laborers without resources and knowledge of the country would risk going to places where there are few of their compatriots? To tell an immigrant that he would be paid a much higher wage in Kansas, Colorado, or California than he receives in New York is to no avail. He arrives with a longing in his heart for his homeland and dreams of returning there one day to live in peace. After two or three years, when he realizes that one can survive in America but cannot grow rich, he sends for his family members or returns to his homeland to get them. The few words of English that he has learned ensure his employment, and every step toward the west, every mile he moves away from New York represents more sorrow because the indefinite, vague, and impossible hope of returning to his homeland slips farther away. The concentration of Italians in large cities is, however, the root cause of all the evils that afflict our immigrants. The first among them is the immigrant's tendency to live a life unto himself in his surroundings, with little or no interest in studying the English language or learning about the country in which he lives. What need, in fact, does the immigrant have to learn English when he lives in the middle of a colony where he has an Italian boss, an Italian theater, an Italian newspaper, an Italian tavern, and an Italian church? In addition, he is content with his lot and has no aspirations to associate with Americans so that one day he may earn a living within the American system. This way of life could be considered to be a fine example of Italian patriotism, especially by those in Italy who do not understand the problem, but to someone who is intimately familiar with life in our colonies, all of this seems to be a painful consequence of ignorance, a primitive state of mind, and a lack of ambition. If this were patriotism, it would be long-lasting, and its effects would be seen in the second generation; as is the case with professionals, merchants, and rich families, the second generation is disastrously lost, not only with respect to citizenship but also to language and ideals.

The filthiest sections of Italian cities are reproduced in American cities, not because the immigrant loves his homeland, but simply because he is absolutely incapable of living in another environment at the time of his arrival. The typical Italian colony in a large U.S. city is comprised ninety percent of workers and their families, half of whom cannot read and write, and a third group represents the fluctuating population of newcomers who must depend on exploitative brokers or supervisors to earn a living. Ten percent is made up of professionals whose goal in most cases is to make as much money as soon as possible; small merchants who import specialties from their homeland for their customers and fellow country-men; and bankers, shipping agents, and notary publics, more than half of whom are absolutely irresponsible and would lower themselves to any level to make money. They are, in short, a great mass of working and uneducated poor, exploited somewhat by all classes; and the so-called leaders, rather than taking charge of their social and moral guidance and the serious problems that plague them, are busy making money in any way possible and spending the rest of their time at parties and banquets. If the hunger for gold in Americans presents a sad spectacle, it is even more repugnant in Italians. Americans love money not in and of itself but rather for the pleasure of making it, so much so that after they have earned it they amuse themselves by giving it away. For Italians, with a few exceptions, the philanthropic spirit does not at all develop with wealth. They love money itself, and they breathlessly seek it at the cost of misery, failure, and the neglect of others; it is nauseating. Left to its own devices, the great mass of ignorant workers essentially creates a serious problem for the host nation and for itself. The forms of primitive and violent crime, the convention of personal revenge, and the traditions that govern the concept of honor—everything is in striking contrast to American civilization and therefore arouses a sense of distrust and repulsion towards Italians, which is especially evident in the higher classes of American society.

This negligence presents serious consequences for young newcomers and for children born in the United States. A boy arriving in America at the age of twelve or thirteen is sent by his parents to work rather than to school as the law dictates. All too often parents state the child's age falsely so that he is able to work in a factory; Italian children of about ten years of age or younger frequently work in New Jersey's glassworks. The boy begins to work at an age when the labor is still too difficult for him. He gives most of the money he has earned to his family, and with the little money that is left he learns to wander around the taverns and gambling houses. For the child born in America, or who has arrived from Italy as an infant, his father cannot avoid sending him to school. As happens quite often, the child is educated in a bright and clean environment with a better and more decent life, while he is forced to live at home in a dirty and unhealthy environment which is at odds with the gracious and beautiful one at school. The child does not know anything about Italy other than the crude dialect spoken at home, the obscene words that he hears on the neighborhood streets, and the primitive methods and thoughts of his illiterate parents. He never sees an Italian book at home because no one knows how to read, he knows nothing about Italy because his father could not tell him anything, and he grows up intelligent and educated with a sense of revulsion for anything that has to do with Italy. When he is older, he Americanizes his name because he is ashamed of being Italian and, if he is inclined to do well, he moves to another neighborhood in the city and becomes an honest American worker.

Frequently, the lack of moral parental influence, through the ill-conceived notion of freedom as a result of ignorance and coarseness, completely abandons children to an environment that is better suited to create criminals than gentlemen. It is significant, for example, that among the Italian delinquents in New York City, the percentage of those who were born in America or who came here before fourteen years of age is much greater than those immigrants who arrived after the age of twenty-five. Italian delinquency, which alarms many Americans, is more a product of an Italian-American upbringing than of Italy, and it certainly will not decline until its causes have been addressed. As far as the ruling class is concerned, until now it has often profited, not through legitimate commerce or professional practice, but by exploiting the ignorance of the masses. There is no shortage of professionals and honest merchants, but the majority is content to advance within a semi-honest system, which unfortunately continues to thrive. The shipping agent and the banker are paid enormous prices for their services; the recruiter sends thousands of laborers to any dangerous job site to work as slaves or to die of poverty while he still receives his commission; the doctor sells imported medicine at outrageous prices; the lawyer, in taking advantage of his clients' ignorance, absorbs what little savings they have, and in cases brought by workers injured on the job, he ruthlessly negotiates with the industrial and railway companies and receives money from both sides; and the newspaper owner fills the newspaper with enticing and misleading notices while tempting the weaknesses of every rich profiteer. What if in the midst of such surroundings honest young people, who represent the future of the colonies, disdainfully rejected them? What if the Italians who knew how to read and write and who could not be exploited, instead of becoming the heart and soul of Italian-American life, were to establish subversive organizations in West Hoboken and Paterson where the spirit of healthy and moderate discontent has degenerated into an atrocious spirit of rebellion and deadly hatred? Two years ago in New York where there are nearly half a million Italians and where fifty thousand Italian students attend school, a few idealists, headed by an Italian commissioner of the city public education committee, persuaded the school authorities to introduce the option of teaching the Italian language in those schools where at least a certain number of students had requested it. This was considered to be a great victory for the city's Italians. The prominent people in the community hosted a banquet in honor of the commissioner, they gave speeches praising their homeland, and naturally the government sent a medal; but when it came to the facts, not one of the hundred thousand Italian laborers asked that his child be taught the Italian language. At this rate, there will not be any traces of Italian immigration to the United States left in the future, except for a few dirty neighborhoods and an increase in crime and disorder.

It would be unfair, however, not to recognize the modest efforts thus far by a few who were motivated by more than money and felt a duty towards the oppressed. Many good works for the benefit of emigrants have been achieved under the direction of various religious groups.

There are currently more than two hundred Italian priests in the United States. While it is true that too many of them left their homeland under the weight of guilt, it is no less true that a considerable number use their positive influence to benefit the social condition of the masses. They have, admittedly, yet to learn that certain noisy celebrations and processions make our people seem to be a superstitious and inferior race to the Americans who have never seen Catholics of other nations do these things, but at least these priests speak our language and have proved themselves to be loyal patriots, since the difficulties of Italian politics do not exist in America. Almost all of the Protestant churches have missionaries and ministers among the Italians; there are about ninety scattered throughout the largest colonies. In many places, proper churches were built for them; and since the main purpose of these groups is to Americanize newcomers as quickly as possible, night schools teaching English are often attached to places of worship, and reading rooms have been opened nearby. Protestantism cannot, however, make the same progress among Italian immigrants that could be expected with other races, since Italians lack the individual, evolved conscience that Protestantism assumes. Nevertheless, it bestows a spirit of enterprise and momentum on the Italian Catholic church that only the United States seems capable of providing. A number of charities have been established in some of the more populated colonies. An Italian charitable institute in New York, mainly through the work of an Italian industrialist to whom Italians in the United States should show their utmost gratitude, has almost completed plans for the creation of a large Italian hospital.

The question of Italian colonial life in the United States is very complex and difficult. Those who have thoroughly studied it agree that it presents many difficulties since things have been allowed to take their own course for too long. In the
United States there is the danger of producing a type of citizen within the Italian-
American colonies who embodies the worst qualities of both races instead of the
best ones. The ideal would be to guide Italian immigrants in a way that, while
becoming citizens of their adoptive homeland, allows them to keep their distant
homeland in their hearts and to educate their children to uphold the ideals of their
heritage. In another chapter of this book discussing Italian-American trade, I have
shown that Italian immigration to the United States fundamentally represents a
commercial failure. It is important to ensure that it does not constitute a moral
failure as well. Two main problems exist with respect to Italian immigration in the
United States: one concerns the distribution of immigrants and the other concerns
their protection and education.

The problem of the lack of concentration of Italians in the agricultural southern
states, where they could eventually become landowners, has been studied by Baron
Des Planches, the current Italian ambassador to Washington. After a long journey
through the South, he summed up his conclusions in an interesting report: "Of
course, while success is not always immediate, it does not elude those who work
and persevere. . . . It seems to demonstrate that in terms of our agricultural emigration, which is fifty percent of total migration, it is advisable for them to go
where they are needed rather than where they are considered unnecessary; where
hands are in short supply rather than where they face competition from many others or they adapt to jobs that others disdain; where the climate reminds us of our
own rather than where the winters are long and miserable; where they rediscover
a morally and physically healthy life in the fields rather than where they cannot
escape from base practices on the streets, or if they work in factories, where the
pernicious air that one breathes alternates with the tempting and voracious stench
of saloons and the noxious dankness of the "slums." It is very doubtful that directing immigrants to the agricultural South could displace the Italian neighborhoods
of large cities, but it is not doubtful that it could prevent further overcrowding.
Without intending to cast a shadow over the optimism of this illustrious man, we
must not forget that there are enormous obstacles. Italians do not want to be isolated and will not go to the South without the most extensive guarantees of safety.
If they are so poorly protected in the North, where they live in large numbers and
where their homeland's governmental agencies are present in major cities, why
would they go to the South where consular services are not only lacking, but one
could assert that they do not exist at all? Moreover, we cannot forget that the in-

habitants of the south, who are accustomed to Negroes, do not pay comparable wages and treat workers as well as they are treated in the North. In many states the laws established to prevent Negroes from voting also prevent white immigrants from doing so, and even an American court was called to decide whether Italian children had the right to go to school with white American children instead of Negroes. While it is true that the cost of living is lower in the South and that those who persevere can prosper and one day own land, they are the exception, and in any case those who persevere can also prosper in the North. If the Italian government, which imports millions of tons of tobacco each year from the South, and the industries in northern Italy, which import millions of tons of raw cotton, were willing to boldly enter into colonization and have Italian hands produce the materials they need, then perhaps the influx of Italians to the South could be a success.

The second problem is one of protection. The Italian government has done something to protect the emigrant during the crossing and has subsidized protection agencies at the ports of arrival to protect him during his entry into America. But the protection ends here, even though it should not only continue as a protective mission, but should also broaden its scope and include an educational mission as well. This basically would serve to protect the immigrant from dishonest speculators while looking for work and to raise the moral level of the colonies to ensure a future generation of honest and industrious Italian workers. Initially, the Italian government attempted to open an employment agency in New York, which constitutes a significant step if only for the good intentions it has demonstrated. The agency, however, places a relatively small number of workers, while there are hundreds of Italian contractors in the United States who employ many more workers each year. It is difficult to remedy the situation. The failed student who reads and writes correctly, knows a little French, and has modest pretensions is not cut out for life in the United States. The labor issue regulates itself for the most part as the recent crisis demonstrated; the worker who needs an agency to find him a job in the United States is more often than not unsuitable to work in this country. It would be more important for the agency to concern itself with the inspection and supervision of contractors. The Italian immigrant always prefers to look for work through one of his fellow countrymen, even paying him a commission rather than going through a government office which would find him work for free. But if every contractor knew that the employment agency monitored him, and that he could not extort money or send an Italian immigrant to become a slave and die in West Virginia, Louisiana, or Florida without being sent to prison according to the country's laws, the situation would somewhat improve. If it were understood that no lawyer could profit from a worker's ignorance without the intervention and protection of a government agency, we would no longer see Italians who have lost an eye, an arm, or a leg at work and receive only a few hundred dollars as compensation. In order to carry out the educational mission, it would be necessary to assemble a group of honest professionals. It would be an excellent initiative for the Italian government to create a number of scholarships at universities in Italy for intelligent young people who were educated in America. They could help immensely by serving as interpreters of the Italians' aspirations for the Americans, among which they live and are now part, if they knew something about the beauty, ideals, and history of Italy that they ignore. In most American universities where the Italian language is taught, why are the professors American? Is this not our field? Why do we want to chase after money if the Americans, who are more energetic and practical, continue to defeat us? But in the field of art and literature, which is our field, why should we not win?

If we could find a way to organize the Italian workers, using the most intelligent workers as representatives, the objections of the American workers' unions could be easily countered. In Boston, something similar has been attempted but the results will not be seen for some time. It is perhaps better to encourage the Italians to join American unions where they can exert their influence to benefit their fellow countrymen, rather than to organize exclusively Italian unions that lack the fundamental principles of democracy and order on which American unions are founded, and quickly degenerate into oligarchies.

For several years, in addition to poor country peasants from southern Italy and Sicily who arrive in the United States, there has been an influx of craftsmen from the cities, students who were unable to finish their studies and find work, as well as young people from well-off families who seek a larger and more profitable area for their businesses. The mission of Italian government officials in the United States should be to ensure that these immigrants are not lost to the great American masses, but that they become the future of a more beautiful and pure colonial life. In order for this mandate to be effectively carried out, the officials need to be carefully selected and the responsibility of protection must be fully placed in their hands. It is clear that a government official who is suited to be a consul in Turkey or China, where the authorities are terrified of him and where he only comes in contact with a small number of wealthy Italian travelers, may not be suited to be a consul in a large U.S. city where he does not inspire any fear and where there are tens of thousands of poor workers to protect, organize, and educate. For countries with large numbers of immigrants, the consular role requires special training that no school other than experience can provide. The Italian government should learn how to create properly a class of consular officials qualified to serve in countries with large numbers of Italian immigrants, and it must give these officials ample resources to supervise the various initiatives aimed at the protection and education of emigrants. The Italian consul in the United States should be sufficiently aware of the environment, language, customs, and ideals of the American nation so that he is understood and respected by the most intelligent persons, and at the same time he should recognize the moral conditions and problems within the colonies so that he may become a vital force in guiding emigrants on their new path. . . .

Until now, we have not been on the right track and the miserable state of many colonies is due in no small part in this neglect. . . .

Under these circumstances, how can the Italian government know the real state of the colonies and their needs? And who will guide the Italian emigrants in the midst of so much neglect and disorganization?

Since the moral guidance and inspirational forces are lacking, immigrants can only look to criminal con-men who have neither the desire to work honestly nor the ability to practice any profession and who improvise as journalists. In weekly newspapers which live and die as quickly as mushrooms, they demonstrate their abilities by praising those who pay and blackmailing those who do not. The ten daily newspapers, which after many years of struggle for survival are now beginning to emerge from the dark shadow of semi-honesty, cannot yet lead life in the colonies, which need far more strength and independent action. And yet, how great, how beautiful is the mission that seems providentially entrusted to the Italians in the United States! The railroads built by poor Italian laborers; the tunnels, bridges, and roads wet from their sweat; the factories where they have largely made the triumph of American industry possible; the mines where many of them died and were ignored; the orange groves and vineyards in California and perhaps the fields in the west and south that will one day be tilled: all of these great and productive things in and of themselves are only temporary contributions to the economic greatness of the richest country in the world. The one great and true contribution that the children of Italy can offer the United States is an everlasting one: it is the sense of beauty, an ideal of life in which the Latin race excels and which the American people lack. Given their work, Italians do not produce what others can do equally well or even better, but the children from the land of the sun have in their blood an ideal, a heart that other people do not have. Poor and illiterate, even looking at the painting of a great artist, hearing the notes of a dear piece of music, lifting their eyes up to the blue of heaven or shifting their gaze to the depths of the countryside, contemplating the infinite ocean or the sun drawing to a close, witnessing a generous act, or listening to a love story their soul experiences emotions, throbs, anguish, despair, passion, and dismay that are and will always be a mystery to Anglo-Saxons. If one day the United States produces great artists or poets, the blood of the poor children of Italy will run through their veins. . . . The American people of the future, with the purity and rigidity of the Puritans, the tenacity of the Germans, the happy optimism of the Irish, and the commercial skills of the Jews will not be complete without the artistic sentiment and the ideal inclinations of the Italic race, and it is every individual's duty to ensure that this contribution can be freely given and gratefully received and appreciated. This will create deep currents of sympathy between peoples which matter much more than treaties and perhaps even more than commerce. If this can be achieved through the elevation and purification of our colonies, then Italian immigration to the United States will not be a failure.

Translated by Giulia Prestia

Neither Foreigners nor Americans

Alberto Tarchiani

Rome, Italy, November 11, 1885–November 30, 1964

Between 1907 and the autumn of 1916, Alberto Tarchiani, one of the most esteemed among the exiles in the 1930s and 1940s, carried out his first profitable journalistic experience in New York, directing the weekly *Il Cittadino* (The Citizen). Administered by businessman Joseph Personeni and of modest means, though of a much higher quality than the average colonial newspaper, *Il Cittadino* published stories in series, such as Gogol's "Taras Bulba," and did not hesitate to enter into debate with the *Progresso* of Carlo Barsotti. It distinguished itself during the First World War for its democratic interventionism, which, among other things, translated into venting a harsh invective against Senator Lodge and the political nativists intent upon impeding the conscription of the children of Italian American citizens ("Un caso penoso" [A Painful Case], June 24, 1915). It also strongly attacked George McClellan, a professor of economics at Princeton, who lived in Venice and was a supporter of neutralism. Tarchiani asked for his expulsion from Italy ("Per l'espulsione di un protettore maldicente" [For the Expulsion from Italy of a Slanderous Protectionist], June 24, 1915). In this context, touching however upon questions of greater breadth, is Tarchiani's article "Neither Foreigners, nor Americans," published in *Il Cittadino* on December 9, 1915.

Repatriated to volunteer for the front, Tarchiani then became an editor at the *Corriere della Sera*. In 1926 he moved to France. In August 1929, he was among the organizers of the rescue of Carlo Rosselli, Emilio Lussu, and Fausto Nitti from their place of internal exile on the island of Lipari. In Paris, with Rosselli, he created *Giustizia e Libertà* (Justice and Liberty), then, with Randolfo Pacciardi, *La*

Giovane Italia (Young Italy). In the United States, where he returned in autumn 1940, he was the secretary general of the Mazzini Society, for which he founded, with Alberto Cianca, first, *Mazzini News,* then, *Nazioni Unite* (United Nations). He reentered Italy in summer 1943, with the Allies, and on April 22, 1944, he was named Minister of Public Works in the second government of Badoglio, whose seat was in Salerno. As Italian ambassador to Washington from 1945 to 1955, he applied himself to the cause of including Italy in the future Atlantic Alliance. Among his books, *Dieci anni tra Roma e Washington* (Ten Years Between Rome and Washington) (1955) describes his ambassadorial experiences.

ESSENTIAL BIBLIOGRAPHY

Tirabassi 1976 and 1984; Torlontano 1984.

Our observations on the phenomena of dual citizenship[1] have provoked the usual chorus of protests and approvals. Of course as always happens when one presses on an open wound hidden under the bandages of oblivion and hypocrisy, the protests were much louder and more resounding than the approvals. We are used to it! . . . Initially, certain nationalists of dubious origin rose up to say that it was a crime to advise Italians to apply for American citizenship (which does not mean, one should note, becoming "Americanized"). Then there emerged, with the scimitar of loyalty, the mamelukes of artificial denationalization and re-nationalization. Between these two extremes there are those who are silent and they are the great majority of naturalized Italians who well know the reasons why and under what circumstances they "legally" renounced their citizenship of birth to acquire their adoptive one.

Random or bellowing nationalists and "Americanists," either out of ignorance, utility, or an instinctive and resolute aversion to the police, have not considered and understood a simple truth: Italians residing in the United States for years— whether naturalized or not—are no longer foreigners even if they are not yet (and nor will they ever be) Americans. They are political and moral hybrids who love their home country from far away and despise it up close, just as they do with their adoptive country. All foreigners despise America when they are there. They praise it when they return to their native country. Thus, for emigrants, Italy, especially the one that they have never seen (since most of them are only familiar with their "hometown" and Naples) is an earthly paradise. When they go there (out of their

---

1. The author refers to a series of articles on this subject that appeared in his newspaper and that addressed the issue of conscription in the Italian armed forces.

own ignorance and the instinctive apish vanity of those who have traveled), they find the Coliseum wretched and Piazza San Marco barely tolerable. The mentality of the so-called "exile" is mixed with disappointed comparisons coupled with the inability to judge fairly and knowingly. It follows that an Italian-American is truly that and cannot be anything else. The "hyphen" (that is, a dash, a unifying line) which is so nerve-racking to self-styled, native-born Americans really does exist and is a normal and incorrigible condition of life for all those born and raised in one country and then, due to circumstances, forced to live in another. We cannot and should not pretend that these individuals who are welcomed as friends and collaborators would change their nature. If they were to change, seemingly to pander, they would be (and there are many who are) hypocrites who are much more damaging to the moral life of the nation than those who are openly and freely loyal to two flags that do not fly in opposite camps and can, for the greater development of human civilization, be called upon to protect the same principles of law and freedom. The Italians of America can only (for sentimental reasons beyond their control) become naturalized half-way—and those who are native-born must be content with this half. It is for the same reason that Italians in Italy are content with the semi-nationalization of foreigners who acquire citizenship, hoping and with good reason (and with magnificent results) that our schools and our environment will make ardent and generous patriots of their children. It is, therefore, useless to delude ourselves; despite the environment, the schools, and the Anglo-Saxon character that reigns here, they do not have such a direct and decisive influence that even the children of Italians who are born and raised in the United States are inevitably destined to become Americans, and unfortunately . . . in many cases, not necessarily model Americans.

Surprised and breathless from the serious phenomenon of the "pronouncement" by "hyphenated" Germans, the most ardent and blustering Americans or those who are Americanized, instead of bothering to study and solve this particularly grave and threatening problem, give themselves over, body and soul, to proclaiming a stolid and quixotic crusade against the windmill of dual citizenship wherever it may hide or freely live. Instead of fighting what is currently and greatly damaging, not only as a moral (and invincible) phenomenon but as an extremely coercive force, they give themselves over to the trouble of launching rambling rhetorical speeches against a deep trench of intangible emotions. Wanting to impose on the foreign-born the absolute renunciation of his homeland for the new land in which he lives is a crime against nature. It is as if one would demand that every foreigner speak English—by law—better than the language or dialect that he learned from his mother.

Arriving at the particular case of Italy and Italians, our hosts and their heralds (either in good faith or in service) should not be alarmed. The natural, immutable human condition that renders Italian-Americans fond of and loyal to Italy on the one hand, and grateful and devoted to America on the other, is not harmful to their immediate interests and does not conceal the terrifying danger of things to come. The children of these Italian-Americans, due to the same inviolable law of nature, will either be more American than their parents or American through and through; with their grandchildren, the transformation will be decisively complete. Why the desire to fabricate people by machine, with inhuman laws of "yes" and "no" that, being absolutes, have no real value in our brief, relative, and ever uncertain and dubious existence? One would ask foreign residents for what they can give, not what runs contrary to certain incomprehensible yet vital impulses of their souls. One cries out against those who become American citizens out of utility and even louder against the others who, having full and solid experience of this fact, dare to frankly assert and recommend it. And what about those who believe in the lofty ideals of the eighteenth century revolution, that the semi-literate or generally uneducated foreigner who lands on these shore can and does realize, in five years of bitter struggle for life, from the wonders of American democratic institutions, that those famous and noble principles are denied and trampled upon in practice every day? If those ideals, rather than bloody and ruthless selfishness in all of its ferocious expression, were the regulators of everyday life, the foreigner would quickly notice it and would be, quite differently, willing to love and perhaps favor this country. But it is not so; everyone finds the same brutal life here that he left on the other side, with purely material differences. And due to these material differences, he seeks and accepts American citizenship. In order to create willing citizens . . . it is necessary for a nation to HAVE, not to boast or pretend to have, an imposing and tangible civic superiority. And this is not the case, despite certain ostentatious appearances and many arbitrary statements by the United States, where public awareness, in general, is in a state of inferiority compared to that of more developed European nations.

The Italians of America are Italian-Americans and so shall they remain. They cannot dissolve their bonds of affection for their homeland regardless of how many naturalization cards they acquire or how many oaths they take. They can, however, be equally obedient, devoted, and productive citizens of the United States, in all instances except for an absolute difference or a conflict between Italy and this country. For in such a case, the best they would be inclined to do, we believe, would be, through an effort of will and discipline, to remain peaceful and neutral. But since no future hypothesis suggests such a possibility between these two nations that are on the same side in the fight for a better social and civil order, it seems pedantic, fussy, unfair, and intrusive to deign to consider a similar case. Let the "Italianists" who defend the deserters and the "Americanists" who hatch Washingtonian ideals in order to make a dollar therefore rest assured: our emigrants—naturalized or not—are not and cannot be anything other than "hyphenated" Italian-Americans. Instead of trying to induce them to become one or the other (a futile and vain undertaking), would that they try—with both intellect and love—to improve them by fostering, toward both Americanism and Italianism, the sentiments of moral integrity, decorum, human sympathy, in a word, "gentlemanliness" that, common to all races and nationalities, are crucial elements for the "true and lasting glory" of all great peoples.

Translated by Giulia Prestia

Public Service Is My Motto

~ *Al Capone*

Naples, Italy, January 17, 1899–Miami, Florida, January 25, 1947

No—he was born here (handwritten margin note)

Prob. 1920 (handwritten margin note)

The son of immigrant parents who came to Brooklyn, New York, when he was a baby, Alphonse Capone is the most famous gangster in American history. From childhood, he was in the ranks of organized crime, in Brooklyn and at the "Five Points" in Lower Manhattan, profiting in the field while he was working as a barman for the criminal Frankie Yale. Bearing a disfigurement on his face, he was nicknamed "Scarface." When the atmosphere in New York became troublesome, Yale sent him to Chicago, where he arrived in 1919, with his Irish wife, whom he had married a year before. In close association with Johnny Torrio, he became the right-hand man leading a racket that controlled prostitution, gambling, and smuggling. When Torrio was constrained to leave Chicago, Capone inherited command of the empire, whose dimensions he succeeded in notably enlarging, thanks even to the support of mayor William "Big Bill" Hale Thompson. After years of complicity, Thompson considered it advisable to rid himself of a partner so compromising who had by now become a national legend. Thus, Capone decided for the second time to change atmosphere (which he discusses in the interview published here), and in 1928, he moved to Palm Island, Florida. From here, he continued to rule his empire smoothly, grounded on an unprecedented violence: the most famous episode is that of February 14, 1929, the so-called St. Valentine's Day Massacre, when four of his hired thugs broke into the liquor storehouse of rival gangster George "Bugs" Moran and killed seven people. The capacity of Capone readily to evade the law was legendary, as was his style, during the hardest times of the Great Depression, when he ostentatiously made known his acts of "beneficence" toward impoverished fellow-citizens, such as opening soup kitchens for the poor and ordering merchants to give clothes and food to the needy at his expense.

It was only in 1931, at the height of his fortunes, that the law succeeded in closing in on him, first for financial evasion and then for violations of Prohibition laws. At the end of an extremely tough judicial battle, in May 1932, Capone was imprisoned in the penitentiaries of Atlanta and of Alcatraz to serve an eleven-year sentence. In prison, Capone manifested signs of syphilitic dementia and was hospitalized. His sentence pardoned, in 1939, he was transferred to the correctional institute of Terminal Island, in California, for one year, then was able to return to his home in Florida.

ESSENTIAL BIBLIOGRAPHY

Bergreen 1994; Kobler 1992; Pasley 1930; Schoenberg 1992.

∾

Al Capone, also known as Al Brown, the chief among Chicago's providers of the forbidden vices—wine, revelry, and games of chance—announced last night from his headquarters at the Metropole Hotel that he is going to leave the city high and dry.

"I'm leaving for St. Petersburg, Florida, tomorrow," Capone said. "Let the worthy citizens of Chicago get their liquor the best they can. I'm sick of the job—it's a thankless one and full of grief. I don't know when I'll get back, if ever. But it won't be until after the holidays, anyway. . . ."

As he gently pursued his muse, Capone rather gently reproached the police who had accused him of being one of the principals of a syndicate which has been reaping profits of $75,000,000 annually in exploiting vice in Chicago.

"I've been spending the best years of my life as a public benefactor," he said. "I've given people the light pleasures, shown them a good time. And all I get is abuse—the existence of a hunted man—I'm called a killer.

"Well, tell the folks I'm going away now. I guess murder will stop. There won't be any more booze. You won't be able to find a crap game, even, let alone a roulette wheel or a faro game. I guess Mike Hughes (Chicago's police chief) won't need his 3000 extra cops, after all.

"Public service is my motto. Ninety-nine per cent of the people in Chicago drink and gamble. I've tried to serve them decent liquor and square games. But I'm not appreciated. It's no use."

Why should he want to go to Florida, land of the rum runners, Capone was asked.

"I've got some property in St. Petersburg I want to sell," he said. "It's warm there, but not too warm.

"Say, the coppers won't have to lay all the gang murders on me now. Maybe they'll find a new hero for the headlines. It would be a shame, wouldn't it, if while I was away they would forget about me and find a new gangland chief?

"I wish all my friends and enemies a Merry Christmas and a Happy New Year. That's all they'll get from me this year. I hope I don't spoil anybody's Christmas by not sticking around. . . .

"My wife and mother hear so much about what a terrible criminal I am, it's getting too much for them, and I'm just sick of it all myself.

"The other day a man came in here and said that he had to have $3000. If I gave it to him, he said, he would make me the beneficiary in a $15,000 insurance policy he'd take out and then kill himself. I had to have him pushed out.

"Today I got a letter from a woman in England. Even over there I'm known as a gorilla. She offered to pay my passage to London if I'd kill some neighbors she's been having a quarrel with.

"The papers have made me out a millionaire, and hardly an hour goes by that somebody doesn't want me to invest in some scheme or stake somebody in business.

"That's what I've got to put up with just because I give the public what the public wants. I never had to send out high-pressure salesmen. Why, I could never meet the demand.

"I violate the prohibition law, sure. Who doesn't? The only difference is I take more chances than the man who drinks a cocktail before dinner and a flock of highballs after it. But he's just as much a violator as I am.

"There's one thing worse than a crook and that's a crooked man in a big political job. A man who pretends he's enforcing the law and is really making dough out of somebody breaking it–a self-respecting hoodlum doesn't have any use for that kind of fellow–he buys them like he'd buy any other article necessary to his trade, but he hates them in his heart."

Pridefully the gangster declared he never was convicted of a crime in his life. He has no "record," as the police put it. "I never stuck up a man in my life," he added. "Neither did any of my agents ever rob or burglarize any homes while they were working for me. They might have pulled plenty of jobs before they came with me or after they left me; but not while they were in my outfit."

Then Capone warmly endorsed Cicero, that village on the southwest of Chicago which has been pictured for years as the cradle of the country's vice. There for a long time Capone and Johnny Torrio, his patron who broke him into the game, made a headquarters from which to direct their vice and booze and gambling traffic.

"Cicero is a city of 75,000 people and the cleanest burg in the USA," declared Capone forcefully. "There's only one gambling house in the whole town, and not a single so-called vice-den."

(Originally in English)

PART II

Colonial Chronicles

Introduction

On September 29, 1880, the first issue of a new daily was published in New York. The founders were Vincenzo Polidori and Carlo Barsotti, a native of Lucca who emigrated to the United States in the early 1870s. After serving (among other things) as "foreman for a number of railroad jobs which employed many Italian workers," Barsotti made his fortune first as a banker and then as a printer and owner of a small chain of cheap boarding houses,[1] which he called hotels but his many detractors would continue to define as brothels. The new newspaper was called *Il Progresso Italo-Americano* and, according to local hagiography handed down in the editorial offices, was conceived as a polemical alternative to Giovanni Francesco Secchi de Casali's old weekly *L'Eco d'Italia*. As a matter of fact, De Casali had not been enthusiastic over Barsotti's reports on the activity of an Italian American committee which had been set up after Pietro Balbo's death sentence (1879). Irritated and surprised that the only Italian newspaper published in New York did not care about the fate of a compatriot sentenced to death, [Barsotti] told the director of the weekly *L'Eco d'Italia*: "The Italians of the Atlantic coast need another newspaper. I'll be its director and it will be a daily."[2]

It seems that at the outset the daily was "run by hand" and consisted of a short account of the trial in Italian, written with a fountain pen and posted at the entrance to Barsotti's "shop" near Mulberry Street. People would gather around the

1. Rossi 1892, 175–176. On Barsotti, see also DBI and DAB. Polidori was an associate of Barsotti for only the first years of the operation. Before long, the two were embroiled in bitter litigation against each other. In 1887, Polidori would give life to a new paper, the *Cristoforo Colombo*, and, according to Gaja (1919, 83), also *Araldo Italiano* (Italian Herald).

2. Rossi 1892, 176. See also Gerbi 1962, 20.

posted sheet, so many that Barsotti decided to multiply the copies, still handwritten, and sell them.[3] The early days of the printed version of *Il Progresso* were recounted with plenty of additional picturesque details by Adolfo Rossi, who by chance and without any previous experience became one of the very first editors-in-chief: "Only in the New World do such things happen. . . . Today one makes eyeglasses, tomorrow he wears the iceman's apron or that of the omnibus driver, and the day after tomorrow he writes the entire issue of a newspaper."[4] The newspaper was "very small": "Two entire pages are reserved for advertisements. Two more remain. The second is filled with news from Italy and various events from the newspapers there. On the first page we translate from English the latest transatlantic dispatches, write a small editorial, and sum up the American news."[5] It might happen that in the absence of the latest Italian newspapers they would recycle news that had been published months before, stealing it from the paper used to wrap a few shirts in a trunk. It was enough to change the date, and one could find there "plenty of thefts, suicides, and armed robberies."[6]

Rossi took on the burden of editor-in-chief on December 6, 1880. On December 23, after a one-day interruption, the daily came out with a new format, a new masthead, and a new title, *Il Progresso Italo-Americano*,[7] which it kept until 1988, when *America Oggi* picked up its legacy. In 1880, the Italian colony of New York was made up of 25,000 people, in great part illiterate; however, the newspaper's adventure was justified by finding "a strong resource in the advertisements." Indeed, due exactly to the increased amount of advertisement, it became necessary to enlarge the format.[8]

There were still evident problems with the editing and the printing of the newspaper: a skeleton staff, printers who did not know Italian and made an endless number of mistakes. But Rossi proved more than capable. He wrote a series of articles in defense of the unacknowledged inventor of the telephone, the Italian Antonio Meucci, who at the time lived in poverty in Clifton, Staten Island, in the small house that had hosted Giuseppe Garibaldi thirty years earlier. On this occasion, even the American newspapers took notice of *Il Progresso* and repeated the salient points of Meucci's case against Edison and Company. Vanderbilt himself, the famous tycoon, took an interest in the case.[9]

3. Barbieri 1967, 232.
4. Rossi 1892, 179.
5. Ibid., 178.
6. Ibid., 184–185.
7. Gerbi 1962, 40.
8. Rossi 1892, 187.
9. Ibid., 193.

It was the beginning of a prosperous period. There were further enlargements of the format, the number of pages increased to twelve, and new editors and contributors were hired. To block his rival's success, Secchi de Casali, in March 1881, turned *L'Eco d'Italia* into a daily, but soon he was forced to return to his original weekly schedule of publication.[10] In 1887, another daily, *Cristoforo Colombo*, was founded. But after a decade of troubles, it was taken over by Barsotti himself. Initially, the fate of the *Araldo Italiano*, a daily launched by the lawyer Giovanni Vicario in 1894, seemed to be more propitious—so much so that in 1899 it was joined by an evening edition, cosponsored with *Il Telegrafo*, a newspaper founded in 1893. (Under the direction of Ercole Cantelmo during the Spanish American War, the hallmark of *Il Telegrafo* was to "scream" the main titles in red.) But the *Araldo*'s success did not last long. The two newspapers were then absorbed by another daily, *Il Giornale Italiano,* born in 1909 thanks to initiatives of the textile entrepreneur Celestino Piva and of Michele Grella. Directed by Cantelmo, it lasted until 1919.[11] Notwithstanding several challenges to its leadership, *Il Progresso* continued to dominate the New York market. Eventually, in 1931 it took over the *Bollettino della Sera*, an afternoon daily founded as a weekly by F. L. Frugone in 1898. In its early years this paper had a masthead slogan that read *"Bollettino della guerra ispano-americana."* Even this modest acknowledgment within an immigrant community can contribute to gauge the extent to which 1898 actually marked the entrance of the United States into a new epoch, the age of imperialism. Only later was the *Bollettino* turned into a daily.[12] Most important, in 1931 *Il Progresso*—as we will see—bought up the very ambitious *Corriere d'America*, a daily founded in 1922 by one of the major figures of Italian journalism, Luigi Barzini. It continued to come out as a separate paper until 1943.

In 1896, on the occasion of the Abyssinian "adventure," *Il Progresso* had its own special correspondent,[13] but its fortunes were mostly linked to reporting criminal news in the Italian community. Barsotti continued his editorial defense of his compatriots who were sentenced to death. He was active in catalyzing the immigrants' frustrations, whetting their pride, and continuously emphasizing the pres-

10. After having passed to Felice Tocci and his family of bankers upon the death of Secchi, in July 1891, *L'Eco d'Italia* (Echo of Italy) would have a serious disagreement with Barsotti, who accused Francesco Tocci of having swindled Buenos Aires customers before moving to the United States. After ceasing operations in 1894, *L'Eco d'Italia*, was resurrected briefly in 1896 by H. A. Pollak as *Rivista Italo-Americana* (Italian American Review).

11. Barbieri 1967, 236.

12. Ibid., 233.

13. Gerbi 1962, 40.

tige and quality of the best manifestations of Italic genius—always within the framework of his initial inclination to favor populist-socialist tendencies. Typical in this respect was his commitment to the erection of monuments celebrating famous Italians. Other successful initiatives involved assisting the victims of natural disasters.[14] Unsurprisingly an interventionist during World War I—which, like the war in Libya had proved a real bonanza for the Italian American press—*Il Progresso* achieved a record edition of 100,000 copies. For a while Barsotti also launched an evening edition of the paper; this edition in turn, reached 30,000 copies but was suppressed in order to avoid damaging the morning issue.[15] During the war, in 1916, a new daily—rather, an "independent daily"—was also founded in Boston. It was edited for a short period by the former socialist congressman Vincenzo Vacirca (see Part IV). Named *La Notizia*, it was later edited by Graziano Lungarini and became a biweekly after World War II.[16] *La Notizia* attracted a remarkable number of readers with a circulation of 24,000 copies and lasted until 1975. In Philadelphia, in the two years 1905–1906, two dailies were published: *La Sera* and *L'Opinione*. Still other newspapers came out in New Haven (*L'Indipendente*) and even in the small center of Calumet, Michigan, where *Il Minatore Italiano*, a local periodical, was turned into a daily for a few years, starting from 1894.[17]

14. In 1914, a long list of initiatives the newspaper promoted began to appear underneath the headline. For example: "By the initiative of 'Progresso' and its director, the Honorable Carlo Barsotti, we have erected monuments to Garibaldi (1888); Columbus (1892); Verdi (1906); Giovanni da Verrazzano (1908)—collected funds for the victims of the earthquake at Ischia and Casamicciola; for the cholera victims of Palermo; for the injured in Africa; for the victims of the earthquake at Liguria; for the distribution of bread to compatriots during the crisis of 1893; for the Italian Home Hospital; for the victims of the cyclone at Galveston (Texas); for the victims of the 28 December 1908 earthquake at Calabria and Sicily (454,256.93 lire); for the families of the dead and injured in Tripolitania—saved many compatriots from foreign gallows, including Giuseppe Giudici, Domenico Bega, M. Trezza, Chiara Cignarale, Maria Barbera, and Anna Valentini—placed the bronze crown sent by Italian Americans on King Humbert's tomb at the Pantheon—sent a bronze plaque to the mausoleum for President McKinley at Canton (Ohio); and, as an homage to the Italians in America, made so many efforts for the betterment of Italian immigrants and the image of their faraway homeland."

15. Gerbi 1962, 44. On September 2, 1914, under the headline "The Supreme Infamy of Pivo's Rag," *Progresso* ran an editorial attacking *Il Giornale Italiano*, which continued to advise Italy to preserve its neutrality so as not to tarnish its honor. *Progresso* also reproduced and praised an article from the German newspaper *New Yorker Staats Zeitung* entitled "An Abominable Step": "It is readily apparent that no German newspaper could have written anything else with as much pride." More research is needed on the rapport between the Italian and German colonies across their respective presses during World War I.

16. Barbieri 1967, 236.

17. See Russo 1972, 504–505.

The years straddling the two centuries—in parallel with the dramatic growth of Italian immigration—thus saw this great, indeed stunning, emergence of "colonial" newspapers: "Even if we take into account the great number of Italian communities . . . the quantity of Italian papers published is on average exceptionally large and superior to that of any other Italian colony elsewhere in the world, even those more prosperous than the American ones."[18] In 1909 there were eleven dailies, eighty-nine weeklies, six periodicals "which come out twice or three times a month," fourteen monthlies, and fifteen more sporadic papers. "As a whole, 135 periodicals were being published (or presumably so) by the end of 1907: let's imagine the number that would result by adding up all those which were born and died before, and how difficult, if not impossible, it would be to trace their history even approximately."[19]

Thus, while *Il Progresso Italo-Americano* became an established newspaper in New York, on the other side of the continent in San Francisco, in 1886, another daily, *L'Italia*, made its appearance. It lasted until 1965. It became the property of J. F. Fugazi, the owner of a railway and shipping agency.[20] In the summer of 1887, *L'Italia* embraced the heritage of Federico Biesta's old, moderate sheet *L'Eco della Patria*, founded in 1859. It represented the fusion of two earlier weeklies, and its purpose was to compete for the readership of the thick-skinned Republican newspaper *La Voce del Popolo*. Even after Carlo Dondero's lengthy stint from 1871 until the early 1930s, *La Voce* was able to find skilled journalists, in particular the equally long-lived Cesare Crespi.[21] When it came to promoting itself, *La Voce* would declare that it was a paper that "does not confuse the Fatherland with the cliques that impose themselves on it."[22] Only in 1944 did the paper actually merge with *L'Italia*.[23] After the initial directorship of Biesta, who died in 1894, and Pio

18. Fumagalli 1909, 129.

19. Ibid., 130.

20. See Loverci 1979, 545n.

21. Before dying in San Francisco on November 26, 1948, at the age of ninety-one, Crespi was an authoritative representative of the Californian radical anarchist left. Author of *Per la Patria* (For the Country), the book of revelations of Carlo Camillo Di Rudio, he also wrote sketches and stories (for example, "Fantasia di Natale" [Christmas Fantasy]) in *La Voce del Popolo* (The Voice of the People, December 25, 1915) and in 1900 gave life, with Enrico Travaglio and then Giuseppe Ciancabilla (see Part IV), to the anarchist review *La Protesta Umana* (Human Protest). Among the other newspapers he founded or oversaw, *Era Democratica* (The Democratic Age) in 1918 attacked the "reactionary insanity" of the Chicago Mooney trials. His pieces would be printed in various Italian American newspapers. In particular, in the last phase of his life, he collaborated on a series for the socialist newspaper *La Parola del Popolo* (The Word of the People).

22. *La Voce del Popolo*, subscription campaign notice, January 10, 1916.

23. See Russo 1972, 498n.

Morbio, *L'Italia* was edited by Ettore Patrizi, an engineer who acted as its soul until his death in 1945. Patrizi used to recount that he had been introduced to journalism by Dario Papa, director of the Milan-based *L'Italia del Popolo*, who supposedly had sent him to the first performance of *Falstaff* at La Scala to write up his impressions of it. Afterward, he collaborated with Teodoro Moneta (who later won the Nobel Prize for Peace in 1907) at *Il Secolo* and won a reputation for his work in various humanitarian associations. During the Chicago World's Columbian Exposition of 1893, Patrizi was assigned to represent various Milanese industries and was appointed a correspondent for the paper *Lombardia*. Thanks to letters of recommendation from Papa and Moneta, he was able to meet Luigi Roversi at *Il Progresso* and Alfredo Barbieri at the other daily, *Cristoforo Colombo*. Under Patrizi's dynamic management, *L'Italia* was initially run like an American paper. Leaving Italian politics aside, the paper focused on life in California and documented the astounding economic growth of the state. It also followed the struggle among monopolies to control the state's resources. Owing to an inevitable Irredentist infatuation, *L'Italia* hosted Arnaldo Fraccaroli and Luigi Barzini's reports from the front, while Patrizi himself crossed the ocean and visited the conquered Gorizia, sending dispatches from there.[24] In the 1920s and 1930s, Patrizi's directorship was characterized by his all-too-eager support of Fascism. The engineer did manage to create an elegant and gentlemanly style of his own which sprang from his belonging to a social class whose worldliness was well above the Italian American average. The scholar Giovanni E. Schiavo has defined him as "the west coast exponent of the best that Italian immigrants had to offer, whether to Italy or America."[25]

Patrizi's *L'Italia* was a good example of the new Italian capitalism in California, which had its major exponent in the resourceful banker Amadeo Giannini and

24. On July 4, 1916, the newspaper came out with an ingenious first page, with two lions of Venice coupled with portraits of Garibaldi and Washington accompanying the grand title: "The Italians, thirsty for liberty and justice, also commemorate the Fourth of July. Also, our immortal hero Giuseppe Garibaldi, the lion of Italy, was born on this sacred day of American independence on which George Washington, the lion of America, played the greatest part." Patrizi's editorial was entitled "Americani ed Italiani uniti nei più alti ideali" (Americans and Italians United in the Highest Ideals). Among the patriotic material published during the war years was a short story by Nerina Patrizi, "L'adolescente volontario" (The Young Volunteer, July 16, 1916). However, Patrizi was not completely immune from literary temptations: see the old-fashioned story "Muori ammazzato!" (May You Die a Violent Death), published in 1896 in Milan's *Farfalla* (Butterfly).

25. Schiavo 1958, 272. Information on Patrizi, generally confused and contradictory, can be found also in Gerbi 1962, 79–103, and in Barbieri 1967, 233–234.

experienced its "heroic moment" in 1906, with the devastating San Francisco earthquake. In fact, the newspaper's new offices had been destroyed by the quake—a circumstance that forms the subject of the interesting poem of its distinguished contributor, Fanny Vanzi-Mussini—but it was able to pull itself together quickly and reengage with its readers as "a sheet of four small pages" included in the Alameda newspaper *The Encinal*. This heroic edition of *L'Italia* won the warmest congratulations from Edmondo Mayor des Planches, the Italian ambassador in Washington, D.C.: "I received that precious relic. . . . It deserves a place in an Italic museum with a section devoted to the valor of our people."[26]

Statistics from the year 1907 mentioned above give some indication—to be taken with extreme caution—on the sales of the main Italian papers of the day. Patrizi's *L'Italia* ran off "not more than 2,250 copies a day," like *Il Progresso* and *La Voce del Popolo*, a Philadelphia daily founded in 1893. *L'Araldo Italiano* had an even stronger circulation of 4,000 copies. The data for the two other dailies, *L'Opinione* of Philadelphia (founded by C.A. Baldi in 1905) and the *Bollettino della Sera*, are missing. Evidently, other periodicals had a wider circulation: 7,500 copies for the weekly *Vesuvio* of Philadelphia, which bears the improbable title of "the oldest and most influential paper in Pennsylvania" and was founded by F. J. Scannapieco in 1886; the Chicago-based *L'Italia*, founded by Oscar Durante in 1886, had a circulation of 30,846.[27]

Many other periodicals were born around the late 1880s and early 1900s. Without taking into account the political and syndicalist sheets, which will be discussed in Part Four, one should mention the following: *L'Unione* (Pittsburgh, 1890); *Il Corriere del Connecticut* (New Haven, 1893); *La Gazzetta del Massachusetts* (founded by J. M. Gubitosi in Boston, 1896, and edited by James Donnaruma beginning in 1904); *L'Unione* (founded by H. Chiariglione in Pueblo, Colorado, in 1897); *Il Pensiero* (founded by Luigi Carnovale in St. Louis in 1904); *Il Risveglio* (founded by Frank P. Mancini at the young age of sixteen, in Denver in 1906);[28] *Il Cittadino* (New York, 1907, directed by Alberto Tarchiani); *L'Italo-Americano* (Los Angeles, 1908); *La Tribuna* (founded by Vincenzo Giuliano in Detroit, 1909). Another weekly deserves special attention: *La Follia di New York*, which lasted until 1996

26. Gerbi 1962, 88–90. On Mayor des Planches, author of the interesting *Attraverso gli Stati Uniti. Per l'emigrazione italiana* (Across the United States: On Italian Immigration, 1911), and on his participation in the immigration debate, see Franzina 1995, 186–214.

27. As given by *Rowell's American Newspaper Directory*, 1907, reported by Fumagalli 1909, 133–134. By 1898, *L'Italia* of Chicago boasted a circulation of 20,000, undoubtedly "larger than any other Italian newspaper in the United States."

28. See Schiavo 1958, 273.

and was established in 1893 by Marziale Sisca and his brother Alessandro. The latter, using the pseudonym of Riccardo Cordiferro (see Part III), was a precocious poet who from the age of seventeen was destined to become a leading protagonist of the theatrical and literary scene in Little Italy. *La Follia*, perhaps the most popular and certainly one of the most discerning and conscientious of the Italian periodicals, took its name from a Neapolitan satirical newspaper of the second half of the nineteenth century. From the outset it distinguished itself as a paper concerned not only with social and political themes (such as the indictment of the fake doctors who exercised their profession in the colony or the bankers who enriched themselves by swindling immigrants), but also, more consistently, with cultural issues. Thanks to the Sisca family's Italian connections, *La Follia* was able to rely on the prestigious collaboration of many famous writers, from Salvatore Di Giacomo to Ferdinando Russo, Nicola Misasi, Carolina Invernizio, Matilda Serao, Neera, Trilussa, Roberto Bracco, and Mario Rapisardi. Moreover, it availed itself of the support and contributions of real stars whose popularity in America was enormous: from Enrico Caruso, who drew his amusing caricatures for the paper (gathered into a volume by Marziale Sisca in 1908), to Tito Schipa and Beniamino Gigli. Nor should one forget that also the signatures of a very young Frank Capra and Rodolfo Valentino appeared in its pages.

Josef Velikonja has recorded 1,804 newspapers up to 1980, fourteen of which were founded before 1880, forty-two date back to the period 1881–1900, and ninety-eight to the period 1901–1915. Pietro Russo goes so far as to calculate 2,344 newspapers, and one should notice that up to 1915 Italian newspapers were established in as many as thirty-five states of the Union.[29] The great number of papers reveals how members of the early business and political elite felt the need to use the press to acquire a further means to consolidate their position within the colony in order to continue to act as its privileged mediators—and hopefully to influence local elections. On another level, the colonial newspaper became the natural training ground for a legion of aspiring journalists and writers. At this early stage there was no Italian American novelist, poet, or playwright who failed to contribute more or less regularly to some "colonial" newspaper, unless he was in fact its founder or director: a circumstance which, given the extreme high rate at which newspapers sprang into and out of existence on the publishing scene, was even more common. We need only page through some of the countless Italian American *Who's Who* collections, printed over the years, to demonstrate that frequently

29. See Velikonja 1983, 38, and Russo 1972.

the biography of practically any significant personage records at least one stint with the newspapers.[30]

As a matter of fact, the "colonial journalist" became a real type, a characteristic figure in the Italian American world. The newspaper became the ideal place for people on the make to try out their often grandiose ambitions, resorting to furious polemics, insults, insinuations, and attacks often at the edge of legality.

> "Vulgar man, misshapen scrivener, newspaper obsessed with common crimes, and empty brain-pan"—these give but a pale idea of the vituperative vocabulary used daily in the colonial editorial offices. One wonders how many casualties are picked up every day from the thresholds of the editorial rooms. The whole staff and all the editors might be continually engaged in fighting a duel or seconding their colleagues; every paper might hire at least one surgeon. No longer: the duel is a barbaric institution, and this is civil journalism.[31]

This extreme form of contentiousness is a rather typical trait of Italian American journalism. If on one hand it can be seen as an abuse of the sudden, great freedom of expression available in a country like the United States, on the other hand, we should always bear in mind that very often both directors and publishers used their newspapers as weapons to establish or defend interests of another stamp. They were *banchisti* (bankers), travel and commercial agents, labor middlemen, and various kinds of entrepreneurs, people who among other things started assuming roles linked to public administration, exactly like their rivals who tried to dethrone them in turn.

When Oscar Durante, director and owner of the Chicago-based *Italia Giornale del Popolo,* handed on the directorship of the paper to Giuseppe Gaja in 1893, he wrote a farewell editorial in which he reminisced with gusto about all the quarrels of the past eight years, and begged his readers pardon for the vehemence with

---

30. Among yearbooks and guides, *Who's Who* is effectively the most numerous and widespread and has changed into a characteristic instrument of the American market in every state. Among the most active compilers of these publications are also authors of works of greater literary or scientific engagement, such as storyteller and poet Lisi Cecilia Cipriani, dramatist Ario Flamma, and historian Giovanni Ermenegildo Schiavo. Among the most prolific publishers is Antonio Frangini, who at the beginning of the century published dozens of newspapers dedicated to various geographic endeavors. Another specialist of the genre was Cleto Baroni of California.

31. See Amy Allemand Bernardy 1913, 119. On Bernardy, a prolific author of travel narratives and an accurate observer of Italian colonies abroad, see Tirabassi 2005.

which "the reputation of the colony" had often been attacked. One point was particularly telling. Durante mentions how he was obliged to interrupt his habitual cordiality when "on the occasion of the first issue of the rival newspaper, these actual words were made part of the agenda: 'We publish *L'America* because so far there has been no honest Italian newspaper in Chicago.'"

Thus, personal matters and grudges came into play besides the rule of free competition. In this case, Durante considered himself discredited by Ginocchio, Olcese, Puccini and d'Auria, from whom he sought $50,000 damages. The cause was a series of articles that appeared in *L'America* concerning the ugly story of how his reconfirmation as an officer for compulsory education in the Chicago schools had been blocked. On the eve of the expiration of his term of office, in fact, a meeting of the representatives of the Italian Society had been convoked in order to draw up a petition asking the directors of the public schools to appoint a more competent person. The Board of Education, according to Durante, had replied sarcastically: "If you do not agree, that is okay. It means we will appoint a Turk."[32]

This reply displays yet another important aspect of the Italian American press: the ambition to establish a benchmark, a link to, and a bulwark of *italianità*. In the first phase of mass immigration, this kind of ambition coincided with the elites' need to control as large a number of newcomers as possible, those who did not need to integrate in the broader American scene. Moreover, almost all of them planned on returning to Italy as soon as they could. Defense of *italianità* and focus on one's own private interests: such was the recipe making up the attitude proverbially defined as "Barsottism," especially by the left.

32. See *L'Italia. Giornale del Popolo* (Italy: The People's Journal), September 30, 1893. On this same day appeared the cited editorial by Durante entitled "Dichiarazione" (Declaration). This controversy lasted a long time and was rekindled by Gaja when, in the November 18, 1893, issue, announcing his resignation owing to health problems caused by Chicago's cold winds, he wrote a stinging critique of Luigi D'Auria, a journalist in the pay of the "prominent" Ronga, accusing him of being a "vile plagiarist," an "imbecile," a "talking animal," and so on. The Turinese Gaja (or Gaya, as he calls himself in his *Ricordi d'un giornalista errante/Memories of a Wandering Journalist*) was especially active in Brazil, Argentina, and other South American countries. He also wrote poetry (*Sacrilegi poetici/Poetic Sacrileges*). Highly typical of Italian colonial journalists—scatterbrained, unprejudiced, and anything but rigorous (for example, "Who for one reason or another has not been jailed in this brilliant and free America?" is the terse comment in the margin on his arrest in Montevideo in 1891; Gaja 1919, 33)—he traveled extensively in the United States, visiting San Francisco the day after the great earthquake. Of his experiences in Chicago, titled "Porcopoli" (Pig City) and written for the purpose of covering the famous problems with the meat industry, he reported chiefly on the attempt to save from the gallows two Lucca fruit vendors accused by an Irish person of murder.

Various newspapers also fought over questions of principle, even if these were hardly relevant, by comparing their respective merits on the grounds of *italianità*. As we have already pointed out, a source of pride for Barsotti's *Il Progresso* was the promoting of the construction of a monument to Giovanni da Verrazzano. Well, in 1909 Cordiferro's *La Follia* contested the newspaper's merits, using one of the Neapolitan character sketches (*Macchiette napoletane*) that its director signed with the pseudonym of "Sandro." It claimed the paternity of the original idea in such an amusing way that we cannot resist reproducing part of that bravura performance, entitled "Verrazzano, Garibaldi and the Fourth of July":[33]

> The other day Filiciello the barber came to my house with *Il Progresso* in his hand, and he was so angry it seemed that something had happened to him . . . This paper, Filiciello said, this paper is worse than an open sewer. A paper like this could only be printed in America where thieves speak of honesty and gentlemen—if there are any—stand with two feet in a shoe, to avoid the danger of being either beaten up or locked up like criminals. Suffice it say that the owner of this paper is one who thirteen years ago was a banker. And he ran away after stripping the poor people of thousands and thousands of dollars (*pezze*). Now he's back in New York and once again is having his way. He directs a newspaper where he sets down the law for everybody. . . .

The fact is, "Filiciello" had read an article in *Il Progresso* about the proposed statue to Verrazzano, and the "five-thousand *pezze*"—the $5,000—that were needed to erect it.

> Feliciello, Master Rafae' (Raphael), Feliciello was right . . . With Barsotti there's not a moment of rest . . . Now for one reason and now for another . . . that's all he does is look for people's money . . . With the excuse of the statue Barsotti is always bothering the person next to him. . . .

In the course of this facetious conversation, it is also noted that the story of Verrazzano and his having beat out "Hudsonno" (Hudson) was stolen from *La Follia*. Barsotti, he and his lackey Agostino De Biasi, had stolen it, "that big crab, that lobster (Aragustino/Agostino), and to me he seems a real lobster. If Barsotti is a knave, then Don Lobster is a soul in hell, because no living person like him could

---

33. *La Follia di New York* (New York Folly) 17, no. 27 (July 4, 1909).

sit at the top of the world." In the same stroke Cordiferro also criticized Agostino De Biasi, since 1901 the editor-in-chief of *Il Progresso*, the future founder of the review *Il Carroccio*, and one of the most important Fascist journalists in America.[34] Moreover, Cordiferro's newspaper always dealt with De Biasi in the harshest possible terms. In an earlier issue it had even celebrated the latter's demise "as a man and as a journalist" after the New York section of the Dante Alighieri Society—then directed by De Biasi—was suspended. De Biasi was defined "as an open sore for our colony" and was renamed "Don Aragostino De' Plagi."[35] The charges leveled against Barsotti were even more malevolent, although they were already common knowledge. "Filiciello" was right: thirteen years earlier (in 1897) Barsotti had in fact declared bankruptcy, and in his fall the savings of many of his fellow countrymen were swept away with him. In addition, in 1901 Barsotti went through another difficult moment exactly when the inauguration of the monument to Dante Alighieri, fruit of the subscription drive launched by *Il Progresso* for that purpose, was to take place. Giovanni Preziosi harshly criticized the way the subscription was set up; this led to a defamation trial that was held in Rome and ended on December 21, 1912, with Preziosi's acquittal.[36]

According to Alberto Pecorini, who directed the newspaper *Il Cittadino*, there was no other community of half a million civilized people in the world with a press that was worse than that of the Italians in New York. All the efforts of this press were aimed at keeping the Italian community ignorant of the laws, the history, and the many opportunities of the host country. Its aim was to foster a colony

34. See the pamphlet *Il Progresso e la missione del giornale fra gli emigrant oltre oceano, per la mostra del lavoro degl'Italiani all'Estero in occasione dell'Esposizione Internazionale di Torino per Cinquantenario dell'Unità Nazionale* (Il Progresso and the Newspaper's Mission for Immigrants across the Ocean, for the Display of the Work of Italians Abroad on the Occasion of the International Exposition of Turin for the Semicentennial Celebration of National Unity, 1911).

35. "Come il tempo è galantuomo!" (How Time Acts the Gentleman), a news item in the column "Cose e . . . cosi" (Things and How) in *La Follia di New York*, June 27, 1909.

36. See DBI (H. R. Marraro). Preziosi, already a follower of Salvemini, in 1909 had published *Gli italiani negli Stati Uniti dell'America del Nord* (The Italians of the United States) and in 1913 would found *La Vita Italiana* (Italian Life), a review of foreign immigration and politics. An echo of Barsotti's judicial transfer is also in Valenti 1924, 300: "In the first days of September 15, Carlo Barsotti returned to New York from Italy. His *Il Progresso Italo-Americano* [*Italian American Progress*], a newspaper that, during three years from 1913 through 1915, and during World War I, during the absence of the director—busy in Italy during the contractual phases of a trial involving moral and civil claims—grew to an unexpected circulation, the gloomy figure of one million, Barsotti's fortune. I say gloomy figure because the ignorant, old millionaire is the saddest, most unhappy man in the world."

completely separated from the American society and make it so that the Italian masses would remain captive to the criminal organizations that exploited them in every way possible. Pecorini was eager to encourage integration as promoted by the Protestants and in 1910 had founded the Italian-American Civic League, which had little success and a short life. On the other hand, *Il Progresso* had attacked the League from the very beginning and accused its founder of having delivered himself into the hands of "four American good-for-nothings" and of thereby having discredited the image of the Italians in New York.[37]

This discrediting activity was a bared nerve: almost all of the newspapers proclaimed the primacy of Italic civilization in reaction to the disdain and underestimation accorded to it by the Americans. They were also uneasy and baffled concerning the misunderstandings, if not scorn, such attitudes provoked in Italy. Already in 1891, for example, *Il Progresso* had engaged in a quarrel with Napoleone Colajanni: "Concerning an Undeserved Insult to the Italian Military Society of New York." In *L'Isola* of Palermo Colajanni had criticized the Italian Americans' picturesque propensity for full-dress parades. On one occasion he had written that "the masquerade that the Italian street cleaners and shoe-shine boys offer on July 4 in New York, dressing up as officers and soldiers of all the different corps of the Italian army and farcically passing them in review, leaves the Yankees splitting with laughter. All this is not only irreverent but humiliating."

Il Progresso replied that they were not "masquerades" but "dignified and serious displays of *Italianità*":

This scornful attitude, this stigma of inferiority, and this sort of "diminutio capitis" which you inflict on New York Italian immigrants is simply an offense to equity, humanity, and justice. There are thousands and thousands of immigrants from the various regions of the "bel paese" who arrive penniless, starved, in rags, ignorant, and practically with nothing but their animal instincts. America then transforms them into productive workers eager to stand up and educate themselves and expressing their interest in the affairs

37. These opinions of Pecorini figure in an article by Frank Marshall White, "The Black Hand in Control in Italian New York," in *The Outlook*, 104, August 16, 1913, as partially reported by LaGumina 1973, 98–108. The judgment of Pecorini on the Italian press is largely shared by intellectual circles, according to whom it was almost a commonplace to equate "journalist" with "con artist" or worse. Indeed, it is useful to remember the most staid opinion of anarchist leader Armando Borghi, when recalling that the Italian Americans were for the most part honest and hardworking before the sharks, adventurers, journalists, Camorra, and Mafia came and spoiled the environment (see Borghi 1978, 341).

of their homeland and public life. Moreover, they learn the language, refine their manners, and become mindful men and good American citizens—but without thereby forgetting their dear and distant mother country.[38]

Already at this stage, a gap appears that in successive decades will become more visible.

Even though they availed themselves of the collaboration of a host of prominent Italian intellectuals, as I have already pointed out when discussing *La Follia*, the papers—which generally had a short lifespan—were written in a rather poor Italian. Indeed, the quality of the language not only did not improve over time but even worsened as the borders were being closed.[39] As a result, the Italian colonies began to crystalize.[40] The papers were quite sloppy, graphically modest, and hopelessly rhetorical. Nevertheless, they reflected the new reality of an uprooted people—the colony. These people were struggling to find themselves and, most of all, to define themselves according to inevitably new parameters, although these were continuously modeled on the traditions of the mother country. (See Giuseppe Antonio Cadicamo's exemplary poem dedicated to the distinguished visitor Giuseppe Giacosa.) Thus, the heavily negative opinion of the "colonial press" expressed by numberless Italian and Italian American observers ended up involving the colony as a whole. As one of the most active of the Italian American journalists, Luigi Carnovale, had fully understood:

According to the hearsay of ninety-nine percent of our immigrants (both illiterate and literate) and a healthy number of Italians in Italy, this poor intellectual and moral organism—Italian-American journalism—is nothing

---

38. *Il Progresso Italo-Americano* (Italian American Progress), December 10, 1891.

39. A systematic count of these recurrences is needed, and perhaps it would be useful and interesting to tackle this difficult task. Anyway, by way of example, only during the years of World War I do we find on the illustrated supplement of *Il Progresso* the signatures of Guglielmo Ferrero, Guido Podrecca, Ada Negri, Trilussa, and Luigi Barzini, in addition to those named in other parts of this text. Emilio Cecchi's signature appears on Philadelphia's *Opinione*. But the importance of prestigious signatures could also be seen in more peripheral periodicals. For example, Baldo Aquilano's Paterson-Passaic weekly *Il Messaggero* (The Messenger) published Benito Mussolini's war diary in installments.

40. The slim to nonexistent syntactical and grammatical quality of the Italian press is an inevitably common challenge for all Italian travel writers in America. The problem was, moreover, abundantly clear to Italian Americans. In the 1910s, *La Follia di New York* adopted a regular column, "La colonia di Dante" (Dante's Colony) dedicated to the worst rubbish-talkers readers could find.

but an ugly parasitical beast, "a filthy, fraudulent image invading the world with its stink." Everybody feels qualified to aim their darts (luckily, less poisonous than dirty) of backbiting, of the worst kind of slander, of the most ferocious persecution and the most vulgar scorn against it. In short, these darts stand for all that stupid and hateful trash that so fittingly characterizes (I painfully admit) the mass of illiterate immigrants.[41]

In 1921, Carnovale led an incredibly generous promotion to celebrate the sixth centenary of Dante's death.[42] In spite of his modest literary resources, he was a very faithful and lively witness of the sense of frustration that marked those Italian Americans who cared most about civil redemption of the poorest of their fellow countrymen. Carnovale's anticlerical patriotism was modeled after Mazzini's. He would commemorate Giordano Bruno and was a warm admirer of the poem *Hymn to Satan* by Giosuè Carducci. He fought the idea of an Americanization that required a person to give up his Italian citizenship, an idea involving the embracing of values foreign to one's original cultural identity. Consequently, his experience as a journalist included many moments of despondency; like David against Goliath, he did not shrink from attacking the English-language press. Above all, he was taken aback by the fact that his initiatives failed to stir any interest in his potential audience. Thus, the "educated colonial" rejected his newspaper "with the same pale and compassionate smile with which he would reject a madman who told him he had found a safe way to reach the planet Mars." And the "newly rich colonial" did the same—"with a glowering glare and barking like the dog Cerberus, the way he would send off a thief who tried to kill and then strip him."

He continued: butcher, barber, tailor, shoemaker, the "colonial hordes crowding the 'shops' in every American city," all

swollen to the eyes with resentment against their fellow Italians and a pride based only on ignorance and money in the pocket—for nothing they would cut your throat and rip open your belly and smash your head with their skivers and their scissors and their axes. They sneer horribly in your face and tell you, in totally vulgar language, that by now they are *Americanized*.[43]

41. Carnovale 1909, 9–10. Born in Stilo, Calabria, Carnovale arrived in the United States in 1902. See Fant 1927.

42. See Carnovale 1921 and 1924. The first is a pamphlet, a sort of appeal to all Italian Americans urging them to commemorate the greatest poet. The second is an enormous volume (over 700 pages) that contains a long, punctilious account of initiatives undertaken.

43. Carnovale 1909, 10.

As for the "noble pick-and-shovel workers," there is even less to laugh about:

> The vast majority are grand marshals and flagbearers of societies whose only aim is to parade every Sunday around the dusty and smoky streets of America's cities amid the jeers of the foreigners, with images of saints and madonnas that do not even appear in the Catholic calendar. They stare into your face with eyes wide open and glare at you as if they were stunned. They grimace with wonder like Barbary apes, they stutter in strange monosyllables, and they end up making you realize that the paper written in the language of their country for them might as well be a mysterious Egyptian papyrus worth displaying in an archaeological museum.

Imagine what he says about "the few generous members of the business and political elite (*prominenti*)! They subscribe to the colonial newspaper but make sure not to read it, "not even when their publisher friend has stirred up their empty ambitions with half a column of patent lies." And "as soon the postman delivers the paper, they throw it away still not opened among the banana peelings."[44]

Here we touch upon one of the most frequently underscored negative aspects of the "colonial" press: reportage on the piddling events of the colony, especially when the *prominenti* themselves are the subject. Thus, we have

> the dinners of the grocer, the tailor's musical soiree, the pharmacist's supper, the marriage between the much beloved *A* with the charming niece of *B*, the "delightful days" spent by the Director in *G*'s home, the birth of yet another young monkey to our friend *X*—already the happy father of five lovely brats, an amazing brood especially when we consider that the mother is still a provocative beauty. Such is the news of more than one colonial paper, which claims that it only accepts news of general usefulness and public importance from its correspondents.[45]

---

44. Ibid., 11. This lack of interest in buying newspapers is a recurring theme in the Italian press. See, regarding the original initiative taken by *Italia: Giornale del Popolo* (Italy: The People's Journal) of Chicago, which on May 14, 1898, launched a dishonorable "List of Freeloaders" that included the names of "those who after receiving the newspaper for months and years, now refuse to send in their subscription money and have not responded to the many letters we have sent."

45. Bernardy 1913, 121. One may find laments of equal tenor in nearly all the books or travel reports concerned with the Italian American colony. See in particular Cianfarra 1904, 173–174, and Prezzolini 1963.

In any case, it is exactly when they start to describe that other world of convulsive transformations, bitter disappointments, unrecountable personal tragedies, and unthinkable fortunes that the journalists of this marginal press begin to invent a new "colonial" literature. It is a truly new literature, both at the level of its production and, perhaps even more so, at that of its consumption. It would be enough to mention the role played by the colonial press in teaching the community to read and write. By readers, we mean the masses of illiterate or semiliterate immigrants, who only spoke in dialect and who by means of the colonial press encountered the Italian language—or at least what was deemed as such—for the first time in their lives. Perhaps for the first time, they experienced the Italian language without the accompanying subservience they suffered in their ungrateful mother country.[46] We are not speaking here of the journalist-poets or playwrights (who will be discussed separately) to whom the newspapers opened up their pages (especially such periodicals as *La Follia*), so much as the real reporters, the editors in charge of following the many appetizing incidents of the day—especially criminal and judiciary cases—that notoriously mark those years.

We have already mentioned that the immigrant Adolfo Rossi, who still could not have imagined the brilliant diplomatic career awaiting him, was among the first editors of *Il Progresso*: and certainly that experience proved central to the writing of his "American" books. He was a contemporary of Ferdinando Fontana and Dario Papa, already famous journalists and writers in Italy, who went to the new world as a team to write on the current scene. Papa remained for more than a year and was appointed editor-in-chief of *Il Progresso*.

According to Rossi, Papa's American experience was fundamental in changing his way of thinking. In fact, "it took [Papa] several years before he decided to get rid of the scapular of the moderate monarchic order; but it was in those months of intense travel and observation that he began to lose his old beliefs"—so much so that he might have written "an autobiographical study" entitled *How I Became a Federalist Republican*.[47] In point of fact, Papa profited from his American experience above all as a professional. *L'Italia*, the newspaper he founded in 1883, when he returned to Milan, was a highly innovative organ compared to the old models of the nineteenth-century press. Primarily, it was a paper no longer "infested" "by a host of literary men who do not feel equipped to report on the ordinary affairs of

46. On this subject, see the keen observations of Robert Park in his study on the American ethnic press (Park 1922).
47. Rossi 1893, 159–160.

the public and who are always coughing up great ideas but avoid the toil involved in making the paper a vehicle of news rather than an academy."[48]

News, facts, a simple language, and a clean-cut editing of the bombastic rhetoric of the past—this was the new style of journalism advocated by Papa and modeled after the American papers. For their part, Italian American journalists went only halfway in adopting this example. On one hand, they were well aware of the requirements of a daily, especially as far as the theme of labor was concerned. On the other hand, the panegyrics about roaming *italianità* filled entire pages in a flowery and improbable style—moreover, reflecting the style used by the "subversive" newspapers to celebrate the exact opposite of *italianità*, that is to say, working-class internationalism. Another aspect, though, distinguished the Italian American newspapers from their Italian counterparts: their attention to the daily news. Popular newspapers focused especially on the criminal and legal news. They followed the American papers' cult of the news and the scoop. There is more than one point of contact with the contemporary phenomenon of muckraking journalism, which explored the multiethnic mosaic of the big cities and found exactly in the Italian communities an overabundance of material to offer its readers. Under such conditions, there was obviously a shift from journalism to narrative.[49] This is what happened to the best American investigative journalists and also to a few Italian American journalists. One might also say, and it is quite obvious, that Italian American fiction was born alongside the new metropolitan American fiction, which was acutely aware of the phenomenon of mass immigration from so many different parts of the world. In this sense, the emergence of writers in Little Italy coincided with the American writers' "discovery" of a new exported Italy and, at the same

48. Quoted in Castronovo 1970, 111. Editor of the *Corriere della Sera* (Evening Courier) from 1879 to 1881, Desenzano native Dario Papa had undertaken with Ferdinando Fontana, already his partner in the "bohemian stronghold" of Via Maddalena in Milan, when he worked gratis for *Italia Agricola* (Agricultural Italy), the first stop in a career that would bring him to *Sole* (Sun), to *Pungolo* (*The Spur*), and toward the direction of *Arena* of Verona, a trip to the United States in order to learn the secrets of American journalism, having already regarded them as an example of modernity and vivacity. Papa discovered them as one of the first chief editors of *Progresso Italo-Americano* and then, returning to Italy, sought to translate his complete experience into the pages of the daily *L'Italia*, the Milanese newspaper founded in 1883, for which he became editor in April 1884, and that effectively represented an innovation in the panorama of the national press: sensationalistic headlines, creative layouts, and, above all, a pro-republican attitude. See also Bandini Buti 1962, Nasi 1958, 51ff.

49. It is none other than a different elaboration of the traditional journey from orality to literacy so characteristic of the Italian American narrative, in particular the "fact in fiction" schema described by Gardaphé 1987.

time, a traditional Italy. The latter, however, was quite different from the one described so frequently in the travel books of the nineteenth century.

The experience of a writer-journalist like Elisabeth Jones Cavazza is a perfect example of the perspective of such travel books. Not by chance, she had been taught to love Italian language and culture and had married an Italian. Her novels and short stories—but also her essays and articles—were mostly set in Calabria and Sicily and reveal a deep and detailed knowledge of Italian life. This knowledge served as a bridge between America and the new immigrants.[50] Yet it cannot be said that the theme of Italian immigration was confined to the contributions of important journalists such as Jacob Riis and other end-of-the-century authors actively engaged in reformist activities. Indeed, already in the 1870s, characters from Little Italy started to figure in American prose fiction published in some of the country's most important reviews.

The most significant example is that of Caroline Augusta Frost, the daughter of John Frost, a professor of the humanities and author of various erudite works. In 1854 she married Count Merighi, a native like her of Philadelphia who was very likely the descendant of a family from the Marche that played some role in the events of the Risorgimento. A poet and translator, she is mainly remembered for two short stories published in *Harper's Monthly*, "My Little News-Boy" (January 1871) and "The Bread-Crumb Artist" (April 1872). These stories are among the first to feature protagonists drawn from Italian immigrant culture in America. What is striking in Caroline Merighi is a conspicuous dose of worldly elegance indicative of someone who loves Italy, thanks to a knowledge (perhaps as a tourist) of its history and culture. It is precisely characters like hers that help to bridge the privileged Italy of high culture and the disadvantaged Italy of emigration. The protagonist in Merighi's story "The Bread-Crumb Artist," one Luigi Vanessa, who at the age of ten copies Michelangelo's *Pietà* using bread, evinces this continuity.

---

50. Born to a rich family in Portland, Maine, Elisabeth Jones Cavazza studied voice and piano. Trained in journalism by Stanley Pullen, owner-editor of *Portland Press* for which Cavazza worked, she wrote poetry, sketches, reviews, music criticism, and distinguished herself in literary circles with a pseudonymic parody of Swinburne's *Atalanta* called *Algernon in London* that caught the attention of members of the Century Club of New York (among others, Bayard Taylor, E. C. Stedman, R. H. Stoddard, and A. R. Macdonough), who, believing the author to be a man, offered her membership; another parody of Robert Browning also earned the Century Club's praise. Married in 1885 to Modena native Nino Cavazza, she was widowed within just a few weeks. In 1894 she married Pullen. Editor of the Italian section of *Transatlantic* and an editorial staff member of Boston's *Literary World*, she assisted important journals such as *The Atlantic Monthly* of Boston and *The New Peterson* of Philadelphia. For her writings on Italian issues, see the bibliography; see also Durante 2004.

He represents the "spontaneous" artist who serves almost naturally as a conduit for the singular creative consciousness of Italic genius. In the character of Luigi Vanessa, who will be "adopted" by a high-society lady, his artistic genius is wedded to a diamondlike honesty and loyalty to his American benefactors, as if to underline the need to confide in Italians and to invest in their capacity to become exemplary citizens.

Merighi's short story reproduces the same moral paradigm as that incunabulum of Italian American literature, *Il piccolo genovese*, which was published anonymously in 1869 in the New York-based paper *L'Eco d'Italia*. In that first narrative representation, however, the protagonist's success is achieved not in the art world but in that of finance. In this sense the two cases are significantly different. The short story in *L'Eco* is the direct expression of the world of immigration and its social expectations, while Merighi's story reveals a rather subdued and more idealistic position.[51] This position is more or less present also in various other American narratives such as Grace Elizabeth King's popular *Balcony Stories*,[52] Henry Cuyler Bunner's *Urban and Suburban Sketches*,[53] and stories by Robert C. V. Meyers[54] and Arthur Willis Colton.[55]

It is appropriate that we insert in the heart of this little vogue the work of Luigi Donato Ventura, considered the originator of Italian American narrative. Being entirely, or almost so, extraneous to the milieu of the colonial press (but not to that of the Italian press of Italy), Ventura was eager to work for the American press. For this reason, his 1880 short stories—including the small masterpiece *Pep-*

51. About Merighi, designated sometimes as "Mrs. Merighi," we know that she completed a difficult translation job of French popular fiction: between 1882 and 1884, the New York house Munro published six titles by Fortuné Hippolyte Auguste du Boisgobey (1821–1891) and one by Émile Erckmann (1822–1899) that Merighi translated. She was also the author of poems of Italian inspiration (see the bibliography). On this subject, see Durante 2004.

52. In 1893, New Orleans native King (1852–1932) published *Balcony Stories*, one of which was entitled "The Christmas Story of a Little Church" and, featuring a "little Dago girl" protagonist, was published in 1888 by *Harper's New Monthly Magazine*.

53. Bunner (1855–1896), author of stories and plays, is actually remembered above all for *Jersey Street and Jersey Lane: Urban and Suburban Sketches* (1896); a piece entitled "Jersey and Mulberry," which is highly pertinent to the present discussion, was published by *Scribner's Magazine* in 1893.

54. A wholly Italian American atmosphere is created by the *Harper's* story "What the Madre Would Not Have" (1895); it is one of the first examples of the extensive literary use of Italian American speech. Robert Cornelius V. Meyers (1858–?) was an author of farces, plays, and the *Life and Adventures of Lewis Wetzel, the Renowned Virginia Ranger and Scout* (1883).

55. Colton (1868–1943), author of several books, published "The Sons of R. Rand" (1897) in Boston's *New England Magazine*, in which the protagonist is an organ grinder named Pietro.

pino, which vaguely recalls Edmondo De Amici's *Il Cuore*—were written in Italian and then translated into English and French.

Up until the 1890s, the space devoted to serialized novels and stories in the Italian American newspapers remained with few exceptions the exclusive domain of those same Italian or foreign writers (especially French) who were also active in the newspapers of the mother country. The colony grew rapidly and filled up with crowds and stories. It became a world finally capable of expressing a life of its own. As a result, the literature produced by these "foreigners," certainly familiar to the readers but by then fatally distant, was flanked more and more frequently by a new kind of narrative drawn from life and on the spot. This can be demonstrated even by a cursory glance at the lists of the titles available in the "Italian bookstores" that were promoted by almost every newspaper in Little Italy. These lists appeared more and more frequently with the passing of time. Thanks to these bookstores and especially the initiatives of several resourceful publishers (first among them Frugone and Balletto on Park Row), colonial journalism became the almost exclusive force driving Italian American literature.

In the Sunday pages of *L'Eco d'Italia*, by then about to close, a story was published in 1891 that had little in common with the more typical serials of French derivation. It was the novella *Lustrascarpe* by Giacinta Pezzana, a famous actress who was also a writer. The story was not, therefore, a product of the colony, but still a piece set in New York whose main character is a recognizable immigrant type.[56] On the other hand, this same newspaper had already hosted stories written by its editor-in-chief, Edoardo Michelangeli, through whose efforts the anonymous *Il Dramma di Mulberry St* (The Drama of Mulberry Street, included here) was published. This title is strictly related to the auspicious début of Bernardino Ciambelli, who was to become the best-known and most prolific of the colonial novelists.

A journalist who wrote for many papers, Ciambelli is the most representative case of the blend of literature and journalism. He was a reporter par excellence; and was even a witness in the notorious trial of Maria Barbella, the facts of which have many points in common with the complicated plots of his novels. Straddling the two centuries, his novels were the most popular serials of several Italian American newspapers.[57] Ciambelli, it seems, first appeared as a novelist in 1893, the year

56. *L'Eco d'Italia* (Echo of Italy), New York, March 22, 1891. Pezzana (1841–1919) also performed in other countries, especially Uruguay; she wrote *Maruzza* (1893), a Sicilian-themed novel that was reprinted by Sonzogno in 1932. On Pezzana, see Pandolfi 1954, 220–226.

57. On April 26, 1895, Maria Barbella, a young immigrant from Ferrandina, Basilicata, cut the throat of her seducer, bootblack Domenico Cataldo, with whom she cohabited in a miserable

in which he published as many as five serialized novels, the first of which—*I misteri di Mulberry Street* (The Mysteries of Mulberry Street)—can be considered his masterpiece. This title unequivocally marks the simple originality of his literary project. In fact, his aim was to transpose characters and plots from the well-established European tradition of the *feuilleton* onto the Italian American scene, in particular the neighborhood and the street best symbolizing Italian immigration in the United States. The book was an instant hit and was read widely; as a result, the author was immediately obligated to dash off four more bulky novels. One of these was commissioned by *L'Italia* of Chicago, with the title *La Città Nera ovvero I misteri di Chicago* (The Black City or The Mysteries of Chicago), which takes place in the heightened atmosphere of the celebrations linked to the great Columbian Exposition then being held in that rapidly developing young city. Ciambelli was already announcing the imminent translation of his works into English, but this never took place. Instead, he was suddenly overwhelmed by an inordinate amount of work. As a result, he was unable to complete the Chicago novel, which he set aside in May of 1894, at the beginning of the second part. Already a month earlier, however, the author had to skip several installments and felt obliged to excuse himself with the publisher and his readers:

> You are a hundred, a thousand times right, and your readers too. Before Monday you will receive a great deal of copy so that you will be able to announce to your readers that as of Saturday, April 14, regular publication of the serial will begin, and you will be able to publish it in double installments. Lately I have had enough work to kill an ox.[58]

---

tenement house on East Thirteenth Street. The man, despite her insistence, refused to marry her and toward the end greatly insulted her. Condemned to the electric chair for first-degree murder—it would have been the first execution of a woman using this then five-year-old technique—she was incarcerated at Sing Sing as she awaited the appeals process. In the meantime, a vast popular movement grew out of the incident, owing largely to the efforts of influential writer Cora Slocomb, who was married to Count Detalmo Savorgnan di Brazzà. Maria thus had the support of some large American newspapers and was able to count on a valuable and great number of defense attorneys who ably mined the evidence surrounding the crime and brought to light the profound discomfort under which Barbella labored, not to mention her epilepsy. On December 10, 1896, the jury rendered its verdict: not guilty. Many newspapers dedicated ample space to the proceedings, and the Jewish dramatist Moyshe Ha-Levi Ish Hurwitz composed a Yiddish-language tragedy in four acts that went on stage at Thalia Theater four days after the sentence and remained on the playbill until the end of January. The whole affair is brilliantly recounted in Pucci 1993.

58. *L'Italia: Giornale del Popolo*, Chicago, April 7, 1894.

"Enough work to kill an ox": this candid admission fits the man like a glove, an authentic athlete of the pen, whose formidable writing capacity became legendary. He was still a workhorse at the moment of his very death, which occurred in 1931 while he was at his desk at the *Corriere d'America*. Ciambelli had been compelled by circumstances to write at night and, as we have seen, to work at several projects at once. He was only able to write muddled novels filled with events that were protracted over months, if not years, and reached such levels of intrigue as to disconcert and puzzle those who might still be willing to apply themselves to them. On the other hand, we should remember that these novels were read serially, in the newspapers or in periodically published fascicles. Thus, they were read differently than books. The author's skill consisted in building an engrossing world that his readers readily recognized, and then recounting the vicissitudes of characters with whom they could easily identify. And to some extent he was courageous in writing stories that included the denunciation of the many sordid and dubious aspects of colonial life. Even a knowing reader like the anarchist leader Carlo Tresca (see Part IV), a thousand miles distant from Ciambelli's small colonial world, recognized his unique merit.[59] With his extraordinary pulp tableau, Ciambelli provides us with a testimony of that world which is all the more alive and breathing because we experience it from within, sharing its life, expectations, difficulties, and frustrations. Certainly, the literary influences are evident, and they can be best summed up in the venerated name of Eugene Sue, the author of the famous *The Mysteries of Paris* (1842). What was most urgent and "necessary" in Ciambelli's novels is also underscored by the fact that experiences like his can be found not only in so-called "American literature" but also in the literatures of every ethnic group that arrived in America. Ciambelli's novels need only be compared to their important German-American precedents, namely the "mysteries" of Philadelphia, St. Louis,

59. Tresca writes in his *Autobiography* (written starting in the late 1930s and held at the New York Public Library): "A well-known Italian editor wrote two historical novels called: 'The Mystery of Mulberry Street' and 'The Mystery of Bleecker Street' in which he gave a mild picture of the disgusting white slave traffic, the daring acts of brigandage and the blackmailing exploits practiced by professional and unscrupulous characters—assassins camouflaged as newspaper workers. 'The Mystery of Mulberry Street' has disappeared from the market, probably because it relates the ugly story of the Campidoglio Hotel where, on the eve of their departure for their native countries, immigrants were murdered during the night by asphyxiation and their deaths reported to the police as suicides the next day, after the victims had of course been duly robbed of their savings from years of labor" (96–97). [Ed.: See Tresca 2003, where this passage does not appear.]

Cincinnati, and New York (studied perspicaciously by Werner Sollors[60]) in order to appreciate the latter's characteristic thematic and even lexical coherence.

The Mysteries of Mulberry Street and the others that followed—but with an increasingly mannered and repetitive technique—represented more than any other novel or literary testimonial the complex reality of the early colonies of New York. From within, we noted, but we could add, without sealing itself off. On the contrary, Ciambelli connected the colony directly to the greater America that surrounded it. By means of countless and bold incursions into the American scene, *The Mysteries* revealed its most spectacular aspects: from the minute description of a criminal's execution in the electric chair and the working routine of the New York fire department to the already pervasive and increasingly relentless advance of technology and the modern in all its forms (electricity, the vast construction sites of the subway, and so on). The novel also investigated the details of everyday life, such as women's emancipation, amusement parks, domestic customs, and shops. This is why *The Mysteries* might have been construed as a useful introduction to American life, not only for the new immigrants but also for Italians on the other side of the ocean. Instead, his novels never served as guidebooks, even if we know that the author and his publishers would have ardently desired it.

Already in the first *Mysteries*, but more noticeably in the later ones, Ciambelli's adherence to the real, to the exact topography of the Italian neighborhood, was increasingly enriched by the addition of real characters from the community who acted out their amusing cameo appearances within his marvelous fictions. This technique was taken from his experience as a journalist and became a constant in *The Mysteries of Bleecker Street* (*I misteri di Bleecker Street*) and *The Foundling of Mulberry Street* (*La trovatella di Mulberry Street*). It is perhaps a clear signal of his decision to fall back upon the colonial setting and of his abandonment of any illusions concerning the possibility of being published in Italy—and, perhaps, of being translated into English. As a matter of fact, several later novels by Ciambelli, published in the 1910s, are based on a decidedly and exclusively colonial paradigm. Moreover, they appear to have been constructed according to a well-oiled formula,

---

60. Antonino, *Die Geheimnisse von Philadelphia* (The Mysteries of Philadelphia, 1850); Heinrich Borstein, *Die Geheimnisse von St. Louis* (The Mysteries of St. Louis, 1851); Emil Klauprecht, *Cincinnati, oder, Geheimnisse des Westen* (Cincinnati, or, Mysteries of the West, 1854–55); Rudolf Lexow, *Amerikanische Criminal-Mysterien, oder, Das Leben der Verbrecher in New York* (American Crime Mysteries, or, the Life of the Criminal in New York, published contemporaneously in New York and Stoccarda). See Sollors 1990, 176–184, with particular attention to Klauprecht.

one that relies heavily on narrative motifs and situations already present in the earlier works and here expanded to novelistic breadth.

Both in America and in Italy there are few libraries or archives that conserve even a small fraction of the many materials published in this period. And yet if we read the advertisements in the Italian American newspapers, we get a very clear sense of a rather intense publishing scene. On this basis, we might hypothesize that besides the names cited by the press, there were still other authors engaged in singularly important narrative adventures. We know, for example, the promising title of a huge novel published by Frugone and Balletto perhaps in 1893, *I Borgia americani, ovvero Gli avvelenatori per denaro* (The American Borgias, or Those Who Poison for Money).[61] But we know nothing about its author, even if it is highly tempting to attribute the whole thing to Ciambelli. Furthermore, we know that the publishers did not limit themselves to big centers such as New York, but also distributed their activities to smaller ones. In fact, not only Italian American but Italian popular novels as well were serialized in the newspapers: such as those by "William Galt" (Luigi Natoli from Palermo), which were published in New York by the Italian Book Co. in Mulberry Street, or those by Guido Bassi, published by the American Premium Book Co., Passaic, New Jersey.[62] Indeed, it is often difficult to distinguish between the two text types. Anyhow, the phenomenon remained rather conspicuous up until the 1930s. Around 1922, for example, the anonymous *Donna contro Donna* (Woman against Woman, a "passionate novel of Love and Hate") was published in Cincinnati in at least 113 weekly installments and counting overall more than 2,700 pages. In 1938 an otherwise unknown Guido Bozzacco published, again in Ohio, *La spigolatrice di Sapri* (The Gleaner from Sapri, a "sensational historical novel") of much more modest dimensions.

Menotti Pellegrino, of whom currently we know only his name, specialized in both genres—the "mysteries" and the costume novel. A cloak-and-dagger novel written by Pellegrino and titled *I tre cavalieri di Trinacria* (The Three Knights of Trinacria) came out in New York in 1929. But already in 1903 this author, a timely follower of Ciambelli, had published *I misteri di New York*, which Martino Marazzi has rightly defined as "muddled and totally disconnected."[63] Published a little later (1905) was the much shorter novel *La 'Mano Nera'* by Adolfo Valeri, which was se-

61. From an announcement in *L'Italiano in America*, a popular weekly edited by Anselmo Bigongiari and published by Frugone and Balletto, New York, September 20, 1893.

62. This author in 1910 published, in about a hundred installments, *Sangue Siciliano* (Sicilian Blood), "a great historical novel set in the era of the Bourbonic domination." The same publisher also issued novels on the adventures of Buffalo Bill and Nick Carter.

63. Marazzi 2001, 22.

rialized in the New York *Bollettino della Sera*. Some decades later, Paolo Pallavicini, practically Ciambelli's "natural heir" and also a journalist in New York before moving to California in 1920, wrote plots that were perhaps even more illogical than Ciambelli's. Moreover, Pallavicini displayed an even more simple-minded, optimistic, and softhearted attitude toward the Italian protagonists of his stories and gave his plots a stronger sentimental twist. The context, too, changed. While Ciambelli wrote from the inferno of the Lower East Side, Pallavicini used as his background the more livable spaces of the "model colony" of California. Perhaps for this reason and also because of his "italianissimo" tone, which did not displease the Fascists, his novels were published in Italy as well.

Italo Stanco then took a further step forward. Stanco, whose real name was Ettore Moffa, and who came from Molise, worked as a journalist for *La Follia* from the 1910s and later became news editor of the *Corriere d'America*. He sought to go beyond the popular context dear to Ciambelli and Pallavicini and sought to develop a poetics of critical realism and social denunciation, coupling it with the description of different social settings, lavish interiors, enormously rich, dark ladies, and impossible loves. Perhaps he was drawing upon the unique Italian "white telephone" convention. On the other hand, in the 1920s the Italian American press loved to serialize the bestselling "harmony" novels then in vogue in Italy. Caterina Maria Avella and Dora Colonna, both short-story writers and collaborators of *Il Carroccio*, promptly moved into this promising field. Their handling of sentimental romance found an unexpected imitator in Clara Vacirca, the wife of Vincenzo, one of the most prominent socialist agitators in America (who, as we shall see, was also a novelist). Clara's novel *Cupido fra le Camicie Nere* (Cupid among the Black Shirts) was published in New York and accompanied by a preface from the bard of the proletariat, Arturo Giovannitti. Nevertheless, it has nothing to do with the Italian American scene and can instead be classified as the extravagant product of the political opposition from abroad.[64]

Corrado Altavilla, another journalist at *Il Progresso* and collaborator at *Il Corriere della Sera*, took a different road in the late 1930s. The critic Martino Marazzi has provided a sophisticated reading of Altavilla's *Gente lontana* (People Far

64. In 1922, *Miraggi d'oltre Oceano* (Transatlantic Mirages) was published in Italy; it is a novel by diplomat Paulo G. Brenna (1881–1943), who, among many diplomatic posts in Europe, Asia, and South America, also worked in Seattle. Here, too, the characters are of bourgeois origin and refined and cultured customs, and the book, in addition to providing various descriptions of that environment as well as social digressions, tells a love story with a strong nationalistic component that will be the cause of the protagonist's parting from America. See Franzina 1996, 182–187.

Away), interpreting it as a sort of elegy for the old colonial Little Italy at the moment in which the second generation of Italian American writers had begun to write in English.[65] In this novel the author passes from the mysteries to the mystery and the legal thriller. In this original development, one breathes the tension of the American detective story set in an exemplary story of failed immigration.[66] Italian Americans were in an ideal position to take advantage of this genre, which offered motifs and three-dimensional characters—both "good," like the legendary Joe Petrosino, and "bad," with the increasingly pervasive presence of criminal organizations growing out of the fabulous "Black Hand."[67] The genre's interesting possibilities had already been tested by Tito Antonio Spagnol, a journalist and globetrotting writer, who worked in Hollywood as a screenwriter for Frank Capra.[68]

Already in the 1920s, however, Eugenio Camillo Branchi, another globetrotter, author of novellas, and collaborator of Agostino De Biasi's *Il Carroccio*, and Ernesto Valentini, journalist at the New York newspaper *L'Araldo Italiano*, had in part distanced themselves from the model of the old *feuilleton*. Valentini based his stylistically vivacious novel *Il Ricatto* (Blackmail, 1924) on a famous trial whose defendants were said to belong to the Black Hand. There is also an interesting case involving Luigi Barzini, the director of *Il Corriere d'America*. Relying on an original editorial coup, he succeeded in launching an author who was hardly credible from a literary point of view but one who had great popular impact: Michele (Michael) Fiaschetti, the man who succeeded Giuseppe Petrosino as chief of the Italian squad in the New York police department. Starting in 1926, Barzini's newspaper

65. Marazzi 2001, 38–40.

66. A notable review of the novel appeared in *Follia di New York* by author Rosario Ingargiola, who placed the novel at the head of the Ciambelli-Pallavicini-Stanco line: a kind of Italian American canon that evidences a certain historico-critical consciousness. See " *'Gente Lontana'* di Corrado Altavilla," *La Follia di New York*, December 11, 1938.

67. Petrosino was a protagonist in many novels and stories, not to mention films, in various parts of the world. In Italian immigrant literature, he peeps in, as we shall see, in the works of many authors, from Ciambelli to Italo Stanco.

68. Veneto native Spagnol (1895–1980) was a journalist in Paris, New York, and Los Angeles. He stayed for a time in Mexico and Canada and, after the war, worked in Italy for *Il Tempo* (Time), *Corriere della Sera* (Evening Courier), and various magazines. In *Memoriette marziali e veneree* (Martial and Venereal Remembrances, 1970) he claimed to have introduced Italy to the thriller short story genre. *L'unghia del leone* (The Lion's Claw), the first of his crime stories, which was published in France in 1932 and, two years later, in Italy. It was about protagonist Alfred Gusman, a detective patterned after classic American private eyes like Sam Spade and Philip Marlowe. In August 1939, Spagnol, who for a long time had written for other Italian periodicals, began weekly correspondence on America for Mario Pannunzio's *Oggi* (Today).

published stories that Fiaschetti based on his own experiences, although they were probably reworked by Prosper Buranelli, a second-generation Italian American from Texas who in 1930 coauthored with Fiaschetti the volume *You Gotta Be Rough*.[69]

One can also find lively narrative material in the work of several poets who had the strength to emerge from the amateur underbrush that sprang up around the many training grounds of journalism. Among the first and most notable, we should include the already-mentioned Giuseppe Cadicamo. There is also Lorenzo Sosso, chronologically one of the very first. A prolific poet, he published his first volume in 1888 in San Francisco and continued writing well into the second half of the twentieth century. Sosso wrote in English and his themes were, so to speak, philosophical; but the results were frankly very modest. His Italian roots rarely surface and when they do, they appear only in his nonpoetic work, such as his collections of proverbs.[70]

Excluded here are those poets who were directly engaged in political struggles (who will appear in Part IV) and those who worked above all for the theater (who will appear in Part III).

Much later, Antonio Calitri would soar above all the other poets of the colony. Calitri was among the circle of friends that gathered around Fiorello La Guardia and collaborated with *L'Araldo Italiano* and several other newspapers. His *Songs of North America* (*Canti del Nord-America*, 1925) reveals a deep and inspired responsiveness to everyday news. But in those same years we also find a popular poet like

69. See Fiaschetti 2003 for biographical and bibliographical information on the author, to which can be added the interesting fact that Fiaschetti (1886–1960?) was given the charge by New York Mayor Fiorello La Guardia in 1935 to supervise, as deputy commissioner, the policing of the city's public markets. It was the "first significant appointment" made by the new mayor and contested by anarchist leader Carlo Tresca, who called Fiaschetti a "fascist" and deemed him "weak, empty, and presumptuous with great roots in the lowest ranks of society," and least able "to drive out the merchants from the temple" and "to exterminate the racketeers." Tresca had continually reported on the mudslinging directed at Fiaschetti, in particular the accusation that he had lent support to the ice industry racket. See Carlo Tresca, "Proponiamo un'altra 'Patacca' a Fiorello La Guardia, 'the man on the flying trapeze'" (We Propose Another "Medal" for Fiorello La Guardia, "The Man on the Flying Trapeze"), *Il Martello* (The Hammer), May 14, 1935.

70. Sosso's first book, *Poems*, was harshly and briefly reviewed in *The Atlantic Monthly* (June 1888): "This poet, an Italian by birth, does not lack patriotic enthusiasm for his adopted country; what he wants is poetic thought and poetic expression. If he would write one line for ten, and then keep his one line a year before printing it, this self-repression might make his verses more acceptable." The same journal, a few years later (April 1892) gave an equally telegraphic and derisive treatment of the ambitious *Poems of Humanity, and Abelard to Heloise*. On the various titles by Sosso, who was born in 1867, see the bibliography.

Calicchiu Pucciu (Calogero Puccio), who in the Sicilian short poem "La Pruittedda" puts into verse a story of emigration that would not have displeased Ciambelli. In some sense this poem has the tone, as well as the liveliness, of the traditional repertory of the storytellers who were so popular in Little Italy with their eternal sagas in the manner of "Il Guerrin Meschino" of Andrea da Barberino. Among the many others who can be mentioned here are two commentators in verse who treat the vicissitudes and humors of the colony: Thomas Fragale, a Protestant minister, and Angelo Rosati, connected to the circle of Cordiferro and *La Follia*.[71] And then we have the simple, delicate, but authentic voice of Severina Magni, perhaps the most inspired lyrical poet of the entire period covering the first half of the century.

Alongside the so-called prose fiction and narrative poetry, there is a flourishing production of lively memoirs, these too generally written by more or less partisan journalists. Among them, besides the already mentioned Adolfo Rossi, we have Camillo Cianfarra, who alternated between journalism and involvement in public administration. He cut his eyeteeth as a journalist at *La Follia* besides working briefly as director for the organ of the Italian American socialists, *Il Proletario*. From this experience of political and journalistic militancy, Cianfarra owes his narrative debut, *The Diary of an Emigrant* (*Il Diario di un emigrato*, 1904), which combines the formality of witnessing in the manner of Adolfo Rossi with a more pronounced narrative fluidity. Obviously, here too his partisan spirit is basic. The writing is, one could say, all of a piece with the author's political personality. But at the same time and in a freer manner, this spirit goes beyond mere politics to tell a story filled with life and studded with typical characters of the colony. This new manner is perhaps a sign that the author had already broken with the Socialist Party. There were already symptoms of such a break in *Those Without a Country* (*I senza patria*, 1899) written by Giusto Calvi, another Socialist party leader (see Part IV). In this book Calvi sought to follow in the path of De Amicis's *On the Ocean* (*Sull'Oceano*). Somewhat later, there will appear a document still more dramatically connected to a break with politics, *In the Island of Tears: Ellis Island* (*Nell'isola*

---

71. The number of Italian American poets, in particular those of the first generation who wrote in Italian, is enormous. Ferdinando Alfonsi, in his 1985 anthology and 1989 listing, counts, respectively, four hundred and about one thousand of them. But the last figure may easily be doubled. For a more general treatment of the subject, see Durante 1994a. However, it should be noted, apart from their qualitative level, that a good percentage of these authors, already active in the 1920s and 1930s, who flourished until recent years, almost create a sense of "fossilized persistence" regarding the historical evolution of Italian American problems, and it was therefore decided, with some regret, that they should not be included in the present work.

delle lagrime: Ellis Island, 1924) by the former anarchist and journalist Ludovico M. Caminita. Here, however, the stinging wound resulting from the abandonment of political militancy is imbued with a grudge—and a rancor—that places the book well within the vicissitudes of the Italian American left (for this reason, I will discuss it in Part IV).

Finally, we have quite a different tenor in the memoirs of Antonio Marinoni, a university professor in Arkansas and husband of the poet and narrator Rosa Zagnoni Marinoni (see Part IV). Marinoni wrote mostly in English and enthusiastically adhered to Fascism. Right from the title of his book of the early 1930s, *How I "Made" America* (*Come ho 'fatto' l'America*), one can guess that the work, while not lacking in a liveliness of its own, belongs to the genre—which will be very popular later on—of the immigrant success story.

Translated by Franca and Bill Boelhower

Peppino

◌ *Luigi Donato Ventura*

Trani, Italy, 1845–San Francisco, California, January 11 or 12, 1912

Luigi Donato Ventura arrived in New York between 1879 and 1880, very probably from France—given that in his pocket he had five hundred francs, as he narrates in *Peppino*. Some years later, he was offered a teaching position in Italian, at Sauveur Summer College of Modern Languages in Burlington, Vermont. Thanks to the encouragement of Lambert Sauveur, president of the institute, in New York, in French, he published the narrative *Peppino,* which was then featured in a series of *contes choisis* (selected stories) for the school. The year after, in Boston, he published *Misfits and Remnants,* a collection of an "etnico" character, representing realistic scenes from the life of the most humble classes of New York. The collection, which opened with *Peppino,* was written in English and in collaboration with the Russian American S. Shevitch, who may have been the author of the non-"etniche" stories in the collection. Meanwhile, Ventura's career as teacher continued; in 1886, for one year, he became docent of Italian, at Boston University, succeeding Giovanni Battista Torricelli, the ex-Capuchin monk who had been the director of the unfortunate Mazzini newspaper *L'Esule italiano.* Ventura resided in New York, in Boston, and in San Francisco. We do not know when Ventura first visited San Francisco, but while he was there he also published *Peppino il lustra-carpe,* which was probably the first version of his novel. A friend of the great actress Adelaide Ristori, he helped her publish her memoir, to which he added a biographical appendix. It is known that Ventura married at an advanced age and had a daughter, and that throughout his life, he struggled against poverty, to the point that he considered returning to Italy. Actually, he had maintained contact with his mother country through his contributions to the socialist review, *Cuore e Critica,* of Arcangelo Ghisleri. An article written for the review, "I negri d'America" (The Negroes of America; February 20, 1889), expressly reveals his disillusion as an emigrant: "The America that you see from afar with the eyes of a dreamer, perceiving it as the champion of civilization, that America that I hoped to find . . . is neither, after all, the America of your dreams, nor the America of my expectation."

The dispersed bibliography of Ventura, a very important author in this critical anthology because he opens the era of the Italian American narrative, classified as such, has been reconstructed by Frank Lentricchia, who has added a good many titles to the very small number cited in the collections of Olga Peragallo and Rose Basile Green. A striking discovery amplified the material on *Peppino*; besides the two cited editions, there is in fact a third one, in French, dated 1913. Other stories appeared in collections of stories, in reviews, and in small editions. Their literary and instructive importance is evidenced by articles written for *Overland* and *Bookman.* Moreover, Ventura was responsible for bringing Edmondo De Amicis (author of *Cuore,* a celebrated children's book) into prominence, providing notes in English for the Jenkins edition, 1889, of *Un Incontro,* intended for schools; and he collaborated with W. A. Nettleton in the translation of Paolo Mantegazza's *L'età di Tartufo* (1890). His friendship with Adelaide Ristori, other than the biographical appendix to the *Memoirs* of the actress, is attested also in the article, "Unpublished Letters of Ristori," issued in the same year, 1907, in *Bookman.*

About the same age as De Amicis, Ventura made his first appearance as a noteworthy narrator a year before the publication of De Amicis's *Cuore,* and he spontaneously approached the very popular author from Piedmont, despite his interest in Mantegazza, author of a contra-*Cuore* for children, brilliantly entitled, *Testa* (Head, in contrast to De Amicis's *Heart).* Ventura himself, in 1888, was the supervisor and preface writer of the American translation of *Testa,* carried out by the Italian students of Bangor, Maine; his preface was reprinted from *Cuore e Critica.* A writer of novelettes more than an authentic novelist (*Peppino* is a notable exception), in his social sentimentalism, he becomes slightly mannered. Even with its many good qualities, above all, its documentation, *Peppino* appears somewhat fabricated. The documentation exposes the phenomenon of labor performed by children procured from Italy. It also pictures daily life in the Italian quarter, already bearing definite characteristics of a southern culture, and Ventura offers a vivid psychological portrait of those emigrants who still perceived the venture into the new world as a temporary phase in their lives. Yet, despite Ventura's emotional involvement, the story discloses a certain distance he maintains between himself and the poor unfortunate protagonists. He, Mr. Fortuna, is the writer, a man of the world and of culture; who every so often speaks in French; who is obliged to distinguish social differences, even in regard to Italians from outside the south; and who therefore can turn to his American readers rendering them the complicit privilege of observation. By now, as Lentricchia noted, "the inhabitant of two worlds, without being at home in either one, Fortuna cannot but speak in an equivocal manner," as when he happens to bless America for having made of so many poor compatriots some very good and industrious citizens. Rose Basile Green has underscored Ventura's choice of the French language as an additional means of social self-promotion, pointing out that the deceit of passing as French was not rare among the Italians (as in a similar comical example in one of the most successful stories of John Fante, "Odyssey of a Wop"). In the case of Ventura, it seems rather that a certain exhibition of French culture acts as a generic ostentation of elegance. It is however certain that Ventura published in French solely for scholastic necessity, but nevertheless signed with his very Italian name.

Misfits and Remnants was received with some interest, and in a certain sense, with divided criticism. If, in fact, *Harper's* magazine underscored the originality of the work, determining it to be "a curious contribution to international fiction," finding it to be "pleasant and amiable," and judging in particular "Peppino" its best part; the *Atlantic Monthly* viewed it instead as rather insignificant: "The music is fairly good, but it is played with one finger."

A few years ago, thanks to the new digital resources of newspapersarchive.com, I discovered that Ventura died of a suicide in the night of January 11–12, 1912. He shot himself with a gun to the heart, leaving a terrible message to his daughter Lillian: "Life is too hard now; I have no brains, no ideas, and you will be happier after this ordeal." The news was published in several newspapers, including *The New York Times* (January 13, 1912).

ESSENTIAL BIBLIOGRAPHY

Basile Green, 1974, 63–64; Cagidemetrio 2000; Fucilla 1967, 155; Lentricchia, 1975; Maffi, 1998; Marazzi 2001, 20–21; Marazzi 2007; Marazzi 2011; Peragallo 1949, 224–228; reviews in *Harper's New Monthly Magazine*, November 1886, 964; *Atlantic Monthly*, November 1886, 719, and May 1889.

ᢒ

If you should ever go to New York, and on some fine day in the month of May should saunter, half on business, half for pleasure, in the direction of the Post-Office, take my advice, do not get into the horse-car which goes through Union Square to Barclay Street, for you will surely be crushed to suffocation in the mass of stout women who seem to frequent these vehicles. Neither should you take the omnibus, that relic of barbarism, that unblushing exhibitor of pretty ankles; but take my advice, I repeat, light a good cigar, and quietly pursue your way on foot, following the right-hand sidewalk.[1]

Not only will you have saved five cents, but you will see the beautiful things spread out to tempt you in the shop-windows; you will meet many pretty women; you will be much amused by the absurd walking advertisements, and edified by the soles of boots at the windows of the reading-rooms of the St. Nicholas and the New York Hotel; and besides all this you will make the acquaintance of Peppino.

For I do not imagine that you are one of those who waste their time by blackening their own boots, but that you much prefer to patronize the poor Italian who for five cents will put so wonderful a polish upon your lower extremities.

For see now, we must all live, in one way or another; and my poor countrymen have a right to exist, were it only by selling melons or by blacking boots.

Do you know Peppino? No? Then I will introduce you to him. Come with me to the corner of Prince Street, opposite of the Metropolitan Hotel. On that corner stands a boy about twelve years old, with a brown skin made yet browner by the sun, a head covered with thick, curly hair, a pug-nose, and a *je ne sais quoi* in his appearance which makes him look very droll as he stands there, with his blacking box strapped across his chest. Peppino is not dirty. He wears a blue jacket with a sailor-collar, trousers rather short, indeed, but clean, and on his feet are slippers of yellow leather.

When Peppino cries out to you "Shine?" you will not be able to resist the fascination, and, like so many others who are passing him, will stop and confide your boots to him while he makes them shine like a mirror. Peppino is an aristocrat in his own way, and has a ruling idea in life. His ambition is to be able to possess, one of these days, by the aid of your boots, a swell-front in his native town, a little America in the heart of Southern Italy.

If you will give me the time, I will relate to you how I came to know Peppino, and will tell you things that you do not hear every day.

This came to pass at that blessed time when I first came to America. At that epoch I was not precisely in intimate relations with the Manhattan Bank; but in three weeks of New York life I had experienced great fluctuations in my own special "Bourse," and in a relatively short space of time I had had my financial Water-

1. This is the English text of "Peppino," taken from L. D. Ventura and S. Shevitch, *Misfits and Remnants* (Boston: Ticknor and Company, 1996), 3–50; reprinted in the Marazzi edition of *Peppino il lustrascarpe*.

loo. Picture to yourself that I had come from Italy with five hundred francs in my pocket and with an idea, even many ideas, in my head: I believed that in America money ran like a river through the streets, and therefore it was not necessary to bring any, but simply to come and gather it up.

With these ideas five hundred francs were more than superfluity; and to say the truth, I got rid of them with an indifference worthy of a nabob.

For instance, I had been led to believe one could be modestly lodged in New York for less than fifteen dollars a week; and in the matter of food there was nothing to be thought of but the bill of fare at Delmonico's or indeed Martinelli's menu. Naturally, therefore, I threw myself into the hospitable arms of Ernest Delmonico's maître d'hôtel, and of Paolo, the aide-de-camp of Martinelli. I was a little surprised to see at these tables only gentlemen in full dress and ladies in the most fashionable attire, and even said to myself: "I wonder where the working people live?" But I answered myself: "You stupid! They probably eat at an hour when you do not happen to be hungry."

As I went on my way, seeing all things as through a prism, and not knowing a word of English, having determined at all costs to discover America for myself, it occurred to me that in three weeks I had descended through all the semitones of the financial scale, and had learned three things: First, that I had been obliged to go from a lodging at fifteen dollars a week to one at ten, and then to one at five, and at last was not able to pay anything at all; second, that I had fallen from the height of Delmonico's to the depths of an underground restaurant, where I paid twenty-five cents for my dinner, beer included; and third, that it had become almost impossible for me to have my boots blacked. The result was that at the end if three weeks I found myself possessed of the appetite of a wolf, that I had un-blacked boots, and a quantity of manuscript with which I intended to civilize America.

Every morning I put these big rolls of paper in my pockets, a political article on M. Gambetta, a criticism on M. Zola, a comedy in three acts with *chansonettes*, and the inevitable biography of poor old Garibaldi. Armed with these, I went to the "New York Herald" office and asked when Mr. Bennett, who was in Europe, would be likely to return, and to the "Sun," to know if perhaps Mr. Dana had finished his breakfast. Then I sought out the editors of the various departments, and emptied the treasures of my pockets upon their tables. It was true the brave fellows could not understand a word I said; but they had traveled the same stormy road themselves, and could at least sympathize.

The following day I would return to find my precious things in the box devoted to rejected contributions, and attached to them this sacred legend: "The manuscript returned, with thanks." It was only after several of these excursions that I found out that I had given my political articles to the "sport" department, and my literary criticisms to the obituary notices.

It was during one of these peregrinations that I first saw Peppino. I had just issued from a grocer's shop, where I had been buying ten cents' worth of crackers and cheese, of which my breakfast for two mornings had been constituted. While I awaited the sale of my first article, to allow me to dream of some sort of dinner, as I was passing the Metropolitan Hotel a boy suddenly started from the wall, and dropping on his knees and calling in a high voice, "Shine! Shine!" without giving me time for resistance, seized one foot, and in a moment my right boot was blacked and polished.

"My boy," I expostulated.

"I will do it very quickly, signorino," said the lad.

It was in vain to protest; my second boot was already in process of cleaning, and soon shone like its predecessor. At last my foot was free; but alas! I was on bonds mentally. I truly believed that I turned pale. Do you guess why? No? Well, the truth was that I had passed through Rabelais' *mauvais quart d'heure* for the want of five cents. My entire property consisted in a bag of crackers in my hand and a biography of Garibaldi in my coat-pocket. I looked at the boy; he stared at me. Several of his customers went by, making a sign to him to black their boots; but he did not stir.

"Five cents!" he sighed at last.

"I haven't a single one!" I ejaculated with some difficulty.

"It is no matter at all; *non fa niente*; the Madonna be with you!" was his reply.

I took hold of his arm with a friendly grasp.

"What is your name?" I said.

"Peppino," touching his cap.

"Thank you, my Peppino; I shall come and see you again to-morrow."

"The Madonna be with you!" he said again, and I walked away with tears in my eyes, saying to myself: "Now I must make some money at any cost, in order to reward this boy for his honest trust in me."

Evidently the boy brought me luck, for on reaching my room I read in the paper that the Ministre de Justice had just died in Italy. In all haste I wrote an obituary in the great man, and took it to the "New York Herald." It was accepted; and better than that, they sent me immediately the money for it, which amounted to the sum of seven dollars! Picture it! Seven dollars! It was indeed like manna in the dessert to poor starving me. My first thought was to seek Peppino. He received me with the smile of an old acquaintance.

"I knew very well that you would come back," he said; and without more ado took possession again of my boots, and polished them as if I had been the best customer in the world. When he had finished, I slipped fifty cents into his hand; whereupon he began to search his pockets for the change, still on his knees. He found forty cents, and would have given them to me; but I told him to keep them. He looked at me with an air that seemed to say: "Don't you think me capable of blacking a pair of boots on credit without usury?"

"Keep the money, my boy," I said; "and if you would like it, come to me every morning at eight o'clock to black my boots."

"Indeed I will; but where shall I go?"

"No. 25, Ludlow Place."

"*Va bene!* All right; I shall be there."

II

I saw nothing of my Peppino the next morning, and I supposed that he had pre-ferred some customer whose pay would be more certain than mine. I was a little disappointed; and scarcely conscious of the direction in which I went, strolled downtown, and came upon Peppino at the corner of Prince Street, where he was busily brushing the boots of a colored man. He made me a hasty sign with his brush to wait, and worked away busily at the larger surface which required to be polished. This finished at last, he turned to me and said in rather an injured tone, pulling the strap of his box over his shoulder as he spoke.

"I went to your house this morning, as I said I would; and after keeping me waiting a long quarter of an hour on the doorstep, an old woman came, and I asked for you. Ah! Signorino, she must be bad, that old woman, for she was very, very cross to me, and if I had not run away, she would have called the police to put me off the steps; she said she would."

"What do you mean? She really sent you away?"

"*Proprio così,* exactly so," said the boy; and then, seeing that I looked sorry and mortified, added: "Never mind; if you want me, I will come again, I am not afraid."

"I believe you, Peppino; and you shall come again, and the old woman shall re-ceive you properly, I promise you."

I wished to shake hands with him; he hesitated a little, and then with some con-fusion began to rub his hands on his trousers, trying to wipe away the stains that the blacking had left on his fingers.

"Well," I said, "are you not going to shake hands with me?"

"With you, a signore?" said he, opening his great black eyes; and then he reached out his hands and put it in mine with great satisfaction.

That afternoon when I returned home I went to the sitting-room of my land-lady. This worthy woman, thin of persona and cat-like of voice, was always installed in a small, dark apartment, furnished with black horsehair chairs and sofa, a marble-topped table, and a large Bible. She was very pious and very grim. When she saw me she asked in sharp tones,

"What can I do for you, Mr. Fortuna?"

"Nothing, madam, except that I wish you would not prevent one of my countrymen from coming to see me."

"What do you mean by countrymen? The only person that has been here to see you was a dirty little Italian brigand. I don't want such people in my house."

"Madam," I replied, "Peppino is a compatriot of mine and an honest gentleman; and as I pay you for my lodging, I wish you to allow my friends to visit me in it. This boy wishes to gain an honest living; he comes to black my boots."

At this my landlady held up her hands in holy horror.

"To black your boots? I should think that it would be much better for you to black your own boots."

Now I had passed through many stages of poverty; I had breakfasted on crackers, and had gone without any dinner to speak of: but it had never entered my head to be the possessor of blacking-box and brushes. I had often put my boots outside my chamber door, thinking perhaps the servant-girl might take pity on them, but with no result; and they were indeed very rusty when I first made acquaintance with Peppino.

Not caring to discuss this point with her, however, I reiterated that I wished her to have Peppino let in whenever he came; and left her, she shutting her door with a malicious slam as I took my way upstairs.

From this time Peppino and I became the best of friends. His entrance into my room every morning was like a ray of warm sunlight from my dear native land, and I could see that he was really pleased with the familiar friendliness with which I always treated him. He was very intelligent, and always respectful and polite, never coming in without knocking at the door and saying, "Buon giorno, signore."

While he was at work he watched me as I wrote at my table, going quietly about the room on the tips of his toes, for fear of disturbing me, when my credit of forty cents was exhausted, and I wished to give him some money, he said in a timid voice, "*Non fa niente*, if you don't have change."

The boy understood my situation, and if he had dared to, would have offered to black my boots for nothing.

"But you must take it," I said, a little provoked.

So he pocketed the pennies without another word.

My affairs went on from day to day in about the same way. My landlady was always sour of aspect, bringing my bill, with a grim and suspicious look on her face, early every Saturday morning. Peppino said nothing, but I had reason to think that his way to me was often interrupted by combats, more or less personal, with the aggressive woman. Once he said to me: How can you live, signorino, in the house of that bad-tempered woman, you a signore?"

"Signore!" I repeated; I live here because I am poor, and cannot find cheaper lodgings."

"But you, a signore!"

Peppino evidently thought that this word "signore" meant many things.

One day, when I was in a talkative mood, I asked him: "How much money do you make a day, my boy?"

"That depends, signore; sometimes I make a dollar and a quarter, sometimes only seventy-five cents. In the summer I have more work, but my winter customers pay me better; so it comes to about the same thing."

"And how much do you spend?"

"*Chi lo sa*? Who knows? Sometimes ten cents, sometimes twenty-five cents."

"Why, then you are a rich man! What do you do with all this money?"

"We send it home."

"We? Who is we?"

"Myself and my two brothers."

"And what do your brothers do for a living?"

"Oh! My brother Antonio is a first-class boot black. He stands at the corner of Union Square and Broadway, and his price is fifteen cents. He is very smart, my brother; sometimes he makes as much as three dollars and ten cents a day. But he plays *mora*, and then he loses his money."

"And do you give your money to him?"

"No, not to him, but to my brother Filippo, il signore; he plays on the violin, he does, and dresses like a gentleman. He plays the violin on the Coney Island boats. It is to him that I give my money, and he sends it home to Italy by Signor Cantoni, who has the bank in Wall Street."

"How much does Filippo make?" I went on.

"Oh! A great deal. Sometimes four dollars a day."

"And where do you live?"

"We live all three together in a little room in Crosby Street, and we cook macaroni every Sunday." He added breathlessly; "Would you come and eat macaroni with us next Sunday?"

"Oh! I thank you, my child, but I think not."

"Ah signore, you must say yes; I have already spoken of it to my brothers, and they want you so much to come."

This invitation seemed a little strange; but I would not have offended Peppino for the world, and I accepted it. The following Sunday he appeared, quite transfigured. He had out on a jacket of black cloth, black trousers, and a pair of laced shoes, much too large for his feet, but resplendently new. He had washed his face until it shone, and had a bright red-and-white handkerchief tied round his throat for a cravat. When I saw him in this attire, with his blacking box strapped round his shoulder, the whole get-up was so incongruous that I could not help smiling; at which the tears came into his eyes, and I hastened to assure him that I did not mean it in ridicule, but was he going to work in those fine clothes?

"Oh no! it is *festa grande* to-day," he said; "and you are coming, are you not?"

"Yes, sir; but it is only half-past eight o'clock."

It is true; but my brother has to go on the boat to-day to make music, and for that we must have our macaroni at about nine o'clock."

Upon hearing this I jumped out of bed and was soon ready, and we set forth together.

The house where Peppino and his brothers lived was of dismal appearance, in the most crowded part of Crosby Street, where human lives and rubbish of every description seem to be thrown together pell-mell, in a heap. As we ascended the steps of the house, I found that I was really in the midst of Southern Italy. Sitting on the ground were little children, dirty and ill clothed; others rolled happily among the mud puddles. Olive-skinned women were combing each other's long black hair; others, of the true Abruzzi type, wore bright petticoats, somewhat ragged, and scarlet *bustini*, according to the custom of their country. They had gold necklaces, with pendant crosses, and long earrings, called *scioccagli*, which almost touched their shoulders. Old women were pulling over rags in baskets, while the men disposed themselves in various attitudes, enjoying the *dolce far niente*, smoking bad cigars and drinking worse beer. When they saw us, the women hastily caught up their children from the ground, and the men made way for us, saying, "Ecco! Here comes the signore."

Peppino was quite triumphant, and laughed until his white teeth sparkled between his red lips. "Yes, indeed, it is the signore," he cried to all of them, and tossed his hat high into the air and caught it again, as he showed me the way upstairs. Making our way with some difficulty through many hospitable people dispersed here and there on the stairways, who asked us cordially to have a drink of beer as we went by, we came at last to the top of the house and stopped before a door which seemed to have for all fastening a loop of cord, which passed through a hole made of wood, and was caught inside. This door opened, and two young fellows appeared, upon which Peppino introduced us to each other as follows, "It is the signore."

The two brothers took me in with a comprehensive glance, from head to foot, and then cried together: "Ben venuto!" "Welcome!" and gave me so cordial an American shake of the hand that my wrist was almost dislocated.

"Keep on your hat," said the musician.

"Thank you," I replied.

"And don't stand on ceremony," added the vicious gambler at *mora* while he got a chair and put it for me in the very middle of the room, as if to put me in possession of the place. At the same time Filippo drew up a table, on which was served in a moment the traditional dish of macaroni, which was evidently all ready and waiting. At nine o'clock in the morning I must confess that I was not enormously inclined to do much honor to the Neapolitan dainty; but it was pressed upon me with such cordiality that I found myself finishing two platefuls, and not finding it bad at all. After the macaroni came a course of candy and peanuts.

Peppino was radiant.

The room was very poor, certainly, but very neat. There were two beds, one for the violinist, and the other occupied evidently by the two younger brothers. On these beds were bright-colored figured cotton quilts. Over the head of each bed was a print nailed to the wall with big black nails. One represented the Crucifixion, and the other the Madonna del Rosario. In one corner was a large wooden chest, once white, but now yellowed by age and weather, wherein they kept all their effects; and four straw-seated chairs completed the furniture of the room. There was a wash-basin on a shelf; here also, leaning against the wall, were two bits of looking-glass. Red cotton curtains hung before the windows, and on one window-seat was a splendid red geranium in full bloom.

"You are lodged like princes here," said I to the three brothers.

"We are contented," said the violinist. "But this is nothing; we shall have a house down there."

"Down there? Where?"

"At Viggiano."

"Are you from Viggiano?" I asked.

"Certainly," replied Antonio; "we are going to have a first rate house on Broadway."

I was puzzled. Viggiano—Broadway! I could not understand, and began to suspect that a very *petite vin de Sicile*, of which my hosts had drunk at breakfast, had gotten into their brains or mine. I laughed, not knowing what else to do.

"I see," said Filippo calmly, "that you know nothing of Viggiano."

III

"Well, then," said Filippo, "would you like to have me tell you all about Viggiano?"

"Now, why should the signore care to know about Viggiano?" interposed Peppino, who feared that it would not interest me, and wished to be agreeable to me at any cost.

To reassure him, I declared that nothing would please me more than to hear what Filippo had to say.

"You must know, then," began he, "that our Viggiano is in Basilicata."

"Yes, I know."

"He knows," said Peppino in a stage whisper.

"And at Viggiano everybody plays on some instrument or other, harp or violin. That comes by nature; no one teaches us that. One fine day some one went away from us to seek his future and see the world, without knowing whither he went; and this some one, always wandering, found himself at last in America. Now, since this first some one returned to Viggiano with five thousand dollars in his pocket, emigration has not ceased for a moment. From father to son, for twenty-five years, it has always been the same story. One leave's one's house a little boy, a harp on the back or a violin under the arm; and always playing as one goes along the roadsides of Italy, one picks up sous. These sous have grown to be many by the time one reached Genoa. Then it is easy to get a passage on board some ship going to America; and if the passage-money is not quite complete at starting, one makes it up by playing on board, and so gaining a little. That is the way we get here. Every month we go to Signor Cantoni's and take the money we have made, some of us by playing, some by blacking boots. When we have sixty dollars, it is sent to the mayor of our village. He is one of us; he has been in America, and now he is a rich man."

"How much money does a man require to be called a rich man?" I asked.

"Oh! With four thousand dollars you are very rich," answered Filippo.

"And what security do they give you for the money you send?"

"We ask none but a receipt, and with that we are perfectly content. With the money they buy for us a lot on Broadway. Broadway is the name of our great street, half a mile long! It was called so by one of our mayors, who had been chief boot black in Broadway in New York for ten years. It is he who had the church built at his own expense. So you see," continues Filippo, lighting a pipe as he spoke, "that thirty years ago Viggiano was only a cluster of poor little cottages, whereas now every one who comes back from America speaks more English than Italian and has a house with a swell-front! Not fine houses like the ones on Fifth Avenue, to be sure, but yet very nice—white plastered with swell-fronts!"

Great emphasis on the swell-front. Peppino clasped his hands in applause, and Antonio puffed away at his cigar with an expression of supreme content, watching me the while to see the impression that all this made upon me. Surely I had never dreamed that there was this curious little reflection, as it were, of American life and manners among mountains of Basilicata.

"Are you never afraid of losing your money?" I ventured to ask.

"Never," said Peppino. "Here we save every sou and live with the greatest economy; but there we have plenty, we want nothing. We had beautiful *festas*, and music never stops at all. My cousin Paolo has a room papered with New Year's cards that were picked up in the streets here and sent to him, and the *curé* has a trunk entirely covered with American stamps!"

"In about a year," added Filippo, "I shall go back to Viggiano and marry my cousin Filomena, who has been waiting for me these eight years. I have paid the schoolmaster to teach her to read; I have paid him a dollar a year."

"A fine salary for a schoolmaster!" I observed.

"Why he is very rich," said Antonio. "There are six hundred inhabitants at Viggiano, and he makes almost four hundred dollars a year. That is a very good income down there."

"You see," said Filippo, with a slightly superior air, "I am a violin player and well-dressed, because, going into the world as much as I do, that is necessary. But Peppino and Antonio only black boots, and of course they cannot dress like gentlemen. No one would give them any work if they knew they had money already. Here we are always poor, for all our money is for the *paese*; here we lay up comfort for our old age. If you only knew how beautiful it is at Viggiano, signore! They have flowers there, and in the evening everybody sits and sings outside of his swell-front." These swell-fronts were evidently the mania of the place. He continued: "I went home last year, because my old father wanted to see me, and besides that he wanted me to promise not to be false to Filomena. Some gossip had written home a story that I was in love with an organ-grinder. She lives in the house just opposite here; but that is nothing. Things have changed a little at home. Nowadays the children go directly from Viggiano to America, without stopping to play by the roadsides in Italy, and there is always an older brother or cousin to receive them when they land at Castle Garden."

Antonio now proposed a game of *mora*, but Peppino reproved him with a severe aspect; and as Filippo was obliged to go to the Coney Island boat, we accompanied him to the foot of Twenty-second Street. That day I invited Peppino to dine with me, and after a little urging he accepted my invitation with delight. We ate our modest repast at a French restaurant in Houston Street, at the sign of "Le Grande Charlemagne."

"People like Antonio," said Peppino, with great gravity, "have a *café* and bar at Viggiano, where they can play *mora*; but Filippo says that if one is going to drink, it is better to drink at home than to patronize the keeper of that *café*, who had a bad reputation in New York for always gaining at *mora*. For myself, I shouldn't think of going there, no, not once in six years." This with an air of reflection.

"That's right, my lad," I said, patting him on the shoulder.

I really almost envied Peppino and went to sleep that night, my head full of swell-fronts and Broadways; and I blessed America, that makes of my poor countrymen so many good and industrious citizens.

My landlady's manner became so very unpleasant that I decided to change my lodging, and was obliged to take one so far from Prince Street where Peppino stood at his work, that although the boy was most anxious to come to me every morning, I persuaded him that he ought not to do a thing so much against his interest. He was quite unhappy; but I promised him that I would go to him twice a week, which I did. I managed, by a little timid advice, to induce him to take more care of his personal appearance, telling him that politeness and neatness should go hand in hand. He was very docile, and promised to take a bath every now and then, and scrupulously brushed his hair every morning. The poor little fellow did most willingly all that I asked him.

"Say, *maestro*," he said one day, "when I go back to Viggiano I shall wish so much to know how to read. How much shall I pay you to give me lessons?"

"Peppino," I answered, "I will teach you to read with much pleasure; but I could not think of taking any money. No, no."

"No? But this is business, signore, no money, no lesson."

"Very well; we will see about it this summer some time." I said.

Just about that time I was called away to the West in haste. I wanted to say good-bye to Peppino, and went to Prince Street for the purpose. He was not there. I was really disappointed, but left New York without seeing him. I was away longer than I had expected to be, and did not find myself in New York again until three months had passed. Almost the day after my return I was seized with an attack of low fever which kept me in the house for a fortnight. At last I recovered, and one of my first thoughts was to see my Peppino. For my first walk I sought him and found him. How glad he was to see me! He left a customer with a boot half finished, and taking me by the arm, led me a little aside. When we were alone, he told me how sadly the time had gone while he had not seen me, and that now I must let him come again to me every morning. So I gave him my address most willingly.

During the fortnight that I had been ill the small sum of money that I had made in the West had flown away like summer flies, so that I was once more almost penniless. But I had learned how to make my way more easily with the editors of the daily papers, and I managed to get on somehow or other by my pen and a few lessons in Italian. One morning when Peppino came to my room I was still in bed, and not in the best possible humor; I fear I did not answer his *Buon giorno* in the pleasantest way. He went to work at my boots; but when he had finished he did not go, but after reaching the door once or twice, came back without opening it.

"Well," I cried, "what is the matter?"

"It is that you seem so sad, are you ill?"

"Yes," I said, "I am ill."

"That is not true."

"But since I tell you so," in spite of myself I was forced to smile at his air of assurance. The child still shook his head, and I could not help a sigh. While this little comedy was going on we heard a knock at the door.

"Come in," I said.

In rushed my landlady with a paper in her hand. Addressing herself to me, she said that I had allowed my bill to go over two days, that I used too much gas, that she must pay the gasman, and that I must either give her the money or leave the room.

"But, madam, I am ill."

"I will give you twenty-four hours," she answered, and she went away.

This was the secret of my bad-humor, I could not pay my lodging bill.

When the woman had gone, Peppino came timidly to my bedside.

"*Sentite*," signore, listen!" said he. "Will you let me come back in ten minutes? I want to speak to you about something."

"Yes, Peppino, I shall not go out at all."

There must have been something quite terrible to the child in my face as I said these words, for he left me quite overcome. At the end of fifteen minutes he was back again. He had in his hand a red handkerchief. In this handkerchief there was something heavy and round of body, like a bottle tied at the neck. He approached the bed half roguishly, half ashamed, and in a tone as if he were imploring a great favor, cried, "You will do me this pleasure, won't you? You can pay me back, you know. Hold!" And at the same moment he untied the handkerchief, and out tumbled a quantity of pieces of money on my bed—quarters of dollars, ten-cents and five-cent pieces, and pennies. All this made a large heap on the bed. A bank-teller would have been puzzled to guess how much money was there.

"And you wish," I stammered, "to lend!"

"To lend you this to pay the *padrona*. Come, now, do take it! I know I am only a poor boy, but I am of your own country, and I cannot see you insulted."

I was not strong, and the tears overflowed my eyes and rained down my cheeks. The poor boy was shocked, and I compelled myself to say, "So be it; I will take it. Count it."

"It is counted," he answered; "these are twenty-five dollars there. Do you really want it counted?"

This with an air which meant that of course he would count it if I insisted, but it would take a long, long time to do it, and his customers were waiting.

"Go," I said, "and come back to-morrow, and thank you."

"*Grazie a voi*," replied Peppino.

The little episode just related surprised and touched me at the same time. That which I had not been able to obtain by the most strenuous and desperate labor, that which men who professed to recognize merit and perseverance had not done for me, was offered to me by a child; and it made me reflect that into the hands of children is often put the gracious work of Providence. Already once before had Peppino brought me luck, at my first meeting with him, and my debt to him of five cents was followed by the sale of my first article in a New York paper. And now again, as you will see, Peppino was to have a good influence upon my destiny.

I counted his money with great meanness, it must be confessed. There was not one cent more or less than the twenty-five dollars. I called my landlady, and as a kind of punishment for her harshness I paid her for one week in pennies. As a slight mitigation the price of another week was added in two-cent pieces, and to cap the climax I gave her a quarter for the servant; and the servant and the land-lady happening to be merged in the same individual, she went from my room with an air of having witnessed a miracle.

Fifteen dollars still remained, which I proposed to return to Peppino when he should come the next morning. He appeared in due season, with an aspect more than usually beaming. The postman had brought a letter for me, and he had taken it from him and bounded upstairs with it, knowing how anxious I always was for the mail. As he opened my door, he held it above his head, that I might see it on the instant. It was a large envelope. My eyes sparkled when I saw on it the stamp of the "World." Opened it, and forthwith began a species of dance of joy around the room. Peppino looked at me astounded, his brush arrested in mid air on its way to my boot.

"Good news!" I cried.

"*Me ne consolo*; that delights me," he said.

"Are you busy today?" I asked.

"Have you an errand for me to do? I am here to serve you."

"Very well; I shall give you a dollar for the commission." Peppino was petrified.

"See, now," I said. "You won't understand about it, but that is no matter. You know that all these words that you see in writing on paper are called an article for a paper. Very well; a paper has bought these words. Do you understand?"

"Yes, signore."

"I shall give you a note to the editor of the paper, or rather his check, and he will give you the money, and you will bring it back to me immediately. No; on second thought, another way will be better. They will give you forty dollars. Take twenty-five, which belongs to you, and put them into your pocket. The fifteen that will remain you will put in an envelope and come and put it here on this table, for I shall not be here probably when you get back. You understand?"

"Yes, certainly, signore."

I wrote a word to the clerk at the paying-desk of the "World" office, begging him to remit the amount of the check to the bearer, who was a person in whom I had perfect confidence. It was pleasant to see how proud Peppino was to be entrusted with his important mission. He told me again and again how quick he would be, and how particular in all details, and I bid him good-bye until the following morning, and put into his hand the dollar, to be earned by the business he was to do for me, which dollar was one of the twenty-five he had so generously lent me.

The boy went; I was very happy, happy in my little success, and happy that I was able to show the child how entire my confidence was in him: in him who had shown so much in me. And I thought of his twenty-five dollars, gathered together cent by cent, and then thrown in a heap upon the bed of a sick man who was not able to earn his own living. And I built enough *châteaux* in Spain that day as I went about my affairs to fill a volume with the telling about them.

I returned to my room quite late in the evening, and naturally my first glance was towards the table upon which I expected to find the envelope that Peppino had left for me; but nothing was there. I searched, I turned over everything. Nothing! It was strange; but I said to myself that probably Peppino did not like to leave the parcel on my table, and had therefore given it to the landlady to keep for me. It was so late that she was doubtless in bed, and it would be cruel to wake her. I would wait, and in the morning I should know all about it. And I went quietly to sleep, and dreamed that I had been offered the head of the dramatic department of the "World." I waked early. It was Sunday. My first thought was to buy a copy of "The World." There was my article, occupying three columns, and looking so very well! It was in a humorous vein, and they had really paid me royally for it. I read it over, and confessed to myself I was very proud of it.

At eight o'clock my landlady knocked at my door. "Ah," thought I, "she is coming to bring my envelope!"

"Have you the 'World,' Mr. Fortuna," said the woman, "and would you lend it to me?"

"Certainly, Mrs. Woodmilken; and with all the more pleasure that you will be able to read my article, of three columns, Mrs. Woodmilken."

"Indeed!" she muttered.

Meantime I waited for my money; but not a word.

"By the by, madam," I said, "if you would be so good as to give me my *Envelope*—"

"What envelope?" she asked.

"Why, you know, Peppino, did he not leave something with you for me?"

"Absolutely nothing," croaked the bird of ill omen; and she went away evidently glad to see that I was troubled a little by something about the despised Italian boy.

"Oh well!" I said to myself, "Peppino will soon be here, and then all will be explained." Nine o'clock struck, and then ten, and so time went on until noon. Then I began to be restless, and went out, walking the corner where Peppino always was. No Peppino. Then I went to Union Square, where Antonio ought to be. Not the shadow of Antonio. This began to be decidedly strange. At three o'clock I knocked at the door of the house in Crosby Street. The door was hermetically sealed. By this time I was seriously anxious. The next day the same search, with the same result. I went to the "World" office. The check had been paid in bills and given to the bearer who brought my letter. What was I to think? I went back to the house where Peppino lodged, and asked the neighbors if they knew anything of him. They had not seen the boy for two days. Antonio had gone to Chicago some time before, and Filippo was also away, traveling with a troupe of Spanish students.

Then I was at the end of my resources, and had to make up my mind, most sorrowfully, that the boy had either been assassinated perhaps, or at all events my money—ah, no! It was horrible to suspect even for a moment the boy, who was honor itself. Nevertheless, I must confess that the idea came to me that perhaps poor Peppino had lost the money and had hidden away in the fear of confessing it.

Two days went by; three; a whole week. Then I put on mourning for my money as lost, and tried to fall back on whatever skepticism I possessed on the subject of Italian boys.

One evening, in loafing about the streets, I found myself in front of the Bellevue Hospital, and in passing the gate I heard a voice calling, "Signore, signore." I turned and what did I see? Peppino, face to face with me. A torrent of questions poured out of my mouth before I could pay attention to anything. Then as he came nearer to me I saw that he was lame in his right leg. I looked more attentively at him. He was pale, frightfully pale.

"But what is the matter?" I asked. "What are you doing here?"

"It is the hospital here," he answered. And he told me how on the very day he went to the "World" office for me he had been run over by a heavy cart, how he had been picked up and carried to the hospital in a fainting condition, and how no one had been able to understand what he said when he revived.

"But you did wrong not to send for me," I said, "you knew so well that I was your friend."

"Yes," answered the child hesitatingly, "but—"

"But—"

"I did not know your name, signore."

It was true. How much these simple words meant to me! He did not even know my name, and he had done so much for me. I learned afterwards that he tried to tell them where I lived; but as he could give no name, and his English was worse than poor, they did nothing about it.

"And the money that you got for me that day, my poor child, of course it was lost when you fell in the street?"

"Not at all," he said. "I never lost a cent of it. I put it, you know, in a book on the table, for fear that the bad, cross landlady would see it. I don't like to have business with her."

"The book? On the table? Ah, I see! You are much better, are you not? Would you like to come away with me? You shall be well taken care of. I will speak to the doctor here about it."

"*Fate come volete.* Do as you please, signore."

And I went to the office of the hospital, and was allowed to claim the boy and take him away. I called a hack and put him carefully in it and carried him home. He was still quite lame, although no bones had been broken. He was able to get upstairs with the assistance of the hack-driver and myself; but when he reached the door of my room he refused all aid, and hoping on one foot, scrambled as quickly as he could to my writing table, and resting the lame leg on a chair, began to turn over all my books. At last, at the very bottom of all, he found an old "Ollendorf," and took possession of it with great joy. He opened it, took an envelope out from between the leaves, and waved in the air."

"*Ecco!*" he cried, his eyes full of delight. "Here is the money! I hope that you never had a doubt of me?"

I embraced him with all my heart, and assured him that I could never think any ill of him.

Will you believe it, my reader? The poor boy had not dared to open the envelope, as I had given him full authority to do. His own money was there, as well as mine, and Ollendorf had taken the best care of our little fortune.

Peppino remained with me a week, sleeping on my sofa and being cared for by a good doctor who would not accept any remuneration for his frequent visits. More than that, when the child was able to work again, and had taken his old stand at the corner of Prince Street, the doctor became one of his regular customers, and never failed to shake hands with him and give him ten cents every time he blacked his boots.

Peppino was very proud of his aristocratic friends, and always declared that it was to me that he owed everything. But, on the contrary, I considered that all the luck was on my side in having met that rare thing in this world—a good and honest heart.

And let me beg of you, my readers, if, indeed, you are of the masculine gender, never to go by the corner of Prince Street without stopping to have your boots blacked by Peppino.

Peppino is modest, and I cannot give him greater pleasure than by putting my own obscure name in the shadow, as it were, of his great honesty.

The Destruction of San Francisco, April 18, 1906

❧ *Fanny Vanzi-Mussini*

Florence, Italy, November 16, 1852–San Francisco, California, April 29, 1914

Descended from a notable family of musicians, Fanny Vanzi-Mussini was bred in a circle of people with international connections and culture. She was one of five children (four girls and one boy) of the famous painter Cesare Mussini and his wife, the Prussian aristocrat Elisa von Blesson. In 1879, she married the journalist Leonetto Vanzi, and they had seven children. In 1895, the family moved to America, and in San Francisco both Fanny and Leonetto—who were to go back several times to Italy and then return to California—were engaged in the milieu of Ettore Patrizi, the editor of the daily *L'Italia*. Leonetto was a staff writer for the newspaper, and also the president of the local section of the Società Dante Alighieri.

In Italy, Fanny was a well-known journalist. Using the pseudonym "Lea," she contributed (and she continued to do so while she was in America) articles, verses and short stories to important newspapers, magazines, and journals as *Fanfulla della Domenica, Capitan Fracassa, La Nuova Antologia, La Nazione, Natura ed Arte*, and *Il Giornale d'Italia*. She was also the author of several books, novels, collections of short stories and "*bozzetti*" (sketches), published by national publishers as Hoepli, Vallardi, Carabba, and Le Monnier. Among them are *La storia di Giulietta* [Juliet's Story] (1889), *A Mezzocolle* [At Mezzocolle] (1892), *Zingaresca* (1894, which Matilde Serao reviewed, saying that it was a "modest" book), *Repubblica letteraria* [Literary Republic] (1894), *Illusioni estreme* [Extreme Illusions] (1899), *Il Natale di Lenina* [Lenina's Christmas] (1899), and *Vecchie ragazze* [Old Girls] (1902).

Fanny Vanzi-Mussini also wrote the lyrics for many songs and "romanze", such as *Canto dell' alba visino* (music by Enrico Bossi), *Bacio vivo* [Living Kiss] (music by Angelo Bettinelli), *Baci d'amore* (music by Cesare Seghizzi). But she is most remembered for her translation of the *Cinquanta novelle* [Fifty Stories] by the Brothers Grimm, whose first edition, of the many released until recent years, was printed in 1897. In San Francisco, in 1914, the year of her death, a small collection of her poems, *Emigranti e altri versi* [Emigrants and Other Verses] (L'Italia Press, 1914), appeared.

ESSENTIAL BIBLIOGRAPHY

Leclerc 2011; Marazzi 2011, 94–104; Trotta 2008, 69.

It's deep night: the city rejoices
In the madness of flowers,
Sounds and whirling dollars.
The colors of the flyers

Shine in every street, in the pearly
Crystal that sparkles and dies—
In the thousand atoms
cloven by the human tides.

It's April—it's Easter. Agape invites
all weary people—a pagan nation—
to nod off drunken
on foolish jubilation.

But a gloomy light now floods the skyline
That does not herald any April day.
And while the sleepy mind now drifts away
Among the reveling phantoms of tea and wine,

Of opium, of wretched conceits,
A terrifying force now runs through the streets. . . .
It shatters and topples the peaceful houses,

The gigantic towers . . . onward and loose
The secret brute force presses on swiftly
And the fire rises now in shuddering fury.

The children sleep. . . .
They fall in the vortex:
The moans are silent
Under the rubble.

Women are running
And have on their shoulders
The silken dresses
Of their last orgy.

Below the ground are left entombed
Dull-witted old men—drunken and doomed,
Through alleys and streets—the crowd scampers off.
The blaze invades—it has not had enough,

It devours all—gloriously shining,
And in a short time–it consumes everything.
In wild confusion—the people run
away from the ruins—towards the ocean.

In that reflection
Of gold and blood
Childhood's nipped in the bud.

One can barely hear
A few faint moans
Soon dying down.

In the constant crash
Of burning timber
In the odd spasm
Of fatigue and hunger,

The sun appears
In the yellow smoke cloud
Like a bloody globe
Tingeing the sea with blood.

The hours race on
In hellish flight.
The fire lights the streets
In the dead of night.

It's a confused melee
Of flames and figures.
Emotions rage on
amid clashes and fears.

In the lovely gardens of the squares
There are people from every land: a mutilated
Blond woman screams—and there,
In silence, a Chinese man lies dead.

They are hospitals and graveyards
Without beds or crosses—
Yesterday oases for children and sweethearts,
Today places of horrible losses.

And in the frightful night
So many new lives awaken
That for an instant beat bright
And soon die, ignored and broken!

Sad childbirths, so called
only for the womb's strain
a brief hour and then fallen
in blood and in pain.

(Because help came too late)!—
And among them dim shadows meantime
Wander in the mystery, to commit before daylight
The contemptible crime:

Cutting the fingers of the dead
to steal jewels and gold,
Searching breasts and thick hair on their heads,
Fighting with the defeated and the old.

And more and more the fleeing throngs
Crowd along the seaboards,

In the teeming of desperate tongues,
Of savage words.

When on the shores, all of a sudden,
The Italians' slender boats come by—
They are the children, the women
That the fishermen take far away

To safety on that sea of fire—
And the nets and clothing
and bedsheets and all their meager
treasure. Quiet, without looking

To see who's left behind in the deep.
Wails of fresh sorrows break out,
Curses. And black courtesans weep
Along with yellow children in swaddling cloth

And blond girls, while down there the city
collapses in the blazes—
And on the rhythmic ripple of the sea
The mothers' stifled voices

Whisper words of comfort still
Urging all to try to be calm as they can,
But mixing with the tears that fill
Their sullen eyes. There, a frail old man,

Holds on to his daughter, and here a little girl
Hugs her little brother . . . The horrible night
Goes by and the next morning early
They are nowhere in sight.

Others have come and many many more. . . .
The big ships have gathered aboard
the wandering crowds–and on the shore,
Dawn no longer carries heavenward

A lovely color tinged with mirth
And hope—it seems to rise
Silently on the deserted earth
With a gaunt and haggard face.

But amid the mists the fishermen
Have landed on a shore out of harm's way
And leave their families without fear. Then
They steer their sails out of the bay

Into the treacherous ocean and cast their nets.
The women stay behind,
And return to the walls of their lost nest
with their faithful mind,

Their dark eyes turning ill at ease
From side to side in their dismay.
They hold their children between their knees. . . .
In silence they observe the day

Rising gloomy and cold within the haze.
Solitary?—No.—A lot
of people gather around them . . . Their gaze
Falls on the wings of the small boat

Appearing once again over the horizon—
The strong men are coming back ashore.
In their misfortune, the multitude of reborn
Raise their heads high once more.

The humble fisherman (unknown to all)
Uncovers the treasure of the sea,
And gives and gives until the hull
Is emptied totally—

A chorus of voices and sobs echoes
"Oh! bless you! . . ." For countless days
The fearless outcasts' shadows
Wander across the ocean, in so many ways

Doing good for all. And meanwhile in their perils
The sacred names of Genoa and Ancona,
Of Palermo and Naples,
Enter their thoughts and spur them on.

O homeland, homeland, your faraway children
to their courage and faith have always been true.

You did not lose them—they are still Italian,
They'll always be worthy—my land—of you.

NIGHT, DECEMBER 12, 1906 — MARIN COUNTY, CAL.

Translated by Luigi Bonaffini

The Five Points

～ *Adolfo Rossi*

Lendinara (Rovigo), Italy, September 30, 1857–Buenos Aires, Argentina, 1921

After high school, which was interrupted by his father's death, and after being employed by the post office, Adolfo Rossi published in *Bacchiglione*, a journal in Padua, a novel "on the condition of young elementary schoolmistresses." Rossi's fellow-citizen Alberto Mario aided him in publishing some novellas in the *Vita Nuova* (Milan) of Arcangelo Ghisleri. One of those novellas, *Lo zingaro* (The Gypsy) was published in the appendix of the first issue of the *Il Progresso Italo-Americano* on December 13, 1880. After founding a bimonthly of family readings entitled *Il Grillo del focolare* (The Cricket in the Fireplace) in 1879, Rossi embarked at Southampton on the *Canada*, bound for New York. In his pocket he had four hundred lire, which were soon stolen. He arrived at his destination with only three and a half lire to his name.

In America, he spent five years, initially supporting himself by working at odd jobs. He worked as an iceman at the Metropolitan Concert Hall, as a vendor of fans at Coney Island, as a waiter. He was hired as a domestic for a family of wealthy Americans. He tried to buy a boarding house. Then he met Carlo Barsotti, who entrusted him with the responsibility of managing *Il Progresso*, founded only two months earlier. Subsequently, eager to pursue adventure in the West, he found himself employed on the railroads in Colorado, at the mercy of contractors without scruples, in conditions of extreme privation.

After three further years of working for the *Progresso*, he returned to Italy, but he continued to travel and publish extensively. His successful *Un italiano in America* (1891), almost a best-seller, reprinted in 1899, is particularly interesting. (In

138

1889, there had been a first version, entitled *Nacociù, La Venere Americana: Avventure degli emigranti al nuovo mondo*. (Nacociù, The American Venus: Adventure of the Emigrants in The New World). In 1893, he published, *Nel paese dei dollari: Tre anni a New York* (In the Country of Dollars: Three Years in New York), which also had a first version in 1891, under the title, *Vita d'America* (American Life), a collection of articles issued in the *Tribuna* of Rome. Other titles of this period, in which Rossi contributed to the *Corriere della Sera* and the *Secolo,* are *Da Napoli ad Amburgo; Escursione di un giornalista* (From Naples to Hamburg: A Journalist's Excursion; Rome, 1893); *Nel regno di Tiburzi; ovvero, Scene del brigantaggio nella campagna romana* (In the Kingdom of Tiburzio; or, Scenes of Brigandage in the Roman Campagna; Rome 1893); *L'Eritrea com'è oggi* (Eritrea Today; Rome 1894); *L'agitazione in Sicilia. A proposito delle ultime condanne* (Agitation in Sicily: The Most Recent Judgments; Milan 1894); *Un'escursione nel Montenegro* (An Excursion in Montenegro; Milan 1896); *Alla guerra italo-turca* (At the Italian-Turkish War; 1897); *Impressioni ed istantanee di un corrispondente* (Impressions and Snapshots of a Correspondent; Florence 1897); a novel set in France, *Il garofano rosso* (The Red Carnation; Milan 1897); *Da Constantinopoli a Madrid (Impressioni di un corrispondente)* (From Constantinople to Madrid (Impressions of a Correspondent; Catania 1899); and *Inglesi e Boeri (1900) attraverso l'Africa Australe e il Transvaal* (Englishmen and Boers: Across South Africa and the Transvaal; Milan 1900). In addition, he published various pamphlets on social and political themes.

Named inspector of emigration "with the unanimous vote of a commission that included among its members the senator Arcoleo and the deputy Nitti" (Prezzolini), he carried out missions in Brazil. His account, *Condizioni dei coloni italiani nello Stato di San Paolo del Brasile* (Conditions of Italian Colonies in the State of São Paulo, Brazil) published in 1902, in the *Bollettino dell'emigrazione*, placed notable weight on the efforts of laws against the exploitation of Italian agricultural workers in Brazil, as well as in the United States, where he produced an outstanding series of letters, *Per la tutela degli italiani negli Stati Uniti* (For the Protection of the Italians in the United States), published in 1904, in a monographic number of the *Bollettino dell'emigrazione.* Rossi was an able and astute official and a brilliant social analyst; among other notable initiatives, in 1908, in the *Bollettino,* he published, "Vantaggi e danni dell'emigrazione nel Mezzogiorno d'Italia" ("Pluses and Minuses of Emigration from Southern Italy"). He progressed to the position of Commissioner General of Emigration. In addition, he was vice commissary and consul in Paraguay and minister plenipotentiary in Argentina, where he died. In 1919, one of the descriptions of his voyages, *Da Asunción (Paraguay) a Buenos Aires con un idrivolante italiano* (From Asunción [Paraguay] to Buenos Aires in an

Italian Seaplane) was published by *Le vie del mare e dell' aria* (Seaways and Airways).

"The world is big, there is America, and New York is a vast metropolis. I will go there, study those famous Americans, learn English. In the beginning, I will work with my hands, but in the country of activity and above all, liberty, I will learn better to understand life and men, and one day I will return to Italy rich at least in experience. Then it will be easier to dedicate myself completely to journalism." In the first pages of *Un italiano in America,* Rossi evoked the sentiments that drove him to take the great step, not, after all, so different from those of the mass of emigrants. A petty bourgeois without great problems of subsistence, he became aware of the tedium of provincial life; in this way, "a little at a time, the discontent that I felt was transformed into a mad will to flee from that prison of the post office, to bestir myself, to travel, to see."

Rossi's dream of America was a very common one for his generation, eager for accounts and narratives of far-off countries. Prezzolini compared his manner of writing with that of De Amicis, and found in his pages a reminiscence of the picaresque, "the human tone of the *Gil Blas*" of Lesage. Prezzolini had a high opinion of Rossi's first American book, to the point of proposing it to be a rare, true model of emigration literature, which was often tainted by rancorous sentiments or by boring melancholy. Rossi was instead "a man without preconceptions, without vanity, without profound passions, but with an eagerness to experience the world." For this reason, the book had the value that belongs to a "credible and uncommon" testimony.

Not only a trustworthy account, *Un Italiano in America* also shines with the natural qualities of narrative. Rossi was inclined to narrate his experiences, not to dull them by presenting them as a documentary. Rossi rendered experiences live and present, absorbing the reader page after page, with a charm that belongs more to the storyteller than to the essayist. His testimony is important in understanding the world of the early Italian colony of New York at first hand: to enter into the squalid hovels of the usurers; into the ill-famed bars of the "Five Points"; into the presence of Irish prostitutes and taciturn bosses, exploiters of laborers. The book is full of curious episodes, of characteristic figures, of personages more or less memorable. Here is the procession of the Barnum circus, "the tremendous show in the universe." Here is the simplicity of the president of the United States, who dined alone at the table in a restaurant, and it happened to Rossi, as he recounts, that he served him. Here is the amusing dialogue, imaginary but not altogether: "What do they think of the Italians in North America?" Here is the story of the first steps of the *Progresso,* and then the meeting with Antonio Meucci, and even the news about the "newyorkese" sojourn of Garibaldi. In 1882, Rossi sent this to the Risorgimento heroine Jessie White Mario, who included it in her biography of Garibaldi. Here are the adventures of the "royal consular agent," of Colorado, Cappelli, with his past as player of the street organ and trainer of monkeys and bears. . . .

Nel paese dei dollari (In the Country of Dollars) takes up the story from the point in which it was left in the preceding volume. Recalled by Barsotti to manage the *Progresso*, Rossi returned from Colorado and thrust himself headlong into his beloved work as editor. Even if *Nel paese dei dollari* is not properly a book of Italian American journalism (Rossi had half a notion to write one), the text originates, nonetheless, in his experience as a reporter, and for this reason, it has a rhapsodic flow, underscored also by the presence of an appendix on the New York life of Jessie White's Italian husband. In fact, the volume opens with the story of Angelo Cornetta, an ambulatory emigrant musician from the province of Salerno, condemned to hang for murder, and it proceeds to describe a masked ball in the house of millionaire Vanderbilt, which affords the author the opportunity to wander through various episodes regarding the story of some immense American fortunes. Following is a chapter on the opium smoking dens of New York and another on the puritanical blue laws, rigorously enforced on Sundays. Among the other themes treated is the destruction of the Indians and an interesting chapter on the voyage of Dario Papa in America, whom Rossi met in New York, along with Ferdinando Fontana, and who then remained for seven to eight months in the city, contributing regularly to the *Progresso*.

ESSENTIAL BIBLIOGRAPHY

Bagatin 1991; Prezzolini 1963, 401–408; Rossi 1892, 83–89.

∾

If Irish immigrants, ignorant, bigoted, addicted to liquor, are regarded poorly, our fellow countrymen do not enjoy higher esteem. In New York being Italian is almost a reason to be ashamed.

The vast majority of our compatriots, comprised of the wretched class from the southern provinces, live in the dirtiest neighborhood in the city, called the Five Points. It is an agglomeration of repulsive, dilapidated, black houses where people are piled on top of each other worse than beasts. Large families live in only one room: men, women, dogs, cats, and monkeys eat and sleep together in the same cubbyhole without air or light.

In some houses on Baxter or Mulberry Street there is so much dirt and foul air it would seem impossible that there would not be a fatal cholera outbreak with the first summer heat every year. Yet many people who never wash their faces and are condemned to live in unhealthy hovels with their squalid wives and their ragged children still work, earn, and save.

There are very many disgraceful scenes to witness in the Five Points. One day, seated on the steps of one of the blackest houses, I saw an Italian woman who, with her breast exposed, nursed a baby monkey as if it were a child. The monkey was ill, and that woman, the wife of an organ grinder, was attempting to cure him with her own milk!

"Those who arrive with a little money," the landlord on Rose Street told me, "all go inland. Those who don't have a penny stay in the cities on the coast—New York, Boston, Philadelphia."

And he told me that seventy-five percent of them are peasants who during the summer are taken to work on the railroad or in the country, and in winter come back to fill the streets of New York where young boys shine shoes and adults are employed in repulsive jobs rejected by workers of other nationalities—loading garbage onto boats and unloading it at sea, cleaning sewers and the like—or even going around with a bag over their shoulders, rummaging through garbage barrels, collecting paper, rags, bones, broken glass.

And since there are more than twenty-five thousand Italians in New York alone, one cannot walk the street without finding a boy on a corner who shouts *Shine! Shine!*, inviting you to have your shoes shined, or a ragpicker bent under a load, walking with an iron hook in his hand. In this way, the Italian is continuously exposed to the poverty of his own country and the degradation of his countrymen.

I was deeply disheartened, humiliated, and wounded in my national pride— and at this stage I had only seen the Five Points in passing. When I visited more closely, I found incredible things. One night, for example, I had the occasion to go down into one of those underground rooms where spoiled, stale beer is sold for two pennies a pint.

Beneath the interior courtyards of the most repulsive *tenement-houses* there are certain dark and foul cellars, lit by a kerosene lamp, where you dance and drink cheap beer. If you are not from the neighborhood it is dangerous to venture into those catacombs of vice and degradation without being accompanied by a *policeman*.

The bad beer is purchased in this way. Every day the proprietor of the cellar buys the beer that has remained on the bottom of the barrels the night before at a dishonest price, often getting it for nothing, from the closest beer halls. Then, when the beer car passes by and takes the empty barrels from every *bar room*, he sends a man back who helps to load them with the agreement that he will collect the drippings into a bottle.

So the leftovers from the beer halls and the drippings from the barrels become the drink that is passed off in these cellars. It is a reddish, bitter, nauseating liquid that intoxicates, upsetting the stomach, and always makes anyone who is able to swallow it even thirstier.

At dusk, when the streets of Five Points are swarming with people, out from the most hidden hovels come shady figures: they are women, mostly Irish, tattered, unkempt, prematurely aged who, along with the bruises from punches sustained the night before, bear the traces of the most despicable debauchery on their emaciated faces. These hags, clutching mud-stained shawls to their scratched chests, stumble down into the *basements*.

The *basement* is usually furnished with a counter, behind which is the owner—Italian—an ugly mug surrounded by barrels of *stale beer*. Against the walls there are some benches where the customers sit. Amid the sound of a harmonica or some other badly-tuned instrument, they dance the dances of distant countries very badly, mostly Irish jigs and Italian tarantellas.

Looking through the doors of these caves around midnight, under a dense cloud of smoke, drunken men and women can be seen on benches; some drink, sing, mumble jokes, argue, and snore while other couples jump and stumble, in scandalous poses, in coarse postures, amid violent jostling.

The patrons are international: Americans, Germans, Irish, Italians. Occasionally, with a word, the competition for one of those women causes brawls to break out, punches to fly, knives to flash. After two, when there is no more beer in the barrels or more oil in the lamps, the scene changes. One by one, they lie down on the benches, they bed down underneath, males and females mixed together, unconscious. The atmosphere is stifling. The wheezing sleep of those creatures is occasionally disturbed by someone who sits up and with unintelligible curses spews the swallowed liquid all over the nearest companion.

The Five Points are at the center of the Italian slavery practiced with impunity by *bosses*, owners. These people are also Italian who, profiting from the country's practices and their own knowledge of the English language, assume work contracts directly, take the number of workers they need, and give them less than half of the wages due.

So it is with all of the physical work on the interior, from excavating rivers, laying railroad track, to building bridges or factories: our laborers are led like flocks of sheep by *bosses*, who exploit them in the most inhumane ways.

There are Italian *bosses* who have taken a large number of laborers from the Five Points or have had them come directly from Italy by paying their passage to bring them to work on some big job site. Besides passage, the companies contract with the owners or the foremen for two to three *scudi* per day of work for each worker, who does not, however, receive more than one from his *boss*. These veritable slave traders have another way of taking even more of their wages from their workers by obligating the men to buy food and clothing from them. Finally, they rob them again when sending money to their families in Italy.

While the workers toil from morning to night, the *bosses* leisurely smoke and monitor them with rifles slung over their shoulders and revolvers on their belts. They seem to be—and are—true bandits.

What if some honorable man, outraged by this Camorra, tried to bring together the peasants from the provinces of Avellino, the Abruzzi, Basilicata, and explain to them the wages the companies pay, two thirds of which go into the pockets of greedy *bosses*, and advised them to tell the owners to go to hell? He would be wasting his time.

"Young man," any peasant would respond with a stupid smile," we are ignorant and don't know any English. It's our *boss* who brought us here, he knows where the work is, and he contracts with the companies. What would we do without him?"

Others would regard the question with mistrust, suspecting that he is one of the *bosses'* rivals. Always used to being fooled, they cannot convince themselves that there may be someone who would advise them selflessly, solely for their own well-being. Between an unknown honorable man and an exploiter from their own, they prefer the latter. Others resign themselves to their sad fate out of fear, as all *bosses* are overbearing, determined, blood-thirsty.

The directors and engineers of the companies are well aware of the Camorra, but do not care. They consider our laborers to be inferior, equal to Chinese *coolies*, and say: "What can we do if, like ignorant beasts, illiterate, incapable of understanding one word of English, they need their owners? Too bad for them!"

The Italian Ministry of Foreign Affairs could have addressed this very sad state of affairs many years ago if the consulates in New York, Boston, Philadelphia, New Orleans had established offices designated to welcome immigrants, to serve as their guide, to put them under the direction of honest men who would lead them to work without cheating them, who would act as their advisors in good faith.

Such welfare, relief, and charity offices would have quickly destroyed the Mafia, the Camorra, the *bosses*. With them, they also would have long since put an end to the veritable white slave trade which is the exportation of shoe shine boys, harpists, ragpickers.

But our government, which spends millions on the so-called Colony of Eritrea and on Italian schools in the East, has never done anything to protect the well-being and morality of the Italian colonies in North America, and it is no wonder that the Mafia and the Camorra flourish there as in the worst times of the Bourbons and that the Italian, illiterate, knife-wielding, exploited or exploiter, is despised more than the Irish and the Chinese.

Translated by Giulia Prestia

To Giuseppe Giacosa

∾ *Giuseppe Antonio Cadicamo*

San Demetrio Corone (Cosenza), Italy, February 2, 1842—New York, New York, 1921

In Italy, Professor Giuseppe Antonio Cadicamo, of whom very little is known, published poetry in a series of pamphlets dedicated to patriotic Italian themes. Poems center on the defense of the betrayed workers in Marsah, Libya, and Marseilles; other poems center on the Balkans, in the vein of anti-Islamic irredentism. Among these is "Davvero è morta? Ode patriottica" (1877), relating to Albania and its early roots. In this last pamphlet, among other things, "a Bosnian novella in five cantos," is announced, entitled *Zulica di Costainitza*. However, it was not published.

The ninth of fourteen children of a notable Arbresh (Italian-Albanian) family in which the father was also the mayor of San Demetrio, Cadicamo was the director of the boarding gymnasium of Corigliano Calabro. He came to the United States in 1887. Subsequently, in New York, for three years he applied himself with intelligent diligence to editing the *Eco d'Italia,* after which, in February 1891, he founded a boarding school, the Dante Alighieri, in Astoria, Queens, declaring that "it is the sacred duty of those born in Italy to conserve the character of the race and of the nationality of the new Italian generation, born and bred in a foreign country." Furthermore, the program of the new institute asserts that "it is enough to give a glance at the major part of colonial families" to become aware of the fact that "compared to Italian parents, the children do not possess anything Italian except their blood and name. All the rest is being lost; by their assimilation into the country of their birth, their Italian language, character, traditions, attachment and customs are being fatally effaced." The issues of *Eco d'Italia* dedicate ample space to the school, where students could attend elementary and upper grades, a technical-commercial section, and a classical section. Cadicamo appears as a benefactor of culture, and as such, besides as a prolific poet, he is additionally remembered by Bernardino Ciambelli in two novels. In *La Trovatella di Mulberry Street* (The Foundling of Mulberry Street, 1919), he figures as composer of a chorus set to music by countess Gilda Ruta, very well recognized as a musician in New York at the time, and above all, as author of a "splendid" poem, "Abba Garima" (evidently, celebratory of the Italian Eastern African enterprises), which is declaimed by Luigina, the principal personage in the book. The news of the short life of the boarding school in Astoria is revealed by an allusion that precedes some of the more diverting pages of another novel of Ciambelli, *I Misteri di Bleecker Street* (Mysteries of Bleecker Street, 1899). Already, by 1897, the period of Ciambelli's novel, Cadicamo's noble project had been bankrupted, and the establishment would be transformed into a bordello renovated to attract an international clientele. In New York, in 1906, Cadicamo published *Visione epitalamica*; in 1909 *Tennysoniane: "Nothing will die," "All things will die," Versione libera* (New York: F. Tocci); in 1910, the collection *Davidica*; and in 1915, nothing less than an actual screenplay entitled *Rosmunda*.

The poem printed here was recited by the author on the occasion of a small banquet in honor of the dramatist Giuseppe Giacosa, who happened to be on tour in the United States and who in 1898, in Italy, would publish an interesting book entitled *Impressioni d'America*. Giacosa was famous as the author of two libretti for Giacomo Puccini, *La Bohème* and *Tosca*. Beyond the subject of the occasion, the poetry exhibits interesting and unusual epic elements, as well as rapid descents from the cosmic level to that of the immigrants, with reference to the internal discord of the Italian community (a reference that was probably obscure to Giacosa). The theme of internal discord reflected concerns expressed in the *Eco d'Italia* and in other newspapers, exhorting for the unity of the colony, a unity evoked again on the occasions of various campaigns for solidarity with the far-off *patria*.[1]

ESSENTIAL BIBLIOGRAPHY

Alfonsi 1989; Ciambelli 1899, 202; Ciambelli 1919, 60 and 378; "Il nuovo Collegio-Convitto, Dante Alighieri, in Astoria," in *L'Eco d'Italia* (New York), February 3 and 4, 1891.

1. I am obliged to Salvatore Bugliano, of the Centro Studi Genealogia Arbesh, for some information reported here. —Ed.

ↀ

By now they're musty legends,
The Crusades, eternally
Caught in the grand pages
Of epic poetry.
With a turbine's driving force,
With the roar of thunderstorms,
Other crusades erupt from
The old world, hapless swarms
Fleeing their native place
Cursing fate, with a few
Curses for the wicked
Tax collector too.

This fever, O Giacosa,
That impels all these
Workers to leave their homeland
To sail across the seas,
Is useful to the wise mind
That guides and regulates
According to a hidden law
And corrects our fates.
Just as the ancient culture
Born of the Latin line
Migrated with the gallant
Warriors in Palestine,
So, on this *nova terra*
Promessa, in weaponless
Fingers of laborers
Migrating seeds progress,
Seeds of Europe's wisdom
That the American sun
Quickly fertilizes
And grafts onto a sovereign
People that disdains
All privilege and degree,

All autocratic rulers,
All popes and royalty.

The torrent of thinking atoms
Swells and roils about,
Shatters dikes and dams,
Giacosa, have no doubt.
It swells and carries over
From the Saturnian shore
So dear to its exiled children
With deities at war,
Intelligent, industrious
And robust pioneers,
And every day another,
Thicker troop appears.
Here the displaced souls
Crush against intense
Rebels, deluded paupers,
And gentle artisans,
And in the clash of varied
Elements, the sky starts
Darkening, and Discord
Roars and poisons hearts,
The struggles of the savage
Sensuality of Cain,
Outbursts when wars are over
Of the hatreds that remain.

But when the raging winds
Turn the sea's surface violent,
The waters down below
Stay calm and still and silent.
Just so, just so, Giacosa,
The Italian colony
Stays calm and steady through
Storms and adversity.
The people work, they work
Under the burning sun,

In harsh and freezing places
They fearlessly work on.
They split the virgin soil
Of vast and empty prairies
They dig out hidden treasures
From lifeless mines and quarries.
Where giant bridges' structures
Rise elegant and tall,
Where hands are shaping statues
Or frescoes fill a wall,
Where the new steam engines
Puff as they pull trains
Encroaching on wild beasts
Across the desolate plains,
Where Prometheus' torch
Is shining splendidly,
Bright emblem of progress,
Guarantor of peace,
Here, focused on their duty,
Not profits, you find bands
Of Italian working people,
Italian artists' hands.

Out of shame and damage
The ugly struggles will
Be swept away, the howling
Tempests will grow still;
Beyond the shuddering of
The dark and angry stream,
Like an Eastern sapphire,
Hope begins to gleam,
And minds, out of the filthy
Social depths, now feel
Themselves rise to the azure
Realm of the ideal.
The blessed love of art
And ardent patriotism
Calm the stupid rages

Of faction and of schism.
And if a sudden squall
Shrieks across the bland
Esperian air, if there
Is a trembling of the land;
If cholera in Naples
And flooding of the Mincio
Bring misery to the people;
If from atop the Pincio
Death hurls his heated darts
At the royal Quirinal,
If at Dogali a dreadful
Slaughter should befall,
Pity pulsating for
Brothers in distant places
Binds all Italians here
Together with strong laces.

If, from Parnassus' slope
Where one day Dante rose
So he might speak the *novo
Idioma* to all those
Of the Bel Paese, a bard
Has come to us, whom we
Revere, as the world envies
The Muses of Italy,
If, on the well-versed boards
A goddess treads, he fashions
A living picture from our
Human faults, the passions
Appear, and through the trembling
Audience they wind,
Inflaming every body,
Igniting every mind;
And if from the stirred public
Applause is showered down,
If on that poet's brows
They place the laurel crown,

Giacosa, there isn't one
Italian here who hasn't
Felt a great consolation
Deep in his soul, who doesn't
Exult as you honor the art,
Steeped in antiquity,
Of the buskin, both within
And far beyond Italy.

Hail, Giacosa! sing
The American multitude
In new and strangely shaped
Huge buildings that protrude
Proudly above broad shores,
Soaring into the sky,
Heights that give perennial
Pleasure to the eye.
In our beloved homeland,
That sweet edenic clime,
Genius finds and shows us
Heights even more sublime,
Those of Italian thought,
Those heights immeasurable
Whose bedrock is the True,
Whose sun's the Beautiful.

Giacosa, to the summit
Of those you made your way,
The muses placed the laurel
Upon your brow that day;
There you were infused
With heavenly inspiration,
To imagine kinds and forms
And give flesh to the creation.
And, trembling with your love
For the race of mortal creatures,
You have portrayed their fault
With Sophoclean features.

So, deeply stirred, the public
Gives its applause to you
With profoundest admiration,
In the old world and the new.

Translated by Michael Palma

Two Stories

⌒ᐃ *Edoardo Michelangeli*

Born Rome, 1860

Little is known of Edoardo Michelangeli, who was born in Rome around 1860. In 1877, he published a booklet entitled *S. Fridolino confessore, protettore e titolare dei Cantoni svizzeri Glarus e San Gallo, ricavata dal testo di San Notkero, tradotta e annotata da Edoardo Michelangeli alunno del collegio francese, diretto dai Fratelli delle Scuole Cristiane in Roma* (Rome: Tipografia Guerra e Mirri). This indicates that his education was of a certain rank, and that he studied with the Jesuits. Another small work he published, also on a clerical subject, was *The Thirteen Pope Leos: Historical* (Rome: Tipografia Forense, 1878). In 1890, thirty-year-old Michelangeli arrived in the United States on a passenger ship from Naples and headed to Chicago, which he found disappointing, even though his occupation was that of "publisher."

In New York, at the beginning of the 1890s, he was the chief editor of the daily *Eco d'Italia*, managed by Felice Tocci. In this role, he was active in the community and delivered speeches at numerous public events, from the banquet recognizing the good services of the Italian Home to the even more obligatory occasion of the mass meeting for the victims of the mass lynching of Sicilians in New Orleans, which took place, at his suggestion, on March 20, 1891, at Cooper Union. On that occasion, he spoke, along with Luigi Roversi of *Il Progresso Italo-Americano*, Bernadino Ciambelli of the *Cristoforo Colombo*, and with Teodoro Palumbo of the *Emigrato Italiano*, affirming that "the calm of the strong is ours," and auguring "that the Statue of Liberty veils her face in darkness just as today the Italian flag is darkened." Michelangeli was always addressed as "professor," perhaps also because he collaborated actively with the Istituto Italiano and with the Children's Aid Society, giving lessons on the history of Italy.

An individual unquestionably well known, he became involved in various typical journalistic polemics pertaining to the Italian colony. He launched notable press campaigns: shortly before the New Orleans massacre, for example, he revealed notorious cases of the exploitation of Italian laborers by unscrupulous bosses in South Carolina. Then, in the inflammatory days after the hanging of eleven Italians, in an editorial in *L'Eco d'Italia* of March 22, 1891, he inveighed vituperatively against New Orleans: "Even devoid of the most humanitarian and civil principles, this is a city that deserves punishment only a cannon can inflict!!!" A threatening letter was published on the first page. "You had better keep your damned mouth shut," it read; otherwise, "New Orleans will be but a picnic compared to what will occur." Added was a series of very heavy insults against Italians in general: "A nation of born murderers"; "the sooner they are exterminated the better for the World—You specially so." The letter, which came from Virginia, concluded with the retort of threatening to take recourse in arms: "Let Italy send on her ironclads. She will never want to try it a second time." It was signed, "Mafia." Michelangeli commented on it with contempt: "If that madman or coward . . . would present himself within the range of my Italian boot, he would return to his forests . . . edified." Shortly after the happenings at New Orleans, Michelangeli orchestrated other important campaigns regarding the problem of the exploitation of prostitution by Italian criminals and the preservation of the house in Staten Island where in 1850 the inventor Antonio Meucci had given hospitality to Giuseppe Garibaldi, who had gone into exile after the fall of the Roman Republic.

Michelangeli interests us above all as the author of one of the first short stories on the Italian American environment, published in the pages of the *Eco*: "Il Miserere del Trovatore," published here. From a clarification by Michelangeli, in response to the critics of the daily *Cristoforo Columbo,* which, among other things, questioned if he were the author of the story, we learn that it had already been published in 1881 in the *Corriere di Firenze* and that the version in *L'Eco* was modified to reflect the specifically *newyorkese* environment.

"Il Miserere" was not the only story of Michelangeli published in that period in the *Eco.* Of subjects not pertaining to immigrants, there is, for example, "Un viaggio nelle mie tasche" (A Journey in My Pockets, February 8, 1891). Other stories are cited, if not certainly attributable to him, certainly having passed through his hands and having been prepared by him for publication. The most relevant among these is "Il Dramma di Mulberry St.," which, like "Miserere," was presented as a true story. Such emphasis on the realistic character of the story makes this material representative of typical products of journalistic Italian American literature. Also, because of the themes treated and the taste for the heavily dramatic, the stories anticipate the large number of romantic narrations of Bernardino Ciambelli.

ESSENTIAL BIBLIOGRAPHY

Michelangeli 1873, 1891a, 1891b.

☙

The Troubadour's Miserere: A True Story

The clock struck two after midnight.[1]

The Brooklyn Bridge was deserted.

The current below broke with a weak murmur against the bridge's heavy arches.

A thick, damp, unwholesome fog darkened the air. The electric lamplight seemed like a nebula lost in immense space.

Giorgio Valieri, bundled in a fur coat, was thinking as he walked to his apartment on the other side of the bridge. He was around forty, tall, slender, with a proud, free stride. His thick black hair framed a face with irregular, pronounced features, which nevertheless formed an attractive whole.

Women went wild over him: few had resisted the mysterious spell of his imaginative, poetic talk, as heated as lava from Vesuvius, in whose shadow he was born. He was well off and bent on enjoying life. Although he didn't brag about it, his friends took him for a Don Juan, a Don Juan who could really count in his amorous archives a growing number of beautiful young wives who had risked an exception to the marriage contract for the first time.

However, once in a while, he wandered mentally through the cemetery of his loves. A blond curl carefully closed in a red silk box caught his attention and with a sigh he kissed it affectionately. Perhaps it was his only memory of a true, sincere love, the only one from a life of adventures. In those lulls he felt approaching old age most strongly; he dreamed of a family, a beloved wife, two lively, curly-haired children with sweet smiles calling him daddy. . . .

That evening he had been up late with high society. More tired than usual from the insipid chatter, he found it a pleasure to walk along his street, to be alone and lose himself in thought. In fact he heard the coming and going of the trains only as one long high whistle.

---

1. From *L'Eco d'Italia*, February 1, 1891.

A young boy leaning with his elbows on the bridge parapet, staring wide-eyed at the water as though measuring its depth, challenged that solitude.

He appeared to be about twelve years old.

The nearby lamplight barely illuminated a patched jacket, torn trousers, and a pointed cap decorated with a bunch of artificial flowers, held by an old colorless ribbon. On the young boy's dark, haggard face, framed with long blond hair falling in ringlets on his bare neck, there was not the extremely beautiful smile or extremely proud look of an Italian child.

You might say he looked like one of those unhappy beings that the cruelty of an unloved father and the greed of a speculator pushed out of the house every morning to search for a bit of bread.

The boy turned away from the river toward the street. He pulled a violin from under his jacket and began to scrape out "The Troubadour's Miserere."

Why play at that hour?

What reward did he expect from that desolate tune? He knew no one was listening. He wasn't even aware of the only person who was coming slowly his way.

The unhappy boy, who could not read music, drew from the small instrument sounds so harmonious, so inspired as to compete with a seasoned artist.

No one had ever explained the title's meaning to him, but the little musician felt that those notes held sobs, farewells, and thoughts of death.

Perhaps he didn't know that that unique harmony in the pain of isolation and sharp torment of the soul supplied his art with enough expressive power to move the most indifferent listener. It seemed that every note broke a chord in the sad little boy's heart, and that he might fall lifeless on the ground clinging to his violin when the tune ended.

Enrico stopped halfway on the bridge to listen. He didn't want to interrupt the "Miserere." He waited for the last note, carried by the frozen night winds, to vanish in the air. Then he went up to the young boy and putting a hand on his shoulder: "Bravo! You played beautifully. Too bad no one heard you. Here, I want to reward you well," he said, handing him a five dollar bill.

The boy politely refused the money.

"Thank you. I'm not asking for charity."

"So much the better. However, I am free to show you my gratitude for the pleasure you brought me."

"No one owes me anything. I didn't play for you."

"Well, then, whom did you play for?"

"For myself," the boy said sadly, resting his blue eyes on Giorgio's face.

"But you live on your daily earnings. Maybe someone is waiting for you at home."

"I won't be going home."

"What's that? You'll stay on this deserted bridge all night? You'll be arrested for a vagabond."

"I'm not afraid."

"Your father will be worried because you are late."

"My father? I don't know him."

"Your mother?"

At this memory the musician winced. Then in a weak voice he added: "She would have killed me."

Giorgio ventured other questions.

The strolling musician was silent. Valdieri understood he had no right to the stranger's confidence, and slipping the money in the young boy's pocket, he quickly walked away.

The boy put his violin on the ground and looked up to the sky.

Not a star . . . nothing.

Solid darkness.

Then he nimbly climbed over the parapet and without taking a breath jumped into the river.

The splash in the water made Giorgio turn. Not seeing the boy he imagined he had fallen, and going to the parapet he yelled as loud as he could. "Help! Help!" And he ran to the nearest bank.

After a few minutes guards, sailors, boatmen gathered around Valdieri asking why he was shouting.

"A boy is drowning, hurry," Giorgio said breathlessly.

But because no one moved: "Five hundred dollars to the one who saves him."

He was fascinated by the mystery of the musician and wanted to save him at any cost.

"Hell!" a sailor exclaimed, his mouth watering at the sum, but the night was as dark as the inside of an oven.

"A boat! A boat!" Valdieri yelled. "I'll go myself with two oarsmen. A thousand dollars to the one who follows me."

He waited a few moments for the boat to be readied. Two robust, willing men took the oars while Giorgio, standing between them, pointed out where he had last seen the violin player.

The boat owner was right. The shore was covered with thick layers of fog. In spite of the lamps there was nothing in view. It was a dangerous proposition.

The oarsmen refused to go.

Valdieri pleaded, promised more money . . . In vain.

Then moved by heroic feelings, he found the energy and resolution.

He had one of those inspired moments when one's strength is doubled under the influence of a dominating will. Something inexplicable, unknown, moved him toward the sad violin player. He believed that that sacrifice could expiate his faults . . . and a beautiful woman's image crossed his mind like a flash of lightning.

In an instant he was free of his fur coat and quick as a wink jumped in the water.

Without thinking the boatmen cried out. The promise of a thousand dollars had made a deep impression. Sure of a large reward they immediately shoved off in two lifeboats.

After a few minutes Giorgio's head appeared on the surface of the water and then vanished again.

A disheartened groan followed that disappearance. Everyone thought he was a victim of his heroism.

The boatmen raised lanterns with tensed arms to shine a light as far as possible. They waited in vain. The boats' rudders were turned toward the shore when every man let out a shout of joy. Giorgio had reappeared holding the young boy's body in one arm. The courageous savior was exhausted by the supreme struggle.

His strength was gone. They threw him a rope and a moment later Valdieri and the little musician were saved.

Taking shelter in a hospitable home nearby Giorgio, after changing clothes, warmed himself beside a large fireplace, and revived his strength with a glass of hot wine while he waited for the boy to regain consciousness.

The strolling musician opened his eyes and looked around.

"My violin," he asked in a weak voice.

An hour after being fortified by a cordial he was sitting by the fire. He stared strangely at those around him, almost as if he wanted to ask them why they had kept him from dying. However, he did not say a word, and hiding his pale little face in his hands, he closed his eyes.

Valdieri understood what the boy was thinking.

God only knows how desperate a boy can be who throws himself into the arms of death, a boy that has an instinct for life more than anything.

What does tomorrow mean to him! The sorrow will soon be replaced by joy, the tears by a smile.

How much unspeakable torment, agony, suffering, he must have had to endure to embrace that final solution.

Valdieri knew money's power to regulate every human activity. Whatever the cruelty of those who oppressed the poor might be, it was sure to be wiped away with a bank note.

An intimate, mysterious voice drew him to that abandoned soul; he would give anything for the right to protect him.

He wanted to question him and so politely asked the others to leave.

"Do you recognize me?" he asked.

"Yes, sir," the little musician replied.

"Do you think I like you?"

"Yes, sir. You gave me five dollars."

"Do you trust me?"

"I believe you are a good man but you did something very bad to me."

"I did?"

"Yes. I wanted to die and you saved me."

"Why did you want to die . . . think of your parents. . . ."

"They turned me out of the house."

"So young. . . ."

"It was my stepfather. He hates me. But he has been punished. My sister Zeffiretta is dead," the boy added, with a sob.

"What is your name?"

"Stecchetto."

"Where do you live?"

"My stepfather turned me over to a certain music master. I live with twenty others who all play an instrument, one the harp, one the guitar, another the violin, and other instruments. If we don't earn a dollar a day the maestro beats us mercilessly in the evening and we go to bed without supper. I never scrape together what he wants. I play badly, I cry while I play . . . one should laugh but who gives me the courage? My little sister is dead . . . I'm always hungry."

"Is your stepfather poor?"

"Very poor."

"Does he work?"

"Two or three times a week."

"Saturdays he comes home drunk; he beats my mother, and she takes what he has left. The next day we eat potatoes."

"And the other days?"

The boy did not answer. Giorgio was moved by the cruel realism of the simple story.

"What misery," he murmured. Then he held Stecchetto and looked at him kindly. "I'll take care of you."

In tears Stecchetto embraced his liberator.

"Now tell me where your stepfather lives."

"On Spring Street."

"Your parents' name."

"Francesco. My mother's name is Carmela."

Giorgio started involuntarily at that name.

"Carmela," he repeated. "But her family name?"

"I don't remember."

"The name of your real father?"

"I never knew it . . . Before mama married Francesco she was a seamstress."

A question passed through Valdieri's mind.

"And then?" he asked anxiously.

"When we were alone mama would often cry and say that they had betrayed her . . . and she would cover me in kisses."

"Go on, go on, for God's sake," Giorgio said, emotionally overwrought.

"One day we met Francesco. He seemed like an honest man . . . and in those days he seemed to love me. He was always giving me candy. Mama was attracted to such a nice man and married him. But it wasn't a month before he hated me and I didn't know why. One evening he pulled me from my mother's arms, who was screaming in desperation, to take me to the music master. But she defended me to the end. She forced Francesco back two times with scissors, but he kicked her in the head so the poor woman fainted in a pool of blood. They'll kill me, they'll kill me." The boy broke into a flood of tears.

"Carmela, Carmela, could it be . . . No, it's not possible," Giorgio shouted, beside himself; and pulling his hair in a frenzy he suddenly stood up, took the boy by the arm and brought him under the light.

"Your mother's maiden name?" he asked in a fit of indescribable agony.

"I don't remember," the little musician replied for the second time, lifting his face that was immediately illuminated by the lantern.

Giorgio stared at him for an moment; then as if those features reminded him of another. . . .

"You! You . . . Are . . . No it can't be." Shaken by nervous agitation he called the cordial family back and asked the head of the family to get him a cab.

It took half an hour for the cab to arrive.

Valdieri saluted those good people and placed Stecchetto in the carriage carefully and sat down next to him.

While they were about to leave the boy asked: "My violin."

"Remember to bring it to my house tomorrow," prompted Giorgio and gave the coachman his address.

Stimulated by his earnings the coachman's thin nag flew to the lower end of the city. In a short time the carriage entered Spring Street.

It stopped at Valdieri's signal. The two descended in pitch black darkness.

To move without danger Giorgio had to detach the lantern from the carriage to light the way.

He went up some steep broken steps with the boy behind him and stopped at the first door.

In the room he heard the even steps of someone who tries to kill time by pacing automatically. Valdieri knocked. No one answered.

"Call," he said quietly.

"Mama, it's me," the boy shouted.

"You? You?" a voice from inside replied.

At the sound of that voice Giorgio had no doubts. He leaned against the wall to keep from falling.

"Yes, me, Stecchetto. Open the door."

They heard a shout of joy but the door did not open. The woman was afraid of another scene.

"Is the maestro with you?" she asked.

"No. There is a gentleman who saved me from the river when I jumped in to kill myself."

The door opened wide immediately.

"Kill yourself. Kill yourself," Carmela exclaimed, embracing her son.

It was a moment of unspeakable joy.

"She . . . She . . . in that condition," Giorgio repeated to himself pale as death, with his hand resting on his heart almost as to suppress the violent beating. The happy-go-lucky, the happy Don Juan now saw the consequences of a bad deed. His numbed conscience rebelled and judged him harshly.

He looked at Carmela. Where was the girl of long ago to whom in a passionate frenzy he had repeated De Amicis' love poems hundreds of times?

"Carmela, Carmela, I'm ready . . . To make it up to you. Forgive me," Giorgio shouted in pain.

"You! You the savior of my—of our—son? You've come too late. One day, desperately hungry and without work, I was forced to provide an existence for my . . . for our son. It's my fault; I wanted to die that day, but I lacked the courage: I was a mother!"

"Carmela, forget the past. I have money. I can do anything."

"Who is asking you for anything?" the woman added, raising her head proudly.

"Don't be selfish. Think of my son's education."

"Never!"

"Let me at least do something."

"Never!"

Then as though regretting those cruel words: "Get me a job." Bowing her head and holding out her gaunt hands to Giorgio she broke into tears.

She still loved him. . . .

Clinging to his mother's knees Stecchetto followed the finale of the domestic drama with tears in his eyes.

The Drama of Mulberry St.: A True Story

NEW YORK, MARCH 14.

"When you receive this I will be back in Italy.[2] There in my native mountains I will try to forget. If some neighbor wants to shake my hand on my return he will hardly recognize me because I have changed so much from the atrocious suffering that torments me night and day. My hair that turned white that terrible night is now falling out, and I will soon be bald. I have lost all self-esteem. I haven't killed myself because an idiot doesn't have the courage. I am nothing more than a walking cadaver. Publish my story. Don't forget names and dates; it will be a mark of shame on the brow of that dreadful woman."

We will not mention names or dates. It's not for us to avenge the unfortunate man; however, we will leave in all the bare facts, which are true human documents.

I

A few years ago we arrived in New York: my wife Luisa, my six-year-old daughter, Enrichetta, and I. We had saved some money from the sale of our household goods, and so we were able to open a little shoe shop on Mulberry Street No. . . .

2. From *L'Eco d'Italia*, March 29, 1891.

and live honestly on my trade. My wife took care of the house; after three or four months our little girl could speak a smattering of English. How sweet she was! She was my love; my love, my future. I could have kissed her all day! During the long hours at work when I couldn't see her because she didn't come to the shop with her mother, I would make a quick visit home, nearby, at No. . . .

One Thursday I ran home; I knocked at the door and no one came.

"Luisa, Luisa," I called. Silence.

I had a bad feeling something might have happened and ran upstairs to ask the neighbors. When we forced open the door of my house, a man wrapped in a peasant's cloak came out. He dashed down the steps and passed me without realizing I had recognized him. He was Giovanni, a fellow Italian. I ran inside. Luisa was smoothing the bed. To fall from paradise into inferno, to have been happy and tranquil for so many years, and in a single moment lose everything . . . everything, it's terrible, it breaks one's heart! I would rather die a thousand deaths than face that horrible, agonizing, moment! Yelling dreadful curses I fell on that woman. I threw her to the floor, kicked her, and covered her with bruises, while that shameless woman kept repeating: "No, I don't want you anymore; we are in America, I am free!"

I would have killed her if our little girl hadn't come back from a neighbor's and shouted: "Papa. Mama!"

I let the slut go . . . Bursting into tears I embraced my daughter. That innocent child was all I had left! That woman lying on the floor who had betrayed me, that woman I had loved so much, had the wicked courage of her sin. Who had stolen that woman's body and soul from me? Quicker than I can write it I took my revolver and ran to look for Giovanni. At the bar the usual drunks said with a sneer: "Giovanni left town and said to tell you hello!"

II

I went back to work. Every day my little girl brought me something to eat in the shop and evenings I put a mattress on the table for a bed. I can't say I slept. I don't think I slept any more than an hour or two after that day.

My Enrichetta often asked me: "Why don't you come home?"

Struggling to hold back my tears I would answer: "No, my little girl, I have a lot to do."

"Yes, it's good for you to work. Anyway mama is calm now even if you don't come, because she knows you must work."

It was the knife in the wound. That innocent child didn't know that those words made me bleed. One noontime my little girl didn't come. I waited nervously until evening with nothing to eat.

"Can she be ill? Doesn't she love me anymore? Dear God, what agony!"

As it grew late, I couldn't wait. I had sworn not to set foot in that shameful house again, but love for my daughter was stronger than my vow. The door was ajar. The whole room was upside down, the dresser drawers empty . . . and neither my wife nor child was there. The neighbors told me that around two in the afternoon they had loaded their trunks in a cab and headed toward the East River.

"Wicked, wicked woman," I shouted, and staggered back into the house.

I don't remember anything else about that dreadful day; I only knew when it was morning again because of the cold air coming in an open window. I put a hand to my forehead and pulled it back covered with blood! I had hurt my head in a fall. To rob me of my only love, my daughter! It was too horrible!

III

I sold the shop; the thought of revenge entered me like a cold knife. It cut into my flesh and brain, giving me relative peace, almost as though that knife sticking in live flesh had stopped the blood flowing from the wound; I could think of nothing else.

I roamed around the Italian neighborhoods in New York with a pistol ready. Not a trace. Evenings my determined, premeditated vendetta turned into miserable obsessions. An Irish neighbor who knew the sad story helped me drown my sorrow in whiskey. From whiskey to unnameable houses. The way from idleness to vice is one short step. One night I went to a tenement house of dubious elegance after a long session at the bar. The "lady," inviting me to sit in a rocking chair, made a sign for me to wait. The whiskey and cigar fumes had gone to my weakened brain. I waited in a stupefied drunken state. A familiar voice startled me. In the dim kerosene lamplight I saw a man embracing a woman as they came out of a bedroom.

A wild animal howl erupted from my breast. I took the pistol from my pocket and aimed it. It was my wife! The man ran away, while the adulteress, white as death, in a frenzy of fear, shouted: "Enrichetta, hurry. It's your father!"

"No, no, she mustn't see; first a bullet in your heart, you foul prostitute!"

The gun went off. But it didn't strike that woman. It struck the child coming toward me, holding out her arms and calling me with the sweet name of Daddy. I loved, I adored no one but her and I killed her!

IV

The next morning some friends dragged me to the bank on Mott Street No. and said to the owner Don. . . .

"What do you mean you don't recognize him!?"

"Oh, poor man!" the banker exclaimed. Overnight my hair had turned white!

"Yes, read this." And they showed him our newspaper. Read it, Don. . . ."

"My God, is this possible? Last night in the tenement house at number . . . on Mulberry Street, a certain . . . 26 years old, playing with a pistol, unfortunately struck his child, killing her instantly. So testified the landlady and some compatriots of the poor woman. But they didn't believe her at the Station House and she was arrested."

"How horrible," exclaimed the banker. "But. . . ."

Then one of my compatriots told him the truth. That good man took pity on me, and shaking my hand, said to me: "You are more unfortunate than guilty." Then with the little amount I still had in savings, he made out a ticket for Italy. Just as I was getting ready to leave America I heard that my wife had been sentenced to three years in prison. Judge R . . . did not want to concede that the little girl had been killed by chance!

Oh! My Enrichetta! My Enrichetta, how unhappy I am.

However, I still have to complete the vendetta. When I have killed Giovanni I will die a happy man. That is why I am going back to Italy where he may be hiding.

Translated by Martha King

A Story, Sketches, and a Play

ᕧ *Bernardino Ciambelli*

Lucca, Italy, 1862–New York, New York, July 2, 1931

Bernardino Ciambelli is a central figure in the colonial culture between the nineteenth and twentieth centuries. A very prolific author, active until the end of the 1920s, Ciambelli was born in Lucca or in the province of Lucca (perhaps at Bagni). He settled in the United States in about 1888. Ten years later, after an experience on the editorial staff of *Cristoforo Colombo*, he was summoned by Francesco Frugone to direct the *Bollettino della guerra ispano-americana* (Bulletin of the Spanish American War), soon renamed *Bollettino della Sera* (Evening Bulletin), a daily.

From this moment on, he contributed extensively to many newspapers, among them *Il Telegrafo* (The Telegraph); *La Voce del Popolo* (The Voice of the People) of Philadelphia, when it was transferred to New York; *La Follia di New York* (The Folly of New York), in which he also assumed his pen name of "Pin Pan," at times using only "Pin" or "Pan"; and, above all, *Il Progresso Italo-Americano* (Italian American Progress), of which he was the reporter par excellence. In addition, until the 1890s, he wrote a curious column, "Here and there, around the colony," made up of short, juicy reports whose subjects were identified by special graphic symbols: for example, a stag represented the small section dedicated to stories "*di corna*" (stories of malevolence and cuckolds). He also contributed to newspapers outside New York, such as the *Unione* of Pueblo, Colorado, which he would go on to manage, in consequence of "a not particularly happy domestic event, exploited by the wickedness of a few of his enemies," according to his obituary in the *Progresso*. In addition, he contributed to the *Roma* of Denver, and *Italia* of Chicago. He wrote a *giallo* (detective novel) related to his experience in Colorado. The Colorado State

Archives reveal in fact that in 1902 Ciambelli was tried and incarcerated, for a little less than a year, because of an ill-defined case of forgery, a fraud or a falsification of an unclear nature. In the judicial documents, he was forty at the moment of incarceration, which is consistent with 1862 as his date of birth.

Ciambelli's role in the events in the life of the Italian American colony was notable, from the mass meeting of protest against the hangings in New Orleans in 1891, where he spoke as representative of the *Cristoforo Columbo,* to the trial of Maria Barbella (1895), where he appeared as a witness. Significantly, he was one of the most active supporters of the institution of Columbus Day, introduced as an official holiday in 1905 in Colorado, and in 1909 in New York. In later years, he was nominated *cavaliere* (knight). He became a Fascist, in the same period in which a "misunderstanding" with Barsotti caused him to move to the *Corriere d'America,* the daily in which he was granted his desire to "die on the ramparts" doing his work.

Ciambelli was "able to turn out in one night a drama of five acts, from the first to the last scene; of writing an entire novel at par with the most sensational ones; of filling eight pages of a newspaper with fresh material" (Bosi). He maintained, in fact, that he preferred writing "by the light of the moon that whitened the hideaway in Staten Island where he lived." (*L'Italia,* September 30, 1893). Novels make up the most conspicuous part of his prodigious production, all published in America, a body of works including a vast cycle of mysteries of a popular appeal and a nineteenth-century character: cyclical narrations, incoherent, cumbersome and effusive, arising from the detective genre. They are sentimental, often superimposing and mixing the historical and social in the same course of action, in the manner of Mastriani, who created the first Italian model of this genre. Also similar to Mastriani is the labyrinthine and multivocal dimension it has, almost as if the true protagonist is the metropolis, with its aspects and quarters of misery and degradation; its continual changes of scene; revelations; flashbacks to past life in Italy; and a cornucopia of personages of the most varied ethnicity. Among these are especially Jews, but also Irish, Chinese, and African Americans, typified according to a range of vices that only at times actually serve to make more noticeable the virtues of the poor, ill-treated Italians. All of this action, plot, and character intrigue moves within the complex stratified reality of the mythical "Five Points," the heart of New York's Lower East Side. But this geography, very well known to the author, is amplified and enlarged according to the exigencies of the narration. In *I sotterranei di New York* (The Underground of New York), for example, the action even shifts to Kiev, in the Ukraine (but then that city, bordering on the sea, is basically a detail of little importance). Recurring in Ciambelli's pages are the names of other authors he considered true and proper masters, among them Georges Ohnet, Eugène Sue, Alexandre Dumas, Emile Zola, and, above all, Xavier de Montépin, who is thought of as a very obscure follower of Sue, but who in the late nineteenth century enjoyed a vast popularity even in Italy and in the Italian American colonies.

The bibliography of Ciambelli is still in need of an accurate, totally reliable cataloging. The difficulty lies in the complicated editorial history of his novels, which appeared in three diverse venues: as appendices in the various Italian American newspapers (which are problematic to reconstruct due to the lacunae in the collections of the first years); serialized in weekly issues (the famous dime novels), and therefore, even in this case, unaccounted for because of other lacunae; and finally, in true and proper volumes. Some of the titles attributed to him are still not located nor are the dates known, as, for example, *La vergine di Trieste: Episodio della guerra Italo-Austriaca* (The Virgin of Trieste: An Episode of the Italian-Austrian War), and *La prostituta di Trieste* (The Prostitute of Trieste). The list of recovered works opens with an amazing production in 1893 of five titles, starting with the long novel *I misteri di Mulberry Street* (The Mysteries of Mulberry Street), followed by others: the novella *Fiori d'arancio o, La moglie del Barbiere* (Orange Blossoms, or The Barber's Wife); an uncompleted novel written for *L'Italia* of Chicago, *La città nera ovvero I misteri di Chicago* (The Black City, or The Mysteries of Chicago); the novella *World's Fare* (i.e., Fair) *ovvero Suicidio con l'elettricità* (World's Fair, or Suicide by Electricity), also linked to Chicago and its International Exposition; and *I drammi dell'emigrazione, seguito ai misteri* (The Dramas of Emigration, The Consequence of Mysteries). From 1894, are *Amore, lussuria e morte ovvero Il processo di Antonio Bianco* (Love, Lust, and Death, or the Trial of Antonio Bianco) and *La bella Biellese ovvero Il mistero di Columbus Avenue* (The Beauty from Biella or the Mystery of Columbus Avenue). Appearing in 1895 were *Il delitto di Water Street* (The Water Street Crime), the first volume of the series *I misteri della polizia* (The Police Mysteries); as announced, there was also a following volume, *Le tane di New York* (The Hideouts of New York) and *I delitti dei bosses* (The Crimes of the Bosses), which completes the trilogy initiated with *I misteri di Mulberry Street* and followed by *I drammi dell'emigrazione.* Following these are *I misteri di Bleecker Street* (1899); *Il delitto di Coney Island ovvero La vendetta della zingara* (The Crime of Coney Island, or the Gypsy's Revenge, 1906–1908); *La strage degli Innocenti; ossia, I delitti di un medico* (The Slaughter of the Innocents, or A Doctor's Crimes, 1908–1909); *I misteri di Harlem; ovvero, La bella di Elizabeth Street* (The Harlem Mysteries, or the Beauty of Elizabeth Street, 1910–1911); *L'Aeroplano Fantasma* (The Phantom Airplane, 1911); *I sotterranei di New*

York (New York Underground, 1915); and *La trovatella di Mulberry Street; ovvero, La stella dei cinque punti* (The Foundling of Mulberry Street, or The Star of the Five Points, 1919). Among the last writings of Ciambelli recorded thus far are some short Christmas sketches, published in the *Follia* in 1926, 1927, and 1928: *Il Natale di Caino; Il Natale di Abele e quello di Caino; Il Natale di un eroe* (Cain's Christmas; Abel's Christmas and Cain's; A Hero's Christmas). In addition, already published in 1915 in the *Follia* was the vignette *La notte di Natale nelle trincee* (Christmas Eve in the Trenches).

Ciambelli's playwriting output is also remarkable, and apparently it includes several adaptations of his novels. He is reported to have been not averse to presenting himself as an actor as well, and sometimes, together with his wife Luigia, performed texts of Grand Guignol, in the manner of the French, or social dramas or even Neapolitan farces. Already in February 1891, as recorded in a review appearing in the *Eco d'Italia,* his drama *Sogno e realtà* (Dream and Reality) was performed in the Germania Assembly Rooms. The following, in succession, are among the many titles: *Figlia maledetta* (Accursed Daughter); *I bellimbusti di Hoboken* (The Dandies of Hoboken); *I Fasci di Sicilia, ossia La rivolta della fame* (The Sicilian Fasci, or The Hunger Rebellion); *Lo scoppio del "Maine" nel porto di Avana* (The Bombing of the *Maine* in the Port of Havana); *Il processo degli anarchici* (The Anarchists' Trial); *Francisco Ferrer; La risaiola di Conselice* (The Rice Weeder of Conselice); *L'invasione del Veneto* (The Invasion of the Veneto); *Ladra* (Thieving Woman); *Pulcinella presidente onorario* (Pulcinella, Honorary President); *Una sfida fra barbieri* (A Challenge among Barbers); and (the only recovered text thus far) the interesting drama in four acts *Il martire del dovere, ovvero Giuseppe Petrosino* (The Martyr to Duty; or, Giuseppe Petrosino) of which one part is published here.

Emerging, just from this list, is the profile of an author who was very attentive to the events of his time, especially news of a sinister or lurid character, which was "a rich genre for his inexhaustible fantasy," as observed in *L'Italia*: Ciambelli drew directly from reality, "enriching it with particularities and adorning it with the most fascinating and flattering alluring descriptions." He was "without literary pretensions," but his writings "vibrated with reality," as is very well seen in the *Martire del dovere,* in which he describes the love of an unfortunate young woman for an incorruptible policeman; they are "endowed with a marvelous fantasy, with a simple attractive form, flowing with ease, with a 'verve' that always delighted and never exceeded the limits of urbanity" (*Il Progresso).* Ciambelli appears perfectly aware of the popular taste of his audience, to whom he offers not only stories of the Italian American colony, but also varied events extracted from Italian and international chronicles: workers' agitations; the great proceedings against the anarchists; the Spanish American war of 1898; and the First World War. On September 30, 1893, a review of the novella *Fiori d'arancio* (Orange Blossoms) appeared in *L'Italia,* signed by a certain Jago. The reviewer effectively captured one of the fundamental elements of Ciambelli's success: his capacity to be perfectly attuned to the public, to share almost confidentially its temper, its spirit, its secrets: "It is necessary to have an idea of the life of the *italo-newyorkese* to understand all the intimacy of the story and understand the pleasures it offers." Related to Ciambelli's instincts is the habit, more frequent in his later production, of inserting into the plot numerous references to real situations and real people. Taking just *La trovatella,* we see references made to "the popular Nannetti of Park Street," a real restaurant, or to the actual publisher Agostino Balletto, and to the impresario of funeral processions Bacigalupo, and the count of Cesnola with his secretary Roversi. It would not be very difficult to outline an accurate map of the Italian colony of New York between the two centuries using only the novels of Ciambelli. In comparison with his undoubted ability to conform to the tastes of the public—among other things, through a capable method of mimicry that permits the Tuscan author to talk to the heart of an audience largely from southern Italy—there is unfortunately an undeniable sloppiness and an inconsistent style that paint Ciambelli as a prodigious writer of first drafts, careless of form, often far too casual even where the logical development of the intricate events he narrates is concerned. His carelessness is manifested in the frequent typographical errors, such that the same names of the characters may change unaccountably in the development of the plot.

A typical serialized story by Ciambelli in a newspaper must be looked upon as representative of a sort of memorial to early Italian American literature. The topics most dear to the author are the orgy; the theme of the pursued girl; prostitution and its world of lost women, sometimes called the "*orizzontali*" (horizontals); and the redeemed; also, the opposition between the unyielding virtue of the good and the diabolic wickedness of the bad; the friction between the world gilded with richness and the criminal underworld, an underworld described with abundant detail and also physically placed in a hellish dimension, subterranean, dark, and mysterious. All these themes already appear in *I misteri di Mulberry Street,* perhaps Ciambelli's masterpiece. The innocent Vittoria, who has come to America from Naples to search for her husband Ruiz, mysteriously disappears and is driven to prostitution by two diabolical natives of Marseilles, self-proclaimed Italians, Margherita and her husband Napoleone, "trafficking in human flesh." While she is under the influence of a drug made available to Margherita and Napoleone by vicious drug dealers, she manages to recognize her husband, who seeks to violate and then to strangle her. He plans, in fact, to marry the American heiress Fanny Spencer. Vittoria does not die, but meanwhile her rescuer, the young Righetti, who has crossed the Atlantic on board the same ship in which she voyaged, is found by the police while he is crying over her apparently lifeless body, and is arrested. Vittoria, who has gone mad, is confined to Blackwell Island. This plot, already rather complex—and this is only the prologue!—spreads into a maze of smaller streams after the first part of the book. The key personage is Boni, formerly, head of the police in Naples, who, convinced of Righetti's innocence, resolves to remove him from prison, and, step by step, follows the trail of Ruiz. A great many astonishing things take place, among which an altercation between Ruiz and Margherita, who, disfigured by fire, becomes a circus attraction, a freak, in a typical roadside show of the epoch, with the name, "Regina Mavaii," an authentic wild woman from the Congo. She ends by manifesting cannibal tendencies at the trial against Ruiz. Eventually, the trial takes place, certifying Righetti's innocence. After a failed attempt to escape, Ruiz is extradited to Italy, but the ship on which he is voyaging shipwrecks. Vittoria, who meanwhile has recovered, marries Righetti. However, it seems that Ruiz escapes death in the sea. And in fact he appears again in the following *I drammi dell'emigrazione*, which narrates new events and, in the first part, memorably denounces the exploitation of Italian laborers; and, moreover, among a thousand other things, offers sensational descriptions, some approaching the limits of pornography, descriptions of the vicious effects of the opium dens managed by the Chinese, "lewd children of the sky," and so forth.

I misteri di Bleecker Street is a spider's web of still greater complexity, filled with intrigues, deeds, situations, and personages. However, set during the Spanish American War, it has a more substantial scenario. One of the principal personages, the Piedmontese workman Enrico, fights in Cuba and is wounded. He is then rejoined by his fiancée Ada, the typical young pursued girl who has succeeded in safeguarding her virtue in the face of a tangle of adventures fraught with danger. In *I sotterranei di New York*, a hardened delinquent, "the Fox," pursues the beautiful Sara, already the prey of exploiters who want to drive her to prostitution; subsequently, she becomes the model wife of a successful construction contractor in metropolitan New York. Then, once again, she is abandoned to a destiny of misery with her little newborn baby boy; at the end, she is rejoined by her husband and discovered to be the heir to a princely house in Russia. The particularity of *I sotterranei*, which is among Ciambelli's most eventful novels (the settings change from New York to Chicago to Nevada, and, indeed, to Russia), is the primary role of the

Jewish Russian American heroine, represented with vivacity, and the concentration on the secret sects fighting against the despotic czar.

The novellas, of course, present more compact plots, given their shorter length. One example, the *Fior d'arancio*, was summarized in *L'Italia*, of Chicago: the narration recounts the story of a young barber, who receives stolen goods from a hag. Desiring to redeem his past with a new period of life of pure love, he marries a gentle, beautiful girl from his town in Italy, who has emigrated to America. But stung with jealousy through the insinuations of the hag, he doubts the virginity of his wife, even the consummation of the bridal night, and flees in despair, abandoning the conjugal nest.

In her ample and accurate analyses of Ciambelli's narrative structures, Franca Bernabei has stressed the "etnico" character of these stories. Ciambelli himself singles out this character in the *Spiegazione* (Explanation) that precedes the first part of *I misteri di Mulberry*, and, in effect, writes a defense against the critics who accuse him of inflicting shame on the Italian colony of New York:

> Writing a novel for Italian readers, it was right, logical and useful, to choose a title that would draw the attention of my fellow countrymen and women and awaken their curiosity. I chose *Misteri di Mulberry*, because the name is popular and also because many scenes take place there, or are prepared there. . . . As to those who speak of shame, who maintain that this work is an insult to the colony, that it is an unpatriotic act to expose the colony's sores, plagues, social ills, they have judged too hastily; if they were to read what I write, they would be convinced that those judgments are rash, unjustifiable, that their fears are exaggerated. . . . But even admitting the case, that in the novel there are some ugly figures deserving to be hung, do you think that this might have a harmful effect on our colony, when contained within it, there are one hundred thousand honest workers, full of good will, and an honor to the country where I was born?
>
> And therefore, to show the plagues that could mar a colony is not to cause insult but to incite it so that the afflictions disappear, because no one can claim that also in Mulberry, in the middle of a population of brave and good workers, with the most honest wives, with innocent children, the plant of vice does not sprout; that the door to the brothel is found in contact with respected families; the gambling house, next to the shop and the workhouse, where one sweats and works to earn a morsel of bread. From my novel, Mulberry will emerge rehabilitated, because that is a place in which beats the

good, affectionate, honest heart of the many, born in that generous land that the valor of Garibaldi united to our country in 1860.

Finally: This work . . . is not a libelous novel; its scope is not to insult, to display dirty laundry, but rather to brand with a red-hot iron of reproof those few who inflict unmerited disgrace upon the Italian name . . . And on that premise, in the name of Italy, which I venerate and love, that name I would not for anything see stained, I continue without any fear whatsoever, certain that I create honest and good work.

ESSENTIAL BIBLIOGRAPHY

Aleandri 1983a; Basile Green 1974, 64–65; Bernabei 1999; Bosi 1921, 408; Ciambelli 2009; Deschamps 1998, 288–290; Gardaphé 1995; Maffi 1992; Marazzi 2001, 22–24; obituary, in *Il Progresso Italo-Americano*, July 3, 1931; Sollors 1986.

The Victim

1. The Arrival

On that October morning the vast reception room of the Barge Office, where the newly arrived file past the visual control of the Immigration Agents, was extremely crowded; the transatlantic steamers had brought more than two thousand immigrants from Europe; some were German, some were Russian Jews, but most came from the Southern regions of Italy.

The Jews, with their cautious demeanor, buttoned up in their long shabby coats all trimmed with fur, formed a group apart from the others, as though they were afraid to mingle with the crowd that swarmed around them. The Germans, serious but satisfied, like those that arrive in a conquered land, remained close to one another as if they were soldiers ready to attack the enemy. The Italians, happy, carefree, loud, lent a cheerful note to the group, giving it life with their observations, spoken in loud voices in the various Southern Italian dialects that range from a barbaric accent to the softness of the Arab tongue.

The newcomers filed past one by one to be interrogated, as was the custom, by the Immigration Agents. More than half of the immigrants had passed, when, from the Italian group, a beautiful young woman stood out clearly, as her dress and manner were nothing like those of her travel mates. In fact, while the immigrant women flaunted showy colored dresses, cloths and shawls, dominated by reds, yellows and greens, the woman that was passing in front of the agents was dressed in elegant simplicity: a black skirt, not new but clean, enveloped her elegant moving body; a waistcoat, also black, imprisoned her supple waist and her full and provocative bosom; a small round hat of the same color covered her head. Her beautiful Hellenic face, framed by her luxurious black hair, was left completely uncovered.

The woman's eyes—two large, deep blue, and almond shaped, with a sweet and kind expression, veiled by long eyelashes—flitted back and forth, timid and fearful; but when they rested on the sweet child that she held by the hand, they took on a loving expression that showed how much this beautiful immigrant woman loved and adored that child, who must have been her son, because only mothers can show such affection in their eyes.

The woman found herself in front of the agent. The civil servant looked at her surprised and, changing the brusque and rough tone that he customarily used, began the usual interrogations; realizing that the woman was Italian, he called the interpreter and had him ask her the questions:

"What is your name?"

"Vittoria Ruiz," the woman answered in a sweet and melodious voice.

"Where do you come from?"

"From Naples."

"Is this your son?"

"Yes" she answered, with a certain pride.

"Do you have relatives in New York?"

Vittoria hesitated a moment and then resolutely answered:

"Yes, my husband!"

"Enough, you can pass."

Vittoria Ruiz started for the door; she did not understand the money changers who were yelling in her ears if she had money to exchange; she did not hear the hotel agents that offered their services; she walked straight towards the door, as if she was in a hurry to touch the pavement of the biggest Metropolis of the American Union. She did not even stop to say good-bye to her travel companions, nor did she see the longing gaze of a young man, who, lost among the immigrants, looked at her with great veneration.

When the woman found herself outside the Barge Office, her bosom rose, breathless, and a sigh escaped her lips along with this word: "Finally!"

II. *The Demon*

The fog enveloped Battery Place. The towers of the Barge Office were lost in the dark and gloomy mist, and the coast of the river had disappeared, as if a large curtain had been spread out in front of her, and the foghorns of the steamships sounded their mournful song.

Vittoria Ruiz—from now on we will call her by the name she gave to the immigration agents—stood for a moment on the threshold of the Barge Room and looked at the fog that was becoming thicker, then took her first steps into the unknown. The fearful boy held on to the skirt of his mother, who, with a steady pace, started down one of the many avenues that cut across Battery Place. Where was she headed? The poor woman had no idea!

All of a sudden, as she was entering State Street, she felt a hand on her shoulder, while a caressing voice said to her in English: "Well, my dear, where are you going?" Vittoria turned, startled and afraid. But seeing in front of her a woman with gray hair and a sweet demeanor, she felt reassured and using gestures made the lady understand that she did not understand the language that was being spoken to her. The old woman understood. Immediately and with great haste she said, this time in Italian.

"Have you arrived from Naples?"

Vittoria hearing the language of her land felt a thrill of joy and answered: "Yes, I come from Naples."

"Well then, we are fellow countrywomen." The old woman replied.

Vittoria did not notice that though the woman spoke Italian she did so with a very pronounced accent; she was just happy to have found a person from her country; she held out her hand innocently, a hand that could have belonged to a duchess.

"And why did we come to America, my sweet dove?" the woman continued in an insinuating way.

"That is my secret, and I will not tell it to anyone."

"Keep your secret; the child, is he your son?"

"Yes, he is my dear Enrico."

"But tell me, where are you headed?"

"I don't know."

"You don't know? Do you have anyone in New York?

Vittoria hesitated somewhat and then answered: "No one!"

"Money. Do you have any?"

"No, Everything I had went for passage on the steamer."

A flash of joy lit up the old woman's face, and for a moment it took on a repulsive look.

"My dear girl, you were born under a lucky star," the old woman said. "I am looking for a girl to be a companion to a fine, rich Italian lady, and if you do not have any objections. . . ."

"Ah! My dear lady, you are my savior. It is God who has sent you."

The old woman smiled maliciously. She was sure it wasn't God that had sent her.

"So you accept?"

"With all my heart."

"But, there is one problem. The lady for whom you will become chaperone is on vacation and won't return until mid-November."

"My God, where will I stay until then?"

"Oh my dear! You will stay with me, my house is not really nice, but for a short time it will do. You'll see, from my house one often and happily goes to live in a beautiful villa, all trimmed in lace . . . that's enough, we'll see if you are reasonable; let's go."

Vittoria, her new companion and the child set out towards the center of the City. The fog came in thicker than ever. People lost their forms and began to look like shadows.

III. Vittoria Ruiz

Before we continue, we will tell you why Vittoria Ruiz and her child landed in New York on the morning of October 15, 1891.

Vittoria was a member of an honest and respectable Neapolitan family, and until the age of twelve she had lived in comfort, adored by her father, a rich businessman who was loved and esteemed by everyone; her mother died giving birth to her. One morning the poor child found herself in front of the body of her father, who had committed suicide to escape from a disastrous business failure. The young girl almost died of grief, and for two months lived in a state of madness. When she began to remember, she was told that to live she had to work. She took up a post in a milliner's shop in Via Toledo for her room and board.

Vittoria, at the age of fourteen, was already a woman and her beauty attracted the stares of all that saw her. More than one dandy became a frequent visitor of the store where Vittoria worked. But it was all in vain, because the young girl didn't seem to notice them.

One day though her heart throbbed, love broke the ice that enveloped her, and made her understand that it is man's destiny to love and to be loved. It was on the day of the feast of the altars at Torre del Greco that Vittoria met for the first time the man that would eventually make her shed so many tears. Her mistress, like a good Neapolitan, had gone to admire the famous flower carpets, genuine exquisite mosaics made by the people of Torre del Greco, and had taken Vittoria along. During the evening, while music played in the piazza, and fireworks turned the dark sky into a magical tapestry of lights, a wayward rocket hit her clothes of light muslin, and her dress immediately caught fire.

A cry of terror escaped the lips of the frightened child as the crowd looked on, paralyzed. The flames were beginning to burn her flesh when a young man hurled himself on her, held her in his arms and, at the risk of burning himself, smothered the flames.

The crowd enthusiastically applauded the young man. Vittoria fainted. When she came to, she saw the young courageous man at her side, held out her hand and whispered, "Thank you!" The girl's rescuer must have been twenty years old, elegant, slender, with a head of black hair that made his pale complexion stand out; he had all the physical qualities to be called a handsome young man; only his eyes, his beautiful eyes, had a steel and sinister gaze; it was an evil look.

His name was Rinaldo Ruiz. His parents, who had been dead for a while, were Spanish. He lived a comfortable life in Naples without anyone's knowing precisely where his resources came from. Some whispered that he was the kept man of a rich older woman, others said he was a gambler, while others ventured that the well-dressed young man of aristocratic manner was a notorious thief. Was there any truth in all the gossip? Maybe Rinaldo Ruiz was all those things, a kept man, a gambler and a thief. Vittoria fell completely and madly in love with her savior; the warnings of her mistress, the supplications of close friends that begged her not to tie her future to an unworthy man, had the reverse effect. Instead of diminishing, her passion for the young man grew.

Ruiz, proud to be loved the by the most beautiful young woman of the neighborhood, hung around the shop where Vittoria worked and tried to make her his lover, but the girl resisted and kept her honor intact. Ruiz, excited by her resistance to his advances, and wanting to possess at all costs the beautiful virgin, gave in and married Vittoria.

The first three months of matrimony were, for the young lady, who was only fifteen years old, a dream of constant joy and happiness that words could never explain. Ruiz rented a small, beautiful apartment in the neighborhood of "Largo della Carità" where the young married couple lived a comfortable life. Vittoria's happiness did not last long. Her husband soon began to stay out all night, and when he returned home he was drunk more often than not. It was during those times that he would experience horrid hallucinations that terrified him, and he would react with violent outbursts. One evening, the same day Vittoria learned that she was pregnant, Ruiz returned home in a horrible state: his clothes were ripped and he was covered in blood and mud.

"I came to change my clothes and pack some underwear because I have to go to Avellino."

When his wife asked him why he was reduced to such a state and where did all that blood come from, he answered in a trembling voice that he came to aid of a painter friend who had fallen from a bridge he was working on. Ruiz quickly packed his suitcase, changed his clothes, and without saying a word abandoned his home. That night and the next and the following nights Vittoria waited in vain for her husband's return.

Two days after that awful evening, Vittoria read in the "Corriere di Napoli" the horrible details of the murder of a rich banker, who, drawn into a deserted house near Posillipo, certainly by a pretty woman, was killed and robbed; the police found the body but there were no clues that could lead to the identity of the assassins.

Vittoria, in reading that bit of news, had a premonition that Ruiz, her husband, the father of the child growing in her womb, was one of the perpetrators, and was overwhelmed by a great fear. Soon, not having money to pay the rent, she had to leave the apartment she was living in, and with the money she made from selling her furniture, about 600 lire, she furnished a small room in Pigna Secca, and returned to work at the milliner's shop. Almost a year to the day that Vittoria met Ruiz, she gave birth to a son, on whom she concentrated all of her love.

Five years passed without any news of her husband; one day, two months before our novel begins, a woman who had just arrived from America met Vittoria and told her:

"I saw your husband in New York, he is a gentleman with class and demeanor, he squanders away money big time, and I believe that he is ready to take another wife."

"Are you really sure of what you are telling me?"

"Sure as I am sure that San Gennaro is the patron Saint of Naples."

Vittoria immediately made a decision. She wanted to find the man who like a coward had abandoned her. She sold the furniture and all her goods, and, with her child, boarded a steamship of the Fabre Line and sailed for New York.

During the long crossing she kept herself apart from other passengers. Completely absorbed by her grief, she barely noticed the disgusting filth that surrounded her. Being of a delicate nature, she tolerated, without noticing it, repugnant contacts, and only reacted when some bold lout dared speak to her in a manner that was less than respectful.

From the beginning, the passengers dubbed her "madonnina" and were very attentive to her needs. But Vittoria, occupied by other thoughts, didn't notice their attention and kindness, so they began calling her the proud one and left her alone as if she had the plague. Only one passenger, a good-looking young man with an honest face, who conducted himself with distinction, developed a great admiration and affection for the poor soul; but he never showed his feelings, well understanding that the beautiful woman was prey to a grief and sorrow that would be impossible to console.

After 18 days at sea the "Neustria" arrived in New York. Vittoria set foot on American soil, where more misfortune and evil awaited her.

IV. *In the Lair*

Vittoria had come to America without even thinking about the dangers that she might face there. Her burning desire to find her husband so occupied her thoughts and directed her actions that it did not even cross her mind that arriving in an unknown foreign place, without money, without friends, without any support, would certainly lead to a series of terrible disasters.

The woman that chance brought her for a companion from the moment she set foot on dry land seemed to the poor thing a blessing from Providence, so she followed her with joy, not suspecting for a moment what birds of prey await the poor immigrants when they arrive.

Vittoria and her son followed the unknown woman across Battery Place, a part of State Street, and found herself on Broadway, the main avenue of New York. In the meantime, neither the immigrant nor her companion was aware that a young man, the same one we saw in the great waiting hall of the Barge Office, followed their footsteps; the sidewalks of Broadway were so crowded that the young man didn't stand out.

The bells rang noon, and from the majestic office buildings a sea of employees swarmed forth, quickly going to the beer halls, the "Lunch Rooms," and the bakeries for their lunch. On Broadway the fog was lighter and more transparent. Vittoria glimpsed, as if in a dream, the elegant stores where the electric lights glowed, while barely hearing the voice of her companion, who, at every chance, repeated: "If one uses good judgment, one can attain anything one wants in New York." The young Enrico shuffled behind his mother, hanging on to her clothes, afraid of losing her. The old woman held out her hand to him, but he did not want to hold it at any cost. After they crossed City Hall plaza, the woman guided Vittoria through Centre Street and then Worth Street, Paradise and Park Street, ending up at Mulberry Street. The fog had cleared and the sun, red as a brass disc, hung over the city giving it an aura of sadness and fear.

When she set foot in Mulberry Street, Vittoria looked around dumbfounded, as though she had just wakened from a long deep sleep. The place reminded her of a street in the beautiful city where she was born; it reminded her of one of the working-class neighborhoods of her beloved Naples, and for a moment she thought that the trip and the arrival in America were nothing more than a dream that had lasted a long time. Around her she heard the picturesque dialect of her city, she saw types and figures seen other times when she, happy and careless, walked through the streets and avenues of Naples. Her companion brought her back to reality, telling her rudely that it was necessary to walk faster and get home because her man would go into a beastly rage when he didn't find lunch ready and on the table by noon.

Vittoria automatically followed the woman, happy to find so many things that reminded her of her native land.

"Here we are, my lovely." The old woman said suddenly, "It's not a palace, but we have to be satisfied."

It definitely wasn't a palace, it was a low two-story house, the front was the color of clotted blood, blackish, and looked like a hovel; on the ground floor there were two shops with dirty windows, broken in a number of places and repaired with paper of an indefinable color. Under the shops, a hollow led to the cellar where a crude sign announced "Italian Restaurant, Maccheroni with Tomato Sauce."

Vittoria and her guide entered a narrow open corridor between two houses into a small courtyard crammed with debris, where a dirty rivulet spread its filthy waters everywhere, making the uneven stone pavement slippery. At the back of the courtyard, a rickety old door led to a ramshackle staircase, where a greasy rope, slimy like the skin of a snake, served to support those that went up and down those unstable stairs.

"Follow me, don't be afraid, my beauty." The old woman said to Vittoria, "In this neighborhood we don't have staircases and courtyards made from marble."

In spite of her disgust at the filth that surrounded her, the resolute young woman made for the stairs. When they arrived on the second floor, the woman knocked on the door; a grunt, not resembling anything human, answered, followed by staggering steps. Finally the door opened.

"Damn . . . whore! You're finally home," he yelled in pure French.

"Shut up stupid, I'm with good company," Vittoria's companion answered in the same language.

"Good company, what do I care!"

"You're drunk again! You brute! Get out of the way and the let this beautiful lady with me pass!"

"A lady? I understand. Make way for the ladies, as we used to say in Belleville in the good old days."

The drunk barely finished his sentence when his wife pushed him and sent him rolling to the middle of the room.

"Come in without fear, my beauty. That animal drank too much today and doesn't know what he's saying."

The disgusting scene left a vivid impression on Vittoria. The woman to whom she had blindly entrusted herself and her son to did not seem good and honest. Not knowing French, Vittoria did not understand the words the couple exchanged, but by their tone she understood that some sort of threat was involved. Nonetheless, she entered the small room with a smoke-blackened ceiling that must have served as kitchen, dining room, and even as a bed-room, because there was a cot in the corner with dirty linens and a torn pillow that spilled its cotton stuffing from its numerous wounds.

On the cast iron stove, in a tin saucepan a sauce made from onion was cooking, emitting an acrid, sharp, nauseating smell that stuck in poor Vittoria's throat, making it impossible for her not to show her distaste. Her expression did not go unnoticed by her protector, who quickly tried to reassure her by saying:

"Don't worry, we are not going to eat that stuff."

"You're not going to eat" yelled the drunken man who had lifted himself from the floor, "This sauce is a nectar, you'll see my sweet princess." While saying this he approached Vittoria and held out his filthy hand to caress her chin.

The young lady pulled back with a shudder; that man revolted her. Indeed, it wasn't possible to have a more repugnant face than his. His eyes were small, yellow, and phosphorescent; the cheeks purulent and scrofulous; the nose, a living red, resembled an armor of disgusting scabs; a thin mustache with bald spots, shaded his big lips, turned inside out, sinuous, and disfigured on the sides by ulcerous sores.

"I don't want to eat you," grumbled the monster, seeing Vittoria's look of revulsion.

"Napoleon, that's enough," thundered the old woman, "leave the child alone, and heaven help you if you dare touch a hair on her head."

Vittoria looked with gratitude at the old woman, who whispered to her: "He isn't bad, my Napoleon, but today he drank a bit more than usual." The young Enrico was deathly afraid of Napoleon and hid in his mother's dress.

"Now, my girl, we are safe, and surely you both need to rest. We'll talk business after we eat, and you will see that the devil is not as ugly as he is painted."

"No, he is beautiful, beautiful like . . . me," grumbled Napoleon.

"Here you will live like a little queen," continued the woman, not paying any attention to her husband's interruption, "We will give you the best room, and we are not as poor as you may think. Look, here is your apartment." She opened a door and pushed Vittoria into a charming room, wallpapered in light blue with gold stars, with an elegant carpet designed with bunches of violets on the floor, and a large bed made from carved walnut, and chairs covered with deep blue velvet.

An oil lamp, with a porcelain bell and crystal pendants, illuminated the room. Vittoria was amazed by the sudden change. On the other side of the threshold, misery, filth, negligence, here elegance, luxury, almost wealth. The old woman saw the astonishment on the young woman's face. And quickly said: "This is the custom in this country, neglect everything to beautifully furnish one room."

"But I can't allow you to deprive yourself of your comfort for me!"

"Don't say it even as a joke. Mamma Margherita knows the duties of a host, and then, after you've settled yourself you will repay me. Now rest, then we will have a good meal and discuss our business. Good bye, my beauty, and think of this as your house."

Vittoria took one of Margherita's hands, brought it with veneration to her lips and whispered, "Thank you."

The old woman had an evil smile on her lips as she left, leaving the young immigrant woman alone. Vittoria fell to her knees and thanked God for having sent her someone who would protect her. The poor thing still did not understand that she had fallen into the most heinous trap.

v. Traffickers in Human Flesh

As soon as Mamma Margherita found herself alone with her worthy husband, in a stifled voice she uttered:

"The bird is in the cage. It is beautiful, and who wants to buy it will have to pay dearly. Spread the word in the usual places you know, speak of it to that half-Spanish, half-Italian merchant you're acquainted with. You know what a libertine he is and how generous. If we do this right, we could have a real gold mine on our hands."

"You're right, the little one is pretty enough, but I. . . ."

"Silence, animal, she is not stuff for your teeth."

"What about the child, wife of mine?"

"Your question tells me that you've sobered up; in time the boy will disappear, but if the beautiful immigrant knows what is wanted from her she can keep him; if she becomes fussy and hard to please, then we'll see. Now don't waste time, go to the shopkeeper Ruizzi and inform him of my beautiful catch. As soon as he smells fresh meat, he runs like a hungry hyena."

"I'll go, but first let me eat my onion stew."

What hands had the bride Ruiz fallen into?

The unfortunate woman had had the bad luck of bumping into one of those miserable human beings that hang around the Barge Office, waiting for some poor young lady, alone from Europe, who can be tempted by seductive words, and taken to wicked places where she ends up disgraced.

These women—whom the police see but do not disturb, because they pay good money in bribes to be free to practice their despicable profession—they lure poor naïve creatures with a thousand promises. These hags look respectable, and they fool even those that are on their guard. They will do anything, with force or love, to make these young ladies available to degenerates, young and old, who, to slake their lust, pay these traffickers of human flesh handsomely.

Mamma Margherita was one of these women, and one of the most dangerous. She was highly thought of in the world of the pleasure-seekers because she had done some masterful things, and in that small room wallpapered in blue, in her house on Mulberry, more than one poor girl had lost her innocence, and taken the first step on that slippery road that leads to a brothel, prison, and eventually the hospital.

Margherita and Napoleon passed themselves off as Mr. and Mrs. Ghirendini from Naples. Their name and country were false, their name was really Gautier and they came from Marseilles.

Margherita had spent her youth in the small wine bars that you find everywhere along the dirty alleys in the vicinity of the New Port of Marseilles, where sailors go to appease their lust after their long voyages. Corrupt in body and soul, shrewd and clever, at the age of sixteen, Margherita negotiated her body as a Jewish merchant negotiates his merchandise. She earned lots of money, but it did not remain long in her pockets; Napoleon Gautier, a member of that revolting breed that in Marseilles they called "nervi," was Margherita's idol, and all the money the wretched woman made went to him. At the age of 25, worn-out and old before her time, Margherita became Gautier's wife and at the same time the proprietor of the popular 100 Rue Bellegarde that the refined world of Marseilles and the surrounding area knew well. For a while, business was good, but when the police discovered that at 100 Rue Bellegarde underage young girls were being sold, they ordered the arrest of the Gautiers. Tipped off by some of their high-ranking customers, the Gautiers took flight and went to Italy.

In Marseilles, the quintessential cosmopolitan city, all languages are spoken but particularly Italian. Margherita and Napoleon spoke this language well, so when they decided to go to America, they changed their name and in New York they passed themselves off as Italians and went to live in that quintessential Italian neighborhood—Mulberry.

In America, they followed their old trade and made plenty of money. Whenever a steamboat arrived, Margherita ran to the Barge Office and, when she thought the moment was right, she would spread her net, and heaven help who was caught in the trap. More than once on Mulberry you would hear of the heinous work of the Gautiers, but nothing certain could ever be said because they were very careful and took all precautions. Anyway, they were rich, and with money all crimes can be easily covered up.

This is the situation the poor wretch Vittoria Ruiz had fallen into, and this the peril that threatened her.

VI. The Lover

The young man that had followed Vittoria from the Barge Office, followed her to Mulberry, and firmly engraved in his mind the place where that woman had entered who had awakened in his heart the most powerful love.

The house did not have a number but the young lover would have found it even in the darkest night. This young man, who by all indications did not fit the mold of your usual immigrant, was named Alberto Righetti. He was from a noble Florentine family and had emigrated to America seduced by the mirage of gold that surrounds the land discovered by Christopher Columbus.

Alberto Righetti, educated, cultured, and well-mannered, would have quickly understood that America is no place for those that are not adapted to manual labor or do not have a trade. Alberto saw Vittoria on board of the "Neustria" and was immediately struck by her beauty. During the voyage he often saw her sad and melancholy, and more than once he tried to console her, but to no end. Vittoria would turn her back to him without saying a word. Alberto suffered from her rejection, he suffered cruelly for not being able to alleviate the pain of the woman he had fallen in love with.

When the steamship arrived in New York, Alberto offered his services to Vittoria. She thanked him but formally declared that she did not need anyone's help. We then saw him follow the young mother to Mulberry where the honor and life of Vittoria were in the greatest danger.

VII. The Contract

Napoleon Ghirendini, having eaten his onion stew, put on a long black overcoat, which had turned a shiny dark red over the years, and hurried to the office of the wholesaler Ruizzi, to whom he revealed the news, in the strictest of confidence, that a morsel fit for a king was awaiting at his house, and that if he desired to sample it, he was the preferred one.

The wholesaler had greeted the happy news with great satisfaction, saying that if the bird was worth it, he would not skimp on the price.

"This is a rare bird," said Napoleon, "but it is necessary to wait until it's more domesticated."

"OK, you'll tell me when the time is right," added the libertine.

Rinaldo Ruizzi was young, he could not have been more than 26. Women found him handsome: his hair, his were eyes black as ebony; and the paleness of his skin highlighted his features that were spoiled by his stare that was icy, evil, inflexible as the blade of a dagger.

Ruizzi had been in America only five years and he had already made quite a position for himself.

His store of Venetian glass was a gold mine, and the number of clients grew by the day. Bold, entrepreneurial, he seized fortune by the horns, and everything was going well for him.

No one knew exactly here he came from, and he was very careful not to let anyone know.

Every once in awhile, the word on the street, immediately stifled, was that the merchant's name was not Ruizzi, and that he wasn't even Italian. But there was no proof to the gossip. The handsome Rinaldo was held in high esteem by everyone, and he brilliantly continued his career, thirsty for good times, orgies, and pleasures.

Margherita was one of Ruizzi's suppliers, money being of no concern when she brought him "a pretty little thing."

Let's imagine then how Ruizzi anxiously awaited a call from the Ghirendini's, a call that meant a night of infinite sweetness in the arms of a naïve woman who had fallen in the clutches of Margherita.

VIII. *The First Signs*

Three days went by. This was all the time Margherita needed to learn why Vittoria had come to New York.

Vittoria's disclosures about her life had dissolved all apprehensions that trafficker of human flesh might have had. Really, what did she have to fear?

Vittoria didn't know what name her husband was known by in America; she had left Naples without even knowing the identity of the woman who had brought her the news of her husband so that she might find her, and ask her more precise questions. The unfortunate Vittoria had given in to a moment of elation, and she believed that once in New York everyone would have been able to tell her where he lived. The old Margherita did not discourage Vittoria; on the contrary, she gave her to understand that with her help it would be easy to know where Ruiz lived. In the meantime, the shrewd woman began to test the waters, and slowly turned the conversation to the unexpected adventures that happened to many young girls who were able to latch on to that unstable Goddess, fortune.

Vittoria, sweet innocent soul that she was, listened in awe, like a child that listen to the tales of the *One Thousand and One Nights*, to all her protectress told her, and not once did she think about what price the conquest of wealth had cost those beautiful girls.

Vittoria lived in that depressing house on Mulberry as a prisoner might, and from the day she arrived she had not gone outside. She didn't even look out the window because Margherita had told her that for her own good she should not to be seen by the neighbors, who, being gossipy and blabbermouths, would have told the whole neighborhood about her arrival and possibly have caused her an infinity of problems and grief.

Every now and then she would hear the echo of a festive Neapolitan song, sung full out by happy people who lived near the Ghirendini and who did not have the faintest idea of the drama that was unfolding right next to them. From the window of Margherita's filthy kitchen, Vittoria saw, through the balcony of the house across the way, a young bride, beautiful, with fresh complexion, in total bliss, admiring the beautiful child she held in her arms, to whom she offered in total grace her breast full of milk. Vittoria looked on the scene deeply moved and would have given anything to embrace that chubby rosy-cheeked child. On the fourth day of her imprisonment, Vittoria had a moment of freedom. Seeing the woman and the child, she opened the window, and yelled:

"What a dear beautiful child!"

The happy mother raised her radiant gaze from her child and thanked the beautiful lady, who, by praising her son, had conquered her affection. Vittoria, hearing the young mother speaking with a strong southern accent, asked her happily:

"Are you Neapolitan?"

"From Potenza. Have you just arrived from Italy?"

"Yes." Victoria answered.

"Who are you staying with?"

"In the home of a kind woman who has offered me her hospitality."

"Are you staying at the Ghirendini's?"

"Yes."

"Be careful and keep your guard up, my dear."

"Be careful, why?"

She couldn't say more. Margherita entered the house and pulled her violently from the window, "Are you crazy?" she yelled at her in a gruff voice.

Vittoria, taken aback by Margherita's violent reaction, did not have the strength to utter a word, but, from that moment she was possessed by a vague fear, her sense of security had vanished, and she promised herself to follow the advice that was just given her and to be on her guard.

In the evening of that same day that had left such an impression on Vittoria, the witch began to show her cards. Supper had ended. Napoleon was already snoring away like a double bass in a corner of the small living room; his face, red from too many drinks, was more horrible than ever. The young Enrico had fallen asleep with his head on his mother's knee. In a sweet honeyed voice, Margherita began:

"My dear girl, as hard as I have searched, it has been impossible to find any trace of your husband; New York is big, and one cannot do in a few days what is quite easy to do in a small town. You know you also have to think about yourself. The woman I had spoken to you about doesn't need a maid anymore, so it is necessary to look elsewhere."

"You are absolutely right, it's necessary that I work, I can't continue to be in your debt."

"I'm not saying this because of that, my angel; what I'm saying is in your best interest, and if you heed what I say, you will be better off for it."

"Dear lady, I will listen to you, as I listened to my poor mother."

"Good! Now listen. In America people are not as scrupulous as we are in Italy. One comes here to make money, then we go back to our towns, and no one thinks about asking you how, where, and in what manner you accumulated your fortune. I know ladies that in Europe are thought of as Grande Dames, who while here they did all sorts of things."

A great fear crept over poor Vittoria as she listened to those strange words, and, though she wanted better to understand the soul of this woman who was beginning to show her true face, she did not say a word to interrupt her. Margherita, corrupt, wicked, and not capable of understanding the real meaning of Vittoria's silence, understood it as a tacit agreement, and began to freely give vent to her talk.

"You," continued the old woman, "don't owe anything to your husband. He abandoned you, and you should consider him dead. Now, widowhood cannot be eternal, you're beautiful, quite beautiful, and more than one man, I am sure, would be pleased to possess you . . . Listen, I know many Italian gentlemen. You could choose one that would comfort you and at the same time avenge the treachery of your husband's desertion."

The mask had completely vanished. Vittoria now had no more doubts that the woman she had believed to be her heaven-sent protector, actually wanted her ruined. She still did not know that they wanted to sell her body, but she understood that they wanted to throw her into the arms of some man. Her sense of feminine decency rebelled. She proudly lifted her head and with a resolute voice said:

"I don't know what the purpose of this conversation is, but understand that I have been and will remain faithful to my husband. If I don't find him, I will work and earn enough for me and my son to live on. I'm not afraid."

"But . . ." the old woman began.

"Enough on this subject. If not, I will leave this house immediately."

Margherita understood. It was useless to insist, and not wanting to lose her victim changed her tactic and said:

"I approve of your pride. I didn't want to suggest anything dishonest. I was only referring to a possible husband who would make you rich and happy. This is not for you? We won't talk about it anymore, finished."

"Dear lady, tomorrow I will begin looking for work."

"My child, now you bear a grudge against me for something I said to try and help you."

"No madam, I don't hold a grudge against you. I am very grateful, but it would be an abuse of your generosity if I remained."

"What are you saying? You are the lady of the house. . . ."

"Thank you, but if you want my eternal gratitude, find, or help me find work."

"I will do all that is within me to make you happy, but now go to bed and don't be so nervous. Good heavens, you look frightened, as if you had seen the devil. Go, go, good night, my child."

"Good night, Madam," and with that she took her son by the arm and started going towards her room.

"What's this? What news is this?" Margherita yelled, "Aren't you going to give me the usual good night kiss?"

"You're right, I was distracted." Vittoria kissed the old lady on the forehead with trembling lips, impotent to hide the disgust she felt in kissing that woman, now that she was aware of her malicious plans.

When the poor wretched girl was alone in her room, she burst out crying.

IX. Conspiracy

As soon as Vittoria was in her room, Margherita approached her husband and shook him brutally. The drunkard woke up swearing but did not have time to show his bad mood, because Margherita quickly began speaking to him in a whisper telling what had just transpired with Vittoria.

"My dear," grumbled Napoleon, "I told you nothing would come of this. That woman has a look that reflects honesty a mile away."

"Fine," the woman replied, "we won't get anything with kindness, but we have other ways."

"Yes, but dangerous ways that can lead us directly to Sing Sing."

"You've been singing the same song for many years now, and if I had listened to you, today we would be dying of hunger."

"That devil of Ruizzi. I painted such a seductive portrait of the girl that he wants to see her at any cost. He seems so restless, and he told me he will come tomorrow evening."

"Let him come, Vittoria will be his."

"Wife, look. . . ."

"Coward!"

"Do as you wish, but I pray you let's go to bed."

They lowered the folding bed and, in that filthy kitchen, the worthy couple soon took their place, continuing their conversation, whispering under the sheets so as not to be understood by any living soul. Husband and wife, before closing their eyes, had plotted the ruin of the young mother, who at that same moment was crying and praying.

x. *The Narcotic*

Vittoria had not closed an eye all night; at the slightest noise she would jump up from her bed, startled and frightened, her heart pounding in such a way that is seemed it would break. At daybreak, tired and defeated, she fell asleep, but not a real sleep, more like a lethargy populated by wicked forms and frightful scenes. Her lethargy lasted until Margherita came to knock on her door to tell her it was time to get up. The old lady, wanting to deceive her victim, told her that in a couple of days she would find her work in a candy factory that belonged to one of the most respectable Italian families.

Vittoria would have preferred to leave the Mulberry Street house immediately, but since she had no place to go she felt that she had to stay put. That day, Margherita did not leave her side for one minute and was kinder than usual. Napoleon did not show his face all day, not even for lunch at noon. A sure sign that his purse was full.

Napoleon returned home around six in the evening, and strangely he wasn't at all drunk. Dinner that evening was most refined and plentiful. Napoleon had even brought home a bottle of Rhine wine, made in California, that when poured gave the glasses an amber color. When the couple lifted their glasses to drink that precious liquor, instead of bringing it to their lips they masterfully threw it over their shoulders. Vittoria did not eat much, but drank a couple of glasses of that Rhine wine with great pleasure. Supper had just ended when the young lady felt a great weight on her head, her eyes began to close, and a general drowsiness began taking possession of her body. She wanted to struggle against the drowsiness, but she was helpless. Her son Enrico had also fallen into a deep sleep. When Vittoria stopped moving, Margherita ordered her husband to pick her up in his arms and take her to her room.

Napoleon didn't have to be told twice. He picked up the sleeping beauty like a feather, hugged her to his chest with a thrill of pleasure and set out for the room. His eyes twinkled like that of a cat, the contact with that perfect body was making his blood go to his brain, and if his wife hadn't been there, poor Vittoria would certainly have been raped by that brute. When Napoleon had set the woman on the bed, his wife made him leave the room, and began quickly to undress Vittoria, who was sleeping ever more soundly. From the ceiling fixture a weak light illuminated the splendid form of the unfortunate creature who was about to become the victim of the most heinous attack.

XI. Sold

When Margherita came out of Vittoria's room, her face was radiant.

"And so?" her husband asked her.

"All is going well. The girl is sleeping like a log, even cannon fire couldn't wake her."

"Ruizzi, when is he coming?"

"He'll be here in a bit. What are we going to do with the brat?"

"Put him in the small room and cover him with this quilt. He'll be fine."

Napoleon obeyed immediately. After about a half hour, hurried steps could be heard coming up the stairs and a few moments later a cautious knock on the door. Margherita hurried to open and Ruizzi, well dressed, elegant and perfumed, entered.

"Welcome, my lord," the woman said, "You are fortunate. I have prepared for you a beauty of the first order, as well as a woman of the highest virtue."

"I know you, Mamma Margherita, and I'm sure that you will treat me like a first class client. Now, can I see the game."

"Certainly, look through that door."

The scene that unfolded in front of Ruizzi's eyes made his blood boil with lust; on the bed, with only a nightshirt to cover her, without hiding her sculpturesque profile, Vittoria was lying on the bed. Her voluminous black hair covered part of her face, making it impossible to see it from the shadows. The ceiling light concentrated its rays on the woman's bosom and showed it in all its opulence and whiteness.

Ruizzi was ready to throw himself on that beautiful body, when he felt himself restrained by Margherita's hand as she closed the door to the room.

"First, let's reason."

"Well, how much do you want?"

"The dangers are many, we are always on the road to Sing Sing, we need to think about what could go wrong. . . ."

"Enough talk." How much?

"O.K. then, it seems that one hundred dollars. . . ."

"Very well. . . ."

"Then you have lodging expenses."

"What do they total?"

"Let's say one-hundred and fifty dollars."

Ruiz took from his pocket an elegant booklet covered in red leather, he opened his fountain pen, and wrote on a 'Check' the sum of a 150 dollars, and gave it to Margherita, who immediately made it disappear in her bosom.

"And now," Ruizzi said, "leave. Leave the house to me."

"Certainly, we're leaving," answered Margherita, "but first I must tell you that the woman is asleep."

"My kisses will wake her."

"I don't think so, she took a narcotic."

"I would have preferred her awake."

"Then she wouldn't be yours. Good luck."

XII. *Husband and Wife*

As soon as Mr. and Mrs. Ghirendini retired to their room, Ruizzi flung himself into Vittoria's room. With unbridled lust, his trembling hands touched her firm and wonderfully perfumed flesh, and, for a long time, pressed his lips to those of the beauty sleeping before his eyes. The bed's canopy blocked the lamp's feeble light and formed a shadow over Vittoria's face. Ruizzi, gasping for breath, with temples pounding, was overcome by a feeling of ecstasy that he was not used to. But he would have preferred that that body would reawaken and respond with equal passion to his caresses.

All of a sudden it seemed to him that Vittoria moved. He waited anxiously, hugging the young woman tightly to his bosom. A few minutes passed when a sigh came from Vittoria's lips, and then her eyes opened. Immediately she didn't understand what was happening, but as she saw herself half naked in the arms of a man she let out a horrible yell, and freeing herself with a violent movement from those arms that held her like the coils of a serpent, she jumped from the bed, asking for help.

Quickly, Ruizzi was on top of her again. A savage fight ensued with Vittoria defending herself by biting and scratching the wicked individual that wanted to possess her. Ruizzi, inflamed and excited by her resistance, did not give ground. In the struggle, Vittoria's shirt was torn and she found herself nude in the arms of the vile libertine. The poor soul was exhausted, and the moment when she would have to yield was rapidly approaching. Ruizzi's triumph was almost certain as he began to lower his victim onto the bed and as he prepared to vent his carnal needs, Vittoria stopped defending herself. . . .

All of a sudden, a ray of light fell on the woman's face. Ruizzi recoiled, scared, and from his lips came the following:

"My wife!"

"Renato!" Vittoria replied.

There was a moment of silence. Then the man broke the silence, with a voice that was full of anger:

"What are you doing in America?"

"You're asking me? Your son and I have been looking for you"

"What are your intentions?"

"To live by your side, not for me, this was the last straw, and my heart will not yearn any more for the wretch that entered this room to commit the most heinous of crimes, but for our son who has the right to a family."

"You will return immediately to Naples."

"Never."

"It's necessary." Ruizzi yelled with a threatening voice.

"I will remain by your side." She answered, not at all intimidated.

"That can't be and will not be, you will return."

"No."

"Do not challenge me. Listen, if you wish that someday I may return to Europe a rich and esteemed man, you must leave me."

"Never, never, I found you and I will stay. Not to love you, that's true, but at least our son will have a father."

"Vittoria, I implore you, leave."

"It's no use, I will not leave."

"Vittoria, be careful!"

"What?"

"Desperation leads to crime."

"It would not be the first."

"What are you saying? Bitch."

"Do you remember why you left Naples. . . ."

Ruizzi became livid, this woman wanted to ruin him as he was ready to assure his future with his forthcoming marriage into a rich family. Her appearance on the scene was about to bring his carefully constructed plan to a screeching halt. It could not be, it would not be.

To escape the danger that was threatening him, his wife had to return to Italy. He changed tactics and tried to convince her with kindness, but to no avail. Vittoria was adamant about not leaving.

Her opposition irritated Ruizzi. He treated his wife brutally, while she, resigned but firm, did not utter a lament.

But when Ruizzi, foaming at the mouth, yelled at her that it took some courage to bring to America a son that was not his, the martyr raised her head proudly, and exclaimed with conviction:

"You're a vile, miserable human being, more foul and disgraceful than I thought could ever be possible."

Those insults hit Ruizzi like lashes to his face. He lost the light of reason and threw himself on his wife, his fingers in a death grip around her white neck.

Vittoria still had the strength to cry "Coward! Murderer!" then the words choked in her throat as Ruizzi maintained and tightened his grip. Her still body folded unto itself and dropped to the floor when the hands of her assailant stopped choking and let her go.

It was then that Ruizzi realized what he had done. He had committed a new crime and was overwhelmed by a great fear. His future flashed before his eyes: the inquest, the trial, the conviction, the electric chair, and again he was overwhelmed by a great and indescribable fear; he quickly regained his cool-headedness and thought of saving himself and not leave any traces of his passage. Furthermore, he was certain that the Ghirendini would not betray him because they would also suffer the consequences. Ruizzi dressed himself and left the room where his wife's body was lying on the bed, without as much as a single glance at the woman who had loved him so. While he was hurriedly going down the stairs, a young man, a little uncertain of himself, was slowly walking up. Ruizzi went right by him without paying any attention. When the assassin set foot on Mulberry, it was one in the morning.

XIII. The Arrest

The man Ruizzi almost ran into while he was running down the stairs after having committed the most horrible crime was Righetti, the young man passionately in love with Vittoria. We will briefly describe why and how he was on the Ghirendini's stairwell at that late hour of the night.

One can say that the young lover, forgetful of everything and attracted by an arcane, mysterious force to the house where the one who had taken possession of his heart lived, spent his life on Mulberry. Moreover, in that Italian neighborhood, much slandered and at the same time so picturesque, he found a piece of his faraway country, and the high spirits that surrounded him rendered the first days of his exile less painful.

Righetti preferred to stay across the street from the house where he had seen how the joy of his heart was brought, hoping to see her as she went out. Asking questions here and there, he became convinced that Vittoria was in great danger. Those countrymen, the majority from the Southern provinces, made him understand, with their brusque candor, that the Ghirendini couple had a horrible reputation and that all honest people should avoid them like the plague. The young man, who came to America with a small sum of money needed to confront the first necessities, had in his wallet about 1,000 francs, not a large sum in America, but he was determined to use those meager resources to help the woman he loved.

Across the street from the Ghirendini house there was a large beer hall, not elegant, patronized by many Italians because the owner was very popular. Righetti made this beer hall his general quarters and basically stayed there from morning till night. The regulars, seeing this new face that no one knew, tried their best to figure out from what part of Italy he came from. The young man, who had no interest in lying, told them who he was and why he came to America.

The Italians, used to the hardest type of work, sympathized with all their hearts because they knew that America was a place suited only for men who had strong arms and backs to work, and understood that the young man, elegantly dressed, with a refined bearing and long white delicate hands, would soon run into the most painful disappointments.

When Ruizzi tried to take possession of the beautiful immigrant Margherita had sold him, Righetti was at his usual place in the beer hall. That evening the owner had kept the bar open longer than usual because of the serious discussion among the small colony of Italians, one of those discussions that always ended in vile battles and murders, where the Italian name would be brutalized and covered in mud. The owner of the beer hall, an influential man and leader of various associations, surrounded by many friends, was discussing the events of the day, and, in the heat of the discussion, did not realize that it was past midnight, the time that all beer halls should close. The policeman on the beat took it upon himself to remind the owner of his duties, and the owner quickly, but courteously, showed his clients the door.

Righetti was one of the last to leave. The weather was not good, it was gloomier than usual. The young man took a long look at the house where the idol of his heart lived, and was ready to leave when he thought he heard a stifled cry that came from the Ghirendini's house. He listened carefully but did not hear anything. He dismissed it as a trick his mind was playing on him and began to leave but an internal voice kept on saying, "It's a mistake to leave, Vittoria needs you."

"Well, I'll take a look." He whispered to himself. He crossed the street, entered the narrow alley, and, like a common thief, he staggered up the stairs that lead to the Ghirendini's apartment. When he heard someone coming down the stairs, he was almost overcome by fear, almost turned around, but love gave him courage and he continued up the stairs.

Righetti reached the landing of the Ghirendini's home and he felt a pang in his heart when he saw the door wide open. Nonetheless, he entered determined to see why. There was no one in the kitchen. He crossed it with a steady step and moved towards the open door to Vittoria's room. As soon as he crossed the threshold, he let out a horrible anguished cry and almost fainted.

The spectacle in front of his eyes was dreadful. The bed was unmade, the furniture strewn about, the curtains ripped, and in the middle of that confusion, like an ancient statue that's been toppled over, was the nude body of Vittoria. Righetti had an intuition of what must have happened, and cursed his destiny that had made him arrive too late. On his knees on the rug, the young man looked for the slightest movement, hoping that the body in front of him was still alive. In the meantime, his desperate cry sounded the alarm, and the neighbors began to open windows and ask each other what could have happened; some said they heard cries, laments, and moans throughout the evening, while others suggested that it would be wise to call the police. That suggestion met with a general consensus, and a young man took it upon himself to complete the mission.

Righetti, in tears, was uselessly trying to give life and warmth to that motionless body that seemed to have already received the cold kiss of death. When the policeman entered the room, Righetti was holding Vittoria's body tight to his bosom, and, overcome by his passion, was furiously kissing the beautiful woman that rested in his arms. He was awakened from his ecstasy by the policeman's rough voice, who yelled at him, "You are my prisoner."

Righetti did not understand the words, but feeling the policeman's hand on his shoulder he understood that he was being arrested. He had entered a house that wasn't his, so the policeman had every right to arrest him. Various neighbors, who entered the apartment behind the officer, saw the naked body of Vittoria and quickly ran to cover her, while giving Righetti, who could not comprehend why everyone was looking at him so menacingly, a look of contempt.

"Follow me," the policeman said abruptly, and to a detective, "John, you stay here until the ambulance arrives."

Righetti did not understand the words of the policeman and remained frozen in front of Vittoria's body, which the women had laid on the bed. The policemen brutally grabbed him by the shoulders and shoved him towards the door; the unlucky young man wanted to protest, but the policeman raised his club and hit him repeatedly.

In the meantime, like a bolt of lightning, the news spread on Mulberry that a crime had been committed. The windows on both sides of the street opened noisily, and everyone was asking questions, asking for details of what happened. Like all news, even this was exaggerated: from one end to the other of the long street, the news was that an Italian had committed a horrendous crime and that he had killed at least four poor souls. The farther one went from the scene of the crime, the larger the proportions that the event assumed. So that, when Righetti, who everyone already assumed was the murderer, came out of the building in the hands of the police, a loud threatening cry went up from the crowd in the street and was repeated by the women at their windows in their nightshirts, oblivious to the cold. The rumbling, always louder, always more insulting and threatening, accompanied the poor man to police headquarters at the end of Mulberry, where, in spite of his protests, he was locked in a small narrow cell, with an iron gate and a filthy table.

To Righetti it all seemed like a bad nightmare. When the iron gate closed behind him, he asked himself more than once if he was sleeping or awake. Unfortunately for him, he wasn't dreaming, what was happening to him was a sad and tragic reality, and soon he would realize that he was being overcome by terrible events.

XIV. *The Accusation*

The hours that Righetti passed in the filthy police cell were for the poor soul an indescribable agony.

Certain that he did not commit any crime, Righetti was not worried. He was sure that, after explaining what had happened, he would be cleared and set free. What anguished him was Vittoria's death, the woman he loved and to whom he had sworn all his affection.

In his heart a sense of vengeance was taking hold towards the individual who had abused and murdered Vittoria. He had no doubts that a crime had been committed and that the author of the crime was the man he ran into while going up the stairs to Margherita's house.

"I'll find the coward," he kept on murmuring to himself, as he paced up and down like a caged animal, "I will find him, and then heaven help him!"

Then he would be overcome with doubts. Find him! How? Without friends, without contacts, with few means, in a large city he did not know, in the middle of an immense population, where even the best policemen lost traces of criminals.

The lover's meditations were interrupted by the yelling and cursing of other prisoners the police were continuously bringing to the station. These were drunks gathered along the way, full of bruises from their falls, or men with black and blue eyes from a beating they had received. Along with these filthy men came women who were even filthier, with their vests and dresses ripped to shreds, muddied from the dirty water on the street. The policemen brutally shoved those poor souls into those miserable cells and answered their cries and groans with nightsticks, contempt, laughter, and a string of obscenities. This was the nightly show that took place among the steel gates, the heavy doors, under the eyes of the guards, who, used to the recurring spectacle, sat with their legs propped up, reading the first news of the day. Finally dawn arrived, the light from the gas lamps paled, and the hallways were suddenly full of people, the janitors began sweeping the pavement, cleaning the gates and polishing the locks.

Around eight a bell sounded, and, soon after, the cells were unlocked and the servants began the distribution of coffee, milk, and bread. It was time for breakfast, welcomed by the joyous sounds of the detained. Righetti wanted nothing to do with his ration. He was anxiously waiting to be interrogated and then set free.

At ten the arresting office came for him. He was very happy, but when they tried to put the cuffs on him he backed off.

The policeman, without niceties, grabbed Righetti's arms, who shivered from indignity and shame when he felt the cold steel that circled his wrists, as if they were those of a common criminal.

The prisoner was brought on foot to the Tombs. All along the way people stopped to stare at him and a group of curiosity seekers followed. The wretch, confused and red from shame, felt he was going to die under the sarcastic looks that followed him without pity. Finally they arrived at the Tombs, a depressing granite building, a frightful edifice that injects a sinister note into one of the busiest streets of New York. Righetti went up the stairs as the crowd moved to the sides, all the while looking at him threateningly.

The hall of the tribunal of the Tombs was also full of people. The morning newspapers had published in great detail the crime that happened on Mulberry

Street. The reporters had also made things up about Righetti and painted him as one of those ferocious animals, horrible in affairs of love, cruel in their vengeance, and bloodthirsty. Furthermore, they added that since he was an Italian accused of being wicked and dangerous, to lynch him would be an act of grace.

Since Judge Trainit did not begin to administer justice until eleven, Righetti had to wait in a holding cell a good half hour before being called to his hearing. That time was well spent by the reporters who took photos of the assassin.

Finally, it was time to go in front of the judge. The poor wretch thought that he would be allowed to explain why he entered the house of persons he did not know, and that since he did it with good intentions he hoped to be pardoned and set free.

When Righetti found himself in front of the judge, the arresting officer went into a long narration. They were words that made no sense to the prisoner. When the policeman finished, the judge said: "Good. Take the accused and bring him to 'City Prison' and kept in custody until further clarification." The policeman was handed a file from the Judge and said to the prisoner: "Let's go!"

What! They were taking him away without letting him speak, without saying a word? Was he free? He interrogated the officer. It was useless, as the man didn't know Italian. The interpreter approached him and said:

"You can't be judged here for your crime, you have to see other judges."

"My crime! What am I accused of? Speak to me. In the name of God tell me."

"You don't know? You are accused of attempted murder, for vengeance, of a young lady recently arrived from Italy."

"Me, a murderer!" He yelled in a voice choked by emotion. He didn't say more, the news hit him too hard, and the poor soul lost his senses and fell backwards as though he were dead.

The people in the hall started whispering, and everyone wanted to see what had happened. The policemen on duty had a hard time controlling the crowd, while two of them took the prisoner and led him back to the cells by the stairwell that connected the Tribunal with the Tombs.

When Righetti woke up three hours later he occupied cell number 69 in the Tombs, one of the more dreary in the dreariest of buildings.

XV. Insane!

The officer who arrested Righetti had called for an ambulance from Chambers Street Hospital. The ambulance arrived quickly and transported Vittoria to the hospital. Since this was classified a crime, the doctors on call made a careful examination of the body which had all of the rigidity and appearance of a cadaver.

The results of their preliminary diagnosis made them aware that the woman was alive but that her condition was serious.

Vittoria remained between life and death for eight days, if you could call it living: she was in a deep coma that the doctors could not explain. The doctors surmised that it was a miracle that poor woman had not been strangled; the nails of the assassin had penetrated the skin around her neck, leaving wounds and bruises all around her neck.

During the ninth day of her hospital stay, Vittoria began to recover her senses, her arms and legs started losing their stiffness and her blood began to circulate. Only her eyes remained shut.

When, after so many days, the poor soul reopened her eyes she began to furiously toss and turn and agonizing shrieks came from her lips that were streaked with white foam. At times she was plagued by terror and wanted to flee from her bed, at other times she begged for pity. She was often threatening, her voice became hard and bitter, and her stare hard and frightful. The doctors did not hesitate to give their diagnosis: Vittoria Ruiz was insane.

When Righetti came to, it took him a while to gather his thoughts, but he finally began remembering. Passionate tears flowed down his cheeks to think that he was suspected of killing the woman he loved! How? Why? Was justice so blind to commit such errors? All of a sudden he let out a cry of joy. He remembered that the interpreter told him that he was accused of attempted homicide, attempted. That meant that there was no murder. Vittoria was alive!

She lived! What a feeling of immense relief he felt. What did he care about being in that cell? Vittoria's deposition would open the prison doors for him, and maybe the event could also serve to bring him the greatest happiness. Righetti, fully reassured, threw himself on the steel cot with the hard straw mattress that occupied more than half of the cell, and slept soundly. He was awakened in the evening by the servers that brought him bread and soup. He was hungry and avidly ate his bread and soup, if you could actually call that mixture soup. That night, Righetti rested peacefully, and dreamt a thousand beautiful things, as though he were sleeping in a palace instead of a squalid cell in the Tombs.

The days passed, and it seemed that everyone forgot about the prisoner. During the two hours of daily exercise, which consisted of walking up and down the narrow terraces that circle the cells of the three floors of the Tombs, Righetti had a chance to speak to other Italians, also awaiting their trial. They advised him to turn to an Italian lawyer, and gave him the address of a young lawyer, talented and with good intentions, to whom Righetti immediately wrote a long letter.

The lawyer accepted Righetti's invitation. He listened attentively to what Righetti had to say and came away convinced that the young man was innocent of the crime he was accused of committing.

"Besides," Righetti concluded, "Vittoria is alive and she will tell them who rally tried to abuse her and kill her."

"Don't deceive yourself, my friend," the lawyer answered, "Vittoria will not vindicate you."

"What, do you also believe that she is guilty?"

"No, no: but there are other insurmountable motives. You see, the young woman you love is. . . ."

"Well. . . ."

"I wouldn't want to. . . ."

"Tell me, tell me. Now I have to know everything."

"Maybe it is better that you know. Vittoria is insane."

"Insane! Insane!" he cried as he burst into tears.

"Do not despair, we'll get you off nonetheless."

"What do I care? I would rather be in a chain gang than know that the woman I love suffers so."

The lawyer did not know how to answer, and to hide his emotions he left.

Two weeks later the Grand Jury indicted Alfredo Righetti[1] for attempted murder in the first degree.

Vittoria, whose madness worsened, was brought to Blackwell's Island.

The small Enrico, who called for his mother with pitiful cries, was turned over to the Gerry Association.

The Ghirendini's were never seen again on Mulberry Street. This made an impression on the whole neighborhood, and Inspector Byrne, who has a nose for these things, took note of this and promised himself to get to the bottom of the mystery of that disappearance.

Renato Ruiz spent those first days after the crime in anguish. When he learned from the papers that Vittoria was not dead, he thought of fleeing, but so many business interests tied him to New York that he stayed despite the danger he faced. When he read that his wife was declared insane and incurable, he felt a delirious joy. He was safe and could complete his plans without impunity.

---

1. In a typical sign of haste, the character Ciambelli first introduced as Alberto Righetti is now Alfredo Righetti.

For the man that was in jail for his crime, Renato had not even a thought of compassion; besides, he had had his trial and was found not guilty. Justice was served and the case was closed.

Vittoria's voice could not be heard from the depths of the asylum. Everything was going as well as could be. Renato was triumphant.

Translated by Paolo Giordano

∾

Up and Down the Colony
(from The Reporter's Notebook)

Giorgio Vestro was having fun throwing a sharp knife against a board to see if he could get it to stay planted straight in the wood just as the jugglers did.[2]

One of his friends, Carlo Aletti, inadvertently passed in front of the board and Vestro's knife went and struck his left thigh.

Because of the loss of blood, Aletti had to be transported to Bellevue Hospital, while Vestro was taken to prison in a pitiful state.

Yesterday morning, the Yorkeville Court judge set bail at $300 bail for the involuntary accidental assailant.

Giancomo Alessandri, 22, appeared before the Special Sessions accused of having given a kiss and a slap to Nellie Smith, 17. The sensual caress progressed to a brutal blow, although briefly I would say. Ten days ago Giacomo, who for a while had been gazing lovestruck at his neighbor Nellie, met her in the hallway and unceremoniously squeezed her within an inch of her life and planted a big kiss on her crimson lips. Nellie responded with a strike of her pink fingernails which produced a bloody gash on the perpetrator's face, who, forgetting chivalry, unleashed a powerful slap on the girl who began to shout desperately.

A policeman arrested Giacomo, and yesterday the judge, considering that Nellie's lips now blow kisses two by two, given the serious provocation for the scratch, acquitted the accused.

Here comes the best part. As soon as Giacomo was set free, Nellie, who was in Court, graciously smiled at him; he approached her, they talked a little and then they both left the courtroom to enjoy a day in the country.

2. All excerpts are taken from *Il Progresso Italo-Americano*.

I'm sure that by now they have exchanged who knows how many kisses, without any scratches or slaps.

[SEPTEMBER 2, 1894]

Luigia Sampietro, wife of Bernadino Ciambelli, happily gave birth at three a.m. on Monday to a little girl that will be called Maria Pia, Elisabetta and Clara.

I went to interview the newborn, but she absolutely did not want to respond. All of my skills as a reporter were in vain; she maintained an eloquent silence. I then read in that rosy face, in those lively eyes, in those crimson lips of that little Ciambelli doughnut good enough to eat with kisses, and I discovered that she is happy and glad to have come into the world just as her daddy and her mommy are so very happy with her arrival.

Breaking with office conventions, all of my colleagues screamed into my ears their greetings and congratulations to Luigia and Bernardino Ciambelli along with a thousand best wishes for their beloved daughter.

I serve my colleagues with such joy that it would seem as if the happy event were my own. . . .

[NOVEMBER 7, 1894]

Slaps, scratches, punches, and kicks were exchanged yesterday amid a crowd delirious with joy. Anna Paletti and Eufemia Rucci, being rivals in love fought a real "rustic duel," ending with the intervention of a policeman who brought them to the police station. In court the two women repeated a violent scene and the judge had to call for back-up to separate them. They were each fined $5 for disorderly conduct.

Geltrude Minocchi, 45, of 121 E. 132th [sic] Street, allowed herself the luxury of deserting her marital home to coo with a pock-marked young dove.

Her husband, Rosario, perhaps, would not have understood the reason for Geltrude's flight if she had not taken $120, a watch, and a gold chain, and for this reason Rosario reported it to the judge, who after hesitating for a moment issued a warrant for Geltrude's arrest.

". . . I want her to rot in prison, that fair maiden," said Rosario, "not because she went with another man, but because she stole money I earned by the sweat of my brow."

Now the poor man, in addition to sweat, has appendages on his brow that would make a deer proud.

Antonio Grossi, 28, was arrested for having brutally beaten his young wife Maria. The poor woman told the judge that in 18 months of marriage she never had a moment of peace, not even on their wedding night when her husband had given her, not what usually occurs in that circumstance, but a couple of slaps for a misspoken word. Antonio claims that his wife is a shady character, and if he gave her a couple of slaps it was because he found the English Channel instead of the Behring [Bering] Straits. The judge, not very well-versed in marital geography, sentenced the savage husband to trial, setting bail at $500.

[FEBRUARY 24, 1895]

Punches, the kind that leave marks, were exchanged the other night by Antonio Marco and Giovanni Santino who were fighting over a whore whose snout does not even deserve a second glance.

The policeman rushed over in the heat of the scuffle and arrested the belligerent parties who got away with paying a $10 fine each.

The two left the Court with black eyes and swollen faces, but at least they satisfied the urge to beat each other senseless.

There isn't any great harm when Italians come to blows, and I have noted with pleasure that for the last few days the tabloids haven't reported any ostentatious incidents with knives or guns; I hope that it continues on like this forever, for the good name of all Italians and to avoid the misfortunes that cause endless tears to be shed and ruin entire families.

Giuseppe Levico, organ grinder, was arrested in Brooklyn and held in custody because he allowed his monkey to behave obscenely in public.

It seemed that the mischievous little prankster gave a not-so-clean performance; this despite the fact that people, especially the little girls, were having loads of fun and weren't even blushing.

The trial will be very interesting, particularly because we don't know what the vulgar monkey's sentence will be.

[APRIL 21, 1895]

Translated by Giulia Prestia

∾

The Martyr of Duty, or Giuseppe Petrosino

CHARACTERS

Antonio

Rosalia, his wife

Alberto, their son

Aurelia, their daughter

Rocco, Aurelia's boyfriend

Don Raffaele, Rosalia's cousin, a brothel owner

Carmela, a madam in his brothel

Lucia, a prostitute in the brothel

Santo, her fiancé

Lt. Giuseppe Petrosino, a Policeman

A Doctor

ACT I

Rosalia and Antonio, threatened with eviction, live in poverty in a slum. He is unable to work and does not receive any financial aid; he has a sick son and a daughter, Aurelia, who earns some money hawking newspapers. It is the last day of the year in New York, and it is snowing. Antonio would like to ask for assistance from Don Raffaele, his wife's cousin, a leader in the Italian community, but Rosalia does not want him to because her cousin makes his money profiting from prostitution. When Aurelia returns, Antonio goes out in the snow in search of help; Aurelia goes out to buy coal, and while Rosalia is alone, Don Raffaele arrives; he wants to possess her, but she drives him away. Aurelia returns, recounting how the coal seller wanted to rape her. And then Antonio returns, out of breath: he had asked for charity; he was mistaken for a thief; so he fled. Petrosino rushes in: he understands the situation, but he must do his duty. Meanwhile, Alberto, the son of Antonio and Rosalia, dies. Petrosino rebels: "My God! What must be will be, but I will not take this man away at such a time. Duty is duty, but the heart demands its rights."

ACT II

In one of Don Raffaele's houses of ill repute, Carmela, the Madam, asks Aurelia's penniless boyfriend, Rocco, to bring Aurelia there in exchange for one hundred dollars. Lucia, another girl in the brothel, has overheard the conversation and wants to prevent Aurelia from the same fate as her own. Disguised as a laborer, Petrosino arrives at the brothel and draws Lucia aside: he tells her he is an agent for the Children's Aid Society, and Lucia discloses to him that they are bringing in a new girl that night; then she hides him in another room. Rocco brings Aurelia in to see Don Raffaele, but Rosalia arrives and she too is captured. They start carrying off both mother and daughter to rape them when Petrosino enters on the scene: "Can I join in the party too?" Then he arrests them.

ACT III

(Time has passed, Antonio and Rosalia have come into an inheritance.)

Scene V

ANTONIO *(entering)*: Petrosino, our good friend, you're here?

ROSALIA: We wanted to send for you; today is Aurelia's birthday, and we've decided to have a party, which you can't miss.

PETROSINO: Well, give my congratulations to your dear Aurelia, but I will not be able to come to your party; I have a lot to get ready before I leave.

ANTONIO: You are leaving?

PETROSINO: I am going to Italy.

ANTONIO: My God, who knows how long you will be gone!

PETROSINO: Two or three months at the most. I can't stay far away from my wife and my baby girl for very long.

ROSALIA: Right, your baby, how is the dear little angel?

PETROSINO: *(with pride)* She is growing, which is a good sign; she is a wonderful gift; she is the ray of sunshine in my house.

AURELIA *(under her breath)*: How happy he is!

PETROSINO: I also have some good news to tell you.

ANTONIO: You are always the man with good news.

PETROSINO: Santo will marry Lucia.

ROSALIA: Good, Santo, I am sure that you will be happy.

SANTO: I think so too.

ANTONIO: We will take care of furnishing the bride's trousseau; she's like our own daughter.

ROSALIA: Aurelia, why are you so pale?

AURELIA: It's nothing, mamma, nothing.

ANTONIO: You stay indoors too much; you need air. Today is such a beautiful day.

PETROSINO: It's true, you should go out.

AURELIA: I am still very weak.

ANTONIO: We'll go out in a coach and we'll ride in Central Park; I will go with you, and Mamma and Lucia will take care of everything for your party this evening.

AURELIA: But . . . I don't know.

PETROSINO: Listen, Aurelia, if you go out and take a nice walk, I promise you that I will come this evening to give you my congratulations.

AURELIA: Really?

PETROSINO: When I make a promise, I keep it.

AURELIA: Then, I will go out.

ANTONIO: Very well. Lucia, go to the coach house next door and have them send a coach.

LUCIA: Right away. (*She exits*)

Scene VI

ANTONIO: Go get ready, my dear child.

AURELIA: I'll be ready right away. I'll be back in a minute. (*She exits*)

ANTONIO: Petrosino, my friend, we are the most unlucky parents.

PETROSINO: Why?

ANTONIO: Can't you see that my daughter is afflicted with a terrible disease that will take her to her grave?

PETROSINO: Don't say that.

ROSALIA: We live in continuous fear. The doctors don't know what to do for us, and she is slowly dying.

(*Santo looks into the street from the window.*)

ANTONIO: You see how cruel fate is. Once we were poor, and our Aurelia was very healthy; now we are almost rich, and Aurelia is dying.

PETROSINO: Let's not exaggerate. It's because of the trauma she experienced over that night in Don Raffaele's brothel, but she will recover; take her to the country to distract her attention and she'll forget.

ANTONIO: God willing. And so what happened to that gangster Don Raffaele?

PETROSINO: They released him on bail, and he fled. He's in Italy, for sure.

ANTONIO: Be careful you don't run into him in the street; that man is despicable and capable of anything.

PETROSINO: I am not afraid.

ROSALIA: And if they should kill you?

AURELIA (*entering*): Kill who?

ANTONIO: Our friend Petrosino, who is going to Italy.

AURELIA (*with emotion*): Don't go, don't go!

PETROSINO: Duty above all else. I'll tell you again that I am not afraid of the few criminals who dishonor our name. After all, we are soldiers, and the soldier must not fear death.

AURELIA: I don't want them to kill you.

PETROSINO: Don't worry, Aurelia, they won't kill me, and I'll bring you back a beautiful gift from Italy.

SANTO (*excited*): What's happening in the street? People are screaming and running all over!

PETROSINO: Some crime maybe. Wait, I'll run and see. (*he exits quickly*)

SANTO: I'm coming with you. (*he exits*)

(*Everyone approaches the window*)

ANTONIO: People are crowding in front of our house.

ROSALIA: My God, what can it be?

ANTONIO: They are coming up the stairs.

FINALE

SANTO (*He carries Lucia in his arms; she has a bandage on her throat*): They murdered her.

AURELIA: Murdered? No, it's not true.

ANTONIO: Who was the killer?

(*They carefully lay Lucia down on the divan and everyone surrounds her.*)

ROSALIA: Run get a doctor.

AURELIA: Lucia, answer me. . . .

LUCIA (*she speaks with great effort*): He took his revenge.

AURELIA: Who?

LUCIA (*slowly*): Rocco.

AURELIA: The bastard.

PETROSINO (*dragging Rocco with him*): Here is the hoodlum who committed the crime.

AURELIA (*to herself*): And I loved that man!!

ROCCO (*boldly*): It is not true; I am innocent.

PETROSINO: Here in the face of your victim, let's see if you have the nerve to deny it.

LUCIA (*Seeing Rocco, she lets out a frightened scream*)

PETROSINO: Don't be afraid, poor child; he will never hurt anyone again. And now, speak Lucia, and you all are witnesses. Wasn't it this criminal who attacked you?

LUCIA (*She throws a glance at Aurelia who seems like she wants to die*): No . . . It is not him.

(*The Doctor runs to Lucia and examines her wound.*)

ROCCO (*triumphant*): You see, you were wrong? Let me go and you, go watch out for your girlfriend.

PETROSINO: On your knees, you bum, on your knees in front of this victim who helped you escape, maybe from the electric chair.

ROCCO (*Under Petrosino's grasp, he is forced to kneel down*)

AURELIA (*to the Doctor*): Doctor, relieve me from this anxiety that is killing me; is there any hope?

DOCTOR: She will live.

(*Exclamations of joy*)

ACT IV

Petrosino is assassinated in Italy. The Doctor advises Rosalia and Antonio to bring Aurelia to Italy in order to find distractions to shake her out of her depression. Everyone tries to keep her in the dark about what has happened, but the girl knows. She receives a postcard from Petrosino, and she kisses it. From the street they hear music for a funeral march. Aurelia goes to the window to throw flowers. Then she dies.

Translated by Emelise Aleandri

෨

An Emigrant's Diary

൞ *Camillo Cianfarra*

Lama dei Peligni (Abruzzi), Italy, 1879–Rome, Italy, August 14, 1925

Camillo Cianfarra was probably born in Lama dei Peligni (Abruzzi) in 1879; the Ellis Island database has a notice of a certain "Cauillo Cianfarra" arriving in 1894 at the age of fifteen. He died in Rome on August 14, 1925, "from heart failure and complications resulting from his arrest and torture by the Fascisti" (*Chicago Tribune*, August 15, 1925). After serving in the diplomatic corps in New York and (probably) Washington, where he also "investigated numerous cases of Sicilian murderers who were given opportunities to go to America instead of having to serve in Italian jails" (ibid.), he went back to Italy, where he was correspondent for several American papers, including, after the beginning of the 1920s, the *Chicago Tribune*. The famous journalist George Seldes, in *You Can't Print That! The Truth Behind the News 1918 to 1928*, narrates that in 1925, CC "died two weeks after my expulsion from Rome, from heart failure, as a result of being beaten by Fascisti, apparently for the reason that he helped me obtain the documents which charged Mussolini's complicity in the Matteotti assassination." The documents here cited are the famous Rossi memorial (Rossi was the head of Premier Mussolini's press bureau of the foreign office). Cianfarra had these documents in January 1925 and sent the news by cable to America, so he was arrested. "Mr. Cianfarra's release was obtained by John Clayton of the *Tribune* staff through the intervention of the American embassy at Rome with the Italian foreign office. However, Mr. Cianfarra's health was completely ruined by his sufferings in prison. When Mr. Seldes was expelled from Rome, the Fascisti openly declared that they would have Mr. Cianfarra's life."

Despite its title, *Il diario di un emigrato* (An Emigrant's Diary), published in New York in 1904, can be considered a true and proper novel, although strongly autobiographical. Yet the novel's purpose is not clearly defined, since it mingles a sentimental story with the socialistic-libertarian denunciations that emerge in its many secondary episodes. Yet precisely these denunciations leap to the fore with major force. The narrator warns that "not everyone will say that what I narrate here is true. Those who deny it will be those whom you and I will meet, the *arrivati*, the ones who have 'made it.'these people, in the name of a false patriotism, weave a web of rosy lies around what is really the true foundation of our colony. These people, at banquets and public places talk this way to the naive and the deluded who will never have occasion to come into contact with reality."

The story begins on April 28, of an unspecified year of the last decade of the nineteenth century. The narrator disembarks in New York and applies himself to looking for work. "For you, a pen is required, not a 'sabre'" (meaning a shovel), people say to him, noting that his hands are free of calluses. The consul advises him to go West; meanwhile, however, he meets Maria again, a woman he met on the ship, and Maria invites him to stay at her aunt's pension. Maria—whose rapport with him is reminiscent of that of Lamartine's *Graziella*—wants to marry him, but his opinions, however much he professes love for her, are incomprehensible to her. This circumstance provokes a libertarian exhortation: "You perhaps have dreamed of me at your side, before the altar in the presence of a benedictory minister: but for me, there is no altar more sacred than that of my conscience, administered more authentically by my heart itself," after which the two kiss.

With "Professor" Savini, a curious figure of colonial intellect who paints a very gloomy picture of the state of affairs, the narrator visits the Italian quarter of New York. In the meanwhile, Maria is seduced by Cesare, a stonecutter, who, with the support of Maria's aunt, wants to marry her. The narrator finds work with a wine merchant and importer of liquors. "Do you want to become a wholesale importer and vendor of Chianti? Do as I tell you: write to Italy and have two bottles of Chianti sent you. The flasks wrapped in straw can be found here, and the labels to attach to them will cost you almost nothing. When you have the wine in hand, take the flasks and fill them halfway; then add a gram of tannic acid, a bit of seltzer water, and then . . . water, until the flask is full" (83). This and other ways of "honestly" making a fortune in a very few years compared with the squalor of the existences of so many derelicts—including the squalor he sees one night on a visit to an Italian bordello—begin to prey on the narrator's mind, to fill him with doubts, and these doubts then corroborated by the occasional customers who are socialist and anarchist activists.

Savini informs Cesare about the culture of the local professors who give Italian lessons to make a living. "I know one, for example, whose literary culture does not extend beyond the poetry of Stecchetti. As soon as one of his pupils is capable of reading, with difficulty, he thrusts before her 'Postuma' (a poem by Stecchetti), and explains some bit of bad taste whose elegance and worth he cannot properly judge. Another friend of mine, who, like me, has so often written 'Professore' on his visiting card, knows only Manzoni's *Inni sacri*" (Sacred Hymns, 91–92).

The book proceeds to excerpt a quantity of short colonial sketches, like that of the subeditor, who in the café goes on and on about the condition of Italians in New York and about the future of Italians; or that of the "out-of-breath singer" who relates wonderful things about himself and his past, and then "at eight in the evening goes to sing light Neapolitan songs in a French café, which pays him fairly"; and that of the anarchist Gigi, with his discourses on free love. The narrator answers him a little pompously, and with the air of transmitting a sort of inner communication to the movement: "Your ideas are fine and good, but you should not touch upon certain keys. To discuss free love and the relations between the sexes requires, unfortunately, a level of understanding you have not reached. Do not think that a pamphlet or two or three newspaper articles are sufficient to exhaust the question: long and difficult studies are necessary, and then one must know how to expound with calm, without presumption, and above all, with clarity. You should limit yourself to dispensing simple propaganda, to saying clearly only that about which you are certain and know quite well; otherwise, repeating uselessly what you have read or heard said, and have not digested at all, ends simply by doing your ideas more harm than good" (103–104).

Meanwhile, the stonecutter, who is unaware of the relation between the narrator and Maria, turns to the narrator, asking him for advice. Cesare is a good boy, but when the narrator begins to talk of him to her, Maria begins to cry until her tears are smothered by their kisses. Christmas arrives, and thoughts travel to the far-off mother.

The diary picks up the story on the first anniversary of the arrival of our narrator in America. Exhausted by so much work, tired of being exploited, the narrator decides to go away. The scene of the story becomes a hermitage, where a gang of laborers works on the construction of the railroad. There is the *bordante* (laborers' mediator) in the pay of a Roman *padrone*; there is the story of a certain Nicola who was a priest but had a lover, and for this reason, must leave the United States; there is the banker Don Raffaele, who visits the laborers to collect debts; and after him other priests arrive, anything but welcome; and black prostitutes ("the possibility of a union between a black and a white—even if he be a starving Southern Italian peasant—I have never imagined," the narrator writes). There is above all the inflamed discourse of a socialist agitator.

The narrator returns to New York to work in the bank of Don Raffaele. As he has advised her, Maria marries. Then Don Raffaele flees with the bank money, and then follow three months of unemployment for the narrator. On the third anniversary of his arrival, he becomes a colonial journalist.

> "No, then I did not know the colony: the prominent men who flatter to obtain good publicity, and those who offer drinks to hold onto friends; the illustrious fleshly and prosperous who notify us of the seventh child, and those who announce to us their forthcoming matrimony; the unappreciated geniuses who bring us manuscripts to read, and the persistent amateur players who pursue us relentlessly; the barbarous poets and prose writers who poison our dinners, and the inventive shoemakers, who want their photographs in the "Supplemento"; the blowhard singers who ask us to announce their next concerts, and the angry swordsmen who want to announce their tournaments." (173–174)

Fortunately, at least Maria is finally married; she has an eight-month old baby, and her husband is considering opening a hotel on Lake Como.

According to De Ciampis, Cianfarra arrived in the United States in 1897: "along the streets of the Metropolis, he talked to the emigrants about socialism, under the aegis of the SLP" (Socialist Labor Party):

> One day, [in autumn 1897] the barber Giuseppe Spallone, called the "red," a native of Macchia Valfortore, found Cianfarra, who was talking to a group of bystanders on a street corner in New York. He liked the impressive speech of the orator and invited him to Waterbury for a conference. Cianfarra came, but found that the police had revoked the permit to have a meeting, and that the door of the hall was blocked by numerous agents. Spallone was not deterred and brought the audience to his own house, angry at the despotic act. Cianfarra spoke and generated great enthusiasm in the listeners. They immediately formed another section, a subdivision, but these first socialists, groundbreakers as they were, had to pay dearly for their boldness, because they were soon ostracized from work by the barons of the local industries. (De Ciampis 1958, 136)

Cianfarra, then, spoke eloquently. In fact, an article in the *Proletario* of December 23, 1899, reveals that he was by now a member of the Circolo Socialista di Bassa Città (Downtown), functioning as organizer and propagandist. In his hectic life, also involving frequent changes of residence, Cianfarra's role as the historical head of the Italian American socialists was not secondary. In 1898, he was the managing editor of the biweekly *Il Proletario* in Paterson, New Jersey. As De Ciampis reveals, his pseudonym was "Walker," under which he polemicized, with the lawyer Gullino Giovanni Vicario's *Araldo Italiano*, of "a survivor of imprisonment in Italy, for intrigues" (138). Notable is that the *Diario* issued from the printing house of the *Araldo*. Cianfarra held his position through June 1899. CC, during his early years in America, had a love affair with Emma Quazza, a twenty-year-old weaver and an anarchist from Mosso Biellese (Piedmont), whose parents sent her back to Italy from Paterson, New Jersey, in 1900 in order to keep her away from Cianfarra, whom they disliked. But on the ship back to Italy, Emma became the lover of Gaetano Bresci, the anarchist who was to kill King Umberto I in Monza.[1] Between 1900 and 1901, Cianfarra was still director of the *Proletario*. He was forced to resign because of the conflicts among the editorial staff in relation to the election of one of two socialist parties, the SLP or the SPA; he remained, however, in the party organization. As he himself confessed in the *Diario*, his political convictions, already developed during his high school years, had almost been a private fact and somewhat academic, until his arrival in America; before then, he was unable to come into contact with actual socialists.

Traces of him are then lost until we find him again in 1907, as a colleague of G. E. Palma of Castiglione, the director of the Bureau of Placement for Immigrant Stabilization established by the Italian Government in New York, an institutional role by now far removed from his political undertakings. As Inspector of the Labor Information Office, he had already signed a report in November 1906 on "La manodopera negra [undocumented laborer] nel concetto degli Industriali del Sud degli Stati Uniti" (Undocumented Labor in the View of Industrialists in the Southern United States) issued in *La Rassegna Nord America*, a review in which a month before he had published a story entitled "My Stenographer and Me." Another of his stories, "A Christmas Romance," was issued in *La Follia of New York* on December 18, 1910. By the end of 1910, however, Cianfarra centered his interest on the problems of assisting emigrants, and in Italy, published the pamphlet, On the Only Possible Protection in America (*Dell' unica protezione possible nel Nord America]* Rome: Unione Tipografica Cooperativa).

1. This information comes from Roberto Gremmo, *Gli anarchici che uccisero Umberto I. Gaetano Bresci, il "Biondino" e i tessitori biellesi di Paterson* (Biella: Storia ribelle, 2000), 17.

De Ciampis claims that he would become for many years the correspondent from Rome for the *New York Times*, but he mistakes Camillo Cianfarra for his son Camille Maximilian Cianfarra, called "Cian," who born in 1907 on Long Island and died in 1956 in the shipwreck of the *Andrea Doria*. Cian was an esteemed *vaticanista* (scholar of the Vatican) and president, in 1951, of the Foreign Press Office, as well as correspondent in Mexico and Spain. He had veritably become the backbone of the Italian American newspapers. Actually, in 1913, his father was nominated correspondent to Rome for the *American* of New York. In 1911, he had already repaired to Italy, to follow the famous trial of Cuocolo for *L' Araldo Italiano* of New York.

In Rome, Cianfarra became director of the United Press bureau, a position he held until 1925.

ESSENTIAL BIBLIOGRAPHY

Cacioppo 1999; De Ciampis 1958; Marazzi 2001, 30–31; obituary in the *New York Times*, 1956; Seldes 1929, 1931, 1935; Vezzosi 1991, 28–29.

Walking along Mulberry Street, Professor Savini looked at the police station and added, "This should guarantee order and morality, but after the black neighborhood, the most turbulent is the Italian. Like Jews, Poles and Russians, we love being among our own. The Germans and Irish instead are scattered throughout the city, and because of this they draw less attention to themselves from the older, longer-standing residents. At one time, the Italian neighborhood aroused as much interest as the Chinese. On beautiful summer nights, when our half-naked people would take to the streets, it wasn't unusual to find groups of American gentlemen returning from sumptuous dinners at clubs and fashionable restaurants. They came to have a good time, to take in all these habits and customs as foreign to theirs as the Hottentot's to the Parisian's.

"It is easy to imagine the impression they formed of us. For them an Italian is by definition as dirty as an ancient monk who is forbidden to use water. And overall they us put on the same level as Negroes. And what should we expect? We ourselves created this reputation of being pigs and illiterates, and it will take time to get rid of it.

"'You see that cafe?' he went on, pointing out shop windows displaying sweets of all kinds, bringing to mind the cafes of Naples.

"'Well, the people that frequent it are convinced the police are useless. From morning to evening, you will see young men there whose wealth will amaze you. They have diamonds on their fingers, chests and wrists that make you think of lucrative professions and fabulous unearned revenues.

"'But don't go beyond that, nor try to know who they are and what they do. You would be ashamed of being a man, and you would want to have the thunderbolt of Jove to incinerate them and rid our colony of them. You see that man entering now, the one with the ash-gray hat who seems the picture of health? Well, once upon a time he was a barber, and at his feet misfortune put a half-ruined girl. She was squint-eyed, short and ugly, and we would never stop and look at her. She was only half-lost, I say, and could have rehabilitated herself. But instead she rented a room here on Mott Street and stood at the door of the house to call the passers-by.

"'Along with the Italian girl was a Jewish girl, and after a few months they opened a brothel. And that other one sitting at the table holding a pack of cards, you see him? That one exercises the same trade with a little addition: he also does loan-sharking. And this is their center. They are products of Mulberry Street. They live on Mulberry Street, and the people of Mulberry give them the means to thrive and buy diamonds. From overcrowded tenements, the most unlikely assortment of people used to give off a pestilent stench that would make you hold your nose. Groups of women would dress in the strangest styles, exiting from corridors of houses where garbage was a foot high. Scantily-dressed women would show their flabby arms up to the shoulders. Others were flat-chested, wearing white, red, or black bodices that barely covered what one might guess were withered breasts hanging down to the waist. Others wore short skirts, without shoes, revealing black and deformed feet hardened by the scourge of adversity, their half-naked dirty feet that ran through the street with small children who slipped between the legs of passers-by, robbing here a handful of beans, there an apple, followed by the blasphemous and vile remarks of the robbed vendors.

"'From other places on whose door would shine in red and gold the word *Ristorante*, there came the strangest and most nauseating odors, along with the yelling of customers as they argued over prices. From basements, songs and sounds would reach the street, while from the windows adorned with vases and jars, could be heard calls in all of Italy's dialects. And from both sides, along the sidewalks, counters and benches of all sizes are loaded with fruits, greens, dairy products, salamis, sweets, cakes, roasted fava beans, boiled chick peas, newspapers, histories of miracles, "The Kings of France," "Neapolitan dream books," "astrological guides," pipes, tobacco, and cigars. It was an exhibition of all kinds of things reminiscent of small towns in Italy.

"Between an ale house and a grocery store, you see a group of individuals, immediately recognizable as new arrivals, leaving a bank. Some stare at the

American money they have just received in exchange for Italian currency. They have never seen it before. Others look around suspiciously, fearful of finding themselves face to face with the famous "American thief" of whom the most clever have already been telling them. Between a grocery store and a restaurant, there is a shop that sells linen and second-hand clothing. At the door a bearded Jew calls to passers-by, employing the twenty or so phrases of dialect learned after months of listening to the Italian ale-house keeper and newspaper vendor."

"You see," Professor Savini pointed out to me, "the Jewish neighborhood always borders the Italian neighborhood, and I leave it to you to imagine how our fellow countrymen are cheated. Besides, our people should know that, according to Moses' commandments, one shouldn't be honest except to those who share your faith. To the infidel "he should lend at 100 per cent," embezzle the stranger, and sell him all his damaged merchandise.

"Along Mulberry Street, in fact, among hundreds of carts, I have accompanied many full of handkerchiefs and pieces of fabric of the liveliest colors, driven by Jewish merchants. They are easily recognizable by their black hair and curls, their oblong faces, their protruding cheekbones and aquiline noses. Near the carts, the lower classes bargain for the fabric or apron, gesticulating wildly, and due to their lack of English vocabulary, making use of signs and head movements in order to make themselves understood. The Jew instead limits himself to looking at them, opening and closing his hand until reaching the amount that he was wishing for. He returns the object being bargained for to its place if the woman has shaken her head to signal her disapproval."

On the already crowded sidewalks are stupefied *contadini*, peasants watching the passers-by push their way through the thick groups of agricultural workers waiting to depart for the countryside. In front of a bank, among a circle of other *contadini*, an individual dressed more decently than the rest talks in a loud voice, gesticulating the whole time, getting angry and calming down by turns, borrowing from all the dialects of countries from which it seems his listeners come.

" 'Not at all,' this man was saying, 'I assure you the work will last for three years. The "bosso" is a *compare* of mine. He keeps his men closer to his heart than his own children. The pay comes once a month. In order to leave, you don't need anything because the company pays for the trip. For the first month, you hang on to your money in order to pay the expenses you need to pay. If not, the *compare* will extend you "credit." The air is good in the 'shanty.' You are given lodging like so many other gentlemen: the company is strong, and there is no danger that you will want to leave.' "

"On the other side of the street, a big strong man with a big red handkerchief around his neck is speaking no less passionately to another group of *contadini*. Like the first group, they listen with their mouths open, and by their expression it is impossible to read the impact of the astonishing promises being made. Do they believe what he is saying? And if they don't believe, why don't they raise any objections, or ask for clarifications?

"What do you expect them to know?" Professor Savini said to me. "They are here for a few days, and the height of New York's factories, like the movement in the streets, has amazed them and rendered them mute. The difference between the environment they left behind and the place they have landed after a 15-day voyage will not become clear to them for quite a while—for some, perhaps never. All they know is that they need to work and make their fortune. Their ideal is to return to their homeland where they will again embrace the wife, pay off the mortgage, and resume the primitive life—a life we will never know, with joys we will never relish.

"With this mirage before them, they have said goodbye to their wives and children. They have seen the last peaks of their mountains disappear from the horizon. They have faced the dangers of the sea, the horrors of the unknown. And they are here, within reach of those who will drag them off to the sulfur mines of South Carolina, where one works in water up to the knees, or to plow the fields of Alabama where there are laws that can still force a worker to labor against his will. And from mining centers in Pennsylvania, from the desolate places of Arizona, from the pampas of New Mexico, from the rocks of Colorado, from all the furthest points of the U.S., their savings flow here, to these banks, in order to be saved without interest or to be transmitted at whatever rate the banker finds agreeable.

"And often one of these banks suddenly closes its doors, and from all over the American Union comes a single scream, a harrowing scream, however impotent, that tells you of the nameless deprivations, of the thousand tricks by which a dollar was taken by the rapacious hand of a contractor and 'bosso,' in order for it then to disappear in the pockets of a monster that will spend it in some remote part of the globe.

"And how many of these cases I have seen! If the sidewalks and streets could talk, they would tell you a story of scrounging, robbery, and blood that the colony's newspapers have scarcely reported and are many times guilty of ignoring. They would tell you how hundreds of our co-nationals have been repatriated with little savings after years of work, plundered here by individuals with whom newspaper publishers have divided their booty. They would tell of the banker that recently converted the American cash of his victims into Italian money. They would tell you of other unfortunates who, with the lure of a better exchange rate, were fooled with counterfeit Italian bills that had been smuggled into New York from Sicily in the packing cases of *maccheroni*—others dazed with 'whiskey' and robbed, others who the next day were found asphyxiated by gas in the hotel room where they decided to pass their last night.

"And the police? But who could penetrate the mysteries of these houses that are such labyrinths? Who could find the guilty parties protected by everyone, and above all, by the families of the dead, people who wish to seek justice on their own? When a crime is shrouded in mystery, the police say it was committed by the Mafia, or some other secret society."

Here Professor Savini kept silent. All that he said had filled my mind with obscene, ugly mugs and bloody ghosts of bandits at the corners of every street lying in wait for naïve passers-by to ambush. The cry of the lemonade seller and the demanding voice of the peddler have shaken me, driving me to look straight ahead. In all the windows were displayed garments in all colors—dirty and clean, old and new. Next to a sheet there is a red slip, ripped and frayed in many places; next to a tablecloth, a row of patched and mended socks.

Ah, I wish my old friends and schoolmates could see me, those who tie America to all their dreams of fortune and glory, and who look with envious eyes at all those whom destiny has forced to leave! Fortune? Riches? Yes, just these: a pot full of glue, a paint brush, a pile of fraudulent "labels," and six dollars a week that, after board and lodging, leaves me two dollars and twenty-five cents I can set aside if I don't smoke and I'm content being alone and resigning myself to being inactive. And how long will this life go on? Two, four, six months, a year? Who knows? The owner, who had a talk with Giovanni, is kinder than the others. Often he tells me to learn English quickly because I will be able to earn more. I can easily get 12 or 15 dollars a week he says. But to study English, where's the time?

Every evening I go home tired, exhausted, and above all I can't see anything but labels white, red, gold—labels I have begun to hate with a passion. Books that were so dear to me lie dusty on the table. The old desire to read has left me. Learning English means studying night and day, and in order to study it is necessary to have that peace of mind that allows one to concentrate without being disturbed by other thoughts.

Instead, robbing my sleep is the little pot of glue always before me, and the thought that I cannot find a better job. How many people who don't have more than a third-grade education, who have never seen the cover of a book by Loria or Spencer, live better than I, and they work less! Giovanni, for example, in two or three hours earns from three to five dollars, and on certain days, when he has some success, he earns 20 or thirty dollars. He works for a firm that imports oil, and he tells me that, on an average, the firm that imports 10,000 lire sells it in New York for more than 20,000. The secret of the fortune lies in there. When I pointed out that it seemed immoral, he responded:

"Maybe so, but we aren't the only ones who do it that way. Everyone 'cuts' the oil that comes here with cotton oil, and that's where the profit is. When I offer it for sale, I always talk about oil imported from Lucca, extra fine, and from every gallon I take 50 cents."

But would I be capable of doing the same thing? Could I get myself to tell 40 lies in order to make 50 cents? No, I couldn't, and for this reason I will perhaps always remain a label-sticker at six dollars a week. . . . This monotonous life between the store and the boarding house weighs on me terribly. For some time I have struggled hopelessly against a past that remains always before me. It happens everywhere, in the store, when I sit at the side of a young man whose education was begun and completed in his father's tavern, and whose culture doesn't go beyond the third grade. It happens when I find myself in touch with individuals whose morals are the lowest and whose career includes time in prison. It happens when I am forced to mix and deal with people who feel, think, and reason in a way that I have never felt, thought, or reasoned.

In the evening, after ten hours of work, I take my seat in an environment that is neither something I need nor something I'm used to. Around the rectangular table sit an average of 20 to 25 people representing all regions of Italy; each of them is convinced, because he pays, that he is in his own house, and thus disregards everyone else. When a plate arrives, they assault it the way a pack of starving dogs would assault a bone. They choose the best pieces, and take so much more than they need that they are forced to put some back on the plate. "I know one guy," according to Giovanni, who eats once a day, "who when the plate of noodles arrives, doesn't have but one aim, taking all the noodles for himself and leaving the broth that isn't very good. Another has a voracious appetite for pasta and unfortunately for those near him, when the plate falls into his hands, they have to resign themselves to his taking everything. What is more amazing is that he eats enough for seven people."

An indescribable racket accompanies this: laughs, screams, blasphemies, and vulgarities of every sort. At the end of the meal, when the wine and a full stomach have put everyone in a good mood, everyone has something to say, and the racket reaches its peak. All political parties are represented, and it is interesting to be present at discussions between Gigi and a socialist who, if he doesn't have the lungs of an anarchist, has the exactness and astonishing effectiveness of one. The debate is always of revolution versus parliamentary struggle.

"All you want," Gigi screams, "is a seat in Parliament. You urge the masses to be calm and resigned. You lull them to sleep while you know that it is only through rebellion and violence that the bourgeoisie will surrender. You want to be in the majority? I'll admit that one day you will have 300 or 400 deputies. Do you believe the King will resign and go into exile, and the bourgeoisie will let itself be expropriated, without protest? You are a bunch of impostors and frauds."

An old man from Piedmont, refined and austere, on whose face one reads a past of great suffering and disappointments in love, quarrels often with Gigi, flinging at him the bitterest epithets. One evening, at dinner, the old man tells of his wonderful days at the side of a cannon of Piedmontese artillery. With words of sincere admiration, he praises the general whose skillful maneuver forced into retreat two columns of Austrian infantry that were about to attack from the rear.

"Bravo, the generals," said Gigi, "but they're butchers!"

The old man fell silent, looked at Gigi for a second and with a stern grimace, put his finger in his face saying, "I'm sixty years-old, but swine like you, I could strangle two a night."

The old man, whose sincere and irrepressible anger has the seductive charm of a magician, is applauded. Gigi falls quiet. He realizes he has committed an indiscretion. The old man believes he fought for a just cause, and this remains among his dearest and most beautiful memories. Afterward, Gigi comes to me to ask if his concept of generals is correct. I tell him that, frankly, I agree with him, but talking to an old soldier, I would have used other words and another manner.

At certain times, some guys whose look and behavior are anything but reassuring come to the boarding house. Giovanni, who knows the life, death, and miracles of the entire Colony, points them out to me with a wink of the eye. One evening, Giovanni tells me in two minutes the story of one of the guys who is now an importer of foodstuffs. "I knew him 15 years ago," he says. "One day he opened an office and for two days ran an ad in a newspaper asking for men for a job in West Virginia. In less than 10 days he picked up 800, made them all pay two dollars for a boss's fee, and two hours before the fixed hour of departure he disappeared. He went to Chicago, changed his name, and did the same thing all over again. Later I don't know what he did. After being gone for three years, he returned to New York. First he worked as a salesman in a grocery store. Then he opened up his own store."

The importer comes by the boarding house only to hawk his goods to Signora Rosa. A beer wholesaler stops in for the same reason, and Giovanni tells me some good ones about him. But the most original type is an undertaker who habitually talks in rhyme and ogles all the pretty girls, to whom he continuously offers drinks. The girls accept and don't even say thanks.

Sunday evening is the most interesting time for the observer in search of human subjects. The undertaker is always at his post among the cuter girls from Piedmont who, Gigi says, are already devoted to prostitution, already precociously impudent, girls Signora Rosa invites to attract clients. The beer dealer sits near a Sicilian piano teacher, and the grocery store owner tactfully pinches the bare arm of the aging *demi-mondaine* from Tuscany. She is still an excellent dancer, more famous on Mulberry Street than San Gennaro in Naples. She, like the other women who come, eats for free, but in exchange is required never to refuse an offer to drink with a man.

Dinner ends, dancing begins. The piano professor skillfully plays a waltz. The undertaker sets a good example and invites one of the women, "Signorina, would you dance with me, a little *ballatina*?"

Even if the *signorina* is a *signora*, he still uses "*signorina*," because the whole point is the rhyme.

The moment of chilliness that follows the clearing of the tables gives way little by little to the most boisterous hilarity and exuberance. The Tuscan courtesan gives the bawdiest caresses to the grocery store owner. One of the women from Piedmont lets a waiter squeeze her waist, insisting on speaking French with her. The other girls smile and make eyes at those around the tables where fumes rise from the punch loaded with whiskey. Then out comes a glass brimming with blended *claret*.

Signora Rosa is radiant. The wine bottles, the glasses of anisette, whiskey, and cognac disappear, spreading the drunkenness. The bustle grows and the witticisms and sweet little words fly, making the eyes of the drinkers sparkle greedily until they can't reason anymore.

At midnight the air is quieter. Cesare, the stonecutter, sleeps on a table. The Piedmontese women sit with a languid attitude on a sofa waiting for the waiter and another servant to lead them home, where they can leave another shred of their decency. The Tuscan woman sits on the knees of the grocery store owner, sipping listlessly a last glass of whiskey that burns and paralyzes her senses. In the kitchen, Signora Rosa lets herself be courted by the undertaker who is left without a lady. She, the lady who keeps letting him into the house, manages him as best she can, granting him some pinches and maybe kisses.

This reminds me how one evening, having had occasion to go into the courtyard, I surprised her alone with Antonio, who having nailed her against the wall, took her by the waist with one hand, and with the other fondled her breasts and neck, covering her furiously with kisses. Signora Rosa, ecstatic from the rough caresses, didn't protest at all, but with an exasperated voice, said, "Enough now, someone might spot us! Later, later!"

I retired without allowing myself to be seen, I knew enough already!

And that's how these dances go. The signora has an extra 20 dollars in her pocket, and all the shameful revelers have only headaches.

The evening was foggy. The drizzle came down relentlessly and further darkened that stretch of Mott Street that goes from Baxter to Esther. Along a slight slope, flanked by tall, four-or-five story buildings, there nestles an Italian population drawn from nearly all the regions of Italy. Halfway up the block my new friend, a young man full of ingenuity and cunning, stops to light a cigarette and says to me, "I'm cautious now. The police, although well-paid, occasionally do roundups to justify their existence. You'll see. They are prone to the same thing with us."

We start on our way again along a low dark corridor. Twenty seconds later, someone who hears us speak Italian, sticks his head out and invites us to enter with the picturesque Neapolitan phrase: "*Trasite signuri.*" On the narrow, muddy wood stairway (who knows how many others before us have passed there?) it is still pitch dark. Before reaching the third floor, I bump against the humid, sticky walls a dozen times. The woman who welcomes us is dressed in white. She has a dark complexion, a mass of radiant black hair carefully combed up high until it seems a continuation of her forehead. It is held together by a tortoise-shell hatpin studded with fake pearls.

The priestesses of Venus, with their long pink and yellow blouses, lie together on the faded sofas in the parlor. There are four—three Italians and one Jew. This last one, having seen that there were two of us, and both Italian, retires to a corner and starts reading again the novel that was interrupted by our arrival. The other three are suddenly upon us, bombarding us with questions, acting interested in us, in a way that seems to me ridiculous and out of place.

One, however, doesn't try to conceal from me this obligation to act happy with the customers. She is the best-looking and perhaps the youngest. Tall and slender, of the whitest complexion, she has, like the owner, black and abundant hair, an almost perfect oval face, and deep, black eyes. The other two are already quite a bit older than thirty. Despite plenty of makeup caked on thick, one can still imagine all the flabby skin and revealing wrinkles beneath. Through their immodest, provocative gazes one can read an entire history of corruption and intemperance; their gestures and words reveal an innate vulgarity. These two do not interest me. The other one who has had moments of dark concentration during which she stares with bulging eyes at the crumpled rug, arouses my interest until she entices me to follow her. The little room where she leads me isn't anything like those of the women I have embraced in the days of my wild and reckless youth.

Narrow and low, it contains a cot covered with laundry scraps, a chair, a chest of drawers on which there is a white metal basin and, at the front of the bed, a great terracotta crucifix at whose feet is a basin for holy water. Upon entering, a musty smell that at first I do not know how to define makes me instinctively bring the thumb and index finger of my right hand to my nostrils. For a moment I am at the point of leaving. When I see the woman has taken off the long blouse that covered her, I enter, with my pulse quiet and a cadaver's pallor.

"I'm not really here for my own pleasure, and I am tired and need to rest."

"Take this," I hurriedly give her, reading on her face the dread of losing 50 cents, "and drink to my health."

"Have I offended you?" she asks, greatly surprised and dismayed, looking at me with her big eyes full of pain.

"No: and what might you have done to offend me?"

"One never knows," she says; "just yesterday that disgusting barber from Baxter Street hit me and left because I didn't want to kiss him the way he wanted."

While speaking she shows me bruises on her fat arms, and another on her shoulders, evidently products of a blunt instrument. While in the room, she said she had to wear a happy face with her clients or else her sweetheart (this is the way she referred to her executioner) would fly into a rage. She is Sicilian but has lived on the mainland for a long time, in a city in Puglia where her father owned a tavern frequented by soldiers. She was victimized by a cavalry sergeant and afterwards married a shoemaker who led her to America, where she met the Sicilian who is now her "sweetheart."

The husband, intimidated, and often beaten, reached the end of his rope and left to open a little store in a village in Connecticut, where he now lives with a baby girl, the only fruit of their love.

"And why don't you catch up with him and ask his forgiveness," I ask when I reassure her, showing my indignation at the litany of cruelties of which she has been the victim.

"I have already fled twice," she says, "but he always takes me back, and now I'm waiting for the right time."

One time a drunkard came in and chose her as his victim. He was filthy and wanted . . . wanted certain things that she would only do with someone she truly loved. She refused and when the drunkard went away muttering, "her sweetheart" punched him and broke his tooth. And after all this she was forced to stay there, "waiting for the right time," forced to endure without protest the blows of that man who took from her the last penny she earned.

When I am about to go away, the girl begs me to tell the owner that I have been satisfied, something which I don't forget to do. In the living room with my friend and two women, I find a small boy who smokes with the air of a mature man. He might be fifteen years old, but in his glazed-over eyes, and thin, pallid face, one can see the early signs of vice. When my friend tells me it was he who invited us to come in, I am amazed. In a few minutes I see in front of me a pimp, a cheat and a convict, dragging at his feet a heavy chain. This I learn on my first visit to that place that flourishes in the heart of our colony, protected by the police, and frequented by our fellow countrymen. Oh, Professor Savini was right. . . .

How much I would pay to feel satisfied and content with my surroundings! Giovanni tells me that eight dollars per week is the median salary one is paid in our colony. And there are some poor young clerks at banks and commercial firms that earn even less. Six of them have to put in ten and eleven hours of work, another seven are obligated to write from 40 to 50 letters per day. And thus I should be content; but whenever I see all these people who know far less of the situation than I do, yet earn three or four times more, an urgent need assails me to try other ways, to bring myself to other places where the possibilities of earning and working are greater.

The other night I was chatting with a Romagnolo waiter, who shouts and curses the fat, vile bourgeoisie along with Gigi. He told me he worked for four months in a luxury hotel and made enough to live comfortably for a year. How did he do it? That is another question that in America seems indiscreet.

How did he earn so much money? It's never necessary to ask it. The fact that he has the money in his pocket should be enough. All this makes me feel conflicted regarding my principles and the reasons I came here. If I don't have any intention "of making my fortune," I can return. The sky of my fatherland is always bluer and the language of my parents smoother to my ears. If I want "to make my fortune," then I shouldn't think about the means, but just the ends.

And that's another moral heresy, another infernal dogma accepted without objection. But who said, "the ends justifies the means?" So if I want to have a thousand dollars in my pocket, is it right for me to take it from someone like myself, perhaps by stabbing him four times in the stomach? If not, should I try rather to save my salary, penny by penny? And there it is, the crux of the heresy: the ends justify only the possible means and nothing else. Oh *parvenus*, illustrious members of our Colony, may you enjoy with a clear conscience your fortunes earned by crime. I won't make a fortune, I'll never know how to get hold of in three months what it would take me a year to earn. I will not put aside 15 or 20 thousand dollars in 11 or 12 years. I'll never win!

Am I perhaps exaggerating?

The number of those unhappier than I is great, and unfortunately, for many of them there is no hope of improvement. In the cafe on Mulberry Street I have known four or five of them who skip lunch or supper, sleeping in the corridor of an abandoned house in the summer, on the bench of some oven in the winter. It is a natural and negligible thing. One, for example, is a unique case. In Italy he was of respectable status and had a splendid fortune, but here he lost both thanks to a series of circumstances resulting from his character and his idiosyncrasies.

Gentle and kind as a baby, he had by nature a temperament that could have been philosophical had he possessed a clear and consistent vision of his aims and goals, or even highly poetic if he had acquired the proper culture and literary background. But he had neither. Once he believed he could be a good farmer and wasted a large part of his fortune on the cultivation of wines. As a result he was reluctant to keep track of his money, regularly spending his last pennies and believing there would always be more.

Tall with a fat, round face, his hair and mustache lightly grizzled, he had a resonant and pleasant voice, with the smooth words and phrases of the classic Southern Italian orator. In New York he found a semblance of the lifestyle he had in Naples. He was only able to accommodate himself thanks to the philosophical part of his character, thanks to his inability to leave, thanks to his fear of new things, of anything that might make him change his ways.

Some other guy who is short, fat, dirty and sloppy has, however, an enormous ego that rests on a foundation of sand. A bit of natural intelligence and a hasty reading of many books allow him to do many things, but all badly. He writes an insolent article that no one wants and pens a poorly-written play, in which he inserts himself in the lead role for his own benefit. He revises the punctuation of the writings of others, and he writes a speech that he has learned and recited by heart. His presumptuousness makes him absolutely ridiculous, and his physical imperfections render him pitiful.

When somebody suggests he should act like himself again, making reference to Bovio, he'll rebut with something like this:

"But why could Petrarch do it and not I?"

Quarrelsome and impudent, he is forced to remain continually on the go—as a promoter in the colony's little theater, as a baker, or even as a carrot picker on some farm outside the civilized world. When he disappears from the cafe, nobody thinks twice. "Edoardo is working," they say. When he returns, he tries to change his ways for the better, but his attempts always remain ridiculous and only garner more pity.

One day, they say, he tells everyone he is the greatest talent in the colony. Being misunderstood, and being kept at arm's length from the editorial offices of newspapers because of the jealousy of those who are there, he says that he'd return to Naples to be elected a deputy. In fact, he collects money and departs. But evidently, not even in Naples can they understand him, since after a while the old-timers who frequent the cafe see him come around again—more dirty, sloppy, and presumptuous than ever.

Another one here makes a living as a barber, but in Italy he did something altogether different. In spite of his trade, he is convinced that he is a poet and his penchant is art and criticism. For him, as for others, all of Italy's poetic patrimony is "Postuma," in which there is a competition to see who can more quickly recite the verses. At times he is aggressive to his displeased audience and he'll go so far as to threaten to have his little poems published; meanwhile, he'll have them corrected, or even written for him, by someone at the colony's humorous newspaper, who then might publish it. These, and two others, are the satellites who rotate around the star of the foremost greatness, the humanist philosopher, the one who offers paternal protection, and who pronounces absolute sentences in their heated disputes, re-establishing the peace and satisfying everyone.

The table where they sit is the center of general attention, and it is invariably surrounded by a crowd that listens, approves and disapproves, yet always concludes that the philosopher Don Alfonso is right. To hear them, when they debate, is evidence that men of letters and artists live only for art and literature. Observing them in their personal lives, we too often find that, because of art, because of literature, because of prose, they sacrifice lunch or supper, often lunch *and* supper, and a good bed, such is their modesty. And frankly, I feel bad for these people because of their present suffering and for an unrelenting future without sunlight.

Yesterday the boss introduced me to a gentleman who is the opposite of Professor Savini, the chief editor of a newspaper that I often see in the hands of frequenters of boarding houses and cafes in our colony. Giovanni, who knows him, has often mentioned his name to me. I had never hoped to meet him, nor to ask him to clarify all those things I hadn't succeeded in explaining to myself, or in having explained to me by others.

This complex and complicated organization which is called the colony isn't, nor could it be, a society of criminals, as Professor Savini and Giovanni, albeit involuntarily, might have me believe; in its bosom there are surely moral and benevolent forces, as well as healthy individuals, who work to raise it to the level of the people who host us. I see the signs of this everywhere in our colony, for there must also be here altruists and courageous, enlightened patriots who display the name and the glories of the fatherland in their every act and pass such pride to their children.

I wanted to know all this, and the gentleman was very kind and spoke to me at length. He spoke to me of the bad humor of those who are displaced and unsuccessful. He himself had the air of the person that has neither regrets or rancor, satisfied with himself and his position, oozing optimism from all his pores.

"Our colony is young," he said, looking as if he wanted to read the future, "but as long as its destiny remains up to us, it will be full of opportunities. I have great faith in the virtue and energy of our people. I am a believer in the resurrection of this supposedly dead Latin soul. It will round off the angular character of the Anglo-Saxon soul, giving it something of the enthusiastic and poetic temperament by which we unconsciously manage to exalt virtue more than one should and consider evil as even more ruinous and painful than it actually is.

"It is astounding that the Irish, whose traditions connect them to a band of shepherds and fisherman, cold and pale as their sky, in which not even the enlivening breath of Roman invaders raised and educated them, and whose history has never crossed the English Channel, have here become a powerful presence; that from such a womb have come financiers and magistrates, literary figures and scientists, philanthropists and politicians; that at the same time they have also contributed the most to poverty and prostitution, to criminality and alcoholism. I see at least in every one of my countrymen, sober and respectful, energetic and intelligent, the father of the citizen of the utmost integrity, a type higher and more perfect than the American of the past. "Today they call us 'dago.' Today they scold us for our lack of cleanliness, for the frequent use of the knife, but all of this is nothing but a repetition of what the Danish herdsmen of Manhattan used to say about the Scotch, of what the Scotch, the Danish, Americanized and blended in, used to say about the Irish, and of what all three groups used to say about the Germans. Today they are four peoples molded into a homogeneous unity, one that insults and derides us. But we will be a part of this unity, and we will begin to make our weight felt, the weight of a healthy and strong race, one whose blood has for infinite generations coursed with vigorous tendencies and inclinations that made it glorious, and that today make it agreeable—a race that stores intact its characteristics across a thousand years of savage internal struggles; that when it seemed dead, knew how to raise itself and to conquer its national independence. The future is ours! The hundreds of dollars put aside from rummaging through barrels, or building chairs for bootblacks, or selling fruit from a cart, will serve one day to educate our sons, to launch them in this American world where we—having arrived too late—will never enter.

"And I already see them, these future lawyers, doctors, engineers, painters, sculptors and architects. I see them carrying their beautiful Italian names into the exclusive groups of science, art and industry, like the Germans and the Irish, elevating the prestige of the fatherland of their origin, discrediting preconceptions and correcting misunderstandings."

All of this was said to me slowly, without excessive emphasis, without the air of wanting to convince me, but only inviting me to look at things the way he saw them. It did me a great deal of good; he eliminated many doubts and convinced me of many truths.

"And if these immoral houses flourish, if these pimps strike their victims with impunity, if some of their fellow countrymen are thieves, some fellow country men. . . . And what about this?" he continued, after my observations.

"There are thieves in Italy, and pimps as well, so isn't it possible that there are also some here? In New York, it seems extraordinary and strange because we are few; but we should take into account not just the needy immigrant, but those who can't remain in Italy for reasons that are less than honorable. But seventy percent of those fellows rehabilitate themselves, and twenty years of honorable life seem to me sufficient to forget an offense whose details, motives, and extenuating circumstances we are often do not know."

While he told me this, I thought of Giacomo, who worked below in the wine shop and who had suffered so harshly for his crime. I thought of all the other unfortunate souls who might have once falsified a banknote, fled after a quick holdup, let off a gunshot in a moment of rage.

"Unfortunately," the gentleman continued, "thirty percent of those who don't rehabilitate often remain victims of themselves. They attract the attention of the Protestant ministers who paint us as a bunch of cannibals, denying us the chance of rising up to the level of their blind followers. But it isn't so, and it can't be. The Protestants hate us because we are Catholics, the way the lower class Irish hate us for prejudices that reveal their primitive sense of morality. But here the enlightened aren't lacking among the great mass of Italians. Oh good Virgin, they see in us the future sons of this great republic.

"But," he added, after rubbing his forehead, almost as if to drive away a bothersome thought, "Woe to us, woe to all Italians, if we don't teach our children respect for our country of origin, if we denigrate and slander it, noting its defects but forgetting its virtues.

"It's true there are those who have a reason to complain. There are others who don't have grounds to be grateful. But the fatherland, that great and unhappy land, shouldn't be confused with the individuals who govern it and often go off course.

There are, unfortunately, also some Italians who have the perverse habit of changing their names, almost ashamed to reveal their origins. There are others who want to be so devoted to their new fatherland that they end up hating their old one.

"But these people are unfortunate and so are we, who by accident sprang from the same soil. They do more to discredit the Italian name than twenty delinquents atoning for their sins on the electric chair. They set a bad example for the poor ignoramuses who are easily made victims, laying the ground for further hardships and struggles, postponing the long-desired moment of triumph." I was at the point of embracing this gentleman when evening led me to go home. I felt less uneasy among the crowd that surrounded me, among the crowd that spoke a language that wasn't mine, that separated me from everything: amidst all this, only the future bound me in some way to the past and present of this place. And in each of those upstanding, well-groomed individuals I seemed to have recognized the Irishman, who hates us out of ignorance of our accomplishments in industry and labor, and the Protestant minister who hates us to appease his myopic followers.

Translated by Gil Fagiani

Two Poems

~ *Thomas Fragale*

Serrastretta (Catanzaro), Italy, 1855–Pittsburgh, Pennsylvania, 1929

Thomas Fragale's book *Poesie* (Poems) was published in Kansas City, Missouri, in 1929, which, according to Ferdinando Alfonsi, is the same year the author died. From Serrastretta, his hometown, to which he dedicates a poem, Fragale emigrated to America in 1892. Diverse compositions dated to the 1890s were composed in Hammonton, New Jersey, where he was pastor of the Presbyterian Church until 1900. Later poems, dating from the first years of the new century, were composed in Pittsburgh, the city in which Fragale was remembered by Gaetano Conte as a Protestant missionary, active in an Italian and English school, a kindergarten, night schools, and an educational association for youth. In 1898, Fragale published the defamatory Protestant propaganda work *Romanism Antagonistic to the Bible*. Frangini also attributes to him a pedagogic treatise for teachers of elementary school and the upper grades, and remembers him as contributing articles and poetry to various newspapers.

The generally patriotic and pro-monarchial tone of his verses separates him from other Italian American poets of the time, whose orientation was usually socialistic. Imbued with the spirit of the Risorgimento and a follower of D'Annunzio, he exalted the grand undertaking, and he wrote poetry in the manner of Manzoni, using the decasyllable, on the occasions of the deaths of Vittorio Emanuele II and Umberto I. He was a convinced interventionist and anti-German, though he did not disdain more ordinary themes tied to episodes in the colonial life. Significant in this respect, together with various compositions composed for special occasions, are the satires on the so-called prominent people and against the "refined cobbler" who pretentiously styles himself a journalist. Finally, of notable interest is the invective, reproduced here, against the promoters of the infamous Johnson Bill, which sanctioned the quota for immigration into the USA.

ESSENTIAL BIBLIOGRAPHY

Alfonsi 1989; Conte 1906, 28; Frangini 1910, 75.

For the Supporters of the Johnson Bill

Between being and not being
There is a sea,
So big and so terrifying
That it cannot be crossed.
Some, for example,
Believe that among all peoples
Some for their blood and their history
Are outstanding and excellent.
And often disparage
Those worth much more than they
In knowledge and merit,
In noble ideals.
The lofty thought
Of Lincoln, of Washington
For these important folks
Is worth nothing;
In their insane haughtiness
Sitting on high seats
They sanction ridiculous
And hateful laws.
Just yesterday, they decreed
With laws and edicts,
That only Anglo Saxons
Deserve honors and rights.
And that to others it is not allowed
To come where
Ironically stands the Statue

Of true Liberty!. . . .
    They claim for their race the men
Who stand above all others,
Columbus is German,
Vico and Dante are English.
    Then they say that the glorious
Northern race
In art, science and letters
Never had an equal;
    And so the Greeks and Italics
Are classified
Among the undesirable,
And quickly rejected.
    But in vain the megalomaniacs
Try to turn night into day,
All the honest glories
Have no value for them.
    To deny the truth, to fight it
Is the work of madmen,
Nor can any bluster
Discount the evidence of facts.
    If any distinguished person
Can't see these beautiful things,
Let it be known that the world still venerates
What is Roman.
    When the deep darkness
Of wicked slavery
Forced all peoples
To a miserable existence,
    It was first and only Italy,
Mother of shining heroes,
Who raised the torch
Of freedom for all peoples,
    And, today, is not D'Annunzio
The best in literature?
And Marconi's genius,
In which country was it born?
    The past and the present attest

That rare genius
Is the indisputable gift
Of the Latin people,
　And savage and barbarian,
With no civil language,
You would still be, had Rome
Not brought you its gifts.

PITTSBURGH, PA., MAY 9, 1924

∾

The Parade of 19 . .

　Move aside, move aside
Here comes the parade,
That our ringleaders
Have so well arranged,
　To show they enjoy
The favor of the powerful,
And are of the colony
The truly PROMINENT ones.
　See their stately gait
And superb march;
As if they had attended the school
Of Orlando and Gradasso.
　But just as a donkey
Cannot hide its tail,
So indolence cannot
Hide under costumes.
　Of little value are clothes,
Poses and hats;
When of science and letters
There is nothing in the brain.
　Behind them come
The unruly colonists,
Who, gabbing, advance
By pushing.

Then having arrived in the square, immediately
The parade leader
Presents to the entire audience
The intrepid orator,
    Who from his high stand
With the gesture and words
Of a poor fanatic
Starts screaming at the top of his lungs,
    Without being able to finish
A point, or an argument,
So that many begin
To lose their patience.
    But the great mass with a single,
Unintelligent voice,
To every great proposition cries out hurrah, hurrah.
    Let's abandon such spectacles
Worthy of the Zulus,
They cover us with ridicule
And nothing more.

Translated by Maria Enrico

Two Poems

୬ *Antonio Calitri*

Panni (Foggia), Italy, June 7, 1875–Lawrence, Massachusetts, July 12, 1954

Antonio Calitri studied to be a priest and dressed in a cassock; then he cast it off and emigrated to New York in 1900. He had taken his degree in letters at the University of Naples, and in America he was an Italian teacher in various public schools. Among other things, he wrote short plays for use in schools. He contributed to the *Araldo Italiano*, and in 1909, he published, among other poems, "La canzone dell'Hudson River," composed on the occasion "of the memorable festivals of Hudson and Verrazzano." Then in 1925, a collection of his poems, *Canti del Nord-America*, was published in Rome in a prestigious edition, prefaced by Giuseppe Prezzolini, a very special honor in view of the contempt that the founder of the *Voce* generally expressed toward the improvised poets across the sea:

> This book, a manuscript crossing the ocean, came into my hands to be printed. I edited it as best I could, according to the intentions of the author. . . . Bear in mind that I met its arrival with a certain skepticism. Stuff of an expatriate! What could be left of Italian in him, after so many years of America? And Farfariello's caricatures, heard in theaters in the Italian quarter of New York, filled my imagination with his Neapolitan-Anglo-Saxon dialect . . . [Yet,] in America, the Italian poet has remained a poet and Italian. . . . In him, one hears again, the knowledge, sometimes of Dante, of Lorenzo, of Pascoli, of Shelley, of Carducci; but even Dante, Leopardi, Pascoli, Shelley, and Carducci had read other poets, and remembered them.

Actually, Calitri translated Shelley, a volume he submitted to the press in 1914. But besides the great Italian authors cited by Prezzolini, Calitri was also familiar with the most modern American literature and also, more in general, with American culture and traditions. In the *Canzone dell'Hudson,* for example, he manifests a profound knowledge of the Indian legends relative to the great river of New York.

Prezzolini exalted the persistence of a strong Italian sentiment in the mind of the emigrant poet, and, undoubtedly, Calitri held strongly to his roots. He did not hesitate to produce a patriotic ode, "Italia!" that "was read by Onorio Ruotolo, November 12, 1911, at the Comizio Protesta, sponsored by the *Araldo Italiano,* against the unfair practices of the American press." In any case, it is not by chance that the *Canti* were dedicated "to the pleasures of the people of Panni and to the emigrants in America, who, laborers like them, grew in gentility." Unlike the literary productions of most Italian Americans, the *Canti* owe their stylistic and literary value primarily to their adherence to Italian literary traditions, such as repetition of schema, modulations of formal units, and small formal artifices, and consequently they were not appreciated. Calitri is among those very rare writers who know how to control the rush of sentimentality, in cases, obviously frequent, in which nostalgia, melancholy, and the drama of separation are placed in the center of the poetic work. And as a specimen of this artistry, *Il Cantoniere,* a "corona" of twelve inspired sonnets, is the clearest example.

In 1913, the Board of Education of New York authorized Calitri to organize Italian courses in night school. He was a friend of Fiorello La Guardia, the mayor of New York, who, like him, had origins in Puglia on his father's side and who shared his reformist vision. Calitri contributed to the *Fuoco* of Giovannitti, and founded and directed *La Favilla* and *Il Convito,* the latter in 1929. *Il Convito* was also intended for the students of P. Hoffman Junior High School, in the Bronx, in which Angelo Patri was the principal. A monthly, dedicated to "studious youth," it featured little stories, single acts, poetry, and various other materials organized with evident didactic purpose.

Calitri was also the author of a novel with poetry, entitled *Dietro la maschera: Diario di Don Bruno,* edited in Italy in 1949. Taking place in the imaginary town of Montefumo and, it seems, largely autobiographical, it narrates the story of a young priest, pure and dedicated to his clerical office, but assailed by doubts. He falls in love with a girl who becomes pregnant. The town is convinced that another is the father of the baby; consequently, Don Bruno, who cannot confess that he is the culprit, decides to go to America, in order not to add another shame to the poor girl. *Fanciullezza a Montefumo* (Childhood in Montefumo) uses the material of the *Diario* more directly in the manner of a memoir.

ESSENTIAL BIBLIOGRAPHY

Fichera 1958, 21–22; Flamma 1936; obituary by Pietro Greco in *La Parola del Popolo* 16 (October–December 1954), 55–56; Schiavo 1935.

༄

The Roadman

They were dark times that made you despair. No day went by without an insult. Poor Italians! Every misdeed in America was perpetrated by us. Almost every morning the newspapers published one of them, in large print. The criminals were very often introduced with barbarian names: German, Slav, Jewish, Swedish, Turkish. Yet the newspaper, before and after mentioning the barbarian name of anyone at all, always stuck in "Italian" or "Sicilian." Italian! The rumor had spread, and nobody took the trouble to rectify, correct, and do justice.

Our people were insulted in every place, especially where they spent their energies in very heavy work. Mistreated by the bosses, disliked by everyone, below the Blacks, below the Chinese.

How many are buried underneath the tunnels, in the stone quarries, in the woods, at the bottom of rivers, lakes, seas? People without names, martyrs of work, vanished like nobody's children.

Oh, the great injustice of being abandoned by their motherland, governed by men without a mind and without a heart! Oh, the vicious criminality of the colonial slave drivers, who trafficked with the blood of their brothers!

I remember, on the train, a Jewish mother who, pointing to a group of Italians burned by the sun and sweating by the rails, said to her blond daughter: "Watch out for them; they are Italians, murderers!" And opened wide her mouth and eyes. And they, tanned, sweating and shirtless, had opened and were opening the track on which ran the train that was taking the two of them to the shore!

A century seems to have passed since that time, and yet it is only a few years, and yesterday, yesterday a student was telling me: "But why this hostility that we encounter everywhere?" "Why? Nothing new, son. It is the old racial hatred, fear of loss of possession. It is the history of America, of the whole world. The Indians against the Pilgrims and . . . so on."

"When will we have possession and rights! . . ."

"We are on the right track, if only we were not distracted by so many extinguished stars coming from overseas! They distract us. What to do? The conquest will be accomplished by you young people."

If you knew about twenty years ago! So much bitterness! So much strife! So much pain!

Speak of today!

All right. Back then we studied not just the classics, but society and the ills of the Colony as well, and we went to vent our bitterness in the woods, when we could, and there Virgin Nature soothed the blood, comforted the heart, and revealed certain of her secrets that brightened even pain and death.

So it was that, one day, after crying over pages 65 and 66 of H. G. Wells' *The Future in America*, I envisioned "The Roadman."

In the page reprinted here below in the original English, Wells is excited about a precipitous journey from Chicago to Washington, but stops to describe the death of an Italian, nobody's son, run over, decapitated, and mangled by the wheels of an express train, on a bridge. A black man was saying to a passenger: "His head is still in the water." "Whose head?" "The man we killed, we hit him on the bridge." "Who was he?" "One of these Italians on the tracks," and he turned elsewhere. The train whistled and started off again, but Wells felt the spirits that were exciting him freeze, and his heart was filled with a sad feeling of pity for the Italians, whom he had seen in the lands of Italy, on the crowded ships that took them to America, to Ellis Island. So many hopes, so many dreams decapitated, buried, mangled in great America! And the black man who insults work and death!

And the poet weeping for the unknown brother, killed, abandoned, insulted, tried to revive him with his art and portrayed him as he saw him in his sorrowful heart.

He saw him in a scorching afternoon, with his head full of dreams, working on the railroad, open in the solitary plains. Alone, poor, a lost brother, he thinks about the joy of the first ray of love on the blossoming hill of his native town.

He daydreams and works. He dreams about his woman's first kiss; in his mind he sees his valley, his mountains, the waking night, the golden harvests, and the image of her, who seemed to fly over the crops the whole day after, with the morning star on her forehead.

With his mind he goes back to the big day of the wedding.

He hears the whispers of the gossips, his mother's anxious voice, the voice of the bell calling and his father's warning.

The golden thread of memories is suddenly severed by the shadow of death. The train has gone by; he is safe, but shaken by the passed danger, he sees in the blazing sky the images of his children, and his wife sheds tears of blood.

He works the rest of the day, and when mists rise from the distant sea and shadows envelop the mountains, he starts on the way back and begins to daydream. He sees his wife with the children against her bosom, at the edge of the farmyard, the day after threshing the wheat.

He thinks about his return. He will be in his town on Christmas eve, the scene of his unexpected arrival smiles in his heart. He knocks, his wife doesn't want to open; he knocks again, his wife opens almost naked and trembling . . . the darkness, the bed, and the tears of joy.

In the church they sing the Christmas novena. He goes in. His old mother is in the church. He passes among the crowd; his name is whispered from mouth to mouth until it reaches his mother, who sees him and recites more fervently the prayer to the cross.

He is oppressed by the emotion of memories and hope. Is it joy or sorrow? He feels exhausted, tired; and when he awakens to the first star in the evening sky, he lies down on the dry grass, falls asleep, and dreams.

What does he dream about? His white little house on a hilltop. His wife tending to the chicken coop. He sees himself in the vegetable garden, at work, and after sunrise he hears his wife's voice calling him to breakfast.

But now he stirs, he turns and turns over the hay. Is he suffering? What was it? A bad dream or a good dream? Did he dream of his wife in his own arms or in those of someone else? He wakes up, hungry, dazed, fearful, and he goes on the bridge and is run over by the train.

The train stops. The rumor of an accident spreads. People cry, shout, hurry. Questions, answers, with the screeching of wheels and doors. What was it?

A black man gets off, holds the head of the poor brother decapitated and mangled and, turning to a passenger, shouts, jeering: "Oh! It is a Dago." He is an Italian!

"It is a Dago" is no longer said today; today they don't even say "it is a wop." But aren't there still people who scorn us because they believe Italians are inferior? When will we get across the fact that Italians are worth more than all the people from other races? Italy has demonstrated it, it is up to us to instill respect for her immigrant children in people from other races.

I

Down from the scorching sky in crowds, in swarms,
blowing from primeval forests far and deep,

into the plain's burning solitude sweep
images serene and well-known forms
    smiling in beauty. While in his head whirl storms
of immaterial ghosts, humble, asleep,
the Roadman tries with his hands to heap
the white gravel on the road without form.
    "O my youth's earliest dreamlike image
in the month of May's most fragrant brightness
over the hill, where twisting, turning, rises
    the road to the last houses of the village.
The spirit wanders under the sweet caress
of love across the blossoming rise.

II

    "She comes the first time, longed-for. She's
a fairy in a lovely June evening. A kiss,
and she flies away; as her light dress
slips through my fingers like a gentle breeze.
    My heart is empty and my veins ablaze.
I dream divinely the whole night, sleepless,
until the morning star, alone, has
full dominion over the clear blue skies.
    All around, proud and bright the mountain tops
rise up, and the valley opens down below
with all its mists, and on the horizon climbs
    the sun. All day long I see, countless times,
my love take flight across the yellow crops,
the morning star beaming on her brow.

III

    In her father's house, already dressed in white
by her *comari*, resplendent, my bride
wipes her cheeks after she has cried
looking about bewildered and contrite.
    —No toll yet? Anyone heard the bell ring out?—
nervously asks my mother by her side.
The whispers stop, and the harmonious tide
from the belfry of the ancient church in flight

sings to the trembling soul in anxious wait
across the limpid sky and slowly dies.
—Twice, children, does the bell toll for us—
    deeply absorbed in thought the father sighs
—now it calls you joyfully to church, straight
to the cemetery in a hundred years.—

IV

    Like a cloud, death's shadow's mournful bane
passes before the Roadman. He has a scare,
he jumps up and stretches with sudden care
his sunburnt limbs twisted by work's strain.
    By the gentle image of his wife, again,
he sees the faces of his children, sweet and fair,
and sees falling through the blazing air
scarlet tears wrung out by grief and pain.
    The earth shakes, and on the barren flatland
the steam train whistles by at a fast pace
enveloped wholly within a cloud of dust.
    In silence, with the back of his hand
slowly the Roadman wipes his bony face
drenched with tears and sweat.

V

    The setting sun is starting to ignite
with rubies the black forest on the high mount
and from the shining shore dissolves the white
faraway haze. The shadow ascends up
    ever so slowly, hiding the coast from sight,
and the Roadman's work comes to a ground
dazed by the voices that in the falling twilight
through the motionless peace begin to sound.
    He talks to himself, leaving the plain behind:
"Maybe, at this hour, with the children tight
against her bosom, the farmyard's rim her seat,
    my Giacinta looks up at the clear sky
and listens to the frogs down in the pond
measuring in her mind bushels of wheat.

VI

On Christmas eve I'll be there and I'll knock,
soon as the dawn of the new day is up,
softly on the door. She'll say: —I won't unlock,
baker, go back to the oven and your shop.

I won't open before sunrise. —Once more
I rap, with the boot: —Giacinta, here I am,
I'm back! —Giacinta's naked at the door,
with her apron in front, and pale with shame.

As on the eve of love, all trembling too,
she gives me a gentle kiss and then runs fast
to the bed looming inside the darkened room.

I light a lamp, the way I used to do,
and while I hold my children to my chest
Giacinta weeps and laughs away the gloom.

VII

What joyful bells the happy people call
to the novena of the early morn!
So clear a sound from a bell so small
by the serene and motionless air is borne.

As I make my way in the crowded church,
elbowing through the people, someone
wonders and says: —Who's the man proudly lurching,
his elbows pushing everyone?

And when my name is whispered all along
the column where, sitting so devoutly,
an old lady is praying in a low voice,

trembling as soon as she lays eyes on me,
my mother rises, her eyes fixed on the cross,
and the priest at the altar sings the song.

VIII

A gentle wave of blood begins to race
up to the throbbing heart through every vein
and is so filled with every loving face
it stops him on the road, crushed by pain.

Is it only joy or is it sorrow,
that powerful inertia felt so clear?
Coming out of the sky serene and hollow
the first star is just now starting to appear.

And the Roadman lays down his head to rest
upon the hay stirred by the gentle hand
of the evening breeze and falls asleep.

Under the stars, in the immense and deep
cry of the night, from seashore to the forest,
the longing dreams look for the native land.

IX

Against the newborn dawn's whitening gleam
O solitary, bright little house that still
stands on the summit of that gentle hill
watching the singing wave of the small stream.

Half-dressed and barefoot, the housewife goes outside,
opens the coop and shoos the chickens, when,
asleep (even in his dreams), the Roadman
throws off his jacket and starts to work in stride.

And the sun rises. Graceful and thin,
the grass before him, hues of gold and silver,
a mist behind him lifts from the black ground,

when the vigilant ear catches the sound
of Giacinta's voice calling him in
to breakfast on the night before's leftovers.

X

What convulsed tremor appearing on his face
shakes the flood of perspiration and then freezes?
In his solitude, what evil phantom seizes him,
or sylph to raise him up to a higher place?

On the crackling hay turned over a great deal
does joy or sorrow escape from the soul?
He rises in the shadows and, staggering: "Fool!"
He says. "They're dreams!" And nothing more reveals.

Then, egged on by hunger, he begins to go,
filled with bewilderment and with fear

and hurries on the road, gets on the bridge.
Wretched man! And death struck him right here!
In the dark, the steam train's whistle and dire woe
from afar echo against the mountain ridge.

XI

The breast of the jolting monster shakes in fits
with shouts, with sighs, with tears, with howling grim,
like a pit of hell filled to the brim
with a host of frightful, whimpering spirits.
Bitten by the brakes the wheels screech and grunt,
and in a flash a hundred ghosts lean out
from the windows, from the doors up front,
men and women trembling with fear and doubt.
With a lit lantern a black man goes ahead,
fixes on the bridge's bars his burning stare,
searches and finds, and takes hold of a head.
He then lifts it by the blood-soaked hair
observes it and to the pale conductor: "Oh!"
he shouts with arrogance, "It's just a dago!"

XII

O Italy's children oppressed by sorrow,
driven away from deserts and dark caves,
tamers of forests and of cliffs, so brave
and fearless in the face of danger's shadow.
What land in harsh exile now draws you,
where by voracious packs of wolves harassed,
a horrid death does not strike you to waste
and tear your flesh with its ferocious claws?
Where Columbus' and Americo's star
shines with its most refulgent glow,
children of Italy, where the land's infused
with your most noble blood aflow;
more cutting than ancient slavery by far
the whip is its ungrateful vile abuse.

∾

The Emigrant Returns

I

He goes on! Goes on! From the impetuous heart
spring up uninterrupted streams
of happiness and strength.
Deep inside he feels
the bloodless vermilion flower of youth
bloom once again, in that endless night.
    In his eyes he holds the gathered light
of all the stars, on the road covered
by fragrant bushes;
and, step by step, he forges on
along the road, that dips, turns, and climbs,
climbs toward the mountain still asleep
    like an erect skeleton. But to keep
a watchful eye there's the morning star alone,
above the black wing
of the castle. Rustling leaves,
mysterious beating wings, soft tears of dew
accompany the moving initial note
    of the nightingale hidden in the briars
of the dog roses, strange interweaving
of phantoms, trunks, branches,
wails of trodden grass,
and echoes of frightful shriekings
from distant darkened thickets.
    The night has not a voice to touch his soul
that reaches forth toward the small house,
already shining in the longing
of the desire so very long
suppressed. He stumbles and falls down on his knees.
"Before daylight I will reach the summit."
    "When will the train arrive up to these slopes?
Jesus! Jesus be praised! He falls again.
Nails, nails you need
for these accursed roads!

I am not tired, but I am not drunk either!
Now there is light!" He trips and falls once more.
    The smile of the star now fades away
little by little, and the sky unveils.
Down the steep incline
the houses sloping down
one upon the other give off flashes
and sudden streams of light. He broods and frets.
    "I'll find her up already, if the dawn
hues the sky orange and interrupts her dream!
I am already tired. . . .
There was a time when
it took less than an hour on this road. . . .
My lazy legs, come on, I am ashamed!. . . ."
    The swollen knapsack flaps against his side;
but his nerves remain as tense as ropes.
He is drenched by sweat, it's nothing,
he gets close to the slope.
The small bell awakens The sky tinged
milky-white: "You are deaf souls, you're deaf!"
    It calls and calls again, and rings out loud:
"Awaken! Awaken! for it's May!"
At every toll a void
opens in the aching heart,
and it is a swell of happiness that spurts
from all the veins, and it's the journey's end.

II

    He throws the swollen knapsack to the ground
and, with his shoulders leaning on the outer
low wall of the main
road of the valley,
he stretches his robust arms a little
and: "Alone!" looking with a smile around.
    He lifts up his forehead moist with sweat
toward the rooftops of the shining houses;
he listens to the roosters'
morning song, as

in a dream, and his soul has a start.
"What am I waiting for? that the people rouse?"
    "The are a few steps left." His own house
is at the end of the street climbing across,
he can barely see it,
and he glances shyly,
hesitates, trembles, and his deepest being
is submerged under a milky cloud
    of vaporous dreams. A door bangs aloud;
the doves gather in flocks up from the rooftops,
and an echo of slippers
strikes him in the forehead
like a club. With his contracted hands
he hangs the knapsack from his neck and rushes off.
    "They saw me! Yes, Giacomino D'Altiero!
Did he recognize me? Why does he smile?
Avoid him?" He comes closer.
"Oh, Carmine La Pressa?"
"Yes" "Good morning; you're an early riser"
"Quiet, don't let anyone see me!" And he laughs.
    "It's a surprise for my wife, you know!"
and laughs good-heartedly, like a child.
"So long, then, go quickly."
An he hears nothing else,
or doesn't understand: "Unless you are
the one to be surprised on this fine morning!"
    Once at the door he feels suffocated
by the anxious joy, trembles and pauses.
"Giorgina's asleep; my dove
is shut inside the nest.
She is lying in her bed so sweetly asleep."
And then he put his eye against the keyhole.
    Everything's quiet. Only the blood roars
inside his ears and almost deafens him;
he is saddened, suffers.
A sudden doubt pulses
under his brow: "Could the house, like a grave,
be empty?" He pulls and pulls the string again,

and a convulsed sound spreads about inside.
"Hey! wake up, Giorgina!" And he pulls and pulls.
He shouts: "It's Carmine,
Carmine coming back!"
From inside only the doorbell answers him,
so that, seized by annoyance and anger,
    he strikes the door with a thundering kick,
and waits for the answer in a daze.
"Nothing! what is it that I hear? subdued voices!
terrified voices! a light
sound of steps, the hurried shuffling of a dress!"
"God, with what fury, what tempest of kicks
    he lunges against that door: "Giorgina, quick!. . . .
I'll put an end to you if you keep stalling
another minute. Behind him. . . .
what is it? Already
people at the windows? I'll kick the door in!"
And that thought enrages and incites him.
    And he strikes with furious fists and kicks,
squealing like a beast inside his cage.
"Ah, you wretch!" The storm
hurls flashes of blood
against his brain. Now he understands
his neighbors' hateful words and laughter. He grasps
a hammer the carpenter had left the day before
next to the threshold. "And this is why
they praised his wife!
Lovely, lovely; unpicked flower
that makes all passers-by drunken with love,
that shines with beauty from her modest nest!
And our dear Carmine living far away
provides the gold for his beautiful woman!. . . ."
His heart gets fiercer, like a thorn bush
in a fire, and strange laughter bursts
from a thousand stab wounds.
"I catch her in the act. Oh, my saintly wife!"
    Sinister flames, sudden fires fan out
high above, and even the road gets red

and redder, and the rickety
door screeches.
"Where is the wretched woman! The neighbors. . . .
let them rush in after I have beaten her!"
  She's there, yes, she's there: a terrified ghost,
and as sweet as he had never seen her
in his thoughts in the America
of exile, that brightens
the visions of human beings who are
the life of life, over the empty road.
  But now who holds him back, so petrified?
Her lover, her lover! As if, fallen
from on high, the sun
had set him all on fire,
he is consumed, he lashes out, he strikes.
His blood bursts in his vein. He strikes! The stranger,
already recognized, falls on his back,
and still half-dressed his wife moans on the ground.
Spirits, black phantoms,
flicking red tongues,
dull menacing voices. The whole house
shudders, filled with dreadful throngs
  of furies with ruinous rage unleashed.
"They're coming, yes, they're coming." "The comare
ran to the *brigadiere*."
"That hammer should
have been for her." "Right! yes, he is a cuckold."
"How old he looks!" "And seems in such a daze"
  To run away, run! Who is nailing his shoes
down to the floor? who took away his strength?
What blind fate brought him
to this horrible massacre?
And what will this bloodshed ever bring?
The lantern of his thoughts is dying out.

  Translated by Luigi Bonaffini

Three Poems

 *Angelo Rosati*

Born Gioa del Colle (Bari), Italy, April 6, 1867

Witty annotator of Italian American newspapers while working as a bank functionary, Angelo Rosati was essentially a satiric poet, often appearing in the *Follia
of New York*. Emigrating to the United States in 1901, an American citizen after
1911, and the father of nine children, Rosati settled in Scranton, Pennsylvania.
Some of the poems contained in *Parole, parole, parole . . . !* (Words, Words,
Words . . . !), his only known collection, published in 1925, date to Rosati's years in
Scranton. The collection also contains older components, as, for example, a poem
on the death of Giosuè Carducci. Rosati also wrote a comedy in verse, *Reginetta*
(1928), which was published by the Tipografia Minatore in Scranton in 1928.

   Rosati satirized President Woodrow Wilson's attitudes toward Italy after World
War I, a favorite theme, treating of such subjects as the laws restricting immigration; he also wrote about Prohibition and the theory that the Vikings, not the Italians, discovered America (see *Colombino lo scopritore norvegese* [Little Columbus,
The Norwegian Explorer]). Other favorite themes centered on lighter subjects: his
satire on the Italian American electorate; on feminism; and on prominent people.
Rosati was a great friend and admirer of Riccardo Cordiferro as well as Cordiferro's brother, Marziale Sisca, owner of *La Follia*.

ESSENTIAL BIBLIOGRAPHY

Schiavo 1938.

To Woodrow Wilson, The Second Solomon

When you inveigh against Italy,
My dear professor, no one listens:
Here and there the colonists shudder,
They know what it means to sweat,
And, sadly, they do get upset, but they're wrong,
as everyone knows it's a dead man talking.

You think you got it right, in your *History*,
When you call us dregs . . . but every morning,
Wrapping "mozzarella" in newspaper and
Eagerly returning to his grinning hell,
It is the Miner who writes the true History.
And with much greater eloquence.

Who, my dear Professor, were your ancestors?
Were they perhaps Indians? . . . Surely you forget
That they too came here like the rest of us,
And now do you pretend you are Indian?
But them you did not call dregs.
Someone might say: this is wrong,
The historian is supposed to be impartial.

It was a strange miscarriage of nature
That saw your name pinned to the Presidency,
And quickly you thought yourself Janus.
But bitter war must have ruined your mind,
For when you drew the bottom line you saw only
Furrows on your forehead and emptiness.

Every one listened quietly when there
At Versailles your lofty speech resounded. . . .
It was the CREDITOR speaking! . . . He cannot be wrong,
Listeners would say with some concern.
But wily as a fox, old Lloyd George
Made you look like a puppet on a string!

Fiume goes to Italy? No, that's too good a deal:
We loaned them a ton of money,
'Tis enough! Let good sense prevail,
You said to yourself with a smug smile,

Italy's been the home to some ingenious heroes,
Does it need further recompense from us?

    You took on the airs of the new Redeemer
And went about preaching; peace, you said,
Peace is what I want, no winners here, no losers,
For fear that someone might audaciously stand up
And claim that the TRUTH of history is that
IT WAS ITALY ALONE WHO HAD WON.

    And what surprise at Versailles you
Did not demand Battisti's executioner
Get a medal for his exploits
At Caporetto! Could it be you recalled
Your dear old France had more
Than its fill of Caporettos.

    Wilhelm, for sure, dropped his breeches,
When he learned what had happened by the Piave!
At the time, even the snails came out to shout
To the world: WE HAVE WON, hail, hail!. . . .
But never ever even mentioned. . . .

    We will erect a beautiful monument
To your famous Points, proudly displayed
THERE WHERE WAS A MONTENEGRO. . . .
And we will pray to GABRIELE so that he may,
Before souring, write an epitaph to remind the World
That you alone have been the second Solomon.[1]

Prohibitionism

    That immortal wise man
Master Anthony used to say,
Wine and beer for the poor
Are not an asset to their health,
And I feel that these fluids

1. This was written after the Boston speech, when Wilson gave another gratuitous slap in the face to our Italy. —Author.

Are not conducive to Freedom.
   Freedom basking still
In the bay of Verrazzano
And it appears to be saying
To the people or the sovereign:
This thing, your living freely,
It's just too much, I mean it.
   Some say that this Law
Was shoved onto those peacocks
Who had already voted it,
Because they confined it
To the water, where we see it.
   But that can't be true.
An idol does not act on spite:
If they placed it on the island, well
Of course, they were forced to do so:
They looked everywhere, these
Practical people, there was no other place.
   Moreover, Freedom's torch
Is to light the channel,
Can't expect it to shine
Upon minds of its children. . . .
Who now have electric light
Which in truth is more beautiful. . . .
   And . . . enough, let's go back
To master Anthony presently
Rationalizing about wine
We can no longer drink, saying:
The poor the law will have to obey.
   Italy, for example,
Which lacks everything,
While friends devour
Biscuits with prosciutto
And the goatskins fill up
With either Rhine wine or Bordeaux,
   Cannot even touch the water
From one of our Rivers!
(But to this strange weirdo

Responds our Diety:
Alone, against Philistine
Iniquities, I will stand alone).
    And yet we must believe
If these prohibitionists
Wish to take our wine away,
They're being humanitarian,
Because they know the poor
Cannot afford the good stuff.
    So they suffer and
Drink wine for us. . . .
Think about it: what noble
Bellies, what great heroes:
These American virtues
Do not come from Europe.

Johnson Bill . . . !

Johnson Bill says to Progress:
Such a fury, my dear friend,
We'll get there just the same
Even if at the slow pace of a donkey.
You're bringing in from the East:
Friends too many and relatives too
Good and charming they may be, but to us
They are a force, they are relentless!
And especially those Italians
They are so quick to invent the new
And things so strange to seal your triumph.
To them, we know, it is a game
To square off against all perils:
Young or old it doesn't matter.
They can make roads and bridges, and . . . children too!
In the war they were massacred
To defend this very land
Which had first bid them welcome.

But we want to keep away
These "dagos" in particular
Though they work both brain and brawn
Like they were super-human.
And because they now nearly feel
They're related to the Indians;
Could it be the day will come
They may all be called pretenders.
Well . . . it could! He was a crazy dago
With three tiny ships landed first
And yes he did, he had children with the Indians . . . !
So dear Progress it should be clear,
Why we must shut down the gates:
Are there enough of us? . . . relax:
So you will proceed a bit slowly, who cares?
The Zulus, who know you not,
Live happy and free
Without the shadow of a calamity,
Without so many pretenders. . . .

Translated by Peter Carravetta

The Poor Woman

෴ *Calicchiu Pucciu*

Santa Margherita di Belice (Agrigento), Italy, September 29, 1876–New York, New York, 1927

Calicchiu Pucciu's real name was Calogero Puccio. A sculptor and carver, Puccio had a studio in Brooklyn. He was also a dialect poet and began to publish verses in *La Follia of New York* in 1906. In America, appointed to a special committee, he sculpted the wooden panels of the principal altar of the parish of Santa Margherita, in Sicily. He was then sent to Sicily to mount the work and was caught up in the war. He went to the front, then came back to America, then, in 1920, returned to his hometown to complete the work he had undertaken. The work, which represents the passion of Christ in various panels, was buried in the collapse of the church in the earthquake of 1968.

In 1922, Puccio was again in New York, "but how tired, afflicted, sick! And no one could ever explain why" (Fichera). Recovered later of an illness, treated in a hospital on Ward's Island, he fell into a depression and attempted suicide, jumping into the East River. Rescued, he died two days later of pneumonia, "in the throes of the blackest distress" (Federal Writers' Project).

In 1909, he had published a volume of Sicilian verses entitled *Triateuco* and the satirical short poem "Lu suonnu di Monsignuri." In 1922, he published *Cusuzzi*, a larger collection in three parts, and in 1923, *Fogghi di lauru* (Laurel Leaves). His long dialect poem "La pruittedda" ("The Poor Woman"), published earlier and perhaps his major work, is strongly in sympathy with anarchy and socialism and sensitive to the entreaties of the needy. (Through *Cusuzzi* there runs an acrostic component pertaining to the anniversary of the foundation of the club Avanti!) Puccio was a friend of Cordiferro and Onorio Ruotolo, to whom he dedicated an ode.

Puccio's experiences were certainly among the most outstanding in relation to the numerous group of "poets of the *sottobosco* [underbrush—that is to say, marginalized]." Puccio was an author of a "fluid, inexhaustible vein," a "vivacious imagination," and a "volcanic mind" (Cordiferro). He was readable, despite a certain discontinuity that was due in part to his refusal to exercise a rigorous discipline in his writing. Often, he knew how to gain his effect, whether by producing rapid and savory colonial sketches or—as in "La pruittedda"—by choosing a more extensive narration in verse. In one case or the other, the consciousness of a genuine rhapsodic popular tradition strongly emerges; apparently, he was willing to be perceived as the spontaneous and congenial interpreter of the Sicilian spirit.

Puccio was at ease in the "fertile country of Santa Margherita Belice, where [he] would saunter all day, living an almost peasant life" (from the preface to *Cusuzzi*), a life that is often invoked in his verses. He was similarly at ease in the diverting metropolitan landscape of Brooklyn and his daily life, which constitute the poems of *Triateuco*, and also a large part of *Cusuzzi*. By this time, he was familiar with life in the city and had memories and regrets, as when he nostalgically declares his longing for "the balsamic air . . . of Brantivuddu," that is, Brentwood, which he briefly came into contact with when he moved to "Brucculinu" (Brooklyn).

Old World and New World are present in "La pruittedda," which relates the story of poor Maria, who, a former prostitute, becomes a nun and, subsequently, a Mother Superior of a convent in Rossano, in Calabria. She then falls in love with Marcantonio, an artist who is sick and committed to her care, and she follows him to America. Mercantonio goes into combat on the Isonzo, a river in Gorizia, and dies. Maria embarks on the sad return voyage, but overwhelmed by sorrow, she jumps into the sea. *La Pruittedda* has the tone and action of a typical story of a ballad singer, except with a contemporary theme. Among other things, it may be partly autobiographical. With roles reversed, it is reminiscent of Antonio Calitri's *Dietro la maschera* (Behind the Mask).

Puccio's popularizing or populist intensions are declared in *Fogghi di lauru*, the book that contains *Centu Ritratti d'Omini Illustri* (A Hundred Portraits of Famous Men) in the form of sonnets. (In titles of works, as here, many Italian American writers adopted the English rules for capitalization.) In the preface, Rosario Ingargiola writes that "the author has written principally for the less cultivated reader or—as he himself expressed it to me—for the worker"; thus was born "a little pocket encyclopedia, containing the poetic medallions of men celebrated for their knowledge and deeds . . . a thing that no one, before Pucciu, had ever thought of." A cursory look at the list of personages, their political tendencies, and their cultural background, closely relate the poet's own, reveals Puccio's predilections. Aside from the ever-present Caruso, Colombo, Garibaldi, aside from the tutelary gods of America, Franklin, Lincoln, T. Roosevelt, Washington, here are Giuseppe Aurelio Costanzo, Olindo Guerrini, Mario Rapisardi, Pietro Gori, Émile Zola, and Nietzsche; and here are Andrea Costa, Francisco Ferrer, and Léon Giambetta. The preferred milieu, then, is that of classic political extremism, even if the authentic theme of Puccio is not political.

ESSENTIAL BIBLIOGRAPHY

Cacioppo 1962; Federal Writers' Project 1939, 77; Fichera 1958, 29.

The poor nun is thirty,
A dangerous and arrogant age;
Her great bosom bellows, she is breathless,
The spine of love does wonders,
And propositions to run away come out
Into the open at every moment.

The nun says yes, then says no.
"The scandal," she says, "will be huge."
She recalls the first escape with don Cocò,
And thinking of it a little feels disgusted.
Her lover is a great sculptor. He offers
To take her to America, and proposes

That he himself leave first from Rossano and head
Straight towards New York, then
Write some letters to the chaplain,
Who knows all, and depart at a gallop.
Having agreed, he again gives her a strong embrace,
And gives her a couple of deep kisses.

Night falls, and dawn appears,
The moon heads toward the sea,
The full sky is a sea of lights,
And a divine air invites breathing,

And the butterfly that circles and circles
Begins its twilight flights.

After five months of waiting
The Prioress receives a letter
That says, "Leave this land,
Land of hunger and wretchedness,"
And other expressions
Perfectly modulated in various tones.

The nun packs up
And on the sly buys the ticket;
She steals out by a side door
Even as the midnight bell rings,
And goes to her trusted friend
Who is both chaplain and curate.

Trembling, she has him read the letter
And the attached ticket;
He says, "May you be blessed!
There has never been a woman like you,
An astute woman,
With sixty pairs of buttons."

The chaplain, who sees her at home
Like a young and vermillion rose,
Embraces her and embraces her strongly,
And kisses her,
Telling her, "I kiss you as a daughter,"
And again kisses her . . . but it's nothing:
He kisses her as if she were his relative.

The priest improvises a small dinner,
And both eat in peace;
The nun is in a little hurry,
But the priest is in no hurry at all;
And he kisses over and over
This relative he has in his house.

Already, the steamer whistles, and all is ready,
The defrocked nun is at sea,

The sea is clear as a wellspring,
The time for sailing is perfect.
It's spring, though there are no flowers,
Yet the sea is lovely with colors.

The sun caresses her and keeps her company,
Reflecting its color over the sea.
The nun goes on and does not complain
Over the nuisances of travel:
And she is joyful and sings and laughs,
Bringing love and faith to Marcantonio.

Marcantonio is the name that we have kept hidden,
So far, of the lover,
A name often celebrated
By both the wise and the ignorant
For the great works of sculpture
He has made, works that surpass nature.

The poor woman amuses herself and has fun
With the people in third class;
She, who travels in second class, higher,
Is far away from all the noise,
From all the garbage,
And from the evil and the mud and filth.

She arrives in New York, and after a couple of hours
Marcantonio comes to pick her up;
The eagerness she had and the great love
Helped her through the swollen sea,
And now that she has embraced Marcantonio,
What happened during the voyage has come and gone.

Marcantonio has a house in an American
Neighborhood (he speaks a little English),
A house worthy of a gentleman
In a kingly place:
Two rooms and a well-adorned living room
Where he sits with his beloved.

The poor woman is happy, and all festive
She tells him of how the voyage went.
She says, "There was a bit of tempest,
But I am not troubled by these tempests:
I often leave the porthole open,
Have fun with the sea, and enjoy myself."

Marcantonio often caresses her,
And holds her tight, and kisses her;
Each kiss stirs his fire,
And so they celebrate the new house. . . .
The bed is quite new, and they stay in that nest
Like two young turtledoves in love.

So they pass the Spring
And part of Summer;
Time sweeter than the grape,
They stay faithful, united in love;
So fully in love these hearts
That words cannot tell how much.

Marcantonio has the studio and works
And always uses her as model
Because her natural beauty
Is not possible to find in any other;
Model and artist live happily together,
And all talk about it and agree.

But fortune is much too capricious;
It's a wind that changes every moment;
Now it fills your sail and the boat moves at a gallop,
And now it stops and barely moves.
Now it lifts you and you reach the sky;
Now it pulls you down and you blend with the ice.

The poor girl enjoys
Her lover next to her, working,
Bad luck hits her,
And she falls in the arms of misfortune,

A misfortune she really does not need,
Our subject, our Maria.

Marcantonio, who is also an avowed anarchist,
While Italy goes to war
Has the idea to run away and be a soldier,
And while fighting, in the middle of a scuffle,
In an advance toward Monfalcone,
Gets hit by a cannon ball.

As soon as Maria hears of it,
She falls down flat on the ground;
And the joy, the liveliness, all the love,
In an instant change into pain.
Poor Maria does not die
Only as a sign that God wants to save her.

And so she remains lost in the world,
Poor, and alone, and without a penny in her pocket.
This Maria has no luck,
And scarcely makes ends meet.
She sings in theaters, and she models
Since she has kept herself beautiful.

Tired of being an art model
And of singing in theaters,
Without guidance from lover or father,
Fearful as she is (moreover),
She decides to return to Sicily.

Oh, had she never had this thought!
Destiny calls you, poor woman.
When something is truly lovely
It is her destiny to be wretched,
Especially if her beauty is incomparable

Like Maria's. Like everything that reaches a certain age,
She is still herself, always the same,
And when she walks, she moves

Queen-like, and all is free
In her perfect and lovable gait.

Aboard the steamer, there is no man
That does not look or smile at her,
But she looks at no one and sees no one,
Nor gives her name as she had done before;
The others are those who look and admire.

All know that aboard there is a beauty,
And this is cause of argument and discussion;
Believing that they are all good people,
She goes here and there in tranquility
Even as she knows the world is disgraceful.

No one ventures to speak to her, all are silent,
No one at all says a word;
They admire her when she comes outside,
No one at all says a word
And then they stay in blessed peace,
Saying, "This girl is an angel."

And the steamer whistles
To announce its departure;
The sailors go to stern and bow
To let those who don't know it is time to depart,
And the steamer enters the ocean.

The sun shines and each element laughs,
Each thing in the world gaily murmurs;
Only our lovable Maria
Is disturbed, a torment in her heart
That truly gives her no rest.

Anxiety grows inside her heart;
With a desperate rush, like a pile of bones,
She loses herself on her bed.
There is no one to help and comfort her,
She is alone in the cabin and thinks and thinks
Of the cruel fate and of her bad luck.
She is a broken soul,

A being lost on earth
That struggles and has no peace in the heart.

Poor Maria
Thinks of her beloved, thinks of his death,
And it rends her soul and her being,
And she loses herself to ugly thoughts.
She thinks of her land, and with pride;
Because she has no money, she reflects.
And once again she thinks of Marcantonio,
And enjoys him a little with her mind,
With her tired and peculiar mind.

And she weeps and struggles and curses
All her past and present;
She curses the people
That brought her close to her lover,
Except for Marcantonio, her god,
The one God she adores on earth
Who, to her misfortune, died in war.

She leaves the cabin and climbs
On deck with anxiety in her heart,
Speaking mighty words
To the stars, to the sea, and to the people,
She throws herself with a great jump
And falls straight into the sea,
And in the calm and starry night
The water, sobbing, swallows her.

Finis

Translated by Emmanuel Di Pasquale

The Little Madonna of the Italians

ॐ *Paolo Pallavicini*

Turin (or Milan), Italy, September 7, 1886–San Francisco, California, January 1938

Paolo Pallavicini's four-act drama *La figlia di Nennè* (Nennè's Daughter, 1914) was perhaps his first published work under the name Pallavicini-Pirovano. Born, according to Ario Flamma, in Turin, and according to Giovanni E. Schiavo in Milan, Pallavicini arrived in New York in 1908. Here, he founded and directed various newspapers and was editor and/or contributor to the *Progresso Italo-Americano*, to the *Giornale Italiano*, and then to the *Corriere d'America*. In 1920, the engineer Patrizi asked him to come to San Francisco to direct the daily *L'Italia*, which he did for some fifteen years.

A very prolific author, a figure in the catalogues of such important Italian editorial houses as Sonzogno and Salani, Pallavicini is a rather distinctive case in the Italian American panorama of the time. Like Ciambelli, he is in need of a definitive bibliography. Currently, however, eight long novels, published in newspapers and later collected in volumes, are recorded. Many of them appeared in the appendices of the *Italia,* of San Francisco, among them, *Il ventaglio di Aquileia* (Aquileia's Fan, 1917); though between 1915 and 1916, the *Ventaglio* had already been printed in the dailies of New York, *L'Araldo Italiano* (The Italian Herald) and *Il Telegrafo* (The Telegraph), by the same editorial group. Other novels include *Nix, il Figlio dell'Austriaco* (Nix, The Austrian's Son, 1920) and *Per le vie del mondo* (Through the Streets of the World), published in California in 1933, in a more extended version than in an earlier publication in its original version, in appendices in the *Corriere d'America*, in 1922–23, with the title, *Il romanzo d'un emigrato* (An

Emigrant's Romance). Following chronologically, are *L'amante delle tre croci* (The Lover of Three Crosses, 1923), which forms a diptych with *Il romanzo d'un Emigrato; Quando Berta filava* (When Berta was Spinning Flax, 1923); *Tutto il dolore, tutto l'amore* (All the Sorrow, All the Love, 1926); *La casa del peccato* (The House of Sin, 1931); and *La carezza divina* (The Divine Caress, 1939).

In addition, Palavicini was the author of a radio drama, *Nella terra del sogno* (In Dreamland, 1936), and of voluminous reportage on World War I, with a heavily dramatized nationalism, collected in the book *La Guerra Italo-Austriaca* (The Italo-Austrian War), published in New York in 1919. In more than five hundred pages, he recounts all the battles of the conflict in detail, according to a scheme that never deviates from the patriotic position, exalting bellicose deeds, whether of humble soldiers or of their commanders, and invariably painting the enemy in the most contemptuous tone. Lacking is a true politico-strategic analysis of the facts, and the unilateral premise impedes the understanding of the tragic aspect of the war. In the preface to the volume, the editors write, "The facts of the huge conflict are in the public domain, but without order, confused, with wrong or uncertain dates. To us, a book in simple popular form seemed necessary. It would narrate all the epic events that have given to our country the greatest victory that the history of the world records. Here it is. The reader will follow it with the same avidity with which he reads a novel of dramatic, passionate interest. And, instead, it is the pure history of yesterday, written by the heroic blood of the sons of Italy." The same bellicose atmosphere is found in his first two novels: *Nix,* especially, is a very complicated story of love and espionage behind the Italian frontline during the Great War.

The Italian American theme is dominant in the other works, where the prevailing interest in the sentimental plot does not get in the way of an attentive look at the social context in which the protagonists find themselves, moving freely among very divergent backgrounds, from the mines of Pennsylvania to the farmlands of California.

Pallavicini's most engaging book is *Per le vie del mondo.* In more than six hundred pages, with settings in California, New York, and Italy, it recounts the story of Bruno Speri, Italian foreman in a California factory, in the neighborhood of which, Oscar Renner, the betrothed of the *padrone*'s daughter, is killed. The Italians in Speri's gang will be held responsible for the crime, and they will be incarcerated, more on the basis of a rooted prejudice than on decisive verification. Speri investigates on his own, and, naturally, after various complicated turns of fortune, he succeeds in demonstrating the innocence of his Italians. At the climax of the story, he marries Adriana Rosenthal, the daughter of his employer, and he reveals the verminous perfidy and viciousness with which the rich Gerardo Lussendhorf, in love with Adriana, has conceived his criminal design, involving the opium dens of Chinatown and the ostentatious lords of the mine industry.

Although Pallavicini was in some ways more middle-class than Ciambelli, and because of the California context—held to be the "model colony"—in which he functioned, he is still far from the international forms of Italo Stanco and Corrado Altavilla. Nevertheless, he, too, openly avoids any obvious ethnic basis to his narratives. He concentrates, rather, on reproducing the various regional types that constitute the Italian colony, therefore making large use of cadences and dialects, with a strong presence (peculiar to the Californian public) of those northern Italians, who often come close to a popular use of American phrases.

Pallavicini had a large following of readers, especially in San Francisco. In the first pages of the *Carezza divina*, he provides a brief autobiographical glimpse, hidden behind the personage of Giorgio Albani. This book is interesting because it provides a close-up and intimate portrayal of the "irresolute dualism of the children of the second generation," who in the final pages, "become temporarily appeased, thanks to the apparition of a hero of art (Mascagni) and of a dramaturgic hero of the new Italy," none other than Mussolini, who is "forging a new Italy" (Marazzi).

ESSENTIAL BIBLIOGRAPHY

Cinel 1982, 191; Flamma 1936; Franzina 1996, 206–209; Ingargiola 1938; Marazzi 2001, 26–27; Pallavicini 1933, 49–56; Schiavo 1938.

The news that Adriana Rosenthal had returned from Italy spread quickly towards evening in the Italian neighborhood of Santa C . . . The bearer of the news was a factory worker, who had gone to the villa and had seen her sitting in the garden with her father, as well as William Fox and two women whom he did not recognize. The first to learn about it were the regulars at the bar *Fra Pacifico*. Among them were Maso Landi and Gaspare Preda, two of the accused accomplices of the murder of Oscar Renner, who were later found innocent along with Rocco Sagri and Antonio Carlusi, thanks to the work of Bruno Speri and Adriana Rosenthal.

None of them had left town. They had all kept their jobs at the factories. Carlusi, *Totonno the Neapolitan*, as he was nicknamed, and Rocco Sangri, whom they no longer called *Sponge* because, since his release from prison, he drank very little, no longer got drunk, and seldom went to the bar. All of them had family lives, and much of their free time was spent at home with their wives and children. The memory of the tragedy that had been about to lead them to the gallows or at best to bury them alive in San Quentin Prison was still so fresh in their minds that they had a holy terror of everything, even of shadows. Therefore, they preferred to live quietly in two little homes nearby, rarely finding themselves in public places.

Maso Landi and Gaspare Preda, the *Scicco*, had no family and, despite being in a boarding house of friends who considered them part of the household, in the evening leaving the factory or after dinner, they headed to Fra Pacifico's to play a little game of cards. Thus, the worker who had seen Miss Adriana related the incident to these men who were the first to learn of it as they stood at the counter of the bar, intent on drinking a cold glass of beer and chatting with the owner who more than ever deserved the nickname *Fra Pacifico* because more than ever he remained white, red, fat, round and smiling.

"Oh my God!" exclaimed Preda, *lo Scicco*, who, despite the violent storm that had burst over him and had been endowed with that stoicism and air of grit and courage typical in Sicilians, dressed always with a special refinement, always *chic*, justifying the nickname of *Scicco* that had been given to him by his companions but no longer made him fly into a rage as it once did. "So Mr. Bruno Speri has also arrived."

"If he hasn't arrived he's about to!" said Maso Landi and, turning suddenly to all the other workers who were spread out at different tables in the bar and intent on eating the meal that *Fra Pacifico* had served by a young lad, yelled: "Boys! Our *little Madonna* has returned!"

Maso had given this name to Adriana Rosenthal one day before her departure for Italy. It was as she passed through the Italian neighborhood and stopped in the middle of a group of children who surrounded her, clapping their hands! Not one of them ignored the role she had played in the release of the four innocent workers: everyone had realized after the second trial that between her and Bruno Speri there existed a spiritual bond of affection that made her more dear to them; everyone had learned from the servants of the Rosenthal household and then from the newspapers that they were to marry. With the artful, warm, and passionate imagination of the Italians, they had created around the two young people a legend, making him no less than a warrior saint who destroys his enemies and makes justice triumph, and her . . . their living Madonna who had saved their companions, victims of a horrendous conspiracy, and had showered them with all kinds of benefits, imposing upon the town a better treatment of the Italian element, and favoring as much as she could the workers in the factory.

When some months earlier the news had spread that they were to marry in Italy, the entire day the Italian neighborhood of Saint C . . . seemed to be in celebration. In the homes, on the doorsteps, at the windows, on the street corners, nothing else was discussed, and their enthusiasm was expressed in hymns to the goodness of one and the other, and exploded in exclamations of joy, of admiration, and amazement.

"Ah! This is a real love story, one of those you read about in books," the women observed.

"Sometimes it's really true that birds of a feather flock together."

"And sometimes good things happen in this world," added someone who wanted to put a bit of philosophy into his considerations.

"How well they will get along!"

"Both are so attractive!"

"She sure is, she looks just like a Madonna, but he will be good, honest, and handsome. . . ."

The women threw themselves into an animated discussion of the physical attributes of Bruno, of that something special that he had in his entire person that, they said, made him the most handsome man of all.

And so they continued to talk, not only that day, but also in those that followed, finding a reason for everything and reconciling in the most naïve and charming way all the obstacles that the disparity of social and family conditions could stir up between the engaged couple.

Maso's cry "Our *little Madonnina* is back!" provoked another general, formidable discussion, and an avalanche of questions asked almost all at once. It seemed that they were trying to out-yell one another.

"Who told you so?"

"How do you know?"

"Where is she?"

"And is Bruno Speri with her?"

"Are they married?"

It took all that was possible to quiet everyone and to allow the worker who had brought the happy news to tell all that he had seen and what he knew.

Miss Adriana was in the garden of her villa. She suddenly appeared while he was delivering a package for Mr. Rosenthal that had to be handed directly to him. She, however, had not seen him because she was reclining in an arm-chair and was speaking with other people. He was struck by her paleness. It was for this reason that, as he was leaving the garden accompanied by the male attendant who came to close the gate, he had asked if she was well.

"She arrived last night," the attendant answered, "She must be tired from the long journey."

"And did she arrive alone?" He dared to ask.

"With some friends."

"Which friends?"

The attendant looked at him with a look that was not very encouraging.

"That is none of your business!" This was his answer as he closed the gate and turned away from him. But he did not give much weight to the response because he knew that this was a new servant, who had recently come from San Francisco, and must have ignored Miss Adriana's orders that the Italians were to be received as friends in the Rosenthal home.

And so, there was no doubt. She had really arrived. No one thought that her return was concealing something painful. How could they imagine the drama that would unfold in just a matter of days that would destroy the dream of love between the two sweethearts.

"Perhaps Bruno Speri is also among those friends," said Gaspare Preda.

"I didn't see him."

"He could have been in the house. . . ."

"Perhaps he had gone some place else for the time being."

"You didn't see him, but no one told you that he wasn't there."

"You'll see that he too has returned."

"And why didn't anyone know about it?"

"Because they probably didn't tell anyone, fool that you are!"

"If they married, is there a need for them to hide?"

"Married, I'd say no, because the newspapers would have written about it and then some one would have mentioned it in the factory or in town. . . ."

"That's true."

"Rather, I bet that they came here incognito, as they say, not to inconvenience anyone and to marry in her home in order to make Mr. Rosenthal happy, who certainly must not have been happy with the idea that his daughter had married someone from so far away."

No one doubted any longer Bruno Speri's presence in villa Rosenthal. The marriage must be imminent. They must have been preparing a big surprise for the entire town. Who knows what festivities were about to take place.

Some folks, who were eager to share the news with other Italians in town, left the *bar*. They set out in different directions and asked whomever they met:

"Did you hear?"

"What?"

"The *little Madonna* of the Italians has returned!"

In just a short time the neighborhood was turned upside down. Hard to say who threw out the idea, for the announcement had stirred up such joyful confusion. Perhaps the sudden thought of everyone. The fact is that they all were in agreement to go as a crowd—women, children, all that could, naturally—to villa Rosenthal to wish the newlyweds well. They wanted to bring them the first good wishes, so that they would immediately learn that they were always remembered, loved, and how much they were expected.

The crowd began to swell as it moved toward the villa. The women and children had their hands filled with flowers pulled from their gardens without much care. If they saw their *little Madonna* they would have showered her with them. She had always been so kind; she had given them so many beautiful things; she had always helped them.

"And without her we would still be in San Quentin!" yelled loudly Rocco Sangri, who found himself at the head of the group holding the hand of his little daughter, whose task it was to remind him of *San Quentin* each time that she saw him drink more than one glass.

Totonno the Neapolitan dragged along his wife and all his children. He felt something greater than all the others. He believed he had more of a right to Miss Adriana's attention, because he had been an innocent man in prison, he had truly suffered the pains of hell. Had his misfortunes continued just a bit more, he would have ended up at the gallows. And at that horrendous thought he quickly made the sign of the cross repeating many times his usual invocation:

"Saint Gennaro, help me!"

Maso Lando was so happy that he ran from one group to the other communicating to everyone an idea that had come to mind and he believed to be quite brilliant.

"Now that all has passed and that dreadful story has ended with a beautiful marriage that will make not only the newlyweds happy but also all of us, one almost feels compelled to thank God for causing that little tragedy."

The first to hear those words shouted cries of protest.

"But what are you saying?"

"Are you crazy?"

And Maso Landi let them vent, then he asked them with a self-assured air:

"Do you think that the Americans would have treated us as they treat us now and that we would have enjoyed so many benefits if Miss Adriana had not come to us as a result of the misfortune that sent us to San Quentin innocent?"

Many responded immediately that he was right.

"She would have continued to consider us what unfortunately many of those like her still believe, and we would have continued to be called *dagoes* and put up with it."

They all ended up agreeing with him and they would have continued this discussion for quite some time had they not arrived at the street of villa Rosenthal.

Night had fallen, one of those enchanting evenings that often descends on the Californian countryside; sweet-smelling nights that send forth with the light breeze certain fragrances that reinforce the Italian soul's longing for those of his distant native land. Though they may not be the same, they resemble each other very much. And with the wave of fragrances came that of dear and nostalgic memories.

The veranda of villa Rosenthal was lit. You could see it most clearly from the street. You could see shadows move: "I'm sure they are close friends who have come to pay their best wishes to the newlyweds," someone said loudly. And those words gave rise to the first cry from the crowd that resonated in the silence of the starry night:

"Long live the newlyweds!!"

In a matter of moments the crowd of Italians was in front of the gate where they renewed their powerful cry, as they began clapping their hands. On the veranda there was a feverish movement of people. You could see some of them enter hastily into the house and others come out, and almost immediately three or four male attendants race down the stairs and head toward the entrance intending surely to stop those cries of celebration and to send everyone home. Maso Landi and Gaspare Preda were again at the head of that sort of procession and were the first against the closed gate. Driven by the enthusiasm and convinced that they were paying their dutiful regards to the *little Madonna* whom they loved dearly and were doing a friendly act that should not have been displeasing to anyone, they did not think it was necessary to wait for the servants to open the gate. They turned the handle of the gate, which, having been left inadvertently unlocked by the gardener, flung open. The Italians in mass entered the garden. They were already half way down the road when they ran into the servants who began to yell:

"Out! Out of here! Quiet! Get out! Go back!"

At first no one paid much attention to the intervention, brutal as it was, and even as the servants tried to oppose with their arms forward the tumultuous advance.

"We want to give our regards to Miss Adriana!" protested Maso Landi freeing himself from the hand of a servant who had grabbed him rather roughly by an arm.

"And Bruno Speri!" Added some others.

And the crowd in chorus repeated the cry:

"Long live the newlyweds!"

The servants were too few to contain the overly enthusiastic throng. Therefore, it was easy for the crowd to drive the servants back up to the foot of the staircase where they repeated their hurrahs. There then appeared on the veranda, which had been momentarily deserted, William Fox, followed by John Miller and by other people, including some women. In that group there was Jule Rhudel, Frank Black, Peter Gontrasky, Rosa White, Helen Lheridan, Doctor Shelling, and Engineer Harold.

On everyone's face there was an expression of indignation as if they found themselves facing something that was both shameful and inconceivable at the same time.

Mr. Rosenthal had understood from the first shouts what was going on, because on other occasions, before the departure of his daughter for Italy, those Italian hotheads, who are only happy when they can make noise, had come to improvise similar demonstrations. He then had his friends, who were on the veranda with him, return immediately into the house. He ordered some servants to secure the gate, while he hurried to Adriana who, having remained calm and composed the entire day perhaps because she was exhausted from so many emotions, had begun to show signs of restlessness and annoyance at the sight of the household's friends from whom it was not possible to conceal an arrival that had taken place under special conditions. The night following her unexpected adventure at the Italian restaurant she had felt so badly not only for what she had seen and for her own state of mind but also because, convinced of chasing away harassing thoughts, of dulling her senses, and of wanting to forget, she had drunk a few more glasses of wine than necessary, especially for someone who drank very little. Dr. Shelling, already frightened by the fact that he let himself be taken in by the girl who left the hotel without his realizing it and who had reverted back to that condition despite his having received the order to watch over her, no longer wanted to hear about such a responsibility. He then telephoned Mr. Rosenthal for instructions, and was told to bring her home if he felt that the trip would not do her any harm and if she was not flatly opposed to it. And Adriana, who felt somewhat relieved after the crisis, had, nevertheless, lost all her strength and will to react, allowing herself to fall into a state of lethargy, resigned, almost as if any reaction was useless. Such was her condition when she returned to her father's home, which she had left not long before with a heart full of hope. Now she crossed the threshold with the most beautiful dream of her life brutally destroyed. And this time forever.

Rosa White and her friends had arrived in the afternoon. Around evening the Millers, William Fox and a few other old acquaintances of the family had asked to see her.

Her calm and patience had surprised her father.

"Are we leaving tomorrow for our sea travels?" she asked graciously.

"Tomorrow, even later, when you'd like . . . It doesn't matter to me."

And the old man had partly consoled himself with those arrangements, thinking that a delay of a few days spent resting at home would have perhaps improved her condition, allowing her to face with greater certainty the hardships of another journey. Though every possible comfort would be provided during the trip, there was still an element of uncertainty.

When the hurrahs shouted by the Italians reached him, Adriana was stretched out on a sofa in the parlor with her eyes half-closed. She seemed to have dozed off.

At the cries of the crowd she suddenly jumped to her feet.

"What do they want?" she asked her father who immediately entered completely flustered for fear that she had heard.

"Nothing, nothing! They're sending them away . . . Listen? No one is shouting any more."

In fact, William Fox, leaning over the railing of the veranda, had waved animatedly to impose silence. Having arrived at the foot of the staircase where they had driven back the powerless servants, the crowd came to a stop, seeing those gestures, understood and grew silent almost immediately. While the servants attempted in vain to prevent the Italians from advancing, Jule Rhudel and Frank Black suggested telephoning the sheriff and the agents of the factory's private service.

"Meanwhile we'll keep them at bay with this" said Frank Black revealing the butt of the revolver that he kept in his pant pocket.

"A handful of clubs is enough to frighten them all off!" exclaimed Engineer Harold.

"Take it easy! Take it easy! Let's not do anything foolish!" screamed a frightened John Miller, as if the group of workers was a rebelling crowd on the verge of rushing the house.

"These ragamuffins are always armed! Remember that they have the blood of bandits in their veins."

Just hearing the word bandits, John Miller's wife and Miss Helen Lheridan let out screams. It seemed that they were about to become prey to ferocious bandits.

William Fox, like old Rosenthal, had imagined the misunderstanding that had provoked that demonstration. A man of good sense, he measured the consequences of a violent act against those workers who, unaware of the events, only wanted to celebrate the young woman who had done them a good service. Hearing the statements and the women's screams, he had an outburst of anger.

"No one move and no one yell; please!" he ordered with a voice that did not allow for any objection, "The women will go into the house and will not cause any useless confusion!" "These people have by no means come to plunder, for God's sake!"

Everyone became silent, and it was then that the director of the factories could ask with a gesture of his hands that the crowd also be quiet.

"Friends!" he then yelled so that his voice could be heard by all, "Go home immediately. Miss Adriana is not well. She has returned ill. It's not the time to do what you'd like. . . ."

A rustle similar to the sound of the breeze passed over that mass of people assembled in the shade of the garden. It was an outcry of painful surprise provoked by the unexpected announcement.

You could hear among the crowd the voice of Rocco Sangri:

"We'll leave immediately, Mr. Fox; but tell our *little Madonna* that we came to say hello and to show her how we always remember her and how we make vows for her happiness."

"Very well! Very well! However, now go home!" responded the director of the factories who was on tenter-hooks.

Maso Landi got up on the tip of his toes and turning toward the crowd yelled with a stentorian voice:

"Go home, companions, but first . . . hurray to the *little Madonna* of the Italians!"

The cry was repeated with enthusiasm by everyone in chorus:

"Hurraayy!!"

That hurray didn't seem enough for Gaspare Preda so he added another one:

"Hurray to Bruno Speri!"

"Hurraayy!!"

The formidable cry resounded in the night. The Italians were about to retire when those who were closest to the steps began to yell:

"There she is! There she is! There she is!"

"Who? What?"

"Miss Adriana!"

"She heard us!"

"She wants to greet us!"

Now no one moved. Everyone made an effort to draw closer and to see better.

Adriana had in fact appeared on the veranda. She was wearing a white dressing-gown and, since she was suffering from sharp headaches, she had her beautiful blond hair loose on her shoulders. From a distance she seemed a Madonna figure because you couldn't see the corpse-like pallor of her face nor the dim flame in her eyes. Her father and Doctor Shelling were by her side, and with soft violence they attempted to stop her from proceeding, and force her to return inside. The friends of the Rosenthal household, who were on the veranda and equally moved by the sight, stepped aside to let her pass by freely. And so she was seen by everyone, but no one uttered a single word. The light of the lamp illuminated her completely. She seemed a Madonna, but a suffering Madonna.

A young child, the daughter of Rocco Sangri, suddenly climbed the stairs and slipped unnoticed through the legs of the servants. She must have been pushed through by her father. She had a large bouquet of flowers. Before someone could stop her, the little toddler rushed toward Adriana and gave her the flowers.

The crowd of Italians expected to see the little Madonna embrace the small child for whom she had a fondness before her departure; instead, they noticed that, after grabbing the flowers from her hand, she pushed her with such a rough gesture that she fell to the ground. She then threw the flowers at her by the handful. The little girl let out a scream of pain and fear. While old Rosenthal and the Doctor took Adriana by her arms and tried to calm her, Rocco Sangri, seeing his poor darling fall, leaped up the stairs with the intention of running to her aid; however, the servants grabbed him, leading to a scuffle.

As a result of that sudden and unexpected scene, the Italians were left stunned and amazed, and did not know what to do.

Overwhelmed by a fit of hopeless agitation, Adriana began to struggle yelling, "Let me go! this riff-raff insults me! I want to beat them! Go away! Go away! I don't want to see a single one of them any longer! Chase them out of town!"

Frightened by the condition of his daughter who had lost control of herself and was no longer responsible for her words and actions, Mr. Rosenthal flew into a rage against those people who had come to ruin all his diligent and patient work to spare the sick girl any emotion.

"Throw those wretches into the streets!!" he yelled. At that point Frank Burke was seen removing his revolver from his pocket and descending the steps with his gun leveled at the crowd.

"Follow me!" he yelled, "in two minutes we'll have them all chased away!"

At that moment however there sprung from the crowd, which was already beginning to disperse and had no intention of reacting, a colossus of a man,

Ammazzasette,[1] who with one leap found himself in front of the youth. He ripped the gun from his hands and hurled it far into the darkness of the garden. Crossing the remaining steps with just two strides, he took in his arms Rocco's daughter, who was so terrorized that she didn't dare to move. He returned down the stairs and with a violent shove he freed Rocco from the grip of the servants. Then turning to the Italians he said loudly with a powerful voice:

"Go home! Peacefully! Immediately! Quietly!"

Once he saw his daughter in the arms of *Ammazzasette*, Rocco Sangri immediately stopped rebelling against the attendants.

No one in that moment of confusion paid any attention, but, among the discouraged and dismayed crowd that was quietly leaving the garden, there was also Massimo Chiaramonte who, having arrived with *Cecchin*, immediately took over and began instructing everyone to stay calm and politely pushed the men and women on to the road.

As soon as they saw from the balcony that the Italians were retreating, the women breathed great sighs of relief almost as if they had escaped some terrible danger and the men, except for William Fox, adjusted with a rapid motion either a tie or a jacket as if they had withstood a struggle to defend the villa from the attack of pillagers.

Adriana was immediately carried to her room and put to bed. The terrible nervous fit was followed by an exhaustion that reduced her to a rag without any strength or thoughts.

Moments later all was calm and silent around the villa. As she was returning to the parlor with the other women, Jule Rhudel said:

"It could have been worse!"

Frank Black touched his wrist numbed by the grip of *Ammazzasette*. Mrs. Miller, who was nearby and who had set her eyes on that fine figure of a young man, felt sorry for him.

"Oh! *poor boy*! Did that scoundrel hurt you!" Everyone had seen *Cecchin* and his action. As usual the giant had made quite an impression by his stature and his strength.

"But that man is frightening!"

"*My God*! What hands!" exclaimed a smiling Frank Black, "Had I held him off a bit longer he would have broken my arm."

"What do you have to say about all this, Mr. Fox?" asked John Miller.

---

1. Seven-time killer.

William Fox, who was the only one in that company who felt a sincere regret for what had taken place, responded sharply:

"Everything could have been avoided. My words would have been enough."

"But the audacity of that little girl who wanted to come all the way up here. . . ." said Helen Lheridan. The director of the factories did not let her finish:

"It was by no means audacity," he interrupted, "The Italians had no other intention but to do a kind action in their own way."

"Thank heavens for that kindness!" grumbled Frank Black as he continued to rub his wrist.

"You had no reason to pull out that pistol!" snapped William Fox, "If that Italian had broken your arm, he would have had every right to do so and I would not feel very sorry for you."

Having said his piece to those people who had become unbearable at that moment, he left the parlor to go inquire about Adriana.

The only person who during the incident had kept an impassive demeanor, and who even now as she lay stretched out on a spacious arm-chair remained extraneous to the conversation, was Rosa White.

Peter Gontrasky immediately approached the small table where different bottles of liquor had been lined up and, pouring himself a large glass of whiskey, said as he winked to Miller and Engineer Harold to join him:

"After all this emotion this is what is needed to calm one's nerves; *you know*?"

Having reached the road, the Italians stopped in small groups. Who knows how long they would have discussed the unexpected conclusion to their naïve, yet noble action, had Massimo Chiaramonte not hurried to give an explanation of the incident and, for the moment, persuaded them to go to their homes, sorrowful but resigned.

"Miss Adriana was in peril of death, and she is still gravely ill. The doctors have said that she needs complete rest . . . If before going to the villa you had asked me, I would have discouraged you."

"But why throw to the ground my little girl?" asked Rocco Sangri who had a knot in his throat and still seemed to be dreaming.

"You don't know what illness she is suffering from."

"She becomes like crazy!" *Ammazzasette* wanted to add in order to come to Massimo's aid.

"Poor thing!" murmured many affected by the scene.

The women, who still had tears in their eyes from fright and humiliation, uttered other exclamations of sympathy and painful astonishment.

"However, those men, to treat us in that way!. . . ." said Gaspare Preda who could not swallow the arrogance of the servants and the action of Frank Black, "To threaten us with a gun because we wanted to give our regards to our *little Madonna*!. . . ."

And he clenched his teeth out of anger.

"Don't say anything to anyone!" advised Massimo as they arrived in the Italian neighborhood, "just pretend that nothing happened. If there is any news I'll keep you informed."

"And where is Bruno Speri?" asked Maso Landi.

"He hasn't arrived yet," the inventor responded evasively.

Everyone parted with a heavy heart. Shortly thereafter, when the street had become calm and silent, the voice of a woman cried out from the window of a house, most likely to a friend at a window nearby:

"*The little Madonna of the Italians* does not love us any longer."

Massimo and *Ammazzasette* heard these words as they were getting into the car of the foreman—the man who had run to alert them at the house of the inventor about the demonstration by the Italians—and they felt that it was a painful but appropriate comment to the entire story, to which they would have preferred an entirely different conclusion.

Ammazzasette had been at Massimo's house that evening, because for several days, having finished his duties in the fields and the stables, he would go down to the town dying of curiosity to come and ask the inventor about their friends from San Francisco and about their research. They had learned nothing new. If the man who had come to take his supposed wife in San Francisco was truly Bruno Speri, he must have left the city without leaving any trace of himself. This was the only thing one could deduce from the whole of the circumstances.

Massimo had no longer dared to speak of his doubt that that woman was really Bruno's wife, but as much as he forced himself mentally to side with Marcella he could not explain that mystery differently. That unknown person was named Anna Speri. That she wanted Bruno there was no doubt, because her first letter was looking for him in the Rosenthal factories. At the hotel, Gigi Zanasso had recognized him from the description given to him by the landlady. The name then, that was also the name. There could then be no mistake. All this was comprehensible, justifiable. The mystery could be reconstructed perhaps to the benefit of Bruno but not on plausible grounds. What was really difficult to explain was the disappearance, escape, or hiding-place in which Bruno had hidden himself. With the others, there could be a reason, but with him, with friends, no! No matter what was the cause of his behavior in the entire matter, he should have shown up. He certainly had duties toward those people who had believed in him as in a God. Those same people who, as a result of moral and material benefits that they received, remembered him with veneration and were ready to die defending him. If anything, he needed not to leave them with the awful doubt that in that mystery there was a flaw that could send the idol into fragments.

When they were again in Massimo's small living room and had explained the incident to Marcella, *Ammazzasette*, who had kept quiet during the ride due to the presence of the factory's foreman who was at the wheel of the car, said with a tone of determination, like someone who had made an unyielding decision:

"Tomorrow morning I'm going to San Francisco."

"To do what?" asked Massimo.

"Because it seems to me that our friends down there did not search very well," responded *Cecchin*.

"What more could they have done?"

"I don't know, but in these situations there are two ways to search: there are those who search because they're sure to find something, and there are those who feel it's a lost cause."

Massimo gave *Ammazzasette* a look of astonishment. Marcella smiled but said nothing. Nana who was also sitting at the small table intent on cutting out pictures from the newspaper put down the scissors and listened.

"Explain yourself a bit more," continued the inventor who thought he had understood but could not imagine that giant capable of such subtle thinking.

"Gigi Zanasso and Carlo Rota have in their heads the bad idea that Bruno Speri is really married and that woman is his wife. And if he has still not been seen, he has on his conscience something that is not very good and he feels ashamed. And so they search, yes they search, but they say: if it's him who does not want to be found why do we have to run after him? I instead don't think that Mr. Bruno has a wife and even if tomorrow I were to hear from his own mouth: Cecchin, this is my wife! No, damn it, that's not true; he's a liar! So, I'm now searching because I'm sure that when I put my hands on the whole thing *what* will pop up is something that we were unaware of and will make us say: look at that! who could have imagined that!"

"Very good, *Ammazzasette*!" yelled Nana clapping her hands enthusiastically.

With the calm and always just intuition of children, the young girl felt herself drawn toward Bruno Speri from the first time that she saw him. She then became tenaciously fond of him. Speaking about him to her mother one day, she said:

"If I did not already have a father, I would have liked to be his child. And would you have been happy to be his wife?" Marcella's face turned a burning red color, as she squeezed to her chest the little child whispering in her hair:

"Hush! dear; one doesn't say these things."

"Why?"

Because it's pointless to think about what isn't possible, never!

Ammazzasette was happy to have the approval of the young child who for him was a miracle of intelligence. He also read in the look of Mrs. Marcella that she was of the same opinion. And this encouraged him.

"I'd like to acknowledge everything you are saying, Cecchino," Massimo muttered with a sigh, "but I must always insist: why is it that Bruno Speri doesn't come out and explain to us the mystery of that woman and her strange behavior!"

"He can't!" a convinced *Ammazzasette* replied.

"But who tells you that he can't?"

"*I* say so and that's all!"

Massimo did not dare insist because he knew his wife's opinion on this and he rightly assumed that each time he raised any doubts about Bruno Speri she would think: "Because you did it this way, you think that others are capable of doing the same thing." But he had no faith in *Ammazzasette*'s work, to the point that he didn't even ask him what he intended to do.

As she was accompanying the gigantic man to the roadside gate, she placed her hand on his shoulder, telling him in a troubled voice:

"Do all you can, Cecchino. I'm sure that you are right; it would be a crime on our part to distrust him and not do anything either to help if it is necessary or to defend him against any accusation of something that he has in no way committed."

"I'll do all that I can," replied *Ammazzasette*, "and if there is someone who is out to do such a dirty trick against him . . . Mother of God! . . . ."

He didn't entirely finish his thought, but he raised his powerful fist. If at that moment the supposed enemies of Bruno Speri had been within reach of that arm, he would have destroyed them with one blow. Nana, who was tied to her mother's apron strings, looked at him with intense admiration, almost as if he was something supernatural. In fact, the colossal figure, standing proudly erect with a threatening air, really seemed to be the god of strength.

With a little, moving voice that was full of hope, the little child said:

"*Ammazzasette*, I'll pray for you, but remember what is written in my prayer book: Do not kill!"

The innocent words of the little girl shot to the heart of the giant like a warning leaving a profound impression on him. Marcella felt her eyes tear up. In a gesture of infinite tenderness, she pressed her daughter close to her. *Ammazzasette* first fixed his boy-like eyes on the sky completely flooded by the silvery light of the moon, then he lowered them to the earth and remained a few seconds in this position: in a silent, intense prayer for Bruno Speri and for the *little Madonna of the Italians.*

Translated by Mark Pietralunga

Bohemian and Detective

❧ *Italo Stanco*

Riccia (Campobasso), Italy, December 20, 1886–New York, New York, 1954

Ettore A. Moffa, who adopted the pseudonym of Italo Stanco, and, on other occasions, that of J. Cansado (*stanco* is Italian and *cansado* Spanish for "tired"), undertook his first freelance activity in Naples, then in Florence. In 1907, he emigrated to Argentina, where he worked for the *Giornale d'Italia e dell'America del Sud* (Journal of Italy and South America). In 1909, he was in the United States. On July 23, Riccardo Cordiferro presented him at the Beraglia Hall, in New York, with the following words: "Still an adolescent, he began to contribute to the literary newspapers of Naples, revealing himself as a poet of no small significance. In Naples, with the printing houses of the Stabilmento Tipografico Tornese, he published one of his first volumes of verse, entitled *Bandiere della miseria* (Flags of Poverty). . . . He published some critical essays, entitled *La penna italiana* (The Italian Pen), in which he reviewed the principal literary productions of that time" (Cordiferro, "Italo Stanco," in *Mondo nuovo* [New World], a New York weekly of politics and art, directed by Italo Stanco). Italo Stanco was, in sum, a true man of letters; his pseudonym is emblematic, and his Neapolitan critical essays, especially *La penna italiana* (whose complete title includes the word *Paralipòmeni*), reveal tastes and knowledge far from banal. In New York, he founded the review, *Maga Arte*, on art and criticism, and from 1916 to 1928, he was subeditor of the *Follia*. From 1925 to 1938, he was a reporter, then subeditor of the *Corriere d'America*. In the 1950s, he was still active as director of the *Follia of New York*, and member of the Circolo di Union Square, a sodality that revolved about the sculptor Onorio Ruotolo, and published a weekly review, *Divagando*, in which the poets Antonio Calitri and Pietro Greco took part. Between 1952 and 1954, it published a hundred or so installments under a rubric entitled, "Questo è il mondo folle and tondo" (This is the mad round world). In 1958, Ruotolo dedicated to him the poem "Notturno di rimembranze" (Nocturne of Memories).

Stanco's production was vast and varied: novels, theatrical works, and translations from Spanish, English, and French, among others, translations of Alarcón, the *Sibylle* of Mirabeau, and various popular narrators. In examining Stanco's production, Martino Marazzi identified four of his American novels in volumes: *Dopo la colpa* (After the Fall, 1913); *Il diavolo biondo* (The Blonde Devil, 1916); *Sull'Oceano* (On the Ocean, 1922, similar to the pathetic and moralistic stories of E. De Amicis, from whom Stanco borrowed the title of the book. But this story treats of a crime); *L'amica del kaiser* (The Kaiser's Lady Friend, 1925). From Marazzi's examination emerge five other novels, published only in *Follia* and *Corriere d'America*: *Il re della pampa* (The King of the Pampas, 1911); *Il nemico del bene* (The Enemy of the Good, 1914–15); *I rettili d'oro* (The Golden Reptiles, 1915–17, reprinted in 1952–53, in *Divagando* (Wandering); *Le piovre di New York* (The Leeches of New York, 1925–26); and *Reginetta di fuoco* (Little Queen of Fire, 1931). Finally, there are numerous novellas, *allegretti* (short comic novels), poetry, and dramaturgic works.

Italo Stanco tended to simplify the popular novel with a colonial background, concentrating the plots in a more modern sense, as if after the models of popular naturalism, represented by Sue, Zola, Mastriani, and Invernizio. He adopted the narrative coming into fashion at the beginning of the twentieth century, represented by Guido da Verona, Pitigrilli, Zuccoli, and the like. His plots, however, abused the situations typical of Ciambelli: pursued girls, disappearances and recognitions, as well as noticeable strokes of theater, like the apparitions of Petrosino in the novel *Il diavolo biondo*. The narration becomes drier and tighter, more observant; it makes more frequent and decisive incursions into the gilded world of the rich and famous, without losing sight of the pertinent subject, on one side, of the events and environments of the emigration, and on the other, of contemporary events. *L'amica del kaiser*, for example, tells an improbable story of German espionage in Manhattan during the First World War; the intrigues of the central powers are foiled by the good Italian American detective. The novel contains an interesting psychological novelty: the happy political ending does not afford an equal fate for the protagonist, who commits suicide for the love of the perfidious spy (who is also of Italian origin). This unfortunate turn is the sign of a certain impartiality and also a pessimistic vision of the destiny of the Italian Americans, a bent of mind that is almost Stanco's constant signature. In reference to his style, according to the poet Joseph Tusiani, who knew him and visited him frequently in the 1950s, "his eloquence . . . was his unquestionable point of advantage."

Stanco's eloquence and pessimism are amply illustrated, in particular, in *Diavolo biondo*. The protagonist of the book is an Italian American detective, James Forley, born in Naples, with the name of Giacomo Forlì, a resident of the Bronx with his young daughter Laurina, the governess nurse Giacinta, and Fox the dog. Forley is dependent upon the celebrated Petrosino. The "Black Hand" abducts Laurina. Orchestrating the abduction is the "blond devil," Lady Ryton, wife of an English baronet, who in New York has recast himself as an influential republican politician. In reality, the woman is none other than the baroness from Palermo, Livia Iamicelli. Years before (in the novel, these circumstances are introduced via a long flashback), in a nocturnal duel, James had killed her fiancé, his rival in love. Livia accepted him and fled with him, then gave birth to Laurina. In the course of the search to recover Laurina, James becomes entrapped in a lunatic asylum of Brooklyn by a very wicked German psychiatrist; Petrosino enters the scene to save him, and in a tragic crescendo, James succeeds in liberating himself from the grasp of Lady Ryton's accomplices. A dramatic recognition scene ensues as mother and child discover their respective identities. The finale is a hecatomb: Laurina is killed, and in sorrow, her young suitor Anthony commits suicide. James also dies, falling from the Harlem Bridge, after having, in his turn, killed his daughter's assassin. Triumphant, beautiful and perverse, she is, naturally, "the blond devil."

ESSENTIAL BIBLIOGRAPHY

Flamma 1936; Marazzi 2001, 24–26; Schiavo 1938; Stanco 1916, 43–47, 55–61; Tusiani 1988, 202ff., 334ff.

∾

One evening, soon after Lucio Fini had returned to his small, monastic room on 106th Street, his friend Claudio came in, much less talkative and cheerful than usual. He had, instead, a serious and contrite look, and he appeared unusually worried. He carried a suitcase, and he flung it in a corner.

"Ah, you're here? A little late, if you haven't already had dinner. The waiters have already cleared the cafeteria; and now, as you can see, they are in the smoking parlor. Can I offer you something?" After saying this the sybarite, with comical seriousness, offered the sculptor a cigarette stub selected from the many that he had in a small tray.

"They are *barba di Sultano*,[1] expressly imported for my private use."

Claudio took the butt, sat down and heaved a melancholic sigh.

"Well then, is it the evening for a *barba di Sultano*?"

"As you see. But what happened to you? It looks like you've returned from having swallowed Aristotle with all his peripatetic treatises."

"It's nothing. You know that I still owed two months rent to my landlady. . . ."

"And so?"

"That shrew, who up to a few days ago promised to be patient, today made me put all my furniture on the street."

"Did you really say your furniture?"

"Don't joke around. I found my apartment empty . . . My poor statues are confined in a basement. What a disaster!"

"And now you've come to ask me to put you up?"

"More or less."

The sybarite pulled a notebook out of his pocket and began to consult it, while he muttered some incomprehensible words between his teeth.

"Very well!" he then added, "I'm happy to have you as my guest, at least for three days. After that, we'll both need to leave this place. My time expires Friday morning at dawn."

"Are you also in arrears?"

"The question is unworthy of you. But we have three days ahead of us and the world belongs to us. I'll have your rooms prepared, and I'll put at your service the most beautiful slaves of my harem. . . ."

Who were those two dear friends who mocked their limited means and made jokes about their own hunger? We have already introduced them to our readers: two artists, a sculptor and a painter. The life of young artists, one knows, is always that of the classic *Bohème* and our friends succeeded in repeating the deeds of the Henry Murger heroes even in such a recalcitrant society as that of America. After their first disappointments and driven by an adventurous spirit, they had left Italy. Claudio Sparta came from a wealthy family in Naples, whose bosom he could have returned to, if his most dear friends and also the shame of returning as a prodigal son had not kept him bound for New York. Lucio Fini had no one, except for an ex-fiancée who had been unfaithful to him and whom he had, in a fit of jealousy, injured on her forehead by throwing a porcelain palette at her. Consequently, a punishment of six months in prison was waiting for him. Both of them had talent, or rather genius, and in New York both could have

---

1. Sultan's beard.

earned enough to live in comfort had they consented to clip the wings of their art within the walls of a so-called artistic workshop. They did their best to seek commissions, and often, by reproducing the noble portrait of a nouveau riche *grossiere* or of an austere *housekeeper*, they resolved life's problem. They created meanwhile wonderful works, awaiting a patron who would enable them to exhibit them. Young, bold, full of energy, equipped with an acute insight and great observation, they completed, without having really meant to, a profound study of the cosmopolitan environment in which they lived.

We have already seen how a spirit of observation led them to discover at times secrets to which they then committed themselves, with their generous carelessness—in very risky ventures.

"By the way," Lucio asked his friend, "would you like to keep me from offering you dinner?"

"The truth is that I have not yet had the time to go to a *restaurant*. Tonight they'll wait for me in vain at the *Martin*."

"Do you have much of an appetite?"

"For several hours, it has yielded its place to its venerable mother, hunger."

"Then we ought to consult our ledger," added Lucio, emptying his pockets. "Between my moveable and immoveable property I have nineteen cents."

"You're as rich as Croesus; I barely have three cents."

"Twenty-two in all, a fortune that we need to spend with good sense. I'll prepare the *menu*, and you go shopping."

"Remember to include among our pressing purchases some wood to throw in that old stove. In these days you can't live any more. It's as cold as winter."

"And to say that we are just at the end of January!"

The painter sat at a small table full of books, paintings, paint brushes, and boxes, and took a piece of paper and began to reflect. After ten minutes of mature reflections he gave his friend the following:

Menu
Assorted hors-d'oeuvre consisting of a salted anchovy, 2 cents.
Meat pie, 5 cents.
Poached egg in the Mercy of God, 3 cents.
Vegetable cheese, 2½ cents.
Horse salami, 2½ cents.
Fresh fruit, 1 cent.
Dessert, 1 cent.
Bread, 2 cents.

Omega Cigarettes, 1 cent.
Rosewood to feed the heating stoves, 2 cents.
Total $0.22.

Claudio read the *menu* and let out in an enthusiastic cry.

"Great! We'll dine like two hedonists. Lucullus, Vitellius, Sardanapalus, and other similar predecessors of ours would shake with envy in their tombs."

"Cleopatra did not offer any better to her friend Anthony," the painter added seriously. "Now go and spend. Here is the fortune, be judicious. On the corner, there is an Italian *restaurant* that gives decent portions of boiled meat for five cents. In the meantime, I'll prepare the table."

Claudio crushed the wide old hat on his head and headed toward the exit. But as he was opening the door, he found himself face to face with a gentleman who was about to enter.

"Doesn't Mr. Fini live here?" he said in perfect Italian.

"Yes."

"A painter?"

"Yes. . . ."

Left alone Lucio got busy clearing the room, piling up carelessly the paintings, palettes, and his clothing; he then stopped in front of the mirror and gave quick primping to his clothes.

It must have been around eleven o'clock.

"It's time to call the little ones," he said to himself "They're probably back from the moving-picture and the snail at this hour has probably gone to bed."

He went out on the landing, where there where three apartment doors, and softly tapped on one of them. The door opened almost immediately, and one of the pretty young girls appeared in the room.

"Were you waiting for me, Miss Maria?" asked the artist, greeting her.

"I had the vague feeling that you might come to call on us."

"Is your daddy sleeping?"

"He's dead drunk. Is there a reception this evening?"

"Actually a gala event. The guests are already crowding the rooms, and the dancing is heating up. Can you hear this intoxicating Strauss waltz."

The girl pretended to listen: then she burst into laughter.

"Then we'll be right over, Mr. Lucio."

"I'll grant you a half-hour, Miss."

Maria and Luisa Monte were two sisters who had recently arrived in America with their father, a good-for-nothing of the first rank, whose golden dream was to live exploiting his daughters. We're not sure how he had planned to exploit them; he was, however, content that they, through their own spontaneous choice, were music-hall singers in the Italian vaudeville. They earned fairly well, and the honest parent had enough money to keep him on good terms with the nearby bar and cigar store. Living in the same house, it was natural that a very warm friendship should develop between the two girls and the painter, who then introduced them to the entire group of penniless artists. There was, however, nothing illicit in their friendship: the two sisters were not exactly little nuns, but they had solid principles and, while staying out all night sometimes in the merry company of young men, they knew how to set boundaries to their . . . generosity.

While Lucio was preparing the room for the guests, Claudio had brought the shopping list to the closest "restaurant," ordering to send everything to the address indicated on the piece of paper. He then headed toward 106th Street, where Betty, a model with whom he was said to be a bit enamored, lived. He urged her to get dressed and to come to Lucio's house.

The night was dark and foggy, but not too cold. The passersby were becoming scarce and some stores were already closing. Claudio didn't have the habit of turning around, so he didn't realize that a man was shadowing him from the time he left the house. That man was wearing a black overcoat with a collar so wide that when raised it covered his entire face. It seemed he had only an interest in following our young friend. Nevertheless, he kept very close to him and often he drew so close that he almost grazed him with his elbow. In returning from Betty's house, Claudio turned toward Pleasant Ave, quickening his pace as the dampness was penetrating his bones.

He had arrived in front of a miserable looking bar when the stick he was carrying under his arm was ripped from him and an imperious voice whispered in his ear: "Not a word, or you're dead!"

He turned quickly and found himself before a man of imposing stature, whose face was covered by the wide collar of his overcoat. A gun glittered in the hands of the attacker. Claudio stopped, more surprised than frightened. However, as he saw several people standing in front of the above-mentioned bar, he did not heed the threat and let out a shout that the man drove back down his throat grabbing his head and shutting his mouth with a hand that felt like lead.

The artist was encouraged when he saw two men running. A logical but vain hope! His surprise had no more limits, when the two new arrivals, instead of defending him, grabbed him by the arms and dragged him into the bar through a little door on which was written: Family Entrance. He found himself in a very spacious room, saturated with smoke and alcohol. It was filled with men and women. Some were intent on gambling, others were drinking away, joking around obscenely with a drunken woman, while others were performing an unruly and obscene dance. Claudio realized that he had fallen into a den of thieves, and he considered himself good as done for.

"And all this for fifty dollars!" he was thinking sadly, since he believed those people had known what he had in his wallet. The three accomplices pushed the artist into a semi-dark small room in which there were stacked cases of empty bottles. Then the man with the raised collar said:

"Raise your arms. You better obey! A person of your intelligence knows that in certain cases it's better to obey."

"You're a funny guy," Claudio answered, raising his arms, "and you talk like a Salamanca lawyer."

The honorable man looked at him, not knowing whether he had been paid a compliment or insulted: then he shrugged his shoulders and did a quick but thorough search of the young man's pockets. He seized the wallet and hurried off.

"You're free," he said returning after a few minutes and handing over the wallet to the artist. "Leave and, if you value your life, don't tell anyone about your adventure."

"Sir," Claudio said, as he did his best to adjust his clothes, "you ruined our party. In return, you enabled me to experience the emotion of a millionaire and for that I am grateful. I won't ask your name because the secret of the office prohibits you from revealing it. I am Claudio Sparta, sculptor, willing also to sculpt you, if tomorrow you become a famous bandit. I'm an admirer of Cartouche."

This said he left, humming as he crossed the room crowded with people who were drunk on crime, wine, and lust. A beautiful, wild-looking girl with tousled hair and disheveled clothes, stopped him throwing herself around his neck:

"Hello, sweetheart, how did the doctor find you?"

"Fifty dollars of fever, my girl," the artist replied without batting an eye. "Ten minutes ago I would have offered you a bottle of champagne; now all I can offer you is a kiss."

"Well, I'll take it at that" the girl replied, offering him her lips, which still had the fresh scent of adolescence.

A drunken voice called the girl:

"Come on, come on! Cut that out!"

Once on the street, Claudio breathed deeply, quickening his pace as he turned the corner. But it was his fate that he was to go from one surprise to another. He had not taken ten steps, when, from a shadow cast by a cart, a man jumped out and appeared in front of him.

"Again!" said this time the artist, in amazement. "I'm not fond of encores. What do you want?"

The unknown man seemed, by his face and clothing, one of those vagrants for whom life passes solely and uniquely in the adoration of whiskey.

"I don't have anything, not even one cent!" Claudio added, in English.

"I don't want anything," answered the other man in perfect Italian. "Don't you know me?"

"I don't have that honor, nor do I regret it."

The other leaned into his ear.

"I'm Sergeant Petrosino and I'm on a trail."

"For Heaven's Sake! Made up like that? You've outdone any famous actor."

"Are there many people in that bar?" the brave Italian policeman pressed him, for it was indeed he.

"Lots."

"Did anything strike you?"

"Yes; a stink of whiskey to make the stomach of a hippopotamus turn."

"I don't mean that. Was there any meeting going on?"

"I don't believe so, at least not in the room where I was taken. Men and women were drinking and carousing."

"That's enough: thanks and good night."

"Good night."

Claudio was about to leave when Petrosino called him back and abruptly grabbed him by the arm and began to laugh crudely, writhing and every now and then slapping the young man's stomach.

"Now what's gotten you?" our friend exclaimed, as he was taken by surprise.

The other, with the skill of a ventriloquist, said, while he continued roaring with laughter: "We're being watched. In a loud voice, tell me to go home and sleep it off."

"Yes, dear friend, she's a fine figure . . . very nice girl!" The policeman continued in a tipsy voice. "I want her . . . *yes*, I want to marry her and when I have married her, yes, good bye!"

"You're dead drunk!" Claudio said, who understood the game perfectly.

A well-dressed young man had stopped under a street lamp, six steps away and appeared intent on lighting a rebellious cigar.

"Me drunk? No, dear I drank only eleven glasses, yes . . . strange, really only eleven . . . She says yes, mama no . . . Ah! Ah! Is mother needed? Must I marry the old lady too? Ah! Ah! . . ."

While the detective acted out this scene, with such art to make the most expert artist turn pale, he had found a way to say to Claudio in a very low voice:

"Go home and be careful. I don't know for what reason, but you've been followed for several nights, actually for several days. Meanwhile, speak naturally, treating me like a drunk."

"Go to sleep!" yelled Claudio, laughing too, and freeing himself from the grasp of the false drunk. "You've got a tremendous crush. If the girl were to see you like this she would no longer think about marrying you. Good night, John!"

"Well, good night, dear! But I tell you that it would be nice . . . No . . . No . . . marry the old lady! Ah! Ah! Ah!"

In the shade of the old apple tree
For the love in your eyes I can see
And the paint on your face
Is a perfectly disgrace.

The cop went off, humming the crude song and stopping from time to time to ponder the stars.

The well-dressed young man had finally lit the cigar and, passing near the drunk, without even looking at him, began shadowing Claudio.

Translated by Mark Pietralunga

Brunori's Fortune

Ernesto Valentini

On October 2, 1912, a pharmacist in the Bronx, Vito Pittaro, received a threatening letter from a criminal organization that designated itself "The Iron Hand." The letter demanded a good sum of money in exchange for the possibility of his continuing his business tranquilly. Pittaro, whose shop was the place for the gathering of a small crowd of Italians in the neighborhood, confided in some of them, drawing diverse impressions and reactions. Immediately, they created two factions: the first was decidedly in favor of telling all to the police and asking for protection; the second was oriented instead toward a more expeditious and private solution of the problem. Immediately, Pittaro began to nurture some suspicion of the most convinced supporters of the second hypothesis: the doctor Nicola Brunori and the veterinarians Giulio Cavazzi and Giuseppe Gaspari Marchese.

Between equivocations and suspicions, in the following days, other threatening letters reached Pittaro, Brunori, and Cavazzi. Gaspari offered to mediate between the blackmailed and the criminals, using certain of his old acquaintances. He would receive sums of money from his friends and use it to pay old debts. Days passed, exacerbating strong tensions in the group, especially between Pittaro and Brunori. At the end, Pittaro would have the police arrest Gaspari, Cavazzi, and Brunori.

The "blackmail of the three doctors" was a cause célèbre in the Italian colony of New York. Brunori, in particular, was a highly esteemed person, and in support of him, a committee was quickly formed, which even marshaled libertarian organizations, like the Circolo Ferrer and the Circolo Pensiero ed Azione, as well as a notorious prominent personality such as Andrea Ciofalo, the anarchist. In 1917, Ciofalo would flee to Mexico with Sacco and Vanzetti; in 1919 he would be arrested, and still a fugitive, flee from forced deportation to Italy, to then return clandestinely to America in the twenties and become the principal collaborator, with Raffaele Schiavina, in the undertaking of the newspaper, *L'Adunata dei Refrattari* (Meeting of the Unwilling), until the 1960s.

Freed on bail, Brunori, however, was condemned in the course of the trial, which found the three accused guilty of attempted extortion. Brunori remained in prison—in Sing Sing, Auburn, and then Comstock—from July 7, 1913 to November 6, 1916. Released from prison, he found old and new solidarity—among others, the support and protection of lawyer and future judge Salvatore Cotillo.

In 1924, in Turin, the lawyer Ernesto Valentini, a journalist for the *Bolletino della Sera* (a newspaper that was one of the few that openly sided with Brunori), published the detailed story of the celebrated case, entitled "Il Ricatto" (The Blackmail), providing it with a significant subtitle: "Eccola, la Giustizia!" (Behold, Justice!). The book, a curious pastiche mixing passages of narrative and trial documents, chronicles, and digressions, is one of the most characteristic results of a colonial literature that crossed personal invective with polemics, originating in the journalistic environment, and occupying itself with the most notorious cases. Valentini, who has no doubt of Brunori's and Cavazzi's innocence, describes the perverse mechanism by which the two were imprisoned. In reality, the procedure was a "parody of the judicial process" (227), during which the judge, Channon Press, did not hesitate to lash out against a person as popular as Brunori, in the prospect of pursuing his own career. (Press coveted the chair of the district attorney for the Bronx, a position that had been instituted in 1912 and was still vacant.) Press, says Valentini, was, in any case, a Republican, like Pittaro, and he expected electoral help from the Republicans. But the spider's web is more complicated and comprises an entire network of personal interests that collide with those of Brunori and Cavazzi, to whom, in addition, the documents that might have helped prove their complete innocence, were never returned. Instead, they inexplicably made their way into the hands of the only guilty one, Gaspari.

The intentions of Valentini were naturally polemical; his big volume, in eight parts, attempted to introduce a vein of disquiet concerning the functioning of American justice. But what most significantly strikes the reader is the fresco that emerges of the old Italian Bronx, of its personages, of the customs of the community, of the gossip its people engaged in. There are felicitous pages of narrative. These pages are more sincere; the rhetorical vein of the author finds a congenial setting to be more expressive, as in the pages published here, which reproduce the profile of the three doctors, protagonists of the story.

Little is known of Valentini. In the 1920s, it was he who published *Zarathustra*, a review of high cultural profile, oriented to the left, of which, however, there is no trace in bibliographies or archives. In that same period, he contributed actively to *Martello*, edited by Carlo Tresca. Giuseppe Zappulla remembers that in 1936, he worked together with him on a WPA project on Ellis Island, and that he did not live long.

ESSENTIAL BIBLIOGRAPHY

Marazzi 2001, 34; testimony of Joseph Zappulla in *La Gumina* 1979; Valentini 1924, 122–124, 126–132.

Doctor Brunori was fortunate. The two rooms of the small clinic were full of people from the early morning hours. In one room the patients waited their turn in order to be examined and were cared for in the other.

The women, especially, adored the young doctor who showed such a patient interest in the pains of those bodies tormented by illnesses, by the brutality of men, or by beastly housework.

Men found him kind; above all, conscientious. They became his friends. They confided in him. Despite his being from Northern Italy, you could talk to him like a brother and he had no airs, the workers from the South used to say, as they were always suspicious and timid toward northerners.

Many felt in that physician the sweet, brotherly spirit of a missionary, who, what's more, asked for modest fees, the lowest possible. When he sensed that someone was poor, he refused payment in a way that would not humiliate that person.

In this way, Brunori began his productive professional life, at 28 years of age and with a high sense of righteousness.

Pittaro, naturally, spread the word as much as possible of the doctor's clinical value and rare altruism. But, at the same time, he balanced, up to the American usurer's standard, the cost of care, by increasing the price of the prescriptions in relation to what Brunori would reduce the cost of the visits. When Brunori was convinced of this, he had at first a sense of disgust, which he repressed.

But even at 50 cents a visit, thanks to his very hard work, Brunori realized great sums of money that in Italy he would have only dreamed of, making him quite satisfied with his life.

However, Brunori's young wife was not happy.

Was this the much-praised America? This the country in which she would have found the longed–for happiness?

When she was leaving Florence, with her heart full of romantic dreams, she used to say to her husband: Who knows what excitement we'll experience over there when we encounter an Italian?

Instead the first house in which they had found shelter was that of a peasant-woman from the province of Benevento, who had them eat in the kitchen. In the apartment on Morris Avenue, surrounded by crude immigrants, the furnishings barely met the most elementary needs. It was a decline in conditions, a reduction that mortified her. During the first days, when Brunori was not practicing, or was beginning to practice medicine, Signora Isolina was curious and amazed as she wandered the streets of New York with her husband. But the puzzling city, full of surprises and incomprehensible signs, struck her as alien and hostile. It seemed to reject her; she felt it hopeless to create for herself, in a land so different, an environment and a nest. Where to live? With whom? How to place oneself among those millions of beings, who whirled about blindly and deafly through the streets, like swarms of elusive birds?

She resigned herself to forgo New York and to enclose herself in the small Italian section of Morris Avenue. She saw herself surrounded only by laborers and small store-keepers from Abruzzo, Campania, Basilicata, Sicily, and Calabria. Good people whose language she did not understand and who barely understood her. With them all community of thought and life was absurd.

The delicately refined Signora Isolina felt as foreign to those Italians from the South as she did to the Americans of Madison Avenue.

Now the profound difference of character and language between the Italians from the ancient kingdom of Naples, and those from the northern regions, from the Marche to extreme Piedmont, is more striking in America than in Italy and constitutes an essential element for the study and explanation of the events that we are about to narrate. . . .

In the typically southern circle of the pharmacy, Brunori and Cavazzi made up the small component from northern Italy.

Among Pittaro, Villamena, Alliegro, Telesca and the two doctors, there prevailed the language of business, the conventional one for social formalities; or rather, the language of everyday chatter; however, the incomprehension between the feelings of one group and that of the other was profound. They thought differently, even when they were in agreement. The mind of the southerners, without even recognizing this difference that was due to the automatic force of the above-mentioned history, remained latently hostile toward the two northerners. It was one of those acrimonious hostilities toward one's fellow man that lies at the core of the human animal.

After many months, Signora Isolina was becoming used to the vulgarity of their dialect and to the exuberance of their naïve and obsequious ways, which were almost servile; however, she was unable to mix with those people, nor to make any friendships with them.

Brunori, on the other hand, allowed himself to be more and more carried away by a professional fever. When was he home? Never. For Signora Isolina, the days were slow and gloomy, as she spent them in the solitude of those small, joyless rooms.

And from a deep past, the memories began to emerge. What memories? Especially one: the expectation of happiness that had changed its direction as the years passed, and had not yet arrived.

Since they were unable to start a family, Brunori's young wife declared that nature had not made her for the home, the primordial nest of the races, but for something quite different. And in the physical and spiritual powers of her being, she explored what exactly was that mission to which she was destined.

Meanwhile, exhausted by the struggle against the nothingness of her existence and overwhelmed by an unconquerable, nostalgic malaise, she wanted to return to Italy. There were no financial obstacles because Doctor Brunori had become the most popular Italian doctor on Morris Avenue. Now he only had time for the sick and for the study of scientific progress.

He was also active in the protestant religious movement as well as in the labor unrest of the Italian American workers, where he gave speeches and doctrinal lectures.

Signora Isolina went to Italy and remained there a few months. Even there she wasn't happy. Where then was her source of support? Where, with the force of intelligent beauty enclosed in that feminine being, would she realize her destiny?

She returned to New York with her sister, who filled the emptiness of the little house on Morris Avenue.

She found the doctor even more absorbed in his work. He studied and was now going to the hospitals in the Bronx. Favor, popularity, and high esteem surrounded his person with a crown of superiority that foreshadowed the flattering caresses of fame.

Who in the Bronx and in all of New York ignored Doctor Brunori, a man of science, a generous physician, and an ideal champion of the proletariat's demands? The missionary had been overwhelmed by the clinic.

Pittaro's pharmacy remained his center of action.

But he, now, oppressed the gang of regulars at the pharmacy and its proprietor with the weight of success and with that of a developed and nourished mind.

It's not true that the human vermin-heap admires the man who is gifted with human qualities. He is not wanted. A highly gifted person, who does not join to these qualities an energetic and combative spirit, is crushed precisely by these qualities.

The world belongs to the mediocre, better yet to the nothings, who, in the struggle for existence, do not alert or awaken the powers of defense.

And so Brunori, as he rose in fortune, was eyed suspiciously by invisible enemies, embittered by envy: this social cancer that so easily attacks the Italians.

Then, one day, there penetrated menacingly from the windows into Signora Isolina's room vague rumors of the gallant adventures of her husband the doctor, whose sweetness charmed the women who trusted in him with loose abandon. This is natural. Just as there are no secrets of the soul for one's father confessor, so there exist no veils for the physician.

Sometimes he pretended not to understand. This reaction was the consequence of a residue in his spirit of that sexual religious lie that imposes a monogamy condemned by nature and violated unanimously by men.

But other times, when the blood of his thirty years heated up, how could he resist the allure of a first embrace that more than once was the last?

A duty of faithfulness? Ridiculous.

When one opens the book of love to the long and hefty chapter on marriage, at only eighteen years of age, it's not possible, unless one dies, to read for one's entire life that one page, without improvising.

The doctor's enemies told, among other things, and had it repeated by the newspapers as well, during the trial, of an hysterical woman who, having been struck by a religious obsession, confessed her sin of love with Brunori, as a form of atonement to her husband who had her then placed under the care of a psychiatrist.

These rumors, made bitter by products of success, led Signora Isolina to a definitive decision.

Despite being hurt in the depths of her heart, she did not get angry. She looked in the mirror, and at the splendor of her pure beauty, and just pitied the decadence of Brunori's taste.

Beauty, which triggers the sparks of love but does not have the strength to keep it burning in eternity, becomes almost dead for a man who has exhausted the magnetism that it had charged. Love, which novelists have wanted to idealize melodramatically, is nothing but a physiological function, subject to inevitable physioelectrical laws. From the adulteration of this sweet instinct is derived an intolerable moral and age-old, tedious literature. Why doesn't there exist a novel or a morality of digestive functions?

"Well then, let's do this," Signora Isolina said to Brunori that day, "I'll devote myself to art. Music, singing, my beautiful voice, the lyrical reproduction of passions, perhaps glory, certainly financial independence and freedom. Oh! This is what I need. I'm asking you. Help me study."

It was settled. They looked for singing teachers. In New York one could choose from among barbers, amateur mandolin players, shoemakers, guitar players, has-been singers, and even among the capable and intelligent who studied music in Italian, French, and American conservatories. Who is the Italian who has any doubts that he knows how to sing or is able to teach singing?

For Signora Isolina the mirage of art meant the reblossoming of life. The past was destroyed. Illusions were reborn, with the wonder of the unknown. To aim toward an imagined and desired goal is to live. It is to feel oneself happy, if that happiness consists of waiting for something nonexistent, the only happiness that is, after all, real.

However, having those singing teachers in the home irritated Brunori. Moreover, they were so mediocre. Mrs. Brunori, who aspired toward the pinnacle of art, needed an excellent school; and it would do her well to breathe the living environment of music. Therefore, it was better for her to continue her studies with the great teachers in Italy. With joy in her heart and her mind set on her dreams, she then sailed off for the third time from New York without regrets and without turning back.

She studied at first in Parma, guided by a cousin violinist of great prestige. Then no less to the world's center of canorous voices, to a Milan of musical opportunities, whence one goes onto the stages of renowned theatres.

With Mrs. Brunori's departure, how many rumors were set off in Pittaro's pharmacy, where every event sparked a foul stream of friendly gossip among the regulars!

This did not keep the companions from their evening conversations, their card games, their festival dinners at the "Criterio," their group excursions in the intimacy of long-time friends.

Deodato Villamena, as interpreter of the Court and a man devoted to politics, considered himself a person of influence due to his many acquaintances.

It was September of 1911. And in the early days of the month, at the Dock on 34th Street, one of the old steamers of the Italian General Navigation, the *Duca degli Abbruzzi*, had anchored.

The master of the house, Mr. Perfetti, asked Villamena, his old friend, if it was possible for him and the other officials of the steamer to visit the famous prison of Sing Sing.

Why not? Villamena knew Kennedy, the then-director of the prison. He received permission.

He spoke about it at the pharmacy, which inspired his friends to want to take advantage of the opportunity. In fact, on a warm, autumn morning, the group, led by Villamena, along with Perfetti, the officials of the steamer, Cavazzi, Brunori, Pittaro, and Gaspari, arrived at the gloomy gates, where murderers are killed and where freedom is suppressed not only for those who commit crimes but also for those who do not commit them.

Villamena introduced the visitors, who were then given a tour of this environment of redemption and social revenge, with its cells, corridors, workshops, recreation areas, library, chapel, infirmary, administrative offices, and finally the bleak death chamber, where, between the silent walls of horror, there dominates the electric chair. Here one fulfills the ferocious wish of salaried judges, who order, between one meal and another, the suppression of life with the mechanical regularity of a phonograph.

Brunori thought: It's here where two respectable executioners, who are paid a salary that in other circumstances would be called a contract for a hit man, shatter the lives of those unknown to them and kill with the passive indifference of bureaucratic routine.

Murder as a result of hate and violence is a vital instinct in us and in all organized beings. Like all forces of nature, even the most sinister, it has something great, the greatness of fatality. The artificial and irrational murder of the law is nothing more than its revolting imitation.

Cavazzi, instead, had a childishly bizarre idea.

He wanted to sit in the electric chair, and strap on his head the metal cap of the condemned.

No one laughed.

Upon their return to New York from Sing Sing, still distraught, the group visited the library on 42nd Street. The walls, not the books.

Then on board the *Duca degli Abruzzi* they were served an Italian meal with savory food and sparkling wines. At the end, the officials remained on the steamer. Instead, the guests, lead by Villamena, having crossed the immense dock crowded with cases of macaroni and cheese, exited into the boundless darkness of 34th Street, broken at intervals by the rays of the electric lamps.

A voice proposed:

"Let's go pay a visit to Madame Lenon, who is here on Seventh Avenue."

The hospitable house opened itself up. Two women wearing low-necked dresses were waiting, smoking cigarettes with their legs crossed.

Madame Lenon, the hostess of the house, introduced Alma, a very young, beautiful creature, with perfect features. She had languid and tired eyes due to her nighttime excesses. She was a running fire of lovable playfulness.

Villamena did some exhibitions: the metal cap, the insignia of the performer's officialness and anything else that could demonstrate his strength as a man and official: he laughed coarsely.

Excited by that angel's face tainted by lust, Gaspari pounced on the young woman with spasmodic frenzy.

He led her to a dark corner of the room, where he spoke to her with burning emotion, while his friends, winking, surrounded Madame Lenon, who explained to them how the young woman could care less about men, whom she found dull and brutish. Madame Lenon then added that ten men were not worth one of Alma's caresses.

Vito Pittaro, foreseeing that at the end of those provocative conversations there might emerge the obligation of a payment, kept quiet and to himself in order not to incur any charges.

After that evening, Gaspari remained so possessed by the vision of that girl that he had to see her the next day, and then again, until he decided to deliver her from the tutelage of Madame Lenon, so that he alone would care for her existence and upbringing.

From here began the financial complications that then ended in blackmail.

Translated by Mark Pietralunga

Hold Up!

ꙮ *Eugenio Camillo Branchi*

Genoa, Italy, 1883–1962

Eugenio Camillo Branchi was a journalist, a contributor to the *Corriere della Sera,* for which he went on a mission to the military operations in Tripolitania, but he was expelled in 1912, for entering prohibited territory without authorization. Shortly before the war he attempted a journey around the world, which he interrupted in Lima, Peru, because he had contracted a tropical disease and because of the looming conflict in Europe. At the beginning of 1915, he was a second in a duel for the anarchist lawyer Merlino, who had challenged the then-director of the *Popolo d'Italia*, Benito Mussolini. Branchi told the story in a long article in the Fascist journal *Carroccio* (named for an ancient Italian war carriage) of New York, in December 1927. After serving as a navy officer during the First World War, between 1924 and 1927 he taught Romance languages and literature at the College of William and Mary, in Williamsburg, Virginia. From 1928 until 1936 at least, he was the secretary of the Italian Chamber of Commerce in San Francisco and taught at the University of San Francisco. In 1950, he moved to Santiago, Chile, but at the end of that year, he returned to Italy with his wife, passing through New York. In 1956, he was made Commander of the Order of the Star of Italy.

Branchi was a globetrotter who wrote and published substantially. His principal Italian American contribution is the book, *Dagoes, Novelle Transatlantiche,* published in Bologna in 1927, but already printed in part in *Carroccio*. The stories were written on transatlantic liners carrying him from France to the United States and from the Caribbean Sea to Rio de la Plata and to New Orleans, as well as on trains in Mexico and even small boats to the Chilean island of Juan Fernández.

The notes on the dates of the stories contribute to creating the idea of a cosmo-politan author, who, in presenting *Dagoes*, affirms that he "interrupted his rela-tions with Italian," in consequence of the continuous voyages, which in some twenty years, took him almost into the regions of the whole world. "But I have since been purged and purified from the influences and from imitations. . . . A cosmopolitan mentality is forged within me, and I have discerned perfection in three qualities, with the accent on *à: 'brevità, semplicità, originalità.'*"

In reality, the genre of the "transatlantic novel" was taking a new shape, and Branchi figured as a popular narrator, not much more sophisticated than Ciam-belli or Pallavicini. He, too, was drawn into the hard lot of poor immigrants. For the rest, as programmatically indicated by the title of the book, there are descrip-tions of certain worldly splendors in gilded environments that hide vices and ex-cessive profits and comforts: a little of all the ingredients, in sum, of the popular narrative of the worlds of the migration, inevitably interested in dramatically de-picting the extremes of the rich in contrast to those of the indigent.

Branchi, who was a good friend of Giovanni Ermenegildo Schiavo, one of the first and most productive historians of the Italian American experience, published a series of articles and pamphlets on the Italian presence in America, among which, *Dante e la scoperta d'America* (Dante and the Discovery of America; Val-paraiso 1921); *Il primato degli italiani nella storia e nella civiltà americana. Brevia-rio degli italiani in America* (The Preeminence of Italians in American History and Civilization: A Reference Guide of Italians in America; Bologna 1925); *Memoirs of the Life and Voyages of Doctor Philip Mazzei* (Williamsburg 1929); *Los enigmas de Colón* (The Mysteries of Columbus; Santiago 1934); *The Birth of America, a Contri-bution to the History of America* (New York 1937). Several of his titles feature sea topics: *Mare* (Sea; Bologna 1909); *La nave e la navigazione* (Ship and Navigation; Milan 1912); *Il Fortunale* (The Storm; Bologna 1913); *La isla de Robinson* (Robin-son's Island; Valparaíso 1922). His bibliography also includes a translation of the *Corano* (Koran; Rome 1912). In Santiago, Chile, he wrote his last work: *Così parlò Mister Nature. Fatti e impressioni di un italiano in America* (Thus Spake Mister Nature: Deeds and Impressions of an Italian in America; Bologna 1953).

ESSENTIAL BIBLIOGRAPHY

Flamma 1935 (article); Franzina 1996; Marazzi 2001, 27–28; Schavo 1944 (article) and 1976, 128–129.

∾

The public knew it by reputation but didn't know exactly where it was located, since the Fifth Avenue Literary Club wasn't on Fifth Avenue. It was called The Millionaires' Club because, as they used to say, only those with an income of at least $500,000 could become members. The title of the club was really in social terms what splendid grooming and tailoring are to the beautiful body of an impure young person. Literature was a flag that unfurled by day in the magnificent and aristocratic halls where an elect group of gentleman intellectuals got together to hear the song of a fashionable poet or the reading of the latest novel of a declining one. At night the beautiful body would strip, and the same halls received the corrupt husbands who as usual had rich and intellectual wives. Then there was nothing literary except the debasement of names: Shakespeare became a synonym for "baccarat," Dickens for "twenty-one" and Longfellow for "poker."

The Fifth Avenue Literary Circle was organized in a perfect way. There one saw the imprint of some clever Wall Street bankers. The "fixed" and cumbersome games had been abolished and those games of chance, the so-called "flying" ones based on cash, were not allowed. No telephones, no electric alarms, no gossipy servants. The staff had to be mute from birth and to respond to orders, by means of lights that used the different colors of the electric bulbs to replace audible signals. When the normal light changed to blue, it was the alarm; and then all the players made the playing cards and the banknotes disappear in order to assume the respectable pose of readers immersed in the reading of ancient illuminated manuscripts and American journals. The night-time "entrances" permitted the day-time "escapes."

If the sunlight increased the literary prestige of the club, its nocturnal darkness fed its passion. Since gambling is not a vice but a luxury and a passion: a passion that exceeds that of love in that it is more morbid, more feverish, more constant, more expensive: a luxury because it is only allowed, with impunity, to millionaires. But the virtuous ladies, by way of expiation, had decreed two annual donations that their husbands regularly paid and that formed the "Metropolitan Foundations:" the first to encourage young authors and the second to intensify the struggle against vice. And the ladies, with Machiavellian intuition, preferred the venial sin that works well, to the virtue that remains passive.

That night William Ross, treasurer of the club, was full of luck.

At eleven, when the club opened, he had begun to play as usual without interrupting a round of baccarat and had collected in front of him a small heap of banknotes that was already troubling him with the thought of his having to pocket it. For Mister Ross was, yes, a fan of the game, but he played for enjoyment, not to win. As all things, even pleasant ones, become boring through constant repetition, thus that luck that followed him, if at first it flattered him, then it later vexed him.

Those always-favorable cards, that continuous mopping-up of the winnings, that invariable accumulation of bank notes with the annoying exclamations of his unlucky companions, made him irritable. He had resolved to lose one hundred dollars every night and was following this plan with the casualness of one who spends a few coins every night to enjoy a stage show. The winnings, from time to time, will serve only to make the game more interesting and to somehow balance the losses. But now it was too much. It was not fun anymore. The players were looking at him with surprise.

"You are on a winning streak, my dear Ross," Sam Morgenthau exclaimed with some envy. "Your bad luck has finally 'turned.'"

"If you had been at Montecarlo you would have broken the bank at roulette!" added Jack Monroe, the son of the famous billionaire.

As his entire answer Ross murmured, "Sincerely, I would prefer to lose."

"Oh, don't say that. We see that you do not have the soul of a gambler. One should never object to good luck."

Ross was not a gambler: he was an artist.

Another round of baccarat was ended and Ross, who was the center of attention, collected from the table another half-dozen notes.

"In what way could I lose?" he asked, feeling the mathematical certainty of winning, of winning again.

"The only way is to abandon the game and go away," Morgenthau let slip to him.

A fat and bald "gentleman," the fortunate majority shareholder of the Texas Oil Company, said to him, "You want me to share your luck? I always lose!"

"Take it!" replied Ross, throwing him a fresh pack of cards. "You're right, Sam. I'm leaving. I've had enough."

And taking advantage of the right to leave the game at any time the gambler wishes, a right that was in force in the club, he got up, resolute, looking in his various pockets for space big enough to hide the bulky rolls of banknotes. He said goodbye in a rather bad mood and passed through the other rooms, heading for the exit. It wasn't yet his usual time, but he preferred to look for diversion in another way, immersing himself in the nocturnal life of the metropolis. He was a slight man, small in stature, with a fleshy face, around forty years old. His fine flat hands, his stout and slightly adipose body, the placid expression of his features and the premature baldness all marked him as someone accustomed to a sedentary life. And in fact he ran "down-town," for fifteen years, a well-regarded real estate office that, it was said, was a real gold mine. He was not a hero. He was a mild and generous soul who loved novels; as a youth, he tried his hand at it but with little success. He had given himself body and soul to gambling because he had found in it the stimulation that his calm existence lacked. He feared one thing above all else: the aggression that infested New York. He often had a foreboding that one day or another an adventure would happen to him, too.

However, if the "hold up" had been bloodless, it would not have displeased him, because it would have been, the adventure, for one time an agreeable diversion. But . . .

He passed through various rooms in which some "gentlemen" in evening dress were playing in silence. He exchanged greetings with two of them He remained deaf to the appeal of a friend who was calling him to complete a hand of "bridge." He assured himself that the husband of the beautiful Lolette—a blond woman from overseas who had entered his placid existence like a meteor—was intent on a game, and passed in the antechamber through a thick door that opened when one pressed the key of a electric button. Just as the rose-colored light scattered in the new atmosphere, one of the waiters in attendance handed him his fur coat and his derby. He exited.

The night was dark. Veils of fog were passing over the electric streetlights, clouding them in a yellowish aureole. The cold was intense. The great nocturnal life of the city seemed to be suspended. It could have been two in the morning. He headed to his automobile, parked a short distance away, and ordered his half-asleep chauffeur to go home. That night he would return alone. He was thinking about Lolette.

The entrance of the subway was about two blocks away. He started off in that direction driven by a secret desire. All his winnings that night were not worth the kiss of a familiar mouth. He was seeking repayment for his shameless luck. He walked fast, close to the wall of the buildings. The street was deserted. The sliding automobiles passed like shadows on the pavement. All of a sudden he heard, from behind, a heavy step and a voice—a voice with a foreign accent made him stop.

"What time is it?"

He turned, instinctively checking his watch, and while his eyes were making out the figure of a wretched-looking man, his heart violently throbbed, the blood surging through his arteries. He had a terrible foreboding. Before he could say a word the man was on him and the blow he received pushed him into a storefront.

An energetic, strange, commanding voice whispered to him, "Hold up! If you scream, I'll shoot." And, from its glint, he saw that the barrel of a handgun was pointed at his heart. New York, also that night the American City—in which sovereigns without crowns and slaves without chains live in the most fantastic splendor and in the darkest misery, which offers to the light the virtue of its marvelous work and to the darkness the mad frenzy of its sin—also that foggy night in the one hundred thousand labyrinths of its avid heart, New York insinuated its slimy tentacles of desire and cupidity, of pleasure and of crime.

New York, the modern Babylon.

New York, the tentacled city with suction cups of human flesh.

The East Side of Manhattan is the shelter of the impoverished. In a squalid room at the end of 112th Street, Tony had not been able to sleep. He had laid down that evening in the single bed that already held Maria and little Joe, who had a fever, in the center. He felt the intense heat of that poor sick body that had barely blossomed, and he was feeling acute remorse over that situation for which he, in his pessimism, did not have a solution. The mines of Scranton had been closed for five months. He had knocked at every door in vain. For a week he looked for a way out. Where to go in two days, when he would be evicted from the only shelter that he still had? Discouragement turned to desperation in the silent night of his brain. He could not resign himself to his destiny because of his obligations to those two creatures who depended upon him and who meant the world to him. The whispering of his wife as she prayed had calmed him a bit. He obsessively felt the touch of Joe's feverish limbs. He must—must—find a solution to his unsolvable problem.

Every day the city's voluminous daily papers brought him horrible news reports. His mind collected them, and he pondered them in his forced idleness. Two things in particular had gotten stuck in his brain: aggression and suicide. All it would take would be to turn on the gas and fall asleep forever without suffering, without pain . . . in such a way, every day, they died, shipwrecks of life, like him, in the great city. But the vision of his two innocents, lying stiff on the table of a morgue, made him reject the idea. It was vile, too vile for a father, for a husband who would have given his life for them.

"Hold up?" And why not? It was by now a common daily occurrence. If the attempt had gone well, it could have prolonged his existence while he looked for honest work . . . if it were to fail, his pitiful case would have gotten public charity to take care of his innocent ones. If the deed was dishonorable and immoral, it was not vile, since he had at stake his life, only his life. His conscience kept quiet. Day by day, in the slow agony of poverty, a small edge of him had darkened. Urgent necessity overcame the barriers of a morality conceived by men with full stomachs. The situation demanded extreme action.

Then, his mind made up, he got out of bed and dressed quickly in the icy room. The pale reflection of a streetlight illuminated the interior of the room. He tried not to make any noise so as not to wake his wife but didn't notice, as he took his cap, that she had placed on it one of those pistols, perfect imitations of real ones, that the bazaars sell as children's toys. It was Joe's, Joe's only toy. The noise it made when it hit the floor woke up Maria. She woke up, frightened.

"Where are you going at this hour, Tony?"

"I'm going to bring you the medicine and milk for the little one," he said in a low voice, trying to avoid her gaze.

Maria, having a premonition, stared at him. "You're not going to do anything bad? Tell me, Tony? You won't do anything bad? Better death than that. God sees us. . . ."

"Don't worry," he lied while putting on his soft cap. "Don't worry. I'm going to the 'docks' to see if I can find work."

"But how can you get work there if you don't belong to the 'Unions'?"

"I'll try another time."

He left his old overcoat on the bed where it was the main blanket, kissed drowsy little Joe on his half-closed mouth, he hid the toy and the cap in his pocket; then, still avoiding his wife's inquiring gaze, quickly left.

Thus it was decided. Let happen what had to happen. He reached Fifth Avenue at the top of Central Park and walked on the sidewalk that points out the fancy residences of the privileged blessed by good fortune. The icy temperature kept company with a veil of fog. One caught only a glimpse, through the park's fences, of the milky underbrush where the snow had not been cleared away.

The way was long and he had to cover it on foot since he did not have the nickel for the subway. He had to cover a mile. Because he had a goal. He had a plan. The next door neighbor, a Polish woman, speaking with Maria had told her that her husband—mute since birth—earned thirty dollars a week as a domestic in a gentlemen's evening club where gold flowed profusely every night. She had committed the address to memory. There he would find his victim. A few dollars from a millionaire, at last. He would wait for one of them to come out alone and would then confront him.

He nevertheless feared the critical moment. He counted on the terror that "hold ups" inspire to easily overcome his victim. He felt, however, that he would not have recourse to violence, lest he himself end up the victim if his victim rebelled. And then how to shoot? And what if the victim didn't have any money on him? It could be an instance of a gambler who had left all his money on the green table. Oh! A few dollars were enough for him to pay the landlord and to buy medicines for his child. Goodness knows that fortune would not have helped him in that circumstance, the fortune that had been up to then his implacable foe? He had an eighty percent chance of success.

He walked quickly with his hands in his pocket to keep them warm. There were no pedestrians on the tree-lined avenue. Occasionally some automobiles sped by. Something struck his imagination. Half-closing his eyes, he saw against his eyelids a black spot that turned, turned around on itself. He observed that this always happened to him in the abnormal moments of his life. In front of the Plaza Hotel, he saw once again the place where a week earlier he had shoveled the snow with other unemployed people. There, exactly there, he had earned his last dollars. And by an association of ideas he remembered the small restaurant on the East Side where the Italian owner charitably had given him the leftovers. That's how they lived, until now. He entered "down-town." The profusion of light brought out all its life. The fog formed luminous nebulas around the large billboards. He encountered more people, mostly couples. It was the happiness, the joy, of others that touched him. Therefore happiness still existed?

He reached the "tenderloin:" the gay heart of the city of theaters and big hotels. Memories flooded his brain. He recalled the sleepless nights spent near the grandest nightclubs in the hope of finding some lost object at the exits. In New York there are people who live off such proceeds. But his search had been fruitless: two dollars knotted in a handkerchief, a pair of gloves, and some cigarette packs.

Therefore, there were people who were still enjoying themselves while his child was on the threshold of death. And he thought about the strange contrast in which the richest city hosts the most dreadful misery: against gold, blood. He passed in front of a building housing the offices of a benevolent society that had promised him a subsidy, but he hadn't been able to obtain it because of a procedural complication he didn't understand. He smiled. But his laugh was nothing but a contraction of his facial muscles. At the corner of 42nd Street, he paused at a crowd of people. A policeman was arresting a drunkard. Since he wasn't curious, he kept walking. Someone observed him, surprised by his wretched figure unprotected from the evening chill. He still had a few blocks more to cover.

Finally he arrived. The address corresponded to a charming little three-story building with illuminated windows. They must gamble up there. He observed oddly that the unknown victim would come to his encounter brought by destiny. Was destiny not already written in the great book of life? He approached the entrance but he did not read any writing there. He was in doubt. But the number could not lie. Some automobiles were parked in front, among them some taxis. He stepped back to check out the surroundings. The subway station was two blocks away and it had four entrances, one of which led to Broadway after one passed through a complex underground passageway in the bowels of a great commercial bazaar. He could not have hoped for anything better. It seemed to him that fortune, good fortune, was lending him a hand. And calmly he conceived his plan.

In order not to attract the attention of the chauffeurs, he placed himself at the far corner of the street, where he could observe without being seen. A long, anxious time passed. His sangfroid faded from the anxiety of the wait. He would have liked to have already gotten past that terrible situation. And he tried to resign himself to the thought that in an hour it all would be over.

A group of three people had already left the club, and they were heading on foot toward Broadway. Some automobiles left and others arrived. He feared that the victim would escape him, but in his fear he tasted a certain contentment in the depths of his mute conscience. He wished that the tragic moment either would come with lightning speed or else would be indefinitely put off. At last he saw a small and fat gentleman wearing a hat and bundled up in a fur coat approach an automobile, and after a moment's pause he headed towards him. He was delighted to observe the visible physical deficiency in that man, while he hid behind the corner of the deserted street. The gentleman, who had the look of a rich man, passed by with a rapid gait, without noticing him.

This was the victim. Tony asserted his courage, murmuring to himself, "You must," like an order that he gave himself, an order he could not shirk. He followed the man for half a block. Then he approached him from behind and asked him the time. The stranger stopped hesitantly and Tony, with a strength he had never recognized in himself, pushed him with the leveled handgun into a storefront.

"Hold up! If you scream I'll shoot."

Some unknown force made him act. He didn't remember clearly what he had said nor what he had done while the pale and trembling victim leaned against the storefront window with his hands in the air.

He found himself running toward the subway entrance with a roll of banknotes in his pants pocket. The danger gave him self-control. He went down the empty stairs, threw away his soft cap, pulled his beret down low on his forehead and passed in front of the ticket booth without going through the turnstiles. He mixed in with a current of people who, having just gotten off the last train, were climbing the opposite stairway and were entering the underground passageway that led to Broadway. When he arrived outside he emitted a deep sigh as if a great weight had been lifted from his heart. He was safe. Fortune had finally come to his aid.

At first he felt relief. He was brimming with joy. With his right hand deep in his pocket he felt, closed in his fist, the roll of banknotes. It seemed to him that the world again was his. He now watched the people passing under the fantastic lights of the billboards as an equal, smiling, barely feeling the cold that he pressed him from all sides. He would be able to live, to buy, to enjoy himself with his loved ones who for a few hours more were still moaning in a miserable bed. How beautiful life was! And it would become honest once again. . . .

His excited mind was now focused on a desire: to know the sum. How much did it amount to? To fifty . . . one hundred . . . five hundred dollars? His nervous fingers rubbed the bills. The paper, sticky to the touch, really was that of American banknotes. Oh, how well he knew it! In Times Square an idea flashed through his mind. And right away he descended into the labyrinth of the subway to seek in the solitude of a toilet stall a secure refuge from the public's prying eyes. He did not abandon precaution. When he locked himself in the small, dimly lit room, he took out his stolen treasure. And he saw wrapped in three bankrolls of ten dollars, another seven he didn't recognize, that bore on their sides the number five followed by two zeros. He looked at them with surprise, as if they were worthless. Were they fakes? He mentally added them up: 3,530 dollars. Was it ever possible that he had so much money in his hands? He was puzzled. Then some papers caught his attention: an envelope and a business card. They both bore a name and an address: William Ross, 214 Riverside Drive.

The gentleman he robbed? Yes! Destiny wanted him to know the name of his victim. Strange. And then? The nervous tension grew when he once again was in the open air of Broadway. Restaurants and drug-stores, all open at that early hour, seemed to beckon him: "Come shop for your little Joe, for your wife." It repeated to him its argument, with a musical charm: "Two years, two years, two years, of beautiful, gay, calm life." But his reawakened conscience cried to him, "Thief!"

Ten times he was at the point of going into those stores that offered him all God's blessings from their radiant showcases, but ten times he held back. By now the reaction to his mad act had taken hold of him. Little by little, like the lifting of a veil, he realized the gravity of what he had done. No more joy but fear; no more fear but dismay. His conscience, aimed straight like an arrow, wounded him.

He had robbed. The bankrolls that he still clutched in his fist burned him. He had robbed. Disdain towards that other self that had done this deed now struck him. He had robbed. He now felt that a deep abyss separated him from the other one—from the thief—as if a new personality had taken the place of his ego. He had robbed out of necessity, but he had robbed! He remembered his father's last words, from over there in his native land, "You must be proud about only one thing: holding your head high."

He felt a tear drop from his eyelash. He was moved. His temples pounded as if he had a fever; he had a lump in his throat. He stopped at the corner of 54th Street. All his thoughts brought back distant memories. Over there in that "dock" five years before, he had left his ship . . . a sultry August morning . . . he resumed his way "up-town." He passed Columbus Circle. It all now seemed like a dream to him, or rather more like a nightmare. But the nightmare was unbearable. He would have liked to become the man he had been two hours earlier. But was it all not a dream, a terrible dream indeed? And he wished to wake from it so that all that "reality" would vanish. Where to go? To throw himself in the Hudson? And what about Joe? And Maria? The innocent creatures entrusted to his man's conscience. . . . Oh, no! There was over there a street and a number: Riverside Drive, 214. And went on his way. And the spot, the famous black spot of his nightmare, turned, turned in the center of his half-closed eyelids.

He didn't wait long on the icy stairs of the large apartment house that gave off from its mass a faint light against the leaden sky. Fifteen minutes later a taxicab stopped and the little familiar gentleman, with the fur coat and the derby, got out. He paid the fare, then while the vehicle drove off, came through the parterre towards the door. Tony, now trembling, stood up straight and extended his hand full of the banknotes, and said in a cracked voice, with his foreigner's English:

"Mister Ross . . . I beg your forgiveness . . . I have brought back the sum I took from you a little while ago."

The gentleman stopped, afraid.

"I am honest!" the man said to reassure him. "I am a miner from Scranton. I've been without work for five months. For two months I've looked in vain in this great city, offering myself to all. I have a baby and a wife at home who are dying from hunger and the cold. I ask your forgiveness!"

The gentleman approached him.

"You are the man who assaulted me?" he said, lowering his voice and looking hard at him. "But don't you know that I reported you to the police an hour ago?"

"I am in your hands ready to pay personally but spare my loved ones. Here's your money."

Ross took the bankroll, observing intensely the miner's troubled face.

"What nationality are you?"

"My action has no nationality. I am a man of the crowd: a wretch who, for you, comes from the unknown."

"How did you know my address?"

"From your papers."

There was a brief pause while the gentleman looked him over. He had by now regained the mastery of himself.

"You have given me the greatest proof of honesty that a man can offer. No, I do not want to know your name or who you are. I take you at your word. There's only one thing I want from you, a precious thing that will represent for me the memory of the most emotional day of my life: your handgun. In exchange I'll give you as much as you need to be free of your troubles." Tony took little Joe's toy pistol from his pants packet and gave it to him.

"With this?" the stunned gentleman asked when he got a good look at it.

"With this!" the miner repeated.

As his reply the millionaire put the roll of banknotes back in Tony's hand and said to him, "I think that your gun is worth more!"

"Oh, no!" Tony burst out, holding back his inner turmoil with the lashes of his dark eyes. "My deed deserves punishment. Let me take only three bills from the tens!" And having taken from the outstretched hand the low denomination banknotes wrapped around the roll, he ran off in a hurry, resolute.

The millionaire, newly surprised, watched him for a moment as he departed, and then called out to him from an impulse of generosity: "I forgive you! I forgive you! Come see me. . . ."

But Tony had already disappeared into the soft curtain of fog.

Translated by George De Stefano

The Two Girlfriends

Dora Colonna

Agostino De Biasi's review *Il Carroccio*, first nationalistic, then openly Fascist, constituted an important literary venue for the colony. This periodical, which published well-known Italian and American writers, early opened its pages to numerous aspiring Italian American writers working in English or Italian. Writings of Silvio Villa, Louis Forgione, Pascal D'Angelo—among the first Italian American writers definitely choosing the English language—appeared in the *Carroccio* with a certain regularity. But besides these authors, there were more numerous writers in Italian, among whom, notably, a handful of women writers, who, however, were not included in the important anthology, *The Dream Book* of Helen Barolini. A little later, we will look at the work of Rosa Zagnoni Marinoni, an eminent poet and author in English, who in this period exhibited an enthusiastic adhesion to Fascism. Here reprinted is a story from the 1920s by Dora Colonna, of New York. Very scanty biographical information about her exists. Known to have been written by Colonna is the volume *Volere è potere; metodo speciale per la lingua inglese, compilato dall'esimia scrittrice Dora Colonna* (To Wish and to Be Able; Special Method for the English Language, Compiled by the Distinguished Writer Dora Colonna; Philadelphia: Germano, 1912). Two of her novellas appeared in the *Carroccio: Le due amiche* (The Two Girlfriends, April 1926) and *Common Clay* (August 1926).

ESSENTIAL BIBLIOGRAPHY

Marazzi 2001, 28.

315

They met just by chance one evening on the elevated train that leads to Long Island from New York.[1] The train at that hour was full, and since Nora, who was older, was standing and reeling with every jolt, Amalia stood up and offered her seat with infinite courtesy.

It happened that the two young women got off at the same station, and once on the street, walking alongside one another in the late evening, they couldn't help speaking to each other.

"Are you Italian too?" Nora observed, petit, elegant, with the face of a little Madonna—who would have guessed, so blond and with those blue eyes!

Amalia smiled and said nothing.

The route was rather long, and Nora felt like talking.

How many years was Amalia in America? Did she speak the language well? Did she like it here? Oh! Amalia had been in America for three years, and she spoke the language okay—but not real well, and—as for liking it here, oh—*well. . . .*

Her sentences were evasive, broken: they seemed like fragments of a hidden thought that did not want to be caught off guard. Only in speaking about her child did the husky voice of Amalia assume a sudden liveliness.

"A child?"—the other said incredulously—"who would have thought it? So young and already married and a mother?"

Yes, Amalia was married and a mother. Edith, the name of her child, was a little doll of about three, this tall, lively, a real little rascal, with such dark, curly hair. Nora's inquisitive gaze flew to the other's face.

"And yet, you are as blond as ripe grain!"

"Edith looks like . . . her father."

There was a brief hesitation between the two words.

"Where is she now?"

"Oh, at a private teacher's."

"Oh!"

"Otherwise, how could I manage to go to the factory?"

"Oh, I see! . . ."

"How I love her, and how I fear for that child!" Amalia added with a sigh.

"Fear? Why?"

"You have to be a mother to understand certain anxieties and fears," said the first with an adorable modesty. "And you do understand, don't you?"

"Oh, well. . . ." said Nora with a melancholy smile.

---

1. Published in *Il Caroccio* 23, no. 4 (April 1926).

"You're not a mother?"

"No. . . ."

"*Oh, that's different. . . .*"

Nora coughed and looked for a handkerchief in her purse.

"Tell me about yourself," Amalia added.

The other shrugged her shoulders. She had come from Italy three years earlier, and did not know the language, except for a few idioms, nor did she care about learning it. For doing the "finishing work" at the factory, one did not have to be educated! And here came a sharp laugh with a slight tinge of irony. That was how she thought, plainly. And then . . . Nora was a spinster, which for her was of greatest importance; she had no one, she had no bonds, no responsibilities, nor did she plan to have any.

The husky voice of the other interrupted her: "Wouldn't you get married?"

"Married? Never!"

But she might change her mind later; love is deceptive, and you never know when it might appear. Nora had not answered. Her pale Madonna-like face had contracted in anguish as if at the memory of a great sorrow. Amalia understood that she had been indiscreet and regretted it.

"You haven't yet told me how you found New York," she said then, just to say something.

"Better than I imagined," Nora answered with sudden animation. "I hated this country before I knew it; but not any more. New York is a vortex. If you carry with you a memory from home that consumes you, throw it into that vortex and you will be sure of having got rid of an enemy. . . ."

"*It is wonderful!*" exclaimed Amalia.

And as they made small talk along the road of the barren countryside, the two women finally discovered that both came from the same province, which delighted them greatly, but they didn't say from what town, they didn't take the trouble to ask themselves, they didn't care to know: the confidences that had been expanding, retreated at that point, remained suspended in the air like a veil drawn to simulate an empty space.

It was perhaps this singularity that joined together the two souls in a harmonious accord of thoughts and feelings.

Each morning the same meeting in the village square, the same walk along the path to the station, the same talk of things abstract and light-hearted, the same exchange of courtesies in the crowded train, until heading in opposite directions, the two friends were swallowed up by the turbines of the metropolis. They met again in the evening, usually at Amalia's.

Some evenings Nora happily spent playing with the child, whom she loved very much, while Amalia read the newspaper sitting before the large Japanese lampshade. Other evenings Nora sat at the piano and Amalia sang in a low and subdued voice, swaying in the "rocking-chair" with Edith half-asleep in her arms. And when the piano stopped playing and the voice stopped singing, the two friends remained in their places in silence, rigid and unmoving, with their heads bent down in a pensive state. Confidences, none, ever.

There remained between the two kindred spirits an unconscious reserve, yet vigilant and tenacious, which put them on guard against any expansiveness, as if in attempting to probe into each other's lives would mean committing a sacred violation.

But one evening that reserve broke down. Nora had entered the home of her friend with heart beating rapidly. She had been called in a hurry, and, not having been told what it was all about, had the strange apprehension that the child was ill. In fact, for some days a harsh wind had been blowing, and in the village several cases of influenza had been reported. But it was not the flu. Amalia was a bit nervous and, as usual, she needed some company, *that's all.*

"You made me worry so much," said Nora, "I was particularly worried above all for Edith. The cold is intense, and one never knows. If you saw how much it's snowing!!"

"Snowing?" asked Amalia, as if such news annoyed her.

"*Yes,* it's snowing *to beat the band*!" her friend assured her, laughing in triumph for having afforded herself the luxury of an idiomatic phrase.

Amalia went to the window, glanced outside and withdrew sighing.

"Where's Edith?" asked Nora, blowing on her numb fingers.

"She is sleeping. The little one was tired."

They both went to the little bed where the child was sleeping.

"Oh, how I wish I were you," Amalia let out.

"Me, why?"

"To live without attachments and responsibilities is a privilege, isn't it?"

Nora leaned over to gaze at the sleeping child, without responding.

"She looks like a cherub," she then said, raising herself up, and after a pause, "If . . . I were a mother I would choose the moment in which my little creature was sleeping to look at her. I don't think that for a woman there can be a greater satisfaction, a joy more intense."

One could see in her eyes glittered with tears. Amalia did not notice, nor did she have anything to add. Her thoughts were absent.

As they were about to distance themselves from the small bed, she said, "How I suffer! . . ."

"Why?"

"I don't know."

As she passed in front of the piano, Nora ran her agile fingers over the keyboard.

"No, *please, no*," Amalia begged her.

They drew close to the blazing hearth.

"Sometimes, you know? . . . I'm afraid of losing her."

"Lose who? . . ."

"Her, my daughter!"

"Why such strange thoughts?"

"Oh, my poor head! . . ." exclaimed Amalia striking her forehead, "My poor head . . ." and again she withdrew into silence.

"Please, speak to me," implored Nora, putting her arm around her waist. "Are we or are we not friends?"

With a gesture Amalia invited the other to sit with her in front of the little fireplace. For a few moments no one spoke. Both seemed fixed on the monotonous crackling of the logs on the andirons.

Nora said, "You have a memory that is killing you."

Her friend raised her head as if to protest and again lowered it.

"To cling to the relics of a past sorrow," continued the other, "it's like letting oneself sink into a morass with them. Forget. And if you cannot forget and if my words can be helpful, speak, I beg you, so that I may be able to understand you. . . ."

The voice that was interrogating the mystery and never been sweeter, never more persuasive and soulful. Amalia was shaken by it.

"It's more than a memory, my dear friend. . . ." Although she was calm, Amalia's hands were trembling. In her tapering little fingers there vibrated a longing to squeeze, to crush, and to destroy. Nora saw this. With a compassionate gesture she placed her delicate hand on those of her friend.

"Talk to me, Amalia."

"You have not known life, Nora. You cannot understand. . . ."

There was a moment of silence. Nora's face lit up with a sudden flame.

"I have also seen how one can suffer and . . . how one dies," she uttered quietly but with a biting emphasis.

"It's not everything, it's not everything," Amalia sobbed, "One must be a mother to understand certain things . . ." Her friend didn't answer. A convulsive tremor shook her lips.   After a moment she said: "Speak."

"Something terrible is happening to me," she said panting.

"What is it?"

"They are threatening to take my child."

"Ah?"

"Do you understand?"

"Criminals?"

"No. . . ."

"What then?"

"Her father . . . the child's father."

A story of passion and of its consequences followed. Amalia had gambled on life and had lost. The only daughter of a wealthy landowner from the mountains, she had been brought up in the city among young women of the aristocracy. And on her return to the mountains she had found life in the hamlet exasperatingly dull. The mountain air, that should have sedated the tumult of the eighteen-year-old, filled her with languor, lured her to incredible temptations, and left her empty and sad. She became ill-tempered and rebellious. She was scornful of the tender guidance of her parents, often made her sweet and good mother cry, and threatened to run away.

It was then that she met the man of her dreams.

Oh, that day! Amalia would never forget it. It was May. She had taken a mountain road. She often went there. The peak enticed her with infinite promises. And it was on the peak that she saw for the first time her Adonis in his hunting outfit, his rifle under his arm, his hair waving in the wind. He was tall, thin like a cedar of Lebanon.

And so love was born.

But in the home of the young woman the news of this encounter raised serious apprehension. No one knew the young mountaineer. He was an adventurer, a hack—her father said—a dowry hunter.

Amalia would not be convinced. Her father changed from warnings to threats: he would shut her up in a convent where she would comb the hair of Saint Catherine for the rest of her life. Vain words.

One day Amalia ran away from home, took the path through the mountains where love was expecting her, and, without even waiting for the young man to make the usual promise to marry her, she offered herself to him with complete devotion.

"We need to go, leave this place," the girl said, fearing her father's wrath.

He hesitated before responding. There was urgent business to take care of. They would leave a bit later, they would go to America.

The idea of living in another country excited Amalia. But when? Perhaps in the winter. Nevertheless they could not remain long in the village. What would they do? The young hunter was ardent and full of resources.

He proposed to his lover to spend their honeymoon in the open countryside, in the mountains, on the opposite side. Amalia found this adventure to be audacious beyond belief. They would take their love, already mature, to the mountaintop where it began. But the idyll did not last long.

Winter arrived. The mountain gusts began to blow violently. The two lovers were forced to seek shelter in the village, waiting for the time of their departure as a liberation.

Until the night of their flight arrived. A stormy night with driving snow and a howling wind. He was in a state of crushing sadness, and Amalia, who did not understand why, kept quiet and stared at him in wonder.

Never had the young man looked so handsome. That air of pensive sadness gave him a new grace: something noble and spiritual that he never had before. On the *steamer* she found out the reason. She learned that on the other side of the mountain, another woman and child had rights to the man she thought was hers!

It was a shocking revelation. For the first time in her eighteen years, Amalia looked at life with the horror that one looks into an abyss.

From deep within her something rebelled, but she didn't dare protest. It was too late.

Love had dug into her heart a fatal breach, and then . . . she was a mother.

The first days in America were not very happy ones. The formidable shadow of New York frightened the youths, it embittered them, it made one hostile towards the other. Then the baby arrived, and things grew more complicated. Life's necessities became even more urgent. He became deceitful. He was reluctant to look for a job. He made it perfectly clear that he would never become part of the herd that killed itself to make the *rich men* richer. And so began the reproaches, the squabbling, the days without bread and without peace . . . until one day he disappeared, just as he had appeared. . . .

And so three years had passed without a word from him: three years of hard work and humiliation for the young woman who had never worked or suffered, until . . . here Amalia interrupted the story.

Her friend had listened to that discourse without batting an eye, motionless, absorbed. Her pale face had acquired an ashen color and appeared here and there furrowed by deep creases.

Before speaking, she held out her hands toward the fire to warm herself.

"Well then?"

The other did not respond.

What is the name of this man? There was a certain bitterness in her thin lips, almost sneering.

"Marco."

A long pause. In the silence one could hear a stifled sound of repressed sobs. With a mechanical gesture Nora patted the back of her friend who was crying and said:

"Come . . . come, these are things of the past."

The other dried her eyes:

"There's more, dear friend."

"Ah!"

"In the past month he has been giving signs of life. He won't leave me alone; all he does is ask for money, all he does is ask for the impossible."

"This too?"

"This and more. He wants me to take him back or . . . he will take away the child. The rogue! Here, read . . . ."

Nora held out her hand, somewhat hesitantly. She read:

My Dear! Whatever you do to escape the dilemma, you won't succeed. Either you consider me yours, giving me the place that is my due near you, or you will lose the child. How and when this happens you need not know. Tonight therefore your final answer, and . . . Watch out because I'll go to any extreme should you become unreasonable—Marco

"I don't know what he means by that 'go to any extreme,'" Nora said, giving her back the letter.

Nora appeared to reflect. "What do you plan to do, Amalia?"

"I don't know. Up to now I've been unable to arrive at any conclusion. For two days I've shut myself up in the house guarding the door, *that's all.*"

"Do you think he's serious?"

"I think he's capable of any madness."

Neither spoke. In the silence the ticking of the clock could be heard. Amalia looked at the time. Eight o'clock.

"Why didn't you tell me about this before?" asked Nora, a slight harshness in her voice—staying closed up in the house won't get you anything, *you know!*"

"I know," the other said with a sigh, as she glanced at the clock again. That incessant ticking was an incredible torment to her.

"Don't you love him . . . anymore?" her friend asked suddenly. Their eyes met.

"Well?" she asked, since the other hesitated.

Amalia shook her head and lowered her eyes, somewhat disturbed by her friend's insistence.

"Don't you think I would have already agreed to his demands if . . . I loved him?" she said all in one breath.

"Would it then be too great a sacrifice on your part to yield?" asked Nora.

"Horror! . . ."

They fell silent. Amalia was agitated.

"Take him back after that wretch of a man left me at the depths of misery and despair! After the neighbors think I am a widow. Horror!"

Nora said nothing.

"And then . . . and then . . . I hate him, I loathe him! . . ."

"Wouldn't you do it for Edith?"

"For Edith? I'd rather see her dead than in his arms."

Again they were silent. Amalia got up. A tenuous color like that of a faded rose tinged the noble paleness of that face that suffered without tears. Seeing Nora start toward the door with her head bent, Amalia went to her, seizing her hands impulsively.

"Nora, dear friend. I have been too harsh in speaking to you of my trouble, isn't that true? . . . You . . . you are suffering."

"I'm suffering knowing you are unhappy!" Her lips were white, but she was calm. There was a pause. Nora said, "Do you think that he is really capable of coming here tonight and harassing you?"

Amalia clasped her hands as if she was praying:

"I don't know, I don't know! It's not the first time that he makes these threats, and yet this evening I feel strangely uneasy," she glanced at one of the windows, and added: "That window there frightens me."

"Why?"

"I don't know."

"Come on, you're a child!" said her friend, forcing a jovial tone, "Perhaps he's doing this to test you. If he finds it as tough as it's been until now, he'll get tired of it."

"Ah, no, Marco is not the type of man who gives up."

"Listen," Nora resumed after a brief reflection, "it surprises me that you have not thought of moving. You've had plenty of time."

"I have thought about it, and I'm sorry about it. But you'll understand. I liked it so much here. In New York life is expensive, *you know*, and then I've enjoyed my reputation."

"Nevertheless you should have foreseen it. . . ."

"If I get through tonight without incident, I'll do it tomorrow. I'll leave every thing that belongs to me to my landlords and. . . ."

"That won't save your reputation," interrupted her friend, "you'll only complicate things, and make it easier for him to be even more audacious."

"Then what would you advise me to do?"

"Confront him."

"Are you crazy?"

"*Yes*, confront him!" cried Nora, vehemently, "Ask him to meet you, and tell him what you think of him."

"Do you believe he will then leave me alone?"

"I don't see why he would persist."

"Nora, your simplicity is exasperating! If I told you that Marco is a dangerous man?"

"I don't understand."

"He belongs to the 'gang,'" cried Amalia, covering her face with her hands: "He is a derelict who lives by exploiting others."

Nora closed her eyes a moment as if seized by dizziness. Shortly afterwards, patting by the back of her friend, she said, "Come, come . . . you'll end up making yourself sick."

"I'll end up driving myself mad."

"Don't be afraid. Tomorrow we'll make the appropriate provisions," said Nora as she headed toward the door.

"But tonight . . . suppose . . ." exclaimed Amalia, trying to hold her back. "Oh, I am a coward, coward. . . ."

"Your fears could be unfounded, Amalia."

"It could be; nevertheless, I can't deny that I am very afraid. It's from there above all that I am afraid of an attack, from the window that overlooks the 'yard.' Oh, this house on the ground floor is a disaster! . . ."

"An extremely tall man couldn't reach that window with the tip of his finger," observed Nora with a sad smile.

"Marco has wings!" Amalia said with her head lowered.

"You, you still love him!!" Nora let slip out, and her eyes flashed.

"I am telling you that I hate him!" yelled the other furiously.

At the door they embraced and kissed as usual.

When she arrived at her small room on the third floor, Nora closed the door and gave a sigh. She was panting. She felt an unbearable weight on her heart. There was a moment in which she would have let out a cry, the weight troubled her so. She wanted to cry, but could not. Her eyes were dry, burning. Her hat in one hand, her gloves in the other, she walked around the room a couple of times; she stopped a moment in front of a painting hanging on the wall, and started again. Weary, she threw the hat and gloves on the bed and let herself fall on a chair where she sat without moving for some time, crouched over as if bent by a yoke.

Marco was his name. And on the other side of the mountain another woman and child had the right to the man Amalia thought was hers!

Nora suppressed a cry. Her heart continued to weigh on her, her eyes were burning in pain.

A vain and hollow man, Marco! He had broken two lives and he wasn't satisfied. He returned to the attack one more time; he waited at the threshold like a bird of prey. A gentleman he never was, but so cruel . . . criminal! God! Oh God! . . ."

Nora rose in agitation. That memory was burning. The memory that she believed to be drowned in the whirlpool of New York, had come to the surface more vivid than ever, it laughed at her face with a chuckling laughter, kindled in her heart a vindictive flame. She approached the window, opened it, looked outside.

It was still snowing. Silence weighed heavily like a tombstone on everything. On the "elevated tracks" the train screeched on the rails, and disappeared shrieking as if it were in pain.

Nora shuddered, turned back, and closed the window. She was again in the dark, isolated, with her memories . . . The child—her child—who died in the cradle, and Marco her unfaithful husband, who couldn't wait to flee . . . her vain attempts to restrain him, her tears, her pleas would have moved a stone; the hand-to-hand struggle between him and her up to the final moment when he slipped out the door. Marco! But he fled, and she behind him! An agonizing race into the dark night, against the snow and wind, onward, always onward, until exhausted she collapsed to the ground. Upon her return to the forsaken home, Nora discovered that her child, even her child, had gone never to return! . . .

Amalia, left alone, had tried in vain to calm her fears and to fall asleep. She threw herself on the bed fully dressed, and just in that moment that she was dozing off the clock struck ten and she leaped to her feet in a hurry.

Edith woke at the sound and asked for water. When she fell back to sleep, Amalia ran to the door to make sure it was locked.

She turned off the night light, went to the window that looked onto the "yard," pulled slightly the curtains and looked out into the night.

It was from there that she feared the ambush; and why she felt that the attack would come from there and not from the front door, she was unable to explain; nevertheless that presentiment tormented her.

The "yard" belonged to the landlords, who lived next door; it was rather large, crowded with lumber and other things, surrounded by a crumbling wall. Behind the yard was an alley that led to the main street.

Amalia continued to look outside with a vigilant eye. The snow persisted. A lamp-post at the corner cast a gloomy light. A little farther at the entrance of a "dancing-hall" a group of youths were shouting and laughing. A woman crossed the alley, light as a shadow, stopped a moment and disappeared.

Amalia reflected. She thought about her broken life; she thought about her uncertain future. No! Tomorrow would not be any better than today! It was pointless to flee or to hide. Marco would have pursued her to the end of the world. Confront him? Oh, *yes*! How easy to say it! Perhaps she would not do it if it were not for the child! Oh, to be a mother is a curse!

Amalia shook her head. This time she would confront him, she would have torn his flesh with her nails.

A woman, the same as before!—emerged, skirting the wall cautiously, and went off with the same hurried pace.

"Oh," exclaimed Amalia, and she pulled the curtains to get a better look. How strange; as if that feminine shadow had, in the uniform whiteness of the street, outlined Nora's "silhouette."

The thought of her friend gave her courage. The clock struck eleven. A train whistled in the distance. The child whimpered in her bed and fell back asleep immediately. Amalia felt tired and seemed sleepy. Oh, to sleep; she wanted nothing more but to sleep, to forget! She withdrew for a moment to close the shutters, casting a quick glance outside. She stood there, staring more carefully. She noticed a shadow, a man under the lamppost.

Who was it? How long had he been there? The snow began to ease. Some one passed by singing. The noisy youths were no longer there. The windows of the "dancing-hall" were dark. The man under the street light crossed the street and disappeared into the entrance of a building under construction. Amalia felt faint, but she didn't move. She would have remained all night behind the curtain and keep watch. The man reappeared. He seemed cautious and uncertain like someone who was fearful of being followed. Amalia sharpened her gaze. The torment of uncertainty made her uneasy. Not a sound could be heard. The night was silent, threatening. The man took a few steps toward her residence, stopped, appeared in the light. Marco! The same Marco of the mountain, fearless, his hair flying in the wind, tall, slender as a cedar of Lebanon.

Amalia was struck by dizzy spell and leaned up against the windowsill in order not to fall. But the vision attracted her as it had that day, and, curious, she pulled aside the curtains, revealing her pale face through the bare glass.

Marco saw the raising of the blind, looked, recognized his lover. And absorbed in that contemplation, he didn't notice the enemy who was following him. Nora, the wife, who was already behind him.

A sudden explosion tore the silence—a cry—and Marco fell heavily, flat on his back, with his arms crossed.

Translated by Mark Pietralunga

The Flapper

 Caterina Maria Avella

As stated in the preceding introduction, Agostino De Biasi's review *Il Carroccio* constituted an important literary venue for Italians in America. Caterina Maria Avella, of New York, was a regular contributor, but not much is known about her, save that she was the author of the novellas *La "Flapper"* (August 1923) and *Patsy e Patricia* (June 1924).

Like Colonna, Avella probes middle-class interiors, ambiances, and customs; they depict a style of life no longer tied to the Italian tradition. And if in *Le due amiche* Colonna treats of the old theme of the drama of emigration in a new style, in Avella that horizon has by now disappeared. In particular, in *La Flapper*, figures of emancipated women emerge with vivacity—even if with malice—sure of themselves, by now middle-class, and what is more significant, perfectly at ease in an Americanized universe of liberty.

ESSENTIAL BIBLIOGRAPHY

Marazzi 2001, 28.

∾

It was a sultry August afternoon when, after much yearning, waiting, and hoping, the woman who was the principal object of Amedeo's existence finally gave him a decisive "no" as an answer.[1]

He changed. Whatever the cost, he had to forget; salve for his wounds could only be found in activity, distance, oblivion. Therefore, he decided to leave his

---

1. Originally published in *Il Carroccio* 18, August 2, 1923.

home town, leave it with all its burden of sweet and sad memories that burned his soul with every recollection.

He wanted to be far away; why not go east as far as the "Suez," in that country Kipling found without "the ten commandments," where every restraint on life and every suggestion of civilization, morals, or decency was lacking? The wildest feelings and craziest emotions would take him far from his deep suffering! What difference whether it was the east of "Suez" or the south of "Gehenna"? To go far away to the most remote and isolated corner of the terraqueous orb, far from human society if possible, where he would not have the opportunity to see other women, another woman; to leave, escape, was the most vital decision. Distance and time, the great moderators of all things, could resolve the tremendous crisis that gripped him; and so he wanted to get away.

After living for two years in a distant town, in the heart of the vast North American continent, Amedeo Villadio was standing on the porch of his little house, looking at the small port nearby where the lights of a steamship shone in the velvety night like tropical stars; but his thoughts wandered far from the lights and stars. In his hands he held an invitation:

Mr. and Mrs. Francesco de Roberti invite you to the wedding of their daughter Lilla Luisa.

So she was getting married! At the bottom of the invitation he read: "Please, please come!" "The eternal woman!" he thought with some satisfaction. Without emotion, however. There had been a time when he was at Lilla's beck and call, but now she raised only a slight smile that faded in a murmured: "Still the same!"

In two years of isolation, without ever returning north, Amedeo had completely changed, not only in temperament, but also physically. The torrid sun had tanned his skin, giving him that special color that suits certain men, making their marked features stand out. Also his former characteristic patter had changed: now he could express himself in brief, concise terms.

And had Lilla changed too? Who knows what impression he would have if he went to her wedding! . . .

A voice from inside the house called to him, and with a shrug, he went inside. Mr. Rocas had come from the main office to verify the accounts, consign everything to the successor, and to notify Amedeo that the general management was transferring him to the main branch in New York in reward and compensation for his zeal and irreproachable cooperation.

"What do you think of that, Mr. Villadio?"

"I would say that such a decision is as unexpected as it is overwhelming, and that I have a right to think it over, don't you agree?"

"You are very fortunate, my dear sir. I had to languish five long years before reaching. . . ."

"I might be fortunate, but I need time to get ready for this repatriation."

"I think you'll be very happy to see how much New York has changed; both its streets and modern life, know what I mean?"

In this moment of indecision, Amedeo was thinking that he might after all accept the invitation of the 26th.

After his arrival in New York, he expected to go work immediately, but he was given a month off before taking charge of the new office. What should he do? Go visit his little town? He had no one there, no relatives, but there was still his house with all the memories . . . outside the station the first thing he saw was a Fiat with a pretty woman who was looking at him, smiling mischievously. Amedeo went up to her.

"Don't you recognize me?" the woman asked, holding out her hand.

"Certainly I recognize you, Vera, the once-upon-a-time mischief maker."

"Exactly." And seeing that Amedeo was looking at her while he continued to shake her hand, she said as though to justify herself: "I'm not Lilla, you know, just her little sister. Oh my, how you've changed!" she went on with total ease. "So you'll come to the wedding?"

"I don't know. I'm just here for a few days."

"It will make Lilla very happy; she's counting on having a great number of 'disconsolate' guests."

Amedeo remembered those words written below the invitation. Who knows to how many others she had written the same thing? But what did it matter anyway?

"Where are you staying?"

"At the Inn." And seeing a taxi arrive, he said quickly: "I'm glad to have seen you after such a long time. . . ."

"I doubt it," Vera blurted. "Let the taxi go and I'll take you. I came to meet daddy, but since he's not here, I'll be your chauffeur. Do you mind?"

Amedeo thanked her. He looked at Vera as she put the car in gear. She wasn't as beautiful as Lilla, but there was something attractive about her. She had always had a sharp wit, and she spoke very frankly and openly, while Lilla was always surrounded in mystery. He noticed she wore her hair short and her clothes were mannish. He didn't much care for that virile look; nevertheless he thought that if Lilla had concentrated less on her femininity and more on frankness, things might be different now!

Right then Vera looked at him and asked: "Do you find me very different?"

"Not much."

"They say that younger sisters, with their long legs, always turn out more beautiful."

"But you don't have long legs. . . ."

"Lilla inherited all the beauty in our family," she concluded without bitterness.

"Who's the lucky man?"

"Luigi Martinis from Philadelphia, a dull forty-year-old, madly in love, and loaded with cash. Lilla will be happy."

"What a gruff way to talk," Amedeo thought. Such frankness in this woman amazed him; but after all she represented modern society. A fine example of a "flapper!"

Vera talked but kept her mind on her driving. Amedeo watched her every gesture. She wasn't an authentic beauty like Lilla, but her almost perfect profile, the brilliance of her blue eyes, bright as stars, and everything together made her a pleasant and interesting person.

Vera caught him looking at her, and: "I think my profile is interesting enough to look at, too, but it's not always so easy to show off!"

Amedeo was shocked; then with a smile he recovered: "I heard that was the way of the new woman, to talk about herself and show off."

"The 'flapper,' right? But you're also very different from what I imagined. Perhaps because you're not wearing the narrow trousers and the big boots you wore at. . . ."

"How do you know?"

"When our friend Pio came to see us he brought some photographs. He gave me one and I fell immediately in love. For almost a month I talked only about you and thought only about you. Aren't you flattered?"

"Absolutely!" he answered, and thought, "What a strange way to act!"

"I told you only because Lilla found the photograph in my drawer, and I'm sure she will tell you at the first opportunity. Besides, she thinks I've always been in love with you. That's why Tommy is constantly at my side."

"And who is Tommy?"

"Tommy is a twenty-three year old Harvard graduate whose father is very rich and. . . ."

In the meantime, by a pure miracle the Fiat did not crash into a car speeding toward them from the opposite direction. There was a moment of confusion that cleared after the close shave.

"It was their fault. They should have honked," Vera defended herself.

"But why didn't you honk?"

"I was thinking about Tommy. And I was thinking that your appearance is somewhat embarrassing because Tommy will believe more than ever that I'm in love with you."

Amedeo didn't reply. Meanwhile Vera had a bright idea: "Will you go along with a little game in the romantic comedy I'd like to perform to make Tommy more jealous?"

"Hold on," Amedeo interrupted. "It's always dangerous to play with fire."

Vera gave him a wicked smile. "Don't be afraid for me, or are you worried about yourself?" And changing tone, she continued, "I would like to get engaged to Tommy, especially since my father is so opposed to it, and I'm sure if you showed a little interest, I could make it happen."

They had now reached the Inn. A bellhop came to take the luggage and Amedeo could say nothing more than, "Thanks a lot, and we'll get back to the subject that interests you so much as soon as possible."

"It's nothing; I was really glad to do it. I'll tell Lilla you're in town, and I'm sure you'll be hearing from her soon."

As a matter of fact, right after lunch Amedeo was called to the telephone.

It was Lilla, "I heard you were back. What a nice surprise. Are you going to the Rivaldi's ball?"

"No, I just arrived, and no one knows I'm here."

"Oh, come with me then. Luigi will be here at nine and if you want to come fifteen minutes earlier, we can talk. I want to hear all about you."

She hadn't changed a bit! But anyway he would have to see her sooner or later. Better now for a few minutes.

Precisely at a quarter to nine, Amedeo arrived at the door of the charming De Robertis home. A well-known voice called his name; in the semi-darkness Amedeo guessed it must be Lilla.

"I'm here. Come closer!" the voice spoke with a good Ethel Barrymore imitation. Amedeo was confused for a moment, but the other one went on without a pause. "You've been very lucky. I hear you've been very successful."

"Let's not exaggerate."

"After all, you owe me a little gratitude," she continued, leaning a hand on his arm. "If it hadn't been for me. . . ."

Amedeo started with surprise; he hadn't expected that.

"At least you should be." And since Amedeo seemed unwilling to respond, she continued, "On the other hand I think it was better that way, because if you had stayed here, who knows. . . ."

"Certainly," Amedeo thought, "it must be an allusion to that August evening."

An automobile turned off the street toward the house and illuminated the darkness for a moment.

"Vera!" Amedeo exclaimed in amazement.

"Oh, well, I almost pulled it off. I could be a good actress if I was prettier. I'm a good mimic. I often did imitations of you in the past, and you should have heard Lilla laugh. Seriously, you really should be very grateful, because otherwise she might have married you."

"So it was you who phoned me?"

"No, Lilla. I overheard her and was sure that she would say what I said to you. Anyway, in a minute you'll see her and can find out for yourself. Tommy is impatient," she added when the horn of the car parked just outside the entrance honked twice. "If he knew you were here, he would pepper me with questions and be a jerk all evening. He certainly wouldn't have imagined that I imitated Lilla." And with a "Have a good evening," she left him standing there.

At that same moment a servant told Amedeo that Miss Lilla was waiting for him in the library.

"You're late," Lilla said while extending her hand. "But I forgive you because you have come so far for my wedding." Amedeo was about to contradict her, but she went on, "I was hoping you would come if only to know you have forgiven me." Amedeo was momentarily taken aback. It seemed her sister's words might be true, and he was happy about that. But just then her fiancé came in, which saved him the need to reply.

Lilla introduced them and taking her cloak, said, "You're not coming with us then?"

"No, thank you."

"I'm happy you made this short visit and hope you'll come again soon," Lilla said as they separated.

When alone, Amedeo could only think about what had taken place. Two such different women: Vera more modern and unfettered, Lilla always the same. After all, he had to admit to himself, Lilla hadn't been a great loss.

The next day Amedeo went to the Club to play a game of golf, and there on the veranda steps he ran into Vera.

"Hello, come for a game?"

"If I can find someone to invite me. My membership expired while I was away."

"I'll invite you on the condition that you play a game with me."

Amedeo hesitated a moment. He was beginning to be afraid of Vera. He didn't feel comfortable because he didn't know what she might say or do from one moment to the next.

"I'm out of practice. I didn't have much opportunity to play golf down there."

"Never mind. Besides, Tommy needs a lesson. He promised to meet me at ten and he's already five minutes late. There's no excuse for that."

"Don't be too hard on Tommy!"

"Quite the opposite. I'll make him pay for last night. It's interesting how ridiculous men become when they are jealous, and Tommy can be terrible every time I mention your name. And so I mention it often."

"I would be very flattered if. . . ."

"Oh, there's nothing to worry about. Tommy thinks everyone wants to steal me away, or something like that. And the strange thing is only last week he told me that it was a real relief to meet a woman he could be friends with without a lot of nonsense."

"And that's why you treat him so badly?"

"Heavens! You're a bright man. You understand it's certainly not a great pleasure to hear you are harmless and admired only for your intelligence."

"He said that?"

"Yes. I have the honor of being the only one who understands him in that lofty atmosphere he inhabits; then he told me he wasn't the marrying kind, and I'll bet he'll eat those words too."

Tommy appeared when Amedeo and Vera were already on their second game. He barely waved from a distance. He wanted to seem indifferent, but barely managed.

"I'll bet he'll ask Emilia," Vera said. "And to think that only yesterday he told me how much she bored him. Maybe he thinks it'll make me jealous," and she casually began to hum the latest ditty as she prepared to tee off.

"Perfect," Amedeo praised her.

"I know. A lot of men don't want to play with me. They prefer women who gush over them with corny compliments. Oh, yes, that's what you men want."

"I have no intentions of contradicting you," Amedeo interposed. "Anyway, I'm sure I wouldn't be able to."

And so Vera won the game.

"Will you ever forgive me for winning?" she said as they returned to the Club House.

"Does Tommy ever win?"

"Absolutely never," Vera exclaimed.

Amedeo smiled.

"Good heavens, here's Lilla," Vera exclaimed again, and with a slight nod she left him.

Once he would have thanked her for doing that, but this time Amedeo felt abandoned. Lilla confessed that she had come for lunch and not to play golf. Luigi, she said, was somewhere around, and when Amedeo offered to look for him she broke into provocative laughter. "There was a time when you wouldn't have been so anxious to leave me."

Even though the woman spoke with feigned indifference, Amedeo had to make a great effort to extricate himself form that sorcery, until Luigi came to liberate him.

"Emma told me she sent you an invitation to her ball this evening," Lilla said while on the point of leaving. "I'm sure I'll see you there because I don't think you'll want to miss it," and leaning on Luigi's arm she left.

"Phew!" Amedeo murmured. "After all, I prefer Vera's direct way. At least you can defend yourself."

That evening Emma called him, begging him to come to her ball, and Amedeo was forced to accept.

As soon as he entered the ballroom, Vera came up to him. She wore a beautiful dress with a bunch of violets at her waist.

"Thank you," she said with a pretty bow, smiling.

"For what?" Amedeo asked.

"These," she touched the flowers. "Very thoughtful of you after I beat you at golf."

Amedeo didn't understand; he was about to stammer something, but a look from Vera shut him up. He turned around and saw Tommy looking at them with a tragic air.

"You are welcome, you're very kind," and he bowed.

Vera didn't answer but looked at him smiling, and after glancing around said in a low voice in English: "You're a sweetheart. Tommy looks like he wants to give it to someone. If you'll insist on at least five dances, he'll surrender."

Amedeo didn't know whether he was pleased or not. Only when their last dance ended did he notice he was sorry he hadn't asked for more. In fact, he was annoyed to think that Vera would dance with Tommy. And yet wasn't it because of Tommy that Vera had danced with him? After all, why take it so to heart? He certainly didn't love Vera. He had only known her for two days. And yet he was happy when he seemed to read in her eyes a certain disappointment in realizing that it was their last dance. And without thinking about it he asked for another two. Vera gave him a strange look; for a moment Amedeo regretted asking, but her words reassured him.

"Then I dance all right?"

"To perfection; but that isn't why I asked for other dances." (What an idiot I am, he said to himself. Why did I say that? Vera will have every right to make fun of me.) And he waited for a sarcastic laugh; instead she looked at him with such sincere joy that Amedeo was almost consoled.

It seemed to him that she held him closer, making herself smaller in his arms; in fact in a turn it seemed that Vera touched his shoulder with her head, brushing his cheek with her hair. At this contact Amedeo felt a shiver, making a sudden movement not in rhythm with the music, and Vera looked at him. It was electric. Amedeo was surprised that that fleeting contact should affect him so much and not wanting Vera to notice, he said, "You're a wonderful dancer."

"Thank you," she replied all dewy-eyed. "Do you mind if I look at you with . . . adoration? Tommy says that the way I look at you infuriates him."

Amedeo smiled, and when she lowered her head for a moment, he brushed a kiss on her hair. When the music ended, Tommy came up to Vera and reminded her he had the next dance. Anyway, it was time for Amedeo to dance with Lilla.

She showed him her completed dance card, but after taking a look, Amedeo crossed out "Luigi" and substituted his name.

"Oh, good. Luigi won't be too unhappy; he is a very proper gentleman."

Fortunately the dance was short, and Amedeo was again dancing with Vera.

"How did it go?"

"Oh, he apologized for being late this morning and for staying with Emilia. He even begged me for a date tomorrow, but I refused."

"Why?"

"Did you forget that we have a date tomorrow?" and she looked at Amedeo with such honesty and frankness that he was baffled. This Vera was amazing!

"Excuse me," he said.

"My fault," she assured him and went on: "I told him that I couldn't go for a canoe trip in the afternoon because you had already asked me for a date. He certainly won't know that you invited me right now." And she gave him another look.

Amedeo was at a loss for words. "Certainly," he managed to say. "I'm pleased to ask you out and am flattered you accepted."

"It seems you're the one who finds it difficult to accept an invitation. I promise not to be so irritating, and I'll also protect you from Lilla, who can't get used to the idea that you have forgotten her so quickly. In fact, I must tell you that she is looking for the first opportunity to entice you again. Oh, it's useless for Luigi to intervene . . . Lilla is Lilla."

And once more Vera's words came true. With a simple excuse, Lilla refused the dance with Amedeo, inviting him instead to follow her into the garden. After settling down on a bench, and though Amedeo tried to keep the conversation on the day's events, Lilla interrupted him at every opportunity, and with her Ethel Barrymore voice said, "Are you really 'healed'? And yet I had hoped. . . ."

And as usual her sentence remained unfinished, suspended. Luigi appeared again, who once more, without meaning to, saved him from embarrassment. It was clear that from now on he had to avoid any encounter with Lilla. But by chance he saw her again a few days later on the Club veranda.

"Are you waiting for Vera? I just left her with Tommy," Lilla said with a hint of malice. "But I think she'll be along soon."

Amedeo bowed simply to avoid prolonging the discussion, but Lilla continued. "What do you want from Vera, if I might ask?" And she smiled slightly.

"You might ask what she wants from with me. . . ." but he regretted it before he had finished.

"Undoubtedly Vera wants to amuse herself at your expense."

This suspicion had entered his mind often the last few days.

"Besides you can't blame her entirely. You've made yourself so available. Even in the past, she never let an occasion go by to make fun of you," Lilla went on.

"I know I was very ridiculous then."

Lilla smiled. "You were then, but not so much as now. Don't you see that Vera is using you to make Tommy jealous?"

"I know. She told me and it amuses me."

"Really?" Lilla couldn't keep herself from exclaiming. "But here she comes," and saluting him, she went away.

"I'm sorry to be late, but Tommy. . . ." Vera excused herself.

"Don't you think it's time to stop and have a little pity on him? You treat him very badly."

Vera looked at him in surprise.

"I seem to remember that Lilla treated you even worse."

"That is perfectly true, but I was very different then."

Vera made no reply, but stared into the distance, while Amedeo, entranced, admired her delicate profile outlined so beautifully.

"Meanwhile," Amedeo added, "I'm sorry to say I have to leave tomorrow."

Actually Amedeo had no idea of leaving; it was simply a little test. But when he saw how shaken Vera was at the unexpected declaration, he had to persist with the story of their immanent separation. Vera's expression grew dark as the sky before a storm.

"It's business. Duty calls me back to the office."

"If your mind is made up, will you at least come to the picnic this evening?"

"Picnic?"

"We're going to Captain Kidd's Island on Tommy's yacht, with Emma and another friend. We'll have supper. It's a full moon tonight, and the evening should be wonderful."

"I'm sorry, but I have to pack my bags."

She was about to insist, but changed her mind. The game lost, she offered to take him to his hotel in her Fiat.

Vera remained silent, and Amedeo took advantage of it to admire her. She was a beautiful woman, he thought; but those eyes enchanted him; they were really beautiful, shining; they projected vivid reflections. Her strange but interesting behavior had made its way into his heart. They were approaching the Inn when Amedeo said, "Goodbye then, maybe this is the last time we'll see each other."

Vera looked at him for a moment, then as though she had made a decision, "No! That will never be. You are coming with me this evening no matter what!"

Amedeo was about to object, but seeing he was powerless in the fast-moving car, he remained still, and as though influenced by a voice that came from her heart he, satisfied and proud of his unexpected display of feeling, was content to let it go. But an instant later he was terrified of falling into a trap.

"Don't feel sorry for Tommy. When I told him that you might not come, he insisted you love me and would come because of that. This will be the last time I bother you, because it's my last chance."

Amedeo started to protest, but Vera's eyes seem to grow moist. He accepted the invitation without speaking. That is how he found himself in the middle of two couples on Tommy's yacht that skimmed over the water to take them to the Island, while the purplish sun spread its last rays of the day. However, Amedeo felt an agitation he couldn't explain. "Why had he come?" he asked himself "Why had he let himself be carried toward such a precipitous slope?" Sometimes he felt totally confused; after all, Vera was interested in Tommy; how could he solve the riddle of this modern sphinx?

The way Emma and her boyfriend had of talking drew his attention in the meanwhile. But he couldn't help but note the different way modern young people had of acting. Emma said: "I'm so sorry I didn't bring my bathing suit. It would be wonderful to jump into the sea in the moonlight."

"Why bother with a suit?" her companion replied.

In other times such boldness would have offended everyone; today, however, even if surprising, it is passed over without a comment.

Amedeo was becoming more and more restless and thought about going ashore; the fragrant sea breeze would distract him and revive him from his heavy torpor.

Thinking about Vera made him very unhappy, because not only was he forced to follow her whims, but he also had to abandon her! And like a reflex action, he was beginning to hate that idiot Tommy. Suddenly he heard someone whisper, "Now we have come to a crossroads and must make a decision. Vera, tell me honestly if you loved me; it's time I finally know!"

"Shhh. . . ." Vera cautioned.

Tommy and Vera were leaning on a parapet under the shelter of a very slender shadow. Amedeo, who just happened to be there, went up to them saying, "I don't mean to bother you, but since we're all here, I'll tell you I want to go back alone and on foot."

"But it's not possible to go back on foot," Vera said. "It's a long walk."

"A little exercise will be good for me. Good night," and he went off without another word.

The moon in all its brightness lit the way; the stars twinkled in their many-colored reflections. The evening was enchanting, but Amedeo felt depressed, uncomfortable, and infinitely alone. Thus he marched along quickly, thinking that after such a long time of serenity and tranquility he had rashly fallen back into love's whirlwind. At a certain point, Amedeo noticed that Tommy's boat also moved away from the shore quickly. He stood still and after watching it grow smaller he continued on the road. From time to time car headlights struck him with their light and he moved to the edge to let them pass. He had gone about half way, when an automobile roared up and stopped two feet from him.

"I felt obliged to come get you." It was Vera.

"Thanks, but I prefer walking."

Without another word, she turned off the motor and got out of the car. "All right. I'll walk, too."

Amedeo stopped decisively, like someone who has something to say. But he couldn't find the right words to begin and stood there looking at her. Vera placed herself squarely in front of him and looked at him intently also. Her face seemed suffused with an aura, giving Amedeo the impression of a divine image.

"Why are you mad at me?" Vera asked.

"I'm not at all, I assure you."

"You're cross with me because I didn't speak to you all evening, isn't that right?"

Amedeo couldn't stand it any longer. He wanted to shout at the top of his lungs that he loved her, loved her so much . . . but he still had the strength to repress his heart's explosion, and pale and trembling, he managed to murmur, "Why do you keep trying to tempt me?"

Vera was desolate; she gave him a long, penetrating look, then said, "Thanks," and started to move away.

At that moment a chastened Amedeo stopped her by taking her hand.

"Tell me honestly, Vera, what do you want from me? You wanted to make Tommy jealous and you did it. Now what else do you want?"

"Do you really think I went to all that trouble for Tommy? Oh, Tommy makes me sick."

"What?"

"Yes," she went on with some warmth. "It certainly wasn't for Tommy that two years ago I worked so hard to make Lilla get married . . . and it wasn't for Tommy that I stole the invitation Lilla addressed to you and wrote in my own hand, 'Please, please come' and. . . ."

"You . . . You . . . you wrote. . . ." Amedeo stammered.

In the moonlight he noticed an unusual expression on Vera's face that made her more interesting and fascinating than ever.

"Yes! I hoped that you would come and at the same time didn't want you to, because you would think the invitation came from Lilla. Then . . . Then . . . then I did what you know, and it wasn't to make Tommy jealous, but you . . . This evening was my last chance, and. . . ." She couldn't finish, and lowered her eyes for the first time.

"Vera. . . ."

"I know what you think of me; you probably consider me too bold, but what can I do? I'm not beautiful. . . ."

"What do you mean, you're not beautiful?" Amedeo almost shouted. "You . . . you are . . ." He couldn't continue, he was afraid.

"Well, go on, hurry, say it!"

"You are simply an adorable creature!"

"Great Scott," Vera shouted with pleasure. "Then you love me more than I thought!"

Amedeo, in total confusion, seemed to be dreaming with his eyes wide open. She came closer to him and her hair brushed his face. Amedeo couldn't stand it any more, "Vera . . . my little Vera! Do you really love me?"

Vera held him tighter and laughed, "Men are so funny."

Translated by Martha King

Seven Poems

ை *Severina Magni*

Lucca, Italy, 1897–Detroit, Michigan, 1954

The simple poetry of Severina Magni (whose surname is that of her husband Gianni) is clearly removed from that of all the other authors included in this section, not only by virtue of her notable aesthetic value but also and above all because she chooses an expressive line, new and different in respect to the dominant classical, restrained style of Carducci and Stecchetti that weighs upon most of the colonial poets. The vein of Severina appears very delicately crepuscular—that is, belonging to a sort of late decadent style—and in the best moments, it would be tempting to define her as approximating the tender pastoral style of Giovanni Pascoli. Her poetry is animated by a sweet melancholy, by the remembrance of a remote world in a rarified atmosphere, a landscape constituted of lights and sounds, "*cantabile*," a childlike, doleful song, more pertaining to memory than to actuality, almost never, in any case, set in any place—and for this reason, far from the longings for Italy of the emigrant poets.

A worker in a textile factory, Severina Magni published her poems in various Italian American newspapers, among which *La Stella di Pittsburgh* and *Divagando*, and she collected them in a small volume, *Luci lontane* (Faraway Lights), published in Milan in 1936. Rodolfo Pucelli translated one of them, "La poesia" (reprinted by Helen Barolini) for his anthology. He also wrote the obituary in the monthly *Il Compasso* (June 1954), enclosed in the *Parola del Popolo* of Chicago, and asked rhetorically, "How could a woman so fragile, and born for song, find herself in a land as averse to poets as America?"

ESSENTIAL BIBLIOGRAPHY

Barolini 1985, 299–300; Cocchi 1001, 9–10; Magni 1937; Pucelli 1954.

∾

Far Away Lights

The lights we see flickering,
lovely, small and far away,
are like stars rising at the limits
of interminable flat solitudes.
    They shine sweetly amidst the deep
purple veil of the dark night,
and seem descended from the immense sky
whose infinite vastness frightens;
    unknown and inaccessible, wrapped
in a light feeling of melancholy,
they are like chimeras longed for
in vain on the eternal path.

Lace

The patient needle wove into the cloth
patterns of infinite loveliness,
like the foam on the white wake
stretching on the sea after a sail;
    like mystical winged prayers
medieval church marbles,
in the garlands that adorn the portals,
in the colors that burn in stained glass windows.
    They are radiated with the true light
of beauty born of pain,
the silent flame and the contained ardor
of silent and severe renunciation.
    With its thread seemingly so slender yet so tenacious
martyrdom created them with tired fingers,
that might have been the dream of a life
of work without cease or peace.

The Flowering Cherry Tree

The sweet vision
of the flowering cherry tree,
white and softened
by the snowy illusion,
    fills the bright pane
of the small window,
with the delicate snowfall
of the lovely petals,
    falling on the thick grass
like the white wings
of tired butterflies,
gathered in peace.

My Mother

The little girl who was playing in the garden
—dear mother! it was so cool and shady—
has wandered throughout the whole world in silence,
crying at her steep path.
    Where are the roses and the violets
of that magic time of life,
where is the newly green hedge
where the talkative child rested?
    And where are you, my sweet mother,
who consoled my childish tears,
with your tender and sweet kisses
and the light touch of your delicate hand?

The Hurricane

The sky became dark and the wind pulled
ferociously at the groves of trees,
the gust passed rapidly and chased
the leaves and branches tossed in the whirlwind.
    A moment of threatening quiet,
then the clouds opened with a bolt of lightening,
the birds crossed the tempestuous
thick fog seeking escape.

The hail fell merciless and white
and the thunder resounded frighteningly,
while the earth lay down tired
in the tumult of the whirling roar.
    But abruptly far away
the fog tore open and the blue skies laughed,
the rainbow arched over the horizon,
radiating the divided clouds.

Nostalgia

    If I could only see the green banks
of my native river
and the clear sky reflected in its waves
and their cool murmuring.
    If I could seek among the white pebbles of the gravel
my lucky stone,
find the laughing and happy voice
of my blissful childhood,
    and see again in the emerald water
my face as then,
transfigured by the warm reflection
of dawn's laughter.

Separation

    Listen, the wild shore
is splendid in the moonlight,
that radiates the pure air
of the silent and dark night.
    The moon, that heard my crying,
the moon, that heard my crying!
It was on a night of enchantment
that you appeared on the beach,
    with your fiery gaze,
your sweet seductive voice,
then you crossed the blue waters
following the nomad's path,
    like the sails

at the farthest edge of the sea,
that vanish into the cruelty of time
and never know how to return.

Translated by Maria Enrico

The Hula Hula Flag

ᕙ *Antonio Marinoni*

Pozzolengo (Brescia), Italy, July 30, 1879–Fayetteville, Arkansas, 1944

Antonio Marinoni, destined to become professor of languages at the University of
Arkansas, is included in this anthology by virtue of a lively book of memories entitled *Come ho "fatto" l'America* (How I "Made" America), published in Milan in
1932, which has a certain interest because of the notably extraordinary character of
the author's personal experience. The book relates that his father had already emigrated to America when Antonio was a baby. Marinoni recounts, in fact, that
when he was nine years old, his mother took him to Brazil in search of his father.
Later, his father apparently moved to the United States, where he was probably
joined by his wife. Marinoni meanwhile was completing his studies (according to
Flamma, he took his degree in Padua), and perhaps in 1900 he himself emigrated.
He became a waiter in Brooklyn. Here the book dwells on a description of Little
Italy, even offering a translation of the poem "Malebolge" by Arturo Giovannitti.
Then he worked in a factory in the vicinity of New Haven, and he began to teach
English to the Italians. He matriculated at Yale and obtained a master of arts degree, then a doctorate. He began to teach at Columbia University, after which he
obtained an assistant professorship at the University of Arkansas, where for more
than thirty years he was head of the Romance languages department. When his
father heard this news, he exclaimed, "Toni, you have made America!" In July
1908, he married Rosa Zagnoni, a fiction writer and poet, a bold, daring young girl
portrayed in the excerpt here.

Marinoni published various books, several of an academic character: *Italian
Reader* (1909); *Elementary Italian Grammar* (1911); *L'Italia* (with E. H. Wilkins,

1922); *España* (1926); *France* (with R. Michaud, 1927); *Andiamo in Italia* (1929); and *Italy Yesterday and Today* (1931).

ESSENTIAL BIBLIOGRAPHY

Flamma 1936; Marinoni 1932; Schiavo 1938.

The separation from my loved ones was less painful to bear, from the start, within that family of decent Calabrians who were waiting for me. I was, in fact, a guest of honor of sorts. When I arrived, there was only the lady of the house to receive me; the two little children had already gone to school, and the cousins and her husband had left for work on time. She welcomed me with the deference that is shown in Italy, particularly by common women, toward the well-educated. This is not inspired and even less imposed, as is erroneously believed, by preconceived class distinctions. It is time to loudly proclaim and dispel the myth widely believed in America, that there are privileged classes in Italy which exist within a closed system of small oligarchies of blood and money and to which the middle-class bourgeoisie and the common people show honor, even bowing down before them like serfs or as in times of Bourbon despotism long ago. It is time to stridently declare that servitude of the spirit no longer exists even in Italy, and it only remains here and there, the mere appearance as a simple oral form, or as a purely utilitarian pretense. A title of nobility without a core of honesty, of virtue in the Roman sense, the upper class that does not understand the gesture of charity but rather keeps to itself—these have finally had their day in Italy. One single superior class now exists in our country, the one that has passed down to us over time and through the most distant traditions, to which all bow without distinction: the class consisting of those who distinguish themselves from others through their good will and intelligence, the class that is moved by the splendor of good works, courage, and thought. This triumph is only for the winners.

"Welcome, sir!" said the good woman from the doorway, bowing slightly. She shook my hand warmly.

She had, like all southerners, the gift of gab, polite manners, an expressive face. Seated at the kitchen table (the main room in all houses in the Colony, used nine times out of ten with the double or triple functions of kitchen, dining room, and living room), I watched my landlady bustling around a huge cast iron stove, ready to remove the coffeepot from the fire as soon as it boiled, which she was making fresh for the guest. In the blink of an eye, she placed a modest place setting on a small white cloth, and when the coffee was poured, she sat in front of me, to keep me company, as she said smiling.

The first hesitation having vanished, the conversation went along smoothly, no sooner than I had reassured the good woman that I perfectly understood her colorful and fluid dialect.

"We don't have, as you can see, many conveniences at home, but in our village, in Villa San Giovanni, life was hard, so much harder than here in America. At least here we have running water and in the winter we keep warm because coal is plentiful. And then my husband has always worked, and we put a few dollars aside, while in Italy we had to sweat just to survive. On a block like this, we can't expect to enjoy the air and sun, and our thoughts go back there often, to our Calabria, but living here also has its benefits. Almost all of the tenants in this tenement are from our village, and for me it's a great comfort to be able to call out to my old friends from the stairs. Our health, thank God, is very good, and my two children are honor students. After all, we live for them. I hardly ever leave the house; I go down to do my shopping and come back home right away.

"Imagine! I've lived in this house for fifteen years and I've never been to New York!" My husband often tells me, "'Why don't you come with me? I'll take you to see the Statue of Liberty, the skyscrapers, the shops on Fifth Avenue!' But, sir, what does he want? I don't feel like going. There are always things to do at home, and then. . . ."

The good woman made a gesture as if to say, "What's the use in going?"

"And maybe you're right!" I agreed, gathering her internal thoughts from her eyes.

In fact New York, with all of its spectacular achievements, surely appeals to the calculating intelligence of men who love a challenge, or to the pleasure-seeking, light-heartedness of those who have no responsibilities, but little can be said for simple souls like hers. Fans of dynamism go to New York or even those who are forced to work there, not those who, like her, feel the nostalgia for fresh air, of peace, of sun.

"Coney Island, yes, sometimes I go there in the summer," the woman began again, "but only to take a ride, for the sea, which is certainly not as blue as the one in Villa San Giovanni, but it's still the sea."

"I see that even after twenty years in America, Villa San Giovanni is always on your mind."

"And how could I forget it, sir? The place where you were born is like a prodigal son; you will always love it. But to go back there, I don't believe so. My husband, though, thinks about it and always tells me, 'Concetta, once our children no longer need us, we'll sell everything and go back there.' I agree with him, to make him happy. But it's a dream. When the time comes to leave them, our children, even he won't know what to do. You'll see them tonight, our kids, how big they are—and how American!" added the woman with visible pride. "You should hear how they speak English!"

"Very well," I interrupted her, "but Italian, or at least your dialect, they speak that as well, don't they?"

"Well, sir, what do you expect? Italian, no, because there are very few in the Colony who speak it well, and they don't want to speak the dialect because they say that it's a barbaric language that makes Americans laugh."

And she was right. Indeed there is no other country in the world where so many languages are spoken as in America and, oddly, where more people laugh upon hearing the inflections of an unknown language. It has happened to me many times on the street that while conversing with friends in Italian I have noticed a giggle escape the lips of a passer-by almost in sympathy or commiseration, in those instances when it was not muttered gibberish or sounds made to mimic or even worse.

But Italian is not alone in arousing this kind of childish laughter, and the privilege of entertaining listeners is without exception also enjoyed by other languages. Especially in the theater, one should see how the general public enjoys it when a character actor impersonates a Jew, a Frenchman, a German, and most amusing of all, a "guaglìò" as if to suggest something even lower than an Italian.

And it is not out of place to recount an episode that I witnessed in those days. One muggy day in July, I had gone to Coney Island to take a dip in the sea with some friends whom I worked alongside every day. We went into a tavern, a sort of café-concert, and sat down.

The place was packed with a diverse crowd of aspiring Americans; this was clearly obvious not only by their characteristic features and faces but also by that indefinable set of mannerisms and inflections that never vanish, typical of foreigners speaking English. The variety show was so weak that we were about to leave a short time later when a magician appeared on stage.

"Let's see what he can do," said someone in the group.

And so we stayed. After a series of games, disappearances and reappearances, the magician began his final number. He had a huge tuba on his head. He takes it off, and he slips his arm inside to show us simpletons that it is empty. Many doubt it, and the artist, to reassure his audience, passes the tuba from hand to hand until it returns to the stage, after a careful and serious examination by the most curious.

"Now I bet," I say, "he'll pull out of a pair of doves, a duck, and a guinea pig!"

Unfortunately he had not been a magician for very long. After a series of futile moves, it's here, it's not here, it's coming out, it's not coming out, he slowly pulls out a corner of a handkerchief.

"Nice work," I said. But no, it's not a handkerchief, it's a flag; in fact, unfolding and unfolding, it really is an enormous flag, so big that two assistants are needed to keep it unfurled. A huge melon is painted on a black background; the melon is broken in half and is so red that I have the urge to bite into it.

"It's the flag of the blacks," the magician declares, amid laughter from the audience.

His hand goes fishing inside the tuba another time, and a second flag comes out.

"Whose will it be this time?"

It's the German flag; there is no need to say it. A ruddy German announces it, painted in the middle with a gigantic glass of beer in his hands. And this one is also greeted with the sound of roaring laughter.

But the magician is not finished. Again he sticks his hand inside the tuba and out comes . . . but this time it's not a flag: the two assistants are busy unfurling something that looks like a sheet in front of the stage, but may not be. And the girl who may or may not be dressed, shown in such an ambiguous position in the center of that sheet, what does she represent? The audience eagerly awaits the answer. Many try in vain to guess, but the magician is here to put everyone out of their misery.

"This," he says, "is the *hula hula* flag."

"It's really too much," I remark with my neighbors' approval.

But judging by the laughter of the crude audience, one could say, as in the game of poker, the sky was the limit.

"Let's go," I said, "before it's our turn!"

But one of my companions, new to this kind of vulgar humor, asked me to explain the riddle. It so happened that while I was explaining to my naïve friend the hidden meaning of that reference, the magician had already taken a fourth flag from the tuba. There was nothing to doubt or even guess. It was ours, with its three beautiful colors. Only, instead of the Cross of Savoy, there was painted in the middle a man in rags, with many earrings hanging from his two lobes. If only it ended there. No, sir. The audience had immediately understood and laughed while the magician did his best to restore some order. When he could speak, he said, "This is the macaroni flag," as he shouted loudly.

My friends were appalled; I felt denigrated. A powerless rage roared within me that kept me paralyzed as if I were seized by an affliction.

"Earth, open up, and swallow me alive."

But suddenly the scene changes. What is it? Perhaps a hero of our people came forward to protest this vile insult? In my soul I felt the remorse of the indifferent who live "without praise and without blame" and leave the task of fighting for God and country to the courageous. We turned to where a strange bustle indicated that something was happening.

Dear and noble creature! After nearly thirty years that you have been my companion in life, my safe guide, and as I referred to you earlier in these pages, always faithful, I still see you in my memory, surrounded by a halo of glory, when with the spirit of an Italic heroine you rose up and put a stop to the destruction and returned that audience of castaways of Americanism to a more dignified concept of themselves more than of others. And man, the eternal child who also harbors an innate righteousness in the deep recesses of his consciousness, welcomed that noble indignation with sincere signs of rejoicing. Even the magician had to give his respectful apologies, and when from that ill-fated tuba he pulled the glorious flag of stars and stripes, the audience suddenly burst out with a fitting demonstration of warm affection for that flag and for all the other flags of the world.

It's not for nothing that all the psalms end in glory.

Of course the American press did not deign to cover the event at all, not even in one of the many local news columns, but a few days later in one of the Italian newspapers in New York, I had the pleasure of reading this note:

AN IMBECILE INSULTS THE ITALIAN FLAG

We learn from a letter to the *Bollettino della Sera* by Mr. Giuseppe Cristosi that at Dreamland's Midget City Theater in Coney Island, a magician, playing a game with flags, pulled out the Italian flag, and to be humorous took the liberty of saying:

"This is the macaroni flag."

A young Italian lady had the presence of mind to get up and, in the presence of over six hundred people, said in English: "Shut up, you're an idiot, that's not the macaroni flag, it's the Italian flag and everyone must respect it."

The courageous young lady, who was able to respond in such an Italian way, bears the name Rosina Zagnoni, and she is the daughter of the eloquent journalist Mr. Antero Zagnoni, correspondent for the *Tribune* in Rome.

Pleased that our beloved colleague was able to provide his daughter with an education in patriotism, we hope that other compatriots follow Miss

Zagnoni's example in order to garner respect for our homeland and the free citizen, so that at a time in the not too distant future we will no longer hear stupid insults repeated by ignoramuses and charlatans who know nothing about our homeland.

Translated by Giulia Prestia

The Verdict

✑ *Corrado Altavilla*

Aversa (Caserta), Italy, 1897–New York, New York, 1950

Gente lontana (People Far Away), the novel that Corrado Altavilla published in Milan in 1938, is a curious, very captivating mixture of narrative voices. Above all, the novel is a *"giallo"* (detective story), in fact, what Americans call a police procedural, a narration that has its moment of greatest tension in the trial phase. At the same time, it is also a metropolitan novel, whose best pages are those dedicated to the description of New York: its mythic underworlds, its affluent sections, and the Babel of people who live there, strongly typified. Although characterized by a rapid pace, a nervousness, wholly concentrated on the development of the plot, carried forward with a skillful montage, through fragments dedicated to the individual protagonists, the novel is not averse to conducting an interesting psychological probing of its personages, from which emerge, in particular, some passages characteristic of the mentality of the emigrant.

Gente lontana is a successful blend of a certain type of Italian narrative of consumption, which typically chooses boldly worldly themes, especially tied to the world of vice, and the American detective narrative, the genre of the hardboiled, with which the author appears to have an up-to-date familiarity. Nonetheless, the novel constitutes a rather singular case. Though a heavily dramatic novel, wholly pivoting upon the sorrowful events of an Italian family, it is not sentimental. It cannot quite be said that "it alternates between melodrama and irony" (Traldi), but certainly, *Gente lontana* is a story of facts, as incontrovertible as a police crime report.

After having spent a considerable fortune in Italy, Stefano Sacchi emigrates to New York, where he starts a family, which includes his wife Maria and children

John and Emma, who at the time of the narrated events are, respectively, eighteen and sixteen years old. Sacchi is employed in the advertising department of a soap works, which evokes a digression on the ruthless mechanisms of the market; he is neither rich nor poor, and he lives in a residential section in the suburbs.

For some time, John has alarmed his family. He has left his studies, he returns to his house very late, and has too much money in his pocket. To his mother who questions him, he explains that he won the money in games. Ultimately, he leaves the house of his parents to live alone. He is by now the accountant of Kelly, an Irish owner of a billiard hall frequented by questionable people. Kelly gives him a pistol and invites him to carry arms.

"By night, following this or that new friend, he had become familiar with strange haunts, brothels and cabarets of the lowest orders, where black and yellow men danced with white women and vice versa, mouth to mouth, reciprocally inebriated by their breath, which inebriation had rendered acrid. He had become familiar with the opium dens of Chinatown, haunts of the perverted of Greenwich Village, the underworld of Harlem" (53). With a pretext, Kelly sends John to the apartment of Kitsy, the beautiful, sensual mulatto of whom he is the lover, and an attraction is soon born between the two young people. In the meanwhile, John's parents are looking for him. The father discovers a note signed by Kitsy, with the address of the place where she works as a B-girl, and decides to go for verification. He finds the woman, and falling in love with her, he does not reveal the motive for his visit: the two pass a night of sex in her apartment. The morning after, Kitsy, by now disgusted with her own life, summons John, but when both are about to yield to their desire, she exhorts him to go. Several hours later, she is found dead, killed by two bullets from a pistol.

An investigation immediately ensues, and various witnesses testify that the last two persons who entered Kitsy's house were a distinguished gentleman and a young man. Returned to Kelly, John reads the news in the evening newspapers; agitated, he takes refuge in an opium den and then, still under the influence of the drug, returns to his parents' house. His father is assailed by a tremendous suspicion. He talks with his son, and together they decide to go to see Kelly, who, however, has already denounced John to the police. Father and son are interrogated, and notwithstanding the attempt by the father to exculpate John, he is incarcerated. The police try to brutally extort a confession from him, but he resists, and he will be incriminated for murder in the first degree. In the meanwhile, his father Stefano, whose license has been revoked, sells the house with the obligation to leave it in six months, and with the proceeds, hires a competent lawyer, Anthony Garra. Two days before the trial, Stefano's wife Maria dies, and contrary to the opinion of Stefano, Garra does not want to ask for the delay of the date of the trial, which will conclude with a verdict of not guilty. The real assassin is soon discovered.

Emerged from the nightmare, the family is now profoundly marked. In a secret drama taking place within the larger drama of the family, Emma has aborted, after being made pregnant by her fiancé, Frederick. The final choice is that of returning to the first steps in the family's life. Stefano decides to embark for Italy with his children. With them is also a bier. In this way, according to Martino Marazzi, who has produced a lucid reading of the novel, *Gente lontana* ideally closes the vicissitudes of the Italian American novel in Italian, almost in the moment in which Little Italy, with the election of the mayor of New York, Fiorello La Guardia (1934), obtains its full consecration, even in politics.

Altavilla was on the editorial staff in Naples, of the *Giornale della Sera* and the *Monsignor Perrelli*. In 1923, he moved to New York, where for years, he was on the editorial staff of the *Progresso Italo-Americano,* and also occasional correspondent of the *Corriere della Sera.* He returned to Italy in his fifties and became a correspondent for the *Tempo* of Rome.

ESSENTIAL BIBLIOGRAPHY

Altavilla 1938, 283–299; DBIO 1948, 337; DBIO 1957, 344; Marazzi 2001, 38–40; Traldi 1976, 246–247.

The jury entered Indian file, just as they had gone out. They returned silently to their places, and Stefano tried in vain to read the verdict in their faces.

Silence returned to the courtroom, and it was frightening. Suddenly he heard a door creak, and the judge appeared and went calmly to his chair. A few more seconds went by.

Then the clerk stood up and asked the jury foreman if a verdict had been reached.

"Yes," replied the silk-stocking salesman, who, being the first to be chosen, had automatically assumed the role of jury foreman. John, at that monosyllable, bent over and gripped the edge of the table. Stefano bit his finger to keep from crying out.

The clerk asked, "And what verdict have you reached?"

Everyone in the courtroom—the public, reporters, the judge himself—bent slightly forward almost as if they wanted to move a little closer to the person's mouth who was about to speak, the better to hear his words.

Standing up, the salesman said in a low, almost indifferent voice, "Not guilty."

"Not guilty!" everyone repeated at the same moment, almost echoing the sworn foreman's words. "Not guilty!" shouted Stefano, running to his son and hugging him to his chest. "Not guilty!" shouted the lawyer Garra to himself, almost congratulating himself for the good work. "Not guilty!" shouted the reporters while dashing to phone booths. "Not guilty!" murmured the public, rising, partly pleased, and partly disappointed.

John, hugging his father, listened to his sobs and did not speak. Then suddenly, bringing to an end a hundred confused and rapid thoughts passing through his mind, he too was seized by an outburst of tears and murmured, "What good does that do? What good does that do?"

It didn't seem to have a thing to do with absolution: who was there to take the good news to, if the house was deserted and she wasn't waiting for him? Once more he thought it would have been better if they had condemned him, and the verdict seemed like a joke, an awful joke. But a little later when he was outside and noticed the fresh evening air, and turning around didn't spot the guards at his heels, he was struck by sudden happiness and thought with horror of the anguish that would have struck at the same moment if by chance the foreman had pronounced a single word instead of two, if he had simply said, "guilty." Lafayette Street was deserted and seemed excessively wide. All the buildings seemed new and more beautiful and everything looked different, as if he had been away from the world for many many years. A taxi drew up to the sidewalk and his father murmured: "Let's go." He got in reluctantly because he needed the sky, and the low automobile made him feel like he was in a cell. They didn't say a word. Stefano no longer felt anxious for his son; other worries came back to haunt him, and he wasn't able to get rid of them to enjoy that brief moment of joy. John looked at the street through the window, at the illuminated signs, men walking on the sidewalk, and everything gave him a strange feeling of pleasure, filled him with an unfamiliar will to live. The taxi went fast, stopped at intersections, and started up again dodging other cars, dodging pedestrians. Suddenly the taxi stopped. John was surprised not to be in front of his own house. He thought his mother was still at home, in the living room blazing with lights. But he didn't ask. He followed his father up the big marble staircase, through the long white-tiled hallway, without a thought in his head, without an emotion gnawing at his soul. When they reached a door his father stopped and said very softly, "She's in here."

They looked uncertainly at each other. That second was enough for John to feel in his heart that sorrow was destroying the joy just as earlier joy had killed the sorrow. "She's here," his father repeated, and pushed the door open.

The room was dark. There was only a tremulous spot of yellowish light in one corner. Two candles were at the head of the casket, and the air was impregnated by the odor of flowers.

John went in on tiptoe, and when he was near the casket, he saw his mother's face. She was thinner and her mouth a little twisted. Her nose had become longer and more pointed. Her eyelids were not completely closed, giving the impression she was not dead.

The idea suddenly flashed through his mind that this was a play, a faked death to get the jury to exonerate him. He bent over, and it seemed to him that her bosom lifted imperceptibly with a light breath. He then looked at her crossed hands, rather high, with the tips of her fingers nearly touching her neck. He looked at them for some time. They were white and tapering. The fingernails looked like wax. He wanted to touch them but as he stretched out a hand, he began to tremble; he turned suddenly to his father. Their eyes were dry. They stood quietly next to each other, and a little later John, overwhelmed again by the same trembling, took his father's hand and squeezed it tightly. Then he asked in a very low voice, "Did you hear that?"

"Hear what?" Stefano asked without understanding.

"She's breathing, she's breathing!" his son said with a quiver in his voice.

They stood close together with eyes staring at the cadaver, holding their breath. They waited.

Suddenly a weak, barely perceptible breathing broke the silence. John grabbed his father's hand more tightly and with the same tremble in his voice, "Did you hear?"

Holding him tightly his father pulled him away from the casket and then said quietly: "It's not her, it's not her!"

In an opposite corner, in the dark, on a chair with her head leaning against the wall was Emma, asleep.

When they went back home after the funeral, the house seemed so different. The furniture was the same, the divan there, the table here, the sideboard and armchairs in the same place. And yet it seemed empty.

A neighbor entered soon after with a big basket and went straight to the dining room, spread a tablecloth over the table, set it for three and took from the basket a boiled chicken, some salmon, a little fruit, and a bottle of apple juice. Then she said in a loud voice, "Come on, there's nothing you can do, what is done is done, sooner or later we all have to go."

Stefano and his two children were hungry, but they didn't move. The woman then went into the living room, took Emma by her hand and led her to the table. The other two got up and followed her.

The woman sat down also, facing John. Then to break the silence, she murmured, "And to think it could have been worse!"

"Worse than this?" Stefano asked without raising his eyes from his plate.

"Oh, yes, worse, it could be worse, they could have convicted that one there!" and she motioned toward John with her chin. None of the three responded and she continued, "Just imagine what pain that would have caused us here! No one ever believed it was him who fired the shot. You just don't do such things with a face like that. And we know how he was raised. But when you run with the devil, you do bad things, and I who have read every word about it in the newspapers . . . what can I say! The facts were all against him because, no matter how you slice it, the last man to go there was no one but him."

John turned pale and his appetite vanished. His stomach suddenly closed as though in a vise and the piece of chicken in front of him even made him feel nauseous.

"Right," said Stefano. And to change the subject, Emma asked, "What kind of fish is this?"

"Salmon," the woman answered, and started up again, "The neighbors even made bets. Louis McQuade, the one in the corner house, bet a hundred dollars that he would be convicted, and he's furious now because he says you bought the jury. But that one bets on everything, even on car licenses. If the sum of the numbers of the first car that passes is odd he wins, if it is even he loses. Gambling is a sickness."

Since no one spoke she also remained quiet. But after a little silence, she asked, "Where will you go now?"

John looked up and asked in turn, "What do you mean 'where will you go?' "

"Where will you go live," the woman explained. "Now that you have sold your house, where do you have to go?"

"Sold?" John asked in dismay.

That question took Stefano by surprise, and he calmly replied, "And where did you expect us to get the money for the trial, the funeral, enough to live on, now that I've lost my job?" After he said that and noticed his son's face grow pale, he regretted his words and added in a tone of voice he hoped sounded calm and natural. "If I hadn't already sold it, I would sell it now: it's too big for the three of us!"

He looked around him and in fact the rooms seemed big without her: was it possible that such a little woman could leave such a huge emptiness? The same thought occurred to Emma, who now looked with resentment and impatience at that woman sitting in mama's place. She stood up to avoid looking at her, hoping she would get up too. John remained silent. One thought was on his mind: to go away, leave everyone, run off to some place far away where no one could find him and no one could remind him of what had happened. He thought, "Staying here means to die. Every day someone will talk about the trial, every day they'll talk about the dead woman, they'll say it was me who killed her, and when we leave the house they'll talk about the house that was sold because of me. Like that for all my life, always always always?"

He got up and followed Emma into the living room.

At that moment, family friends arrived. They had come through the Holland Tunnel to offer their condolences. They were friends from New Jersey who came, as they said, to shed a tear. They entered with contrite faces—Mr. Gandolfi, small and bald; his wife, big, still fresh and rosy-cheeked; their two daughters who were Americanized in everything except their dark, kinky hair. After a round of strong and meaningful handshakes they all sat down without speaking.

John greeted them and went to his bedroom, certain that sooner or later talk about the trial would come up.

After five long, embarrassing minutes Mrs. Gandolfi took her courage in hand and murmured, "Who would ever have thought it!" Her words failed to solicit a response. Then one of the girls asked in English, because she didn't know Italian, "How old was she?"

That question surprised Stefano. He was surprised he didn't exactly remember the age of that poor woman who had lived beside him all those sad and melancholy years without ever complaining. And not knowing what to reply, he said, "She was still young!" As he said that, it occurred to him that he would have to give her age for the death certificate. Why couldn't he remember anymore?

The conversation became more lively, and Emma described her mother's death because she was the only family member with her when she died; Stefano was lost in calculations, looking for points and dates of referral to precisely establish how old his wife was when she left this world. The visitors had become loquacious, and without shedding that tear they had come so far to shed, they began talking about other things, even letting little laughs escape, which they stifled immediately, however.

Mr. Gandolfi said that his business was going to the dogs, and he exaggerated a little because it seemed inappropriate to look like he had no problems when they had so many. The lemons in California "had learned" to grow large and juicy, and now he imported so few of them from Sicily, which barely made a glass of lemonade. "I've got to change businesses," he said; "the tariffs have become impossible, the taxes are going up, you lose money by the shovelful. America is finished. Whoever had the luck to make it has lost it on Wall Street, and whoever hasn't made it yet never will."

His two daughters looked at him and didn't understand a word of what their father was saying because, while keeping a close watch on his lemons, Mr. Gandolfi had never bothered to teach them his language or even his dialect.

Stefano was disconcerted and could only hope that the visit would end soon, while Emma hoped they would stay a while longer, almost as if she were afraid of being alone in the house with her father and brother. What would they do all day, and the day after, and the one after that? The lively conversation continued. When Mr. Gandolfi stopped, his wife would take over; and when she stopped the two daughters would start talking at the same time about the same fashion model, the same movie they had seen the night before, the same picnic they were organizing with a group of friends on the shore of a lake they had heard a lot of good things about.

Then other people arrived. The Rossi family from Staten Island, the Rev. Gennaro Desimone who assiduously frequented cabarets in order to hear and see the sins he had to contend with, the lawyer Colantuono who organized pilgrimages to the Mother country to cadge free tickets for himself and his family, the Marquis Sanzoni who promoted banquets in honor of whoever he came across and then collected a percentage from the restaurateur, Professor Marimpietri who taught everything from singing to algebra, Cavaliere Spaselli who murmured shamefacedly, "To tell the truth I don't know if this is a visit of congratulation or condolences," and he quickly looked at each face to see which expression he should wear.

Stefano thought, "If the verdict had been a conviction, not a soul would be seen in this house!" And whereas previously he had neither hated nor loved those people, now he felt a sense of aversion that made him want to get up and boot them all out.

Up to now he had felt indifferent when around them: seeing everyone at that moment now with those faces of fake sorrow, he felt he knew them for the first time, or rather, knew them well for the first time. They revealed themselves to be small-time swindlers and wheeler-dealers, all people who knew how to take advantage of the ignorance of the poor emigrants who arrive lost and dazed in a new land and blindly trusted them, only to be exploited. Over these long years they had made money by cheating and ripping them off and had grown fat. Then the emigrants had gone their own way and had no more use for them. New ones were no longer arriving. The wheeler-dealers tried other means of earning a living, but they lost their money, and were cheated and swindled in turn. And they ended up as they had been when they arrived, or rather, worse off, with old age creeping up. Stefano took a good look at them: he had known that attorney Colantuono, that Marquis Sanzoni, during their good times—cars, chauffeurs, summer homes.

Now they were in bad shape. The emigrants went to visit the Mother Country on their own without needing to be herded together like sheep. The banqueters had learned to deal directly with the restaurants or with the directors of hotel dining rooms. And if any of them had a son or daughter with a beautiful voice, he sent them to a recognized voice teacher and not to Professor Marimpietri who had ended up in a furnished room he continued to call a "studio," which was also a bedroom, living room, and kitchen. Everyone was talking, at times all at once, but when someone suddenly forgot they were there to make a visit of condolence and let out a boisterous laugh, the others would look at him and revert to silence and sad faces.

During those moments of silence, which were repeated from time to time, everyone's thoughts turned to John who was not to be seen. Colantuono and Cavaliere Spaselli were of the same opinion: "There was not enough proof to condemn him, but he was the killer." If he had been condemned, neither of the two would have set foot in that house, yet even though they were convinced that within those walls was a murderer, they stayed there without moral scruples since the law had had its say, and officially the boy was not guilty. Now they, and with them the others that thought as they did, were assailed by the curiosity to see that person suddenly become famous for all the columns written about him and for all those full-face and profile photographs of him that had been published. However, no one dared discuss what he or she often quietly asked each other, "Where is John?" The Gandolfi girls said he was there, since they had seen him when they came in, and his wish to stay hidden augmented the general feeling that he was not innocent. Why, in fact, didn't he show his face? He was afraid, that was it, afraid to show himself in public because he knew very well (and if he didn't know who did?) that this time the jury, luckily for him, was badly mistaken.

Stefano hoped they would go away, but no one moved; when one topic seemed exhausted, another would be put forward. Everyone would have his say, and the conversation would suddenly be reanimated. Everybody had a secret resolve: to wait for John come down so they could see him and, encouraged by his presence, talk about the trial, a subject which no one had the courage to begin, not knowing where to start.

In the meanwhile time was passing. Emma began to feel very tired and twice was forced to close her eyes because her head was spinning. In her father's head, one thought followed another: he judged those present, hoped they would go away, had the idea of ditching them all and closing himself in his room, thought about the funeral, the trial, the attorney Garra, the twelve jurors. The idea occurred to him to go back to his office, thinking that perhaps they had given him his job back. He made a mental calculation of the money that was left and divided it by twelve.

Suddenly the lawyer Colantuoni asked, "Where is John? Can't we see him to offer our congratulations?"

The others remained in awed silence. Stefano answered, "He's upstairs. I think he's sleeping." Emma, on the other hand, not realizing how morbid their curiosity was, believing instead that the wish to see John was only a courteous and kind desire, got up saying, "I'll go call him."

Short afterward, John entered the living room. Everyone got up and gathered around him noisily. Colantuono and Spaselli embraced him, kissed him on both cheeks and one said "Bravo!" and the other murmured "Finally!" Mr. Gandolfi's girls were more expansive than ever. One stroked his hair, the other pinched his chin.

Professor Marimpietri, after a bit of calm had been restored, loudly intoned like a preacher beginning a sermon, "Once more justice has triumphed!" The others were silent. He was a little embarrassed by that silence, not knowing whether to continue or stop there, and he preferred to say something else—abandoning the solemn tone, however, "And he is really lucky because unfortunately justice triumphs so rarely in this world. In America, then!" he added after a pause, "In America, the more money you have, the more things go your way!"

"But this is not the case!" murmured Signor Gandolfi, under the impression that the professor had made a blunder.

"Certainly, certainly!" the other one said at once. "This time it turned out well."

In the meanwhile they went back to their places; they had John sit in the middle of the divan, as is usually done for people of high standing or for the guest of honor.

"Bravo, bravo!" Cavaliere Spaselli repeated who could find no other words because of his unshakeable conviction, and he looked at John thinking, "He had some guts to kill that woman, and now has the courage to put on that saintly face with his body full of pooh!"

The lawyer Colantuono was the one to begin the interrogation, first looking around: "Something like that could happen to any one of us. You go someplace, you leave shortly afterward, they find a body. Who was the last to leave? Cavaliere Spaselli? And Cavaliere Spaselli is arrested!"

"That's right!" Mrs. Gandolfi murmured with a sigh. Because of the heat her face was sweaty and red.

However, the Cavaliere didn't like that "Cavaliere Spaselli arrested," because once he really was almost arrested on account of trouble over a bill.

"Yes," he said. "It could happen to anyone: who was the last to enter—the lawyer Colantuono? And the lawyer Colantuono is arrested." After saying that, he felt he had put everything in its place.

Colantuono, who had pronounced those words without an ulterior motive, realized he had made a mistake because of the business of the bill, and he wanted to make up for it: "It could happen to any gentleman like you, like me." Then turning to John he asked, "When you saw her that morning, was she worried? Did she feel like something was about to happen to her?"

"Who?" John asked, who was thinking about other things and hadn't heard the last sentence.

"Who? That woman, the mulatto," Colantuono was more precise, looking John in the face.

John thought, "I shouldn't have come down. I knew how it would end up." Then he said, "No. She was calm. Very calm."

One of the Gandolfi girls asked, "Was she as beautiful as the pictures they published in the papers?"

"Yes," John replied pretending indifference. "She was a beautiful woman."

Stefano covered his face with his hand, thinking he might betray himself, given that he could have answered that question better than his son, and he thought, "More than beautiful, if you had seen her as I saw her!"

"She was a beautiful woman," John repeated, and everyone hung on his words, especially the two Gandolfi girls and Emma. "I saw her twice and only for a few minutes," he then said with the same indifferent tone.

"Did she have black skin?" asked Mrs. Rossi who opened her mouth for the first time, looking at her white hands almost as if making a comparison.

"Dark, not black," John said. "A little darker than any brunette."

Cavaliere Spaselli thought, "He knew her well!" and the same thought entered the mind of Attorney Colantuono.

The Rev. Gennaro Desimone, who had remained all that time with his hands crossed over his belly and his head slightly inclined, simulating deep thought, raised his eyes at hearing talk of dark skin and became attentive.

"The mulattos are beautiful when they are beautiful!" Attorney Colantuono said with the air of one who wanted it to be known that he knew certain things. "And they are hot blooded, oh . . . if they are hot blooded!" he added with a snicker.

Mrs. Gandolfi looked down with affected modesty, while her two daughters turned their eager, greedy little faces toward John, expecting him to confirm the thermometric virtues of mulattos.

But John did not respond. That topic was very distasteful, and he was anxious for the conversation to take another tack. He felt all their eyes on him and sensed they wanted to read his thoughts, evidently to learn something more than they were not convinced of his innocence, and that at least a doubt remained in each of them, a question mark that from time to time slipped out in the form of an imperceptible, ironic little smile.

"It it were me," Mr. Rossi suddenly exclaimed, "I would dedicate my life to tracking down the guilty person. What little money I have I would spend down to the last red cent."

"If I had it," murmured Stefano.

"What?" asked Mr. Rossi.

"That little money to spend down to the last red cent," concluded Stefano, who had now finished the mental accounting of his finances. And after a pause he added, "And then to what end? To render a service to society? Do you think it's worth the effort?"

"Yes, yes, that is right," said Mrs. Gandolfi. And the Rev. Desimone murmured: "Not for society, but for the moral satisfaction, to be able to say: 'You will see, you will see what kind of mistake you were about to make!'"

"And don't you think it is enough to have a clear conscience? And then don't you who are preachers believe in God; don't think it's enough to have God your witness to what you do?" Stefano asked slowly.

The Rev. Desimone thought, "It's not enough, not enough, because if they had convicted him, John would be at peace with his conscience." But instead he said: "Oh, certainly, certainly! One's own conscience, most certainly, is what counts, and the only thing that counts, that is true!"

The living room was filled with smoke, and since there were so many of them stuck so close together, they all began to feel very warm. Mrs. Gandolfi kept wiping her face with a lipstick-stained handkerchief, and the Rev. Desimone, feeling a thirst coming on, thought of those dear Irish families who, when there was a body in the house, brought out bottles of wine and whiskey and in the summer large jugs of chilled beer. "It's the only way to forget a little bit," he was thinking, and clicked his tongue against his dry palate.

Finally Mrs. Rossi stood up, saying, "Thank goodness it ended well," and going to John, followed by her husband she shook his hand murmuring, "Buck up, these things happen in this world!" The others also stood up.

"I'm going, too," Cavaliere Spaselli said. "We are, too," the four Gandolfi said all at once.

There was a cordial exchange of good wishes, a loud crisscrossing of empty phrases. They huddled around John, the two Gandolfi girls each holding an arm, then the little group went away, and not one remembered to look contrite. They had forgotten all about the dead woman. From the house they could still hear the confusion of voices. They recognized Cavaliere Spaselli's laugh, a loud outburst, and the fresher laughter of the two girls, whom the Rev. Desimone had taken by the arm with an air of questionable protection.

Emma was very pale. Twice lately she had felt dizzy. When the discussion about conscience had come up she had thought that she, the least expected, was the only one in her family not to have a clear one. Then she had thought of Frederick who had not come around even after John's acquittal, not even after mamma died. While the others talked, she had asked herself whether he still loved her, and her response was vague, imprecise, since she didn't even know what she felt for him.

When everyone had gone, she began putting the chairs back in place and suddenly felt the weight of a great weight of a great responsibility. She picked up all the dirty ashtrays, went to the kitchen, noticed the plate with the leftover chicken and the one with untouched salmon on the polished table. That sight filled her with disgust; then she ran quickly up to her room, and throwing herself on the bed, began to cry.

John heard her sobs and went to her bedside. He sat down next to her and stroked her hair, murmuring, "It's useless to cry, Emma, we can't do anything about these things."

She suddenly turned, looked at him wild eyed, feeling his last words pounding in her brain, "We can't do anything about these things!"

Only afterward did she understand that John had tried to comfort her with those words, believing she was crying for mama.

Translated by Martha King

PART III

On Stage (and Off)

Introduction

"Mandolin players on clear nights filled the salt air with soulful strumming of old folk tunes."[1] With this quietly touching and melancholic image, a novelist of the 1930s portrays a group of emigrants on the deck of the *Conte Bertoldi*, an imaginary transoceanic steamship that is taking them to America. Could one speak of Italians without mentioning music? No, not since the days of Dapontian opera; indeed, even earlier. Since the eighteenth century, music, along with the broader range of staged spectacles, from prestidigitation and pyrotechnics to acrobatics and various other circus performances, puppet theater, and experiments with mediums,[2] was for Americans strictly associated with the name *Italian*. Thomas Jefferson himself had written to an unidentified Italian friend, "If there is a gratification, which I envy any people in the world, it is to your country its music. This is the favorite passion of my soul, and fortune has cast my lot in a country where it is in a deplorable state of barbarism."[3]

The Italians' musical inclination, which hosts of illustrious travelers witnessed for centuries, was a defining element of the people: The language itself, its sound, revealed it. Italians seemed born singers, dancers, and musicians. It was a character trait, both good and bad at the same time. Also associated with violence and ignorance, it evoked an idea of exaggerated theatricality, an inveterate lack of discipline, indolence, and noisiness. On the other hand, it also signaled a deep-seated

1. Lapolla 1931, 1.
2. A delightful anecdote on the various Italian exploits in the artistic field in the United States from the 1870s to the 1880s can be found in Marraro 1946 and in Schiavo 1958, 203–208.
3. Quoted in Marraro 1946, 104. The richest collection of information on Italian American music is found in Schiavo 1947.

tendency to sentimental abstraction. However deplorable with respect to modern living standards, it was still the mark of an ancient civilization that touched the direct experience of everyday life. Music was a romantic way to face it and grasp its simple beauty.

At the popular level, Americans became acquainted with Italian storytellers and street musicians as early as the 1850s, if not before. After the street musicians from Liguria and the peddlers from the Emilian-Tuscan Apennines, the famous *viggianesi*—who in point of fact came from Viggiano, Corleto, and other centers of Lucania—arrived in New York and many other American cities. Not infrequently, they succeeded in redeeming their image as paupers both by improving their social and economic status in various fields of activity and by specializing exactly in the field of music. Giovanni Schiavo has recorded the forthright success on various stages (and in particular those of San Francisco) of a certain Vincenzo Abecco, from Viggiano, who died in Washington in 1869 at the age of sixty-seven. His serenade *La Neapolitaine* became very popular in San Francisco in the 1860s:

> Neapolitaine, I am dreaming of thee!
> I'm hearing thy foot-fall so joyous and free;
> Thy dark flashing eyes are entwining me yet;
> Thy voice with its music I ne'er can forget.
>   I am far from the land of my own sunny home,
> Alone in this wide world of sorrow I roam;
> In the halls of the gay, or wherever it be,
> Still, Neapolitaine, I am dreaming of thee!
> Neapolitaine, I am dreaming of thee!
> *Neapolitaine, I am dreaming of thee!*[4]

On the other hand, Schiavo recalls that Abecco also used to sing a touching *Viva l'America, home of the free!*

In the luggage of the emigrants who landed in New York, one could often find musical instruments. In fact, since the early nineteenth century, music itself has provided not a few Italians with job opportunities in America (one could mention

---

4. From *Sig. Abecco's Sentimental Songster: Containing All the Most Popular Songs*, San Francisco, Appleton, 1961; cited in Schiavo 1958, 10–11. Information on Abecco is also in *L'Eco d'Italia*, February 19, 1869, and in Schiavo 1947, 217. The song was published in 1847 by Atwill in New York as a different "Napolitaine" version by Alexander Lee.

here Piero Maroncelli, a political exile and a musician in the Italian Opera). In the 1870s and 1880s, there was an infamous traffic of child musicians. In addition, we also find a grim and at the same time stereotyped image of the Italian street musician, equipped with his hand organ and monkey. Before being transplanted to America, this image had made the rounds in Europe. However, during the last years of the nineteenth century and the first years of the twentieth century, there emerged—in total or partial autonomy with respect to the tours of the Pattis, the Carusos, and other big names of opera—a certain "ethnic" professionalism. This new class of professionals exported models of popular entertainment already widely tested in Italy and changed them into something original in the new American context.[5] In doing so, they responded to a precise need of the Italian colonies, which wanted to recreate an atmosphere that was as close to home as possible. Music, therefore, and songs, mostly Neapolitan songs, those most popular among the great majority of the nameless crowds of emigration of the fin-de-siècle. That is why instead of a real theater, we have something much more modest. In fact, "the first Italian stage in New York" was a cafe. As Giuseppe Cautela writes in 1927:

> Thirty-five years ago, the Italian actor or singer who landed on this soil with his outlandish dreams of success, found himself confused and lost until, wandering around the Italian quarter, he saw in the sign of a cafe a glimmer of salvation. In the lazy atmosphere of that place drenched with the odor of anisette, cognac, and coffee, he found a seat and, disheveled and starved, began meditating on his destiny. As soon as he mentioned his profession, the owner, with tears in his eyes, prepared to listen to those memories of theatrical life back home, and arranged for him to perform for his customers. In this way the first Italian immigrants began to hear the songs of their mother country in America. The cafe answered to the same social needs which for centuries it had responded to in Italy. It was the only place in which one could find an audience.[6]

At the beginning of the 1890s, a New York café located on Mulberry Street, near Canal, and called Villa Vittorio Emanuele, was among the first to have a regular

---

5. An Italian contribution to the birth of jazz has been hypothesized and documented. On this subject, see Volpelletto Nakamura 1990.

6. Cautela 1927, 106. Schiavo 1958, 203, further reports that, by 1805, an "Italian Theater" existed on Broadway already, and he makes mention of an "Italian Hall" in Cleveland, Ohio, in the 1830s.

space for artists. The owner, Cautela recounts, did not pay these artists, but when they finished performing, the people in the cafe would give them something. A little later, this system was changed and the customers were required to pay a modest fee. Anyhow, the pay for an actor or singer remained low—"seven or eight dollars a week"[7]—and one could round this off with the money tossed onto the stage with a request for an encore. According to Cautela, every evening there was a crowd at the door of Villa Vittorio Emanuele. They came not only to see the show but also, more generally, to "socialize": in a period of immigration for the most part still highly transient, it was exactly there, in the cafe, that one could find one's countrymen, those who might be able to address the problems of the newcomer.

In a short time, quite a few cafe-chantants were opened in New York: Villa Giulia, Ferrando's Hall, later D'Alessio Concert-Hall. The passage from the musical–popular song performance to the first forms of a more structured and complex spectacle, involving acting, was a natural development. Competition was a decisive stimulus, and alongside the various amateur theatrical companies, among them some connected to the activities of anarchist and socialist groups, real professional performers began to emerge. It is possible that Italian theater borrowed poetic and organizational models from other ethnic theaters that, in the same area, had preceded it or grown up nearby. In fact, New York's Lower East Side was made up of just such a mixture or mosaic of different traditions, as Mario Maffi has aptly defined it.[8] This mixture fully emerges from an article in a newspaper of the day concerning the disappearance in 1911 of one of the historical stages of immigration, the Thalia Theater in the Bowery. It was built in 1826 and renovated half a dozen times, "changing its name, owner, the kind of shows, and even the local color bestowed on it by the nationality of the patrons." The history of this place was really checkered:

> First, it was an exclusively American venue; then, Irish; then, German. This was the glorious period of its existence (1879–1888), largely because first-class companies and artists of European renown performed there. The influence of Jewish immigration in the neighboring quarters and the opening of the German Theater in Irving Place led to another change, and the Thalia became exclusively Jewish and open to variety shows. Then the executors of the Kramer patrimony put it up for auction. . . . At the Thalia there were often Italian shows: Maiori, Rapone, and a few amateur theatrical companies

7. Cautela 1927, 106.
8. See Maffi 1992, with interesting remarks and information on the subject.

performed there in Italian and Neapolitan. A few years ago, *Mimi' Aguglia* was produced there and, in November of 1909, Bernardino Ciambelli's *Francisco Ferrer* attracted an audience quite different from that of the usual "habitués" and was a sensational success.[9]

According to Emelise Aleandri, the scholar who has most thoroughly studied Italian American theatre of this period, the amateur phase of Italian American theatricals spanned the years 1878 and 1896 and several of its memorable actors were the no longer young Giuseppe Zacconi (father of the famous actor Ermete), the most successful Pulcinella of Little Italy, Francesco Ricciardi, and Paolo Cremonesi, a worker at a silk factory in Paterson, New Jersey. At the beginning of the new century, Cremonesi formed his own company and remained one of the few interpreters of works in the Piedmontese and Milanese dialects, most dialect pieces being in Neapolitan or Sicilian. After this phase, the first professional Italian American theater company emerged in South Brooklyn in 1889 and was soon moved to Manhattan by another Ricciardi (the Sorrentine Guglielmo) and Francesco Saverio Savarese.[10]

A likeable actor, singer, and entertainer, Guglielmo Ricciardi came to New York along with his father, the captain of a cargo ship. And, as he later recounted in his fragmentary book of memoirs, "It was really in this crazy city among its lost people that I began my life's course. It would take volumes to tell of my *via crucis* and the vicissitudes of my sixty-three years among people from all over the world."[11] We know—Ricciardi himself tells us—that the piece the company chose for his debut on November 25, 1889, was *Lu retuorno da Buenos Aires* (Back from Buenos Aires) by G. Marulli, and that evidently the theme of migration was present from the very beginning in the repertories of the Italian American theater. Very important for the future development of this story was Ricciardi's encounter with the Sicilian Antonio Maiori and the Neapolitan Pasquale Rapone in the early 1890s. Both Maiori and Rapone were skillful actors and dancers. This threesome formed several companies and produced a considerable number of shows. Around them circled a large

9. "La scomparsa del Thalia Teatre [*sic*]" (The Death of the Thalia Theater), *L'Araldo Italiano* (Italian Herald), New York, March 20, 1911.

10. See Aleandri 1983a, 18–56, and, for the history of the Italian-American Dramatic Society, 11–18. There were such societies in other cities before the end of the nineteenth century. In New Haven, Connecticut, Il Circolo Filodrammatico Politico San Carlino, founded in 1897 by Domenico Mazzarella, had in its repertoire various works by Pasquale Mazzacane, one of the founders, among them *I misteri della notte* (Mysteries of the Night) and *Fra i pazzi* (Among the Insane), by Bernardino Ciambelli, of which no other citation has been found. See Frangini 1908, 71–73.

11. G. Ricciardi 1955, 17. Ricciardi was born in Piano di Sorrento on July 12, 1871.

number of actors, *macchiettisti* (character actors), singers, musicians, and various entertainers in the early years of Italian American theater. Companies were formed and dissolved in the blink of an eye, often due to very typical personal complications, as Ricciardi himself was forced to learn when his actress wife, Concetta Arcamone, left him for Maiori. "I didn't kill him only because I always believed in the happy ending," Ricciardi wrote some forty years later.[12] In the meantime their paths were divided for good. Ricciardi returned to Italy for a while and later, back in America in 1900, he was hired by Alessandro Salvini.[13] (Salvini was the son of the famous actor, playwright, and director Tommaso, a celebrity also in America, where Henry James found the time to praise his *Othello*.) Ricciardi found a new wife of German origin, Adelaide Triber, who helped him polish his English pronunciation, and he began a new career in the American theater. Later, he also acted in American cinema, but in between times he returned occasionally to acting on the "ethnic" stage.[14] Cinema offered a territory of maximum artistic affirmation for Italian Americans and soon became a very interesting outlet for a discreet segment of the theatrical and literary community of the colony.[15] This progression would seem to follow the time-tested trajectory that goes from the most ancient to the most modern medium, but at least in one case, that of Rudolph (Rodolfo) Valentino, things worked differently. Of the legendary "white sheik" this volume offers a few poems (known to but a few) written by the very popular Italian American actor.

Maiori and Rapone continued to work together in the Italian Comic-Dramatic Company until July 1903, when Rapone set up a company of his own.[16] Their headquarters was the Teatro Italiano in Spring Street, in the heart of Little Italy, and from there they took short tours to the working-class centers of New Jersey—Hoboken, Paterson, Newark. These tours were the first stages of a success story that increased through the years. Maiori's repertory, albeit clearly popular, was rather

12. Ibid., 135.
13. An unexpected case of plagiarism would be added to this bitter disappointment of love: "The steamboat voyage I described in short story form was stolen without credit by the English writer Mackenzie and sold to *Cosmopolitan* magazine. A sickness of the English. . . . The title . . . is Ludovico's Luck." See ibid., 19.
14. See Aleandri 1983a, 34ff. Guglielmo Ricciardi's is not the only case of Italian actors moving to American film. Among those of this first "heroic" phase, Silvio Minciotti should be remembered, who was for some time the dramatic director of Francesco Ricciardi's company and who performed many character roles in various films, including *Full of Life* (1957) by Richard Quine, which is based upon a John Fante novel.
15. On this subject, see Bruno 1995, Casella 1998, and Muscio 2004.
16. See Aleandri 1983a, 56.

up-to-date, and included, for example, *Il padrone delle ferriere* (The Owner of the Ironworks), which Georges Ohnet had adapted for the stage in 1883. With time, it was enriched with more important texts by Giacosa, D'Annunzio, Bracco, and Verga among the Italians, many from the French (among them Sardou), the German Sudermann, and of course Shakespeare. Each dramatic performance, moreover, was followed by a Neapolitan farce performed by Pasquale Rapone. Rapone's interpretation was enhanced by his appearance; in fact, "Nasone" (big nose) was the nickname by which he was known. Along with Guglielmo Ricciardi, he was one of the first Pulcinellas on the stages of New York's Little Italies.

Cautela has provided a rather indulgent picture of Maiori's successes: the need to find increasingly larger spaces in order to satisfy the demands of a steadily growing public; new artistic ambitions which led him to include plays by Shakespeare in his repertory; and finally, the success which the Italian theater finally obtained with a public that was no longer exclusively "ethnic." When the company settled in the Windsor Theater in the Bowery, it became fashionable for many rich Americans to attend its evenings. This, Cautela observes, "happened during a time when the journalists couldn't stay away from the Bowery."[17] That is to say, at the height of the success of muckraking journalism, when—just to mention a particularly resonant name—Hutchins Hapgood, in his *Types from City Streets* (1910), dug into the melting pot and brought up the many different faces of the metropolis and, along with them, the hidden treasures of the newest ethnic communities.

Everything in that context proved to be a spectacle, on stage and off. One might assume that the opinion of a contemporary Italian observer coincided with that of the astonished Americans: "Sometimes the shows are very amusing, especially for those who observe the audience rather than the stage."[18] Hutchins Hapgood himself provided an entertaining portrait of the Spring Street theaters in the review *The Bookman* in 1900, where

after his spaghetti, chianti, and fernetbranca . . . the suave and polite man with dark eyes and ragged clothes lights his cigarette, and with his black derby hat fixed permanently on his head he goes to see the continued fight between the armoured puppets representing Christian knights and Saracen warriors, at Spring Street, or to see Othello, some melodrama, or farce, at No. 24 of the same street.[19]

17. Cautela 1927, 106.
18. Villari 1912, 222.
19. Reprinted in Moquin-Van Doren 1974, 317–320.

Emelise Aleandri, on the other hand, has documented Maiori's year of grace, 1902, which coincided with a sensational American acknowledgement of his qualities as a tragic actor. Maiori was capable of attracting very qualified audiences, which, even in the following year, competed with each other to host the Sicilian artist in their homes in order to have him recite, read, and stage plays in their private theaters.[20] It was probably this success, with its ensuing economic rewards, that convinced Maiori that the time had come to build a real, new Italian theater. And in 1904 he launched a subscription for its construction.

By then the Italian community was taking root and had acquired the characteristic features of the "colonial" stage of development. The most important of these features was a new "language" of its own, which soon proved to be the most original expressive tool for a theater that went beyond the models of a national or European tradition and began to reflect the very themes of the immigrant experience. Hapgood maintained that one could count on the fingers of one hand the plays written on site and inspired by the real life of the neighborhood. In this regard he quoted Edoardo Pecoraro's *Maria Barbera* and *Jack lo squartatore* (Jack the Ripper) and Ciambelli's *I misteri di Mulberry Street* (The Mysteries of Mulberry Street).[21] To tell the truth, however, there was a considerable production of Italian American plays already before the end of the nineteenth century. Soon there was a veritable outpouring. "A piece of news, a political clue, a bit of gossip provide the stimulus to write a play which the public appreciates," a participant in New York's theatrical scene observed many years later. He also recalled the activism and "knack for business" of Clemente Giglio, actor, author, and, in the 1920s, the chief impresario of Little Italy.[22] At the present stage of research, very few of these works are extant. Most of them were not even published and simply remained in manuscript form. But some of the titles can provide us with an interesting panorama of the themes they treated.

Already in 1887 the Italian American amateur theatrical *Circolo* had staged Rocco Metelli's *Chiara, la condannata* (Chiara the Condemned), which was based

20. See Aleandri 1983a, 62. It is curious to note that among American fans of Maiori, there was, at this time, also William Marion Crawford, son of the famous novelist Francis, who loved Italy and lived near Sorrento.

21. *Maria Barberi* is one of the plays written around the sensational Maria Barbella affair (see Part II, note 57). This incident was successfully performed on stage at Thalia Theater, Lower East Side, not far from the Italian theaters, as well as by Yiddish dramatist Moyshe Ha-Levi Ish Hurwitz. See Pucci 1993.

22. Gatti-Emanuel 1937, 228–229. On Neapolitan Giglio, son of a magician, see Falbo 1942, June 28 and July 5.

on the true story of Chiara Cignarale, a woman who was charged with killing her husband in league with her lover, was imprisoned in October 1886, and was then sentenced to death. The Italian community had launched several petitions and the governor had commuted her sentence to life imprisonment. (Cignarale was subsequently released in January 1900 and promptly returned to Italy.) Here, then, we have a typical example in which news about the colony reverberated on the stage. Edoardo Pecoraro, the author mentioned by Hapgood, specialized in this field. He worked in collaboration with Bernardino Ciambelli, who was then the director of *Il Bollettino della Sera.* In the years 1896–1897, Pecoraro wrote, for Guglielmo Ricciardi's company, various sensational melodramas based on newspaper reportage. The main ingredients were crime and passion. One of these plays was *La tragedia di Bartolomeo Capasso* (The Tragedy of Bartholomew Capasso), the owner of a cafe in Mulberry Street who was killed by an Italian. Italo Carlo Falbo recounted the great success obtained by this play in Fabio D'Alessio's little theater Villa di Sorrento. D'Alessio had the show run until midnight, thereby obliging Ricciardi and Pecoraro to extemporize two entire supplementary acts besides the three in the script.[23]

After such exploits, Pecoraro's promising theatrical career suffered a few setbacks. The author wrote for several newspapers, and several other newspapers wrote about him. In one of them, *Il Corriere di Boston,* the editor Giuseppe De Marco mentioned in 1897 Pecoraro's collaboration with New York's new bimonthly *La Scherma Italiana,* which he defined "a swank newspaper of Chivalry and . . . Asininity . . . under the ballistic and grammatical direction of Prof. Dammit La Rocca Pavese." In the following passage, he abuses Pecoraro in a savory excerpt of ordinary journalistic-theatrical life:

> Speaking is Pecoraro Edoardo, New York's vice-Ibsen, strongly suspected of having been the *strangler* of Mulberry Street, of having committed *the Elisabeth St. murder,* of having been partially responsible for *Annina Fiore*'s death, of having received, as his reward, many ovations . . . and of having poured onto the above-mentioned *Scherma Italiana* an indigestible gruel of inflated apologetic reviews for the honor and glory of Generoso (Dammit) Pavese. Pecoraro speaks, calling his colleague Granata an ass and his colleague Melchiorri an idiot, both of whom, in spite of these epithets, succeed in

---

23. Falbo 1942, May 3. This episode is also narrated very briefly in G. Ricciardi 1955 and retold in Aleandri 1983a, 49–50.

maintaining not a few brains in their skull. After this, I say, he addresses his colleague Cordiferro and sticks between his ribs this languid homily:

"In memory of your most noble actions, I declare to you that I don't want to start an argument *with you*. In no way do I. . . ."

"How could you be so atrocious (Oh! . . .)? Give me your hand, etc., etc. . . ."

"I proved it, I'm proving it, and . . . I'll prove it. . . ."

A bit of decorum, by God! With this sodomitical language you really risk ending up in the chaste arms of Antonio Comstock. That would be a real stroke of luck for Italian-American journalism, indeed.[24]

In point of fact, in 1900 Pecoraro is listed as being the director of the weekly *La Sentinella* of Calumet, Michigan. Then in 1903 we find him in California, where his plays *Maria Barbera* and *Giuseppe Musolino* were being performed.[25] Given the fact that the bandit Musolino had just been put on trial in Italy, we have here another example of a newsman's alacrity. This confirms the broad success news-based plays garnered; Emelise Aleandri mentions that Musolino's life adventures were also given a farcical rendition in *Il brigante Musolino con Pulcinella, bandito per necessità* (The Brigand Musolino with Pulcinella, A Bandit out of Need), a piece perhaps written by Francesco Ricciardi. This phenomenon aroused the theater company directors to pay greater attention to the local scene. And as a natural outgrowth, Italian American playwrights built up an independent repertory by setting their works in both the colony and Italy and by keeping an eye on current events. The lost play *Marta ovvero i drammi dell'emigrazione* (Martha, or, The Dramas of Emigration) was written and performed in 1903 by Guglielmo Ricciardi himself. One of the six acts of the play was set in the Matese Restaurant in Grand Street, one of those locales in Little Italy where plays were staged. But the new colonial authors worked especially for Maiori, who in 1900 put on *L'assassinio di Re Umberto* (The Assassination of King Umberto). In this same period the novelist Bernardino Ciambelli wrote at least a couple of plays for him, and Agostino Balletto, Ciambelli's publisher, wrote (in 1904) the farce *Il campanello dello speziale* (The Druggist's Bell).

Already in 1894, Maiori had begun staging the first texts (in verse) of the author who was to become the most glittering star of Italian American drama, namely

24. *Il Corriere di Boston* (The Boston Courier), September 25–26, 1897. Anthony Comstock was a famous turn-of-the-century preacher obsessed with problems of morality.

25. See Aleandri 1983a, 53–54.

the Calabrese-Neapolitan Riccardo Cordiferro. One of his pieces, the monologue *Il pezzente* (The Tramp, 1895), which was remarkably popular and had a rather distinguished performance run, can be considered a small classic of Italian American dramatic art. This is also true of the social drama in four acts *L'onore perduto* (Lost Honor, 1901), which was staged by a variety of directors, including the author. Its success was so great that in 1906 it called for a sequel, *Giuseppina Terranova ovvero L'onore vendicato* (Josephine Terranova, or, Honor Avenged). It often happened that these plays were performed during evenings that included the recitation of various other shorter works by Cordiferro: songs, poems, and Neapolitan impersonations.[26] Due precisely to his ability to play at different tables—theater, journalism, poetry, and direct contact with a public that was fascinated by his oratorical skills—Cordiferro is truly one of the more outstanding figures in the new Italian tradition of New York. In this city, where already in 1893 he had founded with his father Francesco and his brother Marziale the newspaper *La Follia*, he became a "*prominente*," a member of the cultural and political elite in the culture of the colony. A prodigy at the young age of eighteen, he was able establish himself as a point of reference for all would-be writers. Moreover, he was close to radical groups and was in effect the first, along with Bernardino Ciambelli, to become a professional writer by drawing on the pulsating life of the colonial milieu. Among the many authors and/or theater-company heads who followed in his footsteps, we might mention the versatile Armando Cennerazzo, whose vast repertory included not only the more numerous light comedies but also plays inspired by life in Little Italy.

Among Cordiferro's works that Maiori directed in 1894 is the one-act play *Genio incompreso* (Unacknowledged Genius). This was perhaps the first satire produced by the immigrant amateur theatricals, and it toyed with the theme of the improbable mastery of English, as well as the authentic blunders pronounced both on-stage and off. Thus *Genio incompreso* might be considered a sort of incunabulum of an entirely Italian American genre, the "colonial impersonation" or *macchietta coloniale*. Soon its most gifted interpreters were in point of fact Cordiferro, the Neapolitan Eduardo Migliaccio ("Farfariello"), and the Palermo-born Giovanni De Rosalia ("Nofrio"), but also many other authors adopted the genre and gave it various regional, and even noncanonical, inflections. A sonnet by Antonio Crivello, a poet active in the labor movement, offered a rare testimony of the colony's literary and theatrical bohemia. Here the two main characters, Cordiferro and De

---

26. Ibid., 100–101.

Rosalia, improvised verses in front of their friends in a Mott Street tavern. Cordiferro starts:

> You moved us with your emigrants
> Whose great sufferance you recounted

and the other concludes:

> De Rosalia then played *His Excellence*
> And finally impersonated, among bursts of laughter,
> *Litteriu Trantulia from Calamenza.*[27]

We have here a rather revealing picture: almost as if in a normal evening of the colonial theater, the tragic and the comic coexisted. One should add that while Cordiferro held to his youthful socialist ideas throughout his life, De Rosalia went so far as to sing the praises of fascism, although this did not mean that he was actually a militant.[28] Evidently, their ideological differences did not prevent them from being friends. For his part, the socialist Crivello greatly enjoyed De Rosalia's comic energy.

The *macchietta* is a typical product of the Neapolitan theater. In that same period Nicola Maldacea, Berardo Cantalamessa, Pasquale Villani, and others were its most renowned interpreters in Italy. It was a "total" show including singing, reciting, pantomime, and quick costume changes. Not by chance was it well liked by the futurists. It also became one of the archetypes of the synthetic theater. All in all, each single skit encapsulated an emblematic character, a comic type. The performer's impersonation would include singing verses and reciting, and in the central section there was a more or less lengthy monologue during the course of which he was for all practical purposes entirely free to improvise according to the spirit and mood of the moment. His dress had to bear the distinguishing trait of the character he was impersonating. Moreover, he needed to be remarkably versatile, since he was expected to play a certain number of sketches during the course of the evening. By the end of the century, Migliaccio was not only the best of the character actors, but also he was the first to choose not to limit himself to repeating the repertory of the Neapolitan masters. On the contrary, he invented, often

27. "'Mpruvvisata d'arti" (Improvised Arts), *Il Convivio Letterario* (Literary Conviviality, Milan] 24 (January–February 1956): 30. For Litteriu Trantulia, see De Rosalia in the present volume.

28. See Fichera 1937, 438–439, where a sonnet on Mussolini is cited that says among other things: "You are our father, supreme weapon,/admired and desired by the whole world/at which you hurl words and actions with lightning speed."

in close collaboration with Tony Ferrazzano, the new genre of "colonial *macchiette*" (character sketches). These sketches portrayed the world around him and, in order to reflect it faithfully, had to conform to its newly invented language.

Aware of Migliaccio's success, many performers followed in his footsteps. Migliaccio's Farfariello mask was so successful that it took on a life of its own, independently from that of its author-interpreter. In what is considered the first review of the Italian American theater, it even became a symbol capable of appearing alongside the discoverer of America himself. Among the first was Giulio Capocci's *Cristoforo Colombo e Farfariello*.[29] In the early years of the twentieth century, Pasquale Rapone updated and gave an American twist to his repertory of the Neapolitan farce, derived from Petito and Scarpetta and linked to the character of *Pascariello*. *Pascariello* became *Polisse* in a comedy, and in another, coupled with Scarpetta's mask of Don Felice Sciosciammocca, lampooned the theatrical milieu (*Pascariello e Feliciello scrittori drammatici*, Pascariello and Feliciello, playwrights).[30] Gennaro Camerlingo was the author, among other things, of a comedy significantly entitled *Pascariello a Coney Island, ovvero 'O Pic Nic d'e Sciainature* (Pascariello at Coney Island, or, The Shoeshine Boys' Picnic). Not by chance, it was interpreted by Migliaccio himself.[31] Ettore De Stefano, "*banchista*" and journalist as well as director of *La Rivista Musicale* and *La Gazzetta Legale*, was the author of *macchiette*, among which *Il contabile* (The Accountant).

Some of the more successful character actors and singers were Alberto La Maida, Eduardo Perretti, Gennaro Pisano, Edoardo De Pascale, Aristide Sigismondi (interpreter of Cordiferro's *Polisso*), Gennaro Amato, Giuseppe De Laurentis, and Jefferson De Angelis.[32] De Laurentis's most popular interpretation was that of the "*bommo*"—that is to say, the bum—based on scripts by Frank Amodio. Also worth mentioning is Vincenzo Massari who in the 1920s became a congressman in Colorado and wrote *O Pulisso e 'a taliana*, a 1910 duet set to music by G. De Gregorio. Domenico Porreca, nicknamed "Spaghetti," from Abruzzo, collaborated with the publisher-author Antonio Paolilli from Providence. There was also Ernesto Quadrino, author of *'E Talianelle 'e Brucculino* (The Little Italian Girls from Brook-

29. Capocci, born in Rome in 1893, created the Amauli Duo with his wife, which specialized in caricatures. After World War I in America, he staged this review for the Fourteenth Street Theater. He was the author of scripts in Neapolitan and of subjects and screenplays for the movies, as well as the owner of the Alba movie studio of Newark. See Flamma 1936, bibliography.

30. See Aleandri 1983a, 110–119.

31. Ibid., 168.

32. Of Corsican origin, born in San Francisco and alive from 1859 until 1933, he remained on California stages for some sixty years. See Schiavo 1958, 208.

lyn, 1916). Luigi Donadio was the author of a remarkable *'A Ngresa e l'Ausekip* (The Englishwoman and the Housekeeper, 1911). Filippo Dato collaborated with De Rosalia in the creation of the Sicilian macchietta *Piddu Micca* (Peter Micca). In the 1920s and 1930s Silvio and Ester Minciotti, the former from Umbria and the latter from Piedmont, produced comic dialogues for the radio in various dialects. Among them was *Le avventure di Mincuccio 'o barese* (The Adventures of Mincuccio from Bari). According to some scholars, this last character was launched by Francesco Fanizza,[33] and was also the pièce de resistance of Michele Rapanaro, who in the 1930s won fame for the comic sketch *Minguccio sopra la Tracca* (Minguccio on the Railway). Gino Calza, an assiduous collaborator of *La Follia*, specialized in the Roman dialect. In a Columbia Records catalogue listing the Italian records for the year 1930, by far the greatest space is taken up by the list of "popular songs, sketches, duets, and Neapolitan comic sketches." Here we find the titles of many pieces that clearly derive from Farfariello. For example, *'E Paesane 'a Battaria* (Fellow Countrymen at the Battery) and *'O Sciumecco* (The Shoemaker), interpreted by Gennaro Amato; *Mastu Ciccio Dint'o Muvinpiccio* (Master Ciccio in the Moving Picture) and *Sette Solde P'o Sobbuè* (Seven Cents for the Subway), interpreted by Giuseppe De Laurentis.[34]

But there was also space for the dialects of northern and central Italy on the stage of the Italian American comedy and variety show: at the beginning of the century the farces of Stenterello were played by the Tuscan immigrants of the New York amateur theatrical circle L'Amicizia. The Società Veneta Daniele Manin promoted shows drawn from Goldoni and Gallina. In its turn, during the course of the 1903–1904 season, the Milanini Company staged several farces and comedies based on the mask of Meneghino at Ferrando's Music Hall. It also boldly tried to combine Milanese and Neapolitan traditions by having the masks of Meneghino and Felice Sciosciammocca appear together in the same comedy. It is worth noting that from this group emerged Renata Scarlati Brunorini, the daughter of a Newark actor. According to Emelise Aleandri, she was the first female author of the Italian American theater, with *Lo zio di dieci nipoti* (The Uncle of Ten Nephews, 1904), a text lost to us. Finally, I feel compelled to mention the name—which could very easily belong to one of those fake aristocratic bluffers happily singled

33. Born in Gioia del Colle, Puglia, in 1892, this character actor arrived in the United States in 1910 and by age twelve was already on stage. See Flamma 1936, bibliography.

34. *Dischi Italiani–Italian Columbia Records–General Catalog 1930*, an advertising booklet held at the Immigration History Research Center at University of Minnesota. Several of these performances were placed on the *Cartoline da Little Italy* (Postcards from Little Italy) album, compiled by Paquito del Bosco in the Fonografo Italiano series of Fonit Cetra.

out by Migliaccio—of Ranieri Uguccione Bourbon del Monte, "Marquis of Sorbello, Count of Civitella." He was the author of the one-act play *Con le signore c'e più gusto* (It's More Fun with the Ladies) staged in New York in 1935.[35]

Rocco De Russo was probably Migliaccio's most gifted epigone. Born in Sant'Arsenio in the province of Salerno in 1885, De Russo grew up in Italy in the presence of actors who would become famous later on—Nino Taranto, to mention one of them. As he himself recounts in his autobiography, preserved in manuscript form together with the script of forty-nine comedies at the Immigration History Research Center of Minneapolis, he made his debut in Mulberry Street in 1905. His style was more "Italian" and was influenced by Ettore Petrolini and the genre of the Neapolitan "*sceneggiata*" (melodrama). In spite of serious misunderstandings with Francesco Ricciardi, he was very successful. Urged on by his wife, De Russo returned home in 1908, opened a hotel, and soon went back to writing scripts for the theater. In 1911, after separating from his wife, he returned to America and married a young woman who, however, died in 1917. A third wife, Ria Sampieri, began acting and became his stage partner. The duets of the couple "Ruby De Russo" were very popular and were also recorded on vinyl. De Russo died in 1975.[36]

The comic-parodic ambit provided a notable literary outlet for an Italian American language that became the most effective, as well as credible, tool for representing a small, bizarre world. It recorded the colony's moods, colors, and sounds in a manner that anticipates the linguistic experimentations of many second-generation writers—in particular, D'Agostino, Mangione, and Di Donato. The language question is fundamental in defining a unique Italian American expressivity and in identifying, so to speak, the first and most characteristic literary productions coming from within the colony. Rather than attempt to trace an exact chronology of the phenomenon, it seems more appropriate to speak of a spontaneous and widespread blossoming. Nevertheless, there is no doubt that Giovanni Pascoli's "Italy" is the first instance in which a poet—and what a poet!—shows an interest in the expressive potentialities of this new and peculiar linguistic hybrid. *Primi poemetti*, which ends precisely with "Italy," was published in 1897. Other testimonies of the time show that Italian American was by then a "dialect" flourishing

---

35. According to Schiavo 1935 (see bibliography), Uguccione was born in Florence in 1906.

36. For the history of Rocco De Russo, see his unpublished autobiography, held by the Immigration History Research Center of Minneapolis. De Russo is cited by Cautela 1927. It is noted that with De Russo duets became fashionable, of which the Roma-Borelli couple is another valid example ("Push Your Skirts Down, Marianna" is the title of one of their recordings for Columbia in 1930).

above all (but not exclusively) in the metropolitan areas of the East Coast. Adolfo Rossi dedicated several pages of his autobiography *Un italiano in America* to this subject.[37] Here he gave "an authentic demonstration of the dialogue between two southern Italian peasants who start out from The Five Points for Grand Central Depot." In fact, he put into their mouth a number of typical idioms: *carro* (car), *nipo* (depot), *terza venuta* (Third Avenue), *siti colle* (City Hall), *cecca* (check, meaning ticket), *tronco* (trunk), and so on. Probably he added some instances of smug exaggeration, such as *Giacomo Squea* (Chatham Square), *Morbida stretta* (Mulberry Street), and *Cosimo stretto* (Crosby Street). Giuseppe Giacosa also had an ear for that language, which later on became the subject of the most vivacious chapters written by many travelers to America, Italians but not only. In 1899, for example, Remy de Gourmont recognized not only the practical but also the aesthetic value of this language.[38]

It took almost twenty years for academic scholars to turn their attention to the Italian American language. From its very title, Arthur Livingston's essay "La Merica Sanemagogna" draws on one of the most special Italian American coinages ("son of a gun," in Italian *figlio di buona donna*). The essay was written 1918 and thus belongs to the most dazzling period of Italian American vaudeville, linked above all to the names of Migliaccio and Ferrazzano. In point of fact, the first decade of the twentieth century marked an increase in the use of Italian American in the literary field. Its potentialities were intuited by, among others, Achille Almerini (*La colonia di Dante*; The Colony of Dante, 1912) and Michele Pane (*Lu calavrise 'ngrisatu*, The Americanized Calabrese, 1916). Also worth mentioning is the ingenious and then very popular work of the poet of Irish origins Thomas Augustine Daly (*Carmina*, 1914). Daly was the only author who chose to use the Italian American language "in English" in his poetry, although it was limited to the comic mode. The works of the authors quoted immediately above were not directly inspired by theatrical ambitions. But even so, their expressive power was often highly dramatic.

We should also add that on the Italian American stage language was used above all to construct the umpteenth variation of the classical satire that makes fun of the peasants, here opportunely defined as *cafoni* (hayseeds). But it might easily elicit several other interpretations. In fact, T. A. Daly's poems "concretely express if not the authentic personality of an immigrant, at least an interesting American

37. See Rossi 1892, 82–85.
38. *L'Esthétique de la langue Française* (The Esthetics of the French Language), cited by Livingston 1918, 210, and Mencken 1947, 640.

conceptualization of his personality."[39] They give us the parameters of a still negative, even if benevolent, appraisal. This very "negativity" triggered a curious about-face by which the Italian Americans turned that linguistic uncouthness into an emblem of a social condition and even a tool of struggle. For example, Livingston recalls that Ferrazzano, Migliaccio's collaborator, "made his debut" in 1913 among the ranks of the striking IWW workers as a composer of protest songs. These songs were appreciated by the masses and, although relatively unimportant, "they were more valuable than any other thing produced at the time by the American Association of Manufacturers."[40]

On the other hand, the role of the popular song in the political struggles of the labor unions is, as we will see, well documented. These songs were often in dialect and did not lack Italian American neologisms. Perhaps the most convincing demonstration of the extent to which the *cafone*'s way of speaking was proudly adopted as an ethnic emblem is offered by the sonnet "Vennero i bricchellieri" (Then Came the Bricklayers). Even recently, this sonnet has been reprinted as the work of a not better identified "Rosina Vieni," obviously a pseudonym behind which an old-time socialist, Simplicio Righi, used to hide (see Part IV). This sonnet is by far one of the most interesting Italian American literary creations and was promptly acknowledged by H. L. Mencken as an attempt "to use the Italian-American language at a higher literary level."[41]

With the preceding work we have come a long way and have reached the years in which Pasquale Seneca convincingly used that slang in an extended prose narrative, *Il Presidente Scoppetta* (President Scoppetta). There followed more modest experimentations such as those by V. A. Castellucci, the "consular narrator" Paulo G. Brenna,[42] and Vincenzo Campora. Several poets belonging to the so-called underbrush, who kept writing until the 1950s and beyond, also generously employed the Italian American idiom—in particular, Nicola Testi and, from a clear-cut fascist perspective, Rosario Di Vita (see Part IV). With them the language seemed to lose some of its immediate, vital traits and become an academic exercise, albeit occasionally successful. In an exemplary way Nicola Testi tried to bend it to the Pugliese dialect, which was not his own—or rather, did not pertain to that peculiar lingua franca which took hold in the various Little Italies between the two centuries. Here a transdialectal model found its two main poles of attraction in the

39. Livingston 1918, 224.
40. Ibid., 216.
41. Mencken 1947, 642.
42. Brenna parodied the Italian American slang not only of the United States but also of South America. See Franzina 1996, 190–191.

Neapolitan and Calabrian-Sicilian sonorities. This was obviously due both to their respective and conspicuous regional presence and to the recognized primacy of those two dialects—especially the Neapolitan—in music and the theater.[43]

It is not worth dwelling here on the morphology and syntax of the Italian American dialect.[44] Instead, we should underline its indisputable features, which consist in a communicative code both strongly connoted and connoting. We are in the presence of a sort of thieves' language born somehow out of necessity, in order to allow illiterate peasants coming from different regions in Italy to connect with each other on a linguistic basis that was ultimately national. That basis was capable of providing easy communication within the heterogeneous Italian world of the Little Italies as well as of confronting, thanks to its lexical resources, the new reality, which was so different from the one the immigrants had left behind them. Antonio Marinoni recounted having come across an Italian American barber on the steamship that took him to America in around 1900. "Don Giovà" expressed himself in a funny mixture of American and Neapolitan:

"In Italian you say *Va bene*: in English you say *dazzorai*."

"And how do you spell this word? Come on: how do you write *dazzorai* in English?"

"And how should I know?" he answered frankly. "I *speak* English, but I don't write it."[45]

But the most concrete proof of this oral expedient is provided not so much by the authentic or virtual bits of conversation reported by writers such as Adolfo Rossi as by the "written document." Advertisements, flyers, posters, and the newspapers effectively expressed the need for the immigrants to have an immediate relationship with American reality.[46] Thus, rather than rename its objects or insti-

43. Nicola Testi (Sansevero, Italy, 1884–Trenton, N.J., 1959) had already published in New York, 1939, the collection *Stonature* (False Notes). His poetry most pertinent to this theme is found, however, in two published accounts in the 1950s in Italy. For more information on him, see Fichera 1958, 30–31; Tusiani 1983, 32; and Durante 1994.

44. Other than Livingston 1918 and Mencken 1947, on the subject one should also consult Turano 1932; Menarini 1947; Prezzolini 1963; Ciacci 1972; Ballerini-Chiappelli 1985; Franzina 1996, 187–197; and Haller 1993 and 1998. Among the travel narratives that treat this theme thoroughly, the most noteworthy is Bernardy 1913, in the chapter "La lingua del iesse," 88–122.

45. Marinoni 1932, 34–35.

46. On the language of Italian American periodicals published in Italian, there is a small and rather amusing literature; see in particular Bernardy 1913, 117–122; and above all Prezzolini 1963, 350–354, where, under the title "Un 'direttore smarto'" (A "Smart Editor"), appeared a rather

tutions, they would preserve them in the original English and simply cast them in a more familiar register of pronunciation.

Anthony Turano, a second-generation writer, recalled that he had been consulted to solve a quite revealing case involving the testament (handwritten in a rather incorrect Italian) of a former miner who lived in Nevada. No notary had been able to decipher the words *nota* and *morgico*, which were used in this document. It did not take long for Turano to realize that *morgico* (with its variant *morgheggio*) stood for the word *mortgage* and that *nota* was nothing but the equivalent of the word *note* or *promissory note*.[47] It is easy to imagine that *mortgage* and *promissory note* must not have been familiar terms to the testator. If he had made his fortune in America, he probably never had to face similar proceedings in Italy. As a matter of fact, for the most part the Italian American vocabulary was constituted by terms which had no Italian or dialectal equivalent, or denoted objects, concepts, customs, and institutions unknown in Italy.[48] A modest but quite interesting example of this usage dates back to the 1930s and is included in this anthology: the two "promotional" sonnets in Roman-American by Alfredo Borginiani, a poet-mechanic from Trenton, New Jersey.

Obviously, the comic mode does not exalt the wide spectrum of interest of Italian American dramatic art. A particularly productive sector was that of historical dramas. Among them we can mention the five-act drama *I misteri dell'Inquisizione spagnola* (The Mysteries of the Spanish Inquisition) by Luigi Gualtieri and Alessandro Salvini; *Fabio Romano o La Vendetta* (Fabio Romano, or, The Revenge), four acts that Guglielmo Ricciardi adapted from a Maria Corelli novel; the one-act dramatic poem *La moglie di Putifarre* (Potiphar's Wife, 1922) by Danton M. Fonzo; and

---

sharp satire of Fortune Pope (that is, Fortunato Papa), editor of *Il Progresso Italo-Americano*. "A newspaper," said Papa during an imaginary interview with the author, "can be made only for the people who know the language or to teach it to them. . . . We have adapted ourselves to reality. Don't you know what happened to a naïve Italian who wanted to rent his house, and placed an ad in our newspaper that read: 'House for rent without heat, without a super, long-term lease, made of brick, near elevated train'? Nobody wrote the advertiser. After repeated ads, the naïve Italian brought himself to complain to the head of advertising. He asks to see the ad, and when he does, he bursts into laughter. 'Naturally,' he said to him, 'how did you expect to rent?' Give it to me: I'll write it up. Listen: 'Brick house for rent, no appraisal, without a parent, with long list, near an elevator.'" The next day the house was rented.

47. Turano 1932, 356. On this author, see Durante 2002.

48. Other interesting examples of this Italian American usage not necessarily delegated toward humorous ends can be found in the generous, if not reliable, collection of popular Italian American songs gathered in Marion and other counties of West Virginia by Regina and Roy D'Ariano in 1976. See in particular the song "Nicolo [*sic*] è andato in America" (Nicola Has Gone to America), 82–84.

Giovanni da Verrazzano alla corte di Francesco I (Giovanni da Verrazzano at the Court of Francis I), a four-act play by Antonio Tua (1913). To a certain extent, Tua's play sought to repeat the relative success of the old *Cristoforo Colombo* by Paolo Giacometti (1816–1882), a play that had been repeatedly staged in Little Italy to please an audience that presumably was susceptible to the grandiloquent proclamation that closes the fifth act. Here Columbus, by now almost overwhelmed by a mutinous crew that wanted him dead, finally spots land in the distance:

COLUMBUS: "Land . . . Land! Swear to me, all of you, that you'll respect that
    virgin soil!"
THE CREW: "We swear!"
COLUMBUS: "From this moment the two hemispheres are united . . . and the
    pact of an immortal alliance is sealed!"
BARTHOLOMEW: "Long live Columbus!"
THE CREW: "Viva!"[49]

Verrazzano was written in 1909 and published in 1913 in a plush edition. In the preface Tua defined himself as "a humble amateur," fearful of presenting himself to the readers of Little Italy. In fact, they were used to "reading high-minded works written by eminent literati who, although few in number, emerged in the literary field also among us." His only intention, he declared, was "to help keep alive in our colony the memory of a national glory of our own, namely, the discovery of Hudson Bay and the island of Manhattan by the Italian voyager Giovanni da Verrazzano." Tua was thinking of the celebrations promoted by *Il Progresso* and pointed out the genuinely patriotic character of his drama, dedicated "to the Italians of New York who, animated by a sublime love for their home country, spontaneously and consciously joined in claiming a glory which had been ours for three centuries and had been usurped by the egotism of a foreign people."[50]

Quite obviously, also the colonial theatrical world, given its proximity to that of the newspapers, cultivated patriotic feelings. The tone might change and become more dramatic in the face of events that called for a national (Italian) mobilization. Or it might sustain a more generic and even downright smug complicity. This is the case, for example, of a poem by Cordiferro dedicated to "Garibalde"—

49. This play also exists in a New York edition: *Cristoforo Colombo alla scoperta dell'America* (Christopher Columbus and the Discovery of America, New York), Società Libraria Italiana, n.d., at IHRC in Minnesota, which has a copy that had belonged to Migliaccio.
50. Tua 1913, vii ff. That the publication of the play had more broadly "educative" goals is underscored by the fact that the volume included a "historical outline" and "historical notes."

perhaps the best-loved personage in the colony—and certainly written to be recited in public. An old father warns his son in the following way:

If you forget Garibalde,
You forget your father. . . .
My son, do you remember him?
If you love him, you love me. . . .
He gave his life to Italy,
And he gave his heart. . . .
And then he died like a tramp
And everybody knows it.[51]

One of the events that had a remarkable echo in the theater was, of course, the death of King Umberto I. In spite of the reaction to this news in the anarchist and socialist circles, it also inspired a few plays that were not politically committed.[52] The outbreak of World War I had a far greater effect. It challenged many authors, such as Bernardino Ciambelli, who wrote a sketch titled *L'invasione del Veneto* (The Invasion of the Veneto), which displays the nonchalance with which this patriarch of the colonial literati switched from the anarchist longings of *Francisco Ferrer* to a rhetoric of irredentism. There was also the Sicilian Damiano Bivona, whose three-act play *Prima e Dopo il Piave* (Before and After the Piave) was staged by Maiori in 1919.[53] Finally, Silvio Picchianti, a Florentine author very active from the first decade of the twentieth century, produced the one-act plays *La Madre Triestina* (The Triestine Mother) and *Le trecce di Isabella* (Isabel's Braids).

During World War I, there was a large number of comic-satiric works that were inspired by it. Just to give a few examples of its humor, we might mention "*Telusa mi restar!!!*" (I Was Disappointed) by a not better identified "Spoletta" from Philadelphia or "Blonde Karolina's reply to her poor blond Fritz Kaiseringer." Here a Teutonic couple tries in vain to console themselves after the German defeat in battle:

51. *La Follia di New York* (New York Follies) 27 (Sunday, July 4, 1909).
52. Other than the already mentioned *L'assassino di Re Umberto* (King Humbert's Assassin), produced by Francesco Vela, Maiori, and Rapone, it is worth pointing out *Il Regicidio* (The Regicide), a work that the prodigy Clemente Giglio wrote at age fourteen. He was destined to become the principal impresario of Italian American theater in New York.
53. See Bivona 1919. Bivona was also the author of a collection of "war poems" entitled *Cicca Peppi e Compagnia* (Cicca Peppi and Company).

A beautiful tambourine
I bought for you
Made in Berlin
A big pipe for me. . . .
Oh, how well in my mouth
This big pipe fits!
The little hat with the ribbon
The color of a red poppy.[54]

The inevitable explosion of obscene puns[55] is also present, but with more subtle results, in Ferrazzano's macchietta *Cecco Beppe ha perduto il 'Carso'* (Cecco Beppe Lost the Carso, 1915), where the author plays with the allusions which underlie the numbers of the Neapolitan system for predicting lottery numbers.

Now tell me, how many nights
Do you pray to your Saint Peter
So that you may soon
Take back the Carso?

The 15 didn't work
For you, Uncle Joe; but believe me:
The Carso which you lost
You'll get back in 16![56]

The theater we have been talking about so far was characterized in particular by its strongly inflected ethnicity. But the Italian American stage was also open to a different kind of dramatic art. On one hand, these alternative productions tried to insert themselves in the international classical repertory—we should remember here Maiori's contributions. On the other hand, they tried to make the ethnic scene more bourgeois. We should stress that the Italian theater in New York was

54. *Il Cittadino* (The Citizen), September 26, 1918.
55. A component very much present in the Italian American scene, where were also performed entire "licentious plays," such as *La Mantragola* [sic] *ovvero Il Liquore Di Venere Del Dottore Americano M. Fursterngamberlordzumzum* (The Mandrake, or, Dr. Americano M. Fursterngamberlordzumzum's Venereal Liquor) by E. Rizzo (E. Ozzir), three acts with participation by Pulcinella, who must solve the problem of his padrone Enrico's impotence. The manuscript of the comedy is held in Naples at the Raccolta Cennerazzo of the Biblioteca Lucchesi Palli.
56. *Il Messaggero* (The Messenger) (Paterson–Passaic, N.J.), February 12, 1916.

always—or almost always—an altogether different phenomenon from the Italian American theater. The instances in which actors and authors from Little Italy succeeded in climbing the golden stairs to Broadway were very few. Anyhow, most of these few reached that goal fortuitously, when specific productions called for an authentically "Italian" type.

In his *Memorie* (Memoirs), published in the late 1930s, the actor and entrepreneur Guglielmo Emanuel-Gatti, born in Stupinigi, Piedmont, claims the merit of having founded the first Italian theater of quality in New York. He acknowledges, however, Antonio Maiori's part in founding the theater "of speculation," as he defines it. Emanuel-Gatti arrived in New York in 1915. He had worked in the Thalia Theater in the Bowery and, after the war, he rented the Amsterdam Opera House on West Forty-Fourth Street and founded the Teatro d'Arte Italiana. Subsequently, he became president of the Dante Alighieri Society. A very "official" story indeed. But if we read his personal observations, we get a sense of the constant vitality of the Italian American scene: "Here it would be possible to set up six companies: two of them dramatic, one for Operettas, one Neapolitan, one Sicilian, and two for variety shows."[57]

At the time Emanuel-Gatti was writing his memoir, there was an increasing number of writers for the theater who, as the novelists had done before them, attempted to enrich the ethnic scene with more up-to-date themes. They were concerned with interpreting the last phase of naturalism with a more experimental sensibility. They tried the difficult path of symbolism or perhaps were more simply interested in a "bourgeois" dimension as they sought to distance themselves from the by-then panting, oleographic old world of Little Italy–indeed, almost a museum now. Their work also presented non-Italian characters. Even if not clearly expressed, the aim was to win the interest of the American public by means of translation. Such an ambitious project, however, had little success. Today, the works of authors such as Michele Rapone, Ario Flamma, Picchianti himself, and Armando Romano[58]—to name only some of the most prolific—appear as

---

57. Gatti-Emanuel 1937, 229.

58. Born in Lecce, Puglia, in 1889, Romano arrived in America in 1912. Editor of various newspapers, from 1932 he worked for the Sunday supplement of *Progresso*. He was the author of tragedies (*Fiamme umane/Human Flames*, 1924), plays (*Le nostre vie/Our Ways*, 1926; *L'abisso/ The Abyss*, *Rosa mistica/Mystical Rose*, *Parisina Malatesta*, *Mater nostra/Our Mother*), a book of short stories (*Due donne due passioni/Two Women Two Passions*), a novel (*Il Volto della patria/ The Face Of the Motherland*), and a fictionalized life of Jesus (*Alba nuova/New Dawn*, 1954). See Flamma 1936, bibliography.

the most lifeless products of the Italian American scene in the early twentieth century. And yet we cannot deny them a certain documentary value.

Already in the 1920s Michele Rapone (not to be confused with Pasquale) created a number of "social scenes." In them he showed a peculiar but not openly declared affinity with the experimental work of the theater of proletarian agitprop. In addition he foregrounded the poisonous grudges and private malice of the upper classes. In the one-act play *L'ultimo regalo* (The Last Gift), set in Milan, we have a law student, Alfredo, who falls in love with the Countess Anna, Count Ettore Rolandi's wife. Alfredo is poor and has made up his mind to leave for New York and seek his fortune there. The Count wants to present his wife with a gift for their second anniversary. He asks her what she would like, and she answers that she would like to go to America. Later, however, Giacomo, the Rolandis' faithful butler, reveals to the Count that his wife has betrayed him and gives him the hat Alfredo has lost. On its inner band he sees Alfredo's embroidered name. Then the Count summons his wife and tells her that he is leaving for Rome and that she will have to leave the house before his return. Anna defends herself and proclaims that nothing happened between her and Alfredo except for a pure feeling of love. Given their difference of age, this is understandable; she is in her twenties, and he is over fifty. Ettore takes it all in and decides that Alfredo will be his gift to Anna and in addition he will supply him with a substantial sum of money. As for himself:

GIACOMO: Your bags are ready, Count.
ROLANDI: I have changed my mind, Giacomo; I won't be leaving for Rome.
GIACOMO: Where will you go, Count?
ROLANDI: To America.
GIACOMO: To America?
ROLANDI: Yes, to New York.
GIACOMO: And for how long?
ROLANDI: I will be staying there for the rest of my life. I'll change places with
Alfredo Spina.[59]

Thus the happy ending is triggered by a classical overturning of roles. In this case, however, there is no punishment for the "bad" character. Indeed, the Count is not at all bad. Rather, the ending represents a subtle form of atonement for the original sin of having desired a wife so much younger than himself. The conclusion

59. Michael Rapone, *L'ultimo regalo* (The Last Gift), typewritten MS, Naples, Biblioteca Lucchesi Palli, Raccolta Cennerazzo. No information could be found regarding the author.

of this little drama is thus aimed at recomposing the natural order of things, an order so just that not even a very rich man dare feel entitled to transgress it merely by resorting to his overwhelming wealth.

Another work by Michele Rapone, the one-act "social sketch" *Lettere d'amore* (Love Letters), is pervaded by a similar belief in the generosity of mankind. Here Teodoro Ansperti, a Roman businessman, reveals to Lucia Caretti, the wife of Arturo the banker, that her husband is on the point of ruining him by calling in a number of his bills. Lucia feels sorry for him, but is afraid that she can do nothing to help him. Then Teodoro threatens her. Applying the law of "an eye for an eye," he will tell Arturo that he is the real father of his children. He pulls out a bundle of letters and warns Lucia to go home and fetch the bills. In this way she will learn what is contained in the letters. The dramatic tension is released by the intervention of the good-hearted Maria, Ansperti's wife, who burns the compromising letters and foils Teodoro's attempted blackmail.[60]

Clearly, these were only slight incursions into a world that was fatally different from that of the colony. It was precisely Ario Flamma who more convincingly tried to force the natural limits of Little Italy's dramatic conventions. He came to America in the first decades of the twentieth century. In Italy he had written and published some things but without any success. Even in the New World, he groused, he remained unappreciated:

> I have been in America for ten years, stubbornly following the bitter and harsh path of art. I am still surprised that I have not yet forgotten my Italian, given that the three million Italians in America speak every dialect but Italian. I don't know if I was right or wrong in persisting in a profession which, in America, lends itself to the most bitter disappointments. Here one doesn't know English well enough to write in it as if it were his own language and is forced to live among other Italians: excellent, hardworking, but totally ignorant of art and almost hostile to those who have made it their profession.[61]

As a matter of fact, his plan was to reach beyond the stifling ethnic boundaries of Little Italy. As soon as he settled in America, he printed a very pretentious edition of his *Dramas* in English. Besides, he exhibited complementary letters by personages with high-sounding names as authoritative proof of their enthusiasm. But

60. Michael Rapone, *Lettere d'amore* (Love Letters), typewritten MS, Naples, Biblioteca Lucchesi Palli, Raccolta Cennerazzo.
61. Preface to Flamma 1923.

success was not forthcoming. The quality of Flamma's dramatic art was what it was and perhaps the times were not right. His real mistake was his refusal to draw his subject matter from his own experience. The same mistake was made by those who, like him, obstinately looked beyond their personal horizon for the key that would open the doors to Broadway. This is confirmed by the fact that not many years later, in 1941, Pietro Di Donato, author of *Christ in Concrete*, was able to propose a play based on the novel's plot, *The Love of Annunziata*. In 1950 Italian Americans were able to recognize themselves in Tennessee Williams's *The Rose Tattoo*. Finally, in 1955, with *A View from the Bridge*, Arthur Miller chose to rework a classical love-and-death story of Italian immigration by giving it the solemnity of a Greek tragedy. In those days, many small amateur theatrical companies continued to stage plays in Italian. Above all, these plays were broadcast on radio, in extended serials that usually lasted thirteen weeks—the length of the contract. All in all, these plays repeated the blood-and-thunder formulas of the old colonial narrative. In 1941 someone was already in a position to note that "the only thing surer than death and taxes is that, barring the unlikely possibility of another wave of Italian immigration, the Italian theatre, along with all other similar immigrant-language enterprises, is doomed to slow but certain death."[62]

Translated by Franca and Bill Boelhower

62. Colombo-Adams, 1941, 19.

The Interrogation of Pulcinella

❧ *Francesco Ricciardi*

The Neapolitan Francesco Ricciardi, "prince of the pulcinellos," head of a "Neapolitan Company of New York," was among the leading figures on the scene in Little Italy, specializing in the production of comedies, farces, and other shows in dialect. Already active in 1889 as an amateur (he was a glove maker), in the new century he assumed a more decisively professional position, including as director of the theater Villa Vittorio Emanuele III, on Mulberry Street. More than sixty years later, Rocco De Russo, one of the most acclaimed Italian American caricaturists, would remember him in this capacity. In his still unpublished memoirs, De Russo drew a portrait of Ricciardi that was hardly flattering, a man full of himself and suspicious of the competition of younger actors.

In her pioneering study of the Italian theater in New York City, where she carefully examines the contemporary daily press, Emelise Aleandri notes that Ricciardi performed his last theatrical role of the waning century in March 1895. The ensuing, long hiatus, lasting until the end of 1901, suggested a creative void that may now, in some measure, be filled with works preserved in the Raccolta (Collection) Cennerazzo in the Biblioteca Lucchesi Palli of Naples. Among these is the manuscript of a comedy in three acts, *Pulcinella soldato volontario all'Africa; ovvero, Gli amori della regina Taitù ed il prigioniero Pulcinella* (Pulcinella the Volunteer Soldier in Africa, or the Amorous Affairs of Queen Taitù and the Prisoner Pulcinella, 1897), a characteristic illustration of the attention the ethnic theater paid to current affairs pertaining to the Italians. Perhaps dating from 1898 is another manuscript, the comedy in three acts, *Pulcinella condannato all sedia elettrica* (Pulcinella Sentenced to the Electric Chair), of which a sample is offered here. The manuscript of the comedy in four acts, *La distruzione dei Cristiani in Cina* (The Destruction of the Christians in China, 1902), features a helpless Pulchinello struggling with a bear and an orangutan. Probably of the same period is the comedy set in an Italian American ambiance: *Pulecenella a Nuova York; ovvero, Nu buordo puosto a rummore da Pulecenella e da n'americano* (Pulcinella in New York, or the Noisy Boardinghouse of Pulcinella and the American). Different from the preceding comedies, in this one, the author was not indicated; Ricciardi, however, figured as the principal interpreter, obviously in the role of Pulchinello.

Aleandri recorded a substantial series of other titles, notable among them are *Nu pulicino dint'a stuppa* (The Kid on the Stoop, 1901); *Tanta mbruoglie pe nu matremmonio* (So Many Mix-ups for a Wedding, 1901); *Pulcinella candidato democratico con Farfariello impazzito per la tragedia* (Pulcinella the Democratic Candidate with Farfariello Gone Crazy over the Tragedy, 1904), in which Ricciardi and Migliaccio acted together, as happened other times, whether Migliaccio wrote for Ricciardi (*Pulcinella sindaco di Chicago* [Pulcinella Mayor of Chicago] 1903), or whether Ricciardi wrote for the celebrated Farfariello (*Farfariello truvato dint'a'nu varrile* [Pulcinella Discovered in a Barrel, 1903]). Finally, there are various anonymous titles, but credibly attributed to Ricciardi: *Pulcinella imperatore del Mongol* (Pulcinella Emperor of Mongolia, 1903); *Il brigante Musolino con Pulcinella bandito per necessità* (Musolino the Brigand with Pulcinella the Bandit by Necessity, 1903); *La distruzione dei Cristiani in Cina con Pulcinella giapponese per combinazione ed obbligato a combattere con la Russia* (The Destruction of the Christians in China with Pulcinella a Japanese by Chance and Forced to Fight for Russia, 1905), which seems to be a variation of the title cited earlier.

Ricciardi worked as all the pulcinellos of Naples have always worked: remaking the tradition of the mask (a stock character from the commedia dell'arte) and enriching it with new material, with personal elements, and with progressive expansions that in Ricciardi's case, achieve particularly notable results because of the necessity of transplanting Pulcinello to America. *Pulcinella condannato alla sedia elettrica* is nothing other than an adaptation for the Italian Americans of the popular nineteenth-century piece *Pulcinella Molinaro* of Filippo Cammarano. But in the transposition, the text is expanded and assumes new forms; it becomes unrecognizable. The direction notes, inserted in a copy of the manuscript—which by force of circumstance presents frequent incongruities, such as different styles of writing, orthographic errors, and so on—signal the various departures from the subject. In performance, it was left to the skill of the interpreter and his caprice to vary the dialogue, integrate new meanings, and twist remarks, according to the temper of the occasion or news of the moment.

In Ricciardi, the use of Italian American argot is still moderate, which reveals that the author's work belongs to an earlier period, where it is still possible to distinguish three distinct linguistic categories not integrated, and even suspiciously kept intact: American English; literary Italian; dialect. In the case of *Pulcinella condannato alla sedia elettrica*, before the happy ending, the audience views Pulcinello's misfortunes, due to the underhanded dealings of a petty-thief court officer, Felice Martino, conspiring together with the judge Giacomo (James) Muller, to conquer the beautiful hostess Ketty (Katie). The first two serve as personifications of unjust and corrupt power.

ESSENTIAL BIBLIOGRAPHY

Aleandri 1983a; Falbo 1942; Sant'Elia 1994.

CHARACTERS

> Judge Muller
> Felix, Clerk of the Court
> Guards
> *Pulcinella Cucumber*
> Gerry Barricello, a Policeman
> *Second Policeman*

Scene I

Courtroom.

JUDGE MULLER: Give the order to have the perpetrator Pulcinella brought here.

GUARD (*at the door*): Prisoner No. 39.

VOICE (*offstage*): Prisoner No. 39.

ANOTHER VOICE: Prisoner No. 39.

PULCINELLA (*from offstage*): Straighten your tie.

FELIX: Your Honor, I recommend . . . do not forget, that this guy Pulcinella should be found guilty, and should be condemned.

JUDGE MULLER: Leave it up to me—I promised you I would put myself at your disposal, and in your favor, I will do it, etc., etc.

FELIX: Thanks very much. I will be much obliged to you.

JUDGE MULLER: I'll tell you what I think . . . I am convinced that he must be the murderer . . . because when someone is innocent . . . you know it from their honest, sincere answers . . . etc., etc.

PULCINELLA (*from offstage, then onstage*): I can walk just fine by myself, I don't need you to accompany me, you jerk.

POLICEMAN BARRICELLO: Shut up!

PULCINELLA: I'll give you "shut up"[1] right in your eye.

JUDGE MULLER: Silence.

PULCINELLA: But I only said. . . .

JUDGE MULLER: Enough. If you say another word, I'll dismiss your case . . . and then . . . and then . . . etc., etc.

PULCINELLA: Your excellency, your excellency.

JUDGE MULLER: Do you know why you were arrested?

PULCINELLA: If you don't know, how do you expect me to know?

JUDGE MULLER: You're in contempt! Is this how you respond . . . don't you know that I can . . . etc, etc?

FELIX: Don't you know that he is the Judge?

PULCINELLA: Etc., etc. How come these two little jinxes are so nosey?

JUDGE MULLER: Clerk, swear him in.

FELIX: Stand up here—put your hand on this book and swear to tell the truth.

PULCINELLA: You want me to pick the lottery numbers from the dream book— but I can't read.

FELIX: It doesn't matter . . . repeat after me.

PULCINELLA: Then I would only be saying vulgarities.

FELIX: Shut up, stupid.

PULCINELLA: Shut up, stupid.

FELIX: Keep quiet, you filthy animal.

PULCINELLA: Keep quiet, you filthy animal.

JUDGE MULLER: OK, take him back to jail; the trial will proceed without him.

POLICEMAN BARRICELLO: Come on. (*He seizes him.*)

PULCINELLA: Hey, come on I say, take it easy.

POLICEMAN BARRICELLO: Hurry up.[2]

PULCINELLA: What do you want, ricott'? . . . stop, stop. Tell me what you want, I'll do it.

JUDGE MULLER: You must swear on the Bible to tell the truth.

---

1. "Shut up" sounds to Pulcinella like the Italian word *sciroppo*, "syrup," so he repeats "shut up" as *sciruppo*. Illiterate and limited to his dialect, Pulcinella frequently misunderstands the formal Italian if the others, as he might an English speaker, and responds with attempts at word play. In this instance there is a mixed image of a punch in the eye or syrup (in context, possibly medicinal or poisonous) in the eye.

2. Pronounced *arriòp*.

FELIX: Put your hand here.

PULCINELLA: Here it is.

FELIX: I swear to tell the truth.

PULCINELLA: I swear not to tell the truth.

FELIX: To tell the truth.

PULCINELLA: To tell the truth.

FELIX: Nothing but the truth.

PULCINELLA: Anything but the truth.

FELIX: The whole truth.

PULCINELLA: The whole truth.

JUDGE MULLER: What country are you from?

PULCINELLA: I don't know.

JUDGE MULLER: Where you were born?

PULCINELLA: December 25th, the 26th is the first holiday and 8 days after that is New Year's Day.[3]

JUDGE MULLER: What is your surname?[4]

PULCINELLA: I am OK, nothing is broken.

JUDGE MULLER: I mean what is your name.

PULCINELLA: My name?

JUDGE MULLER: Precisely.

PULCINELLA: Pulcinella Cucumber.[5]

JUDGE MULLER: And your father?

PULCINELLA: Pulcinella Big Cucumber.

JUDGE MULLER: Mother.

PULCINELLA: Whose mother?

JUDGE MULLER: Yours.

PULCINELLA: I thought you meant yours.

JUDGE MULLER: Answer me quickly. And you, Clerk, enter it on the record.

PULCINELLA: Portia Dufus.[6]

JUDGE MULLER: How old are you?

PULCINELLA: 22 years, twenty days, two months and one week old.

---

3. Pulcinella mistakes the word *natali* (birthplace) for *natale* (Christmas), and thus his answer.

4. He mistakes the word *casato* (surname) for *scassato* (broken), and thus his answer.

5. In dialect, *cetrullo* means cucumber. When used in reference to a person, it is one of many expressions used to signify a person of limited intelligence or ability.

6. *Sciabecco* in dialect means someone who is tall and stupid. A. Vallardi, *Dizionario Napoletano* (2009). See www.vallardi.it.

JUDGE MULLER: Which trade do you practice?

PULCINELLA: Your aunt's.[7]

JUDGE MULLER: I do not understand you.

PULCINELLA: I understand.

JUDGE MULLER: I mean what job do you have.

PULCINELLA: Look, I'll tell you . . . I work as a bouncer in a tavern.

JUDGE MULLER: What is the name of the man you work for.

PULCINELLA: I don't have a man for a boss—I only have a lady for a boss.

JUDGE MULLER: What is her name?

PULCINELLA: Katie—Ah, if you saw her, how attractive she is, you would eat her like a dish of macaroni with marinara sauce.

JUDGE MULLER: Enter it on the record, Clerk. Where does she live?

PULCINELLA: On Blicchio Street.

JUDGE MULLER: On Blicchio Street?

FELIX: On Bleecker Street, Your Honor.

PULCINELLA: Honestly, we live on Blayker Street.[8]

JUDGE MULLER: Enter it into the record, Clerk. Tell me, have you ever associated with people who lead bad lives?

PULCINELLA: Bad lives, yes sir.

JUDGE MULLER: Enter it on the record, Clerk—with thieves. . . .

PULCINELLA: Thieves, no sir.

JUDGE MULLER: With murderers. . . .

PULCINELLA: No sir, they were idiots.[9]

JUDGE MULLER: Smugglers?

PULCINELLA: No sir.

JUDGE MULLER: So then, with which people of low life have you associated?

PULCINELLA: With a cripple, a blind man, and a hunchback.

JUDGE MULLER: And these people are somehow low-lifes?

PULCINELLA: Yes sir.

7. This reflexive reference to a female family member in the possessive serves as an all-purpose, extremely crude, and insulting comeback, suggesting the genitalia of the referenced family member and therefore her loose morals or status as a prostitute. This insult, commonly used by men and women with none of the social graces, could be found in as many variations as categories of female family relationships (*'e mammata*, *'e sorreta*, *'e ziata*) and was the last resort of the verbally inept who found themselves in need of a retort or insult.

8. In the Italian original, phonetically spelled "Blecher," suggesting an attempt to repeat Felix's pronunciation.

9. In dialect, *pippa* refers literally to pipes but has a number of secondary meanings, none positive. See Vallardi.

JUDGE MULLER: Have you ever carried on your person weapons, guns or sharp knives?

PULCINELLA: Yes sir, sharp knives.

JUDGE MULLER: A stiletto?

PULCINELLA: A stiletto, no sir.

JUDGE MULLER: A razor?

PULCINELLA: A razor, no sir.

JUDGE MULLER: A stick?

PULCINELLA: No sir, cod fish.[10]

JUDGE MULLER: Enter it into the record, Clerk, cod fish. A knife?

PULCINELLA: A knife, no sir.

JUDGE MULLER: So what weapons have you carried?

PULCINELLA: The scissors, the needle, the thimble and the tongue.

JUDGE MULLER: So these are the sharp weapons?

PULCINELLA: Well, don't you cut with the scissors?

JUDGE MULLER: Cut that from the record, Clerk.

PULCINELLA: Cut that and I'll show you how to cut a ream of paper.

JUDGE MULLER: But what does the tongue have to do with sharp weapons?

PULCINELLA: Your Honor . . . I see that you don't know.

JUDGE MULLER: Would you explain it?

PULCINELLA: Sure: nothing cuts sharper than the tongue—because when it doesn't tell the truth, a person can even be sent to death . . . and then when a woman uses it . . . it can cut sharper than a razor.

JUDGE MULLER: Enough, enough—Enter it into the record, Clerk.

FELIX: But what should I enter?

JUDGE MULLER: Enter it . . . enter it . . . scissors, tongue, etc., etc.

PULCINELLA: I'll let you write for a while.

JUDGE MULLER: You have certainly carried firearms.

PULCINELLA: Yes sir.

JUDGE MULLER: Enter it on the record, Clerk. . . .

FELIX: But which ones?

JUDGE MULLER: Etc., etc. . . . a rifle?

PULCINELLA: No sir.

JUDGE MULLER: A gun?

PULCINELLA: No sir.

JUDGE MULLER: So what firearms have you carried?

---

10. He mistakes the word *stocco* (stick) for *stoccofisso* (stickfish or dried cod).

PULCINELLA: Bait and tackle.

JUDGE MULLER: And these are firearms?

PULCINELLA: Sure.

JUDGE MULLER: Strike that from the record, Clerk.

PULCINELLA: Yes, Clerk, strike that out and I'll send you to Vietri for more paper.[11]

JUDGE MULLER: You were found on a city street, with the knife in your fist . . . covered with blood.

PULCINELLA: But I'm telling you, I was walking in the middle of the street, slowly, very slowly, holding a basket with macaroni and steak on my shoulder to bring to a banker on Centre Street to eat, I tripped and I fell, sure[12] and found myself on top of a dead body. Sure, I got up and the dead man did not move . . . (*he makes the hand gesture to ward off the evil eye*) . . . I was going to leave and I found a knife on the ground; I picked it up, intending to sell it to the hardware store and while I was walking away . . . two faces appeared and wouldn't allow me to . . . one plus one, two (*indicating Felix and the Policeman*) and they started saying that I killed him . . . and they took me to jail.

JUDGE MULLER: Don't deny it, you killed him.

PULCINELLA: You must be dizzy.

FELIX: Don't deny it—I found you at the moment that you were running away with the knife in your hand.

PULCINELLA: But I told you that I tripped on the dead man and fell.

JUDGE MULLER: It's useless to deny it—we even have the sworn testimony of Policeman Gerry Barricello—you are the murderer—etc., etc.—Enter it into the record, Clerk.

PULCINELLA: And you have the nerve to say that I murdered him.

POLICEMAN BARRICELLO: It pains me, poor Pulcinella. I am sorry for you, poor Pulcinella—it breaks my heart, poor Pulcinella . . . I am sorry for you . . . but I cannot deny the truth, you killed him.

JUDGE MULLER: Enter it on the record, Clerk.

PULCINELLA: Enter it on the record, my ass. I did not kill him. And you, you phony (*to the Policeman Barricello*), you'll pay me for this; step outside if you have the courage!

11. A reference to Vietri sul Mare, a coastal village near Salerno, Italy. Pulcinella is wishing he could buy some time.

12. Pronounced *sciò*.

JUDGE MULLER: Silence!

PULCINELLA: But I said I didn't kill him.

JUDGE MULLER: Silence! Enter it into the record, Clerk.

POLICEMAN BARRICELLO: Poor Pulcinella, I feel like crying!

PULCINELLA: First you murder me and then you cry for me.

FELIX: Your Honor . . . it would be better not to waste time and to go right to sentencing.

JUDGE MULLER: O. K. . . . take the perpetrator away.

POLICEMAN BARRICELLO: Come with me.

PULCINELLA: And where are we going?

POLICEMAN BARRICELLO: Where are we going? My friend, I see you're in trouble, so it's causing a knot in my throat . . . it's getting so big it will burst and who knows how many tears I'll cry.

PULCINELLA: Barricello, before you burst, I'll throw something at your head, and I'll make you explode.

POLICEMAN BARRICELLO: Come on, come on. Poor Pulcinella! What have you done now!

PULCINELLA: May every curse come down on you.

POLICEMAN BARRICELLO: Let's go—then we'll come back, to hear your sentence. Who knows what they will give you.

PULCINELLA: Tell me, Barricello . . . couldn't I hear it right away?

POLICEMAN BARRICELLO: Let's go, let's go—poor Pulcinella.

JUDGE MULLER: Are you going, or not? (*They leave at this comment.*) Mr. Clerk, my good sir . . . what do you say . . . do you really believe he is guilty?

FELIX: Certainly, and besides the crime is written all over his face. . . .

JUDGE MULLER: But what would all the newspapers say about us . . . if we condemned an innocent man. . . .

FELIX: But what newspapers, what newspapers? With a few dollars they can be bought—and then listen, Judge—these worries are a waste of time—If this man doesn't die, I'll never know peace and tranquility again. In any event, I will always be here to support you.

JUDGE MULLER: All right then, I consent to it. Write the death sentence.

FELIX: Leave it to me—it's already prepared—I can always foresee the future.

JUDGE MULLER: Bravo–you're a psychic clerk. (*He rings the bell.*) Bring in the perpetrator.

FELIX: Here I am, finally on the verge of total happiness.

Scene II

PULCINELLA: Hey, listen my dear sirs, do me a favor, let me go home . . . because today is the last day of the month, and I need to go and collect my wages.

POLICEMAN BARRICELLO: Poor Pulcinella, you'll get what's coming to you, for sure.

SECOND POLICEMAN: They'll give it to you in gold. Poor Pulcinella.

FELIX: Your Honor, here is the sentence for you to read.

PULCINELLA: But I don't have time to waste . . .

JUDGE MULLER: Silence! (*He reads*)—Having found the accused here present, today on the 25th day of April 1898, guilty of having committed the horrible crime of killing Florindo Pippo, for the purpose of robbing him, and not having been able to deny the crime–because he was found near the corpse still with the bloody knife by Mr. Felix Martino, Clerk of the Court, and by the Policeman Barricello, also here present, and after an investigation according to all the rules prescribed by law. And the court not having found any extenuating circumstances, the court, in its infallible wisdom, sentences Pulcinella Cucumber—son of Pulcinella Cucumber Senior and Portia Sciabecca, to the death penalty—to be carried out by means of the electric chair in Sing-Sing prison.

Translated by Emelise Aleandri

Four Poems and a Dramatic Play

Riccardo Cordiferro

San Pietro in Guarano (Cosenza), Italy, 1875–New York, New York, 1940

The name of Riccardo Cordiferro, a pseudonym for Alessandro Sisca, is tied to that of the *Follia* (Folly) *of New York*. In January 1893, not quite eighteen, Cordiferro was one of its founders, together with his father, Francesco (1839–1928), who was also a poet, and with his brother Marziale.

The Siscas moved from Calabria to Naples, following the head of the family, a functionary of the prefecture. In 1886, Alessandro entered the Seminary of San Raffaele, in Materdei, and it could be that this brief experience was instrumental in forming his successive anticlerical choices. But the Neapolitan sojourn might also have stirred artistic leanings within him, for it was exactly in Naples that he published his first verses and became involved with the literary and theatrical environment of the city. These experiences must have been useful in the composition of numerous caricatures in the manner of Maldacea and other celebrated protagonists of light theater; they also afforded him practice in using Neapolitan dialect in poetry, with notable results. He composed the texts of many Neapolitan songs, performed, among others, by Enrico Caruso, one of which is the very famous "Core'ngrato" (1911), with music by Salvatore Cardillo.

Emigrating with his family to America in 1892, Alessandro resided in Pittsburgh for a year with an uncle; then he established himself definitively in New York. The work for *Follia*, combined with intense literary activity, absorbed him completely; and winning approbation for raising the newspaper to notable success on the whole East Coast led him to make frequent trips to conferences, to give theatrical representations, poetry readings, and to engage in debates, very often with political undertones.

In this period of his life, in fact, Sisca maintained rather close contact with anarchist and socialist circles, which resulted in more than one arrest and constrained him to resign from directing the *Follia*. He continued to contribute to it, however, using pseudonyms—"Corazon de hierro," "Ironheart," "Eisenherz," "Sandro," "Ida Florenza"—there and in writing for other newspapers such as *La Sedia Elettrica* (The Electric Chair, which he edited), *La Notizia*, and *The Haarlemite*.

In 1895, the following theatrical monologues appeared: *Per la Patria e per l'onore* (For the Fatherland and for Honor), in which an exile who returns to his native country commits murder to vindicate his sister's honor, and *Il pezzente* (The Ragamuffin), which had hundreds of performances, and according to the author, was performed even in Italy, France, and South America. In the Americas, in fact, it became a standard in the repertory of amateur players in revolutionary political circles.

The drama in three acts *Da volontario a disertore* (From Volunteer to Deserter) was written in 1897. In 1901, Cordiferro wrote the social drama in four acts, *L'onore perduto* (Lost Honor), which, produced by Antonio Maiori and directed by the author, was received with great favor and continued to be staged until the 1930s. Among those who appreciated it was the famous anarchist agitator Luigi Galleani.

L'onore perduta (whose text is also lost) is set in historic Little Italy, on the Lower East Side. Alberto Rotini, formerly a teller in a bank on Mulberry Street in which Don Celestino works, has lost his job because he is accused, unjustly, of stealing one hundred dollars. He appeals to an old Neapolitan friend Giuseppe Esposito, to intercede for him with Don Celestino and to take care of his wife Sofia and his daughter Ida; Sofia has found work as a seamstress to help support the family. Giuseppe informs him that Don Celestino would be disposed to drop the charges provided that he sign a letter asking for pardon. Alberto refuses, since that would be tantamount to admitting that he committed the theft. The police arrive and arrest him. A month later, Ida is very sick, and in despair of being able to save her, Sofia reveals Giuseppe's transgressions to Pasquale, a friend of the family. In Naples, Giuseppe wanted her to be wife, but having been refused, he emigrated to America, where as boss, he became rich exploiting the poor immigrants, preparing his revenge. It was he who drew Alberto to America, finding him employment in the bank. Giuseppe repairs to Sofia's house, but she chases him out, threatening him with a pistol. He continues to deny that he was responsible for Alberto's imprisonment and reproaches her for her pride. A month later, sick in jail, Alberto writes a letter to Sofia telling her that Giuseppe has opened his own bank and been nominated cavalier and that he has offered to pay the bail to free him. Don Celestino has new proofs of Alberto's guilt, and therefore it is necessary to hire a lawyer and be prepared for the trial. Giuseppe returns to Sofia's house and proclaims his good intentions, but Sofia accuses him of wanting to save her husband at the price of her honor. The woman is in a crisis, such that she entertains the idea of yielding to him. In the final act, Alberto is released from prison and returns home, but Sofia is now dishonored. She drinks poison and dies. Alberto vindicates himself by stabbing Giuseppe to death. Heavily dramatic, filled with invective against the wickedness of the rich exploiters, in particular, the easy life of bankers, and of tirades against religion, *L'onore perduto* achieved such success that in 1906, demands were made for a sort of sequel. Cordiferro then wrote *Giuseppina Terranova; ovvero, L'onore vendicato* (Giuseppina Terranova, or Honor Avenged), which is reprinted here.

From a rereading of these texts, it could be said that, basically, as a committed writer, Cordiferro never wandered far from the genre, though he possessed a very cordial attitude toward the weakest, aspiring to vindicate social justice, which in the contemporary colonial environment, was common territory for all those who wrote at all for publication. In addition, Cordiferro colored the dramas on honor in the gloomy tones dear to Ciambelli. As a person, Cordiferro was perhaps more drawn to satire, the comical, and the sentimental. He wrote poetry all his life, quickly becoming a source of reference for hundreds of amateur poets asking him for criticism and to write prefaces to their volumes, which they might well publish in his family's printing house. Besides writing poetry for many years, Cordiferro dedicated himself to comic theater.

In 1894, Cordiferro was already writing for the famous company Maiori-Rapone-Ricciardi: the comedy *Genio incompreso* (Misunderstood Genius) and the comic skit *Chi ha la testa di vetro non vada a battaglia di sassi* (The Man with a Glass Head Doesn't Fight with Stones) satirize the amateur actors of that time in Little Italy. Following were the one-act *Dio Dollaro* (God the Dollar, 1896), composed in the manner of Carducci's *Inno a Satana* (Hymn to Satan); the comedy *Il matrimonio in trappola* (Marriage in a Trap, 1897); and numerous caricatures, often performed in addition to more serious dramas in the same evening. Other theatrical works were *Il prominente coloniale* (The Prominent Colonial); *Io m'aggio fatto Monaco* (I Became a Monk), interpreted by Eduardo Migliaccio; *Don Vincenzo 'o cammorrista* (Don Vincenzo the Gangster); *Don Vincenzo the Orange Peddler*; *'O guappo (The Cammorista): Muglierema m'ha passato* (My wife passed me by); and "Il 'polisso' italo-americano," reprinted here. All were written in the period extending from 1898 to 1902.

Cordiferro's volcanic activity produced a quantity of flowing works, but in quality they were very irregular. Undoubtedly, in his particular manner, Cordiferro had an ingenious faculty for verse in a spontaneous vein, whose principal characteristic was truly an extraordinary lyricism. Even so, in the various small volumes of his poetry, including the posthumous *Poesie scelte* (Selected poems), published in Italy in 1967, it is difficult to find episodes that are elevated much above the negligible average of the colonial hack writing.

It is known that Cordiferro especially valued his social cantos and planned to collect them into a single volume entitled *Musa rossa* (Red Muse). Notable among the cantos are "Inno alla Pace" (Hymn to Peace), "Cantilena del Primo Maggio" (Lullaby for the First of May), the "Ode alla Libertà" (Ode to Freedom), and many others, representative especially of his early production. A significant example of this period is the collection, touched with Cordiferro's mastery: *Singhiozzi e sogghigni* (Sobs and Sneers), perhaps from 1916, for G. De Marco's review of it was published in the *Follia* on January 16, 1916. Cordiferro also wrote poetry on the most disparate themes. Fichera mentions some thousand compositions in Italian and in dialect (Calabrese, Neapolitan, and Sicilian), and records some significant passages from the author's preface to the collection entitled, *Il poema dell'Amore* (The Poem of Love, 1928), then reproduced in the small volume *Poesie scelte*:

> Always subject to the interruptions and endless see-sawing of the lot of destiny; always gripped by the inexorable tight irons of the cruel necessities of life; and always slave to the heavy hair shirt of journalism, for which I have uselessly wasted my best time and squandered my most healthy and resolute intellectual energies; it is no wonder that I could not wholly live the divine life of poetry and adorn my verses with classical elegance . . . Denied to me was the supreme joy of the spirit. And I have sung life; I have sung love and pain, with simple words turning to the most humble things, and I have not known any other secret than that of rendering, with communicative simplicity, the profound sense of the things surrounding me.

Perhaps hidden in the underlying emphasis on the goading and impelling need that poor, unknown writers have to work to live, is Cordiferro's vague awareness of his limits, an awareness reflected in biographical data, registering his many difficult moments, especially in the auspicious opportunities of being between two centuries. To the police persecutions Cordiferro experienced is added a series of mournful circumstances taking place in the years 1897 and 1898: his wife Annina Belli died, as well as his children Emilia and Franchino (in 1899, he married Lucia, sister of the actor Achille Fazio).

Although interested in English literature (Fichera mentions his translations of Shelley), as a poet, Cordiferro remained well inside the Italian tradition. His principal influence in social compositions is Carducci, together with the other nineteenth-century, "angrier" poets, from Stecchetti to Costanzo, Rapisardi, and others. He achieved a freer, in a certain way, more original manner in his humorous poems and love poems, inspired and "dictated," as he proclaimed, with unconcealed pleasure, "to my lovers, in the trains, in the trolley cars, in the parks, in the cafés, in the restaurants, in the hotels, in all the discretely tranquil corners of our frequent amorous meetings." His Neapolitan disposition with its customs, rhythms, and themes of the city's popular songs and light shows, has undoubtedly influenced Cordiferro's verses.

However, whether because of the aesthetic achievements of his oeuvre, and for better or worse, Cordiferro was principally responsible for the flourishing of colonial poetry. He was the mediator between the average poetic taste of the country of origin and the new literary phenomena of the Italian American colony, of which he became the arbiter and guarantee. Basically, he is the first to be genuinely "other," even staying within the confines of a well-circumscribed tradition.

If the question is put in these terms, it is possible to correct Giuseppe Prezzolini's very harsh judgment of him, which reduced him to a typical exponent of provincial Italian poetry, that of "Farfalla illustrata" (Specimen Butterfly), a poem "that was stranded here and remained as such, as if inside a museum glass of a museum, conserved in naphthalene." This severe judgment conceals Prezzolini's vexation with Cordiferro's long fidelity, first to "subversive" ideals, then to the antifascists: he was among the collaborators of Carlo Tresca's *Martello* (Hammer) even into the 1930s. In that period, he also wrote a good deal for *Il Nuovo Mondo*, an antifascist daily of New York.

ESSENTIAL BIBLIOGRAPHY

Aleandri 1989; Cordiferro 1967; Deschamps 1998, 282–283; Fichera 1958, 18–21; Marazzi 2001, 85–87; Prezzolini 1963, 257–262.

The Beggar

The scene is a bare and dreary cell in a prison in present-day Italy. The actor is pale, emaciated, woeful, shabbily dressed.

A bit of bread! a bit of bread! I beg
a single crust for hunger's sake! . . . Alas!
I'm dying of starvation . . . So I said
to passersby, my hand stretched out to them,
then I began imploring them, eyes wet
with tears, but all my sad and supplicating
words were repelled by their irony, by their
brusque and haughty gestures, by their scornful
scowls, and by their glances of contempt. . . .
Nobody stopped to offer me a cent,
nobody showed any pity for my pain;
nobody even offered me a single
smile of compassion . . . How I would have welcomed
one word at least from anyone, one word
of pity and of hope . . . I bowed to all
the passersby, like this, the way a dog
that has been whipped prostrates himself in fear
at his master's feet . . . I followed after them
hunched and weeping, with my hat in hand,
and everything a needy wretch can say
I said to them: A bit of bread . . . I'm starving. . . .
I haven't eaten for two days, my children
are all at home, they're waiting for me, please
hear my sad tale, o good and generous
gentlemen passing by; a bit of bread
and I ask nothing more of you . . . Ah! please
don't make me go back home with empty hands!
If you have hearts within your breasts and have
the blood of men, if you believe in God,
if you have children too, ah! don't walk past
indifferently in front of me. I'm made
of flesh and blood like you . . . I beg of you,
give me a coin.

(*pause*)

The gentlemen hurrying by
without a word, wrapped up inside their coats,
the ladies wrapped in fur and elegantly

covered with marten and with velvet, all
proceeding on their way, go by without
turning around or giving me a thing. . . .

(*pause*)

    Ah! if there is a coward on the vile
stage of this murderous and wicked world,
if there's a man with no faith and no heart,
one who'd betray his father or his brother,
he is that man who with his silence says
to one in need who's holding out his hand:
"Don't block my way; you fill me with contempt,
contempt that makes me want to call you names,
and not give you a thing!"
      The most outcast
creature on earth, enduring such offense,
should answer such contempt indignantly
and rise in rebellion . . . But instead I smack
this face of mine that's blushed so many times:
when weeping I would look for bread and pity,
without the courage or the pride to call
myself a man, as good as other men.
This slap I give my own face I should give
a thousand times to the arrogant hard faces
of those who hurl insults at men in rags
and laugh at every moaning wretch they see. . . .

(*pause*)

    The snow was coming down in great huge flakes,
the dark and dreary sky above me looked
like a heavy cloak of lead, the cold
was so intense that in my blood I felt
the chill of death; benumbed, with the inferno
burning inside my heart, with bloody lips
and fever too, I dragged myself along
until I'd almost come to my front door.
Under my tattered clothes my naked flesh
was showing through, my teeth were dancing in

my head, and I was shivering like a reed
caught in the wind; I didn't think that I
would make it to my hovel still alive. . . .

(*pause*)

Ah, me! They all were waiting for me there,
starving, my poor young children and the mate
of my sad days . . . Maybe, for all I knew,
death and mourning waited there for me!. . . .
And yet I couldn't bear to go back home
without a crust of bread, without a cent,
I was that close to stealing, turning myself
into a slave and murderer—I don't care!—
to make sure that my children would survive. . . .
You tell me: how could any father not
do it for love of his children? Even if
he had a thousand lives, he'd give them all
to save his children . . . He'd become a villain
to make them good and happy, and provide
nourishment for their bodies and their spirits. . . .
There isn't any pain in all this world
to equal what a father feels who sees
his children waste away before his eyes
and hears them crying "Daddy, we're so hungry!"
The mind can well imagine every pain,
but not this one: it's horrible, it's cruel. . . .
it's a death rattle, it's an open wound
that never can be healed, and it's a shriek
of anguish and insanity: this pain
is so immense that there's no word for it. . . .
The father feels he hasn't any spirit
and life itself is tearing him to pieces,
because his whole life is his children's lives,
because his children's lives are his own life. . . .
I knew the very pain of which I speak,
I had a precise awareness of my torment. . . .
And I went on ahead. . . .

		I saw a lady
walking beside me who was carrying
a bundle in her hands, who seemed to me
beautiful, kind and gentle. . . .
		I took off
my hat and, sobbing, in a pitiful
tone of voice I spoke to her this way:
"I'm hungry and my children haven't eaten,
may I carry your package for you?"
		"Go away!"
that lady answered me, "I am the Countess
del Giglio, and as for you, you tramp, you wish
that I would deign to walk beside you here!". . . .

(*pause*)

There, see how vile is the world, and see the insult
that luxury pukes right into the face
of misery. . . .
		I drew back, silently,
but with my eyes still fixed on her, injected
with rage and venom . . . When that haughty bitch
was far from me, I cried out in my fury:
"May God's anathema fall down upon you!"
God! What an empty word! What lunacy!
What a pathetic irony! What a lie!
For a starving man who takes those insults from
the well-fed and resigns himself to fate,
there cannot be a God!
		And when at last
I had drawn near the entrance to my hovel,
the sky was dark and from the nearby temple
the holy bells rang out Ave Maria. . . .
	I don't know why I didn't want to go
inside my sad and squalid little house.
I don't know why my knees were shaking, why
I felt a tear come rising to my eyes.
I had a premonition in my heart,

I thought some unforeseen misfortune had. . . .
Alas! the heart of a poor wretch is not
very often wrong . . . And no, I wasn't wrong!. . . .

(*pause*)

   I knocked . . . but no voice answered to the sound;
I knocked again, and still there was no answer. . . .
Then finally I threw a hard punch square
against the fragile door and broke it down. . . .

(*pause*)

   Astonished and confused, without a word
I walked into the bare and empty room,
I called my wife and my two children! nothing. . . .
There was nobody there. . . .
     A thousand strange
notions assaulted me . . . And I cried out:
"Where is my heart's companion, and Gino and Lilla,
my poor little children?" And exhausted, pale,
totally broken, aching, stiff and sore,
I let my body fall into a chair
close to the window. . . .
     I could feel myself
practically dying, but nonetheless a flame
spreading like wildfire preyed upon my brain. . . .

(*loudly*)

   I could have wished to hold the world within
my fist, so I could smash it, could have wished
to be God for one instant, so I could
destroy it, everyone and everything. . . .

(*pause*)

   Hunger was gnawing at me; even so,
I could have gone another thousand days
without a crumb, if someone said to me:
"Your wife and children have enough to eat."
This thought had pierced my heart and run it through,

inflicting death upon me. . . .
            Leaning on
the window-sill, face in my hands, I looked
outside, and there came back into my mind
these verses I can still recall, dictated
by an indignant and rebellious soul.

I

   When I am on my way home every day
a wretched beggar asks for charity,
invoking Jesus' beautiful and gay
mother Mary as he speaks to me.
   My heart's inflamed, I want to strip away
my things for that poor man in misery,
and yet, "Get out of here!" is what I say,
"I won't give you a cent! Now let me be". . . .
   Accepting fate, you're glad if someone throws
a hard and moldy crust of bread to you.
Rub shoulders with the rich, the bourgeois, those
   who live well. Steal, because you're able to,
exhausted creature, pluck right from their clothes
the pearls and diamonds glittering like dew. . . .

II

   Yes, steal, and kill, if you can manage to:
Don't grovel, don't show such servility
to me, your brother and a man like you.
Don't tip your hat, a hypocrite's flattery.
   If I have coins and won't give you a few
because I'd rather spend them on a spree
of drinking, or a whore . . . don't say boo-hoo
and beg: poor hungry bastard, murder me.
   Justice compels you to it. Heed the call
and do it, or you're cowardly and base,
a beggar forever. Once you had a small
   stash, and now it's gone without a trace:
priest, bailiff, boss, official took it all.
If you know that I'm rich . . . spit in my face.

III

And I, I am a beggar too, you know,
who has no roof, like you, who has no bread. . . .
I also suffer, toil, have nothing, though
I await the dawn of a better day ahead.

In me, though I am scorned and full of woe,
a furious love of freedom is not dead;
in verse I boldly strike the rabble, so
cowardly, timid and mean-spirited.

I strike their faces hard, more than a few
of those who call us madmen, miscreants,
the faces of knaves, cowards, morons too.

I join the suffering outcasts with no chance
and loudly call to them: O gallant crew
of fighters, the future waits for you, advance!

(*pause*)

Then suddenly I heard the door being opened,
and in a voice so feeble and so faint
that to my ears it seemed the final breath
of someone dying, my forsaken mate,
advancing toward me, said to me: "Enough;
I prefer death a thousand times to shame
and to dishonor . . . but this is too much!
More than four hours we have sought in vain,
weeping and wandering through the avenues,
a bit of bread, please, for the love of God. . . ."
And as she said this, she showed me the children,
hollow-cheeked, skin and bones, in tattered rags.
My two young ones that I love and adore
like nothing else that I have loved or love,
hugging them to my knees: "O daddy, daddy,
give us a piece of bread!" they cried.
    Just then
the light went from my eyes and I could feel
my reason growing dim . . . And like a lion
starving for his prey, I gave a roar,

thirsting for blood and thirsting for revenge. . . .
Then turning suddenly to face my children,
I said: "Wait here for me. I'll be right back:
I'm going to get some bread. . . ."
    "You're leaving us!"
my little children answered me together,
with one voice.
    "No, no, little ones, I swear,
I'll be right back with bread for you!" I said,
and lifted up their hearts. . . .
    The avenue
was dark and silent when I left the house. . . .
I couldn't hear the breathing of a single
living thing, and not one sign of life
appeared before my eyes. . . .
    The night was far
along already, and the snow was still
heavily falling, spreading a white sheet
over the pavement. . . .
    And I walked along
withdrawn and miserable, an unseen ghost,
my wretched heart was pounding desperately
inside my chest. . . .
    After a while I heard
a sound, the tramping feet of someone walking
close to me, going by in great hurry,
all muffled up, his hands inside his pockets,
someone who might have been on his way home. . . .
I turned around and quickly overtook him.
I grabbed him by the arm and stopped him there,
and said in a commanding tone of voice:

(*loudly*)

"Your money or your life!"
    "I won't give you
a cent," the coward answered me. "I'm rich
and powerful, and with a single shout
I could have guards and servants from my house

here in an instant, but I'm not afraid
of you or of your threats."
        And saying this
he pulled a pistol out of his coat pocket
and fired right at me, but luckily
I wasn't hit . . . I tried to run away,
but he came chasing after me. I fell
face-down into the street, and moments later
the cops were on me and they dragged me here. . . .

(*pause*)

    In here there are no criminals, no thieves,
in here are the innocent and the unlucky,
strong and open-hearted spirits, gallant
veterans of sacrosanct campaigns,
apostles of sublime and beautiful
ideas, and pure-souled warriors and rebels. . . .
In here some of the finest of our youth
are slowly worn away, the light of genius
in vigorous and robust minds is spoiled
and fades to feebleness. . . .
        And if I live
to see the day when I can have again
the cherished freedom that I've lost, more precious
than life itself, then I will bow my head
before these walls in reverence and tell
the world: The large of soul and the rebellious
together are imprisoned here, condemned
by this inhuman society. I'll say
to everyone: I have the ugly name
of criminal, because you made me one,
you heartless hypocrites who all refused
to give me a penny and a bit of bread.
You made me a criminal, every one of you
who laughed right in my face, insulting me,
calling me tramp and scum. . . .
        If I at least
had killed a man! If I at least had tasted

the intoxicating ecstasy of blood
for just one single moment! . . .
    Ah! but what's
the use of one existence, when three lives
are wasting away with hunger, the three lives
that are most dear to me, the ones I carry
engraved forever in my heart and mind? . . . .
Alas! what's going to become of them?
How will they let me know if they're alive?
Alive? I fear they're not! For all I know
this very evening they have starved to death,
for all I know my wife has sold her honor
if there's no other way to feed my children. . . .
And what if that were true? . . . Ah, God, then I
would never want to leave this place again;
I would just want to die, die and curse fate,
to die and curse this hard and hateful world
crawling with tyrants, overrun with slaves . . .
And maybe I would find a way to rip
the heart out of my chest . . . If it were true
what I keep seeing, what torments me so,
then this is how I'd die . . . like a damned soul.

(*He tightens his hands around his neck as if strangling himself.*)

Translated by Michael Palma

Giuseppina Terranova, or Honor Avenged

CHARACTERS

> Giuseppina Terranova
> Giuseppe Terranova, her husband
> Gaetano Riggio, her uncle
> Concetta Riggio, her aunt
> Don Bartolo and Turiddu, two members of the Sicilian underworld from
>   Brooklyn

Arturo Romualdi and Domenico Ciccio, two laborers who work for Gaetano Riggio

Giovanni Cuccia and Luigi Borgogna, two other laborers, who work for Gaetano Riggio and are non-speaking roles

ACT I

Scene I

(A modestly furnished bedroom. On top of a chest of drawers a picture of Saint Rosalia is surrounded by withered flowers. An oil lamp burns in front of the picture.)

CONCETTA RIGGIO *(alone, kneeling below the picture, prays)*: Blessed Saint Rosalia, I will never tire of praying to you. You know that I am more unfortunate than I am guilty. I am slave to a man who does with me what he wants; I have neither the strength, nor the courage to rebel against him. Please forgive me, Blessed Saint Rosalia, and do not ignore my humble prayer.

Scene II

Concetta and Gaetano

GAETANO *(watching her with an arrogant look, he approaches Concetta. The woman has finished praying. Her hands are joined together, her head bowed in front of the picture, in an act of devotion)*: Have you finished or not? Do you have to bore that poor Saint Rosalia from morning till night? The saints, my dear, are too high up above us to be concerned with the misery of this world below! . . .

CONCETTA *(almost pleading, without daring to look him in face)*: But I don't believe it does any harm. After all, I feel the need to pray; I feel the need to confide the secrets of my soul, the grief that upsets the peace in my life, to my favorite saint.

GAETANO *(sarcastically; getting closer and closer to her)*: Then you have secrets, eh? Very good, Mrs. Concetta! This I did not know, that you had secrets! But better to keep them jealously hidden inside you, rather than reveal them to Saint Rosalia . . . It's a waste of time . . . The hell our parents spoke about is very far away. Centuries will pass before we get there. And then, the last thing I think about is death. Now, I only think about enjoying myself. Life is so short . . . What happens in the future doesn't matter to me! . . .

CONCETTA (*springing up, because Gaetano's words sharply affect her*): Now you are hopelessly lost. You pretend to be an unbeliever, so you can better enjoy your hateful sin of lust.

GAETANO (*he looks intently into her defiant eyes. Surprised by the audacity of his wife, he now challenges her with his indifference and with his cynicism*): What sin? . . . I am not guilty of any sin . . . I have a clean conscience and I can walk down the street with my head held high.

CONCETTA: First examine your conscience, and then tell me if it is really clean.

GAETANO (*bored: looking her up and down from head to toe*): Now I really don't intend to waste time with you! Tell me, otherwise I'll force you to talk.

CONCETTA (*powerfully; now having decided to speak*): Ah, you want me to talk? Well then, yes, I will talk. (*she grasps his arm; brings him in front of the picture of Saint Rosalia*) Come . . . come here . . . I will stand here and see if you have courage to deny, in the presence of Saint Rosalia, everything you have done.

GAETANO (*who has already understood everything and pretends not to have understood anything*): I am really curious to know what it is that I have done!

CONCETTA (*always squeezing his arm; steadily bringing him closer to the saint*): Listen . . . listen to what you have done . . . You have, with diabolical deceit, abused the innocence of a child, a girl barely 11 years old, and unaware of the dangers that surround her. You dragged her into your bed, you violated her with your poisonous breath, you abused her like an animal. That is what you did. The innocent girl didn't have to say anything . . . it was I who read in her poor suffering eyes the whole depressing tragedy that took place here . . . it was I who forced the horrible secret from her soul . . . (*she releases his arm. She moves away from him a few steps. Now she waits for her husband to speak, to defend himself from the serious accusation*)

GAETANO (*who until this moment has kept his head down, like someone who is listening to a sentence, like someone who is resigned to getting sentenced with an awful punishment*): You know everything, then . . . And it was you who forced her to talk . . . It doesn't matter if I know what she told you. I only want to know how and why she told you.

CONCETTA (*approaching him, now almost satisfied at having humiliated him, of having forced him to confess his error*): Is that it? You hoped, maybe, that nothing would ever be known about your crime? You hoped, maybe, that it would be covered over quickly with a veil? (*Pause*) What? you're trembling?

GAETANO (*he shrugs his shoulders once again; then he sneers derisively*): No, I'm laughing . . . laughing as I hear your words, the words of an ignorant little woman. You're wasting your time, if you delude yourself about converting me!!

CONCETTA: I know well enough that it would be stupid to try to show you the right way, but remember though, Gaetano Riggio, that God does not pay wages on the sabbath and that he who laughs last, laughs best. That girl—it is horrible to say it—is your niece, my sister's daughter, blood of my blood. Now, if there is a God, do you believe that he will not impose justice? If there is a God, do you believe. . . .

GAETANO (*interrupting her, acting like he is about to attack her*): Shut up . . . shut up . . . At this point I've had it . . . I'm tired of listening to you. I am not a fool . . . I couldn't care less about God and the saints . . . about all the punishments, past, present and future. Go . . . Run . . . I'll wait to see if you have the courage. (*Pause. Concetta Riggio cries, again on her knees. Gaetano Riggio, enraged, seizes a stick that catches his eye*) Damn your soul . . . (*He hurls it at her, trying to hit her*) Shut up, shut up, witch that you are . . . shut up, you damned woman, or I'll kill you. . . .

Scene III

Gaetano, Concetta and Arturo, Gaetano's worker

ARTURO (*Intervening as a peacemaker between wife and husband*): Mr. Boss, please now, your screams can be heard a mile away. People on the sidewalk across the street are looking up at the window of this house.

GAETANO (*he calms down a little, but his eyes still smolder with anger. Then he goes to put the stick down in a corner of the room*): It's true; I need patience and calmness . . . you're right, Arturo, you're right . . . But this shrew of a wife of mine forces me to lose first one and then the other. Since this morning she's been tormenting me . . . And she won't stop it.

ARTURO: But why? I don't think you've given her any reason to do that . . . Maybe because Giuseppina. . . .

GAETANO (*surprised more than ever and, at the time same, indignant*)" What? . . . What are you saying now? . . . You too, maybe? . . . (*unexpectedly flying into a rage at his wife*) Ah, that shrew . . . that shameless witch.

CONCETTA (*afraid of getting hit, she protects her head with both hands*):. . . but I didn't say anything . . . I didn't do anything wrong. . . .

ARTURO (*putting himself in front of Concetta to shield her with his body*): But, Don Gaetano, be sensible . . . I don't know anything about your personal affairs. I haven't spoken with your wife for more than two weeks. . . .

GAETANO: And then how do you explain. . . .

ARTURO: What?

GAETANO: That you know. . . .

ARTURO (*surprised*): What? . . . I don't know anything. . . .

GAETANO: That Giuseppina. . . .

ARTURO: I tell you again that I do not know anything. I only know that Giuseppina is sick. . . .

GAETANO (*he calms down. Calm suddenly spreads over his face, which just before had been clouded with doubt and anxiety*): Ah, that's all you know!

ARTURO (*even more surprised*): And what else am I supposed to know?

GAETANO (*who now has resumed is normal demeanor*): So then . . . we don't have to talk about it any more . . . I misunderstood you. . . .

ARTURO: Meantime, I hope the argument is finished. . . .

GAETANO: It's good and finished . . . You can even go down to the bakery and tell the workers not to worry. It was a little squabble, and it ended as usual, without any consequences. You can go, Arturo. . . .

ARTURO: I'm going and . . . They are husband and wife, after all. . . .

GIUSEPPINA (*Her voice is heard from offstage*): Aunt Concetta . . . Aunt Concetta. . . .

GAETANO (*he trembles at hearing Giuseppina's voice. He is surprised at how the girl is outside*): Giuseppina! But wasn't she in bed before?

ARTURO: No; she was downstairs in the bakery . . . She went to give lunch to the boarders.

GAETANO: You go to lunch too, Arturo . . . Your friends are waiting for you.

ARTURO (*turning to Concetta who it is still huddled on the floor*): And you, Mrs. Riggio, get up, and you too should show some patience.

GIUSEPPINA (*Her voice is heard from offstage*): Aunt Concetta . . . Aunt Concetta. . . .

CONCETTA (*she gets up. She is pale, tired, depressed. She goes very slowly towards the window. She shows herself and yells out to Giuseppina*): Here I am . . . here I am . . . I am coming right away . . . (*she exits*)

Scene IV

Gaetano, alone

GAETANO: What does all this gossip matter to me? The only fault I can be accused of is that I took advantage of my niece. Even so, I could say that it wasn't my fault. (*pause*) Besides, I don't know that what I did was so wrong. Giuseppina, sooner or later, would have been intimate with some man. What's the difference if that man was me? If nothing else, I can help her . . .

I have money, thank God. That way I can provide her with a dowry and make sure she finds a comfortable situation. Certainly, no one will ever know that I took her. My wife would have to tell . . . But my wife won't say anything . . . She'll have sense enough not to give me any trouble. (*he turns towards the door, because he hears the sound of footsteps*) Who is it? (*moving towards the door*) Who's there? (*short pause*) There surely must be someone there. (*he opens the door*)

Scene V

Gaetano, Don Bartolo and Turiddu

GAETANO (*very much surprised. Meanwhile he struggles as much as possible to appear calm*): Oh! You're here, Don Bartolo! What an honor this is! (*kneeling awkwardly, as is the custom for people of the underworld, who for the most part are used to ridiculing the common people and giving themselves an importance they do not have. Turiddu follows him and he too kneels awkwardly*)

DON BARTOLO: The honor is all mine . . . but my visit shouldn't cause such surprise . . . You know very well because I came to see you once before.

GAETANO: Then, your visit is not a very pleasant one. It is nothing less than a matter of paying money. But the fact is that I don't have any for you . . . And I don't understand why those fine friends of mine in Brooklyn insist on believing that I have it so abundantly. . . .

DON BARTOLO: That's what it looks like, dear Don Gaetano . . . You enjoy a splendid financial position . . . and all of the leaders of the city know it.

TURIDDU: And besides, what's a thousand dollars to a man like Don Gaetano Riggio?

GAETANO (*like someone who suddenly had a cold shower splash on his head. Looking at the two criminals in a half surprised and half indignant manner*): A thousand dollars! . . . Then you expect a thousand dollars? . . . But where do I go to get you a thousand dollars? I could give at the most a hundred. . . .

DON BARTOLO: One hundred dollars, dear Don Gaetano, is very very little. It's not worth the effort to ask for it, nor to accept it. . . .

TURIDDU (*seeing that Don Gaetano's answer is making him wait, he decides to negotiate. At the same time, he winks at his companion*): Give us five hundred and . . . we will be happy with that just the same. Five hundred dollars is a trifle for you . . . If you find more excuses though, that means that you want to put our good will to the test, at any cost. Up 'til today you've received at least a dozen letters. And you always turned a deaf ear. Understand, though, that I am not the only one involved in this transaction. Our organization is huge and has members everywhere. Besides, you know more than you should know. . . .

DON BARTOLO: And you also know, Don Gaetano, that until today we have treated you like a friend. If we wanted to abuse our power, right now you would be dead and buried. But why spill blood, when there's another alternative? (*with sarcasm, emphasizing his sarcastic words with one of those characteristic sneers on his face that alone is enough to express the thought of the one who is sneering*) And then, Don Gaetano, apart from being our friend, you are also a native of our beautiful province. So you deserve some considerations. . . .

GAETANO (*he doesn't know if he should or shouldn't take seriously the compliments of the two scoundrels. He is trapped like a helpless animal*): I thank you from the bottom of my heart, but what good do they do me, your considerations, all your friendly words, if you nevertheless expect me to give you the fine sum of five hundred dollars . . . just like that . . . for no reason . . . on a simple whim? . . .

TURIDDU: And who should we turn to if not to those who can give it to us? Five hundred dollars is nothing for you, while for us it is a treasure. . . .

GAETANO (*posing as victim, trying gently to arouse compassion from the extortionists*): I beg you not to force me to make this sacrifice. . . .

DON BARTOLO (*bored by the insistence with which Don Gaetano refuses the demanded money. Staring him resolutely right in face*): But you really must be joking, it seems to me! You should give us the sum we demanded and forget about it forever. . . .

TURIDDU: By the way, who's watching out that the police didn't follow us? That devil Petrosino swore to get rid of us all at any cost. . . .

GAETANO: As far as that's concerned, you can be confident about me. In my house, you are as safe as in your own house. I am not Sicilian for nothing, and it is well known, since the world was created, that there has never been a Sicilian who became a spy. Enough . . . Enough . . . Please . . . don't torment me anymore . . . Leave me in peace . . . Do me a favor and leave me alone . . . I need peace and quiet . . . I am sick . . . I am sick . . . leave me alone, please . . . leave me alone. . . .

TURIDDU: We'll leave you alone right now, if it makes you happy . . . Meanwhile, do us the courtesy of giving us the five hundred dollars. . . .

DON BARTOLO: That's what we're waiting for. . . .

GAETANO: Yes, I have it here . . . I will go get it right away . . . Be kind enough to wait a moment for me. . . . (*he heads for the next room*)

TURIDDU: Now where are you going?

DON BARTOLO: Certainly not to the Bank. . . .

GAETANO: I'm going right here, into the next room . . . I'll be back in five minutes.

TURIDDU: Let me come with you?

GAETANO: So you've got doubts about me maybe? I said I wasn't a spy and that should be enough.

DON BARTOLO: Then go and come right back.

GAETANO: I'll be with you in five minutes. (*he enters into the adjacent room. The two crooks accompany him to the doorway*)

Scene VI

Don Bartolo and Turiddu

DON BARTOLO: He was a little difficult . . . but he finally gave in. . . .

TURIDDU: He was forced to give in. . . .

DON BARTOLO: I'm sure we'll be able to get money from him again. . . .

TURIDDU: When?

DON BARTOLO: After we spend what he gives us today.

TURIDDU: Oh, sure . . . but we have time to think about that. . . .

DON BARTOLO: Here he comes. . . .

Scene VII

Gaetano, Don Bartolo and Turiddu

GAETANO (*re-enters with a stack of dollar bills in his hand. He goes to the small table and begins to count them*): Come here . . . come here . . . there are ten fifty dollar bills, brand new . . . Who should I give them to?

DON BARTOLO: To one or to the other makes no difference . . . We are good friends and good coworkers. . . .

GAETANO (*to Don Bartolo*): Then you take them . . . Here. (*handing him the money*) Count them . . . if you want to count them.

DON BARTOLO: No need. . . .

TURIDDU: We're convinced enough that you are an honest person. . . .

DON BARTOLO: And a respectable person. . . .

GAETANO: You gentlemen are too good, much too kind . . . Thank you . . . thank you . . . now leave me alone . . . I need quiet . . . I want to rest a little. . . .

DON BARTOLO: Goodbye, Don Gaetano, and always remember us . . . Also, if we can be useful to you in some matter, we two are freely available to you . . . We'll always be happy to be able to serve you. . . .

GAETANO: Thank you, thank you . . . I hope I won't need anything. . . .

TURIDDU (*sarcastically, with a deep bow*): Let's kiss his hands. . . .

DON BARTOLO: Goodbye. . . .

GAETANO: God dammit! God dammit! The Eternal Father has begun to punish to me already . . . I commend my life to you . . . I commend myself to you . . . Let me die a Christian . . . Help me, Father . . . help me! (*he falls in front of the picture, almost fainting from emotion and from fear*)

ACT II

Scene I

(In the parlor of the elegantly furnished Riggio house.)

GAETANO (*he is seated in an armchair. In front of him, is Giuseppe Terranova who is asking for the hand of Giuseppina. Gaetano seems tired and bored. As the curtain rises, he remains thoughtful for a few moments; then, suddenly, as if he has come to a decision*): No, no, no . . . I said no and that's enough . . . I don't agree, and so I'm absolutely opposed.

GIUSEPPE (*humble, submissive, respectful*): I don't understand why you must continue to refuse me the hand of Giuseppina. (*short pause*) I love Giuseppina with a pure and true love . . . Since the first day that I saw her.

GAETANO (*without moving from his armchair and taking a piece of tobacco now and then*): The best thing you can do, my young man, is to change your mind. You should try to love another woman instead. The nail drives away the nail, as the proverb says, and you will quickly forget about Giuseppina.

GIUSEPPE (*he becomes sadder and sadder at Don Gaetano's refusal. He approaches him in order to better convince him, to evoke his compassion*): No, no, it's not possible . . . This pain you are inflicting on me is a thousand times stronger than I am. I have sworn not to love any other woman except Giuseppina. . . .

GAETANO (*he shakes his head, as if to commiserate with him, to make fun of him*): I am sorry to tell you that you counted your chickens before they hatched. The chicken, in this case, is me. Giuseppina will do what I tell her. I am her guardian; I am the one who takes the place of her father. Before her father died, he entrusted her to me, that is why I took responsibility for raising her, and I saw to her education myself. I took her, an orphan, out of the street, and she found bread, shelter and security in my house. Her mother is a poor fool, who wouldn't have known how, nor would she have been able, to help her in any way. Giuseppina would have died of hunger if

I had not taken care of her. Now you come for her, from who knows where or why, and you expect me to hand over my niece, and you propose to tear her away from me forever, as if she were a worthless object, something not worth the trouble to consider. (*powerfully*) Ah, no, this will never be! The day that Giuseppina leaves my house, I will no longer have any reason to live. . . .

GIUSEPPE (*kinder, humbler, more submissive. He still hopes to be able to convince him, and to be able to achieve his goal*): I understand the affection that you feel for your niece and I admire your love and your sacrifices. But I do not want to deprive you of her, Don Gaetano; I do not want to steal her from you. I want to make her my wife; I want to make her happy; I want to become the companion of her joy and her pain, I want to be, finally, her inseparable friend, her affectionate husband. . . .

GAETANO (*determined, powerful, unshakable*): I repeat no again, and I hope that you don't force to me to repeat it to you again. Giuseppina can not be yours, nor anyone else's, besides. She will never leave this house. She wouldn't abandon me for all the gold in the world. Don't you know she is barely fifteen years old? She is still a girl, Giuseppina, a naïve inexperienced girl. A lot more time must pass before she can decide to take a husband . . . even if she wants to take this step. . . .

GIUSEPPE (*after a short pause. He now wants to make one last attempt, he wants to show Don Gaetano that, after all, he does not mean to make him unhappy*): If it is simply a matter of time, I will wait a year, even two. Provided that you give me preference . . . provided that Giuseppina promises me not to give her hand in marriage to any one else.

GAETANO (*forcefully and in a manner that makes Giuseppe understand that it is useless to insist, useless to say another word*): No, no, I do not want it . . . It's useless to insist . . . I said no and that's enough. . . .

GIUSEPPE (*convinced that all pleading will be of no avail, that it is better to end the conversation, that he has done all he can do and that it is not worth insisting anymore*): So then you really are determined not to give your consent? . . .

GAETANO (*more forcibly than before, white with anger at having been opposed for such a long time, at having uselessly wasted so much breath*): My refusal is final. And nothing, nothing is going to persuade me otherwise. Your words are like spit in the wind.

GIUSEPPE (*resigning himself. His voice is hoarse, his eyes well up with tears*): I won't talk any more, Don Gaetano, I won't talk any more . . . With the name

of Giuseppina carved into my heart, I will go far away. Goodbye, Don
Gaetano. . . .

GAETANO: May good luck go with you. . . .

(*Giuseppe looks at him through his anger and his sorrow. Then he goes away,
crushed and humiliated, with his head lowered*)

Scene II

Gaetano, solo

GAETANO (*He walks back and forth through the room. Now he is finally alone,
and can freely give to vent to the feelings in his soul*): So they want to steal
her away from me . . . But I will not let myself be moved, neither by anyone's
prayers, nor by their tears . . . Giuseppina belongs to me. I would be a fool if
I gave her up to anyone else . . . No, no, a thousand times no! All the
demons in hell couldn't take her away from me. . . .

Scene III

Gaetano and Giuseppina

GIUSEPPINA (*She is unkempt, disheveled, her clothes are powdered with flour.
She speaks softly, the presence of her uncle almost frightens her*): Hello, uncle
Gaetano.

GAETANO (*rough, sullen, angered. He obstinately stares her in the face*): Hello . . .
Where are you coming from?

GIUSEPPINA: I am coming from the bakery.

GAETANO: And you didn't meet. . . .

GIUSEPPINA (*surprised at the question, sure more than ever of being able to prove
to her uncle that she has done nothing wrong*): Who?

GAETANO: You didn't meet anyone a few moments ago?

GIUSEPPINA (*becoming more and more astonished. She does not know what to
think of her uncle's questions*): Where?

GAETANO: Here, at the door. . . .

GIUSEPPINA (*very agitated, she trembles. Her voice is muffled from tears*): I didn't
meet anyone. . . .

GAETANO (*bounding towards her, threateningly, with tightened fists, with his eyes
bulging out of their sockets*): You are lying through your teeth . . . You ugly
creature . . . You witch's daughter . . . Look me in the eyes . . . You see, they
are bloodshot. All the anger, all the anger in the world is in my eyes. I will
tear you apart, understand, I will tear out your insides, before you insult me
by replacing me with someone else. Pay attention, Giuseppina, I spy on all

your movements and I follow all your steps. I am jealous of you, you understand, I am jealous of you to the point of desperation. The thought that someone else might get a smile from you, a word or even a look, that someone else might put his passionate hands on your pulsating flesh, that someone else might possess you, even if only for a moment, this terrible thought makes me tremble with fear and makes me crazy. . . .

GIUSEPPINA: But I don't see anyone . . . I don't talk to anyone . . . I am always alone . . . I am always near you and at my aunt's side. . . .

GAETANO (*getting even angrier, in a louder and more agitated voice*): Ah, don't lie . . . don't lie . . . You go out every day now . . . The day before yesterday Arturo met you while you were walking with a young man. Tell me, tell me, who was that young man?

GIUSEPPINA (*she frowns and remains pensive for a few minutes, struggling to remember*): I don't remember. . . .

GAETANO: He was—Arturo told me—a tall, dark, slim, attractive young man. He whispered sweet words to you and you smiled happily, happily accepting his attention . . . Tell me, tell me, Giuseppina, who was that young man?. . . .

GIUSEPPINA: I don't remember . . . I don't know . . . it doesn't come back to me now. . . .

GAETANO (*overcome with anger. Giuseppina's evasive answer exasperates him beyond words*): Ah, so, you want to brazenly lie . . . Do you understand that I want to be obeyed? Do you understand that I don't want to give orders in vain? (*He has hurt her terribly. He knows he has been very unpleasant with her. He very quietly comes closer to her, he takes her hand, he leads her into the middle of the room*) It is jealousy that dims my reason and makes me see black instead of white.

Scene IV

Gaetano, Giuseppina, Concetta

CONCETTA: Gaetano, some people from the bakery need you.

GAETANO (*almost shaking, he approaches his wife. Giuseppina, pale and sad, is now seated in a corner of the room*): And what do they want? Didn't they tell you what they want?

CONCETTA: They want to see you as soon as possible.

GAETANO: You could have asked them what they want from me.

CONCETTA: I forgot. . . .

GAETANO: Never mind . . . (*short pause*) I'll be back right away.

Scene V

Giuseppina and Concetta

GIUSEPPINA (*desperate, crying, lost, she throws herself into her aunt's arms*): Auntie, my dear auntie . . . I can't go on anymore . . . I can't go on anymore! . . . Protect me, you who are my second mother . . . Please . . . please have compassion on me! . . .

CONCETTA: Me? . . . But I can't do anything, my child! You can't reason with my husband . . . The day before yesterday, thinking he was in a good mood, I dared to tell him that, after all, you couldn't possibly to stay in our house indefinitely, and that the day would also come when you would have to take husband. I had never spoken to him about this!

GIUSEPPINA: All of this must really stop. After being a slave for so long, I finally have to be free to be mistress of myself. If, up until now, the world's inquisitive eyes didn't look through these walls, now that I am no longer a child, they will look in here now. Everyone will point me out as a loose woman, unworthy of any compassion. Everyone, everyone will say that I am my uncle's mistress.

CONCETTA (*She searches for words. She wants to convince her niece that she is making a mistake to think this way, that Gaetano Riggio's reputation is superior to any insinuation or any suspicion*): Listen . . . my child . . . Listen. . . .

GIUSEPPINA: No, no, I don't want to hear anything. You've already told me enough. You know all about the horrible tragedy that goes on in this damned house. You know what your husband did to me . . . (*short pause*) After you learned about everything, I remember you protested to the monster who violated me. But, alas! Your protest was in vain and short! To you he gave all his money, to you all his mortgage titles, to you all his valuables. You agreed to this hellish pact, and your lips spoke no more, your eyes saw no more. You became resigned to it, you put up with all your husband's demands. And now, he kisses me, he embraces me, he violates me right in front of you: now he is free to do whatever he wants to his victim.

CONCETTA (*she tries to speak, but Giuseppina abruptly stops her, with one of those hand gestures that allow no reply*): Listen, Giuseppina, my child, listen . . . Let me just say a few words to you. . . .

GIUSEPPINA: Keep them to yourself, I beg you, please . . . I know what you want to tell me . . . I know everything . . . I know everything . . . But I tell you again that my bondage has continued long enough, that I am tired of putting up with the continuous outrageous abuse; and after robbing me of my honor, now he wants to take my life from me. I love, and you know him, I love Giuseppe Terranova. I saw that young man only a few times, and I already feel that I love him as if I had loved him for a hundred years. He gave me words of comfort, mercy, compassion. But Gaetano wants to hold me in his power until I die? Ah, no, no . . . I am sick to death of this life that shames me and ruins me. I will do anything to win the freedom I have waited for so long, that is now the most beautiful dream of my young life! . . .

Scene VI

Giuseppina, Concetta and Giuseppe

(*light footsteps are heard.*)

GIUSEPPE (*He appears at the threshold of the door. The two women go to meet him, not knowing what the reason could be for his appearance. He reassures them with his words and gestures*): Don't be afraid . . . Don Gaetano has gone to New York on very important business. He won't return before this evening. He also told the young men and Arturo will come to tell you soon.

CONCETTA: But then, Arturo knows that you are here, with us? . . . .

GIUSEPPE: He knows . . . but Arturo is a thoughtful young man . . . He won't say anything . . . I asked him not to say anything. . . .

CONCETTA: Well, then. . . .

GIUSEPPE: Well . . . I came specifically to know what Giuseppina thinks about Don Gaetano's refusal. . . .

CONCETTA: My dear Giuseppe, I have already told you several times what she thinks about it. She loves you and she is ready to follow you anywhere. . . .

GIUSEPPE (*he beams with joy. He finally sees his rosy dream of happiness coming true. It seems that he has reached his sweet, coveted goal*): . . . You're ready to follow me anywhere? Really, Giuseppina? . . . Say it . . . say it . . . I am waiting to hear those words of comfort and joy from you. . . .

GIUSEPPINA (*rushing towards him—almost crazy—in a burst of love, passion and madness*): Yes, yes, everywhere . . . even to hell . . . Let me hold you . . . Let me welcome you, oh my liberator, let me kiss your hands to thank you for the freedom you promised me, for the freedom you will surely give me . . . The slave is here, at your feet, and she begs you and implores you to free her . . . Protect her, since God did not hear her prayers, her lamentations and her pleas . . . Giuseppe, take me away from this damned house . . . let me come with you, Giuseppe, take me with you!

GIUSEPPE (*holding her tightly to instill courage in her, almost lifting her into his arms, like a tired or sick child*): Ah . . . Let's escape . . . let's escape . . . Come . . . don't be afraid . . . come into my arms, come . . . come.

CONCETTA (*she tries to embrace her. Giuseppina scornfully rejects her*): One kiss, Giuseppina . . . one kiss for your aunt, who loves you so much. . . .

GIUSEPPINA (*rejecting her aunt; throwing herself desperately into the arms of Giuseppe*): No, no, no . . . I don't want to kiss any of my tormentors . . . This house is cursed . . . this house is damned. . . . (*holding on to each other, Giuseppe and Giuseppina both flee*)

ACT III

(*The home of the newlyweds, Giuseppe and Giuseppina Terranova. The stage shows a parlor furnished in very good taste. There is a table with a large oil lamp. There is a sofa and several chairs. On the walls hang beautiful oil paintings and pictures. The couple is returning from a visit to Giuseppina's uncle, Gaetano Riggio. They are dressed in the same clothes they wore to their wedding. Instead of the wedding garland, Giuseppina wears a very elegant bonnet covered with flowers. Giuseppe goes to the table and lights the lamp. Then he removes his hat and throws it carelessly on the sofa. Afterwards he removes his gloves, nervously throwing them on the table. He is very agitated. Giuseppina is extremely pale and upset. As soon as she enters, almost as if she were tired from a long and exhausting walk, she collapses on the first seat she finds. It is the eighth day of their marriage.*)

GIUSEPPE: So now, Giuseppina, now that things have come to this point, an explanation is more than necessary. . . .

GIUSEPPINA: Ah, don't you think, Giuseppe, that I have explained myself enough already?

GIUSEPPE (*he paces the room up and down, barely keeping in check the agitation that is overcoming him. He can almost foresee what will happen: Giuseppina's eyes have already spoken eloquently. He has read the secret in those eyes. She has deceived him. Hiding her past sin from him, she gave herself to him. But she will speak. She will make a full confession. And their honeymoon will have lasted only eight days. And he will abandon the unfaithful woman. He will leave her forever*): In what way? You still have not told me. Nothing you have said to me is an explanation. . . .

GIUSEPPINA: Ah, no, Giuseppe, I have said so many sad and terrible things, many things, so many things, that there is almost nothing more left for me to say. (*he continues pacing. Giuseppina, seated, watches him while she speaks*) Listen, Giuseppe, listen to the cry of this bleeding heart, of this heart that will soon stop beating because my cruel fate has not stopped tormenting it for a single moment. (*short pause*) Listen, Giuseppe, there is no woman in the world who has suffered more than me, there is no torment that can compare to mine. I was born under an unlucky star, oh Giuseppe. I was three or four years old when my father died, killed in a quarrel in Tunisia, and I was left without any other support except my mother, a poor simpleminded woman, a paralytic. I was brought here, to America, and entrusted to my uncle Gaetano Riggio, who . . . who . . . alas, has been the cause of all my misfortune. . . .

GIUSEPPE: I already know all that you are telling me . . . The story of your life, I know it . . . I know that your uncle is a scoundrel and that he continuously mistreated you. . . .

GIUSEPPINA: Oh, you cannot imagine, Giuseppe, how he treated me while I was in his house! I was a little girl, weak, pale, sick, when I was brought into my uncle's house . . . so sick that I even believed I would die soon. I became my uncle's servant. For five long years, I had to get used to doing the most menial tasks. I was obliged to get up from bed at three in the morning and go to bed late at night. I worked incessantly, every morning, evening, and night. I put up with it all, waiting for the time I would be free. The day will come—I said to myself—that I will get out of this hell. And the long awaited day, the day so hoped for, finally came. When you appeared in Gaetano Riggio's house, to me you were an angel of freedom. You freed me from my long imprisonment. You restored to this poor slave the freedom she dreamed of. And she came to you more than ever confident about her future. And you made her your wife, and she told you everything, but she didn't tell you the horrible secret of her life. . . .

GIUSEPPE (*approaching her, to encourage her to speak, somewhat bending over her as she sobs anxiously*): It is the secret your uncle hinted at . . . With a single word tonight, he destroyed all my rosy dreams of happiness. "You wanted to marry my niece," he said to me, "but you were a fool and you will repent your stupidity. She is a girl born on Holy Friday and all the girls born on that day cannot be virtuous." And now, here I am before you, Giuseppina, for the explanation. Can you swear to me you will be a faithful wife and that you have come to me pure and without having known other men? (*Giuseppina, who until this moment, has fixed her gaze on her husband, now, full of shame, she lowers her eyes to the ground. Now she cries bitterly. With one hand Giuseppe wipes his forehead damp with cold sweat. His voice is emotional, becoming hoarse from the pain and the anger*) Ah, there it is, there it is, Giuseppina, the explanation! You are crying . . . You are crying . . . Your uncle did not lie after all . . . You are not a chaste woman!. . . .

GIUSEPPINA (*suddenly kneeling down at his feet, giving free vent to her tears and her pain, at last*): Ah, yes, yes, Giuseppe . . . here I am at your feet, to beg for your mercy and your forgiveness . . . Yes, it is true, I do not deny it, my uncle told the truth, I am not a virtuous woman!. . . .

GIUSEPPE: Ah! . . . (*he starts to rush towards her. He would knock her down, destroy her if it were possible. But he retreats like someone who realizes he has stepped to the edge of a precipice. And he bites his hands to repress his anger*)

GIUSEPPINA (*shaking, crying, still down on her knees in front of him*): Mercy . . . Giuseppe . . . mercy! . . . You see me here, at your feet, ready for anything, ready for everything, even to die for you . . . You could drive away me from this house . . . and I would go away . . . I would go away without holding a grudge against you . . . you could kill me, if you wanted to kill to me, and I would die without any regrets, without saying any words of sorrow or grief to you . . . But, listen to me, Giuseppe: before I go . . . before I die . . . you have the right to know everything, my whole painful story . . . My uncle didn't lie when he told you that I wasn't a chaste woman . . . but he didn't tell you . . . he didn't tell you that he was the rapist . . . This he didn't tell you . . . that despicable man . . . that wicked man . . . he didn't tell you, he didn't tell you!. . . .

GIUSEPPE (*Giuseppina's declaration is for him like lightning across a quiet sky. The statement is so unbelievable, that he is left surprised, perplexed, overwhelmed, stunned and unable to utter a syllable. A long pause follows. Then he decides to speak and it is like an outcry that escapes from the very depths of his soul*): Is it possible? . . . Is it possible? . . . Ah, what a disgrace! a disgrace! . . . Unspeakably shameful!

GIUSEPPINA (*she still cries, sobbing. With a white silk handkerchief, she wipes the tears that fall profusely from her eyes*): Listen, Giuseppe, listen . . . and then tell me if it's my fault . . . I was eleven years old . . . I was a poor innocent child. I cried and I protested. But all my protests were useless. And his wife, instead of his wife making him stop the torture, she saw everything and she kept quiet and she let him do it. He would have kept me in his house forever. And who knows how long I would still have been his servant, his slave, his mistress, if you had not come to free me. But since it is my fate that my life ends tragically, tomorrow Gaetano Riggio will pay the penalty for his lechery and for his crime.

ACT IV

Scene I

Gaetano and Giuseppina

(An elegantly furnished room. Gaetano Riggio is alone, holding an open letter in his hand, and he rocks on a rocking chair. Giuseppina enters stealthily, notices her uncle seated on the rocking chair, watches him steadily for a few minutes, almost as if she could strike him with lightning from her eyes.)

GAETANO (*The uncle is not aware of his niece's presence. He is absorbed in his thoughts and continues rocking.*): But if they try my patience, I will end up pressing charges against them in court. I haven't done it 'til now, but I will do it, sooner or later, for sure.

GIUSEPPINA (*who has remained motionless, near the door to listen to him, approaches him step by step. She is pale, distressed, nervous. Her eyes flash with contempt*): Good evening, uncle.

GAETANO (*turning around suddenly and hiding the letter in his shirt for fear that someone might have heard him; it falls from his hands*): You are here? And you come sneaking in like the enemy! What is it? You don't feel well, perhaps? Have you seen your aunt?

GIUSEPPINA: Yes, I saw her a few moments ago. She is downstairs in the bakery. I think she has a lot to do. She told me to wait here.

GAETANO: Too bad she happened to be at home! It has been a long time since you paid a visit. (*he gets up and goes towards Giuseppina; he caresses her brow, he rests his hand on her shoulders, he tries to pull her as close as possible to himself. Giuseppina, frightened, backs up. The lecher's words are like so many poisoned darts stabbing her in the chest. Overcome with anxiety, she listens to him. She trembles like a sapling blowing in the wind*) I was very sure you wouldn't be through with me after your wedding. And, you know, that was the reason I didn't want you to take a husband. I would have showered you with gold, with jewels and with diamonds, if you had stayed at home with me forever. . . .

GIUSEPPINA (*who at this point can take no more, furious like a wounded wild animal*): To be your servant, is that it?

GAETANO: My servant? Really . . . I don't know how you can say such a thing . . . I treated you like the lady of the house. It was you who attended to my business transactions, it was you who arranged my affairs, it was you who handled my money. Even my wife depended on you. And she and I both did so much to satisfy your every desire, to give in to your every whim, to please you in every way. One fine day I will die and all my wealth would have been left to you. You would have been, without a doubt, my one and only heir.

GIUSEPPINA: This is a lie too, because ever since aunt Concetta became aware that you were molesting me, you—because she kept quiet, because she did not cause a scandal—you went to an attorney to make her the sole owner of your properties and your money.

GAETANO: Nonsense! Nonsense! You are just confused, that's all. So much so that, maybe to pay me back for the many sacrifices that I made, you come here to tell me, right to my face, that you were my servant. . . .

GIUSEPPINA: Yes, your servant and your lover.

GAETANO: That too?

GIUSEPPINA: And you dare deny it, too! Ah, no, you will not deny it! I was your mistress, the instrument of your pleasure and your whims. I was, for you, no more no less than a toy. You did everything that you wanted with me. . . .

GAETANO: And perhaps, you yourself never resisted my will . . . my desires . . . my advances? Did you maybe reject me sometimes, did you perhaps push me away from you? Maybe you told me that you found me repulsive . . . that our affair would mark your life with dishonor and shame? Docile and passive, you always gave in to my wishes, you always said nothing, and your guilty silence was more eloquent than any words of consent. It was not I who should have retreated from the path I took, it was not I who should have feared the consequences of my actions. You, woman, should have resisted . . . you, woman, should have thought about your future. If you didn't do that, why is it my fault?

GIUSEPPINA (*she has her eyes glued to the ground while her uncle talks to her this way. From time to time she looks at him with sullen eyes; then she remains pensive; then once again she seems distracted. It seems that an unknown and terrible God within her tells her that the time to attack has not yet arrived, that the final hour has still not struck*): Oh, shut up, shut up . . . you want to pose as the victim too! You want to lay the blame for the shame of your crime and your betrayal on me too . . . I, yes, it is true, I submitted to you like a slave to her owner, I gave myself to you every time you wanted me;

without a resentful word from my lips, without letting a hateful look flash from my eyes. But would it have been worth the effort to rebel, since I was in your house, since I was considered by everyone to be your daughter? I stayed quiet in the sweet hope that the world would always ignore my shame, I stayed quiet because my poor mother would surely die of suffering, if I revealed to her the horrible secret of my life. I stayed quiet, every day repressing my soul's desperate cry for revenge. But, oh Gaetano Riggio, here I am, the timid lamb transformed into a tiger, and here is the tiger, ready to tear you to pieces, ready to torture your body, as you tortured mine. (*in an instant, Giuseppina pulls out of her blouse a revolver that she carried with her, to put into action the unhappy plan she made the night before. She shoots quick as a flash. But the shot misses. Gaetano Riggio, recovered from the first unexpected shock, seizes a chair to hurl at his niece, who, quicker than he is, goes after him and shoots a second time. Then he falls face down on the ground. Giuseppina stands over him, and with a large knife she brought with her, anticipating that the gun might fail, she stabs him savagely*) Bastard . . . Tyrant . . . Murderer . . . Die . . . Die . . . Die . . . (*she repeatedly stabs Gaetano Riggio with the knife; Gaetano collapses heavily to the ground*)

Scene II

(*Attracted by the screams of the struggle, Gaetano Riggio's workers run in. There are four: Arturo Romualdi, Domenico Ciccio, Giovanni Cuccia and Luigi Borgogna. They stand aghast before the horrible spectacle. The scene is atrocious and terrible.*)

ARTURO (*approaching his boss who lies on the ground gasping for air*): Boss, sir . . . Mr. Riggio. . . .

CONCETTA (*she arrives gasping, panting, also attracted by the loud noise. A piercing scream bursts from her throat when she sees her husband on the ground and Giuseppina smeared all over with blood, with the revolver in one hand and the knife in the other. In an instant she understands everything. Gaetano Riggio moans in a weak voice. She desperately throws herself over his body*): My poor husband! My poor ruined house!

GIUSEPPINA: And now for you, Concetta Riggio . . . (*her action is so quick that nobody can hold her back. Concetta Riggio screams her last breath. Those present watch the tragic scene horrified. Nobody dares move now. Nobody dares speak*) This is how God makes even you pay the price for your crime.

DOMENICO: You miserable girl . . . you wicked thing . . . what have you done now. . . .

GIUSEPPINA: They destroyed my life, my happiness, my future. (*She gives one last look at Gaetano* and *Concetta Riggio who are contorted in spasms of agony on the floor. And they lie one beside the other in a pool of blood; she throws the bloody knife down next to the dying couple, then turning to the bystanders*) And now they will surely arrest me, and let death come too. At least I will die happy that I have avenged my honor.

Translated by Emelise Aleandri

∾

Macabre

But was there one day then
The sun on this earth?
Were there roses and violets,
Light, smiles, ardor?

GIOSUÈ CARDUCCI

I

   And they tell me I am still virile,
that my heart should be cheerful:
and they invite me to enjoy friends
since for the young the world's beautiful.
   And they point out the road to pleasure
requires songs from my smiling mouth:
they don't know my songs are sorrowful,
and that a snake is concealed in my soul.
   My heart has ceased beating
and in my skull there's no more brain
there's no longer blood in my veins
and I can't remember ever living!

II

   I've forgotten that once they crowned
my furrowed brow with laurels;
I'm oblivious to my mother's guileless
and tender words, her merciful countenance.

I've forgotten my dreams of glory,
and the anguish I endured once.
I've discarded all illusions, the crying
I unleashed for my dead son.
    I've forgotten that once I beheld men,
that women loved me unhindered
My mind is a pile of worms
My delicate heart a tomb!

Translated by Peter Covino

∾

The Feast of September 20th in New York

Oh! today the houses are festooned for the feast,[1]
the streets are more lively . . . What kind of novelty is this?
    Here and there everyone's marching, grinning haughtily,
all the illustrious and the prominent of our colony
    They are decked out in uniform. Look . . . It's natural
For everyone who doesn't know, today is Carnevale.
    He goes pompously and broad-chested on an agile stallion,
ahead of every one, the upright and immobile grand marshal.
    As a hierarchic rule they trail behind him in single file
all of the locals . . . (like hoodlums from the town of Sila)
    There are some colonels and there some generals,
there's a vast number of soldiers and officials.
    Get a look at that guy who . . . seems to be a captain,
Everyone recognizes him, he's a well known thug.
    That other one carrying a sabre as if it were a cane,
he wields his authority priggishly as a lion.
    That rotten drunk who just fell out of rank and file
mumbles prayers from morning to night; he's fanatical.
    That skinny thing, tall as a canopy,
is a professor, but nonetheless a miserable cretin.

1. This poem describes an annual parade celebrating Garibaldi's taking of Rome on September 20, 1870, completing the Unification of Italy.

And that pygmy who yells with all the breath in his gullet
is a doctor who should really still be in school.

And that strange eccentric type with a face of clay
is the director of the "Bed Bug," an oafish notary.

There's also a real Don Puppet, an illiterate banker
who in his native village worked as a shepherd.

There's Father Pigsbloodspie and Father Peasanteater,
there's the lawyer Mr. Robyoublind, and the king of all cheaters.

There's the one everyone calls the cavalier Carlino,
in the company of that celebrated writer Don Agostino.

There are Papa Luigi, Mr. Pumpkin, Vito, Cambria,
the ambassador, the consul, Mr. Babywalker and his chums.

Today is a feast day! It's September 20. It's a spectacle
passing by. Listen what a brouhaha, a racket.

Listen! Listen . . . They're playing the hymn to Garibaldi
Ah! damned race! Imbeciles and scoundrels!

Perhaps this is the Italy of which you dreamed,
O Lion of Caprera, figure full of dread.

Perhaps this is the Italy that you boldly and with strength
fought for a hundred times, shouting: "Either Rome or death?"

Here, Italy passes by . . . Look at all these prominent men,
as if delighted the crowd salutes grimacing.

Look how they squeeze their Durandel swords
while another gives a speech and barks like a dog.

Look how they listen to the orator so attentively
as he wipes his sweat with his elbow occasionally.

Oh how many, how many veterans of this jailed country,
speak of honor, of country, of honesty. How merry!

And how many, how many in Italy were condemned
to an island, today are applauded and commended.

Here Italy passes by . . . Tip your berets. . . .
Could a spectacle be more beautiful and tempting?

Without paying a cent, you will see
things that in other times are difficult to believe!

The "Saint Rocco Society" goes ahead of everyone,
"Bruno's" society is next. You're laughing and . . . Then—

There's no reason to laugh . . . The one now in process
is the Club identified in the name of "Progress."

It's followed by another, the club of the "Banner"
quickly proceeded by that of the "Prayers."
    Look it's all silk. Oh! What an opulent pennant!
"The Holy Virgin of Meta" is written on it.
    And this other belongs to the society, even richer,
Of the members of "The seven chains of the mother."
    Here Italy passes by . . . And you all laugh! It's true:
these are things the whole world would ridicule!
    If at the sound of these booming and harsh trumpets
the martyrs who made Italy could rise up
    for awhile from their tombs, what would they say?
Who could ever be sure? They'd likely exclaim
    we must repent: this has to be some bacchanal.
Who knows! perhaps we've been resurrected in Carnevale.

    Translated by Peter Covino

The Italo-American "Polisso"

I

I am the most prized *pulisso*[2]
no one can act too fresh with me,
I've arrested more than one son of a bitch
and there're more thieves and loafers!
    My billy club's always at the ready,
it's always in hand and I'm a champion
if I'm in a fight, I'd send even Corbett
to Brooklyn, oh yeah, because I'm *strongo*. . . .

---

2. Policeman. Translation and explanations of much of the Italian American slang is
included: many of those terms are rendered in italics; several other slang terms were rendered in
English in order to preserve the integrity of the poem, without compromising the obvious
humor and are explicated below. *Io songo lu pulisso cchiu apprezato* is the first line of the
original; note the play on the word *songo = sono*, I am, with a play also on song, or the heightened music of the poem. The strict ABAB rhyme scheme of this poem was not preserved, though
clear sound linkages, off rhymes, and some sight rhymes exist throughout. Other clever original
dialect phrases, sometimes rendered phonetically, that were not rendered literally include,
Sanamangogna = son of a bitch; *ai em strongo* = I am strong.

I'm a fine *pulisso*
and *veri* smart too
I know my job
and I need respect.
You want a *naisa giobba*?[3]
I'll ask Dick and Harry;[4]
I'll tell everyone to Wait awhile
I'll tell everyone: Hello.

II

Every *barì*[5] will tell me: This *menno*[6]
isn't afraid of anybody
Aidonchè[7] if someone's a *riccimenno*.[8]
If he's a *toffepipelo aironchè*![9]
   The Black Hand has got to keep quiet,
if not I'll have to get out my club
goddamn blackmailers . . . go to hell
you know . . . all you troublemakers. . . .
   When I came to *a Mereca*,
I went to work the shovel,
and then I was able to stomach
working on the trash.
   I was always part
of the political pool
of Tammany Hall,
and now I'm a policeman.

III

Well som taime, ai se di tru,[10] the sergeant
gives me the business, because I'm talian. . . .

---

3. Nice job.
4. Ai esk a Tizio e Caie = I'll ask Tizio and Caio, an Italian idiom that became "I'll ask any Dick and Harry" in colloquial English.
5. Everybody, with a play on the southern Italian city of Bari.
6. Man.
7. I don't care.
8. Rich man.
9. If he's a tough guy I don't care.
10. Well, sometimes, to tell the truth . . .

Sciarap,[11] he yells, and I don't say nothing,
if not *ai luse di giobba e gubbai gian*.[12]

 I make good money, and the grocers,
caffe and bar owners, you know . . . business
folks, give me good tips. They like me,
even the stones on the street in this city like me.

 Now in political circles
I'm a big deal,
I'm a big boss,
during elections.

 I'm a fine policeman,
who does my job,
and, I hope, soon to become
a roundsman, hurray!

  Translated by Peter Covino

11. Shut up.
12. I lose the job and good-bye Jack.

Five Poems

Eduardo Migliaccio

Cava de' Tirreni (Salerno), Italy, April 15, 1882–New York, New York, March 29, 1946

Emelise Aleandri is the first scholar to attempt to organize the imposing legacy of Eduardo Migliaccio, the famous "Farfariello," without doubt the most popular figure in the Italian American theater at the beginning of the twentieth century. Thanks to Aleandri, there is emerging a systematic arrangement of manuscripts made up of scores, newspaper articles, loose sheets, and pamphlets, but no books or collected works. Among the difficulties of construing Migliaccio's legacy is a scholar's imperfect knowledge of the Neapolitan dialect and the varying theatrical texts, continually modified, lengthened, or shortened, according to the exigencies of the interpreters and the taste of the public.

With great precision, Aleandri has also begun to distinguish the difference between texts Migliaccio interpreted and those he actually wrote, and consequently to reveal what part of his vast repertory was the contribution of other musicians or writers. Many of the texts normally attributed to Migliaccio were, in fact, composed by other poets, no less talented but obscure, in particular Tony Ferrazzano. To distinguish the author from the interpreter, including the interpreter who through virtuosic performances makes the material his own, alters the evaluation of Migliaccio's merits.

For a long period, Eduardo Migliaccio was a leading actor of the vaudeville of Little Italy, on the Lower East Side of Manhattan. His *Neapolitan Caricatures*, or "colonial caricatures," constitute one of the first original fruits of the Italian American theater, documenting the colony's way of living, of thinking, of speaking, of singing. His art set the standard, so that, within a few years, every regional group of Italian immigrants could rely on artists to perform based on the Neapolitan-American original and to create new versions reflecting the differing geographical regions of Italy.

Migliaccio was only fifteen years old when his father, already in America, made him emigrate from Naples to the United States. It is not reasonable to think that at this age, the future Farfariello would have already been able attentively to study the style of Nicola Maldacea, who, in about 1890, with the help of the poet Ferdinando Russo and the musician Vincenzo Valente, in the celebrated Salone Margherita, had transformed himself from a traditional singer into the highly praised first interpreter of the new genre, the character caricatures (the *macchiette*, historically related to the *commedia dell'arte*). Maldacea was often cited as the maestro of Migliaccio, and, in fact, in the Migliaccio Papers at the Immigration History Research Center (IHRC), of the University of Minnesota, there are two volumes of *Macchiette e Monologhi* by Maladacea (1907). A line of progression from Maladacea to Migliaccio is clear, but there were other models as well. For example, Berardo Cantalamessa, another contemporary Neapolitan performer, is credited with introducing into the genre a more marked taste for the obscene double-entendre, which Migliaccio later did not spurn. Cantalamessa ended by establishing himself in Buenos Aires, where he died in 1917. Other examples included the caricaturists already operating at the end of the century in New York, where every manner of theatrical work arrived from Italy, including, on a regular basis the musical scores of all the Neapolitan Piedigrotte, often reproduced in local editions. New York also produced original Neapolitan caricatures, thanks to the inspiration of Cordiferro and others. In Naples, where Migliaccio studied at the Istituto di Belle Arti and perhaps attended the first year of an academic high school, he could see Maldacea on the stage of the Teatro Nuovo, but he would become passionate about the art of the caricature once he was in America. In Hazleton, a small mining center in Pennsylvania, he worked in the same Italian bank as his father, who was the director. The latter, as it seems, had once been wealthy, but was then ruined by a failed investment in the mining business. The task of the boy was to write letters for illiterate clients of the bank; he did not like it, but the contact helped him develop his extraordinary ear for the spoken language.

His move to New York was a step forward. He worked in the Banca Avallone of Mulberry Street at the same sort of job he had in Hazleton. While he was working at the bank, where he continued for several years, he took to frequenting the theatrical and artistic environment and soon became part of it. In fact, already in 1898, he performed the caricature, *Io me so' fatto Monaco* (I Became a Monk) of Riccardo Cordiferro, though it seems that his official debut took place in April 1900, when he acted in minor roles in two productions of Antonio Maiori: *Amleto* (Hamlet) and *La jena del cimitero* (The Cemetery Hyena). According to Aleandri, these are "his only two attempts as a dramatic actor." More interested in the profession of singer, Migliaccio then succeeded in finding an opportunity to interpolate short melodious Neapolitan numbers in Mulberry's theater of marionettes, but without much success, even provoking the anger of the public, which was more interested in the deeds of the paladins than in his voice. He therefore moved to one of the already numerous café chantants of Little Italy, the Pennacchio music hall on Mulberry Street (formerly Sala Umberto I and later Villa Vittorio Emanuele III, politically motivated name changes), and he soon obtained a contract for modest compensation of four dollars a week. It could be said that it was in this first period that Migliaccio found his theatrical persona, adopting the pseudonym "Farfariello" (Little Butterfly), derived from the ritornello of one small comic song: "Oi Farfarie' nficchete llà, / nficchete, nficche, e falla schiatta" (O little butterfly, slip in there . . . and make it burst). Perfectly evidenced is the taste for the malicious double entendre.

Modestly appreciated, Migliaccio offered a robust, very current repertory of songs and Neapolitan caricatures, but his real success arrived when, on the base of a caricature à la Maldacea (or à la Cantalamessa, or still further, à la Villani), he grafted the lively experience of the transplanted immigrant world. His method was predicated on two fundamental elements: an exquisite musicality, with a sensitive shift from traditional Neapolitan rhythms and melodies toward American meters, close to ragtime and to the first forms of jazz; the other, more decisive, of linguistic character, with the timely adherence to the daily jargon of the colony, whose Southern Italian dialects mixed with American English produced an original pidgin, which despite its function as an authentic language in use, possessed comic aspects. One of Farfariello's first colonial caricatures was opportunely entitled, *'Na parlata inglese* (An English Conversation). In 1914, his repertory comprised some one hundred and fifty caricatures, and he performed several of them every evening, thanks to his now mature talent as a performer and to the assistance of a troupe that made outfits for him that could be changed very quickly. Shows with vigorous rhythms and high amusement, marked by the lively participation of the public, soon attracted the attention of numerous critics, journalists, and American writers. The fact is that the characters appearing in scenes were often perfectly recognizable not only as types but also as particular persons, sometimes even present in the audience, like the ex-teacher Teodoro Palumbo, immortalized in the caricature, *L'impresario di pompe funebri; ovvero, L'Ondertecco* (The Impresario of Funeral Services, or, The Undertaker), whose reaction, which Migliaccio portrayed as indignance, was instead, as recalled by Italo Carlo Falbo, one of pure delight.

But Migliaccio was not only a caricaturist. Even in his smiling good nature, he often very effectively applied himself to satires of conspicuous figures in the Italian community. The nouveaux riches, improbable patriots, feigned aristocrats, and swindlers of every kind entered his repertory along with the ignorant boors just disembarking onto America soil. He impersonated an entire gallery of personages of most varied species, and was very often asked to interpret diverse traditions: with the Compagnia Comica Napoletana, of Francesco Ricciardi (with whom Migliaccio collaborated intensely at the beginning of the century), Farfariello performed side by side with Punchinello, and for Giovanni De Rosalia, he interpreted the Sicilian caricature *Piddu Macca*.

By the end of the 1910s, Migliaccio was in a position to direct his own companies: Eduardo Migliaccio Vaudeville Company; Compagnia di varietà Farfariello; Italian Comic Opera Company; and others; of aptly staging scenes based on his most notable songs; of participating, with alternating fortunes, in theatrical undertakings; of making long tours throughout the United States, including the West Coast. He became one of the first performers on radio programs for the Italians of America, and in 1936, he appeared in Italy, performing among others, the piece, *L'Imperatore Selassié* (Emperor Selassie). In 1940, the king conferred upon him the title of Knight of the Order of the Crown of Italy. Already a contributor to the *Carroccio,* he clearly did not oppose, as is evident, Fascist propaganda. But later, he assumed a position of wholehearted loyalty to America. In 1942, he created "Suldate americane" (American Soldiers), a patriotic song with the intention of emphasizing the Italian presence in the U.S. Army.

ESSENTIAL BIBLIOGRAPHY

Aleandri 1983a, 130–174; Cautela 1927; Durante 1993a, 1994b, 1999; Falbo 1942; Grillo 1971, 193–194; Parker 1914; Primeggia-Varacalli 1988; Sogliuzzo 1973; Van Vechten 1919; Wilson 1925.

ॐ

The Sport of Mulberry Street

What a roughneck I am . . . I used to say[1]
in Mulberry Street night and day,
as if no other street existed in New York City
just this one street and no other.
Now I spend my time in more elegant places
where in order to get in people have to dress up,
where everyone is weighed down with diamonds,
and everyone has lots of them. . . .
Only on forty-second street
life is not luxurious
where I am surrounded by cars
and the smell of gasoline,
on Broadway they appreciate you
if you walk with a walking stick,
but down here they think
I'm just another hick.
Let's not even talk about the suits,

---

1. *I* I am such an animal . . . I would be there in Mulberry Street night and day, as if no other
street existed in New York City just that one and not other. Now I spend my time in more elegant
places where in order to go in people have to dress up, where people are loaded down with
diamonds, and everyone has them in the same way . . . Only on forty-second street (*forisecone
stritto*) life is not luxurious and I spend my time among cars and the smell of gasoline, on Broadway
(*Broduè*) they appreciate you if you walk with a cane, but down here for them I am the usual hick.
Let's not even talk about the suits, there they appreciate them, there they know style (*staile*), but
down here every time I head out for the club, I hear them call out: stand up straight, you plug. . . .

II And what shows (*sciò*) there are . . . last night, I went to a play. It was all about seeing a
black woman in the way her mother made her . . . but she wore a straw skirt, and danced a south
American dance . . . it made my hair stand up, sure . . . just my hair . . . forget it. With all the
millionaires there I was, and everyone staring that bit of God's bounty. She made you feel like
kissing her on the forehead, on the lips. I went back to Mulberry . . . thinking: go to bed? Who
can sleep? I was restless . . . I felt like dancing. Those are the best women when she moved: tra la
la. I shouted out loud: Encore, Miss! and was kicked out by a cop. Those are shows. One time I
got it into my head to go to the Metropolitan. They were showing the "Cavalleria of the Oyster
Seller" and the fellow Alfio who had been offended sang and said at least twenty times: I'll have
my revenge, I'll have my revenge, I'll have my revenge . . . Tell me when a Sicilian ever made a
song of something he was going to do over and over, he would just tell you straight out and that's
that. Then I also went to see the Traviata. The father didn't want the son to marry the Miss
Ballerina . . . but tell when did a father's opinion ever count? The son throws the girl a bag of gold

there they appreciate them,
there they know style,
but down here
every time I head out for the club,
I hear them call out: stand up straight, you fool

II

And what shows there are . . . last night,
I went to the theater.

---

but she doesn't take it, you can't fool me, what woman ever turned down money? Then they
made it known that the girl had typhus and she died. Screaming so loud that the whole theatre
shook . . . and then they think that people don't understand. But I didn't go there to get to know
nobility. Are you kidding, those that I have met up to now are all millionaires. I am looking to
squeeze into the society of the four-hundred, so what? They are four hundred and I am one,
four-hundred and one. Who knows that I won't get lucky and get to marry a millionaire. I
could use a title, baron or marquee. They give me titles of all sorts, but no-one has said to me
yet: Here you go, Baron . . . Those people don't care about money because they didn't have to
work for it. Just think, they don't even take baths in water, like everyone. Some bathe in
champagne, some in milk, some don't bathe at all, and other have the sea brought to their
home. A few days ago I was at a millionaire's house, a certain Mr. Brok, we sent out for a pint
of beer, I acted like one of them and sent the last of all of them. I took the car that was waiting
downstairs and left. The police chased me and shot at me, what a laugh . . . Because that car
wasn't mine . . . but the police understood that it was a joke . . . if it had worked out it would
have been alright. There is an old woman who is in love with me. I am going to marry her and
take a trip around the world. I want to show her all the ruins . . . the museums . . . then I'll
leave her in some museum and come back home. It's a fact that to be in high society one must
speak a lot of languages, and I do alright with languages. I speak Sicilian, Barese and Neapolitan and I think that's enough.

But you need money. I'll rob my father. I am the son of Pasquale C. Father has an emporium
and doesn't understand . . . there are no more cans and no more cold-cuts but there is no money
in the cash box. He says: if I had a stranger here, but I have you . . . and that's the problem. What
can I do, I want to be a millionaire. I like this life because there is no jealousy among those
people, not like among you Italians you get riled up for nothing, and pull it out to shoot. There
the wife of the husband goes with he who would be the husband of the wife, who has a husband,
and that's the beautiful thing that it's all one big community. But among you it's no use you don't
know how to live, for women it's over as soon as they marry.

One time for a pinch that I gave my comare the compari bit and hit me and more. But there
no one makes a big deal, with a lot of charm, as soon as they know you, all they want is money.
This is the life that can make one happy, but a thought seems to call to me . . . don't even try it,
stay where you are, don't even try it, you'll get in trouble. If you make it with those, thieves
good-bye. For even just saying: how-are-you. They'll take the shirt off your back and you won't
even know it. Don't even bother. If Mary finds out, god-forbid . . . One time when I wanted to
leave her she beat me. Don't even bother what a mess not even in jest Don Ciccio bullet man.
What a pain. Don't even bother. Better stay where you are.

It was all about seeing a black woman
in the way her mother made her . . . but
she wore a skimpy straw skirt,
and danced a South American dance. . . .
it made my hair stand up,
sure . . . just my hair . . . but let's move on.
There I was,
with all the millionaires,
and everyone staring at
that bit of God's bounty.
She made you feel like kissing her
on the forehead, on the lips.
I went back to Mulberry. . . .
thinking: go to bed?
Who can sleep? I was restless
. . . I felt like dancing.
Those are the best women
When she moved: tra la la.
Then I shouted out loud: Do it again, Miss!
and was kicked out by a cop.
Those are shows. One time I got it into my head to go to the
    Metropolitan.[2]
They were showing the "Cavalleria of the Oyster Seller"[3] and my fellow
    countryman Alfio
who had been offended and sang and said at least twenty times: I'll have my
    revenge, I'll have my revenge, I'll have my revenge . . . Just tell me when a
    Sicilian ever made a song of something he was going to do over and over, he
    would just tell you straight out: four plus four is eight'
that's that, no song, and no chit-chat.
Then I also went to see Traviata. The father didn't want the son to marry
the Miss Ballerina . . . but tell me, when did a father's opinion ever matter?
The kid throws the girl a bag of gold but she doesn't take it.
Who are they kidding? What woman ever turned down money?

2. Metropolitan Opera
3. *Cavalleria Rusticana* is of course the title of the opera. The misunderstanding and
transliteration of the title into Neapolitan transforms it into 'Acavallaria 'e ll'ustricaro. An
ustricaro is an oyster seller (P. Verdicchio).

Then they made it known that the girl had typhus and she died
Screaming so loud that the whole theatre shook . . . and then
they think that people don't get it. But I didn't go there
to get to know the nobility. Are you kidding? Those that I have met
up to now are all millionaires. I am looking to squeeze into
the society of the four-hundred, so what's the big deal? They are four hundred
and I am one, four-hundred and one. Who knows that I won't get lucky
and get to marry a millionaire. I could use a title,
baron or marquis. They call me all sorts of names, but no-one has ever said
to me: Here you go, Baron . . . Those people don't care about money
because they didn't have to work for it. Just think, they don't even take
baths in water, like everyone else. Some bathe in champagne, some in milk,
some don't bathe at all, and others have the sea brought to their home.
A few days ago I was at a millionaire's house, a certain Mr. Brok, he sent me
    out
for a pint of beer. I walked out like I was one of them and sent another guy out
    to get it.
Then I took the car that was waiting downstairs and left. The police chased me
and shot at me, what a laugh . . . because that car wasn't mine. . . .
but the police understood that it was a joke . . . but if it had worked out it
    would
have been all right. I've got this old woman who is in love with me. I am
going to marry her and take a trip around the world. I want to show her
all the ruins . . . the museums . . . then I'll leave her in some museum
and come back home. It's a fact that to be in high society
one must speak a lot of languages, and I do all right with languages.
I speak Sicilian, Barese and Neapolitan and I think that's enough.
But you need money. I'll rob my father. I am the son of Pasquale C.
Pop has a grocery store and he doesn't understand . . . there are no more
    canned goods
Or cold-cuts left to sell, but there is no money in the bank either. He says:
if I had a stranger here, but I have you . . . and that's the problem.
What can I do, I want to be a millionaire.
I like this life because
there is no jealousy among those people,
not like among you Italians
you get riled up for nothing,

and pull guns out to shoot.
There the wife of the husband goes
with a guy who would be the husband of the wife,
who has a husband, and that's the beautiful thing
that it's all one big community.
But with you people it's no use
you don't know how to live,
for women it's over
as soon as they marry.
One time, for a pinch
that I gave my friend's wife,
my friend bit and hit
me and worse. But there
no one makes a big deal,
with a lot of charm,
as soon as they know you,
all they want is money.
This is the life that can make one happy,
but a thought seems to call to me. . . .
don't even try it,
Watch where you're going,
It's better to stay where you are,
Watch where you're going.
Otherwise you'll get in trouble.
If you go in with those guys, good-bye
For even just saying: how-are-you,
They'll take the shirt off your back
and you won't even know it.
Watch where you're going.
If Mary finds out, god-forbid. . . .
One time when I wanted to leave her
she beat me.
Watch where you're going
what a screw-up,
a real mess,
Don Ciccio,
A bullet he'll send

What a problem
Watch where you're going.
Better stay where you are.

Translated by Pasquale Verdicchio

∾

Let's Go To Coney Island

I

Hey, Mamie, it's a beautiful day[4]
and you lock yourself up in some shop?
Forget that. Let's take off
and afterwards we'll have a drink. . . .
Let's go, your mother is out doing the shopping,
with her basket; and your father
I saw him–no offense Mamie–
at the corner shining shoes.
I want to show you Luna Park,

4. "Let's go to Coney Island" is a song in the style of the tarantella, with music by N. Bonsanti. The manuscript text is as follows:

I Hey, Maime, it's a beautiful day and you lock yourself up in some shop (*scioppa*)? Don't bother, let's take off and afterwards we'll have a drink . . . Let's go, your mother is off doing the shopping, with her basket (*baschetta*); and your father I saw him—no offense Maime—at the street (*stritto*) corner shining shoes (*sciaina*). I want to show you the Luna Park, all electrical! I want to walk you beneath an arch with shining lights all around! This is a beautiful life! What do you say, will you come? And in a little boat we'll bump along (*bombalò*). . . .

II Your brother is a shoemaker (*sciù-mecco*), and doesn't count: and by now he's already drunk on whiskey! In the trolley, me on one side and you on the other, we'll understand each other with a whistle . . . I'll wait for you under the Brooklyn Bridge . . . Who'll notice us in the middle of that crowd? If the boy is a nuisance, Tonino, give him candy (*chente*), and you'll see him go. I want to buy you a chicken, a spring-chicken (*sprinche-cik*), Mamie! And you can eat it all on your own: but then know what I would like? Only a little of the thighs and breast! Come on, let's eat . . . you have to fill your belly to bursting!

III When we're there, if you like, we can go down the slide, we'll laugh like crazy. Careful though on the rides, especially on the corners: get in and out but don't get hurt . . . When it gets to the top . . . right at that moment . . . what a great pleasure! Then it ends . . . and slows down. If you go riding in the merry-go-round, I'll take you to the loop-the-loop (*luppo-luppo*) and dancing too, follow me. If your mother complains, tell her: Ma! Didn't you and Pa go into the fields together?

all electrical!
I want to walk you beneath an arch
with shining lights all around!
This is how life is beautiful!
What do you say, will you come?
And in a little boat
we'll bump along. . . .

II

Your brother is a shoemaker, and doesn't count:
and by now he's already drunk on whiskey!
In the trolley, me on one side and you
on the other, we'll understand each other with a whistle. . . .
I'll wait for you under the Brooklyn Bridge. . . .
Who'll notice us in the middle of that crowd?
If the boy is a nuisance, Tonino, give him candy,
and you'll get rid of him.
I want to buy you a chicken,
a spring chicken, Mamie!
And you can eat it all on your own:
but then do you know what I would like?
Only a little of the thighs and breast!
Come on, let's eat . . . you have to fill
your belly to bursting!

III

When we're there, if you like,
we can go down the slide,
we'll laugh like crazy.
Careful though on the rides,
especially on the corners:
go up and down but don't get hurt. . . .
When it gets to the top . . . right at that moment. . . .
Before the plunge . . . What a perfect ride!
Then it ends. . . .
and carries you more slowly.
If you ride the horse on the merry-go-round,
Be careful not to fall!

I'll take you to the loop-the-loop
and dancing too, follow me.
If your mother complains, tell her:
Ma! Didn't you and Pa
go into the fields together?

Translated by Pasquale Verdicchio

∾

The Bumpkin in a Tuxedo

I

I like this land, America,[5]
Because here we are all the same.
The President has to shake my hand
As he does his brother's.

5. *I* I like this land, America, Because here we are all the same. The President has to shake my hand As he does his brother's. Now that I know America I have no more manners.

I go along with the belief that no one is better than I. Whether you are born a prince, or if you are a scientist, I have a tuxedo and I am just like anyone else. Frank, that's because I like this country.

II In order to make love in my town, You have to carry a knife in your pocket, Or else the father or brother for their honor Will flatten your nose. But love here is alright (*orraite*), It's really beautiful, The father thinks only of dollars, And the brother thinks of girls (*ghelle*) So the road is free, The doors are open. You call her: Come down (*come daune*), You pick her up and take her away, That's because (*dezze bicos*), Frank, I like this country (*mi laiche dis contri*).

III If you get married in our parts, You get into deep trouble and that's that, You can't do anything about it, compare, You pay a dear price, whether good or bad. But, here in America, If you're not happy with her, You break the marriage, And go get another one.

You say: Mr. I don't like it (*misto no laiche*), Fill out a few forms, So the mayor can make another one. That's because, Frank, I like this country.

IV I always hear it said that an Italian Discovered this country but it's not true. That Christopher was the first man Who took it. He was the first passenger. I talked with someone who Really know and he says that A certain fellow from the Bronx Found this place. Do you think that in America Where they know their business That they would let that guy Find their land? . . . That's because, Frank, I like this country.

V And in the summer you go to Coney Island Heaven . . . so many beautiful things The loop-the-loop (*lupo il lupo*) . . . In dreamland (*drimilando*) you see So many strange things . . . The mirrors really stupefy you Gosh what a laugh Staircases that bounce around, The wheel goes like this. What a mess. Men and women Shouting, pushing Hugging, kissing In the dark in the tunnel. That's because, Frank, I like this country.

Now that I know America
I have no more manners.
I go along knowing that no one's better than me.
Whether you are born a prince,
or if you are an educated man,
I have a tuxedo
and I am just like anyone else.
And that's why, Frankie
I like this country.

II

In order to make love in my town,
You have to carry a knife in your pocket,
Or else the father or brother for their honor
Will flatten your nose.
But love here is all right,
It's really beautiful,
The father thinks only of dollars,
And the brother thinks of girls,
So the road is free,
The doors are open.
You call her: Come down,
You pick her up and take her away,
And that's why, Frankie,
I like this country.

III

If you get married where we come from,
You get into deep trouble and that's that,
You can't do anything about it, buddy,
You pay a dear price, for better or worse.
But, here in America,
If you're not happy with her,
You break the marriage
And go get another one.
You say: Mr. I don't like her,
Fill out a few forms,
So the mayor can make another one.

And that's why, Frankie,
I like this country.

IV

I always hear it said that an Italian
Discovered this country, but it's not true.
That Christopher was the first man
Who took it. He was the first passenger.
I talked with someone who
Really knows and he says that
A certain fellow from the Bronx
Found this place.
Do you think that in America
Where they know their business
That they would let that guy
Find their land?. . . .
And that's why, Frankie,
I like this country.

V

And in the summer you go to Coney Island
It's Heaven . . . so many beautiful things
The loop-the-loop . . . In Dreamland you see
So many strange things. . . .
The mirrors really stupefy you
Wow what a laugh
Staircases that bounce around,
The wheel goes like this.
What confusion. Men and women
Shouting, pushing
Hugging, kissing
In the dark in the tunnel.
And that's why, Frankie,
I like this country.

Translated by Pasquale Verdicchio

∾

Unlucky Pasquale

I

I am not blaming the blessed memory of my mother[6]
Who made me ugly as I am
And I don't blame the family either,
That my bad luck is in everything and with everything.
From when the ship left and was about to sink
Deep into the sea, I crossed myself thinking,
If you die Pasquale your suffering is over.
When I arrived here at the Battery,
They found, I don't know, something wrong
And turned me back around along my way. . . .
But then I came back here for spite

6. *I* I am not blaming the good soul of my mother Who made ugly as I am And not even with the tana, That my bad luck is in everything and with everything Since the ship left and was about to sink Deep into the sea. I crossed myself thinking If you die Pasquale your suffering is over. When I arrived here at the Battery, They found, I don't know, some mistake And turned me back around along my way . . . But then I came back here for spite And discovered these American lands . . . I alighted on this noisy land . . . Trams, elevated (*alivete*) roads, cars and bells . . . After six months I was still unemployed . . . Then one day I had my first chance (*accianza*) . . . I was run over by a police car. . . .

II As soon as I left the hospital I went to visit with all those from my town. I did not want to forget compare Pasquale Who lived uptown. I was searching around on 70th street . . . It was getting dark . . . and I couldn't see well, or else the directions were wrong. . . .

When I hear a boom . . . like thunder A bomb . . . a bomb . . . and I like a dummy, but anyone would have done it, ran away. That's when people started to chase me: There he is, catch the wop (*checce de wop*) The police shooting from behind. They caught me, took me to jail Wrote up a report and Took a nice picture . . . And that very night the paper carried . . . Pasquale, head of the black hand . . . Good thing that when the Italian paper came out They gave me back my honor. I have it put away a piece of The Telegraph for some compatriot who might not believe me (he reads slowly and carefully): "The usual police crabs. Pasquale Fortunato, nicknamed, Unlucky, arrested for black-handedness was yesterday absolved of all charges. Police suspicion was aroused after the sensational capture because Fortunato could only stand there like an imbecile—it's true—and could not give any plausible explanation of why he found himself in the area on the night of the explosion. We have done our own investigation and can affirm that Mr. Unlucky is a hard worker . . . a good man . . . and for all his goodness back home they used to call him Pasquale the D . . . —OK, I get it. We would like to make it clear that Mr. Unlucky has never been Involved with any bombs. . . ." Yes, sir, all these years in America and no bombs. So, after this disaster I went to work in Pennsylvania in a carbon mine. Brothers, I don't recommend it . . . when you see that dark cave it's scary and thump thump with the metal pole. There are gasses

And discovered these American lands. . . .
I landed in this noisy place. . . .
Trams, overheads, cars and bells. . . .
After six months I was still unemployed. . . .
Then one day I had my first chance. . . .
I was run over by an ambulance. . . .

II

As soon as I left the hospital
I went to visit with all those from my town.
I did not want to forget my old buddy Pasquale

---

there and they blow up . . . and one day Kabbbuuum . . . and they had to dig me out like a piece of coal . . . the dust blew in my face and now my eyes don't always see. But the company won in court because they said they were right and we should go to jail . . . and we split with the lawyer the middlemen and so on . . . I ended up with a buck and a half for this eye . . . I tried to figure things out: and if I lose the other one would I also get a dollar and a half? And for a buck and a half I decided to keep it and left. I started working pushing a spade. An Irish foreman (*formene airesce*) kept bothering us . . . one day all the Italians ganged up on him. I alone ran away for fear of being arrested . . . and I'm the one who got nabbed . . . They took me in front of a judge and I gave my story: Mr. Judge I always worked (*evri uorche*) and that's all and the Irishman . . . dig you dig dig (*dinghe dinghe*) more you and we lost our head (*mecco luse de nervature*) and somebody broke his head (*brecco di edde*). Okay, six months for you (*sicchese monze fore iu*) . . . I did not work in the subway (*subuè*) long the first day I started at seven and as seven thirty I was in the hospital where they were fixing (*ficchessianno*) my leg . . . The foreman came to see me and said: You're lucky you're lucky . . . as he looked (*locchi*) at the other leg. Don't look don't look this one I'm taking home with me. In a sawmill I left these two fingers to the boss in a machine (*mascina*) and I left. The lawyer told me not to sue it was my fault. And now if I come back I come back happy because I'm the one who made America. If machinery works it's because I dug the coal, if walls and buildings are strong it's because they're made with the blood of this Italian worker everything is in place and I can leave.

III I went to say goodbye to my town-folks My suitcase is ready and I want to say

To you as well: Goodbye! Let's shake hands! Good luck! What has been has been

I don't want to think about trouble! Happy! . . . I found a man in the park at Mulberry who kept looking at me and then he said: Hey! Aren't you Marco? No sir! I'm Pasquale!—I made a mistake. I know you—what's up, you leaving? Me too . . . finally I have found someone from my hometown . . . Be careful around here There are thieves, robbers! Have any money?—Three hundred dollars! Careful where you put it! Dear Pasquale, don't let anyone rob you, It just happened to another guy. Then he said: Goodbye, and kissed me.

My name is Francesco and he hugged me. What a fine man Francesco! Careful!

He said: don't let them rob you! Where is it! Blessed Saint Pasquale! The money was right here . . . He hugged me, kissed me and robbed me He was the thief Police! Arrest everybody (*evri bari*) Police! And now I no longer see . . . dear Francesco . . . and the little girl . . . Dear me! I didn't think this would happen to me I am really Unlucky Pasquale! Police! Arrest everybody Police!

Who lived uptown.
I was searching around on 70th street. . . .
It was getting dark . . . and I couldn't see well,
or else the directions were wrong. . . .
When I hear a boom . . . like thunder
A bomb . . . a bomb . . . and I, like a dummy,
but anyone would have done it, ran away.
That's when people started to chase me:
There he is, catch the wop
The police shooting from behind.
They caught me, took me to jail
Wrote up a report and
Took a nice picture. . . .
And that very night the paper carried. . . .
Pasquale, head of the black hand. . . .
Good thing that when the Italian paper came out
They gave me back my honor. I have it put away
a piece of The Telegraph for some compatriot
who might not believe me (he reads slowly and carefully):
"The usual police screw-ups. Pasquale Fortunato, nicknamed, Unlucky,
arrested for black-handedness was yesterday absolved of all charges.
Police suspicion was aroused after the sensational capture because
Fortunato could only stand there like an imbecile–it's true–and could not
give any plausible explanation of why he found himself in the area
on the night of the explosion.
We have done our own investigation and can affirm that
Mr. Unlucky is a hard worker . . . a good man . . . and for all his goodness
back home they used to call him Pasquale the D . . . —OK, I get it.
We would like to make it clear that Mr. Unlucky has never been
Involved with any bombs. . . ."
Yes, sir, all these years in America and no bombs. So, after this
disaster I went to work in Pennsylvania in a coal mine.
Brothers, I don't recommend it . . . when you see that dark cave
it's scary and thump thump with the metal pole. There are gasses there
and they blow up . . . and one day Kabbbuuum. . . .
and they had to dig me out like a piece of coal . . . the dust blew
in my face and now my eyes don't always see. But the company won
in court because they said they were right and we should go to jail. . . .

and we split with the lawyer the middlemen and so on . . . I ended up with
a buck and a half for this eye . . . I tried to figure things out: and if I lose
the other one would I also get a buck and a half? And for a buck and a half
I decided to keep that eye and left. I started working as a ditch digger.
An Irish foreman kept bothering us . . . one day all the Italians ganged up
on him. I alone ran away for fear of being arrested . . . and I'm the one
who got nabbed . . . They took me in front of a judge and I gave my story:
Mr. Judge I always worked and that's all and the Irishman . . . dig you dig
dig more you and we lost our head and somebody broke his head. Okay,
six months for you. . . .
I did not work in the subway long. The first day I started at seven and
at seven thirty I was in the hospital where they were fixing my leg. . . .
The foreman came to see me and said: You're lucky you're lucky. . . .
as he looked at the other leg. Don't look don't look
this one I'm taking home with me.
In a sawmill I gave these two fingers to the boss
in a machine and I left. The lawyer told me not to sue,
it was my fault. And now if I go back home I go back happy
because I'm the one who made America. If machinery works it's because
I dug the coal, if walls and buildings are strong it's because they're made
with the blood of this Italian worker. Everything is working, so I can leave.

III

I went to say goodbye to my town-folks,
My suitcase is ready and I want to say
To you as well: Goodbye! Let's shake hands!
Good luck! What has been has been
I don't want to think about trouble! Happy!
. . . I found a man in the park
at Mulberry who kept looking at me and then he said:
Hey! Aren't you Marco?
No sir! I'm Pasquale!–I made a mistake.
I know you–what's up, you leaving?
Me too . . . finally I have found someone from my hometown
. . . Be careful around here
There are thieves, robbers! Have any money?
–Three hundred dollars! Careful where you put it!
Dear Pasquale, don't let anyone rob you,

It just happened to another guy.
Then he said: Goodbye, and kissed me,
My name is Francesco and he hugged me.
What a fine man Francesco! Careful!
He said: don't let them rob you!
Where is it! Blessed Saint Pasquale!
The money was right here. . . .
He hugged me, kissed me and robbed me
He was the thief
Police! Arrest everybody Police!
And now I no longer see. . . .
My son Francesco . . . and the little girl. . . .
Dear me!
I didn't think this would happen to me
I am really Unlucky Pasquale!
Police! Arrest everybody Police!

Translated by Pasquale Verdicchio

The Funeral Director

I

What do you want, some people,[7]
they think that to be an undertaker
doesn't take much.
But that's why they make a big mistake.
One needs to know how to deal with his countrymen,
if you don't make friends you'll have no work

7. *I* What do you want, some people, they think that to be an undertaker (*ondertecco*) it doesn't take much. But that's why they make a big mistake (*dezze uaie de mecco big mistecco*). One needs to know how to deal with his countrymen, if you don't make friends you'll have no work (*giobba*) and you can sit there with your hands in your pockets, even with all your service and proper goods. In the bars, in cafes, take note how I treat everyone well, I shake hands, why? Because among so many acquaintances six or seven a week will die.

II Business is not going too well now of course, everyone is in good health. When the holidays come around they help a bit: accidents, fights, someone dies from overeating.

and you can sit there with your hands in your pockets,
even with all your service and the good work you do.
In the bars, in cafes, take note how I treat
everyone well, I shake hands, why?
Because among so many acquaintances
six or seven a week will die.

II

Business is not going too well now of course,
everyone is in good health.
When the holidays come around, they help a bit:
accidents, fights, someone dies from overeating.
You think that I gain from other people's suffering.
No sir! Rather than going to someone who will cheat you
I will treat you with great decorum and honor,
I bury people with great satisfaction.
Luxuriously and carefully prepared
with fancy carriages for the family.
A widow was once so satisfied of my work
that on the following day she called me
to introduce me to her daughter.

III

I sit on all the committees,
I am a well-known big shot.
Have you ever seen me in the parades?
I have been in them on foot and on horseback.
I am the true, one and only savior

You think that I gain (*gagno*) from other people's suffering. No sir! Rather than going to someone who will cheat you I will treat you with great decorum and honor, I bury people with great satisfaction. Luxuriously and carefully prepared with fancy carriages for the family. A widow was once so satisfied of my work that on the following day she called me to introduce me to her daughter.

III I sit on all the committees, I am a well-known big shot. Have you ever seen me in the parades? I have been in them on foot and on horseback. I am the true, one and only savior of the Italians. Of course, if one is born, is married, I take them to church, and if one dies I am the first one to get the caskets ready. If someone gets into a mess and ends up in court I have friends and will help him until I see him condemned to death; after that I pick him up and take him to the graveyard.

of the Italians. Of course, if one is born,
is married, I take them to church, and if one dies
I am the first one to get the caskets ready.
If someone gets into trouble
and ends up in court
I have friends and will help him
until I see him condemned to death;
after that I pick him up
and take him to the graveyard.

> *Translated by Pasquale Verdicchio*

The Blowhard

More than one person who knows me[8]
has asked, surprised: Marquis, what are you doing here?. . . .
I have come without telling my family
to have a look at America.
This land cannot impress me
with its large buildings.
It will take more than this,
my castles reach much farther into the sky. . . .
Half of Naples is mine,
Four-horse carriages . . . what beautiful animals.
I have a hundred servants . . . Some people say:
You have all this and you disdain it! I can't help it.
I've lit cigars with

8. More than one person who knows me has asked, surprised: Marquis, what are you doing here? . . . I have come unbeknown to my family to have a look at America. This land cannot impress me with its large buildings. It will take more than this, my castles reach much farther into the sky . . . Half of Naples is mine, horse carriages . . . what beautiful animals. I have a hundred servants . . . Some people sai: You have all this and you disdain it! I can't help it. I light cigars with thousand lira bills And the way I dress still makes heads turn. Make sure that they know I have landed here they'll send me to italy that can't be done. I am looking for a millionaire a woman to whom I will give my title. And if she should refuse me I'll tell her: You miserable, I'll write my father, you gossip . . . I will buy up all of America . . . Does anyone have a cigarette?

thousand lira bills
And the way I dress
still makes heads turn.
Make sure that they know
I have landed here,
they'll send me to Italy
We can't do without him.
I am looking for a millionaire,
a woman to whom I will give
my title. And if she should refuse me
I'll tell her: You miserable, I'll write
my father, you gossip. . . .
I will buy up all of America. . . .
Can I borrow a cigarette?

Three Poems

❧ *Tony Ferrazzano*

Died 1926

In the period in which Migliaccio appeared at the Caffè Ronca, relates Cautela, Tony Ferrazzano presented himself to him, pleading with Migliaccio to take a look at Ferrazzano's writings, and Migliaccio obliged him. Despite noticing many errors, Migliaccio recognized Ferrazzano's talent and encouraged him. In this way, a very fertile collaboration was born, producing some of Farfariello's best caricatures, among them *Il cafone patrioto* (The Patriotic Bumpkin); *Lu cafone che ragiona* (The Thinker Bumpkin); *La lengua 'talian* (The Italian Language); and *'O sunatore 'e flauto* (The Flute Player). Generally, the loose sheets of text stated "Versi di T. Ferrazzano" (Verses of T. Ferrazzano) and "Riduzione e creazione del cav. Eduardo Migliaccio" (Dramatization and Creation of Mr. Eduardo Migliaccio). The maestro undoubtedly contributed his part, but Ferrazzano is to be credited with some ingenious intuitions and verbal solutions. It is rightly held that this popular figure must be retrieved from obscurity and placed alongside the most celebrated Neapolitan actor.

As mentioned in the introduction to Part 3, the texts of Ferrazzano had the honor of being studied by Arthur Livingston. The author was also an actor with the stage name "Totò," with which he signed some of his compositions, published in the *Messaggero*, a weekly of Paterson and Passaic, New Jersey, directed in that period by Baldo Aquilano. On April 22, 1916, when the weekly came under the direction of Ermete De Fiori, Totò inaugurated a less successful rubric of poetry, "For the Women," of which only the first issue is known to exist.

The 1910s were Ferrazzano's most fertile period. In the pieces not conceived for Farfariello, Ferrazzano appears to try his hand at the use of Italian American jargon, as exampled in this passage, accompanied by the mandolin: "'Na serenata llaica helle!. . . ." A Serenade like hell! (1911). Besides "llaica helle," like hell, jargon colors other parts of the song: "*crese,*" crazy, "*tuosto,*" toast. He left his brother uptown to go to Bronx Park ("*lassato a frateme oppettano/pe dinto'o bronze parco [Bronx Park] pe vveni*"). Ferrazzano published his musical sheets in collections of songs and caricatures, but also in volumes. His poems on patriotic-satirical themes, on the Italo-Turkish war, and on the First World War, appeared in editions (rare today) of 1911, 1915, 1916, and 1919.

ESSENTIAL BIBLIOGRAPHY

Aleandri 1983a, 190ff; Cautela 1927, 110.

The Italian Language

What a beautiful thing is the Italian language[1]
Whoever invented it should live a hundred years
But I can not understand English or American
even if my life depends on it.
But there is no other tongue
more beautiful
than when my wife
insults me. . . .

I

It's more than twenty years now
since I arrived here directly from my home town
more like twenty one and still I haven't learned
even half a word of English.
Because I don't like[2] contorted tongues

---

1. Center for Migration Studies (CMS), Staten Island, looseleaf, undated. The music of the comic is by Raffaele Grauso, the redaction and creation by Eduardo Migliaccio.
2. "*Biccosa mi no llaico*"

that are not Italian, and that's why[3]
I will stay here until I die
without knowing a word.

Not that it is an ugly language,
American; it's probably very nice,
but it's not Italian. . . .
When they promised me
the citizenship card
I had to wait two years, and in the morning
I went to city hall[4] and didn't get it
because the judge[5] spoke to me in English.

II

My wife, instead, that good for nothing,
talks to me almost always in American
when I call her, she says: "What do you want?"[6]
But "what do you want?" is not Italian!. . . .
And she answers, oh "you jackass!"[7]
Jackass? But "jackass" is also English.
And she often says "I break your face!"[8]
And back home they don't say this.
I know that all of Italy
up and down
talks and reasons
in Italian.
Whatever dialect
an Italian speaks
if you don't understand him
he'll make himself understood
with his hands.
And that's why I wouldn't exchange

3. *"tezzo guai"*
4. *"seti holo"*
5. *"giogge"*
6. *"guario guanne"*
7. *"iu giacchese"*
8. *"ai brecche iu fesse"*

English for the Calabrian dialect.
And this is what we were talking
about in the basement. We were all Italians
and Calabrese and we were saying that Neapolitan
is the most beautiful language! For its beautiful words
as well as for its bad words; if you really want to talk
then American is Italian broken up, turned upside down,
so that when we say *donne* here they called them *uomine*.[9]
And then Italian is smooth! What it says it means. *Pane* means bread[10]
not here where they call it *bread*! I used to have a parrot
who only spoke American; he never wanted to learn Italian
so I cut his head off. Now I have another one that I really like
because he speaks Italian, and in fact I call him Brother.
He too, when he sees me, begins to call: Brother! Brother!
And, you know, some of the greatest men in history spoke Italian:
Alighieri, Garibaldi, Ciccio Cappuccio. And, when Americans argue,
when they have a fight, they only use four or five bad words and that's it!
We know thousands of them . . . even without counting those my wife knows.
And so, when my wife slams me with bad words I console myself
because they're in Italian, and Italian is a smooth tongue!
"You piece of this, you piece of that!" and I enjoy it! "I'll do this,
I'll do that!" "I can't wait for the news that they've killed you down
in some basement before you could find an Italian priest to confess you."
Ah, it's just delightful! because they are Italian words
and the Italian tongue is smooth. . . .

III

One night it was after midnight
and I found myself at a corner
where there were about a dozen young men
who started to insult me for no reason.
They said some very disrespectful words
in American. I thought I should scare them

9. "Women" to the author's ear sounds like the dialect term "*uomene*," meaning men (in Italian, *uomini*).
10. "Bread" to the author's ear sounds like the dialect term "*preta*," meaning stone or rock (in Italian, *pietra*).

and without speaking English
I put my hand behind my back and stopped.
Thinking that I was holding some sort of weapon
those good-for-nothings stopped talking
and I moved on.
But as soon as I was
half a block away
they blew me a Bronx cheer
but I felt better
because from a distance I recognized it
as an ITALIAN CHEER!

Translated by Pasquale Verdicchio

The Thinking Bumpkin

I

Today the American is the one[11]
who runs this land and does what he likes;
so when he sees an Italian,
acting like a king,
he calls him dago.
What gives him the right
to insult Italians?. . . .
If I am a bumpkin,
I have countrymen,
who are masters of science,
who are to you professors,
who could really tell you
a few things!. . . .
So my friend Antonio
am I right or not?! . . . Eh!. . . .

11. CMS, sheet music, copyright 1910 by Antonio Grauso. Music by Paolo Bolognese; correct assignation: "Lyrics by E. Migliaccio and T. Ferrazzano—Special creation by the divo Farfariello."

II

What Americans do here
you don't even see pigs do where I come from;
they blow their noses in their hands,
in the middle of the street . . . and they call us guinea?!
They eat with
chewing tobacco in their mouth!. . . .
You'll see a drunken woman
on every corner!. . . .
If Rosa were to do that
I'd eat her alive!. . . .
But this race is . . . powerful
Tell me it's imaginary!. . . .
Tell me, my friend Antonio,
am I right or not?! . . . Eh!. . . .

III

American women, even when they're married,
have fun with all sorts of people,
and at times stay out all night. . . .
. . . and the dumb husband just goes to bed.
And then, if you want to make love here
it's not a problem!. . . .
As soon as you meet someone
they all get really friendly:
"How are you? Come in! Sit down!"
and you are part of the family:
a pint of beer for the father,
and you have fun with the daughter.
So, Antonio, my friend
am I right or not?! . . . Eh!. . . .

IV

They say that we are sons of maccheroni!
And they who fill their bellies with coffee?!. . . .
After they eat they're hungrier than before
potatoes, milk, cake and tea.

They stuff themselves with potatoes
and then throw up in your face!. . . .
But they're Americans
and no-one will kick them out!
We're sons of maccheroni?!. . . .
Well, then Americans are
a bunch of sons of . . . potatoes.
It's true, no, Antonio my friend,
am I right! or not? . . . Eh!. . . .

Translated by Pasquale Verdicchio

ᘐ

The Women at Coney Island

I

It's a great pleasure to go to Coney Island,[12]
among so many beautiful and sweet young ladies;
there are things you see there
that make your blood heat up.
All the beautiful girls go there
to go swimming and cool off!. . . .
And round and round it goes
the wheel is fine and sure,
only in Coney Island
can one enjoy nature! . . .

II

American girls courageously dive
(and smile) up to their chest
without thinking of the impertinent fish
who could play some trick on them! . . .
And so many of them have let the fish bite
as they were there swimming! . . .

12. From "Musical Ditties by Maestro Del Colle," *Il Messaggero* (Paterson-Passaic), February 19, 1916.

And turn the wheel,
American women
are not afraid of water
or even sharks!!!

III

After a swim, the Jewish woman
stretches out on the sand all smiles;
her beautiful swimsuit sticking to her body,
showing off her wares to everyone!
Young men stare and walk by
otherwise they'd get arrested!. . . .
And the wheel turns and goes,
the cart wheel,
the Jewish woman holds God's gifts
all on her chest! . . .

IV

Italian women at the seaside
wait for the sun to burn their faces;
they like to have their feet
and arms turn dark;
but never let themselves be stared at
when they go in the water to refresh! . . .
And turn the wheel,
Italian women, in august,
when they go swimming,
they do it on the sly! . . .

   Translated by Pasquale Verdicchio

Nofrio on the Telephone

∾ *Giovanni De Rosalia*

Palermo, Italy, 1864–New York, New York, 1935

Nofrio La Fardazzi, figghiu di don Saullu e niputi di Cuticchiuneddu, the comic masque (in Sicilian dialect) invented by Giovanni De Rosalia on the Italian American vaudeville scene, is the equal of Migliaccio's "Farfariello" for ingeniousness, popularity, and success. Nofrio was the type of newly rich immigrant, proud of achieved prosperity and the many status symbols that surrounded him, and at the same time uncomfortable in his close contact with the objects of that bourgeois respectability because of his bottomless ignorance. A stupid fool, nonetheless, he gave substantial proof that he was not devoid of peasant cunning.

De Rosalia, who in Italy had been part of professional companies like that of Scandurra and in 1890 had published a small volume of *Versi siciliani*, broke onto the New York scene in 1903, shortly after his arrival in America. In 1904 he became a teacher in the New York public schools, and he also gave English lessons to Italians. At the Villa Mascolo Concert Hall of Canal Street, on a tiny stage, and then in various other theaters and small theaters, De Rosalia performed parts in classical and modern drama, from Alferi's *Oreste* to Giacometti's *La morte civile*. From the summer of 1904, he was the proprietor of the Compagnia Comico-Drammatica Giovanni De Rosalia alla Villa Napoli, succeeding Francesco Ricciardi; but a year later the Villa Napoli changed ownership and was converted into a music hall. After various changes of fortune, De Rosalia formed the Nuova Compagnia Filodrammatica De Rosalia–Perez–Picciotto, but even this experience did not last long. And at a certain point, he was faced with the serious problem of changing his style and repertory. Writer Italo Falbo imagined De Rosalia's solution to this dilemma as follows:

> Even I had begun with drama, in fact, with the tragedies: *Otello, Amleto, Saul*. Much applause, little money. And I changed my manner. I became Nofrio, the comical fool, buffissimo Nofrio. And for me the sun broke out.

While Migliaccio already dominated the scene and remained fundamentally a great entertainer, a brilliant author and performer of little scenes, caricatures, and songs, De Rosalia's comic theater was somewhat different. It was oriented toward an extension, in a dramatic sense, of the farcical material, and was therefore not very removed from the orientation of his coeval Nino Martoglio, author of *Aria del continente*.

Nevertheless, De Rosalia also performed the same genres as Migliaccio. A catalog of Italian records for the label Italian Columbia Records of 1930 lists some twenty "little Sicilian songs and comic scenes" performed by him with his company. Actually, Fichera notes that De Rosalia "has cut more than three hundred records with 'little farces,' comical poetical little scenes executed by him together with his wife, and with two other comedians." Even so, the texts published in the late 1910s are distinguished by a knowledgeable theatrical writing. Despite considerable marginal directions for histrionic improvisation, reserved for the head comedian, De Rosalia himself, who "acted in rumpled clothes and with a big artificial nose" (Sogliuzzo, 67), the rest of the texts (as published from the very beginning), appear predisposed toward achieving a rigorous and faithful execution, and of organizing the manuscripts into a repertory.

In the manner of so many other comedians more or less great, whether they be Italians or Italian Americans, even De Rosalia, writes Fichera, wrote a memoir, *Avventure di palcoscenico*, which has not been traced.

However, De Rosalia, like Migliaccio, was also a vernacular poet. Fichera mentions his volume of verse, *Amuri chi chianci*, published in America, of which, however, he found no trace. Leonardo Dia defines De Rosalia as "Granni vati [poet bard]" in his reference to him in a pamphlet celebrating the Sicilian artistic literary Cenacolo Vincenzo De Simone, a sodality of which De Rosalia was an associate founder. Even in poems, however, De Rosalia favored the comic vein, with the same extraordinary effects of linguistic hybridization, which are so typical of his theater. In the novella in octaves, *Litteriu Trantulia ovvero Lu Nobili sfasulatu*, which according to Emelise Aleandri would have appeared in 1903–1904, a bailiff, precisely, Litteriu Trantulia di Calamenza, is possessed by a veritable obsession for blue blood. He affects elegance, speaks (obviously badly) in Italian, and convinced that the heroine Rosina is of noble origins, falls in love with her, defining her as, "custurera" daughter of a "donna baccalara." He directs the following letter to her (in hybrid Italian):

Madamuself, vu sete treggiulì	Madmezel, you are tres jolie
Io pere vu son diventè pazzò;	I for you am going crazy
Pa possible potire piò dormì!	Pas possible for me dormir!
Ce soir a mezzannò io passerò	Ce soir at midnight I will be
De sotto le balcone per sapì	to find out under your balcony
Se vu mi amit o puramente no!	If your amour you will give to me! . . .
Se la votre respò sarà affermè,	If your response will be affermè,
Vi prè, mandatemè lu vo retrè!	S'il yous plait, send me your portrait!

To which Rosina replies, saying "nun so parlari infrancisò" (I do not know how to speak in French); to then cut him short:

E ti respundo, in quanto a lo ritrè,	And I respond about my portrait,
Aio lo càntaro e quillo serve a me!	I have a chamber pot, and I need that!

Of great enjoyment are also the "scherzi poetici" (poetic amusements) *Lu Socialisimu* and *Lu Ciarlatanu.* In the first appear the two personages of "Nnappa Minicu mudestu munnizzaru e Peppi Coppola miseru siminzaru." Peppi asks Nnappa what is socialism, and the other responds, for example:

Dicemu, per esempiu,	Let's say, for example,
Ca semu tutti uguali;	that we're all equal;
Non c'è cchiù riccu e poviru	There's no more rich and poor
Spartennu beni e mali.	If we distribute good and evil.
Ti divi dari un prìncipi	A prince owes you
Mità di la ricchizza	half his riches
E tu ci duni in cambiu	and, in return, you give him
Mità di la munnizza.	half your garbage.

The protagonist of the second scherzo is a charlatan who extols the virtues of his "cirotto enciclopetico," an "encyclopedic Band-Aid." Here, the regional dynamics of the Italian American colony come to the fore, perfectly traced to the traditions of the mother country. The fact that the charlatan expresses himself substantially in Neapolitan is required by his theatrical type.

Illo non vi guarisce solamente	That doesn't just remove
Lo callo che lo piedi v'ha accioncato;	your foot callus;
Exempio: se ci avete mal di dente,	For example: if you have a tooth ache,
Se il dente è rotto a pure è spertosato,	if your tooth is broken or rotten,
Non c'è bisogno mettere l'unguente	you don't need to use the ointment
Che l'àvotre dottori hanno insignato.	That the other doctors prescribe.

This amusing tone does not, however, override the emergence in the piece of a certain typical populism—the Russian socialist movement—of the epoch.

De Rosalia demonstrates a profound understanding of the life that flowed before his eyes on the streets of Little Italy, the same understanding displayed in his theatrical representations. This ethnic culture finds its most fulfilled expression in the small theatrical saga of De Rosalia's Nofrio. In Nofrio, De Rosalia mirrors the entire community, which identifies with him and the events that happen to him: the upsets, the difficulties, but also the many novelties and the small pleasures of an existence that is uprooted, and yet obstinately searching for a new estate, for an identity to superimpose on, if not substitute for, the original one.

The comedy of Nofrio consists exactly in this hiatus, in the excessiveness engendered by the experience of emigration. Almost in every farce, the comical mechanism is actuated by this conflict: the "modernità" not well assimilated in the present condition of the protagonist struggles with the persistent tenacity of the traditional inherited elements from his world of departure.

Nofrio ai bagni (Nofrio at the Seaside) is composed of the customary misunderstandings of comedy, in this piece prompted by the action of Nofrio's beautiful wife Caterina, who has kissed her courtier Ernesto simply to prevent him from committing suicide for love. Interposed are fragments of conversations that mark Nofrio's estrangement in respect to the context—a luxury hotel—of where he is. (The following dialogue gently satirizes Norfrio's ignorance, even of *The Divine Comedy*.) Camillo, the hotelkeeper, opens the dialogue.

CAM.:: . . . L'ha letto mai la *Divina Commedia?* (Have you ever read the *Divine Comedy?*)

NOF.: Nun mi ricordu beni! Catarina, l'haiu liggiutu mai sta Divina Commedia? (I don't remember! Catarina, have I ever read this *Divine Comedy?*)

CAT.: (*seccata*) Non lo so! ([*upset*] I don't know!)

NOF.: (*al locandiere*) Nun mi ricordu beni! Ma ricordu d'aviri liggiutu lu *Mischinu di Custantinòbbuli;* la storia di Fioravanti e Rizzeri; lu libbriceddu di Santa Ginuveffa; lu tuppi tuppi, ma sta storia che diciti vui nun l'haiu liggiutu mai! ([*to the hotelkeeper*] I don't remember! I remember I read the *Mischinu di Custantinòbbuli,* the story of Fioravanti and Rizzeri, the little booklet of Saint Genoveffa, the *tuppi tuppi,* but I've never read this story you're talking about!)

In *Nofrio arriccutu,* the eponymous protagonist, heir of the classic uncle in America, is introduced by Carpanzio to his daughter Elvira, who does not want him, for though rich, he is profoundly ignorant. Nofrio is accompanied by a maestro, Ernesto, who reproaches every foolish thing that comes out of his mouth. At a certain point, what Nofrio tells him is almost an epitome of the somewhat schizophrenic condition reflected in the preceding dialogue.

Ma tu ài ad aviri 'n'anticchia di pacenzia: e t'ài a ricurdari ca iu prima era panillaru ed ora sugnu luminuaru! (You have to be a little patient: and remember that, before, I used to sell *panelle* and now I turn on street lamps.)

In Sicilian dialect, Nofrio uses the word *prima* (first). "*Prima*": This is the key word; better, the suitcase word that contains a whole world.

Finally, besides productions in verse and those for the theater, there exists another notable type: "little scenes," closely connected to the theatrical productions. The scenes were published in the *Follia,* Cordiferro's weekly. For a good period of time, starting from the end of 1910, De Rosalia had a rubric entitled, "Sicilian Scenes," printed on the page that also contained two other columns, among the most appreciated in the newspaper: the *Macchiette Napoletane* of Sandro (Cordiferro), and the *Schizzi Romaneschi* of Poco de Bono (Gino Calza). De Rosalia's work had an impressive discographic release for the Victor Company, with comic scenes, songs, and farces, always with his theatrical Compagnia and sometimes together with Migliaccio.

ESSENTIAL BIBLIOGRAPHY

Aleandri 1983a, 222–235; Falbo 1942 (September 13); Fichera 1958, 15; Sogliuzzo 1973.

ᴄᴡ

CHARACTERS: Cicca, Nofriu, Turi, Annirìa

The stage is divided into two parts, a big bedroom and a small one. A telephone in each bedroom.

Scene I (Turi, alone)

TURI (in the bigger bedroom, facing the other room): Cicca, put some beers in the *àisi bòchisi*.[1]

Scene II (Cicca and Turi)

CICCA (*entering*): I put them there this morning.

TURI: How many bottles?

CICCA: As many as I could fit!

TURI: My cousin Cola is coming tonight, so put in some strong set-up too; you know that he doesn't drink beer.

CICCA: Good for him. I don't understand how one can like beer. It's like drinking straw water!

TURI: That's the problem: you think beer is straw water and you take it out on Italian wine!

CICCA: Wine is better than beer. As the old saying goes, "water is bad for you, and wine makes you sing!"

TURI: Yeah, and while singing, you down a barrel in two days! But you're purebred: your father, God rest his soul, died because of his drinking!

CICCA: Yeah, right! He died because of his drinking! My father died from a disease in his throat.

TURI: Sure, because your father was full of wine up to here (*he points at his throat*). Enough with your father already. Let's talk about my *cumpari* Nofriu who got a telephone installed in his home.

CICCA: Really? What does he need that for? Who is he going to call, his sister?

TURI: What do I know! He's like a kid: when he sees someone doing something, he has to do it too. The funny thing is that he thinks that I don't know that he got a telephone and says he's going to give me a prank call.

1. Icebox.

CICCA: So don't tell him that you know! Just go along with it.

TURI: *Sciua.*[2] I won't tell him anything. But it's gonna be fun when he calls me, because he doesn't even know how to make a call. A couple of weeks ago he called the market and fought with the operator. You know why? Because he doesn't know that to call someone, you have to give his number to the operator. Plus, when he speaks American it sounds Chinese.

CICCA: Yeah, that's true! How is it possible that he's been living here for so many years and he still can't speak American?

TURI: Go figure!

CICCA: While you and I, eh, Turi, no more than six months after we arrived here, we started speaking American. And now, when we speak, people think we're Americans!

TURI: *Sciua! You tocchi veri nàisi!*[3]

CICCA: *Ma you tocchi cchiù nàisi!*[4]

TURI: *When you tocchi, mi stenni.*[5]

CICCA: *Orràitti!*[6]

TURI: *Azzòl!* (*someone knocks at the door*) *Cominni!*[7]

Scene III (Nofriu, Annirìa, and said characters)

NOFRIU (*entering*): Can I say hi to my *cumpari* and *cummari*?

TURI: *Cumpari* Nofriu, is that you?

NOFRIU: Yeah, that's me!

CICCA: Oh my God! We were just talking about you!

NOFRIU: What about?

CICCA: Oh God! I forgot! Turi, you tell him!

TURI (*a little embarrassed*): I forgot it too.

NOFRIU: What a good memory you both have! *Cumpari, cummari,* excuse me for taking the liberty of bringing this friend of mine here, but I wanted you to meet him.

TURI: It's our pleasure!

CICCA: Absolutely!

2. Sure.
3. Sure! You talk very nice!
4. You talk more nice!
5. When you talk, me understand.
6. All right!
7. That's all! Come in!

NOFRIU: Annirìa, sit down; *cummari, cumpari,* we don't have to stand! Let's have a seat! (*they sit down*) Anniria, my *cumpari* is a real friend. He's been in America for a long time and he knows how to mind his own business.

ANNIRÌA: How long have you been here?

TURI: *It is ebbàuttu fortinni iersi.*[8]

ANNIRÌA: What's he saying?

TURI: *It is ebbàuttu fortinni iersi.*

NOFRIU: *Cumpari,* you can speak American as much as you want, but he doesn't understand you! He's a *grin orni.*[9]

TURI: Oh! You just arrived from Italy?

ANNIRÌA: Yes sir. I got here three days ago.

TURI: How was your trip?

ANNIRÌA: Bad, very bad! We all nearly drowned.

NOFRIU: *Cumpari,* these seas are always rough; that's why they're always moving.

TURI: Why?

NOFRIU: Because the world is round, and as you get closer to here, the sea leans on one side.

TURI: Yeah, that's how it must be! (*To Annirìa*) And how long did the trip take?

ANNIRÌA: Twelve days.

NOFRIU (*in a low voice*): Cippi, cumpari, veri cippi.[10]

TURI: *Sciua*!

ANNIRÌA: When we got to the *gulfu strimpa,*[11] the sea was really rough. It was night. The captain, realizing it was getting too dangerous, sent a message through the cordless phone and an hour later we saw a light.

TURI: What was this light?

NOFRIU: It must have been a lighthouse beacon.

ANNIRÌA: No! It was the light of a steamboat that came to help us. But by the time the steamboat arrived, the sea had calmed down, so it turned around and left.

NOFRIU: *Cumpari* Turi, I have not quite understood yet how this cordless phone works that lets you talk from one end of the sea to the other, even at night!

8. It is about fourteen years.
9. Greenhorn.
10. Cheap, cumpari, very cheap.
11. Gulf stream.

If it were during the day, I would let it go, but not at night! What do you say?

TURI: *Cumpari* Nofriu, I say that there must be a cord!

NOFRIU: Absolutely! Otherwise how could the word walk? Does the word know the way? Annirìa, you really went too far this time!

ANNIRÌA: On board I heard it was cordless.

NOFRIU: They told you that it was cordless not to scare you, but there must be a cord! You need a cord just like you need bread.

TURI: *Cumpari*, let's forget about the cord and talk about something else. Would you like a glass of wine?

NOFRIU: No, *cumpari*. You know that I never drink on an empty stomach; plus, it's been three days that as soon as I drink some wine, I feel a sharp pain in my throat.

TURI: This is exactly the disease my father-in-law, God rest his soul, had!

NOFRIU: What disease?

TURI: When wine got to his throat, he died.

NOFRIU: *Cumpari*, are you jinxing me?!

CICCA: Don't listen to him, *cumpari*; you know he's always goofing around!

NOFRIU: I know, I know, I'm joking too! (*looking at the telephone*) *Cumpari*, that's beautiful! (*to Annirìa*) Annirìa, did you see what my *cumpari* has?

ANNIRÌA: What does he have?

NOFRIU: A telephone! With this thing here you can talk to whomever you want! Annirìa, you wanna see how it works? See this eardrum? You put this into your ear and then you speak. The word gets into this little funnel, it grabs the cord, it starts walking slowly, and finally it arrives into the eardrum of the person who's on the other end.

ANNIRÌA: And how long does it take to get there?

NOFRIU: It depends on the distance! It takes some time for the word to walk all along the cord. One speaks from here, someone else hears from there, and the conversation just goes.

ANNIRÌA (*in a low voice to Nofriu*): Let me ask you something: isn't this machine like the one you have at your house?

NOFRIU (*interrupting him, in a low voice*): Keep quiet, because my *cumpari* doesn't know that. (*To Turi*) *Cumpari*, it's a great convenience and I want to get one installed! As soon as I get one, we're gonna have so much fun calling each other all the time!

TURI: Whenever you want!

NOFRIU: *Cumpari*, my friend would like to see how it works. Do you wanna show him?

TURI: (*walking towards the telephone, which is located on the actor's right*) Of course. I want to call my cousin Cola. (*he calls*) *Spring tri, tu, fo, nàinni! Aló!*[12] Cola, is that you? It's me, Turi. Tell me, what time are you coming tonight? At eight? *Orràitti!* Wait, my *cumpari* Nofriu is here and wants to talk to you. *Cumpari*, help yourself!

NOFRIU (*on the telephone*): Cola, how are you? Good? It's me calling! Can you hear me? Can you hear me well? Can you tell it's me calling? Am I good at it? Be honest! Cola, wait, let me introduce you to a friend of mine. Shake hands!

TURI: *Cumpari* Nofriu, you think they can shake hands?

NOFRIU: Oh, yeah, that's right! *Cubbai*,[13] Cola. See you later tonight (*he lets go of the phone*) I swear on my grandma's soul it feels like you can actually see the person. Anyway, *cumpari*, we gotta go now.

TURI: What? Your friend is leaving without drinking some strong set-up? (*to Annirìa*) Would you like a glass of strong set-up?

ANNIRÌA: What is this strong set-up?

NOFRIU: Never mind, *cumpari*, don't worry; we're going to eat soon, and it's not a good time for strong set-ups. I'll see you tonight and we'll all set ourselves up with some wine. *Cubbai; cubbai, cummari.*

CICCA: *Cubbai!*

TURI: *Cubbai!*

ANNIRÌA: I kiss your hands.

TURI: *Cubbai!*

ANNIRÌA: *Cubbàita!*[14]

TURI: What an ass my *cumpari* Nofriu is! He wanted them to shake hands on the telephone!

CICCA: Oh God! I was about to burst out laughing! What a stupid *cumpari* you have! Where did you find him, in the garbage?

TURI: Really! It's a good thing the son we asked him to baptize died!

CICCA: Not only he's an ass, but he's also cheap! He asked you to make that call but he didn't give you the five cents! And you didn't even ask him!

TURI: Well, it's just five cents!

CICCA: Turi, come here. Come help me take the pot off the stove. (*They leave*)

---

12. Spring three, two, four, nine! Hello!
13. Good-bye.
14. A pun on the words *cubbàita*, a Sicilian nougat, and good-bye.

Scene IV (Nofrio and Annirìa)

NOFRIU (*entering from the other side of the stage*): Come in, come in, Annirìa. My *cumpari* Turi doesn't expect me to call him now! It'll blow his mind when he finds out that I have a telephone! You gotta know that my *cumpari* Turi is a little jealous. He wants to be the only one to have a telephone in the house. Enough, I'm gonna call him now. (*he reaches the phone*) *Alò tu, tri, fo, faivvi, sìchisi, sèven! Alò! Plisi, col mai cumpari, ondred ad fiffittinni stritti, 'ncostu lu cascavaddaru. Ah? Alò! Plisi, col mai cumpari Turi; ondred e fiffittinni stritti, bituinni cascavaddaru e chiancheri. Ah? Se, uazzimara? No stenni mi? Ai vanti tocchi cu' mai cumpari Turi! Alò! Alò! Alò!*[15] What happened? I swear on my honor, if I catch him I'll pull his eyes out!

ANNIRÌA: Who are you talking about?

NOFRIU: The guy of the telephone: he thinks he's funny! *Se, mister central, you want col my cumpari?*[16]

Scene V (Turi and Cicca)

TURI: (*entering from the opposite side*) Cicca, do you think my *cumpari* is home yet?

CICCA: *Sciua!* There are only two blocks between here and his house.

TURI: Well then I'm gonna call him. He certainly doesn't expect me to.

CICCA: Yeah, go ahead. Let's see how he reacts.

NOFRIU: *Se, missare e schifiusu, plisi col mai cumpari Turi.*[17] (*pause*)

TURI (*on the phone*): Harlem, fo, nain, tri, seven, tu, fàivvi.[18] (*small pause*) Yessa! (*the phone rings on Nofriu's side*)

NOFRIU: See? As soon as I called him fussy, he got upset and now he's ringing the bell to call the ambulance. I swear on my honor, if he says anything, it'll get ugly. (*pause*)

TURI: *Alò!*

NOFRIU: Hello and you're a skunk!

TURI: Ah! (*pause*) Who are you talking to?

---

15. [Hello, two, three, four, five, six, seven! Hello! Please, call my *cumpari*, hundred and fifteen street, near the grocer. Ah? Hello! Please, call my *cumpari* Turi. Hundred and fifteen street, between the grocer and the butcher. Ah? Say, what's the matter? No understand me? I want to talk to my *cumpari* Turi! Hello! Hello! Hello!

16. Say, mister operator, you want to call my *cumpari*?

17. Say, Mister fussy, please call my cumpari Turi.

18. Harlem, four, nine, three, seven, two, five.

NOFRIU: I'm talking to you, big second-hand jackal! You're lucky I'm not there, because I would have hit you a thousand times already!

TURI: You would have hit me?

NOFRIU: Yes, you! (*to Annirìa*) The phone system is getting upset!

TURI: And you're saying all these bad words to me?

NOFRIU: Yessir, to you!

CICCA: What is he saying to you?

TURI: He's offending me.

CICCA: Well then you offend him.

NOFRIU: My friend suddenly got quiet! Are you done talking, you skunk?

TURI: Are you calling me a skunk? (*to Cicca*) Did you hear he just called me a skunk?

CICCA: Call him a thief!

TURI: If you call me a skunk, it is my honor to call you a thief! You think I don't know that back in your hometown you stole the merchant's son's gold watch and then sold it in America?

NOFRIU: How is it possible that the phone system knows what I did? That's impossible! Who are you?

TURI: It's me, Turi Iannimoddi, and next time I see you, I'm gonna slap you silly!

NOFRIU: You've got some guts to call me a thief when you're a first-class rascal! Wasn't it you who broke into the jewelry store so that you could fix a few things in the house?

CICCA: (*taking the phone from Turi's hands*) Wait, let me talk to this sleazeball. (*on the phone*) Hey, you, who do you think you're talking to, your wife?

NOFRIU: Oh, my *cumpari* the buffoon sent you to talk to me? Go knit a sock and let the men talk!

CICCA: You call yourself a man? Go throw yourself into the sea!

NOFRIU: If you don't stop now I'll say the rosary to you too!

CICCA: What can you say to me? Who do you think I am, your wife?

NOFRIU: Remember when you were with the sexton?

CICCA: Who? Me? With the sexton?

TURI: (*surprised*) What sexton?

CICCA: Who knows what he's talking about, this slanderer.

TURI: (*snatching the phone from Cicca's hands*) Give it to me! (*on the phone*) Look, I seriously don't know how you can talk like that about my wife when your wife fools around with all the shoe-shiners!

NOFRIU: This is not of your business!

TURI: You're right, it's not, but if you say that my wife was fooling around with the sexton . . .

NOFRIU: Well, why did you call me a thief?

TURI: You were the first to insult: you called me a skunk.

NOFRIU: But I wasn't talking to you! I thought I was talking to the phone system!

TURI: But I thought you were insulting me!

NOFRIU: No way! Why would I do that? You know I've always respected you.

TURI: And I've always respected you! Well, then, I apologize!

NOFRIU: Don't worry! No big deal! Let me talk to my *cummari* so that I can apologize to her.

TURI: Cicca, he wants to talk to you.

CICCA: What do you want?

NOFRIU: *Cummari*, I apologize for calling you names.

CICCA: *Dazzorràitti!*[19] Say hi to my cummari! (*she gives the phone back to Turi*)

NOFRIU: I certainly will!

TURI: *Cumpari* Nofriu, will I see you tonight?

NOFRIU: *Sciua! Cubbai!*

TURI: *Cubbai!* (*he hangs up the phone*)

NOFRIU: (*hanging up the phone*) Annirìa, you see how convenient the telephone is?

ANNIRÌA: Yes, I see that!

Translated by Chiara Mazzuchelli

19. That's all right.

Child Abductors, or, The Black Hand

Armando Cennerazzo

Tufo (Avellino), Italy, January 3, 1889—New York, New York, 1962

Armando Cennerazzo, an actor and author of theater, poetry, songs, and Neapolitan caricatures, arrived in America at twelve years old. Self-taught, he collaborated with Francesco Ricciardi, performing duets and Neapolitan songs. Ario Flamma maintains that he performed with Maldacea and Mimì Aguglia. Franco Scozio remembers one of Cennerazzo's cinematic experiences, in which he performed with Marion Davies. They were engaged by the Vitagraph Company, with studios in Fort Lee. Already celebrated, Scozio adds that Cennerazzo entered theater later in his life. Aleandri relates that he worked at the Coccè Press, the printing house founded in 1922, by Adamo and Attilio Coccè, launchers of the second printing house of the *Progresso Italo-Americano* (Flamma 1936). According to Scozio, in the last period of his life, Cennerazzo (whose name, as published, appeared sometimes in this form, other times with only one *n*) would return to Naples every year toward the end of spring, and as often, repair to his hometown in Irpinia. In Naples, in 1949, he published his Neapolitan poems, with the indication, "Volume primo"; actually, another volume of poems, edited by Alfredo Guida, would be issued later, with the title, *Rose rosse e rose gialle* (Red Roses and Yellow Roses). After the war, his compositions appeared in the pages of the *Follia*.

His poetry—whose quality is not at all to be scorned—usefully indicates the environment he frequented. There are some poems of "famigliari" (familiar figures), dedicated to his wife Rosarie, and then to Mimì Aguglia; to Enrico Caruso; to Riccardo Cordiferro, upon whose death he wrote the sonnet "Suldato 'e ll'ideale" (Soldier of the Ideal); and many other poets of Naples, some of whom were certainly his friends, like Pasquale Ruocco, who signed the preface to the volume of 1949; Libero Bovio; Ernesto Murolo; Eduardo Nicolardi; and Ferdinando Russo. Cennerazzo was head comedian of a company of modest fortune, active in New York and on the East Coast until the 1910s. In a sonnet of the collection of 1949, "Vi' che triato!" (87), there is an amusing reflection on the theatricality of life itself, which concludes this way:

> Ma che schifezza è vita! Vi' che 'nguacchio!
> Fernuta 'a parte mia, cu'tutt'o core,
> voglio murì allazzanno 'nu pernacchio!

> Life is loathesome, it's a mess
> As for me, I'm done, with all my heart.
> I want to die raising a plume.

Of great importance for the study of theatrical activity among the Italians of America is the Raccolta Cennerazzo of the Biblioteca Lucchesi Palli, an independent section of the Biblioteca Nazionale Vittorio Emanuele II of Naples. It contains a very rich collection of manuscripts and published works, among which abound copies with many stage directions, cuts, and reductions. This collection is the richest of its kind in Italy; not even in America is it possible to consult an equally outstanding totality. The Raccolta Cennerazzo contains, for example, the texts of the works—like those of Francesco Ricciardi—normally only cited as titles in announcements in newspapers and such.

A cursory examination of the material reveals that Armando Cennerazzo's company functioned in a rather ample and decisively varied repertory, moving from Punchinello farces to social and historical dramas, with significant ventures into a cultivated theatre extraneous to the colonial environment. Nonetheless, the company favored texts having a major impact on the current scene, texts relative to things, problems, and sentiments typical of the Italian American world of which Cennerazzo—a resident of the Bronx, at least in the last years—was an attentive and sensitive interpreter. Emblematic of this dynamic adherence to the facts of the colonial chronicle is the text (one act only) chosen for the present anthology: the unpublished, *Rapitori di Fanciulli; ovvero, La Mano Nera* (Kidnapper of Children; or, The Black Hand), written with Guglielmo Vitrone and dated 1912, and ascribable therefore to the first phase (the more socially involved) of Cennerazzo's activity.

Beside his poetry, a few of Cennarazzo's edited works, published in Italy, exist: from 1914, *Odio e vendetta; scene napoletane* (Hatred and Revenge: Neapolitan

Scenes), in one act; from 1924, the dramatic Sicilian monologue, 'A cerenara (The Charwoman); from 1931, the musical drama in three acts and one intermezzo, *Senza mamma* (Without Mamma), written with the maestro F. Nino Pen (Francesco Pennino), maternal grandfather of Francis Ford Coppola; still from the 1930s, *I figli abbandonati* (The Abandoned Children); the radio reductions of *Fiori d'arancio* (Orange Blossoms) and *Tobia il gobbetto* (Tobias the Hunchback) by Francesco Mastriani. Decisively richer is the body of manuscript works, in which figure various reductions of the comedies of Scarpetta and the dramas of Ario Flamma; A. Rosi; Washington Borg; John Sterling; Giacometti; and Wolf-Ferrari. Other reductions are of novels and novellas of Mastriani; of single original comic acts; *Una Camera fittata a due* (A Room for Two); *La mamma si marita* (Mamma Gets Married); *Il ladro e il poliziotto* (The Thief and the Cop); or of the social dramas: *I delitti dell' alcoolismo* (The Crimes of Alcoholism); *Aneme e fango* (Soul and Mud); *Il destino! ovvero, Tenebre e luce* (Destiny! Or, Darkness and Light); and of dramaturgical works that develop the theme of Cennerazzo's single songs, like "Angela Mia!" (My Angel) and "Pusteggiature" (The Parking Attendant), or of other authors, such as Libero Bovio's "Brinneso" (The Toast).

ESSENTIAL BIBLIOGRAPHY

Abbamonte 1940c; Aleandri 1983a, 188; Flamma 1936; Scozio 1971, 42–44.

∾

CHARACTERS

> Luigi, kidnapper
> Marco, kidnapper
> Pasquale, kidnapper
> Annie Del Gaudio, 10 year old kidnapped girl
> Uncle Carlo Moretti, leader of the gang
> Carmela, Carlo Moretti's sister

(A half lit room in a basement. A few barely usable chairs. A small coarse wooden table lit by an oil lamp. Sheets of white stationery, some envelopes, an inkwell, a pen. Two daggers driven into opposite angles of the table. Upstage, to the right of the audience, a pallet of straw on the ground; on the walls, some pictures of the Madonna and the Saints. Door on the left. Upstage in the middle, a hallway with a stairway that leads to the street.)

Scene I

Luigi, seated at the table, is intent on writing. Marco, standing, rudely smoking a pipe, watches him. Voices offstage of Pasquale and Annie.

ANNIE (*groaning from the blows*): No . . . No . . . please, you're killing me!. . . .

PASQUALE (*cynical, alternating words and blows*): Shut up, damn you to hell! . . . or I'll rip your tongue out, I'll rip it out!. . . .

MARCO (*going toward the door*): Hey! When are you going to stop, in there! . . . Hey! . . . I'm telling you, Pasquale, leave her alone to scream herself hoarse and you come out here with us. . . .

ANNIE (*during the above before Marco has finished*): Did I ever do anything bad to you, anything bad at all?! . . .

PASQUALE (*during the above*): To me? . . . Nothing . . . And it's not me doing this to you. It's that lousy miser of your father, who cares so little about you! (*A slap is heard*) He should send us the money, he should send it! (*a choking moan from Annie. Silence follows. Luigi tears up a letter and begins to write another; Marco approaches him.*)

LUIGI: Son of a bitch! That screaming is giving me a splitting headache.

MARCO: And what do you want to do? . . . If you cut her throat we lose the ransom money her father has to send us for her.

LUIGI (*still writing*): But what if the money doesn't come?!

MARCO (*getting worked up*): If it doesn't come! . . . That's bullshit, like Pasquale says! . . . The money will come, it will come, I'm telling you! . . .

LUIGI (*during the above*): In the meantime, this morning's *Telegraph*. . . .

MARCO (*quickly*): What does the *Telegraph* say, huh! . . .

LUIGI (*during the above*): It says the police have learned, what do I know . . . they are finding out . . . in other words, they probably already know. . . .

MARCO (*interrupting him*): What?!. . . .

LUIGI (*he pulls out the Telegraph from his pocket and hands it to him*): Here! Read it yourself.

MARCO (*taking hold of the newspaper, he scans it rapidly with his eyes, then he calls out in the direction of the door*): Come here a minute, Pasquale; this concerns you too.

PASQUALE (*appearing*): What is it?! . . . ?. . . .

MARCO (*sitting down*): Listen to what this morning's *Telegraph* says.

PASQUALE (*coming closer*): So what can it say?! . . . It's bullshit. . . .

LUIGI (*sealing the letter*): No, no, it doesn't sound like bullshit this time.

PASQUALE: Then let him read it.

MARCO (*he puts his pipe down on the table and begins to read out loud*): "THE 10-YEAR-OLD GIRL, ANNIE DEL GAUDIO, STILL NOT FOUND!—VICTIM OF THE BLACK HAND?. . . . The police are certain that the disappearance of the girl, Annie Del Gaudio, the daughter of a wealthy importer from Brooklyn, happened around six months ago or so, under very mysterious circumstances, as our readers will remember; it may be attributed to the usual, unpunished audacity of that corrupt gang of criminals, known by the name of The Black Hand. In fact, despite the reticence of Mr. Del Gaudio, the diligent investigation by several policemen of the Italian Squad has uncovered the terrible truth, and it became known that the aforementioned young girl disappeared from her house, after which her father received three ransom letters; the demands did not bring about the desired effect. In spite of this, Mr. Del Gaudio has remained shrouded in an impenetrable silence ever since, for fear that something worse might happen. (*At this point Annie appears at the door, and unnoticed, stays to listen, watching every move of her captors.*) But the police, even without the aid of the individual most involved, are already following a hot trail and will soon catch the gang that holds the poor girl, and who are tarnishing the most respected reputation of the Italians in America. God does not want these murderous scoundrels, who may be disappointed in their demand for the money, to spill the blood of the delicate Annie."

ANNIE (*frightened by these last words, she runs toward the hall, screaming a long, agonizing, terrified shriek*): Ah! Mother of God. . . .

PASQUALE (*with a leap he grabs her, and covers her mouth with his hand. A moment of fearful silence. No one moves*)

LUIGI (*he whispers, gesturing to the others to be quiet*): We have to tie her up. . . .

PASQUALE (*cruelly, to the girl, without letting her go or move*): I'll choke you!. . . . (*A stifled groan and fitful movement from Annie*)

MARCO (*he goes over to the door. After looking through the keyhole and listening with his ear to the door*): No one! (*Reassured*) That's something!. . . .

PASQUALE: (*during the above*) Should I strangle her?. . . . (*he gestures*)

LUIGI: No. . . . (*he holds him back with a gesture*) We are waiting for Uncle Carlo! . . . Bring her back inside!

PASQUALE (*during the above*): Yeah, but if I stay alone with her, I swear I'll kill her!. . . .

MARCO: So then you did intend to do what the *Telegraph* says?

LUIGI: I intended to, but it doesn't seem possible to me how the police could have received information about our plans. What do you think, Pasquale?

PASQUALE: It's bullshit; I don't believe it . . . They're doing it to scare us, but they're making a big mistake if that's what they think. . . .

LUIGI: What do you know? Police spies are everywhere, my dear friend, all it takes is one slip of the tongue. . . .

PASQUALE: But they can't always rescue people . . . spies know their limits . . . and if I happened to come face-to-face with one of them . . . I would kiss his filthy heart with the tip of my dagger.

MARCO: He's right. . . .

LUIGI: I can't figure out why Uncle Carlo is late.

MARCO: His daughter is sick and it looks like it will be difficult to save her life—she has a case of meningitis. . . .

PASQUALE: Ah!! . . . And what does Uncle Carlo say?. . . .

MARCO: Suppose it was your only daughter. This morning when he looked into her face, she looked like a corpse, poor Uncle Carlo.

LUIGI: But I can't believe that he would forget about our business arrangements.

PASQUALE: What does it mean? . . . He should have been back by this time.

MARCO: What time is it?. . . .

PASQUALE (*taking out his watch*): It's 10 o'clock.

MARCO: He's late!. . . .

PASQUALE: Did you finish the letter? (*To Luigi*)

LUIGI: Yes. . . .

PASQUALE: And did you put everything in it?. . . .

LUIGI: Everything. The skull and cross bones, the dagger, the. . . .

PASQUALE: I'm not talking about that, that's bullshit; they know the deal well enough; it's time for action, friends; you don't just paint daggers, you have to use them . . . What I'm asking is did you put in everything we demanded.

LUIGI: At least I think so, listen: (*he takes out the letter and reads*) Dear Mr. Del Gaudio, this is the third or fourth time that we have made you aware of our demands, and if by Sunday, at 11 p.m., on top of the new Brooklyn Bridge, you don't hand over $1000 to a woman who says "Greetings" to you: on Monday morning you'll find your daughter slaughtered, right in front of your store. (*three knocks are heard at the door. Luigi hastily hides the letter*)

MARCO: Three knocks . . . it's Uncle Carlo.

PASQUALE: Go open it (*Marco carries out the order*), let's hear what he has to say. . . .

Scene II

Characters already noted and Uncle Carlo

CARLO (*coming forward, and without looking at anyone, dryly*): Good evening.

PASQUALE, LUIGI, MARCO (*all on their feet*): Let's kiss his hands.

CARLO (*during the above*): Did you make sure it's closed?

MARCO: Don't worry. (*Carlo gets out of his overcoat, and keeps his hat on his head*)

LUIGI: Don't you want to sit down? (*he brings a chair forward*)

CARLO (*he sits; leans an elbow on the table, and his head in the palm of his hand. He is gloomy*)

LUIGI: And so can you tell us, aah, how your daughter is doing?. . . .

CARLO: She's always doing poorly. . . .

MARCO, PASQUALE, LUIGI: Oh!!!

CARLO: And she's getting worse! (*with a sorrowful sigh*)

LUIGI: Don't talk like that, Uncle Carlo! It's her suffering that does this to you.

CARLO (*angrily*): The suffering is mine, because I see her dying day by day . . . I am just about hopeless . . . (*pause*) My only daughter, my only girl, and God is taking her from me. Ah! God damn it . . . (*he wants to curse but he holds back*) I have to put my mind at rest, I'm not going to worry about it anymore . . . I'm not going to think about it anymore . . . he wants her, let him take her, there's nothing I can do about it. Carlo Moretti should not have children, he doesn't have the right because he kidnaps other people's children.

MARCO: Has the doctor seen her?

CARLO (*during the above*): A doctor? . . . 10 doctors have seen her, they've seen her all right! But they're all a pack of thieves . . . worse than . . . (*biting his hand, he holds back the words*) They're bandits! And then they say that we break the law. . . .

PASQUALE: When a doctor robs you, or kills you, no one says anything, because he has a piece of paper from the University! For us it's different.

CARLO: This morning my wife wanted to call in an American specialist. (*Railing*) He is more disreputable than the others. . . .

MARCO: And what did he say?. . . .

CARLO: He robbed me of $25, to tell me what all the others have already told me . . . The thief . . . and he even wanted to rob me of more . . . he told me we needed the opinion of other doctors.

PASQUALE: Of course, it needs to be done.

CARLO: The truth is, my daughter is dying.

MARCO: And did you call for a consultation?

CARLO: Ah, no! For God's sake, they won't rob me again. Tomorrow I'll send her to the hospital . . . It will cost me a lot less than if I tried to cure her at home.

LUIGI: You're better off this way, Uncle Carlo!

(*Carlo covers his eyes with his hand. A short silence. The others don't know whether or not to disturb him, and they gesture to one another for someone to speak*)

MARCO (*making up his mind*): Uncle Carlo. . . .

CARLO (*rousing himself*): Huh. . . .

MARCO (*not knowing what to say*): Have you read this morning's *Telegraph*? . . .

CARLO (*immediately attentive to the new thoughts*): Yes exactly. (*listlessly*) But they're lies!. . . .

PASQUALE: It's bullshit; I said so; isn't it true, Uncle Carlo? You said so too.

CARLO: Yes, it's bullshit, that's true; but it's always good to keep your guard up. Before, they didn't know the girl had been kidnapped for ransom, and the police investigation had no specific direction. But now they have discovered our letters. . . .

LUIGI: We have to move to some other location. . . .

CARLO: I'll take care of that right away. But how are we going to take the girl with us?

PASQUALE: Do you think it's dangerous to stay here?. . . .

CARLO: I think so. I also suspect someone was following me.

PASQUALE: If that's the case, as you said, the girl . . . (*he mimes slitting her throat*) Like that! . . . And we'll leave her where they can find her.

CARLO (*after listening attentively*): And . . . the father hasn't been told that she is still alive?. . . .

LUIGI: No. . . .

CARLO (*as if demanding*): And. . . .

LUIGI (*interrupting*): Yes sir, just like you ordered, here is the letter. (*he hands it to him*)

CARLO (*taking it*): That's good; I'll take care of it. (*he puts it in his pocket*) And the girl?

MARCO: She's still in there. She screams, every once in a while. . . .

PASQUALE: She was driving me crazy, before you came. But (*he hints at the punches that he gave her*) and I wanted to rip her heart out!

CARLO (*rising*): Don't worry . . . by the day after tomorrow either we get the father's money by nightfall or. . . .

PASQUALE (*surmising*): Or we spill the daughter's blood, you got that right, Uncle Carlo, that's the way it has to be. We have to make an example. And Mr. Del Gaudio, isn't he the crook who got rich selling dirty water as Sicilian wine and cotton oil as olive oil? He's more of a criminal than we are.

(*Five separate knocks on the hall door. Immediate silence. Uncle Carlo and the others arm themselves, some with knives, the others with revolvers, and they watch the door*)

CARLO (*relieved, putting his gun away, and returning to his seat*): Five knocks; my sister's signal. You can open it.

Scene III

Characters already noted, Carmela, then Annie

(*Carmela enters worried and upset, covered with a shawl up to her nose and, unveiling herself, she bursts out into choking sobs*)

CARLO (*alarmed, running to her and pushing away the others who have surrounded the woman*): Carmela, what is it? (*he screams*) Why don't you talk?!

CARMELA (*breathless, she can only stretch out her hands*)

PASQUALE, MARCO, LUIGI: Let her talk!! What's happened?!

CARMELA (*sobbing*): Nica. . . .

CARLO (*understanding, with a savage shriek, raising threatening fists at his sister*): No! . . . Watch out . . . I'll cut your throat! . . .

CARMELA (*she nods yes with her head, then drops into a chair, giving in to her anguish with bitter weeping*)

CARLO (*imploring*): She's dead!! (*defeated, he falls into a chair*)

(*A sorrowful silence. The others, stunned, somewhat touched, watch the scene; Annie reappears at the door, seizes the moment to attempt an escape and starts for the hall, moving sideways with small steps*)

PASQUALE (*turning around suddenly, with a leap like before, he grabs her, chokes her throat and covers her mouth with his hand, until he forces her to her knees*): You're trying it again, huh! But this time it's over for you, and that coward of your father, I'll strangle you this time.

CARLO (*watching them with a cruel sneer, hissing through clenched teeth*): Yes . . . (*he takes out a knife*) Yes . . . (*getting up to seize the girl with his arm*) She's mine. (*He takes her from the hands of Pasquale and raises the weapon in his trembling fist*) May your father also feel the pain of losing a daughter.

ANNIE (*imploring him with a terrifying scream, as she falls to her feet and stares him in the face with panic in her eyes*): No, on the soul of your daughter.

CARLO (*he drops the knife and steps back as if he were hit squarely in the chest, he moans through his choked up voice*): My daughter!! . . . (*holding his heart and continuing to back up, he looks at Annie*) My daughter. (*to the others and always with a hoarse voice*) Do you hear her? On the soul of my daughter who is dead.

(*Carmela wails even more loudly*)

MARCO AND LUIGI: Poor Uncle Carlo!! What suffering! . . .

(*Pasquale has not moved more than an arm's-length away from the girl so he can get back to grab her*)

CARLO (*he sees him and goes after him, he forcibly seizes his hand, dragging him away*): No. (*dryly*) I don't want to anymore. (*emotionally and with a tearful voice*) On the soul of my daughter (*with a sob*), of my daughter who is dead!

(*Annie unsure and not understanding, watches him*)
(*Luigi, Marco, Pasquale look at each other inquisitively*)

CARLO (*to Annie*): Get away from here . . . And . . . (*Annie bolts for the door, but Carlo pursues her and holds her by the arm*) Pray for the soul of my daughter.

PASQUALE: Uncle Carlo, for the love of God.

LUIGI: Pay attention to what you're doing.

MARCO: Close the door.

CARLO (*he pushes the girl out and authoritatively plants himself in front of the door to block the entrance*): This is the way I want it; everyone shut up! (*pause*) If they had murdered a daughter of yours, ah!

PASQUALE: Uncle Carlo!

CARLO: I'm not listening to you, you can leave here. (*he gets out of the way of the door and points to the exit*) It's dangerous to stay here now. *His hesitant partners don't move; Carlo orders them with a threatening voice*) I said: get out of here! . . . Doesn't anyone understand me?

PASQUALE: Uncle Carlo!

CARLO (*planting himself in front of him and staring him right in the eye*): What? Aaaah!

PASQUALE (*he nods his head and sets out towards the hall; the others follow him except for Carmela*)

Scene IV

Carlo and Carmela

CARLO (*moved and suddenly humble*): Carmela. . . .

CARMELA (*in a weak voice, choking with emotion*): Carlo. . . .

CARLO (*bending to embrace her*): She had a father too! I did it because of my suffering . . . for the soul of my daughter I did it, so it will now show God that I did a good deed!! . . . And I will never steal other people's children again . . . No!! I know how a father suffers, Carmela . . . I know how a father suffers (*he draws her to him, bursting into bitter tears*).

Translated by Emelise Aleandri

Two Poems

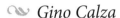 *Gino Calza*

Born Rome, December 14, 1883

For the Italian American colony of New York, the fresh Roman vein of Gino Calza, author of witty sonnets in dialect, was a meteor that expressed itself for a few years in the *Follia di New York*. He was an esteemed columnist whose signature was "Poco de Bono," writing the *Schizzi romaneschi* (Roman Sketches), which, together with the *Macchiette napoletane (Neapolitan Portraits)* of Sandro (Riccardo Cordiferro) and the *Scene siciliane* (Sicilian Scenes) of Giovanni De Rosalia, constituted one of the most popular parts of the newspaper. Besides his rubric, Calza also presented poems to the reader, which he signed with his true name. One of his collections of sonnets, *Su la vena* (In the Vein), was published in New York in 1908 with a preface by Alberto Tarchiani. He, Tarchiani, and Fausto Maria Martini (later author of the novel *Si sbarca a New York* [Arrival at New York]) arrived in the American metropolis together, shortly after the premature disappearance of his friend and companion Sergio Corazzini, to whom he dedicated the poem, "Vita tua è vita mia" (Your Life is My Life), which contains the following verses: "Tu m'ai detto:—Ov'io mi reco / Voglio che tu venga meco" (You told me: Wherever I go / I want you to come with me). Curiously, the name of Calza does not figure in any of the collections of Italian American poetry. In 1912, after he returned to Italy, he published his Roman Sonnets, in the collection, *Dal marciapiede alla soffitta* (From the Sidewalk to the Roof); another collection, *Sonetti romaneschi e una cordiale chiacchierata di congedo* (Roman Sonnets and a Cordial Conversation of Farewell), was published in 1962. Younger brother of the well-known architect Alberto, Gino Calza, who was at the front with the rank of lieutenant during the First World War, was among the contributors to *Tradotta* (Troop Train), the newspaper of the Third Army. After the war, having made a choice diametrically opposed to that of his old companion Tarchiani, he became, along with Bottai and Polverelli, one of the leaders of Rome's Fascist action squads; he was indeed the incarnation of its radical wing, was secretary of its battle squads before and after the March on Rome (1921–23), and was present in the Chamber of Corporations, representing the Corporation of the Theater (1922). He also dedicated himself to notable activity as a movie director: *Buon Natale!* (Merry Christmas, 1916); *Quando gli altri dormono* (When the Others Are Sleeping, 1918); and *Mia moglie si è fidanzata* (My Wife Is Engaged, 1921). He also wrote for the theater: *I paladini della dama a lutto* (The Widow's Suitors, 1921) and *I volontari* (The Volunteers, 1923).

∾

Among the Eminent

They stood on Grand Street, at the corner, one
who had come over seven years ago
and runs a fruitstand now and I don't know
what other business he's got going on.
    They were talking and they said: "Well, all right then,
but my family's here, and it suits me perfectly,
it makes the bonds much stronger, and makes me
by nationality an American!
    Of those still there in Italy, you know,
nobody's waiting for me, so you see. . . ."
But taking all this in, I thought: go slow,
    you didn't leave there yesterday, but stop
and let your noggin cool down and you'll see
somebody's there who still wants you–the cops!

Translated by Michael Palma

∾

If It Weren't

I

   Would you have given me a consolation
if it weren't for my sister and my mother,
knowing as you do what inclination
I have in all the world over any other?
   I'd like to take a trawler, with a rudder
and sails that are just immense, and bring a few
provisions when I take possession of her,
a bit of bread, a bit of water too. . . .
     . . . and one day full of clear and bright blue sky
and a barely blowing breeze to carry it
with the gentle motion of a swing, then I
   will be right where you want me, leaving from
Anzio's port, and in a little bit
look out, America, 'cause here I come!

II

   And when the wind had brought me far from shore
to where a much more distant sea is found,
that holds, since God the father made it, more
dead than Campoverano's burial ground;
   if it were meadow-smooth, with playfully
lapping waves all around, then I'd begin,
instead of thinking you'd abandoned me,
to study how to talk American!
   But if a breaker billowed from the water,
and then the sail were whipped and torn in two,
and then the wild waves carried off the rudder,
   and the sea was howling mad and the wind went
Roaring . . . in all the world what could I do?
Well, damn me dead, but I would die content!

Translated by Michael Palma

The Americanized Calabrian

∾ *Michele Pane*

Adami di Decollatura (Catanzaro), Italy, March 11, 1876–Chicago, Illinois, April 18, 1953

The poetic endowments of Michele Pane, writes Pier Paolo Pasolini,

> exceed that of his contemporaries. [He] portrayed his birthplace in the tender, poetic style of Giovanni Pascoli and within the traditions of an effortless romanticism (the Byronic, romantic scenery of English landscapes of the first half of the nineteenth century, which is among the most perfect images of nature in Italy) . . . . [He] does not succeed in transcending that theme. His poetry conveys an authentic nostalgia, which motivates his description, assuming that when he was young, he went to America to settle there, only to regret his quiet Calabria. Even, perhaps the most noted poem, "Tora," is actually a clear limpid translation, in the mode of Pascoli, in an older language, close to the nineteenth century to which he would allude. (Pasolini, 45)

This judgment has long encumbered the work of Pane, together with the judgments from opposite points of view of his many provincial appraisers, but founded on the same arguments. The circumstance that an entire ocean separated the author, who emigrated to America, from Calabria, the center of all his poetical interests, accounts, in a large part, for his marginality. As would happen to other writers in dialect, this distance served him, moreover, to refine his nostalgic sensibility and to preserve, in some way, the purity of his expressive craftsmanship.

Thus, today, his work is accounted one of the most notable representations of Calabrese dialect in the twentieth century.

Recently, Antonio Piromalli has detached himself from that critical tradition that has tended to praise Pane's lyricism within the limits "of a conventional and unreal *calabresità*" and "an aestheticism of the region and of regional sentiments." Instead, Piromalli has placed emphasis on the historical foundation of this poetry, which originated in the tragic theater of the great postunitary crisis, caused by brigandage, repression, and substantial refeudalization of the land and by consequent emigration. He concludes that the poetry's point of departure is an ideological Garibaldian experience and the great hopes of redemption that it ignited. Pane's poetry, therefore, can be seen, in the first place, as an adhesion to a world of the oppressed, and only in consequence of that, "as painting and as music."

In effect, Pane's debut, the satire, *L' uòminu russu* (The Red Man), 1898, written during military service in Foggia, is precisely a denunciation of the Bourbon (the kings of Naples belonged to the Bourbon family) transformation, which as a representation of the epoch, clothed itself in Garibaldian colors and pretended to cancel its embarrassing past with one stroke. His last work, *Garibaldina—Rapsodia in dialetto calabro* (Garibaldina: A Rhapsody in Calabrian Dialect, 1949), emerges perfectly consistent with his first. Moreover, it reveals a very precise cultural retrospective (above all, familial): his father and Garibaldian uncle, and his mother, the sister of Francesco Fiorentino and a minute knowledge of that very particular "*risorgimentale*" vein, which, tied to the figure of the hero Garibaldi exiled in Caprera, opens a vision of social redemption already of a socialist stamp. It is not by chance that Pane allied himself with the socialistic ambience of Chicago and contributed to *La Parola del Popolo*.

The new century found him in America, in Brooklyn. In 1901, he returned to Calabria to marry and to publish the collection *Trilogia* in Nicastro. Soon after, he departed again. Teacher in an elementary school in New York, but also an importer and seller of wine and, later, the representative of a notary, in 1924, he moved to Omaha, Nebraska, and finally to Chicago, where he worked in a bank. He contributed to various Italian newspapers, among them *La Follia di New York*, *Il Progresso Italo-Americano*, and *Il Corriere del Connecticut*. He founded the review *Il Lupo*, and in 1906 he published the collection *Viole e ortiche* (Violets and Orchids), followed by *Sorrisi* (Smiles, 1914), *Peccati* (Sins, 1916), *Lu calavrise 'ngrisatu* (The Americanized Calabrian, 1916), and *Accuordi e suspiri* (Agreements and Regrets) (Catanzaro: Mauro, 1930). In 1930, Mauro also published the anthology *Musa silvestre* (Forest Muse), edited by Gabriele Rocca, with whom Mauro initiated the Italian success of Pane, who in 1938 returned to Italy for a year on the occasion of the wedding of his daughter, who was baptized Libertà.

"I have always had an aversion for the English language (this was my great ruin)," wrote the poet in 1930 to Giovanni Tucci (Piromalli, 28). This affirmation comprises his world, in which the personal experience of the emigration counts very much in regard to the nourishing of his nostalgia but very little in regard to thematic autonomy: for him, "the terrible condition of those living in the other world is a given" (Crupi), and, in any case,

> Che val per me se in questa gran metropoli
> vi sian cose giammai da me sognate?
> Ponti sul mare come quei di Brooklyn,
> palagi in marmo e ferrovie elevate?
> Che importa a me se ne la baia d'Hudson
> giungan navi ogni dì da tutto il mondo,
> quand'alla vita e al moto io resto estraneo
> e tra la folla resto un moribondo?
> Che val per me se nell'immensa America
> ci sian miniere inestinguibil d'oro,
> quando non vedo mamma e il fiero Atlantico
> mi separa da Lei, ch'è il mio tesoro?

> What does it matter to me if in this great city
> there are things I never dreamed of? Bridges on the water, like those of
>   Brooklyn,
> palaces in marble and elevated trains?
> What do I care if in the bay of New York
> arrive ships every day from the whole world,
> when I remain estranged from life and activity
> and amid the madness I remain moribund?
> What does it mean to me if in this vast America
> there are inextinguishable gold mines,
> when I do not see mamma, and the fierce Atlantic
> separates me from her, who is my treasure?

Actually, one large exception is *Lu calavrise 'ngrisatu*, one of the most notable examples of the linguistic hybridism that was forged by the caricaturists Migliaccio and Ferrazzano, and it is only because of this text that Pane is included in this present section, which otherwise would be uncomfortable for him. Even here, nonetheless, in a composition that adapts the form of a letter written to his father in Calabria, his strong "calabrocentrica" perspective in some way confirms the typical totally colonial experience.

ESSENTIAL BIBLIOGRAPHY

Borrata D'Angelo 1991; Crupi 1979; Fichera 1958, 23–25; Migliaccio 1953; Pane 1987, 5–30; Pasolini 1960; Rocca 1953.

∾

To Peppino Lo Russo
Fraternally

How I rejoice all alone with myself
now that I too am Americanized!
Laugh, Peppino, if you want to laugh;
but don't call me impolite.
If I need to buy a pail of coal,
here—think of it—I have to say:
. . . .
there is no need, you'll get it by yourself!
DEAR TATA,
    I am writing you this letter
to tell you that I'd like for you to come
to America too, where your son is,
for in Italy there's nothing you can do.
Your Michele, whose name is *Màicu* now
—Americanized—is in *'mbisinissi*,[1]
he is a Notary, *Fùrmine*,[2] and Court
'Ntrepitu[3] tata, just so that you know.
    He is *Brodu*, that is brother, and Venerable
of the Freemasons of the Mazzini Lodge;
he is also member of the D'Annunzio *Grubu*,[4]

1. Business.
2. Foreman.
3. Interpreter.
4. Club.

and President of so many Societies:
he has *'nzurata*[5] his *laif* for *Ten-Tàusi*
and *sikstini* dollars, which amount to:
ten thousand dollars and sixteen;
what do you think of your own son, tata?

    He lives at a hundred-twenty *Murberry*
Strittu, that's how the street is called;
he *spicca*, it means talks, better than a *lòjaru*
—a lawyer—and already has *mocci monì*;
he is a *polìtiscinu*[6] among the *fòisti*[7]
politicos of the island of *Manata*;
he knows the *ghenghe*[8] and all the *lòfani*,[9]
who are in this *serì*, meaning city!

    Made for the sly this *contrà*[10] of America,
where the lingo is twisted and two-faced!
Look: *fimmine*[11] here are called *'uomini*,[12]
amore is *lova*, tata, and *la scarpa* is *sciù*.[13]
The *cavallo* is *ursu*,[14] and *la carta*
is *pàpara*;[15] the chef is *cuccu*; *la porta* is *door*;
chiesa is *ciuccia* and *pristu* is the *prete*,
faccia is *fessa*,[16] tata, can you believe that?

    If you want to say *capito*? You have
to say *stend-jù*?[17] The *stivali* are called *butti*[18]
and the *guai* here are called *trubuli*[19]
and you say *guai* to mean: how come?

5. Insured.
6. Politician.
7. First.
8. Gangs.
9. Loafers.
10. Country.
11. Women.
12. Men.
13. Shoe.
14. Horse.
15. Paper.
16. Stupid.
17. You understand?
18. Boots.
19. Troubles.

Fitti—with all due respect—means *piedi*,[20]
and a single *piede* is called *futti*.
Americans call us *Taliani pipuli*
ddecòni[21] and *ghinì*![22] And *l'erba*
is called *grassu*, the *pettine* is *comba*;
dente is *tuttu*;[23] the cop is a *sceriffu*,
a tall bulding a *scaiscrèpalu*, *sindaco*
is *meo*,[24] tata, and *l'albero* is *trii*.
Mamma here is called *the mòdera*,
a *bue* is an *uossu*[25] when alive, *biffu*[26] if dead;
legno is *vuda*[27] and *il toro* is *bullu*;
cielo is *scai*, *il mare* is called *sii*!

    Iessu means I agree, *men* are *uomini*;
young kids are *boja*,[28] tata, and *il lago* is *leccu*.[29]
There are cities with really curious names:
Dimòniu-Juda[30] (let's stay away from there!)
It's *nais*—bello: *Lubucchìnu*[31] and *Monaca*[32]
—with *Luvurpìle*[33] in the state of *Fai*[34]—*Cecacu*[35]
and *Pisciacchìlli*,[36] *Cazzachilli*[37] and *Piritu*[38]
and *O'mà-fadi*,[39] with the . . . *Miscìccà*![40]

20. Feet.
21. Dagoes.
22. Guineas.
23. Tooth.
24. Mayor.
25. Ox.
26. Beef.
27. Wood.
28. Boys.
29. Lake.
30. Des Moines.
31. Hoboken.
32. Monaca (New Jersey).
33. Liverpool.
34. Ohio.
35. Chicago.
36. Peekskill.
37. Catskills.
38. Pyrites (New York).
39. Omaha.
40. Michigan.

My dearest tata, here work has a bad
name, that frightens: *uorcu*, the Indian
is called *corn*, and the hoe is *sciàbula*
la vacca is *cau* and *la vite* is *scrù*!
formaggio is *accìsu*[41]; *lapis* is *pènsalu*,[42]
chichina is *gallina*; *pigg'* is *maiale*.
to say to someone: what is wrong with you?
you say: *Guazza-marra-vajù*[43]?
   A female pig is *sàu*, the ABC is *spèllalu*,[44]
dear tata, *pilu* is the bucket and the carbone
is *culu*;[45] can you imagine? Earthenware
is *crocc'*; a female deer is *doo*.
Who would have thought, (not even from an angel!)
that the son of a Tied-Foot would one day
—don't be offended, my dear tata—
be just behind *Roccufalò*![46]
   I remember that when I was a child
I would go through town with bare feet and legs,
shirtless, and everyone called me "Bull nose,"
first of all you—who looked just like an ogre—
this little devil, you'd say, cannot be tamed,
so I have to send him off to America
because I can no longer deal with him.
   Blessed be the day, and those tears also,
—but every cloud does have a silver lining—
that I left the place where I knew hunger,
and I came ashore to this *Fricontrì*![47]
Had I remained there, I would have been killed
by now, or ended up in jail, while here
I'm having a good time with the black *misse*,[48]

41. Cheese.
42. Pencil.
43. What's the matter with you?
44. Speller.
45. Coal.
46. Rockefeller.
47. Free country.
48. Misses.

and with the *Airisci 'nghelle*[49] and the *Scinì*!
 I take a *raid* with the *automobilia*,
go to the *movi-'mpicci* and the *saluni*;
I'm number one at every dance I go to,
because I do the tango with a pirouette.
Americans are not jealous and mean
—like us Calabresi—they are boneheads:
if you caress their *guaif*—which means spouse—
before their very eyes, they say *hurrè*.
 I go to the *sciò* and the *Grandopera*
on certain nights to listen to Caruso,
who has a voice that thunders like an organ
and sends everyone there to paradise.
Just think whether your son will show you
a real good time, my tata Hairy-Foot,
but I'll tell you in one ear—remember it—
throw out your rag shoes when do you come here.
 I often visit the laboratory
of an old Sorcerer they call *Diosonnu*;[50]
the one who invented the electric light,
the *movi-'mpicciu* and the *grammpfomò*.[51]
I have *bracchifesti* with Mayor *Micciu*[52]
and correspond with *Guillisonnu*,[53] tata;
I'm *arsu*[54] a close friend of the *Cùnzulu*[55]
who says *alò* when he runs into me!
 And pretty soon I will set up a trap
—that here they call a Bank—because the Bankers
—now that the war has made the exchange go up—
are making money like there is no end;
that's the reason why, tata, I am practicing
to learn how to take people to the cleaners;

49. Irish girls.
50. Edison.
51. Gramophone.
52. Mitchell.
53. Wilson.
54. Also.
55. Consul.

the art is easy and it takes little study,
you barely need to manage how to spell!
   Here we are all alike: rich, poor,
educated, dunces, and even *Ministri*;
it's a Carnival without any masks,
that's it, tata, Americans say: *Dazzò*!
How many cons and jailbirds have become
cocks of the walk here, among the *Pulistri*;
whereas Italy's blackmails and its swindles
are covered by a merciful *overcò*![56]
   As soon as this letter reaches you, tata,
make sure you get the passport *raduè*;[57]
write to the *Làina Fràbica*[58] in Naples
for the very best cabin that they have
in the newest ship called Patria, which is
a *festa-stima*:[59] sell the kitchen garden,
hand over the house key to the Mayor, and,
arioppu,[60] get yourself over here!
   Don't forget to say hello to the *Dottor*
and the *Chemist* and the old Engineer;
Give *tu meni chissi*[61] to the parish priest,
and to the *Ticcer affezionatelì*.[62]
If you see the Honorable Colosimo,
tell him I want to be a Cavaliere;
hug him for me, along with don Eugenio,
and remind him that Adami is *Frì*!
   And, tata, say hello to the Post-Master
—who's compare Zuccariello—Amaro—
to my brother-in-law Gianni—Impareggiabile—
and all those who ask you about me;
to brothers-in-law Thomas and Gregorio,

56. Overcoat.
57. Right away.
58. The name of this ocean liner company is not transparent.
59. Fast steamer.
60. Hurry up.
61. Too many kisses.
62. Teacher affectionately.

and to Giose, my dear Cantàru, to everyone,
but one name only will suffice: Cesare,
who is no doubt the king of all the sacristans!
    Stop-rattu, I mean I've to stop writing,
I hear an *allarmi* on my *telefune*;
leave happy, tata, do not hesitate,
don't be afraid, Americans say: *no-fred*
When you get to Gibraltar let me know
with the signal of the Marconi telegraph;
cubai,[63] everything else leave to your son
who hugs you now and is waiting for you.

MAICU BRED[64]

Translated by Luigi Bonaffini

63. Good-bye.
64. "Michael Bread" is a translation of Michele Pane's name.

Dante's Colony

∾ *Achille Almerini*

Garlasco (Pavia), Italy, September 12, 1880–February 1947

In 1902, Achille Almerini took his degree in medicine in Turin, and in 1907, he emigrated to America and established himself in New York, opening an office for ear, nose, and throat diseases, frequented mostly by Italian clients. A volunteer in the Italian military during the First World War, he was stationed at the front as a medical army officer and later was nominated supervisor of the health office. Returning to America, he married and had one son, whom he named Achille. Before the Second World War, he returned to Italy for reasons of health. (According to Prezzolini, "He left America to settle in Italy, three or four times.")

In 1912, in New York, with the anagrammatic pseudonym of Michele Alliarni, he published a collection of humorous sonnets entitled *La colonia di Dante* (Dante's Colony) at his own expense, followed by the undated collection *Il Canzoniere di Cicché* (The Cigarette-Butt Songbook). Almerini was among the very first to publish a work entirely written in Italian American jargon, whose ironical intent, with respect to the emigrated and newly rich *"cafoni"* (boors), is the openly declared purpose of the title and its suggestion that America is an outlier of Dante's geography. In other sonnets, he used a successful mix of Italian and English.

An able versifier, a more able manipulator of spoken language, he has left a brilliant testimony of the epoch, one of the most frankly characteristic, destined in some way to instruct, also in virtue of the notable social rank of the author. Prezzolini describes him as "a typical example of the chronic discontent that afflicted many emigrants, who being in America, felt nostalgia for Italy, but when they return there, feel they cannot do without America, which is like a drug addiction."

ESSENTIAL BIBLIOGRAPHY

Alfonsi 1989; Peragallo 1949, 3–4; Prezzolini 1963, 330–336.

൏

I

    I have my *storo* in the downtown area
and whenever you want, just telephone;
please come and see me, what time I don't care,
day and evening my nose's stuck to the grindstone.
    Is it far? Eh! A hundred blocks, I swear,
but the distance is nothing to bemoan.
Don't care, with all the comforts offered there
by all the trains and *carri* you can get on.
    It's no big *trubel,* try it and you'll see;
on Third Avenue there's the *oliveta;*
you take the train and get off on *Aussonstritte,*
    walk four blocks to the right and you'll see written
between the *andeteca* and the *rialesteta*
"Italian spoken here" and there you'll find me.

II

    Look at Italy, even if you have *moneta,*
maybe they won't consider you at all:
and people know, because the towns are small,
your most private affairs from A to Z.
    With a *realestèta morgheg* it's more *isi*
for you to become *prominente,* on the ball,
and the easier the societies can call
you *presidente,* the more ignorant you'll be.
    And then with the friendship of a big shot
politiscia, bartenda or attorney
from *Mister so end so* you're *bosso* or whatnot;
    then they'll give you a banquet, just the same
as back where we come from for a deputy,
and in all the papers you will see your name.

III

But *sciùa* it takes time, and I wrote you so
(it's better to say certain things right up):
when just off the *stima* you'd better stop
believing you'll find *pezze* in the *stritto*.

Don't be in a hurry to get to the top:
whoever runs too much can't walk straight also,
in the *bisniss* you begin quiet and slow,
and only if you sow you reap the crop.

America and your town are far apart:
do not be *stingi*, because *guarda male*
but try to save some money if you can.

Eniuè,[1] let me repeat to you again,
because this is what is most essential
you have to learn some English from the start.

IV

Difficult? Less than you bargained for:
you will learn very fast, young as you are:
Ollrait, detsòll, sciaràp, go hom, gherare![2]
(if you happen to run into a bore).

And when you think something is bizarre
you ask: *Uazz de matter?* And of course you're
obliged to say *ledi* to a girl, to be sure,
and call *mistar* even your compare!

But learn to speak English, because if you
ask where's your street speaking Italian
to a *scianatore*[3] or the *fruttistendo*

he, whether a Piedmontese or a Sicilian,
to show you that he knows more than you do
will answer: *ai du not anderstendo*.

V

Look at the others: *germanesi, scini*

1. Anyway.
2. Get out of here!
3. Janitor

(but yes, the Jews!) see if they speak American:
you should be happy that you are Italian
but *spicca* the language spoken by *vicini*.

    Nevaiorca was found by Verrazzano!
True, it's common knowledge even for bambini
so that if someone ever calls you *ghini*!
Don't pay attention, it's a *lofar* or vulgarian.

    Don't try to change his mind or what he does.
It's no use! For in the end that bumpkin
will give you a *blecch'ài* or break your nose.

    And keep in mind! When there is a *fait*
if you lose you're wrong and if you win
you're a *smart fello end evritongsollrait*.

VI

    By now it's a legend old and stale
that we're a bunch of bums, a total loss:
the *airisc*, everyone knows he is the boss,
for love of the Pope drives in another nail.

    You'll never get out of their head the tale
that Rome has brigands with their blunderbuss.
You have to sympathize . . . they came across
as settlers too and have dimwits nonpareil.

    What do we care? So much energy spent
to establish our *Italianness*
and now we erect a monument to Dante!

    Will you say hello to him? would say Oronzo,
but in a colony, you need to worry less!
If the ideal is *cip*, then more *cip* is bronze.

    Translated by Luigi Bonaffini

The Pichinicco

🌿 *Pasquale Seneca*

Pontelandolfo (Benevento), Italy, 1890–1952

In 1927, in Philadelphia, *Il Presidente Scoppetta; ovvero, La Società della Madonna della Pace dalla sua fondazione al suo scioglimento* (President Scoppetta, or, The Society of the Madonna of Peace from Its Foundation to Its Dissolution) was published. It was described as a "satirical-burlesque *bozzetto* [a short novel on themes of daily life] on Italian-American customs, in Italian prose, and . . . 'scoppettiana' [adventures of President Scoppetta], written to entertain all and offend no one, by Professor Pasquale Seneca." In addition, it was illustrated by the pleasing drawings of Alfredo Melina. Seneca, an instructor in Romance languages at Lafayette College, Temple University, and the University of Pennsylvania until the early 1930s, had joined his father in Philadelphia in 1903. An organizer of youth groups, he was an active member of the Sons of Italy and of other civic and social associations.

In this case, *bozzetto* is an inadequate definition, since *Il Presidente Scoppetta*, some eighty pages long, with a good variety of situations, is almost a short humorous novel, and therefore one of the most congenial examples of the Italian American literature of the 1920s. The book relates events in the life of Francesco Saverio Scoppetta, a type of unscrupulous emigrant speculator who is aiming to climb the social ladder and consolidate his economic well-being. After having founded the newspaper *La Calzetta d'Italia* (Italy's Stocking), he becomes a promoter of a typical Italian American association, composed of emigrants from an imaginary village in southern Italy named Brigantello, and he takes pains to become its president. The misfortune is that the society becomes very difficult to manage, given the litigation, the ignorance, and the envy that reign unopposed among the members. In this way, between the laughter and *"picchinicchi,"* weddings and processions, bizarre affirmations of Italianità, and funerals, Scoppetta's initiative inexorably leads to bankruptcy.

Il Presidente Scoppetta was dedicated, not by chance, "to the Cav. Eduardo Migliaccio (Farfariello), creator of colonial caricatures, author-singer-actor-protean artiste, a refined humorist, an elegant performer of variety shows, definitely 'a Maldacea, a Pasquariello, a Villani, a Giglio,' perennial inexhaustible dispenser of gaiety, the only one eulogized by American scholars and critics, the only one who knew how to castigate jokingly, the idol of the public." Seneca's Presidente Scoppetta was born in the same environment that had produced Eduardo Migliaccio's *Neapolitan Machiette*, an ingenious American transposition of theatrical Parthenopean plots (Parthenope was an ancient Greek name for Naples). Even if reduced to narrative form, President Scoppetta's malapropism is superbly theatrical in his constant use of the spoken word, which is obviously the hybrid language of the transplanted *cafoni* (boors), directed toward very effective farcical results.

In his humorous use of equivocal verbal forms, of bungling grammatical forms, and in his definition of a small crowd of comic personages, Seneca reveals a profound knowledge of the Neapolitan tradition, from Petito to Scarpetta to Maldacea, revivified upon crossing the sea, and precisely by Migliaccio. *Il Presidente Scoppetta* causes a reader to wonder what results would be obtained if a Totò, so to speak, would impersonate Scoppetta.

Despite denying that *Scoppetta* should be classified as a work of art, Giuseppe Prezzolini acknowledges the value of its content, all the more because "the facts were drawn from the current events of the local newspaper, the *Opinione*, of Philadelphia." He notes that the work "mirrored the conditions of the society that was formed in the stagnant centers of emigration in the peripheries of the great American metropolises almost everywhere, having the same results." Deepening the sociological examination, he adds that "the ability of the few cultivated members to observe social phenomena that lends itself to caricature signaled a conscious detachment between the citizen and the rude countryman ("paesano"), which constitutes an old separation in relation to Italian literature." Prezzolini's attention to Seneca's work is due to the circumstance that a brief chapter was dedicated to it in the repertory of his student Olga Pergallo, according to whom "the dialectal Italian-American buffo adds hilarity to the already entertaining anecdotes and situations."

Seneca also engaged himself publishing literature on themes of pedagogy and education, and was in contact with Leonard Covello, the famous teacher of Italian Harlem, who had a great influence on a whole generation of Italian Americans, among them Fiorello La Guardia. His articles appeared in diverse newspapers, among which was *Il Popolo Italiano* of Philadelphia.

ESSENTIAL BIBLIOGRAPHY

Biaggi 1967, 70; Peragallo 1949, 200–201; Prezzolini 1963, 336–338.

∾

It was seven in the morning and one could already see the first signs of movement in front of the headquarters of the society. It was the prelude to another grand adventure, the annual *pichinicco* of the well-deserving "Lady of Peace" Mutual Aid Society.

It is a Sunday in August. The sky appears beautiful and clear, and everything leads us to believe that it will be a day of great enjoyment for all the participants.

An hour later the crowd is gathering in the streets and making it difficult for traffic. There are the yelling of children and the warning cries of mothers. A cry of jubilation greets the arrival of the *trocchi* [trucks], some of which are half full with provisions and drinks of all kinds for the grand excursion into the country. A few minutes later the cars are filled with people, who are waiting for the departure with feverish impatience.

Meanwhile President Scoppetta is preparing to emerge. As usual, he wants to bestow on this festival all the importance and solemnity of the other ones and, therefore, he has decided to come out in full dress. This time he plans to go on horseback at the head of the society, with the others behind him. To this end he has borrowed the horse of Pezzi, his baker, and the poor animal has been waiting patiently at the door. It appears, however, that Scoppetta is not destined to ride out. The President has already put on the high-ranking uniform of general that he wore at the banquet; however, he is looking here and there for the saber but cannot find it. Meanwhile the people are quivering and growing impatient. A half hour passes and they are still waiting. Nine o'clock arrives, but the *trocchi* do not move. Finally, prompted by the cries and curses of the people, vice-president Pizzafritta steps down from one of the *trocchi* and calls secretary Fasulo who is in the lead car.

"Secretary," he asks him, "can you tell me why we're not leaving, yes or no?"

"Sorry, Mr. Vice-President," the secretary replies, "President Scopetta has given orders that we must wait and that we cannot leave until he arrives. He said that he must go in front."

"Oh please, front or back!" responds a very irritated Pizzafritta, "Tell Maico, the driver, to proceed, and whether Scoppetta likes it or not, he can bear up. Jesus, he takes us for a bunch of fools!"

And so they leave.

President Scopetta arrives a half hour later by automobile, not having been able to come on horseback because he was missing his saber, which was impossible to find. This prevented him from dressing as a general. Thus he comes in civilian dress, but with much regret, as one might easily guess. Along the way, he has thought of nothing but the "military saber," as he calls it. He swears that if he could get his hands on the person who stole it, he would rip him to pieces. Imagine, therefore, how angry he is.

On his arrival in front of the society, he gets out of the car, and, not finding a soul, he begins to swear like a sailor.

"Jimmy," he says to his driver, "I think that this 'pichinicco' today will end up a 'pichinicco!' Here either Pizzafritta or Fasulo has 'tricked' me, and you'll see that before today ends I'll box the ears of both the secretary and the vice-president!" and with this philosophical observation, they leave.

Around eleven the *trocchi* reach the spot, that is the farm of Nick Facciatagliata, president of the *Principe di Piemonte Billone Sucièscene* (Building and Loan Association), and a half hour later the automobile carrying Scoppetta arrives. We've already mentioned that the latter was in a very bad mood that morning. However, the fact is that before he arrived, an unpleasant scene had occurred, so that all the souls were rather upset and the atmosphere was overcharged with electricity, as one would say. This was the problem: since the cars in which the people were traveling included the food and drink, a good part of this was consumed during the trip; and when this was discovered, all hell broke loose.

"Mr. Treasurer," one of the drivers says, "more than three hundred 'sanguiccio' and around twenty 'boxes' of 'situata' are missing."

"That they could throw down all three hundred barrels of blood!" declares the treasurer. And he was about to put the blame on the people who traveled in the cars. But he then reconsiders and decides to hold the drivers responsible, convinced that this is the most practical and straightforward means.

"Listen, friends," he says, "I don't want to know anything about this. You're the 'bossi' of your 'trocchi,' and therefore you're responsible for all the things that are missing!"

"And I'll," replies one of the drivers with an accent from Bari, "have blood heave from your throat and from all your dead!" and with this threat he hurls himself at the society's minister of treasury, with the other drivers following suit. The poor devil would have ended up in bad shape had the other brothers of "The Society of Lady of Peace" not rushed to make peace. This is the spirit of things upon President Scoppetta's arrival. Fortunately, it is almost time for lunch, that is for the *feeding trough*, which brings with it a much needed truce and calm.

Toward the end of grub time, there arises some commotion among Scopetta's closest friends: "We want to hear the President. Give the floor to our Presssssidentttt!" they insist so much that Scoppetta, no longer able to resist, stands up and begins to speak:

"Rise, brothers male members and female members."

"This 'pichinicco' is a 'pichinicco' that I don't believe there has ever been a 'pichinicco' like this 'pichinicco.' I assure you that on this amazing day, this feast is a feast that I believe that there has never been a feast like this feast that we are feasting in these days of festivities. I assure you that the day of today will always be in my guts. (Applause) First of all, you must forgive me if I came dressed in such an indecent manner like all of you. But what can I tell you? I wanted to put on my uniform this morning, but I could not find my military saber, and so I had to come dressed like an imbecile. But that's okay. I will never be able to forget the magnificent banquet that you gave me not long ago (applause), because I know very well that all would have gone very well had that cowardly brother not stolen the compliments that the society had paid to me (Silence). But on this feast of today, however, let's hope that with the help of God there will be no 'trouble.' And I beg you: if someone wants to insult you, keep calm, and don't start fighting. In fact, let me know because if someone gives you a punch I'll give him three, and I'll make him spit blood. You know very well that your President has never abandoned you. For example, who gave you permission this morning to 'stardare' before me? Now if you do not want to obey me and, instead, you want to treat me like a fool, that's another kettle of fish. In the Society of the Lady of Peace there must always be peace and harmony; and that's good. But your President is by no means a scrub or a fool, and he must be respected. Therefore, if I catch that person who 'stardato' this morning without my permission, I'll stuff the 'pichinicco' down his throat!"

The speech, or rather, the threat of the President draws loud applause from his friends and also from the other table companions, who are more attentive to their glasses than to what Scoppetta has to say. Since they are drinking excessively, and not just situata, which is being consumed almost exclusively by the women and children, but also good red wine. For this reason, toasts to the occasion were not lacking, some were rather witty, such as what follows:

This wine is superb and dry. . . .
Long live always our pichinicco!
This drink is superb and lively. . . .

To the health of the Lady of Peace!
This wine was sent to us by Bacchus. . . .
And who does not drink it
Is a big coward!

A member belonging to the anti-Scopetta party, gives a jeer toward President Scoppetta, who certainly is not pleased. Here it is:

Our President wants harmony and peace. . . .
But it is Zinfandel that is much more pleasing to me!

Scopetta is taken by surprise, and he seems to find in this toast a clear lack of respect. But the laughter that the toast has provoked is so boisterous that even Scopetta ends up laughing. And so this crisis is avoided. However, as soon as calm has been restored, another brother, one of those that Scoppetta loved to call "cowardly brothers," evidently prompted by some enemy, stands up drunk, and said:

This wine is bright as the sun. . . .
But Ciccio Saverio Scuppetta is a huge scoundrel!

Heaven forbid! Good-bye *pichinicco*! Good-bye harmony and brotherhood! Glasses, plates, bottles, and chairs begin to fly, and all you can hear is the cursing of men, the cries of women, and the shouting of children. Fortunately, just in that moment a hurricane-like storm is unleashed which, as if it was intentionally ordered by providence, extinguishes the combative passions of the brothers in arms and puts an end to the fierce struggle. All the people take cover in the *trocchi* and return home. And so no one is killed; however, a number end up in bad shape, and for the second time in the history of the "Society of the Lady of Peace," President Scoppetta takes a bottle in the face.

Translated by Mark Pietralunga

Spaghetti House

∽ *Vincenzo Campora*

Born Naples, Italy, 1889

Taking his degree in economics, freelance journalist Vincenzo Campora moved to New York in 1914 and the following year initiated the publication of the monthly *Columbus*. Signing himself at times as "The Man in the Street," Campora would allude to the need for the common sense that animated his journalistic work. For the rest, *Columbus* proposed to contribute to "a major reciprocation of comprehension between Italians and Americans," supporting "the diffusion of the knowledge of Dante and of his language among the Americans." He wanted to "encourage economic relations" as well.

Richly illustrated, even in its modest number of pages—in time, and especially during the Fascist period, when it openly supported Mussolini —*Columbus* became a sort of alternative to the *Carroccio*. It was more disengaged, which did not deter Campora from publishing articles, poetry, and diverse contributions by important Italian journalists and, above all, Americans, among them H. L. Mencken, who printed Campora's poem "Spaghetti House" in *The American Language*.

ESSENTIAL BIBLIOGRAPHY

Flamma 1936; Mencken 1947.

∽

    —Tell me, Sir, you want them al dente, don't you?
"Tomato sauce" and "Parmigiano cheese";
all Italian, you know, even the pan,

the basil, the "chef," and the "assistant" too.
   Now they sell them cooked in the pharmacy
(The sons of bitches!) I mean the "drug store,"
in all the "presto luncheons," "luncheonettes"
of this land of water wands and rhabdomancy.
   But here, at my place, a friend and servant
to every Italian and every good custom
you find the culinary art of the Old Country,
where every flower smells ever so fragrant!
   My words can sound nostalgic to these gents,
I know. But never mind! We'll talk about it
another time over a good dinner.
—Monzù: an espresso for the gentleman—al dente!

   Translated by Luigi Bonaffini

Two Poems

Alfredo Borgianini

Rome, Italy, 1882–Trenton, New Jersey, 1955

A collection of *sonetti* and Roman poems published in Trenton, New Jersey, in 1948, along with another sonnet sequence in Roman dialect, *Cani der core* (Songs of the Heart), constitutes the work of Alfredo Borgianini, who was Roman, or, in any case, from the region of Lazio. The two sonnets published here, composed by the author to publicize his business, were printed in 1935 by *La Sampogna*, edited by Filippo Fichera. They had appeared earlier in the *Nuova Capitale*, the newspaper of the Italian colony of Trenton, the capital of New Jersey. In Rome, Borgianini had studied, possibly, engineering at La Sapienza and was married in the first years of the twentieth century. In 1907, he migrated to the United States (his wife was to join him a few years later). In Trenton, there was a populous Italian colony and, apparently, Borgianini was invited to join them with the offer of a position as designer of automobiles at the Walter Automobile Company, which later became the Mercer Automobile Company, for which he worked until 1917, even travelling as head mechanic with the Mercer racing team, achieving notable successes at the Indianapolis track in the 1910s. Afterward, he opened his own workshop in Trenton, becoming a popular figure with the nickname "Fritz," and achieving notable success. After the premature death of his wife in 1935, he moved to Hamilton, on the outskirts of Trenton, building a new house with an attached workshop that still exists. He was very active in the Italian community, and was among the founding members of several institutions in the fields of finance, sports, and religion.

Alfonsi 1985, 412; Marazzi 2001, 96–97.

The Best Gas

My gasoline, I'm not just saying that,
is the best of all, it's really the flower;
and, as soon you hit the accelerator,
the automobile jumps forward like a cricket.
Going uphill, now anyone can hack it,
under the power given by the motor
and the troubles with the carburetor
are a thing of the past, count on it!
If you should ever need to travel far,
buy this gasoline, try it and you'll see
that not even a plane will catch your car.
Do what I just told you, listen to me,
and like everyone else you will have found
that my gas is the best gas around.

To Those Who Have a Car

When you need to buy some gasoline
a tire, a tube, a jack, an oilcan, or
a fine-brand sparkplug that's the best you've seen
or otherwise a first-class carburetor,
and a headlight for your fine machine
or the oil to lubricate the motor
come to Fritz, 'cause through the window screen
you can see everything you're looking for.
If your automobile should have some malady
so that after it starts it comes to a dead stop,
what I will do is recharge your battery.

And to do that I've a tool, my friend,
that after I have charged it in the shop
the automobile runs faster than the wind.

Translated by Luigi Bonaffini

Six Poems

∾ *Rodolfo Valentino*

Castellaneta (Taranto), Italy, May 10, 1895–Hollywood, California,
August 23, 1926

By 1923, Rodolfo Valentino had been in America for ten years, and he was at the apex of his fame. It is said that at that time, the congressman Fiorello La Guardia had the famed actor's photograph in his office, and not that of the president of the United States. In that year, in New York, Valentino published a small volume of poems, *Day Dreams*, which by now has become a bibliographical rarity. The quality of the compositions is very disputable; the language, inadvertently comical in effect, summons to mind that of the aspiring writer Arturo Bandini, in John Fante's *The Road to Los Angeles*. *Day Dreams* is composed of somewhat abstruse congeries of high-sounding terms, of an affected vocabulary, of conceptions whose sound is more appreciable than the sense. Despite these shortcomings, it should not be concluded that Valentino's poetry is a mere creation of the press agents, a falsity to engage his admirers.

Aside from their rarity, these verses, all written in English, offer a small insight. They seem to correspond perfectly to the image of the actor, veined as they are by a passionate and distressed sentimentalism, as if they were the medium of a vague presage of his death.

∾

You

You are the History of Love and its Justification
The Symbol of Devotion
The Blessedness of Womanhood
The Incentive of Chivalry
The Reality of Ideals
The Verity of Joy
Idolatry's Defense
The Proof of Goodness
The Power of Gentleness
Beauty's Acknowledgement
Vanity's Excuse
The Promise of Truth
The Melody of Life
The Caress of Romance
The Dream of Desire
The Sympathy of Understanding
My Heart's Home
The Proof of Faith
Sanctuary of my Soul
My Belief of Heaven
Eternity of All Happiness
    My Prayers
    You.

∾

A Baby's Skin

Texture of a butterfly's wing
Colored like a dawned rose
Whose perfume is the breath of God
Such is the web wherein is held
The treasure of the treasure chest
The priceless gift–The Child of Love.

∾

Dust to Dust

I take a bit of bone—I gaze at it in wonder—You
O bit of strength that was. In you today I
See the white sepulcher of nothingness—but
You were the shaft that held the wagon of life. Your strength
held together the vehicle of man until God called and the Soul
   answered.

∾

Italy

(To Caruso)
The earth is earth–and that is its worth
To men who walk below
But to the soul that seeks its goal
Each land is all they know.
One calls it Home, another Heart, another Prosperity
But to the one who loves the Sun
He calls it Italy.

∾

Money

Money—you Harlequin of the great masquerade of life
You wear the dollar sign as your mask
I may hide you—yes, for a time,
But when at last grim reality stalks into the midst of the
festivities,
The mask is ruthlessly torn away
and then—is seen
The true expression behind it—the cruel visage of
discordant greed.

∾

Day Dreams

(To The Friend)
Yesterday—in contemplation
We dreamed of love to be
And in the dreaming,
Wove a tapestry of Love.
   Today—We dream our dream awake
Realization
   Coloring our Romance
With all the glory of a flaming rose.
Tomorrow—What awakening lies before us
Our tapestry
In shreds perchance
Or mellowed—glorified
   By love's reflection?
I wonder—

Domestic Court

∾ *Silvio Picchianti*

Among the colonial dramatists, the Florentine Silvio Picchianti explored the whole gamut of popular themes, preferring plots about exiled families, middle-class interiors, and stories of love and adultery; but he did not omit the patriotic and social muse, nor musical comedy and poetry. In fact, before emigrating at the very beginning of the twentieth century, after having read the ode *In Morte di Umberto I* (On the Death of Umberto I) in the National Arena of Florence, in January 1901, he dedicated himself to the musical theater. In America, he wrote, among others, a melodrama in four acts, *Varvara*, set to music by the harpist Cesare Sodero, and a vaudeville, *Il trust dell' amore*, with music by Luigi Prisco. Picchianti was also the author of songs: his "Moonlit Night," composed together with A. Seismit-Doda, was cut by Beniamino Gigli for a 78 Victrola record.

The First World War inspired two single-act plays: *La Madre Triestina* (The Triestine Mother), performed in West Hoboken (now Union City, New Jersey) on May 27, 1916, by Silvio Miniciotti, and based on the story of Anita, the mother who repaired to Galicia in search of her son, an Austro-Hungarian soldier; and *Le trecce d'Isabella* (Isabella's Braids), performed December 20, 1918, in New York, by Mimì Aguglia, set in the Venetian campaign in the first days of the Austrian invasion, in which the evil von Kein prepares to violate Isabella after having her kill her grandmother. She pretends to undress, as he has ordered, but then manages to strangle him using her braids, which he had cut off.

Two one-act plays, of a more social character, appear to date from the last years of the 1910s or the first of the 1920s: *Il ritorno*, on the theme of migration, is narrated by Giuseppe, who, returning to his hometown in southern Italy after three years in America, discovers that his father, Vincenzo, has impregnated his wife,

Concetta; *Il figlio di Toto* is a story of a redeemed ex-thief, Stefano Magni, called simply Toto, who, torn with pain, kills his very son when he discovers that he has a stolen watch in his pocket.

Of Picchianti's copious production, several later published titles are recorded. Distinguished is a comedy in three acts in vernacular Florentine, *I' zio d'America* (The American Uncle); a single musical act, *Il gran detective*; and the dramatic poem in three acts *La stanza di Cupido* (Cupid's Room). The first book Picchianti published in America is the collection of verses *Nostalgie* (Nostalgias, 1908), intimating bits of biographical information: a Garibaldian grandfather; Picchianti's presence in Pueblo, Colorado, in 1903, then the longer stay in Chicago, and, in all probability, the move to the metropolitan area of New York.

Reprinted in this anthology is the finale of Picchianti's one-act play *Tribunali domestici*. The play's text, as clipped from an unknown publication, is preserved in the Raccolta Cennerazzo in the Biblioteca Lucchesi Palli of Naples. A typical example of middle-class theater, which intends to represent the attitudes and values of the American upper classes, the play opens in a courtroom with the acquittal of stockbroker James Murray, thanks to the testimony of William Oakley, an expert calligrapher, who was once in love with Diana, Murray's wife. From William, Diana wants to know if Murray's absolution was justice or generosity, but while the two are in James's office, the telephone rings, and a woman asks to talk with the office-holder, calling him, "Darly." Diana convinces William to pretend to be James and tell the woman to come. Understood from the telephone call is that the unknown woman reminds the presumed James of his promise to give her a pair of diamond earrings should he be absolved.

Picchianti composed much music, including a song, "The Song of the Swan," that was interpreted by the great tenor Beniamino Gigli. Picchianti also recorded for Victor Company a great number of comic scenes featuring the Florentine mask of Stenterello, Tuscan "stornelli," and patriotic pieces during World War I. For the mentioned Sodero, he also wrote the libretto for the grand opera *Ombre rosse* (Red Shadows), which in 1929 was the first full opera to have its world premiere on the radio (NBC). The following year, the opera was represented at the theatre La Fenice in Venice. Picchianti was also editor of the newspaper *La Patria* (The Fatherland) in Chicago.

ESSENTIAL BIBLIOGRAPHY

Picchianti 1908, n.d.(a), 1919.

∾

Scene IV

Lucie and Diana

LUCIE (*enters happy and skipping*): Hallo James! (*upon seeing Diana, she stops in the middle of the room as if petrified. Diana places herself in front of her. Her demeanor is cold, her head held high. She stares at Lucie with an expression of pride and noble indignation. Lucie, confused, lowers her head*).

DIANA: Mr. Murray is not in. What do you want from my husband?

LUCIE (*with surprise*): Your. . . .

DIANA: My husband, yes. In fact, due to no fault of my own, Mr. Murray is my husband. And you, pardon me, who are you to enter here and as if he were an old schoolmate, call out to him "Hallo, James?"

LUCIE (muddled and confused): I have business with him (she starts to leave). But if he is not here, I will come back.

DIANA (*grabbing her by the arm and forcing her to stay*): No, Madame, no. Since you came, you will stay. I will take care of my husband's business, unless it is too intimate.

LUCIE (*trying again to leave*): But you cannot know. . . .

DIANA (*proudly, blocks her*): I know everything, everything (we hear the sound of approaching steps in the hallway). But after all here is James, your James . . . I will ask him what your business might be . . . Madame.

Scene V

James, Lucie and Diana

JAMES (*enters calmly, but confronted by the two women he turns pale and staggers as if he has received a blow to the head*).

DIANA (*smiling ironically*): Tableau! (*to James*) James, do you not see your lover? (*James makes a gesture and seems to want to speak, but a terrifying glance from Diana stops him in his tracks*). Come on, why don't you run to hug her, to kiss her? Oh, that's right, your kisses you send over the telephone. (*looking at them both fiercely and barely restraining herself*) What? You have both become mute? Does my presence bother you? I will leave! (*a joyful gesture by Lucie, one of surprise by James*) Just one moment however, dear Madame! Do not be so quick to smile. Before I leave I want to yell at him to his face, to your James, to him first, only one single word, this one: Coward!!

JAMES: Diana!

DIANA (*turning next towards Lucie*): And to you . . . to you . . . (*restraining herself*) Nothing, nothing to you. (*with a tearful voice and wringing her hands convulsively*) My lips can only repeat prayers to saints and on those prayers blossom words of love and charity. If I were to talk to you, therefore, you would not be able to understand me. For you to comprehend me I would have to speak the language that hisses in vice's depths, in life's gutters, in infamy's stench, but I do not know how, I cannot lower myself to those levels, no I cannot: I would suffocate!

LUCIE (*offended*): Madame!

JAMES: Diana! There has been a misunderstanding. The lady is. . . .

DIANA (*interrupting him*): Your lover! I know . . . Do you wish to introduce her to me? There is no need. She has already introduced herself over the telephone. (*gestures by Lucie and James*) She also expressed her desires. The lady is a passionate collector of . . . diamonds, did you know that? (*in a cold, ironic and terrible tone*) But they must be gifts. You do not have the means to buy them, and finding a way . . . too easily could bring you bad luck . . . Think about it! (*meaningfully*) Judges are not always merciful. . . .

JAMES (*perceives her insult and answers proudly*): Diana! You are insulting me!

DIANA (*ironically*): You stand next to your lover and say *to me, your wife*, that I am insulting you . . . (*she would like to say more and looks at him with disdain*) Oh, if only I didn't . . . pity you. (*for a moment she looks at the two of them*)

LUCIE (*makes a gesture of vexation and in leaving, when at the door, turns back with a challenging look at Diana*): Ta ta, James . . . I'll see you later.

JAMES (*throwing himself at Diana's feet*): Diana! Diana! . . .

DIANA (*She looks at him for a second. Then shaking her head, she moves towards the chair, upon which is her hat. She takes the hat and puts it on. James looks at her anxiously, in surprise. She lifts the telephone and places a call*): Morningside 3296.

JAMES (*stands up, frightened, and moves towards her*): What are you doing? Diana, for God's sake, what are you doing? . . .

DIANA (*she does not answer him. Speaking into the telephone*): Hallo, is that you mother?

JAMES (*trying to take the telephone from her*): What are you going to say to your mother?

DIANA (*pushing him away and not answering him, speaks into the telephone*): Yes, mother, it is I. I will be with you in half an hour . . . For lunch? Yes for lunch, for dinner, for breakfast, to sleep, with you, with you, dear mother, always with you; for my whole life I will be with you because you will not betray me, and you love me, don't you, mother? (*sobbing uncontrollably*) Oh

mother, dearest mother, prepare my lovely little childhood bed, my virgin
bed where I want to once again dream with your caresses and kisses . . .
Why are you crying? . . . But no, mother, I am not crying, I am laughing,
laughing, dearest mother, laughing (*she laughs convulsively while crying and
not being able to stand it anymore, hangs up the telephone*).

JAMES (*pale, upset, beside himself, sees Diana about to leave and throws himself
at her feet while trying to encircle her knees to stop her from moving*): Diana,
Diana! . . . Do not leave . . . No, no forgive me! Listen . . . I will tell you
everything, everything, but do not leave, no, no. . . .

DIANA (*trying to free herself from him*): No . . . Good bye forever!. . . .

JAMES (*desperately blocking her at the door*): No, no, Diana! . . . Did not the court
acquit me? So!. . . .

DIANA (*freeing herself from James, fiercely screams at him*): The court of law, yes,
but the personal one of family has judged you guilty, and given you a life
sentence . . . for all eternity! (*she leaves*).

JAMES (*holds his head with his hands and collapses on a nearby chair*)

Curtain

Translated by Maria Enrico

Leaves in the Whirlwind

∾ *Ario Flamma*

Catamossetta, Italy, 1882–New York, New York, 1961

All that is known of Ario Flamma is drawn from a not quite authentic biography, reconstructed below, aided by notes which are hardly reliable, given the commercial sources of the publications: notices in some *Who's Who*, and even less reliable, supplied by the author himself in his publications. In any case, a typical self-portrait of an aspiring Italian American writer emerges, possessed of unrealizable ambitions, and a bit of a boaster. Yet Flamma gained a curious preeminence for having pioneered attempts to draw middle-class themes onto the popular stage of Little Italy (though he also boasted of improbable successes on Broadway). In the preface of *Foglie nel turbine* (Leaves in the Whirlwind), his 1923 comedy in three acts, a part of which is reprinted here, Flamma narrates an episode that frankly expresses his sense of frustration:

> Several months before sailing to New York, I engaged in a literary hoax, in order to gauge my intellectual limits and that of some directors of various newspapers of the divine, unforgettable Rome. In some mere thirty days, I turned out a novel entitled, *Sorge il sole* [The sun rises], which took place in the red [Communist] days of Saint Petersburg . . . and some brief novellas of Russian life, falsely presenting the novel and novellas as translations from the Russian by the author, a certain Emanuele Baranine, who never existed. The novellas were published in *La Tribuna illustrata*; I was paid, and I was very pleased. The novel, of which the excellent Raimoni absolutely wanted the

original Russian, was published in *Il Messaggero*, of Rome, six months after my departure for the United States of America.

Flamma first emigrated to the United States in 1909. During the First World War, he was a volunteer with the American army. He lived in Chicago, where he worked as secretary of the Italian Chamber of Commerce, and then in New York, where between 1922 and 1924, he was the director of *Vaglio* (Screen). He wrote much, tenaciously following

the bitter and harsh path of art, even today surprised at not having forgotten Italian, for the three million Italians in America speak all the dialects, but not Italian. If I have acted rightly or wrongly in persisting in a profession that in America renders one subject to the most bitter delusions—not knowing English in a manner of being able to write it as one does one's own language, constrained to live among Italians, good people, industrious workers, but completely lacking in art, and almost hostile to those who become masters of it—I do not know.

One of his volumes of *Dramas* was issued in New York, in 1909, in a luxurious edition enriched by a letter (little more than a note) from Anatole France, by a note by Prince Trubetzkoy, and a preface in which Felix Rem states that the author "is a keen observer and analyzer of human nature and of the problems which excite the present society." The book contains three one-act plays, translated into English: *The Queen's Castle*, a philosophical work that "reveals the artificial foundation upon which society has lived and still adheres to, and points out very clearly why real happiness is not attainable in our life-time"; *Don Luca Sperante* (1906), "a vivid portrait of Sicilian character and customs [*sic*]"; *The Stranger* (1908), the story of an old man forgotten in the world, like an autumnal leaf. *Fiamme* (Flames), Flamma's first work, was published, privately, by Nicoletti in New York in 1903; it also includes the one-act *Nuvole rosee* (Pink Clouds). Other dramas by Fiamma are, *Piccole anime* (Little Souls), in three acts (New York 1912), a middle-class story set in the environs of Milan; *La maschera di Amleto* (Hamlet's mask, 1922), a play in three acts; *Dopo la guerra* (After the War, 1923); *La Potenza* (Power, 1926); *Gli ebrei* (The Jews); *Suor Maddalena* (Sister Magdalene), in three acts; and the one-act *All' ombra della croce* (In the Shadow of the Cross). Among his other writings are the poem "La Guerra" (The War), with a preface by Giovanni Bovio (Rome, 1906) and a biography of Fiorello La Guardia.

Federal Writers' Project 1938; Schiavo 1935; Schiavo 1966–67.

ॐ

GIANNI: Forgive me.

CINZIA: Who are you?

GIANNI: Who am I?

CINZIA: What do you want?

GIANNI: What . . . do I want?

CINZIA: I do not know you.

GIANNI: That is true . . . you do not know me.

CINZIA: And so?

GIANNI: I came . . . because . . . to make you go back . . . to your mother's, immediately, on the first train, it's leaving in a few minutes.

CINZIA: Why? What happened? Is my mother not well?

GIANNI: She is not . . . well.

CINZIA: Oh God!

GIANNI: We must not delay, we cannot miss the train.

CINZIA: I spoke to her on the telephone just two hours ago. She was perfectly well. Perhaps . . . Tell me, what happened to her?

GIANNI: Gather together all your things. Do not leave any trace that might reveal your presence in this place.

CINZIA: What happened to her? Tell me.

GIANNI: I already have the tickets for the trip.

CINZIA: Is it serious?

GIANNI: There is no time to lose.

CINZIA: I will hurry, but meanwhile tell me what this is all about, what is the matter with her. I am trembling with anxiety, with fear.

GIANNI: When you are in New York with her, you will bless the person who . . . rescued you from serious danger.

CINZIA: Danger?

GIANNI: Yes. Do not tarry, I beg you. The police could arrive at any moment.

CINZIA: What?

GIANNI: I meant that . . . with every passing moment, the danger increases.

CINZIA: Oh! You do not want to tell me. Perhaps . . . Oh God, no, no! (*She begins walking toward the door on the left*)

GIANNI: Where are you going? . . . Listen . . . A moment . . . Oh! *(But Cinzia exits.* Perplexed he remains, listening and looking towards the garden fearful that someone might be approaching. Then Cinzia's voice is heard—she is talking on the telephone)

CINZIA: Yes, yes, New York. I am ready. Yes . . . Mother! Is that you? . . . Are you well? . . . Oh God! . . . Nothing . . . I wanted to tell you . . . yes, Saturday. Fine . . . Good bye. *(Returning to the room)* I telephoned my mother. She is fine. Why did you lie? Who are you? What do you want?

GIANNI: Forgive me . . . You did not . . . did not give me time to explain myself. I did not tell you . . . I did not mean to say . . . Your mother is very upset because you are so inexplicably far away. She wants to see you, and immediately.

CINZIA: Thank you. We agreed that I will go to New York on Saturday.

GIANNI: Saturday? You must leave now, immediately, without delay.

CINZIA: Why?

GIANNI: Why? . . . Because . . . You do not know the danger that threatens you.

CINZIA: What danger?

GIANNI: I will tell on the way. Time is running short, and every minute hastens your safety, your ruin. *(Cinzia laughs ironically)* I speak as a father, a father . . . who cares for your happiness, your future.

CINZIA: Sir, I do not know who you are, what you want from me. It seems to me that you speak in riddles, that your brain is a bit . . . addled. There must be a misunderstanding. I beg of you, before continuing, reveal yourself, tell me what moved you to come here. It is not true that my mother sent you.

GIANNI: Your mother . . . does not know me.

CINZIA: Ah!

GIANNI: I meant . . . she will not remember me, but I have known her since . . . before she married. We are from the same town.

CINZIA: The same town?

GIANNI: There was a very old friendship between our two families. For this reason I took the liberty to come here—I am doing this, for your own good—to advise you to return to New York as soon as possible, because . . . if you are here, there could be no remedy. Tomorrow the scandal would be in all the newspapers, and your mother in finding out that you have deceived her, that you have been with a man who has taken advantage of your inexperience, of your credulity. . . .

CINZIA: Sir!

GIANNI: Is it not true that your mother believes that you are with a girlfriend?

CINZIA: Who informed you of such details. . . .

GIANNI: I do not blame you, condemn you, but the wretch who promised to marry you. . . .

CINZIA: He married me the very evening we arrived here.

GIANNI: He has ignobly deceived you.

CINZIA: Sir!

GIANNI: What reason would I have to lie?

CINZIA: Who sent you?

GIANNI: Who?

CINZIA: His father?

GIANNI: His father?

CINZIA: This is machination by his father to separate me from Torvaldo.

GIANNI: I do not know his father, and it is a lie that his father is against your marriage.

CINZIA: Did my mother send you?

GIANNI: No, your mother did not send me. I will tell you the truth now. I was wrong to lie, but . . . so . . . so suddenly, the emotion, the rush, the fear of discovery . . . That. . . .

CINZIA: It is useless to resort to further lies. I am warning you that you will not be able to penetrate my soul. I am more experienced than I look, than my age would allow.

GIANNI: Experienced!

CINZIA: Kindly inform Mr. Faversham that he is terribly mistaken if he thinks he can separate me from his son.

GIANNI: Poor girl!

CINZIA: It is true that our marriage was performed in secret, but Torvaldo is determined to make it public in a few days.

GIANNI: In a few days!

CINZIA: I will make him confirm it to you.

GIANNI: He no longer . . . speaks.

CINZIA: You will see.

GIANNI: Poor young thing!

CINZIA: There is no need to pity me.

GIANNI: If you could only understand what you have done. . . .

CINZIA: He loves me, and this excuses and explains everything.

GIANNI: He never loved you.

CINZIA: Ah! Ah!

GIANNI: Do you wish for tangible, undeniable proof? His name is not Torvaldo Faversham. His wife has just returned from Europe. She is in New York. Telephone her. Her telephone number is. . . .

CINZIA: Do not trouble yourself, sir. Thank you. I do not understand, I do not see the reason why you are so greatly interested in a matter that has nothing to do with you, that does not concern you. I truly cannot explain your eagerness, your perturbation over a deception that ultimately concerns me, and I, and my mother, can handle my life.

GIANNI: Your mother lives only for you, and if she knew. . . .

CINZIA: She will soon know that I have married Torvaldo, and she will be happy.

GIANNI: You know how much your mother suffered for having disobeyed her parents.

CINZIA: Sir. . . .

GIANNI: Listen to me, my dear . . . young lady. You are not at fault. I do not accuse you. One hundred other girls could have fallen into the same error in which you have fallen, in which your mother fell. . . . If you truly love your mother, who sacrificed her entire youth so that the past would not darken your horizons, leave this house, immediately. Your mother would become insane from shame, she would die of a heart attack if she found out that you have fallen into the same abyss in to which she was dragged as a young girl. You do not know the slenderness of the thread from which hangs the reputation of a girl. You do not know with how much perfidy and thoughtlessness men judge and condemn women; with how much criminal ease they abandon them once their brutal desire has been quenched. All it will take is for them to find you here, in his house, to unleash against you the most obscene, the most atrocious slander; and since his family is rich, since human hypocrisy favors those who are disinclined to protect us, those who do not. . . .

CINZIA: But you are you? You seem. . . .

GIANNI: Who?

CINZIA: Who are you?

GIANNI: Who . . . am I?

CINZIA: Yes.

GIANNI: I . . . knew you when you were a child. You were only two years old when . . . the first time I took you into my arms. The memory has never faded for me; the years only made in stronger in my heart. But . . . I am talking, talking, and meanwhile time is flying, meanwhile. . . .

CINZIA: You knew my father?

GIANNI:. . . Yes.

CINZIA: Really? Is he still alive?

GIANNI: I do not know.

CINZIA: Oh! If he were still alive, I would want to meet him to throw in his face all of my repugnance, my hate. He made my mother suffer so much!

GIANNI: Do not do to your mother what . . . your father. . . .

CINZIA: There is a difference!

GIANNI: True, a great difference, but in persisting in your error, you would cause your mother the same harm, the same suffering that your father . . . No. This is not possible, it must not happen! It would be monstrous, terrible! Every minute is precious. They will be here at any moment, and before they arrive. . . .

CINZIA: Who?

GIANNI: Who? . . . The police.

CINZIA: The police?

GIANNI: They will subject you to a humiliating, brutal interrogation. . . .

CINZIA: Why?

GIANNI: Because they will want to find out who . . . why . . . why you are here.

CINZIA: This is his and my house.

GIANNI: You have no rights over his possessions.

CINZIA: A wife has no rights. . . .

GIANNI: Wife? . . . He has deceived you ferociously.

CINZIA: The Rev. Hegon will tell you the day and time of our marriage ceremony.

GIANNI: Yes, he married you, I know. . . .

CINZIA: And so?

GIANNI: But he could not, should not have, and it was a diabolical sham.

CINZIA: Sham?

GIANNI: Yes. When a man is blinded by passion, he can justify any crime.

CINZIA: Is marriage a crime?

GIANNI: He had a wife; he knew he was deceiving you and the pastor's good faith.

CINZIA: Ah! Ah!

GIANNI: You do not believe me?

CINZIA: How can I believe you if the first thing you did when entering here was start telling lies?

GIANNI: I believed that your love for your mother would have convinced you more easily to break the chain of deceit that he. . . .

542   *On Stage (and Off)*

CINZIA: The chain of love, you mean.

GIANNI: Love? Fraud, lust, lies!

CINZIA: Please moderate your language. I think it is time.... (*She rings an electric bell*)

GIANNI: What are you doing?

CINZIA: Giorgio will escort you to the gate.

GIANNI: Oh no! I will not leave you unless first....

CINZIA: Kindly inform the person who sent you that it is an ignoble meanness to use such devices, to force a girl to separate from a man she loves and who loves her just as much, and to whom she is indissolubly tied by marriage.

GIANNI: No one sent me here. That is a strange idea of which you have convinced yourself. I am here because ... for the friendship that ties me to your mother.

CINZIA: How did you find out about this address?

GIANNI: How did I find it?

CINZIA: Yes!

GIANNI: I got it....

CINZIA: Ah! Ah!

GIANNI: I got it from your mother.

CINZIA: Enough, enough! But where is Giorgio? Doesn't he hear? (*She rings the bell again*)

GIANNI: Don't ring! You will be lost, you will be ruined!

CINZIA: Sir, it is time for you to take your leave.

GIANNI: Take my leave?

CINZIA: You do not agree?

GIANNI: Do you think I could leave you here in danger, under threat....

CINZIA: What danger, what threat? You are dreaming. And anyway, I do not need any protection.

GIANNI: This is how you repay your mother's suffering and sacrifices?

CINZIA: Leave my mother out of this.

GIANNI: Do you think it honest to remain in the house of a stranger, of a married man?

CINZIA: Why not? Since he loves me....

GIANNI: Since he....

CINZIA: Naturally.

GIANNI: And his wife?

CINZIA: Divorce was created to correct matrimonial errors.

GIANNI: What if she does not agree to a divorce?

CINZIA: Why shouldn't she agree?

GIANNI: For many reasons.

CINZIA: Too bad for her.

GIANNI: What?

CINZIA: Since he loves me and I love him, our union is above any law, convention, or morality; it is above everything.

GIANNI Are you saying that you do not care that you are living with a married man?

CINZIA: You have bothered me enough and I must tell you once again that your lies have accomplished nothing. . . .

GIANNI: I swear on what is most holy, most dear to you, on the life of your mother, that I have told the truth, that a terrible misfortune will befall you if you remain here.

CINZIA: Fine. When Torvaldo gets here . . . But why is he late? It's evening. (*She turns on a lamp light*)

GIANNI: Oh God, it is evening and we are still here, on the edge of an abyss, faced with an increasing danger that is getting closer by the minute. I beg you. . . .

CINZIA: Enough, I said. There is the door.

GIANNI: For the love you have for your mother. . . .

CINZIA: Do not make me repeat it for the third time.

GIANNI: You will kill your mother.

CINZIA: Leave.

GIANNI: I am begging you on bended knees. . . .

CINZIA: But you are insane.

GIANNI: Insane? . . . I will certainly become insane by prolonging this agony, this tempest that for the past two months has been raging in my head, never endingly, implacably overwhelming my thoughts. If on that evening I had carried out my vengeance, what happened would not have happened, your innocence would still be intact, I would not be frantic in my inane efforts to convince you to flee from the impending disaster, the threatening wings of death would not be approaching your mother. . . .

CINZIA: Of which evening do you speak? What vengeance?

GIANNI: What vengeance?

CINZIA: I think . . . I think . . . Your face reminds me of. . . .

GIANNI: Who?

CINZIA: I am not certain . . . I think . . . Oh! Yes! You . . . one evening, at my home . . . Oh God, why did you come? What do you want?

GIANNI: I want you to return to your mother and nothing more.

CINZIA: That evening you were armed . . . you wanted to kill him.

GIANNI: It would have been better if I had nailed him to the ground that evening!

CINZIA: Ah!!

GIANNI: Seeing you made me lose all courage, it completely vanquished my will.

CINZIA: Why did you want to kill him?

GIANNI: Why? . . . You cannot figure it out? You don't know?

CINZIA: Because of money?

GIANNI: Ah! This is the calumny he coined so that I would be imprisoned while he accomplished his deception, certain that I would lose all trace of him. And I spent days, terrible nights in the silence of my cell, because I knew that with every dawn and every sunset he was plucking another petal from the corolla of your virginity, without my being able to the stop the crime because in revealing his misdeed I would have harmed you and your mother, and this I could not do, could not allow! If only I could describe to you how much I suffered then, the ferocious joy that overcame me the day I became free and able to take my vengeance. . . .

CINZIA: Ah!

GIANNI: If I could only describe to you my dejection, my desperation when I became absolutely certain of your fall. . . .

CINZIA: But who are you? . . . Who are you?

GIANNI: Who . . . am I? . . . Can you tell? A finished man, the detritus that a stream drags into a bottomless vortex, the leaf that a whirlwind pushes into the void, into nothingness.

CINZIA: But why . . . that evening . . . why are you still looking for him?

GIANNI: For him? . . . No, I no longer seek him.

CINZIA: And what do you want from me?

GIANNI: Haven't I told you, haven't I been repeating it for hours with trepidation in my soul, with desperation in my heart? Because if they find you here, it will not be possible to avoid scandal, it will not be possible to avoid that people will suspect you of complicity. . . .

CINZIA: Complicity in what?

GIANNI: Oh God, do not ask this of me now . . . I will tell you on the way. Can't you see how late it is? I am amazed that they are not yet here. But they will not delay. Perhaps they have taken him to the hospital. . . .

CINZIA: What?

GIANNI: I meant . . . perhaps . . . well . . . but we must not waste any more time. Your safety, your future, the life and happiness of your mother depend on this moment, on your immediate departure.

CINZIA: Who has been taken . . . to the hospital?

GIANNI: To the hospital?

CINZIA: Yes!?

GIANNI: To the hospital. . . .

CINZIA: Stop repeating my words. Tell me, if you do not want me to start screaming, to call for help. Who? . . . Who?

GIANNI: Who?

CINZIA: Yes, yes!

GIANNI: The man who soiled your virginity, who ignobly betrayed you.

CINZIA: No, no! It's not true! You lie! It is not possible! (*She moves toward the door*) Giorgio . . . Giorgio! Marina! . . . Marina . . . God! There's no one. They have left me all alone. But he should have been here a long while ago. Why this unusual delay? You lied; you are resorting to another stratagem to make me . . . Ah! Ah! I am so foolish; I've fallen into your trap. Ah! Ah! Ah! What a fool, what a fool!

GIANNI: You still do not believe me? How can I prove it to you? Must I die? Well then, I will kill myself, here, at your feet, to convince you of the truth, but promise me that you will leave now, immediately, if not for your honor, your safety, your future, then at least for your mother who will go mad or die of shame and desperation knowing that you have fallen into an error greater than hers because the man who betrayed her, who abandoned your mother, was her legitimate husband. But the man who has betrayed you had a wife, and the ceremony he took part in was done to induce you to the most sacred act of love. It was a tragic farce, a crime two times over, worthy of the most inexorable punishment.

CINZIA: Are you telling . . . the truth?

GIANNI: May God strike me dead if I am telling a lie!

CINZIA: Ah!!!

GIANNI: Poor girl . . . Fate has woven its web of deceit, of pain also for you. But time will heal your wound. Youth will sing again the hymns of joy, of happiness in your soul. Do not despair! You will find comfort, peace and oblivion with your mother. Calm yourself. Time is running short. There is not a moment to waste. It is lucky, very lucky that no one has yet arrived. Except for him, no one knows your name, where you live. If we leave immediately, there will be no trace of you. And, as always happens in

New York, in time people and the police will completely forget what happened. But we must not tarry. If they have not yet arrived, it means that . . . But they will not delay much longer. Gather up your courage. Hurry! The night protects us. Let's go. . . .

CINZIA: I . . . cannot!

GIANNI: Courage . . . I will lead you.

CINZIA: No! . . . First I must see him, ask him. . . .

GIANNI: Ask him? . . . For what purpose?

CINZIA: Because . . . Why. . . .

GIANNI: But he will not come. He cannot come.

CINZIA: I will wait for him.

GIANNI: You will wait in vain.

CINZIA: What do you mean?

GIANNI: Haven't I told you? Didn't you understand?

CINZIA: What?

GIANNI: He . . . He . . . Today, I . . . I was the one who telephoned him, telling him, pretending I was his secretary. . . .

CINZIA: Ah!!

GIANNI: And while he was approaching the station by car, together with his friend, laughing, confident of his ephemeral power, I . . . I took aim, I fired, and I saw him slump. . . .

CINZIA: Ah!!!

GIANNI: Was I not right? Was it not my right to punish him? Doesn't a father have the right . . . (*Cinzia screams desperately and faints on to the nearby sofa. Gianni remains stunned for a moment, and then runs towards his daughter*) Cinzia . . . Cinzia! . . . My daughter, my daughter! . . . I love her so much . . . she is so lovely! . . . To be able to see you up close, to touch your soft, adored hands, oh what joy, what happiness! But only for a few more moments and then I will have to give up this love, this joy, forever! . . . Disappear . . . in the night, in the shadows. Life is so cruel! . . . Daughter . . . My daughter! (*He breaks into tears. There is a sound of voices and footsteps. He hears them, a tremor runs through his body; he jumps to his feet, waits terrified for a moment and then gathers the fainted girl in his arms. He is about to move towards the door when he hears the voice of Torvaldo calling for Cinzia from the garden. He is overcome with terror and loses grip of his daughter's body which falls back onto the sofa. Torvaldo's voice becomes louder.*)

TORVALDO: (*in the wings*) Cinzia! (*Gianni quickly pulls a revolver from his pocket and moves toward the door, hiding in the shadows. Now Torvaldo, the valet, and Johnson, whose arm is bandaged and in a sling around his neck, enter, while Johnson, leaning on the valet, moves toward one of the doors, Torvaldo says)* Where is Cinzia? . . . Oh! Here she is. Is she sleeping? . . . Poor love. She looks so pale . . . She seems to have fainted. Cinzia . . . Cinzia . . . Yes, Yes, open your eyes. It is I, can you see me? Are you ill?

CINZIA: Who . . . who is it?

TORVALDO: It is I, your Torvaldo. Tell me! You were tired, frightened.

CINZIA: Where . . . am I?

TORVALDO: Ah, you are dreaming. You were dreaming. Poor love! Wake up. I have good news for you. I sent for your mother and she will arrive tonight. Tomorrow we leave for Italy and your mother will come with us. Are you listening?

CINZIA: Torvaldo? . . . Is it you? . . . It's not true?

TORVALDO: What?

CINZIA: It wasn't true!

TORVALDO: What was not true?

CINZIA: He lied . . . I dreamt. . . .

TORVALDO: What did you dream?

CINZIA: There is no one . . . You are alone. . . .

TORVALDO: You are a bit delirious. You are not well.

CINZIA: My love! Torvaldo! (*She pulls him to her breast, convulsively, while both crying and laughing. Meanwhile Gianni silently goes into the garden and vanishes in the shadows of the night. So ends the stage fiction.*)

Wilkes-Barre, PA. May–June 1923

Translated by Maria Enrico

PART IV

Anarchists, Socialists, Fascists,
and Antifascists

Introduction

The anarchist movement constituted what Nunzio Pernicone has very appropriately defined as a "unique subculture."[1] In his view, the behavior of the anarchists should be seen in a much broader context than a strictly political one. Rather, it amounts to a complex, variegated lifestyle, a system of values that deeply marked an epoch in America. The years Pernicone is referring to run from the last decade of the nineteenth century to the aftermath of the Sacco and Vanzetti trial (1927). In these years, Italian American anarchists were able to forge their own political line, perhaps more "conservative" than the parallel developments of the anarchist idea in Europe, and yet able to retrieve a special freshness, a sort of juvenile, uncontaminated exuberance. This quality was due to the persistence of a "fin-de-siècle mood"[2] inherited from their Italian masters.

The Italian American anarchists established "a sort of alternative society. . . . They had their own circles, their own credos, and their own culture. They built their own world in the very heart of the system which they detested and opposed. In place of millenarian expectations, they preferred the everyday practices of an anarchist life in the interstices of American capitalism. In effect, they formed small enclaves or small nuclei of freedom . . . and hoped that these would spread and multiply worldwide.[3] But this lifestyle did not prevent them from carving a lasting mark in people's awareness. Furthermore, some groups, such as that which formed around Carlo Tresca's paper *Il Martello* (The Hammer), succeeded in maintaining sus-

1. Pernicone 1972, 1.
2. Ibid., 4.
3. Avrich 1991, 53–54.

tained but problematic relations with the other forces of transplanted radicalism. This did not mean, though, that these groups accepted a professional, bureaucratic view of political action. The salient trait of the Italian American anarchists was indeed their radical opposition to any form of organization that might have represented a threat to the single individual's free and vital self-expression. This form of opposition allowed them to be closer to the spiritual foundations of America, an America traditionally suspicious of any "foreign" ideas.[4] As has been pointed out from within the movement itself, this repeated denial of the value of any political doctrine noticeably influenced the development of Italian anarchism.[5]

We are speaking here of that form of thorough anarchism heated by the communard fires of 1871: atheist, anticlerical, antiauthoritarian, fiercely adverse to any form of state government or political and unionist power, collectivist but certainly not in the sense of the dictatorship of the proletariat. Indeed, class discrimination was completely absent. This movement was rather attracted to the glaring light of a kind of universal resurrection guaranteed by the most radical form of communism, capable of embracing free love, women's emancipation, reciprocal economic assistance according to one's needs, and so forth. Umberto Postiglione struck the note of a radical critique of the labor unions. As he forcefully wrote in this regard: "The Union is a State within the State. It is a form of government, with its executive officers and police force, its bureaucracy, its laws, and its courts. Anarchy is rebellion, and nobody has ever seen priests or cops, regardless of their kind or color, who tolerated or favored heretics.[6]

The anarchists widely shared the belief that revolution was imminent. This is why Bakunin and the leaders of Italian anarchism held that the current conditions of the Italian masses were ideal. From a strictly Marxist point of view, in fact, they were not yet ready for the class struggle owing to their backwardness. But the anarchists' assumption was simpler. The conditions of extreme poverty in which these masses were forced to live would trigger the revolution. Italy lacked a real industrial system, so that it could not breed an authentic class-consciousness. This absence of class consciousness meant that in the proletariat, which was rigorously kept at the margins of society, would not develop the desire to emulate the bourgeoisie.

This same proletariat, consisting predominantly of peasants, would soon face the Great Migration to the Americas. When this exodus began, Italian anarchism

4. See, on this subject, the keen observations developed by Dore 1964, 311–315.
5. See Cerrito 1969, 270.
6. "Su un vecchio chiodo" (On an Old Obsession), *Cronaca Sovversiva* (Subversive Chronicle), July 8, 1916; reprinted in Postiglione 1972, 28–29.

was a heterogeneous aggregation of small, autonomous groups whose chances of influencing social struggles were very few. This was partly due to their traditional hostility to the labor unions, which were increasingly dominated by socialists. Furthermore, these anarchist groups were zealously persecuted by the historical left, which treated them like common criminals.

A new vital phase began when Errico Malatesta returned from exile in South America in 1889. It was he who urged the movement to abandon its aversion to organization and to devise an effective strategy. It was necessary to carry out the revolution, and isolationism was an obstacle to that goal. Thus, there was an urgent need to reconnect with the working classes and take part in the struggle—if for no other reason than to stop the pernicious influence of reformist and parliamentary socialism. These are the recommendations that emerged from the convention of Capolago, the outcome of which in January 1891 was the Revolutionary Anarcho-Socialist Party. The ensuing turmoil in Rome on May 1 provoked the firm reaction of the police and led to a massive wave of arrests throughout Italy. Many interpreted this as a demonstration of the inadequacy of this organizational model, which instead underlay the contemporary rise of the Italian Socialist Party (PSI) in 1892.

Crispi's repression of the Sicilian *Fasci* (Fasces) and the quarry workers' attempted revolt in Lunigiana led to a total setback of the movement, highlighted by Francesco Saverio Merlino's and Errico Malatesta's escape (1894).[7] In this same year the anarchists started taking isolated initiatives and carried out several assassination attempts (often successful) against the lives of the powerful. On June 24, 1894, Sante Caserio killed the French president, Carnot. In that same year Paolo Lega tried to murder Francesco Crispi. In 1897 Michele Angiolillo killed the Spanish prime minister, Canovas del Castillo, and Pietro Acciarito made an attempt on King Umberto's life. In 1898 Luigi Lucheni killed Elizabeth, the empress of Austria. But these were also the years of the harshest repression of the working classes, which culminated in General Bava Beccaris's actions in Milan in May 1898, when soldiers under his command shot and killed hundreds of demonstrators. There followed a massive use of the penalty of internal exile to Lipari and other islands. Thousands of anarchists were interned, and somewhat paradoxically, those places of punishment were transformed into centers of political indoctrination for the

---

7. These events were the motive for the expatriation of numerous leading activists, among them Bernardino Verro, who, from America, sent some interesting correspondence to *Avanti!* See Testi 1976. In 1894 in New York a committee for solidarity with I Fasci was formed, which gathered funds that were delivered to Italy by the engineer Caggiano of Scranton, Pennsylvania (see Ferraris 1968, 49).

following generations of activists. Finally, when the repression let up and the anarchists were beginning to catch their breath, on July 29, 1900, one of them—Gaetano Bresci—shot and killed King Umberto in Monza.

Bresci came from Paterson, New Jersey, the center of a textile-manufacturing industry, where he had arrived in 1897. Later on, an anarchist circle was named after him. In 1899 Bresci had distinguished himself by disarming Domenico Pazzaglia, the man who for some reason—either political or private—had shot in the leg and wounded Errico Malatesta during a public meeting in nearby West Hoboken. After Bresci died in prison in Italy, his widow opened a restaurant at Cliffside Park, in New Jersey, and for a while this served as a meeting place for anarchists.

According to several scholars, in that period, Paterson was in point of fact the most important center of anarchism in the Western Hemisphere. Luigi V. Ferraris estimates that at least five hundred of the ten thousand or so Italians who lived there joined anarchist associations.[8] The New Jersey Center for Workers was the scene of many clamorous events: Malatesta's pedagogical activities in the winter of 1899–1900, his presumed attempt on the life of Giuseppe Ciancabilla, and a number of his other feuds. On hearing about the regicide during a crowded meeting held on July 30, 1900, the beautiful Ernestina Cravello, a legendary activist, burst out, "We did not plan to kill King Umberto . . . but we are happy that someone did." One of Ciancabilla's group sent a telegram to Minister Saracco that expressed the group's exultation. The Francisco Ferrer Modern School—a libertarian institution named for the Spanish anarchist martyr Ferrer—was kept running for a long time.[9]

The first anarchist group in the United States, the Revolutionary Anarchist Socialist Group Carlo Cafiero, had been founded in New York in 1885. Two years later another group with the same name was established in Chicago. In 1888 it started up the newspaper *L'Anarchico* (The Anarchist), which was published by the New York group, and was followed by *Il Grido degli Oppressi* (The Cry of the Oppressed, New York, 1892). Then there came *La Questione Sociale* (The Social Question, Paterson, 1895); *L'Aurora* (The Dawn, West Hoboken, 1899), which was founded by Giuseppe Ciancabilla, Malatesta's fierce adversary on the issue of organization; *La Protesta Umana* (Human Protest, Chicago, 1902); and many others. The movement had rapidly spread in the cities of the East Coast. In the early 1890s

8. For Paterson and the life of Gaetano Bresci in America, see also Ferraris 1968 and Cerrito 1969, which add to the controversy on the subject.

9. See Adolfo Piccinni's article "Una visita alla scuola moderna Francisco Ferrer di Paterson, NJ" (A Visit to the Francisco Ferrer Modern School of Paterson, NJ) in *L'Era Nuova* (The New Era), February 12, 1916.

groups of anarchists were active in Boston, Philadelphia, and Baltimore. Later, new cells were created in Pittsburgh, Cleveland, Detroit, and, in 1894, San Francisco.

In 1886 there was the famous Haymarket episode. The explosion of a bomb caused the death of several policemen in Chicago, leading to the hanging of four anarchists (a fifth committed suicide in jail). This incident revealed how widespread anarchism was in the United States and caused a great stir. The newspapers followed the trial, which lasted well over a year, with a great outpouring of passion. They underscored its aberrations and aroused popular feelings similar to those that accompanied the trial of Sacco and Vanzetti many years later. But the growth of the anarchist presence among the Italian immigrants in the United States was primarily due to the presence of the movement's leaders, and the more or less prolonged permanence in America of a number of important agitators. In 1892–93, Francesco Saverio Merlino, the founder of *Il Grido degli Oppressi* and *Solidarity* (published in English, a language which he spoke fluently), preceded Malatesta to America. In 1895 Pietro Gori, the bard of anarchy, passed through and left his imprint on those whom he met. In 1898 Ciancabilla arrived. In 1901 it was the turn of the forty-year-old Luigi Galleani, who was the soul of the *Cronaca Sovversiva* (Subversive Chronicle). Moreover, along with Tresca, he was the most important personality of the Italian anarchist movement in the United States. For almost twenty years his role was crucial.[10]

Paul Avrich has calculated that between 1870 and 1940, one hundred of the approximately five hundred anarchist newspapers published in the United States were produced by Italians—that is, the ethnic group that was the most active in anarchist movements. To this number, we must add the myriad printed volumes, leaflets, and pamphlets that were distributed through subscriptions or during public meetings.[11] Undoubtedly, these publications have a great historical-documentary value, but they are equally interesting from a more strictly literary point of view. Since Italian American anarchism was characterized by a strong, pervasive, and at times almost mystical spirit, these publications generally tended to transcend the political or social contingencies that gave rise to them. They modeled themselves on a by then consolidated rhetorical tradition that, from *scapigliatura* (a literary and artistic movement founded in Lombardy in the late nineteenth century) passes into *verismo* (realism) and the late nineteenth-century mood of

10. For this rapid reconstruction of events relative to the origins of the Italian anarchist movement in the United States, see Avrich 1991, 45–48. For the complex history of the various newspapers, see in particular Dadà 1976.

11. See Dadà 1976, 54.

rebellion embodied above all in the poetry of the time. Along this line we can mention Carducci with his *Giambi ed epodi* (Iambs and epodes), Guerrini's *Civilia*, and first and foremost, Rapisardi, the poet of socialism. But one should also mention the "radical" writers from France, such as the Valles of *Refractaires* and a poet who is currently forgotten, the Sicilian Giuseppe Aurelio Costanzo. Constanzo was the author of the short poem *Gli eroi della soffitta* (The Heroes of the Attic, 1880), which can be read almost as a "catalogue" of

> Those who disdain to bend
> Their back to the pack saddle,
> Their neck to the halter.

This poem was greatly admired, for example, by the anarchist poet Pietro Gori. Such, in effect, was the background of the anarchist literary subculture. Gori's speeches and fiery poems, Galleani's contemptuous chronicles and Tresca's irresistible invectives relied on the same rhetorical tools. By coining expressions that soon became proverbial, they made their works resonate with mythic allusions. Their writings strike our imagination because, beyond their political content, they are conceived in a literary manner. Its very detractors implicitly acknowledged this distinctive trait of the anarchist press. In particular, with respect to *La Questione Sociale*, even its critics understood that its subversive force was accompanied by the will to reshape a whole world. Never mind if it was precariously based on a mixture of Proudhon, Reclus, Bakunin, Kropotkin, and Stirner:

> The periodicals deploy all their criminal propaganda in order to determine what they call "propaganda exploits." Instead, *La Questione Sociale*, although it does not lose sight of this immediate aim . . . soars to the level of general ideas. It attempts to discipline all that chaotic jumble, the most savage and criminal impulses, into a fictitious logical and systematic order. In this way, the entire lot of the various tendentiously anarchist articles which appear in the journal acquires an apparently organized doctrinal flavor.

The preceding observations come from a timeless study of the anarchist groups in the United States by Ettore Zaccoli, an observer close to Filippo Turati, founder of the Italian Socialist Party, and reveal an interest which, in Italy, concerned not only the various police headquarters but other observers as well.[12]

12. Zoccoli 1901, 7–9.

Antonio Margariti's case is emblematic of the allure that, in agreement with Bakunin's theories, the anarchist apostolate exerted on the masses of destitute peasants who had come from southern Italy. Margariti was the typical semiliterate immigrant harried by an almost feudal system at home and forced to confront a harsh, difficult, and ruthless world in America. Significantly, his memoir begins with a quotation of some lines by Pietro Gori, which he had evidently committed to memory—interjected, one might say, as a precious gem worth preserving for life:

I do not write for art or glory,
I write for what boils in my brain,
I write and rebel against the old world
And the old History.

These lines continue in an extraordinary language that had accumulated in layers over the years on top of its original Calabrian peasant base. Margariti warns that "the subject of my humble piece of writing is nothing but what I remember about my long, rather sad life, if it can be called a life. That is, my tough past." Ultimately, he prefigures a future of universal brotherhood, but one in which there resonates a note of deep sorrow:

The GREAT amount of money spent nowadays to destroy properties and kill millions of poor innocent people will be used for the well-being and progress of those human beings who produce it. This world is worth bringing into being, but I shall no longer be here to be a part of the human family.[13]

For Margariti and many other immigrants, the anarchist circle represented therefore a social occasion that, for the first time, allowed them to attend theatrical events, concerts, picnics, and dances. It also offered educational opportunities, a school for critical thinking (often a *real* school, with teachers, courses, and classes).

13. Margariti (Ferruzzano, Reggio Calabria, Italy, 1891–Willow Grove, Pennsylvania, 1981) published his memoirs under the title *America! America!* in 1979 at age eighty-seven. This savage and touching book awakened a vast interest, so much so as to be a finalist for the Viareggio Literary Prize. One could say that the education of the poor Calabrian immigrant took place entirely in America through his frequenting of anarchist circles; Margariti committed himself, among other things, to the circulation of *Adunata dei Refrattari* (Gathering of the Unwilling) and of *Il Martello*, as well as to committees for Sacco and Vanzetti and to antifascist initiatives. The excerpts of the memoirs mentioned here are quoted in the author's original version. The typescript is reproduced at the end of Giuseppe Galzerano's "translation" in the 1991 edition, with the purpose of facilitating its comprehension.

Here one could better define and give historical breadth to those spontaneous and rebellious inclinations that the helpless confrontation with priests, bosses, and all sorts of profiteers had nurtured for a long time. Workers from all over the country became *galleanisti* (followers of Galleani), even if this did not mean that they were strict observers of the famous leader's doctrine.

Paul Avrich has pinpointed four main ideological currents in the Italian American anarchist movement:[14]

(1) The anarcho-communists like Galleani, who rejected not only the state but also private property. To this category also belonged Nicola Sacco and Bartolomeo Vanzetti. Vanzetti's newspaper article "Cose a posto e le menzogne in gola!" (Things in Order and Lies in the Throat), on the Plymouth strike, disagrees with the politics of the IWW (Industrial Workers of the World) and the socialists.[15]

(2) The anarcho-syndicalists, who in strong opposition to the anarcho-communists were in favor of an organic relationship with the labor unions. The most important figure of this current was Carlo Tresca.

(3) The anarcho-individualists, of nihilistic and Stirnerian faith, who decidedly believed in solitary action, and they too were equipped with their own newspapers, such as *Nihil* (Nothing) and *Cogito, ergo sum* (I Think, Therefore I Am). Both were published in San Francisco at the beginning of the century. In 1922 these groups found their ideal forum in the long-lived *L'Adunata dei Refrattari* (The Gathering of the Unwilling), whose heart and soul was Raffaele Schiavina, formerly on the staff of *La Cronaca Sovversiva* and follower of Galleani, who kept the latter's spirit alive. Indeed, the *Adunata* proved to be totally solitary and impervious to any attempt at striking up an alliance among the scattered cells. Its goal, in fact, was "a spontaneous and inevitable revolution carried out by those subjects whose possibilities of individual fulfillment were crushed by capitalism and the state."[16] Armando Borghi and Virgilia D'Andrea also wrote for the *Adunata*, which was constantly fighting with Tresca's *Il Martello*. The *Adunata* maintained a position of unshakeable detachment even on the issue of antifascist alliances. In 1931, it financed a sort of repeat of Gaetano Bresci's solitary action—namely, the anarchist Michele

14. Avrich 1991, 52–53.
15. *Cronaca Sovversiva*, March 11, 1916.
16. Dadà 1984, 350.

Schirru's attempt on the life of Mussolini (Schirru came from the Bronx, but he was arrested before going into action and was shot in Rome on May 29).[17]

(4) The anarcho-Malatestians, those "without adjectives" and pragmatically committed to spreading the anarchist idea as widely as possible.

The profile of these currents is obviously more nuanced than any zealous sectarian spirit might lead us to believe. The various articulations of anarchist thought at the end of the nineteenth century continued to be influential well into the following century. But they were progressively enriched as the anarchists continued their struggles and strikes and endured acts of repression. A pamphlet like *Perché siamo anarchici?* (Why Are We Anarchists?) by Francesco Saverio Merlino, printed in Patterson, expressed its clear-cut opinion on some basic themes. It stated, for example, that "the 'right to property' is an obstacle to progress and an enemy of the worker's well-being. It is a source of vices, conflicts, crimes, and usury. It is an institution that has become incompatible with the needs, ideas, and sentiments of our times."[18]

Evidently, this assumption was particularly challenging; even more so, if inserted in the reality of the United States, where the buying power of the proletariat had slowly but steadily grown, especially in the large metropolitan industrial areas. This undeniable fact led to a number of transformations and produced new consumer habits much more quickly than in Europe. Opinions such as those expressed by Merlino might have a stronger hold over peripheries like the proletarian hells of the mining fields. Or they might affect those situations where, in point of fact, the labor unions did not have the power to stop the bosses and the vigilante squads from brutally exploiting and oppressing the workers.

Luminaries like Carlo Tresca became central in the more general panorama of American radicalism. They went beyond their own ethnic enclave and built bridges among the diverse currents that made up its tormented history. "At various stages of his career," Tresca "defined himself as a socialist, a syndicalist, and an anarchist."[19] As a matter of fact, Tresca passed from revolutionary socialism to anarchy and then to IWW syndicalism. He was an enthusiastic supporter of the October Revolution and later a merciless opponent of Stalinism. An intransigent socialist, he ultimately formulated a radical critique of unionist profiteering and

17. On this subject, see Fiori 1983. Between 1926 and 1932, Mussolini suffered four assassination attempts by anarchists Gino Lucetti, Anteo Zamboni, Michele Schirru, and Angelo Sbardelloto.
18. Merlino n.d., 9.
19. Pernicone 1989, 216.

became a hard and fast anticommunist. The breadth of his popularity in each of the above-mentioned circles is underlined by the quantity and tone of the comments that appeared in newspapers and literary journals after his tragic death in 1943. All in all, as Max Nomad, the author of *Rebelli e rinnegati* (Rebels and Renegades) and *Apostoli della rivoluzione* (Apostles of the Revolution), pointed out, he was really "the last of the Mohicans" of independent radicalism.[20] A true-born revolutionary and always restless, he embodied a nineteenth-century spirit which in America had found a new ideal impetus thanks to its coming into contact with the problems of the proletarian masses.[21] On the other hand, America had allowed him to purge himself of certain ideological toxins that were typically European. A famous writer, John Dos Passos, nicely summed up this shift as follows:

> In his early years his writings were inspired by the Revolution. He was still inebriated by the grandiose dream of an international working class destined to bring peace and freedom to the world. As the years passed, his dominant concern became the defense of the freedom of the masses. The revolutions which nineteenth-century agitators had dreamt about finally took place, but instead of freedom and peace they brought to Europe wars, oppression, and the most hateful form of despotism which history records.
>
> Within the circle of the new Italian world in which he moved, Carlo Tresca fought to keep far from America the fascist and communist organizations that had turned Europe into a hell.[22]

Appreciated by liberal intellectuals, Tresca had become already ten years before his death a very popular public figure. In the *New Yorker*, Max Eastman had dedicated a portrait-interview to him with the promising title "Troublemaker Number 1: Carlo Tresca." Let us peruse the beginning of it:

> Carlo Tresca is the despair of all those young men whose idea of success and glory is to get arrested and sent to jail in the cause of the working class.

20. See "Max Nomad commemora Carlo Tresca" (Max Nomad Commemorates Carlo Tresca), *La Parola del Popolo* (The Word of the People) 1 (January–March 1951): 28–29.

21. In the teachings of Errico Malatesta, Tresca seemed, at a point, to have found his most firmly ideal reference point, so much so that in the 1930s he dedicated a running column in his newspaper *Il Martello* to "Parola del Maestro" (The Teacher's Word), that teacher being Malatesta.

22. Preface of John Dos Passos in the booklet of the Tresca Memorial Committee 1947. On Dos Passos and the anarchists, see, among others, Baker 1972.

Tresca holds the international all-time record in his field. He has been arrested thirty-six times. He has been tried by jury seven times. The crimes charged against him run all the way from shouting "Viva Socialismo!" in a cop's face to first-degree murder, taking in on the way blasphemy, slander, libel, disturbing the peace, sedition, disorderly conduct, criminal obscenity, conspiracy, unlawful assemblage, and incitement to riot. He has had his throat cut by a hired assassin, been bombed, been kidnapped by Fascisti, been shot at four times (once by an Ohio sheriff from a distance of eight feet), been marked for death by the agents of Mussolini, and snatched from death's jaws by the magic power of the Black Hand.[23]

Eastman went so far as to write that, after Eugene V. Debs's death, Tresca had become "the most universally esteemed and respected man in the revolutionary movement." "If he had learned English, he would have been one of the greatest men in the history of the labor movement in America." But even enclosed in Little Italy as he was, he was still the only Italian capable of deserving the respect of all the 117 different currents of that movement. Eastman portrayed Tresca as a typical southern gentleman, one whom the railway workers of Sulmona used to call "Don Carlo" while marching with him behind the red flag. Eastman brilliantly described the various features of his face and his person, noting "the warm smile addressed to anybody who at the moment was not shooting at him." Eastman tried to reproduce his characteristic way of speaking: it was not English with a marked Italian accent, rather it was "Italian sprinkled with English words." In his conversations with Tresca, Eastman captured one of the most typical aspects of his inimitable personality of a born fighter: "It's wonderful to have friends. But when the moment of battle comes and my dearest friend is on the wrong side, I give him no quarter, I have no pity for him." It was like an urgent and uncontrollable need. For Tresca, who had never asked labor unions or political parties for money, "to fight for the workers' rights is an art, not a profession." Eastman tried to figure out the motivation behind Tresca's way of life: a difficult life, spent in straitened circumstances and in an extremely dangerous and troubled environment—a life that might have been infinitely more comfortable since he could count on the economic prosperity of his family back home. The only answers he could find involved Carlo's desire to roam about the world and fight. Moreover, Eastman offered a rather hazy

23. The *New Yorker* article was reprinted in *Il Martello* on August 17, 1935, a special edition celebrating the fifty-fifth birthday of Tresca and the thirtieth anniversary of his political activism.

perception of a certain Italian type, and he was not totally off the mark. In his view the Italian was a solitary hero, tormented by his inner demons, who on the other hand stood out clearly against the background of the America of the Great Depression:

> There is something peculiarly Italian in the position occupied by Carlo Tresca. He is not the head of a political party or any formal league or union, but an individual revolutionary chief, or *duce*, with his own personal following, devoted and ready to die for him. So is the head of the Black Hand. So in a way is Mussolini. The big black felt hat that Tresca wears . . . is an essential accessory to this role. Absolute personal courage is another essential.
>
> During the great strike of the iron miners in the Mesabi Range, Tresca . . . approached the next town . . . saw that the main street was lined from one end to the other with deputy sheriffs, strike-breakers, and irate citizens. . . . It look[ed] like a lynching party. . . . He walked slowly, and with formidable dignity in that big black hat, through a block and a half of these armed enemies, who shouted their taunts at him but stood still in their tracks.[24]

Arturo Giovannitti, the impassioned poet of the Industrial Workers of the World, had the gift of a charisma equal to Tresca's and had a similar capacity to cut through the divisions of the left. "Because he was dear both to the anarchists and the more moderate unionists, everybody tried after his death to appropriate him."[25] Also in his case, therefore, the perspective of a leftist militancy was not confined to the protocols of a single party. But Giovannitti was not a fighter like Tresca. Rather, he was a poet, an orator, a man who knew how to confer a metapolitical, almost messianic depth to the fortunes of the labor movement. Among other things, Giovannitti was moved by a religious consciousness that was completely absent in Tresca, who was anticlerical in the old sense. Before landing in New York's subversive circles, Giovannitti was a Protestant minister in Canada. His shift to politics was as deeply motivated as a conversion experience. And yet he was often in the forefront of the labor struggles after his arrest and trial, owing to the events surrounding the Lawrence Strike (1912). A strong consensus coalesced around him and Joseph Ettor, and it was Tresca, among others, who orchestrated it. His self-defense was reported in many newspapers and was subsequently col-

24. See the excerpt from Tresca published in this volume.
25. Vezzosi 1991.

lected in pamphlets published for the occasion. Indeed, it became a small classic of Italian American radicalism, second only to Vanzetti's famous closing defense.

A perfectly bilingual poet, in his day Giovannitti was practically the only first-generation Italian American (except for the very different case of Emanuel Carnevali) to avail himself of a language—English—that was perfectly tuned to the contemporary scene. He sang the heroic deeds of the working class, a song that vibrates with an excruciating insight into modernity. Curiously, the Italian language helped him to compose in a solidly traditional manner. His was almost a language of memory that allowed him to employ images of a world quite different from the one he was living in.

The various forms of sectarianism of the nineteenth and twentieth centuries often led to violence, as on the occasion of public debates like the one that took place in Paterson on May 1, 1898, between the anarchist Pedro Esteve and the socialist Camillo Cianfarra. But, even more prominently, violence exploded in Barre, Vermont, in 1904. In the course of a fight begun during the farewell party for Giacinto Menotti Serrati, the director of *Il Proletario*, an anarchist was killed by a socialist.[26] After Tresca's death in 1943, the tone, especially at the theoretical level, had become more moderate. But this was not the case when it came to everyday politics. There was, however, a general attempt to overcome difficulties and misunderstandings and join forces against the fascists. Still, when all is said and done, the debate remained quite lively. The fact was, the communist party was ruled from Moscow and was always ready to dominate antifascist committees and leagues. The anarchists and the democratic socialists had denounced Stalinist repression. Anarchists in particular used a brand of scornful language that harked back to nineteenth-century historical motifs. In 1929, at the end of a lecture on "Anarchist Effects on the Idea of Class and the International," someone asked the Malatestian exile Armando Borghi if socialism was a necessary transition to anarchism. Borghi replied peremptorily:

If socialism means pooling the goods of society under the management of free associations of producers, this is nothing but anarchist communism. In fact, the first internationalists called it *socialism* and later on it was called anarchy. But if socialism means the state organization of production, then this can only be the utmost anti-anarchist phase and it won't lead to anarchism.

26. From this episode came the long, venomous series of articles by Luigi Galleani on "methods of the socialist struggle," later collected in one volume (Galleani 1972), of which one essay is offered in this collection.

In point of fact, it will be an obstacle of the worst kind. It will inevitably end up in dictatorship.[27]

By 1959, the date of Giovannitti's death, those divisions survived mostly as a nostalgic recollection of youth.[28] From this point of view, one may say that the arc of Italian "subversive" history in the United States thoroughly covered the time-span of the first Italian American generation. "The socialist propaganda of the Italians resident in the United States started in New York in 1871 through the agency of the French section of the First International."[29] However, the first Italian socialist circle was established in Brooklyn in 1882. Its secretary was Matteo Passa, who was affiliated to the maximalist SLP (Socialist Labor Party), the only one existing in America at the time (maximalists were those who demanded the full implementation of the revolutionary program). Only later, in 1901, as the result of a long and painful split, was the SPA (Socialist Party of America) founded. Meanwhile, the SLP started up a new circle in Chicago. Other circles were then established in Kansas City, Missouri, in 1888 by the Sicilian Lo Sardo, and in Latrobe, Pennsylvania, by the political refugee from Modena, Paolo Mazzoli. Mazzoli was able to create a network of branches that federated in the Italian Socialist Party of Pennsylvania.[30]

27. Borghi 1930, 141. Authoritative statements by Borghi against Soviet communism, but also against the socialist vision of the "constituents," can be found also in the same source (219–230), in the transcript of the anarchist leader's speech contradicting Vincenzo Vacirca on the subject "I problemi della rivoluzione italiana dopo l'abbattimento del fascismo" (Problems for the Italian Revolution after the Fall of Fascism). The speech was given in New York on February 6, 1930, and resulted in a tragic shooting as a result of FBI intervention. See, in this volume, the Brani excerpt, which narrates these events.

28. Leafing through *L'Adunata dei Refrattari* at the beginning of the 1960s, Giuseppe Prezzolini was able to read there more than anything else announcements "of picnics held outdoors or in restaurants." However, "the perennial deficit revealed by their administrative reports proves that they are not making it. Their Italian is that of fifty years ago. They write better than Pope's [Fortune Pope, proprietor-editor of the Italian daily] *Progresso Italo-americano*. I could say that they seem like old professors, if I didn't fear offending them" (Prezzolini 1963, 66). This statement, which appeared in an article in the Florentine magazine *Nazione* (Nation) and was later retold in the cited volume, provoked a reaction in *Parola del Popolo* 55 (December 1961–January 1962), which did not miss the opportunity to counter with a recollection of, for the umpteenth time, Prezzolini's many ambiguities regarding fascism. Already some ten years before the same newspaper had harshly attacked him; see Bruno Serenis's article "Relitti. Giuseppe Prezzolini: un povero vecchio infelice" (Wreck: Giuseppe Prezzolini—A Poor, Miserable Old Man), ibid., 12 (October–December 1953).

29. Velona 1958, 19. See also Molinari 1976.

30. Velona 1958, 19.

In these years socialists in Europe began to consider the United States as a formidable incubator of revolutionary ideas and actions. In 1887, in the wake of the general strike for the eight-hour working day and the Haymarket riots, Friedrich Engels pointed out that only a few months had been needed for the workers in America to acquire that class-consciousness that it had taken years upon years to achieve in Europe.[31] In the Italian socialist press the American struggles were often portrayed in terms of a grandiose epic. One of the first to report on them in the pages of *Avanti!* was the Sicilian exile Bernardino Verro, during his rather short stay in America in 1896–97. The fact is, as Arnaldo Testi had observed, that firsthand information was scanty, and a certain pseudo-philosophical rhetoric prevailed over news events and reportage. On the other hand, as Elisabetta Vezzosi has pointed out with regard to the first Italian socialist experiences in America:

> A common trait of almost all the socialist groups of those years was the absence of definite political programs and strategies. They also lacked precise ideological connotations. This is why they often looked like mutual aid societies committed to generic socialist propaganda and a form of ethnic solidarity which, in some circumstances, might become class solidarity.[32]

This ideological weakness, among other factors, may explain the kind of socialist inclinations that may be found in the most varied places and personalities between the end of the nineteenth and the beginning of the twentieth centuries. Here we might cite as an example the first years of Barsotti's *Il Progresso Italo-Americano*, which later came to be regarded as the voice of bourgeois nationalism. This also explains why in the colony it was quite easy to reconcile attitudes which, strictly speaking, should have been poles apart: socialism and love of one's country, or even devotion to monarchy. Alongside the party proper there was, in short, a broad zone of "sentimental" complicity, stirred by feelings of philanthropic solidarity with the immigrant masses, their poverty, and the exploitation they inevitably encountered. This complicity was never organically related to the party itself and yet the sympathies were there. As in part we have already seen, some of the most interesting journalistic and literary experiences flourished in this very environment. One may above all recall here Riccardo Cordiferro.

31. See Testi 1976, 313ff. Conveniently, Testi recalls how Marx's and Engels's attention to the United States began as far back as the Civil War.
32. Vezzosi 1991.

Like the anarchists, from the very outset the socialists felt the need not to integrate but to aggregate. In addition, their political models—Turati and Prampolini—were borrowed from Italy. The socialists considered their ideal of society an alternative one, and it bore the typical traits of the subculture. But the differences between the anarchists and the socialists were profound. Certainly, the socialists, too, gave great importance to a sort of "permanent formation" based on reading, the staging of social dramas, and also precise indications (supported by the appropriate manuals) in the fields of hygiene and health. Furthermore, they made wise use of anticlerical, free-lance publications.[33] Nonetheless, there are more lucid documents—the rather common "decalogues" or the like—that outlined the qualities and the virtues a good activist needed in order to act properly. These documents reveal a precise strategy for penetrating American society—practically a kind of "Americanization" process—which the anarchists totally ignored. Alberico Molinari's *Discorsi brevi* (Short Speeches) are exemplary in this regard. They were published on the front page of *L'Ascesa del Proletariato* (The Rise of the Proletariat) between 1908 and 1909. In them the author recommends education, respect for women, sober grooming, and tolerance. He exhorts his readers "not to envy those who are well off" because "hate and envy are negative feelings. Instead, the desire to improve your condition is a positive feeling."[34] In the early 1920s, when times were hard and the vital phase of American socialism had come to an end, Domenico Saudino elaborated "I dieci comandamenti del compagno socialista" (The Ten Commandments of the Socialist Comrade) for *La Parola del Popolo*. Here precepts meant strictly for internal use stand next to bits of advice of a more general import.[35] But, above all, this author wrote in Girolamo Valenti's *Avanti!* a frank exhortation with the significant title "Americanizziamoci" (Let's

33. But with greater prudence and more significant openings. "Anticlerical and anti-religious propaganda constitutes a highly important function of the Socialist Party; but it is a function that should be accomplished with good methods and many tactics; if not, it degenerates into empty rhetoric and ends up in the most deplorable failure," one reads in a pamphlet dedicated to the subject (Agatodemon 1909). Also worthy of note are the numerous socialist activists—including Bertelli and Tresca—who contradicted the arguments of Catholic priests, positions that were at times also published in select pamphlets.

34. These texts by Molinari are reprinted in the present volume.

35. *La Parola del Popolo*, January 28, 1922. In brief, the ten "commandments" are: pay your dues punctually; help at the meetings; support our press; be polite; be disciplined; love your comrades; try to educate yourself; don't betray yourself; be practical; don't be unilateral. One could in fact say they used and condensed Molinari's *Discorsi brevi*. Domenico Saudino (1889–1964), polygraph and journalist, was the author of *Fra i Roseti di Eros/In Eros' Rose Gardens Saggio Popolare di Sociologia Genetica/Popular Essay on Genetic Sociology*; and other works that will be cited later.

Americanize Ourselves): "Let us once and for all set aside the slim excuses we use to justify our absenteeism, excuses which are based on our misunderstood patriotism and natural indolence. As men and socialists, it is our right and duty to consider ourselves—and most importantly to *be*, without restrictions and innuendoes—citizens of the country that is hosting us."[36]

This perspective can be found in one form or another almost everywhere in the literature under discussion here. In particular, drama became the privileged genre for spreading ideas and encouraging the adoption of new lifestyles. In this way the audience might see reflected in the merciless mirror of the stage the shortsightedness of a way of being and of thinking that needed to be radically changed. For example, the playwright Gaspare Marrone, heart and soul of the amateur theatrical club *Avanti* in Brooklyn, tried his hand at a series of "social scenes." Their purpose, underscored by the use of the Sicilian dialect, was obviously didactic. One of them, the one-act play *Eppuru e veru!* (And Yet It Is True, 1914), stages the slow wasting away of the little dressmaker Cuncittina, a flower who withers under the very eyes of her parents Masi and Narda. On one hand, they do not want to lose the wages she makes from her *giobba* (job), but on the other hand they do not feel it is necessary to spend money on pills and doctor's visits. A friend, Giovanni, tries in vain to open their eyes. Why on earth, he asks, did you come to America?

> To have a better life, because there you couldn't get by ... not to die here. We work ... a lot! But without overdoing it. That's right! And we must eat ... not like you who work like dogs and go the whole day on a piece of bread and a tomato. And in the evening, a dish of pasta with beans or escarole ... and off you go! Do you see the results now? You have become so greedy that you forget to take care of yourselves.[37]

Another socially minded playwright, Vincenzo Mortara, from Indiana, took up the issue of sexual morals. In the four acts of *Amore e Fede* (Love and Faith, 1911), we witness the arrest of Davide Vallari and Lina Verne, who are charged with "free cohabitation." The overly zealous cops haul them in and, faced with a hypo-

---

36. *L'Avanti!*, official organ of the FSI, Chicago, August 28, 1920. The exhortation, despite obvious differences, aligned with the campaign for the Americanization of Italians launched by *Progresso Italo-Americano* (Italian American Progress) during spring 1919 to combat the serious risk of the ghettoization of foreign communities, and of the Italians in particular. The issue is discussed again further on in this volume.

37. Marrone 1914, 11–12. The play was performed for the first time on September 1, 1912, at Schwaben Hall in Brooklyn.

critically Puritan world, Davide cries out the truth of his unsullied feelings: "We are indeed guilty of loving each other with all the strength of our heart and soul, and of living together happily, without asking for the approval of an idiot dressed in a robe."[38]

Other and much more colorful manifestations of the vitality of the Italian American socialist "subculture" would seem to contradict this "educational" orientation. Consider the following verses drawn from a *macchietta* (impersonation) by Tony Ferrazzano, a poet who participated in the great strikes of the 1910s:

I am a socialist, and no longer a *cafone*:
The priest no longer makes a fool of me.
I want to get a job (*giobba*) from the boss
With a red tie and this waistcoat. . . .
I don't know how to read and I can
Tell you the entire life of that—
What's his name—yes—Giordano Bruno
From the day he was born to the day he died.[39]

The moment of struggle is indeed liberating. It represents a unique celebration, one that inflames and moves and leads to the realization that one is part of a world that is marching toward a radiant future. American May Day observances, immortalized in countless poems published in special issues of leftist newspapers and journals, were somewhat different from their European counterparts. They displayed a sort of epic zest because it was clear to everybody that right there, in America, a unique modern proletarian culture was being built. At the same time, these celebrations were more sentimental and romantic than in Europe because of the enduring dimension of adventure that was intrinsic to the transoceanic experience of immigration. The negative experience of uprooting was offset by the hope of finding even in the Babel of the new world, an ethnically compact environment where one might live one's militancy within an "ancient" familial culture.[40]

Certain festive features belonging to the European tradition of May Day found in America a style of celebration that exalted their vaguely picturesque character.

38. Mortara 1911, 86. The author writes from jail in Newport, Indiana. Mortara, author also of the four-act play *Momento Fatale!* (Fatal Moment, 1914), lived in Clinton, Indiana.
39. *Lu cafone sucialista* (The Socialist Lout), cited in Livingston 1918, 220.
40. On the May Day of Italian American militants, see Vecoli 1988a.

The various national traditions joined with the all-American custom of the picnic and the parade, and in doing so they underwent a cultural transformation that strengthened, so to speak, their salient traits. The field of political activism, like any other field, proved that America was becoming a "hyper-Europe." It is a serious mistake to treat it as a caricature. Here everything is bigger, more violent, and more impressive: poverty and wealth, sorrow and celebration.

In Italy, Camillo Prampolini composed a hymn to May Day. It was meant to be sung following the melody of the famous popular song "Funiculí Funiculá," evidently to convey the most pressing social issues and thanks to a very well-known musical tune. In the fin-de-siècle United States, that song landed on the front page of an "ethnic" newspaper in New York that was not really in line with the socialist movement:

The populace, under the yoke of the bourgeoisie,
Is languishing—is languishing,
Struck by hunger, hardship, and pellagra,
They are dying—they are dying,
But from the bloodless populace united by a pact
The day will come—the day will come!
The solemn, great day of liberation
Soon will come—soon will come!
Come on, comrades, let's arise in freedom!
Come on, comrades let's raise our heads![41]

But it is not only the "institutional" moment of May Day that inspires this kind of "ethnic" fantasy.[42] The struggle itself, as we have already pointed out, is in a way "festive." The great IWW strikes of the early years of the twentieth century fueled a vast mythology and gave rise to an impassioned and bellicose literary produc-

41. "Il 1° Maggio" (May Day), *Cristoforo Colombo*, May 1, 1894. The text of the Prampolinian hymn is printed also in Mortara 1911, 61–62.

42. Even union agitation fliers promoted these productions. For example, *Lotta di Classe* (Class Struggle), the "Official Weekly Organ of the Italian Branch of the Cloak & Skirt Makers Union of New York," edited by R. Rende, published in the special May 3, 1918, edition poems by Giovannitti, Michele Pane, Pietro Gori and Pietro Greco; a prose poem by G. Procopio; and the first scene of the play *La Figlia* (The Daughter) by Vicenzo Vacirca next to material by traditional authors such as Lorenzo Stecchetti. A constellation of poems by Bartoletti appears on the pages of *Difesa* (Defense), the "weekly periodical in defense of the working class" and the official organ of the FSI of Chicago, a city that celebrated the famous Mooney trial; the name of the newspaper referred, in fact, to this event.

tion. Among its representatives there were the miner-poet Efrem Bartoletti and other proletarian poets such as Simplicio Righi, alias Rosina Vieni, who with varying degrees of success went beyond the old models of Pascoli and De Amicis, which were dear to older leader-writers such as Giuseppe Bertelli. In point of fact, those strikes represented a moment of extraordinary solidarity, not only internationalist but in particular Italian American. They allowed the Italian national group to stand out—alongside the Jewish, the Russian, the Greek, and other groups—as the bearer of unique forms of struggle. Once again, among these forms were music and song: certainly a national patrimony but enlivened by the encounter with the great mass rituals in sheer IWW style. One need only think of the legendary songs of Joe Hill, which were a model for the compositions of Bartoletti. There were also more plainly popular songs.

It is worth quoting another example here—the text of the song "O sciopero d'e sarti di Chicago" (The Strike of the Chicago Tailors), which was composed during that strike in 1910 by Giuseppe Ambra, the owner of the Vittoria restaurant (the meeting place of the socialists at 852 Blue Avenue), and set to music by L. Quaglia:

I
See how happy we'll be
If the Union wins,
Then the Boss
Will no longer command.
It's not like it used to be
When they'd order us about:
Now we are Unionists,
And they must respect us!
Chorus: We are so merry
Deep in our heart;
If they are caught in the net
Giving orders with their "please"
All of us will run
With friends and relatives:
This breed of vipers
We must defeat.

II
Bertelli and Grandinetti
Distinguish themselves

By convoking meetings ("*miinghe*")
Everywhere and at all hours.
Let's clap our hands
Let's applaud and make noise,
With sounds, songs and din
We want to shout.
(Chorus)

III
And you, dear little girls
Like May rose-buds,
Take heart
For we will win.
For us it's sugar-coated almonds,
For the bosses ("*bosse*") it's ruin;
They're nice and fried
And they must sign.
Chorus: We are so merry
Deep in our heart
With these mackerels (mazzuni) freshly caught
We have to make a soup.
Long live the Committee,
Look what it can do!
We tell each other heartily
It must last one hundred years.[43]

I stress these popular productions not so much because they are picturesque but because they underscore how closely the colony and the political-syndicalist headquarters were connected. In the preceding song, for instance, we find the names of two famous political organizers, Giuseppe Bertelli and Emilio Grandinetti. Their names, like those of many other activists, became stars in a small but by no means ephemeral proletarian firmament. Their lives consisted of self-denial, sacrifice, fighting, arrests, and unceasing travel; and through it all, they became models for others to follow. Along with the most intensely dramatic events—the great strikes, the time spent in jail, and the trials—the party organizers' travels

---

43. The song lyrics were printed in *La Parola del Popolo* 28 (May–June 1958), an issue celebrating the fiftieth anniversary of Emilio Grandinetti's time in America.

became a rather productive "genre" with considerable documentary value. They were condensed in countless reports, stories, and articles that appeared in the American socialist press. Contemporary lay missionaries such as Gioacchino Artoni, Arturo Culla, Domenico Saudino,[44] and many others described the life and aspirations of the Italians in the mining districts of Colorado and Pennsylvania as well as in the great areas of the Atlantic and the Middle West.

In comparison with the anarchists, who never passed up the opportunity to point out the socialists' intolerable willingness to compromise, the socialists were obviously more pragmatic and mindful of the real aspects of social life.[45] If they believed in anticlericalism and promoted amateur dramatic performances, readings and poetry, they also provided mutual aid societies and consumer cooperatives. Furthermore, they debated concrete issues such as the organization of labor, wages, and the conditions of the working class. But this model appears substantially closed, the more so in that their membership was very modest. In New York, for example, there were only about two hundred socialists out of an Italian population over half a million. This situation did not change that much in the entire arc of the history of the American socialist movement. Its Italian component was inevitably affected by its originary flaw: a sectarianism that had its roots in the Risorgimento. For their part, the Italians were unwilling to take orders from those Americans who were in charge. In turn, the Americans looked at these newcomers with suspicion because they feared that if the Italians were too independent, their reformist strategy would fail. Finally, more politicized ethnic groups manifested a not unfounded prejudice against the Italians, at least up to the strikes of the 1910s,

44. Gioacchino Artoni (1866–1937), born in Pieve Saliceto in the municipality of Gualtieri (Reggio Emilia) and having arrived in America in 1896, was among the founders of *Il Proletario* and was a greatly popular figure both as a laborer and as an organizer ("Papa" Artoni). On Artoni, see Giacomo Battistoni, "Ricordando i settant'anni di Gioacchino Artoni" (Remembering the Seventy Years of Gioacchino Artoni), *Stampa Libera* (*Free Press*), August 16, 1936, reprinted in *La Parola del Popolo/The Word of the People* 7 (July–September 1952). Arturo Culla, of Rocca Canavese (Turin), emigrated in 1903 and joined the SPA. In 1908, he went to Chicago to join *La Parola* (*The Word*). In 1924 he joined the Columbian Federation, presided over by Vincenzo Massari, a state senator in Colorado. In 1937, he was attacked by fascists who wanted to take over the federation. In 1952, he returned to Italy and died in 1957 in Turin; see the obituary by Tommaso Toselli in *La Parola del Popolo* 29 (July–August 1957).

45. Harshly criticizing the plans of the Third International, Umberto Postiglione, for example, comes to the conclusion that "redirecting the international workers' movement to the worthy path of yellow socialism—from which it had been suddenly thrown off track by the impetuous tremors of the earthquake that had been devastating Europe for two years—was for the anarchists akin to landing on two feet." See "La Terza Internazionale" (The Third International), *Cronaca Sovversiva*, April 29, 1916, reprinted in Postiglione 1972, 17–18.

and were always inclined to consider them genetically impervious to class discipline. Worse than that, they considered them potential strike-breakers. "They'll bring their Italians over here,/ And the Negroes from the South,/ Thinking they can do our work,/ Take the bread from a poor man's mouth," as an Irish protest song of the late nineteenth century eloquently declares.[46] Indeed, it points to a rather common feeling that is also present in the American fiction of the day.[47]

Il Proletario was founded in Pittsburgh in 1896; it was a newspaper destined to last until 1947. In those years socialist ideas were spread among the immigrants by renowned exiles such as Dino Rondani, who had come to the United States after the 1898 crisis, and Giusto Calvi, among others. These exiles took up the challenge of giving a more stable organization to the socialist movement.[48] In 1899 Rondani became the newspaper's director. Previously it was run by Alessandro Mazzoli, and after it suspended publication in 1897 (and the editorship was moved to Patterson), by Cianfarra.[49] Rondani moved the offices to New York, "thereby increasing the newspaper's circulation and giving it a more precisely anti-anarchist and unionist perspective."[50] In less than two years he was followed by Cianfarra and then by Simplicio Righi. Meanwhile, the conflicts between the SLP (Socialist Labor Party) and the SPA (Socialist Party of America) affected the Italian socialists: *L'Avanti* (The Forward) was founded in Newark, in strong opposition to *Il Proletario*.

In 1902, Giacinto Menotti Serrati arrived and founded the Italian Socialist Federation (FSI), which affiliated forty-five circles in one year. Serrati's idea was to

46. "The Poor Man's Family," in Guthrie-Hill et al. 1977, 138–141.

47. In Harold Frederic's novel *The Damnation of Theron Ware* (1896), a boss blames the discontented Irish workers for their low wages, while the Italians are "sensible fellows: they know when they're well off—a dollar a day, an' they're satisfied, an' everything goes smooth." The theme is also taken up by Jack London in *The Valley of the Moon*. See Gossett 1980.

48. Many personalities of the Italian socialist movement crossed the ocean in this period. Rondani (1868–1951), at the time of his arrival at New York from Switzerland (where he had taken refuge after the 1898 events in Milan), was already a member of parliament. In addition to others, of whom more will be discussed during this reconstruction, worthy of mention are also Nicolò Barbato (1856–1917), Sebastiano Bonfiglio (1879–1922), Lorenzo Panepinto (1865–1911), and Bernardino Verro (1866–1915), the last of whom was among the principal leaders of Sicilian fascism. The first, elected to parliament in 1900, was in the United States between 1904 and 1908; Arturo Caroti (1875–1931) was in America from 1905 to 1913, went off to fight with the revolutionaries in Mexico, and then returned to Italy, where he was elected to parliament. In 1914, he returned to the United States on a propaganda tour.

49. For the tormented story of this newspaper and of *Parola del Popolo*, the source followed here is De Ciampis 1958.

50. Vezzosi 1991.

enhance the "ethnic" independence of the Italian American socialists, underlining the experience they were already familiar with in Italy. In exchange he allowed them to choose between the SLP and the SPA. With little success, Serrati's people tried to turn *Il Proletario* into a daily (from May 1, 1903, to January 1904) and, with even less success, they sought an ongoing relationship with the SLP. The first congress of the FSI was held at West Hoboken, New Jersey, in 1903, and opted for "neutrality" between the two American socialist parties. Serrati judged it a regrettable decision because it effectively excluded the Italians from an active role in the American socialist movement. He then returned to Italy, where he founded *L'Avanti!* in 1904, the same year Carlo Tresca arrived. Tresca took over as director of *Il Proletario* in October, 1904, after an "interregnum" in which the paper had been run first by Suprema Tedeschi and then, from Philadelphia, by Giovanni Di Silvestro, who later would become a supporter of fascism. Tresca immediately set out to give the paper a unionist-revolutionary orientation.

In 1905 the IWW was founded in Chicago and decidedly outstripped the "racist protectionism" of the American Federation of Labor led by the famous Samuel Gompers. As a matter of fact, the AFL was corporative and closed to unskilled workers (those without any specialization, which was the case with most Italian immigrants) and particularly to categories such as the miners.[51] The foundation of the IWW was an important occasion for the FSI, and in fact Tresca—and soon after, Giuseppe Bertelli, who succeeded him as director of *Il Proletario*—worked toward joining the two. Galleani's response was enthusiastic. When Bertelli began as director of *Il Proletario*, Galleani reminded him that Tresca "had never hidden either his clear-cut mistrust of the Tolstoian *miserere* of parliamentary reformism or his passionate approval of revolutionary action." On the contrary, Galleani acknowledged that "the emancipation of the proletariat depends on the expropriation of the bourgeoisie. In no way can this expropriation take place in a peaceful manner. Therefore, the spirit of revolt remains still and always one of the most active sources of proletarian action. No doubt, it is the most ener-

---

51. Appearing again in a 1923 propaganda pamphlet for the IWW, the socialist activist Mario De Ciampis wrote: "To say . . . that industrial unionism like that supported by the IWW is none other than the classist syndicalism that has inspired and supported the minority workers' movements of the many countries of Europe would seem strange to many. But the truth, which can be suppressed neither by force nor by the dirty dealings of career politicians, in this case is on our side and flows spontaneously and beautifully from our comrade's pen." See Giantino 1923, 3–4.

getic of those currents capable of inducing social revolution and, consequently, it is one of the most active factors of emancipation."[52]

The encounter between the IWW and the FSI was sanctioned by the Boston congress of the latter in November–December 1906. All FSI members had to adhere to the IWW, but they were left free to choose between the SLP and the SPA. Bertelli rejected his confirmation as director of *Il Proletario* and later passed to the reformist ranks of the SPA. As usual, Galleani had properly reprimanded him for his obsession with staying on the right side of the law.[53] On the other hand, integration between the two parties was quite problematic. In spite of the fact that the International congress at Stockard (1907) reconfirmed its internationalist stand toward immigration, the leaders of the SPA did not miss chance to relaunch their restrictive policy on this very subject. The Italians, who as a matter of fact were discriminated against as a group, in turn discriminated against those who were even weaker than they. Still, in 1910 *La Parola dei Socialisti* wrote: "Nobody can expect advanced and organized workers to sacrifice and delay their redemption for several centuries in order to wait for the Hottentots, the Kaffirs, the Kurds, the Hindus, and the Chinese." As a matter of fact, members of the IWW were deeply shaken by the internal rift between pure and political syndicalists (like Daniel de Leon, who clung to the old SLP line) and were incapable of backing the Italian federation either politically or financially. The latter was in crisis due to the continuous

52. "La nuova redazione del "'Proletario'" (The New Editorial Staff of *Proletario*), *Cronaca Sovversiva*, June 30, 1906. Regarding the mention of "Tolstoyism," see the pamphlet *Tolstoismo e anarchismo* (Tolstoyism and Anarchism), translated by Ciancabilla, containing the report presented to International Revolutionary Workers' Congress of Paris by the group of socialist revolutionary internationalist students of Paris in 1900, and published by the Biblioteca del Circolo Studi Sociali di Barre (Library of the Social Studies Club of Barre), in Vermont, which is the same as saying by *Cronaca Sovversiva*.

53. "Per un appunto polemico" (For a Controversial Point), *Cronaca Sovversiva*, July 21, 1906: "When the powerful are reassured that we don't want their death, so much so that we make sure they know, and without any betrayal, that they should not be afraid, should not take defensive measures, should not ready their weapons . . . on whose corpses do you want to step over if not your corpses?" Needless to say, from this moment on the relations between Tresca and the Social Democrats also became very difficult and stayed that way for a while. In 1921, *L'Avanti!* of Chicago would compare Tresca to Barsotti: "Nella colonia italiana di New York regnano due Carli. Un Carlo vive e specula sui terremoti, l'altro Carlo vive e specula e se la gode sui prigionieri politici" (Two Carlos Reign in the Italian Colony of New York. One Carlo Lives and Speculates on Earthquakes. The Other Carlo Lives and Speculates and Rejoices in Political Prisoners), September 3, 1921. Bertelli would have dedicated a sonnet to them that began: "One day there was a useless Hammer, / That banged crazily / to the right, to the left, mindlessly / banging out one mistake after another" ("L'Uomo che piange, *Martellate a marmellate*" [The Man Who Cries "Hammered and Jammed Up"]), *La Parola del Popolo*, November 12, 1921.

shifts of its members over the difficult economic situation and the more and more frequent defections from its ranks. Besides, *Il Proletario* had somehow lost its grip and kept changing directors without any noticeable results.[54]

The Italian American socialist movement was chronically fragmented. To this we must add the standoff between New York and Chicago, which led to the foundation in Chicago (on February 17, 1908) of *La Parola dei Socialisti*. Directed by Bertelli, it was institutionally linked to the SPA. However, the socialists continued to elaborate—in a contradictory and discontinuous way—original positions and to develop an independent line that occasionally contrasted with that of the national SPA. For instance, other newspapers besides *La Parola* were founded. Among them was Alberico Molinari's *L'Ascesa del Proletariato* (1908–1910) which Prampolini praised in this way: "I don't recall having ever seen a periodical so attractive and popularly socialist."

The problem of the independence of the local federations within the party was becoming critical. The more so because the 1910 SPA congress established that the necessary condition for forming a new federation within the party was a minimal number of five hundred dues-paying members. This was only one of its exorbitant demands. The Italians sensed how little they were held in esteem and realized that they hardly had a say in the party. But to be part of it was of vital importance if they wanted to count more and to avoid closing themselves up like a clam, relapsing into the blackmailing spiral of the old but still very much alive *padrone* system.[55] As to the party, it sought to abandon its ethnic structure and recover the foreign federations by "naturalizing" them and thus insuring electoral benefits. For this purpose, a number of campaigns were launched.

These efforts led to a clean break with the Italian PSI, which had decreed "that members of the PSI who went abroad should become members of the labor unions active in the countries of immigration and oppose any attempts at secession." Either with the PSI or with the SPA: for those who remained in America there was

54. In the period from April 1907 to September 1909, the editorship of the journal changed as follows: E. Mombello, Eligio Strobino, Antonio De Bella, Strobino again, and then the triumvirate Poggi–Mazzia–Rosa with Raimondo Fazio as administrator, then Poggi alone, and finally Arturo Giovannitti. See De Ciampis 1958.

55. Indicative of the American understanding of the scourge of exploitation effected by various Italian bosses is the well timed study "'Bosses' e 'banchieri'" (Bosses and Bankers) by John Koren, published first in America in 1897 in the *Bulletin of the Department of Labor*, and reprinted the same year in *Riforma Sociale* (Social Reform) in Italy. It was republished in Ciuffoletti-Degl'Innocenti 1978, 1:239–247.

not much of a choice. The Federation Socialista Italiana was founded at the end of July 1910.

The best—the most "heroic"—moment in the history of American socialism began now: in 1910, in fact, Victor Berger was the first socialist to be elected to the United States Congress. In 1912, Eugene V. Debs, who was a candidate for the presidency, obtained 6 percent of the vote. The foreign language federations gave a notable contribution to the successes of these years. But as always, there were problems. To start with, the Indianapolis SPA congress of 1912 condemned sabotage—efficaciously defined by the Wobblies as the attitude of "withdrawing efficiency from work" or also of "withdrawing goodwill from work"—as a method of struggle. As a result, something like 10 to 15 percent of the membership abandoned the party, following in Big Bill Haywood's footsteps. Haywood had been expelled from the socialist ranks and became an IWW leader.[56] He was also very popular among the Italians. Giovannitti, who became the director of *Il Proletario* in September 1909, was reconfirmed by the Utica congress in April 1911. When the poet was arrested, the paper was momentarily run by Edmondo Rossoni, who later became minister of corporations in Fascist Italy. After he got out of jail, Giovannitti remained as director until the summer of 1913, when he was replaced by Flavio Venanzi and later, once again by Rossoni. The two-year period 1912–1913 was important for the workers' movement. It was marked by the great strikes of the textile workers in Paterson, New Jersey, and Lawrence, Massachusetts, and of the miners in Pittsburgh, Pennsylvania, the Mesabi Range in Minnesota, and in Westmoreland and Calumet.

This story has been told many times.[57] For my purposes here, I will only underline the fact that participation in these struggles, which are now part of the history of the workers' movement, projected the Italian Americans onto a wider stage. Now they were no longer strictly ethnic. Joseph Ettor and Arturo Giovannitti were accused of inciting violence during the Lawrence Strike. Their trial was a *cause célèbre*. The vicissitudes of Ettor and Giovannitti, like those of Sacco and Vanzetti,

---

56. It is interesting to note how *Cronaca Sovversiva*, glimpsing in these events the seed for the renewal of a more radical initiative, evaluated—through the writings of Umberto Postiglione—the substantial failure of the IWW, which had kindled hopes of being "an organization that was decentralized, antiauthoritarian, and revolutionary in aim and method," but had repeated "the error of all organizations in which the necessity of governing is a sharper and more assiduous concern than facing the enemy." See Postiglione 1972, 131–132.

57. See, in particular, Fenton 1975; Dore 1968; Martellone 1978; Cartosio 1983, a first-rate article that has the merit of extreme clarity in its exposition of rather confusing events; and Vezzosi 1991.

led to a new visibility of Italian workers, which was won at a very dear price. They also introduced a new and more expansive dialectics, due above all to the new atmosphere created by the IWW. It was in this shared breeding ground that exchanges and collaborations, unthinkable a few years earlier, took place. In this climate of forward-looking internationalism, national differences seemed for a moment to fade away. In Lawrence, 25,000 textile workers went on strike, and almost half of them were women; it was they who launched the famous slogan "We want bread and roses too." This adherence was indicative of a remarkable growth of the union's strength. Altogether, these workers spoke forty-five different languages: rather than a strike, it was "a social revolution on a reduced scale."[58] No wonder, therefore, that at the height of the Red Scare it was the Wobblies who became the chosen scapegoat of the establishment when the time came to close the doors of a hospitable America for good.[59] In fact, the IWW believed programmatically in internationalism, and the "foreign" membership—especially the Italians—were enormously a part of it all. During the trials, in the jails, and in the often-fierce debates, the Italians distinguished themselves as one of the most prominent groups. In spite of their reputation for being strikebreakers, they were eager to accept the spirit of a truly new epoch.[60]

With the coming of World War I, *Il Proletario* moved once again to Boston, where it was published by Giuseppe Cannata and later by Angelo Faggi. In 1917 it was suppressed. Faggi then founded *La Difesa* (The Defense) in Chicago. Soon after, in that same city, there appeared *Il Nuovo Proletario*, directed by Antonio

58. Bock 1976, 91.

59. *Il Rosso Bagliore d'Oriente ovvero "Rasputin"* (The Red Glow of the Orient, or, Rasputin), a three-act play from 1920 by Saverio Piesco, was dedicated to "all the prisoners of the IWW; to all the unavenged victims; to all the deported and all those who suffer for an ideal of justice and proletarian emancipation."

60. See Iacopo Tori's pamphlet *Il processo muto di Sacramento, California* (The Mute Trial of Sacramento, California; 1919), in which forty-three IWW activists were condemned to long prison sentences and responded with an unrepentant silence at the formalism of a court whose bias was obvious from the beginning. Three of those charged—the same Tori, Pietro De Bernardi, and Vincenzo Santilli—were Italians; each received ten years in jail. The day on which the grand jury rendered the indictment, the Wobblies staged a prison revolt, protesting for better treatment. "Some," writes Tori, "suggested they sing: 'Allright, fellows, let's have a song.' And one voice after the other sang 'Hold the Fort, for we are coming.' Almost every day the chorus sang the proletarian songs. Some of the preferred ones were: 'Workers of the World, Awaken'; 'Rebel Girl'; 'The White Slave'; and 'Scissorbill'—all by Joe Hill—as well as 'Dump the Boss off Your Back,' 'We Are Coming Home Farmer John,' and others. Whenever the mood arose, it was time for 'Rang-tang! Rang-tang! Zin-zuh-bah! Who in hell-you think we are! . . . Wobblies-wobblies-rah!-rah!-rah! Rough-tough-we never take a bluff—Of free speech, we never get enough. Who!—We Wobblies!!!'" (Tori 1919, 10–11).

Presi. The latter was practically next door to *La Parola*, which in 1910 had been handed over to Molinari and Vincenzo Vacirca. *La Parola* had become *La Parola Proletaria* and was published by T. Lucidi, Pietro M. Camboni, and Vittorio Buttis.[61] In October 1917, it was put into the hands of Girolamo Valenti and changed its name from *La Fiaccola* (The Torch) to *L'Avanti!* In 1920 it became definitely *La Parola del Popolo* and was published again by Bertelli (more than once), Serafino Romualdi, Giovanni Pippan, Buttis, Vacirca, and Matteo Siragusa. It closed in 1948 and started up again in 1951 with Egidio Clemente and Emilio Grandinetti as directors. In 1976 it celebrated the bicentennial of the United States.

To understand what this sarabande of names and relocations means, one needs to go beyond the "damned divisions among the followers of the socialist ideal," which were retrospectively recalled by a prominent leader.[62] This was nothing in comparison to the problems of trying to run a newspaper that, during the Red Scare, was relentlessly subjected to the restrictive measures of the Espionage Act. The years between 1918 and 1920 were terrible for many and especially for the group centered on Galleani. Not only did they witness the arrest of Sacco and Vanzetti, but they also gave rise to a real "crusade against the unruly," as *L'Adunata dei Refrattari* defined it years later. This crusade led to Galleani's expulsion (June 1919) and the end of *Cronaca Sovversiva*. In addition, there were the mysterious, presumed defenestrations of two anarchists—suicides, according to the authorities. The first, Pietro Marucco, was thrown overboard from the steamer on which he was being deported to Italy in March 1919. The second, Andrea Salsedo, a printer who went to America from his native Pantelleria after becoming friends with Galleani, was framed and beaten up by the police in the first stage of the investigation which later led the capture of Sacco and Vanzetti. He fell from the window of the fourteenth story of the FBI building in New York (May 1920). On June 2, 1919, the day in which seven bombs exploded in seven different cities, Carlo Valdinoci had also died. He was mangled by the powerful explosive device he was trying to place in front of the Washington residence of Attorney General A. Mitchell Palmer. Palmer was the key figure behind the Red Scare, which had one of its

61. Born in Venice in 1866, arrested many times, and expatriated to Switzerland in 1894, Vittorio Buttis was sentenced in 1897 to exile in Ventotene and then Pantelleria, defended by Francesco Saverio Merlino, and again imprisoned, then was a fugitive and expatriate in Switzerland and Germany, expelled from there in 1900, was active in workers' struggles in Italy, was again imprisoned, and was again a fugitive (Switzerland, Brazil). In 1915 Buttis arrived in the United States and settled in Chicago, where he died in 1950. In 1940, he published the interesting *Memorie di vita di tempeste sociali* (Memories of a Life of Social Tempests).

62. Buttis 1940, 137.

most zealous interpreters precisely in a second-generation Italian American, Anthony Caminetti, then commissioner of immigration.[63]

No doubt, the bombing attacks, like the dagger or gun attacks, were not a vague threat: the anarchist press had often mentioned them. Among the most radical writers in this context, we should mention the legendary figure of a woman, Paolina Breccia. Born in Locorotondo (Bari), she was the author of several pamphlets that she signed with different pseudonyms. In one of them, the theatrical monologue *Lo zingaro giustiziere* (The Avenging Gypsy, 1915), she complacently describes the murder of a "multimillionaire" who is responsible for starving the people. As if it were celebrating her personal fate of having to go underground, the text closes with a sort of oath to go on fighting:

I will go on being a gypsy, a free citizen of the world. And without a passport. A passport is like a policeman who incriminates you wherever you are. My only passport is human rights. Armed with these rights, I'll always be present wherever rebellion and acts of justice are called for! Goodbye![64]

Among the many activists hit during the "crusade," there was also Ludovico M. Caminita, former editor-in-chief of *Cronaca Sovversiva* and director of *Era Nuova*. He is one of the most interesting anarchist-memoirists. He was arrested, detained, and threatened with expulsion. And in the process, it seemed, he expressed his irredeemable existential plight by revealing many names and incidents. His was a peculiar case of conscience, which makes his testimony from Ellis Island one of the most intense and desperate of texts.[65] Individuals were arrested, expelled, and persecuted. Against the newspapers there were even more effective means, such as denying them

63. Emilio Franzina has read in Caminetti's attitude toward his "subversive" conationals the sign of a more general restrictionist attitude prevalent among the Italians of California, who were of northern origins, often Americanized by then, and little tolerant toward the new immigration. See Franzina 1995, 335–336.

64. Breccia 1915, 12. Paolina Breccia—who every year compiled a *Calendario Storico Scientifico Moderno* (Calendar of Modern Scientific History) that was published by the printer Perrini in East Harlem—used many pseudonyms, such as P. Cratere, Una Madre, and P. Aloop. Among her titles, in addition to the ones cited, are the theatrical sketches *Tenebre e luce* and *Sulla breccia* (Darkness and Light and In the Breach, 1918); the four-act *Fiaccole nel buio* (Torches in the Dark), halved into two little volumes, *Il prete* and *Il process dei processi* (The Priest and The Trial of Trials); and *La patria dei poveri* (The Homeland of the Poor), *Spiritismo . . . sventato* (Reckless Spiritualism), and *La sfida* (The Challenge).

65. For the activities of the Italian anarchists in this period, see the masterly, detailed reconstruction of Avrich 1991.

the use of the mails. Glancing through these papers also means going through an uninterrupted series of appeals to the activists asking recipients to contribute to their circulation and to partake in the countless calls for subscriptions. Those who were politically active were invited to do their utmost to help the newspapers to survive, as well as the structures of the party and the movement itself.

Fascism reached the Little Italies by riding the sense of frustration over Italy's failure to win any territories after the War, a failure generally attributed to President Wilson. Furthermore, Fascism capitalized on the broader need of the masses—which for too long had been affected by a deplorable loss of self-esteem—for some kind of redress.[66] Many Italians in America gave their support to Mussolini thanks to the brashness of his new slogans, some early successes, international recognition by other countries, and the many and various deeds carried out in the course of the last two decades: De Pinedo's transatlantic flight, the blue ribbon won by the *Rex*, and Primo Carnera's triumphs in boxing, not to mention the Abyssinian adventure. On the other hand, for many years there was also a nationalistic movement in America. One of its champions was Agostino De Biasi, a journalist who had founded the ambitious theoretical-cultural monthly *Il Carroccio*. His campaign against a supine acceptance of Americanization was not without a modicum of originality, even if there was some ambiguity in the journal's stance, which would be intensified with the coming of Fascism. Already in 1916 De Biasi's journal warned its readers about the risks of Americanization:

There are Italians who accept Americanism fatalistically, as the only way to fill their lost, empty, and money-grubbing souls. They think about their home country from time to time, according to the contractions of their gastric juices. They bargain away their nationality and get rid of their old identity in order to adapt themselves to whatever is new, foolishly attributing a similar moral deficiency to the Americans. Like foxes, they premeditate changes, renunciations, and falsehoods. Faced with the problem we have raised, these Italians, a sub-species of the real ones, become disheartened, caught in the trap they themselves have set, victims of that very flippancy which seemed to endow their tightrope act with the most stable sense of civility. Thus, they find themselves dreadfully isolated. . . . The Americans are right to reject them because . . . they retain the typical traits of the abhorred hyphen. The Italians repudiate them because they are not *Italians* and, with their fraudulent

---

66. Exemplary of this state of mind is the *"poemetto di rivendicazione"* (poem of vindication) *Italia* (1923), by Vincenzo Ingrao, who retraces the entire history of Italy, up to postwar demands.

intrusions on foreign ground, taint the reputation of their frank and loyal national character. Ultimately, they can even produce material damage to that same element which they have sworn—just think of it!—to protect.[67]

Grazia Dore has studied the reactions of the colonial press to the rise of Fascism. Its response was not perfectly linear. It was strongly influenced by the Red Scare and, parallel to it, the "red biennium" in Italy. Due to the climate of the period, Italian Americans were subjected to considerable psychological stress, especially when they had to face the dangerous equation *foreigner* = revolutionary. This popular equation sprang from the strong dislike of the IWW, which was considered the headquarters of Bolshevism on American ground. *Il Progresso* and other newspapers were hoping for a strong government in Italy, one that would be able to keep the various parties of the left at bay and guarantee a more reassuring image of Italy abroad. Such a government should also have provided a safe foothold for the Italian community in America, which felt helplessly insecure. An article in *L'Araldo Italiano* nicely sums up the paradoxical situation of these foreigners. They were public enemies if they insisted on remaining in America, "pickpockets" if they left the country with the "gold of the republic," strikebreakers if they worked at low cost, Bolsheviks if they fought for better conditions.[68]

The role of the Fascists in Italy began to appear similar to the role played by the fierce opponents of the feared Bolshevik conspiracy in America. However, the colonial press had not yet really aligned itself with Fascism. On the contrary, the press looked with suspicion at Fascism, and a certain proletarian sympathy led the newspapers to criticize measures taken against the strikes.[69] (In particular, *Il Progresso* continued to publish clearly antifascist articles by Arturo Labriola and Guglielmo Ferrero.) Once again, it was the reaction of American public opinion, which was quickly in favor of Mussolini, that determined its gradual alignment.

67. Alberto di Giussano, "L'Americanismo e gli emigrati" (Americanism and the Immigrants), *Il Carroccio* 3, no. 2 (February 1916): 116–117.

68. "Cose di questo mondo dell'altro" (Things from This World and the Other), July 7, 1919, cited in Dore 1964, 339.

69. This did not, however, stop the critical attacks from the socialist camp. During the detention of Eugene Debs, for example, Girolamo Valenti's *L'Avanti!* was able to abuse Barsotti with these quatrains: "Barsotti's 'Il Progresso' / The other day proclaimed / That in Italy Bolshevism / Died right after being born. / It is not the right land / for such a cruel doctrine; / there in eternity will reign / King Vittorio Gennariel. / And Barsotti is right, / That's how things are, / That idea just born / Has dropped dead. / And Barsotti also said: / How lucky, how pleasing! . . . / But a thief Bolshevism never / Would knight!" E. Migrato, "Il trionfo di Barsotti" (Barsotti's Triumph), *L'Avanti!*, April 19, 1919.

Paradoxically, Mussolini had once been a collaborator of the American *Il Prole-tario*. According to Tresca, who had met him in Switzerland and had lived with him when he was in hiding, Mussolini himself had been on the point of migrating to the United States. Soon *Il Duce* posed the problem of the Italian colonies abroad and in particular those in the United States. But Luigi Barzini, former collaborator of Albertini's at *Il Corriere della Sera* and sympathetic to Italian nationalism, was the first in 1922 to invent the idea of a great Italian daily in the United States, one capable of outstripping the existing press. Initially, he cast an eye on Barsotti's *Il Progresso*. Pio Crespi, the Texan in charge of Barzini's group of financiers, authorized Barzini to make an offer of one million dollars to buy the paper. After Barsotti refused, Barzini decided to found a new paper, *Il Corriere d'America*, which started on December 27, 1922, with circulation—a year later—that stabilized at around 50,000 copies. Meanwhile, Crespi was often worried and on several occasions expressed the will to sell. Thanks to a loan granted by the Banca Commerciale Italiana, Barzini obtained a conspicuous share of the journal's stock, thereby keeping Crespi's apprehensions at bay. All the same, Crespi curbed any attempts to expand, including the acquisition of *Il Bollettino della Sera* in 1926. When Barzini died in 1927, it seemed that there was an inversion of roles. Angelo Bertolino, executor of Barsotti's will, stepped forward to acquire *Il Corriere*, but the deal fell through due to the opposition of his heirs. Barzini's other plans to unite the two newspapers went up in smoke, even though in 1928 he had the backing of the banker Amadeo Giannini. But precisely at that moment *Il Progresso* was put up for sale. It was bought for the goodly sum of two million dollars by the entrepreneur Generoso Pope, who beat out the International Paper Company, a giant in the production of paper. Initially, the latter was planning to acquire *Il Corriere*, unite the two dailies, and appoint Barzini the director. As a result, this company ended up trying to acquire only *Il Corriere*, but Crespi refused the offer. Then Pope himself came forward, and in January 1928 the deal seemed done. However, primed by the Italian government, the Italian embassy in New York judged this concentration of newspapers undesirable. Pope was advised to back out, and new buyers were introduced to Crespi. The choice fell on the Order Sons of Italy, and the contract was written up and signed by both parties. Owing to Crespi's hesitations, again things came to nothing. Finally, Pope succeeded in the enterprise, taking advantage of his solid connections with the government in Rome.[70]

70. On these events, see as an appendix to Castronovo 1970, 421–429, an interesting exchange of letters between Barzini and Mussolini. Generoso Pope, a typical self-made man, a native of Arpaise (Benevento), came to America in 1904 and found a job as a construction worker. His

This vast concentration of newspapers also included *Il Bollettino della Sera* (New York) and *L'Opinione* (Philadelphia). Once the circle was closed, Pope was free to orchestrate an effective Fascist propaganda, availing himself of formidable means, to which must be added many radio stations and countless other local sheets, besides newspapers and journals. Among these there were the former anarchist Domenico Trombetta's *Il Grido della Stirpe* (The Cry of the Race), renamed by Tresca *Il Grido della Trippa* (The Cry of the Potbelly) and De Biasi's already mentioned *Il Carroccio*. The latter was assigned the task of giving cultural dignity to the movement. Inflexibly Fascist in its political perspective, the paper was indeed one of the liveliest Italian American literary platforms. It also published the works in English of some of the most interesting authors of the first generation, such as Silvio Villa, Louis Forgione, and Pascal D'Angelo (see Part V). San Francisco, California, was another stronghold of the Fascist press. Here Ettore Patrizi, by then the publisher not only of *L'Italia* but also of *La Voce del Popolo*, had early on fallen in line with the directives of the regime. According to his opponents, he openly posed as the "little Fuhrer of California."[71]

Gaetano Salvemini and others underlined the imbalance between the means available to the Fascists and those of the antifascists. Among other things, Fascist propaganda was able to draw upon a widespread circulation of books, pamphlets, and cheap publications that could be found in the bookstores attached to the many newspapers of proven loyalty.[72] It is also true that the story of Italian American antifascism is characterized by its chronic inability to establish a solid, united

---

ascent to success began in the sand quarries of Long Island and resulted in his founding the Colonial Sand and Stone Company. Within a few years, the company cornered many of the public works contracts in the New York area, becoming a colossus in the field and the coffer for all of Pope's later activities, including newspaper ownership. Pope died in 1950, and his son Fortune succeeded him at *Il Progresso*. See, among thousands of other contributions, Agostino De Biasi's commemoration in *La Follia di New York* (New York Folly), May 1960.

71. See Gino Neri, "Ettore Patrizi—Duce's Head Man in California," *La Controcorrente*, March 1942. In this article, the author retraces Patrizi's first steps toward fascism and, in particular, quotes one of his letters from 1924 (published in *Corriere del Popolo*), in which, dedicating to Mussolini a book published by the Società Fascista Italiani all'Estero (Italian Fascist Society Abroad), Patrizi, recently returned to the United States after one of his frequent Italian sojourns, declared himself ready "to take once more my place in the battle and, saluting you, I place myself under your orders for any task, for any mission, for any effort aiming at the welfare of the Fatherland. Believe me, my dear and illustrious president, your devoted servant, Ettore Patrizi."

72. From an announcement appearing on July 3, 1926, in *Grido della Stirpe* we learn, for example, that it was possible to buy one hundred copies of *Discorsi di Mussolini all'Augusteo* (Mussolini's Speeches at the Augusteo) for only three dollars.

front. In practice, the only concerted effort was that of the Anti-Fascist Alliance of North America (AFANA), founded in April 1923, with Giovannitti as secretary. It brought together socialists, republicans, libertarians, and various currents of anarchists. Furthermore, it was supported by the New York Federation of Labor, and above all by the Amalgamated Clothing Workers and the International Ladies' Garment Workers Union. It also included the communists of Enea Sormenti (which was one of the many names of the controversial activist from Trieste, Vittorio Vidali, who had come to America from Algeria in 1923). AFANA had a "short but highly militant life"[73] and distinguished itself for its restless combativeness. These were the years of raids and rallies that turned into colossal brawls followed by clamorous trials. The most famous was the one against Calogero Greco and Donato Carillo, two tailors from Brooklyn who in 1927 were charged with having killed Giuseppe Carisi and Nicola Amoroso, two blackshirts on their way to a demonstration in Manhattan. In *Il Carroccio*, De Biasi commented that "Cain's murder was not less abominable." In the same tone of passionate appeal to unity that was often used by the Fascist propaganda, he then asked himself:

> What is this misfortune that persecutes us Italians throughout the world? We are eternally enemies among ourselves, enemies of ourselves, condemned to blood and ignominy. We pass among other peoples, and we see how close-knitted they are against us and around us, and yet we continue to disgrace our common homeland. . . . When will we get rid of this implacable curse?

But the appeal to unity did not prevent De Biasi from dealing a much less conciliatory blow to his opponents. He also implicitly involved Salvemini:

> Now the Bronx massacre offers the clearest proof of the existence today of a pack of wild beasts in the shape of men who speak Italian, live among Italians, and are eager to extinguish in blood all those who live in the world and are proud to be Italian, devoted to defending their hearths and their altars. . . . The iniquity of the Bolshevik beast which is lurking in the antifascist political exile who execrates and curses Italy at the very moment he dares to proclaim himself its defender and avenger.[74]

On the other hand, De Biasi had already expressed with absolute clarity his opinion of Salvemini in an article of the year before: "He should be killed like a

73. Montana 1976, 116.
74. "Il massacro del Bronx" (The Bronx Massacre), *Il Carroccio* 5 (May 1927): 545–547.

rabid dog."[75] The Greco-Carillo case turned into a severe defeat for the Fascists when during the trial the famous lawyer Clarence Darrow, convinced that the two defendants had been arrested arbitrarily, availed himself of the testimony of Giacomo Caldora. Caldora was president of Mussolini's old Fascist Alliance, an association that was in conflict with the Fascist League of North America. According to him, Count Thaon di Revel, leader of the League, had offered him money in exchange for testimony against Greco and Carillo. Moreover, Caldora revealed that the Fascists were planning to place a bomb in the offices of *Il Martello*. On occasions like this, Tresca was able to manifest his unscrupulous skill in ridiculing his opponent. In 1932 Caldora also helped to overturn the outcome of the trial for the homicide of Salvatore Arena, and then that of the Terzani trial.[76] His denunciation of the Fascist League, with its transoceanic blackshirts, was carried out with equal skill. Mussolini had finally decided to dissolve this organization in 1929. The antifascist movement had, in fact, succeeded in having its theses published in the major papers and had also pushed Congress to set up an inquest into Fascist activities in the United States. In these same years, however, there were also more urbane public confrontations on the issue of Fascism. The most famous among them was the debate between Gaetano Salvemini and Bruno Roselli, professor of Italian Language and Literature at Vassar College and former attaché at the embassy in Washington. It took place in New York on January 22, 1927, and was organized by the Foreign Policy Association.[77]

In 1927 the ILGWU broke off from the antifascist Alliance. One of its more influential leaders was Luigi Antonini, from Avellino, who was then head of the famous Local 89. The split took place because many of its members dissented over

75. De Biasi 1927, 371.

76. On Staten Island in 1932, the fascists tried to prevent the antifascists from laying a crown on the Garibaldi monument. In the clash there was one death, Salvatore Arena—a blackshirt who later was implicated in a Montreal bank robbery and an old alliance fascist who, duly prompted by Tresca, had accused no less than Trombetta, who was tried and acquitted. A delightful recollection of this episode can be found in Montana 1976, 120–124. The Terzani trial, in 1933, concerned the killing of young antifascist Anthony Fierro during a Queens assembly of Arthur J. Smith's khaki shirts as they were about to begin a "march on Washington." The shooter was a fascist, but in the confusion a heckler from the opposite party was arrested. A defense committee organized by Tresca and Norman Thomas, putting pressure on the rather lazy district prosecutor, succeeded in exposing the true culprits thanks also to "penitents" among the many "khaki shirts" present at the incident.

77. The text of the debate, under the title *L'Italia sotto il Fascismo. I suoi aspetti economici, politici e morali* (Italy under Fascism: Its Economic, Political, and Moral Aspects) was published as a pamphlet by *Martello*.

the use of violence and, above all, because of the communist presence. The socialists, too, considered the Alliance domineering and in February of that year they founded the Anti-Fascist Federation of North America for the Freedom of Italy.[78]

In August 1928, AFANA made public a document that framed the struggle against Fascism within the broader movement of the struggle against capitalism. Consequently, the battle against Mussolini was bound to be a battle against the capitalist foundations supporting him. *Il Lavoratore*, the Italian American communist newspaper, launched a relentless campaign aimed at denouncing Fascist intrigues in the United States. These intrigues were widespread and sought to convert Italian Americans to Fascism by taking over "ethnic" institutions, hospitals, schools, and the Order Sons of Italy (with its 300,000 members in the 1920s, and lodges in every city). The support of the Catholic hierarchy and the diplomatic corps was decisive. The antifascists went so far as to establish a link between Fascism and organized crime, which was defined "*la Mano Nera del Fascismo*." This link was more than allegorical. But it was exactly in 1928 that the communists and the most prestigious libertarian leader, Carlo Tresca, split up. Already the year before, Armando Borghi had urged Tresca to take this step.[79] Now it was Tresca who denounced Stalinist methods and the danger of a Stalinist dictatorship even more oppressive than the Fascist regime.

The success of AFANA was short-lived. The dissolution of the Fascist League was more formal than substantive, and this Fascist organization was then replaced by the less binding *Federazione littoria* established by Trombetta and not in line with Fascist headquarters. Nevertheless, antifascism never had a significant impact on the people. It "remained rigidly intransigent, hostile not only to Fascism proper but also to the greatness and well-being of the mother country."[80] Very rarely have scholars reflected on the sense of frustration and isolation that beset the antifascist, political-intellectual vanguards of America. For example, never

78. Antonini (1883–1968) had spent time as a communist: after coming out of the SPA and founding a small independent socialist federation of New York, he joined the Workers Party, but soon he withdrew with Bellanca. Because of the fuss caused by his "renunciation" he was forced to speak about it publicly: "No metamorphosis has occurred for me; who has changed, moving backward like shrimp, are the others, the high priests, sole holders of the revolution patent and formulators of NEP strategic tactics." See "Perché sono uscito dal Workers Party of America" (Why I Left the Workers Party of America), *La Parola del Popolo*, November 15, 1924. On anticommunism in the IGLWU, see Zappia 1986.

79. With the polemical pamphlet *Gli anarchici e le alleanze antifasciste* (The Anarchists and the Antifascist Alliances).

80. Montana 1976, 116–117.

as in these years can one detect the great distance, almost the feeling of dispar-agement, that separated this elite from the immigrant masses. The Tresca of Mus-solini's heyday at the beginning of the 1930s offers us a striking example here. He violently contested those criminal *cafoni* like Generoso Pope, as well as the many dishonest *banchisti* who succeeded in making even Al Capone credible.[81] Even further, he now included in these detestable categories a much larger crowd, the masses of immigrants themselves. His polemics are pervaded by a feeling of dis-couragement and almost shame with respect to situations in which Fascism had a much harder life, as was the case among the Italians in South America. Thus, in commenting on the umpteenth bankruptcy of the *banchista* Raffaele Prisco (a worthy advocate of Mussolini's cause), Tresca furiously exploded against the stolid victims of that system, "those Italian workers who have slabs of lard on their brain and gather in big whimpering crowds behind the Madonna of Seven Sorrows, in processions which exhibit all the degrading and shameful bigotry of the Italic people; or cry out like wild beasts their subjection every time some ham actor brandishes a *tricolore* [the flag] in front of their eyes."[82] As always in Tresca's arti-cles, the tones of the invective reach a hyperbolic crescendo. In this case, the great libertarian leader almost ends up cursing in front of those victims who do not know how, and do not want, to redeem themselves:

> This ignorant, backward mass jealously preserves its prejudices. It does not elevate itself, even if it comes into contact with superior races. Any weapon of civil propaganda smashes itself against it. It is the *vendée* [a region in France famed for its royalist sentiments]. Let it be robbed, let it bleed to death. *Cavaliere* Prisco! As long as *cafoni* exist, there will always be room for frauds like you. . . . As long as monarchist Italy casts pack animals instead of men onto these lands.[83]

Certainly, this pessimistic aura was aggravated by the American scene at large: from the Great Depression to the convulsions of the syndicalist movement, which by then had spent its revolutionary fervor. In his memoir Armando Borghi recalls that from the time of his arrival in the United States, at the end of 1926, he had been seized by a feeling of dismay on noticing the general "neglect of ideal values."

---

81. Carlo Tresca, "Cafoni e criminali" (Louts and Criminals), *Il Martello*, August 15, 1931.
82. Ibid. Tresca would create a "Sir Brisco," a prototype of the fascist buffoon banker, in his play *L'attentato a Mussolini* (The Assassination Attempt on Mussolini).
83. Ibid.

This inert materialism triumphantly succeeded in deluding even the most savvy of European observers, like Arturo Labriola, who anticipated that "American over-production represented the overcoming of socialism."[84] Furthermore, the Wall Street crisis had disillusioned everybody. Meanwhile, the reactionary journal *La Vandea* (The Vendée) sang the praises of the regime from the columns of the major newspapers. And it guaranteed considerable space to a veritable deluge of "amateur" writings that—albeit quite modest in quality—testify to the broad range of consensus they were able to garner. There were a number of relatively skilled poets and writers such as Rosario Ingargiola, Rose Zagnoni Marinoni, Umberto Liberatore, and a few others. Through them the colony expressed its enthusiasm and its faith in the new Rome, but there were also countless more modest figures. Emblematic here is the case of Rosario Di Vita, who promoted an extraordinary poetic homage to the Duce by editing a hefty album of all the good things the Italian Americans had said about him.[85]

In 1925 a new daily was founded in New York, *Il Nuovo Mondo* (The New World). It was located on that East Tenth Street that Vanni Montana later defined as "the citadel of Italian American anti-fascism." Next door there was the weekly *Il Lavoratore* (The Worker), whose moving spirit was Vittorio Vidali, until he was deported from the United States in 1927. Across the street were Tresca's *Il Martello* and the headquarters of another group of radicals.[86] *Il Nuovo Mondo* was programmatically antifascist and was founded through the efforts of the Italian leaders of two powerful textile labor unions, Augusto Bellanca of the Amalgamated Clothing Workers Association and Luigi Antonini of the International Ladies' Garment Workers Union. These two leaders were supported by the socialist Yiddish daily *The Forward*, and they put together a sizable group of influential professionals. Worth mentioning here are the medical doctors Matteo Siragusa, a socialist, Nino Firenze, a follower of Mazzini, and first and foremost Charles Fama, a second-generation Italian American who was well connected in Protestant, Republican, and Masonic circles.

Vincenzo Vacirca was one of the first directors of *Il Nuovo Mondo*. (Formerly, he had been a socialist deputy in Italy and was deprived of his citizenship by

84. Borghi 1954, 335.
85. This album turned out to be of great usefulness to Filippo Fichera in compiling the equally extraordinary collection *Il Duce e il Fascismo nei Canti dialettali d'Italia* (Il Duce and Fascism in the Dialect Songs of Italy, 1937). An entire section of it is reserved for "poesia fascista degl'Italiani nelle Colonie e all'Estero" (Fascist poems by Italians in the colonies and abroad), with an ample selection of lyrics.
86. Montana 1976, 98–100.

Mussolini.) He was followed by Frank Bellanca, Augusto's brother, and in 1928, for a short term, by Arturo Labriola. Girolamo Valenti, former secretary of the FSI and director of *La Parola del Popolo*, was its administrator and more.[87] On the editorial board there were Carmelo Zito, Serafino Romualdi, and Raimondo Fazio.[88] Vanni Buscemi Montana joined the board in 1930 and recalled the paper's fight for survival, due in part to the difficulty of rounding up advertisements because the storekeepers were scared to appear in the paper. To these problems were added the fact that there were several currents of antifascism among the editors, which led to a very serious crisis in 1931. "The three Jews"— the lawyers Filippo Bongiorno, president of the *Ospedale Italiano* of New York, Santo Modica, grand master of the Order Sons of Italy Grand Lodge, and Michele Albano, secretary of the Fondo Unico Mortuario of the same order— became shareholders. The three of them were "pure-blood *tammanisti*" and behind them Tresca glimpsed the omnipresent specter of Generoso Pope. According to the pugnacious libertarian leader, their presence handed the paper over to the Fascists. As a result, what Girolamo Valenti had called "somewhat boastfully" "the ultimate trench of antifascism," was broken through. As usual, this was due to the chronic financial difficulties that, to someone like Tresca, seemed all in all a negligible problem that had always vexed the press "on our side." From his point of view, poverty "is not shameful." Then Tresca identified in Augusto Bellanca the "evil" spirit, the man who had brought to the newspaper the methods of the Amalgamated Clothing Workers. He attached *bellanchismo*, a disturbing coinage which years later became the title of a series of articles in *Il Martello*. His target was this new and suspect "liberal antifascism,—Masonic,

87. Valenti (Valguarnera Caropepe, Caltanissetta, Italy, 1892–New York, 1958), who was of a well-to-do family (owners of a sulfur mine), immigrated in 1911 for unknown reasons and joined the Social Democratic wing of the FSI. He had a successful career in the union and as the founder and manager of many journals. Equally hard on fascists and communists, he directed the socialist secession from AFANA and the establishment of the Anti-Fascist Federation for the Freedom in Italy. He then collaborated in the establishment of *Il Popolo*, the organ of the Italian American progressives (1937–39), whose president was Congressman Vito Marcantonio. Valenti was a consultant of the Office of Strategic Service on the Italian question and then a militant active in the anticommunist struggle of the Cold War era. His epic battle against *Il Progresso Italo-Americano* lasted until his death (his libelous article "Fascism, Anti-Semitism Rampant in Editorial Room of *Il Progresso Italo-Americano*, An Open Letter to 1st Editor and Publisher Fortune R. Pope" is dated to 1958).

88. Fazio (Seloreto [Catanzaro], Italy, 1897–Pittsburgh, 1957), a tailor by trade and an American soldier during World War I, distinguished himself as a literary enthusiast, preface writer for various volumes, and translator.

moderate, *tammanista*, priestling, at times popish, and other times Protestant. A sort of minestrone."[89]

Behind this initiative was a faction of the Order Sons of Italy, the widespread, ethnic-Masonic organization that openly opposed Giovanni Di Silvestro, who, already in 1922, had gone to Rome to declare his loyalty to the Fascist regime. As a consequence, the group split up when the New York State sections seceded.[90] Now Di Silvestro made a profession of "subservience" to the king and adhered to a Columbian celebration in sheer Fascist style. In his interesting memoir, Vanni Montana later quickly dismissed the question. *La Stampa Libera*, the paper of those who deserted *Il Nuovo Mondo*, claimed the right to represent the original viewpoint of the latter. However, its birth was simply "the result of the editorial board's rebellion against the attempt of some 'generous' financial backers to force us to stop attacking certain Italian American Fascists."[91]

The crisis occurred in the fall. But the history of that year—1931—was longer and eventful. To tell the truth, in his opening editorial, lawyer Bongiorno had solemnly reasserted the original role of *Il Nuovo Mondo* as the only alternative to a press that marched according to the Fascist drum-beat and reduced itself to it:

> I believe that no impartial and intelligent person will deny that the other three dailies published in this city daily conform to those indisputable journalistic beauties. On the contrary, they are called everywhere not "the Italian press of New York" but instead "the Fascist press" or, even worse, "the *cafoni*'s press." The latter definition does not at all refer to the readers of these newspapers but to the policy and distinguishing mark of the newspapers themselves.[92]

Bongiorno was particularly harsh toward Pope's press. The purchase of *Il Nuovo Mondo* responded to a very specific need: to make a newspaper "capable of appealing not only to a well-defined political group but to all the liberals who

89. Carlo Tresca, "La commemorazione di C. Colombo e la penetrazione fascista all'estero. 'Il Nuovo Mondo' nelle mani di Generoso Pope?" (The Commemoration of C. Columbus and the Fascist Penetration Abroad. "The New World" in the Hands of Generoso Pope?), *Il Martello*, October 17, 1931.

90. The leaders of the secession movement were Fiorello La Guardia and Judge Salvatore Cotillo. On this subject, see Diggins 1972, 117.

91. Montana 1976, 100.

92. Philip Bongiorno, "Il nostro direttore, avv. F. Bongiorno ai lettori" (Our Editor, Atty. F. Bongiorno to the Readers), *Il Nuovo Mondo*, March 22, 1931.

today have a common enemy, Fascism, and one interest: the freedom, well-being, and progress of the Italians and the Italian Americans."[93] Then Bongiorno listed the seven cardinal points of his program: the struggle against Fascism and its diffusion as well as the intrusion of Fascist authorities and agents in colonial activities, opposition to dual citizenship, support of "organized labor" (that is, the labor unions), understanding between the American and Italian peoples, and promotion of the Americanization of the Italians. These goals were repeated again and again and triggered the campaign of *Il Corriere d'America*, with Barzini's accusations against the *Ospedale Italiano* for the presumed political nature of its antifascist management and the pressing surveillance of the Order Sons of Italy, another great institution which Fascism sought to convert. An editorial by Vincenzo Vacirca, merely the first act of a bitter battle between newspapers, vibrantly replied to these maneuvers.[94] On April 5, *Il Nuovo Mondo* came out with a full-page title: "The Fascist Scribe Caught Redhanded." The article furiously attacked Barzini, who was accused of anti-Semitism among other things. The editorial was published in English to underline the national scope of the question. It discussed the dominating topic of antifascist propaganda in America: in short, the risk that the Italian colony and the entire country were running, due to the ongoing penetration of Fascism. The *Ospedale* and the Order Sons of Italy were the two most recent examples. Barzini was singled out as Mussolini's representative in America: a "public enemy," as General Butler might define him.[95]

The battle over the *Ospedale Italiano* offers a good observation point for this case, which, after all, is quite marginal and now forgotten. Barzini mustered the patriotically oriented public and published letters from the readers, who in an improbable "plebiscite" called for the elimination of the "traitors to the Fatherland." *Il Nuovo Mondo* fired a series of hard-hitting attacks against Barzini and some of his supporters, like lawyer Rosario Ingargiola. The latter was a literary figure with a certain reputation in the colony and was a grand master of the Ordine Indipendente Figli d'Italia (Independent Order of the Sons of Italy). On May 17, *Il Nuovo Mondo* published for a second time a series of excerpts chosen from some of his collaborative pieces (heatedly antinationalist and anti-interventionist) written during the 1910s for two anarchist newspapers, *Il Corriere Libertario* of

93. Ibid.

94. "Barziniana," April 4, 1931.

95. Smedley Butler was the man who revealed how Mussolini ran over a six-year-old girl with his car and killed her on September 14, 1930, in San Quirito, in the province of Grosseto.

Barre and *La Questione Sociale* of New York.[96] Evidently, one of the most effective topics among those that perennially stirred up the colorful and always contentious Italian American political scene was the extreme nonchalance with which many *"girella"* ("spinning tops"; this was the standard term) had been—and still were—willing to become turncoats. Tresca often made use of it, and to Ingargiola, Giovanni Di Silvestro, and once again Trombetta, he dedicated a vitriolic piece precisely entitled "Girella."[97] Barzini, among other things, was blamed for having betrayed his liberal past and even his Jewish origin.[98] In his case the campaign was relentless, and it is worth lingering over a bit longer. In fact, 1931 was also the year in which Barzini resigned as director of *Il Corriere d'America*, and this paper, too, was then taken over by Pope. Meanwhile, as a prologue to what the antifascists of *Il Nuovo Mondo* considered a real debacle, the "plebiscite" over the issue of the *Ospedale Italiano* was deflated. A brilliant commentator of the antifascist paper who signed his articles "Il Signor Manga Nello" (Mr. Bludgeon),

96. "Un 'Fratello,' Era sincero quand'era anarchico, o è sincero ora ch'è fascista?" (A "Brother," Was He Sincere When He Was an Anarchist, or Was He Sincere Now That He Is a Fascist?), *Il Nuovo Mondo*, May 17, 1931. It is worth citing some verses from Rosario Ingargiola's ode "Impeti" (Impulses), published in *Questione Sociale* on September 15, 1915: "The bristling Janissary rabble grumbles / with the blood and hate that fills their guts, / and at our standard of Life / laughs, and twists the griffin. / But you will fall, O cracked heroes / of the sword, thieving soldiers / of disgrace, savage harpies of a sort / who die. Brother, is it true?" *Corriere Libertario* (Libertarian Courier) was edited by Vincenzo Panizza, "a despicable type of anarchist, who" as Riccardo Cordiferro remembered him, "after having for many years sponged off the subversives of New Jersey and Vermont, changed point-blank into a fanatical interventionist." That same fall he founded *La Rinascenza Italica* (The Italic Renaissance) in New York. He who "ended up later imprisoned in Italy for having killed, after having ignobly exploited, with the complicity of his wife, a young American woman, who apparently was his lover." Cordiferro, "La triade della cricca" (The Gang of Three), *Il Nuovo Mondo*, November 21, 1931. The editor of *Questione Sociale* was then Aldino Felicani, a personality of quite another idealistic coherence, to whom we will later turn.

97. *Il Martello*, August 22, 1931: "Rosario Ingargiola, the ex-subversive who with writing and words incited the holy rebellions and invoked the revolutionary apocalypse, is the head of the Ordine Indipendente Figli d'Italia. Giovanni Di Silvestro, the ex-subversive who with us endured the rigors of prison when the tyrants made his soul tremble with suffering, is the head of Ordine Figli d'Italia [Order of the Sons of Italy]. Both are fascists. Both are rascals of the worst kind." In *Corriere d'America* (*American Courier*), Ingargiola "spit out an article, or better still pissed his bile" commenting on the convention of the Sons of Italy of Niagara Falls, noting also with sorrow that the Vittorio Emanuele III Lodge had changed its name to Vittoria, and commented on the event thusly: "It is a sign that fully confirms the suspicion that no respect for all that is Italian is held in the soul of these men."

98. *Il Nuovo Mondo* labeled him "the circumcised ex-globetrotter" on April 5, 1931, and held against him the unfortunate comments of the "Jewish quacks" who, as he said, could have replaced the Italian doctors of New York Hospital.

namely Edmondo Raiola, ran a satirical column entitled "Con dovuta modestia parlando" (Speaking with Due Modesty). Here, on May 29, he published the following verses on this subject:

Like pigeons called by the cuckoo,
The devoted flocked in hundreds,
But all at once they have all run off.
The plebiscite which stirred up fear
And advanced full of revenge,
Awesome, swifter than the wind,
Has lost its destructive power
And taken the shape of a quagmire
Generated by a monstrous slacker.
The *prominente* grumbles, the gim-crack
Fails to get the game and the Fascist
"Alas!" is left empty-handed.
And the *Cavalier*, like a famous journalist,
Following the Sun, along with his newspaper,
Has turned the corner and is . . . a popist:
"Yes, let Pope build the Italic hospital,"
He said. "He has my support,
Both material and spiritual."
But Pope has dressed up as a sucker,
And brandishing the incensory at once,
He has politely thanked
And fooled the *Cavaliere*.

Finally, on Sunday, September 6, 1931, *Il Nuovo Mondo* was able to announce with a full-page title, "L'ignominiosa fuga dall'America di L. Barzini" (L. Barzini's Ignominious Escape from the Editorial Board and the Bitter Surprise of his "Plebiscitarians), which took place while *"Il Corriere d'America* falls into Generoso Pope's hands." *Il Nuovo Mondo*, which Barzini had so often sarcastically criticized for always being in financial straits, was understandably pleased.

Meanwhile, the verbal exchange between *Il Nuovo Mondo* and *Stampa Libera* was becoming almost as heated. As we have already seen, Carlo Tresca added fuel to the fire. However, *Il Martello* also used to host bylines that did not share its positions. For example, Pietro Allegra, an old activist of the antifascist Alliance, deplored those very same disagreements "that brought Fascism to Italy." He stood for the need to support *Il Nuovo Mondo* in that "even with its defects, it is still an antifascist weapon." Luigi Quintiliano was a tailor-journalist, former secretary of the committee for the political victims of the Red Scare crackdown, and an old comrade-in-arms of Tresca's. He replied to Allegra that it was the supine attitude of the heads of *Il Nuovo Mondo* that had weakened the movement. Indeed, they were scared of the crowds, as they had already shown in *La Parola del Popolo* (the reference was to Valenti) when they had stigmatized the most courageous forays of the antifascist Alliance and condemned the participation of the communists. *Il Martello* also published a letter by Charles Fama, who suavely hailed the birth of *Stampa Libera* as a new weapon against Fascism and exalted the two dailies: "Don't waste your strength in a Cain-like fight among brothers."[99] On the contrary, they should combine forces in a common effort. His words fell on deaf ears. It was open warfare between the two papers. The old Riccardo Cordiferro, who was asked to collaborate on a regular basis with *Il Nuovo Mondo*, launched a number of attacks against the members of the editorial board of *La Stampa Libera*. He denied as pure fantasy that Pope had offered any kind of support to *Il Nuovo Mondo*. He questioned the fact that lawyer Modica had wanted to dismiss for unclear reasons the regular column by Manganello-Raiola, stating that it was only boring and repetitive. As for Valenti, "firmly feeding at the trough of antifascism, he does not have the least intention to change his way of life." But for him, the gravy train has come to a halt. It is useless for him to holler because anyway, "This new enterprise will end like all the others, including the monument to Giacomo Matteotti. Nobody knows, nor will anybody ever know, what happened to its subscription of about 7,000 dollars."[100]

Il Nuovo Mondo interrupted publication on November 29, 1931, but the quarreling went on. As usual, it was Carlo Tresca who took it upon himself to keep the conflict alive. However, he brought it to a higher level of debate, by showing how a valid antifascist activity in the United States might be resumed. According to Tresca, the antifascist struggle must have the character of class struggle. This was

99. All three of these exchanges in *Il Martello* on October 31, 1931.

100. "Il pubblico vi conosce, mascherine!" (The Public Knows You, Masked Ones), *Il Nuovo Mondo*, November 8, 1931. A short poem by Cordiferro, "I tre compari" (The Three Friends)— they being Valenti, Domenico Marino, and Manganello-Raiola—came out November 6; "Stornellata a Girolamo Valenti" (Rhymed Song to Girolamo Valenti) the next day; on November 12 the poem dedicated to the trio was entitled, with the frankness of spoken Neapolitan, "Cricco, Crocco e Manicangino"; another poem, "*A Manganello*" (To Manganello) came out November 13; and a harsh article, "La triade della cricca" (The Gang of Three, the same as the first), on November 21.

why the workers' organizations had been drawn into the orbit of the old Alliance, but with disastrous results. "Once the Alliance was destroyed, these labor organizers, these Fascist party officials of the workers' unionism, completely withdrew from the struggle." Here, once again, a theme dear to Tresca surfaced, and it would become more and more obsessive in the years to come. Namely, the theme of a kind of activism capable of setting aside the cloying syndicalist patronage of the salaried bureaucrat: "The union, for him, is not the labor union, a weapon to fight capitalism, a cell of the future society, a force from which the fire of liberation will burst out. The union is the means and end of an existence spent in search of a job. To keep that job, any cowardly action, any compromise, is worthwhile."[101]

No doubt, this denunciation was to some extent justified. At this time the America of the labor unions presented a rather dramatic panorama of unconfessable transactions and complicity with the underworld. The underworld had happily adapted itself to act as the *longa manus* of the bosses, and now it might as easily become the *longa manus* of labor.[102] Tresca was an irredeemable anarchist and could not have warmed to that world. A theater of real ghosts began to fill up before his very eyes, a theater which would make of his death the terrible crossroads—almost a symbolic sacrifice—marking the apex of the Italian American experience. This stage was missing just one character, the sinister Stalinist presence. Soon enough and inevitably, news arrived of the Spanish deeds of Commander Carlos (his former comrade Vittorio Vidali) and of the violent communist repression of the anarchists. Meanwhile, the battle had to strike at the heart of organized labor, the more or less triumphant *bellanchismo* and its colonial intrigues. Italian American Fascism acknowledged the generalized consent of the masses to Mussolini's Italy. As a consequence, it tried to fight with generosity. But it stirred up a great deal of confusion and got so entangled in its complicated past that it brought to the heart of the battle the dead weight of stratified relations and problems that had, as it were, become gangrenous. In a few years, these

101. "L'antifascismo negli Stati Uniti" (Antifascism in the United States), *Il Martello*, January 16, 1932.

102. Among the three victims of this battle conducted by "professionals" of crime included Giovanni Pippan, founder and secretary of the Italian Bread Drivers league of Chicago, former editor of *Parola del Popolo*, killed by the revolver shots of two hired assassins on August 28, 1933. Born in Trieste in 1894, Pippan immigrated to America in 1924 to avoid Fascist violence; he was at the head of the FSI, then joined the Communist Party, from which he was driven in 1931 for returning to the socialist ranks. He then worked with Paterson weavers and Illinois miners. See Antonio Camboni, "Venti anni dopo" (Twenty Years Later), *La Parola del Popolo* 12 (October–December 1953), and MOI.

problems had set up a formidable barrier between the activism of the Italian Americans and that of the political exiles. The two poles of antifascism were already separated by an inverse perspective: one pole looked to America, the other addressed all its thoughts and actions to Italy. A real integration between the two headquarters proved impossible. Gaetano Salvemini was the only Italian antifascist who, thanks to his long residence in the United States, and perhaps a different political point of view, succeeded in establishing a dialogue with the Italian Americans. It was not easy. The others remained substantially distant from this narrative.

No wonder, therefore, that three years later Tresca returned to the old question in *Il Nuovo Mondo* and embedded it in a story which in serial form "cast light" on *bellanchismo*. In undertaking *La veridica storia del 'Nuovo Mondo'* (The True Story of the *Nuovo Mondo*), Tresca promised to explain "how antifascism had been cheated, exploited, divided, and torn to pieces by his Grey Eminence, Augusto Bellanca." In the multiform maneuverings conceived by this syndicalist leader, Tresca found all the stings of that brand of transformism that he so hated. At first, there was a flirtation with the Bolsheviks based on the successful business of the Amalgamated Bank, the only joint-stock bank to have financial relations with Soviet Russia. Then Bellanca backed down. Finally, he—"illiterate in two languages"—yielded to the irresistible temptation to become "the Pope of labor journalism." Hence the countless times he tripped up Vacirca (he too not appreciated by Tresca, who called him "the honorable provolone") and the family-styled management of the enterprise, which led him to trust his inept brother Frank with its direction.[103] The intensity of Tresca's antifascist vigilance was by now legendary. In 1934 *Il Martello* presented its subscribers with the bulky volume (400 pages) *Sotto il segno del littorio. La genesi del fascismo* (Under the Sign of the Fasces: The Genesis of Fascism) by Domenico Saudino. Soon after, he published the articles that John Spivack wrote in Rome for *The New Masses*. Then came Ignazio Silone's original novella *Don Aristotile* and Salvemini's articles on the causes and effects of the war in Ethiopia. Finally, a special number (June 14, 1937) was dedicated to the murder of the Rosselli brothers. Generoso Pope, the tycoon of the Italian American press, became Tresca's main target, owing to his steady backing of the Fascist cause. Around this sun rotated infinite planets, almost all of them guilty of laxity and lukewarm commitment. One of them was the mayor Fiorello La Guardia,

103. See the articles of the "Bellanchismo" series, signed Ergo Sum, in *Martello* on November 14 and December 14, 1934, and February 28, 1935.

whom Tresca defined "a scoundrel"[104] or "the man on the flying trapeze"—the acrobat who does not hesitate to change his tactics and in view of the 1936 election, gets himself portrayed alongside "my brother Pope."[105] Then there were the labor unions, that is, both Bellanca and Antonini, who continued to use the *cafone* press to circulate their statements, and a whole series of minor figures like the sculptor and poet Onorio Ruotolo. The latter was a close friend of Giovannitti's, and his foggy commitment to democracy did not prevent him from modeling a bust of Mussolini (with La Guardia's continuing financial support).[106]

During the Spanish Civil War, Tresca's relationship with the communists became increasingly complicated. His split with the third Internationalist position was clear-cut. From then on *Il Martello* detected in the activity of the American communists—as exemplified in the pages of *The Daily Worker*—their shadowy alliance with the Fascists. According to Tresca, the communists were ambiguously seeking an agreement in America with the "honest Fascists"—the pope, the clergy, and the people at the consulate.[107] They were driven by the diabolic will to "destroy" everything that the party was not able to "control." This was the case of the daily *La Stampa Libera*, which eventually led to the tacit assent of the sphinxes of Italian American syndicalism.[108] Now Tresca's stubborn anticommunism and strenuous opposition to any scheme leading to a united front became more adamant. The various antifascist organizations heatedly debated the idea of a united front until the end of World War II. *Il Martello* had resumed publication in February 1940, after the short-lived experience of *Intesca Libertaria* (Libertarian Understanding), which was concluded in the summer of 1939 by the Italian anarchist groups in an attempt to join forces around the new initiative. In March of 1942, the

104. Because he guaranteed, during the course of the Ethiopian War, the gathering of funds for the Italian Red Cross launched by Generoso Pope, despite the opposition of the American Red Cross, which had sole rights to fundraising. See Carlo Tresca, "Il rigurgito delle fogne cafoniche invase il Madison Square Garden" (The Overflowing of the Buffoonish Sewers Overran Madison Square Garden), *Il Martello*, December 14, 1935.

105. See "Proponiamo un'altra 'Patacca' a Fiorello La Guardia" (We Propose Another "Medal" for Fiorello La Guardia), *Il Martello*, May 14, 1935.

106. Ruotolo, moreover, would remain loyal to the figure of Tresca. His portrait of the libertarian leader adorns the cover of the special issue of *Martello*, *Manet Immorta Fides*, published on the occasion Tresca's death.

107. See Carlo Tresca, "*È ora di farla finite!*" (Time to Stop), *Il Martello*, July 14, 1937, which comments upon a speech by communist Tancredi Angeli that had appeared in *Stampa Libera*.

108. See Carlo Tresca, "Fronte unico–Unione popolare–Unione democratia. Perché fu stroncata 'Stampa Libera'" (United Front–Popular Union–Democratic Union: Why *Stampa Libera* Died), *Il Martello*, May 16, 1938.

newspaper began attacking the Stalinists' attempt to join the Mazzini Society, which was created between the end of 1939 and the beginning of 1940, thanks to the efforts of Gaetano Salvemini.[109]

At this point it is important to recall that the attitude of the American government towards Fascist Italy had been substantially favorable throughout the 1930s. And this despite the fact that Italy's Ethiopian adventure had triggered serious criticism, especially in Harlem, where the Italians lived side by side with the African Americans.[110] This attitude was heavily influenced by a number of factors: Roosevelt's prudence; the importance of the Italian American vote, which *prominenti* such as Generoso Pope funneled into the Democratic Party; and finally, the short-lived and popular "identification" of the American president with Mussolini.[111] It did not matter that in Miami, on February 13, 1933, a mentally disturbed Italian immigrant, the Calabrese Giuseppe Zangara, tried to kill the president with a handgun. He only succeeded in mortally wounding the mayor of Chicago (who stood near Roosevelt) and being sentenced to death in the electric chair. The execution took place on March 20 of that same year. In short, politics required the ability to maneuver and a good dose of unscrupulousness, neither of which pertained to the anarchist-libertarian tradition. Instead, such political scheming was abundantly deployed by organized labor, to which Roosevelt gave a boost as well as a sense of prominence they never knew before. This situation was indirectly confirmed by an anarchist of proven loyalty, Armando Borghi. Years later, in assessing this period, he traced a discomforting parable of the history of American labor:

When they were forced to fight seriously against the bosses, they were tragically repressed. The episode of the Chicago Martyrs is famous. Later, with

109. See "I pretoriani di Stalin all'assalto della Mazzini Society" (Stalin's Praetorians Storm the Mazzini Society), *Il Martello*, May 14, 1942. The anarchists of *Adunata dei Refrattari* had a different opinion of Mazzini; for them, it was simply the case of a government in exile formed by the same leaders who "after years of dictatorship and exile still have the same fear of liberty and revolutions that led them to hand over the Italian people without even a shadow of resistance to fascist despotism," *La rivoluzione in livrea* (The Revolution in Uniform), February 27, 1942.

110. See Venturini 1990.

111. See the interesting considerations on the subject in Diggins 1972. Ettore Patrizi in 1932 had gone so far as to say that "a dictator is what the United States needs." And Generoso Pope in 1938 sang the praises of corporatism and forecast that it would be adopted in America. The propaganda played on the many similarities: Fascio (Fascist League): American Legion; *balilla* (Fascist Party Youth): Boy Scouts; Programma di Lavori Pubblici e di Assistenza (public works program and welfare): New Deal; Mediterraneo (Mediterranean): Caraibi (Caribbean); and so on.

Gompers, the organizations ended up as fiefs of the leaders. Lastly, with Roosevelt's New Deal, the organizers did not really have institutional ties with the government as was the case with Fascism and Bolshevism. Neither were they linked to the government or the political parties by special treaties or "programs." All the same, they were co-interested in the government's program inasmuch as they owed their fortune to it.[112]

We must add to this picture the Italian American antifascist psychodrama and keep in mind that things changed radically in a very short period of time. The first reason for this was Roosevelt's speech in Charlottesville, Virginia, of June 10, 1940, in which he condemned "the stab in the back" that Mussolini's Italy had inflicted on France.[113] The second and definitive reason was the declaration of war against the United States by Germany and Italy on December 11, 1941, four days after Pearl Harbor. Italian Americans were forced to choose sides even if it was difficult and inevitable. On Columbus Day 1942, the status of enemy aliens for non-naturalized Italians was invalidated; the measure had forced some 600,000 immigrants to "register" as such and brought about the internment of around 10,000 of them.[114] But the major colonial papers themselves also changed course. By then, Generoso Pope was urging the antifascists to accept him. The most savvy politicians and syndicalists, like Luigi Antonini, could not but point out the advantages that would ensue. Stray dogs like Tresca shut themselves up in firm opposition. As Max Ascoli, president of the Mazzini Society, noted, the war had dealt a final blow to the isolation of the Italian community in America. But none of this took place without deep lacerations.

Anticommunist discrimination (the communists remained neutral until the German attack against Russia in 1941) was also a major problem for the organizations of political exiles. In addition, there was the problem of how to deal with those who converted at the last minute. When the Mazzini Society was founded, it seemed natural to keep the communists out. In 1941 Alberto Tarchiani and Alberto Cianca joined the Mazzini Society, and Max Ascoli became the president. At this point the group became an instrument in the hands of Count Carlo Sforza and sought to ally itself with Antonini and Bellanca, whose headquarters was con-

112. Borghi 1954, 335.
113. This speech, which was also subtly interpreted as a return to old anti-Italian stereotypes, among other things caused Roosevelt a palpable reduction in Italian American support in the 1940 election. See Mammarella 1984.
114. See Distasi 2001, Fox 2000.

sidered the only reliable seat for the antifascist organization. The Society was also interested in politicians like La Guardia and Charles Poletti, the lieutenant governor of the State of New York.

However, this politics was at times blatantly contradictory. The syndicalist leaders were more interested in undermining the power of the profascist *prominenti* and therefore tended to give the association a largely Italian American connotation. The exiles who presided over it sought to use both the unions and the Italian Americans themselves to carry out a strategy focused mainly on Italy and the international context.[115]

Such contradictions did not prevent the Mazzini Society from opening dozens of branches and signing up some thousand new members. Antonio Varsori has analyzed Sforza's strategy, which sought in vain to take over *Il Progresso Italo-Americano* and favor relations with the heads of the Western powers. It was a strategy that Salvemini and others disliked and, to tell the truth, not even the American government was particularly in favor of it, preferring as it did an interlocutor among the syndicalists of Antonini's and Bellanca's Italian-American Labour Council and the converted *prominenti*. Thus, there arose the problem of underscoring the Italian American character of the Society. The June 1942 congress marked the defeat of the faction that fostered a dialogue with the communists and the removal of Randolfo Pacciardi, who, like Cianca and the republican Aurelio Natoli, had favored it. In August of that year, Sforza seemed to acquire new prestige, after being proclaimed the leader of antifascism at the Montevideo congress. But once again, he failed to overcome his organization's isolation and to convince the Americans to accept his agenda. The latter called for the formation of a national committee—seen as a sort of ministry in exile made up of members of the movement Justice and Freedom, Republicans, socialists, and *popolari*—and the Italian Legion of Volunteers. The anticommunist discrimination persisted. Giuseppe Berti and Ambrogio Donini, the only PCI leaders present in the United States at the time, relied on the journal *Lo Stato Operaio* of New York to make their availability known. They also expressed their interest in being involved in the planned National Committee. Nothing came of it. An influential Italian American communist, Peter Cacchione, became the first communist city councilor of New York. Patently referring to Antonini's schemes, he wrote in the May 31, 1943, issue of *The Daily Worker*: "If all the democratic forces must be united, anyone who works to prevent these democratic forces from getting together is doing a

---

115. Varsori 1984, 357.

disservice to the cause of unity and the war effort."[116] With Ascoli's resignation in June of 1943 and the departure from the United States of Cianca, Bruno Zevi, Garosci, Tarchiani, and later on, Sforza, the Mazzini Society virtually collapsed. Giacomo Battistoni, an old Italian-American Social Democratic leader, became its president. He continued writing for his newspaper *Nazioni Unite* until 1946.

We have already discussed the difficult relationship between political exiles and the Italian American colony. In the newspapers, the evident lack of communication between the two groups was overcome in few instances, and then always with Salvemini's mediation. Such is the case of *Il Mondo*, Giuseppe Lupis's monthly, which was founded in September 1938. Before the war it provided an important platform for the Italian liberal-democratic culture, with contributions coming from Ferrero, Silone, Lussu, Nenni, Sforza, Salvemini, and then Giovannitti, Antonini, Romualdi, Alberto, Cupelli, and other Italian Americans. *Il Mondo* distinguished itself for its obstinate denunciation of the *prominenti* and its attempt to get out of "the shallows of the ideological standoff which had often locked many antifascist newspapers into a sterile and sectarian form of polemics."[117] On the other hand, it was exactly the old question of anticommunism, which Lupis would have liked to drop, that led to a split between him and Vanni Montana, the influential secretary of Antonini's ILGWU.

Another newspaper of notable interest was *La Controcorrente* of Boston, directed by Aldino Felicani, an old anarchist militant.[118] It was a monthly and began publication in July 1938. Between 1940 and 1941, it published in installments Salvemini's important piece on "Italian Fascist Activities" and was close to the professor from Molfetta, who in the Mazzini Society bitterly criticized the U.S. government's policies, which were favorable to Badoglio and the monarchy. It was in this paper, in June 1944, practically in parallel with *Life* magazine, that the "Manifesto italiano contro la politica alleata" (Italian Manifesto Against the Allies' Policies) was published, signed by Borgese, Giorgio La Piana, Randolfo Pacciardi, Gaetano Salvemini, Arturo Toscanini, and Lionello Venturi. *La Controcorrente* proved a very aggressive presence also in matters concerning the Italian Americans, committed as it was to unmasking "male whores" and "turncoats," and in particular to pursuing the truth

116. Cited in Gerson 1976, 139. Cacchione, born in 1897 in Syracuse, New York, was elected three times in Brooklyn starting in 1947.

117. Torcellan 1984, 318.

118. In the United States, Felicani gave life to *Questione Sociale* from 1914 to 1916, then promoted the Sacco and Vanzetti defense committee, creating for that purpose the newspaper *L'Agitazione* (Agitation, 1920–25), then edited *La Protesta Umana* (1926–27). *La Controcorrente* (The Countercurrent) debuted in July 1938.

about Tresca's assassination.[119] This murder is indeed the symbolic end of the line of our narrative. For this reason, we have chosen to include also a literary version of it, the memoir of Ezio Taddei, a former comrade of Tresca's, then a communist militant engaged in countering any evidence that might lead to the Stalinists.

Translated by Franca and Bill Boelhower

119. Noteworthy are the semiamateur contributions, for example, in verse—in particular those of the assiduous Giggi Mogliani of Roxbury, Massachusetts, who celebrated in Romanesco "Er Duce" (November 1938), but also those of young second-generation Italian American writers such as the novelist Guido D'Agostino (*"I consolati—Trappole fasciste"* [The Consulates—Fascist Traps], December 1938). Among the controversies of major resonance, those facing the old James Donnaruma and his *Gazzetta del Massachusetts* (Massachusetts Gazette, March 1940) and those against Pope and his call for peace among the factions (January 1943), resumed punctually after the war, with indignant articles on the participation of Pope at the banquet in honor of Saragat and Matteo Matteotti on July 1, 1947, and even with an obituary (May 1950) reminding the reader that the deceased was a true fascist.

The First of May

Giuseppe Ciancabilla

Rome, Italy, 1872–San Francisco, California, 1904

After 1890, Giuseppe Ciancabilla created the position of socialist propagandist and editor of *Avanti!* In 1897, he volunteered for the Greco-Turkish war, sending correspondence from the front, an experience that inspired the novella *Verso la morte* (Toward Death) and marked his turn toward pacifism, which translated into an adhesion to the anarchism of Errico Malatesta. He was exiled in Switzerland, where in Neuchâtel he founded the newspaper *L'agitatore*; subsequently, he was expelled from Switzerland for having defended Luigi Lucheni, the anarchist who assassinated the Austrian Empress Elisabetta. He then exiled himself to Belgium and France, where he encountered Jean Grave's group of anarcho-communists, which made him decide to distance himself from Malatesta. At the end of 1898 he went to America, where he succeeded Pedro Esteve as director of the *Questione Sociale* of Paterson, New Jersey, imbuing it with an anti-organizing philosophy that was strongly opposed by the group Diritto all'Esistenza (The Right to Exist). Replaced in August 1899 by the same Malatesta, fleeing from confinement in Lampedusa, in September 1899, Ciancabilla founded *L'aurora,* first published in West Hoboken, New Jersey, then in Yohoghany, Pennsylvania, and finally, in Spring Valley, Illinois, where its publication ended in 1901. The polemics with Malatesta enraged him for several months, and in November 1899 they had dramatic consequences during a conference in West Hoboken, when the celebrated anarchist leader was wounded in one leg by a pistol shot. For a long time, it was said that Ciancabilla shot him, but the allegation seems unfounded.

In close collaboration with Enrico Travaglio and Cesare Crespi on the editorial staff of the *Protesta Umana*, of San Francisco, a communistic-anarchist periodical of a theoretical nature, in 1902, in Chicago, Ciancabilla founded a monthly with the same title, which dealt with the social sciences and art and literature: a year later, this monthly *Protesta Umana* became a weekly, changing its main office to San Francisco. Ciancabilla maintained himself with the proceeds from his contribution to various Italian newspapers: *Il Caffaro* of Genoa; *Il Messaggero* of Rome; and *La Vita Internazionale*, a Milanese newspaper published by Teodoro Moneta. Translator of Kropotkin (*La conquista del pane* [Winning Bread], 1899) and of Grave (*La società all'indomani della rivoluzione* [Society on the Morning After the Revolution]), he was also active as a trade unionist, battling against the corporative racism of the AFL. His pamphlet *Fiori di maggio* (May Blossoms), published in New York in 1900, is dedicated "To the friends in North America, who were my brothers in the fight," and contains the poem published here. This poem marks the tenth anniversary of the first May Day celebration, held on May 1, 1890, in accordance with the decision of the Paris Congress (July 1889) of the Second International to commemorate the Haymarket Riot martyrs of May 4, 1886, with mass demonstrations and strikes throughout Europe and America.

ESSENTIAL BIBLIOGRAPHY

Carey 1985; Dadà 1976; Fedeli 1965; MOI; Nomad 1932, 30ff.; Pernicone 1993b, 477–478.

༄

Into the gentle night of springtime, all at once
a cry erupts, excited, resolute, immense,
from a thousand heaving breasts: "We want our solemn day
to be in May again, we want a tender ray
to descend, on the oppressed, of feast and gaiety,
we want, we outcasts, trapped in a vast misery,
plunged into the dark of filth and barrenness,
a scorned and unloved rabble, now we want for us,
whose souls are torn apart by sorrow all the while,
on our holy day we want to wear a smile.
One day for the oppressed, in the season of flowers,
a symbol of bold hopes, one single day that's ours,
a solemn, fearless respite, arms across our chests,
a threat that strikes cold fear in lords' and tyrants' breasts. . . .
One day of rest, forgetting, festival, and love,

one day when we're allowed to lift our heads above
the painful work of our sold labor, and from there
away, on wings, to quickly scatter everywhere
the good word of serene hope, certain liberation
from the ranks of the defeated, with tears and exultation. . . .
For us, on whom the golden sun bestows no light,
for us, who can no longer thrill to the delight
of nature's deep vibrations when springtime is new,
for us, whose sunset falls before the day is through,
no love to call our own, no kiss, no soft caress,
no flowers bursting forth, no gleam of eagerness,
for us enslaved, condemned to an eternal chain
of an eternal torment, and of horrid pain,
even for us we want one happy holiday,
the festive celebration of the First of May!"

    And then (a decade's gone by since) the innumerable
phalanx of the suffering and the sorrowful
had their own day at last, had their prophetic day,
lit gently by the sunshine of the First of May.
From one to the other pole, from one to the other ocean,
as through a magic pact, as through a single notion,
behold the multitudes, assertive now and proud,
lifting high the heads that previously were bowed;
behold the metropolis along the smoky Thames,
an ever-growing band of ragged marchers claims
in one great resonant, defiant voice the right
to respite from the toil that grinds them day and night;
behold, along the Seine, the strong and roaring stream
of the rebellious Parisian workers as they dream
of new and valiant days in epic poetry
that commemorates the Commune's tragic history.
And, everywhere, a rustle that winds to the soft ray
of the tender golden sun, the golden sun of May.
And, everywhere, the people, bent beneath the stroke
of abject slavery, cast off the wretched yoke.
And they stretch out their arms, fraternally welcoming,
brothers in lives of pain, brothers in suffering.
Sturdy arms that form a strong chain of alliance,

that rise into the sky in a gesture of defiance!
And yet how brief the struggles, a quick insurgency,
the frightened cowardice that fills the bourgeoisie
opposed the wave of bold rebellion with a fence,
a stubborn barrier of blind acts of violence,
and the feast day of the happy folk who, overjoyed,
had sung a hymn of hope to the future, was destroyed
in the spiteful orgy of vengefulness, amidst
the rifles' roar, the scrape of manacles on wrists.
While roses smiled and opened, drinking the sun's rays,
while violets and lilies burst out in a blaze
from fields and gardens in the soft air tenderly,
the slavish rabble in its rabid ferocity
pounced on the unarmed like a panting animal,
and weapons began hissing, and there flashed a wall
of bayonets pressed to their breasts and shattering.
O hours of evil woe, sad hours of suffering
when the resplendent golden beams of May sun found
the bright blood of the sons of toil spilled on the ground!
O radiant noon at Santa Croce, tragic hour
in Rome, O voice that echoes even now with power
to rouse the feeling of affection in my breast!. . . .
O fallen brother, with your lacerated chest
and the sublime vision your dying eye could see
of a booming harvest of peace and liberty
sprung from your sprayed blood, —O fallen brother, dead
by the hideous salute of fratricidal lead,
your murder closed the epoch of the First of May,
and when you fell, the sun went down on our great day.

    Blood that is watered down is flowing in our veins,
weak words have given us intoxicated brains:
rhetorical bonbons, of *love* and *brotherhood*,
have stuffed our spirits with false hopes of coming good.
And all the while our dead are hanging horribly
from gallows unavenged, slaughtered in savagery;
vendettas, tortures, bloody assaults are taking place;
unpunished, unresisted, they smash us in the face.
While more and more in craven idleness we laze,

swaddled in sweet dreams of happy carefree days,
lost within ethereal mists where we acquire
honey and milk and roses, all we could desire,
and call each other brother with carelessness and ease,
and extend the olive branch of forgiveness and of peace,
The skillful bourgeoisie seize the ripe hour (without
the hesitation and the lassitude of doubt),
and with cold treachery, and with the trap well laid,
they stab us in the back with the envenomed blade.
O shining First of May, come gloriously, no hour
of rest for the weary, but a day of strength and power;
not gazing skyward in dull mystic contemplation,
not with arms folded in impotent resignation,
but bold exertion that propels us to the goal,
but holy vengeance that repays and calms the soul.
O shining First of May, deliver us the best
and crowning hour implored by all of the oppressed,
the hour of justice, the hour of the great victory,
when from life-giving blood comes the new history
to wash the shames and insults of servitude away. . . .
That day and that alone will be our First of May!

Translated by Michael Palma

Two Poems

∾ *Simplicio Righi*

The two short poetic texts that follow were absolutely among the most popular in the Italian American colony during the first years of the twentieth century. Both circulated under the name of a mysterious "Rosina Vieni," behind which was concealed Doctor Simplicio Righi, a physician very well known in the Italian colony of New York, who in 1901, for a brief period, was the director of the socialist newspaper *Il Proletario.* The first poem, in particular, had an extensive circulation. It was printed in a large number of newspapers and even merited the attention of H. L. Mencken, who included it in his great work *The American Language* as a classic example of Italian American linguistic hybridism. After having composed many other social cantos, among them "Gli emigranti dell'ideale" (The Emigrants of the Ideal), which on March 1, 1901, appeared on the first page of *Proletario,* Righi would gradually distance himself from politics, as is demonstrated by the fact that his poems were published by a Fascist monthly, *Il Carroccio* (see, in particular, *I sonetti di Manhattan* [Manhattan sonnets], of 1924, dedicated to Onorio Ruotolo). Significantly, Righi was the father-in-law of Achille Almerini, among the most able cultivators of an Italian American creole in poetry.

ESSENTIAL BIBLIOGRAPHY

Alfonsi 1985, 400–401; Corsi 1952; De Ciampis 1958; Gerbi 1962, 108–109; Mencken 1947, 642; Prezzolini 1978, 1:439–440.

∾

The Bricklayers Arrived

The bricklayers arrived hundreds at a time[1]
a whole gang with callused hands
to build the house of forty stories
not counting the roof or the basement.
   Now it seems to challenge the firmament
to the honor and glory of the Americans;
but who cares about the greenhorns, our citizens,
dead by a sudden blow, without sacrament?
   What's it worth, if by bad luck or mistake
   you shatter your bones on the floor below–
   miserable guinea, wretched dago?
      In front of a half pound of steak
   the boss shows off his gold teeth and sneers:
   Who's dead is dead . . . I'm alive and jeer.

༄

Today and Tomorrow

Today. . . .
   Today, discipline and handcuffs
on our pulses and in our brains
and if slaves become rebels
rifles and bayonets.
   Today, in other furrows,
with wrinkled brow and bathed in sweat,
the laborer agonizes,
and inside the mines,
in the depths of unexplored lands,

---

1. The words in italics below appear in the original version, entitled "Vennero i Brichchell-ieri" and are "Itaglish" corruptions of English: *bricchellieri* (repeated in the first line) = bricklay-ers; *ghenga* = gang; *ruffo* = roof; *basamento* = basement; *grinoni* = greenhorns; *mistecca* = mistake; *floro* = floor; *ghinni* = guinea; *ponte* = pound, with a pun on the Italian "bridge"; *bosso* = boss; *io vivo e me ne frego* = literally, I'm alive and I could give a damn or could not care less, was translated as above to preserve rhyme integrity in this fine sonnet.

cursing the pickman dies.
    Today, a world of masters and slaves
of lions and lambs!

Tomorrow. . . .

    Oh, tomorrow no more bowed heads
no more chains and fetters,
from humanity's veins
blood of redemption will flow.
    Tomorrow we'll be brethren
with united hearts
and poets will sing only of love,
and to redeemed souls
the new May day of laborers
will laugh eternally.
    A whole world of free men, tomorrow
holding hands.

    Translated by Peter Covino

Methods of the Socialist Struggle

Luigi Galleani

Vercelli, Italy, August 12, 1861–Caprigliola (Massa), Italy, November 4, 1931

Exiled from Italy, France, and Switzerland, then imprisoned for five years in Pantelleria, from which he succeeded in escaping in 1900, and then taking refuge in Egypt and London, Luigi Galleani arrived in New York in 1901, at forty years old. He established himself in Paterson, New Jersey, assuming the direction of the *Questione Sociale*, and started an intense activity of propaganda and agitation, whose first serious test was the strike of the silk manufacturers of Paterson, in 1902. Wounded in an encounter with the police, he was accused of subversion. He escaped to Canada, then returned clandestinely into the United States and hid in Barre, Vermont, where since 1894, an anarchist circle had been actively engaged in political causes among the workers at the stone and marble quarries.

A teacher's son, Galleani had studied law in Turin and upon just emerging from adolescence, became an anarchist. An orator of legendary eloquence, a bearer of very radical ideas of an anarcho-communistic stamp, he was a convinced supporter of the need to overthrow the government, even in armed struggle. In 1905, he published a pamphlet entitled *La salute è in voi!* (Health Is in You!), which in truth was a manual on how to make explosives. He incited great enthusiasm and was not averse to an almost mystical faith in the virtue of regenerating liberty versus every form of regimentation. In sum, he was in favor of the most absolute resistance against the system. Galleani would sustain a fundamental part of the American anarchist movement for almost twenty years, causing the seething FBI to perceive him as "the most dangerous element in the United States." (Sacco and Vanzetti themselves were his followers.)

In 1903, in Barre, Galleani began to publish *Cronaca Sovversiva* (Subversive Chronicle), moving the editorial staff from time to time, first to Lynn, Massachusetts, then to Providence, Rhode Island, and finally to Turin, Italy. The *Cronaca*, which lasted until 1920, was one of the longest-running anarchist newspapers in America and undoubtedly the most combative and widely circulated. It numbered 56,000 copies, which thanks to activist distribution even reached Europe. Galleani gave the best of himself as journalist to the pages of the *Cronaca*, in which he continued to publish hundreds of articles, collected before and after his death in various volumes.

Galleani was more a fiery individualist than a sectarian; his criticism became ruthless against all those who could not agree with his positions, even only occasionally, and who were then quickly accused of betrayal. An example of the fight among the diverse factions of radicalism was the episode in which anarchist Elia Corti was killed during a meeting held by socialist leader, Giacinto Menotti Serrate—the meeting that inaugurated Galleani's famous series of articles on the *Metodi della lotta socialista* (Methods of Socialist Struggle, 1903), collected in 1972. Significantly, many things happened to Galleani in 1906, always in connection with Serrati. At the culmination of a stinging polemic with the followers of Galleani's group, known as "Galleanisti," *Il Proletario* published the hideout of the anarchist, who was arrested and tried for the actions in Paterson, but then released, because of a hung jury.

The following year began a harsh ideological duel with the deviationist Francesco Saverio Merlino, following the latter's conversion to socialism, certified by an interview with *La Stampa* of Turin, published under the significant title "La fine dell'anarchismo" (The End of Anarchism). To respond to Merlino's thesis, according to which anarchism had no future, Galleani wrote an essay published in the *Cronaca Sovversiva*, in ten installments, between August 1907 and January 1908. The apt title of the series (collected into a volume in the 1920s) was in its turn very eloquent: "La fine dell'anarchismo?" Galleani then stated his thesis. Far from being historically exhausted, the role of anarchism found new reasons for existing, right in that historic moment, in an epoch of monstrously expanding centralized organizations, whether at the political or economic level.

At the outbreak of World War I, Galleani naturally assumed a firmly antimilitaristic position. "The war," he wrote in the *Cronaca* on December 6, 1914, "is nothing more today than an operation of the purse, a business . . . a disavowable and shameless fraud." He engaged in a sharp polemic with Kropotkin, the Russian anarchist and political philosopher, for choosing to go to war, justified by the need to restrain Germany. And when, in 1917, the United States entered the conflict, he dedicated himself to a hammering campaign, crying, "Against the war, against peace, for the revolution!" soon became in the explicit invitation, published in the *Cronaca*, to eliminate oneself not only from obligatory conscription (which did not consider foreign immigrants, unless they had already begun the procedure of naturalization) but also simply from *immatricolazione* (registration), extended to all men of recruitment age. "Matricolati!" was the title of the memorable article, May 26, 1917, in which Galleani, signing with the habitual pseudonym of "Mentana," implied that eliminating oneself was possible only by hiding; many of his followers did just that, among them Sacco, Vanzetti, and Postiglione, who ran off to Mexico. Galleani himself took a change of air, going to work, incognito, in the countryside.

In June 1917, the distribution of the *Cronaca Sovversiva* was prohibited. Several days afterwards, on the day following the promulgation of the Espionage Act, the FBI broke into the editorial office of the newspaper, temporarily blocking publication. In his refuge in Wrentham, Galleani was arrested, brought to Boston, and then released on bail, together with the printer; in the following trial, he was condemned to pay a fine of three hundred dollars. Naturally, the *Cronaca Sovversiva* resumed publication.

However, the FBI's surveillance of the newspaper and Galleani's circle of followers remained strict; and after the discovery of the plot to dynamite Youngstown, it became even stricter. In May 1918, Galleani was arrested again and again released, but in the following July, the newspaper was definitively outlawed. Nonetheless, the press was transferred to Providence, and Galleani published two further issues, in March and May 1919.

In the meantime, however, facilitated by the special law of October 1918 that gave the law jurisdiction to expel foreigners involved in seditious activities, the judicial mechanism was put into place that would deport the anarchist leader and eight of his followers. Galleani was arrested in June 1919, transferred to Ellis Island, and deported to Italy on the *Duca degli Abruzzi*, the same ship on which Pietro Marucco went to his death (also an anarchist, he supposedly jumped overboard). Galleani's wife and five children were left in America.

In January 1920, the *Cronaca Sovversiva* was reborn in Turin, thanks also to the contribution of subscribers from America; in October, it was definitively suppressed by the authority of the police. With the advent of Fascism, things worsened. In fact, the surveillance of anarchists became more rigid, and the Italian authorities collaborated with those of America, exchanging information on the more dangerous subjects. Arrested in 1924, Galleani spent fourteen months in prison. Released, he assumed the old polemic with Merlino in the pages of the

American newspaper, *L'adunata dei refrattari* (The Meeting of the Unwilling), which even printed a volume of his writings. Arrested still again in November 1926, he was then confined in Lipari and from there at a prison in Messina, Sicily.

In February 1930, by now in a precarious condition of health, he was freed, and he retired to Caprigliola, in Val di Magra, where, always under the eye of the police, he died after a fall.

The excerpts included here originally appeared in *Cronaca Sovversiva* on October 17–31, 1903.

ESSENTIAL BIBLIOGRAPHY

Avrich 1991; Dadà 1976, 182–183; EAL; Fedeli 1956; Galleani 1972, 196–212; Masini 1954; MOI; Molinari 1974, 1981; Nejrotti 1971; Pernicone 1993b.

∾

Espionage, Defamation, Ambush, Murder

We never would have wanted to return to that bloody tragedy which left two faraway elders, a young wife, three children—three honest working families—mourning, and because of an unexpected death, inconsolable grief has enshrouded them for a week and will forever more.

The obscene impudence of our *camorra* and *mafia* enemies brutally forces us out of the self-imposed silence we would not have wished to break until after the judicial investigation. Those who premeditated and executed cold-blooded murder add to the hypocritical impudence which tramples upon the dead, insults the suffering of the survivors, and threatens the freedom of the living.

So much the worse for those incorrigible troublemakers who, lying about the truth, threw away the revolver that gunned down Elia Corti and concealed the treachery of those who were armed and lying in wait and who would now want to pose as victims of that "anarchist violence" on which the wrath and the curses of the aberrant common people and of sectarian blindness so easily converge.

For once the truth will not put up with the shamelessness whetted by extreme audacity, abuse of power, or deception; we will restore the truth as incontrovertible, entirely on the basis of clear, consistent, irrefutable evidence. Demonstrating that even if thugs can rely on police protection and the strength of false allegations—strange method of reprisals and compensation!—that they murmur by the hour, they will never confuse, never distort the judgment of public opinion, whether it is of law and order or the socialist party.

The general outline of the drama is well-known: Elia Corti attended a lecture held by the Socialist Section on the evening of Saturday the 3rd *where without provocation, he was duplicitously killed by the socialist* Alessandro Garretto. This fact cannot be dared to be disputed, not even by the socialists who were present at the mournful scene.

The material responsibility for the murder is therefore attributed to the socialist Alessandro Garretto who turned himself in to the police for protection out of fear of being lynched, as was loudly demanded by the local population; he showed some minor bruises, some superficial lacerations sustained during the public outcry *after* committing the murder of poor Corti, and was recognized *twice* by them as the sole assassin.

For those who preach decorum, resignation, calm, the civil weapons of discussion, for those who take pleasure in retracting the claws of rage under the banner of "better to be victims than murderers," the blow is harsh, the failure is public, and there is an insistent need is to find within the incoherence of murder a broader justification in the precedents.

And it would be acceptable conduct if it were intended to save the men and methods of the party from catastrophic disaster; it would be a merciful, humane act if it were the gallows, prison, a penal colony—useless and ferocious reprisals of a society at war with itself—that would do away with the head, the life, the liberty of a poor wretch. And this deed, which Elia Corti so generously initiated, on the threshold of death forgiving the perpetrator of the murder, perhaps would not have counted us as allies in the hour of agonizing pain, but it would not have counted us as enemies.

We are not enemies, even now, except that a painful necessity of defense calls us to charge against the *deliberately, knowingly false allegations* made by *opponents in solidarity with the murderer that are directed against comrades* in solidarity with the truth and with the victim but disdainful of stooping to allegation, of requesting any weapons for protection and revenge from the authorities and the law.

But it would be foolish to allow this lie to spread with impunity, covering up the murders and those who ordered or instigated them, insulting the dead, and denouncing the living without at least refuting it with the hard truth of the facts. We therefore object to this deliberate and cleverly spread lie, letting it be known *that for every one of our statements there are supporting documents, irreproachable testimonies*, not only from fellow comrades but also from outsiders, *from opponents, socialists themselves, in the most serious instances.* These are documents and testimonies which we do not hide and that we make available to all those, friends or foes, who have the intention of conducting their own independent investigations.

We therefore challenge the most skilled manipulators of words and circumstances to impugn the irrefutable truth.

And since the *Daily Dirt*,[1] taking delight in the murder, *the hard and painful lesson that has disillusioned us*, insinuates that comrades entered the socialists' hall through fraud or violence in order to incite unrest and *remains silent about the public invitation*, publicly distributed in the handbill on Saturday afternoon, which we publish here just to clarify things a bit.

ITALIAN SOCIALIST FEDERATION
BARRE, VT. SECTION

Workers,

You are cordially invited to attend a lecture given by comrade G.M. SERRATI to be held this evening at seven o'clock in the headquarters of the Socialist Section on the topic METHODS OF THE SOCIALIST STRUGGLE

The Committee
Barre, Vt. October 5, 1903.
(E.W. Cumings Printer, No. 75 North Main Street, Barre, Vt.).

We were therefore invited: as far as how "cordially" we will discuss later on; attendance was therefore within our rights as it was within the rights of those attending to ask, fifteen or twenty minutes after the appointed time, if by chance the lecture would be postponed to another evening.

What did not fall within anyone's right was to raise his hands and strike peaceful people who remained in the hall with the serious and respectful demeanor of guests, or to constantly shout the foul-mouthed vulgarities of a whorehouse at those who kindly requested information. This, instead, is the only response from a socialist—always free, always unmoved and always to remain so because none of us will ever steal his job as accuser—a bestial and idiot socialist opposes a question courteously posed by a comrade that was not directed to him; the response given to the brotherly recommendation of someone who begged him to keep calm and quiet: "We are here in our house; get out, all of you, from first to last."

None of the comrades, NOT ONE! to be clear, threatened to disrupt the meeting to impede the freedom of speech of the speaker who was awaited in vain.

1. The reference is to *Il Proletario* (The Proletarian).

The violence against the *invited* comrades was brutal, boorish, and exclusively socialist, and as long as the socialist troublemaker, backed by twenty or so mercenaries, did not raise his hands to strike two comrades, no one noticed the provocation.

And here again it becomes opportune to refute another legend of the *Daily Dirt*, that the anarchists from the start of the disorder until the tragic moment of Corti's murder were *twelve* in number; the socialists, as we will see from the lists to be published, if necessary, were between twenty-two and twenty-five in number, the peaceful ones, *all armed with revolvers*, while the anarchists, "the delinquents, the insane, the criminals who reason with clubs and razors," did not even have a pin in their pockets.

And this, too, will be proven, if necessary, *with testimony from socialists*!

There is indeed a socialist who, beating his fists at the height of the uproar, got a beating for himself and for his own kind, and the *next day*, influenced by one honest Don Basilio, had comrade Martino Rizzi arrested at his home, accusing him of having stabbed him with a knife during the tumult, thus obtaining the arrest of our comrade who was subject to bail of 4,000 dollars [*scudi*] for armed assault; but the imbecile had stated the evening before, *in the presence of many*, that the graze was nothing more than the result of a having a chair thrown at him, as confirmed by expert medical opinion as testified in public records.

It is, therefore, *under false accusation* that comrade Rizzi was arrested and placed on bail! This honest deed of socialist pacification will see its conclusion in court when a bright light will shine on the hidden purposes that drive it.

Until now, only a weak, weak ray of light has shone on them, that of a telegram sent from the Prisons to the *Daily Dirt* in which the editor, saying nothing about Corti's murder at the hands of Garretto the socialist, announced that "two anarchists had fatally wounded two socialists." Remaining silent about the truth can be practical; speaking the opposite of the truth is one more honest method in the socialist struggle.

A copy of this telegram is in good hands!

We can, then, summing up, establish the evidence at hand:

1.   —That the anarchists in attendance were invited to Socialist Hall and that it is a lie that they entered by force or by violence!
2.   —That none of the anarchists threatened, at the meeting, to challenge the speaker's right to freedom of speech;
3.   —That the provocation began within the ranks of "socialists and was not returned" until violent language turned into deplorable acts, and so defense became legitimate as well as necessary;

4. —That none of the anarchists present was armed, that no socialist could show any weapon wounds as such. Brusa, who accused comrade Martino Rizzi of stabbing him, "lied, knowing full well he was lying" since the night before the accusation, the evening of the actual event, stated, "with many people present," that the graze to his scalp sustained during the scuffle was the result of a punch, then of being struck by a chair. The medical report has condemned the foul sectarian lie;
5. —That the socialists were in the majority at that meeting;
6. —That they were, from first to last, all armed with revolvers;
7. —That they were the first to provoke and to strike;
8. —That if anyone had come to the Saturday, October 3rd, meeting at Socialist Hall with the resolute and calculated intent to crush the exercise of civil rights with violence and weapons, with the precise and calculated purpose—this, too, will be seen—of "disabusing with a long anticipated, hard and painful lesson," any naïve preconceptions about the honesty of our so-called opponents—it was the Socialist Section of Barre, Vt., and these were exactly their dirty deeds.

In the next issue we will return to the resolute, precise, and calculated intent with which Elia Corti's murderer carried out the ambush.

The impudence of the bastard cousins is not in evidence:

It is the slow, consistent, constant socialist provocation that has sowed hatred, spite, anger, and murderous rage here;

It is with the trap of a supposed socialist lecture within the socialist Block that a socialist duplicitously murders one of our friends without provocation, finally giving us "the long anticipated, hard and painful . . . and instigated . . . lesson" . . .

And the *Daily Dirt* strokes the hypothetical sections of the party to vote for solidarity measures—they being the civilized enemies of violence!—with Garretto and with . . . that other one; he writes that it really was us who transform noble battles of ideas into brutal conflicts, and that we finally achieved our goal: bloodshed!

Oh forsaken Maria Corti, oh poor children whom a reckless brute has wrapped in tears and mourning within the grim span of an hour; old people defeated by time and by work who wait in vain among the cliffs where they saw him as a child, their strapping son bursting with life, intelligence, and hopes—so haven't you heard the latest news?

It is not him—the glad husband, the father, your son who, in the last gasp of extreme agony, touched again by an ineffable ideal of goodness and love, forgave the hired killer—he is not the victim of the bloody drama over which all the good people around you are crying.

The victims are poor Garretto, the ringleaders, the accomplices. . . .

The murderer is Elia Corti.

El Vecc
(October 17, 1903)

II

In our last issue we concluded that the supposed lecture held by the Socialist Section was an ambush directed at our good faith and that the socialists had come to that meeting with the resolute, calculated intent to respond to our first objection with pistols and murder.

It is incontrovertible truth that emanates from the facts as they occurred and which were also detailed in the first issues of the *Daily Dirt*: it is also truth that certain circumstances shed even more light, to which we once again direct the attention of our readers.

The announcement of the lecture was a cunning and extreme act of daring. After the provocation, after the slander, after three months of daily defamation . . . from a distance, when almost the entire Italian colony, *most of them socialists themselves*, labeled the vile smear campaign with their own scathing opinions and had nothing more than an epithet for those who led it with shamelessness equal only to their depravity: spies! Pagnacca thought that it would have ended there, as a last resort, the final blow of audacity: to come here quietly, to announce, as a matter of form, a lecture which no one would have attended except for the tame audience of his cohorts, to defend himself against the indelible reputation of a spy, to spew again poisoned spittle on those absent, on those who were far away, and the next day write in the *Daily Dirt* that, here, those lambasted by his devious and reactionary prose had threatened, cursed, challenged him from far away, and that, with him here, they had cowardly backed down.

It would have been the resurrection, the rebirth of his audacious political platform! And perhaps it would have succeeded if the clandestine suspicion with which the invitation to the lecture was distributed, had he not encountered infidels. Because Pagnacca yells so loudly, the anarchists were the first to get the handbill; here even the cobblestones know that *all of the anarchists' homes were carefully avoided in the distribution*, and that *no anarchist obtained the handbill from his* socialist distributor. They obtained it in every other way, even at second and third hand, and they attended the lecture, albeit in very small numbers, confident that Pagnacca would not show up.

Bark! Scream and make those braggarts in their consular dens in New York do what all cops know how to do with enough enthusiasm that is in direct proportion to their salaries, but in this situation, eye-to-eye, face-to-face, certain obscenities never escape from even the most brazen lips.

Someone, in fact, on River St. between five and six p.m. that same day asked him if he dared to repeat that the anarchists in Barre were forgers, thieves, and murderers, slapped him twice on his yellow cheeks, and refreshed them with some spit. Pagnacca stammered pathetic apologies, useless whimpers of a whore, cowardly distinctions, all the spineless artifice of his professional dirty tricks, while at his side there was a low-level mobster snitch, an illustrious representative of the "*annurata sugietà*"[2] who drew his *camorra* revolver on the courageous who, one against three, armed only with his hands and his legitimate grievance, swallowed his scorn and disgrace for the contemptible pamphleteer.

When from the neighboring houses, none of which was inhabited by anarchists, women and children came down, and recognizing him, shouted in unison: *disgraceful spy*! Go throw yourself in the "river" if you have any shame left! The mobster[3] put the revolver back in his pocket and Pagnacca took his leave in anger with a blatant threat: *tonight we'll settle the score!*

From that instant until the lecture, though, he carried in his heart a solemn grudge, a steadfast renunciation.

Two of our friends, among them an exceptional and serious comrade, entering an acquaintance's house for a drink, found at twenty minutes past seven—the conference was to take place at seven o'clock sharp—Pagnacca with several cohorts sleeping off their rage; from that house to the location of the lecture it is a good quarter of an hour's walk.

It was, at this point, quite clear that he would not be going to the lecture.

Meanwhile in the socialists' hall, the thugs were justifying the *alibi* with provocation and murder; Bernasconi was to begin, Garretto to end, and Pagnacca would have been a nuisance and he was late.

Because at 7:25, he finally got going, sure that he would not find any more trouble and that the inconvenienced spectators would already have dispersed due to the delay . . . and their friends. On the way, the mobster, one of the "*annurata sugietà*," made him lose a few minutes by getting in a few more punches; pro-

2. The Camorra is known to its members as La Suggietà Annurata, the honored society.
3. *Guappo*, a member of the Camorra.

tected as a group of three with two others following behind, they had wanted to insult two boys, two *arrogant* boys according to them, and despite the magnificent display of pistols, all three were taken down, a little muddle of furious punches.

This, in short, is the point: that when Pagnacca arrived at 7:40 at the Granite St. Bridge, people poured out into the street from the socialist Block where three other cries spread the word of Elia Corti's murder.

It therefore remains a fact that while the lecture was scheduled for seven o'clock, at 7:25 Pagnacca was still taking a nap; that Pagnacca arrived at the socialist Block when the audience of anarchists had been dismissed by the provocations of the thugs and the gunshots of comrade Garretto.

The simpletons won't touch the apparent contradiction between Pagnacca's threat: "we'll settle the score tonight!" and our expressed belief that "he did not want to attend that meeting," to arrive at either the vanity of the threat or the absurdity of our conclusions. The threat remains: only to settle the score—since in these instances there is give and take, something is always at risk—either it was ordered or someone else volunteered.

Was it not known for months that someone in Barre had yearned for "the opportunity to act as the anarchists' executioner," prepared, if the opportunity arose, "to pick three off all by himself"? Was it not known that someone was hiding under the civilized banner of peaceable socialism who because of his violence and brutality "toward the comrades" had been expelled from the Section "after public deliberation;" who on a very recent occasion had in a public forum given proof of his socialist brotherhood by rearranging the face of one of the Section's comrades?

The man, therefore, was predisposed by a wild nature to the most sinister undertakings cultivated with slow, assiduous, daily, nurturing of venom and spite: it was enough to show him a bruised, ashen face, with broken glasses, and shout at him about anarchist violence and brutality because the blind sectarian anger unleashed a storm of wild fury to give us the hard, painful lesson that had been anticipated for a long time.

The murder was inevitable!

I will not add that Garretto was an agent, but to deny that the murder was hatched with savage and vigilant care one must be an accomplice or an idiot!

Garretto was standing alone in the doorway, without speaking to anyone, without anyone speaking to him, absent-minded, resolute in one single obvious purpose: not to abandon at any cost his post at the entryway; and it was a surprise to everyone when from that location, the only quiet corner of the hall, two revolver shots resounded; the most distressing surprise came when the most peaceful in the group, Elia Corti, mortally wounded, fell backwards into the arms of his brother.

What demon of madness, then, moved him to fratricide, this villain whom no one had provoked or offended? Who seemed absent, estranged, impervious to that passing but dramatic clash of passions?

To what sinister notion had he succumbed in order to act so brutally, so unexpectedly, with gun in hand in a conflict with unarmed men; he could have imposed order with superior, Herculean vigor, but how could he keep shooting even the most rowdy men who were unarmed?

It is, for now, an impenetrable mystery to us but perhaps not to the one who entered the hall that evening and uttered to Garretto this meaningful saying in French: "Garde-à-vous!"[4] almost immediately after which the general, unrelenting melée erupted!

In any case, the following is well-established: that the supposed lecture on the "methods of the socialist struggle" was an evil trap laid for our comrades, who were unprepared because they had no experience of this sort of thing, and because their consciences were clear; they met the cunning arts of experienced cops and professional criminals, all used by the so-called socialists of Section no. 2 of Barre, who use this civility when they fight the noble battles of ideas with their revolvers loaded.

The sugar barrels of the socialist cooperative do not speak, but the very next day after the murder the fact was confirmed by irreproachable "socialist" testimony from neutral parties and against whom those revolvers had been drawn.

It has still been proved, documented—as we shall see in the next issue—with an abundance that goes beyond any doubt, that if Garretto could be the perpetrator of the murder, the moral responsibility rests entirely, squarely, dreadfully on the obscene opportunists of slander and betrayal, on the dirty snakes, on the abject souls, on the sewer rats, who by putting ideals, their vile [political] appetites, and the arduous educational task above all else instead of igniting the sacred passion for truth and justice in the minds of others—which makes us equally respectable and good on different sides—stimulate, irritate, arouse something dormant within us that is primitive, medieval, and barbaric.

For magistrates, not noticing or acquitting the filthy breed that conceals our divisions, our mourning, and our wounds with boards that it paints with the figures of Judas and Cain, the obvious command center almost always escapes, elusive.

4. Stand at attention!

And this is supreme tragedy!

Before the world that fights and works, that suffers, believes, and hopes; before the world of the poor that love guides them, compels them, and marshals them to the generous rebellions of faith, the threatening and underhanded breed must pass naked, unattached—an ineffable symbol of horror and disgust—the dirty face on which invincible proletarian honesty has been etched, an otherwise terrible stigma that not even the treachery of bourgeois verdicts could condemn this way.

Translated by George De Stefano and Giulia Prestia

An Editorial and a Dramatic Play

∾ *Umberto Postiglione*

Raiano (L'Aquila), Italy, April 25, 1893–San Demetrio nei Vestini (L'Aquila),
Italy, March 28, 1924

Attending technical schools in Sulmona and Rome, Umberto Postiglione graduated in 1910 in L'Aquila as an accountant, and in October of that same year, after
having participated in student irredentist demonstrations, he embarked at Le Havre
for America. From New York, he moved to Chicago, where he was employed in a
bank, on the editorial staff of newspapers, as a librarian, an accountant, a clerk, a
worker in chemical factories, in factories making musical instruments, in glassworks, and in foundries, besides as a miner and excavator. In the United States, his
humanitarian ideals found an outlet in frequenting anarchist circles. Venanzio
Vallera relates that upon arriving in Chicago, Postiglione was welcomed as a guest
of his relative Ettore Boverini in an apartment of a building owned by Giuseppe
Bertelli, who lived on the floor above and who was the director of the *Parola del
Popolo.* Postiglione did not hesitate to attend Bertelli's meetings and to oppose him
openly. His militancy in subversive circles soon became assiduous. He became a
propagandist, traveling in the mining camps of Illinois, Wisconsin, and Iowa, and
he contributed to the *Cronaca Sovversiva,* with particular frequency in 1916, when
in Barre, Vermont, he accepted the post left by Luigi Galleani during the strike of
the miners in the anthracite basin in Pennsylvania.

The year before, in Chicago, he had founded *L'Allarme,* an anarchist newspaper
in a popular vein, in which he published the important article, "Madre ritorner-
emo" (Mother, We Will Return), dealing with an Italian emigrant whose mother
recalls him to Italy to fight in the war against the Austrians, and who responds by

saying that he would return, but to start a revolution. Galleani had written an analogous piece, "Figli non ritornate!" (Sons, Do Not Come Back!) in the *Cronaca Sovversiva*.

Postiglione traveled all through the United States, from New England to California, holding meetings from which people emerged electrified by his oratory. But in 1917, the government imposed the draft for foreigners of military age; failure to appear for draft enrollment incurred confinement in prison and deportation to the country of origin.

Like many others, Postiglione went to Mexico, and from there, wandered for two years through all, or almost all, of the villages of Central and South America, contracting malaria in Nicaragua. In 1918, in San José (Costa Rica), he founded a school of languages, and in this way, he discovered his true vocation. Traversing the Andes on foot, in 1919, in Buenos Aires, he embarked to reenter Italy, and in Salerno, in autumn, he began military service. Subsequently, in 1921, he obtained his license from the normal school of Avezzano and teacher's qualification in L'Aquila and found a job in a cooperative in Genoa. Then he reentered Abruzzo to teach in elementary schools, dying shortly afterward of pneumonia.

Postigione has left eight poems in the dialect of Raiano: a small collection of lyrical poems, interrupted by his premature death, which nevertheless are enough to place him among the most authentic voices of the twentieth century from Abruzzo, and to make him an inspiring singer of nature. In 1925, Paravia published his book *La Terra d'Abruzzo e la sua gente* (The Land of Abruzzo and Its People). His *Scritti sociali* (Social Writings) appeared in a volume, edited by Venanzio Vallera, in 1972: they are articles from the *Cronaca Sovversiva,* dedicated to workers' struggles and political and economic themes. Postiglione reveals the great ardor of the polemicist, a lashing sarcasm turned against the compromisers in the socialist and syndicalist circles, and in moments, almost mystical tones that make him one of the most genuine writers of the anarchism of the 1910s.

He also wrote for theater. One of his social plays, in two acts, *Come i falchi* (Like Hawks), was published in Philadelphia in 1939.

ESSENTIAL BIBLIOGRAPHY

Del Ciotto 1997; Marchesani 1925; Postiglione 1960; Postiglione 1972: 269–273.

ა

Blood and Gold

The praetorian guards of the whorish republic do not stop at the elimination of every constitutional right nor at the suppression of freedom of thought, assembly, speech, and press.

But they bestow their consent on heartless attacks by swinish bullies in Cain's trade of spies and assassins; but they incite the obstinate recurrence of "wholesale murder" on the starving proletariat; but they deny those in rags the right to request a crust of bread that is less hard, less bitter, less steeped in blood and sweat; but they justify the torture and the destruction of proletarian flesh that has been torn, consumed, burned in volcanic ovens, in pits of extreme labor. But they hole up in bunkers; for a quick execution they grant the republican executioner the heralds of the future and the knights of freedom to atone for the crime of having benefitted from a right that has been consecrated a thousand times in the constitutions of States, a right sanctioned by the supreme code of the nation, by the Declaration of Independence: the right a thousand times trampled with impunity by the manservants of the state hierarchy, by the police of the bourgeois monopoly.

The greedy vampires and the pirates of the bank and finance will not settle for draining gold from the sweat of the destitute plebeians. This is not sufficient payment if they are to spend life in the sweetness of doing nothing, if they are to seize all of life's best, every pleasure, every joy, if they are to take all of the fruits from the earth and all the smiles of heaven. They not only want gold and pleasure from serfs, from factory inmates, from those buried in mines, but also flesh and blood to dampen their unsatisfied, insatiable lust.

They want to squeeze blood and gold from the veins of the proletariat, and with the ferocity of a hyena they throw Point Creek, Calumet, Aguilar, Ludlow, and Virginia to the lions.

The strikes and the massacres at Point Creek, Calumet in Michigan, Kawawka in West Virginia were the day before yesterday.

It was yesterday's massacre that was horrible, atrocious, Cain's Aguilar: the winds still have not scattered the ashes of the wild fire in Ludlow; the sun still has not dried up the puddles of blood on the streets of Elizabeth.

Today's assassinations were in Derby, Connecticut, and in Virginia, Minnesota.

And in every massacre there is a cautionary warning and in every new tragedy we welcome this sad, bitter lesson: that uncontrolled outbursts, and the merciless wrath of the demigods cuts deep; and the hordes of mercenaries hired by owners show the most bestial ferocity where the resignation of slaves is most supine, where the herd has remained deaf to the calls of the bold and generous guardians, where the helots are most scrupulous in their respect for the law, the most blind in their faith in fetishes. In America as in Europe, in Ludlow as in Bugerru, in Bilbao as in Colliers, in the mining camps of the wild West, as in little towns perched between the gorges of the Sila, on the peaks of the Apennines, scattered along the plateaus of Puglia, anywhere that is medieval in terms of methods of production, in thought, and in aspiration they have remained both slaves and slave-traders, in every aspect have remained closed off from the innovative breath of the emerging civilization of work, impervious to the interruptions of revolutionary forces.

Capitalism has been more compliant and long-suffering, and no longer provokes killings, nor incites lynchings, nor organizes attacks; but in large industrial centers and in sprawling cities where the pulse of a new life is stronger, there are more frequent contacts, and the fever of new ideas is more contagious.

The king of money and the king of law both want gold and blood. In Europe, drunken brothers lash out against each other, unleashing the fury of devastating war; in America, the fury is the premeditated killing of the plebeians who want bread.

And the cannibals of capitalism will follow, to suck blood and squeeze gold from the inexhaustible veins of the proletariat; and after the massacres, the murders, the lynchings from the day before yesterday, yesterday, and today, will follow those of tomorrow and then tomorrow, if the everyday battles do not make us see that peace and well-being, health and joy cannot come from heaven, a sovereign grace of an impossible god, nor from earthbound heavens, the pitying largesse of bourgeois philanthropy, nor from the protection of the established order dominated by political scoundrels, nor from the Sanhedrin unionists, filthy dens of ruffians and Judas Iscariots, but from revolt, from open, armed, violent, and ruthless insurrection by battalions of workers who in their unrelenting force overthrow idols old and new, break the levees and dams of every empire, cross the borders of property and law, casting the supporters of bourgeois society into the abyss. Our pledges are sterile, our anger in vain, our anathemas insipid, our struggles will remain fruitless, if we do not bring the war to a wider field, towards the higher goal, with less fragile but tougher weapons, with less weakened faith, with warmer enthusiasm, with fervor, with vigor, with renewed tenacity.

If to the anguished soul, if to the dark minds of the losers of life, we fail to bring a touch of audacity, to open a glimmer of light.

If we are not going to uncover them in their hovels as starving, abandoned, ridiculed, and isolated to shake their apathy and awaken their consciousness, to enliven them to our faith and warm their enthusiasm.

If victory grows increasingly more distant, if we leave the hostages in the hands of the enemy that caught us, if the law does not support itself, it does redeem itself, it does not defend itself with courage, boldness, and strength.

If before the enemy surrounded by weapons and hatred, we will not think to arm ourselves, to taste the hatred.

If to the latest new attack, we will not respond immediately and with equal force; if on the battleground, we are about to fight for the ransom of old and new hostages, of all the victims of the bourgeois reaction, then we will only be selling tickets for the circus or the specialties of the shop, but not for our shared salvation; if presumptuous partisan vanity is mortified, then we will not rally all the opponents of the established order, the allies from across the border and overseas for the avant-garde's attack warning, who fear the hordes of the enemy's mercenaries, and spur the great proletarian army of one hundred homelands onto war.

Translated by Giulia Prestia

Like Hawks

The action takes place in a mining town in Pennsylvania. Present time.

CHARACTERS

Lina, 25 years old, Enzo's wife
Enzo, miner, 30 years old
Cecco, old miner, 50 years old
Tonio, foreman of the mine, in his 40s, chubby, with a curly moustache. He is a
classic bosstype, arrogant and parasitic.

ACT ONE

The scene takes place in the main room of a miner's house. In the center is the front door. To the left of the entry, there is another door that goes to the bedroom. To the right is a window. Tools and kitchen utensils are present.

Scene I

Lina alone

LINA (*entering, while taking off her shawl*): Nothing, not even today . . . Not even a word! (*sitting down, taking up some crochet work*) Poor Enzo . . . he must still be going around looking for work! . . . And if he's found it? Oh, no; that's impossible. He would have written me. No, he's surely still unemployed . . . Oh god, how will he manage without even a cent in his pocket? (*brief pause*) Because by this point he must have surely used up the little money that he'd brought with him: everything we had. And how will he manage to travel? . . . by foot? . . . illegally? At times like these!? And if he gets sick? . . . Oh mother of god, protect him! (*she hears the sound of a wagon getting nearer, as is common in mining camps. A trumpet sounds and a bell rings announcing the arrival of the grocery wagon*)

LINA (*getting up*): It's the grocery wagon! (she looks around) Where's the booklet? (*she sees it, picks it up, while from outside a voice cries out: Lina . . . Oh Lina!*)

LINA: I'm coming . . . (opens the door) Hello!¹

THE VOICE: *Hello*, Lina!? I'm sorry . . . but I don't have anything for you this evening.

LINA (*shocked*): But why . . . since I ordered some stuff this morning?. . . .

THE VOICE: I know you did, Lina, but while I was there getting ready to leave, the captain of the mine came and he ordered the shopkeeper to take away your booklet, because your husband doesn't work for the mine any longer.

LINA (*discouraged*): This is all we needed! . . . Oh, dear god, it's just one thing after another.

THE VOICE: I'm sorry, Lina . . . if it were up to me . . . But, you have to understand, I'm a servant . . . I don't count nor do I accuse . . . and I'm forced to do what others tell me to do.

LINA: I don't blame you or the others . . . not I. The will of god be done.

THE VOICE: Let's hope for the best. *Good bye*, eh!. . . . (*tells the horse to get moving*)

LINA: *Good bye!* (*closes the door, dropping onto the chair*) Oh, I can't take it any longer! . . . I can't last like this . . . What is my terrible fate? . . . (*knocking on the door*) Who is it?. . . .

---

1. Italicized words in the text were in English in the original.

Scene II

Lina and Cecco

CECCO: (*entering with a bundle under his arm*) It's me, Lina . . . Cecco!

LINA: Come in, come on in, Cecco.

CECCO: (*moving closer*) *Hello*, Lina! How ya doin'?

LINA: Bad, real bad, Cecco . . . And you, how are things?

CECCO: Let's not talk about it, dear Lina . . . How should things be after thirty
    years of working on my back? (*getting worked up*) An old man like me, who
    still goes into the mines, it's an insult to Christ. Well, some day I'll die
    down there, and so I won't even have to pay for a gravedigger and a funeral.
    (*he sits down*) Enough . . . News from Enzo?

LINA: Since the letter from the day before yesterday, nothing new, Cecco.

CECCO: And what did he say?

LINA: He told me . . . that he still hadn't found work . . . that he was going to
    look around some more . . . and in the meantime I shouldn't worry.
    But tell me, Cecco, how can I be relaxed with so many troubles on my
    shoulders?. . . .

CECCO: Oh it's a rotten world, a dog's life, I know . . . I know this well, I who
    have moved around half of it without even a moment of peace. What have
    you done wrong? What did I do, then, that I've had to endure more than Job
    from the time I was a child. (*pithily*) Our crime is to be poor . . . *that's all*!

LINA: But why is it our fault if we were born poor?

CECCO: Born poor? . . . Well, I don't buy that any longer. I've seen desperate folks
    I could turn upside down without them even having a match fall out of
    their pockets, and now they count money by the shovelful.

LINA: And how'd they do it?. . . .

CECCO: Huh! They stole it from others! Believe me, Lina, working doesn't make
    you rich. (*with a familiar tone*) Tell me . . . wasn't Antonio Rossi a miner
    once? . . . He was more wretched than wretchedness itself . . . But now he's
    the *boss*, and he lives it up like a gentleman . . . Ah . . . one's born poor! . . .
    Lies! lies, my dear Lina.

LINA: Oh . . . that boss, how dreadful! He threw my Enzo out of the mine
    without a reason, Enzo, the best miner he had. And as though that weren't
    enough, now he has ordered the company shopkeeper to take away my store
    credit. And he has the nerve to greet me, that shameful man! . . . He has the
    nerve to flatter me, when he sees me, that face of a pharisee. . . .

CECCO (*disturbed but to himself alone*): Hmpf! . . . when the devil caresses you, it means he wants your soul.

LINA: What did you say, Cecco?

CECCO: Oh . . . nothing, nothing. I meant to say . . . I know the swine, you know? It's been many years, I know it . . . He's capable of anything. He did hurtful things to me too! And a lot of them too. He makes me stay home for weeks at a time, and me with that brood of children that I have . . . And he gives others work. But what can I do . . . I'm old now too. And even my wife is old. . . .

LINA: Your wife? . . . What does that mean, Cecco? What's your wife got to do with the mine?

CECCO: Oh . . . I know perfectly well what I'm talking about. Enough, enough! (*offering the bundle*) Listen, Lina, I brought some things . . . take them. . . .

LINA: But why, Cecco? . . . No . . . I don't want to . . . I can't. . . .

CECCO: What are you saying? . . . Don't be so formal. Oh, no . . . by god! Even I've needed help at times, and my friends helped me . . . If we poor folks don't help each other . . . And then . . . it's nothing. I'd like to help more if I could. But I've also got a lot of debts . . . and the butcher, when I buy a half a pound of meat he gives me a look, that scoundrel . . . and then he thinks he can clean his corrupt soul with a prayer on Sundays in church. Oh . . . if I were to pay in cash it'd be a different story . . . Damn poverty!. . . .

LINA: Who are you blaming, Cecco?

CECCO: Who am I blaming? . . . Damn . . . I know perfectly well who I should blame . . . Enough, enough . . . I don't want the little bit of soup that's waiting in that hovel to be poison for me . . . (*leaving*) Good evening, Lina, and cheer up. . . .

LINA: Good evening, and say hello to Rosa. . . .

CECCO: (*leaving*) Hell, it's raining!

[. . .]

Scene IV

Lina, and then Tonio

(*someone is knocking on the door, Lina goes to open*)

TONIO (*entering*): It seems my visit surprises you . . . Did you forget that the rent is due today?

LINA: I know very well . . . but the thing is . . . see . . . I don't have even a penny. . . .

TONIO Hmpf!. . . .

LINA: Anyway, you should know . . . money doesn't rain down from the sky after all. And when the men don't work, we don't even have anything to eat at home. You should know this, you who were a miner once, before you were the foreman of the mine.

TONIO: I know that well . . . And I also knew that you wouldn't be able to pay me. . . .

LINA: And if you knew that, why then did you come?. . . .

TONIO: But . . . I have to do my duty. I have to bring the bill and the money to the office, otherwise. . . .

LINA: Fine . . . then tell the office.

TONIO: Tell . . . tell them . . . Oh my sweetie, they don't go looking for stories at the office . . . they want money!

LINA: But if someone doesn't have any?

TONIO: Oh, sweetie . . . one gets some, by god! If not, they lose their house. [. . .]

TONIO (*insinuatingly*): What do you want . . . This is life. The world's like this . . . And if I were to pay attention to certain fixations . . . one would surely be worse off . . . see . . . one time, I was just a miner, you know that. I worked like a mule . . . I wanted to be an honest man. But at the end of the month, I would barely make it . . . then a crisis came . . . unemployment . . . and it went on and on . . . I got to a point where I couldn't take it any longer. I prayed to Christ over and over again . . . But Christ doesn't listen . . . if you don't work, you don't eat. You try to be honest . . . But honesty is surely not something you eat! . . . I sent my wife to talk to the supervisor of the mine . . . She came back with the order that he'd give me back my section.[2] At first I didn't understand . . . then I understood. I understood all too well . . . I closed an eye . . . and then both of them. And now I'm the *boss* . . . I don't work hard . . . I have money in the bank . . . and I have a good time.

LINA: You're the boss, that's right, but you're also a big crook!. . . .

TONIO: That's . . . what people say. But in the meantime, people starve to death . . . and I enjoy myself.

LINA: Well, but I prefer. . . .

2. In the original, the word used is *piazza*. I thank Tim Baker, a former coal miner from Pennsylvania who now works for the United Mine Workers of America, who suggested the term "section" or "working section" as the most likely equivalent.

TONIO: . . . to starve to death? Oh, don't say that. It's really not worth it. Especially when that can be avoided. . . .

LINA: At that price . . . Never! You can feed yourself by working too.

TONIO: Working, you say? . . . But you can't always find work. Your husband doesn't have any work, and unless I'm mistaken, it seems he has little chance of finding any. Winter is already here . . . Come on now, I'll tell you one more time . . . let go of your scruples. In any case no one will ever find out. Your husband's not here . . . and he won't be back tonight for sure. . . .

LINA (*with disdain*): No one will know, you say? . . . And won't I know? Won't my conscience know?

TONIO (*with a cynical smile*): Your conscience? . . . But if we were all to listen to our conscience, sweetie, we would all be in trouble . . . come on now. . . .

LINA (*resolutely*): No, not for any reason!

TONIO (*with the tone of a veiled threat*): Well then, that's your choice! But watch out, you'll regret it . . . and it could be too late . . . (*moving as if to leave*) So, you can't pay the rent, huh? . . . .

LINA: I told you! . . . .

TONIO (*with a commanding tone*): Well then, start to pack up these few things because later. . . .

LINA: Later what? . . . .

TONIO (*serious and peremptory*): The company guards will come and put you out . . . (*he opens the door, the hissing sound of the storm can be heard*)

LINA: Tonight? . . . With this bad weather?

TONIO: I'm going to give the order.

LINA (*shocked*): But the law . . . the judges . . . they won't allow it!

TONIO (*ironically*): The law? . . . Judges? . . . Don't make me laugh. You think you're so smart! . . . We make the laws. Here, we are the judges. (*he opens the door, a big gust of wind comes in that brings in the sleet*)

LINA (*a stifled voice*): For pity's sake close the door, close that door . . . Oh, poor me! . . . My poor Enzo!

TONIO: Enzo . . . he will never know a thing, I tell you! . . . .

LINA: But I'm full of love. . . .

TONIO (*insinuatingly*): That's fine . . . you're full of love. But you'd be doing it for him too. Do you like to see him go wandering, so far from you, always poor, without work? . . . Come on now . . . I'll give him a good working section, I'll say it again . . . And you'll benefit from it, here, among yourselves. . . .

LINA: So . . . you're set on satisfying your lust at any cost?

TONIO: You guessed it! And you're set on persisting in your silly refusal?

LINA: Yes!

TONIO: Well then, good bye until I return with the guards in an hour. (*he opens the door*)

LINA (*with a hasty voice*): Wait, wait . . . So you'll throw me out of the house like a rag, or else I have to satisfy your lust like a bitch?. . . .

TONIO (*shrugging his shoulders*): You can decide: either wretchedness, hunger, desperation; or well-being and happiness!

LINA: Oh . . . don't talk of happiness!

TONIO: And so? . . .

LINA: And so (*putting her face in her hands, cursing*) . . . and so bitch for bitch . . . others sell their muscle, I sell my flesh for bread . . . You'll have me!

TONIO: Oh, finally!

LINA (*trying to buy time*): Yes, yes . . . you'll have me! But in the meantime leave . . . Come back later . . . I want to be alone now. . . .

TONIO: Fine . . . I'll whistle before I come in. You'll make a sign with the lamp, and then come and open. . . .

LINA: (pushing him out, re-locks the door, then, beside herself with frustration sobs loudly. She slowly moves towards the chair and lets herself fall into it, stammering Enzo's name between sobs) Enzo . . . Enzo . . . Enzo . . . my Enzo!

(*curtain falls*)

ACT II

The same scene as the first act. Lina finds herself seated on the chair with her head in her hands and leaning on the table as though sleeping, when a knock is heard.

Scene I

Lina, then Enzo

LINA (*she jumps up*): Already . . . Who is it?

ENZO (*from outside*): It's me, Lina . . . Enzo! Are you already in bed?

LINA (*surprised*): Enzo! . . . (*she runs to the door happily, and then as though taken by a thought all of a sudden, says to herself*) And if he comes? . . . Oh . . . what will I do now? . . . Mother of god, help me!

ENZO (*impatiently*): But aren't you coming to open?. . . .

LINA (*hurrying*): Here I am! I'll turn the lamp on and come . . . (*she turns the lamp on, goes to open, they hug*)

ENZO (*candid and smiling*): Surprised, eh? You weren't expecting me, right?

LINA: Me, no . . . You'd written me to say you would never come back to this town, and that when you'd found work you'd call for me. . . .

ENZO: Sure, aren't you happy to see me again, eh?. . . .

LINA: Do I seem . . . But. . . . (*confused*)

ENZO: But . . . but what? Do you mean did I find work? . . . Yes, yes . . . I found work not far from here, in the Black Diamond mine.

LINA: How? . . . you wrote and told me how hard it was!

ENZO (*confirmingly*): It is hard! But you know, I made a friend, a brother, like they, those miners, say down there. In short, a good man, who will share his section with me.

LINA (*as though speaking to herself*): So there are good people in the world too.

ENZO: There are bad ones and then some . . . and oh how bad! But there are good people also . . . Oh . . . yes there are! (*as he says these things he takes off his coat and cap and hangs them on a nail*) It's cold here, you know?. . . .

LINA: I do know . . . but what can I do? We don't even have a pail of coal in the house. . . .

ENZO: And you think that's a good thing? . . . We miners dig coal every day and we don't even have any to keep us warm. That's right . . . they said the same thing in our old towns: the shoemaker has the worst shoes, the bricklayer lives in hovels that are worth less than the match needed to burn them. It's a dog's life . . . (*Lina sits down listlessly and sighs*) You sigh . . . (*he approaches her*) What's wrong? . . . You seem strange . . . You're not yourself . . . That's it! Tell me . . . you don't feel well?

LINA: But no, Enzo, I feel fine . . . Why do you think that . . . for no reason? Why don't you tell me something about your trip instead.

ENZO: What can I tell you . . . I have so many things to tell you I don't know where to start. I saw a new world . . . there, that's it!

LINA (*laughing*): Hee . . . Hee . . . Hee! . . . How you exaggerate! A new world a few miles from here . . . and in a week?. . . .

ENZO (*with conviction*): That's right . . . a new world. Those friends I made down there . . . they opened my eyes.

LINA: And before were they closed maybe?

ENZO (*lively*): Exactly . . . They were closed, like yours are and like those of all the workers who continue to die from hard work and hunger mumbling Hail Mary's and Our Fathers.

LINA: What's gotten into your head, Enzo? . . . What . . . did they bewitch you, maybe?

ENZO: That's right, that's right . . . bewitched! More than bewitched! . . . In an hour I saw what I'd never seen in my entire life.

LINA (*curious*): But can you tell me what you saw? . . . .

ENZO: Here, this is what I saw . . . The other evening at Black Diamond I happened upon a room attracted by the voice of a person who was speaking to a group of miners. I feel like I still hear the voice now . . . And those words have already entered deep into my soul . . . But you see . . . I don't know how to repeat them or otherwise I'd be doing so throughout the whole world!

LINA (*as above*): And what, then, was this person saying?

ENZO: What was he saying? . . . Words of gold, dear Lina, words of gold! When I went in, he was talking about the life of the miners, about our beastly work, the dangers that we expose ourselves to . . . Do you know what he called miners? . . . Human moles, he called them . . . Just like that, by god! We're like moles . . . We live underground and a small landslide can bury us at any time, without even a last kiss from our mothers . . . from our wives . . . Human moles! . . . (*a brief pause. Thoughtful, then he nears Lina and puts his hands on her neck*) And he spoke about all of you, Lina . . . about our women! . . . Oh, when he said that many women, in the face of suffering, threatened by hunger . . . are forced to give themselves to the boss in order to keep their husbands' jobs . . . (*Lina sobs*) Lina, you're crying? . . . Oh . . . I was crying too when I heard that young man . . . Even he had tears in his eyes. (*brief pause*) You know, Lina, I was so taken by those words, that I stood there as though under a spell. I thought of you, Lina . . . I saw you here, alone . . . without a cent . . . afraid. I imagined that someone, taking advantage of my absence, could have attacked you . . . tricked you. My temples pounded . . . My blood boiled . . . I wanted to come back here right away . . . to fly . . . and grab the boss by his neck . . . that vile man who forced me to leave you, and . . . ring his neck like a chicken. . . .

LINA (*screams instinctively*): The boss? . . .

ENZO: Yes, the *boss*! . . . But what's wrong with you? . . . .

LINA (*faking*): Nothing, nothing. With those dazed eyes of yours you scare me.

ENZO: Oh . . . don't be afraid, Lina. Thanks to those good friends, now I can work. We'll leave here right away . . . And we'll live another life, you'll see! . . . Of course we won't be happy . . . because I realized that none of us workers can be happy as long as we are slaves to anyone . . . But you see, I'm sure that from now on, life, for me, will be more beautiful; even though it may also be more difficult . . . But now . . . we need to leave this place. I can't see myself here any longer.

LINA: Yes, go away . . . You're right, but in the meantime. . . .

ENZO: In the meantime, what? . . . Oh . . . I know, I know . . . You're worrying about the rent that we have to pay. But you see . . . those friends were so good to me, they practically forced me to take some money. Between us poor folk, we all know our needs . . . Everyone knows that when you move you need some money . . . and they offered me some.

LINA (*amazed*): They really must be good people! . . . To offer you money the first time they met you!

ENZO: You know, for anarchists, every worker is a brother.

LINA: These people are anarchists?

ENZO: Of course! Oh . . . you're surprised, you're almost afraid . . . because you don't know them. But you'll meet them too and you'll learn to respect and admire them . . . So tell me, did the *boss* come and ask about the rent?

LINA (*confused*): Yes . . . that is, no, no . . . he didn't come. I ran into him but . . . Enzo, it's already late. You should go to sleep . . . I'm going to stay up a little while longer . . . I still have a little work to do. . . .

ENZO (*indifferent*): I'll wait. I'll keep you company . . . I feel like smoking . . . Where's my pipe?

LINA: It must be there, in the drawer where you usually put it. (*Enzo walks towards the table. All of a sudden a whistle is heard and then, little by little, the sound goes . . . Lina jumps and while the whistle gets softer, whispers*) It's not him! Dear mother!. . . .

ENZO (*who was about to open the drawer turns quickly*): What's wrong with you tonight? . . . You seem so mysterious . . . Every little noise makes you jump.

LINA: That whistle . . . all of a sudden. . . .

ENZO: And you're afraid of a whistle? Maybe if you were alone . . . But you're with me now. Come on . . . (*he opens the drawer and pulls out a diaper and other things needed for a newborn*) What, do we have children in the house maybe?

LINA (*timidly*): Not yet, but soon. . . .

ENZO: If that were true? . . . Oh, my love . . . come here so I can give you a kiss . . . (*they embrace, then, all of a sudden*) I want a boy, you know, I want a boy!. . . .

LINA: Oh, sure! . . . I want a boy! That's easy to say . . . And if it's a girl?

ENZO: Oh . . . it'd be the same. Wouldn't it still be the fruit of our love? I'll love it just the same . . . I love it even now, so, so much . . . I'll make whatever sacrifice is necessary to raise him healthy, sturdy, strong . . . so that he can fight next to others . . . so that this weed is removed from the face of this earth . . . so that there are no longer swine like . . . (*asking himself*) . . . Like . . . Antonio Rossi, the boss of the mine. (*a high-pitched whistle is heard*)

LINA (*dismayed*): It's him!. . . .

ENZO: . . . Him? Who is he? . . . (*brief pause. Enzo seems to reflect on things for a moment, then*) Oh . . . you were waiting for your loverboy! . . . Now I understand your fear . . . your sighs . . . Truly . . . I didn't expect this! While I was suffering far from you . . . you were planning with your lover. Oh . . . you disgust me (*he pushes her and she falls on to the chair*).

LINA (*crying*): What are you saying, Enzo? . . . No, I don't have a lover! . . . Listen . . . Listen!

ENZO: What's going on, then? . . . Talk!. . . .

LINA (*hesitating and confused*): It's about . . . it's about. . . .

ENZO (*agitated and pressuring*): It's about what?

LINA (*as above.*): . . . it's about . . . Antonio Rossi, the boss of the mine.

ENZO: Oh . . . it's about him! That miserable man! (*he starts to leave*)

LINA (*she blocks his way, placing herself against the door*): Kill me if you want to, but listen first. . . .

ENZO (*furious*): Talk, talk!. . . .

LINA: He came this evening, a little before you arrived . . . He asked me for the rent . . . Naturally, I couldn't pay him . . . So he told me that he was going to throw me out of the house tonight . . . with the snow. . . .

ENZO (*very angry*): Oh . . . that scoundrel!

LINA (*continuing her story*): Then. . . .

ENZO: . . . and then? . . .

LINA: Then . . . no! I don't want to . . . I can't say it. . . .

ENZO: You can't say it? . . . (*commanding*) Speak, I tell you!. . . .

LINA: . . . Alright . . . then he says to me that he was ready to give you your job back . . . on the condition that. . . .

ENZO: On the condition that?. . . .

LINA: . . . On the condition that I give myself to him.

ENZO: Shameless! (*extremely angry, he goes to leave, but Lina holds him back again, blocking his way. So, very angry, he turns to Lina*) And you?. . . .

LINA: (*blushing, hesitating and troubled*) Me? . . . I hate him . . . I rejected him . . . but then. . . .

ENZO: Then . . . what?

LINA: Then . . . I promised.

ENZO (*with his face distraught, he stares at her strangely, he grabs her by the shoulders and pushes her violently on to the chair*): What horror! . . . Listen to what I have to hear! . . . (*he puts his hands to his face in shame and disgust*)

LINA (*getting up again from the chair walks towards Enzo; begging on her knees at his feet*): Enzo . . . Enzo listen to me! I swear . . . I didn't promise because I loved him . . . I did it for you, Enzo . . . for our child that is not yet born . . . so as to not die of cold . . . to not die of hunger . . . I was stunned . . . beside myself. Now I understand . . . Forgive me, Enzo, forgive me.

ENZO (*pause. The actor must express the internal fight that is going on inside him, not knowing if he should decide to pardon his wife or exact revenge; but then love prevails, and not without bitterness he says*): Get up, Lina, get up! . . . Come here! . . . (*he sweetly helps her up and pulls her to him*) If it were in the past, maybe I wouldn't have forgiven you . . . I wouldn't have been able to forgive you . . . But now I live with the thought of a new world . . . and I know that you . . . Me . . . all of us poor destitute, are the victims of the times. You women even more than us men . . . (*another whistle is heard. Changing the tone of his voice*) He's still here! Go and open the door for him!

LINA: He's waiting for the sign. . . .

ENZO: Do it right away!

LINA (*begging*): Enzo!

ENZO (*imperious*): Go!LINA (*she goes to give the sign. Enzo hides. After a little while Tonio comes in, greets her and takes off his hat*)

Scene II

Tonio and the above

TONIO (*to Lina reassuring her*): Don't be afraid of anything. No one saw me. (*approaching her*) You don't respond? Oh . . . those scruples! . . . Come here! . . . come on! (*he goes to hug her*)

LINA (*pushing him away*): Don't touch me, swine! You make me sick!

TONIO: But why this change all of a sudden? Your obstinate refusal only makes my desire to have you grow. (*He grabs her, puts his arms around her body. Lina defends herself, fighting. She falls on the couch, while Tonio beside himself with lust, screams*) Oh . . . you'll be mine!

ENZO (*coming out of his hiding place*): No, she will not be yours!

TONIO (*turning around surprised*): Enzo!!

ENZO (*with contempt*): Enzo, yes . . . Surprised, eh? You'd arranged this trap well. But now you're in the net, miserable man. And you won't get out clean, believe you me. (*brief pause*) You took away my bread . . . and then you wanted to take away even my heart. I have the right to take away your rotten miserable life!?

TONIO (*shocked and humbled*): Enzo . . . in the name of god, forgive me!

ENZO: In the name of god? . . . In the name of god you rob us and starve us . . . in the name of god you kill us like dogs in the street . . . in the name of god you massacre us in wars . . . in the name of god you take everything from us and you leave us nothing . . . And in the end in the name of god you also want us to resign ourselves to all of your infamies! Ah . . . certainly not!

TONIO (*as above*): Take pity on me, Enzo, forgive me!

ENZO: Pity? . . . And did you take pity on this woman who begged you to leave her in peace? . . . Should I then take pity on you? Oh . . . no! I'd be a coward! It was not enough that you took away my bread, you came to rob me even of my love and you want me to leave you unpunished? . . . You, who positioned yourself like a hawk to capture your prey when she was alone! . . . (*remembering*) Oh, the hawks . . . down there in the old villages! . . . Do you remember, Lina? . . . When a peasant killed a hawk, he would nail it up on the door of his house as an example to the others. (*blind with rage*) The hatchet, the hatchet! . . . (*goes around the room looking for the hatchet*) Where's the hatchet? . . . (*he finds it in the corner near the door, he takes it and goes menacingly toward Tonio, who is terrified, as if to hit him*) I want to cut your head off, you miserable man, and nail it to the mouth of the mine just like the hawks are nailed!

(*Curtain closes*)

Translated by Laura E. Ruberto

A Letter and a Story

≈ *Ludovico M. Caminita*

Palermo, Italy, March 5, 1878–1943(?)

From a dispatch sent out by the New York Italian consulate in November 1905 we learn that Ludovico M. Caminita was active in the anarchic circles of Barre, Vermont. In this period, he published the dramatic novella, *L'idea cammina* (The Idea Travels), with a preface by Raimondo Fazio. Warned that he was being investigated by the police of Palermo, Caminita wrote a vibrantly intense letter to the police headquarters, published here. The letter contained news in regard to him, in particular, clarifying the equivocation of his name. He is in reality Michele Caminita. Ludovico was his brother, who failed to appear for military enrollment and died in Canada in 1903 after falling from a train. Caminita assumed his name "in memory of a victim of greedy and villainous capitalism." (According to consular documents, it is possible that he could have changed his name to hide his brother's death from their father.) Caminita contributed to the *Cronaca Sovversiva* of Barre and was editor of the *Questione Sociale* of Paterson, New Jersey, where he also published *L'Era Nuova*, which was suppressed by the authorities in 1917. At that time, he founded the clandestine newspaper, *La Jacquerie*. He published libelous pieces on various themes. *L'educazione de' fanciulli* (The Education of Children, 1908), which profiles a non-authoritative school, is curiously dedicated "to J. Montalbano barbitonsore [barber], in Old Forge, Pa.," given that "the dishonest writers [*pennivendoli*, writers who compromise substance for better pay] have by now understood that the belly is filled better licking the feet of the successful." Later works are *Che cosa è la Religione* (What Is Religion), with a preface by Guido Podrecca (1906), and *Free Country!* (1917). He also contributed to not openly militant newspapers, among them *La Follia of New York*, with poems and essays.

In the middle of the "Red Scare," Caminita was arrested on February 14, 1920, with twenty-eight other persons in the raid that destroyed the entire group of the New Era. The group was to be deported on May 22, but the provision was suspended for six months. On its expiration, Caminita was a resident of Hawthorne, New Jersey, and an editor of the *Bolletino della Sera* (Evening Bulletin). The consulate informed the Department of the Interior that Caminita did not fight any longer for anarchy and did not write anymore for *La Questione Sociale*; it concluded that "in the articles that he often publishes, he professes patriotic sentiments," even if it was noticed that the change was due to the threat of expulsion. It could be, however, that Caminita had evaded the deportation thanks to the information he provided to the investigators in the course of the various interrogations, and that, as Paul Avrich recalls, he was responsible for getting several militants into trouble, among whom were Roberto Elia, the Calabrian printer, companion of the imprisoned Andrea Salsedo and Aldino Felicani.

A further ascertainment in September 1930 found that Caminita was not a dangerous person; he lived in Hawthorne for years with his wife and son Lucifero. The consular representative of Paterson even reported that he was now "a great admirer of the Duce and of Fascism," and that for this reason he had incurred the hatred of his old trusted companions, who were not sparing with public attacks. In this period, Caminita moved to Scranton, Pennsylvania, to publish the weekly *Il Minatore*, of which he figured as director and proprietor. According to the consul of Philadelphia, the former anarchist would now justify his past participation in the *Questione Sociale* as a necessity to oppose the heavy restrictions "during a great economic crisis that troubled this country." He could hardly find another occupation. He left publishing "and because of this, he drew the hatred and persecution of Carlo Tresca, the noted subversive leader of North America." Caminita, then, was an apostate. But to complicate the picture, his name was included in the list of "fellow countrymen politically dangerous as propagandists or instigators of criminal acts," prepared by the Italian consul in Scranton, Tiscar, and revealed by Tresca himself in the *Martello* of August 22, 1931.

In May 1921, in New York, Clement Giglio presented a production (performed by Mimì Aguglia) of Caminita's drama *Sonata Elegiaca*, in which social themes were anything but abandoned. The story depicts a rich American writer, Errico Parson, who ends up supporting the workers during a great strike, because of his love for a typical militant of the proletariat cause, Lillian Owen, who is imprisoned, accused of being the perpetuator of a dynamiting attempt. Her imprisonment is due to the conspiracy of Emma, Parson's jealous wife, and the manufacturer Giovanni Oliver, who wants to be Emma's lover. Lillian dies in prison. The drama, dedicated to Italo Stanco, has an ambiguous finale. After being completely cleared of the plot, Parson basically resumes his habitual work. Is such an indication enough to postulate a revision of the old revolutionary ideas? Or, on the contrary, does the drama intimate a typical anarchist message on the impossibility of every mediation? In fact, *Sonata Elegiaca* remains a social drama, originating from the ambiance of the revolutionary left, nor is it his only one. There was still at least his older social drama, *L'idea cammina*, which, as testified by an announcement in the *Parola del Popolo*, was still being performed in January 1922. Perhaps the most interesting episode of the literary career of Caminita is tied to his memoir, *Nell'isola delle lagrime* (On the Island of Tears), whose title makes reference to his detainment at Ellis Island, in 1924, and is also therefore posterior to the presumed "turning point" of 1920. In this book, marred by a series of typographical errors, which rendered the pagination confusing and even caused the exclusion of some pages of notable importance, in order to reconstruct some of the facts narrated, Caminita recalls events tied to the year in which he was arrested and put on trial for subversive activity, as it seems (according to what he relates), by the intervention of Fiorello La Guardia. Not sparing with attacks on the heads of the movement, Caminita nevertheless attempts to modify his militancy, but various indications incline one toward a different interpretation. In 1943, Caminita was also the author of a biography of Amedeo Obici, the multimillionaire "king of hazelnuts," of Venetian origin.

ESSENTIAL BIBLIOGRAPHY

Avrich 1991, 181–182; Caminita 1924; Fumagalli 1909, 90; Marazzi 2001, 31–32.

∾

I Know That Your Watchdogs. . . .

PATERSON, N.Y. [*SIC*]

OCTOBER 12, 1906

To the Police Commissioner of Palermo.

I know from letters that have reached me from the city that your watchdogs have repeatedly visited my parents' home, pestering my old mother with annoying questions about Ludovico Caminita, a draft dodger seeking refuge in this country for several years or so.

The poor old woman has always responded that her boy died far away from her, without the comfort of one last maternal kiss. But the blind tools of robbery that for a handful of beans have undertaken the repulsive task of torturing neighbors also insist on harassing the poor woman, claiming that Ludovico is alive.

Allow me to ask, were it not a useless question, if police headquarters knows more than the pitiful mother, then why torture the poor woman with the painful memory of her lost boy?

My mother does not understand the insistence of the policemen and cannot understand it because she ignores the reality of things.

I come, once and for all, to act as a disinterested *informer*, renouncing in advance any compensation drawn from those famous secret funds that secretly end up in the throats of secret bloodsuckers.

So Ludovico Caminita, the draft-dodger, *died* on February 12, 1903 in the general hospital of Winnipeg (Canada) from a fracture of the right leg. That Ludovico who you think is still alive because he edits the socialist-anarchist periodical *La Questione Sociale* of Paterson, N.I. [*sic*], is the undersigned brother of the poor dead man. I use that name as a pseudonym in memory of a victim of capitalistic greed and evil.

Do you want more? My mother ignores that I am an anarchist, just as my old father ignores the death of old Ludovico.

I would hope that you will now leave those two old people in peace who have as much to do with the fight between me and the bourgeoisie as you have to do with the mysteries of the Virgin Mary.

And I will not complain about the many letters sent to me from my wife that the Post Office has lost, but that could have been left on some police director's shelf.

MICHELE CAMINITA
Editor
LA QUESTIONE SOCIALE-PATERSON. N.I.
THE SOCIAL QUESTION–PATERSON, N.J.

Translated by Giulia Prestia

∾

L'arresto

On Saturday, the 16th of February 1920, I was working in on a short literary piece in my small study. It was about midnight and a violent storm blustered outside. Just as in the novels of Carolina Invernizio.

During that miserable February the so-called Spanish influenza raged on. My son, who had not yet turned ten, slept, convalescing in his little room. My wife, in bed, burned with fever. I heard a knock at the door. Some of my friends, knowing that I am nocturnal, often came to visit me at that hour, and so I answered convinced that it was one of them.

Opening the door, I was threatened with the mouth of a black automatic pistol and a hoarse voice that ordered, "Hands up!" I looked the brute in the face and saw that he was a detective whom I did not recognize.

To me it seems that a policeman carries the trademarks of his occupation stamped on his forehead. It is certain that, despite his disguises, ninety times out of a hundred, I recognize him. Behind that gentleman there were others of his kind, all with their automatic weapons drawn. Since I hesitated to raise my hands, the same voice repeated angrily, "Hands up!" and the barrel of the gun was planted in my abdomen. I raised my hands, and the gang—there were eight—burst into the house, stamping their feet on the floor to shake the snow from their galoshes. Among them I noticed a man whose manners were too courteous for him to be one of them. He was about fifty, well-dressed, with spectacles, and had the appearance of a gentleman.

I was frisked, and an amber cigarette holder and a tortoise cigarette case imported from Italy were confiscated, neither of which I saw again.

My wife called me and asked the reason for the noise. In order not to alarm the poor woman, I told her that it was an unimportant search. Then my wife closed the door of the bedroom to dress, but two of the tough guys, alarmed by who knows what imaginable danger, began to push the door to enter, ordering my wife to open up.

"Let me get dressed," the sick woman was saying, but the thugs wanted to enter immediately and were pushing the door and cursing. I protested. It was worse. One answered me with vulgarities, threatening to rearrange my face; another made a motion of breaking the door with a powerful blow from his shoulders. And he would have done it, had it not been for the "gentleman" who stopped him, looking at him threateningly.

"In that room," he told him, "is a woman. Before you enter, let her get dressed."

Speaking to my wife, he added, "Don't be frightened, ma'am. Please hurry because the federal agents must search the house."

He made me go into the small study and ordered me to sit down on the sofa. The agents ransacked every corner, looking in every opening, beating the walls with the butts of their weapons. One of them, a real hoodlum from the slums of New York, was tossing books in the air, throwing aside those that had either a red cover, a red binding, or were a shade of red. Every so often he snorted, "Gee, how many books!"

It seemed strange to him that in the poor house of an Italian there would be so many books. As they were going in and out of the rooms, the thugs would ask in a low voice, "Any booze?" No! It was a disgrace that in an Italian's home there was nothing except books with red covers or bindings and not even a drop of wine or liquor! An agent carried four empty suitcases from the attic, and the hoodlum started to fill them at random with books.

My wife came in and sat down next to me. From her face, it was obvious that she was burning with fever.

"What is this about?" she asked.

"Who knows?"

Her glance settled on the desk.

"And the fountain pen?"

"It should be on the desk," I replied.

My wife began to look for the pen on the desk, in the drawers, on the floor.

"Are you sure it was here?"

"I was writing with the fountain pen when these people came in."

The "gentleman" asked the agents if they had seen the pen. No one had seen it. With a look, I accused the hoodlum. He noticed.

"I swear to God, I don' know nothin' 'bout it."

Then, seeing that the "gentleman" glared at him hard, he unbuttoned his overcoat and said, "If you don't believe me, frisk me." But he quickly went back to throwing books into the suitcases, adding, "All dangerous stuff."

That stuff really should have been dangerous! Those books included *The Greatness and Decline of the Roman Empire* by Guglielmo Ferrero, *History of the French Revolution* by Taine, *Commentaries* by Julius Caesar, *Universal History* by Cantù, and the most dangerous of all, because it had the reddest cover of them all, *Primitive Man* by Figuier.

"Even this stuff is dangerous?" my wife asked him, taking out a half-dozen opera librettos from one of the suitcases.

The "gentleman" looked at the librettos and put them on the desk, electrocuting the wretch with a look full of contempt. That is to say that it would have electrocuted him if that criminal's skin was not harder than a rhinoceros's hide.

The agents turned everything upside down in the cellar, rooms, and attic; they dumped the contents of drawers, closets, and trunks onto the floor, which was worsened by the disappointment of not finding I do not know what. In my son's small room, a squabble began between two of them and the "gentleman." My wife went to protect her child. A few minutes later, she returned to the study with the "gentleman" who was holding the boy in his arms. From the expression on his face, one understood that he was outraged. My son, in his pajamas and his bare little feet, looked around in dismay. To comfort him, he smiled, calling him, "big man." The man covered him with a woolen blanket.

"What a beautiful angel!" said the gentleman, sitting on the couch with the boy in his lap.

"You don't seem like a police agent," I told him.

"Thank God I'm not! I am an official with the American Legion. The Department of Justice asked me to help with your arrest because these agents do not know the area and do not trust the local police. I regret coming. I never imagined that I would have to witness such a humiliating scene in the name of American justice."

When the agents were tired of rummaging, they showed me an arrest warrant from the Department of Labor, and they ordered me to dress and follow them. I did not take any money, because I was certain that it would have been taken from me later on. I took some cigarettes, kissed my loved ones, and urged my wife not to become discouraged, and promised the boy—drying the tears in his eyes with my lips—that I would be back in a few hours, and I left on the doorstep the poor sick woman burning with fever with a sob in her clenched throat and the boy who did not cry because he had to be a "big man."

I found myself on a country road surrounded by agents, in the darkness of night and in the middle of a blustering storm. The wind was very strong and the snow was blinding. To get from my house to the bus, one had to go down a small hill covered with ice. The descent was quick and dangerous because one risked slipping and falling into a ravine. The detectives told me to lead the way. We descended, frequently sliding on our overcoats and gloves. There was a moment when even I, someone who recognized every inch of the terrain, ran the risk of breaking my neck in a ditch. One detective who was carrying one of my suitcases full of "dangerous stuff" slipped, but had the quickness and the presence of mind to use the suitcase as a sled and arrived at the foot of the hill in two minutes, with a ruined suitcase, bloodied hands, ripped overcoat, open galoshes, and in a pitiful state. His partner revived him with a sip of a liquid which had the strong odor of whiskey, but could not have been whiskey because one assumes that the police detectives were the first to respect the laws of Prohibition.

"Drink," he told him. "It's the good stuff; it was given to me as a gift, in Washington, by a congressman."

Two other detectives lost their caps; I lost one of my galoshes.

After a half-hour of tormented waiting, the bus arrived. We got on. I was made to sit in the rear. The official from the American Legion sat next to me and did not say a word during the trip. The detectives talked, laughed, and drank that stuff that stank of whiskey but could not have been whiskey.

Arriving at the municipal building in Paterson, we got off and headed toward the Postal Building where the Department of Justice was located. Having arrived there, the official from the American Legion took his leave of me, shaking my hand and wishing me good luck. He turned away without saying good night to the detectives. We climbed the steps until we reached the second floor, and I was taken to a large room lit by many electric lamps. I looked around and saw a scene which I had not expected.

There were about twenty Italian workers whom I recognized, all standing or leaning on the walls and guarded by many federal agents. They all looked as though they were in mourning. I understood that they had all been arrested like me, and tried to cheer them up a bit, as if to say: Have courage; this is an error that will soon be cleared up. Tomorrow we will have a little party. But no one seemed to cheer up. A few of them were members of an education club, a kind of informal university that offered free lectures on history, geography, Italian, and English, but most of all there were interesting domino and pinochle matches. Others did not even know that such a club existed. I, because of my solitary temperament, was not a member of the club but I was invited by the board of directors to give free lectures on Spencer and Darwin, which did not have the slightest bit to do with politics.

Only one of those arrested men, one Alberto Guabello, professed to be a philosophical anarchist. But his anarchy was more harmless than the arioso of "Andrea Chénier"; an arioso that sends the audience into ecstasies if sung by a great tenor, but does not create revolutionaries, not even in the peanut gallery. Alberto Guabello's anarchic propaganda was a waste of time; it was woven together by so many ifs, buts, and howevers that it allowed him to agree with both the devil and Saint Michael. Alberto Guabello spoke of his own anarchism when he was at the table with friends, between a bellyful of dried almonds and a bottle of Gragnano, topped off by a Cuban cigar. That philosophical anarchist was as harmless as a lamb, incapable of harming a hair on someone's head, ready to commit murder and die in the electric chair if he had the fortune of coming face to face with the person who had the perverse idea of inventing work. Because Alberto Guabello was a bigger enemy of work than of the state. I think that for him anarchy was no more than a pretext to stay as far away as possible from the factory and to live off his woman, a weaver, and his "comrades in ideals." When he was in dire straits, when he did not know where else to sponge, he schemed to be named an assistant organizer in any local labor organization. Having made a small nest for himself, he spent his time curling his mustache, reading the newspapers, courting the organizers, and completing his education at the cinema. Like Mazzini, he always dressed in black as a sign of mourning for the fallen victims on the altar of the motherland, and in this way our philosophical anarchist always had nails rimmed in black, perhaps as a sign of mourning for "all of the pallid victims bleeding from the class struggle." He had a virtue that is the same for both for men and mules: that of kicking those who had been good to him. I could not understand why the federal agents had arrested him. I thought: had he, for our and his misfortune, finally met the person who invented work? A printer from Calabria was also among those arrested; he was of a very short stature, very fat, very dark, and with very alert black eyes. His name was Beniamino Mazzotta and he was incredibly intelligent and terribly witty. Although he was a naturalized American citizen, he was interested in politics as much as politics could have interested the mother-in-law of the cook of the butler of a Chinese imperial official. He had no passions except for hunting, and he had never killed anything, not even a goose or a rabbit accidentally. Why had they arrested him? The others were passive workers, big spaghetti and polenta eaters, and were therefore dangerous at the dinner table. None of them had been questioned yet. They were waiting for me, the leader. And so they gave me the honor of going first. A door opened and I was pushed into the interrogation room.

It was a big rectangular room. The interrogator was sitting at a desk. He was a small Jew, a lawyer. Later on I learned that his name was Stone and he suffered from diabetes. On the left there was a stenographer. All around, along the walls, standing, there were about forty colossal, brutal-looking men. I was made to sit down in front of Mr. Stone. Two of the huge men were stationed at my back; one guy was a big, perfect, blonde German; the other was dark and must have been Spanish or Spanish-American.

Mr. Stone was thin, nervous, tortured by the sickness that gnawed at his life, and had a cruel countenance. Behind him, seated on his heels, was a man of medium stature, with a cap pulled over his forehead, his face hidden by a plant. His odd posture caught my attention and I guessed who he was.

He had lived in Paterson for a few months and he went by the name of Joe Termini. He said that he was the son of Sicilians, born in Tunisia, and immigrated to the United States with his parents when he was a boy. He was about twenty-five years old and claimed to be a war veteran. He alleged that he had been injured on the front lines: he, in fact, showed off a scar on his leg. He joined the club and diligently attended. Always the first to arrive, he swept, cleaned, looked after the stove, and was always the last to leave. When I was at the club, he never spoke; he sat in a corner of the room and listened to my lectures attentively, with the smile of a good little boy on his lips. But when I was not there he was quite a chatterbox. He would say that his mom was well-off, lived in Boston, and that he did not get along with her. He had a close friendship with a weaver who was as generous as he was slow-witted. Moved by the poverty of the son with the well-off mom, the weaver gave him lodging, food, change for cigarettes, and taught him the art of weaving.

This poor weaver loathed politics and education in general; he attended the club more because of Joe Termini's prodding than to listen to the lectures. And yet even he was among those arrested! . . .

"I hope you understand that we are not here to waste time. I have proof that you are the director of this underground newspaper. Here it is. *Il Martello*, revolutionary periodical of New York, declares that the director of *La Jacquerie* during the war worked at number 226 Lafayette Street in New York. *La Follia*, the official instrument of the Italian Socialists in the Eastern States, published that you are the director of this underground periodical, and who ironically calls you Mr. Jacquerie."

He was silent for a moment and then began again:

"As you can see, this is not the Department of Justice. It is not I, it is not my agents who accuse you; it is an anarchist and a socialist, who accuse you publicly, in their own party's newspapers. Do you still have the impudence to deny the truth?" . . .

I could not take it any more. I was overcome by people who struck me coldly, without knowing me, for a miserable wage. A primitive man was awakened within me, repressed by human progress over the millennia. In the few seconds that were available, I bit a hand, a finger, a piece of living flesh to vent the anger that blinded me. But I was no more than a tiny plaything in the hands of huge brutes, against whom I was completely powerless to defend myself. How long did the torture last? I do not know. I do know that during that period of time, that I thought would never end, I fiercely hated all, all, all of humanity.

When Mr. Stone tired of my stubbornness, he shouted, "Get this son of a bitch out of my sight, or I will set his head on fire."

I was dragged into an adjacent hall. The agent to whom I was handed over leaned me against a wall, dried my face with a handkerchief, tidied my hair with his fingers, had another agent bring my spectacles, cleaned them and gave them to me, repeating, "I am sorry, very sorry."

Little by little, that man's voice, which reassured me that the physical and moral torture inflicted on me also pained him, restored some small, infinitesimal part of my humanity. When he saw that I had perked up a little, the agent offered me a cigarette that he lit himself. I began to smoke it greedily. The nicotine refreshed my nerves and spirit.

After me the other prisoners were led into a hallway, one at a time. Their interrogation had been very short.

"What is your name? Are you an American citizen? Do you know Ludovico Caminita? Have you ever received *La Jacquerie*? No? Go?!"

Only one of these, a guy of about nineteen, born and raised in the United States, got a slap and a kick for having said that he was annoyed by this arbitrary arrest. A few hours later he was set free, not because he was annoyed, but because as an American citizen he could not be deported. Beniamino Mazzotta was also freed because he was a naturalized American citizen. That bandit left us with a thumb of his nose and still laughs at what he calls his only non-amorous adventure. But I cannot say that he laughed when, upon returning to his print shop, he found everything turned upside down. It took him over a month, after overcoming his laziness, to put it back in order. Joe Termini was also led into the hallway. An agent put him in line with us, and he gave the agent a shove. This was necessary to show everyone that Joe Termini was not a spy! I was put into an automobile, along with an old weaver from Piedmont, one Firmino Gallo who accepted the adventure stoically, and was brought to the local police headquarters, just two blocks from the postal building. The others were led on foot.

Halfway there, Joe Termini slipped away, right under the under agents' noses; he cut and run, and disappeared. All of the prisoners saw it, but not the agents!

I did not hear anything more about him. If he had really been injured on the frontlines, I blame the Germans who did not know how to shoot straight.

We were frisked again at the Paterson police station. In handing us over to the local police, the federal agents gave them strict orders to not allow us to communicate with anyone. While they frisked us, I understood that there should have been bad blood among us.

As soon as the federal agents had left, the local agents returned our cigars, cigarettes, tobacco, pipes and matches, and locked us in the cells, two in each cell. It was about four in the morning. We began to call each other by name, to describe how each other's interrogation was carried out, to speculate on the cause of that sudden, unexpected arrest. And we all had profound contempt for Carlo Tresca and Gerolamo Valenti.

Every cell was about seven feet long and three and a half feet wide; the floor, the walls, and the ceiling were all thin sheets of steel; there was an iron "bidet" with water that ran in short intervals; a metal net for a bed. On that bed, without a mattress, without a pillow, without a cover, one suffered from the cold and a stiff neck. So this is why we stayed seated or stood up. And we smoked, we whistled, and we sang until a guard shouted, "Shut up!" We were quiet for a minute, and then we were even louder than before. We could not remain quiet: the silence would have been too oppressive. Every one of us felt the irrepressible need to amuse ourselves, to cheer ourselves up, to banish from our minds the painful images of our loved ones in extreme misery at home. . . .

Once we arrived at the train station, the officers did not let us enter because the waiting room was too crowded. They made us stand against the wall under the canopy, and planted themselves in front of us so as to prevent us from approaching anyone. Behind us there was a window that opened onto the waiting room. I looked through the glass and I saw that people rushed to look at us. A man had a folded newspaper in his hand, and I could read a few words of the headline, "Arrest . . . Deport . . ." Without a doubt that newspaper article referred to us. The man guessed what I wanted and explained the first page. I read the headline printed in enormous red letters,

"King of the anarchists arrested with twenty of his gang—Will be deported from the United States."

A subheading in black:

"For eighteen years he escaped police capture."

Another in italics:

"Weapons, hand grenades, and dynamite hidden in his house."

The king of anarchists, according to the newspaper, was I! And there was the picture of an ugly mug with a cap and without a collar, obviously dug up from the slums of the Bowery, which the newspaper passed off as my photo. After about ten minutes the other prisoners arrived on foot and were lined up under the canopy. I knew that American reporters attending universities took special courses in journalism where they studied the best methods to tickle the morbid curiosity of readers. But I had never imagined that their audacity had no limit. The crowd was looking for the human beast surrounded by his terrible minions and found neither one. The crowd saw well-dressed people who seemed very civil, in handcuffs.

What disappointment! All of a sudden there was a scuffle. I saw Grandi's petite wife, Pietro Baldisserotti's tall, robust wife with strong muscles, and the woman who had brought cigars for her husband and cigarettes for Joe Termini, struggling with federal agents. The three women wanted to break the police line to get closer, and it seemed that they had lost their minds. They must have suffered so much that they could no longer restrain themselves. They had spent more than eight hours on the sidewalk in six degrees below zero! All they wanted was to be near their spouses for a few minutes and give them some words of comfort. The crowd expressed its sympathy for those poor women by launching scathing remarks and sharp insults against the officers. They stood up to the women, but did not dare to react violently.

In the end, one of them drew a "blackjack." For those who do not know, this insidious weapon is a lead ball tied with a flexible leather handle. By law, this weapon is strictly prohibited even for use by the police, but practically every officer carries one without even hiding it. The agent, visibly exasperated, threatened Baldisserotti's wife, but the women became even more enraged. But they were three against a group of brawny men armed with weapons, including the strongest weapon of all: the assurance of impunity.

The crowd began to scream; someone, one of the more audacious, showed his fists to agents. Then an investigative sergeant from Paterson, one Billy Hughes, known for his great courage, ran to me.

"Mr. Caminita, tell your friends to signal to their women to have patience. What would happen if the federal agents drew their automatic weapons?"

"Let them pass and everything will be fine."

"But the officers have strict orders. I'm afraid there will be a massacre."

"Ask them, on our behalf, to resign themselves for the well-being of their own spouses."

The sergeant ran to relay our request and did it so that our women could see us. We gave them a signal to calm down by showing our handcuffed wrists to indicate that we could not help them. They understood. Grandi shouted to us in English so that the agents would understand: "We want to enter the station to buy tickets. What right do these brutes have to stop us?" An Italian-American investigator from Paterson, one De Luccia, also went to calm him. The police officers exerted much effort in subduing several men who threatened to strike them. Finally calm was restored.

I looked everywhere, searching for my wife. I saw her. We greeted each other with a smile. And we continued to smile, but all of a sudden she could no longer sustain the effort to control herself. She hid her face in a handkerchief. Knowing that she was so sick, it seemed to me that exposing herself to this intense cold was a veiled attempt at suicide. Paterson's police officers began to criticize the federal agents, calling them troublemakers.

"It's unnecessary cruelty," one said.

"It's a stupid set up," concluded the investigative sergeant.

Finally, the train arrived. We exchanged a glance and a smile with our relatives and left. Along the way—an hour into the trip—my companion, a cheerful young man, whose friends call him by a name that I cannot repeat, was no longer cheerful. Like a dog that peeks out from under the table expecting a beating from his owner, he was casting sidelong glances at the agent who had threatened to kill him once they arrived on the island. He did not dare to speak. Finally he said in a whisper, without turning his head toward me, "When we are on the island that ape will get back at me, right?"

"I don't think so."

"Oh, yes, he is going to beat me good! How he looks me over suspiciously! But I didn't want to offend him. I don't even know myself why I told him to shut up. For the damned habit of always saying 'You shut up' when someone tells me to be quiet."

I was tormented by his whimpering throughout the trip. Once in New York, the agents lined us up and led us to South Ferry on foot. People stopped to look, perhaps thinking that we were at least a gang of highway robbers who had been captured in the far west. The ground was covered with ice, and to avoid slipping we had to work wonders to keep our balance, giving each other fierce tugs on the wrists. The handcuffs stuck to the skin like pieces of ice. My hands were frozen. My gloves did not give me any relief. I feared that the tips of my ears would freeze, so I occasionally rubbed them with my free hand. The agents cursed the cold and they took it out on us. That march of one and a quarter miles would not end. When we boarded the ferry boat which was heated and warm, it seemed as though we had entered paradise.

The ferry departed and along the crossing, with heaviness in my heart, I saw New York fading in the distance; New York, the great, immense, beautiful metropolis where I had enjoyed so much and suffered so much; New York that I loved as one can only love one's hometown!

When we were near Ellis Island, from the window I saw the beautiful, magnificent, gigantic Statue of Liberty that stands near the Island of Tears. The words of Madame Roland came to my mind, those words that she pronounced before she placed her head on the guillotine as she looked at the statue of Liberty before her.[1]

Translated by Giulia Prestia

1. "O Liberty, what crimes are committed in your name!"

Six Poems

༄ *Giuseppe Bertelli*

Empoli, Italy, October 1869–Chicago, Illinois, 1943

A "lover of novelty," Giuseppe Bertelli enlisted in the French Foreign Legion in Algiers in 1887, but a year later he deserted and entered the Italian Royal Army as a volunteer. Accused of theft, he was demoted from the rank of sergeant, put on trial in Naples, and acquitted. He was discharged in 1893 and returned to Empoli, where he joined the PSI (Partito Socialista Italiano) and edited *Il Pioniere* (The Pioneer). In 1900, he participated in the sixth socialist congress of Rome, then edited *Il Lavoratore* (The Worker) in Trieste and *Il Secolo Nuovo* (The New Century) in Venice. In his first writings, collected in *Chi siamo e cosa vogliamo* (Who We Are and What We Want, 1902), he perceived the United States as an example of a multinational country, almost in anticipation of his destiny, because in 1906, he emigrated to Philadelphia, where he joined the FSI (Federazione Socialista Italiana), from a position on the left, supported by the SLP (Socialist Labor Party). Successor of Tresca as the director of the *Proletario*, he proceeded to assume an orientation that favored strong ties with the IWW (Industrial Workers of the World); at the same time, he departed from the idea of the necessity of constructing one sole socialist party. His political vision began to become more reformist. In 1908, in Chicago, he began to publish the *Parola dei Socialisti* (The Word of the Socialists), which the Italian members of the SPA (Socialist Party of America) transformed into the *Parola del Popolo* (The Word of the People). In October 1909, he ceded rights in the newspaper to a cooperative under the management of the party, but he continued to contribute his work gratis until 1913, when Alberico Molinari succeeded him as director (though Bertelli again reassumed directorship twice during the 1920s and 1930s). In 1913, The Italian Labor Publishing Bureau was created, with its cooperative printing office and annexed bookshop. In those years, Bertelli's activities as propagandist were intense, especially when, after the Socialist Party of America's congress of 1910, he expounded the necessity of proselytism to achieve the organized levels required by the individual federations. With equal energy, he carried out the campaign for the naturalization of Italian laborers. Bertelli singled out the "enviable harmony" of the multiethnic community of cigar makers of Tampa–Ybor City, Florida, as a valid model. As a result of all these efforts, in July 1910, the Italian Federation of the SPA was founded; Bertelli was among the five members of the executive commission.

Bertelli played a prominent role during the strike of the clothing workers of Chicago. For three months, he refused the accommodations offered by the AFL, and then experimented with a method of fighting used during the strike at Lawrence, Massachusetts, moving the strikers' children to the homes of families of socialists who lived in other cities. In Italy, in 1918, he published the pamphlet *Ai conservatori in buona fede* (To Conservatives of Good Faith), in which he augurs an interclass dialog with a humanitarian scope. Bertelli also worked extensively in antifascist militancy. In 1929, with Vincenzo Vacirca, he edited *Il Nuovo Mondo* (The New World) and in 1936, he was president of the Statuary & Novelty Plaster Union.

In the political efforts of Bertelli, Elisabetta Vezzosi has identified significant constants. A capable ethnic mediator ("ethnic broker"), precisely in virtue of the instruction he delivered and the professionalism he gained from it, Bertelli became a leader who was listened to in America, while in Italy, his role in the workers' movement had not been particularly brilliant: "His was a hasty and superficial cultivation, in which Marxism figured only secondhand. He was a good-natured devil, adorned with a big, very decorative beard, and had the typical mentality of the petty bourgeois lover of a quiet life" (Piemontese). Equally disparaging judgments of him were made by the adversaries of the revolutionary wing in America, like De Ciampis, for whom his work had been "inconclusive."

Bertelli's other writings include an ardent anticlerical pamphlet, *Gesù Cristo, i preti e noi* (Jesus Christ, the Priests, and Us). A tract from the *Parola del Popolo* was another text reprinted in pamphlet form: *Dibattito sulla "Esistenza di Dio" tra il Rev. Amadeo Santini e il Prof. Giuseppe Bertelli* (Debate on the Existence of God Between Rev. Amadeo Santini and Prof. Giuseppe Bertelli) In relation to the latter, *La Fiaccola* (The Torch), of Detroit confronted him with his own phrase, upon closing a conference on atheism: "All may make mistakes, only God is perfect." The phrase is perhaps an indication of a "natural" religious sense, which may be found in the ending of one of his poems, "Signore Iddio!" (Mr. God):

If it were true that one day you will judge
All men, I would not be afraid;
I am certain that you will not damn me.
Omnipotence! I was your creature;
I was only your instrument, nothing more;
Not I was guilty, but you!

In 1940, Bertelli published a book of poetry, *Rime d'esilio–Il bacio* (Rhymes of Exile: The Kiss). "The genuine truth," he wrote in the preface, "is that I have always had the conviction of not being a poet, also because I am an admirer of the greatest poets of the four nations whose language I know. And I have always held that before them, I would make a very poor impression." Nonetheless, he kept in his house a "trunk sheltering kilograms of manuscript paper . . . rhymed," a sign that to compose verses was an old pastime. In fact, on the occasion of his seventieth birthday, his companions-in-struggle (the class wars), such as Battistoni, Camboni, Sacchini, Buttis, and Silvestri urged Bertelli to publish his poems. The collection of *Esilio* (Exile) poems principally manifests the typical characteristics of social poetry. Not lacking, however, are more intimate moments, like those of "Io son l'autunno, tu la primavera" (I Am Fall, You Are Spring), dedicated to his poet friend Plinio Bulleri; or of "Alla finestra" (At the Window), pertinent perhaps to the first period of his stay in America, when he was still filled with nostalgia for Italy.

ESSENTIAL BIBLIOGRAPHY

Bertelli 1940, 73–74, 87–88, 111, 129, 133; DBI; De Ciampis 1958; MOI; Piemontese 1974, 192; Vezzosi 1991, 141–149.

May First

The furrows watered by your sweat
produce harvests for your bosses,
down down, underground, in the dark terror,
you mint coins for the rich barons.
    You live in hovels, erecting palaces,
for those who do not fight you die in battle,
at great banquets, waiting on the tables,

you serve submissively, you blessed rabble!
    Hoping, hoping you wait for something
from new bosses, from new parties,
but you remain victims used,
for days, for months, for years betrayed.
    Forward! The oppressed straightened their backs,
pushing forward serenely, an era is dying,
they broke in fury the old chain,
to an era raising hymns of peace and love.
    Arise, comrades, we are millions,
we are life, we are history,
arise sounding the red songs,
arise comrades, we are victory!

I Am Fall, You Are Spring

To my friend Plinio Bulleri

    Of the land where flowers
perfume the air all year, and nightingales
    warble in the shadows,
where the sky is blue and the soil is green,
where oranges and sycamores grow
    on the slopes of the Apennines,
where man is poet, woman poetry,

    the language harmony,
you make me hear the songs again!
    Oh! The household gods
my first youthful illusions!
The first dreams of my mind!
    I thank you, O Plinio,
for you remember what I loved so greatly.

    Yet I no longer know how to sing.
I am prey to a tedium that constricts my heart
    I who dreamt of glory
of dying in battle, triumphant,

I have long learned to despair.
   Speak to me of songs,
that I may dispel the shadow of dishonor.

On the Gallows

   Are you vacillating? What? Are you trembling, executioner?
The soapy rope is around my neck,
The crowd is inpatient and yells "die"
so satisfy the depraved throng!
   I know you, you rabble, and I despise you,
beggars brutalized by serving;
I am accustomed to your ferocity,
but you cannot make me die!
    I am a giant compared with you pigmies,
for I am mind and will,
I am justice and frighten the guilty,
I am strength, rights and duties.
   Come! Pull the rope, you wretches,
I laugh at you! Make me die?
I am eternal in boundless time,
no one can kill me: I am the future.

Italy in Black Shirts

   From the Alps to the sea, where in other days shone
the city of Scipio and Catullus sang,
the divine Raphael painted
and whose marbles Vinci immortalized,
   where the fugitive Ghibelline wrote,
and a Genoese the world contemplated,
where every science and every art resided
and the great Enotrio of liberty sang,

Lanzichenecchi[1] with daggers armed,
from the Monviso to the Sicilian cliffs,
martyrized the chained slaves.
    Leader of the thousands, from your Caprera
arise and awaken the red shirts,
from the Alps to the sea that shame now rules!

❧

Nighttime on a Street Corner

    She said: "You're not wrong, you're old,
and I am little more than a girl,
but in my small room there is a mirror
that every day tells I am pretty."
    "You can reject me, but the moral,
please keep it to yourself, I have to eat,
I don't want to die of hunger in a hospital,
and virtue doesn't feed me."
    "What I sell is all I have,
is that why you consider me disgraced?
My sweet mother lived honestly,
just to die at thirty of hunger."
    She stopped, lowered her head, whispered
then in pity: "Go, I am the one who is wrong,
your wife must be waiting for you, when
you kiss her think of me!"

❧

At the Window

    All alone I look at
the mud and filth on the street,
while rain falls
and tedium descends upon my soul.

1. The Lanzichenecchi were German mercenaries who sacked Rome in 1527.

People pass by, and are silent;
not one child's cry is heard,
not one flower is on any sill,
not one house has a balcony or garden.
Not one person singing or smiling,
they are all deep in thought, they are all in a hurry,
smoke is everywhere,
that damned mud is all around!
Oh! golden sunsets
of beautiful May, that adorns the hedges with flowers!
Oh! perfumed nights,
shimmering with the light of the moon!
Oh! shining stars,
like the bright eyes of a dark haired girl!
Oh! almonds in flower!
Oh! hawthorns with a delicate perfume!
Gentle violets,
Symbols of modesty and candor!
Ah! I am so far away
from that sweet, eternal springtime,
in this new homeland
that feels so foreign to me!
Flowers of my mother country,
on the hills I loved so greatly,
sweetly perfumed flowers, tell me,
will I ever pick you or smell you again?
I dream of you while here,
sweet poetry of another land,
while rain falls
and tedium descends upon my soul.

All translated by Maria Enrico

Brief Discourses

ᗐ *Alberico Molinari*

Cremona, Italy, November 1876–Bardonecchia (Turin), Italy,
September 15, 1948

"For eighteen years, I have fought at your side in a whirling alternation of enthusiasms, of dejections, of warlike episodes, and I would not exchange these eighteen years for any other period in my life." Thus, in July 1921, Alberico Molinari, departing for Italy, took his leave of the columns of the *Avanti!* of Chicago, and from his socialist companions. In Italy—or better, in Turin, where he would establish himself in 1923—many difficult times were anticipated. Meanwhile, in the harsh struggles in the socialist battlefield, Molinari vigorously supported the Second International in contrast to the communistic direction of the Third International. Molinari also took part in the congress of Rome for the formation of the Unitary Socialist Party of Turati and Matteotti. Subsequently, upon the advent of Fascism, Molinari was imprisoned in Turin, Milan, and Rome, then underwent five years of confinement in Sardinia for having participated in the secret association Giovane Italia (Young Italy). His daughter Medea was also arrested. Molinari continued his clandestine activity until his liberation, and finally, he was subjected to a brief but agitated postwar period in the PSIUP (Partito Socialista Italiano di Unità Proletaria), then in the PSLI (Partito Socialista dei Lavoratori Italiani).

   Born to a family of landed proprietors and taking his degree in medicine in Modena, in 1903, Molinari completed his studies in mental illnesses, in Turin and Paris. By 1900, he had already begun to contribute to the socialist press and, in particular, to *Brescia Nuova* (New Brescia). He was arrested the first time that very year, and in 1902, a second time. In the autumn of 1903, he departed for New York, leaving his wife and one daughter in Italy.

Molinari succeeded Serrati as leader of the Federazione Socialista Italiana (FSI, Italian Socialist Federation) and director of *Proletario*. Joined by his family in 1905, he combined his propaganda work with medical activity among the miners of Wilkes-Barre and of Scranton, Pennsylvania. In 1908, he founded the fortnightly *L'Ascesa del Proletariato* (The Rise of the Proletariat), of which he published thirty-nine issues. Very active, he did not fail to catch the attention of the consular authorities of Philadelphia, who in 1909, as Rudolph Vecoli writes, noted how "in all the places Molinari visited, there were socialists and anarchists; there, where several years earlier, one did not know any person not filled with reverence and love for the country."

In 1911, in Chicago, Molinari assumed direction of *Parola del Popolo* (Word of the People), and for a decade was still occupied with militant journalism and immigrant health. Reformist, supporter of gradualness, tenacious adversary of the anarchists, he opposed the invasion of Libya, in the name of an ideal of international solidarity of the proletariat; and on this theme, he composed the one-act play *La bandierina di Carlo Marx* (The Flag of Karl Marx), printed in Chicago. On the occasion of World War I, he allowed that socialists might fight in defense of the independence of their own countries, convinced that the defeat of the central commands would signify a democratic awakening in all Europe. In that period, *La Parola* had much trouble with the police and, in an effort to avoid scrutiny, was renamed first *La Fiaccola* and then *L'Avanti!*

The salient trait of Molinari's personality, however, was that of the educator. From this point of view, *L'Ascesa del Proletariato* provided clearer examples. In *L'Ascesa*, actually edited wholly by him, Molinari concentrated material whose end was to "arm the brain" of the oppressed workers, or better yet, first "arm them with anger"; therefore, the newspaper published articles on themes like the private American monopolies; the history of the American workers' movement; scientific discoveries; the theories of Marx, of Darwin, of Lombroso; writings about pedagogy; and so on. An example of this production is the *Discorsi brevi* (Brief Discourses), reproduced here, writings originally published on the first page of the newspaper and then collected into a volume. Other collected writings include *I martiri di Chicago: Episodio storico* (The Chicago Martyrs: Historical Episode); *Ai primi albori del movimento rivoluzionario negli Stati Uniti d'America* (At the Dawn of the Revolutionary Movement in the USA); *Teorie di Cesare Lombroso spiegate agli operai* (Cesare Lombroso's Theories Explained to the Workers); and

Catechismo della Costituente (Constitutional Catechism), published for the political Italian elections of 1946.

ESSENTIAL BIBLIOGRAPHY

MOI (article by Rudolph J. Vecoli); Toselli 1951; Vezzosi 1991, 149–151.

Shake Off Inertia

Socialism is yet to come. The essence of the socialist movement lies in the preparation of consciousness in even the smallest ways.

The word propagandist is assimilated into the word socialist.

Today he who is not a propagandist is not a socialist either.

Are you awake to what matters while others are sleeping?

Your need in this world is not to sleep—it is to awaken him who sleeps;

Because your liberation and the liberation of your comrades must be your own effort and that of your comrades.

Shake off inertia–sharpen your mind–strengthen your will.

Become a propagandist.

Do You Know That Type?

Do you know that type of "half-consciousness"?

That type of socialist—yes, but a friend to priests and bosses?

Lion in word—lamb in deed?

The first in line when the flag and the music come out—absent in the struggle for strikes, elections, propaganda?

Do you know this "half-consciousness"?

That type of—socialist, yes, but above all a friend to his own interests?

Strident for battle–but afraid to expose himself to fire?

A great subversive, yes, at the bar, where the more he drinks the more revolutionary he becomes?

Poor "half-consciousness!"

Simple, light-weight, flimsy, a half-man.

No, do not rail against him—but do not count on him.
Poor "half-consciousness!"

∾

Knowledge and Courage

Two things form the socialist consciousness: knowledge and courage.
   Two things block socialist propaganda: ignorance and cowardice.
   Many do not know.
   Many play roles in the world that oppose their own positions.
   Many know and rightly feel it, but fear annihilates them.
   Knowledge is something that is acquired.
   Courage is something innate.
   Help will come from awakened know-nothings.
   Never from cowards.
   Let us abandon the cowards and nurture the know-nothings.

∾

Your Woman

Your woman has the right to all of your respect.
   Do not commit wrongs against her that you would not accept from her. She is not your subject nor your subordinate nor your servant.
   She is the good partner of your life. Keep her high at your level and she will be persuaded to have a mission in life and at your side. Ask her for cooperation not obedience.
   Ask her for advice not submission.
   Love and respect your woman.
   Within the family, she is just as useful and necessary as you.
   She struggles and suffers as much as you. She has as many rights and duties as you. Your aspiration for equality among men is something sacred.
   But in the meantime begin to establish equality within your family. Respect, love, sacrifice, mutual support.
   At the very least, do not do to your woman what you would not want her to do to you.

～

Your Own Person

Take care of your own person.

It is not only a question of health or decency; it is a question of self-respect.

As soon as you return from work, make one last effort to conquer your fatigue.

Undress and wash up and put on your best clothes, and immediately you appear clean and different during the last few hours of the evening. They can say that you are illiterate, but not that you are a slob.

They can say that you are afraid of guns, but not that you are afraid of water. So that people do not avoid you, twisting their mouths and thumbing their noses.

Methodically devote even twenty minutes a day to yourself. Your hair, face, teeth, body, clothes, shoes only need quick attention. You will feel your morale uplifted. You will feel more human.

Spending time with your comrades, you will feel their respect increase.

The person on the street, the boss, the person in-the-know will address you in a completely different tone.

Try it today.

～

Your Reward

Your efforts towards intellectual advancement entitle you to a reward.

This reward is someone's admiration. But the question is this: whose admiration do you want to inspire? Do not strive for the admiration of someone who knows less than you.

This kind of admiration is too easily achieved and is unproductive.

It keeps you down—it does not raise you up. Strive for the admiration of those who know more than you. Its cultivation is arduous—but the fruit is delightful. It is a sharp prod to always do more.

It is proof positive that you are worth something.

Always look to the best within yourself and take sweet satisfaction from their assent, the reward of your efforts.

～

Emotion and Reason

Watch out for him who is ruled by emotion.

Tomorrow he will change if a different and stronger feeling appears in his field of consciousness. He will be a pendulum that swings, not due to changing external events, but due to his own internal shifts.

Do not trust emotion.

The concrete foundations, to which you must apply your subversive consciousness, are logic and reason. If your convictions are a correct and reasoned interpretation of the facts, they will not be the honey or the wax that melt with a ray of emotional heat. They will be eternal, because in this world facts obey laws that do not change.

Emotion is like alcohol—it gives one courage and fervor but dulls the mind. Emotion is the atavistic and negative faculty of our brain.

Man has but one sincere friend: and it is reason.

Distrust emotion. Stick to reason.

Talk to Your Child

Talk to your child continuously. And talk to him seriously, as you would an adult.

Teach him all that you know—at home and outside draw his attention to every fact and thing, large and small.

Even if he does not understand, your words are not wasted—a few traces will remain in his mind.

Carefully cultivate your child's mind.

Give him the impression that you are his friend and his teacher, and he will follow you.

Take charge of his mind if you do not want strangers to take charge of it.

Do not abandon your child—the priest and the boss lie in wait.

Take pleasure in his company and devote your free time to him.

Mould his character with extreme care—as you would with a statue.

Make him a hardy soldier of your ideals if you do not want to see him—one day—marching under your enemies' flag.

Today's neglect will become your pain and humiliation tomorrow.

Do not forsake your child to others—cultivate his mind and make him in your own image.

∾

To Defend Socialism

Speak if you thoroughly know what you are talking about.

If you talk about socialism, be sure you understand it.

Because to defend socialism one needs to understand it, and to fight against it one also needs to understand it.

For you nothing is more important than to understand socialism.

For it is true that it holds your redemption and the redemption of all slaves like you.

∾

Act Methodically

Act methodically.

Do not warm yourself before straw fires.

Do not be the braggart for a single day every now and then.

Become the methodical woodworm that gnaws all year round.

Act methodically.

Method means order, consistency, and precision.

In science, method is everything.

And industry advances as much as the method advances.

And the farmer loses his crop if his method is defective.

Spreading an idea is work like any other.

It requires method, that is, order, consistency, and precision.

Map out the plan for your work, and be mindful of your efforts and your environment.

Then study every minute detail—and work on each detail with diligence.

If you want to be an effective militant for your idea, it is true, work is required.

But work is not enough—it requires method, that is, order, consistency, and precision.

∾

Do Not Have Any God

Hold neither any god nor any man above you.

Grant that above you there is only "human society."

Because it is everything—and you are part of it.

Because its interest is also your interest;.

Because if you are its servant, it is and will always be your servant.

If you meet with a man who is superior to you in physical strength or intellect or character,

Do not think that he has any right over you.

Human dignity is not humbled in front of those qualities.

It is equally sacred in him and in you.

Do not ever bow down—do not ever humble yourself.

Let alone before the boss who exploits you.

Worker! They have chained your arms, don't let them chain your mind.

Prisoner of war, at least save your honor and your dignity.

❧

You Will Become Tolerant

One sprout has grown tall and robust—another has grown small and thin.

The mysterious reasons were contained within the two seeds and the soil.

In both sprouts there is neither merit nor guilt.

You have become a socialist while your comrade has become a bigot.

The mysterious reasons are biological through heredity, and social through the environment.

Neither you nor he is to be praised or blamed.

This is positivism.

Look at your bigoted comrade from this point of view,

And the hatred and contempt and anger will fall from your mind.

You will become tolerant. Learn to not get angry. Do not take offense if others do not think as you do.

Do not isolate yourself. Surround yourself with the ranks of the slaves; sit with them; reason with them, and preach your faith. Respect them and they will respect you. Call them and they will follow.

❧

We Do Not Want to Hate

Do not envy those who are doing well. Only wish that you too will do well.

Hatred and envy are negative feelings. Instead, the desire to improve your condition is a positive feeling. In fact any social progress grows out of this positive desire of the human soul. The same thing appears in nature.

The root fearlessly turns toward the good soil; the leaves decisively turn toward the brightest light;

The wild beast risks its life a hundred times for a better meal. And you, what will you do for yourself, for your children, for your class? We do not ask you to hate or envy. We ask you for the desire to do better.

Do you have this desire? If you do, come with us, and we will teach you how to fight and win.

Your Class

You belong to the "class" of the exploited. Your boss belongs to the "class" of the exploiters. You will steadily improve your condition only by improving the condition of your "class." If you are a believer in this principle, you have "class consciousness." If, individually, you extract an improvement from your boss, the improvement is the emptiest thing in the world.

It will be taken away tomorrow—or it will be taken from your children.

But if your entire "class" plants a flag over an enemy trench, the achievement goes down in history. The improvement remains stable over the centuries. When you think of the best, do not think only of yourself or your family. Think of your "class"—worldwide army of victims. Fight, suffer, and push with "class consciousness."

Do Not Ever Settle

Do not ever settle but sow discontent. Christ brought war and discontent. War and discontent brought philosophers, scientists, reformers, all the pioneers of advanced civilization. He who settles sleeps.

Humanity would still be in a primitive state without discontent, the demon scourge. Discontent is initiative, desire, faith, progress, and conquest. Do not ever settle but sow discontent. A worker who is content with his lot is his own enemy, your enemy, and the enemy of the entire working class. He is blind and deaf to his misfortunes and those of his comrades. He is the boss' ally—and dead weight on the feet of the liberated worker. For you there is neither peace nor truce until you have made him discontented.

Translated by Giulia Prestia

Four Poems

Arturo Giovannitti

Ripabottoni (Campobasso), Italy, January 7, 1884–New York, New York, 1959

A complex intellectual figure, perennially astride two worlds, Giovannitti is one of the rarest cases of an Italian American writer who, despite the extraordinary reception accorded him within the American culture, strictly speaking, did not ever abandon the ambiance of the Italian community. His case, similar to that of Emanuel Carnevali, in reality differs exactly because the latter, a full member of the circle of American poets, had no rapport, in practice, with Italian American poets, though he did have one with Italian poets. Giovannitti was an ethnic mediator; his companions of the various socialist locals were close to him, and some of them, in particular, Antonino Crivello, often dedicated themselves to translating his English poems into Italian, or even Sicilian dialect. Giovannitti, moreover, never abandoned the Italian language, in which, in fact, he wrote some of his most beautiful pieces.

The son of a pharmacist, Arturo Giovannitti left home at seventeen years old. He emigrated to Montreal, Canada, where he attended McGill University and became a Protestant pastor. In this role, he moved to Pennsylvania and worked with the miners. In Springfield, Massachusetts, he began to be attracted to socialism. Finally, in 1905, he arrived in New York, where he attended Columbia University and joined the Italian Socialist Federation (FSI). From that moment, he began his period of maximum political and syndicalistic commitment. Even further, he took directorship of the *Proletario*, but above all, he undertook an intense activity as propagandist in the most heated phases of the workers' war. In 1909, he was in Westmoreland, with Joseph Ettor; in 1912, again with Ettor, he participated in the textile strike of Lawrence, Massachusetts, where he was accused of homicide and arrested, along with Ettor and Joseph Caruso. Put on the stand in the legendary trial of Salem, he delivered an apologia, in English, that became famous and was published several times, in Italian as well, and which identified him as a charismatic leader. In prison, meanwhile, Giovannitti had composed, "The Walker," perhaps his most famous piece, which in 1912 appeared in the *Atlantic Monthly*, and was judged by Louis Kreymborg as better than Oscar Wilde's *The Ballad of Reading Gaol*. Highly esteemed in the milieu of the political and intellectual left, eminent exponent of the IWW, he contributed to *The Masses* and *The Liberator*; founded and directed *Il Fuoco;* and was included in histories and in anthologies of American poetry, for example, as compiled by Untermeyer. Giovannitti underwent a new arrest, for anti-American propaganda, that is, for being a pacifist. After 1920, he was among the organizers of the committee for the defense of Sacco and Vanzetti, and then, without interruption, one of the acknowledged leaders of the anti-Fascist movement and of the committee formed after the assassination of his friend Carlo Tresca (who, like him, had always been intolerant of every rigid military discipline).

The distance between the two veins of his production, English and Italian, constitutes a problem of no small moment for the critics. Giovannitti, the American, has a potent voice, a visionary and solemn eye, liberal meters, a tone recalling Whitman, but tempered by more modern experiences, like the themes and tone developing in *Poetry* magazine, which was born in Chicago in 1912, the very year of the strike at Lawrence. Giovannitti, the Italian, expresses himself in a voice that has something older—a private lyricism, one might say, with the force of a natural effect. It is not by chance that he preferred the mother tongue for its more elegiac and intimate components. In every case, he displayed a mastery of the meter and a lexical richness and meticulousness really rare in the Italian American panorama.

In the last years of his life, when, he was sickly and forgotten, he lived in retirement with his companion Flo and had reduced his public activity to the periodic meetings of the Circolo di Union Square (Circle of Union Square) promoted by sculptor Onorio Ruotolo and composed of Antonio Calitri, Italo Stanco, Pietro Greco, and a few others. He also contributed to newspapers such as *La Parola del Popolo* and *Divagando*. Giovannitti formed a friendship with a young poet from Puglia, recently emigrated, Joseph Tusiani, who left a moving remembrance of him, and who is in some way his inheritor, also struggling between two worlds, two languages, "*due parole*" (two ways of expression), that can never quite be mutually exclusive.

Giovannitti's first book was the collection *Arrows in the Gale,* which was published in 1914 and presented by Helen Keller. It was followed as late as 1957, by *Quando canta il gallo* (When the Rooster Crows), this publication a sort of tribute rendered for him by his old companions of the *Parola del Popolo.* A large volume of his poetry, *Collected Poems,* was prepared posthumously in 1962. In the forty years that separated his first from the second book of verses, Giovannitti dispersed his poetical production in a myriad of newspapers, by and large political and syndicalist, and committed some writings to pamphlets of political propaganda, even those not his, issuing from the IWW and from other organizations. This was the case, for example, of *Come era nel principio (Tenebre rosse)* (As It Was in the Beginning [Red Darkness]), a pacifist drama in three acts, performed in New York, by Mimì Aguglia, in October 1916, and published in 1918. It is set in France in the Argonne, at the beginning of World War I.

ESSENTIAL BIBLIOGRAPHY

D'Attilio 1994; Giovannitti 2005; Peragallo 1949, 124–128; Pernicone 1999; Prezzolini 1964; Sillanpaa 1987; Tedeschini Lalli 1981; Tusiani 1988; Untermeyer 1919.

∾

"O Labor of America: Heartbeat of Mankind"

Come, then, come now, sweat, sooty red-eyed,
flame-scorched vestals of the eternal fire of
steel and coal and steam and wood, and stone
and tools that make bread and surcease from want and woe.
Human machines actioned by hope and ambition
and oiled with blood, miners, stokers, hammersmiths,
builders, converters, puddlers, engineers of chasms,
escalators and defiers of the Babylon heights—
O Labor of America, O heartbeat of Mankind,
Come before and beyond all authorities, rules, edicts
ukases, injunctions and excommunications and
foregather and proclaim yourselves in the great
deed of Liberty.
For you have lightened the night of your dream
Even to the humbling of sunrise.
Welcome, dark, fierce cities, daughters of volcanoes,

hearts and matrices of the new world—
Duquesne, Homestead, Calumet, Buffalo, sleepless and
tortured and flint-faced.
And you, Braddock, fevered with an endless
Contemplation of the Satanic glow,
And you, Pueblo, titan-limbed, monster biceps
bursting in the almighty effort of gestation and
agony of the implacable fecundity of our
ferocious industry.
And you, McKeesport, mountain-ribbed, and you
Akron and Youngstown, rubber-thewed, washing
your stolid blank faces in your rusty creeks,
And you, astraddle the Styx and the Acheron,
Pittsburgh, wrathful resting grave of
spent meteors, gateway of Hell,
All ye, unhallowed grails of the last eucharist of sweat,
Welcome to the home of Labor, the last stricken
Archangel,
For your resurrection has come.
Detroit has its hand on the lever,
Gary maneuvers the brakes
And Chicago, feeder of the world,
Rules the switches of the two-fisted earth.
If this is not the fullness of your glory,
O American Labor, there is your New York,
Cosmopolis of Mankind,
Whose towers you raised to mock the hurricanes
and to shame and debase the clouds,
Whose harbor swallows the nations, whose
people, myriad-tongued,
absorb and reshape and amalgam
all creeds, all races in one humanity.
Stand up, then, and take the earth unto your bosom,
Gather the oceans in your mighty cupped hands,
Cleanse the heavens of the scourges of the black demons
Of war, hate, fear and death and destruction,
Remold and reshape the soul of mankind
Into brave exploits of compassion and the dazzling

splendor of reason and brotherhood.
Take most of our bread to the starving,
Whoever they be, wherever they be,
Fill your countless argosies with milk and honey
For the livid parched lips of the children
Of your erstwhile enemies and your detractors,
Uprise the fallen heroes, sustain the weak,
Comfort the widows the orphans and the bereft
Tear down the gateways to freedom to the imprisoned,
Turn the flood gates of light upon the entombed in darkness
Dry up the tears of shame and remorse
From the eyes of the harlot and the thief,
Smoothe the scowl of hate and revenge from the brow
of the earth
And make of all her children the new, eternal united
Israel of mankind.

And now we as Italian-Americans bow in
both humility and pride as we ask you
to stand by and acclaim
your brothers from the land that
gave a new hidden world to the world.

From that venerable mother of
America, from the land of
ecstasies and sorrows, of
Ancient glories and unbearable
humiliations,
From the garden of the earth, from the
only land of many tender and mystic names:
Etruria, Augusta, Enotria, Esperia,
Saturnia, Vulcania, forever Italia,
we call upon you to stop her weeping over
earthquakes, eruptions and floods,
and the desolation of ancient and new battlefields,
to mingle with you in an everlasting embrace
in amity and liberty and love.
Let our two nations, the Mother and her

last Child march on together indissolubly until
we weave forever
A shroud to all oppression
A bridal gown for the young earth,
Till we build together,
The city of the Sun,
The new Jerusalem,
The Peaceful House of Man.

∾

To Mussolini

A man may lose his soul for just one day
Of splendor and be still accounted wise,
Or he may waste his life in a disguise
Like kings and priests and jesters, and still may

Be saved and held a hero if the play
Is all he knew. But what of him who tries
With truth and fails, and then wins fame with lies?
How shall he know what history will say?

By this: No man is great who does not find
A poet who will hail him as he is
With an almighty song that will unbind

Through his exploits eternal silences.
Duce, where is your bard? In all mankind
The only poem you inspired is this.

∾

Malebolge: Mulberry Street

Despots behold! The desolate houses lean,
Hell's innest barbicans, against the skies
Along the tortuous moat of his latreen.

The archangels that rebelled against your wise
Commandments are here tortured in this pit,
As you may hear from their discordant cries.

The damned are these who sinned against your writ,
The wayward who in their wild errant modes
Did all the things for which you were unfit.

Piling above the clouds your white abodes,
Plowing the earth for you, filling your marts
And burrowing through your subterranean roads.

Hark now unto the creaking of their carts,
The calls of ear-ringed bawlers, and the sturdy
Whistles of your policeman who imparts

Your penalties to them; list to their wordy
Quarrels and bargains, and above the din
The plaint of the sad-throated hurdy-gurdy.

Smell the foul wind of woe that blows within
Their cells, whence even the daylight recoils
At the polluting stenches of their sin.

The fetid garlic of the brew that boils
Between the sunfire and the stove beneath,
The vats where fume the sweats of unclean toils.

The crusty lips of babes that gasp for breath
Torment them so, that tho' be great their guilt,
So bitter is their doom that less is death.

Mulberry Street is this. The domes they built
Are not here, Despot! Here is where they mold
And shall decay until their last seed wilt.

Pursuing their mad dreams through ways untold,
They spread through all your lands and all your seas,
Eating black bread and lavishing bright gold.

Peddling their dreams, their songs and fantasies
And quickening with the fevers of their blood
The pulse of your ferocious industries.

All that they made they never thought it good.
All that they loved, they never could revere,
All that they wished they never understood.

Slothful and sleepless, lustful and austere,
Gloried by death, made deathless by rebirth,
The progeny of Rome, Despot, rots here!

Yet pity not, for here dwell faith and mirth,
And to the future still they reach their hand
That thrice led forth mankind and held the earth.

Their house of bondage is within their land
Of promise—but their haven they'll attain
When blares the clarion of the last command.

If they pay now in full with shame and pain
The price for having shunned your monstrous feast,
Tomorrow they shall rise and win again;

For they who gave the most and asked the least,
But dwelled in royal state in every sense
Of their fierce flesh, are all men the freest.

And if they seek nor praise nor recompense
'Tis that they have all things in their grim lot;
The memory of an old magnificence,

The pride of earth-old glories unforgot,
A strength unsapped, a dream inviolate,
The power to see beauty where 'tis not.

The magic of the lyre that softens fate,
For their new love a flower and a song,
And a stiletto for their ancient hate.

And lo! out of this evil maw erelong,
Born of their indestructible desire
And nurtured with the bitter milk of wrong,

Passing invulnerate through flood and fire,
Shaking the sloth of ages, they'll convoy
The chariot of the Hound who from this mire

Will lift them to their heritage of joy.
He will heal all their wounds and blot their scars,
And with red tongues of wrath he will destroy

You, Despot, and the trophies of your wars,
And lift the young Republic's head above
The diadem of her reconquered stars!

For though she closed her door to them and drove
With chains of want and scorn their august clan,
She still remains the daughter of their love.

Aye and of all the names the lips of man
Have uttered since the day they set to roam
And their long quest for the free land began

On which to build at last their gateless home,
America, no word of glowing fame,
Nor even the eternal name of Rome

Beats faster in their bosom than Thy name.

Samnite Cradle Song

Lullaby, baby, mamma's own child!
Who sang the evil dirge about thee?
Thou camest in March time, wee as the tart
Berries of hedge thorns, pale, as the wild
Roses that have a wasp in their heart.
Who has to thee the witchy words spoken?
Who read to thee the malevolent star?
Who cast on thee the spell of the dead?
A hunchbacked wizard thy cradle has broken,
A lame old fairy embittered my teat,
And the blind priest with unblessed water wet
At the font thy poor, innocent head.
Thou art so sleepy, but numb are my arms;
Thou art so cold, but chilled is my breath;
Thou art so hungry, but dry is my breast.
Lullaby, hush-a-by, baby mine, rest,
Sleep for thy mother, who is tired unto death.

Lullaby, baby! The corn was so full,
The vines were so heavy, the season so pleasant,
And happy, so happy, the heart of the peasant,
Who was preparing and sweeping the bin
For the new wheat that was bristling so fine,
While his nude youngster was laughing within
The casks he was scrubbing to fill with new wine.
But God dislikes them whose heart is content,
God loves only them who starve and bewail;
And so he sent us the wind and the hail.
All has been carried away by landslides;
All has been buried beneath the brown mire;
All has been ruined by storms and by tides,
Nor vineyards nor orchards the water did leave.
The mice now dance in the empty meal keeve;

The ashes are cold of the last cauldron fire;
The dams and the flood-traps the torrent has torn;
And poor we! the mill that once ground our corn
Now grinds away the last hope of the land.
Lullaby, baby, the morning is nigh.
Hush-a-by, baby, thou must understand,
The tale of my woe is as long as thy cry.

Lullaby, baby, thy grandfather plowed
And thy father mowed the grain,
And thy mother winnowed the chaff,
And at evening many a spool
Spinned with spindle and distaff,
Threads of hemp and threads of wool.
But granddaddy was broken and bowed,
The land was hard, the winters were cold;
But thy father was twenty years old,
So they took him away and sent him to war.
One was old and one was young,
One was weak and one was strong,
One was too tired to till the sod,
One was fresh in the heart of spring.
So thy grandpa was killed by God,
And thy daddy by the king.

Lullaby, hush-a-by, baby mine, sleep,
    Lullaby, softer than thine is their bed!
Mother will sing thee, mother'll not weep,
    Mother'll not mourn for the dead.

Lullaby, baby, grow strong and brave!
They are no longer hungry now;
Only us two the bad luck smote.
The gravedigger took away the goat,
For digging an eight-foot grave;
The curate has taken the sow,
For saying mass by the biers;
And the Government for its toll
Has taken the earrings from mine ears,

Lullaby, baby, they took our all,
The walnut chest, the iron bed,
The silver brooch, the marriage ring,
The black fichu in which I was wed;
I have not even a scarf to mourn
And honor my young love forlorn
And the faith I swore to him.
I have only the sack of straw,
The bident with the broken horn,
And the medal which the law
Has sent to thee, an iron thing,
Which in his honor bears the trace
Of his young blood upon one face,
And on the other side the grace
Of God about our gracious king.

Lullaby, hush-a-by, baby mine, sleep,
    Lullaby, softer than thine is their bed!
Mother will sing thee, mother'll not weep,
    Mother'll not mourn for the dead.

Lullaby, baby, the winter is near,
The mountains put on their clean hood of snow.
What shall I do? Where shall I go?
In the sieve there is no more flour;
In the bin there is no more coal;
In the jug there is no more oil.
What shall I do, my desperate soul?
Am I to die of hunger and cold,
Or beg for bread from door to door,
Or be a wanton about the inns?
Ah, what do I care what I shall be,
What do I care, so you do not die?
My grief shall stop where your joy begins
And our good day shall surely come by.
And when it comes, and I am in my grave
Or past the age of thy pride or blame,
If I keep true to all that aid me,
Give back a hundred for one they gave,

But if I rear thee with sweets and with shame,
Lullaby, hush-a-by, harken, my life,
For every dollar of silver they paid me,
Give back a stab with your father's keen knife.

Lullaby, hush-a-by, baby mine, sleep,
    Lullaby, softer than thine is their bed!
Mother will sing thee, mother'll not weep,
    Mother'll not mourn for the dead.

Lullaby, baby, the rope is so frayed
That down the well soon the bucket will dart;
The whip is broken, the yoke torn in twain;
But see, how sharp is the hatchet's blade!
The ass has broken away from the cart,
The hound has shaken and slipped from the chain
And I am singing away my fierce heart
Just for the rage of the song, not the pain.
Behold, the dawn fingers the shadows dispel,
Soon will the sun peep at thee from the hill;
The cocks are crowing, the starlings grow shrill.
Wait, and my song with the matin's glad bell
Shall fill the mornings with omens of glee.
For now no longer I sing unto thee,
Mamma's own wolflet, the tale of my woe,
But now that the sun is near, my man-boy,
The night is gone, and my sorrow will go;
List to my prophecy, vengeance and joy.

Lullaby, baby, look! Our great king
With all his princes and barons and sons,
Goes to the church to pray to the Lord.
Ring all the bells! Fire all the guns!
For all the chapter is wearing the cope,
And the bishop himself will sing the high mass.
How came this vision to me, my wild hope?
How came this wonderful fortune to pass?
Behold, the bishop lifts up the grail;
The king is kneeling upon the gray stone;

The trumpets hush, the organ heaves deep:
"*Te Deum laudamus*... We praise thee, O Lord. . . .
For all thy mercies, Lord, hail! all hail!"
Hush-a-by, lullaby, listen! Don't sleep!
Lullaby, hush-a-by, mark well my word!
Thou shalt grow big. Don't tremble! Don't fail!
The holy wafer is but kneaded dough;
The king is but flesh like the man with the hoe;
The axe is of iron, the same as the sword;
This I do tell thee and this I do sing.
And if thou livest with sweat and with woe,
Grow like a man, not a saint, nor a knave;
Do not be good, but be strong and be brave,
With the fangs of a wolf and the faith of a dog.
Die not the death of a soldier or slave,
Like thy grandfather who died in a bog,
Like thy poor father who rots in the rain.
But for this womb that has borne thee in pain,
For these dry breasts thou hast tortured so long,
For the despair of my life, my lost hope,
And for this song of the dawn that I sing
Die like a man by the ax or the rope,
Spit on their God and stab our good king.

Sleep no more, sleep no more! Show me you know,
Show me you listen, answer my sob!
Drink my blood, drain my heart! Just one sign . . . so!
Bite my breast, bite it harder, mother's tiger cub!

Four Poems

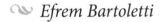 *Efrem Bartoletti*

Costacciaro (Perugia), Italy, 1889–Scranton, Pennsylvania, 1961

Miner, poet, and revolutionary syndicalist publisher Efrem Bartoletti emigrated to America in 1909. He worked in the mines of the Iron Range and fought in the Western Federation of Miners. In 1919, he went back to Italy and became mayor of his hometown, but then abandoned the responsibility, together with all the communal socialistic administration, to avoid the continual violence of the Fascists.

Bartoletti's "heroic" season coincided with the epoch of the great strikes of the IWW—first of all, in 1916, those of the miners of the Mesabi Range, about which he reported to the readers of the *Proletario* in a series of letters from Duluth. In 1919, Bartoletti, who was also the shop boy of a baker, published his first collection of poetry, *Nostalgie proletarie*, made up of poems that for the most part had already been printed in the *Proletario* and were dedicated "to the proletarians, to the martyrs, who work in two hemispheres and sweat, work and die, victims of the predatory bourgeoisie." Already represented in the book are the two principal themes of Bartoletti's poetry: the first, Umbria, its landscape, the vivid emotions it evokes in memory; the second, a decisive, inflamed social inspiration, a song of battle dedicated to registering the most memorable events in the history of the proletariat. Here are, therefore, compositions against the war in Libya, against World War I ("Ecatombe italica"), but also, for example, "In morte di Giovanni Pascoli":

Hail! From the hearts of all, even the rebellious,
Rise and resound over the ocean the shout:
Only he said it to us; he called us brothers.

The "function" of Bartoletti, who "to the proletarian cause . . . contributed with his poetry and other writings, which themselves drove a nail into the heart of emboldened capitalism" (as was written in 1919 in *Il Nuovo Proletario*; cited by Vezzosi, 59), is evidenced by the fact that some of his compositions, like the "Canto dei minatori del ferro" (Song of the Iron Miners) and the "Canto dei minatori del rame" (Song of the Copper Miners), were written for music and used as true and actual revolutionary hymns.

> It was the period when the Russian rebellion was taking place:
> . . . A people of giants
> Worthy of a future, certain that it is that one
> That emancipates itself, emancipating
> Suffering humanity. . . .

And, in fact, Bartoletti dedicated sonnets to Lenin and Trotsky.

After his return from Italy, he established himself in Scranton, Pennsylvania, also a mining zone, and joined the socialists, "militating in the anti-Fascist field, at least until 1940" (Vezzosi, 59); then he turned his efforts to the Italian constituency of the SPA (Socialist Labor Party). According to Mario Pasquale De Ciampis, in 1938, the congress of Italian American trade unionists of Brooklyn proposed him as the director of *Proletario*, but Bartoletti declined the offer. He continued to write poetry, accenting perhaps a more intimate vein, without, however, forgetting his revolutionary past—in fact, always honoring the figures constituting his heroes. In 1955, in Italy, he published *Riflessioni poetiche* (Poetic Reflections), which also contains sonnets dedicated to him by Rodolfo Pucelli at the beginning of the 1950s, and by Pasquale De Amicis, publisher, in 1912, of the *Operaio Italiano*, a weekly of Altoona, Pennsylvania:

> Distinguished carver of sonnets,
> Of green Umbria sings the Sun of May,
> And signs himself, Miner Bartoletti.

Over time, Bartoletti used various pseudonyms, among which, "Etrusco." In 1959, he published his last collection of poetry, entitled, *Evocazioni e ricordi* (Evocations and Memories).

Alfonsi 1989; Bartoletti 1919, 70–71, 88–90, 117–118; Bartoletti 1959, 66–67; Comune di Costacciaro (Perugia), 2000; M. P. De Ciampis, "Un cantore proletario," *La Parola del Popolo* 54 (October–November 1961), 50; ; Marazzi 2001, 92–95; Vezzosi 1991, 59.

The Mays

May returns, the May of the brave
of red flowers and green flowerbeds:
toward the East, it seems, we lift our gaze;
let's look at the new Sun!

    Here, he rises! On his golden beams,
engraved in great gleaming letters,
glows the motto of destiny: Bread and labor;
respite of pain and privations!

    Let's rise up therefore. Liberty, flare up
in hearts drugged with foolish inertia:
soar above the infertile fields
in a howl of revolt.

    We suffered too much! Lacerated to pieces
we were and are wretched cadavers;
from thousands of strong human torsos,
Hunger grimly roared.

    Vain was the howl, since then they served
lead for bread seasoned with bludgeon;
and in that squalid and dark prison
the betrayed pariah died.

    Lawrence the undefeated proletarian voice,
Ludlow and Mesaba the daring and warlike;
Calumet starving and derelict
and Paterson the audacious.

    Voices also of the equally obscure heroes
of scorned and fallen humanity,
the young widows and the orphans who

afterward were raised in sorrow,
    how rabid you were and what an enemy
of America, o villainous, bourgeois wolf,
who starves and murders to satiate your
ancient wrathful hunger.
    But the day will come, even if in a distant future,
when the great May completes this vengeance:
tremble, because a vigilant and righteous eye
lies in wait every hour.

HIBBING, MINN., 30 APRIL 1917

∾

In Memory of Joe Hill

    Joe Hill falls. The bullet-riddled corpse
is now received by the land of the Mormons,
it reproaches the evil, and warns the powerful,
of Salt Lake City.
    He rests, the murdered singer, rests,
young Gracchus, in the mute grave;
never again will melodious rebel songs
gush from his lips.
    Who killed him, what brute force
severed the lifeline of such a courageous soul?
Who would boast in this deadly age
of murdering prophets?
    The sacred were praised in those good remote days,
and surrounded by golden myrtle or laurel,
never found guilty in front of a firing squad
and assassinated.
    Infamous age, that in red blood
falls into the abyss of time,
go, mark yourself with your shames
and crimes.
    Go, he banishes you, and don't ever return,
murderous age, iron age, era

without justice in which Capitalism
rules with force:
    innumerable are your martyrs, your dead;
and among those not forgotten, rises up
Joe Hill the prophet of rebels, proud
agitator.
    Tall he stands, and to the proletariat shouts,
naked he reveals his bullet-ridden chest:
Rise up, o laborer, may your rights
be avenged!

Not for nothing did I fall. From the murderous
lead of Spry that crushed my heart
the reiterated portentous challenge
is taken on by gods!. . . .
    Oh yes, trust, o Martyrs! Your cry
is the legacy of every rebellious slave:
you too will see from your sepulcher
the day of vengeance.
    Be placated for now, gentle bard. Let
your thoughts fly freely beyond that place,
where next to the Great Salt Lake your
lifeblood rests.
    By the thousands flowers grow on the pious
sod that re-encloses your mortal remains,
your flowers ardently yearned and sighed over,
hero of Utah.
    You will not die! The ferocious bourgeoisie
tore your heart, but couldn't tear your solemn songs;
for these your name will appear eternally next
to Ferrer and Bruno.
    Shade of Morrison, governor Spry
tremble therefore; and you cheerless Mormons,
turn pale even in your temples:
Joe Hill will not die!

HIBBING, MINN., 15 NOVEMBER 1916

༄

The I.W.W.

To be or not to be
among beings with life;
to live, or not to live;
that's the bold question!
    Free acts and thoughts,
conform to the existence
of the entire human race
and to human knowledge.
    Reclaim for the destitute
their violated liberties
and shatter the chains
of all their dereliction.
    Wash the shame of centuries
suffered by the oppressed;
make the mighty and humble even,
emancipate themselves.
    Equal work for men,
and equal compensation;
sons of a free world
wherever you walk.
    And eternal war on despots,
on the Rich, and Capitalists;
on hypocritical religions
on the sword and the pastor.
    Death to Bellona: emerge
from nothing to unity;
Announce peace among people
Equality and Liberty.
    The untamed iconoclast
who prepares to demolish;
the Great Union, the Enemy,
the I.W.W. that's who!

∾

Remembering Carlo Tresca

To cry for the dead was never a shame
especially if the dead was worthy of lament
from the common people who suffer
under every oppressor's blow.
    To cry for the dead, out of ancient instinct,
was the custom, and crude death commends
flowers for the coffin, the grave or the urn
for every lost human.
    In diverse and salient assembly,
we bring therefore a fresh crown
of red flowers sadly to the urn
of the proud Carlo Tresca.
    For the tireless unbeaten Agitator,
struck by the furor of an unknown hand
in the uproar of a street where pitch black
rendered it almost distant.
    In the great heart of New York where unpunished
too often they go and remain, these hired killers
today much better off than bandits,
accustomed to massacres, to gunfire.
    O battler Tresca, I remember you
when you were our brother and leader
in Minnesota in that fatal endeavor
with the King of iron miners.

I see you again across the continent
in America going there wherever
a workers' battle was rising up
in a factory or a mine.
    I remember you then when in the conflicts
of Lawrence you excited wretched crowds
where Ettore and Giovannitti were saved
from the infamous pyre of planks.
    We remember you when you tried to tear
Sacco and Vanzetti from the legal gangs,
together with others who know how to hate

violence in every street.

    We are reminded hourly of when you agitated,
with the fluent urgency of your sermons
in a Franciscan beard, and you confronted
with calmness the threat of prisons.

    You also, like every other tormented mortal,
had your flaws and unfounded biases,
but these in good truth generally
became eclipsed.

    You deserved therefore another fate
that is, one of time-honored veneration,
a placid sunset and not a violent
and execrable death.

    We are reminded of you . . . But from such
vibrant vitality now nothing remains
but only a little mourned ash,
that sad remembrance.

    Rest, o great Apostle! He will not escape
from Justice who acted to murder you
and was motivated to carry out
this ignoble mandate.

    All translated by Peter Covino

The Fire

∽ *Vincenzo Vacirca*

Chiaramonte Gulfi (Ragusa), Italy, 1886–Rome, Italy, December 25, 1956

Vincenzo Vacirca was born into a middle-class family in 1886. By 1902 he was a member of the Socialist Party of Italian Workers. That year he organized the first union of peasants in Ragusa, and he was arrested and imprisoned for about a month. Editor of *Azione Socialista* (Socialist Action) of Brindisi (1904), *Parola Socialista* (The Socialist Word) of Ravenna (1905–1906), and *Secolo Nuovo* (New Century) of Verona (1907), he also wrote the social novel *L'apostata* (The Apostate). Condemned for subversive publishing, he emigrated to Brazil in 1908, and there directed the daily, *L'Avanti!* (The Advance) and published the novel, *Disertore* (Deserter). Arrested and expelled from Brazil, he went to Argentina, where he remained until 1911, and published *Gli italiani nella provincia di Mendoza* (The Italians in the Province of Mendoza). Imprisoned, he was released through the intervention of the socialist deputy Enrico Ferri. Reentering Italy illegally, he fled to Trieste and Pola, where he published *Istria Socialista* (Socialist Istria). Expelled from Austria, he then left for the United States.

In New York, between 1913 and 1919, he published *Lotta di classe* (Class Struggle); in Chicago, *La Parola del Popolo* (The People's Word); in Boston, the daily *La Notizia* (The News) and socialist weekly *L'Internazionale* (The International). In New Orleans, in 1915, during a meeting to oppose the war, he was hit by two gunshots fired by Italian nationalists. On May 5, 1918, in New York, he debuted his pacifist drama, *Figlia* (Daughter). In 1919, after having published the pamphlet *L'Italia e la guerra* (Italy and the War) in Boston and the book *La Russia in fiamme* (Russia in Flames) in New York, he returned to Italy, where he was quickly arrested.

697

He was released through the pressure of Turati on Nitti, the head of the government, and in November, in Bologna, he was elected deputy. In 1920, he went to Russia, where he interviewed Lenin, Trotsky, and other Communist leaders for *L'Avanti!* Between 1921 and 1924 he was attacked by the Fascists, but he escaped unharmed from a long series of attempts on his life in Ragusa, Modica, Noto, Avola, Vittoria, Bologna, and Alessandria. After he was reelected deputy in April 1921, Matteotti sent him on a mission to London in 1924. On his return, he stopped in Switzerland, where he founded the *Libera Stampa* (Free Press), the socialist daily of Ticino, and published *La monarchia e il fascismo* (The Monarchy and Fascism).

Condemned to five years in prison by the judges of Siracusa, Vacirca returned to the United States, where the Fascists did not cease to pursue him. In Newark, in 1925, one of his meetings turned into a brawl, with gunshots and a knifing. In 1926, he was deprived of Italian citizenship, and his goods and property were confiscated; in 1927, he fled for the *n*th time from the ambushes of hired Fascist assassins. In that same year, in the newspaper *Il Solco* (The Track), which he founded in New York—where he had already founded and directed *Il Nuovo Mondo,* the first anti-Fascist daily abroad—he published the novel *Il rogo* (The Pyre). He also wrote the anti-Fascist dramas *La ragnatela* (The Spider Web), which premiered in Old Forge, Pennsylvania, on March 13, 1932, and *Madre* (Mother), which premiered in New York on March 1, 1935, and was published in Chicago. In addition, he contributed to the *Stampa Libera* of Boston.

In 1933, he was constrained to leave the United States, pressured by the Italian Embassy, and he went to Spain, but six months later, he was in America again. Between 1933 and the end of World War II, he engaged in an intense propagandistic activity, founding and/or directing newspapers and reviews, among them *Il Minatore* (The Miner, 1934) and *La Strada* (The Street, 1938), through whose presses he published *La crisi americana* (The American Crisis, 1940). In that book, which dealt with the problems of the Great Depression, he concluded that the Depression would last as long as there existed a regime based on the monopolistic ownership of the means of production, distribution, and exchange, and that the workers' movement, being limited to a unionist function, was unable to attack the root of the evil. For this reason, it was necessary to establish a great labor party with branches in all the forty-eight states. In 1942, he published a biography of Mussolini, *Storia d'un cadavere* (History of a Corpse), written in 1933.

In 1943, recruited by the Office of Strategic Services, he was among the first to disembark in Sicily, where he was engaged in the local socialist federation, oriented toward reform and semi-secession. In January 1944, he presented a project for regional autonomy to the Allied administration, but it was greatly criticized. It constitutes a chapter in the history of Sicilian independence. In 1946, he established himself definitively in Italy. In Palermo, he published *La Sicilia Socialista* (Socialist Sicily) and in Rome *La Giustizia* (Justice). He participated in forming the PSLI (Partito Socialista dei Lavoratori Italiani), and from a rigorously anticommunist position he directed the party nationally from 1949 to 1952.

Among his various novels, *Il rogo* is the most representative of his long experience in the United States. He narrates the love story between Sirio Campesi, a socialist activist, and the sophisticated, fascinating Elena Mauri. A second woman also enters the action: Lucia Turlà, daughter of an Illinois miner killed by a gas explosion in the mine. Remembering the friendship between her father and Sirio, Lucia visits Sirio in New York, where he is in search of employment. The friendship between Sirio and the young woman reaches the point of being transformed into a more profound connection, but Sirio's tie to the dynamic militant Elena is too strong. Lucia finds work in a textile factory together with Chiaretta, Elena's sister, and both die in a suspicious fire, set for motives of speculation that destroys the factory. In this plot, Vacirca includes some powerful descriptions of the metropolis and the peripheries where the working class lives. *Il rogo* strongly aspires to a distinct modernity, though clouded by a certain obsolescence in the language. It passionately probes into the psychology of the personages and devotes great attention to the urban landscape of New York, to the masses, to the traffic, and to the topography, which is delineated with punctilious precision.

ESSENTIAL BIBLIOGRAPHY

Marazzi 2001; MOI; Terranova 1965.

They came out from their nightly refuge as dawn was beginning to light the city. A cold and foggy dawn that seemed to be born from the deserted streets, quietly chasing away the last remaining shadows gathered in street corners, under arches of doors and the corners of the window sills in the homes of men, around the leafless trees in the deserted piazzas.

They moved towards the first newspaper stand and loaded themselves with printed paper that still smelled of fresh ink.

All the front pages of the various newspapers were studded with large titles forcing themselves to express in weighty words of dread and terror the horror of the tragedy. The first stories on the tragedy, a variety of dramatic episodes in nervous narratives, were confusing. They were written quickly with the professional preoccupation to be the first to inform the public and to give the greatest number of facts, details and particulars.

Elena and Sirio's eyes ran rapidly along the newspaper columns, skipping lines, devouring words, quickly stopping to read titles, looking in silent apprehension at the names of the victims, the dead and the wounded, whose names appeared here and there in the lines of the paper. They could not find the names they were looking for. The ones they came upon were unknown to them.

They learned that the number of the dead had grown to around two hundred, mostly girls. The wounded were twice that number. All the hospitals in the area had admitted some patients. Some firemen had died in their heroic work to save the victims. The losses were estimated to be in the millions. The building was literally destroyed. Enormous quantities of goods were reduced to ashes. The surrounding buildings were damaged and on the verge of collapse. The wind, that in the early hours of the morning had finally calmed down, and the excessive cold that froze the water in midair, made it difficult to extinguish the flames.

A first rapid inquest had created the suspicion that the fire was due to arson. A firm, in precarious financial conditions and heavily insured, had caused it. The flames had spread too fast, more rapidly than expected, while on some floors of the building the workers were lagging behind. The elevators were the first to catch fire. The exits were insufficient. The fire escapes, old and not in good shape due to lack of maintenance, collapsed under the weight of the mob that was trying to escape. The lack of human responsibility made the horror of the tragedy even worse.

The morning newspapers only had vague indications of what really happened. Elena, reading those vague sentences and guessing at what those words could reveal about what had really occurred, felt the pain that was breaking her life apart multiply within her. She pointed the incriminating words to Sirio, while from her throat, hoarse from the cold, and weary from insomnia came the accusing word:

"Murderers!"

There was almost no human quality left to her voice. Sirio heard it echo within himself while a shiver ran through his veins. He looked at the woman and she seemed profoundly changed. Her face, so sweet in the proud beauty of its oval shape illuminated by two clear sparkling eyes, had abruptly changed. The lines of her face became suddenly drawn and frozen in an expression that made her look harsh, almost ferocious. Her narrow lips had erased any sign of softness from her beautiful sensual mouth. It wasn't only pain that sculpted itself on her face but a new will and passion, maybe dormant within her spirit for some time, that bloomed, freed by the burning echo of the homicidal fire.

"Sirio," she continued, clinging desperately to her friend's arm, "They murdered them. I now feel that all hope is gone. Most of the names of the wounded and the bruised are here. What are missing are the names of the dead. Because the dead don't speak."

After a short pause, while Campesi listened to her in silence, unable to find words to express his pain and to alleviate those of his loved one, she added, with a decisive tone that meant more than the words themselves,

"We will speak for them, for all of them. We, the living, the ones left behind. This crime cannot go unpunished. Gold! Gold! Gold! Damned, cursed gold! To go after it, men walk over bodies. Avarice and greed killed them. Ah! That factory! It was a deadly trap. They attracted poor young girls with the promise of bread, like a small mouse with a small piece of cheese. Then the trap is closed. The flames enveloped it and the girls were roasted. Murderers! Murderers!"

She was so excited, and her cries had such a subhuman quality that Sirio began fearing for her sanity. He tried to calm her down.

"Be strong, Helen. Remain calm. Maybe fate was less cruel to these two, at least, than we fear. Let's go. There is a hospital nearby where many of the victims were taken. Let's go, we'll ask."

They began moving towards the hospital.

"Now I understand, Sirio, now as never before, only now. I understand your passion, your work, and your efforts to awaken the sleeping, to give energy to the listless, to shake up the indifferent, and to inflame the cold souls. I was one of them. Love had attracted me to you, breaking the crust of my egotism. It was, however, a tough and tiring effort, an act of will, a fragile construction of my conscience. Now, instead, it is pain that binds me to you, that pain that has destroyed any vestige of my old egotism, the fire, the fire that incinerated my sweet Chiaretta has freed me of all the residue of my past. Sirio, Sirio, now, only now, purified and renewed by these flames, I feel that I am yours, worthy of you, your friend and your partner—forever."

The words came rushing out of her mouth, with a new eloquence, moved and excited by a new miraculous strength, suddenly born in her, overflowing with an irrepressible and overwhelming force. They walked quickly, almost running, the soles of their shoes echoing on the asphalt of the deserted sidewalks, their steps springy and strong. Sirio listened to her speak, dazed by the inner turmoil awakened in him by her words. The immense tragedy filled him with inexpressible anguish, but the revelations of this woman, that he now felt was definitively his, sent a shiver of joy through him that remained stifled and restless in the whirl of his thoughts.

At the hospital the reality of the tragedy came into focus again and with it new signs of cruelty. In the atrium groups of people, men and women, young and old, waited. A small crowd, pained and tearful, their faces undone from suffering, from lack of sleep, from weariness and, above all, by the anxiety punctuated by cruel doubts.

Some were arriving while others left. In groups of four, six, eight, an intern accompanied them along the corridors. The majority returned to the atrium, their faces devastated, their shoulders bent, their eyes bloodshot from crying as they left in silence, while others arrived. Now it was Elena's and Sirio's turn. They were shown a register with names: these were the names of the wounded, the injured, and the ones that almost suffocated but were reanimated. They both read avidly: nothing. They then re-read the names with more care, still nothing. Then the nurse brought them to the ward where the critically wounded and the unconscious were, those impossible to interview, and the dead who, having passed into the kingdom of the afterlife, were waiting to be identified by the living.

Stretched out on white cots, grouped in small rooms, some in twos, some in fours, lay the bodies of young girls, mature women and the occasional gray-haired older person. Some had their heads bandaged, some an arm, or chest, or a leg wrapped, some had faces as white as sheets, while others had black faces covered with sores. The eyes of the young couple rapidly scanned each bed, looking away from one bed with a definite sense of pity and horror, to stop and look at other faces and other bodies. They did not see the faces they were looking for. With a heavy heart, rapidly and violently beating, that felt like it would explode and leave a hole in their chests, they entered and exited a number of rooms, leaving behind them a wake of moans and sighs.

The spectacle of the dead young girls, suffocated or burned, or horribly deformed in their mad attempt to escape death by jumping from a window on the eighth or tenth floor, was unbearable. More than once Sirio, who was holding Elena by her arm, felt her waver to the point of losing consciousness.

They left that first hospital as the city was beginning to come to life. The trolleys drove by with that deafening noise that sounds like a long roar, the trains rolled by on their elevated tracks with that horrifying sound of screeching metal, the cars were sliding along the asphalt filling the morning fog with the strident and hoarse sounds of their horns, while the sidewalks filled with working people on their way to their daily labors, and the cafes and lunch-rooms opened for business. The city was awakening, still a touch drowsy, and began to resume the daily rhythm of its feverish life.

For a few hours, the young couple suffered a veritable *via crucis* as horrible as that of the carpenter from Nazareth, laden with the heavy cross of his crucifixion on Calvary. They visited three other hospitals, and each was a renewal and a worsening of that first spectacle of pain and horror.

At every stop, Elena felt a bit of her life evaporating away. She felt as though her body was bruised and wounded, and that she was losing blood from the invisible wounds that left her veins empty. Sirio, more used to the strain and the pain of the situation, had more strength to resist, but he felt himself beginning to lose all the courage and tenacity that he had called up from within himself with a supreme effort of will. Finally, that which they feared and expected happened. They found them in the same room, laid out on linen cots next to each other, as pale and white as lilies, their eyelids closed by the attending nurses, their hands crossed across their chests, with a serenity that gave them the appearance of two sleeping saints who had returned to the womb of their maker. Lying there they seemed happy to have abandoned a place that is only a waiting station, waiting for that invisible and swift train that will carry us to our eternal life, the final destination of our earthly voyage.

"Chiaretta! Chiaretta! My adored little sister."

Then, a scream cut through the air and Elena threw herself on the inanimate corpse of the child. Sirio, shivering throughout his whole body, had bent over Lucia's corpse caressing her cold and pure forehead with his lips. The fate of the Turlà family manifested itself to him in all its tragedy. The father killed in a coal mine in a poor village in far away Illinois, the daughter killed in a factory in the middle of a city that was full of work and pleasure, sin and wealth.

He then approached Chiaretta's cot, on which Elena, having regained her senses and aided by the two nurses, sat, bent over, staring at Chiaretta's motionless face with hard bloodshot eyes. The two young girls had been found side by side on the floor, in a corner of the vast laboratory, suffocated by the smoke. The flames had not even touched them. The firemen who had picked them up and brought them out had hoped that they had only fainted. At the hospital, doctors and nurses tried their best to bring them back to life. But their motionless bodies never took another breath. Elena and Sirio remained in that small bright white room for a long time, the pure translucent whiteness forming a cornice around the two innocent creatures that Death had kidnapped in the Youth of their Life.

All hope and illusion had vanished forever. The terrible reality was there, simple and inescapable, incredible and certain.

Chiaretta and Lucia. Yesterday two vibrant lives, two beating hearts, two worlds ready to sprout and flower, rich in infinite possibilities of the unknown, looking to the future. Now, two lifeless little bodies, cold and still, two colorless faces, one under a halo of blond hair, the other under a velvety shadow of black curls. And in a short time, even those relics of what they had been, would be swallowed into nothingness, returned to the womb of the Earth. . . .

Two days passed. Two days that Elena and Sirio continuously lived suspended in a nightmarish atmosphere that did not seem real, an atmosphere of desperation. The friends who rushed to help, Rodrighero, Francesco Delmi, the Burkes, Elena's brother Paolo, and Elena's exuberant friend, Miss Mira Adams, with their affectionate presence, were not enough to separate them. The tragedy that had just played itself out under their eyes, all the hours full of anxiety and anguish they had suffered together, had formed new and lasting bonds between them. Then came the hour of separation and of uttering a final good-bye, the hour in which the pain of the crowd resurfaced to boil over and seemed to spread across the cruel city, envelop her in its funerary mantle, and win its ferocious indifference, subdue its brutal egotism, thaw its heart of steel and stone in a torrent of lava, burning with anger and pity.

All the bodies of the victims, the ones sacrificed, were arranged in a long procession of funeral cars covered with garlands of flowers. All the flower shops of the neighborhood, of the city and states near and far were emptied, and those flowers flowed into New York, to render homage to those poor girls, many of whom had never received the gift of a rose.

The emotion and excitement had first affected the working class of the East Side, and then, in various waves, it had engulfed all the social classes.

For a moment, New York seemed to have reacquired its humanity. The incessant and savage hunt for the almighty dollar appeared, at least for a short time, forgotten. The wild chase after pleasure was suspended. The thousands of small but fierce individual egotisms, forgotten. The city became of one heart, magnanimous, immense, gigantic, and full of love. The spectacle of two hundred girls who had died such a cruel way, in one immense catastrophe, had created a unified current of human passion, in which all individual reactions were lost in a vast oceanic tremor of communal agony. The funeral procession was greater than any emperor, than any leader, than any victorious soldier, than any universal poet had ever received. The whole city had interrupted its incessant work, placated its feverish movement, to embrace the bodies of those unknown children killed by that work and by that fever. It seemed that the collective soul of the city unknowingly felt the burden of that dreadful crime. That one and all took on a certain responsibility for the massacre; that one and all were suddenly overwhelmed by the burning need to make amends.

In the boundless crowd Elena and Sirio stood, confused and lost in it like two drops of water that have fallen into a muddy river. Around them, all their friends of happier days were now sharing in the common grief. Mr. John Burke had lost the boyish smile that brightened up his round, blonde face, and his wife, Mrs. Bessie Burke, maybe because she forgot her makeup and lipstick, looked ten years older. Paolo Mauri was silent and gloomy, so much so that no one would have imagined him to be the raucous and joyous friend of Mira Adams, whose usual rose colored cheeks had become pallid and the radiance of her eyes clouded by her weariness. Rodrighero was walking with his shoulders hunched over and his eyes looking at the ground, a look of anger rather than pain across his face. Francesco Delmi was the most depressed of the whole group. The refined characteristics of the musician showed traces of depression and anguish. That air of light sweet melancholy that never abandoned him had changed to a feeling of desolation that is only brought on by irreversible disasters.

Elena and Sirio kept moving within the circle of affection that surrounded them, immersed within the mourning multitude, almost unable to gather unto themselves their own intimate and personal suffering, so much did the agitated wave of the great collective drama hold them in its grip, confining them, removing them from themselves. Heavy, slowly, oppressively, the procession went on for many hours. Masses of black flags, gardens of flowers in procession, music that permeated the air with metallic sobbing and rhythmic laments. And above all an atmosphere that was heavy and humid and a gray sky . . . The funeral cars advanced slowly, a long black meandering procession, and behind and around them the crowd. The crowd, the crowd. It seemed that those two hundred bodies came forth from its bosom, detached from its flesh. In those faces one could see the tragic sensation of a common destiny, of the profound identity of the individual and the species even in the infinite variety of the single lives. The pity that they felt for the victims was nothing more than pity for themselves. The sense of a refound collective brotherhood for an hour, was nothing more a more vigilant love for themselves, a more reasoned egotism. But nothing took away from the sincerity, the spontaneity, and the majestic beauty of the sorrow that enveloped the countless multitude like a sacred work that cleansed it of all its vices, all its obtuse stupidities, and all its baser animalistic and hedonistic instincts. A long shiver diffused itself along the immense procession that rippled uncertainly like a sea ruffled by the wind and then stopped.

The funeral cars had stopped at one of the large steel bridges that stretch out over the East River connecting the island of Manhattan with Brooklyn. There the funeral procession had to stop. The crowd, having finished its rite, dispersed flowing back into the streets and houses of the metropolis. The bodies were to proceed alone from there to the various cemeteries, accompanied only by family members and intimate friends that wanted to complete the homage of pity and render them back to mother earth.

And the rite was completed. The last shovel of dirt fell on the two little corpses of Lucia and Chiara. Bundles of flowers fell on the black earth. A last, gracious gesture that concluded the swift drama of their young lives.

And then, inside a car, racing across the city that slowly returned to its daily frenetic pace, Elena and Sirio, alone, having escaped the suffocating embrace of the crowd, had become themselves once again. Alone, facing each other, mirroring each other, each reflecting the other's wounded soul. They did not say anything because words were useless. They both felt the sensation of having survived a ship-wreck. Around them, everything had collapsed, humanity had vanished, perished. Alone, on a barren rock in the middle of an angry sea. Alone, like Adam and Eve after having lost the Eden of their innocence. And the car continued on its course over the asphalt street, breaking suddenly, darting through and around traffic jams, slowing down and quickly speeding up as soon as the road in front cleared.

Where were they going? To them, it seemed that they had lost all sense of reality. It felt as though an unknown hand had cut all the invisible and tenacious threads that tied them to life. The automobile they were riding here appeared to them more fantastic than Charon's vessel. Towards what frozen destiny, what fiery fate were they being driven? The automobile stopped. It had arrived in front of Elena's house. They got out and entered the main door. Sirio stopped in the hall-way. He stretched out his hand towards Elena in an indefinite gesture that even he could not say if it was to take his leave, or if it was a gesture of supplication or of brotherly affection. Elena took his hand and looked into the eyes of her friend. Then, on her face a smile began to appear, light, like the breath of a bird.

"Are you coming up?" she said to him. Together they went up to her apartment, where they had not been alone in a long time. They entered the empty house. In the living room, in a corner was the marble bust of Elena that he saw molded by the hands of Rodrighero. He remembered that evening in April when he had entered that house for the first time. It had been almost a year. And all that had passed between them during that year appeared rapid and lucid to his memory, awakening drowsy echoes, and rekindling in his blood the flames that the anguish of the last few days had turned off. He looked at Elena who was standing, watching him and seemed animated by the same thoughts. She again broke the silence that weighed over the room, buried in the twilight of a dying gray winter day.

"Stay, don't leave me alone."

The words rang clear and distinct. Sirio caught them in all their meaning. His heart beat violently. He approached her slowly and took her in his arms, and their lips met in a first, long kiss where their pent up passion of flesh and spirit broke through all the stops, pulled down all the obstacles in an instantaneous, violent and joyous explosion born of the depth of their grief, and, in an uncontrollable rush, all the force and power of Life flowered from the disintegration of Death.

Translated by Paolo Giordano

In Union Square Park

 Onorio Ruotolo

Cervinara (Avellino), Italy, 1888–New York, New York, 1966

Onorio Ruotolo spent his infancy in Bagnoli Irpino, Campania, and then went to
Naples, where he was a student of the sculptor Vincenzo Gemito. In 1908, Ruotolo
moved to New York, to exercise his art and to win notable fame. In 1925, together
with Attilio Piccirilli, he founded the Leonardo da Vinci Art School, which constituted an important point of reference for the Italian American community, even
though Ruotolo was accused several times, by Carlo Tresca, of holding an ambiguous attitude toward Fascism. Soon, the members of the Circolo di Union Square
were frequenting the art school, gathering in Ruotolo's study, which, upon occasion, also drew all the intellectuals of the first generation. In 1988, Tusiani rendered
a lively, affectionate description of this association.

   Ruotolo was a person of distinction in the Italian community. Jack London
and Theodore Dreiser, Enrico Caruso and Rodolfo Valentino, Giuseppe Antonio
Borgese and Helen Keller all posed for him. Ruotolo was also celebrated by, among
others, Frances Winwar, who in 1947 wrote the monograph *Ruotolo: Man and Artist.* Aside from sculpture, Ruotolo engaged in other artistic activities, becoming a
promoter of many initiatives. He edited the *Quaderni* of the Circolo di Union
Square, the first number of which presented a new Italian translation of Giovannitti's English language poem, "The Walker." He participated intensely in political
debates, representing typical issues of his cultural environment and his generation, always standing midway between a strong patriotic Italian identity and an
equally strong socialist adherence. Among others, Ruotolo was a very good friend
of Arturo Giovannitti, whose work he translated and defended in arguments with

the writer and critic Emilio Cecchi, who had not understood the value of Giovannitti as a poet. He published poetry and articles in the *Parola del Popolo*, *Divagando*, and other periodicals. He also published historical-critical writings in
pamphlets and reviews on the Sacra Sindone (Christ's Shroud) and such figures as
Michelangelo, Canova, Jacopo della Quercia, Donatello, and Leonardo, as well as
Antonio Meucci and Fiorello La Guardia. One collection of lyrics, entitled *Accordi
e dissonanze* (Harmonies and Dissonances), was published in 1958 by Convivio
Letterario.

ESSENTIAL BIBLIOGRAPHY

Fichera 1958, 41–43; Marazzi 2001, 97–99; obituary of Bruno Zirato in *La Parola del
Popolo* 83 (February–March 1967): 43–44; Schiavo 1965; Tusiani 1988, 201–205.

∾

Those who have never seen you
Or don't know you very well
Are almost afraid of you,
Little privileged park
In Union Square;
Where the New Deal's wise rebuilders
Gave shelter to the statues
Of Washington, Lincoln, and Lafayette.

Writers have painted you
A den of red madmen,
Fomenters of strikes and treasons,
And instead you are nothing more
Than a sweet shadowy oasis
For the disappointed, bewildered, unruly,
For the conquered, for survivors, for the destitute,
And for all the weary travelers
In that endless desert
Of hot human sand,
Manhattan,
The chaotic imperial city:
Oh shunned and slandered!
Little green and wooded island
In Union Square.

A hundred languages and accents
Change places, cross paths
And mingle freely
In the most diverse debates,
Among the most foreign ethnic groups,
Shouted every day,
Assembled in the shade
Of the beautiful Starred Flag
That flaps in the wind, in the sky above
That narrow but free space
In Union Square.

At the sides of the white paths
Making a cross that shapes
The grassy esplanade—
There are, sitting or even lying down
On wood-and-concrete benches,
Drunks and the homeless,
Snoring with open mouths,
The starving, the weak, the dull,
Scattered among the pairs of lovers,
Of every color, age, and costume,
Smooching, embracing,
Murmuring words of love
In the traditional manner
Of Union Square.

Here, a pale and slender poet,
Staring wildly, yes, but surely in love
With a beautiful notion or a beautiful woman,
Entrusts to his frail papers
His inspired thoughts:
Writes, blots, rewrites;
Pauses; contemplates for a bit
The scatter of little white clouds
Behind the great Edison Tower;
Smiles to himself, happy;
He pets a friendly gray dog,
And then, deaf to the hubbub,

Turns to write, for hours more,
Under the limpid blue sky
Of Union Square.

There sits, shabby and uncommunicative,
A bearded, plump old man
With the skull and face of Socrates.
He eyes and lips half-shut,
He seems always rapt . . .
He is a misanthrope philosopher, a madman;
Who is he?—A famous model,
Sought after by painters and sculptors,
And even well known to the regulars
In Union Square.

Further on, a group of the curious
Stare in wonder
At the pleasant improvisations of a shaggy artist,
Quick in tracing likenesses
In graceful or grotesque profiles,
Price twenty-five cents.
He is the most admired,
And, after the pigeons, the best . . . fed
In Union Square.

Strewn in every direction,
They are crouched on the steps
Or leaning against the handrails,
Standing still,
Or dawdling with slow steps,
There's one who smokes a pipe, one who reads,
One eats fruit, or chews gum,
Or slakes his thirst
At the cold spurt of the drinking fountain;
And there's one who only has care and love
For the little winged creatures and for the dogs
Of Union Square.

Around the three circular terraces
Of red granite that form the base

For the bronze "Emigrant Pioneers"
And for the neglected
"Tableau of Independence"
On the gilded monument to the Flag,
Children and toddlers, some pretty, some not,
White girls and black urchins
Cling together, run crazy in circles,
Egg each other on, make a huge racket
In pure brotherhood,
Drunken with innocent gaiety. . . .

Only the fatherly eye
Of the Martyr, liberator of the slaves,
Humble, caped,
And ruefully smiling,
Immobile, watches them, protects them,
From high upon the broken pyramid
Of his unadorned pedestal,
In Union Square.

Under the heroic statue
Of the noble Father of the United States,
First Soldier and First President—
Rather, under the rump of his horse
From its arched and flowing tail,
Crowd the most heated radicals.
It seems this is the site
Best loved
By the Tribunes of pure American blood,
For in that place they speak only English
To the wildly varied listeners:
Too often objecting,
And rarely applauding.

There, the most loquacious, the most learned.
The most fearless, the reddest,
The best able to convince,
The best prepared to win by a mile,
To make speeches and examine at length

The most abstruse international problems
Of war and of peace,
Of politics, of economics, of religion,
Of new heresies and of old utopias.

There, the most cunning to put questions,
And the wiliest to reply,
They struggle, they howl,
Booming and threatening.

But, in truth, in truth,
This harmless verbal combustion
Scares no one;
Not even the pigeons, well-fed,
Roosted and drowsing
On the hospitable poplars
Of Union Square.

Why never, never does there take place
Nor perhaps will ever take place—
Without a policeman anywhere—
The simplest scuffle,
The briefest fistfight,
The commonest crime,
Or even the rumor of a robbery
In Union Square?

Maybe because this oasis, an island
Little known and ill regarded,
Out of the way, forgotten,
In the heart of the boundless City,
That seethes with greedy and rapacious beings,
Is a true and complete democracy:
Such that wandering pilgrims
Of every age and race;
Of every faith and of all ideals,
Like its hundred gaily-colored doves,
Find a place of refuge, expression, and peace
In Union Square.

Ah, if they knew you better,
Little park, with no other laws
Than free fraternal tolerance
And mutual respect
For the civil liberty of all! . . .
Then they might then discover,
Your ignorant detractors,
That shining America, wished for
By Jefferson, Mazzei, Washington,
Franklin, Lincoln, and Whitman,
Is honored every day only in you,
Little space of greenery and trees,
In Union Square, in Union Square!

Translated by Robert Viscusi

Fascism in America

〜 *Agostino De Biasi*

Sant'Angelo dei Lombardi (Avellino), Italy, 1875–New York, New York, 1964

A precocious journalist, in 1893, Agostino De Biasi recommenced a local newspaper, *L'Eco dell'Ofanto* (The Echo of the Ofanto, a river that rises in Irpinia and flows to the Adriatic), founded twenty years earlier by his father Giuseppe. Joint director of the *Popolo Irpino*, he initiated a career that carried him to Naples and Rome, contributing to *Il Mattino* (The Morning), *La Tribuna*, *Don Chisciotte* (Don Quixote), and *Il Giorno* (The Day). In 1900, he arrived in New York, was employed by the *Progresso*, and a year later, became subeditor. In 1905, already joint owner and director of the *Telegrafo*, with his brother Pasquale, he founded *L'Opinione* in Philadelphia, and then went to work for the *Araldo Italiano* (Italian Herald) of New York. Involved in various colonial initiatives, among them the Società Dante Alighieri, he polemicized sharply with the socialists—in particular, with Giacinto Menotti Serrati. Nationalist and interventionist, De Biasi was an early Fascist. In 1912, he was the promoter of the first Italian Fascist association abroad, which was in New York City. In 1915, he founded the monthly *Il Carroccio* (an ancient Italian war carriage), which he directed until 1937, with a period of suspension at the end of the 1920s, owing also to his disagreement with the Fascist hierarchy. In 1923–24, he was the secretary general of the Consiglio Centrale Fascista del Nord America and was nominated the Knight Commander of the Crown. In 1927, he published a collection of articles, *La battaglia dell'Italia negli Stati Uniti* (The Battle of Italy in the United States), composed predominantly of polemic articles against the syndicalists and the enemies of Fascism. Reappearing during World War II as a journalist on various minor newspapers, and greeted with sarcasm by the antifascist newspapers (see Glauco, "Il ritorno del maestro," in *La Controcorrente*, March 1947), he contributed to the *Uomo Qualunque* (Unremarkable Man) of Giannini, and in the last years of his life, to the *Follia of New York*, where he republished pages of his recollections and wrote articles on international politics. His biography, in Ario Flamma's 1949 edition of *Italiani di America*, is expurgated of all references to Fascism.

Despite the limits of a rigorous Fascist militarism and a certain patriotic extremism, *Il Carroccio* was the best cultural review produced by the Italians in America. In the review, De Biasi persisted in the defense of "italianità," which he perceived as being always in the breach, as expressed in the title, "Sulla breccia, sempre," of one of his leading articles, published February 16, 1913, in the *Araldo*, against the attempt to introduce heavy limits to immigration. The review, featuring great Italian and American writers, launched a continuous series of Italian American writers, whether in Italian or English.

ESSENTIAL BIBLIOGRAPHY

De Biasi 1927; Flamma 1936 (article) and 1949 (article); Frangini 1907; Franzina-Sanfilippo 2003; LaGumina et al. 2000 (article by N. J. Falco); Schiavo 1966–67 (article).

ↄ

The core of North American Fascism was first established in New York, and the same day Mussolini sent a cable there from Milan. He gave the transatlantic outpost the place of honor in his newspaper and entitled the article: "The Future" (May 1921).

Future! Yes: future.

Fascism once again had to prove its vitality. Not because of its history, nor because of its aims. It did not lack for action. Rather it was because of the peculiar precipitating circumstances in which it manifested itself, the way it burst out and spread rapidly, in its domineering way, throughout the country's life. Precipitating circumstances that, on the surface, could have crystallized into a sharp reaction against the internal disorder in its national structure, and the unstable activity of its rallies.

It is clear that reducing Fascism to mere punitive actions against Bolshevik violence, and to simple functions of electoral seats, would have exhausted it like an empty sack the day after elections. Authority and force would have returned to the State guarded by the very Fascism that had aided Italy when she was perishing from within.

It was easy for Italy's enemies—surprised, terrified and cowardly before the Fascist-nationalist onslaught—to assume that the development was purely ephemeral. Then things would have returned to the way they had been before. Anarchism would change tactics. The necessity for Fascist beatings would disappear. The assault on the State would go better, once the improvised forces sustained by the nation had been dissolved.

The same guardians of order, incapable of defending themselves, constrained by the instinct to conserve their weak flesh and consumed by the Fascist whirlwind—benefited, that is, by Fascism—denied recognizing in "the new force" that part of the eternal truth that comes from the imperious law of the moment, the law of the war Italy had won, the law of its victory, the national and international law of its life. Any blessing had to come through war, if the war was waged for Italy's regeneration and for the renaissance of the Italian people.

Because to win the war would guarantee a new life for Italy—Italy, that before the war was so lost and defeated, so defeated, and so lost, in fact, in spite of Vittorio Veneto, the return of the government of the defeatist scum was tantamount to the dashing of Victory, to the absurd of the absurd, to the horror of horrors.

And yet, Fascism was not really an improvisation, nor a reactionary expedient, nor an electoral expedient of the political moment. But who recognized it?

The Fascists were unable to judge their own cause. The anger of the dispute yielded to the opposite bad faith of throwing shade on—truly, this time—"the sun of the future." Its adversaries denied it; those who benefited from it were still frightened by Fascist violence, they did not pass judgment. Did not the most cowardly desert the voting booths—not because of their fear of Fascist violence, for the Fascists were their protectors, but for fear that their enemies would catch them?

And the shadows continued to obscure the dazzling star on the horizon. But there was *the future*. Fascism crossed the Atlantic. Fascism reproduced itself in the immigrant heart. The distant brothers felt that it was something of their own making, something in their own heart and destiny. Reflecting on their Fatherland, the exiles began to feel that it was truly their Nation.

Not five thousand miles of distance, not the vastness of the seas, not even the corrosive force of all the bitter salt of its immense waters, was mighty enough to challenge the great integrity of the new force that plows the waves and suddenly conquers the distant soul. It is a sign that the vitality of Fascism is incorruptible and ever-lasting. It is a sign that the duty of Fascism does not end at the exact or inexact borders of the country. It does not finish in an electoral dispute, does not limit itself to rejecting violence and the punitive expedition. But it adheres instead to the mission of Italian pride operating in a foreign land, in peaceful forms, honest and civilized, in its culture and work, and in its supreme purpose of making the most of the Victory.

As yesterday, all the Italians of America experienced the rights of Italy in the case of Fiume, so today, following the same ideal line, Italy tastes her joy in Fascism, which has for its cornerstone the vindication of all the rights of Italy's sons, wherever they may be found, with Fiume at the summit.

This adherence of the immigrant soul to the new soul of the Fatherland is nothing new. We must repeat that we emigrants were the precursors of that genuine and disinterested love of the Fatherland that, in the peninsula's outskirts, among many—the exhibitionists in particular—was just "a vain word in flight?"

Nothing new.

What does Fascism want?

Internal order. That is, an Italy that works, that prospers, that inspires its sons overseas with the pride of being a vital part of her esteem from strangers, respect, awe.

The ancient dream of us immigrants, it is the dream that made us suffer humiliation, discouragement, in *diminutio capitis* [loss of status] planned by a foreigner not better educated than us, but always treating us unjustly and arrogantly.

What will Fascism want in America?

The dispatch sent by the Fascist organization of New York and Mussolini's article reveal the general lines of the program that could, and we assure ourselves, *will* be carried out. Other indications found in the local program, were set and established by the founders of New York Fascism. But it is not the details we want to talk about, since program is not the will to action. And it is Fascist action—very Italian that is—that our platform calls for, from whoever is thinking of taking part in the national work, in whatever place he finds himself, high or low.

We demand that emigrants have the right to participate in Italy's national restoration and reconstruction. We intend to link our action, needless to say, in limits set out by American hospitality, *to the action of true Italians in Italy*.

Today we do not see *true Italians* except in Fascism, except in those who under the emblem of Fascism have put an end to the Red terror, to the inconceivable Russian nightmare that the audacity of the Fatherland's enemies, and the cowardice of the Nitti government, made appear inescapable, catastrophically destined, and about to throw into ruin the marvelous architecture of civilization and glorious rebirth of Italy.

We should defend abroad the Fatherland's institutions, that are the proofs of Italy's national nobility and the banners of centuries-old struggles, of sacrifices, of martyrs, of blood. It's the historic right of the race and the uninterrupted continuity springing from the greatness of Rome.

We hold ourselves to be citizens of an Italy upheld by a plebiscite Monarchy, by a Monarchy that is sworn to the constitutional charter of the state and that cannot but serve its most sacred and legitimate wishes. We are subjects of a King who has been the First Soldier at the front with the enemy, and who has the right and duty, on the throne, to feel "the sensation of Victory," the same right that belongs to the most humble of his subjects, the most obscure of his emigrants.

In the company of foreigners, it is not permitted to reflect on differences of parties and factions that are already deplorable at home. It is this understanding that we want to clarify above all, even before the idea that Fascism means the Republic takes root here as well. It is easy to guess that all Italians in America experience themselves as Fascists. Minus the very small minority that does not welcome Fascism, whether in good or bad faith, being at the same time outside the repudiated Fatherland, belonging to no country.

There is the suspicion of that same internationalism that, blind, serves in reality, aside from propagandistic chatter, as a force for other nationalisms in conflict, each predatory and exclusive on its own account. "The Patriotic Revolution" has liquidated the anti-Italy. When we say the anti-Italy, we mean to refer to all that was anti-nation before the war, that was anti-nation before the slaughter, and raged anti-nation after the triumph.

Italy should be judged by the spirit that gathers the spent lips of its 500,000 Dead, the spirit of the trench, not a militaristic spirit, not that of an arbitrary, invading imperialist, avaricious, brutal spirit, but a new spirit of liberty, democracy, civilization—for Italy and for the world.

It is the spirit of the Fasces that is valued. It is the nation's will that prevails. It has followed the destructive spirit and the sense of decomposition with a sense of unity and harmony.

Mussolini says, "We are a movement, not a party, not a museum of dogmas and immortal principles."

He also says, "It is necessary to break the closed circle of Italian political life. To sweep away the old, obsolete, decrepit Italy that is obstinate and does not want to die."

And again, "We should mobilize our forces to create a new ruling class for Italy born from Vittorio Veneto. We should carry out an active and relentless work of selection and refinement, wake up and encourage the energy of new men. We should operate at the head of all the hierarchies without thinking of individual interests or our own ambitions, aiming only at the collective interest of the people and the nation. . . . Italy's tragedy is in a solution of necessity." ("May 4th Speech at the Great Electoral Meeting of the Constitutional Block of Milan").

You may say, have we emigrants not always wanted this new order of things for the Fatherland? Witnesses and participants in life of other States, we were always constrained, in confrontations with others, to blush at some of those holding political power in Italy. There is another salient point regarding the basic national Fascist problem. The political program of Fascism abroad is, in a word, expansionism. We are tired of the rickety policy of being at the bottom of the barrel. Italy should be involved in all those things that interest human kind. Now is also the time to stop living off the glories of the past. It is necessary finally to live and struggle and work for the future.

Foreign policy. This concerns us directly. Yes, government men and diplomats should be involved. But we Italian emigrants should also in great measure be involved. Foreign policy should not be made without the foreigner's having an exact understanding. It should be accepted voluntarily and not imposed. If the Nation is not strong internally, if it is not infused with a national discipline, if it does not project its strength abroad, in its sons, in an action always in a quick, shrewd, determined way, then the only result will be a succession of defeats, derisions, and humiliations. It will be discredited, causing misery to the body and soul.

Foreign policy is something that involves our most exquisite faculties as militant Italians abroad. Therefore, we vindicate our right to participate in the elaboration of it, in so far as it is consented to each person. But it's not enough in the United States of America for foreign policy to be just for colonial consumption. It is necessary that Washington be affected by Italian diplomatic action that is virile, robust, honest and imposing. Now, this should be generated and established by the government, and for that matter, by the Parliament and the People.

From here derives the necessity for Fascist directives. Italy was the victim of an interminable succession of diplomatic errors. We abroad are the most reliable witnesses of the results of those errors. We constantly have seen our Italy relegated to the sidelines, always more absent on the world stage. Washington, London, and Paris decided the destiny of the world. Therefore, the destiny of Italy was sealed and Rome was always silent. Not because silence was golden, but because behind the tongue, the brain was empty, the ganglia did not vibrate, and the back was spineless.

They wanted to erase the United States from our international horizon! What blind folly! What guilt! What crimes, indeed, against Italy. Sonnino could be absolved for everything except the responsibility he assumed in neglecting to consider that America arbitrates war and peace. From that responsibility that not even we, defenders of the Pact of London and Fiume, neglected to denounce *when there was still time to do something about it*—from that responsibility was set in motion the odyssey of our troubles up to Versailles and thereafter.

And with our policy we always remain in the circle imposed upon us by the Treaty of Versailles. The policy of Harding's Administration does not allow room for our errors. It is clear. Furthermore, there is a persistent, rigid, invariable policy in the United States, that has made war in its defense, and wants to see reestablished peace in every corner of the earth according to its interests. If Rome had understood even a tiny part of the foreign policy Washington had forged, how differently things might have happened!

Is it a fact—yes or no—that the settlement of all European affairs will depend on America? Is it a fact—yes or no—that only America has the means to attend to our economic-industrial renaissance? Can we establish an autonomous and independent policy? No. It is clear, we should depend either on America or England. And should we expect understanding in America? Italy should extricate herself from the meshes of the foreign policy in which she is entangled. Italy should give new direction to her proposals concerning international life. Italy should make herself an earnest friend of America.

American supremacy does not frighten us. That is a reality beyond debate. It's a force that cannot be restrained. It's a law that should be accepted. England and France accept it, and we should accept it, especially where it corresponds to our essential interests. What is in the essential interest of Italy is to break the chains of servitude to England, and to leave France, which does not deserve our respect, to the devil.

Finally, there is the debt that Italy owes the United States. In the United States we possess the means of excellent persuasion that can allow us to address the question of Italy's war debt *in a manner different from that of other nations*. If we Italians knew how to speak to America, if we knew how to act towards America, we could liquidate our debt on favorable terms, and find the way to free ourselves from English usury. Fascism will be vigilant in Italian foreign policy towards the United States.

When we have organized Fascist organizations in the colonial centers—the lookouts, the observers for the Fatherland—our ambassador will then find the masses better prepared to collaborate with him. The vanguard of invincible Fascism overseas promises this to Italy from all Italians to Italy.

All this we wrote in May of 1921, in full agreement with the Leader of Fascism. We found, as one sees from his widely reported article, immediate adherence to our proposals. Mussolini understands the foreign policy of the emigrant, that he enhances the value of Italy's forces in the world. When a minister—Crispi and Mussolini are synonyms with this matter—identifies the internal discipline of the country with its influence in the events of the world, Italy will no longer be an isolated, rotating satellite, on its own, in the void, but a complete, luminous, great star in the constellation of equilibrium and world peace.

In May 1921 our ideas were very clear. Should we formulate today another program, with different words and attitude? Yesterday's article is just as good. It is reproduced literally, except some line about a current event that took place that day.

We simply want to observe this. We took a Fascist position immediately in the summer of 1921, and then in the fall during the Washington Conference. We had proposed that the Fascist Party make the basis of foreign policy the action of that parliamentary committee which had wanted to send Washington directly an account of the work of the Conference, *where they had been able to really and truly resolve Italian problems*, removing French and British influence that up to now had muddled things and done severe damage. Instead, in Washington prevailed the stupid policy of that dull-witted midget of Italian politics, Carlo Shanz, with his fearful, cowardly, Jewish-Austrian sentiments.

If Fascism had acted during the American Conference, following the Fascist line indicated by *Carroccio*, Italy would not find itself, apparently by extreme necessity, allied with France, as opposed to the American spirit which is adverse to the foolish French adventure.

Fascism in America, whether it is organized in squads or professed as a national creed, promises solidarity to the rulers of the Fatherland's destiny. It asks corresponding solidarity. Fascism means justice and fidelity, union and harmony.

Translated by Gil Fagiani

The Lighthouse

 Rosario Ingargiola

Born Marsala, Italy, 1898

In 1931, Rosario Ingargiola was the object of stinging invectives flung at him by Carlo Tresca and other leftist polemicists for his subversive past and his writings for the Fascist journals *La Questione Sociale* and *Il Corriere Libertario*. In 1923–24, Rosario Ingargiola was the editor of and then contributor of critical literary articles to the *Corriere d'America* and other newspapers. He brought many colonial poets to prominence and was himself a poet, publishing a book of verse, *Io canto la vita e la morte* (1926). He emigrated at eight years old to Brooklyn, where he took his degree in law. He practiced law there and was greatly venerated by the Ordine Indipendente Figli d'Italia (Independent Order of the Sons of Italy).

ESSENTIAL BIBLIOGRAPHY

Flamma 1936.

Deep is the night, clear is the moon,
Starlight and murmuring sea,
Vast solitude and thick shadows.
On, on toward fortune,
Under the arch of a full moon sky,
O Ship of the Homeland, O immense Ship!

Over the entire Atlantic, here, stretches
a shudder of dream and fear,
a canticle of love and hope.
Peaceful is the wave the Ship cuts,
High is the night that darkens space,
Full of light is the approaching end.

In this immensity of sky and wake,
Where the eye loses itself and my heart trembles,
The Mediterranean aura gives me wings
And murmurs to me, in noble harmony,
The breath of a mystic poem
That blares in my soul: Italy! Italy!

And the Ship proceeds. But, from the sea,
Here suddenly a thread of light surges
That fully lights up the black horizon:
Quickly it appears and quickly it leaves,
It rises, sparks, dies, and is then reborn. . . .
Oh, thread of light in the mystery!

Oh, luminous lighthouse of Sardinia,
First vision of the ancient Motherland,
Star of Italy at the outposts, O Lighthouse
Of Sardinia, that for the thoughtful exile
Shows the way with friendly light,
Because of you the sky becomes clear this night.

Oh, lovely Lighthouse of Italy, in the misty
Night and vortex of the sea—sun, air,
Symbol and numen of the Great Goddess—
If you burn, the shadows, here, are broken;
If you light up, the abyss clears up;
And if you shine, the exile rejoices.

When, in the sea of our lives, it happens
That deceit, darkness and insult
Descend on us humble and unaware,
Star of Italy, Lighthouse of Sardinia,

Then do raise your burning faith
And from there hurl her to all the seas!

Translated by Emmanuel Di Pasquale

To Mussolini, the Immortal

∾ *Rosa Zagnoni Marinoni*

Bologna, Italy, January 5, 1888 (or 1891)–Fayetteville, Arkansas, March 26, 1970

Rosa Zagnoni Marinoni is the fiery, patriotic young woman described in a passage in part V of Antonio Marinoni's autobiography. She would become his wife in 1908 and would move with him to Fayetteville, Arkansas. She was an author of numerous collections of poetry in English, among which, *Behind the Mask* and *Pine Needles* (1927); *In Passing* (1930); *Timberlane: Selected Verse* (1954) and *Radici al vento / Roots to the Sky*, published in Milan in 1956. She contributed regularly to the *Carroccio*, in which she published diverse stories, always in English, and for a period, ran a rubric of aphorisms, also in English, entitled, *Piccole cose* (Small Things). Poet laureate of Arkansas, she founded Arkansas Poetry Day and was part of numerous cultural societies. She used various pseudonyms, among them Ross Zane Morrison, The Jester, Dawn Star, and Rosca. She wrote "To Mussolini, the Immortal" in English.

ESSENTIAL BIBLIOGRAPHY

Alfonsi 1989; Fiamma 1936; Peragallo 1949, 148–151; Schiavo 1966–67.

∾

There is the lure of jungle in your eyes.
Eagle wings have swept your pensive brow.
You have the untamed majesty of lions

Who scorn to follow, but unconscious reign.
You remind me
Of breakers crashing against wind swept cliffs
Rising to meet the sun.
You are a man such as is born but once,
But that once born
Shall never taste of death.
Your name shall be as a phosphorous torch
That glows out of the night
Casting eternal light upon your sons.

Two Poems

〰 *Rosario Di Vita*

Palermo, Italy, 1879–New York, New York, 1939

Rosario Di Vita suffered a tormented childhood and was made to work right after elementary school. Subsequently, he enjoyed a happy period with an adoptive family in Brescia, followed by a return to his native Sicily and then a stay in Naples in the house of his godfather, studying on his own. Finally, in 1906, he made the "leap" to America and found new work as an employee with managerial responsibilities. He directed several literary newspapers and contributed to many others, and in 1933, in New York, he founded and became president of the Cenacolo Artistico Letterario Vincenzo De Simone. Di Vita published several poetry collections: *Prime stille* (First Teardrops), *Fiori e sorrisi* (Flowers and Smiles), *I nostri fiori alla patria* (Our Blossoms for the Fatherland), *Perle azzurre* (Blue Pearls), and *Vuci d'oltrimari* (Voices from Abroad; published in Milan, in 1934, with a preface by Vincenzo De Simone). He also wrote for the theater: *Chiantu di Galiota* (The Galley Slave's Lament) (New York, 1925) and *Scenette umoristiche e drammatiche* (Humorous and Dramatic Scenes) (New York, 1926). According to Filippo Fichera, he composed a Sicilian rhyming dictionary, "rich with two hundred thousand words." In 1933, he offered the Duce the *Raccolte del Decennale (Collections for the Tenth Anniversary)*, "an exhaustive detailed documentation of all published works in the two Americas, pertaining to Fascism and to the corporative idea in the world" (De Simone). Di Vita's production is generally in Sicilian dialect, though not lacking are poems composed in a Sicilian American jargon or based on a very curious phonetic transcription, some of which were published in the *Rivista italiana di letteratura dialettale (Italian Review of Dialectal Literature)*. Among these are themes celebrating the invasion of Ethiopia; the "five sanctions"; and the *italianità* of the Ladino people and of the Maltese archipelago. In the poems published by Fichera, in 1937, Di Vita celebrated the Duce, calling him "cògnitu Pilotu" (conscience and piliot) "Novu Cesari" (new Caesar) and "Cesari mudernu" (modern Caesar) and deeming fascism "simbulu d'unioni" (a symbol of union).

ESSENTIAL BIBLIOGRAPHY

De Mattei 1933; Fichera 1937, 432–441, 449–450; Fichera 1958, 25–26.

O Italy! O lighthouse of every arcane brightness

O Italy! O lighthouse of every arcane brightness,
You who know the weight on those who suffer,
Ease the mind, and with your hand
Show to those who have offended you,
Say it, that your FATHER is Italian!
Rebuke your changed face,
And that you are reborn—*not in vain*—
Daughter of Eternal Rome newly risen!
Say it, that there is a CAESAR that watches
Jealous, over you, and that it wants you *great*!
That he wants the *Italian family* to
Follow his work and be truly admired. . . .
Say it, that by obeying the DUCE,
We will give you, great Motherland, LIGHT AND VOICES!

With the passing of time, your glory marches on

With the passing of time, your glory marches on,
Rises higher, enchanting people everywhere;
That you are great has not been said often enough,
My beloved Duce, known in every sphere.

Human, most noble your heart, and good your soul,
Resembling a God with Your virtue,
From where the ray of hope (the dream of all of us)
Was given to us, in true reality.

Because of you, my Fatherland is like a garden
With flowers, plants, fruits, and opulence;
Building yard of activity and work; and still yet:
Songs, joys, happiness, and providences.
Because of you, now the Peninsula is strong,
Envied and feared, as it never was:
For its potential of arms and of throngs
Of exuberant, Roman-tempered "Youth."

Italy, because of You, has her name,
A new history, new glory and presage;
Her liberty, her new Fascist rebuke
With her Fasces from the ancient age.

Italy, has in You, the omnipotent Duce,
The new immortal Caesar Augustus;
In her Fascism, she has the Life and the Light
And the universal Flag of Justice.

Translated by Emmanuel Di Pasquale

Two Poems

ை *Umberto Liberatore*

Umberto Liberatore was born in Alghero, Italy, as we learn from his biography. According to the bibliographic list provided by his biographer, his oeuvre is composed of the pastoral poem "Mariangiola"; the historical tragedy *Beatrice Cenci*; the dramatic poem, "Le tre sorelle" (The Three Sisters); the poetry collections, *Vortici di luce (Vortexes of Light)* and *Solitudini* (Solitudes); the collection of historical and literary writings, *Profili storici* (Historical Profiles; Rome, Formiggini, 1936), with profiles dedicated to Virgil, Dante, Petrarch, Ariosto, Tasso, Leonardo, Galilei, Alfieri, Garibaldi, and Sebastiano Satta; and a series entitled *Poemi storici* (Historical Poems), consisting of the one-act pieces, *Faust perduto* (Faust Doomed), *Cyrano de Bergerac*, and *Pia de'Tolomei*. Fascist poet and celebrator of the "Italic genius," Liberatore infused his poetry with a species of patriotic mysticism, which he applied to contemporary experiences forgotten today (among others, making reference to Pietro G. Varvar, another Italian American, who in 1939, published "Alma Mater," a poem dedicated to Sicily). His versification is generally inflated and grandiloquent, even when he turns to more modest and domestic themes. Nonetheless, he merits recognition for his metrical skill, his varied lexicality, and for a tone not common among the other marginalized literary Italian American authors: all signs of a higher literary awareness, characteristic of the texts of a twentieth century that had already gone beyond D'Annunzio.

ESSENTIAL BIBLIOGRAPHY

Fichera 1958, 46; Liberatore 1939, 35–39, 109–110.

ை

The Hudson

Sky and sea like melted tin,
And the coastlines a great green ribbon;
The people, under the sun, in the confusing
Bustle, disperse on deck. . . .
From the other shore comes the croaking
Of crows that lingering
Flash through the air. . . .
Below, birds caw on the sea. . . .
   The sun is at its height and far away.
As if a mirage, it dissolves
Things, leaving in the distance
A polychrome of fabulous coastlines. . . .
I see turrets and dwellings covered
With flowering vines,
I see on dark mountains
Stretches of turquoise and gray crags. . . .
   Profiled under the sun are shady maples,
Willow arbors, poplars and pine trees
Conscious of their life on rocky
Hills, or of the Alpine land at their borders. . . .
There, where in the night of origins
Lay the memories
Of what is the debris
Of time, one can see aboriginal races. . . .
   And you think of what was, of what you dream
Should be! Of the vast crossing
Of faiths from which you desperately desire
A great miracle! Of the already designed plan
To erect the great and powerful city
Using the cross
And fearful swords
Of an invading people in tumult!
   You think of Verrazzano, seaman
Without compare, who first the mouth
Of the beautiful river touched! And the most savage

Lenapes glimpsed! And the world filled
With terrible and beautiful deeds
Pain, sarcasm and oblivion!
All that is wondrous
Is handed on the wind by Time to the people. . . .
    Yet think of a faith that is
Filthy fetishism! Rising again
From the abyss of Time is the sun so that
A savage people will still believe
In vain things, in inert matter,
While it repudiates the truth;
A people that worships,
Genuflects before symbols and ignores them!
    A progeny of foolish people
Constantly screeching and wanting and losing itself
In a crazy and savage history of the gods. . . .
And believing and dreaming in vain! Oh! one loses
The gift of intellect when thinking
Of the times when the ship
Followed your banks Oh beautiful river
And you were given the name of a great god!
    Today you are, after centuries of waiting,
Beautified with bridges and avenues;
Along your two sides run in an extended
Spiral the rapid trains, for which
Tunnels were excavated . . . Look around
And see the majesty
Of the road that winds
Around the mountain, high up, for those who gaze. . . .
    How from everything is renewed incredulously
The life that had been, the life extinguished!
    How from everything also surges the thoughtful
Forest kept alive by the slow
Activity of man! Everything returns
To life and everything to dust
In the eternal journey
That discerns, overwhelms and evolves everything!
    But just as everything is set when one builds

With faith and raises high! So with the thought
Of those who wanted to erect and with faith
Did what they could, the truth
Then leaps to one's eyes. Just as
You see and so hope
To see true things,
So you will also see those that are not! . . .
 After many years, today, the city
Built at your lovely borders rises,
Its peaks reaching towards immensity!
So it lives again, so it still leaps
Under the blue mystery! The majesty
Of the powerful work
Is revealed to the minds
Of aware and grateful men. . . .
 O noble men Verrazzano and Hudson!
If your sublime spirits were to return
To the places you explored,
With great wonder they would learn
That because of your deeds
Of centuries ago
Here lives a people in daily ascent!

Fascists

From the war front on the Alpine
Peaks wrapped in clouds, to where
The sea sleeps in the sun's radiance
–And the kiss of the Tyrrhenian the Adriatic
Salutes–we rightfully earned
With pain, with wounds, with lives,
Our country, which had for so long been lost.
And insatiate, meanwhile, is the rage
Of our friends; insatiate is the enemy
Who attempts to incinerate the laurels
Of the still smoking battlefield,

And wants to turn chaos into eternal night.
Enough! The she wolf's pups arise!
The fasces, that the Roman lectors carried
And the legions' eagle, are symbols
That today we revive for love
Of our country, for law and for justice.
Faith, our daring, whatever
Sacrifice we will accept, as death
Elevates fate to the sublime and renders it certain.

Translated by Maria Enrico

The Failed Ambush

Armando Borghi

Castel Bolognese (Ravenna), Italy, April 6, 1882–Rome, Italy, April 21, 1968

Armando Borghi was a merchant's son, first a follower of Mazzini, then a follower of Bakunin. Through his maternal lineage, he was the descendent of a patriotic Mazzinian who died in 1896 in the papal prison of Paliano. Very early in his life, Armando Borghi became an active anarchist orator, modeling himself on the teachings of Errico Malatesta. In 1898, he moved to Imola, then to Bologna, where, working irregularly, he took various classes at the university. After publicly defending the anarchist Bresci, who had shot and killed Umberto in July 1900, Borghi hid for some time in the country, but in 1901 he returned to Bologna, and the next year was arrested for the first time for having delivered speeches that incited resistance to military enlistment. Released from prison in 1906, he assumed the direction of the *Aurora* (Dawn) of Ravenna, and in 1907 he participated in the first anarchist congress that was held in Rome. In that year, he published *Il nostro e l'altrui individualismo* (Our Individualism and That of Others), where he affirmed the necessity of the organization of polemics with the anarchist followers of Max Stirner, the German satiric philosopher, a theme Borghi took up again at the congress in Rome. In Bologna, he organized union activity as secretary of the union of building workers, a union independent of the national federation and the CGdL (Confederazione Generale del Lavoro, General Labor Confederation), and he also launched the editions of the Biblioteca Lux (Light Library) specializing in antimilitaristic pamphlets.

Incriminated for defending a crime (praising the act of the anarchist Masetti, who had shot his colonel), he went into exile in Paris, where he contributed to various newspapers and became friends with Sebastien Faure and other influential exponents of anarchism. In Switzerland in 1912, he was quickly expelled, and later, given amnesty, he returned to Italy, only to be arrested again in January 1913.

Borghi immediately supported the Unione Sindacale Italiana (Union of Italian Syndicalism) of Alceste De Ambris, founded in 1912. In 1913, in Bologna, he published the book that contained his thoughts on the theme of unionism: *Fernand Pelloutier nel sindacalismo*, in which he praises French unionism, capable of maintaining itself independent of parties. In June 1914, during the *"settimana rossa"* (red week), he was very active in Emilia Romagna. In September 1914, at the congress of the USI, he succeeded in passing his agenda, which, in contrast with De Ambris's, was anti-interventionist, and consequently, he became the secretary of the USI and director of the newly founded newspaper *Guerra di Classe* (Class Warfare). Arrested and given amnesty in August 1915, he moved to Modena, then to Piacenza. In 1916, he was confined in Florence with his girlfriend, a typographer who died of consumption in 1917, with whom, in 1912, he had had a son, Comunardo. Betrayed in Isernia, he succeeded in eluding surveillance and in meeting two socialist directors, Serrati and Morgari, in Rome, to found an alliance among anarchists and socialists, the *"intransigenti."* In this period he met Virgilia D'Andrea, who became his inseparable companion.

Borghi believed in the theory of a general revolutionary strike. Under the pressure of incipient Fascist violence, in April 1919, he proposed the formation of a committee made up of the USI, Unione Anarchica Italiana, PSI, CGdl, and Sindacato Ferrovieri (Railroad Workers Union), but meanwhile the dissension among the socialists was increasing. Already a fervent supporter of the Russian Revolution, in 1920, after a venturesome voyage, Borghi arrived in Russia and made the acquaintance of Zinoviev, Lenin, and Kropotkin, who opened his eyes to the torturous road that led to the revolution.

Upon returning to Italy, he was arrested again after the occupation of the factories; and in prison with Malatesta, he initiated a hunger strike. On July 26, 1920, he was acquitted. In 1921, at the UAI congress of Ancona, he delivered a successful speech urging separation from Bolshevism. His anti-Stalinist, antiauthoritarian stance, contrary to an organic alliance with the communists, was received even more favorably at the USI congress in 1921. Shortly before the Fascists' march on Rome, Borghi left Italy. He went to Berlin, Paris, Madrid, and Santarem, Portugal. At the end of 1923, he moved with Virgilia to Paris. Invited for a round of conferences, on November 19, 1926, he arrived in New York by train, boarding in Canada. Borghi was an already known personage in the United States, where in 1925, the IWW press had published one of his collections of writings on the murder of

Matteotti, *Il banchetto dei cancri* (The Banquet of Cancers). Nevertheless, in his memoir *Mezzo secolo di anarchia* (A Half-Century of Anarchism, 1954) he describes his arrival in that world, so new, in highly dramatic colors. Borghi was amazed by America: "For a long time, I did not understand it. I was attracted by it and at the same time repelled by it." Given hospitality by a friend in Brooklyn, in an environment that reminded him of Sicily, he quickly began his political work, taking part in a round of conferences for the committee for Sacco and Vanzetti; he visited Vanzetti, in Charlestown, and Sacco, in Dedham. The communists of the Alleanza Antifascista, AFANA, were seeking to boycott his conferences. Borghi hurled accusations at Vittorio Vidali and engaged in polemics with Carlo Tresca (see his pamphlet *Gli anarchici e le alleanze antifasciste* (The Anarchists and the Antifascist Alliances, New York 1927). Arrested on June 1, 1927, and detained for a month at Ellis Island because his residence permit had expired, he was released on bail on condition that he leave the country, but instead he stayed in New York, where after a year Virgilia rejoined him. In New York, in 1927, he published, in Italian, his book *Mussolini in camicia*, which had a very large circulation and was later translated into English as *Mussolini Red and Black* (1938). Other editions were published in Paris, Amsterdam, and London. He was employed in various jobs: as a salesman of cigars, oil, and neckties. As he relates, he was dismissed from a doll factory. He knew the anarchist Schirru and was largely employed in political activity, participating in various meetings and writing intensely for *L'Adunata dei Refrattari*, with the pseudonyms of "Girarrosto, "Etimo Vero," and "Biarmando."

On April 6, 1930, he participated for the first time in a public debate at Cooper Union, in New York, on the theme "I problemi della rivoluzione italiana dopo l'abbattimento del fascismo" (The problems of the Italian revolution after the overthrow of Fascism); his antagonist was Vincenzo Vacirca, freed, like him, on bail. He discussed the passage published here, a tract from *Mischia sociale* (Social Brawl), a book published that same year in New York. Escaping arrest, he resumed a clandestine vagabond life, which took him to many American cities, in particular, in California. In 1929, his mother died; a year later, his father died; Malatesta died in 1932; and Virgilia D'Andrea died in 1933. For a decade, as he relates in his memoirs, Borghi held discussions within a Brooklyn circle every Tuesday and Friday. He also wrote a drama, *La tragedia fascista nella scuola* (The Fascist Tragedy in the Schools). It is not clear if he went to Spain during the civil war. In his memoirs, he writes that his son, who was there, dissuaded him, because of the intrigues of the Communists and of the "governmental anarchy"; the murder of Camillo Berneri was proof enough. Nevertheless, his presence in Barcelona between April and May 1937 is attested by police documents. In 1940, finally, following the directives of Roosevelt's administration,

Borghi registered. Arrested, he was again conducted to Ellis Island, where he found himself in a cell with the ex-Fascist deputy Casagrande; he managed to change cells and after four months was released thanks to the good offices of Gaetano Salvemini and Walter Toscanini, son of the celebrated orchestra conductor, and bail of five thousand dollars, which was reduced to a thousand dollars.

He returned to Italy in 1945 and found a very different situation from that which he knew, and in 1948 he resumed life in the United States. In 1953, however, he definitively repatriated, and the Federazione Anarchica entrusted him with the editorship of *Umanità Nova* (New Humanity).

ESSENTIAL BIBLIOGRAPHY

Andreasi 1971; Borghi 1930, 1954, 1966; DBI; Emiliani 1973, 193–224; MOI.

∾

This was yesterday's headline.

It was all over the newspapers and I will discuss it with some difficulty, with much delay, and from so far away.

To illustrate a few details of the story.

To give a few psychological and personal political "snapshots" of it.

To conclude—book and chapter—with my speech that day. My speech, although interrupted midway by fascist police violence, I think fits in well alongside these pages and which, in my opinion, has value as a succinct commentary despite changing circumstances and changing times.

The preliminaries of the debate date back to the previous year.

Here is a brief history.

In March 1929, I was speaking at the Galileo Temple on "Fifty Years of Socialism in Italy." It was an unpleasant lecture for socialists, in which I was documenting the half-century, sweat-filled struggle to replace the fetishism of the ballot with the spirit of revolt. A socialist defended his ideas. I replied.

Without anger and without stammering.

There followed an exchange of letters between other socialists and a group of us.[1] The idea of a debate crept in. Dr. Nino Firenze—a republican, a spirit open

1. Ruggeri of the *Nuovo Mondo* [New World] wrote this for a group of socialists: "Last Friday, given the late hour and the confusion, not one of us had taken the floor to rebut the speakers. Therefore I implore you to confirm for next Friday, April 12 (1929) a lecture by Vacirca on the topic: 'Why the Italian Proletariat was Defeated.' If you want, you can advise Borghi." The response letter from our comrades reads: "If you really want to pursue the matter it seems that it would be right to take it up with Borghi for a regular debate at our meeting hall but not at the

to the broad views of social struggle. and a regular at the "Galileo" evenings— grew fond of this idea. He himself was a speaker at that sort of People's University that a group of anarchists and sympathizers there had set up.

Everything remained suspended until January of this year ('30) when I again spoke at the same location, this time on the topic of "Life and Miracles of the Antifascist Alliance."

From then on, Dr. Firenze was given the mandate to conduct negotiations for the final agreements. And it was done.

No defiant challenges.

No polemic restrictions.

No—yes, even this—verbal jabs!

I arrived at Cooper Union late that day. Several faces were already darkened.

I could not explain why.

I will now say that there was a detail which the honest press had to overlook in being thorough. One then could offer a reason for the petty treachery of the republican judiciary, ready to pile up minutiae and impressions of every kind, even successfully swelling up the charges to "complicity in murder. . . ." Oh, no doubt, not against the policemen-murderers but against the five arrested, the one dying, and the rest of us who are wanted. The balance was soon tipped in our favor, either because of the garish evidence of the despicable fascist-police trap, or because it so happened that the only ones shot were on our side, or above all because of the moral outcry from the newspapers in every language and color. Not unless we mean the toads of fascist Barsottism and several red under-toads . . . but nothing shameful, which they did do later on. . . .

Everyone knows that several comrades had some vague suspicion of a threat against me at the entrance of Cooper Union. But there were prior instances, and there had been many previous warnings which were always empty; and it seemed, and it would have been, childish to take them seriously. And so? What if they were fascists? Should we leave the podium whenever real fascists show their intimidating mugs at our lectures?

There were prior instances. For several months the comrades with whom I lived warned me that thugs were looking for me. What for?

I was *out on 2500 dollars bail.*

Even from Boston comrade-friends had warned me that after my departure from that State, a few weeks before the debate, they had suspected that in nearby

People's University. If you want, the same [anarchist] group will take the initiative if you write back."

Providence a definite police attempt to injure me had failed because of a federal agent's delay (*Piaggio*? . . .) in getting an arrest warrant (?!). In this last city, in fact, at one of my lectures a state police truck had been overturned, and as we know, state police cannot carry out their duties unless they call for "back up" in federal cases (oh! longed-for Italian federal republic. . . .). But at the time we didn't give it a second thought!

Shadows or reality?

I did not understand and gave up trying to understand anything, shooting straight ahead, without posturing, and without that fear which is the only way to always get the worst out of the risky things in life.

Later on everything became clear.

They were living shadows of a decayed reality, inconceivable unless one understands the troubled waters that lead to the corruption of officials in this American world of wheeling and dealing, where everything has a price in gold, cash, or checks, and everything, in every field, is bought, sold, rented, extorted, or blackmailed. In this shocking fantasy world of bandits up for auction and illustrious pimps, in which legality and illegality merge and blur together and lose all meaning and are only appearances of the same putrid reality; a world of multiple police forces—public and secret or pseudo-secret or authorized or permitted; all are instruments, often in competition, of profiteering and supremacy in the hands of lodges, clubs, pandering journalists, even self-styled workmen, low-class lawyers to troubled clients and devious "games"; always unreliable means for whoever buys or sells them, always entwined in the slimy branches of the underworld, and always prone and face down before the golden calf of capital and the principle of authority.

On April 6, someone had the impression of noticing at the entrance of the meeting hall the same gentlemen who had recently come to ask for me several times on Fourth Avenue, number . . . this, in Brooklyn, where for two years, in a group with four others, and sometimes six, poor but unforgettable comrades, I stayed in a luxurious apartment with three rooms, heated in winter only by our "steadfast" faith in the everlasting presence of the future sun. But *who* were these "gentlemen" who were looking for me?

A deft surveillance team was improvised to study the moves of those individuals inside the meeting hall.

And here I can still see in my mind that comrade's thin figure, panting from the run, jubilant for having caught up with me; I see him again at the subway exit—a hundred yards from the meeting hall—with his arms up waving nervously as if to say, "We saw certain faces . . . What to do? It would be best to be careful."

These, and others like it, were his words.

All my life had I paid attention to all the false alarms given to me in the most sincere good faith by comrades, often subject to exaggerate the danger for the sake of the cause, I do not know how many lectures[2] I would have missed giving, adding to the propaganda that arises when people wait and do not see the face of the longed-for speaker and end up no longer believing even the most legitimate reasons. Instead, I mention it here in passing, am known as one of the most punctual speakers, and in three years, out of several hundred lectures in the United States, I have missed *three*: once for real illness, another because I was detained elsewhere by comrades who had misjudged the distance, and once I was absent in Brooklyn because I wanted to remain in Boston, where the fascists had threatened to *skin me alive* if I did not leave that city.

Shadows or reality?

The conversation was short:

"Are there people?"

"The meeting hall is full. . . ."

"Is Vacirca here?"

"He arrived early."

"Calm down and follow me if you want . . ."

I was relying on myself.

On my own experience.

On my—how shall I say?—training in this field.

Because—can I allow myself to forgive certain indiscretions on my embarrassing criminal record?—I carry on my back at least seventeen political convictions, quite a larger number of charges against me (most of which were thrown out after protective custody), and so many arrests that I gave up trying to keep count. But what is more scandalous for police officers and their friends and sympathizers of every color, is that I can count at least *five* rather sensational escapes, six with the one at Cooper Union (and I promise to continue if I can and when it is necessary).

First escape: —I ran away 27 years ago—September 20, '03 in a square in Bologna, when during the speech by our poor, great Pietro Gori, we waved the first

---

2. I took it upon myself to circulate the letter from Boston to all those interested in the debate, just to be absolutely certain. But I was out on bail and I realized that it seemed almost ridiculous to give substance to certain . . . shadows. In fact it passed, as it should pass, as a fantastic alarm, and such was the opinion of Firenze, Vacirca, and others present at the final meeting for the debate.

anarchist flag, on the occasion of the unveiling of the bronze statue honoring the fallen of August 8 '48.

Second escape: —I ran away from the podium (still in Bologna) surrounded by cops, even jumping into the audience (January '05), after having spoken at a very agitated rally held at the Hall of Notaries to protest the historic massacre ordered by the Czar in Petrograd.

Third escape: —I ran away from the patrol wagon (Castel Bolognese, October '05) while they were taking the 12 of us to the prisons in Faenza. And from the same car *three other comrades* ran away as a result of my escape because the police chased me, who, while attempting—in vain—to recapture me, abandoned the other prisoners.

Fourth escape: —I escaped from my house through a window (July '06 in Bologna), where half a dozen cops were already in my presence to arrest me.

Fifth escape: —I escaped from the station in Geneva (October '11) where I was headed to give a scheduled lecture, although some comrades had arrived several railway stations before me, to warn me that one of us had already been put in the clink as soon as the train arrived, having been mistaken for me. In the evening we escaped from the People's House, where I was headed to give the lecture. And I gave it, and it was only that night that I was arrested and expelled.

One memory leads to another . . . And I will say that sometimes I was taken for a big fool, and I realized it, as when, after Red Week, I was one of the few who remained in Italy and I was blockaded in one of the processions as part of the conspiracy.

The amnesty of the good war saved us, which then gave us four years in a prison that was called "internment". . . .

I had every reason to trust my previous experiences.

"Do what you must; come what may." An old but great maxim! Missing the debate, *no*! Sneaking in—even if it was an excess of caution—talking, at the exit, settling my own accounts with the gentlemen police officers, outside the audience.

This was my plan.

Inspecting the surroundings of the building—"sealed off."

Lots of policemen at the two regular entrances.

Another inspection.

We discover a back door on one side. In four passes, through a network of corridors, we are in the meeting hall.

Brief "introduction" by Dr. Firenze. A moment to pause—which he suggested—standing, to commemorate our martyrs.

Poor Gino Mazzola, he was already memorializing himself. . . .

It is not within the scope of these pages to reproduce the speech by the other speaker, Vincenzo Vacirca. He certainly found his eloquence, as I found mine, and by all accounts one of my best moments.

It is not about that!

It could have been a day of only sensible emotions. The audience experienced moments of intense joy that could be seen on all their faces, for all the speeches.

There was anticipation, anxiety, passion, desire for knowledge, profound enjoyment of the unusual calm, unaccompanied by the usual posturing of false programmatic uniformity—which is only amorphous thought—of false harmony and often false esteem.

There was all of the good and perhaps all of the bad of the major assemblies. No one however encouraged or provoked negative emotions. After the first "question and answer," our president turned to the appeal for the cost of the meeting hall (it was agreed by the parties to donate the surplus to the political victims).

Absolute quiet . . . We come to the tragic moment.

A gentleman among others, tall, thin, sallow, is on the stage behind us. He does not open his mouth. He tries to smile, but only succeeds in giving me the impression, which still persists, of an animated skull in a hard hat, planted on one of those straw puppets from one of those "five balls a penny" booths at the fair.

He motions with his finger for me to come closer.

I do not move.

He repeats the gesture.

I do not move.

I notice that the area behind the stage is crowded with uniformed policemen.

The man-skull approaches.

"Do you know that man?" I ask Vacirca.

"Not at all!"

The man-skull is now face to face with me.

"Are you," he tells me in English, "*Mister* Armando Borghi?"

"Me? . . . and you, who are you? . . ."

He repeats the question.

"Are you Mister Armando Borghi? . . ."

I gave up trying to describe what I glimpsed in a flash at that moment. I now know this better than then: the human mind can in exceptional moments perceive in a flash, with mathematical precision and absolute lucidity, that which in normal moments it would not know how to unravel even after careful consideration. . . .

Perhaps from my previous memories the escape from Bologna came to mind, twenty-five years before at the Hall of Notaries. . . .

I do not know. . . .

Of course I guessed what caused me to be arrested, there, at that important point. For me, we are in agreement, dispatch to that beautiful country, where one becomes famous *escaping* abroad at the risk of one's life.[3] And the others? The comrades present who most certainly would not *let them do*? . . .

They were there, around me and our friends and comrades, even our adversaries, with blood in their veins, although certainly unprepared in every way for such a surprise.

What would have happened if policemen had gotten their hands on me, there, in plain sight of two thousand enthusiastic spectators?

What would have happened if I had wasted a few minutes in discussion or if I had turned to the audience to apologize for not being able to continue "because I was under arrest?"

This is what shook the press, even the American press. And fortunately it so happened that it was not in a remote village where criminal police behavior occurs, but it occurred at the center of New York, in that old, austere meeting hall used for solemn occasions where incidents or conflict had never occurred, and which obliged everyone to not ignore it.

We try to reflect on all of this. We will learn that those who hired Piaggio and the other moral bare-footed dogs in his gang for that undertaking; there—I repeat—in that place, at that hour, in those circumstances, having carefully considered and calculated their plan and did not waste the money of poor Italian donors.

"Disappear."

This idea struck me. But how? Two minutes of indecision and I was lost, thereby avoiding the hell that broke loose.

"Borghi for you." I answer, "*no!*" And I'm already off the stage with a quick jump that plunged me, fortunately but not on purpose, in perfect balance and in one of the open areas between the rows of stationary chairs. One tumble and I would have fallen into the hands of Mazzola's murderer who eyed his weapon (and was not alone) down there without anyone's knowing it. No sooner said than done, I put my hand on the first hat and the first overcoat to cover myself with the collar turned up to my chin, and in the stupor of surprise in which everyone saw things differently

3. The matter at Cooper Union forced Buffalo Bill in Rome to grant an interview which has been around the world, like all of his farts, where, after saying that the behavior of men like Armando Borghi in America shows what we wanted to do and did do in Italy, he ended with the assurance that he "does not shoot" his enemies, but limits himself to *arresting* them! Good Time Buffalo Bill, who, in truth, also arrests his friends like Dumini, after the customary torture. But does Mus . . . that is, the Dogface—get it, that we will go to Italy when he wants the opposite?

from the other and no one was able to see them in their own reality, I made it to the exit.

I learned after the hundred hypotheses formulated by comrades: that I had been carried away with the others in the clash with the police; that I had been blocked at the exit. . . . I least of all could see what was going on behind my back and after the jump. The greatest act of courage—this memory—cost me the obligation of being arrested cold in the hallway, moving me out to the street, showing me off in full view of the other police officers, the surly indifference of an inconvenienced spectator. It was like suddenly applying the brakes on a car going full speed. The secret of success is almost always in these cases knowing how to take over at a given point.

It is difficult to predict what would have happened if the cops had not found the resistance that they effectively found. It is also likely that the lightning resistance did eclipse "other" tools that did not take the audience's quick response into consideration.

It bears repeating over and over again. I was *out on bail*. Vacirca was in the same situation. Everyone knows that this means that under American law if an individual is out on bail, subject to the money deposited, and until the termination of bail by the government, *he cannot be harassed*. What then, was *behind* this attack? There was more to it. An agency in Washington—the Federated Press—a few months before the debate shocked us with some news that would have given me an even greater sense of security, just at the time when the above mentioned sinister visits were initiated by sinister figures. Mysteries of the capital's "coulisses": this same agency published the . . . good news that I reproduce here, under the title *The Right to Asylum Granted to Armando Borghi*:

"Washington, D.C., November 9—The State Department has decided *to withdraw* the order of deportation issued against Armando Borghi, anti-fascist refugee, persecuted by Fascism in Italy. The order states that 'as long as Armando Borghi's life is endangered by his deportation to Italy, he will have the right to stay in the United States.'"

"The fascist consul in Boston, Mass., confiscated Borghi's passport, so that it is currently impossible for Borghi to travel abroad. Behind the accusations made by fascist organizations, Borghi was once arrested in the United States on the charge of being a *philosophical anarchist*."

I will go no further.

Nino Mazzola—yesterday the name of a comrade, today a martyr; Salvatore Vellucci—young militant, but an old friend—who, dripping blood from his chest even shouted amid the cops who were . . . helping you, long live our anarchy; your blood, like the blood and sacrifice of all those who struggle for freedom, will neither be forgotten nor unavenged. None too soon for our readiness to fight. None too late for our revolutionary foresight.

The supreme executioner knows us from personal experience—he—as we know him very well; and he knows that those of us "missing" were not ever and nor will we ever be. He knows that we were ahead of and not behind him, when he, without faith, assumed the posture of grimaces and screams of anti-Tripolism and of Herveismo. In front of him, and without his begging constituency, during Red Week. Indomitable against him (and his accomplices and his bosses), in his bootlicking Rabagasism, from the first day when he was contracted by the directors of war. Against him after the war and never seduced by his brazen two-facedness.

And he also knows that he owes his survival at that time to his cockroach-like prudence, and the vile price at which they all hired him—rightly so, if it were not about him and the four toadstools that pump him up—without having unfortunately *foreseen* that at the times of great fear it is on the dung of renegades that the gallows, the crosses, and the crucifixes have always been planted! He knows—the bragging executioner of a cowardly race—that we will meet again on the same road as in the past, at the hour in which we can harm him up close, without forgiveness. And we will see that hour. We will greet it rejoicing and only those who doubted it will repent.

We will "live it" in the struggle.

It now still seems worthwhile to live for that hour.

When "they" long for us to stay away, we will pursue them.

When "they" want us exiled, we will flock there.

When "they" will try to hide in a sewer, the Italian people and all of the drains will drown them.

And nitric acid will disinfect the drains![4]

Translated by Giulia Prestia

4. The same agency has reopened Borghi's case dated September 17, 1930, repeating that the case had been closed allowing him to remain here unharassed . . . ; this (added the proletarian agency . . .) while Guido Serio (a communist) was to be deported to Italy! The *Nuovo Mondo* then recognized the detective novel tone of the communication. The agency in fact— proletarian!—said that it had drawn on sources from the Department of Labor's chief of police. . . . Needless to say that both the Borghi Panel as well as the lawyer knew that things were just the opposite and denied them.

Remembering Michele Schirru

∾ *Virgilia D'Andrea*

Sulmona (L'Aquila), Italy, February 11, 1890–New York, New York,
May 11, 1933

Virgilia D'Andrea was Armando Borghi's loyal companion. Orphaned at the tender
age of six years old, she was placed in a religious boarding school, where she remained until she obtained a teaching diploma, and then taught for several years.
Very soon affiliated with anarchism, she became a fascinating orator as well as a
poet, but as Borghi wrote to Pietro Gori, in intimacy with her, "she did not store the
literature in the refrigerator." Her verses, collected in Paris, in 1929, in the collection
Tormento (Torment), prefaced by Errico Malatesta, are all of a social tone and feature the international struggles of the 1910s and 1920s, celebrating personages like
Karl Liebknecht and Rosa Luxemburg. In Italy, Virgilia D'Andrea carried out intense propaganda activity "in raids that extended from Milan to Florence, Ancona, Bari," and all of the kind, as Borghi emphasized, where "the meeting was
not a peaceful conference in the hall." Involved in 1920 in the trial that led to the
arrest of Borghi and Malatesta, but soon released in Milan, she was also involved
in the investigations into the assault on the Diana Theater on March 23, 1921,
which caused 21 deaths and wounded 172 people, and in which, moreover, her
companion was condemned to prison. Until the summer of 1922, she continued to
carry out political work in the Marche and in Romagna, at the side of Borghi. In
Bologna, she was threatened with death by the *arditi* (special forces soldiers).

   Exile brought her, together with Borghi, to Berlin, then to Paris, where she dedicated herself, among other things, to editing the review *Veglia* (Vigil). In 1928,
Borghi, who had already been in America for several years, convinced her to come to

America, where she continued her activities in contact with many personalities of the movement, among them Michele Schirru, the subject of the following essay. Borghi writes of his disagreements with his family, who did not approve of his union with Virgilia, which was not sanctioned by a regular marriage; he was in particular disagreement with his brothers, nationalists who, remaining in Italy, had become Fascists. Virgilia remained with him through numerous moves, notwithstanding her poor health. She went to California, where she gave numerous lectures. In 1932, learning of Malatesta's death, Borghi rejoined her in Boston, where, however, he found her being treated in a hospital. Operated upon by a daughter of Luigi Galleani, she returned to New York, but in the spring of 1933, had a relapse that brought her to another hospital, where she died of cancer. Borghi relates that just before dying, on the very same day, she saw the newly issued first copies of her last book, *Torce nella notte* (Torches in the Night).

The production of Virgilia D'Andrea is composed of varied books and pamphlets on political propaganda, all of a fragmented structure, and collections of various pieces dedicated to political themes, characterized by an inspired and solemn writing. Among these are, *L'ora di Maramaldo* (The Villain's Hour), printed in New York, in 1925, which contains a section dedicated to the trial of Sacco and Vanzetti ("While the executioner waits"); *Chi siamo e cosa vogliamo* (Who We Are and What We Want), together with *Patria e religione* (Fatherland and Religion), which collects the texts of two lectures and was published posthumously by the Biblioteca dell'Adunata dei Refrattari (Library of the Meeting of the Unwilling) in 1947; also posthumous is *Richiamo all'anarchia* (Call to Anarchy, 1965). In her American period, she contributed amply and continuously to various periodicals, especially to *L'Adunata dei Refrattari*, edited by Raffaele Schiavina-Max Sartin, who was her good friend from her Paris days and who published her diverse contributions, even poetry.

Michele Schirru, the subject of D'Andrea's essay, was an Italian antifascist executed on May 29, 1931, in Rome for having threatened to assassinate Mussolini.

ESSENTIAL BIBLIOGRAPHY

Armando (Borghi), "Virgilia D'Andrea," in *L'Adunata dei Refrattari*, May 15, 1943; Borghi 1954, 353–356; D'Andrea 1933, 193–208.

∾

Sadness, that sweet and intimate, slow and subtle illness that lies at the back of all my thoughts, had oppressed my soul more than usual that evening, and my lips refused to speak of the secret bitterness.

My friends, clustered in small groups, talked animatedly, filling the room with smoke, evocations, hopes, phantasms.

Excited snatches of their talk came to me, concealed behind the wide window curtains.

"Fascism? Exactly . . . a colossus with clay feet: it should collapse of its own weight."

"It should . . . it should . . . But up to now it is our leaders who fall, and people like Lucetti end up in jail . . . when not condemned to death."

"Whoever dies for truth and justice is not the vanquished, but the victorious."

"Fine, good," many applauded, and a fresh, young voice softly intoned:

E noi cadremo in un fulgor di Gloria
Schiudendo all'avvenir novella via.

And we fall in a blaze of glory
Opening new ways to the future.

"Words, always words . . . and meanwhile this Biblical language, like the Sermon on the Mount, doesn't change a bit of hard, cruel reality. The dead lie unavenged: the islands and prisons are full of comrades, and we ourselves, overcome by misery and torment, humiliated, abject in our helplessness, are still wandering around the world . . . and look at us . . . we grow old here . . . in exile." His voice broke in the grip of emotion.

"And the rest, why don't you tell the rest?"

The mob, the miraculous mob, the so-called brood-mare of heroic events, the cowering dog that licks the hand of the one who beats him; it prostrates himself, more and more servile, to hail a mad tyrant, plumed like dancing redskins, white-faced like an awkward clown calling fools to his fair booth.

Now a silence more eloquent, warmer and more effective than words hung over us like a threat and promise: a horizon dense with clouds: the secret depths of an ocean that breathes, rumbles, and swirls in impenetrable abysses.

Silence . . . memories pass in flocks under the sky of the soul: wings of gulls passing over the sea, flights of swallows fleeing November's icy breath.

Exile! That word made me feel more bitterly the evil that was expanding in grim melancholy. The enormous and fantastic city flung itself toward the lofty and sublime with a prodigious boldness of networks, towers, spires, tentacles, arrows in gigantic clusters of gold. Tired of the worries, the troubles, the concerns of the earth, discouraged by feeling its roots caught in a corrupt chasm of crimes, barbarism, revenge, the siren mirrored in the immense luminous bay, thirsty for purity, flung her refulgent hair to the kiss and embrace of the stars.

Exile! The solitude of anguish in the noisy multitude; the solitude of the desert and of the unknown in a vast and fickle crowd that swarms, shouts, bumps into you, pushes you, ignores you, overwhelms you.

Exile! That most exposed and flagrant poverty in a superabundance of colors, elegance, refinement, luxury, alternating between squares and streets that shimmer with every gaudy and dazzling opulence; the most exacerbated poverty among a succession of enormous and mighty buildings in which swirl, among future and chimerical dreams, fantastic fortunes; under which, buried in granite sureness, are amassed mountains of pure gold, in a labyrinth protected by corridors, dungeons, traps, caverns.

Exile! Forced inactivity, a dull and penetrating rasp that gnaws at you and destroys you, while around you the flight of thought and works pulses, trembles, sparks. Flares, changes, gains everlasting fame.

Exile! The impossibility of understanding the new world around you, so foreign, so varied, so changeable. A world so near, and yet so far from being yours: for its potential for seeing and hearing that is not equal or similar to yours; for its manifestations of thought, sorrow, joy, love, that do not resemble yours in any way; for its artistic creations that find no conformation or echo with the rhythm of your song, with the visions and fantasies of your sight, with the accent and sensitivity of your poetry.

Exile! And you vainly try to cling to this reef; to engage your existence in the gears of this formidable machine: it throws you back, pushes you off the road, and you are alone on a river bank, a miserable regurgitation from the storm waves, tired scraps to toss in the refuse, while deep inside you feel that you are still worth something, that you are still someone.

Exile! The emptiness, the incurable emptiness, the unseeing stare, along a course of bridges, streets, squares, monuments, buildings, in which no stone, no angle, no remote corner has a sigh for you, a voice, a fondness, a memory. . . .

That mountain path, smelling of thyme and broom where you, a little girl, sitting on the bare white boulder, sang a popular refrain to the little snail you picked up along the way, inviting it to poke its shy, black little head out of its shell.

Those green, rolling hills and knolls that in the quiet, rosy May sunsets were decorated with flocks coming from afar with slow, engrossed shepherds in that solemnity of sun and silence.

Those secret, winding lanes among fragrant crags and hedges, where at night you would chase golden fireflies, and with little trills of joy catch some to put under a glass on the bedside table. And what a flood of tears the next day when you no longer found magic falling stars but shapeless little insects, black and motionless. Thus it was all your life! A moving, a tenacious moving toward lights and dreams, and always finding shadow and frost, and always finding the cruel sneer of ambush and deception.

And those singing woods . . . those mighty chestnut trees . . . the torrents foaming between rocks and cliffs, and over all that magnificence of water and color, the garrulous and industrious spinning mill, and the centuries-old Dominican convent, now a teacher training school where, with your little closed and austere face bent over books and your work, uncaressed by maternal hands, you were becoming prepared alone, all alone, for life's drama.

Someone laid a hand on my shoulder. Tall and thin, a soft helmet of blond hair waving over a calm forehead, a healthy, easy smile on the pure, open arc of his young lips, the new arrival was looking at me closely.

"Why all alone, Virgilia?"

I didn't reply: my thoughts were still immersed in the mist of the past.

"Certainly," he added, "you must feel uncomfortable in a new land. And then . . . someone who has seen fascism, who has suffered because of it, who has lost friends over there, must be brokenhearted, and every word must seem empty."

That fraternal voice, spontaneous, full of care and concern, was good to hear after so much disappointment and bitterness. In the meantime a slow, sad song was lifted in the hall: the nostalgia and effusion of a piteous, unknown romantic heart.

Ai sedici d'Agosto, sul far de la mattina,
Il boia avea disposto l'orrenda ghigliotina.

On the sixteenth of August, at daybreak,
The executioner set up the ghastly guillotine.

The shade of the young Caserio had returned to us, full of fascination and charm, and I, tugged by that wave of heroic memories, believed I saw him living again in those big blue eyes that were sweetly looking at me, and in the beautiful blond head that was bent, thoughtful and kind, over my worries and solitude.

"Do you hear?" he resumed, while something—scorn, protest, revolt—passed, lightning quick, to darken his look. And yet it is not the time for lightheartedness and song: it is the time for action.

I looked him in the eyes, and they seemed full of tears and ardor.

"Today heroism is needed; a generous sacrifice of someone who knows how to face death."

I was a bit dumbfounded and remained silent in the face of the exuberance of that young man whose name I did not even know.

"Yes, he must defy life," he went on in a low voice, almost as if trying to penetrate, to hammer all the syllable of those serious words in his soul.

"What is your name?" I asked him then.

"Michele Schirru."

"Sardinian?"

He answered me with a cutting "yes" like a thin sharp knife.

A fleeting vision of superb bleak and barren peaks against the infinite: a roar of violent, angry water: a mountain of foam spraying a rain of blue and white flowers against Neptune's rock: the eagle's shriek from the powerful mountaintop: the moan of wolves in the deep valley.

In the hall the choir voices were rising at the refrain's crescendo:

Disse Caserio: Che cosa c'è?
È giunta l'ora, alzatevi in piè.

Caserio said: What is it?
The time has come, get up.

Outside . . . flames, flashes, interlinking shining beams in the city of gold, commotion, magnificence: inside . . . in that modest meeting place, a seething of hatred and scorn; enflamed memories, promises, hopes, which soon, unexpectedly, would become the highest and hottest of flaming bonfires.

A jolt: a lurch of the heart: a crazy fluctuation of thoughts, then just one word: *Schirru!*

I picked up the newspaper that had brought me unexpected news, and I stood still to swallow the cowardly, useless tears that collected in my throat. Friends entered excitedly.

"Have you seen the papers?"

My reply was a gesture; but I remained silent in order to see and hear only Him. Anguish, consternation, admiration, and rebellion: all of us feel it.

"So young, so strong and healthy. . . ." sobbed one of his dearest friends.

I follow the intimate thought that is awake and appears in every look, in every expression.

The blind and sincere believer in an immortal God that punishes and rewards can in the hour of supreme sacrifice find strength and exaltation at the thought of the *beyond* that awaits him in an awakening glory.

The pauper, the beggar, who has come to find a crust of bread wherever he can; the maimed whose enormous weight of misfortune grows heavier every day, depriving him of love forever, getting cold, mortifying looks of pity in compensation; the sick who waste away and slowly die, can never know delight, ecstasy, wild happiness; this disabled being, this tragic submersion in the waves of life who flings to a secret, cruel will the agony of that tormenting Rapisardian[1] "because," can anticipate, possibly without regret, the meeting and embrace of death.

Or che un cieco poter sì m'ha distrutto,
Perché salda alla terra ho la radice?
Perché se più non devo esser felice,
Pietoso Iddio, non mi distruggi tutto?

Now that a blind power has destroyed me,
Why are my roots secure in the ground?
Why, if I can no longer be happy,
Don't you destroy all of me, merciful God?

The long, bitter suffering, the acrid trickle of every day, of every hour, can explain, in this eternal shipwreck, Brutus' spectacular gesture; they can illuminate the mystery that encourages it and supports it in the face of the supreme holocaust of everything.

But He . . . this loving and beloved man, this healthy and vigorous father. This handsome, smiling man, who could have become intoxicated with dazzling frenzies of pleasure and oblivion, who could have enjoyed the warmth of his sound, tranquil nest, and looked with indifference upon the misery of the crowd, and mocked their timid, servile resignation, from what source does he draw such superhuman energy and such bright splendor that keep his heart steadfast and strong?

Another one . . . another one, on those very days had surprised the entire world with his strong and proud demeanor: another one, his sea-green eyes fixed on the stars that were going out in the sky, had walked haughtily, solemnly, chest bared and forehead shining, toward his tragic death.

1. Mario Rapisardi, Italian poet (1844–1912).

These are the flames of an Idea that has roots in the land, but with foliage that breathes blue immensity.

They are secret, uncompromising forces of the oppressed, the rejected, the abandoned, the disillusioned that suddenly, when the air grows grayer and night seems imminent, shoot a homicidal arrow at the suffocating pain.

They are the radiant springs that blossom from time to time from the handful of bold forerunners accused by the idealists of fraud, selling out, of grinding materialism at the elevation of human spirit.

"Now I understand . . . he disappeared and didn't even say goodbye," someone murmured.

The enormous mass of skyscrapers rising on the shoreless bay slowly dissolves before his eyes: memories of the past drift from land and assail his spirit, while the splendor of the statue of Liberty, a lie clothed in light, fades in the fog settling on the dark water.

The sea's obscure and insidious desire beats against the sides of the ship.

He is alone between that slap of water and propeller and the immobile sky. He is alone, far from everyone: burned, consumed by a persistent thought: closed like a tomb over his secret.

In the evening, when the sea seems calm, at night when everything is tinged with pale moonlight, he feels again his woman's head in his arms, his daughter's little hands, the wing chair that trembles with every embrace, every kiss, every caress; but the iron will that carries him away does not vacillate. Elegant, supple couples, captivated by excitement and desire, dance in the ship's belly, amid the splendor of banners, lights, flowers, and wild jazz; but he, the handsome young blond who drags behind him abysses, immense deserts, the people's destiny, is not excited, is not watching that fleeting ravishment of nerves and feeling.

Thus . . . Thus . . . in the same way—like the pale weaver from Prato on a day long ago—He will pass, mute and absorbed, amid the glamour, beauty, beauty, and luxury of Paris that the sensuous, smiling, charmer will show him, her whirlwind of pleasures, her whirlpool of mad and delirious mirages.

To others . . . to others that fatuous life of adventure, ease, vice; to others that life of binges, sensuality, frivolous and ephemeral drunkenness: for Him . . . life is something else for Him.

Life is the passionate, violent drama that the martyrdom, agony, heartache of those buried in prisons injects into his blood; that fixes like burning nails into his soul the names, faces, look of the fallen; that arms and flings him, alone, against the tyrant.

Life is the incessant, unending tempest that shakes, seizes, pierces, transfigures, exalts him, and finally tears him from the resigned human herd to shape him in the eternity of time and love.

He is no longer a man: he is an emblem of the sun that advances through darkness.

He is not someone about to die; He is the creator of tomorrow.

He is not alone and abandoned, he is the herald of a storm that rages, swarms, builds, expands, and roars in the swirl of winds, in the crash of waves, in the din of thunder, in the rumble of abysses.

Tomorrow, when He, steady and majestic, will move through hundreds of armed men with satrap faces and hyena hearts toward his execution, all this dark, toiling martyrdom of a people that has captivated and stripped his heart like boiling lava flowing down a mountainside; all this violent, oppressed passion of souls on which human beasts, covered with slaver, blood, and mud, paddle and row for years believing themselves on sure, calm waters, he will overthrow in radiant flame in the ardor of his blue eyes, and He will shout out his grand Idea: *Viva Anarchy!*

Then pale, trembling, the faces and lips of the living: serene in the ecstasy of the dream the face of the dead, while slowly, in the sadness of the dawning day, his beautiful, wounded body transforms and dissolves in red-hot vapors.

Vivere un'ora, un attimo solo, un palpito ardito,
Poi tuffarsi nell' onda dell'azzurro infinito.
Ecco la vera, intensa voluttà della mente,
Ecco il desio gagliardo di chi medita e sente.

To live an hour, only an hour, a daring moment,
Then leap into the wave of infinite blue.
That I the true, intense will of the mind,
That is the brave desire of one who thinks and feels.

One after the other his friends arrived, and their eyes showed the traces of tears.

"And now . . . wounded, chained; how He must suffer from the crew of drunken whoremasters!" everyone is thinking.

Not a word of cowardice, weakness, renunciation; but dull, dark torment while his flesh aches; while his head in the bloody bandage is splitting; while his spirit struggles in the chains: only one thought, only one regret: *Not being able to kill him!*

He is a hero; the supreme hero if the most tragic Greek concept.

Chained on a high mountain, suspended between earth and sky; in the howling wind and lightening, not a word of humiliation and exhaustion. This conquered superhuman remains impassible in his anguish, insult and torture, awaiting his hour of death that will be a liberation.

The marvelous, powerful vision passes through, strikes, and revives in his eyes wild with fever and delirium.

"And now down with all enemy powers: fall on me, strike lightening from the tortuous furrows and murderous places: unleash your rage, thunder, and furious winds over me; uproot the earth and mix it with the fearsome swirl of the sea and the fiery stars; oh Jove, hurl down into the black bottomless pit my body dragged from overwhelming and pitiless violence: *Today I am Immortal.*"

Translated by Martha King

What to Do?

∾ *Raffaele Schiavina*

San Carlo (Ferrara), Italy, April 8, 1894–New York, New York, 1987

Raffaele Schiavina was a peasant's son, but he was able to earn a diploma as an accountant, which was useful to him in obtaining his first employment in America, where he emigrated in 1913, settling in Brockton, Massachusetts. Initially an adherent of socialism, he was influenced by reading Kropotkin's *Memorie* (Memoirs), and in 1914 he began to frequent anarchist circles. He subscribed to the *Cronaca Sovversiva* (Subversive Chronicle) and became acquainted with Galleani. In 1916, the latter committed the administration of his newspaper to Schiavina, together with Carlo Valdinoci. Schiavina established himself in Lynn, Massachusetts, and began to write articles and give lectures. On September 25, 1916, he experienced his first arrest, with Mario Buda and Federico Cari, for an antiwar demonstration in Boston, and was subsequently released. In 1917, on the occasion of the arrest of Galleani, he hid the list of subscribers to the newspaper. In 1917, soon after delivering an antiwar speech in New York, he was also arrested and then, being released again, was able to return to work on the newspaper, which he did not abandon, even when the main part of Galleani's group became expatriates in Mexico to avoid conscription. He was suspected of being involved in the plot to dynamite Youngstown, and after the arrest in Chicago of Ella Antolini in January 1918, he was put on trial and was condemned to a year of hard labor for failing to appear for the draft. He served his sentence in the prison of East Cambridge, after which on June 24, 1919, he was sent to Ellis Island to be deported to Italy, together with Galleani and seven other anarchists.

In 1920, along with Galleani, he brought the *Cronaca Sovversiva* back to life in Turin, succeeding also in circulating the newspaper clandestinely in the United States, but in October of that year, the Italian police authorities definitively suppressed the newspaper. With the advent of Fascism, Schiavina decided to expatriate. In March 1923, after having passed through Ferrara to see his mother and sister for the last time, he left for Paris, where he established contacts with Italians in political exile. He created the newspapers *La Difesa per Sacco e Vanzetti* (The Defense of Sacco and Vanzetti, 1923) and *Il Mondo* (The World, 1925–28) and published the volume *Sacco e Vanzetti: Cause e fini di un delitto di Stato* (Sacco and Vanzetti: Causes and Aims of a State Crime, 1927).

In New York, meanwhile, conceived as the heir to the *Cronaca Sovversiva*, on April 15, 1922, *L'Adunata dei Refrattari* (The Gathering of the Unwilling) was initiated as a fortnightly. Directed by Costantino Zonchello and then, briefly, Ilario Margarita, its purpose was to support Sacco and Vanzetti and to serve as an antifascist bulwark. Upon his return from Paris in 1928, Schiavina became its editor, using the pseudonym "Max Sartin." He was able to reenter the United States clandestinely, thanks to the good offices of some old comrades, among whom was Emilio Coda.

Schiavina personally developed *L'Adunata,* which in 1934 changed from a fortnightly to a weekly, and he edited it until 1971. Andrea Ciofalo, who also illegally reentered America and who died in the 1960s, served as the principal collaborator for the administration of the newspaper and for contacts with the press.

L'Adunata , from which the following is excerpted, remained faithful to the old ideals of Galleani—the anarchism that sanctioned the use of dynamite and the motto "salvation is within you." In 1931, the newspaper provided help to the anarchist Schirru for his projected attempt on Mussolini. In 1936, it was the point of reference for volunteers willing to fight in Spain against Franco.

With an unshakable faith in an ideal that was by then passé, and with the gradual disappearance of all the old political associations, in 1982 Schiavina ended his political life. Assisted by Robert D'Attilio, he published his last work, the translation into English of Galleani's small book *La fine dell'anarchismo?* (The Purpose of Anarchism?). According to Schiavina's intentions, the book, addressing the young generations, would be "of great help today, tomorrow, and always," until the "evils of oppression, of exploitation, and ignorance would be removed from the face of the earth." After fifty-nine years of living clandestinely, Schiavina shifted from place to place continually, obsessed, as Paul Avrich recalls, with the fear of being discovered and with recurring nightmares that displayed "the bulldog face" of J. Edgar Hoover, director of the FBI. Schiavina, who underwent a pacemaker implant in 1972, deteriorated in health, until even he, the last Italian American anarchist, passed on.

ESSENTIAL BIBLIOGRAPHY

Avrich 1991, 123–124; Dadà 1976, 212–214; Dadà 1984; Sartin, in *Bollettino dell'Archivio G. Pinelli*, August 13, 1999.

❧

What to do? The question is no longer ours alone. It is no longer only for moral avant-gardistes and progressive intellectuals, making work for pioneers within this bourgeois society corrupted by vice and rotten to the core, which marches heartless and aimless toward its rapid, inevitable downfall. Yesterday, no one was asking, except for a few sentimental liberals troubled by liberalism's organic inability to reconcile the irreconcilable: man's liberty with the subjugation of the citizen; justice for the producer with the privileges of the owner. Today the leaders ponder it, those whom fate and the calculus of privilege have elevated to the supreme hierarchy of the existing social order.

What to do? In truth, the question is warranted. Things are happening that are likely to bewilder the most tenacious lovers of dogma. The day before yesterday at the corner of 42nd Street and 8th Avenue in New York, in front of a stately bank building, one of the few that still thrive, under the indifferent eyes of the crowd looking toward nearby Broadway for diversion, entertainment, and oblivion, a middle-aged man, pale and haggard, staggered and fell, exhausted, on the sidewalk. The policeman on duty rushed to lift him up: "My name is Christopher Christ," he said, "and I'm starving to death."

The case is typical, but not unique. From the coal mining regions, death notices continue, with the monotonous regularity of the sun: "In the Renton mining camp, near Pittsburgh, Pa., the child John Love, two years old, died of starvation. In the camp there are four other children who are in grave danger." If children die of hunger, what extreme deprivation will befall adults? The "Department of Hospitals" of the City of New York announces that since the beginning of the crisis city hospitals have noted an influx of patients, more than 25 percent above of the normal average.

It is currently estimated that there are ten million unemployed and thirty million needy individuals. Meanwhile the condition of the working class is increasingly worsening, following the reduction of wages announced last week by all of the major industrial companies in the country.

The expert statistics of accountants in service to the State and to plutocratic Christian philanthropy announce that in 1928, at the height of so-called prosperity, the average American worker's real wages had increased by 35.9 per percent in relation to 1918, while the cost of living in comparison had increased 70.7 percent. Later, from 1928 onward, wages have fallen in proportions ranging from 20 to 40 percent—and even more in some industries—while the cost of living has not declined more than 10 percent. Also note that these percentages refer to the hourly rates of those who are actually employed; one third of American workers are currently out of work and most of the remaining two thirds work part-time. Therefore the famous American standard of living on which so much of Herbert Hoover's electoral demagogy was based has become a myth, pure and simple. In fact, it is estimated that this year, American workers receive a total sum of salaries of over twenty billion less than those received in 1929. That is to say, a lot less than half of what was paid in wages two years ago, and it explains in facts and figures the rampant poverty, the cause of unimaginable suffering and death.

By contrast, the mood of this impetuous aristocracy of the dollar does not know despair. The day when large corporations, led by the steel trust, announced a reduction of ten percent on the wages paid to their employees, prices on the New York Stock Exchange rose from one to fourteen points. And it is logical: reducing wages means incrementally docking workers, which increases capital "profit," shareholder dividends, and thus encourages holders of liquid capital to buy shares, assuring the continuity of the profits that permit them to surrender, without a hint of concern, to joy and debauchery.

The lavishness and opulence flaunted by the stars of Hollywood cinema for the "première" of a drama depicting the horrific ordeal of two innocent men condemned to a slow agony of life imprisonment because they were detested by the golden gang of bandits who on their own whim pass laws in California, are undoubtedly an atrocious insult to the desolation and infinite anguish of Rena Mooney.[1] But the extravagant and crazed orgies from the mountains to the sea, in every American city and in every cosmopolitan locale in the rest of the world, drown out boredom and squander the treasures of American plutocracy without restraint and without any concern but for satisfying the caprices of disordered senses; they are a daily, mocking insult to the poverty and misery of an entire people. When it is read that, while in mining camps children are starving to death, a few days and a few hundred meters away from the time and place where Christopher Christ was falling down on a sidewalk, exhausted from starvation, in the heart of the metropolis, in a hall in the Biltmore Hotel that was transformed into a

---

1. The reference is to the opening of *Precedent*, the drama inspired by the Mooney case. *L'Adunata*'s source in Los Angeles is the writer Louis Adamic.

race track, three hundred students "invited" twenty-five horses to a banquet, and the city administration and the army of the republic officially participated in the senseless revelry; indignation rises from the heart to the throat, the horror is accompanied by contempt. Not only does the ruling class make a spectacle of its own recklessness, but also its insensitivity: one seems to be reading a description of a Roman orgy of imperial decadence.

Men have lost track of the precise notion of material and spiritual values. The senseless waste by some highlights and exacerbates the extreme misery of others. The head of a great railway corporation proclaims theft to be last resort for someone dying of hunger; three hundred unemployed in Henryetta, Oklahoma, march armed en masse on the village shops, not to beg, but to demand the food they need for themselves and their families; an ex-serviceman miner in Kentucky spends his "bonus" just paid by the government to buy arms and ammunition with which to fight the assassins hired by the mine's top brass; the most fanatical academic of the confederation, N.M. Butler, advises a far-fetched salvation for capitalist society, the Socialism of the State; while Herbert Hoover, head of State, persistently repudiates him in the name of his "American individualism" that the progressive development of trusts has annihilated for at least thirty years. Evidently, something so excessively large that it cannot be perceived by the incurable blindness of men, surrounds us. What is it?

Some will tell you that it is the State. Aware of its secular sins, of the moral emptiness on which it is based, equal only to the emptiness left in its coffers by the abuse of power and the wages of war, the great pirates of finance see it as booty, teetering on the edge of a precipice, and they run for cover creating below it the imaginary support of a universal providential function. It is almost as if the State, which was the worst administrator of political justice and could not assure freedom for its citizens, revealed itself to be an impeccable administrator of social justice, an instrument adept at assuring bread for everyone, at exactly the most lasting moment when it announces its own ruin, whether it falls into the predatory hands of an absolutist plutocracy or surrenders to a coup by the proletarian revolution.

Others will tell you that the economic structure is in ruins: it lacks direction, method, order. The capitalist economy is a failure: cause of savage wars, of indescribable disasters. It is necessary to socialize wealth, to modify the mechanism of production and distribution, to entrust its management to the most competent and most honest, who at the same time will be both skilled directors and executives of economics and politics of mankind. . . . Again the Providential State! If the political ways of so-called bourgeois progressivism are followed, or the economics of Marxist socialism, it invariably leads to the rehabilitation of the State, relieved of its own moral ruin and placed high on the pedestal of a new faith, rededicated away from authority and privilege and toward the veneration of men.

And then there are the moralists who in Christ's name look to mortgage the future by launching anathemas on the evils of today. The pope wants "fair wages." But who will determine the limits of "fair wages" in a world where the profits of those who monopolize capital is necessarily in direct proportion to the intensity of exploitation of the "goods" of labor? The fear of God or the law of the State? Father MacEachen has actually seen the misery of the miners and discovered that the evil is social injustice. "The crimes committed by all the Czars," he writes indignantly, "are no less heinous than the crime of social injustice perpetrated against the American workers of our time . . . What does social justice require? It requires, undoubtedly, recognizing the worker's right to work: it is because his right to life depends on his right to work. In addition, all workers have the right to work at all times because they have the right to live at all times." Words of gold: but who will guarantee workers this inalienable right to work in a world where all of the means of production and trade, all of the wealth accumulated by the painful effort of dead generations is the monopoly of a privileged minority that does not allow its use except upon payment of predatory usury? Again: the fear of God or the providential State?

In ruin is all traditional order with its political fratricide, its pirate economy, its wild morality. And they have endless reasons to worry about tomorrow as long as they harbor enough intellectual light to see the precipice.

The old order is dissolving. Democracy—pride of the fathers—has degenerated into a squalid and ruinous plutocracy. . . . The economy, full of all imaginable material and intellectual resources, has created chronic unemployment, pauperism, and pellagra. Christian morality, hypocrisy, corruption, fraud on a scale never before seen. And the dispossessed have ceased to respect a government that will gun them down, an economy that starves them, a morality that deceives them. Until when will they peacefully bear the heavy burden of the costs and pains that the privilege heaps on their backs every day?

The unknown haunts the nights of prophets, who know that there is nothing left that is alive, healthy, and fertile to support this unjust social order. More than anything, besides the traditional ancestral resignation of the underprivileged masses on which the scourge of poverty and the relentless glare of progress beat together to hasten the awakening.

May it not delay.

Translated by Giulia Prestia

Two Articles

Carlo Tresca

Sulmona (L'Aquila), Italy, 1879–New York, New York, 1943

The fourth of eight children, Carlo Tresca was born to a family of landed proprietors, whose mode of living, "because of some unfortunate speculations," would greatly worsen within a few years. In his formative years, Tresca bore the weight of the anticlerical ideas of his father, fiercely opposed to those of his mother, who would have had her son become a priest. Tresca attended the technical institute, renouncing thereby a more defined course of studies that would have concluded with a degree in jurisprudence.

Already, in Sulmona, the boy adhered to the socialist circle of the railroad workers, and through the weekly, *Il Germe* (The Seed), which he founded and directed, he began a series of engagements on ideal themes but also on more concrete questions, like those tied to the social redemption of the peasants. His first sentencing, for defamation, occurred in 1904 at the end of a trial that was epochal, during which he was assisted by two renowned defenders, Enrico Ferri and Arnaldo Lucci. He was threatened with twelve months of imprisonment, six months of close confinement, and a fine of one thousand lire. Tresca appealed and left Italy. First he went to Lugano, where the mayor's friends wanted him to stay. In Switzerland, he made the acquaintance of, among others, Benito Mussolini, at that time an exile.

After several weeks, Tresca embarked for America, to which his older brother Ettore had already emigrated. Tresca's wife Helga Guerra, whom he married in 1903, probably joined him shortly thereafter. In Philadelphia, Tresca was already known in the small circle of those who read *Il Germe*, and who, meeting in the association Circolo Risveglio Giovanile Italiano (Circle of the Young Italian

Awakening), had given a theatrical performance and collected the money necessary for Tresca's voyage.

Arriving in America August 1904, Tresca began to write for various newspapers, among them *Mastro Paolo* (Master Paul), *La Voce della Colonia* (The Voice of the Colony), and *Il Popolo* (The People). He then joined the Federazione Socialista Italiana, assuming the direction of the *Proletario* (Proletarian), a newspaper that, as he stated, was practically "dead." "But I gave the *Proletario* life again. I directed it for some time without pay; then I earned four dollars weekly; then eight, and finally, twelve. With personal sacrifices, I saved the newspaper. I relieved it of all its debts. To galvanize the discouraged masses thereabout, I threw myself headlong into a very dangerous battle against the consular camorras of America, a battle that cost me three months in prison."

In 1906, perhaps tired of the interminable political disputes of the socialistic environment and attracted by the anarchic Communism of Errico Malatesta, Tresca distanced himself from the newspaper, passing first to the *Voce del Popolo* (Voice of the People), then founding the weekly *La Plebe* (The Common People), and, simultaneously, a "Università popolare," among whose speakers was Luigi Galleani. In 1908, condemned to three months in prison for defaming the Italian consul in Philadelphia, he had to move to Pittsburgh. The following year, permission to publish his paper was revoked as the result of a further condemnation to six months in prison for calumny: in publishing a compromising photograph, he had, in fact, revealed the love affair between a Catholic priest and his housekeeper. "Tresca has been condemned," commented *L'Internazionale* of Philadelphia, "but he remains luminously certain that the photograph published by *La Plebe* is actual and that as a consequence, the Reverend Di Sabato is a true and actual filthy person." Compelled to make another move, thanks to the help of a friend from New Kensington, Pennsylvania, Tresca was able to launch a new newspaper, *L'Avvenire* (The Future), in Steubenville, Ohio.

After these various experiences and accomplishments, Tresca embarked upon the most legendary stage of his life. His popularity among the immigrant workers greatly increased with the echo of his battles against the bankers, labor intermediaries, consuls, and priests. It was also the period in which Tresca drew close to the IWW and utilized his very popularity as a charismatic leader during the great strikes of Lawrence (1912), Paterson (1913), and the Mesabi Range (1915). On this last occasion, he was arrested for the murder of a policeman. In America and in Italy, however, numerous public demonstrations were organized to obtain his release. The FSI (Federazione Socialista Italiana) went so far as to launch an appeal to the Italian government, calling upon it to defend "the honor of his [Tresca's] country before history and humanity," and Arturo Caroti, among others, published the pamphlet *Per Carlo Tresca* (For Carlo Tresca). Subsequently, the accusation was dropped. In the meanwhile, Tresca drew close to Elizabeth Gurley Flynn, activist of the IWW, and his wife requested and obtained a divorce.

The United States entered World War I, and in 1917, shortly after his arrest under the imputation of conspiring to have violated the Espionage Act, Tresca became defined in the *New York Times* as "one of the most fanatic among the agitators of the IWW." Subsequently, *L'Avvenire* was banned. But Tresca found money to acquire another colonial newspaper, *Il Martello* (The Hammer) and transformed it into "a publication of scientific propaganda." In time, it became the principal limelight of radicalism, even if, as Vecoli notes, it comported itself with a certain prudence in respect to the problem of military intervention. "Even so," remembered the companions of Tresca in the published celebratory pamphlet on his death, "he underwent much distress during that period of persecutions and of relentless physical and moral brutalization."

Tresca became somewhat cumbersome for all the directors of the party, and for him, the postwar years signaled a phase of curious isolation. On one side, he felt the emptiness he created around himself; on the other, he was aware of the zeal of the people, desiring to have him back at their very side. "In economical organizations, my progress is blocked. Tresca? Too radical. Too persecuted by the police. . . . During the strikes of the waiters, of the young dressmakers, the shoemakers, the weavers, I felt like taking up the direction of the masses again: 'No, you cannot talk; excuse us, but you are the black beast of the padroni and agents of the police.' And the people, the people, who know and appreciate my spirit of devotion, the people wanted me."

Those postwar years also signaled a progressive distancing from prohibited positions, defended with so much fervor in the period of revolutionary purity. However, Tresca carried on a tempestuous and always increasing antifascist opposition, attested by the fact that already in 1923, under pressures of the Italian diplomatic complex, he was put on trial, accused of sending obscene material by mail, a pretext as bizarre as the imputation that the *Martello* announced the publication of a book on birth control. Such was the reaction of the public that President Coolidge was induced to commute the condemnation from one year to four months of detention.

By the 1930s, Tresca was a champion of the anti-Stalinist left. In accord with the orientations of other important radical leaders, among them Emma Goldman, he denounced the Moscow trials and the abandonment of the anarchists in the Spanish civil war, and he was a member of the Dewey commission, which was investigating the Soviet accusations against Trotsky. For Max Eastman, after Eugene Debs, Tresca was, "the most esteemed and respected personage in the revolutionary movement."

In the final heroic stage of his life, he took as his insignia a militant antifascism, even including physical skirmishes among opposite factions. On his left cheek, Tresca already bore a deep scar, the memory of an attempt on his life (not the only one) he suffered in Pittsburgh, in 1918. Now Black Shirts organized punitive raids on the office of the *Martello*, as did the New York police, in the days following the assassination of two Black Shirts on Memorial Day in 1927. In exchange, Tresca and his faction were always in the first ranks in occasions of violent actions disturbing the meetings promoted by the Fascist League of North America. Tresca became a member of the Mazzini Society, and as such, opposed the admittance of Communists and ex-Fascists. At the outbreak of World War II, he collaborated with the Office of War Information in organizing the Italian-American Victory Council; and in 1942, with Giovannitti and Valenti, he was among the promoters of the Italian American League against fascism.

On the night of January 11, 1943, while leaving his office, he was shot and killed by a hired gunman. The crime remained unpunished. Among the possible conspirators were the Communists, the Fascists, or some unknown economic power. Among the possible executors were activists under the orders of Moscow; spreading reports indicated Vittorio Vidali. Other possible executors were Mafioso elements; reports indicated Carmine Galante and Frank Garofalo, with the eventual complicity of Generoso Pope, the Fascist editor of the *Progresso Italo-Americano*. The homicide was defined by the *New Republic* as "the case of Matteotti in America." For ten years, a commission, presided over by the socialist Norman Thomas, investigated the case without success.

The figure of Tresca quickly entered into legend. The booklet *Rimane salda la fede* (Keep the Faith), edited upon his death by Arturo Giovannitti and Onorio Ruotolo, gives a sufficiently precise idea of his fame, with ample testimonies. James T. Farrell, who wrote an obituary, "In Remembrance of Carlo Tresca," defined the principal enigma of Tresca's fame. "I think that Tresca's politics can be defined more or less as anarchic-Communism. His ideal of liberty leaned toward anarchy. He was not an organizer, not in the sense in which the Marxist revolutionaries are, but he saw with clarity the necessity to work together with the organizations and through them, while still maintaining his own independence of action, not—as some do—to have an excuse to do nothing, but because this position imposed upon him his convictions; the precise consciousness of his own role in the workers' and radical movement, his liberal and generous personality."

Instead, touching upon another undoubtedly basic element of Tresca's fame, John Dos Passos emphasized the American interpretation of the myth: "When the great European revolution was transformed into an immense war by unruly bands, Carlo, whether fighting against the Communists or the Fascists, became a preserver, in the best sense of the word, fighting to protect the people he loved from a new influx of the brutal European logic. . . . It can be said that he died in defense of America."

Tresca, then, an American hero: a free man, a personality not encapsulated in a political or syndicalist role bureaucratically defined, appears truly as "a Free Lance of labor" (as defined by F. Guadagni), who "held formal coherence to be of no account," and, paladin of the weakest, "rushed where the masses were fighting, and in the fight, he was never among the last." Carlo Tresca was a personage very dear to the American imagination. Besides being the subject of many important historical researches, he was also a personage of romance. He is, in fact, Paolo Polizzi, protagonist of Jerre Mangione's *Night Search* (1965), and the vicissitudes of his life are also at the center of Joseph Arleo's novel *The Grand Street Collector* (1975).

Tresca's writings are almost exclusively journalistic; apparently, there are no organized collections in volumes. Excerpted here is a passage from *The Autobiography of Carlo Tresca*. Among Tresca's political texts are the anti-Fascist dramas *L'attentato a Mussolini; ovvero il segreto di Pulcinella* (The Attempt on Mussolini's Life, or, Pulcinella's Secret) and *Il vendicatore* (The Avenger). Many other writings, among which, for example, the celebrated debates with Catholic priests, are to be found in various collected pamphlets.

ESSENTIAL BIBLIOGRAPHY

Eastman 1942; Giovannitti-Ruotolo 1943; Gallagher 1988; MOI (article by Rudolph J. Vecoli); Pernicone 1989; Vezzosi 1991 and 1994.

ᖇ

Carlo Tresca's Hellish Day in the Mesabi Range

The day broke.[1] I arose with the firm resolution to get Andreichin out of prison. At that time I was leading the strike of the iron miners on the Mesabi Range in the State of Minnesota. George Andreichin was still being held in jail in Grand Rapids, but he was needed in Hibbing, Minnesota. This young idealist was the only one

1. The date was probably July 3, 1916.

who spoke a Slavic language, and the striking miners were almost all Italians and Slavonians. In fact, there were more than ten thousand Slavic miners who had gone on strike, and none of us could make himself understood by them except Andreichin. The success of the strike depended in large part on the return of this comrade of ours to the large group of his countrymen.

It was a beautiful August morning and the hills of that section of Minnesota were in a haze. The sun was shining and the prospects of the strike seemed to be bright. In Hibbing we had comparative freedom, and contact with the courageous fighters was always a source of inspiration to me. That morning I was inspired with a bright idea. In a flash I decided to take the bull by the horns: to go to the city judge and ask him to lift the seven-hundred-dollar bond he had imposed on Andreichin after another local accusation, and to release him on parole. George had been incriminated in two places: in Hibbing, he had already been released under a bond of $700, and in Grand Rapids, he was still in jail for the lack of $1,000.

Jauntily, I walked into the chamber that was full of deputy sheriffs and strange-looking mine guards. His Honor was sitting on the bench. I approached him, and upon his asking, "What do you want?" I told him that we needed Andreichin in the interests of peace. "The Slavonians," I said, "are very restless, the situation is serious. Andreichin's imprisonment in Grand Rapids has only increased the tension." If the judge were to release the seven-hundred-dollars that had been paid in Hibbing, I would go to Grand Rapids, I said, and bring him back. I knew the proposition was a bold one, but . . . the judge looked squarely into my face and then turned his gaze to the mine guards and deputy sheriffs. In a low tone he told me, "Well, I guess we'll have to do to it, but don't let them know what it's all about. Come later, I will fetch the money for you."

One hour later I had the seven hundred dollars. In a few more hours I had collected three hundred more and was on my way to Grand Rapids to ransom our comrade.

Our delegation consisted of three: a local lawyer by the name of White, myself, and the chauffeur, who was a friend of the strikers and the owner of an Italian grocery store in Virginia, Minnesota.

It was about three o'clock in the afternoon when we left Hibbing and three hours later we entered the county court building in Grand Rapids. Our way led us to the District Attorney's office where we found one clerk. The clerk politely replied that the District Attorney would be back in a few minutes and asked us to take seats. Soon the telephone rang, and there was a short conversation between the clerk and somebody on the other end of the wire. I cannot explain why that conversation stirred me. Is it because the tense situation made me hypersensitive? Is it because I was in fear of danger, or did I actually overhear something? At any rate, I felt that there was danger in the air. This sense of lurking danger was nothing new to me. I had experienced it hundreds of times in similar situations. I leaned over to White and told him. "This clerk has received orders to arrest me." To which White replied, "Nonsense." "They cannot do anything to you here." My assurance, however, was so great that I offered immediate proof. Whispering to White, "Watch," I took my hat and started toward the door. The clerk immediately jumped up and told me, "Mr. Tresca, the sheriff wants to talk to you." That was sufficient proof of danger. But such is human nature that I almost triumphantly turned my face to White as if to say, "I told you so."

Just then the District Attorney stepped into the office. He was a young, nice-looking American type, very polite, very correct, very officious. Mr. White introduced me to him. He shook hands with me.

"Glad," he said, "to see the dangerous leader of the strike."

We sat down and had a nice chat. He expressed surprise at my insinuation that I was about to be arrested. He was all courtesy and decorum.

Presently, however, while this polite conversation was going on, we heard a noise outside like the tramping of soldiers' feet. Turning to the door we beheld a dramatic scene. The sheriff, in shirtsleeves with a belt of cartridges around his belly, with one gun on his hip, ferocious looking, stepped into the office with two husky deputy sheriffs at his heels. The man was red in the face and, without introduction, began to shout, "You goddam agitator, what did you come here for?"

"For business," I replied.

To which the deputy sheriff in a still more rasping voice said, "And it's my business to run you out of this County as quick as I can." Facing me at close range, he peremptorily ordered, "Give me that gun."

Tense as the situation was, I didn't fail to realize the comic side of it. I did not reply. The man approached me very closely shouting into my face, "Give up the gun."

"Why don't you take it?" I asked.

The sheriff hurled at me a number of very ingenious insults and only after giving vent to his temper did he order a deputy sheriff to search me. Of course, no gun was found on my person. This only increased the sheriff's ire.

I looked at the District Attorney. I was really interested to watch his reactions. He finally interfered. He took the sheriff by the arm, led him to another room where they had a brief consultation. Presently, the young, polite fellow returned and informed, me first, that I had no business to come to his county; second, that

White had nothing to do with the case; third, that he would not let me see And- reichin, and fourth, that I must go out of Grand Rapids and back to Hibbing as fast I could. I tried to protest. In fact, I exchanged a very few sharp and unpleasant words with the Sheriff, but I decided to go back promptly. There had been three mass meetings organized for that night in Hibbing, and I couldn't really stay away. In turning toward the door I said goodbye to the District Attorney in a courteous way, to which that polite and charming young officer replied, "Get the hell out of here, you S.O.B." This was about too much for me; I stopped, looked squarely into his eyes, and told him. "Look here, you are many and I am alone. You are armed and I am unarmed." But before I finished, I felt the muzzle of the sheriff's gun at my back and the sheriff shouting, "Get out, get out!" There was nothing to do but leave.

There begins now our journey back to Hibbing—a trip I'll never forget as long as I live. It was more than a trip. It was a procession. Our little truck was followed by two other cars with the Sheriff in one and a number of armed men in the other. At a distance of three blocks from the Court House three more cars appeared from a side street, filled with men holding rifles in their hands. The three cars joined the procession. Soon we had left Grand Rapids and the country stretched on either side of us. We were alone—three men followed by five cars filled with armed, hostile keepers of the law.

In a few minutes we were approaching the mining town of Mishaevaka. Mr. White again seized my arm and nervously pointed at something ahead. There, at the entrance to the town, two columns of men—many of them armed with rifles— were lined on either side of the street, watching in silent gloom. White said to me, "This is a lynching party for you." The only thing I could say was, "The sooner, the better."

There was no misjudging the character of the groups that awaited us. My chauffeur-friend became very excited. Mr. White was becoming whiter and whiter. Both were speechless. I saw that it was up to me to take the initiative, I said to White, "Let me get out of the car and walk back of it very slowly, while the chauffeur and you remain in your seats. Let's go through the crowd facing them calmly. Never mind what happens to me. Take care of yourselves. If this is a lynching party, let me be the victim. If we escape, then we'll get into the car after the danger is over."

Thus our strange procession entered the space between two lines of enraged, armed men. We heard curses on either side. "Damned agitator." Fists were being clenched; distorted faces emitted words of insult; some of the men in the lines were about to throw themselves on us, but I soon discovered one element in the picture which made me breathe more easily. Behind the lines of armed men I noticed groups or miners in threatening postures. I heard shouts from the distance: "Courage, Tresca! We won't let 'em hurt you. Hurray for the strike!" I presume that this and our composed demeanor held the crowd in leash.

Amidst the storm of shouts, threatening gestures, curses and general bedlam, we proceeded to the end of the town. The imminent danger was over. We soon reached the county limit. By this time I was back in our truck. The sheriff stood up in his car surrounded by the four other cars and gave us the last warning, "Remember forever that this place is not fit for you. When you come again I will kill you. Go, and keep going." I certainly did keep going for more than an hour until we reached Hibbing late in the evening with my mission unaccomplished.

I was almost ready to say, "This is the end of a perfect day," when I realized that the end of the day was not yet. Passing through Main Street, opposite the office of the local paper, we saw boys rushing with shouts "Extra, Extra!" There it was, printed with fresh black ink, "Clash in Biwabick. Deputy Sheriff Murdered." Biwabick was another mining town where the strike was on. The murder of a deputy sheriff was not to be disregarded. There seemed to be more trouble ahead.

While I was reading the paper, a crowd of strikers and sympathizers surrounded me, only to confirm the alarming news. Three strikers had been killed, they told me, and the situation was very bad. I hastily took leave of Mr. White and rushed to the local strike headquarters, only to find the place deserted, closed and dark. I had the creeping feeling of impending danger. I couldn't rest. I had to go to Virginia, which was the headquarters of the strike committee and also my own headquarters. I asked the chauffeur to drive there. The poor soul replied, "I'll be damned if I do. For God's sake let's stay here; I'm afraid." I didn't blame the man, but I had to go and was about to take the trolley car. The faithful soul didn't let me go alone, however, "I don't care what happens," he said, "I must go with you." And so we started out for Virginia, the very same evening.

What a deserted city! What gloom! What an eerie feeling! All stores closed. Headquarters deserted. Dark. Nobody walking in the streets. I was looking around for anyone from the committee. I could find none. I could only think of the dreadful city of night of James Thompson and of Dante's fierce city of Dis. Nothing remained for me to do but go to that one-story frame structure owned by one of the strikers. I used to sleep there because I felt protected: eight young, strong Italian strikers always slept with me in the same house, all armed with guns and ready for action. They did not sleep all the time, either; they kept vigil in turn. I found them on the spot.

My first question was about Frank Little,[2] who was among the leaders of the strike. I was particularly concerned about Frank because he hadn't been feeling well; besides, he was practically alone since the strikers were either Italians, Slavonians, or Finns, with hardly a native American among them. To my consternation I learned that he had gone to sleep in a hotel, contrary to the advice of my Italian friends. Under the given conditions this was a foolhardy step, to say the least. The only thing I could do was to go to this hotel and beg him to go into hiding. I explained to him that, owing to the Biwabick situation, there was every likelihood that we would be arrested; that the only thing to do was to stay away. Frank, half asleep, muttered, "You are seeing red, Carlo! You mustn't get excited."

When I insisted, he said, "Oh, go to sleep. Let me alone."

"They will come, Frank, and take you."

"Aw, let 'em come. What do I care?"

It was rather amusing to see this fighter displaying such a degree of equanimity. He turned his back to me and fell asleep. Still, I did not want to leave him alone; I sent my Italian bodyguards back and took a room in the same hotel, keeping only one man with me, the I.W.W. organizer, Gildea, a native American.[3]

It was about four o'clock in the morning when I heard loud knocks at my door and harsh voices shouting, "Get out there." I jumped out of bed, asking who it was. Through the window that opened into the corridor (the room was dark while the corridor was lighted), I saw two searchlights playing and the muzzles of two guns pointed into my room. It was a very interesting play of silhouettes against the opaque glass. I cannot say that I felt very comfortable, yet I knew that I had to be firm. I said, "I won't open before I am told who it is."

To which a still harsher voice shouted, "You are wanted by the sheriff."

When I asked about a warrant, a strange voice replied, "We don't need no warrants for fellows like you."

Whereupon I said, "If that's the case, you might as well break the door at your own risk."

And thus we stood in the room, Gildea and I, without lighting the lights, ready to meet the assailants in case they should break the door. It was the better part of wisdom to stay inside away from the window, through which the guns were stretching their threatening muzzles. Soon new voices were added to those out-

2. Frank Little was an important IWW organizer who was lynched by vigilantes in Butte, Montana, on August 1, 1917, because he spoke out against the war.

3. James Gilday. Tresca uses the term "native American" in the sense of "old immigrant" stock, not American Indian.

side. There was a tramping of feet, a hubbub of conversation and a woman's voice screaming at a high pitch, "For heaven sake, Mr. Tresca, come out and spare us the trouble, or else our hotel will suffer damage."

To which I replied with all the gallantry I could muster, "Well, Madam, I never fail with ladies. If you tell me who is there, and tell me the truth, I will open the door."

There was some whispering and shuffling behind the door, then the lady imparted to me the cheerful news that there were outside the door eighteen plainclothes men with a chief. The information made it advisable for me to surrender.

"Well, Madam, if you tell me to open the door, I obey."

In the county jail where we were temporarily interned, we found Sam Scarlett, an I.W.W. Organizer and Frank Little, without a coat, but in a very cheerful mood. "You see," Frank said, "they did spoil my good sleep, those rascals."

Before long, detectives and policemen invaded the jail, handcuffed all four of us and took as out without telling us where we were going. As I looked around, I realized that we were being escorted by a large number of policemen and deputy sheriffs, armed with rifles.

There was little time to meditate, however. It was not long before we reached the little railway station where we found a special train consisting of an engine and one car. We were ordered to enter the car where we found four men, three of them handcuffed to each other by the wrists, while the fourth was lying on a bench badly torn and bespattered with blood; the head of one was all bandages. Other police were keeping everything quiet in the car, and the whole thing bore the marks of something very mysterious.

As soon as we entered the coach, our handcuffs were removed and we were seated, each on a bench with two detectives on each side.

It was all very queer. I was used to all the vicissitudes of labor struggles, but this journey in the early morning in a special train was something new. I asked my "companions," "Where are we going?"

The reply was, "I don't know; I don't care to tell you. But be sure you won't see Virginia any longer."

As the train sped on through meadows sprinkled with dew, among clumps of trees swaying in the light morning breeze, under a clear sky that looked bathed after the night's gloom, the tension relaxed. We began to talk to each other. The guards relented, and we soon learned what happened in Biwabick. Four deputy sheriffs had gone to the house of a striker by the name of Philip Masonovich with a warrant for the arrest of one of the boarders. The men of the law were very rough and they beat up Philip's wife. There were three Montenegran workers boarding in the house. The fellows were former soldiers who had participated in many a war in the Balkans. They were courageous fellows. They could not allow the deputy sheriffs to continue their dastardly acts. So they dashed against the four deputy sheriffs, took away their guns, killed one and severely wounded another. It was a real battle between deputy sheriffs and the strikers, and they were all arrested. These were the four men that we had found in the railway car. They were all being conveyed to Duluth to be imprisoned on a charge of murder in the first degree. As to Little, Gildea, Scarlett and myself, we also were charged with murder as accessories before the fact. This is why we all were in the car. We were being accused of a murder that took place in our absence in a different town. We were being attached artificially to the murder case in order to eliminate us from the strike picture.

It was about ten o'clock in the morning when we finally landed in the Duluth jail and I could tell myself that one day of my life had been completed. 'Twas a crowded day, indeed.

∾

The Fascist Gene Pope Is a Man of Straw

Generoso Pope, proprietor of the *Progressor* and the *Corriere* of New York and the *Opinione* of Philadelphia: I believed he was a man with guts.[4] Now I learn that instead he is a man of straw.

I have openly put before him, like a lashing that makes its mark, a precise, detailed accusation: that of being a racketeer and a gangster.

In fact, no sooner was my accusation published, than a certain gentleman, one of two that Pope uses to intimidate his opponents,—*his name is known to Pope and to my friends*—came to pay a visit to the offices of the *Martello*, 94 Fifth Avenue.

Really.

A courtesy call. He was all politeness, and he requested, with exquisite good manners, a copy of the *Martello* in which my prosecutorial summary against Pope had been published.

Pope and I both know the meaning of such visits, and how much they resemble the methods that gangsters use.

It can be considered as an act of bravado, a harmless show of courage. I will make it clear to them that we have the courage to flush them out even at home.

4. From *Il Martello*, November 14, 1934.

I do not doubt the courage of such people.

I only say that I too have courage and that I do not fear them.

They can take this as a warning.

But I say that we are in open battle, and between forces in open battle there is no need for warnings.

And I wished to give Generoso Pope this advice (even in English, so that the many American friends I have interested in this dispute for preventive reasons might understand me, and so that they might be able to learn who would be more or less responsible for what might take place):

"Keep your men at bay. This is not a game that can be defined like those you have played with Giordano and Sisca and Bernabei. If I fall, you inevitably follow me."

But now I see that I have before me . . . a straw man.

He offers an olive branch. And he has someone write, but this time he does not sign it, a tear-jerker article "For the peace of our community" (*Progresso*, 14 November), with which he wishes—see how far human imbecility can go—to invite all and sundry, reds, blacks, yellows, catholics and atheists, bosses and workers, not to poke the fires of political visions, not to divide the immigrants into fascists and antifascists, and not to create "disputes that disturb our collectivity."

Since Generoso Pope, in addition to being a racketeer and a gangster, is an illiterate quadripede, even if he signs editorials in his newspapers, it might be well to tell him straight out that such a peace can never be.

Instead, I wish to argue here with the writer in *Progresso*, convinced that he will take care to explain to Pope—hopefully in dialect, to be sure that Pope can better understand—the things I am going to say here.

Above all, how can one talk about peace when one writes: "Who seeks to make noise with violent individual attacks, in the vain hope of strengthening one's own position or to wait a little for manna from heaven or from the earth? One is speaking generally of old figures that the great majority of conationals know well and profoundly despise?"

Here shoots out, involuntarily, the real evil that corrupts Pope, that undermines him in all his essential humanity: the self-conceit of an ignorant and presumptuous peacock.

So that, after nearly forty years that I am in harness and have never bent before the violent forces of two governments; after never having lowered even a single hem of my flag, I, who even believe that I have a mass of followers, intelligent and devoted, not to me personally, because idolatry is not an attribute of intelligent people, but to the ideal that is my only motive force, I have the need to attack Pope, as if Pope were the sort of star in the human firmament to spread around himself light and heat.

Do you come down from your pedestal, you gilded ass? From the pedestal down to where, since you are a golden calf, you have placed the vile and amoral crowd of your servants; come down and even plunge your snout into the foul dregs of the colony, if you wish, but do not try on before me, or before my friends, these postures of "great man," which might even be tolerated in someone truly great in talent and in moral fiber, but not in one such as you, a presumptuous jackass without even the intellectual capacity to know the difference between good and evil.

Yes. Even Barsotti knew me well. More than once I nailed him to the pillory, making him suffer, and not just a little. I would attack Barsotti with a violence that was dictated to me by the imperious will not to save an enemy from any blows—the same reason that I attack you Generoso Pope.

Personal reasons? No. Like you, Barsotti incarnated the exploitation of man by man, political, religious, and economic.

Through your newspapers, you, represent everything we subversives hate: the state, religion, capital.

You yourself say just this, in the articles that others write and you sign.

It is for this that I and my comrades attack you. For this, and for no other reason. You personally do not interest us. We subversives despise you, believe me, perhaps less than you despise those who adore you, those who crawl around you.

Violent individual attacks, my specialty, formidable accusations. And why do you not bring suits for libel to show that you are not a racketeer and a gangster? This would be the only civilized reply possible in a country where it is not yet permissible, to do what the fascists do, to stab someone to death with impunity.

Why not ask the court to punish whoever it is that attacks you unjustly?

Even "your friends" are awaiting this.

You speak of *peace in our community.*

Now you say this. Now that I have forced you to pull in your horns. But yesterday you wanted to dictate this peace in the fascist manner: You wanted to use the methods of gangsters and racketeers, to intimidate and to silence your adversaries, the antifascists.

The antifascists will never give you any peace so long as you continue using your newspapers to make propaganda in favor of fascism.

And you disgust us. Like Prezzolini and Bigongiari.[5]

5. Giuseppe Prezzolini, director of the Casa Italiana, Columbia University, 1933–1937; Dino Bigongiari, Lorenzo DaPonte Professor of Italian, Columbia University.

You say, "We are not the ones who demand the fascistization of the United States." You lie, because you are a coward. If you had the courage of your convictions, you who claim that Mussolini has given to Italy "a regime that has assured regular employment to the masses of Italy even through drastic curbs of freedom that were rather often the causes of disorder and of wretchedness," then you would say to the jackasses who bray for you in the *Progresso,* those out-and-out jackasses who believe freedom can be the cause of disorder and of wretchedness, you would tell them that "drastic curbs of freedom" are wanted even in the United States. And you would say this, if for no other reason, just to silence my own rather modest voice. And I have mentioned Prezzolini and Bigongiari. These are cultivated people. And so they remain as mute as fish.

You don't even know how to be quiet.

And what a pitiable spectacle! The cultivated people, along side you, a four-footed animal! While the Casa Italiana stands accused of being a den of fascist propagandists, a home for fascist propaganda in the United States, Prezzolini and Bigongiari remain silent, like cowards. If they had the courage of *their* convictions, they would say, "True, we are fascists, and we make use of the Casa Italiana to make propaganda for fascism, which is our faith."

Now that criticism and public accusation touch them, they pull in their horns, like snails.

And Pope, whom I have put against the wall because he wanted to employ the methods of racketeers and gangsters to silence any voices of antifascism, has neither the courage to silence us with the hands of his hired assassins, nor to bring us before the magistrates, and he offers us, in the name of the Italian community, the olive branch.

Coward.

Peace? Not now, not with the black shirts. Neither with cowards nor even with those who are not cowards.

One day there will be peace. But only when we shall have hung Italy's tyrants from the highest lampposts in Rome and the revolt of the proletariat shall be an accomplished fact. Who knows? Maybe then we will be able even to talk of peace. Before that, no.

Once Again Tresca

∾ *Ezio Taddei*

Livorno, Italy, October 2, 1895–Rome, Italy, May 16, 1956

Born to a well-to-do family in 1895, from 1903 Ezio Taddei lived in Rome, and at twelve years old, spent a night in Regina Coeli Prison for having participated in an illegal meeting. From that moment, his father repudiated him, and Ezio Taddei began his life as a vagabond, employed in an infinite number of occupations, from shop boy to furrier and from upholsterer to workman in the steelworks of Terni. He went to Milan and Livorno and worked as a shepherd, carpenter, typographer, electrician, mechanic, baker, and gardener. In 1915, he enlisted in the *bersaglieri*, a corps of the Italian army, and at the front earned a bronze medal for having saved a companion wounded in the arm. After his discharge in 1918, he was committed to the military prison of Savona for counterfeiting documents. He succeeded in escaping but was seized again.

The first writings of Taddei appeared in *Avvenire Anarchico* (The Anarchist Future), published in Pisa. In 1921, he was arrested in Genoa in relation to an investigation against an anarchist group, followers of Malatesta, who had perpetrated a series of attempted dynamite attacks. Taddei assumed the entire responsibility for the affair and was the only one to remain in prison, but more than that, to be sent afterward from prison to prison to discharge the sentence of eight years that was meted out to him. He was in Porto Santo Stefano, Procida, Nisida, Finalborgo, Porto Longone, Alghero, Civitavecchia, and Pozzuoli and spent two years in Ponza. In 1933, he was sent into confinement in Bernalda, in Basilicata, where he remained until 1935. In prison, he read widely. In this period, he wrote, among other things, his first story, *Fra le tenebre* (Amid the Gloom). After the confinement, Taddei went to Switzerland, where he was also arrested and released, and then to France. From Paris, he began to contribute to the *L'Adunata dei Refrattari*, and in 1938, embarked clandestinely at Le Havre, for New York.

In the United States, he quickly bound himself to Carlo Tresca and began to write for *Il Martello*; he also enjoyed relationships with various intellectuals of the American left, among them Samuel Putnam, translator of Pirandello; Frances Keene, student of Salvemini and translator of Vittorini; and Arthur Miller, who in 1955, would visit him in Rome. After Tresca was assassinated, Taddei wrote the pamphlet *The Tresca Case* (1943), in which he charged the Fascists with the crime and not the Communists, a position supported by Luigi Antonini. As a consequence, he was attacked by the members of the ILGWU (International Ladies' Garment Workers' Union) as an agent provocateur in the service of the Stalinists. In fact, Taddei entered the Communist camp and became an editor of the *Unità del Popolo* (Unity of the People) of Ambrogio Donini. He returned to Italy in the autumn of 1945, establishing himself in Rome with a sister and working on the *Unità*. In close communication with Corrado Alvaro and other intellects, in 1955, he founded the review *raccontanovelle* (Telling Stories), a monthly issued for just eight numbers.

Taddei's literary career was actually initiated in America, with the publication in 1940, of the *carceraria* (prison) autobiography *L'uomo che cammina* (The Man Who Walks). Following were the stories in *Parole collettive* (Collective Words, 1941); *Hard as Stone* (1942), translated by Frances Keene; *Alberi e casolari* (Trees and Cottages, 1943) and *Il pino e la rufola* (1944), translated in 1945 by Samuel Putnam as *The Pine Tree and the Mole*; and *The Sowing of the Seed* (1946), translated by Putnam. Then published in Italy were *Le porte dell'Inferno* (The Gates of Hell, 1945); *Rotaia* (Track, 1946); *La fabbrica parla* (The Factory Speaks, 1950); *Ho rinunciato alla libertà* (I Have Given up Freedom), (1950, this too on an American subject); *Il quinto Vangelo* (The Fifth Gospel, 1951); *C'è posta per voi, Mr. Brown!* (You've Got Mail, Mr. Brown, 1953); and an installment of the novel *Michele Esposito*, excerpted from *raccontanovelle*. In the collections of stories on the resistance, *Il secondo risorgimento d'Italia* (The Second Italian Risorgimento, 1955), appears his *Potente* (Powerful), together with works of Calvino, Viganò, Joyce Lussi, Carlo Bernari, and others. Taddei also wrote for the theater and political pamphlets propagandizing Communism. In the pamphlet, *De Gasperi consiglia gli italiani ad emigrare* (De Gasperi Advises Italians to Emigrate, 1953), he ironically describes De Gasperi's visit to the United States, warmly welcomed by Generoso Pope, by the labor leader Luigi Antonini, and by the Mafioso Frank Garofalo, but staying a good distance away from the poor immigrants of the East Side.

Taddei's work, which has recently been the object of an intelligent critical appraisal by Martino Marazzi, can be divided into two principal veins: one pertains to the robust realism of the Tuscan tradition, to which belong, for example, *Il pino e la rufola* and *Alberi e casolari*; the other, autobiographical, especially as represented in *Le porte dell'Inferno* and in *Ho rinunciato alla libertà*, is most relevant to the subject matter of this anthology. Emerging from the autobiographical works is a bitter portrait of America, kingdom of illusions and burning disillusions, of insupportable contrasts between nabobs and the miserable, of inexpressible vexations to which the needy immigrants are subject. Even if a certain prejudicial attitude, which has political origins, is a recognizable constant, these pages, expressed dryly and with cold, objective descriptions, above all of nocturnal interiors, sometimes evoking the paintings of Edward Hopper, constitute one of the most original and notable contributions of the Italian American narrative of the 1940s, and they place Taddei among the most interesting, if less known, personalities of Italian neorealism.

ESSENTIAL BIBLIOGRAPHY

Dizionario degli italiani illustri e oscuri; Fusco 1962; Javarone 1958; Marazzi 2001, 67–81; Peirce 1956; Umbrella 1967.

∾

There was a banquet at the Manhattan Club. The major figures of the Italian Colony had to be there. Washington was represented by a high functionary of the Treasury Department, along with the usual deputies and political figures.

Carlo also received an invitation, and I had a conversation with him that same evening.

"Don't go," I said.

"Of course I'm going. What excuse can I give?"

"What are you going to do there?"

"Nothing, I don't know, at least make an appearance."

"You will find yourself in bad company. Pope will be there and who knows who. . . ."

"In that case I'll leave immediately. In fact, you know what we should do? You go to Mary's on Bedford Street, and I'll meet you in about an hour."

In the Manhattan room, Carlo Tresca went and sat in a seat by the side, gave a glance to those invited and began to come up with a pretext to leave, then saw by the front door two people enter arm-in-arm. One was a woman, the Deputy District Public Attorney of the Federal Court, and the other was a man that everyone knew, the head of the Marese gang. The judge's name was Dolores Fecondi, the gangster Frank Garofalo. The two lovers took their seats at the table of honor among the representatives of the Treasury and other VIPs.

Carlo Tresca found an excuse. He raised himself from his seat.

"This is too much," he said, "besides Fascists, there are also representatives of the underworld."

He left the room, and rushed to the restaurant where I was waiting and told me everything.

"You will see tomorrow," he told me.

"What?"

"I don't know, but certainly something new. Come early to the newspaper. I implore you."

The following morning the telephone calls began. The first was the City Treasurer who asked Carlo Tresca not to say a word about what happened. Then another, and in the end the door opened and she came in. I saw her dressed in gray with black gloves, real tight, a bit of hair on her lip. She took a seat at the side of Tresca's desk and began to talk. At times she smiled, at times she wanted it understood that this was all nonsense.

Tresca instead remained listening with a grave, unchanging look on his face. When his turn came, he talked with a paternal voice. "Naturally, I won't say anything... But what the hell! A married woman! A judge!" His voice became animated. "A judge appears in a place like the Manhattan Club, and in whose company? Frank Garofalo's. But do you know who he is?"

"Yes."

"And do you believe you are the only one who knows him? Think a little: At the door the police recognize him. You can't get away from him. One day he will do something and it will be impossible to cover it up. And then? Tell me something, you might find yourself in court, in the midst of journalists who will come to interview you. And then your family...."

Dolores Fecondi didn't respond. When she left she moved in a way very different than when she entered and left us locking the door very softly.

Poveruomo

Talking about some things with an old friend, at a certain point I asked him. "How did it happen, ending up in the hands of that gangster?

"How did it go?... You remember that Poveruomo. Have you heard me mention him?

"But is that really his name?"

"It sure is."

"Well?"

"He used to do this work when he was younger, now he's not up to it anymore. He used to bring girls to the big shots."

I kept listening.

"You understand," my friend continued, "there are some rich men who have a bit of a family, a bit of a position, so it doesn't please them to go with just anyone. Also, in order to avoid being blackmailed. In short, there is always something to fear. Then there is the one who procures her for him. Poveruomo does this. He used to frequent the houses of Italians that had daughters, and became a friend. He knew thoroughly what were their hopes, and since every immigrant wanted their children to study, Poveruomo began to say he could get them a scholarship, and with the scholarship everything else followed.

My friend looked at me then resumed. "You're surprised? . . . What can you do when that kind catches a 15 year-old girl! Often the father and mother didn't know how to read or write. He brought her to a meeting place where there are big shots. It's the stuff to turn people's heads! Nothing could be done . . . I will tell you something else. To him it became a trade and he began to cultivate his business when they were very young. He was the godfather, and so it was like a type of breeding. This really happened to Miss Fecondi. First he brought her to Pop who gives her the money to continue her studies, and of course she was his. Sometimes he used to introduce her to Americans to show off . . . and even gives her to them . . . Imagine that! And this poor *guagliona* was able to continue to study."

"And then?"

"Ms Fecondi isn't a fool. . . . She scarcely had that piece of paper in her hand! He sticks her in the office and Pop passes her to Garofalo. Garofalo was from Pop's gang. He had her named a judge, and you can easily imagine the outcome between a gangster and that one in Federal court.

They Are Communists

We don't know what Generoso Pope and Frank Garofalo said after the banquet. The fact is that from that moment Carlo Tresca felt in danger and informed the F.B.I. of this. The evening of January 11, 1943, I had a telephone conversation with Carlo Tresca and it went like this:

"Where are you?" he asked.

"In the Bronx. Do you want to come?"

"No, no way. There are people here. Do me a favor, please come tomorrow."

At 9:30 Tresca went into the street. When he was on the sidewalk opposite the newspaper office, a man fired a pistol shot into his back. Tresca turned, the man fired another shot under his left eye. Tresca fell. It was 9:30, at 9:45 Luigi Antonini transmitted the news by telephone: "They killed Tresca. The Communists did it."

Someone telephoned him.

"Antonini, they killed Tresca."

"I know, the Communists did it."

At midnight I went home. I passed by 5th Avenue at 15th Street and saw the windows of the newspaper office lit up. And how could that be, I said to myself? I went up and tried to enter. The door was locked from inside. I knocked and the door suddenly opened and two policemen with revolvers in their hands said, "Who are you?"

"Me? I'm the editor of the paper."

"Who are you looking for?"

"Nobody, I want to come in. Why are you here?"

"Do you know Carlo Tresca?" they asked.

"Certainly."

"He's been killed."

I remained lost in thought.

"Enter," the police said.

One of them went to the telephone, called, and after a few seconds a police car arrived that brought me to the homicide squad. As soon as I entered, the room filled with people, and from everywhere I heard them say to me, "You saw the Communists, what did they do?"

The Interrogation

The room on the first floor of the homicide ward was emptying. The interrogators said goodbye and returned home because it was late. Now there remained in the offices, and along the corridors, the special detectives who came from every part of the city.

I was still waiting. I looked at my watch, it was three. The room remained empty, full of cigarette smoke. I should have been pleased that at least I wasn't really the last one. Instead I was worried, and tried as much as I could to figure out what to do, and not to make any mistakes. And although I had had a few hours at my disposal, I still hadn't succeeded in coming up with a plan. I discarded ideas as soon as they came to me.

"No, not this."

I then returned to the starting point.

"It is necessary to get out of here without them suspecting anything." The whole history of gangs in the United States remained there in front.

"If they come to understand that I know things, they'll shoot me. Them! . . . I won't even make it home . . . then they'll say it was the Communists . . . I'd be a fool, I'll tell them. . . ."

A door opened. "Let's go!" they said.

"We're here," I said to myself. Behind the desk was the District Attorney, surrounded by a dozen special detectives, police captains.

"Sit."

The District Attorney began: "Who killed Carlo Tresca?"

"It is difficult to say," I answered.

"Who do you think?"

"There are many possibilities."

Then we continued to go back and forth. He resumed. "Do you believe it was the Communists?"

"I'm not in a position to say."

"Did you have a close relationship with Tresca?"

"Yes."

"And was it true you were his closest collaborator?"

"I believe so."

"You're with the paper, *Il Martello*?"

"Yes, the editor."

"Did you know that Tresca had a violent dispute recently with the Communist Party?"

"Yes. There are copies of the newspaper you could check."

"Had Carlo Tresca ever said to you that he feared being killed because of such disputes?"

"No, he never said that to me."

"Do you know Vittorio Vidali?"

"I have heard the name."

"Do you know where he is?"

"In Mexico."

"Do you know if he came recently to New York?"

"I don't know."

"Do you know if there is a Communist named Grieco hiding in New York?"

"I don't know."

"Do you know where Palmiro Togliatti lives?"

"Where he lives?" I asked, astounded.

"Yes," he insisted.

"I believe in Moscow."

"Not in New York."

"I don't believe so."

"Have you ever heard the name Umberto Terracini?"

"Yes."

"Do you know if he is in New York?"

"No, he isn't."

"How can you be so sure?"

"Because he's in jail."

"Where?"

"In Italy."

"And how do you know."

"I left him there."

"Who is it that killed Carlo Tresca?"

"Many people could have."

"Why?"

"Because Carlo Tresca had disputes with everyone."

"With whom?"

I exercised more self-control by saying nothing.

"He couldn't live without causing disputes."

The interrogation lasted a couple of hours. Then the District Attorney said that for security reasons I had to go to a nearby hotel to get some sleep. The detective who accompanied me told me in the car. "We'll take you to it. The Communists could kill you to get rid of a witness."

I was very tired. In the porter's lodge of the Grand Hotel, the detective gave two false names, one for him and one for me. This worried me because one never knows what is going to happen at night. There were two beds in the room, one for me and one for the agent. I did everything in a matter-of-fact way, but no matter how much I tried, I didn't succeed in getting any sleep.

It was scarcely morning when another detective entered the room and said it was necessary to go immediately to the District Attorney's Office. During the night many things might have happened. Perhaps the great figures of the city had already acted. I realized this entering the office, as soon as I saw that the one who was going to interrogate me wasn't the Assistant District Attorney of the night before. They had changed him. I heard him talk in a low voice to his friend.

"I've taken the case. These are a bunch of idiots." He nodded his head to the other officials sitting around him. He greeted me politely, then told me his name. Cagnucco. Afterwards, he took a photograph out of a yellow envelope on the table.

"Do you know who this is?"

I saw him smiling. Then I looked at the photograph. There was a line of writing in German, Red Front. There were also some men, a table, and other more distant men.

"This is Vittorio Vidali," said the District Attorney, and he put his finger on the figure of a man. I thought, how could they have made this photograph? Is it possible, in just a few hours? There it was, already done! I decided to remain even more on guard, and suddenly he began interrogating me again. This time in Italian, more courteously, but also more clearly.

"No, no, there isn't any doubt. We will examine all aspects of the case, but this is where we should strike. Vidali will be extradited. In the meantime the Mexican border is being watched, and the ships leaving for Russia are under surveillance."

In the afternoon he finally told me I could go, that I was free. But he gave me some advice and warned me to be careful. I stayed in my house for a long time, then went out and walked all night. I bought the newspapers that came out after the killing, and they were full of opinions, interviews, photographs, all with the same theme. Carlo Tresca was dead. Now I really felt alone, and further burdened with a very grave responsibility,

They are really capable of holding a serious trial and sending a pair of innocents to the electric chair. What can I do? I turned to my friends to see which one I could ask for advice. But what good what would it do, that one is going to tell that other one. The other one is in contact with so-and-so.

My head was spinning, there wasn't an escape. But the idea never left me for a minute, I would tell at any price what I knew. The next day I went to meet with my friend. I confided in him, left him some documents, a hand-written declaration, and then I went to meet with the District Attorney Luis Cagnucco. I told him briefly, without giving too much importance to it, what had happened between Carlo Tresca and the group made up of Pope, Fecondi and Garofalo during the banquet at the Manhattan Club. But while I talked, I noticed the District Attorney was annoyed by what I was telling him.

He tried to persuade me that these incidents were of no importance, and they couldn't have had much impact. In the end, he said he would keep my speculation in mind. At any rate, what mattered to him at the moment was to remain on the trail of the Communists, because soon he would make an announcement that would eliminate any doubt.

Several days passed. I continued to gather information. I got in touch with a journalist friend of mine from the *New York Post*, and even Carlo Tresca's friends decided to hold a public meeting to commemorate the thirtieth day of his death. I announced I would speak and make a public accusation.

February 14, 1943, was the date fixed for the meeting. On the night of the 11th, I was summoned to a restaurant and the same people I dined with tried to persuade me to back off my resolution, making it clear the dangers I was going to encounter. I said I would speak anyway, and that same night my house was broken into by gangsters who entered by the steps of the fire escape and got into the building hoping to surprise me.

The next day District Attorney Cagnucco called me into his office. He warned me that if I spoke at Sunday's meeting he would arrest me and take me to court. On February 14th, I spoke anyway.

Translated by Gil Fagiani

PART V

Integrated Apocalyptics

Introduction

Many Italians did not try to maintain their connections with Italy. They arrived in America as children in family groups or alone, as young immigrants in search of fortune. The moment they came into contact with this new reality, they immediately entered into a process of radical cultural change. Some of them fully espoused the new language and culture, and they tended to abandon their Italian roots. Their adhesion to an evidently superior lifestyle was either natural or the result of a courageous bid for autonomy. This implied many challenges. For one thing, it meant testing their own capacity to express themselves with new tools. In some instances this choice coincided with their entrance into the world of written culture: Pascal D'Angelo (as we will see in detail) and his compatriot from Abruzzo, Francesco Ventresca, were almost illiterate when they came from Italy, and in America they made up for that lack by learning to read and write directly in English. In the case of Constantine Panunzio and Giuseppe Cautela, they had to undergo a psychologically more courageous and lacerating experience. They were compelled to abandon their fathers' language in order to acquire, as Joseph Tusiani put it, "the difficult word," that is, the first stage toward mastering the "new word."[1] Only this new speech could grant them full citizenship, visibility, and the possibility of being read, understood, and appreciated. I have decided to define this group of authors "integrated apocalyptics"—combining the two terms of Umberto Eco's famous antithesis—precisely because of their double role. As apocalyptics, they upset the precarious colonial balance; as integrators, they were experimenting with the process of assimilation. Thus, they inhabited an interme-

1. See especially the titles of the first two volumes of Tusiani's autobiography, 1988 and 1991.

diate zone between Italian Americans who were well rooted in the Little Italies and second-generation writers who were rooted elsewhere. The former maintained an uninterrupted bond with Italy; the latter, especially from the 1920s onward, were able to give a full American literary voice to the oral heritage of their culture. Somehow, these integrated apocalyptics succeeded in expanding the scope of *la storia grande* (history on the grand scale) and enriching the notion of the American melting pot with the ancient experiences of mass immigration. In so doing, they made radical change, breaking the protective shell of the colonial egg, of those besieged enclaves in American cities where the old Italy continued to exist in a self-sufficient and marginal way. Actually, this is what the old Italy has been doing almost up to the present day.

These writers, then, correct the Great Emigration with the stabilization—even if problematic and not definitive—of the Italian component within the checkered panorama of a new nationality and a new sense of belonging. They close the colonial experience and seek to separate themselves from it in a highly visible way. At the same time, they often take the responsibility of being among its proudest witnesses, as if they were seeking to mediate between that world which had come to an end and the broad new horizons of Americanization. They believed in the myth, then in full force, of the melting pot that was still able to dissolve racial differences and mold the new American type by containing and harmonizing them. However, they were conscious of being different and remained legitimately themselves, however difficult that might be. Contrary to what the second-generation writers later asserted, these writers felt no shame in being Italian, the exponents of a disadvantaged group heavily stigmatized by prejudice. Indeed, from time to time and in the midst of the fumes and convulsions of the American metropolis, they were often nostalgic for the skies and the light of Italy. They did not yet manifest that characteristic love-hate relationship toward their new country. They did not articulate the splitting of a self driven by the need to return to Italian traditions and, simultaneously, the need to shake free of them. In fact, only the latter drive defined them. As first-generation Italian Americans, they did not feel they had to come to terms, almost fatally, with their origins. By contrast, a second-generation writer like John Fante had to commit what I have elsewhere called "a ritual patricide"[2] in order to revitalize the old culture within the new. But, these first-generation authors acknowledged the fatal erasure of a culture (the Italian one) and the need to update their models and adapt them to the surrounding environment. This was the only way they

2. Durante 2003, 26.

could establish a contact, otherwise inhibited, with their American audience. It made sense that the first step in this direction should be the adoption of the English language, in spite of the difficulties and sacrifices this entailed—a real challenge indeed.

Admittedly, the categories of first and second generation are simplistic. Strictly speaking, a first-generation Italian American is born in Italy and then settles in America, taking up citizenship there. On the other hand, a second-generation Italian American is an American born in America to Italian parents. But clearly, this rather linear scheme is upset by all kinds of distinguishing conditions. Some "first-generation" writers, like the novelist Garibaldi Marto Lapolla,[3] thought to all effects like "second-generation" writers. As a matter of fact, these immigrants completed their full educations in America. They had left Italy at a very young age and had not had the time to absorb a culture worthy of its name, except for the poor, exclusively oral lore of the domestic circle. In other cases, such as that of Frances Winwar (Francesca Vinciguerra),[4] her slightly longer stay in Italy and membership in the bourgeoisie had already provided her with a rather well-defined cultural framework. But after coming to America, this framework proved to be advantageous as she made the leap into the new culture without hesitating.

In the perspective of the present work, therefore, the rigid generational scheme is modified according to the individual case at hand. This section of the anthology will not include writers—like Lapolla and Winwar—who belonged to the "first generation" and yet anticipated a later phase. On the other hand, the inborn elusiveness of the generational dynamic is precisely due to the way it functions in different historical periods. The attempt to modulate and order the vast production of Italian American writers must necessarily reckon with this not insignificant critical problem. In other words, can we group together three writers like Gino Speranza (born in 1872 and already active in the second decade of the twentieth century), Jo Pagano (born in 1906 and active since the 1930s), and Mario Puzo (born in 1920 and active since the 1950s) simply because they all were "second generation"? Likewise, does it make any sense to put the writers who will be introduced in Part IV in the same group as, say, Joseph Tusiani? Like them, he was

---

3. See Durante 2002; Marazzi 2003.

4. On Winwar and her time publishing in Italy—*La vita del cuore. George Sand e i suoi tempi* (The Life of the Heart: George Sand and Her Times; Milan: Longanesi, 1947; *L'ultimo amore di Camilla* (The Last Love of Camille) (Milan: Mondadori, 1955); *Con D'Annunzio di fuoco in fuoco* (Wings of Fire: A Biography of Gabriele d'Annunzio and Eleonora Duse) (Milan: Mondadori, 1960)—see Peragallo 1949, 233–242.

"first generation," but he arrived in America only in the late 1940s rather than at the beginning of the twentieth century.[5]

Clearly, inclusion in the first or the second generation entails psychological problems that have persisted even beyond the different historical periods. But obviously, in time the Italian presence in America went through different stages and along a slow but inevitable path of emancipation and assimilation. Those who arrived at the end of the nineteenth century or the beginning of the twentieth century were faced with a reality much different from the one encountered by those who came a decade later. The former might even have thought that the Black Hand was the most remarkable Italian novelty. The latter discovered that the mayor of New York had an Italian name. And although, at bottom, the feeling of estrangement might have been the same, these very different contexts could not but strongly reverberate in their works.

Rose Basile Green was the first scholar (1974) who tried to draw a map of the Italian American novel (almost entirely) in English. She was well aware of these problems and set out to solve them by weaving together the datum of generational belonging with more cogent historical and thematic considerations. In this way, she outlined a critical framework within which she successfully—although with some difficulty—grouped her materials. I almost totally disagree with her scheme. Nonetheless, we need to keep it in mind, inasmuch as it successfully shows her bewildered response to a literary phenomenon the complexity and breadth of which was only partially known at the time. Basile Green's study is preceded by a prologue of sorts entitled "Entering a New World." Here she deals, among others, with the work of Constantine Panunzio and Pascal D'Angelo and relates it to definitely more extravagant texts like Antonio Arrighi's and Rocco Corresca's autobiographical narrations and to much later works like those written by Angelo Pellegrini and Bernard Ficarra. The main partitions of Basile Green's scheme are articulated in the following way:

> The "early impact." For obvious reasons of precedence, here she includes
> Ventura and Ciambelli. But also Villa, Cautela, Lapolla, and even John
> Antonio Moroso, a third-generation author whose production has little or
> nothing to do with Italian American themes.

5. It is not by chance that the "ancient word" would be the title of the final act of Tusiani's autobiography (1992): the Italian language regained from the new American position, meaning the final stage of this story of encounters and conflicts between cultures, on a wide open, almost multicultural, horizon in which perhaps it no longer makes sense to design complete geographies of literature. See Siani 2004.

The "need for assimilation." Curiously, none of the authors dealt with in the present anthology is included here.

The introspective phase of "revulsion," into which falls, among others, Winwar.

The "counterrevulsion" (obviously in opposition to the previous phrase), which more or less includes all of the major second-generation narrators of the 1930s and 1940s.

Basile Green's contribution certainly represents a milestone in the study of Italian American literature. However, her scheme does not stand up to the slightest historical-critical assessment. First of all, it is based on a documentation that, however voluminous for the years in which it was collected, presents many, and often serious, lacunae. It also reflects a certain "pro-ethnic" optimism. For example, she is right in pinpointing, as central to the first-/second-generation problem, a moment of "revulsion," that is, of the choice of "non–Italian American themes." This attitude should be related to the general one of an ethnic group's seeking to identify with the broader American culture. In my opinion, the phase of revulsion was articulated in complex and highly nuanced ways. The trouble is that Basile Green includes in this phase not only Winwar (a perfect choice) but also three authors like Bernard DeVoto, Paul Gallico, and Hamilton Basso. Elementary considerations based on the sociology of literature would have suggested their total extraneousness to literary representations of "Italian American themes."[6] This said, the ensuing phase of "counterrevulsion" is hardly credible, defined as it is as "a return to old sources in which the Italian-American, like the frontier back-trailer, returns to his distinctive heritage and resumes Italian-American themes on a more artistic level of American fiction."[7]

This remark is made with reference to a writer like John Fante, who, together with Jerre Mangione and Pietro Di Donato, should be the most representative of

---

6. DeVoto, novelist, historian, and essayist, was a third-generation Italian American, born and raised in a Mormon community in Ogden, Utah; his Italian heritage was for him little more than an ornament. Gallico, sports journalist and storyteller, son of an Italian musician and of a Viennese woman, was born in New York in 1897 and shortly thereafter, one could say, was entered into an international environment for which the problem of Italian immigration and, in general, of Italy was only one of many possibilities. Basso, journalist and storyteller, was a third-generation Italian American, belonging to a family of complex ethnic roots; his principal contact with Italian culture was his activity as a correspondent in Rome during fascism. On these three authors, see among many possible sources, the profiles by Peragallo 1949, respectively 76–88, 109–116, and 13–18.

7. Basile Green 1974, 23.

the phase of "counterrevulsion." But while it recalls Arturo Bandini's tyrannical father, it does not suit Arturo Bandini himself, the young American hero in search of an *ubi consistam*, who is the novelistic double of the author—the other side of the problem in which love and hate are fused, as already pointed out, in equal doses. In reality, if the "counterrevulsion" of which Basile Green speaks appropriately defines Mangione, it would be more fitting if it referred to authors who arrived after the generation of the 1930s, prone to more tolerant and pacific tones, those of a sort of *cantabile* "that's *amore*."

In a certain sense the personal trajectories addressed in Part V mostly concern, to borrow from the title of Constantine Panunzio's best-known work, the investigation of "the soul of the immigrants." These trajectories express the need to query one's own experience by recording its intermittencies, emotions, stumblings, and drives—all of which are aimed at achieving a goal that in some cases was professional, but more often than not was first and foremost existential. The goal coincided with a sense of satisfaction for having successfully transformed oneself and for having emerged from one's shell with a new mental outlook. In this regard, we have the exemplary cases of Louis Forgione and especially Silvio Villa, whose first real American book was published in 1922 with the title *The Unbidden Guest*. This narrative not only comes to grips with his migratory experience but also anticipates a more complex narrative season. Indeed, what the author mostly cares for and what best embodies his hopes for literary success was a fictional work truly freed from ethnic branding.

Thus, from a certain point of view and at least in theory, the authors who belong to this phase are the "noblest" and most important in the entire arc of the history of mass migration. They pioneered a new reality and were the first to venture out into the American sea without the safety net of the colony, a colony that might have welcomed, nourished, and consoled them. Restless spirits in search of another self, for the most part they wrote their books driven by the urge to communicate to the American public the reasons for their existence. Only indirectly were they interested in fiction. If anything, in the cases of Emanuel Carnevali, Pascal D'Angelo, and Arturo Giovannitti, poetry was the means through which they succeeded in expressing the compelling solicitations of that drive.

On the other hand, it is interesting to note that the colony did not remain indifferent to the efforts and, in some cases, successes of these authors. Reviews such as *Il Carroccio*—not to mention the many *Who's Who* volumes that recorded their biographical profiles—published some of their work and often became interested in their cases by presenting them (with characteristic exaggeration) as grand affirmations of the Italian spirit. But the fact remains that the experiences of these writers remained entirely, or almost entirely, beyond the pale of the colony. Significantly, in the case of Panunzio, the only real contact with that world took place not only in the context of his work—typically, the work of a cultural broker—but also in the political arena of the Mazzini Society. This context represented a different form of emigration, that of the political exile, whose cultural status, although thoroughly Italian, placed them incommensurably beyond the colony. The case of several Italian American politicians, in particular Edward Corsi, was different. They were forced by their very profession to "commute" between the two cultures and, therefore, the two languages, even if the American language was obviously predominant. Finally, there were the educators, the most important of whom was Angelo Patri. In this case, too, the problem of mediating between diverse cultures was clearly preeminent. However, as an authentic protagonist of the crucial period of the melting pot, Patri confronted it from a perspective that was, yes, deeply rooted in the Italian humus, but also embraced a fertile ethnic pluralism. He acknowledged that he was the descendant of a specific group, but also that he was only one of the many who happened to weave their lives into the fabric of the new world. At the beginning of his *A Schoolmaster in the Great City*, Patri writes:

> I remember sitting with the family and the neighbours' families about the fire place, while the father, night after night, told us stories of the Knights of the Crusades or recounted the glories of the heroes of proud Italy. How he could tell a story! His voice was strong, and soft, and soothing, and he had just sufficient power of exaggeration to increase the attractiveness of the tale. We could see the soldiers he told us about pass before us in all their struggles and sorrows and triumphs. Back and forth he marched them into Asia Minor, across Sicily, and into the castles of France, Germany, and England. We listened eagerly and came back each night ready to be thrilled and inspired again by the spirit of the good and the great.[8]

This might seem the foreword to a list of national claims or, at most, the overture to a fond, elegiac reevocation of the domestic circle, as at times happens in the second-generation writers.

In 1907, however, Lisi Cecilia Cipriani published *A Tuscan Childhood*, a warm recollection of an Italy and a way of life that seemed to spring from a fairy tale.[9]

---

8. Patri 1917, 1.

9. A sister of Cipriani's, Charlotte Jane, who lived until 1932, was a children's author in addition to a teacher. Her works, recalled by Olga Peragallo, are *The Child Vixen* (Chicago/

But in Patri's observations we find rather a more mundane declaration of his belonging (which, at any rate, is beyond question). Moreover, Patri sought to pinpoint a primitive phase of pure orality that the educator was obliged to fill with new contents. Patri chose to tackle this new phase by availing himself of that ancient way of transmitting knowledge; he grounded his pedagogical method on the fascination and stimulation that storytelling exerted on children's imagination. Thus, he became a "schoolmaster in the great city," namely, in that universe where all the ethnic groups that composed it shared the common problem of having to learn to read and write and painstakingly adapt themselves to a new way of life.[10]

From the 1920s onward, Italian Americans inevitably moved toward a new culture that in fact turned its familiar roots upside down. It was at this point that the Italian community started to realize that it was high time to give form and depth to its history in America. Up to that moment, this task had been delegated, in a casual and episodic way, to the feature columns, literary appendices, and Sunday supplements of the colonial press. As we have seen, the latter played an important part in celebrating the home country's glories by erecting monuments and whatnot.

The first noteworthy compilations of Italian American history appeared in the 1920s. Adolfo Bosi's *Cinquant'anni di vita italiana in America* (Fifty Years of Italian Life in America, 1925) was the first book of some substance. But it was only in the 1930s that we can find two writers of superior stature: Giovanni Ermenegildo Schiavo and Howard Rosario Marraro. Schiavo devoted his enormous erudition to every aspect of Italian American history in his ambitious project eloquently titled *Five Centuries of Italian American History*. But he did not live long enough to com-

---

New York, 1905), *The Little Captain* (an account of the life of Gerolamo Savonarola; Chicago/ New York, 1906), and the academic textbooks *Etude sur quelques noms propres d'origine germanique* (A Study of Some Proper Nouns of Germanic Origin, 1901) and *Exercises to Accompany Armstrong's Syntax of the French Verb* (1915).

10. A narrower pedagogical horizon, in the religious sense, also characterizes the commitment of authors like Antonio Mangano (Acri, Cosenza, 1869), the Protestant minister who, having immigrated to the United States in 1875, in 1917 published the volumes *Sons of Italy* and *Religious Work among Italians in America*. From him it was a case of giving to his church—the First Italian Baptist Church of Brooklyn—an instrument able to understand the social and individual dynamics of the vast Italian settlement, a base of operations for the apostolate, so that its penetration could have been greater than it would have been otherwise. To do it, a book was necessary that succeeded in shortening the enormous cultural difference between the Anglo-Saxon world and that of the new immigrants. The result, when compared to these goals, must be deemed as modest; yet, in the work of Mangano there emerges with vivacity the intent of the author—he too trying to mediate between the two worlds—to redeem a certain image of the Italians, and to call upon the Americans, through a lively narrative approach, to know them better.

plete it. The volumes that were published were somewhat muddled and tendentiously uncritical, but they still constitute an indispensable mine of information and an obligatory source for the scholar who, even today, sets out to study any question dealing with Italian American culture.[11] Contrary to Schiavo, Marraro was a professional academic. He focused his attention on the Italian Risorgimento and the founding fathers in America. We owe him the first, still extremely useful systematic study of emigration during the eighteenth and nineteenth centuries, before the exodus of the fin-de-siècle.

Giuseppe Prezzolini, who for many years was the director of Casa Italiana of Columbia University, contributed significantly to the launching of studies like those mentioned above. To start with, Prezzolini was the first to alert Italian intellectuals to the existence of an autonomous Italian American literary activity, even if his attitude was generally derogatory. Moreover, he was also the first to be in contact with the best writers of the second generation, from John Fante to Pietro Di Donato. We should also add that he not only imported and translated their work into Italian but also encouraged scholars to do research on them. From Prezzolini's circle came Olga Peragallo's pioneering study *Italian-American Authors and Their Contribution to American Literature*, posthumously edited by the author's mother, Anita, in 1949. We must also mention the work of academics like Salvatore Eugenio Scalia, a good deal of which was published in the pages of *Italica*. This meritorious journal was founded by Rudolph Altrocchi and carried on by Olga Ragusa. Among Ragusa's best collaborators was Antonio Pace, who had the merit of producing exceptionally valid studies like the richly documented *Benjamin Franklin and Italy*.

Translated by Franca and Bill Boelhower

11. On Schiavo (1898–1983), see Pane 1985.

A Story and a Poem

ᕱ *Lisi Cecilia Cipriani*

Lisi Cecilia Cipriani was the daughter of the count Giuseppe Cipriani, a brother of the Risorgimento hero Leonetto Cipriani. The count moved to the United States following financial reverses. In 1903, Lisi Cipriani entered the faculty of languages of the University of Chicago. A polyglot (she spoke six or seven languages), she was the governess to the children of numerous rich families in Chicago. Soon Lisi became an instructor of French and comparative literature at Chicago. A skilled philologist, in 1907 she published an interesting essay, "Studies in the Influence of the *Romance of the Rose* upon Chaucer" in the *Publications of the Modern Language Association of America*. In 1917, the Italian government gave her the task of carrying out war propaganda in the United States. To this end, she returned to Italy and visited the front, to gather useful material for the mission, but upon her reentry, she met with grave difficulties at the consulate, which refused her any sort of help. Cipriani denounced an attempt to discredit her, one that claimed "she was a spy or an adventuress" and that negated the validity of her titles. Without lawyers, she initiated a defamation suit against the consul Giuseppe Castruccio and his colleagues, demanding an indemnity of three hundred dollars, but she lost. Shortly after, relates Olga Peragallo, she declared that the Italian government had sent her a pension for services rendered. Later, she engaged herself in compiling an annual almanac dedicated to shops, firms, and Italian professionals of Chicago (*Italians in Chicago and Selected Directory of the Italians in Chicago*, various editions, 1928–1934), with corresponding biographical profiles, and shortly before 1939, she returned definitively to Italy. According to Schiavo 1975, she was also the president of the Italian section of the Chicago Council for Education.

In 1906, in Chicago, Cipriani had published *The Cry of Defeat,* a collection of short poems, largely melancholy and sentimental; one section was named, "Words of Love and Sorrow." The *New York Times* singled out the collection, regarding it with a certain sympathy. One year later, in New York, Cipriani published *A Tuscan Childhood*, a book of memories of her infancy, passages of which had been published in *The Century Magazine*. Even this book gained a rather large critical recognition on many newspapers, magazines and journals. As clearly revealed from the passage presented here, one of Cipriani's characteristics was to describe the dress and customs of a life typical of an Italian family very different from the poor families of more recent immigration. In short, graceful novelettes, set in an almost fable-like landscape, and veined with a pleasing humor, the author's work relied mostly upon the effects provoked by the distance between the life described and the informal modernity of the Americans.

ESSENTIAL BIBLIOGRAPHY
Peragallo 1949, 48–52.

ᴓ

The Child-Bride and Her Doll

Leghorn, where my mother was born, is the ugly duckling among the hundred cities of beautiful Italy that our poets praise. We consider Leghorn a new place, because its existence as a real city is recognized only for four or five hundred years, and we are apt to ascribe its lack of artistic interest to its newness.

Toward the middle of the last century, my grandfather was the German Consul General at Leghorn. He was a most remarkable man; and not only remarkable, but distinctly original.

He came of Saxon parentage, and, as far as I can make out, of small landed nobility. He was the youngest of twenty-four children, all of one mother, and nineteen of whom sat at the table at one time. The child who lives through being bossed by twenty-three brothers and sisters, surely may be accepted as an instance of the survival of the fittest, and naturally develops abnormal characteristics of defense and offense.

His childhood coincided with the terrible Napoleonic wars. Three of his brothers fell in the battle of Lützen. Moreover, the French were once quartered on his father's little estate, and some brutal, drunken soldiers kicked his mother downstairs, causing injuries from which she never recovered. All of this made the

Consul-General hate the French, and, in fact, all the Latin races. If he had not hated the French and the Latin races, this story of my mother and her doll could never have been written.

Foreign military service being almost the only profession open to the impecunious young nobleman, he entered the English navy, in which he served creditably for several years, finally leaving it to join a brother at Leghorn, where he had great luck, for he married a pretty, rich young Italian girl of good family. They had a little girl—my mother.

I have said that the Consul-General was an original man; in some ways, indeed; he was distinctly odd. He left home before the child was born, saying that if it was a boy, he would come back; if it was a girl, he would not. He evidently did not plan to have as large a family as his father had had before him, and considered this first experiment final. The child, as I have said, proved to be a girl, and the Consul-General would not come home. He stayed away for eighteen months, until they sent him a beautiful miniature of his daughter. The sight of the baby face—an exceptionally beautiful one, too—evidently awoke the Consul-General's paternal feelings, and he returned to his own home, relieving the vice-consul of the extra duties the poor fellow had been compelled to carry.

I have tried to show how environment in early youth developed certain characteristics of resistance, and made of him, as a German friend of mine puts it, "a very obstinate person." He gave in a little, but very little. When he came back, he allowed himself to be fond of the child, but he controlled the situation by bringing her up exactly as though she had been a boy.

Now, at Leghorn, seventy-three years ago, to bring up the daughter of an Italian mother as a boy was a fearful thing to do. Yet he did it, and not only did it bravely, but successfully. The child learned to speak four languages with equal fluency, an unheard-of thing for girls to do in those days. She learned to tramp for miles through the country, to ride horseback and to swim, though in those days young ladies hardly ever took long walks, rode, or swam. Just as soon as she was old enough, she was even made to study book-keeping and the elements of law. Yet the crowning masculine accomplishment was acquired when every Sunday morning the Austrian drum-major was summoned to make her beat the drum. Then the Consul-General was satisfied, for he had got the best of destiny.

Evidently, however, there was a lurking Germanic sense of the proper sphere of woman, and this showed in one phase of the child's education. Part of the day she was given in charge of two genteel Englishwomen, who taught her the English language, and what they considered the best of English manners. Incredible, though true, she was actually taught to shape her mouth by saying "prunes, plums, and prisms." She had to lie flat on her back one hour each day; and she was taught a primness in speech of which the Italians are blissfully ignorant. For instance, once when, on returning from a long walk, she remarked, "Oh, my legs are so tired!" she was solemnly informed, "Young ladies never have legs, they have only feet." Since nature had endowed the child with exceptional beauty and exceptional intelligence, the result of her extraordinary training was at once charming and unusual.

Since the Consul-General hated the Latin races with such fervor, it will be thought strange that he should have married an Italian wife. Probably he did not consider a woman of enough importance to give her nationality much thought, and if he paid such attention to his little daughter, it was to make her as little a woman as possible. Still, as the child grew in beauty, strength, and intelligence, he realized that the time would come when she might by marriage fall into the clutches of some man of the hated Latin race. This he was determined to prevent.

He thought long and hard and finally succeeded in solving the problem to his satisfaction. He decided, to marry her to a man of his own race. But in those days Germans were scarce in Italy, and especially at Leghorn—at least Germans who could be considered proper suitors for the daughter of the Consul-General. He had a friend who would have made an ideal husband, save for one serious drawback: he was thirty-five years older than my mother. Still, a husband thirty-five years older than his wife, and German, seemed preferable to an Italian, even though the latter were of a more suitable age. So the Consul-General used his superior will to persuade his friend of the desirability of such an arrangement.

The friend was a lovable man. He had known my mother all her life. Indeed, when she was weaned, he had carried her up and down in his arms all night, and this because he was the one who could best subdue her wailing. He had often done the same for her when she cut her first teeth. Moreover, ever since she was a mere baby he had given her two fine Paris dolls each year. My mother was exceedingly fond of dolls—a feminine perversity in the face of the efforts her father had made to give her masculine tastes and inclinations—and these presents had established a particularly friendly relation between the two, though it scarcely paved the way to marriage.

Yet the friend was persuaded to overlook all difficulties, and on New Year's Day, in the fifteenth year of my mother's life, he sent 'her a formal and elaborate letter in which he requested her hand in marriage. It was written in German, and requested the high-born young lady to do him the honor of conferring her hand upon him.

As usual, his Christmas gift had been a doll, and a particularly fine one. No wonder, therefore, that my mother was not prepared for an offer of marriage, and all the more as she was young for her age, and had not the slightest tendency to let her thoughts rove in this direction. When the letter came, she was delighted at the mere fact of receiving it, for fifty-nine years ago correspondence was not as commonplace as it has grown now, and for a little girl a letter was an exceptional treat. Her first delight was followed by an impression of surprise and bewilderment. She did not understand what her good friend meant, nor why he wanted her hand. She willingly would have given him both hands any time he came, and saw no reason for his writing a letter about it. At fourteen she had not philosophized as to life and marriage as much as I had at ten.

She took the letter to my grandmother, and asked for an explanation. My grandmother, who did not know German, but did know the contents, made the matter clear to her in the following way, "Harriet," she 'said, "wouldn't you like to go to Paris?"

"Yes," my mother answered promptly; "but what has that got to do with the letter?"

Then my grandmother, who in true Italian fashion overlooked everything in her pride of marrying off her daughter when she was only fourteen, replied, "The letter means that if you'll marry our good friend, he will take you to Paris."

This decided the matter. My mother was delighted at the idea of going to Paris with her good friend. She says that she had secret visions of an unlimited number of dolls. The betrothal was announced to friends and relatives, and my mother found herself suddenly grown up.

Consequently she had to put on long dresses. The effort to masculinize her had made her an active, restless child, and confessedly she was somewhat of a tomboy. Moreover, she was small for her age, and did not appear as old as she actually was. She had no desire whatsoever to grow up, and when she found that giving her hand in marriage involved wearing long skirts, she wept and wailed, declaring that under such conditions she would never get married.

But the Consul-General was a man of iron. He convinced her that once she had consented, nothing on earth would justify her in breaking her word. Even if she did not want to get married, she would have to wear long skirts as a punishment, so the poor child found there was no escape for her: her choice now lay between long skirts and a trip to Paris, or long skirts and staying at home in disgrace. No wonder she decided for the former.

In May, only a few days before she entered on her sixteenth year, the marriage took place, and her husband immediately fulfilled his promise to take her to Paris.

It was before the days of railways and the journey through Central Italy was beautiful beyond description. My mother, who had not often left home, and to whom driving from Pisa to Leghorn was a great delight, enjoyed the beginning of her travel very much. But when they reached northern Italy, and had to drive for days and days over long, dusty roads, bordered with dreary, monotonous poplars, she began to be bored. She regretted her bargain. She was sorry she had ever married, even if it did mean going to Paris.

What her husband thought, I do not know. He had married my mother with the understanding that he was to save her from the possible calamity of marrying into the Latin race. He fully recognized the fact, as did also the Consul-General, that my mother was altogether too young to be treated as a real married woman, but he expected that time and patience would make her into something that would brighten and bless the last days of his life. My mother admits that he had his hands full during their wedding trip, for she proved a most restless, trying traveling companion. I think that he must have felt more like a governess than a bridegroom.

He was a sweet-tempered man, and very kind to her. In fact, during this whole trip he lost his temper only once, and then he had some excuse for it. They had been stopping over night at some small inn in northern Italy. My mother, who had grown to dread the long days in the closed carriage, made the most of her opportunity, and, rising with the sun, ran into the fields to catch butterflies. Later in the morning the inn-keeper saw her and called out to her, "Signorina, will you please tell your grandfather that the post-horses will be ready in a short time, and that breakfast is waiting for you?"

My mother rushed to her husband in perfect delight, crying, "They have taken you for my grandfather; the horses will soon be ready, and breakfast is waiting for us."

They finally reached Paris, and both were glad of it; my mother, because she would not have to sit still so much of the day; and her husband because he found some one to help him in his pedagogical duties.

In those days a newly married woman had but little more liberty than an unmarried girl, and that means almost no liberty at all. My mother found a chaperone ready for her, a Countess de Montmorency, who was a dear friend of my grandmother's.

The countess was a reactionary aristocrat. What I mean by this is that she belonged to the class of French nobles who, after the Revolution, spent their life in due contemplation of the privileges of which the Revolution had deprived them, and which the restoration of monarchy had at least nominally brought back to them. During the Revolution her family had been among the unfortunate emigrants who had known the worst poverty and distress, and, while still a mere child, she had been compelled to sell *petits pâtés* in the streets of London. But what interested my mother most was that as a child the countess had been a play-mate of the unfortunate Dauphin, the little son of Marie Antoinette.

My mother admitted that the countess was sincerely interested in her, and that she got her clutches on her with the intention of doing her much good. She taught her things which even the genteel English women had not taught her. She taught her that no woman who had not been contaminated by modem ideas, and had not lost her self-respect, would allow pink and blue ribbons on the underwear of her trousseau. She taught her that even the tiniest bit of a flounce was not permissible on a skirt that was to be worn on the street in the sight of plebeians. My mother submitted patiently to these counsels, and regretfully told her maid to take all the pink and blue ribbons out of her underwear, and to rip every flounce from any skirt which a plebeian eye might see.

The countess did not stop at this. She taught my mother to bow from the waist and not from the head, and to curtsey three times backward without getting en-tangled in a skirt. For, dear American readers, do not forget that we curtsey once to a person of quality, twice to a princess of the blood, and three times to a crowned head. My mother claims emphatically that curtseying has been the hard-est thing she has ever had to learn. Book-keeping, law, beating the drum, and, later, bringing up seven children, have been nothing as compared with that.

The days went on. My mother was learning manners and being bored. Between her good husband and the good countess, she had no fun at all. She longed for her father, for her mother, for her friends, and, last but not least, for the drum-major.

Nor was she at all consoled by the fact that her husband was showing himself most munificent. He spared no money, and the countess spared neither time nor interest, to fit my mother out with all kinds of rare and beautiful things to wear. Her husband was even planning to give her a whole set of Chantilly laces, which the countess had promised to select with every possible care.

A day was chosen on which my mother, accompanied by the countess, was to make a final choice of these laces. The husband left the money to pay for them with my mother, and the countess was to call for her at the hotel and take her to the shop where the laces were to be bought.

On the morning of the appointed day my mother was alone at the hotel. Her husband had left her. The countess had not yet come, sending word that she could not come until considerably later than she had expected. A coupe was waiting at the door-and my mother was bored to death. She felt bitter and rebellious. She had thought that getting married meant going out alone, eating whatever she liked, and doing just as she pleased. And now she was kept much more strictly than she had ever been kept at home. She decided to show her independence as a married woman, to go out alone, and to satisfy the longing which had made her so anxious to come to Paris—a longing which the countess and her husband had declared childish, and had not gratified. The child wished to go to Giroux's, the world-famed shop from which for years she had received her Christmas toys.

It was easy to get into the carriage and order the coachman to drive to Giroux'. It was just as easy to get out there, and to ask an affable clerk to show her the finest dolls they had in stock; but it was not so easy to come away without buying anything. The clerk smirked, bowed, explained, and persuaded "Madame"— for the long dresses, and the wedding ring which showed through her little mitt, proved her right to this title—that she could not possibly leave without taking one of the handsomest dolls.

"But I have no money with me," said my mother, half in self-defense, for she was well aware that her husband and the countess would not approve of such a purchase.

"We shall send some one with Madame, and Madame can pay when she gets to the hotel," suggested the clerk.

And so she fell. She purchased a doll that could speak and walk, and had real eye-lashes and finger-nails. She wanted the doll, but she really would have refused if the clerk had allowed it. Down in the depths of her heart, however, she was grateful to him because he compelled her to do what she knew she should not, but dearly longed, to do.

She reached the hotel only a few minutes before the clerk came to deliver the new acquisition, a doll which was meant to be given in homage to some little royal princess, and for which Giroux charged the modest sum of one thousand francs!

My mother paid without hesitancy. She had a lot of money for the laces, and she did not think that a thousand francs more or less would make much difference. Her book-keeping had not been of the kind to teach her the value of money. The clerk left, well-satisfied with the promptness of the payment, and my mother remained alone with her doll. It was the first time since she left home that she had been perfectly happy.

When the countess arrived, she was horrified. How could a young married woman who fully understood the responsibilities of her position, and what she owed to propriety, go alone to Giroux, buy a doll, and play with it like a little girl of three?

Her husband also soon returned, and he was not only amazed, but was very angry at the waste of money, and the childishness of his bride. He scolded her, and he scolded her long and hard.

My mother was heartbroken: she was a very little girl, she had been exceedingly homesick, and she was not accustomed to have her "good friend," as she still thought of him, speak harshly to her. Until he married her there had, of course, been no necessity for discipline. But she could not reason this out then as she did many, many years later when she told the story to me. She wept and she wailed. She wanted to go home. She wanted to see her father and mother. She did not want to be married. She wanted to go back to her short dresses, and to be allowed to play with dolls.

Her description was vivid, and I can almost see her as she lay there in a big armchair, her arm pressed tightly over her eyes, her feet stretched out straight and stiff, and her whole little body shaken with sobs. I can almost see the countess and the husband, distressed and perplexed at the situation. It seemed almost impossible to comfort her.

Indeed, what she needed was a mother to take her on her knee and wipe her eyes. Neither the husband nor the countess thought of doing this, and the child kept repeating that she wanted to go home; she wanted to go to her father and mother; she did not want to stay in Paris another single day.

It was her husband who finally comforted her, but this only when he told her that they would leave Paris, that nobody should take the doll from her, and that she might keep it with her in the carriage for the rest of the journey.

And so it happened that the little daughter of the Consul-General finished her first wedding trip with a doll on the front seat of the traveling carriage.

Several years later my mother was left a widow. Then (and I think it served the Consul-General just right) she married my father, a brilliant young Italian, a characteristic representative of the hated Latin race.

Italian-American Hymn

Per Aspra Ad Astra
Dedicato all'Italica Gente di Mare

The Christ bearing dove Columbus
Brought the cross unto this shore,
Hallowed us for love and duty
Evermore and evermore.

Refrain: We are coming, oh Columbus,
For we hold this country dear.
Glad to work and strive as you did.
Oh Columbus, we are here.

Heaven granted through Vespucci
The baptismal holy flame
When he brought this wondrous country
A prophetic, lordly name.

Refrain: We are coming, oh Vespucci,
For we hold this country dear.
Glad to work and strive as you did,
Oh Vespucci, we are here.

At the call of God, Cabotto
Forged the path across the sea
For the troubled Pilgrim Fathers
To be great and to be free.

Refrain: We are coming, oh Cabotto,
For we hold this country dear,
Glad to work and strive as you did.
Oh Cabotto, we are here.

Westward, forward, Verrazzano
Landed with his daring band.
Where New York now proudly rises,
Greatest city in the land.

Refrain: We are coming, Verrazzano,
For we hold this country dear,
Glad to work and strive as you did,
Verrazzano, we are here.

Let us follow in your footsteps,
Let us seek your blessed fate.
Our great Italian Fathers,
You who made two countries great.

Refrain: We are coming, Our Fathers,
For we hold this country dear,
Glad to work and strive as you did,
Our Fathers, we are here.

CHICAGO, 1923

A Schoolmaster of the Great City

ல *Angelo Patri*

Piaggine (Salerno), Italy, November 27, 1876–New York, New York,
September 13, 1965

In 1881, when he was not yet five years old, Angelo Patri (whose real surname was Petraglia) and his family joined his father who had emigrated to New York. His education, therefore, took place in America. In 1904, he graduated from Columbia University, continuing with a specialization at Teachers College the following year, and then in 1920 received a Ph.D. from Tufts College, in Massachusetts. Even so, the memory of infancy in Italy remained alive in him; and if we are to believe the initial pages of his most famous book, *A Schoolmaster of the Great City* (1917), this memory played an important part in his life and, above all, in his long and happy experience as a teacher, one of the most famous and influential of his time. At eleven years old, Patri entered a public school in New York. Until then, his principal educator had been an uncle who taught him Italian; he had learned English in the street. At this time, however, he began to grow aware of the typical condition of the sons of emigrants. His father, Nicola, had only one purpose in his life: to ensure that his son live better than he. Nicola had plans; he wanted Angelo to become a priest. As Patri wrote,

during all the years in which he worked for me, I worked for myself. While his hopes were converged upon the family, mine went beyond it. At night, I worked until late, living a life of which my father had no part. And this living alone tended to make me forget, and truly to undervalue, all that was good in my family. At times, I was ashamed of the fact that they did not seem nor talk like true Americans.

Still, when I felt very depressed about that way of living, so hard and so miserable, I would go to see my father at work. I saw him high above, on a scaffold one hundred feet above ground, and then I became dizzy and my heart was in my mouth. In this way, I would think about him as a poet of ballads, singing in a strong and cheering voice and his gaze lost in a far-off point, and the poet that was in his soul bound his spirit to mine. I understood then why, with a salary of two dollars a day, he had never sent me to high school.

Patri began his career as a teacher in 1897, the very same year in which his father fell from a scaffold fifty feet high, an accident at work that constrained him to endure a long period of inactivity. It could be said that the son benefited greatly from the unconsciously assimilated teaching of his family. All his resolve pertaining to teaching—as emerges from the pages of *A Schoolmaster,* vividly woven with anecdotes and episodes—pivots upon two sustaining elements: the first element is the attempt to excite the interest of schoolchildren, even at the cost of violating the iron rules of the scholastic tradition based on the three canons, the three *R*s (reading, writing, arithmetic), in favor of a less formal approach, and, above all, open to the playful and "existential" necessities of the children. The second element is the need for involving families in the management of the school, in the conviction that taking family environment into account should be an absolutely pressing priority in order to create uniform educational criteria and to guarantee the children equal opportunity at school. In those districts in which year after year, the number of inhabitants grew dizzyingly, paralleled by an increasingly complex multiculturalism, creating great problems, family involvement was a special priority. Patri's pedagogical approach and elaboration were decisively influenced by the ethical-pedagogic philosophy of John Dewey's *School and Society,* in which the school was obliged to teach men to adapt themselves to their environment, searching within themselves to remodel it and render it the most consistent way with their necessities and desires. Patri declared that his objective was not so much, and not only, to "Americanize foreigners"—though subsequently he was convinced of this compelling necessity—as much as, more ambitiously, to "fulfill our destiny and Americanize America" (219), holding as certain that "the attitude in relation to school and children is the founding element of every future judgment of America. And truly the original contribution that America can give to the progress of the world is not political, economical, religious, but educational, the children being our national energy, and the school the means through which adults can readjust" (217).

In 1908, Patri became, as far as is known, the first Italian principal of a public school in New York, namely, PS 4. In 1910, he married a teacher who worked in his institute and who enthusiastically shared the directorship with him. In 1913, he assumed the direction of PS 45, in the Bronx, which "became, in short, the model for the schools of America" (Flamma). *A Schoolmaster*, a book translated into many languages (though not into Italian), brought him fame and made him a point of reference in national pedagogic discussions, besides being a voice much listened to by families. Numerous other titles followed, all issued by important publishers: *Child Training* (1922; Italian edition, *L'educazione del fanciullo,* 1954); *Talks to Mothers* (1923); *School and Home* (1925); *Problems of Childhood* (1926); *What Have You Got to Give* (1926); *The Questioning Child and Other Essays* (1931); *Parents Daily Counselor* (1940); and *Your Children in War Time* (1943). Interesting, and in part revelatory of his original Americana vision, was also Patri's activity as a writer for children: *Spirit of America* (1924); *Pinocchio in America* (1928); and translations of Collodi (*Adventures of Pinocchio,* 1937), Cherubini, and Bertelli. Patri also wrote the syndicated column "Our Children" for newspapers and magazines.

ESSENTIAL BIBLIOGRAPHY

Flamma 1936; Patri 1917; Peragallo 1949, 177–182.

I had met a few, a very few parents who had come into the school on rare occasions. They had come for the most part objecting to something the school was doing. But what of the great mass, who were they?

There were parents who were ignorant, almost, of the school's existence. Some of them did not know the teacher's name, nor the child's class, nor the number of the school. They hardly knew where the school was. Perhaps they had sent a neighbour to register the child in the "baby" class and had never been near the school. What did they know of the school? What did they care?

What did we know of their homes? What did we care?

We would know, we would care, I determined. We would go to them and learn what was beyond their closed doors.

There was Hyman. He was dirty, more than dirty. Word was sent home that Hyman should have a bath. No bath was given. Dirt reaches a climax. It did in this case.

Then the teacher said, "Hyman, if no one else will wash you, I will. But washed you must be."

Hyman led the way cheerfully. There was a short journey through crowded streets, a dark hallway, long flights of stairs, then Hyman's home. The living room was kitchen and dining-room as well. Hyman's mother was at the tubs. On the table in one corner was a cut up chicken, the night's dinner; close to the chicken was a pair of newly mended shoes. There was a loaf of bread with the heart pulled out of it and a dish of butter showing finger marks. Odd dishes, a coffee pot with streaks of coffee down its sides and some freshly washed clothes filled the rest of the table. Children's clothes were all about.

There were five school children in this family. Each on his way from school dropped his belongings, helped himself to a chunk of bread and a dab of butter and made for the street, the only available place to pursue his right to "life, liberty and the pursuit of happiness."

"Yes, I know, teacher," said the mother limply, "I know Hyman is dirty. He won't wash for me. Maybe he will for you."

Through the kitchen into the bathroom went Hyman and his teacher. The bathroom was the family store-room. Everything was there that anybody discarded—a couple of hats, an empty box or two, shoes, old clothes. These were piled on the floor, the tub cleaned and Hyman with the teacher's help got into the bath, the first in many days.

Then the teacher went home, thinking, "What's the good of school, just school, to Hyman? He needs to grow. He needs to learn to be clean more than he needs to learn to spell. Congestion, tenements, dirt, neglect! What chance has Hyman to be a fine American citizen?"

"I want to tell you about a home I visited yesterday," a teacher said. "Percy hasn't done any real work since he entered my class so I thought I'd call on his mother. She made an appointment for me and I went. She was dressed as though for a party and when I apologized for detaining her she said, 'Oh, not at all. It's my bridge club day but it's early yet. What about Percy? Bothering you? Children are a bother, aren't they? How do you ever get on with forty or fifty of them? One kills me.'

"Percy isn't doing any school work," I said bluntly. "He acts as if he needed sleep too. He never does his homework."

"Oh, Mercy! What's homework? Lessons? Of course he doesn't do any at home. Isn't school enough?"

"It is for some boys who work. But Percy works neither at home nor at school."

"M'm. It's too bad. You see we entertain a lot. We are fond of having our friends about us; good for children to meet people, don't you think? Gives them an air."

"But does the child sleep?"

"Oh, of course, you silly child, he sleeps. Let me give you a cup of tea. No? Maybe you'd have a cocktail? What can one offer a school marm? So glad to have seen you. Thanks so much for your interest in Percy! He comes from a good family. He'll come out all right. Don't worry. So glad. Good-bye."

Then there was Ruth. The teachers found her intractable at times because of an overwhelming desire to take control of the classroom. On the whole she was worth while and intelligent. What was the trouble with Ruth?

Ruth was ten and very, very wise. She had glorious red hair, braided and bound like a coronet. She looked at you out of beautiful, green eyes and talked in slow, monotonous tones, the result of much experience with the direct facts of life. Once Ruth had taken off her little red flannel petticoat and waved it in the faces of the Cossacks who had come to search the house for revolutionary literature. This little demonstration had hurried the family's departure from Russia. Somehow she had grasped the idea of going straight to headquarters when she wanted anything.

"I hope you won't mind, but I want to ask your advice," she announced one day. "It isn't about school."

Ruth really never wanted advice. She always felt competent to give it so I waited in silence.

"Well, you see, it's this way. There are eight of us at home and father, he sits home and won't go to work only when he likes it and then he gives my mother only two dollars a week. That isn't much for a room and meals, especially now. Well, I wouldn't mind his not paying more money, if he would only leave my mother and the children alone. No, he sits there and complains and swears to my brothers and sisters. Such language isn't good for children to hear. He is getting worse and worse every day, and my mother cries and I can't bear to see my mother cry. You don't know how hard my mother works.

"There is Abe. He is eight, but he is a little stupid and very weak and can't eat regular food. And my big sister that goes to work in the fur shop downtown and gets home all tired out. You could hardly believe how hard she works.

"And my father makes all this trouble. He plays cards at night with his friends that came from the other side with him, the same country he came from. When the men come to play cards, we must stay up late, and that's not good for us. I can't stand it any longer."

Here Ruth stopped talking and looked at me expectantly.

Still I waited, merely lifting an inquiring eyebrow. "I took advice," she resumed, "and went before the judge and told him everything. Now had I right? The judge asked me if we wanted to put him out. I said no, he was my father, but I wanted the judge to make him stop using bad languages. The judge did, and told me to come to him in case there was any more trouble."

"How has your father been since?" I asked her when I had sufficiently recovered.

"Very well. He does not talk much, but he looks as if he wanted to. I don't care. I know what's good for him."

"Is he to give you any more money?"

"Yes, the judge said he must give at least half his salary and he must work, and be good, and be proud of his children."

I found a boy in a classroom after school hours. His shirt was full of flowers that other children had brought to the teacher.

"What are going to do with them?"

"I'll take them home and hide them."

Why hide them? His mother would not let him take the flowers home. She did not want him to steal flowers.

I went to see his father. He knew his boy took flowers not only from the teacher but from the florist and from the park. He would punish the boy as he had done many times before. I could see for my self by examining the boy's body. He would whip him now more than ever.

"What can I do?" he went on. "I go out to work all day. I have three children that go to school. I make a dollar and a half a day when it does not rain; I have to pay fourteen dollars a month rent. I want my boy to learn. I give him plenty to eat though beans are ten cents a pound. I try to make him study and he goes out stealing flowers and disgraces me."

"A dollar and fifty cents a day, when it does not rain." I saw the man's torn shoes, his shabby clothes and knotted fingers. I saw the boy's skinny body and his starving soul craving for the sweet earth flowers. Was it the children's fault?

"Please help me. Do something for me," pleaded a sixteen-year-old girl just out of school. "My little brother makes such a fuss at home. When he does not like his food, he pulls the table cloth on the floor and breaks the dishes. When a young man comes to see me, my brother makes such trouble that he never comes back. Now I am getting along in years. I'll be seventeen next birthday. I am losing my chances. He threw the sofa pillows out of the window. I must take from my savings to buy more pillows and dishes. How can I save up for a husband?"

"Please make my boy clean himself before he comes to school. He won't do it for me."

"Please talk to Herbert about hitting his little brother. You have such influence over him."

"Put my boy away. He is no good. He steals my money."

"Solomon is at home stamping his feet. He will not go for me. Please send the officer."

"Please tell Dorothy she must take her medicine. She will do it for you. It's a bother to you I know I but I'll make it all right with you."

Inadequate, isolated homes, forever closing their doors and forever begging us to come in!

On one side of the school was the road, dusty, badly kept and constantly used. Across the street was the park, beautiful and fresh at first but as the population increased, abused and neglected more and more.

On the other side ran the elevated trains that disturbed us all. Assembly exercises in the morning had to stop to let the trains go by. Classroom recitations had to stop too for there was no competition. The children and the teachers got the habit of waiting in the middle of a sentence as the roar began, swelled—ceased.

The school district reached across the park to the east where lived many families who owned their own houses. These were the first residents, the lovers of grass and open spaces, of home and family traditions. It extended westward four blocks to the tracks of the railroad and north and south almost a quarter of a mile each way. A wide area this. Scattered about were empty lots, fences, long stretches of fences, empty houses and flats. The neighborhood was in a state of transition from a dignified provincial suburb to a mass of tenements. There was a group of people who came from the southern part of the city each spring that their children might enjoy the open spaces of the neighborhood. They remained until fall when they returned to their steam heated flats. This made an unstable community in the school and in the neighborhood. Each time they came fewer of them returned and the tenements grew in number.

This meant that most of our children came from little two, three and four room flats, strung along block upon block. In such homes there was little time or room for play, work or fun. As the crowds came the tenements increased and poured their tenants out upon the sidewalks and streets. The street corner, the curb, the candy shop, the pool room, the dance hall were becoming the social centres of the district.

There was a mixture of races. These were people who had come from various countries of Europe and they differed in their attitude towards ethics, society, religion, education, cleanliness. These differences isolated the various groups, the families, and the blocks.

These parents did not understand the newer conditions of life. They did not understand the city. They did not understand the school. They did not understand the older residents.

In their turn they too were misunderstood even by their own children. The child saw in the rush of the school life the idea of getting on. In school he saw life in a white collar, fine clothes, and an easy job. Home was not like this.

Michael was one of the brightest and most promising among the boys. He was a yard monitor. He came to school early and stayed late. He helped the teachers attend to supplies and hang pictures. Whatever the work in hand, Michael was first assistant.

A neighbor brought Michael's mother in to see me. She turned to her friend and spoke in a foreign tongue and the neighbor answered, and turned to me saying, "She speaks no English. I have come to talk to you for her."

"That's too bad. I thought Michael was born in this city?" I said.

"Oh, yes, they've been in this country fifteen years, but she never learned the language. She's religious and doesn't go around much."

Michael's mother was anxiously watching our faces while we talked and now she spoke again to the neighbor.

"She says to tell you that she wants to see Michael."

Michael was sent for and came into the office with his usual cheerful willingness. When he saw his mother he stopped. She went toward him. Michael backed against the wall, his face sullen and embarrassed. His mother talked pleadingly, she put her hand on his shoulder and he pushed it off rudely. Then his mother sank into a chair and began to cry softly.

Michael stood against the wall scowling down at his shoes. I looked on wondering what it could be about. The neighbor began to talk.

"It's a pity. It's a shame. Mickee, you shouldn't treat your mother that way."

"She shouldn't come here," muttered Michael. The neighbor looked from Michael to the weeping woman and anger shone in her face as she turned to me.

"You think Michael is a good boy, don't you? You like him. Well, I don't. You think you do a lot for him by keeping him in school all day long and letting him run all over for the teachers. You're just spoiling him. You're only making him selfish. He thinks he's too good to talk to his own mother. That's what you're doing if you want to know the truth."

Then turning to Michael she said, "If you belonged to me you wouldn't act like that. I'd fix you."

Michael lifted his head ready to answer but catching my eye resumed his sullen attitude again.

"You can go to your room now, Michael. Come in to see me after hours," I said to his great relief.

"I'd wish," the neighbor broke in, "you would take a stick to that kid's back. His mother can do nothing more with him. I'm sorry for her. She came from Russia years ago. She was quiet and stayed in the house. Michael is ashamed of her because she can't talk English. He makes fun of her clothes. When there is a school party he doesn't even tell her. Her husband learned English and all the American ways quickly. So did the children. Now her husband is ashamed of her and he lives by himself. Michael goes to see him and lots of times he stays two or three days. His mother hasn't seen him this week. That's why she came here, to beg him to come home to her."

Here were children and parents living their lives apart. These children were ashamed because their parents did not speak or look like Americans. How could I help the children in my school respond to the dreams of their fathers? How could I get the fathers to share in the work of building a school for their children?

Viola

∾ *Silvio Villa*

Villanova Canavese (Turin), Italy, 1882–1927

Silvio Villa had just taken his degree in engineering at the University of Turin when, at twenty-four years old, he decided to depart for America, where his brothers, owners of a silk factory in New Jersey, made him an associate in their company. His brother Alfonso P. Villa was the chairman of A.P. Villa & Brothers Inc. and a member of a number of boards, including Villa, Stearns & Co. in Broadway and the Lincoln Trust Co. of New York (a New York *Who's Who* for the year 1947 calls him "a retired capitalist born in Turin"). From the moment of his arrival, Silvio's goal would become that of a man who wanted to be an American in all senses of the word. He therefore attended an evening commercial school in Passaic and studied the English language. It was not an easy period—"the most unhappy," Villa would say, "of my life"—torn between his need to become an American and his nostalgia for Italy, where, besides his father, a doctor (his mother died shortly before his departure), there remained his fiancée. The occasion to cross the ocean again was presented to him with World War I. Villa departed voluntarily and for three years, as second lieutenant of the Corps of Engineers, fought in the Italian army. After the war, he returned to America and his partnership with his brothers.

It was actually the experience of the war that inspired his first literary attempt, *Claudio Graziani*, a story of some thirty pages published privately in New York, in 1919 (and later reprinted as chapter XXIII of his second book). The protagonist is a young captain of the *arditi* (special forces soldiers) who is shot for insubordination following his refusal to send his men to attack on a suicide mission. The story is based on fact: Graziani was an old friend of Villa, whom he met again by chance at the front and with whom he resumed their former friendship. Villa then touchingly narrates the tragic fate. *The Boston Transcript*, as Rose Basile Green relates, spoke of it as a book that, "should stand among the masterpieces of the English language," praising the conciseness and strength in a polemical key in respect to the presumed superficiality of the current American production. Moreover, Green dwells on the value of this testimony, which brings to prominence the fate of forgotten men in a corner of the world, after the disorderly retreat in Caporetto, discussing it as if it were a sort of precedent for Hemingway's *Farewell to Arms*.

In 1922, Macmillan published Villa's "autobiographical novel," *The Unbidden Guest*, which is dedicated to his brother Alfonso P., "whose twenty-five years of intelligent work in America exemplifies [*sic*] the virtue of modern progressive Italy." *The Unbidden Guest* is among the first fully American books written by Italians in the period of the Great Emigration. The fruit of seven years of labor, the book evokes the happy years of Carletto (the author) in Italy and the difficult ones spent in America, urged by his brother Beniamino (then struck by paralysis) to prepare himself to become a citizen of the country. The book was received with curiosity. Generally, it was praised for its freshness and poetical intonation, capable of touching the hearts of readers. It deals, in effect, with a typical story of development, which in the case of Villa, consists of transforming oneself from an Italian into an American, even if Villa needs to justify the clearly "Latin" nature of the story, observing that he had not tried to correct it in the conviction that only in that mode could he communicate the emotions that nourish the book. Interesting, in particular, was the reception reserved for it by the review *Il Carroccio*, which, in the original English, previewed the chapters regarding an inspired description of Florence and a reevocation of the glories of Garibaldi (in the issues of October and November 1922). *Il Carroccio* then published a long review of it by Gabriella Bosano (May 1923), in which the accent was obviously put on the spirit of the natural Italianism of the author, who, speaking of Carletto (himself) wrote for instance that "his conception of Italy is something almost supernatural." (Just in that period, the review was deliberating the problem of Americanization, from positions of radical Italian nationalism.) In the review, it was not possible for reviewer Bosano to omit Carletto's conclusion, which *Il Carroccio* at least sought to temper: "The machine, not the mechanization, the industry, not the industrialization—I am not able to explain it—the thousand easy pleasures that American progress throws in front of its craftsmen, do not satisfy them; their Italian spirituality leaps free and intact from the struggle, and—that which is more difficult—from the triumph [of progress]."

Almost in a sort of crescendo, increasing in equal pace with the acquisition of a growing American dimension, in 1927, Villa would then publish the stories of *Ultra-Violet Tales,* three novellas, which with a certain continuity in respect to his debut in 1919, further developed inspiring motives and enlarged the universe into fantasy. In fact, the actions narrated in *Where Is She, Viola,* and *Ripe Fruit* reach beyond human experience. Thus, the first, in which the protagonist is a certain Michele D'Albara, has to do with spiritualism; the second, published here, a story of love and telepathy, possibly has some autobiographical elements; and even the third deals with a love affair in which the protagonist is by now a mature man.

Olga Peragallo perceived the book as limited, since it runs the risk of approaching the absurd. In another criticism, better founded, she maintains that the very elaborate style suggests a sense of artificiality. Villa was probably aware of the possibility of such observations, for in the preface to the volume, he stated:

> My stories could appear absurd, upon the occasional moments when I was propelled beyond the confines of the possible; nonetheless, the reader will recognize in the creations of my imagination a humanity that is equal to the reader's, and will remember Viola and Alba and Pierantonio di Galleda long after their action in the book is forgotten . . . The ambition of the author is not that of writing well-constructed stories, but to create personages that will have a place in the heart of the reader. A human being that emerges from the pages of a book is a contribution to life; a novella, no matter how long, will be nothing else but fiction.

ESSENTIAL BIBLIOGRAPHY

Basile Green 1974, 65–68; Bosano 1923; Peragallo 1949, 229–232.

∾

I

When the lifeless body of Viola Redley was discovered one night last June in Central Park, some suspicion was aroused by the fact that a letter from Livio Pieri, addressed to her, was found the next day floating on the lake not far from the scene of her death. It was dated two weeks earlier, and had evidently come from Como, Italy.

The writing of the letter, as well as the signature, was plainly readable. Neither afforded any clue to the cause of the girl's death.

The police investigation which followed brought out the fact that, on the same night, Livio Pieri had died, as mysteriously as Viola, in his native Italy, on the Leghorn shore of the Mediterranean.

Remarkable as this coincidence was, the strangest feature of it was that in neither case did the closest scrutiny reveal mark of violence or trace of poison. The cause of death, in each instance, was set down in the official records as "unknown."

On both sides of the ocean the police and the newspaper reporters busied themselves for a week or two, and then, no results having been obtained, both mysteries dropped into oblivion. Pieri was laid to rest in the land of his birth; Viola, among the green slopes of peaceful Woodlawn. No flower marks her grave, but a simple white slab bears her name:

VIOLA REDLEY
MAIDEN
1895–1920

II

Viola Redley and Livio Pieri had been friends for five years. He had met her, one night, at a little fancy dress ball at an art students' club in the vicinity of Gramercy Park, and they had become acquainted in a rather unusual way.

She wore, that night, a Dalmatian costume and a black velvet mask. He, wearing a purple cape with ermine collar, was supposed to be a Venetian Senator.

Between dances they chanced to be sitting on the same sofa, and as he looked into her eyes, sparkling through the holes of the mask, he thought he recognized a girl whom he knew. He spoke, and she answered, taking it for granted that she knew him, and trying to discover his identity.

They talked to each other for a few minutes, each puzzled about the other. When they removed their masks, they realized that they had never met before.

A fancy dress ball is supposed to do away with formalities. So he simply asked to be excused for his mistake, and seized the opportunity to introduce himself: Livio Pieri, an Italian architect in normal life, at present a Venetian grandee of the golden days of the Republic.

She acknowledged this introduction with a smile, and told him that her name was Viola and that she earned her own living designing gardens for a landscape architect, a lady whose Dalmatian costume she had borrowed for the evening.

This lady herself appeared a few minutes later, in the attire of Bianca Cappello. Being apprised by Viola of the circumstances under which she and Livio had met, she sanctioned the acquaintance by inviting them both to sit at her table for supper with other friends.

The supper was gay. Viola proved to be a delightful girl, very bright, very stunning-looking in her Dalmatian dress and with her mask off.

Livio and Viola became friendly at once. He inquired with evident interest about the art of landscape designing. She answered his questions, adding that her specialty was Italian gardens.

Livio said he himself knew a thing or two about Italian gardens, so he would be interested in seeing her work. Perhaps he might offer her some suggestions. She invited him to call on her any day at her studio on Nineteenth Street, not far from the club. The studio was on the top floor of a little two-story building she said. Here she lived with her father and a younger sister.

A few days later Livio dropped in at tea time. He found Viola at her drawing-table, looking charming in her blue apron. She was pleased to see him again, stopped her work and began to prepare tea. While the water was heating, he looked at her drawings, they were good, though rather conventional; she had never been abroad, and in her work one could detect the lack of direct contact with the things she was trying to represent. Livio complimented her, but he couldn't help adding, "Too bad you haven't been there; I wish I could show you those gardens!"

She smiled, observing that it was her dream to go to Italy some day, but how could she? First, she didn't have the money; then, she had to take care of her father and look after her young sister.

They sat down at the tea table and talked. It appeared that her father was an invalid, helpless from paralysis. He had his room on the ground floor of the house, so that on fine days he could be wheeled out to Gramercy Park to get the sun. The younger sister was just eighteen, very pretty, and gave Viola a lot of worry, being flirtatious and light-headed.

Livio took a great interest in all that Viola told him. She spoke freely of her life. While still very young she had lost her mother from acute heart disease; her father had a small pension as an ex-naval officer, but not sufficient to support his family, so she had to go to work. Apparently she was doing well; there were evidences of a certain ease about the place. She loved her work; her studio was full of sunlight. In the spring, she told him, she spent some of her time in the open air, inspecting the works carried out from her drawings.

For a year Viola and Livio saw a great deal of each other, He went often to her studio for tea, and now and then he took her out to dinner or to a dance. They talked a lot about the subject that interested her most—gardens. She knew Boboli, Villa d'Este, the gardens of Frascati, the Venetian villas along the Brenta—Livio knew them better than she. Most of them he had visited in the course of his studies; occasionally he had walked in some of them in the springtime, with a girl by his side!

So he told her.

She laughed. "It must have been fine!" she said.

He answered, "Like a dream!" and then added, "We must try it some day, you and I."

He suggested plans. They could meet in Rome—it appeared she had friends there; she might be visiting them, he would come and join her—wouldn't it be delightful? She smiled at the vision. He went into details; the gardens of Rome first; Villa Medici, Villa Wolkonsky, Villa Pamphili. In the spring the sunlight is warm and pleasant there; it breaks through the foliage, thrusting hundreds of spears into the shadow below, drawing glitters of life from the waters gathered into the concave urns. Shrouded in a gauze of gold, the statues stand ever still! All is mystery and peace; from afar comes the murmur of Rome, from the marble balustrades now and then the note of a peacock. Under the pines, through the bushes of laurel, runs a tremor of life!

They would go to Venice, too, in the autumn when the placid waters reflect the golden tints of the vines overhanging the walls. Little gardens he knew over there on the Grand Canal; inaccessible bits of Paradise, through the gates of which he had gazed for hours, for some shadows of days past. Golden fruits were ripening in the solitude of the deserted places! Now and then one thudded softly on the mossy ground; now and then, from a marble loggia, a flight of doves arose! Light steps seemed to sound on the gravel—some loving girl of yore. In his youthful folly he shook the gates—ever closed—trying to get at the visions beyond, at the white forms fading with the enchantments of the coming night! What mystery in those little gardens, what deep peace, what voices bidding him "Come!"

Viola smiled at his foolish talk. "You were a dreamy boy, weren't you?" she asked him.

"Yes," he answered. And he told her of his dreams, his youthful dreams of the silent towns of Italy, of the old deserted gardens.

Day by day a bond of deepening sympathy grew up between them, as they evoked the visions of those places connected with the memory of his past, with the aspirations of her art.

Italy was ever present in their talks—Italy sublime, the garden of the world, stretched between sea and sea, fragrant with oleanders in bloom!

Viola's life had been simple and uneventful. She had been born in a little town of New England and had grown up there with her sister, under the care of an old aunt, their mother being dead, and their father most of the time at sea. Then, after misfortune had overtaken him, they had come to New York. She had been fond of drawing ever since her school days, so she accepted with joy the opportunity offered her by a relative of the family, the landscape architect for whom she was now working.

She put all her soul into her work. Living in that secluded section, she seldom came in contact with the gay life of town; all the time that she could spare was given to her father and her younger sister Lucy, the pretty girl whose light-hearted attitude kept her worried. Viola had known little joy, no love. Once, when Livio looked at a snapshot of a family group, taken years before in the little New England town of her youth, he realized how cheerless her life must have been!

Still, she had a natural sense of gayety; she was a brave girl, always active, thinking of every little thing that might make the life of her father less sad; arranging parties for her sister and seeing that she got some fun out of life, though somewhat worried at her ways with the boys. Lucy was a little too free, judged by the old New England standards.

Livio and Viola often had discussions on the subject. He advised her to be liberal, "Let the girl have her fun," he urged; "a couple of kisses more or less will not spoil her complexion; she will never be so young again!"

Viola was horrified at his views. "Fine advice! No, no, no! Girls must look out!"

She was very strict about kisses. He teased her; what was the use of being young? If he were a pretty girl he knew well enough what he would do! He exposed the boldest theories, with the happy-go-lucky ways of the Latin, for whom life is a jolly adventure anyhow. She retorted with the most sensible reasons. He didn't believe in being sensible. At some of his daring statements she didn't know whether to blush, to get angry or to laugh, She just kept on saying: "Oh you crazy, crazy boy!" and hit him on the lips with her ruler.

Thus they went on. He seemed to find it amusing to tease this prim New England girl; she took an interest in trying to reform him.

Little by little, though, Livio's happy go-lucky arguments had the best of it; Viola became more tractable; she began to doubt whether life was as serious a proposition as the Massachusetts Puritans make it. She took a broader view of things, felt a deeper sympathy for Livio's attitude.

They grew intimate. After all, they were not so far apart from each other, when it came to the fundamentals of life. Both had the right blood in their veins, and good blood will get along with good blood, no matter how far apart the sources from which each sprang!

Out of their intimacy grew a splendid friendship (they called it friendship; but perhaps it was love!)

He admired in Viola her devotion to her father, her tenderness toward her younger sister; he liked her delicate sensitiveness, her feminine sentimentality, just tempered by the traditional restraint of her blood.

Of all the girls whom he had met in America she was the one who reminded him most of some ideal girls who had been dear to him in Italy. She reminded him of his sisters—and of a girl Marcella, who had been the first love of his youth.

III

About a year went by. The European war had broken out; when Italy went into it Livio was called to the colors.

Before sailing he went to say goodbye to Viola . . . In the familiar studio, where they had met so many times, they sat together for tea. Both were visibly affected at the thought of the imminent separation. She had prepared for him a lot of little things—a muffler, a sewing outfit, a pair of woolen gloves. She gave them to him. She gave him motherly advice, "Take good care of your health, don't take unnecessary chances, don't get killed!"

He smiled, played the strong-hearted, talked rashly, "What of it, if he were killed? What difference would it make?" She shivered nervously, pressed his hand, said, "Don't be foolish!" When they parted, she put her lips to his forehead, in a kiss like that of a sister.

That kiss kept Livio a-guessing on the boat all the way over. It was the first that he ever had from her, for they were not supposed to be lovers; it was not a kiss of passion, though her lips had trembled in bestowing it.

He said to himself that perhaps it might not altogether be meant for him. She was a romantic girl, and was naturally moved at the idea of his going away towards the unknown, towards those great tragic fields where men were being killed. He almost felt that he had stolen a token of sympathy due to those who had died there. He felt ashamed to have taken it; but in the depths of his heart he cherished the memory.

On opposite sides of the sea, Viola and Livio thought of each other—very often, at first. They exchanged a few letters. He kept her posted about his actions; sent her a few snapshots to illustrate, just as everyone does at the beginning. Then, little by little, their correspondence dwindled. Livio was completely absorbed by his new task; Viola was busy with her work, with some canteen service that she had taken up when America went into the war.

For about two years they did not communicate with each other at all.

IV

Early in 1919, when the war was over, Livio returned to America. He didn't go to see Viola at once. He felt rather shy at the idea of appearing before her, as of playing the part of a returned hero. It was not until about two weeks after his return that, one evening, he called upon her.

He found her downstairs with her father and sister, and they all sat together, in the living room. Livio was glad of this, since it simplified matters for everybody. He was greeted, feted, made to tell about his experiences, Viola spoke but little, somewhat *froissée* for his having waited so long before calling upon her.

Livio would have liked to explain it; to say that it was not negligence on his part but reluctance to accept from her any manifestation of joy for his return that might be exaggerated by a thought of his deeds on the battlefield. No one should rob those who were killed or crippled or gassed or made insane by suffering, of even a grain of the admiration and sympathy due them. He couldn't quite convey this idea to Viola in a general conversation, so she got the impression that he had returned cold and indifferent.

A few nights later he invited her out to dinner. He thought they might have then a good chance for a tête-à-tête talk, as in times past; but it happened that a mutual friend walked into the restaurant just as they were sitting down for dinner. Out of politeness they asked him whether he wouldn't join them, which he did; so again they missed the opportunity for explanation. Some weeks later Livio was called to Europe on a business matter, remaining away six months; and it was not until his second return in the autumn that he really got the opportunity of seeing Viola again.

V

Even in his early youth Livio had had a decided penchant for girls in general and for the pretty ones in particular. Love is a national sport in Italy; good for indoors and for out of doors, for every place and every season of the year. Livio had practiced it quite efficiently at home in his student days; and during his life in America, though most of his time was taken up by more serious occupations, he had not neglected it altogether.

But for the period of the War his life was entirely devoid of sentimental experiences. The only human beings he met were gunners, bombardiers, sharpshooters and shock-troops, a disappointing lot for a man of romantic instincts to chum with! When he came back to civil life, he found the ladies more attractive than ever. He had a flirtation coming over on the boat; another with a little widow, during the time he spent in New York; and when he went back to Italy, he had a full-fledged affair with a lady in Rome.

These incidents of course did not interfere with his relations with Viola. First of all, they were not supposed to be lovers; and then, there is in the make-up of the Italian man a certain spirit of liberality that permits dispensing a little sentiment here and there still remaining true to the main object of his heart.

With Viola he made no mystery of his little escapades. They were a part of his happy-go-lucky ways. She listened with benevolent indulgence to the foolish tales of her light-hearted friend. Her sound New England training put her so much above this semi-irresponsible Latin, that his amorous exploits rather amused her than otherwise. She was too proud to feel jealous of those girls who were so easily won.

So, the first night they met again in her studio, after his second return from Italy, he couldn't help letting slip a few hints about his affair in Rome. He mentioned a picnic on the Lake of Nemi, a promenade in the Coliseum at night, and added jokingly,

"I was thinking of you, Viola, but I had the attractive girl by my side, and in the dark, by mistake, I gave her a kiss."

Viola was listening in silence—sunk in a big armchair facing him. He could hardly see her face, for the lamp-shade kept it in shadow. He was engrossed in his own tale, evoking the memories of that delightful night.

At one moment, though, he thought he caught a strange light in her eyes. She was gazing at him with an intense expression, as though absorbed in some deep inner thought, she did not hear his light talk. She shivered a little. He stopped and asked, slowly, "What is it? don't you feel well?" looking into her eyes.

She made a nervous gesture, "I am cold," she said; "let us light the fire."

They got up; Viola knelt by the fireside, put in some logs, broke a fagot or two, struck a match, fussed for some time without succeeding in making the fire bum. Livio stood beside her, trying to help. She had on a black dress, a little décolleté in the back. The lamp threw a vivid light on her bare neck. The fire wouldn't start. She flung her head up. He saw her eyes. A sudden truth dawned upon him. "Come" he said, "never mind the fire!"

He took her by both hands and drew her to her feet . . . Their lips met. With a sudden impulsive movement, as of one drowning, she flung her arms about his neck and gave him the most passionate kiss he ever had from any woman in his life.

They parted that night without alluding in any way to what had occurred. They met again the next day, went to the theater together, spoke of every subject on earth, but made no reference to the incident of the night before. For a few weeks they met often, either outside or in the studio, resuming their old conversations, as though nothing had passed between them. They talked gardens, talked Italy, talked memories of the war. They sat, calm and apparently indifferent, side-by-side, while Viola served tea or showed Livio some of her work. Now and then, in the midst of the most casual conversation, or during a walk in the park or in a taxicab going home, as though by some unknown force they were thrown into each other's arms, to lose themselves for a long moment in a wave of passionate emotion.

How it could have happened was utterly inexplicable. Was this love? If it were, neither of them was prepared to acknowledge it.

Viola would not admit, even to herself, having fallen in love with this light-headed, light-hearted Italian, whose conception of love was essentially that of the land of his birth—an odd mixture of sensuality and sentimentality, extreme but ephemeral; unreliable, never steadfast.

She knew well enough what type of man she *ought* to love! Pure and noble, he should gather within him all the virtues of the thoroughbred American—force of character, pluck, inflexible will, devotion. Now, how could she ever love Livio, her light friend, so far from the ideal conceived by her through the influence of her girlhood readings or of her home teachings?

Livio, on his side, could hardly imagine himself in love with Viola. It was well enough to joke with her, to be friends, to discuss principles, but, what Italian wants to be in love with a New England girl? Simply absurd! He wouldn't want to renounce his free-and-easy ways; his right to give a kiss, here or there, when the chance came, to forget the blonde for the brunette, to do away with prejudices. That would never do if Viola and he were lovers; she would be bringing into the case that element of New England character that kills the freedom of fancy and joy! Oh no, no, no! He couldn't even see the picture of a Puritan without a chill going through his bones. How could he imagine himself tied up to Viola of West-field, Massachusetts, related to some of the oldest New England stock?

So they dismissed even the idea of being in love with each other, didn't want to think of it! How absurd! How entirely out of the question!

Those kisses were strange, though those strokes of folly that hit them, now and then, without apparent reason, without logical explanation. Well? Why investigate?

They were a great joy. Why worry? So they let things go their way for those three months of autumn; those three months, from September to November, which are delightful in America, and were, that year, the most wonderful of their lives.

At the beginning of the winter Livio was taken sick. One evening, coming home from his studio, he had a chill and was ill all night. The next morning he tried to get up, but he felt dizzy and had to go back to bed.

The doctor who was called in found him burning with fever, and declared it influenza.

It didn't seem to be much of an illness at first, but, after a week or so, it developed rather serious complications. The infection spread. Pneumonia threatened. For a while things looked bad.

However in a couple of weeks Livio was out of danger; but now his lungs appeared to have been somewhat affected. The doctor, after keeping his patient in bed for a long time, made plain to him that the safe thing to do was to go back to Italy and live there. The climate of New York was not to be trusted.

Livio was rather disconcerted at the news. He felt depressed, impatient; he couldn't adapt himself to the idea of any limitation to the freedom of his movements.

He thought of Viola a great deal. She kept in touch with him, sent him flowers, wrote to him.

The winter was a severe one. From his window Livio gazed with dismay on the slush and dirt in the streets, piling up worse and worse every day. When at last he became convalescent, he decided to follow the doctor's advice—give up his business and go to Italy.

No sooner had he reached this decision than the idea of asking Viola to marry him presented itself to his mind.

He was in love with Viola! In those long hours of enforced separation he had learned how much he loved her, how much he needed her!

What was the object of fooling himself with the idea that they were not suited to each other? He was of a somewhat light turn of mind, to be sure; but he was open to her sobering influence. As to Viola, she would no doubt soon respond to the liberal ways of Italian life. Love would do the rest . . . there was no reason to be worried.

There was one matter, however, to be worried about—his lungs. The doctor had taken for granted that a careful life in the proper climate would bring him back to perfect health; but, for the time being, Livio knew, there was something decidedly wrong with him. Under such conditions, was it fair to ask Viola to marry him?

One day he questioned the doctor, "If I should decide to take a wife to Italy with me, do you think it would be wise?"

"Well," the doctor answered, "it would be wiser to wait. Your recovery might be slow. You shouldn't take any risk. The important matter for you now should be your health." Livio was perplexed. For a few days he was quite unhappy.

He did not like the idea of mentioning his trouble to Viola. It occurred to him that there might be a way out.

Ever since Viola and he had met, they had cherished the dream of being some day in Italy together. Now, Viola had those friends in Rome, an American couple, connected in some way with the American Academy and living in a little old villa on the Gianicolo hill, next to the Academy grounds. Viola could visit them early in the spring. Livio might go over to Rome a little later. By that time he ought to be pretty well posted about his health and could the more readily decide about asking Viola to marry him.

He had never met Viola's friends but she had spoken of them so much that he almost felt he knew them. He had seen books which they had sent to Viola, pictures of landscapes, drawings, maps of Roman gardens, material for her work. Also he had read some of their letters. They were eager for Viola to come and spend a few months with them. Just recently, in writing her for Christmas they had insisted again, "Come next spring; things are straightening out in Italy after the war; we have a new little car of our own. We will take you out for a tour to Assisi, to Siena, to Florence—come!" She might not have answered yet; now was the time to accept, to fix a date for her coming, then she and Livio would be able to meet. He would join the party, arrange for a beautiful trip.

Livio waited a few days to communicate his plans to Viola. He didn't quite know how to go about it; he didn't like to write, being afraid of not presenting the proposition properly; she might begin to say "No," and get stubborn.

So, the first time he was able to go down to the telephone, he called her up. She was happy to hear his voice again, greeted his coming back to life, cheered him, wanted an account of his illness, expressed her good wishes for his full recovery. Livio asked her about herself, said he wanted to see her soon, as soon as he was able to go out.

Then he said: "I am going to Italy, Viola."

"What!" she exclaimed; and then: "When?"

"In April."

She said, "Oh!"

Livio was going to say more, but was afraid.

Again she said, "You are going to Italy! For how long?"

He said, "Perhaps forever!" and again he dared not go on.

He heard her repeating, "Forever!"

He added, "Viola, I want to see you soon. I will call you up in a few days, and we will have lunch together, I want to talk to you."

She said, "Yes" slowly. She knew what he wanted to talk to her about.

VII

A few days later they met. He had made an appointment with her at one o'clock in the Della Robbia room at the Vanderbilt Hotel. She was there before he arrived. When he came down the steps she rose from her chair and walked to meet him; the sweetest smile was on her face. For over six weeks they had not seen each other. They had been torn apart just when the passion of those kisses was beginning to overpower them. While he was thinking of her those long hours in his bed, she must have been thinking of him in her studio. They hardly exchanged a word as they walked to their table at the end corner of the balcony. Then he gave the order for lunch.

As the waiter walked out, Livio took her hand and said "Viola!" They smiled again, and then they talked. About his illness, her work, a number of other things; but all the while they knew that they were there to talk about something else.

She first broke the ice, "When are you going to sail?" she ventured.

"Middle of April," he answered abruptly. "What are you going to do?"

She replied, "I am going to stay home."

"Oh, Viola!" Livio exclaimed "you know that your friends in Rome are waiting for you!"

He looked into her eyes. He saw that she had made up her mind, and that he would never be able to persuade her to go.

"Don't be foolish, Viola," he protested; "this is a chance which will never come again."

She repeated; "No, no, no!"

Again he took her hand, "Viola, we have been waiting for this opportunity for years, now it's here! Do you know what it's going to mean?"

Her head drooped. "I do, that's why I will not go," she said; adding in a low, tense voice, "I can't, I can't!"

He said, "Viola, you must!" and again she added, "No."

She sat with carefully averted gaze, while he held her hand, trying to get her to look into his eyes.

For a moment he thought of explaining everything to her; the condition of his health and his decision to ask her in marriage as soon as he would be sure of his recovery. Then he thought it would not be right and kept silent.

The waiter had come back and was serving something. When he left them again, Livio leaned over the little table and lifted her head with a gentle pressure of his finger under her chin, "Viola, be sensible!" he begged. "Why do you act this way? You know you must come; your friends are there. Oh, Viola, May in Rome! It's the fulfillment of one's heart-desire. You will be crying with emotion, those soft evenings! Pine trees on the hills, and the noise of the fountains, and those great skies which seem larger there than anywhere on earth then the slow nights full of rhythm: full of deep calm and fragrance! Viola, I shall be there, at your side, and we will walk together, and talk softly. I will repeat to you the poems that gather all the harmonies of the place, and we will never get tired of looking and listening and feeling our nearness to each other. Be there, Viola, be there! You will see that you will not be sorry! There are feelings which I shall never be able to convey to you but there. Soft emotions which I have known in these days of convalescence, which I will find again there, for you. You will learn what the spell is of those things long dead; you will feel the oblivion there, the profound oblivion; then, amongst those ruins a sudden blooming of life, where the sun strikes! Do come, Viola! It's the chance of our lives; don't let us miss it!"

The orchestra below had begun a soft familiar tune, an old-time waltz which both Viola and Livio knew and loved. He stopped talking. The melody arose from the violins below, evoked memories of nights of gladness. They had danced to that waltz together many a time, lost in the wave of poignant melody.

Now both were silent. Viola, with her elbow resting on the table, bowed her head in her hand. Livio watched her, but the melody carried his thoughts far away. He seemed to be losing the sense of the place; had the feeling of his own great plains—of home, the mountains in the distance, the fragrance of violets, pale face, and tears. When Viola lifted her head a misty haze covered her eyes like a veil. He gazed at her, clasped his hand about her wrist, and whispered, softly, "Viola, Viola!"

She had a painful spasm, startled by his call, swung her head quickly to one side, while the moist film on her eyes broke and a tear flew off, hit his hand.

He said, "Don't cry, don't cry, Viola!" Putting his hand on her arm, he called her sweet names, trying to calm her. But she was sobbing violently, her face sunk into her palms. He said again, "Be reasonable, Viola; people are watching us." She raised her head and tried to smile. "I am sorry," she murmured, and tried to regain her composure, eating mechanically from the food on her plate. Livio followed her example, and for a while they kept up the pretense of eating, silently, their thoughts racing.

The corner where they sat was quite dark. In moving his chair, Livio had detached the connection of the electric lamp. By the time the waiter had returned Viola had dried her tears and regained her usual appearance of calm.

They began to talk again. She said, in timid apology, "I am nervous; I have been working hard." Then: "I wish I could go, Livio, but it can't be done! Really, it can't be done! You know it better than I! I am a weak girl, Livio; I am not built for strong emotions! Leave me alone at my task. I have my father to take care of. He is getting worse in these days; nobody but I can attend to him; he doesn't want anybody else around!"

Livio said, "What about Lucy?"

"She is too young," Viola returned "she needs care herself, I could never leave those two alone here. Then, you see we are not rich. I can't leave my work at this season. Besides," and she smiled wearily, "You don't want me there; you will be busy with your little friend!" and she tried to smile again.

She was alluding to the, girl of the moonlight episode in the Coliseum.

He smiled in his turn. "Let's forget the little friend! I wish you would come; Oh! see, it can be done—you may get a nurse for your father. As for the expense, we may find a way of arranging that."

"No, no, no," she said, "we are good friends, Livio, let's not spoil our friendship!"

It was now she who was pressing his hand and she talked on about, this friendship of theirs, and how fine it was, and how valuable it was to her, while the pressure of her hand was expressing much more than friendship, gliding around Livio's wrist, conveying to him an infinite tenderness and regret and passion, raising in his heart an immense emotion at such noble self-sacrifice and self-denial!

VIII

So, a few weeks later, Livio sailed alone, without making any further attempt to persuade Viola. He knew she had determined that she wouldn't go. He had therefore formed a plan to be patient for a few months, to take the strictest care of himself, and, as soon as his recovery was complete, to come back for her. He would certainly know how to win her consent then. It was inconceivable that the matter of her father and her sister couldn't be arranged in some way.

Livio and Viola met often during the period that preceded his sailing, but they talked no more about the trip. They were both calm; the nervous scene of the first meeting was not repeated. Viola had acquired again her gaiety, they were 'pals' once more, as of old. He promised that in the course of a few months he would come back to New York, for a visit, anyway. When he left, they said *au revoir* to each other, like friends. . . .

Just like friends, but the next day, on the boat, he missed her as he had never missed any friend before. He couldn't think, but of her. Before him were the violet seas of April, sweet France, Italy all-in-flower. He couldn't think of them; he wished to close his eyes and see nothing but Viola. His cabin was on the top deck of the boat. Every morning a boy of the crew woke him up. Perched on a crossbar of the bow mast, at the first break of dawn, he cried out, "The dawn! The dawn!" and Livio woke up. Through the porthole, he saw the boy swinging back and forth among the ropes, and behind him the sky, all pink, and, silhouetted against it, the image of Viola; and then again, lying all day on his deck chair, Livio thought of Viola; and at night, gazing through the black *extente*, he said Viola! He saw her, and thought of her, and was torn by regret because of her absence. The whole trip was an exquisite, mad desire for the missing happiness.

And when he arrived in Italy, and his train was running along the shore of Lago Maggiore, between the blue waters on one hand and the bushes of roses and azaleas on the other, he felt an acute pain for so much beauty being thus wasted while Viola was far away, out of sight, out of reach!

IX

During the first few days of his sojourn in Italy, Livio consulted some of the best doctors in the country. All agreed that the prospects of a complete recovery were good, but that it might take a long time to get him back to normal condition. They advised him to spend the spring on the Riviera or in some other equally genial climate and to go to the mountains during the summer. The probabilities were that by the autumn he would be all right.

He spent six weeks in a small village at the seashore; then feeling quite well and being somewhat tired of the place he decided, about the middle of June: to make a change before going to the mountains. First he thought of Rome. He had always enjoyed Rome! But this time, because Viola would not be there, he feared he would miss her too sorely—after all his dreams. To be sure there was his little blonde friend, who had made his sojourn there so sweet the year before; but he had no desire to see her again, just now. . . . So he dropped the idea of Rome and decided, instead, to spend a couple of weeks at Villa d'Este on Lake Como, not far from Milan: where some of his relatives lived.

But at Villa d'Este a great surprise awaited him. His little friend from Rome was there! . . . Stepping from the boat which had brought him in from Como, he found himself face to face with her on the pier. Both stopped short, stricken dumb with astonishment for the moment; then together they exclaimed, "Well, well, well! What a surprise!"

It appeared that she had suddenly decided, a few days previously, to visit friends at Villa d'Este; her husband being somewhere in France, or England, busy with one of those peace commissions that have been meeting all over Europe, during the last few years, to settle the affairs of mankind.

Under other conditions Livio would have been decidedly happy to meet her; but in his existing frame of mind the unexpected encounter disquieted him. The lady evidently detected his ill-concealed embarrassment; but, mistaking the cause she said, chidingly, "Well, well! You here in Europe, and didn't let me know! Shame!"

He apologized. He had been compelled to keep quiet on account of his health. He intended to give her a surprise. Planned coming to Rome, one of these days, unexpectedly. She introduced him to her friends. They all walked together a little distance to the Hotel. She expressed the greatest delight in seeing him again. Livio was glad himself, after all, in a way.

Being in love with Viola should not prevent him from enjoying the company of a pretty friend, he decided. There was no need of going back to the tricks of the year before. They might enjoy the lake, the beautiful places, the company of the people, who were extremely agreeable.

So they did. For a few days they shared the most delightful companionship and behaved remarkably well. Now and then she squeezed his hand or slyly showed him a devilish glance; but Livio was too much a man of the world not to know how to answer with a little tap on her cheek when nobody was looking; or with one of those schoolboy tricks that grown-up men sometimes like to play with beautiful woman, when the opportunity offers.

But they never went any further. It was a genuine recreation; every one was gay, the weather was splendid, showers now and then kept the air cool; never had Villa d'Este been so lovely!

Villa d'Este, in her magnificent attire of early summer, was royally beautiful. The gardens were perfect; the house, just restored after having been used as a hospital during the war, had acquired again its primitive splendor. Often the blond woman and Livio sat outside together, watching the lake; or climbed up the gardens on the side of the mountain or floated on a flat boat just off the bulkhead.

Seldom they made any reference to what had occurred in Rome the year before. That was supposed to have been forgotten. It had been a sort of a lark, anyhow. Then, too, her husband had been busy somewhere in Europe, helping men of good will to make peace among themselves, while Livio happened to be in Rome on a holiday. One night, after a party with friends, he had taken her home. Passing by the Coliseum they suddenly decided to get out of the carriage and take a walk through the arena amid the great shadows. It was a moonlight night, very still . . . she was a little frightened. In the dark passages she couldn't help drawing closer to her companion with a delicious quiver of fear. The pressure of her arm was soft; her voice was low and sweet; she was asking Livio questions about Nero; then she told him that in the moonlight he looked like her husband . . . that was a dangerous thing to say . . . in the Coliseum at midnight . . . in the moonlight. . . .

When they got outside the old ruin the carriage was gone. The driver, after his long waiting, had evidently given them up as a "bad fare." They walked home. Before leaving her, Livio asked her to meet him the following afternoon at four o'clock, in Piazza di Spagna, for an automobile ride somewhere in the Alban hills. She said "No." Nevertheless at four o'clock she was there. They motored to Genzano. The little lake of Nemi, set deep within the ring of its sloping shores, looked like a jewel, that day. They sat on the terrace outside the hostelry overlooking the lake and ordered some fruit and a bottle of wine. It was windy. The surface of the lake was all rippled; the swallows were flying below them over the water with a silent, gliding motion; when one passed near them, she tried to catch it with her hand, laughing like a child, like an adorable little child. Then the sky grew dark; a mass of black clouds blew in from over the top of the hills and a thunderstorm burst upon them. Livio and his friend had to take shelter within the hostelry. The ground floor was full of village people, so he had to help her upstairs to a room. Through the rain-blurred window panes, they watched the storm; their arms were intertwined. Perhaps, in the vivid glare of the lightning, Livio again looked like her husband; so much this time that she actually mistook one for the other. (What delightful mistakes those Roman ladies make!)

When the rain stopped, they started back for Rome. After the storm, the evening was filled with splendor. Whipped by the wind, the last clouds fled into the western sky, leaving shreds of gauze caught in the tops of the cypress trees. The sun, now out again and near to setting, threw a red light against the tower of Nemi. As they passed over the aqueduct by Villa Chigi, an immense roar seemed to rise from the forest below, lashed by the gale. On the mountain far off, Rocca di Papa shone washed by the rain, all white like an Asiatic town.

They sat silent in the car, full of those sweet regrets that, though supposed to redeem one, in reality make the sensation of guilt last long after the escapade is over.

Livio took the lady to her home, and there said good-bye. He left Rome the same night. Since then he had neither seen her nor written to her. It had been tacitly understood between them that the incident must be forgotten. . . .

And now here they were, together again, amid the perilous beauty of Villa d'Este! . . .

However, nothing but those occasional slyly devilish glances offered the suggestion that the episode was still remembered. . . . The lady must have thought it strange that Livio maintained fidelity to their tacit pledge—Livio, the carefree, the light-hearted! Perhaps she was a little *froissée*; perhaps she understood that, since last year, something new had entered into his heart.

One evening they dined together, alone. Her friends had gone to Como, to some social affair. She, pleading headache, had remained at home. They dined outside, in the loggia. Her headache was gone; she looked very charming in her dress of white gauze. Wine was brought; and as she offered Livio a glass of the sparkling beverage, she gazed at him with languorous, eloquent eyes.

"To our health," she said, "and to our memories!"

There was a pause. They rose from the table. The evening was calm; not a ripple on the lake. A tinge of infinite softness was cast by the dying sun over the mountain on the opposite shore. Como, within its circle of hills, lay still, by the still waters.

She led Livio across the rustic bridge to the extreme end of the garden, "It's damp," she said; "let's sit under this arch," and she walked to a seat set within a niche in the rock.

It wasn't damp at all; in fact, the air was as clear as crystal; but the seat was out of sight of the house, facing the lake. Facing the lake, and the harmonic mountain beyond, and Como at the far end of the gulf. They sat side by side.

"Don't you feel this beautiful evening," she said, "spread its charm upon your heart? I am thirsty for this soft light. I feel worn and languid. What is this strange sensation that comes upon us these nights of June?" In her voice was an infinite tenderness, her soft arm pressed upon Livio's, her head leaned against his shoulder.

What did he feel? Against him she leaned, this woman who had once been the object of his desire. He had but to stretch out his arm and take the gift that she offered him. . . .

Livio stretched out his arm . . . but the virginal image of Viola rose silently between . . . In the mute light, under the sky of rose and pearl, she stood. Solitude and silence all around, and the divine vision standing forth alone!

The blonde woman gave a little cry, and, shivering, drew closer. Throwing her head back, she looked into Livio's eyes:

"What is within you?" she cried; "what shadow covers your forehead? What obscure shadow wraps your heart?"

He did not answer. His dream was a greater thing than she could understand. Nothing else he could do, but gaze at the mute image growing against the pearly sky. A divine calm was setting in around him. No small voice of a light woman could break it.

Again she said, "What dream is within you greater than this dream here? Come!"

She pulled Livio up by both hands. He followed like a man walking in a trance! She led him to the shore of the lake. "*Look!*" she exclaimed.

The image of Viola was all that Livio could see! It was between him and her, between him and the lake, between him and everything! Again the blonde woman uttered a cry and fled.

Long after she was gone and the light had faded in the sky, Livio stood there dumb, alone, gazing at the stars!

Thus the image of the virgin girl whom Livio loved made him thrust aside the gift that was offered to him that warm night of June, in the enchanted garden, by the still lake, under the sky of Italy, full of stars!

x

Livio awoke the following morning feeling a little ashamed of his conduct. He wondered if he had not acted rather unfairly towards his little Roman friend. He wrote her a note apologizing for his queer behavior and sent it up to her room. Then he wrote to Viola!

He intended to give her a humorous account of the event, as he had done on former occasions, turning into ridicule his most delicate feelings. But the impression that he still had of her vision was so vivid and strong that he had not the heart to make light of it.

In his letter, he must have imparted to Viola something of the havoc wrought upon his senses by the occurrences of the evening before. Without mentioning the facts, he conveyed the impression that a woman had been close to him. No garden, no lake, no starry sky could give a man the emotion that throbbed through his lines!

"Viola," he wrote, "I am leaving Villa d'Este! I don't want to stay here any more. I want to go away, to lose myself somewhere. I want to seek those towns of oblivion—those silent towns of Italy which rise alone on the top of a hill or lie deserted upon the banks of a river, wrapped in a divine melancholy, listening to the melodies of the nightingales in the solitude of their cloisters, and dreaming of the life which lies buried under the arches of their cathedrals. I want to think of you there, Viola, of you who should be with me! Oh, Viola! I wish I could take you to Pisa, that we might look together through the gates of the Camposanto and see the sun glimmering upon the marbles of the Dome, and drive with you at sunset towards Ferrara, along the wide road lined with poplars, while the swallows glide by thousands through the skies, and over the vast land all is melody and song. I would bring you to Orvieto, and walk with you through those long streets that seem to lead into the infinite; gaze with you at the towered walls of the palaces and at the immense shadows which they cast upon the silence of the deserted squares. Grass and moss grow there, everywhere; but suddenly, at the turn of a corner, the rays of the sun playing over the mosaics of the great cathedral, blind you with their magnificence!

"I wish I could show you, from the top of Monte Orfano facing east, Brescia, grouped below Cidnean hill, at the feet of the sturdy castle; facing west, Bergamo, spread over the side of the mountain between the two valleys alone, down upon the vast plain, Cremona by the river, and Mantova, far off in the distance; and far south, if the day be clear, the towers of Parma emerging from the plain against the dark mass of the Apennines. And go to Tuscany to see the towns of medieval glory, now silent! Lucca, where Ilaria del Carretto sleeps on the cover of her tomb, wrapped in her vest of marble. San Gemignano of the many towers! Siena, the dream! Fiesole, overlooking the valley below, within which lays Florence. Then, descending into Florence itself, seek in tower and loggie, palaces, churches, memories of the days gone by! In Verona I could show you, through the railing, the white tomb of Giulietta, who, hearing the song of the lark in the tragic dawn, said it was the nightingale, hoping with the sweet deception to hold her lover. In Ferrara I would tell you of Parisina; and in Padova, of Thisbe; and in Rimini of Francesca; and in the desolate land of Maremma, of Pia dei Tolomei, who made the sweet prayer to Dante! Oh, come! You should know these girls of Italy, you, Viola, who are a sister to them! Oh Viola, come!"

XI

Thus Livio wrote to Viola, and the same day he left Villa d'Este, mailing the letter as he passed through Como. In Milan he stopped a few hours; then went straight on to Florence.

He thought that Tuscany would be the place best suited to his spiritual frame of mind. There, amongst those hills that for centuries have been the home of human ecstasy, he might find, from things and creatures, a response to the immense desire of love that burned within him. He stayed in Florence, then for a few days in Siena, then he went down into Umbria, to seek the vestiges of St. Francis. The man who had gathered within his breast the throb of universal love might come as a present spirit into his soul and soothe his passion. Livio was ready to receive him! He was fain to retrace, through him, the path to those summits of inner joy which make us forget our human passions and which he, the saint, had discovered for us!

Viola, far from him, unattainable, was acting upon Livio's senses as the apparition does upon the senses of the devotee. Had not St. Francis, in the fervor of his faith, received one night the tangible signs of the presence of his God? By what sign would Viola manifest her presence to Livio? Couldn't he evoke her out of space, as the saint had evoked his God, by the sheer power of desire? All the time that he spent in Assisi Livio was haunted by this fervent wish. Then, once more, he took his way back through Umbria into Tuscany, to the coast of the sea, obsessed by this desire of Viola, led by her image.

He went to Leghorn. He had made arrangements to have his mail forwarded there. There were letters from New York, but none from Viola. This lack of news rather unnerved him, made his desire keener. He thought of her constantly, all that first day! He couldn't think of anything else.

That night he walked out along the seashore towards Antignano, by the beautiful walk of the Ardenza. The road runs between the sea and groves of oleanders. The scent of the plants in bloom and of the weeds on the rocks was inebriating. All the coast was dark; not a light on the sea but the red glare of the flashlight on the island of La Meloria appearing and disappearing, like a human eye opening and shutting in the night. He walked, and then stopped, listening to the soft breaking of the waves; then walked again, then sat on a stone bench by the oleanders in bloom. All his thoughts were of Viola, all his mind was bent towards her. With wide open eyes he gazed upon the sea, listless, hypnotized by the red flash appearing and disappearing out of the dark. He felt the soft breeze through his hair; he felt the warm night of June taking possession of his senses, and, within him an intense desire for Viola. All his body, all his will, was tendered towards the sea as though from over the water he felt something gliding towards him in the dark as though a living wing impetuously brushed over him. As he lifted his hand he felt Viola's soft hair against his cheeks, her lips pressing upon his, her body clinging to his with superhuman force.

He sprang to his feet, groping blindly in the dark, with Viola's hair twining about him . . . He could feel it . . . he called "Viola! Viola!" and ran frantically to the edge of the sea; then back to the bushes of oleander, still crying "Viola! Viola!" He could not see her, could not grasp her; but he knew that she was there, drawing him to her with irresistible power. . . .

Mad with passion and terror, again he called "Viola! Viola!" But no answer came—only her lips pressing upon his, her long hair binding him, coiling itself with deadly tenacity about his chest around his neck, in a passionate embrace robbing him of breath, of energy, of consciousness; until-dumb, inert, lifeless—he fell to the earth, and lay prone among the oleanders.

On that same night, in New York, Viola Redley was found dead in Central Park.

XII

Upon Livio's departure for Italy, Viola had begun to realize how closely her destiny was bound up with his. She knew that they were no longer friends, but lovers. For months the subtle poison of passion had been working its will upon her. In her fundamental ignorance of the ways of the flesh she had allowed it to permeate her being, take full possession of her. The emotion that she had mistaken for friendship, deceiving Livio as well as herself. now that he was gone revealed itself in its true nature. She was aghast at the revelation. She had let him go back to Italy; to the girls he had loved, saying coldly, "Go, you don't need me there, you will be busy with your Roman friend!" Now, she couldn't bear to think of him somewhere in those gardens of their dreams, making love to another woman. The terrific jealousy that had seized her that night six months before, when, sunk in her armchair, she had listened to the tale of his adventure in the Coliseum, tortured her again now.

Oh! If he ever came back with another tale like that, it would kill her to listen to it! Yet he probably would! She knew Livio! She had no confidence in him, nor in the men of his race! A soft glance from a pair of blue eyes, a smile showing a flash of white teeth, and he could easily forget her and their friendship. And, after all, wasn't he free? They were not supposed to be lovers; she herself had told him, "Go and have a good time!" Too proud to confess her inward terror at the idea of his being free, there, in those gardens of Italy, where even the scent of the roses is a snare, and every lovely woman a temptation!

Alone in her studio, she sat in that same armchair for hours, turning over these thoughts in her mind. She wished she had not been so proud. Why had she let him go in that chilling, unresponsive way? Why hadn't she listened to his plan of meeting in Rome, where her friends were ready with a welcome? After all, it wouldn't have been impossible for her to leave her father for a few weeks in the care of a nurse; and as to Lucy, it was simply absurd to think her unable to care for herself. Lucy was straight enough; what of it if she did get a little amusement out of life? What good had it done her, Viola, to be so strait-laced? . . . Livio was right, life ought to be a jolly adventure; why complicate it with scruples that only clouded its happiness?

Brooding thus, for hours at a time strange thoughts took possession of her. She lost interest in everything and everybody. Her art was her only consolation. Out on Long Island she had some work in course of construction, and went there often to supervise it; she spent a great deal of time in her studio. It seemed to her that in that studio, where she and Livio had been so much together she missed him less.

She was constantly expecting to hear from him. Every day, at the time the postman came around, she became eager and excited. She had a little flutter when she heard the bell ring, hoping to get news . . . but Livio didn't write. He sent her a postal card or two, each with some banal greeting. He never seemed to find just the right thing to say . . . Could he write to her of love, when they had never spoken of love to each other? Commonplace accounts of his doings, his goings and comings, wouldn't satisfy either him or her. So, as time slid by, she began to lose hope. His long silence seemed to confirm her fears that he had forgotten her; that there was someone else. . . .

Then, after an eternity of suspense, came Livio's letter from Como. It was awaiting her, one Saturday afternoon, when she returned from the country.

"There is a letter from Italy for you upstairs," Lucy announced, as she let her in.

Viola's heart fluttered; she stood breathless, while her sister looked at her with a little smile. Walking up the stairs, she stumbled, so nearly was she overcome. Once in the studio, she let herself down into the armchair, gazing long at the envelope before her on the table. Then, rising swiftly, she seized it and tore it open.

She read the tell-tale lines. Profound emotion gripped her from the beginning. Before she could grasp the actual meaning of the words, the passion evoked by them overcame her, "Viola, those silent towns of Italy which rise, alone, on the top of a hill, or lie deserted upon the banks of a river, wrapped in a divine melancholy, listening to the melodies of the nightingales, in the solitude of their cloisters. . . ."

The vision of herself and Livio walking hand in hand through the streets of Ferrara, along the river in Pisa, in the shadow of the great cathedral, appeared vividly before her eyes. She and Livio, and around them the things of pure beauty, the land of love!

Love! Love! She knew now what the emotion was that had shaken her in reading his words! Above the life that she had lived, above her pride, above her duty, above everything stood one supreme truth: Love! One ecstatic joy, to be with him, there! And this joy had been offered to her, and she had said, "No!"

Over and over again she read Livio's letter; but one thought only occupied her mind, the realization of her terrible mistake in uttering that fateful "No!" in denying herself the joy that had been within her reach.

What absurd ideal had prompted her to deny her love? Why had she stubbornly ignored the voice of her heart?

In a spasm of nervousness, she sprang up and went to the window. Leaning on the ledge, listless, apathetic, she looked stupidly for awhile to the street below, deserted at that hour of the day; then, returning to her chair, burst into tears.

She wept like a child, worn, broken, under the burden of her tortured soul.

She considered her life. A flat stretch, a long way, bare, arid, walled in on both sides! She thought of her home and her early days in New England under her aunt's strict joyless rule. Ever since those days, the chastened spirit of her race had subdued every breath of passion in her heart, and she had developed amongst those austere people and things, as plain as a piece of Colonial furniture. Then, in New York for those last eight years, she had ignored the call of the stirring city around her, had lived her life of work and devotion in her studio, or beside her father's chair. Was it going to be so forever? Her youth was well ripened; the best of it was past. Was she going to let the rest go by, without enjoyment, without love? Was she going to let her beauty fade, her flesh wither, while her drab existence spun itself out? She was worthy of love, she wanted love; she could have had it . . . Why had she refused it?

A wave of passionate despair shook her. She sank her teeth in the flesh of her arm, then started crying again bitterly, hopelessly.

The voice of Lucy downstairs called "Viola!" She tried to get up, but sank back into her chair; without force, without will, a prey to her emotion.

Lucy appeared at the door. "Aren't you coming down for dinner, Viola?" she inquired; then, seeing her in tears:

"What's wrong?" she said, "Why are you crying?" She ran to her, and sat beside her on the arm of the chair, gently lifting her head. "Viola, Viola, what is it? What did he write you, to hurt you so?"

"Nothing, Lucy; I am a fool! I had a little spell of melancholy, but it's all over now! I am coming down with you!" but still she wept, her head sunk in Lucy's lap; the younger girl caressing her hair, her cheek, softly murmuring "Viola, Viola!" frightened by the sight of her sister's distress.

"I am afraid he has hurt you with his letter: he is bad! What right has he to make you suffer so?"

"Oh, no, Lucy, he isn't bad, it's I who am a fool. He is good, and you are good, too, little Lucy! I was wrong to treat you harshly! Oh, Lucy, Lucy!" and she drew her sister's face against hers, kissing and fondling her; moved at the idea of being consoled by her little sister in this debacle of her will, in this crisis of her being!

For awhile the two sisters were in each other's arms, Viola sobbing while Lucy kissed her and consoled her in the awkward way of those who have no experience with sorrow.

Then Viola got up. "Let's go downstairs," she said, "Father is waiting!" And, picking up her courage, she smoothed her hair before the mirror, and the two sisters walked down together arm in arm to the dining room.

XIII

That night Viola could not sleep. She tossed feverishly in her bed, had long spells of tears; then for hours she lay motionless, apathetic, worn into stillness!

She couldn't close her eyes without seeing at once the vision of happiness that might have been hers, that now, perhaps, belonged to some one else! Nothing could take from her mind the thought that some woman in Italy had Livio in her grip and would never let him come back. A spirit of revolt shook her of jealousy for this imaginary rival who might be stronger than she! She choked back her sobs, hiding her face in her arms, her lips pressed against the bare flesh.

A slow strife between her passion and her character was in process within her all through the night. She said to herself, "I am a fool! Who is he, after all, that he should upset me in this way?" Her pride came to her aid; she sat up on her bed, appealing to her reason, trying to strengthen her sturdy New England will.

Then, the tide of discouragement overwhelming her again, she fell back exhausted, vanquished! "No! no!" she cried. "It is all wrong, all wrong! Nothing can be right that leads into misery like this!"

In her infinite unhappiness, she disowned her blood and her principles. There was bitterness within her, a supreme despair, a conviction that she had made a failure of her life!

As morning approached, she fell into a heavy slumber. It was late when her sister Lucy awakened her. "I have been worried about you," she said, "Father has asked for you twice; I was afraid you were ill."

"I am all right, Lucy, I am ashamed for being so late; how did I ever sleep so long?"

She jumped out of bed and began to dress, saying, again and again, "I am ashamed," while Lucy, sitting on the edge of the bed, watched her.

A heavy fatigue was upon her limbs; she felt broken all over. She sat down for breakfast with the family, but could eat nothing.

She decided to go to church. It was Sunday morning, and the idea of the whole blank day before her terrified her. In church she followed the service indifferently, listening to the sermon without hearing a word, singing the hymns mechanically with the rest.

Again at lunch she couldn't eat; there was a knot in her throat . . . Lucy tried to urge her; her father, too, noticed that something was wrong, but wisely made no comment.

After lunch she went back to her studio. She was calm, now; a sense of peace and order prevailed again in her heart. She thought she might do some work to distract her mind, got her pencils put on her apron and climbed on her stool.

For a while she was busy, drawing on a plan. She was trying to get the right curve for a staircase leading from a terrace down to a pool. In search of a suggestion, she opened an album of photographs and her eyes fell on a picture of Villa Falconieri, on which one day Livio had jokingly drawn two doves wooing on a balustrade.

He had often done such foolish things, hinting at their love in a facetious way and, because these little jokes betrayed a sentiment, they both got a thrill out of them. It was a sentiment too delicate to be expressed in words; a sentiment which must be kept vague and indefinite lest it be spoiled or hurt by one of those sudden shocks that often occur between lovers of different character, of different race.

Viola looked at the doves with a smile. She remembered the day Livio had drawn them while she was working, the tone in which in handing her the sheet he had said, "Here we are, you and I!" And she had scolded him for spoiling her sheet, and hit him on the fingers with her ruler as she often did, treating him like a bad boy caught by the teacher in a mischievous trick.

She smiled and looked at the doves, pleased to have come across that naive testimonial of his tenderness; then, suddenly, her smile was clouded with tears; she left her work and took refuge in the armchair. That innocent little drawing had brought back with full force the troubled thoughts of the preceding night.

Villa Falconieri in Frascati was one of their dream-places. Once Livio had told her, pointing to the picture, "One ought to live in one of those palaces to know what perfect life is! Only there can it be attained, under the sky of Rome!" and then he had added, with a sidelong glance, "In the arms of one of my passionate countrywomen!"

It was one of the crazy things that he was so fond of saying, partly for the love of hearing himself talk, but more for the fun of startling Viola's New England simplicity. Now, the idea of those "passionate women" haunted her like a specter.

Until lately "passion" had been simply a word to Viola. The best years of her youth had been passed in indifference to emotion; it was that first long kiss of Livio's that had brought to her lips the warm taste of life.

She had felt strangely ever since. At times, she had queer dreams, at other times, a confused warning that above the routine feelings of everyday life, there is a force that can shake the body as the storm shakes a tree. But Puritan to the core, she had steadily refused to acknowledge it.

Now her mind filled with forbidden thoughts. She began to recall the startling sensations that had sometimes assailed her when Livio was with her. She remembered one night being with him in a restaurant, when across the room they saw a man whom they both knew dining with a chorus girl. The girl wore a daring décolleté, and her arms were bare. Under the rosy light of the lamps she looked really beautiful, "desirable," as Livio expressed it, directing Viola's attention to the man's eager gaze.

Viola made a movement of disgust.

"Oh," she said, "he ought to be ashamed!"

Livio had defended him. "Oh, Viola, don't condemn what you don't understand!" he exclaimed.

He had spoken very simply, for the desires of the flesh were an everyday topic with him.

For a minute Viola and Livio had looked into each other's eyes across the table. His were softly worn. She must have seen in them vestiges of things unknown—mysterious!

She turned her head away, feeling uneasy, bitter, sad; as though she had breathed the scent of some narcotic flower of lands unknown.

Now that same uneasy feeling was upon her again. She connected it with Livio's words about Villa Falconieri, and with the memory of their kisses, ever fresh on her mouth, and with what she had seen in his eyes that night in the restaurant?

"Is there anything wrong with me?" she asked herself, and sat for a while contemplating the vague, disturbing visions within.

Her glance fell on her blue cambric apron. It seemed like a symbol of her dull, unlovely life. She got up and looked at herself in the mirror; looked again at her apron, plain, ugly, shapeless, with a flat belt fastened unbecomingly around her waist! . . . She took it off quickly, a little blush stealing into her cheeks . . . Underneath the apron, she wore a plain blouse of muslin purple, with white dots. Slowly she unfastened the hooks and let it glide off her shoulders to the floor. Then she tried to undo the knots of her silk slip; but they held fast, and, with sudden impatience, she roughly tore the garment open. . . .

Her bosom appeared white, pure, as that of a Phidian goddess. . . . Under her disfiguring blue apron she had kept her virginal beauty hidden, useless; unknown even to herself. For a moment she stood still, panic-stricken at the audacity of her action, pressing her lips between her teeth to check the passionate tide rising within. Then she flung herself on her bed, her face rigid against the pillows. Her body shook; her throat throbbed.

"Oh, good Lord!" she thought. "Am I going mad?"

Several minutes passed. . . . An immense fatigue overcame her. The storm was spent; and now she lay supine, worn, her eyes closed, her ears dull. She had no energy left to lift her head or open her eyes.

Without moving her body she reached for a scarf which hung at the head of her bed, pulled it down upon her bare shoulders, drew its folds over her bosom. Her cheeks flamed suddenly . . . What madness had possessed her? she wondered, in an access of shame.

She grew calmer after a while. Taking up Livio's letter she read it quietly though. She couldn't see now why it had disturbed her so . . . It was the sweetest letter she had ever received from him. How foolish she had been to work herself into such a fit of frenzy. He would soon return; in a few months they would meet again, and, oh, this time! This time it would be different! . . .

She smiled at the image of Livio, coming back. . . . But a sting of fear was in her heart. Somehow, she couldn't rid herself of that fear!

She said to herself, "He loves me, I know. . . . Certainly he must have loved me, when he wrote that letter! But, oh! who can tell? How can I trust him? Livio is so careless with his love! Weak as water where girls are concerned! . . . Some day he will come back and tell me of some new adventure, declaring that it wasn't his fault; putting the blame on the landscape, on the moon, on the nightingales' song!"

She was calm enough now to smile at the idea. She knew Livio so well! But she had better forget! She rose and dressed, repeating this to herself. She did not put on the blue apron. . . . Instead, she put on her hat; she wanted to get out into the open before supper.

As she passed by the living room, on the floor below, she told her father that she would soon return. With a little sign of relief, she went out into the pleasant June evening.

XIV

She thought, at first, of walking over to Gramercy Park and resting on one of the benches there. She felt too tired to go far. But when she reached the little enclosure, she couldn't get enough air; the tall buildings over on Fourth Avenue shot out the crimson glow of the sunset. Viola wanted to see more of the sky, so soft and warm and tender at that hour.

Her watch told her that it was seven o'clock. She decided to walk over to Fifth Avenue and ride uptown on top of a bus. Perhaps that would give her the air she needed.

It was something of a walk for one as weary as she. When she reached the Avenue, she was almost too exhausted to go further; but while she waited for the bus, a Victoria came along, one of the few such vehicles that may still be hired on a summer evening. The driver, with an eye to a possible fare, slowed down as he approached. After a minute of hesitation, Viola signaled him to stop. Riding in a carriage appealed to her more, just then, than being jolted on the upper deck of a bus. She climbed in.

She directed the "cabby" to drive up the Avenue as far as the Plaza, then to make a tour of the Park.

"I want to be back in Gramercy Park in about an hour," she said, "but you need not hurry." She thought of arranging the price with the driver; then she said to herself, "Oh, what's the difference!" and let it go for the moment. She enjoyed that little extravagance, riding in her carriage, like a princess!

The broad Avenue looked magnificent, though its great palaces were all closed. Viola observed everything: the library, the Cathedral, St. Thomas' Church, the stately clubs. On the sidewalk people were walking, leisurely, in groups, some of them dragging their children along. She seemed to be the only person alone. She felt a sting of bitterness, riding in her carnage.

At the corner of the Plaza the imposing mass of the Hotel across the square captured her eye. It was an impressive sight, that great building clean cut against the vivid sky! The sky was gorgeous, all rosy, clear as crystal full of light.

Again, in the Park, she looked with envy at the groups about her. Everybody had friends, it appeared, but herself. In the large field across the road from the Mall, all was life and glamour; boys playing baseball, chasing each other; shouting, wrestling on the grass!

She stopped the carriage for a while to look, but so much life and joy seemed only to reawaken her misery. She lost all interest in her ride. Alighting, she paid and dismissed the driver; she could take a taxi back, she reflected.

She walked slowly over to the lake. On the east bank there is a little slope; It was all covered with rhododendrons in bloom. Livio and she had walked up that slope one night in the spring. Now she wanted to see the place again. But she was too weary to walk uphill. She returned to the lake. Just by the edge of the water, she found a bench under a willow tree, and let herself down on it. She felt weak and faint. It occurred to her then that she had eaten nothing all day. Her head was dizzy; she wished she were home!

It was a quiet spot, out of the beaten way. There was no one in sight but a couple of lovers in a boat, drifting idly on the lake; no noise, except the rumbling of the elevated trains far away.

The light was fading. Suddenly, against the western sky, the great sign of the Hotel Majestic flashed out; then, on the roof of the Century Theater, ran a streak of red lights. Viola followed those lights with incurious eyes, intent on her inward thoughts. She remembered that she had once been in the place with Livio. It was the night they had walked over the rhododendron slope. They had wandered through those labyrinths of little paths, then they had found themselves by the lake. The night was calm; in the intense blue of the sky, one by one the stars were blossoming out. He had drawn her dose to his side. . . . In the softness of the still spring night she had experienced a sensation that she had never known before, sweet and cruel, languid, like a dream! She had nearly swooned in his arms, for very sweetness.

Now she consciously tried to recapture that sensation, concentrating all her will upon the effort; closed her eyes and leaned against the back of the bench, her relaxed arm dangling by her side. Livio's letter, which she still held in her hand, slipped unheeded to the ground; the wind blew it into the lake. But she was not aware of her loss. Her mind was too intent upon the effort of recalling the sweetness of that night, two months before! She tried to exclude every other thought, but she couldn't. Her ideas were confused. The noise of the elevated trains, far away vaguely disturbed her. It was like a long, broken rumbling, now indistinct, now defined, or was it perhaps, the wind, or the falling of waters, or a flight of wings in the air? . . . Or the distant murmur of Rome?

Livio's words came back to her, "The sun is warm and pleasant there; it breaks gently through the foliage, thrusting hundreds of spears into the shadows below . . . all is mystery and peace . . . from afar comes the murmur of Rome from the marble balustrades, now and then, the note of a peacock! . . ."

She could see those great gardens now, could hear the rustling of the leaves and Livio's voice! She was dreaming . . . where was he, where was he, her beloved? On what blossoming hill? By what blue lake? In what silent cloister of his native land? It must be night now, in Italy; perhaps he was wandering under his starry sky thinking of her, or sitting on the shore of the sea, amongst the oleanders in bloom! Could it be his voice that she heard calling her. . . . From far away, far, far away, she heard a voice, his voice, from across the seas! . . . And her body was sinking, sinking, she felt herself slipping to the ground, but her spirit was reaching out, with intense yearning, towards that voice, that vision, *over there*!

She gathered all that was left of her failing energy in one superhuman effect to reach to him, across the sea, with her passionate soul, to clasp him to her heart, to press upon his lips her last breath! . . . A terrific spasm shook her; her body stiffened tensely. . . . Yet all the while her spirit was reaching, reaching. . . .

Convulsively she flung out her arms. . . . Time, space, slipped away from her. She was conscious only of the nearness of her beloved. . . . An ineffable peace took possession of her, he was so near! So near! One more effort, one supreme effort, and she would reach him at last!

And in that effort, she died!

In an Immigrant Community

∾ *Constantine Maria Panunzio*

Molfetta (Bari), Italy, October 25, 1884–Los Angeles, California,
August 6, 1964

Constantine (born Constantino) Maria Panunzio was the son of Don Colì (Nicola),
a lawyer and teacher, and the namesake grandson of a patriot grandfather who was
murdered by poisoning in the Bourbon prison of Montefusco. He was the first
male of a group of four sisters and as many brothers. His grandmother, as he wrote
in Italian, in *The Soul of an Immigrant*, had very clear ideas about his future: "You
must become a great man, like your grandfather," she would repeat to him, and she
already saw him first as a priest, then a teacher, and, subsequently, a political man.
But Costantine revealed himself much too lively for those expectations. Following
an accident while he was setting off firecrackers with other children, he lost the
use of his left eye. The sea and boats were his only real passions. His father soon
resolved to punish him for his continual delinquencies by sending him to work
instead of to school. In Molfetta, where he spent all his childhood and a large part
of his adolescence, and which is vividly described in the first chapters of *The Soul
of an Immigrant*, Panunzio entered a *ginnasio* (a junior high school) in a seminary,
but he discontinued his studies, unwilling to be subject to the rigid discipline of
the religious institution. In April 1898, he embarked as a hand on a ship that
shuttled between various Italian and Dalmatian ports. His father died, and in
1899, his mother and grandmother went to Genoa, where they embarked on a tour
of Europe and the Mediterranean. It was in that moment, as the book relates, that
for the first time, he conceived the idea of seeing America.

On July 3, 1902, Panunzio disembarked in Boston. His voyage was supposed to proceed from there, in time, for Montevideo, Uruguay; instead he decided to desert and remain in Boston. "Pick" and "shovel" were the first words of English he learned; his first period in America was characterized by an extremely hard apprenticeship as an underpaid laborer, when he was paid at all. He suffered cold and hunger, the experience of American contempt for the "dagoes," and a series of woes that developed in him the idea of scraping money together to return to Molfetta as soon as possible. He worked in a textile factory in Boston. Then, in the Maine woods, he joined a gang of woodcutters, only to discover that that work was no more than a kind of slavery, and he decided to flee. Subsequently, he fell into the waters of a frozen lake; he found temporary refuge as a worker in a factory in Stacyville, where he became aware, once again, of having been deceived; and he fled, climbing clandestinely onto a train. Discovered, he was arrested, incarcerated, tried, and sent back to his dishonest employer. Fleeing again, thanks to the mother of his employer, he settled at some distance, in Sherman, in the house of the Richmonds, a family revealed to him as the first group of "authentic Americans" he met until then.

Under the influence of the Richmonds, Panunzio began to revive and with renewed spirits, started the process of Americanization. It was an "awakening," which found its moments of major intensity in reading the Bible and being admitted into a Baptist church, as well as in attending the local school. From here onward, his progress was constant. In 1904, Panunzio entered the Maine Wesleyan Seminary, where, after initial difficulties in comprehension, he became a model student, enchanting all with his perfect performance, in the final course, as Shylock in *The Merchant of Venice*. In 1907, he entered Wesleyan University, in Middletown, Connecticut, took his degree in 1911, and subsequently entered the School of Theology at Boston University, with the intention of becoming a Protestant minister. He was naturalized in 1914.

He was assigned various missions in the suburbs of Hartford, Connecticut, and then in the North End, the Italian quarter of Boston. Panunzio also continued his studies, in Washington, perfecting himself in political economy. In the meanwhile, during World War I, he was sent to Europe by the YMCA (Young Men's Christian Association), which brought him to France and then Italy. After visiting his relatives in Puglia, he traveled extensively throughout the country, finally arriving at Mogliano Veneto, the general quarters of the Third Army; but he firmly decided to remain an American citizen.

In 1921, Panunzio published *The Soul of an Immigrant*, an important book, which, as composed, resembles in certain ways the edifying old autobiographies produced in the Protestant ambit—such as, for example, that of Antonio Andrea Arrighi. However, *The Soul of an Immigrant* decidedly differs from others of its kind, in virtue of the varied and deepened context from which Panunzio's whole oppressive emigration emerges powerfully and, above all, because the personality of the author is more fully revealed, as well as his particular independence of judgment in respect to the methods, the strategies, and the culture of his religions companions. The first half of the autobiography is the story of a life: tense, eventful, and fascinating, with its accounts of Panunzio's misfortunes and despair, which summon up similar experiences of Lorenzo Da Ponte, recounted in his *Memorie*. For the rest, the book is a reflection on the theme of immigration in its multiple aspects, always, however, related to actual experience. Even in the more exclusively narrative parts, Panunzio does not forget to refer to the general problem of immigration; he compares his personal experiences to the cases of immigrants in general, synthesizing the possible good and bad turns that could befall each one of them. Ensuing from these reflections are very interesting ideas in relation to some converging questions: on the reasons why the Italians in America do not choose agricultural work; on the distorted idea of the *padrone* system; on the racism that pollutes life; on the unconscionable practice of changing the name of newly arriving immigrants (something that affected him for some time); on the necessity for Italian immigrants to distance themselves as much as possible from the colony in order to accelerate their veritable admittance into American society; and on the grave wrongs to which they are exposed, wrongs that justify the origin of certain criminal attitudes. This reflective part of the book is actually a continuous questioning, a departure from the facts of lived experience to arrive at a kind of theory of assimilation; in here, he can address the less attractive parts of the system: pretenses relative to Americanization, the fallible zeal of Protestant missionaries preoccupied solely with making converts, and police abuse of poor people. Panunzio dedicates an entire chapter (XI) to an analysis of what he lost by becoming an American. Yet, underlying these dispassionate analyses, his love for his acquired country is not lessened; rather, in the final pages, this theme is colored by a solemnity and an emphasis completely disproportionate in respect to the total balance of the work.

For all these reasons, *The Soul of an Immigrant* is a complex and important book, perhaps "the most important sketch of the immigrant's relations with the adjustments to America," as the reviewer of the *Boston Transcript* wrote, in 1921. It was of such importance that it would be republished in 1924 and again in 1934.

Panunzio, who in 1931 became a professor of sociology at the University of California, Los Angeles, applied himself unflinchingly to a profound study of the themes of multiethnic society. Besides his autobiography, another of his important contributions in the field of similar studies is represented by the volume, *Immigrant Crossroads* (1927), in which he narrates the story of immigration from its origins to the restrictive measures of the 1920s. He also wrote a series of academic publications and many articles on prominent themes, among which, particularly interesting, is an essay on the consequences of Prohibition among the Americans of foreign origin ("The Foreign Born's Reaction to Prohibition," 1934) and an analysis of the Fascist influence on the immigrants ("Italian Americans, Fascism, and the War," 1942). Panunzio's anti-Fascist activity is also testified by his adherence to the Mazzini Society.

After retiring from teaching in 1952, Panunzio became a leader in the national campaign for a better economic treatment for emeritus professors and a promoter of the National Committee on the Emeriti, which was formed in 1956. He also continued his sociological work, and in particular he put together a large collection of printed materials relating to the interment of Japanese Americans during World War II, now at the UCLA Library.

ESSENTIAL BIBLIOGRAPHY

Basile Green 1974; Boelhower 1982; Panunzio 1921a; Peragallo 1949, 173–176.

∞

Lo, Lord, the crowded cities be
Desolate and divided places.

Men who dwell in them heavy and humbly move
About dark rooms with dread in all their bearing
Less than the flocks of spring in fire and daring
And somewhere breathes and watches earth for faring
But they are here and do not know thereof.

And children grow up where the shadows falling
From wall and window have the light exiled,
And know not that the flowers of earth are calling
Unto a day of distance, wind and wild—
And every child must be a saddened child.

There blossom virgins to the unknown turning
And for their childhood's faded rest light fain,
And never find for what their soul is burning,

And trembling close their timid buds again.
And bear in chambers shadowed and unsleeping
The days of disappointed motherhood
And the long night's involuntary weeping
And the cold years devoid of glow or good.
In utter darkness stand their deathbeds lowly
For which through the creeping years the gray heart pants
They die as though in chains, and dying slowly,
Go forth from life in guise of mendicants.

RAINER MARIA RILKE (TRANS. BY LUDWIG LEWISOHN)

Chapter XV

Through a series of circumstances, then, as strange as those which twelve years before had in a day snatched me away from it, I now returned to the very community in which I had first set foot on landing in America. But in those twelve years a revolution had taken place in my outlook on life. I had seen some of the best aspects of American life; I had come in contact with some of her best people; I had felt something of the high aspirations of a soul which has come to really understand American ideals. Naturally I would now see things in this community from a viewpoint which would have been impossible had I remained buried within its bounds all these years.

As I looked about me I said to myself, "Well, this is a real immigrant community, of which I have heard so much in the American world!" From the moment I first set foot in it, I began to be conscious of the tremendous difficulties which on the one hand confront America in her desire and efforts to assimilate immigrant groups; and which, on the other, are in the way of the immigrants themselves in their need, and often their desire, to become an integral part of the body American.

For one thing, here was a congestion the like of which I had never seen before. Within the narrow limits of one-half square mile were crowded together thirty-five thousand people, living tier upon tier, huddled together until the very heavens seemed to be shut out. These narrow alley-like streets of Old Boston were one mass of litter. The air was laden with soot and dirt. Ill odors arose from every direction. Here were no trees; no parks worthy of the name; no playgrounds other than the dirty streets for the children to play on; no birds to sing their songs; no flowers to waft their perfume; and only small strips of sky to be seen; while around the entire neighborhood like a mighty cordon, a thousand wheels of commercial activity whirled incessantly day and night, making noises which would rack the sturdiest of nerves.

And who was responsible for this condition of things, for this crowding together? Were the immigrants alone to blame? Did they not occupy the very best tenements available, the moment they were erected and thrown open to them, even though at exorbitant rates?

Not only was all this true, but every sign of America seemed to have been systematically rooted out from this community as if with a ruthless purpose. Here still stood old Faneuil Hall, the Cradle of Liberty; here the old North Church still lifted its steeple as if reminding one of the part it had played in the Revolutionary War; here was Copp's Hill and many other spots of the greatest historical importance; not far away was State Street (old King Street), where the first blood of the Revolution was spilled; and here too, the spot where the Boston Tea Party, which had contributed so much to the making of America, had taken place. But while these monuments stood like sentinels reminding one of what this neighborhood had once been, now every last vestige of America was gone! All the American churches, homes, clubs and other institutions. which once had graced these streets were gone forever; gone to some more favorable spot in the uptown section of the city, leaving this community to work out its own destiny as best it could. There *were* churches here, to be sure, Catholic and Protestant and Jewish, but they were representative of other than America; they were under the leadership of men who, consciously or unconsciously, stood for other than American sentiments and ideals. In the homes and on the streets no English language was spoken save by the children; on the newsstands a paper in English could scarcely be found; here were scores if not hundreds of societies, national, provincial, local and sub-local, in which English was not usually spoken and in which other than American interests were largely represented. There were schools also in which the future citizens of America were taught in a language other than English. Here, when on a certain patriotic occasion, the American flag was raised a moment sooner than another flag, the person responsible for such a "crime" was nearly rushed out of the community. Above the stores and over those infernal institutions which are permitted to bear the name of "banks," the signs were mainly in a foreign language. In a word, here was a community in America in which there was not a sign of the best of American life. Had it not been for three well-organized and splendidly equipped social service houses and for the public schools, all of which consistently upheld American traditions and standards, this might well have been taken for a community in some far-off land.

Nor was this the whole story. Not only were all the constructive forces of American society absent from this community, but also some of its very worst features seemed to have been systematically poured into the neighborhood to prey upon the life of the people in their all too apparent helplessness. Here within this half-mile square were no less than 111 saloons, not because the people wanted or patronized them to any great extent, but because saloons were needed for revenue, so it was claimed. If one section of Boston would not have them, was it not necessary that they should be established in another? When Dorchester decided to turn out the saloons from its precincts, as a matter of course, additional licenses were granted to the "saloonists" in North End. Who would care? Here in this neighborhood were also 53 of the worst imaginable institutions; poolrooms and bowling alleys, dance halls and gambling dens, brothels and the like; again, not patronized in the main by those living in the vicinity, but chiefly by out-of- and up-towners. Within or in the immediate outskirts of the community were also located eleven moving picture theaters in which, according to an actual investigation, 95 out of every 100 films exhibited depicted the lowest of practices, the vilest of scenes, the worst of crimes; and to these houses were admitted children and adults alike, the law notwithstanding. In this community were committed some of the most atrocious of crimes; once more, according to police records, not committed mainly by the inhabitants of the neighborhood, but by those who from every unheard-of place came to this vicinity for their misdeeds.

And while this was in no way a typical American community, neither did it resemble Italy. No one with the least amount of Italian pride in him would want to boast that this was in any sense an Italian community. In fact, more than one investigator from Italy had pronounced it the very contradiction of all that Italian society stood for; the pictures which they painted would have made blush the worst descriptions given by American sociologists. For in this city within a city it was the misfits of Italian society who were "i prominenti" and held dominance; it was those who could "bluff it through," who were the "bankers" and the publicists; it was the unscrupulous politician who controlled things; it was the quack who made his money; the shyster lawyer who held the people within the palm of his hand. True, there were some persons who could really be classed as Italian gentlemen, but they were few and could easily be counted on the fingers of both hands. Again, here were thrown together by the hand of fate the humblest elements of Italian society, who though leading a peaceful existence, still were representing and perpetuating in a miniature way the interests of a hundred petty little principalities and powers in the limits of a single community. Here a thousand trifling, provincial and local animosities and controversies were brought together and fostered in a way that out-Babeled Babel. This conglomeration of folks would have been as much an anomaly in Italy as it was in America. The best of all that Italy stood for was not here. You might hunt in vain for the least sign of that sense of the beautiful, that refinement, that leisureliness, that culture, that courtesy of manner so typical of Italy and the Italian. A sad and sordid picture this; it may displease some, I fear, but it is as true as a correct mental camera could photograph it.

But why paint it at all? Because as a native of Italy and a lover of all that is beautiful in her, I should like to have every Italian and every lover of Italy see it in its true sordid colors; look at it until his fixed gaze would reveal to him that this is not representative of the real Italy; look upon it until he shall come to hate it and every other community like it as I hate it. Because as an adopted American I should like to see every American lover of America look at this picture and every similar picture in all its ugliness, consider the causes that gave it birth and keep it alive; until beneath the intensive and penetrating gaze a determination shall be born in every heart to destroy such communities throughout the country by cutting the roots that give them life.

And yet, strange as it may seem, I came to love the people of the community as deeply as I came to abhor its communal life; I came to love them for the simplicity of their characters and lives, for their hidden capacities, for their jocundity, for their sincerity of purpose, for the beauty of their home life, for the indomitable courage with which they faced the most untoward circumstances in which they were placed.

It was the children who first beckoned to my affections. I came to love them as I saw them, through no fault of their own, separated in thought and life from their parents, and equally separated from all that was America. I loved them as I looked upon them at play in the littered streets. I loved them as I saw them in a thousand unconscious ways express their yearning for the beautiful, the true, the lovely, and all that child life so yearns for.

I recall how my heart went out to them one day, as I entered the community with a cluster of roses in my hand, which I was intending to take to my institution. As I passed down the street the children gathered around me as they once gathered about the Pied Piper of Hamelin Town:

There was a rustling that seemed like bustling
Of merry crowds jostling and pitching and hustling;
Small feet were pattering, wooden shoes clattering,
Little hands clapping and little tongues chattering;
And like fowls in a farmyard when barley is scattering

Out came the children running.
All the little boys and girls
With rosy cheeks and flaxen curls,
And sparkling eyes and teeth like pearls,
Tripping and skipping, ran merrily after,

as they shouted one after another, "Please, Mister, give me a flower." How else could it be, with their love for the beautiful as expressed in flowers, and so seldom permitted to see it! I had no roses left when I reached my destination.

And I loved them for the songs I so often heard them sing. One evening, standing upon a roof, my attention was drawn to little voices singing, their clear notes rising above the tumult below. I listened. From one direction came the strains of the most popular song of the time, "It's a Long, Long Way to Tipperary, but my heart's right there." Over to my right I could hear the music and could almost distinguish the words of "Santa Lucia." While from a third direction I heard a baby voice singing in strains supremely sweet,

O Little Town of Bethlehem,
How still I see thee lie;
Above thy deep and dreamless sleep
The silent stars go by;
Yet in thy dark street shineth
The everlasting light;
The hopes and fears of all the years
Are met in thee to-night.

It almost seemed as if the sweet little voices and the baby hearts were conscious of yearnings unrealized.

I came to love the children, the boys and girls, as I saw them bend beneath heavy loads in their efforts to help their parents in the struggle to make a living. Often I saw them in after-school hours as they went out to gather wood for the hearthstone fire. One afternoon I saw what seemed to be a pile of boards walking on two little human legs and feet. I touched the boards and gently stopped them. Looking under them I saw a baby face, a boy not over seven years of age. And one evening as the sun's last rays were kissing the water of the Charles River, I saw a boy pulling a load too heavy for his small shoulders, up the steep incline toward the State House on Mount Vernon Street. Brave little hearts these, that shared the burdens with those who could not bear them alone, in their efforts to eke out an existence.

I came to love the mothers of this community, more lonely than all the rest, yet putting up brave faces against the most tremendous odds. I remember one especially, a widow. I had heard of her need and called upon her one day. I knocked at the door. Back came the sound of baby voices, the pattering of baby feet. The door did not open. I knocked again, then tried the door; it was locked. The baby voices and the baby feet were locked in while the widowed mother was out in search of bread for her brood. I returned at night. In the desolate room in which she lived a small kerosene lamp was burning. It was dark and damp and dreary. She told me her story. Left alone with three children, she had struggled long to keep them alive, earning nine dollars a week washing dishes in a restaurant, paying five of it for her one room, and locking her children in it while she went out each day to her toil. One of her children had succumbed, the baby. It had died only a short time before and had been buried in a nameless grave. As she told her story back to my mind came the picture of her struggling soul as painted by Daly. Had he known this woman's sorrow? It seemed as if he was uttering her very words,

"Da spreeng ees com; but O da joy
Eet ees too late!
He was so cold, my leetla boy,
He no could wait.
I no can count how many week,
How many day, dat he ees seeck;
How many night I seet an' hold
Da leetla hand dat was so cold.
He was so patience, O so sweet!
Eet hurts my throat for theenk of eet;
An' all he evra ask ees w'en
Ees gona com' da spreeng agen.
Wan day, wan brighta sunny day
He see, across da alleyway,
Da leetla girl dat's livin' dere
Ees raise her window for da air
An' put outside a leetla pot
Of–w'at you calla–forgat-me-not.
So smalla flower, so leetla theeng!
But steel eet make hees heart a-seeng:
'O now, at las', ees com' da spreeng!
Da leetla plant ees glad for know

Da sun ees com' for mak' eet grow;
So too, I am grow warm an' strong.'
So, lika dat he seeng hees song.
But, ah! da night com' down an' den
Da weenter ees sneak back agen,
An' een da alley all da night
Ees fall da snow, so cold, so white,
An' cover up da leetla pot
Of–w'at you calla–forget-me-not.
All night da leetla hand I hold
Ees grow so cold, so cold, so cold.
"Da spreeng ees com'; but O da joy
Eet ees too late!
He was so cold, my leetla boy,
He no could wait.

And I remember a mother who late one night knocked at my door, as if in a frenzy, and sent me out in search of her boy, the boy of her love, the boy who had gotten beyond the power of her control. Sad indeed was the picture I saw long past the midnight hour when I came back to her home without her boy.

I came to love the fathers too, many of whom were putting up a brave battle to make a living for their families. One I remember well. He had been in this country for fifteen years. He had done all in his power through the years to eke out an existence. He had five children, all born in America. One day he was telling me of his struggle when he broke out, "If only I had no children I would go back to Italy. I was poor there, but even poverty is better in one's native country. But I cannot take my children back to my native land. They were born here, they are Americans, they have been brought up in this country. Work as I may, I find it ever more difficult as I grow older to make a living for them." He was a man of fine sensibilities; his heart was breaking beneath the load.

For all their beauty, their simplicity, their patience and endurance, for all their native intelligence and sensibilities, for all their sense of propriety and their law-abiding tendencies, for the wholesomeness of their lives, for the immaculate characters of the mothers, for the unconscious aspirations and loveliness, of the children, I came to love these people.

It was into this community and into this condition of things that my American superiors sent me. As they gave me instructions, what they did not utter seemed to say, "Go quickly, encompass the earth, go in a day and 'Americanize' and

'Christianize' them." They sent me into a building which was anything but representative of the American conception of orderliness, cleanliness and beauty; and anything but suitable for a work of uplift and inspiration. The building was very old and had been used for every imaginable purpose, from a monastery to a storage house, and was sadly in need of repairs. It was a monstrosity, dark, dirty, damp, ill-lighted and poorly ventilated. Forgetting that even the humblest Italian has a love of the beautiful deeply ingrained in his consciousness, my superiors thought this building altogether adequate for the work of transforming all these people in a day from "heathens" to "Christians" and from "foreigners" to full-fledged "Americans." When we came to actualities, we found it difficult to make our constituency believe that this was a church, or even an institution. Moreover, the building had been acquired in an indirect way from certain Catholic interests, and this created a feeling of antagonism from the very outset toward it and toward the institution housed in it. Under the urge of the impulse to speedily "Americanize" and "Christianize," the work had formerly been conducted in such a manner as to arouse the antagonism not only of the people of the community, but also of those persons who should have been its strongest allies, the leaders of the social service institutions to which I have already referred. Antagonisms had been aroused and conflicts created which were conducive to anything but the best social welfare of the neighborhood.

Again, my American superiors kept ever before me the *quantitative* idea of things. To them it was not a question of how solid a foundation we were laying, or how far we were benefiting the community and its people in those unseen ways, through inspiration and amelioration; their one idea was "How many?" Nothing seemed to please like a crowd. How it was made up, what the objective might be, the outcome in terms of social life, were secondary considerations, if considerations at all. I often heard it said, "We must make a good showing." *Showing*, not *doing*. This tremendous pressure was felt not only by our institution, but by others as well. It gave rise to a competitive, duplicating and wasteful system of things. For one thing, the triangle of those little, almost insignificant institutions known as "Protestant Missions," of which ours was one, was on the one hand ever competing for the negligible Protestant following of the community, and, on the other, so inter-related as to form a vicious circle. The services at these missions were held at different hours. One Sunday I attended them all and found the same constituency, meager as it was, swelling the ranks of all three.

Later, by mere accident, I learned that seventy-five per cent of the membership of one was enrolled on the books of the second, and thirty-five per cent on the books of the third. One might say that no harm was done by this triple alliance; yet loyalty was not being fostered thereby, and what perhaps is more significant, the American superiors of each of the three missions were content with their apparent "much serving," when in reality it was the same one-course dinner served up three times. Even more interesting than this was the discovery that on the occasion of the opening of the third mission, which had recently taken place, the pastors of the other two had come to the rescue of the new and enterprising pastor by a "professional" understanding with him, whereby he could count on their membership until such time as he had built up one of his own, and in that way make a good "showing." In the meantime, the people went on pretty much their own way, practicing their Old World customs and habits as if nothing American were within a thousand miles of them.

The fact was that this community, by the will of the American people and that of the immigrants, or more correctly speaking, in the absence of the constructive will of any one group of people, was leading a life almost completely separated from the life of America. What this separation of foreign-born people of any nationality signifies is fully illustrated by the remarks made several years later by a leading American. Though they describe an entirely different community and deal with a different racial group, yet the fundamental principles are so much the same that I quote it here.

It was in the autumn of 1919, at the beginning of the far-famed Steel Strike. I had been assigned by a certain institution to go down to the Pittsburgh region and endeavor to discover at first hand some of the facts underlying the whole situation. I went from village to village where trouble was brewing in its most acute form, and at last I reached Monessen, Pennsylvania. On approaching the little city, upon the hill across the river and overlooking the town below, I saw two men with guns strapped to their shoulders and with binoculars before their eyes, carefully scrutinizing the scene in the distance. As I passed over the bridge leading into the town two armed guards, one standing at each side of the bridge, looked me over as I passed. In the city itself men were walking two by two silently watching every passerby. Here and there were special deputies, some of them negroes, their badges prominently displayed. I was informed that the night before, under the cloak of darkness, two thousand American men, under the lead of a major, a veteran of the World War, had gathered on the plateau overlooking the city to receive instructions and to drill, as if to prepare for a new war. I was told that in this community lived some 16,000 foreign-born people, mainly of Slavic origin, and that all this preparation was being made on their account. The whole aspect of the community reminded me very much of villages close up to the firing lines, which I had seen in Italy not long before.

I had a letter of introduction to one of the leading men of the town. This man was one of the oldest residents of the city and had seen it grow from nothing to what it was then. He was a business man of good standing, the president of a bank, the editor of one of the papers, and a loyal American citizen, whose sympathies were first and last with America and with law and order. The strain of the situation had been so intense that he had been ill in bed from it. Learning of my errand, however, he courteously came down and gave me an interview. In answer to my questions as to the causes underlying the whole situation, this was what he said:

The present situation, sir, can only be met by armed force. I regret to say this, but it is absolutely true. I am ashamed to think that such a thing should ever have been necessary in our town. Ten or even five years ago we could have done anything we wished peacefully; a simple method of education would have prevented all this. But we are primarily to blame; we have forced a feeling of separation upon these people. We needed them for the growth of our industries, we wanted them to come and we did see them come to us by the hundreds. But we refused to admit them to our civic and social life; we gave them no access to our societies, our schools and our churches. We called them "undesirable aliens," we forced them to segregate into sections of their own and to organize into separate groups in which only their own language is used. First they organized for the purpose of giving expression to their social cravings, and then those very groups served as centers of self-defense when we showed antagonism to their segregated life.

When first they came to us they were as innocent as children; the better elements of our community neglected them. Radical leaders, taking advantage of this, had their day and did anything they pleased with these people. We only looked on, laughed at their doings, and called them 'Hunkies.' Now they have us by our throats. Only last Sunday, 'Mother Jones' addressed a great crowd of them on the outskirts of the town. They have been raised to a high pitch of excitement. They have been taught that by means of this strike they can take possession of our mills and our town. Our lives and our property are unquestionably in great danger, but the fault is ours. If we suffer, we do so for what we ourselves have left undone in the years gone by.

The Day of Summer

∾ *Emanuel Carnevali*

Florence, Italy, December 4, 1897–Bologna, Italy, January 11, 1942

"I began to write in English when I was nineteen years old. I will remain in America to write. This is my country. The judgments that the Italians generously make about America are as equally imbecilic as those that Americans make about Italy. There is no actual connection between Europe and America."[1] Writing to Giovanni Papini in 1919, Emanuel Carnevali boldly, and with astonishing insolence, resolved the unresolvable cultural difficulties of emigration. Europe (even more so than Italy) and America are two distinct planets, and it is useless to lose time trifling with old-fashioned sophisms. Carnevali becomes the American; he has encountered a truly different world, more wild and vital than the one he left in Italy, which for him, aside from his having come from a wealthy family, had consisted of oppressive institutions and spiritual poverty. In this new world, he talks of the small portion of Italy that he still admires and is entirely there, across the ocean: the Italy of the Croces (men of the stamp of Benedetto Croce) and of the outspoken dissenters. He also felt little affinity for what he encountered in America. In the slow process of adaptation, he worked for a month in the summer of 1919, as an editor of the *Cittadino di Chicago*, directed by the Presbyterian pastor Pasquale Ricciardi De Carlo. Even when he learned to elevate himself above the average tone of the colony and express himself in poetry similar to that of Arturo Giovannitti (with whom he was associated in 1934, by Alfred Kreymborg, in *A*

---

1. The last sentence was written in English.

History of American Poetry), he still felt that what he gained was far from the thousand miles of projects he had in his head.

Carnevali is truly a separate case in the history of Italian American literature, whether as an artist or a man. Emigrating in 1914, "without any goal," he adapted to the typical and humble work of the emigrant, shoveler or waiter and dishwasher in Italian restaurants. For a short time, he was the secretary to Joel Spingarn, future proprietor of *The New York Times* and a historian of Italian literature. Carnevali was also Spingarn's Italian teacher. For Spingarn, he translated, among others, Croce's *Aesthetica in nuce*. However, he was dismissed for apparently stealing books and then selling them to survive. In 1916, he married Emily Valenza, a young women of Piedmontese origins. Managing to live on her salary and working only occasionally, he was able to dedicate himself to literature, frequenting the bohemia of Greenwich Village, where, to the despair of his wife, he led a dissipated and rebellious life in a sort of artists' commune. Despite all, she remained close to him and helped him in the most difficult moments, for example, when it appeared that Carnevali was liable to the possibility of being repatriated for reasons of his precarious state of health. In 1917, Carnevali presented his first poems to the review *The Seven Arts*, edited by James Oppenheim, which ceased publication shortly afterward. Carnevali made his debut in January 1918, in *The Forum*, with the poem "Colored Lies." From then on, he became a leading figure in American poetry, first in New York, where he remained until June 1919, then in Chicago, where, abandoning his wife, he became a friend of Sherwood Anderson and Carl Sandburg and experienced his period of major inspiration. He also contracted grave maladies that would cause his premature death: syphilis, Spanish influenza, encephalitis, and Parkinson's disease.

His writings appeared in the review *Others* (New York), directed in turn by such writers as William Carlos William and Alfred Kreymborg, and in various other publications: *Poetry: A Magazine of Verse* (Chicago), edited by Harriet Monroe, beginning from March 1918; *The Little Review* (New York, then Chicago, and subsequently Paris), edited by Margaret Anderson and Jean Heap, in 1919–20; *Youth* (Chicago), edited by Samuel Putnam and H. C. Auer, in 1921; and *The Modern Review* (Winchester, Massachusetts). Even after his definitive return to Italy in 1922, Carnevali published his texts in American reviews edited in Europe: *This Quarter*, edited by Ernest Walsh and Ethel Moorhead, and *The New Review*. He continued to receive critical recognition and prize money from America for his work, but had little contact other than visits from, among others, Robert McAlmon, who called on him in 1924.

In 1920 Carnevali became associate editor of *Poetry*, to which he committed his most provocative texts. Critiquing these poems, Ezra Pound summoned up the word "fury." That year, though, Carnevali wrote a slashing criticism of Pound and was consequently banned from the *Little Review*, for which Pound was a correspondent. Carnevali's provocative texts elicited other strong comments: Carl Sandburg spoke of explosions of "pure enthusiasms"; William Carlos Williams (who in March 1919 had borne Carnevali's attack on the group of "Others"), spoke of a "black poet," cursed, satanic, and self-destructive. However, according to Williams, beginning with his attack on the "Others," Carnevali would henceforth be responsible for his subsequent career as a poet.

Other criticisms cited a radical opposition to the artificiality of American poetry through a "shout" with which Carnevali proposed to "disturb America," one that "defecated on the bourgeoisie" (Edward Dahlberg). It was not only an inheritance of Rimbaud, a typical attitude of adolescent revolt, or a generic aspiration to "draw the magic of beauty from things that are more sad and vulgar" (Linati), but also the result of maturing reflections on literature, above all Italian, as is demonstrated by Carnevali's letters to Croce and Papini, published by Gabriel Cacho Millet. (Carnevali had discovered *Voce*, in New York, in 1918.)

In the pages of *Poetry,* between 1919 and 1920 (the period of Carnevali's letters to Papini, a Florentine writer), Carnevali manifests a singular harmony with Papini. He translated passage from Papini's *Un uomo finito* and *Cento pagine di poesia*, but above all, he and Papini had a mutual taste for slashing criticism. And it was in this period that, as expressed in his letters to Papini, he determined the form and content of a projected new poetry review, *New Moon*, modeled on *La Voce*. Actually, he never saw the review realized, for it would founder along with him, after an unhappy love affair with the beautiful Annie Glick and his collapse, caused by his illness. For a time, Carnevali was transformed into a kind of ballad singer wandering into theaters, reciting his poems and singing popular Italian and Neapolitan songs, presenting himself as a subversive, but then was reduced to begging in the streets for his living.

Finally, in September 1922, Carnevali returned to Italy and found hospitality in the psychiatric clinic of Baruzziana, near Bologna, where he remained until May 1926. Still in a shelter, he passed long years of intermittent lucidity without ever quite being wholly restored to himself. In 1925, his *Tales of a Hurried Man* was published in Paris, a collection of material already published in American reviews, put together through the initiative of Robert McAlmon and prefaced by Dorothy Dudley Harvey. In 1932, in the Hague, Peter Neagoe published the initial pages of

The First God, a work to which Carnevali had dedicated himself from 1923, intended to be a sort of autobiographical novel. In 1967, it was published in New York in a complete version with the title *Autobiography of Emanuel Carnevali*, edited by the poet Kay Boyle, in which, however, she intervened obtrusively. A philologically correct edition was finally published in 1978, in Milan, as *Il Primo dio*, edited by Maria Pia Carnevali and with an essay by Luigi Ballerini.

Carnevali belongs fully to the history of American poetry, even if he wrote in Italian and if, as of 1926, Ernest Walsh had foreseen that fifty years after his death, America and Italy would contest his glory. In fact, in his debut in *Poetry*, in 1918, Carnevali asserted that he wanted to become "an American poet," because he refuted the "Italian standards of good literature" and did not esteem Carducci, much less D'Annunzio. The Americans were of greater interest to him, and Whitman was one of his idols. Moreover, after his decisive reading of *Voce*, Carnevali applied himself to translating, for *Poetry*, some of the best Italian poetry, including Palazzeschi, Govoni, Saba, Jahier, and Salvatore Di Giacomo. He was propelled by a strange tension, not completely resolved, which, for example, in 1920, provoked him to become indignant with Thomas Augustine Daly and his very popular "McAroni Ballads" as being culpable of ignoring all pertaining to the Italians, and of prophesizing the future coming arrival of someone who would finally know how to talk about the Italian emigrants and do them justice. For McAlmon, one of his many friends who left a vivid, moving portrait of him, "he was a one-hundred-percent Italian," in that he did not deal in the rhetoric of "morals," of the "soul," and of "conscience." This immunity, as is understood, was one of the reasons for Carnevali's strong impact on the circle of the poets of New York and Chicago.

ESSENTIAL BIBLIOGRAPHY

Carnevali 1978 and 1981; Fink 1973; Linati 1934; McAlmon 1996, 114–117; Peragallo 1949, 36–40; Prezzolini 1963; C. Ricciardi 1981.

ॐ

To Waldo Frank

Morning
How long ago was it
The dawn pleased Homer?
And Petrarca—was it among flowers
Dew-full, tearful for the love of the dawn,

That he sang his best song
For Laura?
Did the eyes of joy of Prince Paul Fort
See it well once,
And was it then that he
"Took pleasure in being a Frenchman"?
In New York,
These summer days,
It's a swollen-faced hour,
Sick with a monstrous cold,
Gasping with the death of an expectance.
Houses there
In a thick row
Militarily shut out the sky
Another fence
In the east;
Over this one a shameful blush
Strives upward.

> Nevertheless I go to perform the ceremony
> Of purification—to wash myself. . . .
> Oh, dear water . . . Dear, dear soap. . . .

Because I am poor
No ceremony will clean me;
In this crowded room
All the things touch me,
Soil me.
To start a day
Feeling dirty
Is to go to war
Unbelievingly.

> A little happy pause here
> For me to think of what I shall be doing in the day.

Now has the deep hot belly of the night
Given birth to noises.
The noises pass
Over me,

I lie
Insensible,
Under.
Work, milk, bread, clothes, potatoes, potatoes. . . .

> This is
> The big
> Beauty rumbling on.
> Is this
> The world's
> Music forevermore?

This and the irrevocable peddlers
Who will come in an hour
To hurl loose:
"Pota-a-a-t-o-u-s, yeh-p-l-s, waa-ry meh-l-n?"
Little apocalyptic faces,
Faces of the end of all faces—
Are they the chief musicians?
Please, listen, I have a small, dear soul; and all I want is a noiseless
    beauty, any little thing, I was born for a sylvan century, may I claim
    to be left alone? . . . I will not even expect you to understand–only. . . .
Under this, like a cold hating prostitute,
I lie
Insensible. . . .
And my face is sad because
Once
There was. . . .
Ah, there was a time. . . .
Now go look for the mail—
Go glean the thoughts they drop before your door,
You eternal gleaner,
Love thoughts, too. . . . ?

> Out in the hall
> The gas jet
> Doesn't give a damn that it is day already.
> Stench
> Of drenched clothes

And snore
Of married men.
Who shall ask the furnished-room poets to write
A song for the dawn?

Oh, MAIL!

Ah, beggars:
"I-am-though-I-refrain-from-saying-it-better-than-you-in-the-end. I-am-
    perfectly-honest-evidently-nothing-up-my-sleeves . . . It-is-out-of-my-
    bounteous-goodness-that-I-like-you-a-little-in-spite-of. . . ."
These scanty rights to live—
A clear day, an articulate moment, may take them from us;
So we advance
At every chance
Our stuttering claim and reference.

Dragging my soul along
I go to the window.
The sun-fingers reach slowly
Over the face of the house in front.
This is the hour they go to their work
Eastward and westward—
Two processions,
Silent.
Shapeless the hats,
Too large the jackets and shoes—
Grotesques walking,
Grotesques for no one to laugh at.
Are they happy perhaps?—
For, of course . . . but do they
Really know where they're going?
Has the first of them
Found
Down there
Something for his happiness?
And has he telephoned or telegraphed to the others
That they are going,
Without looking around,

Without knowing one another,
ALL
TOGETHER
Eastward and westward?
The world has decreed:
These men go
Acknowledged
Eastward and westward.

    Sit down and take the rest of your life,
    o poets!

All my days
Are in this room
Pressing close against me.
I know what I have done, misdone, mistoken, misunderstood, forgotten,
    overlooked,
And I have lost my youth.
Everybody knows me,
No one wonders at wonders at me;
They have placed me in their minds, made me small and tied me up
To throw me in a little dusty corner of their minds.
All my days are huddled
Close against me;
My youth is but a regret and a madness—
A madness . . . Jesus Christ! I am not old yet, never mind what I have
    told you, what I have been!
I have not irremediably committed myself, I am not lost–
For pity's sake
Let me go,
Let me go free!
For pity's sake
Let me go
With my youth!

    Ah, the old days are huddled
    So close against my chest
    That no great freeing gesture
    Is possible.

After the tears,
Cool, new, sensitive,
Under my body hushed and stiff,
I open the door
Quietly,
I close the door behind me
Carefully.
The street's greeting:
I'm out of work—

Damn work—to work and come home in the evening hungry for all the
    things that could have been done instead!

    But to go
    Unemployed
    Without hunger
    At all!

Oh, listen, O Street,
Let your word to me be a delicate whisper:
I am young,
Nice day,
I look
Straight ahead,
Staccato steps,
Stiff and cool,
I walk.
(Sweet morning soeur de charité!)

It is the light mood in the streets of the morning,
Bouncing on the roofs, kicked
By the rosy foot of the wind.
Ah, we—ah, we are chained to the sidewalk but we hold our eyes
    upward,
Lightly, lightly.
Do blow away the dust of our dead,
And save us all from them who are smoldering inside our houses!
See the fine dust from those windows, see the dust angry at the sun!
Who threw these kids here among us, them and their fun and war.
   "GIMME—GIMME!"

King of the triumphing mood, the iceman cracks easy puns with a landlady of the dust!
Kaiser of the lightness of the morning, the policeman, swinging his stick,
  writes sacred hieroglyphs.

Furtively I steal,
From what and whom
I know,
A little youth
For myself.
I know nothing,
I forget nothing,
I'm glad enough to live
In the morning.

Son of Italy

∾ *Pascal D'Angelo*

Introdacqua (L'Aquila), Italy, January 20, 1894–New York, New York,
March 17, 1932

In 1924, an important American publisher, Macmillan, sent *Son of Italy*, the autobiography of a poor Italian worker, a simple "man of shovel and pickaxe," to bookstores. The author, Pascal D'Angelo, had arrived in America with his father in 1910
and had had the courage and the perseverance to study the English language by
himself until he became a poet and writer. After a long series of unsuccessful attempts, he emerged successfully. In January 1922, Carl Van Doren, editor of the
daily newspaper *The Nation*, had finally discovered him. He had listened to
D'Angelo's story, and he had esteemed his verses. He published some verses and
recommended others to colleagues of other newspapers, stirring, in short, a notable interest in that strange figure of a poet-peasant, completely self-taught. "In the
space of a few weeks," Van Doren subsequently wrote in the preface to *Son of Italy*,
"the name of Pascal D'Angelo became known wherever there was a lover of poetry." All of that, however, did not induce D'Angelo to accept uncritically some of
the many editorial offers raining down upon him. "After having paid such a high
price to become a poet," wrote Van Doren, "he did not want his recompense to be
paid him with such low coin."

The price D'Angelo had paid was effectively very high: years of indescribable
privations, of moral and physical humiliations. These conditions, most probably,
contributed to his premature death, occurring in the ward of a Brooklyn hospital,
after an appendectomy. In any case, commented Van Doren, "the fact that he
gradually succeeded in overcoming all the obstacles makes his career one of the

most moving episodes in American literature." Van Doren proceeds to recognize in the poet of Abruzzi, "another son of that Ovid whose fame is still the glory of Sulmona"; to the point that "from now on, no American who observes a gang of dark Italian workers working in an excavation could do less than ask if among them there is not some Pascal D'Angelo." Contradicting the paradigm of the national myth of success and integration, the case of D'Angelo soon became a banner for the colony. All the newspapers were writing about him; one of the reviews was even by Luigi Barzini in the *Corriere d'America*, significantly entitled "Il libro della nostra vita." At the same time, Romolo Angelone, who in April 1922 had already introduced the poet in the Italian monthly of New York, *Il Carroccio*, wrote an article entitled "Dalla Vanga alla Poesia" (From the Spade to Poetry):

> Three months ago, he was one of the thousands of Italian workers who are met in throngs in the cars of the subway, at night, one hour after offices are closed, and who in dialects of their natal villages, review the happenings of the day and comment on them, construed from an Italian journal that one of them reads many times with great difficulty. His was one of the most modest among the Italian male faces, on which the heavy and fatiguing work had left visible signs of the destruction of youthfulness. Now he is the poet of the slums [the last five words written in English]—the poet emerged from the hovel."

Angelone described the poet as follows: "Conversing with this young man with a rather rough appearance, one quickly has the impression of encountering an iron will, which has fought against all adversities, now firmly decided to win and completely affirm himself. He talks by fits and starts, and while he is talking, his restless and very black eyes attentively scrutinize and register vivid and rapid splashes of light that raise your curiosity to inquire into the explanations of the phenomenon." The journalist then proceeded to recapitulate the already mythic story of D'Angelo's childhood. He was a shepherd of the Maiella (a massif of the Apennines) who in winter, after the first snow fell, could attend school, but could not finish the year, because at the first signs of spring, he had to return to pasture the flock. All his education stopped in the second year of elementary school.

D'Angelo was sixteen years old when his father brought the family to America. They went to Hillsdale, New Jersey, where other compatriots had settled. In 1913, his father returned to Italy, and his brother went to find his fortune in the West. As the lowliest of laborers, Pasquale started to move among all the states of New England, sleeping in cattle cars, often prey to dishonest contractors "who ran off the day before payday." In its recapitulation of the story, *Il Carroccio* placed a certain emphasis on the mode in which D'Angelo began to approach literature: filled with patriotic fervor, he would read to his work companions the news of the Italo-Turkish war, which the *Evening Journal* published in a small section in Italian. Here was, then, the slow conquest of the English language; slow and stubborn, impervious to the mockery of his companions and to the presumptuousness of occasional American interlocutors.

The success that came at the end of such a tormented journey was read as a prize earned by the genius and honest application of the Italian race other than by the individual. And, in fact, "we Italians should be proud of this modest, clever son of Abruzzo; but, however, we have the sacrosanct duty of reducing his distressful destitution and helping him in his efforts to complete that success that will add another page to the history of Italian intellectual development in America." The recognition of D'Angelo came above all from the esteem of Americans. Olga Peragallo cites the particularly interesting appreciation in the *New York Times Book Review* (January 4, 1925): "He is one of the few Americanized immigrants whose success has been decisive even without being secular. Edward Bok, Jacob Riis, to mention only two of our most successful national conversions, represent conquests of a practical nature, solid, that constitute worldly success. Pascal D'Angelo is a man of that rare type in America, whose success is so spiritual as to be achieved almost without material frippery."

It is a fact that D'Angelo died very poor; that his friends and admirers paid for of his burial; and that after his death, which occurred in a hospital in Brooklyn after an appendectomy, Mrs. Clarence Browning Smith instituted a "D'Angelo Society," with a special "D'Angelo Medal," to be awarded annually to the best young poets of America. These circumstances, correlated with the enlightening article in the *Times,* and the intuitions of Van Doren in relation to the uniqueness of D'Angelo's book in the already vast panorama of biographies of successful immigrants, contribute to delineate the particulars pertaining to a singular American legend.

In *Son of Italy*, William Boelhower has traced, as he interpreted it, an original ideological strategy. D'Angelo would affirm his American credo not by imposing a new mental perspective upon his very identity, but by actually detaching from it. He would jealously affirm it when, in the first four chapters, he talks about the deterioration of his conditions of life once he arrived in the new world. Then, as a portent of what American society would effectively be after the definitive end of the melting pot, he would confirm it, placing emphasis on belonging to a group, not only Italian, but more precisely "paesano" (native, made up of compatriots): "We formed our small world, one of many in this country," with a lucid individualization of that ethnic mosaic that was already America. The vindication of an autonomous ethnic status is clear, unequivocal: "We people of the mountains of Abruzzo are a race apart. The inhabitants of the sweet plains of Lazio and Puglia, where in winter we go to pasture our flocks, regard us as a people of prophets and poets. We believe in dreams. There are strange creatures who wander through our villages, whose existence we know is pure fantasy. Where we live, there are men capable of foretelling the future, and hags who instinctively know the secrets of the mountain and can cure every illness, without effort, simply by pronouncing some word."

With such a fundamental presupposition, the experience of modernity that D'Angelo underwent in America irreducibly results in the customary figure of the self-made man, from which stereotype, however, we distinguish him not only because of his disinterest in material success, but also, and perhaps above all, because of his poetic distance. He consciously remains the proud "peasant" observing that American world. D'Angelo asserts that the city where he disembarked, the city that assailed him with a thousand visions of abundance, is the "incarnation of the brutal vanity of the human species." For him, to write became the attempt to create a new world as a refuge from the horror of the real world. To write was to pursue the dream of a "reidentification." It was not to enter the ivory tower of literature. D'Angelo says, almost shouts, very clearly, he will remain "a pick and shovel man." To be recognized as a poet was of value for him, as Boelhower writes, in order to pass from a condition of invisibility to one of visibility in the context of American culture. A poet in, not of, the metropolis, "D'Angelo, as a laborer-victim and poet-hero, incarnates, therefore, the dilemma of the immigrant descending into the urban condition and simultaneously transcending it. The ethnic ghetto is a current and homogeneous fragment of a cultural space that belongs to the Old World, but its homogeneity is not enough to organize the metropolitan chaos that surrounds it."

ESSENTIAL BIBLIOGRAPHY

Angelone 1922; Basile Green 1974, 37; Boelhower 1982, 97–135; D'Angelo 1924; Mangione-Morreale 1992; Peragallo 1949, 66–69; Prezzolini 1943.

∾

XII

That night I lingered a long time outside the shanty, thinking. And darkness made the vast solitudes of heaven populous with stars.

At first my mind was turbulent.

And I thought to myself, "Why, I am nothing more than a dog. A dog. But a dog is silent and slinks away when whipped, while I am filled with the urge to cry out, to cry out disconnected words, expressions of pain, anything, to cry out!"

I looked around. I felt a kinship with the beautiful earth. She was like some lovely hardhearted lady in velvets and gaudy silks—one whom we could gaze at in admiration, but never dare approach. I felt a power that was forcing me to cry out to this world that was so fair, so soft and oblivious of our pains and petty sorrows. Then I had to laugh to myself. "After all," I thought, "what are my tiny woes to the eternal beauty of those stars, of these trees and even this short-lived grass?"

For a long time I paced the soft green in front of our shanty. Then I entered. The men inside were grumbling mournfully to one another, barely visible in the gloom. I had resigned myself to my fate. I was a poor laborer—a dago, a wop or some such creature, in the eyes of America. Well, what could I do?

Nothing.

Thereafter, for a long while until my numbed soul was again awakened, my prime interests were food and jobs. First of all I had to escape back to headquarters in New York. My credit was very bad.

I left the shanty with a couple of others; and we began to trudge aimlessly down the long road. At several farmhouses we paused to ask for work. None of the farmers seemed to care to give us any.

"What are you going to do?" asked a young bright-faced lad.

"Walk," grumbled my other companion, a Sicilian.

And walk we did. That night we slept in a most beautiful countryside. But the mosquitoes and the gathering damp prevented our admiring the splendor of the broad starlit night.

Rising a little stiff-jointed the next morning we walked on. We were hungry; for a drink of water at a clear spring had not done much to soothe us. We had a little money between us, and on reaching a placid hamlet nestled amid soft green hills we made a quick run on the general store.

And who should be conducting the store but a *paisano* of mine! We shook hands long and vigorously and in a few minutes I was giving him a detailed account of everything that had passed in our village from the time he had come to America to the day, years later, when I left.

This good fellow-townsman of mine made the three of us sleep in his house that night. In real beds, too. And the next day he even loaned us the fare for New York, which I dutifully returned in time, as I hope my two companions did.

Back again to the railroad yard in Shady Side I went, humbly begging for a job. Fortunately for me, they needed men. And so it was that after my disastrous trip, I was again an inhabitant at our old box car.

Little by little a few other fellow-townsmen drifted back from unsuccessful jobs, and our original gang was in a way re-established.

Strange to say, I had become light-hearted after my troubles. Foremen would shout at me, and I laughed as soon as their backs were turned. I didn't care. I had resigned myself to the gradual eking out of my life. Work and food.

Up on Hudson Heights, on top of the Palisades, was a boarding house kept by a *paisana*. And there I would spend the evenings, joking and fooling. I walked up and down with a broad smile on my face. And it was just by accident, and from this same sense of joking that my life took an upward turn.

First of all, a crowd of Mexican laborers were brought up from the south to work with us in the yard. At first they were kept separated from us, living in long shanties. But gradually a general mingling of laborers took place and we fraternized wonderfully with them. And I found some of them real gentlemen. There was one, a wiry young man, who had been with Villa and had been taken prisoner by the Americans. Besides Spanish he could speak a strange Indian language that sounded very queer to me. That winter he and another older man came to live in our box car and our quarters, already crowded, became packed. They were lively fellows and would sing and play on a discordant guitar. Then at times the older one, Don Tomas, would start off reminiscing and put us all to sleep with his monotonous semi-comprehensible stories.

I began to learn some Spanish from these two Mexicans. The younger one received a Spanish weekly from some town in Texas. To my amusement he would sit hours at a time reading it. Little by little I became interested in the paper, and tried to pick out words that were like Italian. I had gotten to think of a newspaper as something to start a fire with or to wrap objects in. But now I began to read again, very little at first, I must confess. Somehow, I found English more to my liking than Spanish. And about once a week I even bought an English newspaper to look at. There was very little in them that I could understand, even though I spent many a puzzled hour trying to decipher the strange words. When I did learn a word and had discovered its meaning I would write it in big letters on the moldy walls of the box car. And soon I had my first lesson in English all around me continually before my eyes.

One day a friend of mine who was a bartender in one of the many saloons that lined River Road took me to an Italian vaudeville show in a theater on the Bowery,

New York. Included in the program was a short farce. I heard it and decided to myself that I could do better.

I went home and tried to write something after work. I began it in Italian, but unable to manage the language, on a sudden thought I decided to attempt it in English. After a few Sundays of hard work I had about three closely written pages of the most impossible English one could imagine. In triumph, I showed it to a couple of brakemen. They laughed long and loud. There was some doubt whether it was the jokes or the manhandled English which caused their hilarity. However, I gave myself the benefit of the doubt, and agreed with myself that I could write English.

Though I have long since burned most of these "prehistoric" attempts at English, I still have a few among my papers of which the following is an example:

A farmer had not bean in this city very long beefore he-falled in love with sumthing. And this sumthing happen to be a woornan whoo disliked him just as passionately he liked her. Now, please do not think that this turns out to be a joke. Farther from it. This is a seerious story in witch throbs the most violent of human passions. The life of an unfortunate farm swolled up by the whirlpulls of evil. Revealing the futile struggles of a mother who fites to save her son drunkard by liquor which he had not yet drunk. He was like a drunken staggering alung the city streets and falls in some undignfied gutter out of which he emerges with his face embellished by mud and clothes smelling with heretofour unknown perfumes, made out of the too old manure and many other effective ingredients pertaining thereto.

He knelt beefore the wooman he lovd. Being largely dispose to obesity (fatness) whenver she moved away which she did it on purpose—he would go after her (walking) on his knees. Most people become eloquent when drunken or in love and this farmer was not therefour exseption, "I love you" be begined, "I love you so much. I love you! Please come near! come nearer. You are my hope, my quween, my all! You are like a goddes beefore witch I am never tired of kneeling. You are the most beautful wooman in the world you are moor beautful then beauty. More beautful then one of our newly washed pig!" she went way and he called her back "At least help me to git up if you don want marry me." She went and he had a hard difficult job to get up.

So I began to write jokes in "English," most of them of my own invention or paraphrased from some paper. My jokes became known around the yard as great curiosities and things to laugh at. Several good-natured lads who worked there even brought me writing paper so that I could put down a few jokes for them. The things I wrote were not refined at all, but only of the type for my class of people.

Later, when I had learned to manage the English language a little better and could write with some degree of clarity, I put a prize of five cents on some good jokes. That is, if they could keep a straight face while reading a little collection of jokes that I presented them I would give them a nickel. But of course they always refused the nickel. Thus was my first climax in the role of English author.

One day I bought a small Webster's dictionary for a quarter (second-hand, if not third), half torn. But I thought I had gotten a treasure for the price. And I proceeded to memorize it.

Thereafter I was continually going around the yard using the most unheard-of English words. But, insistently, I made them understand what I meant by spelling each word or writing them on a railroad tie.

From that time on I was continually asking questions and writing jokes and riddles— which were for me the heights of intellectual attainment.

One glorious winter night I was coming back toward the box car from a trip to Hudson Heights. With me were a couple of brakemen who were on a night shift and were going to work. They were young light-hearted American lads, always ready to joke with me.

I looked up. The sky was thick with stars. I remarked, "The stars are marching over the deep night. With whom are they going to war?"

"Eh? With whom. . . . ?" they asked.

"With the emperor of Eternity."

"And who is he?"

"Death," I said.

They both laughed and took pains to make me understand that I was crazy. I walked ahead to my box car.

Shortly after this I began to project—ambitiously—a heart stirring tragedy. There was a small hall in back of one saloon on River Road owned by a Hungarian whose daughter I often spoke with. They were not bad people either, and she had beautiful blue eyes. Vaguely I made plans for producing a soul-rending show there, and charging admission, and making a good deal of money. Of course, I was to be the author of the sad play.

Now, just because I knew so little about the city, I determined to put my scene in the great metropolis. And the play was to start with a poor outcast who had to sleep in the subway. But when I sat down to write the speech of this poor being whose rest is disturbed by the rumbling trains, I didn't know what to say. Accordingly, I decided to investigate and spend a night in the subway, which I did very successfully in the matter of sleep. And I never wrote the sad tragedy, either.

But work, continual, hard, fatiguing work, made my attempts at writing few and short lived. I always was and am a pick and shovel man. That's all I am able to do, and that is what I am forced to do, even now. Work with my arms.

Wrecks in the yard were a daily occurrence. I could hardly concentrate my mind, when a man would come shouting, "All out! A wreck!" in the tunnel or away down the tracks toward the sugar refineries. Out I would have to go. And in a few minutes I would be starting long spells of intense, hurried labor to dear away the wreckage or repair the damaged tracks, in the red glow of flickering lanterns.

The superiority of my English was first recognized by the Italian laborers of my gang. Then brakemen and conductors who were practically all Americans began to notice me. And finally rumors of my accomplishments reached even the yard officials. I became quite celebrated in the Shady Side yard of the Erie Railroad as "that queer Italian laborer."

Then a group of young brakemen began a campaign to put down my little local fame. What they did was to bring new and difficult words every morning for me to define. Usually they would come about half an hour before working time, and cornering me would ask the meaning of some difficult word. If I could answer, all was well and they kept judiciously quiet for the rest of the day. But if I failed, then they would make it hot for me.

When noon came they would call me over to the space in front of the office where clerks, yard officials and girls were. And there they would, with plenty of noise, try to show me up to those who liked me.

But their efforts and mental ambushes were all useless—as useless as I could make them. One day they brought me before the whole crowd just to have me ridiculed, perhaps because they were high school lads. They gave me five words to define and I only knew the meaning of three. Throwing up their hands they began to proclaim themselves victorious.

But I calmly gave them two words that they had never heard of. Then I bet them that I could give them ten words and two more for good measure none of which they could understand.

I began, "Troglodyte," "sebaceous," "wen," "helot," "indeciduity," "murine," "bantling," "ubiquity," "cırthrophobia," "nadir," and instead of adding two for good measure I added seven to make their debacle more horrible. And with a pencil against the office facade I wrote the seven words so that everyone might see their eternal defeat, "abettor," "caballine," "phlebotomy," "coeval," "octroon," "risible," "anorexia," "arable," then to complete, I added, "asininity." The defeat of these educated youths was, is and will be an eternal one, because there is no other pick and shovel man that can face them like that.

From the day of that triumph they nicknamed me "solution," and we all became good friends.

And so the months passed, with plenty of joking and foolishness and no end of work.

But at times I would stand in front of the box car on a clear night. Around would be the confusion, whistles, flashes and grinding sounds of the never-ending movement in the yard. I would steal a glance up at the stars. The stars have always been the wonder of my life. I had but lately learned, to my utter surprise, that there were other worlds besides this earth. And I had also discovered in a newspaper article that the stars were other suns with unseen worlds around them. And as I gazed upward I thought that perhaps there were other eyes in those viewless worlds that were gazing wondering in my direction. And how our glances must have met in the black mid-darkness of the infinite.

Such reveries were always broken by a rough shout from some of my fellow laborers to "come in and go to sleep!"

XIV

It was on a November morning in 1919 that I made a hasty decision. It was a quick, yet inevitable decision. I would give my future a chance. I would no longer dream and hope—I would act. Hurriedly eager, to execute my plans before I should change my mind, I went to my friend Saverio.

"Saverio," I announced, "I am going to leave this place. I am going to live in the city and write poetry."

"Pascal," he commented, "you will starve."

"I shall."

I reflected: what was one little starvation more or less in a man's life, especially in that of a self-anointed poet? Within a few years we would be gone, so why not sing our songs in the meanwhile?

My friend looked sadly at me and slowly shook his head, making me understand that we of the uneducated class have more relations to swine and should therefore keep on nuzzling the ground without raising our heads to cast wistful glances toward unwritten beauties.

The next morning, oblivious of the trials ahead of me, I came to New York with my tumble down valise in which were being transported my shirts, books and a cosmopolitan colony of insects gathered from the various corners of the vast

Americas. With little misgivings I turned my back to the ditches and tracks in order to explore a new life.

When I first arrived in America the city through which I had passed had been a vast dream whittling around me. Gradually it had taken shape and form, but had still remained alien to me in spirit. Now, however, as I walked through its crowded streets, I felt a sort of kinship with it. I felt that I was an integral part of this tremendous, living, bustling metropolis.

For several days I wandered about, getting better acquainted with my chosen abode. I felt happy. I had hopes for the future, I had a sort of goal, however vaguely defined. "Nothing," I swore to myself over and over again, "will turn me back from my chosen career of author, nothing will drive me back before I have accomplished something that will justify my starting."

So, wandering through the metropolis, I drifted down to the slums along the Brooklyn waterfront. There I could cut my expenses to a minimum. I took stock of my earthly possessions, and realized that I was in no position to stand a long period of physical idleness. In the first impetus of enthusiasm, however, I wrote continuously for several weeks. It seemed to be a great relief to have all my time free for my beloved poetry.

The winter of 1921 was approaching. Times were bad. Recognition seemed utterly impossible, in spite of my set resolve. A literary future for me was the densest, sunless, moonless, starless gloom the human mind could ever conceive. How far would my scanty savings of the preceding months take me?

I tried to save money in all ways possible. I went to live in the cheapest hole that I could find in the slums of Brooklyn. It was a small room which had previously been a chicken coop and wood shack. That hovel was the main tryst where all the most undesirable inconveniences held their meetings. The entrance to it was through a toilet which served ten families besides unwelcome strangers and dirty passers-by. Often the overflow of that ordure would come running beneath the door and stand in malodorous pools under my bug-infested bed.

There was no stove in the room, and many a freezing day I had to remain huddled in the bed in order to keep warm. The most dyspeptic and indigestible moments were those when I had to shave. I could scarcely shave with my overcoat on—which served me as a quilt at night and as an overcoat during the day.

All those who knew where I was living could hardly refrain from saying, "Are you crazy to live in that room without a stove and toilet water always coming in? You will easily get sick."

I shrugged my shoulders in resignation and tried to make them understand that the price of a better room was beyond my financial compass.

Meanwhile, I would go to the Library—the only refuge opened to me—and write. At least if my body was living in a world of honor I could build a world of beauty for my soul.

Having little money left I set out to master the situation. The easiest thing to cut was food. I searched every possible corner for cheap food. I went into several bakeries and asked for the lowest price on their bread. Too high, too high, always too high. But my search continued. I went into one place and asked the same question. The lady there told me, adding, "Unless you want stale bread." I smiled and jested solemnly, "How much must I disburse for your stale bread before I can proclaim it mine?"

Open-mouthed she stared at me, though she understood "how much." And I became a steady customer for stale bread, although very often I would call it "steel bread" which really was an appropriate name.

Poverty, the eternal torturer, tightened its hold upon me. As days of hopeless darkness followed each other I felt myself constrained to cut down expenses in all possible ways. It was a war for an ideal. For my part I began to live on the most frugal basis imaginable. My daily meals during that winter consisted of stale bread and cold soup in which I put stale bread broken into small pieces and waited until they became soft enough to he eaten, costing, in all, about ten cents. At times I would get reckless and squander a few pennies for bananas, if I could get them cheap enough.

Do not think that I bought those finely assorted bananas with which the corner fruit stands so allure the passer-by. Not by any means. Those which I ate—delicious food—were sold to me, not one cent each, but twenty-five, and sometimes even more, for a nickel. These were not daily occurrences, only Saturdays made them possible. One can easily imagine in what state of decomposition they were to fetch such a low price. For me, in my struggle against poverty, they were a rare delicacy. A banana vendor once, the first time I approached his stand, asked me, "Are you buyin' this bananas for your dog?"

"No," I replied promptly, "for my wolf." Several times on my way home with soup I would begin to tremble—and there was a good reason for it—for if the Prohibition agents ever inspected my soup they would arrest me. Because my soup, in its state of fermentation, would far surpass their constitutionalized one-half of one per cent. Sometimes besides being sour and burnt—at times so badly damaged that I had to throw it away and bemoan the nickel which I had lost in that bad investment—my soup was full of bones, bones that did not belong there. Meatless bones, chicken feet which were dead, but alive enough to scratch my soul with deep humiliation. But the more things turned against me, the more I stood my ground.

I had faith in myself. Without realizing it, I had learned the great lesson of America: I had learned to have faith in the future. No matter how bad things were, a turn would inevitably come, as long as I did not give up. I was sure of it. But how much I had to suffer until the change came! What a thorny, heartbreaking road it was!

XV

As the winter grew more severe my condition became desperate. My books and papers were moulding from the damp. I too felt that I was mouldering. The sufferings, colds, wet and damp were beginning to harm me. Many a freezing night, unable to remain in bed I had to get up and walk about three miles to the Long Island Depot at Flatbush Avenue where I might find a little warmth.

Once I had to stay three days without washing because the lavatory pipes were frozen. On the morning of the fourth day I thought it was worthwhile going to the Main Library at Forty-second Street and Fifth Avenue where I could wash not only my hands and face but my handkerchief also.

I took some stale bread with me and five or six bananas, because that was all I had left. Wrapping the remainder of the bread, destined to last at least two more days, in a sheet of newspaper; I threw it under the bed. Usually, on going out, I would place my bread on the bed rather than under, fearing lest the unwelcome toilet overflows would pay a visit during my absence and render it uneatable. But now that the pipes were frozen I needed no such precautions.

While I was in the public library, several hours later, I had occasion to go from the main reading room to see about a book in the files outside. During my absence some conscientious gentleman inspected my overcoat which I had left on the arm of my chair believing that the library was only frequented by honest people.

Finding it too old to repay him for the trouble of taking it away, he searched the pockets and took the few pennies that I had left.

I was unaware of this until I was approaching the subway station, when my hand instinctively began to feel for the fare.

The lady in the booth—though I did not ask her for anything—made me understand that the B. R. T. was not a philanthropic society.

I turned away from the booth and went up to the street.

Without wasting more time I set out on my long tramp home. It was about half-past ten when I left Times Square. The weather was somewhat cloudy, though I could see no visible signs of either snow or frozen rain.

"It is not so bad after all," I thought, "especially if it does not snow." By two o'clock I ought to be in my hovel. Why did I try to go in the subway, anyhow? Why was I in such a hurry to reach my room? Was there a woman's brightening smile and a child's love-woven da! da! to greet me after their alarm on account of my delay? What was there home for me? Only cold and overflows. Well, they could overflow without me.

I walked.

The wind began to make itself more arrogant. As I was about to reach Canal Street some cold sharp rain began to fall from the sluggish clouds, with increasing rapidity.

Just as I was in the middle of Manhattan Bridge the rain and sleet began to pour full blast upon the city. My face ached from the sharp biting sleet. Two minutes were sufficient to get me wet through to the skin. My clothes became bright and studded with the frozen rain. I could not pause for if I did my water soaked underwear would freeze me. I hurried on head-bowed.

Reaching the Long Island Depot on Flatbush Avenue I entered in order to warm myself a little. I stood there shivering in my cold wet clothes.

Snow could be seen through the glass windows pouring down as intense as the clouds above that threw it.

It was about one a.m. Besides feeling cold and extremely wet, I was hungry. I could not go into a restaurant. I did not have a cent. Neither could I eat snow.

After a while I hurried home under the piercing blows of the ice-pointed wind. There at least I had my stale bread under the bed. It was home after all.

I reached my room a little after two. As I opened the door in the dark I could hear a splashing on the floor as if water were there. The window was open. Snow poured in. The children of the neighborhood had opened it during my absence in order to look at my books and papers. Rain and snow had wet a good half of the bed and quilt. Someone had also tried to warm the pipes in the lavatory and they had burst. Before the water could be turned off enough of it had flowed under my bed to spoil my stale bread and my extra pair of trousers and underwear.

Half of my bed was wet. I could not use it. My underwear was also soaked. The stale bread gave such an evil toilet smell that I could not eat it in spite of my hunger. Shivering, sleepy, hungry, tired, I huddled on the dry end of the bed and pressed my face in anguish against the quilt. How long, O God, how long was this going to last? Would I ever get out of this gulf of sorrows?

I must have fallen asleep, for just as the gray tumult outside was whitening into dawn, I awoke aching and coughing, with fits of fever. I did not feel myself able to plunge through the snowdrifts that filled the streets and so sat shivering in my room while the day cleared and an icy wind blew against my window.

What an immense distance stretched between me and my goal! What an impossibility it appeared to see even one word of mine in print!

Somehow, the sufferings and discouragements which I received during those terrible months only spurred me to greater efforts. Systematically, I made a list of all the newspapers and magazines in New York. And I decided to pay personal visits to all of them. I selected about a score of my poems and divided them into four equal groups so that I could cover several offices in one day. My visits to the newspapers proved useless and discouraging. Some made me leave the poems, saying, "You will hear from us soon," though three or four weeks usually passed before the unfavorable news came. One newspaper, out of pity, I suppose, offered me a dollar for my favorite poems.

Late in December, while the happy populace were beginning their festive squandering, I went to the office of a large, internationally known newspaper. Downcast and sad, I sat on a chair in the receiving room waiting for someone to come and reject my poems. All at once a young man who was passing, stopped abruptly and opened his eyes with amazement at my queer presence.

I rose to my feet and gazed pleadingly at him. "What's the matter, are you sick?" he asked in a semi-jesting voice.

"No, though I have some poems that are from lack of recognition."

A sardonic grin passed over his face at the mention of "poems." "Well, you are in the wrong hospital then, John," he said, walking on.

After a minute or two a solemn looking gentleman came out to lend dignity and weight to the antechamber.

"What can I do for you?" he inquired as if he were the doctor sent out to feel the pulse of my poems. I showed him my poems.

"I am very sorry, sir," he began austerely, "but I can do nothing for you. Our policy or rather the policy of this paper does not enable us to print anything except what is written by our editorial staff. I wish you luck. Good-bye."

Similar receptions did not deter me. There was always the goading thought that if ninety-nine offices rejected my poems the hundredth might accept them.

When I went home at night, there was nothing to cheer me in the freezing, stoveless room, save the encouraging thought that I had not yet visited all the editorial offices in New York. Why then should I buy the coffin before my hope was dead? At times, seized by fits of enthusiasm, about an imaginary success, I would sit down and write, forgetting hunger and cold which beset me.

Toward the end of the year I went into a magazine office from which my poems had been twice expelled and asked the information girl if I could see the editor. I wanted to make sure that it was the editor and not the office boy who had read my poems.

"I am not sure, but I'll try," she said.

After a while I was brought into the presence of a quiet looking old gentleman around whose eyes there seemed to be a touch of sadness.

In a voice whose harshness startled me, coming as it did from such a mild looking man, he asked, "Well, what brought you here?"

I told him that I had come to ask about my poems. His office had held them for such a long time that I had almost begun to hope for their ultimate acceptance, and then they had been suddenly returned to me.

"To tell the truth," he began, "I am editor, and the poems which we print are selected by a special reader out of the large quantity that pours into our office. Therefore you can easily understand that I have in no wise ever seen yours or anybody else's poems except those which the reader hands to me for the magazine. And that is about all I have to say. Good day."

Such receptions were repeated over and over again with sickening monotony. And still I persisted.

During the time I was working in the Under-cliff yard of the Erie I had written a poem called "Light" which summed up my indecisions and doubts about the future. And the light had not yet come. . . .

Toward the end of the year, as one of the last few hopes. I submitted my poems in a contest which *The Nation* was holding. It was a desperate move, a clutching at a straw.

The year ended and no answer came. I became anxious; I wanted to know what had befallen my poems. I knew that recognition was practically impossible. It was a new year of sorrow and suffering. As a sort of despairing gesture I sent a letter to the editor.

To the Editor of The Nation,

Dear Sir:
I have submitted three poems, "For The Nation's Poetry Prize" within the established period as described in the column of The Nation! Not having heard anything from your editorial office, I would be much obliged if you should inform me on the matter.

I hope you will consider them from a viewpoint of their having been written by one who is an ignorant pick and shovel man, who has never studied English. If they do not contain too many mistakes I must warmly thank those friends who have been kind enough to point out the grammatical errors. I am one who is struggling through the blinding flames of ignorance to bring his message before the public—before you. You are dedicated to defend the immense cause of the oppressed. This letter is the cry of a soul stranded on the shores of darkness looking for light, a light that points out the path toward recognition, where I can work and help myself in the literary world. No! No! I only want to express the wrath of their mistreatment. No! I seek no refuge! I am a worker, a pick and shovel man, what I want is an outlet to express what I can say beside work. Yes to express all the sorrows of those who cower under the crushing yoke of an unjust doom.

There are no words that can fitly represent my living suffering. No, no words! Even the picture loses its mute eloquence before this scene. I suffer: for an ideal, for freedom, for truth that is denied by millions, but not by the souls who have the responsibility of being human. For yesterday, New Year's Day. I only had five cents worth of decaying bananas and a loaf of stale bread to eat. And today: a half quart of milk and a stale loaf of bread. All for the love of an ideal. Not having sufficient bed clothes for a stoveless room like mine, I must use my overcoat as blanket at night and as a wrinkled overcoat during the day. The room is damp, my books are becoming moldered. And I too, am beginning to feel the effects of it. But what can I do? Without a pick and shovel job and without a just recognition. And besides the landlady has notified me to evacuate her room on or before January the tenth. She may have someone who can pay a little more than I. So I must go and search for another room. Perhaps it will cost more than this. How can I afford it? Without work and without a recognition that will allow me to work?

Please consider my condition and the quality of the work I submit. And tell me if I can be helped without any expense on your part. You can do something for me. Even in this horrible and indescribable condition I am not asking for financial aid. I am not asking for pity, nor am I asking for an impossibility. I only ask for a simple thing—a thing which you are giving away free. While you are giving it away free, why not see that it goes where it can help the most? I am not coveting the prize because of the money. No but because it will give me the recognition that I cannot do without. If it's given to me I can go around to all the editors, and I can say to them that I have been awarded "The Nation's Poetry Prize." When I say that, they will listen to me—they will consider my works—they will begin to accept them. Then, dominated by an impulse of encouragement, I will write: a novel, two, three, who knows how many! But how can I go now without an introduction of this kind? They don't hear me. If I ask them to see my manuscript they say they are busy, or else they let me leave some poems which they consign to oblivion, in an obscure corner of their editorialocratic drawers. When after a certain time they might accidentally happen to see my poems they glance at the name and see it's an unknown one. Therefore they return them without much consideration. Must it continue like this forever? That is why I am asking this help from you. If it costs you nothing, then why not help me? If the prize is given to a well known writer it does not give him the same aid that it gives me.

There is no writer who exists under such conditions. Let this prize break those horrible barriers before me, and open a new world of hope! Let this prize (even if it is an honorary one) come like a bridge of light between me and my awaiting future. Let me free! Let me free! Free like the thought of love that haunts millions of minds. If it's without expenses on your side then, give, give me an opportunity. Give me an opportunity before colds, wet, sleets, and many other sufferings will pitilessly distort my physical and mental shapes into a monstrous deformity. Give me an opportunity while it's not too late. I can work hard and am hoping to make enough money to have a musical education. For I want to compose music. And yet I do not know the difference between one note and another. What bars me from doing so?

Oh! Please hear me! I am telling the truth. And yet who knows it? Only I. And who believes me? Then let my soul break out of the chrysalis of enforced ignorance and fly toward the flower of hope, like a rich butterfly winged with a thousand thoughts of beauty.

Remember! without any expenses on your side you can help me! This is what I want: to be one sharer (though honorary) of the prize, the honor of the prize, a winner of the prize! For I have no friends who can help me in the literary world. I am a poor worker but a rich defender of truth.

Oh please! The weights of duty crush me down and yet I can not perform. I am not a spendthrift. With a hundred dollars I can live five months. I am not asking an impossibility.

Lift me, with the strength of the prize, out of this ignoble gloom and place me on the pulpit of light where I too can narrate what the Nature-made orator has to say in me.

The miracle happened. All at once I found myself known and talked about. Almost immediately my plea found a sympathetic response and the two editors of two influential weekly publications in America became interested in my work. Henry Seidel Canby, editor of *The Literary Review of the New York Evening Post*, was one of them. Poems of mine were published. Other magazines followed. Soon the newspapers began to print my story and word about me appeared in Europe and throughout America.

The literary world began to take me up as a great curiosity and I was literally feasted, welcomed and stared at. Letters of congratulation and appreciation came from various sections of America: from Boston to 'Frisco. But more sincere and dearer to my heart were the tributes of my fellow workers who recognized that at last one of them had risen from the ditches and quicksands of toil to speak his heart to the upper world.

And sweeter yet was the happiness of my parents who realized that after all I had not really gone astray, but had sought and attained a goal far from the deep-worn groove of peasant drudgery.

(Originally in English)

Incipit Vita Nova

 Francesco Ventresca

Born Introdacqua (L'Aquila), Italy, May 1, 1872

As a townsman of Pascal D'Angelo, it is not far-fetched that Francesco Ventresca decided to write his autobiography, *Personal Reminiscences of a Naturalized American* (1937). As a result of the relative success of *Son of Italy*, a second, definitive edition of Ventresca's autobiography, amplified by three chapters, was published in 1951. The seventh of eleven children, Ventresca arrived in America on May 1, 1892, at nineteen years old. He did not come from a wealthy family, but was driven toward emigrating primarily by the desire to undergo new experiences, as revealed in his book, where he relates that the day after his arrival, he obtained an English grammar and began to study the language, since he wanted to understand it as a true American. In Italy, he had completed elementary school, and was immediately put to work in the fields. In America, in the evenings, which his labor companions, largely Italians, spent in chat and pastimes, he would study English. At twenty-one years old, he entered elementary school, and, in addition, took private lessons in French. In 1900, he entered Northern Indiana Normal School, received his diploma, and returned to Europe with the intention of continuing the study of languages. Having visited his relatives in Italy, he availed himself of the opportunity to see the great cities of art for the first time; he then went on to Paris, where the Universal Exposition was in progress, and remained for one year, finding various jobs as an interpreter, waiter, and guide. Subsequently, he went to Germany, where he taught modern languages at the University of Freiburg for four years and also mastered German. He returned to America in 1905, and pursued his studies first at the Valparaiso University, in Indiana, and then at the University of Chicago, from which he graduated in 1919.

Between 1910 and 1914, he was a professor of modern languages at Washington State College, and he successively found work as an interpreter with the departments of the navy, of war, and of the treasury of the United States. Between 1929 and 1944, he taught at Crane Junior College, and between 1933 and 1937, he was president of the department of foreign languages of Manley High School, in Chicago.

Retiring from teaching after having reached the status of professor emeritus of European languages, Ventresca still found work as an agent of an insurance company in Chicago, in whose environs, Western Springs, Illinois, he had established himself with his American wife, whom he married in 1914.

The first edition of Ventresca's autobiography covered his life up to 1920, but subsequently, upon receiving requests from his readers, Ventresca covered further decades. The autobiography is characterized by an optimism, a smiling, vital impetus, revealing an iron will to emerge from, and free oneself from, the unfavorable conditions of emigration. A writer stubbornly intent upon providing every possible detail of his experience (though burdening the book with frequent citations of documents), Ventresca presents well the problem of his own identity and the division that took place in him following his migration experience. Upon his first return to Italy, in fact, he understood that Italy was no longer his world, that in the misery of the town in which he was born, there was no more space for a man who, like him, was opposed to the already numerous emigrants who returned after achieving prosperity, directed himself toward culture, a self-liberation more spiritual than material. Therefore, Marilena Giammarco has read the *Reminiscences* as an itinerary toward the construction of a more profound identity, realized precisely in America. In fact, it is there that Ventresca would consciously master, for the first time, a true knowledge of Italian culture, and from his American viewpoint, he could finally enjoy the treasure of his own spiritual inheritance, study it, and as early as 1910, completely dedicate some writing to it, among which an essay, "On the Origin of the Type 6–10 in the Italian Endecasillabo," as well as essays on Dante and Leonardo da Vinci in the appendix of the second edition of the *Reminiscences*.

All Ventresca's experience took place substantially outside of the colonial circle, even if a certain Italian spirit was always in force in him, as when he actively raised funds among his townspeople for the cause of a flood.

ESSENTIAL BIBLIOGRAPHY

Giammarco 1997; Peragallo 1949, 221–223; Ventresca 1937, 1951.

ↄ

Incipit vita nova. Here begins the new life. Dante at the age of nine met Beatrice and was inspired to achieve eternal fame. I, at the age of twenty-one, entered an elementary school in Illinois and by sheer determination changed completely the course of my life (if we may compare a little thing to a big thing).

One beautiful sunny morning I was going to the post office to get the mail. It was recess time at the school. The children were playing marbles on the sidewalk. They looked as happy as children could be. It occurred to me that it must be a great thing to go to school here, compared to Italy, where we went to school shivering out of fear lest we would not be able to recite faultlessly the memorized lesson, and would have to kneel down till school was out.

One little tot took me to the first grade teacher, Mrs. Brockway. She directed me to the principal, Mr. Cox, who inquired about my age and told me to come back Monday morning. He was very courteous and seemed much in sympathy with my decision to enter school and learn English.

I must mention here that during the time I remained with my countrymen they often asked me to write their letters home, and they thought so much of my hand-writing that they called me *Il Piccolo Notaio* (The Little Notary). In those days eighty per cent of the Italian people were still illiterate. Oh, how thrilled I was with the pros-pect of actually getting into an American school and learning English first hand!

Monday came and I presented myself to the friendly principal with a respect-ful, "Good morning, Sir," and then asked further, "What news it is?" He answered, "Oh, nothing especial," and informed me that the chairman of the Board of Edu-cation had granted me permission to attend school, as I was not yet twenty-one years of age. To be exact, I was within three months of my twenty-first birthday, but nobody was going to be so scientifically accurate about vital statistics. When once I got started in my school work, no one paid attention to the time that was passing, and I enjoyed work that year and three years more, till June 1896, cover-ing the course to the end of the seventh grade, the eighth grade being considered only review work.

The first day I was assigned to the first grade. It was fortunate I was not an awkward big thing, but a medium-sized young fellow. I was not assigned to a seat, but given a chair and told to sit near the window, not far from the teacher. But when she asked me to read, she made me come near her and sit by the table to her left. She asked me to read and I read *tah-kay* for take, and *tah-blay* for table.

The patient teacher said, "No, that is pronounced *take* and *table*." And thus I was initiated into the secrets of the English written language. Another thing I remember was when the teacher asked me to put my tongue between my teeth to pronounce th in *thought* and *through*, and *these* and *those*.

I meant business. I went home and got busy studying with a fixed purpose. I immediately asked Mr. Knowlson, our neighbor of happy memory, to buy me an English dictionary, Webster's high school edition, and prepared all my lessons for school, by looking up all the words for their definition in English, which means that I acquired my knowledge of English as a native and not as a foreigner.

From now on I was living with my countrymen in body, but not in heart and mind. While they chattered and played and sometimes cursed, I was busy reading my lessons as loud as I dared and looking up definitions in the dictionary. My neighbors watched and watched and then one said, "Francesco, if you keep on at that rate, you'll soon go crazy." I was not frightened by that prediction. I kept on reading nevertheless. I have read an immense amount since, and in many languages, and have not gone crazy.

I had been in the first grade but a couple of weeks, when I was told the work there was too elementary for me and I should be studying in the third grade, so the work done in the second grade does not appear in my memory.

In the third grade I was inspired by the work the class leaders, Enid, Bessie, James, Ray and Justin, were doing. I listened with tense ears to the thorough, deliberate reports James made; to the dignified, well-worded reports of Bessie, and to the loquacious, spirited, endless reports of Ray. One would have thought that Ray had swallowed the newspaper before going to school in the morning.

One fine day that spring I was watching the boys play tops, and when one boy's top knocked off a chip from another's top, the other boy would say, "You did it. You did it!" I learned then and there, in a practical way, that in English the past comes right up to the present, whereas in Italian and most European languages, we would say, "You have done it" (*Tu l'hai fatto!*).

During this same little game, perhaps because I was defending the interests of a weaker, younger boy, a certain boy named Ralph got mad at me and called me "Dago." I gave him one on the jaw right there, and he never indulged in derogatory names after that.

When I was transferred to the third grade James Knowlson, who is now the president of a manufacturing concern, having graduated from Cornell University, invited me to read with him at home. His mother was pleased to have us read together. Along with the assigned school work, we read *Black Beauty*. That was doing well for a pupil who entered the school only a few weeks before. In the course of reading, a dipper was mentioned. I asked, "What is a dipper?" Mrs. Knowlson said, "James, get a dipper and show it to Frank." This same lady reminded me years later that when her son asked me what books I liked to read, I answered, "I don't want to read books; I want to study my dictionary!"

It was a bright day in March that year 1893, and Fred, Harry, James and I were playing ball on the driveway in front of the barn, when James asked, "Frank, who's your girl?" I, expressing in English the answer I would have given in Italian, replied, "My girl is yet to be born." Strangely enough, my wife was born the following month, or within two weeks of that prediction. That fall I was sent to the fifth grade and there I had plenty to do carrying a full program: grammar, arithmetic, history and geography. Once at recess time I meant to say "heat" but said "hit," when Florence Jones corrected, "Frank, it is not 'hit'; it is 'heat', *he, he, he!*"

One day Justin Hayes and I were walking to school. I was now in the fifth grade and he in the fourth, when out he came with the pertinent remark, "Do you know, Frank? You are doing very well. Last year we laughed at you because you did not know English. This year you know English and your own language, too."

The school I was attending was not the usual "Little red school house around the corner" we read so much about, but a first class two story stone building at the conspicuous corner of Chestnut Street and Grand Avenue. Notwithstanding the fact that two new schools have been built since, the old stone school house still remains the best school in the place.

When I went to the post office at noon, the girls in the third and fourth grades would ask me to give them a ride on their sleds, which I did gladly. Who wouldn't under similar circumstances? Then I noticed they all liked candy, so I generally managed to have some in my pockets. I can still see those girls, three, four, five of them, scrambling after me, hanging on my coat. They were all happy and laughed for joy, and so did I.

When spring came my countrymen went away, looking for work. I decided to stay in Western Springs and earn a living there. James' father was kind enough to write a letter of recommendation in my behalf to the manager of a greenhouse. The manager read the message and offered me seven dollars and a half a week, which was not bad those days for a steady job. But I was too ambitious. I had come to Chicago to earn a dollar and seventy-five cents a day. And I had set my price now at twenty cents an hour, because I had learned enough English to take orders. So I declined this offer with thanks.

Some of my countrymen living in Chicago had so much confidence in my knowledge of English that they suggested I should go to live in Chicago, get votes for politicians and make an easy living that way, or even get rich! No, that luring proposition fell on deaf ears. Fancy me a vote-getter in Chicago and for a living!!!

I first got work with the village engineer doing odd jobs connecting water about town. Then the chairman of the board of education engaged me to grade the yard of his new home, plant the garden and do a little building, which kept me busy for over three weeks. When I asked for my pay at the rate of twenty cents an hour, he remarked that in Italy I would have to work for twenty cents a day, and so I never received my money from him. The total loss amounted to about forty dollars.

I did house painting and cut lawns and split wood. By this time I was living in a little new shanty not bigger than a one-car garage, and before retiring at night I invariably knelt down for over half an hour and said prayers. I believe to this day that was good for me. It developed in me staunch faith and tenacity of purpose.

This was that terrible year of 1893 which combined the splendor of the Chicago World's Fair with the misery of unemployment and railroad strikes. Some of the residents of Western Springs said to me, "Frank, you are lucky. You do not have to go to Chicago to earn a living."

Before the summer was far advanced I saw fit to visit the Exposition at Hyde Park. I can still see the big inscription across Fifty-Fifth Street, way up high: MID-WAY PLAISANCE.

I saw many buildings with grand statues and extensive machinery, but most of this is like a dream to me now, except the Turkish Palace, where I saw Turkish women dance in all sorts of contortions. Yes, I saw the Exhibition of Scotland and the bare knees of the Highlanders for the first time that day. The main thing was that I should not miss seeing the Chicago Columbian Exposition.

When summer came, work about town became slack and I secured work on sewers which were being excavated along Brainard Avenue, La Grange. I was assigned to the bank on the surface and had to remove alone what two men threw up from below. The temperature must have been a hundred degrees in the shade. Not a bit of breeze from any direction. The sun was scorching hot.

I worked and worked and worked, until I collapsed exhausted, fainted! The next week I went back to get my fractional pay. That was the only time in my life when I was compelled to be a "quitter." There was no help for it. I have never been taller than five feet and four inches and have never weighed more than one hundred and forty-five pounds. Though I have always been wiry, my going to school and doing work in houses and gardens had unfitted me for strenuous labor.

I am grateful to James' mother who recommended me to Mrs. Blount, with whom I secured work to do chores and take care of horse and carriage for room and board. The son and daughter in the family were both attending the same school and knew me well, and I think, at heart, they liked to see me make progress in education.

That year I learned that Irish people have a language of their own. A Catholic girl named Mary was the housemaid and she spoke very broken English. I asked her why she did not speak English fluently and she replied that at home they spoke their own language, which the old Britons spoke before the Anglo-Saxon invasion.

A neighbor and I dug a soft-water cistern for Mrs. Collins, a neighboring lady, who must have recommended me to her husband, for the splendid Civil War veteran—he had been a major in the Union Army—engaged me to take care of his horse and carriage, his two cows, lawn, and chores about the house, all for twelve dollars a month, room and board. Yes, I learned to milk cows. That was not hard, though, because in Italy I had milked goats and sheep from my earliest boyhood.

My, the fun I had those days! I once went out in the field to get Jerry, a bay horse. There was no saddle. I jumped upon the horse and rode home. It is lucky the present concrete pavement was not laid. We galloped southward along the street for over a block. When we arrived at the driveway, Jerry, without giving the least warning, turned suddenly half way on his hind legs and ran west to the barn. I, impelled by the momentum, continued straight southward to the ground. It all happened so quickly I thought it was great fun. I rolled in the dust like a circus man. The next moment I was petting Jerry. My previous reading of *Black Beauty* came in handy.

But the story was quite different when, in a terribly cold winter weather, the major told me to go to La Grange to have the horse shod. The exceedingly cold weather drove the horse almost insane. I was trying to check him. He jerked. The right tug broke, and I saw my doom with bitter tears in my eyes. The snow was knee deep. The wind in the blizzard bit ears, nose, chin and hands, not to mention the feet. I think here again it was a miracle the horse stopped; and then with numb hands I could not get the harness in order for a long time. I finally got the horse shod and was mighty glad to get home.

Mrs. Collins, who was a scholar in general and spoke French and German fluently, asked me to give her Italian lessons, which I did gladly. One day as I was explaining the agreement of the article and adjective with the noun, she remarked, "Frank, I think you are a born teacher. You love so to explain grammatical rules." Her words encouraged me all the more in my school work.

I used to go to the mill-dam, at Fullersburg, to get feed for the horse and cows. Gray Brothers' feed store was located where Ogden Avenue, cross-country road No. 24, now goes through. But at that time the ruts along Ogden Avenue were knee deep.

As I was driving one day past an old, plain two-story frame house, I was told it was the Lincoln Inn, so called because Lincoln used to stop there when out campaigning. Now, I had seen at school the pictures of Columbus, Washington, Longfellow, Lincoln, Grant, and others; but the historical touch brought Lincoln's life and reality much closer to me. After that, whenever I saw on school tablets the words "Honest Abe," I always thought of the man who really lived and when out campaigning in this part of Illinois, putting up at the Lincoln Inn at Fullersburg.

Those who are acquainted with the anecdote about the Irishman who, when warned to look out, immediately stuck his head out of the train window, will not be surprised at the following experience. One evening Mrs. Collins told me to put out the light. I took the lamp and put it on the sill outside of the kitchen window.

Early one afternoon Mrs. Collins sent me on an errand to Miss Virginia Jackson, of Hinsdale, Illinois. Miss Jackson, a young lady in her twenties, was so accomplished and versatile that she could meet any situation most agreeably. She kindly invited me to her parlor, took her place at the piano and, to her own accompaniment, sang for my benefit, *Per Tutta l'Eternità* (For All Eternity), by Tosti, that Italian composer who became one of the leading entertainers of Queen Victoria's household and was knighted by her. The song was written for Adelina Patti and dedicated to her. In those days Madame Patti was still living and very much in the minds of people fortunate enough to have heard her. Her reputation equalled that of Enrico Caruso, and she died a few years ago at a very old age.

The Italian language, Miss Jackson's beautiful voice, the charming young woman, the sentiment expressed in the song, all united to delight my heart and to make me feel America was not so far from my home after all. Ten years later, when I was at the Crystal Palace, near London, England, I had occasion to buy *Per Tutta l'Eternità*. I sang it frequently and with feeling in Germany and elsewhere, always being reminded of the young lady in Hinsdale who first called my attention to that beautiful song and sang it for me in Italian.

The year 1893 was an eventful year for me. Mrs. Collins had a Parisian lady, a teacher of French, come out to Western Springs to give her lessons. Mrs. Collins did not need French lessons, as she knew the language well, but she was ambitious to aspire to a high degree of proficiency in the language.

On one occasion the teacher, whom I shall call Madame Delcassé, a really re-fined French brunette, inquired of me, if I knew where Mrs. C. was. Noticing my broken English and my foreign appearance, she asked, "Parlez-vous français?" I did not know any French then, but in Italian we say, "Parlate voi francese?" To me that was an opportunity. I asked the lady if she would teach me French, supporting my inquiry, before she had an opportunity to reply, by offering to pay her two dol-lars a lesson, which I knew was the current price for good teaching then. The lady politely declined, feeling perchance that she would be stepping down a bit, if she taught at the same time the lady living in plenty in a mansion, and the Italian boy who did chores around the mansion. I felt disappointed, but bided my time.

Soon this Parisian lady came no more to teach French. Mrs. Collins secured a tall, refined, Parisian lady in her thirties, by the name of Madame Philippe. This name has remained since dear to me, for she kindly condescended to introduce me to her mother tongue, which I was very eager to learn. Madame Philippe, with her daughter, Bianca, came to Western Springs to live. The mother at eighteen had married an Oriental merchant and for fifteen years they had lived in Constanti-nople. It was there that Bianca was born. The mother and the daughter spoke Ara-bic, Turkish, Greek, German, French, and English, with some Italian and Spanish. These are the nationalities represented in that metropolis of the Near East.

The father had died, throwing them upon their own resources. They were both beautiful and had the most genteel manners. Bianca found a place to take care of the children of Mrs. Hoffman.

Madame Philippe could also teach German, for she had spent part of her life at Lausanne, Switzerland. But she did not like German. She first informed me that after the Franco-Prussian War, the French-speaking pupils in the schools in Alsace-Lorraine were told that, beginning with Monday next, they should speak only German, and that, if they were caught speaking French, their tongues would be cut out. The vivid way she told the story left the impression upon me that some tongues were actually cut out. Readers of Alphonse Daudet's *La Dernière Classe* (The Last Class) will, of course, understand the situation.

Seven years later, in August 1900, I learned a few things for myself. I was in Strasburg that year and at a store I asked for soap, in German. Nobody answered. I got impatient. I yelled: "Monsieur, je désire du savon!"—"Ah, vous désirez, mon-sieur?" was the quick reply. I obtained my soap and went my way. Thirty years of German rule had not made the French-speaking Alsace-Lorrainers change their mentality and their dislike for German, whatever fuss they may make today.

Either Madame Philippe volunteered to teach me French, she being sympa-thetic and broad-minded about nationalities, or she showed willingness upon my request. The fact remains that I received French instruction from her, and she would take no pay. My appreciation of her lessons, however, was so great that, when Christmas came, I went to Chicago and bought for five dollars a rich black muff as a gift for the dear French teacher. I did not know it was imitation fur. What did I know about furs? But the good lady appreciated the muff as if it had been genuine. Indeed, she did not want to accept it, for she knew I was working for twelve dollars a month!

With Madame Philippe I did not use a French grammar with English explanations. Whitney's, Ahn's and Sauer's were practically the only French grammars on the market those days. I did not use any of them. I immediately bought Fontaine's *Livre de Lecture et de Conversation*, all in French, and read and reread those lessons until I knew them by heart. I could recognize many words, but the pronunciation was so different from Italian—and the *ü* and the *on* and the *an* and the *eu* and the *ain*! I did not know then what had happened in the days of Julius Caesar and his battles of conquest in Gallia. I bought for six dollars (a half month's pay) a large edition of Ferrari-Caccia: *French-Italian and Italian-French Dictionary* which has traveled all over Europe and all over America with me and still occupies an honorable place among my books.

When I had taken but a few lessons, the teacher asked me to write a composition in French. I wrote the sentences in French as I thought them out in Italian and the result was gratifying to the teacher. She showed the composition to Mrs. Collins, who said to me, "Why Frank, I think you are doing splendidly!"

My instruction may have lasted from four to six months, but my love for the study was so great that the benefit I derived therefrom proved incalculable in years to come. With my determination, I could master the theoretical part of the language. What I needed most was much oral reading and I had so much of that and of fluent conversation that, a few years later, in 1898, I began to teach French in Indiana.

Sometime that fall, Professor Howland, of the University of Chicago, came to Western Springs to deliver a lecture on Monaco, Monte Carlo and San Marino. Madame Philippe suggested that I should not miss that lecture as it dealt with Italian life and would prove of interest to me. The professor was then in his thirties, an inspiring personality. His lecture was highly interesting. He often used Italian expressions, which pleased me very much, for it reminded me of my old home far away. At the end of the lecture, Madame Philippe introduced me to him. He told me in Italian that he was pleased to know there was in the audience someone from Italy. I later learned that the professor was making one thousand dollars a year. As compared with twelve dollars a month, that sounded to me like all the gold mines in Colorado and California.

Mrs. Eggleston, a cousin of Professor Howland, said to me one day, as I was tacking down her carpets, "Why, Frank, of course, you can go to college and make good. We have a friend in Chicago who began to study law when he was forty and he is now a successful lawyer."

The meeting of Professor Howland had set me thinking seriously. "I must learn English and learn it well, for I need that as a background," said I to myself, and studied deep into the night.

One day a man over fifty was shoveling coal into Mrs. Hoffman's basement. He was just an ordinary Irish tramp, in spite of the fact that he had been a student at the University of Notre Dame, Indiana. Someone pointed out to me that there was no use striving for a higher education when that fellow, despite his university training, was shoveling coal, but that comment did not deter me from my set purpose.

On another occasion, we were making hay on the south side not far from the Western Springs depot. Andy Gustafson, an emigrated Swede, was on the top of the hayrack, stamping down and distributing the hay which I pitched up to him from the ground. Said Andy, "Frank, de ye blieve in an ejication." I told him I did. "Well," said he, "an ejication nowadays ain't much account. Ye can make as good a livin' without an ejication." But neither did Andy's wholesome dissuasion influence me. I am perfectly convinced there never was a time when a man could not use an education to advantage. The very feeling of being educated makes one strong in the face of all adversities!

Sometime in 1895, Principal Edgar suggested to me that, if I aspired to a higher education, I could do no better than go to Valparaiso, Indiana, to study at the Northern Indiana Normal school, where there were no entrance requirements and where ambitious young men and women with limited means could get an education and prepare for life. In two years I could get my Bachelor of Science degree and in three years I could get my Bachelor of Arts degree. He even mentioned that I might take up dentistry and that my languages in a city like Chicago would help me secure an abundant clientele. I was determined to get a general education, whatever I was going to do next.

During these few years I had saved as much as I could. I sent some money home, three or four hundred dollars, and put some aside to pay my expenses through school. It is with deep regret that I state here that Principal Edgar, in whom I placed the greatest confidence, betrayed me. He borrowed two hundred and seventy-five dollars from me, promised to pay it back with interest at six per cent, as I would need it to pay my expenses at college and then, intentionally or unintentionally—or, I think, due to lax moral and ethical standards—he never paid it back.

I saw Principal Edgar in Davenport, Iowa, in 1913. He was lecturer, preacher, teacher and poet—beware! From his mode of thinking, he had suggested that I go to college, and two hundred and seventy-five dollars was not too much as commission! I leave it to the judgment of the reader if that was nice for a man who read the Holy Bible before beginning the recitation in the morning at school.

In 1896, Victor Hinshaw, a teacher of dramatic art, with studio in Chicago, came with his wife to live for some months in Western Springs. I took a few lessons in elocution from this young man, who in bodily make-up, in general appearance and in brilliancy in his chosen field, was an inspiration to the listener. He first taught me this important principle in public speaking, "Speak clearly, if you speak at all; carve every word before you let it fall."

Years later, in London, England, I reaped the benefits of this lesson. Miss Annie Jones asked, "Why is it, Mr. Ventresca, that we understand everything you say, whereas we cannot understand the native Americans when they speak English to us?" My answer was that I was a teacher of languages and took pains in the choice of words and in pronouncing them clearly.

It was during this time and in Western Springs that Professor Victor Hinshaw introduced me to his brother, Professor W. W. Hinshaw, for many years a vocal teacher in Chicago, and the efficient Head of the Conservatory of Music of the Northern Indiana Normal School.

Young Victor introduced me as a young Italian full of pep and ambition, who was planning to land in Valparaiso by September of that year. Professor Hinshaw, who was taking training from an Italian grand opera coach in Chicago, Professor Marescalchi, said to me, "Frank, if you come to Valparaiso, I want you to teach Italian to my pupils for me." I am sure I was tickled pink to hear that, and I must have answered that I would consider it a privilege to teach my mother tongue to his pupils.

As a matter of fact, not only did I teach Italian to his pupils, but was also privileged to help him a little bit, and I wish I had had an opportunity to help him more. He was always busy teaching and coaching the chapel choir (to which I belonged) and preparing the operetta "The Captain of the Pinafore" (to which I also belonged). In subsequent years I have occasionally entertained my classes by singing:

I am the Captain of the Pinafore,
And a right good captain, too! I am
very, very good,
    And be it understood,
    I command a right good crew! etc.

In the meantime in Western Springs I joined the Glee Club, consisting of ten or twelve young men I knew, and directed by Professor Frank Perry, a University of Michigan graduate and the son of the Congregational minister. We learned by heart:

The merry month of May is here,
And all is clear and bright, etc.

also,

I see my love at the window, la, la.
Look, you can see her now, etc.

And when the end of the season came and mention was made of the Glee Club in the local paper, there was the statement that Frank Ventresca "had held his own."

In June 1896, the graduating class gave a one-act play for community entertainment. As there were not enough qualified pupils to complete the cast, a few were taken from the seventh grade; I was one of them. I was supposed to be an Irishman, the servant of the family, who spoke very broken English. I just filled the bill. That was my first experience on the stage.

I must have acted very awkwardly, indeed, but I did my best. A few people who knew me, thinking a little boosting would do me good, went so far as to congratulate me. All I can remember is that I, to show my genuine willingness, kept on repeating: "At yer sarvice! At yer sarvice!"

That happened forty-one years ago in the beautiful stone schoolhouse, standing at the corner of Grand Avenue and Chestnut Street, Western Springs, Illinois. It is the same school which my wife attended a few years later, as a first-grader. It is the same school which my daughter and my son have attended during the last decade. I love the place. It has played a major role in my life. It is the birthplace of my renaissance.

The Torture of the Soul

∾ *Louis Forgione*

Babylon, New York, June 21, 1896–Brooklyn, New York, July 1968

Undoubtedly one of the most interesting and complex Italian American authors flourishing in the 1920s, Louis Forgione is also one of the most mysterious. Biographical data regarding him are very scanty, and almost all that is known was published in the *Carroccio*, the periodical of Agostino De Biasi, with whom Forgione corresponded between 1922 and 1924, and who published his poetic and dramaturgical texts in English. De Biasi identified him as a naval engineer of notable success, active in the zone of New York, a position he obtained at the price of great family and personal sacrifices. Forgione had probably been a friend of Pascal D'Angelo, also by virtue of their common Abruzzian ancestry: his mother, in fact, was probably from Sulmona. The origins of his father are not known, though he was probably from Avellino. Also probable is that Forgione was an Italian American of the second generation (an opinion held by Olga Peragallo).

In the Italian American canon, Forgione is remembered for three novels published within the span of only four years by Dutton: *Reamer Lou* (1924), *The Men of Silence* (1928), and *The River Between* (1928). Before these three notable proofs, there were poetic essays published in *Carroccio*. Peragallo rightfully considers the essays "of mediocre literary value." Apparently—and inexplicably—there are no references to further works with the exception of his English translation, from about 1935, of the libretto written by Armando Romano for an obscure opera, *The Gilded Gate*, put to music by Alberto Bimboni.

His debut novel, *Reamer Lou*, could, at least in part, be autobiographical, since it narrates the story of a young son of Italians working in the navy shipyards of

Staten Island. The labor is hard, and the environment is rough, subject to explosions of violence and fostering hazardous games, alcoholism, and women of bad repute. Forgione seizes upon the opportunity to create a credible picture of the conditions of the life of the immigrant laborers; but in a manner contrary to that of John Fante, who some ten years later would apply himself to a vivacious, and grotesque, treatment of the material in the pages of *The Road to Los Angeles* dedicated to fish conservation in California, Forgione chooses the road of a sententious morality that encumbers the development of the narrative and limits its strength.

More successful was *The Men of Silence,* a book that Fred Gardaphé places among those that conceptually more than chronologically arrived at the Italian American tradition through the creation of the heroic figure of the godfather-gangster as the key of an identity that acts as a bridge between Italy and America. From another standpoint, this book is also the least American of Forgione's works, starting from the moment when it relates the happenings of the celebrated Cuocolo trial held in Viterbo, in 1911–12, against the heads of the Neapolitan camorra. If Italianism is the theme, the treatment appears to be very American. Olga Peragallo asserted that the story was "as exciting and gripping as any fictional bestseller mystery of to-day." Starting with the title, she reveals how the book draws out its themes, like those tied to the criminal code of solidarity, which would then meet with great success not only literarily but also in the American imagination.

However, perhaps the book that represents Forgione's artistic personality most fully is *The River Between.* The novel is set in a community of Sicilians in the tenements of the Palisades, on the west bank of the Hudson River, in New Jersey, which the river separates from the dazzling lights and richness of Manhattan. It treats of a painful generational episode, involving the old man Demetrio Lyba, the big leonine *padrone* of a past time, made up of the same volcanic substance as that of his natal Lipari Islands. Demetrio is becoming blind and half-mad and is losing his former domination of the workers and of his own son, Oreste, as well as his fierceness, and his paternal feelings. Oreste is married to Rose (the most memorable personage in the book), a young woman with a much larger perspective than the narrow colonial horizon, and who has left the house because of her very bad relations with Demetrio. But suddenly Rose returns to the Palisades, gladly received by her husband, despite her unconventional behavior. However, when Demetrio learns of it, and upon ascertaining that his son now holds full control over the property once his, he decides to leave. He will become a graybeard, a vagabond. But destiny, with a coup de théâtre reminiscent of the old Italian American serial stories, predetermines that he should meet Rose, who in the meanwhile has left Oreste again and become a prostitute, rushing into a state of irremediable brutalization. In a dramatic finale, Rose brings Demetrio back to the Palisades, and despite his insistence, she resumes the lonely road of the city. The tragedy is consummated in the old house of the patriarch. Demetrio routs the aggressors—his ex-employees—who have stabbed Oreste. But he cries over the body of his son, whom he never really understood, supplicating him to believe that never, never had he been an enemy; meanwhile, all about him, the house is burning.

In the plot, Rose Basile Green has read the relations between Rose and Demetrio in terms of a typical paradigm of migration: conflict, isolation, and assimilation, leaving Oreste out, since he has not been touched by any "internal change." Certainly, Rose, who describes herself as, "the noisy 'Americanized' brat of a plodding 'Wop,'" represents America—that is, complete Americanization and the consequent negation of the world of her origin, a circumstance well underscored by her heavily idiomatic manner of expressing herself. Demetrio remains an archaic and distant force; and despite the reconciliation between the two, in between them, separating them, is always the river.

The novel also includes a series of minor personages, among whom Serafina, daughter of the *padrone* Ntoni. Despite being married to Renato, Serafina is secretly in love with Oreste and is therefore the rival of Rose. Effectively, the whole novel is conducted on a note of tragic solemnity. The same language, adopted especially in the initial part, maintains a tone, a patina, of persistent affectation, which suggests not a possible ingenuousness on the part of the author, but rather the contrary. To detach this drama of emigration from its ascertainable historic context and remove it to the rarefied atmosphere of an ancient Greek tragedy, would, with some imagination, suggest an affinity with Arthur Miller's *A View from the Bridge*.

ESSENTIAL BIBLIOGRAPHY

Anonimo, "I Poeti del Carroccio," in *Il Carroccio* (New York), 17 (1923): 125; Basile Green 1974, 81–85; Gardaphé 1996, 118; Peragallo 1949, 105–108.

Her one delectation now was to torture Serafina, to behold green in the lovely woman's eyes. Viciously, mercilessly, Rose proceeded to vent her spite upon Renato's wife.

As a rule, Rose and her husband made very little display of affection, usually addressing one another with "Hey, say, hello, ho." Serafina, instead, stepped out of her way to demonstrate dutiful love for Renato. Her words were a smear, honeyed, golden, spurious, "Dearest love, *carino*, sweetheart. . . ."

But when Serafina was present Rose outdid the enchantress, assailing Oreste with affectionate language, cooing noisily, "Sweetest boy! Angel! Honeybug!"

Usually the big husband, grinning good-naturedly, would respond to the amorous assault. Twining arms around his neck, drawing his head down, she would kiss him loudly on the lips . . . smack! smack! . . . again and again . . . whereupon Serafina, white-faced, in a huff, invariably retreated to the Purgatory of her room. How Renato's wife must have suffered during those terrible days! At times there seemed to hover around her a sense of those pale white souls of passion moaning and writhing, like mists of spring on the grass, torn by every breeze, born only to be wounded, gnashed and finally scattered to the four winds.

In her set purpose of torturing this lovely, passionate woman, Rose spent many an otherwise tedious afternoon plotting and planning.

The Lyba household was invited en masse, late in September, to the wedding of a truck driver who had formerly worked for Oreste. As Rose would say afterwards, it was the "dopiest, dullest excuse for a party" she had ever been inveigled into. The liveliest thing they played was a mazurka. The dancers bobbed up and down, in peculiar old-country style, separated, sweating, without that soft swaying together of limb to limb, voluptuous, exquisite, resolving existence into a similar rhythmic purpose, which Rose had learned to love so well.

Serafina came too. All she did was to stand for an instant in the doorway, tall and gleaming in the passionate whiteness of her robe, and one thought purple things. She had twined large yellow flowers in her hair and they gleamed in mystic contrast to her eyes. On a second glance, however, one noticed that her dress was of cheap stuff, that she was, after all, nothing more than a menial's wife. And the flowers, what were they but a few black-eyed susans plucked from the edge of the cliff behind the house?

The dance dragged on. So disgusted was Rose that she didn't feel it worth-while annoying Serafina. She sat to one side and munched some sticky pink pastry, licking the cream from her fingers, listened to the doleful music, and grinned when Oreste danced a lumbering round with the lithe daughter of Ntoni.

When he came home the following night, they stood for a moment staring at one another like enemies. First glancing peculiarly, almost sharply, into her eyes, the husband mumbled, yawning, "I'm tired—damn tired." Pulling off his boots he threw them into a corner.

She watched him as he sprawled on the bed and her stomach turned.

"Isn't dinner ready?" he grumbled, all at once, shifting to his side and yawning at her.

Rose, leaning against the bureau, had fallen into a reverie.

Aroused, she asked sharply, "What are you going to do—sleep or eat?"

"I'm just resting a moment. Get something ready."

Neatly, deftly, the little wife set the table. He sprawled, from the bed, stretched his limbs, yawning again, ho-hum, sank into a chair, gulped all the food she placed before him, got up, tumbled back on the bed . . . and in an instant he was snoring.

How could she stand this any longer? She remained staring at the big fellow as he slept noisily, his massive limbs thrown out on the coverlet. An impulse, like a whirl of dust that dies within itself, shook her for a moment. Was she chained to this creature for the rest of her life? What kind of a future did such an existence promise her? This husband of hers was always so quiet, so plodding, so dull, so childishly moral! She sighed, her nerves quivering. It wasn't that he tried to hurt her—far from it. Oreste had noticed the change in his wife and had sought in many simple ways to please her. And it was because of this fact, because of his evident pains to be kind and considerate, that Rose's nerves were on edge. She understood it now: he didn't—couldn't possibly—care for her; his attitude toward her was nothing but pity, nothing but charity adulterated with a little passion. She was a beggar in his house—and worse—worse still!

All at once, frantically, angrily, Rose lurched toward the bed. She grabbed his big shoulders and shook them vigorously, madly. At the same time, from her lips lowered to his ears, escaped that metallic voice which seemed to ring at times from the black, rebellious depths of her being, "Wake up! Wake up! Why—God!—Why don't you do something bad? You—always trying to be so kind, so damn goody-goody . . . why don't you be a little human? Why don't you do something bad? Why—God!—Why don't you act real mean sometimes? . . . Why don't you even put me out?" and blabbering incoherently, Rose buried her face in the bed.

"Ww–w–what's–happened?" Oreste sat bolt upright. In surprise he stared at her.

She was panting, shaking her head, the curls all twisted like the fingers of drowned slaves. "I don't know—I don't know. At times I think you are too darned goody-goody, too darned considerate . . . I don't understand it myself—but— God!—I don't know . . . I don't know . . . I—" Stopping abruptly, she raised her head and fixed brilliant eyes on him, the points of which shining gold, should have needled his very soul.

But the big, tired man was unable to understand. At first he thought she desired a little caressing; the wildness of her language, however, deterred him. So he merely stared at her, falling half asleep again, his lips parted and ready to curl into a smile . . . for Oreste had suddenly concluded that this outburst out of her tortured soul was simply a jest!

Miracle

Giuseppe Cautela

Orta Nova (Foggia), Italy, June 8, 1883–June 12, 1951

Giuseppe Cautela's biography is another typical romance of the self-taught man. Orphaned at six years old, his father a shoemaker, Giuseppe was entrusted to the harsh care of a maternal uncle. He was able to attend elementary school up to the third grade, when the second husband of his mother decided to interrupt his studies and place him in a shoemaker's shop. His stepfather, with whom Giuseppe had very difficult relations, subsequently decided to bring the family to America, and in 1897, Cautela arrived in New York, where he worked as an apprentice to a barber and for three months succeeded, with great effort, in attending night school. He then returned to Italy during World War I and served three years in the infantry.

Returning to America, he began his first literary attempts, in Italian. Olga Peragallo affirms that at the end of four years, he succeeded in composing a comedy, which however had no result. Discouraged, Cautela decided not to write any more and returned to his trade as a barber, but was tempted anew by literature, and this time he made an effort to write in English, but on Italian American themes. Thanks to the support of American friends, he succeeded in publishing some poems, then essays and articles, in important reviews, such as *The American Mercury* of H. L. Mencken and *Plain Talk*. He also contributed to periodicals in the Italian language, in particular, *Americolo*. In 1925, he debuted as a narrator with the novel, *Moon Harvest*, followed by various other novels (Peragallo cites two: *Everything Goes By*, 1926, and *Half Moon Diggers*, 1927), but *Moon Harvest* remains his only published book.

A resident of the Bronx, Cautela married a woman from Rimini, who died in 1934 after bearing five children. Always straitened financially, he continued to practice the barber's trade, which inspired the unpublished novel *Half Moon Diggers* ("the first book ever written about life as it unfolds in that picturesque American institution, the modern barber shop," Peragallo).

The novel *Moon Harvest* narrates the vicissitudes of Romualdo and his wife Maria, who have come to America right from Orta Nova. In the new social context, the couple engages in a hard battle to survive and become used to the rhythms of an existence completely diverse from their city of origin. Romualdo succeeds in becoming integrated; Maria, whose adjustment is intensified by her responsibilities as a housewife and mother, remains in the past. Finally, her husband betrays her with Vincenza, an Italian American of second generation, with refined ways and cultural interests akin to those of Romualdo. Maria becomes the mute witness of the relations between the two; Romualdo is tormented by the split between his social and cultural integration and his feelings. And when his wife dies of a broken heart—almost a ritual sacrifice, a necessary and symbolic martyrdom—he refuses to marry Vincenza, deciding to return to Italy, though the reader intuits that before long, he will return to America, to that mode of life, that is now the only possible one for him.

The novel contains various autobiographical hints, especially in Cautela's emphatic description of Romualdo's efforts to adapt to the new language and culture, but also the emphasis on the inner struggle between nostalgia for the old roots and the desire to become integrated, a burning reflection that is interspersed through the whole book. In this sense, *Harvest Moon* represents one of the most convincing examples of the classic Italian American dilemma, as it is also representative of the more dramatic first phase of the search for an identity. And it sends a very bitter message, demonstrating that in actuality this identity is impossible and is resolved rather in a condition of inextricable restlessness.

The bitter balance of an experience described by Romualdo seems much more authentic when applied to the personal life of the writer, to whom it was not conceded to thoroughly exploit the potential literary possibilities of that conflictive situation, as others could. Fante, for example, centers the very narrative on that conflict, like an obsession that far from seldom touches upon the picturesque, the grotesque, the comic, even these vivid elements of that psychologically disturbed portrait.

In his stories, however, Cautela reveals that he knew these tones and how to avail himself of them, even if with a more firm moral adhesion to the world of his Italian colonists and with frequent insertions of reflections, also critical, on the tenacity of certain cultural and behavioral survivals, by now void of sense in the American context. In sum, being and feeling himself part of the world, Cautela cannot describe it without intense participation between himself and his personages; he cannot put the distance possible for a writer of the second generation. His role is that of a witness, a valuable witness, as illustrated by the revealing descriptions offered by his essays, for example, on the Italian quarter in Gravesend Bay, in Brooklyn, or on life in the Bowery, and, in particular, the Italian theater in New York.

The following story, "Miracle," was originally written in English.

ESSENTIAL BIBLIOGRAPHY

Basile Green 1974, 68–71; Flamma 1936, 76; Marazzi 2007c; Peragallo 1949, 41–44.

༄

One morning at ten o'clock several years ago a father and his daughter of sixteen walked into the office of Dr. Sante Naccarati.

Dr. Naccarati met death last summer in an automobile accident while traveling through the Abruzzi mountains. Every year during the summer he returned to Europe for study and recreation, principally for study. He was a great neurologist and highly cultured, combining two rare qualities in a doctor, the scientific and the artistic. Where his scientific knowledge could not guide him, his artistic intuition brought marvelous results. He was tall and slender, and I often thought of him as a kind of rod that could sense the most imperceptible disturbances. One became quiet, soothed, in that modest studio of his on Park Avenue. There was understanding gentleness in this man of 35 who listened to you sympathetically, smiling, and with that great indulgence that comes only to those who have the gift of meditation.

Though the girl was but sixteen, she looked twenty. She was like a rose in full bloom. She entered the doctor's office and sat in a corner, never raising her eyes, as if ashamed of her physical exuberance. She had tried with a tight bodice but in vain to flatten her generously developed breasts. She had rich, golden hair. Her father remained standing.

"Have a seat, please," the doctor said; but the man did not sit down. He was too impatient for sitting. In the last six months he had been in a dozen doctors' offices. It had cost him a tremendous amount of the money he had made in real estate; worse yet, he had lost faith in doctors, so much so that he had heeded the pleas of ignorant women friends of his wife to allow his daughter to go to witch doctors and faith healers. Francesco Traisci was not over-intelligent himself. He said so, too, whenever he felt that people had taken advantage of his good nature. The doctor invited him to sit down a second time. He took a seat reluctantly.

"Signor Traisci, please tell me, what is the matter with your child? Her name is Rosa, I believe."

"Yes, sir," answered Signor Traisci, eagerly. "She began to act that way about six months ago."

"You mean she became melancholy?"

"Yes."

The doctor apparently was observing Rosa more than he was listening to her father.

"Do you know of anything that might have happened to her?"

Rosa lifted her head a little and then looked at the floor again.

"No. That's just it. I don't know of anything that happened to her."

"Does she go to school now?"

"No, we have not sent her since she has not been well. She shuts herself up in her room, and there she prays all day on her knees before a picture of the Madonna."

"What do you say, Rosa when you pray?" the doctor asked her quickly.

Rosa was startled and for a minute looked at the doctor, then lowered her gaze again. He asked her no more questions. He called her over, watching her with a far-off gaze as she walked across the room from him; and when she stopped near him he lifted her lids and examined her eyes. Then he began to talk on different subjects that apparently had nothing to do with the patient before him. Signor Traisci began to move uncomfortably in his chair. He soon got up, thinking that he was about to be skinned out of ten or twenty dollars without any result, when the doctor said to his daughter, "Do you mind, Rosa, looking at the pictures in the next room while I write a prescription for you?"

The girl went out, escorted by the doctor; he closed the door behind her. Then he turned to her father.

"Signor Traisci," he began, "do not be offended if I touch a delicate subject in regard to your daughter. She is a very precocious child. Our girls develop early, and through this exuberant flowering of nature, a little disturbance very often is the cause of a case like your daughter's. She needs no medicine, but get her out as much as possible. If she were older, I would say marry her as quickly as possible." Signor Traisci made a sign of disbelief. "But we can afford to wait. She will get over it slowly. You need not to be alarmed. The less she is left alone the better. You must have lots of patience with her."

Signor Traisci returned home more dejected than ever.

"What did the doctor say?" his wife asked.

"I told you those doctors don't know anything." He answered angrily.

"Did he give her any medicine?"

"No. I believe he's honest, though. He told me something that makes me think that maybe he's right." He went over and closed the door of his room.

"Do you think," he asked timidly, "that Rosa loves Dominick?"

His wife flushed. "It may be possible, but he has never encouraged her. Dominick is the despair of his father, who has been trying to marry him for the last three years."

"Don't you think he's old enough?"

"Yes, but what can you do if he does not want to?"

"His father asked me about Rosa."

"Well?"

"The doctor told me that if Rosa were older it would be better to marry her."

"Is that so?" exclaimed Signora Maria, not knowing exactly what she meant.

"Why?" countered her husband. "Does it sound so strange to you? I felt the same way when the doctor first told me, but then upon reflection. . . ."

"And you told me the doctor knew nothing. I think he talks sense. My mother often told me . . . whenever a girl got melancholy in the old country the parents went off and married her right away. But Rosa is only a child."

Signor Traisci began to scratch his head. He did not like to think long on one subject.

"Give me a cup of coffee, please," he said to his wife.

Signora Maria, large and heavy, walked slowly toward the kitchen.

During the daytime Thompson Street from Bleecker to Spring Streets, New York City, is a food market. Pushcarts from early morning line up both sides of the street. Fresh vegetables of all kinds, many imported and grown by Italian farmers, like chicory and broccoli, are sold. Fruits of all descriptions fill baskets. Fish kept in excellent condition make you stop and wonder. And then Roman cheese, the best for macaroni. And cheese from Moliterno and other villages of Potenza, which, according to experts, is better than the Roman. Also you can buy tasty *provolone* if you have good wine to wash it down. Every American should eat *provolone*. It is cheese made for men and women who are not afraid of a sharp bite on the tongue. If you prefer a perfumed aristocratic taste, but substantial and wholesome, ask for *caciocavallo*. Ground up, goes well on the minestrone and on thick soups.

Italian housewives come out with baskets and bags to do their marketing. To them it is an adventure, it is a theatre more alive that any other. They stop on street corners to chat with friends, while children tug at their dresses. It is family matters they talk about, principally of marriages and deaths. If a young daughter happens to be along, the first question put to her mother is, "When are you going to marry her? Hasn't she a sweetheart?"

And the girl blushes, exclaiming in English, "My God, give me a chance. You people always talk of the same thing."

Then comes the haggling over prices with the pushcart men. All the Italian dialects are heard. The Sicilians predominate in the fruit and fish trade. They are courteous; they give you a princely feeling while they address you, and their language sounds like bits of classic poetry. The Neapolitan sells a little of everything. His language is sweet, to soothe and charm the listener. He sings his merchandise, he is full of melody; but he is also a born clown. His remarks provoke laughter and many times sharp retorts from his customers.

So up till noon in Thompson Street, also in Mulberry Street and Elizabeth Street, life is picturesque. The air is full of sounds not totally Italian, modified by American customs and climate and mode of living.

But at night it is different. I went there while Thompson Street was celebrating the Festa of the Madonna. What strange conflicts arose in my mind! You simply cannot revive certain traditions. The feeling is not there, the sky is not there, the cool breeze of the evening relieving the enervating warm air of the afternoon with its buzz of flies, is not there. Better, much better, let those memories die sadly within you than let them clash stridently against an atmosphere of jazz.

The odors of decaying vegetables, fish, fruit, and cheese left by pushcarts in the street created a terrible stench. The street was littered with broken boxes and paper bags, while above shone the modern arched decorations of red, white, green, and blue electric lights. For the first time I saw how ghastly and ugly and forbidding those rusty brick tenement houses are. People were at the windows, on the balconies, on the sidewalks, and in the street. You had to elbow your way through. I followed the committee of the Festa; they were making the money collections from the storekeepers. I began to envy the nonchalant air that some of my people keep to their dying day even in a foreign land. We stopped before a store that was neither a cafe nor a restaurant. Four small square tables covered with much-used oilcloth attracted my attention against the nudity of the dirty green walls. Seated around little tables were customers playing cards. They seemed to belong to another world. They still had Italy on their faces. What went on around them did not interest them. The proprietor was standing behind a small counter on which were a few bottles of dark, green and yellow liquids. A tripod gas-stove with a hissing burner kept the coffee-pot steaming at full force. After a few greetings intermingled with jokes, the proprietor, with a small black mustache and shining white teeth, gave his contribution.

We passed on to a grocery store. A young mother, fagged by the heat, sat by the entrance. Her breast was beautifully and innocently bare. Her pale two-month-old baby girl lay asleep on her knees. I looked into the store where on the marble counter lay in one glorious confusion bread, salami, cheese, *provolone*, *caciocavallo*, olives, sardines, *pepperoni*, and macaroni. There was a delicious aroma coming from the shop. Right against the counter was the baby-carriage. The boss was out.

We approached an undertaker's place, but for some reason the committee did not go in.

Finally we came to the real-estate office of Signor Francesco Traisci. The committee found him dejectedly seated behind his desk.

"*Buona sera, Signor Traisci, buona sera, buona sera*," sounded in chorus the committee.

"*Signori, buona sera.*" gravely answered Signor Traisci.

"How is your daughter, Signor Traisci?" asked the oldest member of the committee. He came from the same town that Signor Traisci did, and with them it was all a family matter.

"No better, Rocco," Signor Traisci answered sadly. The other members of the committee assumed a sympathetic expression.

"But don't they know what is the matter with her?" persisted Rocco.

"No one knows, except our God in heaven," said Signor Traisci tragically.

"*Ma come!*" exclaimed another member of the committee, "what has become of all the modern medical science?" Signor Traisci lifted his eyebrows and shrugged his shoulders, then with deep significance he almost whispered, "Yesterday I went to see a great doctor!"

"What's his name?" interrupted Rocco.

"Naccarati. He said something . . . I cannot repeat."

The members of the committee looked scowlingly at one another.

"It must have cost you a world of money," said Rocco.

"Yes. I have tried everything—even the witch doctors."

"Oh, those I don't believe*: mi perdonate, ma. . . .*" interrupted the youngest member of the committee.

"But a father will try anything," interjected Rocco.

"True, true, *ma io non ci credo.*"

"I am still paying my bill to him; five hundred dollars, *miei cari signori*," finished Signor Traisci. They all scowled.

"Why don't you make a last appeal to the Madonna?" pleaded Rocco.

"That I want to do tonight when her glorious image will be borne in procession," said Francesco with fervent hope.

There were those who, still alive with traditions of similar celebrations in Italy, displayed their red, yellow, crimson, violet, blue, cream, and green silk coverlets from their balconies. The American and Italian flags cut into the gay array with their ordinate arrangement of colors. Venetian and Chinese lanterns were strung from windows to balconies and fire-escapes, and people looked down to the street from everywhere. As in Italy, relatives had come to see the *Festa Della Madonna dell' Immacolata Concezione*. They all stopped by the gaily decorated pushcarts to buy sweets, such as *torrone*, shelled almonds hanging like beads on strings, and nuts of all descriptions. And as in the Italian *Feste* of Italian villages, you saw the typical vendors of such merchandise. Faces like classic Italian madonnas with hair parted in the middle, straight delicate noses, black soft eyes and a sweet mouth. One has to be beautiful even in selling sweets. A jolly cry came now and then from a fat, round, dirty-faced vendor of watermelons. He had a good voice, a little rusty from too much hawking. "Meloos . . . Mellmellloooni . . . Mello . . . Mello . . . Mello."

The café was crowded. Delicious aromatic smells floated on to the sidewalks. *Spumoni* paste, *dolci*, made just for one sweet bite, and then black thick coffee with a reviving something in it.

Before the procession the musicians came in for un *sorbetto* or *una granatina*. And the *cameriere*, obsequious, came and went with a smile on his lips. A gentleman came in with a basket full of arms, legs, and hands made of wax, to be donated to the Madonna as an evidence of faith by those cripples who had been cured by miracles after many years of suffering.

A bugle call was the signal for the musicians to assemble. The procession was about to start. A big crowd was pushing toward the niche of the Madonna. This is unusual, a breaking away from tradition. In Italy a saint is never taken out from the church and placed in a niche on the street. Here American publicity has had something to do with it. The niche was made of cardboard nailed on wooden slats and covered with white paper.

This was decorated with silver hands and red trimmings. An immense red heart adorned the top. Another heart with a burst of sunrays formed the background of the niche. The effect was not so bad as might be imagined. The primitive ingenuity of the whole design had the divine touch of simplicity that can be found in anyone who has a feeling for art. Flowers in great quantity gave a fresh vivid softening effect. Against all this came a rustic note of contrast in the plain wooden bench on which were burning huge candles.

The Madonna was taken out of the niche by four members of the committee *della Festa*. Swaying back and forth a little, they raised the Madonna to their shoulders. The band began to play the Chopin *Funeral March* and the procession started. Here everyone rushed forward. It soon became evident that the spectators lacked that respect, that feeling of awe that characterizes and holds in check people who participate in similar functions in Italy. Still, despite the confusion, there was evidence of a prearranged plan.

First came little girls, "the angels," all dressed in white, with veils and green wreaths on their heads. They all carried candles and some carried baskets of flowers, which were strewn along as they went. Then came members of the *Festa* with tricolored sashes across their chests and on the lapel of the jacket a badge with the button of the Madonna. Some of them tried to move back and forth, giving orders as Barsotti used to during his famous parades.

Now the offerings of the faithful to the Madonna. The statue came to a halt every few feet, while men and women pinned gold chains and watches, gold earrings, and bracelets on the silk dress of the saint. It was not long before the Madonna was entirely covered with gold and money bills.

Such was the spectacle when the figure came to a halt in front of Signor Francesco Traisci's real-estate office. The place was crowded with relatives and friends who had come from surrounding towns. Amilcare Cantatore, Francesco's lifelong friend and the father of Dominick, was also there. He kept a grocery store across the street. People hardly recognized him. He very seldom dressed in good clothes. His best dress-suit was his big white apron, and his chief assets a thick head of black curly hair parted on the side and a flowing long mustache. He was rather fat and excitable, becoming very red in the face as he spoke loudly, holding his hands on the counter. His son Dominick resembled him only in looks. He spoke very little, never got excited; and his answer to an angry customer was a soft whistle, which irritated his father so that he ran out of the store to seek relief in Signor Traisci's office.

Dominick was not present. Rosa was seated in a corner, brooding. Her mother had besought her earnestly. "Pray, child, pray the Madonna. She will make you get well." But Rosa tonight was in no praying-mood. She looked like a smoldering fire. Every few minutes she lifted her head, looking across the street right into the grocery store of Amilcare Cantatore, where Dominick was waiting on customers.

Signor Traisci, emotional as he was, when he heard the first strains of the music became deeply affected. Tears began to roll down his cheeks, and his friends tried to console him. People from outside were heard to say:

"Signor Traisci is going to give his gift to the Madonna."

"His daughter, Rose, is sick."

"That big fat thing! She's no more sick than you are."

"She was so stupid at school!"

"What has that to do with it?"

"I know what is the matter with her," said a blonde to a friend. "She's in love with Dominick."

"Go on!"

"Yes, I'm telling you."

Signor Traisci came out, led by his friends. He walked as if going to a sacrifice. His expression showed the importance of the act he was about to perform. Members of the committee made a way for him. As he came near the Madonna, he bowed his head, said a few words of prayer. Then he took out of his pocket a thousand-dollar bill and pinned it on the breast of the Madonna.

The priest who assisted at the ceremony from under the baldachin gave his benediction, and the senior member of the committee for the *Festa* said: "May the Madonna grant you your wish. Her grace is unlimited."

"A thousand dollars he gave!"

"My God!"

"*Ma queste son cose d'altro mondo, l'avesse dato ai poveri,*" were the remarks heard by the people.

The return of the Madonna to the niche was a triumph. A surprise was in store for the spectators. The realistic imagination of Rocco, senior member of the committee, had prevailed in convincing his co-workers to include a stunt in the program.

At the return of the Madonna to her niche, a real angel in flesh and bones would welcome her back by sliding on a wire strung from a balcony opposite the niche. The pushing, expectant crowd saw a girl of about sixteen years dressed in white with wings made of papier-mâché. A wreath of white roses circled her head of flowing black hair. An angel she appeared really—erect on the balcony as if ready to fly.

The people watched breathlessly as she was lifted out of the balcony and held in midair by four strong members of the *Festa*. An iron wheel, like that of a clothes-line, was attached to a stout strap around her waist. Slowly and uncertainly the angel began to descend, guided by ropes from her waist, her feet gradually released by the men on the fire-escape.

"Oh, how beautiful!" women began to exclaim. A young man with musical traditions, to the delight of his friends, began to sing *con mezza voce*: "*O bell Angiolo inamorato.*" As it turned out, the angel was really in love.

"My God, I hope the wire will not snap like it did to that girl who broke her leg two years ago," said a young woman.

"Oh, shut up, you make me nervous!" shouted her friend.

The angel arrived safely on the ground and knelt before the Madonna. The people gave release to their nervous tension by bursting into wild applause.

It may seem strange to learn that the angel really flew away. For two days the girl could not be found. She had run away with her sweetheart.

"You could not do any more than you have done, Francesco," remarked Amilcare Cantatore. "You have done your duty."

Then they all went upstairs to have dinner. While they were eating the band began to play the concerto. The first piece was *Mefistofele*. The cornet sounded like an echo. During intermission, the musicians took refreshments that had been brought to them by one of the committee. Then a placard was hung announcing that *Faust* would be the next number.

"The maestro must be in sympathy with the devils," commented the young man with the musical traditions. The appearance of the maestro was anything but Mephistophelian. Nor did he show any musical sensitiveness. His broad shoulders and thick neck denoted the strength of a bull. But he became transformed the minute he called his musicians to attention. Then it became evident that music to him was like a bottle of generous wine. He did not rush to gulp it down like a coarse drinker. He admired its color, intensely sniffed its fragrance and slowly sipped it like the maestro that he was. He came from Abruzzi, where strength goes with gentleness.

The street was not so crowded now. It was getting late, and the *Festa* was assuming more spiritual significance. The Madonna looked thoughtful, sweet and resigned in her niche. I gathered immense strength looking at her. A young woman, tired from her daily toil, had brought her white pillow to the window-ledge and laid her dark head on it. For a night the factory could be forgotten.

The band began to play *Faust*. The audience was composed of the typical music-lovers you see in all the piazzas of the little cities of Italy. When the band plays they don't eat, they don't sleep; the world is forgotten. Silence is imperative. But it was different in Thompson Street. A yellow and red roadster occupied by a half-dozen youths, hatless and in shirt-sleeves, came tooting down the street right in the middle of Mephistopheles' serenade. It stopped a few doors away from the niche of the Madonna. An old couple seated alongside the niche, who held the tray for the offerings, looked on the boastful young generation with a deeply resigned expression. The yellow and red roadster repeated the same performance three times.

And then during the Garden scene the street-cleaning department intervened. The auto sprinkler tank came through the street, gushing water right and left, and the spell of *Faust* was broken by a fanfare of swearing from the audience.

Dominick Cantatore had been engaged to every eligible girl in Thompson Street. The list's exhaustion gave the older Cantatore a feeling of bitter disillusion and resentment. Most disappointing of all, his son did not encourage Rosa in the least though the girl had given him every opportunity. Adding to his humiliation now was the conviction that the girl was sick because of her love for Dominick. His anger knew no bounds the night of the *Festa* when Dominick failed to appear for dinner at the home of Signor Traisci. He had found it hard to excuse his absence when everyone had expected him. The music had stopped playing.

It was after twelve o'clock: when Amilcare Cantatore left Signor Traisci's home. He went directly to his store. Dominick was still selling *salame* to his customers. He saw his father enter in an ugly mood. Almost against his will he began to whistle softly, irritatingly. It seemed a provocation to the old man, and while Dominick's mind kept saying "Why don't you stop?" his father broke out, "Why did you not come to the dinner? Are you not a member of my family?"

Impulsively Dominick answered, "I am and I am not."

His father stared at him with mouth open. It was the first time his son had answered him like that.

"What—what do you mean, *corpo di Dio*," he said, angrily.

"Oh, just like that," his son said.

"Just like that?"

"Yes, just like that!"

"Well, you get out of here!" roared the old man. "I have been humiliated enough by you."

Dominick did not answer, nor did he move from behind the counter. He looked at his father as might a shy boy who had said something he had not wanted to say.

"And the house I gave to you on your birthday remains mine," thundered the old man.

Dominick raised his head and calmly said, "I don't see how you can do that. You can't do that."

"I'll show you," came back his father.

"Well, I'll tell you," began Dominick slowly, "The house does not belong either to you or to me. It belongs to my wife and to your two grandchildren."

Signor Amilcare Cantatore sat down on a bag of nuts and tried to wipe the sweat from his brow.

"Who—who did you marry?" he stammered finally.

"Now I'll show you," said Dominick with a smile. "Frances! Frances!" he called. Frances had arrived an hour ago from Brooklyn.

"Yes, Domenico," came a voice from behind the store. Frances came out with a boy and a girl; the boy four years old, blond and with deep blue eyes like his mother's, and the girl two, with dark curls and eyes like two black beads. Signor Amilcare Cantatore recognized in Frances a former school chum of his son, an Irish girl whom he had often chased away from his store a few years ago.

He rose, terrifically overcome by emotion.

"Signorina, oh, signora," he quickly corrected himself, "I welcome you into my family."

"Amilcare," called Dominick to his boy, "kiss grandpa!" Signor Cantatore did not know what to do, what with his daughter-in-law and his grandchildren.

He celebrated the event in a manner worthy of him. It recalled one of those feasts in which only people with heroic stomachs participated. He had relatives with him for a month, while every day the discussion of the subject continued unceasingly in the store. All the girls came in and poked fun at Dominick, and the old man gave presents to everyone.

But another thing happened that made Thompson Street hold its breath. Rosa, Rosa Traisci, whom medical doctors, witch doctors, faith healers, and priests had given up, suddenly got well. Soon after she learned the news of Dominick's marriage she began to show signs of improvement. She no longer shut herself up in her room praying to the Madonna for half a day at a time. Instead, she went out on the street to meet her friends again. Her parents watched her with apprehension, lest her moods of depression should return. At last they had to believe that Rosa was entirely well.

When the news of the cure got abroad, Thompson Street began to shout "Miracle! The Madonna has granted a miracle to Francesco Traisci!" And his home became a Mecca. Faithful people came from all over to see the girl who had been the object of such a miracle. And all wanted to know from her how she felt when the Madonna had granted her *la grazia*. Then it became apparent to Francesco Traisci that if he did not take his daughter away somewhere, she would get sick again. So he put a stop to the pilgrimage by sailing for Italy.

A Picture of 1907

Edward Corsi

Capestrano (L'Aquila), Italy, December 29, 1896–New York, New York, December 13, 1965

Edward Corsi was the oldest son of Filippo Corsi, a militant of Mazzinian persuasion and an enthusiastic supporter of the newspaper *La Democrazia*. Edward followed his father into exile in Switzerland before the latter expatriated the rest of the family. When his father was elected deputy in Tuscany, his son could reenter Italy with him. Filippo Corsi, however, died soon after of a heart attack, and the family was divided. Edward was sent to live with a paternal uncle in L'Aquila. His brother Giuseppe was sent to a college in Venice; he was destined to become a director of the INPS (Istituto Nazionale Previdenza Sociale). And his mother and two sisters settled in Sulmona with relatives. Some years later, his mother married another Corsi, a former army officer and distant relative of her first husband. Reunited, the family emigrated to America in 1906 and settled in Italian Harlem, in New York.

The beginnings of the new life were marked by misfortune: occasional work for the head of the family and a grave form of depression for the mother who, not quite two years later, returned to Italy and soon died. The sons worked and made an effort to contribute to the meager domestic budget, yet without interrupting their studies. Edward started to frequent the Harlem House, which at that time was called Home Garden, and later, La Guardia House. Home Garden, established by the Protestant missionary Anna C. Ruddy in 1908, was an important center of sociocultural activities and a veritable hub of prominent political personalities, among them Judge Salvatore Cotillo and Congressmen Vito Marcantonio and

Fiorello La Guardia. Corsi, who personally knew the people and problems of the quarter, later described his experiences there as an actual turning point in his life, the moment in which he became aware of a need to participate. As a result, he became the director of Home Garden, a duty he covered from 1926 through 1931, though he collaborated with that institution for practically all his life. Soon after, upon the nomination of Hoover, a Republican like himself, Corsi made the great leap and became the Commissioner of Immigration at Ellis Island.

Corsi was the right choice, a new countenance for a position of responsibility that up to then had been touched by repeated scandals. He worked at Ellis Island from 1931 to 1933. The next year, he went on to direct the Home Relief Bureau, the office providing emergency aid to meet the social problems of the Great Depression, where he remained until 1935. In this year, he published *In the Shadow of Liberty,* the book born from his experience at Ellis Island, and founded *La Settimana,* a bilingual newspaper publishing correspondence from the most influential Italian journalists in America, such as Amerigo Ruggiero of the *Stampa,* Beniamo De Ritis of the *Corriere della Sera* and then the *Corriere d'America,* and Alfonso Arbib-Costa, as well as prominent exponents of Italian American culture such as Angelo Patri.

Corsi had written for *Outlook* and the *New York World,* and until the 1920s was a correspondent for the *Carroccio* and *La Follia,* as well as for small colonial publications such as, in the 1950s, *Divagando,* and others connected to the literary Italian American marginalized world, like the Milanese journal *Il Convivio Letterario* of Filippo Fichera. Corsi was a brilliant and informed journalist. In full sympathy with most people in the Italian colony, he tolerated the Fascist regime. But it would be a mistake to attach excessive ideological significance to these choices, or, worse, to link them to activity to promote them, as was also indicated by Corsi, in particular, through a long series of radio broadcasts in 1941, treating cultivated themes on Italian and American history and culture. The texts were published successively in the *Follia,* and ultimately collected in the volume *Edoardo Corsi Parla* (1942).

Corsi's political career suffered a heavy loss in 1938, when he lost the election for senator. In 1950, he lost the election for mayor. From 1943 to 1954, he was head of the New York State Industrial Board, occupying himself with political issues pertaining to industry, and two years later, he became special assistant for immigration in the Eisenhower administration, encountering deeply contentious relations with Secretary of State Foster Dulles. Corsi discussed those relations in an article in *The Reporter,* the weekly of one of the most influential spokesmen for the Italian exiles, Max Ascoli. Giuseppe Prezzolini also discussed the subject in an article, "L'affare

Corsi," later republished in the book *I Trapiantati*, confirming that he had become of aware of Corsi and appreciated him as of the 1930s, when, as Martino Martazzi recently recorded, Prezzolini translated and published first in *Omnibus* and then in *Oggi* two passages from *In the Shadow of Liberty*.

Typical of a professional mediator between diverse cultures, Corsi, it seems, maintained equal relations within the colonial community and the more expansive landscapes of American culture and politics. On the cultural plane, his chosen field was never well defined, even if *In the Shadow of Liberty* remains his most important work. The book is dedicated to the history of immigration in the United States, a theme that inspired another book, *Paths to the New World: American Immigration Yesterday, Today, and Tomorrow* (1953). However, the *In Shadow of Liberty* is also, and above all, an autobiographical work. The book relates how Corsi put Ellis Island in order and his ideas on the most efficacious strategies to resolve the problems, but it dedicates much space to the human aspect. "Every person, black or white, in this country, is an immigrant descendant of immigrants," Corsi says very simply. His book, as an important multiethnic American writer, Louis Adamic, noted, is reparation for the sufferings and abuses endured by many hundreds of thousands of persons who passed through that fateful place.

ESSENTIAL BIBLIOGRAPHY

Corsi 1935; Marazzi 2001, 130–137; Peragallo 1949, 53–57; Prezzolini 1963, 376–381; Schiavo 1964–65 (article); obituary in *La Parola del Popolo* (Chicago) 16, no. 77 (February–March 1966).

Many friends and officials of the Immigration Services called at my office during the first few days after my arrival to take up my duties at Ellis Island.

One day, when the flood of visitors had subsided somewhat, and I was discussing various phases of the work with the Assistant Commissioner Byron H. Uhl, the conversation happened to turn to the year 1907.

"Who was here," I asked him, "when I came though the Island?"

"Well, I for one," he replied, laughing. "I'm nearly as old a fixture as the first buildings. I've been in the Service about forty years, you know."

"But an Italian immigrant boy coming through in 1907," I said, "surely wouldn't have seen *you*."

Again he smiled. "We couldn't see the individuals for the crowds we had in those days," he said. "But wait—Martocci! Why didn't I think of him before! He probably admitted your family."

Seeing my eager interest, he explained, "He's the same Italian interpreter we had when you came through the Island. Wouldn't you like to talk with him?"

A few days passed before I had the opportunity to see Frank Martocci. He came into my office and congratulated me in Italian, having already read in the papers of my appointment and my immigrant background. When I asked if he had escorted me personally into this country, he paused reflectively, going over in swift review his many years as Ellis Island. His merry dark eyes twinkling, he ran a stubby hand through his shock of iron-gray hair, which, despite the years, had not thinned. Finally he said,

"Of course I can't remember whether I inspected your family, but I can tell you that the millions of other Italians who came through Ellis Island and now live in America are glad to see you here."

I thanked him and we chatted for some time. Finally I said, "Tell me, what do you remember of those days when I came in? What were the conditions in those days?"

Eyes twinkling, he rubbed his hands together and leaned forward.

"We went to work, of course, from the Barge Office at the Battery. From there the ferryboat took most of the employees to Ellis Island at nine in the morning. Hundreds of other people were always eagerly awaiting and clamoring to get on the same boat. These were friends and relatives of immigrants expected during the day, or already being detained on the Island.

"Fortunately—I was a native Italian, knew the language, and had already been in the service a long time. This combination made me a sort of godsend to many of these people, who, recognizing my nationality, would seize me by the coat, by the arm, and even by the neck, and insist on following me everywhere I went, babbling out their problems and pleading for aid. I did my best to keep clear of them in a kindly way, but sometimes I couldn't help but lose my patience. Waiting for friends, brothers, mothers, fathers, or sisters, they looked at me so hopefully, so anxiously, that my sympathy for them was quite a strain on my nerves.

"Once at the Island, we employees had to plunge immediately into our work, for in those terrifically busy days whole boat loads of immigrants were waiting to be inspected every morning. They came from everywhere: from England, Germany, Russia, Italy, France, Greece and other countries.

"At quarantine, inspectors had already boarded the boats to examine the first- and second-class passengers. Those found eligible were landed at the pier. Many less fortunate, who were considered ineligible, were brought to Ellis Island, where they had to undergo the experience of being judged by the immigration authorities on the following day."

"How different the inspection routine must have been in those days," I mused.

"It certainly was," he answered, "I can well remember, for at that time I was in the registry department, assigned to decide the eligibility of aliens to land. To make things run fairly smoothly in that mixed crowd of poor, bewildered immigrants, we would tag them with numbers corresponding to numbers on their manifest, after they had been landed from the barges and taken into the building.

"Here, in the main building, they were lined up—a motley crowd in colorful costumes, all ill at ease and wondering what was to happen to them. Doctors then put them through their medical inspection, and whenever a case aroused suspicion, the alien was set aside in a cage apart from the rest, for all the world like a segregated animal, and his coat lapel or shirt marked with colored chalk, the color indicating why he had been isolated. These methods, crude as they seem, had to be used, because of the great numbers and the language difficulties.

"All the other aliens were passed down a long line and grouped according to their manifest numbers, and the inspection continued. There were twenty-two lines of inspection, as well as a number of side sections where the aliens were grouped according to letters.

"Every manifest held thirty names, but one inspector never got all thirty. Some were detained by the doctors at the medical inspection, and others were held back for other reasons. Those aliens who were passed were told by the principal inspector to follow the line to a point where another inspector sat with his manifest before him."

"And there, no doubt, occurred the essence of the work," I interposed. "You had to question the aliens to find out if they were eligible to enter the county."

"Yes, and that's where most of our headaches began. If, for example, a woman with three children came before the inspector, she was asked her name. Then she had to produce her vaccination card, which the inspector would compare with her name on the manifest and the line number of the manifest. Her age was asked, and again the manifest was consulted. These manifests, of course, had been prepared by the purser or some other official of the ship, so that they were all ready when the alien came before the inspector.

"Before a barrage of questions such as: Sex? Married status? Occupation? Where born? Where last resided? Where going? By whom was the passage paid? Is that person in the United States or not? If so, how long? To whom is the alien going?— the alien would do his best, wondering what it was all about and when and how it would end. These crowds, this pushing, this hurrying to get things done, this red tape, those cards containing he knew not what damning information against him—it was not at all like his peaceful life back in his native country. Would he get along in this new and strange land? Maybe he should never have come. These thoughts must have been in the minds of most of them.

"With those who were being detained matters were still worse, for it was almost impossible to provide strict sanitation. One Sunday morning, I remember, there were seventeen hundred of these women and children kept in one room with a normal capacity of six hundred. How they were packed in! It had to be seen to be appreciated. They just couldn't move about, and whenever we wanted to get one out it was almost a major operation.

"For example, I was one of the four employees whose duty it was to distribute their detention cards. That day it took us all of four solid hours to distribute the cards to the seventeen hundred people because, added to the general noise in several different languages, we were simply unable to work our way through the massed crowd.

"With so many people packed together under such conditions it was naturally impossible for them to keep clean, for the clean ones were pressed against aliens infested with vermin, and it was not long before we were all contaminated.

"As for the sleeping quarters, please don't imagine they were anything like what we have now. Not only were they inadequate, but what we had were not of the best. There were iron bedsteads, which folded like a pocketbook, and these were in three tiers. The aliens who were unfortunate enough to be without beds had to sleep on benches, chairs, the floor, or wherever we could put them. Today there are usually about two hundred detained every night, but in those days we averaged about two thousand. It was an endless affair, like filling a trough at one end and emptying it at the other.

"And the feeding of the immigrants! It was a sight, back in those days, and I hate to think of it. One employee brought out a big pail filled with prunes, and another some huge loaves of sliced rye bread. A helper would take a dipper full of prunes and slop it down on a big slice of bread, saying, "Here! Now go and eat!"

"There were quite a number going back, too."

"Plenty. And in the case of aged people it was particularly pitiful," he acknowledged. "You see, in nine cases out of ten, an old person was detained until called for by some relative or friend. At the Island, these poor unfortunates would wander about, bewilderment and incomprehension in their eyes, not even knowing where they were, or why they were being kept. It was touching to see how, whenever they saw anyone who spoke their language, they would ask hopefully, "Have you seen my son? Have you seen my daughter? Do you know him, my Giuseppe? When is he coming for me?"

"There were times, of course, when all our efforts to locate the immediate relative failed. Sometimes a married woman had come to join her husband, or a young woman to marry her fiancé, and the man could not be located. Perhaps he had died, or moved, or the correspondence hadn't reached him—who knows? In any event, the results were tragic indeed, as I well know from personal experience. There was no way of soothing these heartbroken women, who had traveled thousands and thousands of miles, enduring suffering and humiliation, and who had uprooted their lives only to find their hopes shattered at the end of the long voyage. These, I think, are the saddest of all immigration cases.

"Sometimes these women were placed in the care of a social agency which agreed to be responsible to the Commissioner, caring for them or placing them in some appropriate occupation. But if everything possible had been done, and the missing husband or fiancé still could not be traced, the poor alien, despite all her tears, had to be returned to her native country.

"Occasionally cases of this kind did not have the element of tragedy, but were queer and hard to handle. There was, for instance, the second-class passenger from Vera Cruz booked under the name of Alejandra Veles. Boyish in appearance, with black hair and an attractive face, she proved to be, upon examination, despite her earlier insistence to the contrary, a young woman. Vehemently she insisted that her identity had not been questioned before. When Dr. Senner asked her why she wore men's clothes, she answered that she would rather kill herself than wear women's clothes. Perhaps some psychoanalyst can explain it, but she said she had always wanted to be a man and it was no fault of hers that she had not been born one!

"Finally she broke down and pleaded with us not to expose her. Then, being threatened with arrest for her defiance of rules, she sent for a very prominent lawyer of the city, who, it turned out, had received a fund for her support. He identified her immediately, after having exacted a pledge that the girl's identity would not be revealed, he told her amazing story.

"'Alejandra Veles' was the daughter of a cultured Englishman who had married a wealthy Spanish woman, and then had been sent to represent his government in the Orient. The girl had been born in the Far East and, when a little child, for some reason or other unhappy at being a girl, she had insisted on dressing as a boy. Although her parents did all they could to discipline her, she would tear her dresses to shreds. She defied all control and finally was allowed to grow up as a boy.

"At the age of fifteen she deserted her parents and started drifting. She came to this country and for two years worked as a hostler in a New York stable, after which she went to the West Indies and bossed men around, nobody ever suspected she was a girl. Her father, frantic and at wit's end, had provided this lawyer with a liberal sum for the girl's support. Was there anything else she wanted, she was asked, 'Yes—give me two plugs of tobacco and a pipe.'

"These were given to her, and she was allowed to leave the Barge Office on her promise to leave the country at once. This she did, sailing for England to visit her parents."

"Did she," I wondered aloud, "sail for England in a man's outfit, or dressed as a woman? But I suppose, having seen thousands of cases, she was just another case to you, and no doubt you are already thinking of someone else."

"Right you are," was his response. "I'm thinking of another strange human specimen we once had detained on the Island—José Maria, who baffled all our officials. Until then I had thought among all of us interpreters we could find someone speaking the language of most every alien. But José Maria was more than our match. He understood none of the many languages we tried on him. Even the Chancellor of the Japanese Consulate, who had a reputation for speaking and understanding almost every dialect of the Orient, and whom we called on for assistance, could make nothing out of José Maria, who looked like a mixture of Japanese, Chinese, and Malay. All he ever said to anyone was, 'Me no sabe.'

"There was nothing about his person by which he could be identified. The newspapers got hold of the story and played up its human interest. They even went so far as to offer us suggestions. One paper guessed offhand that the man was Burmese, and he may have been for all we knew, but he was the only one who could tell, and he couldn't or wouldn't.

"In his satchel he had two envelopes, one addressed to 'José Antonio Chins, Rua de Mancel, Rio de Janeiro, Brazil,' and the other covered with Chinese characters which told a lot about a restaurant somewhere, but nothing of himself. He had $1.50 in German money, and he was heading for Brazil. We never found out anything definite, and my memory is a little vague now as to what became of him, but I do remember that Dr. Senner decided that, in sailing from Bremen, José Maria had taken the wrong steamer, and had landed in New York, when in fact he had meant to take the boat for Rio de Janeiro."

"Tell me," I said, "do you remember particularly any case of a man being deported back to a country that refused to take him back? A man without a country is a tragic person."

"There were many such cases, but none more strange or more tragic than that of Nathan Cohen, who came to us again in 1916. He was insane, and try as we might we could not establish his nationality. As a result, he was shipped back and forth, again and again, between South America and the United States.

"Although we had but few facts to go by in this case, we did manage to find out that he has been born thirty-five years before in Baush, a little village in the province of Kurland in Russia. As a boy he had left home and gone to Brazil. Three years previous he had landed in America, married, and gone into business in Baltimore with several thousand dollars. All seemed to be going well with him. Then his business failed, followed closely, as happens all too often in life, by other catastrophes. His wife ran away with another man, and Cohen lost his memory and his power of speech, and had to be taken to an insane asylum in Baltimore.

"Now he was a public charge within three years of the time he had first landed in the United States and, under the alien law, had to be sent back to the country from which he had come, by the line which had brought him originally. The Lamport Holt Line was therefore instructed to return him to Brazil.

"The Brazilian authorities, however, could not accept Cohen, and the Argentine, where he was sent next, also refused him entrance. Back he was sent to the United States, which promptly shipped him back to Brazil. Since the steamship company could produce no evidence of his Russian birth, he could not be returned to Russia. Such a situation might be funny in fiction, but in real life it was too tragic for humor.

"At last the Knights of Pythias found that he had joined their order in Jacksonville, Florida. With the help of former Justice Leon Sanders, the immigration authorities were induced to let Cohen land, on condition that he be deported to Russia after the war if he is proved to be a Russian citizen.

"So Cohen finally was sent to the sanitarium at Green Farms, Connecticut, as a charge of the Hebrew Shelter and Immigrant Aid Society and the Knights of Pythias. It was there he died.

Of course it wasn't all tragedy in those days. Now and then bits of humor and comedy drifted in at the Barge Office and on the Island. For instance, there was something about the Italians, especially the women, that would not let them leave their pillows behind. No matter what else they relinquished, they usually brought along bulky pillows and mattresses. And very often this was just about everything they did bring!

"But whether they were Italian or Russian, Swedish or Spanish, German or Greek, many of the immigrants came in their native peasant costumes—a strange and colorful procession of fashions in dress from all parts of the world. One would think we were holding a fancy dress party, judging by the variety and oddness of the styles. And the gypsies—I mustn't forget the gypsies!

"The Cunard liner, *Carpathia*, brought them in September of 1904, two hundred and eighty of them, in all the picturesque gorgeousness of their tribal costumes. But what wasn't so picturesque was the fact that forty-eight gypsy children had measles and had to be sent by the immigration doctors to the Kingston Avenue Hospital in Brooklyn.

"This taking of the children was what started things; and what fanned the fire was the fact that several members of distinctive families were taken from the detention room and placed before the Board of Special Inquiry.

"More and more gypsy forces arrived—gypsies from Long Island, New Jersey, and other adjacent points flocked into the Island to meet those detained. Then some gypsy spread the rumor that all the children taken by the doctors had been drowned, and you can imagine what happened!

"At eleven o'clock that night a doctor, who tried to feel a gypsy child's pulse, was attacked by the gypsies as a murderer. This started a riot which could not be checked or stilled, and which raged all night. Every time the gypsies saw anyone wearing an immigration uniform or cap they opened fire, using as weapons anything on which they could lay their hands.

"But at last a way of explaining things was worked out. The next gypsy child who developed measles was sent to the hospital like the others, but the parents were allowed to go along and see how the other gypsy children were being cared for. They brought the news back to the other gypsies, and this was successful in appeasing them. But as long as I live I shall never forget the picture of those gypsy women pulling off their heavy-soled slippers, and sailing into us inspectors and the doctors with a fire in their eyes!

"It seems to me now as I look back that on those days there were crying and laughing and singing all the time at Ellis Island," he recalled. "Very often brides came over to marry here, and of course we had to act as witnesses. I have no count, but I'm sure I must have helped at hundreds and hundreds of weddings of all nationalities and all types. The weddings were numberless, until they dropped the policy of marrying them at the Island and brought them to City Hall in New York.

"Incidentally, as you may have heard, there is a post at Ellis Island which through long usage has come to earn the name of "The Kissing Post." It is probably the spot of greatest interest on the Island, and if the immigrants recall it afterward it is always, I am sure, with fondness. For myself, I found it a real joy to watch some of the tender scenes that took place there.

"There was a line of desks where the inspectors stood with their back towards the windows and facing the wall. Further back, behind a partition, the witnesses waited outside for the detained aliens. As the aliens were brought out, the witnesses were brought in to be examined as to their right of claim. If the inspector found no hitch, they were allowed to join each other. This, because of the arrangement of the partitions, usually took place at the 'Kissing Post,' where friends, sweethearts, husbands and wives, parents and children would embrace and kiss and shed tears for pure joy.

"I have shown how the routine was held up and how complications arose when an alien was unable to give the information required of him. When an alien refused to give this information, the complications that resulted were still more serious. Take, for example, the case of Joaquin Nabuco, the Brazilan Ambassador at Washington, who arrived in November 1906 on the White Star steamer, *Baltic*, from Liverpool.

"Senhor Nabuco refused to answer the following questions which were put to him by immigration authorities purely as a matter of routine: 'By whom was your passage paid? Have you fifty dollars in your possession? Have you ever been in prison or in an almshouse or in an institution for the care and treatment of the insane supported by charity? If so, which? Are you a polygamist? Have you come here under the promise, offer, or solicitation to labor in the United States?'

"Although it was explained to Senhor Nabuco that these were certain set questions, the answers to which were required by the immigration laws, he persisted in his refusal to answer, drawing himself up to his full height and saying:

'I have answered every question which I believed would add to the necessary statistical government information; but these other questions are different. I am not a visitor to this country in the implied sense of the word. I am here as the representative of another power, and as such I am to a certain extent the guest of this nation. This is the ground I take, and for this reason alone I refuse to answer certain questions. There is no friction over the affair, and I should like nothing said about it.'

"Lord Curzon, the English statesmen, who was also a passenger on the *Baltic* at the time, and he had answered the same questions, although this did not establish a precedent, for Lord Curzon was not an official representative of a foreign power.

"At any rate, the purser of the *Baltic* reported the matter and the desired information was asked of E. L. Chermont, secretary of the Brazilian Embassy, but Mr. Chermont could not provide it. Again the information was requested of Senhor Nabuco, and again he refused to supply it.

It was then that Secretary of State Root, upon being unofficially notified of the situation, got in touch with the Department of Commerce and Labor and requested that the courtesies of the port be extended to Senhor Nabuco and his secretary.

"There was talk for some time of an apology being made, and for all I know it may have been; but under customs regulation, a country sending a diplomatic representative to this country is required to notify the Secretary of State in advance, and the State Department then informs the Secretary of the Treasury, who orders that the customs laws be suspended in the instance of the incoming individual. Brazil had not given such notice, and we, as a result, had received no word to suspend such questions in the case of the Ambassador."

(Originally in English)

Bibliography

James J. Periconi

The primary decisions of any bibliographer are to define the scope of inclusion (and, therefore, exclusion) of the field to be covered, and the type of bibliographic apparatus to append to each work. The decision on the latter question I considered made by Francesco Durante, that is, to list merely author(s), title, year of publication, place of publication, and publisher's name of what scholars call the "ideal" copy of the work (that is, a complete copy but not any particular copy). On the former question, it may also appear to readers of this translation of Durante's monumental work that that decision of inclusion and exclusion was made in some final sense by him, and thus that the task of the bibliographic editor was simply to reformat entries in the original bibliography to conform to American citation style. That is not and could not be the case here.

As for primary works: First, I took as a challenge (and a charge) Durante's prescient observation that his bibliography was undoubtedly incomplete, and his happy anticipation that new works—especially new primary works published in Italian during the period in question—would be found after publication of his work. As he stated in his introduction, in 2005:

> I am perfectly aware that [this anthology] is "provisional," a sort of permanent workshop constantly open to new research and further discoveries. . . . The book looks forward to other scholarly research that will go even deeper into the libraries and archives that I have visited (some seventy of them between Italy and the United States). And—why not?—perhaps a new author or title will be miraculously discovered. There are still thousands of attics to pick through and perhaps in a few of them a surviving copy of some lost novel by

Bernardino Ciambelli or the typescript of some play by Riccardo Cordiferro or an unfindable volume of some lost Italian-American newspaper awaits us in silence.

In expanding the body of works, my focus was virtually exclusively on the Italian-language work. In this task, I was very fortunate to have tools—an ever-expanding set of online resources—that were simply not available so fully (if at all) to Francesco Durante as they have been to me. As for English-language authors who were omitted from the original, or previously unknown works by included English-language authors, I did not add them even when those works fell firmly within the 1880–1943 time period of the book.

Other criteria arise from the definitional problems of "Italian American." I continued (and thus added to) Durante's practice of including Italian, as well as American, imprints, of primary works, so long as those reflect the experience or observations of those writers while in America and about their American experience. Italian-language writers and speakers in America undoubtedly found it easier to find and deal with publishers and printers in their native Italy than with those in America. I agree with Durante that publication outside of the various United States should not be any kind of disqualifier from an "American" bibliography. Nor, for these purposes, was it relevant whether or not those writers themselves are considered (or considered themselves) "Italian American."

As for those writers or observers firmly rooted in Italy, who published in Italian with their regular Italian publishers, based on their brief or somewhat brief tours of America, I was less assiduous in adding their works, except as to those whose writings had already commanded attention in Durante's original for the perspicacity or literary qualities, for example, Edmondo Mayor des Planches and Amy Bernardy.

Furthermore, I added to Durante's original bibliography any Italian-language American imprints that I found (and more selectively those published in Italy by the same author also publishing in America), whether those of authors already cited by Durante in the book or not. These include principally those several authors of Italian language works whose work is either exclusive to or more central to Martino Marazzi's *Voices in Italian America*, such as Federico Mennella.

As a result of this expansive approach, therefore, readers should be aware that particular works (and even particular authors) will now be reflected in the bibliography that are not discussed either in the Durante text, or even in the voluminous footnotes to the chapters. As to the latter, on several occasions, works mentioned in the notes in fuller discussions of the author in question did not gain entry into the bibliography proper, for no discernible reason; those works have also been added.

I also tried to ensure that I included any English-language American imprint of an Italian language original work, where the Italian edition alone had been cited by Durante, to make a copy of the work easier to find and more accessible for English-language readers.

For English-language original books, I ensured that the original work only was cited rather than the typically later Italian-language translation cited by Durante for his Italian audience, since the English original would be more available as well as accessible to English language readers.

Secondary works or scholarship: The original bibliography in *Italoamericana* is rich in secondary works—particularly useful with the political literature—and I have expanded that, with one limitation: The explosion of such work just in the last eleven years (since actual preparation by Francesco Durante of the core of his bibliography) made it impractical, if not impossible, to include all such newly published scholarly works on the "*history and* literature of the Italians in the United States." However, I have included as much of the new scholarly literature as possible where the focus of such new work is on the *literature* of the Italians in America (as opposed to their *history*) with particular attention to those works that treat the literature written and published in Italian (whether in the United States or in Italy or elsewhere).

I excluded "republished" citations to works in most cases. Because of the explosion of reprinting by digitization of even relatively obscure works printed in Italian in the United States, I decided that searching for and adding an entry about the republication by Kessinger Publishing, Nabu Books, Kirtas Publishing or, of course, Google Books—to name only the most prominent companies in this business—of individual works would be unduly time-consuming and, more important, would surely become outdated by the time of publication because of the rapid expansion of this practice, and the availability in about two weeks time of so many out-of-print (and especially out-of-copyright) works. I urge readers looking for the entire texts of both Italian-original as well as English-original works excerpted in this volume to look to these providers of reprints for what may be a very pleasant surprise.

So, to sum up: To Francesco Durante's original observation that "perhaps a new author or title will be miraculously discovered," I say simply that I have been lucky enough in the years since he wrote these words to be blessed by quite a few such discoveries. It is a measure of the gracious and generous man (as well as redoubtable scholar) that Francesco is—as well as a huge personal pleasure for me—that he always expresses his excitement and pleasure at such discoveries of any "work not in Durante," and sometimes I am able to observe that excitement and the care with which he cradles in his hands any such new find of which I have been fortunate enough to have the opportunity to show him a copy. *Grazie mille, Francesco!* Those works are now among "works in Durante."

∿

Abbamonte, Salvatore. 1907. *Patria e donna: Episodio della guerra italo-austriaca del 1859. Dramma in un prologo e 4 atti.* New York: Cappabianca.

———. 1919. *Sacrificio: dramma in tre atti.* New York: Bagnasco Press.

———. 1940a. *Nella colonia di quarantacinque anni or sono. La Follia,* January 14.

———. 1940b. *Nei primordi del teatro coloniale. La Follia,* February 11.

———. 1940c. *Attori e filodrammatici della vecchia Colonia Italiana di New York. La Follia di New York,* March 24.

———. 1940d. *I figli dello Spirito Santo, ovvero, Le avventure di due trovatelli. Storia rustica siciliana.* New York: Eugene Printing Service.

Adams, Joseph H. [1903]. *In the Italian Quarter of New York.* New York: [n.p.]. (Facsimile reprint in *Italians in the United States: A Repository of Rare Tracts and Miscellanea.* New York: Arno Press, 1975.)

Agatodemon. 1909. *Dalla propaganda anticlericale alla propaganda antireligiosa.* Buffalo: Tipografia Cooperativa Italiana.

Aiello, Rosa. 1940. *La cucina casareccia napoletana.* New York: Italian Book Co.

Aleandri, Emelise. 1983a. *A History of Italian-American Theatre: 1900 to 1905.* Ph.D. dissertation, City University of New York.

———. 1983b. "Italian-American Theatre." In *Ethnic Theatre in the United States,* ed. Maxine Schwartz Seller. Westport, Conn.: Greenwood Press, 237–258.

———. 1989. "Riccardo Cordiferro," in Juliani-Cannistraro 1989, 165–178.

———. 2006–2011. *The Italian-American Immigrant Theatre of New York City, 1746–1899.* New York: Edwin Mellen (11 vol.).

Alfonsi, Ferdinando. 1985. *Poeti italo-americani/Italo-American Poets: Antologia bilingue/A Bilingual Anthology.* Catanzaro: Carello.

———. 1989. *Dictionary of Italian-American Poets.* New York: Peter Lang.

Altavilla, Corrado. 1938. *Gente lontana.* Milan: Medici Domus.

Ambrosoli, Solone. 1878. *Partendo da New York. Versi.* Como: Franchi.

———. 1882. *Poesie originali e tradotte.* Como: Franchi.

Andreasi, Anna Maria. 1971. "Anarchismo e sindacalismo nel pensiero di Armando Borghi (1907–1922)." In *Anarchici e anarchia nel mondo contemporaneo,* 242–260. Turin: Fondazione Luigi Einaudi.

Angelone, Romolo. 1922. *Dalla vanga alla poesia. Il Carroccio* 15 (April 4): 520–522.

Anonymous. 1899. *Colonia Italiana: Tontitown, Arkansas, Stati Uniti D'America*. St. Louis: Frisco Lines. (Reprint in *Italians in the United States: A Repository of Rare Tracts and Miscellanea*. New York: Arno Press, 1975.)

———. 1902. *[Constitution of] The Society for the Protection of Italian Immigrants*. New York: Powers & Stein Press.

———. [1904]. *Consigli agl'immigranti/Advice for Immigrants*. [n.p.]: [n.p.]. (Reprint in *Italians in the United States: A Repository of Rare Tracts and Miscellanea*. New York: Arno Press, 1975.)

———. 1905. *All'anarchia si arriverà passando per lo stato socialista?* Barre, Vt.: Tipografia della Cronaca Sovversiva (Biblioteca del circolo di sociali, opuscolo no. 4).

——— [A.M.G.SS.C.J.]. 1918. *In memoria della Rev. Madre Francesca Saverio Cabrini, fondatrice e Superiora Generale delle missionarie del S. Cuore di Gesù*. New York: A. Bernasconi; Rome: Scuola Tipografia Salesiana.

———. 1922. *Donna contro donna. Romanzo passionale d'amore e d'odio*. Cincinnati: Nielsen.

———. 1923. *Che cosa è l'I.W.W.?* Chicago: I.W.W.

———. [n.d.]. *La morale di Arlecchino*. Chicago: Tipografia "la Parola" [dei Socialisti].

———. [n.d.]. *I tre inni rossi*. West Hoboken, N.J.: Clinton.

———. [n.d.]. *Mussolineide: Poema antifascista e di rivendicazione sociale*. [n.p.]: [n.p.].

Aquilano, Baldo. 1925. *L'Ordine Figli d'Italia in America*. New York: Società Tipografica Italiana.

Arbib-Costa, Alfonso. 1906. *Lezione graduate di lingua inglese*. New York: Francesco Tocci.

———. 1914a. *Italian Lessons*. New York: Italian Book Co.

———. 1914b. *Advanced Italian Lessons*. New York: Italian Book Co.

Avella, Caterina Maria. 1923. "La 'Flapper.'" *Il Carroccio* 18, no. 2 (August).

———. 1924. "Patsy e Patricia." *Il Carroccio* 20, no. 4 (October).

Avrich, Paul. 1984. *The Haymarket Tragedy*. Princeton: Princeton University Press.

———. 1988. *Anarchist Portraits*. Princeton: Princeton University Press.

———. 1991. *Sacco and Vanzetti: The Anarchist Background*. Princeton: Princeton University Press.

Bagatin, P. L. 1991. "La grande emigrazione e il Polesine di fine '800 nella pubblicistica di A. Rossi." In *Chiesa e società nel Polesine di fine '800*, ed. G. P. Romanato, 215–259. Rovigo: Associazione Culturale Minelliana.

Baker, John D. 1972. "Italian Anarchism and the American Dream: The View of John Dos Passos." In Vecoli 1973, 30–39.

Ballerini, Luigi, and Fredi Chiappelli. 1985. "Contributi espressivi delle scritture e parlate americo-italiane." In *L'espressivismo linguistico nella letteratura italiana*, atti del convegno di Roma, 16–18 January 1984. Rome: Accademia nazionale dei Lincei.

Bandini Buti, A. 1962. "Dario Papa." In *Aspetti e figure della pubblicistica repubblicana italiana*, Atti del convegno organizzato dall'Associazione Mazziniana Italiana a Torino, 13–14 October 1961, 59 ff. Genoa-Milan-Turin.

Barbato, N. 1908. *Scienza e fede*. Philadelphia: Social Printing Co.

Barbieri, Carlo. 1967. *Quarto potere negli Stati Uniti*. Bologna: Cappelli.

Barolini, Helen, ed. 1985. *The Dream Book: An Anthology of Writings by Italian American Women*. New York: Schocken Books.

Bartoletti, Efrem. 1919. *Nostalgie proletarie. Raccolta di canti poetici e di inni rivoluzionari*. Brooklyn, N.Y.: Libreria Editrice dei Lavoratori Industriali del Mondo.

———. 1924. *Un'escursione all caverna di Monte Cucco*. Fabriano: Tip. Economica.

———. 1931. *Nel sogno d'oltretomba. Antico libero*. Scranton: [n.p.].

———. 1955. *Riflessioni poetiche*. Milan: Gastaldi.

———. 1959. *Evocazioni e ricordi*. Bergamo: La Nuova Italia Letteraria.

———. 1999. *Documenti e poesie* [CD-ROM]. Costacciaro: Perugina.

———. 2001. *Poesie. Alla scoperta delle nostre radici storiche*, ed. Martino Marazzi. Costacciaro: Comune di Costacciaro.

Basile Green, Rose. 1974. *The Italian-American Novel: A Document of the Interaction of Two Cultures*. Madison, N.J.: Fairleigh Dickinson University Press.

———. 1983. "Italian-American Literature." in Di Pietro-Ifkovic 1983, 110–132.

Bassi, Guido. 1910. *Sangue siciliano. Gran romanzo storico dell'epoca della Dominazione Borbonica*. Passaic, N.J.: American Premium Book Co.

Baucia, Camillo. 1909. *I miei ragli. Raccolta di sonnetti*. New York: Nicoletti Bros.

———. 1932. *La colonia italiana di Baltimore*. New York: Società Tipografica Italiana.

Becchetti, Nena. 1928. *La figlia dell'anarchico. Dramma sociale in tre atti*. Jessup, Pa.: Il Gruppo Autonomo.

Bello, Vincenzo. [n.d.]. *Rose e spine. Versi*. New York: Bagnasco Press.

Benanti, Salvatore. 1926. *La secessione della "Sons of Italy Grand Lodge." Studi polemici su diversi problemi degl'italiani in America*. New York: Colamco Press.

———. 1928. *Studi critici di dinamica sociale*. New York: La Follia di New York.

———. 1941. *Follie e questione del giorno*. New York: Eugene Printing.

Bergreen, Laurence. 1994. *Capone: The Man and the Era*. New York: Simon & Schuster.

Bernabei, Franca. 1999. "Little Italy's Eugène Sue: The Novels of Bernardino Ciambelli." In Boehlhower–Pallone 1999, 3–56.

Bernardy, Amy A. 1907. *Emigrazione di lungo corso. La Lega Navale*, June.

———. 1909. "Perché gli italiani si addensano nelle città americane." In Sheridan et al. 1909, 33–40.

———. 1911. *America vissuta*. Turin: Bocca.

———. 1913. *Italia randagia attraverso gli Stati Uniti*. Turin: Bocca.

———. 1923. *Paese che vai. Il mondo come l'ho visto io*. Florence: Le Monnier.

————. 1942. "Contributi italiani alla formazione degli Stati Uniti d'America." *Il Giornale di Politica e Letteratura* 18 (January–February), 20–39.

Bertelli, Giuseppe. [n.d.]. *Dibattito sulla "Esistenza di Dio" tra il Rev. Amedeo Santini e il Prof. Giuseppe Bertelli*. Chicago: Italian Labor Publishing Co.

————. [n.d.]. *Gesù Cristo, i preti e noi*. Philadelphia: Tip. Coop. Socialismo.

————. [1908?]. *In difesa di Giordano Bruno contro un parroco italiano*. Chicago: La Parola dei Socialisti.

————. 1940. *Rime d'esilio. Il bacio*. Chicago: Silvestri Printing Co.

Bertellini, Giorgio. 2009. *Italy in Early American Cinema: Race, Landscape, and the Picturesque*. Bloomington: Indiana University Press.

Bevilacqua, Piero, Andreina De Clementi, and Emilio Franzina, eds. 2001. *Storia dell'emigrazione italiana. Partenze*. Rome: Donzelli.

————. 2002. *Storia dell'emigrazione italiana. Arrivi*. Rome: Donzelli.

Bezza, Bruno, ed. 1983. *Gli italiani fuori d'Italia: Gli emigrati italiani nei movimenti operai dei paesi d'adozione (1880–1940)*. Milan: Franco Angeli-Fondazione Brodolini.

Biagi, Ernest Louis. 1961. *The Purple Aster: A History of the Order Sons of Italy in America*. [n.p.]: Veritas Press.

————. 1967. *The Italians of Philadelphia*. New York: Carlton Press.

————. 1970. *Italian Name Places in the United States with Historical and Descriptive Annotations and Information*. Philadelphia: Adams.

Bivona, Damiano. 1916. *Ciccu peppi e cum pagnia: Versi satirico in dialetto Siciliano*. New York: Polyglot Publishing House.

————. 1919. *Prima e dopo il piave, dramma in 3 atti*. New York: Polyglot Publishing House.

————. 1921. *Il dottor Aurelio, romanzo*. New York: Polyglot Publishing House.

Bock, Gisela, Paolo Carpignano, and Bruno Ramirez. 1976. *La formazione dell'operaio massa negli USA 1898/1922*. Milan: Feltrinelli.

Boelhower, William. 1982. *Immigrant Autobiography in the United States (Four Versions of the Italian American Self)*. Verona: Essedue Edizioni.

Boelhower, William, and Rocco Pallone, eds. 1999. *Adjusting Sites: New Essays in Italian American Studies*. Stony Brook, N.Y.: Forum Italicum.

Borghi, Armando. 1907. *Il nostro e l'altrui individualismo*. Brisighella: [n.p.].

————. 1913. *Fernand Pelloutier nel sindacalismo*. Bologna. (Undated edition published in Brooklyn by the Libreria Editrice Lavoratori del Mondo; new edition, Turin: Assandri, 1977.)

————. 1924. *L'Italia tra due Crispi*. Paris: Libreria Internazionale.

————. 1925. *Il banchetto dei cancri*. New York: Libreria Editrice Lavoratori Industriali del Mondo.

————. 1927a. *Mussolini in camicia*. New York: Edizioni Libertarie. (1935: *Mussolini Red and Black,* London: Wishart Books Ltd.; 1938: *Mussolini Red and Black,*

New York: Freie Arbeiter Stimme, trans. from 1932 French ed., *Mussolini en Chemise*, Paris: Rieder, by Dorothy Daudley, with an epilogue: *Hitler: Mussolini's Disciple*. New edition, Naples: Edizioni Scientifiche Italiane, 1961.)

———. 1927b. *Gli anarchici e le alleanze antifasciste*. New York: Circolo Operaio di Cultura Sociale.

———. 1931. *Mischia sociale (Da . . . alla Cooper Union)*. Brooklyn, N.Y.: Edizioni Sociali.

———. 1933. *Errico Malatesta in 60 anni di lotte anarchiche*. New York: Edizioni Sociali.

———. 1939. *Il tramonto di Bacunin*. Newark, N.J.: Biblioteca de "L'Adunata dei Refrattari."

———. [1943]. *Due bozzetti contro il fascismo. Dante processato all'inferno. Italiani che ascoltano la radio dall'America*. Newark, N.J.: L'Adunata dei Refrattari.

———. 1947. *Errico Malatesta*. Milan: Istituto Editoriale Italiano.

———. 1949. *Conferma anarchica (Due anni in Italia)*. Forlì: L'Aurora.

———. 1954. *Mezzo secolo di anarchia (1898–1945)*. Naples: Edizioni Scientifiche Italiane.

———. 1964. *La rivoluzione mancata*. Milan: Azione Comune.

———. 1966. *Vivere da anarchici. Antologia di scritti*, ed. Vittorio Emiliani. Bologna: Alfa.

———. 1978. *Mezzo secolo di anarchia (1898–1945)*. Catania: Edizioni della Rivista "Anarchismo."

Borgianini, Alfredo. 1948. *Sonetti e poesie romanesche*. Trenton: White Eagle Printing Co.

Borrata D'Angelo, Benedetta. 1991. *Memoria e scrittura di Michele Pane, calabrese d'America*. In Marchand 1991, 413–422.

Bosi, Alfredo. 1921. *Cinquant'anni di vita italiana in America*. New York: Bagnasco Press.

Botta, Luigi. 1978. *Sacco e Vanzetti. Giustiziata la verità*. Cavallermaggiore: Gribaudo.

Boulard, Garry. 1988. "Blacks, Italians, and the Making of New Orleans Jazz." *Journal of Ethnic Studies* 16, no. 1 (Spring): 53–66.

Bozzacco, Giovanni. 1938. *La spigolatrice de Sapri*. Massilon, Ohio: [n.p.].

Braida, Albino. [n.d.]. *La società proletaria*. Brooklyn, N.Y.: Libreria Editrice dei Lavoratori Industriali del Mondo.

Braida, Albino, and Giovanni Baldazzi. [n.d.]. *L'unionismo industriale*. Brooklyn, N.Y.: Italian I.W.W. Publishing Bureau.

Branchi, Eugenio Camillo. 1924. *Il primato degli italiani nella storia e nella civiltà americana*. Bologna: Cappelli.

———. 1926a. "Sarete mia, Laura." *Il Carroccio* 23, no. 1 (January): 94–104.

———. 1926b. "Hold Up!" *Il Carroccio* 24, no. 8 (August): 169–176.

———. 1927. *"Dagoes". Novelle Transatlantiche*. Bologna: Licinio Cappelli.

———. 1928. "L'opera del fiorentino Carlo Bellini." *La Nazione*, July 26.

———. 1953. *Così parlò Mister Nature. Fatti e impressioni di un italiano in America.* Bologna: Licinio Cappelli.

Brandenburg, Broughton. 1904. *Imported Americans: The Story of the Experiences of a Disguised American and His Wife Studying the Immigration Question.* New York: Stokes.

Breccia, Paolina. 1915. *Lo zingaro giustiziere. Monologo sociale rappresentabile in teatro e all'aperto.* New York: Perrini.

Bruno, Giuliana. 1992. *Nel mosaico della città. Differenze etniche e nuove culture in un quartiere di New York.* Milan: Feltrinelli. (Translated as *Streetwalking on a Ruined Map: Cultural Theory and the City Films of Elvira Notari.* Princeton: Princeton University Press, 1992.)

Buel, Elizabeth C. Barney. 1930. *Manuale degli Stati Uniti: Istruzione ad uso degli Immigranti e Stranieri.* Washington, D.C.: Società Nazione Figlie della Rivoluzione Americana.

Bugiardini, Sergio. 2005. "Il Freelance della rivoluzione. Note all'inedita autobiografia di Carlo Tresca." In Various Authors 2005, 45–59.

Bulleri, Pinio. 1922. *Versi diversi.* New York: Italian Labor Publishing Co.

———. 1930. *Fantasie nomadi.* Chicago: Italian Labor Publishing Co.

Burton, Clay C. 1972. "Italian-American Relations and the Case of Sacco and Vanzetti." In Vecoli 1973, 65–80.

Buttis, Vittorio. 1940. *Memorie di vita di tempeste sociali.* Chicago: Comitato Vittorio Buttis.

Cacioppo, Marina. 1999. "'Se i marciapiedi di questa strada potessero parlare': Space, Class, and Identity in Three Italian-American Autobiographies." In Boelhower–Pallone 1999, 73–87.

Caccioppo, Vincenzo. 1962. "La tragica fine di Calogero Puccio." *L'Araldo di Santa Margherita Belice* 8 (October 15).

Cadicamo, Giuseppe. 1875. *Dèlia, romanza orientale.* Milan: Treves.

———. 1877a. *Il voto d'una derelitta. Storia bulgara.* Milan: Treves.

———. 1877b. *Davvero è morta? Ode patriottica.* Milan: Treves.

———. 1879. *La necropoli monumentale di Sibari scoperta dall'Ingegnere Cav. Saverio Cavallari. Impressioni e studii.* Milan: Tipografia Letteraria.

———. 1881. *Mascah e Marsiglia. Io triumphe!* Milan: Treves.

———. 1885. *I Daitjas. Poemetto novo.* Corigliano Calabro: Tipografia Letteraria. (Second edition, Rome: Tipografia Centenari, 1886.

———. 1886a. *Canidio. Scena romana.* Corigliano Calabro: Tipografia Letteraria.

———. 1886b. *Natura ed arte (da Les feuilles d'automne di V. Hugo). Versione a fantasia libera. Versi.* Corigliano Calabro: Tipografia Letteraria.

———. 1891. "A Giuseppe Giacosa." *L'Eco d'Italia*, November 8.

———. 1906. *Visione epitalamica*. New York: Emporium Press.

———. 1909. *Tennysoniae, "Nothing Will Die." "All Things Will Die."* New York: Emporium Press.

———. 1910. *Davidica. Nova lirica*. New York: Emporium Press.

———. 1915. *Rosmunda*. New York: Nicoletti Bros. Press.

Cagidemetrio, Alide. 2000. *Peppino*. 1885. In *The Multilingual Anthology of American Literature: A Reader of Original Texts with English Translations*, ed. Marc Shell and Werner Sollors, 214–269. New York: New York University Press.

Calitri, Antonio. 1925. *Canti del Nord-America*. Rome: Alberto Stock.

Calvi, Giusto. 1901. *I senza patria. Note dal vero. Da New York a Napoli*. Valenza: L. Battezzati.

———. 1949. *Dietro la maschera. Diario di Don Bruno*. Milan-Rome: Gastaldi.

———. 2006. *Fanciullezza a Montefumo*. With writings by Francesco Durante and Cosma Siani. Castelluccio dei Sauri (Foggia): Lampyris.

Calza, Gino. 1908. *Su la vena*. New York: Francesco Tocci.

Caminita, Ludovico. 1906. *Che cosa è la religione*. Paterson, N.J.: Libreria Sociologica; Chieti: Tip. Ed. C. Di Sciullo.

———. 1908. *L'educazione de' fanciulli; con una lettera del dott. O.D. Battendieri*. Philadelphia: Social Printing Co.

———. 1908. *Il diritto d'amare*. Philadephia: Social Printing Co.

———. 1910. *I delinquenti*. Latrobe, Pa.: Ed. Gruppo la Demolizione.

———. 1917. *Free Country! Gli Stati Uniti sono un paese libero*. [n.p.]:[n.p.].

———. 1921. *Sonata elegiaca. Dramma*. Brooklyn, N.Y.: Tartamella & Co.

———. 1924. *Nell'isola delle lagrime (Ellis Island)*. New York: Stabilimento Tipografico Italia.

———. 1927. *Augusto Crovelli, romanzo*. New York: Stabilimento Tipografico Italia.

———. 1936. *In Nuova York*. Scranton, Pa.: Il Minatore.

———. 1943. *Obici. Biografia*. New York: Tipografia Editrice Scarlino.

Cammett, John M., ed. 1969. *The Italian American Novel*. Proceedings of the Second Annual Conference of the American Italian Historical Association. Staten Island, N.Y.: AIHA.

Cannata, Giuseppe [G.C.]. [n.d.]. *La tattica sindacalista in America*. Brooklyn, N.Y.: Libreria dei Lavoratori Industriali del Mondo.

———. [n.d.]. *La Tecnica industriale e la rivoluzione proletaria*. Brooklyn, N.Y.: Libreria dei Lavoratori Industriali del Mondo.

Cannistraro, Philip V. 1999. *Blackshirts in Little Italy: Italian Americans and Fascism 1921–1929*. West Lafayette, Ind.: Bordighera Press.

Caporale, Rocco, ed. 1986. *The Italian Americans through the Generations*. Proceedings of the Fifteenth Annual Conference of the American Italian Historical Association. Staten Island, N.Y.: AIHA.

Carey, George. 1985. "'La Questione Sociale': An Anarchist Newspaper in Paterson, NJ (1895–1908)." In L. Tomasi 1985, 289–297.

Carlevale, Joseph William. 1936. *Leading Americans of Italian Descent in Massachusetts*. Plymouth, Mass.: The Memorial Press.

——. 1942. *Who's Who Among Americans of Italian Descent in Connecticut*. New Haven: Carlevale Publishing Co.

——. 1950. *Americans of Italian Descent in New Jersey*. Clifton, N.J.: North Jersey Press.

Carnevali, Emanuel. 1925. *A Hurried Man*. Paris: Contacts Edition.

——. 1967. *The Autobiography of Emanuel Carnevali*. Edited by Kay Boyle. New York: Horizon.

——. 1978. *Il primo dio*. Edited by Maria Pia Carnevali, with an essay by Luigi Ballerini. Milan: Adelphi.

——. 1981. *Voglio disturbare l'America. Lettere a Benedetto Croce e Giovanni Papini ed altro*. Edited by Gabriel Cacho Millet. Florence-Milan: La Casa Usher.

——. 1994a. *Saggi e recensioni*. Edited by Gabriel Cacho Millet. Bazzano: [n.p.].

——. 1994b. *Diario bazzanese e altre pagine*. Edited by Gabriel Cacho Millet. Bazzano: [n.p.].

Carnovale, Luigi. 1909. *Il giornalismo degli emigrati italiani nel Nord America*. Chicago: Casa Editrice del Giornale L'Italia.

——. 1920. *Soltanto l'eliminazione della neutralità potrà subito e per sempre impedire le guerre*. Chicago: Italian-American Publishing Co.

——. 1921. *Esortazione ai direttori dei giornali italo-americani, a gli emigrati italiani tutti, per commemorare degnamente negli Stati Uniti d'America il sesto centenario della morte di Dante*. Chicago: [n.p.].

——. 1924. *Il secentenario dantesco 1321–1921 negli Stati Uniti d'America suprema purissima gloriosa imperitura affermazione di italianità intellettuale spirituale morale*. Chicago: Blakely-Oswald Printing Co.

——. 1926. *Il supremo ideale umano raggiunto*. Chicago: [n.p.].

Carpi Sartori, Daniela. 1985. "Emanuel Carnevali and Guido Gozzano." *Rivista di Studi Anglo-Americani* 3, nos. 4–5: 315–328.

Carr, John Foster. 1910. *Guida degli Stati Uniti per l'immigrante italiano*. New York: Società delle Figlie della Rivoluzione Americana, Sezione di Conn./Immigrant Education Society.

——. 1911. *Guide to the United States for the Immigrant Italian: A Nearly Literal Translation of the Italian Version*. Garden City, N.Y.: Connecticut Daughters of the American Revolution.

Cartosio, Bruno. 1983. "Gli emigrati italiani e l'Industrial Workers of the World." In Bezza 1983, 359–395.

Caruso, Enrico. 1908. *Caricatures in Four Parts*. New York: La Follia di New York.

Casella, Paola. 1998. *Hollywood Italian. Gli italiani nell'America di celluloide*. Milan: Baldini & Castaldi.

Castronovo, Valerio. 1970. *La stampa italiana dall'unità al fascismo*. Rome-Bari: Laterza.

Cautela, Giuseppe. 1925. *Moon Harvest*. New York: Dial Press.

———. 1927. "The Italian Theatre in New York." *American Mercury*, September, 106–112.

———. 1928. "Italian Funeral." *American Mercury*, September–December, 200–206.

———. 1929. "Miracle." *Plain Talk* 4, no. 3, 309–317.

Cavazza, Elisabeth Pullen Jones. 1892a. *Don Finimondone. Calabrian Sketches*. New York: C. L. Webster & Co.

———. 1892b. "Rocco and Sidora, a Calabrian Story." *Atlantic Monthly* 70, no. 420 (October), 476–495.

———. 1893. "The Man from Aidone." *Atlantic Monthly* 72, no. 432 (October), 433–448; no. 433 (November), 577–596; no. 434 (December), 721–741.

———. 1894a. "Jerry: A Personality." *Atlantic Monthly* 73, no. 438 (April), 498–505.

———. 1894b. "At the Opra di li Pupi." *Atlantic Monthly* 73, no. 440 (June), 797–802.

———. 1894c. "Some Recent Studies of the Sicilian People." In *Atlantic Monthly* 73, no. 441 (July), 838–844.

Cecchi, Emilio. 1940. *America amara*. Florence: Sansoni.

Cennerazzo, Armando. 1914. *Odio e vendetta: scene napoletane in un atto*. New York: Commercial Printing Co.

———. 1931. *Senza Mamma—Senza perdono (seguito a "Senza Mamma")—Povera canzona. Tre lavori drammatici ricavati dalle canzoni omonime di Francesco Pennino*. New York: Francesco Pennino/Italian Book Co.

———. 1934. *I figli abbandonati, di Francesco Mastriani*. New York: Eloquent Press Corp.

———. 1936. *La canzona della Madonna. Dramma*. New York: A. Cennerazzo.

———. 1949. *Poesie napoletane*. Naples: Ciro Russo.

———. 1957. *Rose rosse e rose gialle. Nuove poesie napoletane*. Naples: A. Guida.

———. [n.d.]. *A cirinara: monologo drammatico siciliano*. New York: V. Foti.

Cennerazzo, Armando, and G. Vitrone. 1912. *Rapitori di fanciulli ovvero La Mano Nera. Scene coloniali in un atto*. (Ms.) Naples: Biblioteca Lucchesi Palli, Raccolta Cennerazzo.

Cerrito, Gino. 1969. "Sull'emigrazione anarchica italiana negli Stati Uniti d'America." *Volontà* 22, no. 4 (July–August), 269–276.

Ciacci, Margherita. 1972. "Note sul comportamento linguistico di emigrati italiani negli Stati Uniti." In *Gli italiani negli Stati Uniti, atti del III Symposion di studi americani*. Florence: La Nuova Italia. (Reprint, New York: Arno Press, 1975.)

Ciambelli, Bernardino. 1893a. *I misteri di Mulberry*. New York: Frugone & Balletto.

———. 1893b. *Fiori d'arancio o La moglie del Barbiere*. New York: Frugone & Balletto.

———. 1893c. "La città nera ovvero I misteri di Chicago." *L'Italia: Giornale del Popolo di Chicago*, July 15. Incomplete.

———. 1893d. *World's Fare, ovvero Suicidio con l'elettricità*. New York: Frugone & Balletto.

———. 1893e. *I drammi dell'emigrazione, seguito ai Misteri*. New York: Frugone & Balletto.

———. 1894a. *Amore, lussuria e morte, ovvero Il processo di Antonio Bianco*. New York: Frugone & Balletto.

———. 1894b. *La bella Biellese, ovvero Il mistero di Columbus Avenue*. New York: Frugone & Balletto.

———. 1895a. *I misteri della polizia di New York. Il delitto di Water Street*. New York: Frugone & Balletto.

———. 1895b. *I delitti dei bosses (cosidetti padroni)*. New York: Frugone & Balletto.

———. 1899. *I misteri di Bleeker Street*. New York: Frugone & Balletto.

———. 1906. "Columbus Day." In *Gli italiani negli Stati Uniti d'America*, 153–155. New York: Italian American Directory Co.

———. 1906–1908. *Il delitto di Coney Island, ovvero La vendetta della zingara*. New York: La Follia di New York.

———. 1908–1909. *La strage degli innocenti, ossia I delitti di un medico*. New York: La Follia di New York.

———. 1909. *Il terremoto in Sicilia e Calabria*. New York: Florence Publishing Co.

———. 1910–1911. *I misteri di Harlem, ovvero La bella di Elizabeth Street*. New York: La Follia di New York.

———. 1911. "L'Arcibanchettone." *La Follia di New York*, February 19.

———. 1911. *L'aeroplano fantasma. Romanzo contemporaneo*. New York: La Follia di New York.

———. 1915a. *I sotterranei di New York*. New York: Società Libraria Italiana.

———. 1915b. *I viaggi*. New York: Società Libraria Italiana.

———. 1919. *La trovatella di Mulberry Street ovvero La stella dai cinque punti*. New York: Società Libraria Italiana.

———. 1926. "Il natale di Caino." *La Follia di New York*, December 19.

———. 1927. "Il natale di Abele e quello di Caino." *La Follia di New York*, December 18.

———. 1928. "Il natale di un eroe." *La Follia di New York*, December 23.

———. [n.d.]. *Il martire del dovere, ovvero Giuseppe Petrosino. Dramma in quattro atti*. Typescript. Naples: Biblioteca Lucchesi Palli, Raccolta Cennerazzo C889; 2009 Pironti.

———. [n.d.] *L'invasione del Veneto*. Monograph, Biblioteca Nazionale Vittorio Emanuele III, Naples.

Ciancabilla, Giuseppe. 1900a. *Fiori di maggio*. New York: Ruffo & Ciani.

———, trans. 1900b. *Tolstoismo e anarchismo*. Barre, Vt.: Biblioteca Circolo Studi Sociali.

———. 2002. *Fired by the Ideal: Italian American Anarchist Responses to Czolgosz's Killing of McKinley*. London: Kate Sharpley Library.

Cianfarra, Camillo. 1900. *Dell'unica protezione possibile nel Nord America*. Rome: Unione Tipografica Cooperativa.

———. 1904. *Il diario di un emigrato*. New York: Tipografia dell'Araldo Italiano.

———. 1906a. "Io e la mia stenografa." *Gli Italiani e l'America* 16, no. 4 (October).

———. 1906b. "La manodopera negra. Nel concetto degl Industriali del Sud degli Stati Uniti." *Gli Italiani e l'America* 16, no. 5 (November).

———. 1910. "Un'avventura di Natale." *La Follia di New York*, December 18.

Cinel, Dino. 1982. *From Italy to San Francisco: The Immigrant Experience*. Stanford, Calif.: Stanford University Press.

———. 1991. *The National Integration of Italian Return Migration, 1870–1929*. Cambridge: Cambridge University Press.

Cipriani, Lisi Cecilia. 1907a. *A Tuscan Childhood*. New York: The Century Co.

———. 1907b. "Stories of a Girl in Italy." *The Century Illustrated Monthly Magazine* 52 (May–October), 638–646.

Ciuffoletti, Zeffiro, and Maurizio Degl'Innocenti, eds. 1978. *L'emigrazione nella storia d'Italia*. 2 volumes. Florence: Vallecchi.

Clark, Francis Edward. 1919. *Our Italian Fellow Citizens in Their Old Homes and Their New*. Boston: Small, Maynar & Co.

Cocchi, Raffaele. 1984. "In Search of Italian-American Poetry in the USA." *In Their Own Words* 2, no. 1 (Winter): 28–30.

———. 1991. "L'invenzione della letteratura italiana e italoamericana." *Altreitalie* 5 (April): 7–13.

———. 1992. "Rosa Zagnoni Marinoni: From the Bolognese Hills to the Ozarks." In *Bologna. La cultura italiana e le letterature straniere moderne*, 313–321. Ravenna: Longo.

———. 1992. "Selected Bibliography of Italian American Poetry." *Italian Americana* 10, no. 2 (Spring–Summer), 242–261.

Colajanni, Napoleone. 1909a. "I non desiderabili (The Undesirables)." In Sheridan et al. 1909, 83–113.

———. 1909b. "La criminalità degli italiani negli Stati Uniti." In Sheridan et al. 1909, 117–192.

Colombo, Arrigo, and Mark Adams. 1941. "Blood-and-Thunder." *Common Ground* (Spring): 14–19.

Colonna, Dora. 1912. *Volere è potere. Metodo speciale per la lingua inglese*. Philadelphia: A. Germano.

———. 1926a. "Le due amiche." *Il Carroccio* 23, no. 4 (April): 429–437.

———. 1926b. "Common Clay." *Il Carroccio* 24, no. 8 (August): 178–186.

Conte, Gaetano. 1903. *Dieci anni in America. Impressioni e ricordi.* Palermo: Spinnato.

———. 1906. *Le missioni protestanti ed i nostri emigrati.* Venezia: Tipografia dell'Istituto Industriale.

Cordiferro, Riccardo [Alessandro Sisca]. [n.d.](a). *Giuseppina Terranova, ovvero L'onore vendicato, dramma in quattro atti.* New York: Nicoletti Bros.

———. 1895. *Il pezzente. Monologo in versi.* New York: Coccè.

———. 1910. *Singhiozzi e sogghigni.* New York: L'Araldo Italiano.

———. 1915. *Il prete attraverso la storia.* Barre, Vt.: Circolo di Studi Sociali.

———. 1917a. *Brindisi ed auguri per ogni occasione.* New York: Società Libraria Italiana.

———. 1917b. *Canzone d'a guerra.* New York: Società Libraria Italiana.

———. 1917c. *Gli stornelli della guerra.* New York: Società Libraria Italiana.

———. 1919. *Ermete novelli.* New York: Manhattan Printing Co.

———. 1924a. *Scugnizzo. Poemetto napoletano.* New York: Coccè Press.

———. 1924b. *Il prisco cavaliere, scherzo satirico in versi.* Brooklyn, N.Y.: F. Sparacino.

———. 1928a. *'O ritorno d'a guerra. Dramma napoletano in un atto.* New York: La Follia di New York.

———. 1928b. *Il poema dell'amore.* [n.p.].[n.p.]

———. 1933a. *Ode alla Calabria.* Buenos Aires: La Voce dei Calabresi.

———. 1933b. *Mater Doloroso, dramma in un atto.* Brooklyn, N.Y.: Union Press.

———. 1938a. *Gabriele D'Annunzio. Nella vita e nell'arte.* New York: Cocce Bros.

———. [Alessandro Sisca]. 1938b. *A Giacomo Leopardi. Per il centenario della sua morte.* New York: Scipio di Dario.

———. 1967. *Poesie scelte.* Campobasso: Pungolo Verde.

———. [n.d.](c). *La vendetta. Lirica in versi liberii.* New York: La Follia di New York.

Corresca, Rocco. 1902. "The Biography of a Bootblack." *The Independent,* December 4.

Corsi, Edward. 1935. *In the Shadow of Liberty.* New York: Macmillan.

———. 1952. "Il dialetto italo-americano." *Convivio Letterario* 20, nos. 10–12, 61–62.

Covello, Leonard. 1934. *The Italians in America: A Brief Survey of a Sociological Research Program of Italo-American Communities (Bulletin No. 6).* New York: Casa Italiana Educational Bureau.

———. 1967. *The Social Background of the Italo-American School Child.* Leiden: E. J. Brill. (Reprint, Totowa, N.J.: Rowman and Littlefield, 1972.)

Cratere, P. *See* Breccia, Paolina.

Creagh, Ronald. 1984. *Sacco et Vanzetti.* Paris: La Découverte.

Crespi, Cesare. 1906. *San Francisco e la sua catastrofe.* San Francisco: Tipografia Internationale.

———. 1913. *Per la libertà! (dalle mie conversazione col conte Carlo di Rudio, complice de Felice Orsini).* San Francisco: Canessa Print Co.

————. 1939. *Il tallone di ferro*. San Francisco: Gene's Print Shop.

————. 1943. *Fascismo, masnadieri antichi e moderni*. San Francisco: [n.p.].

————. 1944. *La stirpe martoriata. Spigolature storiche e brevi commenti*. San Francisco: Lanson & Garfinkel.

————. 1946. *In attesa della pace*. [n.p.]: [n.p.].

————. 1947. *Per intenderci meglio*. San Francisco: Self-published.

————. [n.d.] *Tempra italiana, dramma in quattro atti*. San Francisco: Tipografia Lanson & Lauray.

Cunetto, Dominic J. 1960. *Italian Language Theatre Clubs in St. Louis, Missouri 1910 to 1950*. M.A. thesis, University of Florida.

Cupelli, Alberto. 1973. "Trentesimo anniversario della uccisione di Carlo Tresca." *La Parola del Popolo* (March–April), 24–27.

DAB. 1928–1936. *Dictionary of American Biography*, ed. Allen Johnson, 20 volumes and two supplements. New York: Scribner.

D'Acierno, Pellegrino, ed. 1999. *The Italian American Heritage. A Companion to Literature and Arts*. New York: Garland.

Dadà, Adriana. 1976. "Stati Uniti." In *Bibliografia dell'anarchismo, volume primo, tomo secondo: Periodici e numeri unici anarchici in lingua italiana pubblicati all'estero (1872–1971)*, ed. Leonardo Bettini. Florence: Crescita Politica.

————. 1984. "La stampa anarchica." In Varsori 1984, 349–370.

Daly, Thomas Augustine. 1912. *Madrigali*. New York: Harcourt, Brace & Co.

————. 1914. *Carmina*. New York: John Lane.

————. 1936. *Selected Poems*. New York: Harcourt, Brace & Co.

D'Amato, Gaetano. 1908. "The Black Hand Myth." *North American Revue* 629 (April), 543–549.

Damiani, Gigi. 1927. *La bottega. Scene della ricostruzione fascista*. Detroit: Libreria Autonoma.

————. 1927. *Cristo e Bonnot*. Chicago: Germinal.

———— [Simplicio, pseud.]. 1928. *"Fecondità". Commedia sociale in due atti*. Newark, N.J.: Biblioteca de "L'Adunata dei Refrattari."

————. 1930. *Del delitto e delle pene nella società di Domani*. Newark, N.J.: Biblioteca de "L'Adunata dei Refrattari."

————. 1939. *Carlo Marx e Bacunin in Spagna*. Newark, N.J.: Biblioteca de "L'Adunata dei Refrattari."

————. 1939. *Razzismo e anarchismo*. Newark, N.J.: Biblioteca de "L'Adunata dei Refrattari."

————. 1940. *Attorno ad una vita (Niccolò Converti)*. Newark, N.J.: Biblioteca de "L'Adunata dei Refrattari."

———— [Simplicio, pseud.]. 1946a. *Sgraffi*. Newark, N.J.: Biblioteca de "L'Adunata dei Refrattari."

———. 1946b. *Stato e commune*. Newark, N.J.: Biblioteca de "L'Adunata dei Refrattari."

———. 1991. *Saggio su di una concezione filosofica dell'anarchismo*. Pistoia: Fondazione-Archivio, Famiglia Berneri.

———. [n.d.]. *Viva Rambolot! Bozzetto in un atto*. Newark, N.J.: Biblioteca de "L'Adunata dei Refrattari."

D'Andrea, Virgilia. 1925. *L'ora di Maramaldo*. New York: Lavoratori Industriali del Mondo.

———. 1929. *Tormento*. Paris: La Fraternelle.

———. 1933. *Torce nella notte*. New York: [n.p.].

———. 1947. *Chi siamo e cosa vogliamo*. *Patria e religione*. Newark, N.J.: Biblioteca de "L'Adunata dei Refrattari."

———. 1965. *Richiamo all'anarchia. Protesta e proposta anarchica in otto conferenze pronunciate in terra d'esilio durante la dominazione fascista*. Cesena: L'Antistato.

D'Angelo, Giacomo. 2008. "L'emigrazione abruzzese e la letteratura." In *Emigrazione abruzzese tra Ottocento e Novecento* 2, ed. Lia Giancristofaro, 263–325. L'Aquila: Regione d'Abruzzo.

D'Angelo, Pascal. 1924. *Son of Italy*. New York: Macmillan.

———. 2001. *Canti di luce*. Mercato San Severino: Il Grappolo.

D'Ariano, Regina, and Roy D'Ariano. 1976. *Italo-American Ballads, Poems, Lyrics, and Melodies*. Parsons, W.V.: McClain Printing Co.

D'Attilio, Robert. 1982. "La salute è in voi: The Anarchist Dimension." In Various Authors 1982, 75–89.

———. 1994. "Arturo Giovannitti." In *The American Radical*, ed. Mary Jo Buhle, Paul Buhle, and Harvey J. Kaye, 135–142. New York: Routledge.

DBI. 1960–. *Dizionario Biografico degli Italiani*. Rome: Istituto della Enciclopedia Italiana.

DBIO. 1948 (5th ed.), 1957 (6th ed.). *Chi è? Dizionario biografico degli italiani d'oggi*. Roma: Scaranno.

De Biasi, Agostino. 1927. *La battaglia dell'Italia negli Stati Uniti. Articoli e note polemiche*. New York: Il Carroccio.

De Ciampis, Mario. 1958. "Storia del movimento socialista rivoluzionario italiano." *La Parola del Popolo* 37 (December 1958–January 1959), 136–163.

De Clementi, Andreina. 1999. *Di qua e di là dall'oceano. Emigrazione e mercati nel Meridione (1860–1930)*. Rome: Carocci.

De Fiori, Vittorio E. [Guido Podresca]. 1923. *Mussolini e il fascismo*. New York: Italian Publishing Co./ Il Carroccio.

De Gubernatis, Angelo. 1880. *Dizionario biografico degli scrittori contemporanei*. Supplement to vol. 2. Firenze: Le Monier.

Del Ciotto, Antonella. 1997. "Umberto Postiglione 'americano.'" In Moretti 1997, 149–183.

Del Giudice, Giuseppe. 1928. *Canti della sorgente*. New York: Bronx Standard Press.

Del Giudice, Luisa, ed. 1993. *Studies in Italian American Folklore*. Logan: Utah State University Press.

Della Vesa, Virginio. 1924. *Qualcuno guastò la festa*. Brockton, Mass.: [n.p.].

DeLuise, Alexandra. 2012. "The Italian Immigrant Reads: Evidence of Reading for Learning and Reading for Pleasure, 1890–1920s." *Italian Americana* 30, no. 1 (Winter 2012): 33–43.

Del Vecchio, Giulio Salvatore. 1892. *Sulla emigrazione permanente italiana nei Paesi stranieri avvenuta nel dodicennio 1876–1887. Saggi di statistica*. Bologna: Civelli.

De Martino, Antonio [pseud. Duchesa X]. 1944. *L'assassinio della Contessa Trigona*. New York: Italian Book Co.

De Mattei, Rodolfo. 1933. "Incontro con i siciliani d'America." *Quadrivio*, December 11.

De Rosalia, Giovanni. 1890. *Versi siciliani*. Caltagirone: Sciuto.

———. 1917a. *Nofrio eroe del 3 febbraio. Farsa*. New York: Casa Editrice Biblioteca Siciliana.

———. 1917b. *Nofrio locandiere. Farsa*. New York: Casa Editrice Biblioteca Siciliana.

———. 1917c. *Tre mariti e una moglie. Farsa*. New York: Casa Editrice Biblioteca Siciliana.

———. 1918a. *Il duello di Nofrio. Farsa*. New York: Italian Book Co.

———. 1918b. *Nofrio ai bagni. Farsa*. New York: Italian Book Co.

———. 1918c. *Nofrio al telefono. Farsa*. New York: Italian Book Co.

———. 1918d. *Nofrio in pericolo. Farsa*. New York: Italian Book Co.

———. 1918e. *Nofrio sindaco. Farsa*. [n.p.]:[n.p.].

———. 1919a. *Nofrio sensale di matrimonio. Farsa*. New York: [n.p.].

———. 1919b. *Nofrio si deve tirare. Farsa*. New York: Casa Editrice Biblioteca Siciliana.

———. 1919c. *Tre mariti ed una moglie. Farsa*. New York: [n.p.].

———. 1920. *Nofrio arriccutu*. New York: Casa Editrice Biblioteca Siciliana.

———. [n.d.]a. *Litteriu trantulia, ovvero Lu nobili sfasulatu. Novella in vernacolo siciliano*. New York: Stamperia della Follia.

———. [n.d.]b. *Lu socialisimu e lu ciarlatanu. Scherzi poetici*. New York: Società Libraria Italiana.

Deschamps, Bénédicte. 1998. "La letteratura d'appendice nei periodici italo-americani (1910–1935)." In Martelli 1998, 279–294.

———. 2001. "Il Lavoro, the Italian Voice of the Amalgamated, 1915–1932." *The Italian American Review* 8, no. 1 (Spring–Summer): 85–120.

———. 2007. "Feuilleton et presse sindacale italo-américaine: Le cas de *Velia, l'histoire d'une petite couturière* dans le journal *Giustizia* (1925–1928)." In *Au bonheur du feuilleton. Naissance et mutations d'un genre (Etats-Unis, Grande-Bretagne, XVIIIe–XXe siècles)*, ed. Marie-Françoise Cachin et al., 197–210. Paris: Creaphis.

Deschamps, Bénédicte, and Stefano Luconi. 2002. "The Publisher of the Foreign-Language Press as an Ethnic Leader? The Case of James V. Donnarumma and Boston's Italian-American Community in the Interwar Years." *Historical Journal of Massachusetts* 30, no. 2 (Summer): 126–143.

Diggins, John P. 1972. *Mussolini and Fascism: The View from America*. Princeton: Princeton University Press.

Di Pietro, Robert J., and Edward Ifkovic, eds. 1983. *Ethnic Perspectives in American Literature*. New York: Modern Language Association of America.

DiStasi, Lawrence. 2001. *Una Storia Segreta: The Secret History of the Italian American Evacuation and Internment during World War II*. Berkeley: Heyday Books.

Di Vita, Rosario. 1915. *Prime stille*. New York: Società Tipografica Italiana.

———. 1922. *Perle azzurre*. Genoa: Milanta.

———. 1922. *Semiramis*. New York: [n.p.].

———. 1924. *I nostri fiori alla patria*. New York: Società Tipografica Italiana.

———. 1925. *Chiantu di Galiota. Sceneggiata siciliana in 3 parti*. New York: V. Grassi & Co.

———. 1926. *Scenette umoristiche e drammatiche*. New York: Tipografia V. Grassi & Co.

———. 1931. "Corruzioni di vocaboli inglesi sicilianizzati." *Rivista Italiana di Letteratura Dialettale* 3, no. 3.

———. 1932. *Matri: esito del Consorso; poetico siciliano d'America sotto gli auspici del Po'T' 'U Cuntu: New York, N.Y.: febbraio 1932*. Palermo: Po' T' 'U Cuntu.

———. 1934. *Fiori d'oltremare*. Milan: Edizioni Siculorum Gymnasium.

———. 1934. *Vuci d'oltrimari*. Milan: Edizioni Siculorum Gymnasium.

Dondero, Carlo A. 1992. *Go West! An Autobiography of Carlo Andrea Dondero 1842–1939*. Eugene, Ore.: Garlic Press.

Donini, Ambrogio. 1984. "L'Unità del Popolo"/"Lo Stato Operaio." In Varsori 1984, 331–348.

Dore, Grazia. 1964. *La democrazia italiana e l'emigrazione in America*. Brescia: Morcelliana.

———. 1968–1969. "Socialismo italiano negli Stati Uniti." *Rassegna di Politica e Storia* 14, nos. 159–161, and 15, nos. 171–172.

Dos Passos, John. 1927. *Facing the Chair: Story of the Americanization of Two Foreign-born Workmen*. Boston: Sacco-Vanzetti Defense Committee.

Dubofsky, Melvyn. 1972. "Italian Anarchism and the American Dream: A Comment." In Vecoli 1973, 52–55.

Durante, Francesco. 1993a. "Little Italy, la riscossa dei 'cafoni' (with three texts of Eduardo Migliaccio)." *Il Mattino*, March 12.

———. 1993b. "Paisà. Anzi scrittore." *Il Mattino*, March 21.

———. 1994. "Partono i bastimenti. L'emigrazione e le esperienze della canzone napoletana in USA." *Euros* 1 (January–February).

———. 1999. "'Farfariello': due 'macchiette coloniali.'" *Acoma: Rivista internazionale di Studi Nordamericani* 16 (Spring): 54–60.

———. 2001a. *Italoamericana. Storia e letteratura degli italiani negli Stati Uniti 1776–1880*, vol. 1. Milan: Mondatori.

———. 2001b. "Viviani nella letteratura dell'emigrazione." In *Viviani*, ed. Marcello Andria. Naples: Pironti.

———. 2001c. "'Avventura' versus 'Flusso'. La letteratura come strumento per capire l'emigrazione." In *Le letterature popolari. Prospettive di ricerca e nuovi orizzonti teorico-metodologici*, Atti del convegno di Fisciano-Ravello, 21–23 November 1997. Naples: Edizioni Scientifiche Italiane.

———. 2002. *Figli di due mondi. Fante, Di Donato & C: Narratori italoamericani degli anni Trenta e Quaranta*. Cava de' Tirreni: Avagliano.

———. 2003. "Uno dei 'Big Boys.'" Preface to John Fante, *Romanzi e racconti*, ed. Francesco Durante, ix–xxxi. Milan: Meridiani Mondatori.

———. 2004. "Giunte ottocentesche al canone letterario italoamericano." In *Merica. Forme della cultura italoamericana*, ed. Nick Ceramella and Giuseppe Massara, 31–39. Isernia: Cosmo Iannone.

———. 2007. "Vernacolari d'America." In *Appunti di viaggio. L'emigrazione italiana tra attualità e memoria*, ed. Ornella De Rosa and Donato Verrastro. Bologna, Il Mulino: 271–286.

EAL. 1990. *Encyclopedia of the American Left*. Mari Jo Buhle, Paul Buhle, and Dan Georgakas, eds. New York: Garland Publishing.

Eastman, Max. 1943. *Heroes I Have Known: Twelve Who Lived Great Lives*. New York: Simon & Schuster.

Ebert, Justus. [n.d.]. *L'I.W.W. nella teoria e nella pratica*. Chicago: I.W.W.

Ehrmann, Herbert B. 1969. *The Case That Will Not Die: Commonwealth vs. Sacco and Vanzetti*. Boston: Little, Brown.

Emiliani, Vittorio. 1973. *Gli anarchici*. Milan: Bompiani.

Ettor, Joseph, and Arturo Caroti. 1912. *Unionismo industriale e trade-unionismo: Può un socialista e industrialista far parte dell' A.F. of L.?* Chicago: I.W.W.

Fabbri, Luigi. [n.d.]. *Le dittature contro la libertà dei popoli*. New York: Il Martello.

Faggi, Angelo. [n.d.]. *Uno storico processo di classe: I precedenti e lo svolgimento del processo dell'I.W.W. a Chicago, Illinois*. Chicago: I.W.W.

Falbo, Italo C. 1942. "Figure e scene del teatro popolare italiano a New York." *Il Progresso Italo-Americano* (May 3, 10, 17, 24, and 31; June 7, 14, 21, and 28; July 5 and 12; September 13 and 20).

Fant, Pietro Antonio (Marius). 1927. *Luigi Carnovale, l'eroe della italianità negli Stati Uniti d'America*. Rome: Tipografia delle Terme.

Fedeli, Ugo. 1956. *Luigi Galleani: Quarant'anni di lotte rivoluzionarie (1891–1931)*. Cesena: Antistato.

———. 1965. *Giuseppe Ciancabilla*. Imola: Galeati.

Federal Writers Project. 1938. *The Italians of New York*. New York: Random House. (Reprint, New York: Arno Press, 1969.)

———. 1939. *Gli Italiani di New York*. New York: Labor Press.

Felix, David. 1965. *Protest: Sacco-Vanzetti and the Intellectuals*. Bloomington: Indiana University Press.

Femminella, Francis X., ed. 1973. *Power and Class: the Italian-American Experience Today*. Proceedings of the Fourth Annual Conference of The American Italian Historical Association. Staten Island, N.Y.: AIHA.

———, ed. 1985. *Italian and Irish in America*. Proceedings of the Sixteenth Annual Conference of the American Italian Historical Association. Staten Island, N.Y.: AIHA.

Fenton, Edwin. 1957. *Immigrants and Unions, A Case Study: Italians and American Labor, 1870–1920*. Cambridge: Harvard University Press. (Reprint, New York: Arno Press, 1975.)

Ferraris, Luigi Vittorio. 1968. "L'assassinio di Umberto I e gli anarchici di Paterson." *Rassegna Storica del Risorgimento* 55, no. 1 (January–March): 47–64.

Ferrazzano, Tony. 1911a. *Nuove canzoni popolari sulla guerra Italo-Turca e su Trento e Trieste*. New York: Società Libraria Italiana.

———. 1911b. " 'Na Serenata llaica helle! . . ." In *Raccolta di canzoni. Macchiette e duetti coloniali*. New York: Società Libraria Italiana.

———. 1915. *Poesie umoristiche sulla guerra fra l'Italia e l'Austria*. New York: Società Libraria Italiana.

———. 1919. *Nuove canzoni sulla guerra Italo-Austriaca*. New York: Società Libraria Italiana.

Feurlicht, Roberta Strauss. 1977. *Justice Crucified: The Story of Sacco and Vanzetti*. New York: McGraw-Hill.

Fiaschetti, Michele. 1926a. "Caccia grossa." *Corriere d'America*, January 19–31.

———. 1926b. "Le tre veglie." *Corriere d'America*, February 10.

———. 1926c. "Le due sorelle." Retitled "La prova del fuoco." *Corriere d'America*, February 19–27.

———. 1926d. "La lotteria della morte." *Corriere d'America*, March 6.

———. 1926e. "La scomparsa del sepolto." *Corriere d'America*, March 12–16.

———. 1926f. "Il mistero della perla." *Corriere d'America*, March 14.

———. 1926g. "Le spie e i confidenti." *Corriere d'America*, May 5–June 14.

———. 1928. *The Man They Couldn't Escape: The Adventures of Detective Fiaschetti of the Italian Squad as Told to Prosper Buranelli by Michael Fiaschetti*. London: Selwyn & Blount. (Reprint, *You Gotta Be Rough: The Adventures of Detective Fiaschetti of* the Italian Squad as Told to Prosper Buranelli by Michael Fiaschetti, Garden City, N.Y.: Doubleday, Doran & Co., 1939.)

——. 2003. *Gioco duro*. Ed. Martino Marazzi. Cava de' Tirreni: Avagliano.

Fichera, Filippo. 1937. *Il duce e il fascismo nei canti dialettali d'Italia*. Milan: Edizione del "Convivio Letterario."

——. 1958. *Letteratura Italoamericana*. Milan: Editrice Convivio Letterario.

Fink, Guido. 1973. "Le bugie colorate di Carnevali." *Paragone* 280 (June): 85–88.

Fiori, Giuseppe. 1983. *L'anarchico Schirru, condannato a morte per l'intenzione di uccidere Mussolini*. Milan: Mondadori.

Flamma, Ario. 1909. *Dramas*. New York: Ario Flamma.

——. 1911. *Fiamme. Dramma in un atto. Memorie di un suicida*. New York: Self-published.

——. 1912. *Piccole anime, dramma in tre atti*. New York: Italian Press Publishing Association.

——. 1923. *Foglie nel turbine, commedia in tre atti/Don Luca Sperante, dramma in un Atto*. Wilkes-Barre, Pa.: Modern Publishing Co.

——. 1928. *Flames: and Other Plays*. New York: The Stage Publishing Co.

——. 1934. *Fiorello La Guardia*. New York: Worthy Printing Co.

——. 1936. *Italiani di America. Enciclopedia biografica*. New York: Casa Editrice Coccè Bros.

——. 1941. *Italiani di America. Enciclopedia biografica*, Volume II. New York: Casa Editrice S. F. Vanni.

——. 1949. *Italiani di America. Enciclopedia biografica*, Volume III. New York: Coccè Press.

Foerster, Robert E. 1919. *The Italian Emigration of Our Times*. Cambridge: Harvard University Press.

Fontana, Ferdinando. 1882. "Dario Papa." *Il Progresso Italo-Americano*, January 19, 1882.

Fontanella, Luigi. 1998. "Poeti emigrati ed emigranti poeti negli Stati Uniti." In Martelli 1998, 299–319.

——. 2003. *La parola transfuga. Scrittori italiani in America*. Fiesole: Cadmo.

Forgione, Louis. 1922a. "A New American Poet From Italy [with six poems]." *Il Carroccio* 16, no. 2 (August): 173–177.

——. 1922b. "Nero." *Il Carroccio* 16, no. 3 (September): 255–257.

——. 1923. "Lines (from The Triumph)." *Il Carroccio* 17 (January): 101.

——. 1924. *Reamer Lou*. New York: E. P. Dutton & Co.

——. 1928a. *The Men of Silence*. New York: E. P. Dutton & Co.

——. 1928b. *The River Between*. New York: E. P. Dutton & Co.

Foster Carr, John. 1910. *Guida degli Stati Uniti per l'immigrante italiano*. New York: Doubleday, Page & Co. (Second edition, New York: Immigrant Education Society, 1913.)

———. 1911. *Guide to the United States for the Immigrant Italian.* Garden City, N.Y.: Doubleday, Page & Co.

Fox, Stephen. 2000. *Uncivil Liberties: Italian Americans Under Siege During World War II.* New York: Universal.

Fragale, Thomas. 1898. *Romanism Antagonistic to the Bible.* Hammonton, N.J.: McCalls.

———. 1929. *Poesie.* Kansas City, Mo.: Tipografia Mario Porretti.

Frangini, A. 1907. *Italiani in Filadelfia. Strenna nazionale. Cenni biografici.* Philadelphia: Tipografia dell'Opinione.

———. 1908. *Italiani nel Connecticut. Strenna nazionale. Cenni biografici,* vol. XLIX. New Haven: Tipografia Sociale De Lucia Jorio.

———. 1909. *Italiani in Buffalo, Niagara Falls e Rochester, NY. Strenna nazionale. Cenni biografici,* vol. LI. New York: Tipografia R. Beraglia.

———. 1910. *Italiani in Pittsburg, Pa. e dintorni. Strenna nazionale. Cenni biografici,* vol. LIV. New York: Tipografia Commerciale.

———.1912a. *Italiani nel Centro dello Stato di New York. Strenna nazionale. Cenni biografici,* vol. LIX. Utica, N.Y.: Tipografia della "Luce."

———. 1912b. *Italiani in New Orleans, La. Strenna nazionale. Cenni biografici,* vol. LX. New Orleans: Tipografia dell'Italo-Americano.

———. 1913. *Italiani in Los Angeles. Strenna nazionale. Cenni biografici,* vol. LXI. New Orleans(?): Tipografia dell'Italo-Americano, G. Spini.

———. 1914. *Colonie italiche in California. Strenna nazionale. Cenni biografici,* vol. LXIII. Stockton, Calif.: Tipografia Stamper e Ciari.

———. 1915. *Colonie italiche in California. Strenna nazionale. Cenni biografici,* vol. LXIV. San Francisco: Tipografia Lanson-Lauray.

———. 1917. *Colonie italiche in California. Strenna nazionale. Cenni biografici,* vol. LXV. San Francisco: Stamperia Italiana M. Castagna & Co.

———. [n.d.]. *Italiani in Chicago, Ill. Strenna nazionale.* New York: Tipografia Commerciale.

Frankfurter, Felix. 1927. *The Case of Sacco and Vanzetti. A Critical Analysis for Lawyers and Laymen.* Boston: Little, Brown & Co.

Franzina, Emilio. 1995. *Gli italiani al nuovo mondo. L'emigrazione italiana in America 1492–1942.* Milan: Mondadori.

———. 1996. *Dall'Arcadia in America. Attività letteraria ed emigrazione transoceanica in Italia (1850–1940).* Turin: Edizioni della Fondazione Giovanni Agnelli.

Franzina, Emilio, and Matteo Sanfilippo. 2000. *Il fascismo e gli emigrati. La parabola dei Fasci italiani all'estero (1920–1943).* Rome-Bari: Laterza.

Fucilla, Joseph G. 1967. *The Teaching of Italian in the United States: A Documentary History.* New Brunswick, N.J.: American Association of Teachers of Italian.

Fumagalli, Giuseppe. 1909. *La stampa periodica italiana all'estero. Indice dei periodici tutti o in parte in lingua italiana, che si stampavano all'estero cioè fuori dei confini*

politici del Regno, negli anni 1905–1907. Preceduto da uno studio storico a cura di G.F.
Milan: Libreria Fratelli Bocca.

Fusco, Giancarlo. 1962. *Gli indesiderabili.* Milan: Longanesi.

Gaja, Giuseppe. 1919. *Ricordi d'un giornalista errante.* 3d ed. Turin: Bosio & Accame.

Gallagher, Dorothy. 1988. *All the Right Enemies: The Life and Murder of Carlo Tresca.*
New Brunswick, N.J.: Rutgers University Press.

Galleani, Luigi. 1904. *Verso il comunismo.* Barre, Vt.: Tipografia della Cronaca Sovversiva.

—— [pseud. Mentana]. 1913. *Madri d'Italia! (Per Augusto Masetti).* Lynn, Mass.:
Tipografia della Cronaca Sovversiva.

—— [pseud. Mentana]. 1914. *Faccia a faccia col nemico. Cronache giudiziarie
dell'anarchismo militante.* East Boston, Mass.: Edizione del Gruppo Autonomo.

——. 1925. *La fine dell'anarchismo?* Newark, N.J.: L'Adunata dei Refrattari. (Reprint,
Cesena: Edizioni l'Antistato, 1966.)

——. 1930a. *Medaglioni. Figure e figuri.* Newark, N.J.: Biblioteca de "L'Adunata dei
Refrattari."

——. 1930b. *Contro la guerra, contro la pace, per la rivoluzione:* Newark, N.J.:
Biblioteca de "L'Adunata dei Refrattari."

——. 1935. *Medaglioni. Aneliti e singulti.* Newark, N.J.: Biblioteca de "L'Adunata dei
Refrattari."

——. 1947. *Una battaglia.* Rome: Biblioteca de "L'Adunata dei Refrattari."

——. 1954. *Mandateli lassù.* Cesena: Edizioni l'Antistato.

——. 1972. *Metodi della lotta socialista.* Rome: Biblioteca de "L'Adunata dei Refrattari."

Galzerano, Giuseppe. 1991. "'America! America!': La testimonianza di un emigrato
calabrese." In Marchand 1991, 437–447.

Gambino, Richard. 1974. *Blood of My Blood: The Dilemma of the Italian Americans.*
Garden City, N.Y.: Doubleday.

——. 1977. *Vendetta. A True Story of the Worst Lynchings in America.* New York:
Doubleday.

——. 1981. *Bread and Roses.* New York: Avon Books.

——. 1990. "Wellsprings of Italian American Art: The Italian American Experience As
Literalism, Myth, and Surrealism." *Italian Americana* 9, no. 1 (Fall–Winter), 43–58.

Gardaphè, Fred L. 1987. "Fact in Fiction: Oral Traditions and the Italian American
Writer." In Krase-Egelman 1987, 165–174.

——. 1995. *The Italian-American Writer: An Essay and an Annotated Checklist.*
New York: Forkroads/Spencertown.

——. 1996. *Italian Signs, American Streets: The Evolution of Italian American
Narrative.* Durham, N.C.: Duke University Press.

Gardaphè, Fred L., and Periconi, James J. 2000. *The Italian American Writers Association Bibliography of the Italian American Book.* Mount Vernon, N.Y.: Shea and
Haarman.

Garosci, Aldo. 1984. "Dalla Francia agli Stati Uniti." In Varsori 1984, 19–34.

Gatti-Emanuel, Guglielmo. 1937. *Memorie. Cinquant'anni d'arte scenica*. New York: S. F. Vanni.

Gentile, Maria. 1919. *The Italian Cook Book: The Art of Eating Well*. New York: Italian Book Co.

Gerbi, Ernesto e Aluisius. 1962. *L'eterna lotta*. Milan: Nuova Editrice Internazionale.

Gerson, Simon W. 1976. *Pete: The Story of Peter V. Cacchione, New York's First Communist Councilman*: New York: International Publishers.

Giacometti, Paolo. [n.d.]. *Cristoforo Colombo alla scoperta dell'America. Dramma in cinque atti*. New York: Società Libraria Italiana/Teatro Italiano.

Giacosa, Giuseppe. 1892. *Impressioni d'America*. Milan: Cogliati. (New ed. 1908.)

Giammarco, Marilena. 1997. "Italia e America in *Personal Reminiscences of Francesco Ventresca*." In Moretti 1997, 129–148.

Giantino. 1923. *Unionismo industriale e sindacalismo*. Brooklyn, N.Y.: Casa Editrice Lavoratori Industriali.

Giovannitti, Arturo. 1912. *Ettor and Giovannitti Before the Jury at Salem, Massachusetts, November 23, 1912*. Chicago: I.W.W.

———. 1913. "Syndicalism—the Creed of Force." *The Independent*, October 30, 209–211.

———. 1914. *The Cage*. Riverside, Conn.: Hillacre Press.

———. 1914. *Arrows in the Gale*. Riverside, Conn.: Hillacre Press.

———. 1918. *Come era nel principio (Tenebre rosse). Dramma in 3 atti*. Brooklyn, N.Y.: Libreria Editrice dei Lavoratori Industriali del Mondo.

———. 1938. *Parole e sangue*. New York: The Labor Press.

———. 1950. *Il camminante (The Walker)*. New York: Morgillo.

———. 1957. *Quando canta il gallo*. Chicago: E. Clemente & Sons.

———. 1962. *The Collected Poems of Arturo Giovannitti*. Chicago: E. Clemente & Sons. (Reprint, New York: Arno Press, 1975.)

———. 2005. *Parole e sangue*. Ed. Martino Marazzi. Isernia: Iannone.

Giovannitti, A., G. Gianformaggio, and E. Goldman. 1930. *Pagine scelte*. Brooklyn, N.Y.: Libreria Editrice I.W.W.

Giovannitti, Arturo, and Onorio Ruotolo. 1943. *Rimane salda la fede*. New York: [n.p.].

Gori, Pietro. 1915. *Senza patria*. Brooklyn, N.Y.: Club Avanti. (Republished in Gori 1968, II, and in Savona-Straniero 1976, 360–389.)

———. [n.d.]. *Prigioni. Versi. Al popolo ed a quanti combattono per l'umanesimo*. Chicago: Libreria Sociale.

Gossett, Thomas G. 1980. *Cinquant'anni di propaganda restrizionista: 1865–1915*. In Martellone 1980, 221–235.

Griel, Cecile L., M.D. [1919]. *I problemi della madre in un Paese Nuovo*. New York: YMCA. (Reprint in *Italians in the United States: A Repository of Rare Tracts and Miscellanea*. New York: Arno Press, 1975.)

———. 1920. *Il bambino.* New York: YMCA.

Grillo, Giacomo. 1971. *Pagine di un giornalista italo-americano.* Pisa: Giardini.

Guadagni, Felice. 1924. *Il Caso Sacco-Vanzetti: Una mostruosità giudiziaria. Esposizione sintetica dei fatti più importanti inerenti al caso.* Boston: Comitato Centrale di Difesa.

Guglielmo, Jennifer. 2010. *Living the Revolution: Italian Women's Resistance and Radicalism in New York City, 1880–1945.* Chapel Hill: University of North Carolina Press.

Guthrie, Woody, Joe Hill, et al. 1977. *Canzoni e poesie proletarie americane.* Ed. Alessandro Portelli. Rome: Savelli.

Haller, Hermann W. 1993. *Una lingua perduta e ritrovata. L'italiano degli italo-americani.* Florence: La Nuova Italia.

———. 1998. "Verso un nuovo italiano. L'esperienza linguistica dell'insegnamento negli Stati Uniti." In Martelli 1998, 233–245.

———. 2006. *Tra Napoli e New York: Le macchiette italo-americane di Eduardo Migliaccio.* Rome: Bulzoni.

Handlin, Oscar. 1941. *The Uprooted: The Epic Story of the Great Migrations that Made the American People.* Boston: Little Brown.

———. 1980. "Per una rivalutazione del ruolo dell'immigrazione nella società americana." In Martellone 1980, 125–139.

Hapgood, Hutchins. 1900. "The Foreign Stage in New York III: The Italian Theatre." *The Bookman* 11 (August), 545–553.

Hartley, Benjamin L. 2011. *Evangelicals at a Crossroads: Revivalism and Social Reform in Boston, 1860–1910.* Durham: University of New Hampshire Press.

Haywood, William D. 1912. *Speech of Wm. D. Haywood on the Case of Ettor and Giovannitti.* Lawrence, Mass.: Ettor-Giovannitti Defense Committee.

Higham, John. 1971. *Strangers in the Land: Patterns of American Nativism, 1860–1925.* Revised edition. New York: Athenaeum.

Hughes, H. S. 1977. *Da sponda a sponda. L'emigrazione degli intellettuali europei e lo studio della società contemporanea 1930–1965.* Bologna: Il Mulino.

Ingargiola, Rosario. 1923. *Io canto la vita e la morte!* New York: Il Carroccio.

———. 1930. *Il primato della civiltà italiana.* Brooklyn, N.Y.: Union Press.

———. 1938. "'Gente lontana' di Corrado Altavilla." *La Follia di New York*, December 11.

Ingrao, Vincenzo. 1923. *Italia. Poemetto di rivendicazione.* New York: Società Tipografica Italiana.

Javarone, Domenico. 1958. *Vita di scrittore (Ezio Taddei).* Rome: Macchia.

Juliani, Richard N., ed. 1983. *The Family and Community Life of Italian Americans.* Proceedings of the Thirteenth Annual Conference of the American Italian Historical Association. Staten Island, N.Y.: AIHA.

———. 1998. *Building Little Italy: Philadelphia's Italians Before Mass Migration.* University Park: Pennsylvania State University Press.

Juliani, Richard N., and Philip V. Cannistraro, eds. 1989. *Italian Americans: The Search for a Usable Past*. Proceedings of the Nineteenth Annual Conference of the American Italian Historical Association. Staten Island, N.Y.: AIHA.

Kampf, Leopoldo. 1917. *La vigilia. Dramma in tre atti*. East Boston, Mass.: Edizione del Gruppo Autonomo.

Kobler, John. 1992. *Capone: The Life and World of Al Capone*. New York: Da Capo Press.

Krase, Jerome, and William Egelman, eds. 1987. *The Melting Pot and Beyond: Italian Americans in the Year 2000*. Proceedings of the XVIII Annual Conference of the American Italian Historical Association. Staten Island, N.Y.: AIHA.

La Guardia, Fiorello. 1948. *The Making of an Insurgent*. New York: Lippincott.

La Gumina, Salvatore J., ed. 1973. *Wop! A Documentary History of Anti-Italian Discrimination in the United States*. San Francisco: Straight Arrow Books.

———. 1979. *The Immigrants Speak: Italian Americans Tell Their Story*. New York: Center for Migration Studies.

———. 1986. "Francis Barretto Spinola, Nineteen Century Patriot and Politician." In Caporale 1986, 22–34.

La Gumina, Salvatore, Frank Cavaioli, Salvatore Primeggia, and Joseph Varacalli. 2000. *The Italian American Experience: An Encyclopedia*. New York: Garland.

Lalli, Franco. 1925. *Fireflies*. Translated by Giulietta Talamini. New York: E. P. Dutton & Co.

———. 1944. *La prima santa d'America*. Brooklyn, N.Y.: Fortuna.

Landi, Leonora. 1932. *Tre cose belle ha il mondo. I segreti della felicità*. New York: Coccè Bros.

Lapolla, Garibaldi Marto. 1931. *The Fire in the Flesh*. New York: Vanguard Press.

———. 1935. *The Grand Gennaro*. New York: Vanguard Press.

Lentricchia, Frank. 1975. "Luigi Ventura and the Origins of Italian-American Fiction." *Italian Americana* 1, no. 2 (Spring): 189–195.

Leonard, J.W. 1907. *Who's Who in New York City and State*. [n.p.].

Liberatore, Umberto. 1939. *Solitudini. Poesie*. Milan: La Prora.

Livingston, Arthur. 1918. "La Merica Sanemagogna." *The Romanic Review* 9, no. 2 (April–June): 206–226.

Lo Presti, Luigi Salvatore. 1920. *Messidoro. Versi*. Boston: Ausonia.

Lord, Eliot, John J. D. Trenor, and Samuel J. Barrows. 1905. *The Italian in America*. New York: Buck & Co.

Losito, Leonardo. 1985. "An Approach to Italian-American Poetry." *Rivista di Studi Anglo-Americani* 3, nos. 4–5: 365–383.

Loverci, Francesca. 1979. "Italiani in California negli anni del Risorgimento." *Clio* 15:469–547.

Luconi, Stefano. 2000. *La "diplomazia parallela". Il regime fascista e la mobilitazione politica degli italo-americani.* Milan: Franco Angeli.

———. 2004. "Becoming Italian in the US: Through the Lens of Life Narratives." *Melus* 29, nos. 3–4 (Fall): 151–164.

———. 2009. "La stampa di lingua italiana negli Stati Uniti dalle origini ai giorni nostri." *Studi Emigrazione/Migration Studies* 66, no. 175 (July–September): 547–567.

Lyell, Earle, E. 1899. "Character Studies in New York's Foreign Quarters." *Catholic World* 68, no. 408 (March 1899): 782–793.

Lyons, Eugene. 1927. *The Life and Death of Sacco and Vanzetti.* New York: International Publishers. (Italian translation, *Vita e morte di Sacco e Vanzetti.* New York: Il Martello, 1928.)

Maffi, Mario. 1998. "The Strange Case of Luigi Donato Ventura's Peppino: Some Speculations on the Beginnings of Italian-American Fiction." In Sollors 1998, 166–175.

———. 1999. *Gateway to the Promised Land: Ethnicity and Culture in New York's Lower East Side.* New York: New York University Press.

Magni, Severina. 1937. *Luci lontane. Liriche.* Milan: Editoriale Moderna.

Malatesta, Errico, Max Nettlau, and Luigi Galleani. [1927?]. *Organizzazione e anarchia.* Paris: L. Chauvet.

———. [1933]. *A Talk between Two Workers.* [Oakland, Calif.]: [n.p.].

———. [n.d.]. *Al Caffè: Conversazioni dal vero.* Paterson, N.J.: Libreria Sociologica.

Mammarella, Giuseppe. 1984. "Gli Stati Uniti verso la guerra." In Varsori 1984, 55–68.

Mangano, Antonio. 1917a. *Sons of Italy: A Social and Religious Study of the Italians in America.* New York: Missionary Education Movement of the United States and Canada. (New edition, New York: Russell & Russell, 1972.)

———. 1917b. *Religious Work Among Italians in America.* Philadelphia: Board of Home Missions and Church Extension of the Methodist Episcopal Church.

Mangione, Jerre, and Ben Morreale. 1992. *La Storia: Five Centuries of the Italian American Experience.* New York: HarperCollins.

Mantovani, Vincenzo. 1979. *Mazurka blu. La strage del Diana.* Milan: Rusconi.

Marazzi, Martino. 2001. *Misteri di Little Italy. Storie e testi della letteratura italoamericana.* Milan: FrancoAngeli.

———. 2003. "I due Re di Harlem." *Belfagor* 58, no. 5 (September), 533–550. (Translated as "King of Harlem: Garibaldi Lapolla and Gennaro Accuci 'il Grande,'" in *'Merica: A Conference on the Culture and Literature of Italians in North America,* 2006, ed. Aldo Bove and Giuseppe Massara, 190–210. Stony Brook, N.Y.: Forum Italicum.)

———. 2004. *Voices of Italian America: A History of Early Italian American Literature with a Critical Anthology.* Madison, N.J.: Farleigh Dickinson University Press.

———, ed. 2007a. *Peppino, il lustrascarpe.* Milan: FrancoAngeli.

———. 2007b. "L'*Autobiography* di Carlo Tresca." *Belphégor* 6, no. 2 (June): 1–21.

———. 2007c. "Introduzione." In trans., G. Cautela, *Moon Harvest*, 23–36. Castelluccio dei Sauri (Foggia): Lampyris.

———. 2009. "Lacrime e libertà. Profilo di Ludovico Michele Caminita." *Nuova Prosa* 50 (May): 105–128.

———. 2011. *A occhi aperti: letteratura dell'emigrazione e mito americano*. Milan: FrancoAngeli.

Marchand, Jean-Jacques, ed. 1991. *La letteratura dell'emigrazione. Gli scrittori di lingua italiana nel mondo*. Turin: Edizioni della Fondazione Giovanni Agnelli.

Marchesani, Vincenzo. 1925. *In memoria di Umberto Postiglione. Profilo biografico e ricordi*. L'Aquila: Secchioni.

Margariti, Antonio. 1979. *America! America!* Ed. Giuseppe Galzerano. Casalvelino Scalo: Galzerano Editore.

Mariano, John Horace. 1921a. *The Italian Contribution to American Democracy*. Boston: Christopher.

———. 1921b. *The Second Generation of Italians in New York City*. Boston: Christopher.

———. 1925. *The Italian Immigrant and Our Courts*. Boston: Christopher. (Reprint, New York: Arno Press, 1975.)

Marinoni, Antonio. 1911. *An Elementary Grammar of the Italian Language*. New York: W. R. Jenkins Co.

———. 1923. *An Italian Reader*. Philadelphia: David McKay/Brentano's.

———. 1932. *Come ho "fatto" l'America*. Milan: Edizioni Athena.

Marinoni, Rosa Zagnoni. 1930. "Grain of Pepper." *Il Carroccio* 16 (August): 45–56.

———. 1938. *Side Show*. Philadelphia: David McKay.

———. 1956. *Radici al vento (Roots to the Sky)*. Milan: Bazzi.

Marraro, Howard R. 1946. "Italian Music and Actors in America during the Eighteenth Century." *Italica* 23, no. 2 (June): 103–117.

Marrone, Gaspare. 1911. *L'api a Coney Island, Commedia coloniale in un atto con personaggi dal vero*. Brooklyn, N.Y.: G. Abbene e Figli.

———. 1914. *Eppuru è veru! Scene coloniali in un atto*. Brooklyn, N.Y.: Stabilimento Tipografico Luigi Finocchiaro Scuderi.

Marshall White, Frank. 1913. "The Black Hand in Control in Italian New York." *The Outlook* 104 (August 16): 857–865.

Martelli, Sebastiano, ed. 1998. *Il sogno italo-americano. Realtà e immaginario dell'emigrazione negli Stati Uniti*. Atti del Convegno dell'Istituto "Suor Orsola Benincasa," Napoli 28–30 November 1996. Naples: Cuen.

———. 2009a. "Rappresentazioni letterarie dell'emigrazione italiana in California tra Ottocento e Novecento." *Forum Italicum* 43, no. 1 (Spring): 155–191.

———. 2009b. "La scrittura dell'emigrazione." In *Italiani e stranieri nella tradizione letteraria*, 283–340. Rome: Salerno.

Martellone, Anna Maria. 1969. *Storia degli anarchici italiani da Bakunin a Malatesta (1862–1892)*. Milan: Rizzoli.

———. 1978. "Per una storia della sinistra italiana negli Stati Uniti: riformismo e sindacalismo, 1880–1911." In *Il movimento operaio italiano dall' unità nazionale ai nostri giorni*, ed. Franca Assante, 2: 181–195.

———, ed. 1980. *La "questione" dell'immigrazione negli Stati Uniti*. Bologna: Il Mulino.

Masini, Pier Carlo. 1954. "La giovinezza di Luigi Galleani." *Movimento Operaio* 3, no. 3 (May–June): 445–458.

———. 1975. *Una Little Italy nell'Atene d'America. La comunità italiana di Boston dal 1880 al 1920*. Naples: Guida.

Massara, Giuseppe. 1976. *Viaggiatori italiani in America (1860–1970)*. Rome: Edizioni di Storia e Letteratura.

———. 1984. *Americani. L'immagine letteraria degli Stati Uniti in Italia*. Palermo: Sellerio.

Mayor des Planches, Edmondo. 1904a. "Gli Italiani in California." *Bollettino del Ministero degli Affari Esteri* 284.

———. 1904b. *Della convenienza che l'Italia artistica ed industriale partecipi all'esposizione di Saint Louis (Missouri)*. Turin: Tipografia Roux e Viarengo.

———. 1911. *Attraverso gli Stati Uniti. Per l'emigrazione italiana*. Turin: UTET.

McAlmon, Robert. 1938. *Being Geniuses Together*. London: Secker & Warburg.

Meledandri, Enrico. 1922. *La crisi del socialismo*. Chicago: "Il Proletario."

Menarini, Alberto. 1947. *Ai margini della lingua*. Firenze: Sansoni.

Mencken, H. L. 1947. *The American Language: An Inquiry Into the Development of English in the United States*. 4th edition. London: Routledge and Kegan.

Mennella, Federico. 1944. *Rapsodia napoletana*. New York: Cocce Press.

———. 1944. *Napule d'aiere*. New York: Cocce Press.

———. 1945. *Le canzonei de l'ora*. New York: Edizioni Sirena.

———. [1945]. *Partenopea. Poesie napoletana*. Naples: Ciro Russo.

Merighi, Caroline A. 1871. "My Little News-Boy." *Harper's New Monthly Magazine* 42, no. 248 (January): 271–277.

———. 1872a. "The Bread-Crumb Artist." *Harper's New Monthly Magazine* 44, no. 263 (April): 696–701.

———. 1872b. "One Night in Venice." *Harper's New Monthly Magazine* 45, no. 265 (June): 82–84.

———. 1874. "Roses of Florence." *Harper's New Monthly Magazine* 49, no. 292 (September): 486–488.

Merlino, Francesco Saverio. [n.d.]. *Perché siamo anarchici?* Paterson, N.J.: Libreria Sociologica.

Michelangeli, Edoardo. 1873. *I tredici Papi Leoni. Memorie storiche*. Rome: Tipografia Forense.

———. 1879. *Un viaggio nelle mie tasche. La porta è chiusa. Monologhi (dal francese).* Rome: Riccomanni. (*Un viaggio nelle mie tasche* reprinted in *L'Eco d'Italia*, February 8, 1891.)

———. 1891a. "Il Miserere del Trovatore. Storia vera." *L'Eco d'Italia*, February 1.

———. 1891b. "Il Dramma di Mulberry St. Storia vera." *L'Eco d'Italia*, March 29.

Migliaccio, Eduardo (Farfariello). 1922. "Padre Taliano." *Il Carroccio* 16, no. 2 (August): 220–223.

———. 1945a. "Il Bacio di Mezzanotte." *La Follia di New York*, February 1.

———. 1945b. "Bacilogia." *La Follia di New York*, April 14.

———. 1946. "Don Leopoldo. Annunziatore Radiofonico, Chiaroveggente, Grafologo, Astrologo, e altre sciocchezze." *La Follia di New York*, January 15, 1946.

Migliaccio, Vito. 1953. "Michele Pane." In *La Parola del Popolo* 11, July–September 1953, 32.

Moffa, Ettore. *See* Stanco, Italo.

MOI. 1975–1979. *Il movimento operaio italiano. Dizionario biografico 1853-1943* (6 volumes). Ed. Franco Andreucci and Tommaso Detti. Rome: Editori Riuniti.

Molaschi, Carlo. 1959. *Pietro Gori.* Milan: Il Pensiero.

Molinari, Alberico. 1909. *Discorsi brevi.* Chicago: Libreria Sociale. (Contains writings appearing in "L'Ascesa del Proletariato" between 1908 and 1909.)

———. 1910. *I Martiri di Chicago. Episodio storico ai primi albori del movimento rivoluzionario presente.* Chicago: Italian Labor Publishing Co.

———. 1920. *Le teorie di Cesare Lombroso: spiegati agli Operai.* Chicago: Libreria Sociale.

Molinari, Augusta. 1974. "Luigi Galleani. Un anarchico italiano negli Stati Uniti." *Miscellanea Storica Ligure* 11: 261–286.

———. 1976. "L'Internazionale a New York e gli internazionalisti italiani." In *Italia e America dal Settecento all'età dell'imperialismo*, 279–295. Venice: Marsilio.

———. 1981. "I giornali delle comunità anarchiche italo-americane." *Movimento Operaio e Socialista* 2, nos. 1–2 (January–June): 117–130.

Montana, Vanni B. 1976. *Amarostico. Testimonianze euro-americane.* Leghorn: U. Bastogi Editore.

Moquin, Wayne, and Charles Van Doren, eds. 1974. *A Documentary History of the Italian Americans.* New York: Praeger.

Moretti, Vito, ed. 1997. *Nei paesi dell'utopia. Identità e luoghi della letteratura abruzzese all'estero.* Proceedings of the Conference of Chieti, 29–30 April 1997. Rome: Bulzoni.

Mortara, Vincenzo. 1911. *Amore e fede, commedia in 4 atti.* New York: Nicoletti Bros.

———. 1914. *Momento fatale! Dramma in 4 atti.* New York: Nicoletti Bros.

Murray, Robert K. 1955. *Red Scare: A Study in National Hysteria, 1919-1920.* Minneapolis: University of Minnesota Press.

———. 1980. "L'Arca dei Bolscevichi." In Martellone 1980, 265–278.

Muscio, Giuliana. 2004. *Piccole Italie, grandi schermi. Scambi cinematografici tra Italia e Stati Uniti 1895-1945.* Rome: Bulzoni.

Musmanno, Michael A. 1965. *The Story of the Italians in America*. Garden City, N.Y.: Doubleday.

Mussolini [Benito], [Libero] Tancredi, and [Gustavo] Hervé. [n.d., c. 1924–25]. *Dio e patria nel pensiero dei rinnegati*. New York: [n.p.]

Nasi, Franco. 1958. *100 anni di quotidiani milanesi*. Milan: IGIS.

Neidle, Cecyle. 1967. *The New Americans*. New York: Twayne.

Nejrotti, Mariella. 1971. "Le prime esperienze politiche di Luigi Galleani (1881–1891)." In *Anarchici e anarchia nel mondo contemporaneo*, Atti del Convegno promossa par il Fondazione Luigi Einaudi (Torino, 5, 6 and 7 December 1969), 208–216. Turin: Fondazione Luigi Einaudi.

Nelli, Humbert S. 1970. *Italians in Chicago 1880–1930: A Study in Ethnic Mobility*. New York: Oxford University Press.

———, ed. 1976. *The United States and Italy: The First Two Hundred Years*. Proceedings of the Ninth Annual Conference of the American Italian Historical Association. Staten Island, N.Y.: AIHA.

Nettlau, Max. 1913. *La responsabilità e la solidarietà nella lotta operaia: rapporto letto alla "Freedom Discussion Group" il 5 dicembre 1899*. Barre, Vt.: Casa ed. "L'Azione"; Stamp. ed. C.A. Bottinelli.

———. 1922. *Errico Malatesta, vita e pensieri*. New York: Il Martello.

Nicotri, Gaspare. 1928. *Dalla conca d'oro al Golden Gate, studii e impressioni di viaggi in America*. New York: Canorma Press.

———. 1934. *Storia della Sicilia nelle rivoluzioni e rivolte*. New York: Italian Publishers.

Nicotri, Gaspare, and Franco Nicotri. 1942. *Freedom for Italy!* New York: Italian American Press.

Nomad, Max. 1932. *Rebels and Renegades*. New York: Macmillan.

Novasio, Pietro, Franco Lalli, and Elisa Odabella. 1946. *La strada della gioia*. New York: Liberal Press.

Novatore, Renzo. 1939. *Verso il nulla creatore*. West New York, N.J.: Virginio de Martin.

Pacciardi, Randolfo. 1984. "L'antifascismo italiano negli Stati Uniti. Una testimonianza." In Varsori 1984, 5–17.

Padovano, Giorgio. 1984. "Appunti sulle origini e gli sviluppi dell'Office of War Information e della 'Voce dell'America.'" In Varsori 1984, 69–74.

Pallavicini, Paolo. 1914. *La figlia de Nennè. Dramma in quatro atti*. New York: Italian Press Publishing Assoc.

———. 1917. *Il ventaglio di Aquileia*. Florence: Salani.

———. 1919. *La guerra italo-austriaca (1915–1919)*. New York: Società Libraria Italiana.

———. 1920. *Nix, il figlio dell'austriaco*. New York: Società Libraria Italiana.

———. 1923a. *L'amante delle tre croci. Romanzo. Seguito a Per le vie del mondo*. San Francisco: L'Italia.

———. 1923b. *Tutto il dolore, tutto l'amore.* Milan: Sonzogno. (Reprint, San Francisco: L'Italia Press Co., 1926.)

———. 1923c. *Quando Berta filava.* San Francisco: L'Italia Press Co.

———. 1929. *Lascia che piova. Commedia in tre atti.* MS in San Francisco Public Library.

———. 1931. *La casa del peccato. Dramma in tre atti.* San Francisco: L'Italia Press Co.

———. 1933. *Per le vie del mondo.* Milan: Sonzogno.

———. 1938. *I salici e le acque.* Los Angeles: J. Rethy.

———. 1939. *La carezza divina.* Milan: Sonzogno.

———. [n.d.] *Nella terra del sogno.* Radiodramma in 24 episodi. San Francisco: L'Italia Press Co.

Pandolfi, Vito. 1954. *Antologia del grande attore. Raccolta di memorie e di saggi dei grandi attori italiani dalla riforma goldoniana ad oggi.* Bari: Laterza.

Pane, Michele. 1987. *Le poesie.* Edited by Giuseppe Falcone and Antonio Piromalli. Soveria Mannelli: Rubbettino.

Pane, Remigio U., ed. 1983. *Italian Americans in the Professions.* Proceedings of the Twelfth Annual Conference of the American Italian Historical Association. Staten Island, N.Y.: AIHA.

———. 1985. "In Memoriam Giovanni Schiavo (1898–1983)." In Femminella 1985, 5–11.

Panunzio, Constantine Maria. 1921a. *The Soul of an Immigrant.* New York: Macmillan.

———. 1921b. *The Deportation Cases of 1919–1920.* New York: Federal Council of Churches of Christ.

———. 1927. *Immigration Crossroads.* New York: Macmillan. (Reprint, Englewood, N.J.: Jerome S. Ozer, 1971.)

———. 1930. "The Contribution of New Immigrants." *World Tomorrow* 13 (July), 301–303.

———. 1934. "The Foreign Born's Reaction to Prohibition." *Sociology and Social Research* 18 (January–February): 223–228.

———. 1942. "Italian-Americans, Fascism, and the War." *Yale Review* 31 (June): 771–782.

Papa, Dario. 1880. *Il giornalismo. Rivista estera ed italiana.* Verona: Franchini.

———. 1895. *La donna in America e la donna in Italia.* Milan: Aliprandi.

Papa, Dario, and Ferdinando Fontana. 1884. *New-York.* Milan: Galli.

Park, Robert E. 1922. *The Immigrant Press and Its Control.* New York: Harper & Bros.

Parker, Robert Allerton. 1914. "Farfariello, Most Popular Italian Impersonator, Who Scorns "Big Time" For Ten-Cent Shows." *New York Times,* January 4.

Pasley, Fred D. 1930. *Al Capone. The Biography of a Self-Made-Man.* Garden City, N.Y.: Star Books.

Pasolini, Pier Paolo. 1960. *Passione e ideologia.* Milan: Garzanti.

Patri, Angelo. 1917. *A Schoolmaster of the Great City.* New York: Macmillan.

———. 1922. *Child Training.* New York: D. Appleton.

Patri, Giacomo. 1940. *White Collar: A Novel Told in Pictures*. San Francisco: Pisani Printing & Publishing Co.

Patrizi, Ettore. 1896. *Muori ammazzato!* Milan: Aliprandi.

———. 1911. *Gl'Italiani in California. Monografia*. San Francisco: Stabilimento Tipo-litografico del Giornale "L'Italia."

Patti, Samuel J. 1986. "Autobiography: The Root of the Italian American Narrative." *Annali d'Italianistica* 4:242–248.

Pecorini, Alberto. 1909. *Gli americani nella vita moderna osservati da un italiano*. Milan: Treves.

———. 1911a. "The Italians in the United States." *The Forum* 45 (January), 15–29.

———. 1911b. *Grammatica-encyclopedia—italiano-inglese*. New York: Nicoletti Bros.

Peirce, Guglielmo. 1956. "Addio ad Ezio." *Il Borghese* 26 (June 28).

Pellegrino, Menotti. 1903. *I misteri di New York*. New York: Tipografia Italiana U. De Luca & Benedetti.

———. 1929. *I tre cavalieri di Trinacria*. New York: [n.p.].

Peragallo, Olga. 1949. *Italian American Authors and Their Contribution to American Literature*. New York: S. F. Vanni.

Pernicone, Nunzio. 1972. "Anarchism in Italy, 1872–1900." In Vecoli 1973, 1–29.

———. 1989. "Carlo Tresca: Life and Death of a Revolutionary." In Juliani-Cannistraro 1989, 216–235.

———. 1993a. *Italian Anarchism, 1864–1892*. Princeton: Princeton University Press.

———. 1993b. "Luigi Galleani and Italian Anarchist Terrorism in the United States." *Studi Emigrazione/Etudes Migrations* 30, no. 111 (September): 469–489.

———. 1999, "Arturo Giovannitti's 'Son of the Abyss' and the Westmoreland Strike of 1910–1911." *Italian Americana* 17, no. 2 (Summer): 178–192.

———. 2005. *Carlo Tresca: Portrait of a Rebel*. New York: Palgrave Macmillan.

Petacco, Arrigo. 1969. *L'anarchico che venne dall'America*. Milan: Mondadori.

———. 1972. *Joe Petrosino*. Milan: Mondadori.

Picchianti, Silvio. 1908. *Nostalgie. Versi*. Chicago: Galbraith Press.

———. 1919. *Le trecce d'Isabella. Dramma in un atto. Episodio tragico della invasione austriaca in Italia*. New York: Società Libraria Italiana.

———. [1930s]. *La "Montanina."* New York: typescript.

———. *L'zio d'America*. [n.p.].

———. *Il gran detective*. [n.p.].

———. [n.d.]. *La madre triestina. Dramma in un atto. Episodio tragico della guerra europea*. New York: Frugone, Balletto and Pellegatti.

———. [n.d.]. *Tribunali domestici*. Naples: Biblioteca Lucchesi Palli, Raccolta Cennerazzo, C566.

Piemontese, Giuseppe. 1974. *Il movimento operaio a Trieste. Dalle origini all'avvento del fascismo*. Rome: Editori Riuniti.

Pierantoni, Augusto. 1903. "Italian Feeling on American Lynching." *The Independent* 55 (August 27), 2040–2042.

———. 1904. "I linciaggi negli Stati Uniti e la emigrazione italiana." *L'Italia Coloniale* 4 (April–May), 423–447, and 6 (July), 37–52.

Piesco, Saverio. 1920. *Il rosso bagliore d'oriente ovvero "Rasputin." Dramma con prologo e tre atti.* [n.p.]:[n.p.].

Pizzorusso, Giovanni, and Matteo Sanfilippo. 2004. *Viaggiatori ed emigranti. Gli italiani in Nord America.* Viterbo: Sette Città.

Podrecca, Guido. 1923. *Il fascismo.* New York: Italy Publishing Co.

Postiglione, Umberto. 1925. *La terra d'Abruzzo e la sua gente.* Turin: Paravia.

———. 1939. *Come i falchi*, bozzetto sociale in due atti. Philadelphia: Circolo d'Emancipazione Sociale.

———. 1960. *Antologia, con ricognizione di alcuni manoscritti, e testimonianze.* Ed. Ottaviano Giannangeli. Raiano: Edizioni del Circolo di Cultura.

———. 1972. *Scritti sociali.* Prefazione di Venanzio Vallera. Pistoia: Collana V. Vallera; Catania: Edigraf.

Preziosi, Giovanni. 1909. *Gl'italiani negli Stati Uniti del nord.* Milan: Libreria Editrice Milanese.

Prezzolini, Giuseppe. 1933. *Come gli americani scoprirono l'Italia (1750–1850).* Milan: Fratelli Treves.

———. 1934. "Scrittori italiani nel mondo—Stati Uniti, Autobiografia e romanzo." *La Gazzetta del Popolo*, December 19.

———. 1943. "Voci di poeti nostri negli Stati Uniti." *La Gazzetta del Popolo*, December 12.

———. 1963. *I trapiantati.* Milan: Longanesi.

———. 1964. "Elogio di un 'trapiantato' molisano bardo della libertà negli Stati Uniti." *Il Tempo*, May 10.

———. 1978. *Diario 1900–1941.* Milan: Rusconi.

Primeggia, Salvatore, and Joseph A. Varacalli. 1988. "Pulcinella to Farfariello to Paone to Cooper to Uncle Floyd: A Socio-Historical Perspective on Southern Italian and Italian-American Comedy." *ECCSSA Journal* 1, no. 5 (Winter): 45–53.

Pucci, Idanna. 1993. *Il fuoco dell'anima.* Milan: Longanesi. (New edition: *La signora di Sing-Sing: No alla pena di morte.* Florence: Giunti, 2002.)

———. 1996. *The Trials of Maria Barbella: The True Story of a 19th Century Crime of Passion.* New York: Four Walls Eight Windows.

Puccio, Calogero (Calicchiu Pucciu). 1909. *Triateuco. Poesie siciliane.* New York: Gutenberg Printery.

———. 1912. *Lu sonnu di Monsignuri X: Poimettu in lingua siciliana (prima edizioni).* Brooklyn, N.Y.: Tip. Italiana del Rinascimento.

———. 1922. *Cusuzzi. Poesie siciliane in tre voll: I cusuzzi; II storia di 'na lira d'argentu; III Sturnetti siciliani.* Brooklyn, N.Y.: Tipografia Editoriale F. Sparacino.

———. 1923. *Fogghi di Lauru. Centu ritratti d'omini illustri. Sonetti siciliani.* Preface by Rosario Ingargiola. Brooklyn, N.Y.: Tip. Ed. F. Sparacino.

———. [n.d.]. *La Pruittedda. Poema in dialettu sicilianu.* Brooklyn, N.Y.: Tipografia Editoriale F. Sparacino.

———. [n.d.] *Rimasugghi.* Brooklyn, N.Y.: Tip. Ed. F. Sparacino.

Pucelli, Rodolfo. 1918. *La canzone d'Aquileia.* Isola d'Istria: [n.p.].

———. 1921. *Canti all'aria aperta.* Trieste: Susmel Co.

———. 1928a. *L'addio dell'emigrante (Polimetri in cinque lingue con prefazione in latino dell'autore).* Trieste: [n.p.].

———. 1928b. *Ellis Island (Poemetto polimetrico).* New York: [n.p.].

———. 1938. *Canti d'oltreoceano.* New York: Edizione A. Nicoletti.

———. 1947. *Poesie vecchie e nuove.* New York: Creative Printing V. Grassi.

———. 1950a. *Sonetti biografici di italo-americani.* Milan: Gastaldi.

———. 1950b. *Lungo il cammino.* Milan: Gastaldi Editore.

——— (trans.). 1950c. *Comments by Italian Writers on the "New Universal Order"/ Commenti di Scrittori italiani sul "Nuovo Ordine Universale".* New York: Coccè Press.

———. 1954. *Anthology of Italian and Italo-American Poetry.* Boston: Bruce Humphries.

———. 1955. *Verso i'ignoto (Liriche).* Milan: Gastaldi.

Rapone, Michele. [n.d.]. *L'ultimo regalo.* Typescript, Raccolta Cennerazzo, Biblioteca Lucchesi Palli, Naples.

———. [n.d.]. *Lettere d'amore.* Typescript, Raccolta Cennerazzo, Biblioteca Lucchesi Palli, Naples.

Rasi, Tintino [pseud. Gold O'Bay]. 1940. *La grande rivoluzione in Marcia. Quaderno No. 1.* Newark, N.J.: Gruppi Riuniti dell'Antracite.

———. 1940. *Le Basi della societa e del diritto. Quaderno No. 2.* Newark, N.J.: Gruppi Riuniti dell'Antracite.

———. 1942. *La Produzione: Le sue basi—I suoi mezzi/Le sue funzioni/I suoi scopi. Quaderno No. 3.* Newark, N.J.: Gruppi Riuniti dell'Antracite.

Ricciardi, Caterina. 1981. "Le tentazioni di Calibano: Emanuel Carnevali e il rinascimento poetico americano." *Letterature d'America* 2, nos. 9–10 (Autumn): 173–215.

Ricciardi, Francesco. 1898?. *Pulcinella condannato alla sedia elettrica.* Ms., Naples: Biblioteca Lucchesi Palli, Raccolta Cennerazzo, C12.

———. 1902. *La distruzione dei Cristiani in Cina, con Pulcinella impalato vivo e lottatore con un orso e un orangtane, Commedia in quattro atti.* Ms., Naples: Biblioteca Lucchesi Palli, Raccolta Cennerazzo, C14.

———. [n.d.]. *Pulecenella a Nuova York, ovvero Nu buordo puosto a rummore da Pulecenella e da n'americano.* Ms., Naples, Biblioteca Lucchesi Palli, Raccolta Cennerazzo, C31.

Ricciardi, Guglielmo. 1955. *Ricciardiana. Raccolta di scritti, racconti, memorie ecc. del veterano attore e scrittore Guglielmo Ricciardi*. Preface by Pasquale De Biasi. New York: Eloquent Press Corp. N. Morgillo.

Righi, Simplicio. 1924. "I sonetti di Manhattan." *Il Carroccio*, February.

Riis, Jacob. 1890. *How the Other Half Lives: Studies among the Tenements of New York*. New York: Scribner's.

———. 1901. *The Making of an American*. New York: Grosset & Dunlap.

Rimanelli, Marco, and Sheryl L. Postman. 1992. *The 1891 New Orleans Lynchings and U.S.-Italian Relations: A Look Back*. New York: Lang.

Rocca, Gabriele. 1953. "Rievocando il grande poeta calabrese" (Michele Pane). *La Parola del Popolo* 11 (July–September), 28–30.

Romano, Armando. 1914. *Abisso, dramma in quattro atti*. Milan: Barbini.

———. 1961. *A Child's Dream of Music*. Rome: Bodoni.

Rosati, Angelo. 1925. *Parole, parole, parole . . . !* Hazleton, Pa.: Union Printing Co.

Rossi, Adolfo. 1892. *Un italiano in America*. Milan: Fratelli Treves. (New edition, Milan: La Cisalpina, 1899.)

———. 1893. *Nel paese dei dollari (Tre anni a New York). In appendice: Alberto Mario a New York*. Milan: Max Kantorowicz.

———. 1904. *Per la tutela degli italiani negli Stati Uniti* (Letter of Inspector Adolfo Rossi, written to the Commissioner's office for emigration in the course of his mission in the United States of (North) America). *Bollettino dell'Emigrazione* 16.

Rossi, Carlo. 1936. *In the Dungeons of Mussolini*. New York: Italian Patronati to Aid the Political Prisoners of Italy.

Roudine, Vittorio. 1914. *Max Stirner. Un refrattario (traduzione di "Mentana")*. Boston: Biblioteca del Gruppo Autonomo.

Roversi, Luigi. 1898. *Luigi Palma di Cesnola and the Metropolitan Museum of Art*. New York: Metropolitan Museum of Art.

———. 1901. *Ricordi canavesani. Luigi Palma di Cesnola a Rivarolo Canavese e a Cesnola*. New York: [n.p.].

Rubieri, Ermolao. 1878. *D'Italia in California. Racconto*. Florence: Stabilimento di Giuseppe Civelli.

Ruddy, Anna C. 1908. *The Heart of the Stranger*. (Reprint, New York: Arno Press, 1975.)

Ruggiero, Amerigo. 1937. *Italiani in America*. Milan: Treves.

Ruotolo, Onorio. 1926. *Mother America*. New York: [n.p.]

———. 1948a. *Geremidade al bambino Gesù*. New York: Casa Editrice La Lucerna.

———. 1948b. *Il mio primo maestro (Poemetto)*. New York: Casa Editrice La Lucerna.

———. 1949a. *Nel fuoco del rimorso*. New York: Casa Editrice La Lucerna.

———. 1949b. *Convito d'amore (Poemetto)*. New York: Casa Editrice La Lucerna.

———. 1958. *Accordi e dissonanze*. Milan: Convivio Letterario.

Russell, Francis. 1962. *Tragedy in Dedham: The Story of the Sacco-Vanzetti Case.* New York: McGraw-Hill.

———. 1986. *Sacco and Vanzetti: The Case Resolved.* New York: Harper & Row.

Russo, Pietro. 1972. "La stampa periodica italo-americana." In Various Authors 1972, 493–546.

Sacco, Nicola. 1920. "Nicola Sacco (Note autobiografiche)." *L'Agitazione,* December.

Salerno, Eric. 2001. *Rossi a Manhattan.* Rome: Quiritta.

Salomone, A. William. 1972. "The Italian Anarchists in America: Comment and Historical Reflections." In Vecoli 1973, 40–51.

Salvemini, Gaetano, and Bruno Roselli. [1927]. *L'Italia sotto il Fascismo. I suoi aspetti economici, politici e morali discussi in contraddittorio dal prof. Gaetano Salvemini e dal prof. Bruno Roselli.* New York: "Il Martello" Publishing Co.

Salvetti, Patrizia. 2003. *Corda e sapone. Storie di linciaggi degli italiani negli Stati Uniti.* Rome: Donzelli.

Salvo, Carlo. 1916. *Fiamme alitur.* New York: Nicoletti Bros.

Sanfilippo, Matteo. 1998. "La grande emigrazione nelle pagine dei viaggiatori italiani in Nord America." In Martelli 1998, 351–376.

———. 2009. "Araldi d'Italia? Un quadro degli studi sulla stampa italiana d'emigrazione." *Studi Emigrazione/Migration Studies* 67, no. 175 (July–September): 678–695.

Sant'Elia, Edoardo. 1994. *Pulcinella condannato alla sedia elettrica.* Naples: Pagano.

Sartorio, Henry Charles. 1918. *Social and Religious Life of Italians in America.* Boston: Christopher. (Reprint, Clifton, N.J.: Kelley, 1974.)

———. 1919. "Don't Push So Hard: A Criticism of Americanization Methods." *Boston Evening Transcript,* May 28.

———. 1920. *Americani d'oggigiorno.* Bologna: Zanichelli.

Saudino, Domenico. 1933. *Sotto il segno del littorio: la genesi del fascismo.* Chicago: Libreria Sociale.

Savona, Virgilio, and Michele Straniero. 1976. *Canti dell'emigrazione.* Milan: Garzanti.

Schiavina, Raffaele. 1927. *Sacco e Vanzetti—Cause e fini di un delitto di stato.* Paris: Jean Bucco.

Schiavo, Giovanni Ermenegildo. 1928. *The Italians in Chicago.* Chicago: Vigo Press.

———. 1929. *The Italians in Missouri.* Chicago: Vigo Press.

———. 1934. *The Italians in America Before the Civil War.* New York: Vigo Press.

———, ed. 1935–1967. *Italian-American Who's Who: A Biographical Dictionary of Italian-American Leaders.* New York: Vigo Press.

———. 1947. *Italian-American History,* vol. I (*Italian Music and Musicians in America since 1757 — Dictionary of Musical Biography — Public Officials*). New York: The Vigo Press. (Reprint, New York: Arno Press, 1975.)

———. 1949 *Italian-American History*, vol. II, *The Italian Contribution to the Catholic Church in America*. New York: Vigo Press. (Reprint, New York: Arno Press, 1975.)

———. 1951. *Philip Mazzei: One of America's Founding Fathers*. New York: Vigo Press.

———. 1952. *Four Centuries of Italian-American History*. New York: Vigo Press.

———. 1962. *The Truth About the Mafia and Organized Crime in America*. New York: Vigo Press.

———. 1966–1967. *Italian-American Who's Who: A Biographical Dictionary of Italian-American Leaders*. Vol. XXI. El Paso: Vigo Press.

———. 1976. *The Italians in America Before the Revolution*. New York: Vigo Press.

Schlesinger, Arthur M. 1980. "Il ruolo dell'immigrazione nella storia americana." In Martellone 1980, 91–106.

Schoenberg, Robert J. 1992. *Mr. Capone: The Real—and Complete—Story of Al Capone*. New York: Morrow.

Scozio, Franco. 1971. *Napoli e napoletani di ieri*. Naples: Agar.

Scura, Antonio. [1912]. *Gli albanesi in Italia e i loro canti tradizionali*. New York: Ed. Francesco Tocci.

Seneca, Pasquale. 1927. *Il Presidente Scopetta ovvero La Società della Madonna della Pace*. Philadelphia: Artcraft Printing.

Sensi-Isolani, Paola, and Anthony Julian Tamburri, eds. 1990. *Italian Americans Celebrate Life. The Arts and Popular Culture*. Selected Essays from the 22nd Annual Conference of the American Italian History Association. Staten Island, N.Y.: AIHA.

Sheridan, Frank. [n.d.]. *Italian, Slavic and Hungarian Unskilled Immigrant Laborers in the United States. Bulletin of the Bureau of Labor* 72.

Sheridan, Frank J., Amy A. Bernardy, Emily Fogg Meade, and Napoleone Colajanni. 1909. *Gl'italiani negli Stati Uniti*. Rome-Naples: Biblioteca della Rivista Popolare. (Reprint in *Italians in the United States: A Repository of Rare Tracts and Miscellanea*. New York: Arno Press, 1975.)

Siani, Cosma. 2004. *Le lingue dell'altrove. Storia testi e bibliografia di Joseph Tusiani*. Rome: Cofine.

Sillanpaa, Wallace P. 1987. "The Poetry and Politics of Arturo Giovannitti." In Krase-Egelman 1987, 175–189.

Simboli, Cesidio. 1917. "When the Boss Went Too Far." *The Outlook*, October.

Sisca, Francesco. 1913. *Lu Ciucciu*. New York: Tipografia Sisca. (Reprint, Cosenza: Pellegrini, 1968.)

Sogliuzzo, Richard. 1973. "Notes for a History of the Italian-American Theatre of New York." *Theatre Survey: The American Journal of Theatre History* 14, no. 2 (November): 59–75.

Sollors, Werner. 1983. "Between Consent and Descent: Studying Ethnic Literature in the U.S.A." *In Their Own Words: European Journal of the American Ethnic Imagination* 1, no. 1.

———. 1986a. *Beyond Ethnicity: Consent and Descent in American Culture.* New York: Oxford University Press.

———. 1986b. "The Invention of Otherness: The Creation of 'Immigrant' and 'Indigenous' Identities." In *L'immigration européenne aux Etats-Unis (1880–1910)*, ed. Jean Cazemajou. Bordeaux: Presses Universitaires de Bordeaux.

———, ed. 1998. *Multilingual America: Transnationalism, Ethnicity, and the Languages of American Literature.* New York: New York University Press.

Sormani, Giuseppe. 1888. *Eco d'America.* Milan: Tipografia degli Operai.

Sosso, Lorenzo. 1888. *Poems: "Ripples on the Tide of Thought."* San Francisco: West End Printing and Publishing House.

———. 1891. *Poems on Humanity and Abelard to Heloise.* San Francisco: E. B. Griffith & Sons.

———. 1902. *In the Realms of Gold: A Book of Verse, 1891–1901.* San Francisco: D. P. Elder and M. Shepard.

———. 1904. *Proverbs of the People: A Cento of Aphorisms Reasonably Rhymed.* San Francisco: A. M. Robertson.

———. 1907. *Wisdom for the Wise: A Book of Proverbs.* New York: Dodge Publishing Company.

———. 1946. *San Francisco and Other Verse.* Larkspur, Calif.: Self-published.

———. 1952. *The Last Roundup: A Book of Verse.* San Rafael, Calif.: Self-published.

Spataro, Pasquale, ed. 1957. *Poeti calabresi in America.* Bergamo: Nuova Italia Letteraria.

Speranza, Gino Carlo. 1903a. "Inchiesta sugli abusi contro gli italiani nel West Virginia." *Bollettino dell'Emigrazione* 14:10–23.

———. 1903b. "É l'immigrazione italiana una minaccia?" *L'Italia Coloniale* 9 (September–October): 1010–1015.

———. 1903c. "The Italian Foreman as a Social Agent." *Charities* 11 (July 4): 26–28.

———. 1904. "How It Feels to Be a Problem." *The Survey* 12 (May 7), 456–463.

———. 1909. "Effetti d'ordine morale e civile dell'affollamento degli emigrati italiani a New York." *Bollettino dell'Emigrazione* 8, no. 17.

———. 1913. "Crime and Immigration." *Journal of Criminal Law, Criminology, and Police Science* 4 (November): 523–547.

———. 1914a. "Marco Baldi, Owner." *Atlantic Monthly*, June.

———. 1914b. "Wander." *Atlantic Monthly*, July.

———. 1914c. "The Alien in Relation to Our Laws." *Annals of the American Academy of Political and Social Science* 51 (March): 169–176.

———. 1925. *Race or Nation: A Conflict of Divided Loyalties.* Indianapolis: Bobbs-Merrill Co. (Reprint, New York: Arno, 1975.)

———. 1941. *The Diary of Gino Speranza.* Edited by Florence Colgate Speranza. New York: Columbia University Press.

Speroni, Gigi. 1993. *Fiorello La Guardia. Il più grande italiano d'America.* Milan: Rusconi.

Stanco, Italo (Ettore Moffa). 1902. *La penna italiana. Paralipomeni.* Naples: Stabilimento Tipografico degli Editori Fratelli Tornese.

——— (using the pseudonym J. Cansado). 1911. "Il Re della Pampa." *La Follia di New York*, September 24.

———. 1913. *Dopo lu capo* [?]. New York: Fratelli Nicoletti.

———. 1914–1915. "Il nemico del bene." *La Follia di New York*, July 5, 1914– August 8, 1915.

———. 1915–1917. "I rettili d'oro."*La Follia di New York*, September 26, 1915–December 9, 1917.

———. 1917. (Riproposto.) *Divagando.*

———. 1916. *Il diavolo biondo.* New York: Nicoletti Bros. (Published under the pseudonym J. Cansado and with the title *Lady Ryton, il diavolo biondo*, in episodes, in *La Follia di New York* in 1914).

———. 1917–1918. "Sull'oceano." *La Follia di New York*, December 23, 1917–November 3, 1918.

———. 1918–1919. "L'amica del Kaiser." *La Follia di New York*, December 22, 1918–December 21, 1919.

———. 1921. *Sull'oceano.* New York: Tipografia Ed. L. Scarlino.

———. 1925–1926. "Le piovre di New York." *Corriere d'America.* (Reprint, *La Follia di New York*, October 1, 1944–November 1, 1949.)

———. 1931. "Reginetta di fuoco." *Corriere d'America.* (Reprint, as "La figlia del dittatore," *La Follia di New York*, November 15, 1949–March 1, 1953.)

Stein, Leon, and Philip Taft, eds. 1971. *Workers Speak: Self Portraits.* New York: Arno Press.

Stella, Gian Antonio. 2002. *L'orda. Quando gli albanesi eravamo noi.* Milan: Rizzoli.

———. 2004. *Odissee. Italiani sulle rotte del sogno e del dolore.* Milan: Rizzoli.

Strafile, Alfonso. 1911. *Memorande coloniale.* Philadelphia: La Forbice.

Taddei, Ezio. 1940. *L'uomo che cammina.* New York: Edizioni L'Esule.

———. 1941. *Parole collettive.* New York: S.E.A. (English translation, *Hard as Stone*, New York: New Writers, 1942).

———. 1943a. *Alberi e casolari.* New York: Edizioni in Esilio.

———. 1943b. *The Tresca Case.* New York.

———. 1944. *Il pino e la rufola.* New York: Edizioni in Esilio. (Reprint, Rome: De Luigi, 1946; English translation, *The Pine Tree and the Mole*, New York: Dial Press, 1945.)

———. 1945. *Le porte dell'Inferno*. Rome: Mengarelli. (English translation, *The Sowing of the Seed*, New York: Dial Press, 1946.)

———. 1946. *Rotaia*. Turin: Einaudi.

———. 1950a. *Ho rinunciato alla libertà*. Milan: Le Edizioni Sociali.

———. 1950b. *La fabbrica parla*. Milan: Milano Sera.

———. 1951. *Il quinto Vangelo*. Rome: Mengarelli. (Reprint, Vicenza: Edizioni della Locusta, 1970.)

———. 1952. "I crimini del titismo. Vittorio Poccecai (Biografia d'un evaso dall'inferno di Tito)." *Il Lavoratore* 8, no. 1048.

———. 1953a. *C'è posta per voi, Mr. Brown!* Rome: Edizioni di Cultura Sociale.

———. 1953b. *Hanno assassinato i Rosenberg!* [n.p.]: [n.p.].

———. 1955. "Potente." In *Il secondo risorgimento d'Italia*. [n.p.], Centro Editoriale d'Iniziativa.

———. 1956. "Michele Esposito." *Raccontanovelle* 2, 8–9.

———. [n.d.]a. "De Gasperi consiglia gli italiani ad emigrare." *Propaganda* 47.

———. [n.d.]b. "Salviamo i Rosenberg." *Il Seme* 5.

Tagliacozzo, Enzo. 1984. "Il gruppo de L'Italia libera' di New York tra il 1943 e il 1945." In Varsori 1984, 371–384.

Tamburri, Anthony. 1989. "To Hyphenate or Not to Hyphenate: The Italian/American Writer and 'Italianità.'" *Italian Journal* 3, no. 5: 37–42.

Tarchiani, Alberto. 1915a. "Gli imbelli, i bruti e i traditori." *Il Cittadino/The Citizen*, August 12.

———. 1915b. "I disertori." *Il Cittadino/The Citizen*, September 25.

———. 1915c. "I disertori e il patrio governo." *Il Cittadino/The Citizen*, October 28.

———. 1915d. "La doppia cittadinanza." *Il Cittadino/The Citizen*, November 25.

———. 1915e. "Né stranieri, né americani." *Il Cittadino/The Citizen*, December 9.

Tedeschini Lalli, Biancamaria. 1981. "La metapoesia di Arturo Giovannitti." *Letterature d'America* 2, nos. 9–10 (Autumn): 43–79.

Teresi, Matteo. 1905. *L'ultima menzogna religiosa. La Democrazia Cristiana.* Palermo: Tipografia Coop. Fra Gli Operai, 1910; New York: Luigi Florio Press.

———. 1914. *Love and Health: The Problem of Better Breeding for the Human Family.* New York: Shakespeare Press.

———. 1925. *Con la patria nel cuore. La mia propaganda fra gli emigranti.* Palermo: D'Antoni.

———. 1932. *Il sogno di un emigrato*. Rochester, N.Y.: Pioneer Printing and Publishing Co.

Teresi, Matteo, and Salvatore S. Romano. 1948. *Love Lights the Way*. Cleveland: L'Araldo Publishing Co.

Terranova, Lorenzo. 1965. "Gioielli da musei: Vincenzo Vacirca, fulgida ed interessante figura del socialismo umano e romantico." *La Parola del Popolo* 70 (December–January): 37–39.

Testi, Arnaldo. 1976. "L'immagine degli Stati Uniti nella stampa socialista italiana (1886–1914)." In *Italia e America dal settecento all'età dell'imperialismo*, 313–347. Venice: Marsilio.

Testi, Nicola. 1954. *Arpe, mandòle e pifferi (in tre tempi)*. Milan: Gastaldi.

Tirabassi, Maddalena. 1976. "La Mazzini Society (1940–1946). Un'associazione degli antifascisti italiani negli Stati Uniti." In *Italia e Stati Uniti dalla grande guerra ad oggi*, ed. G. Spini, G. G. Magone, and M. Teodori, 141–158. Venice: Marsilio.

———. 1984. "'Nazioni Unite' (1942–1946). L'organo ufficiale della Mazzini Society." In Varsori 1984: 295–330.

———. 2005a. *Amy Bernardy e l'emigrazione italiana negli Stati Uniti*. Turin: Quaderni della Fondazione Luigi Einaudi.

———, ed. 2005b. *Ripensare la patria grande: gli scritti di Amy Allemand Bernardy sulle migrazioni italiani, 1900–1930*. Isernia: Iannone.

Tomasi, Lydio F., ed. 1972. *The Italian in America: The Progressive View, 1891–1914*. Staten Island, N.Y.: Center for Migration Studies.

———. 1985. *Italian Americans: New Perspectives in Italian Immigration and Ethnicity*. Staten Island, N.Y.: Center for Migration Studies.

Tomasi, Silvano M., and Madeline H. Engel, eds. 1970. *The Italian Experience in the United States*. Staten Island, N.Y.: Center for Migration Studies.

Topp, Michael Miller. 2001. *Those Without a Country: The Political Culture of Italian American Syndicalists*. Minneapolis: University of Minnesota Press.

Torcellan, Nanda. 1984. "L'antifascismo negli USA: 'Il Mondo.'" In Varsori 1984: 315–330.

Tori, Jacopo. 1919. *Il processo muto di Sacramento, California*. Brooklyn, N.Y.: Libreria dei Lavoratori Industriali del Mondo.

Torlontano, Giuliano. 1984. "Alberto Tarchiani fra intransigenza e pragmatismo." In Varsori 1984, 167–180.

Toselli, Tommaso. 1951. "Nel terzo anniversario della morte di Alberico Molinari." *La Parola del Popolo* 4 (October–December): 19–20.

Traldi, Alberto. 1976. "La tematica dell'emigrazione nella narrativa italo-americana." *Comunità* 30, no. 176: 245–272.

Tresca, Carlo. 1920. *Le falangi rosse al lavoro. La rivolta degli schiavi*. New York: Biblioteca Rossa.

———. 1925. *L'attentato a Mussolini, ovvero Il segreto di Pulcinella*. New York: Il Martello.

———. 2003. *The Autobiography of Carlo Tresca*. Ed. Nunzio Pernicone. New York: John J. Calandra Italian American Institute.

———. [n.d.]. *Il vendicatore. Dramma antifascista*. New York: Il Martello.

Tresca Memorial Committee. 1947. *Chi uccise Carlo Tresca?* New York: [n.p.].

Trombetta, Domenico. 1931. *Pervertimento. L'antifascismo di Carlo Fama*. New York: Grido della Stirpe.

Tropea, Joseph L., James E. Miller, and Cheryl Beattie-Repetti, eds. 1986. *Support and Struggle: Italian and Italian Americans in a Comparative Perspective.* Proceedings of the Seventeenth Annual Conference of the American Italian Historical Association. Staten Island, N.Y.: AIHA.

Tua, Antonio. 1913. *Giovanni da Verrazzano alla corte di Francesco I, Dramma storico in quattro atti.* New York: Italian American Printing.

Turano, Anthony M. 1932. "The Speech of Little Italy." *The American Mercury* 36, no. 103 (July), 356–360.

Turcato, Davide. 2007. "Italian Anarchism as a Transnational Movement, 1885–1915." *International Review of Social History* 52, no. 3 (December): 407–444.

Tusiani, Joseph. 1983. *The Making of an Italian American Poet.* In Pane 1983, 9–40.

———. 1986. "Garibaldi in American Poetry." In Caporale 1986, 64–76.

———. 1988. *La parola difficile. Autobiografia di un italo-americano.* Fasano: Schena.

———. 1991. *La parola nuova. Autobiografia di un italo-americano (Parte II).* Fasano: Schena.

———. 1992. *La parola antica. Autobiografia di un italo-americano (Parte III).* Fasano: Schena.

Umbrella, Belfiore. 1967. "Ricordo di Ezio Taddei." *La Parola del Popolo* 84 (April–May): 40–41.

Untermeyer, Louis. 1919. "Arturo Giovannitti." In *The New Era in American Poetry.* New York: Holt.

Vacirca, Clara. 1938. *Cupido fra le Camicie Nere.* New York: La Strada.

Vacirca, Vincenzo. 1915. *L'Italia e la guerra.* Boston: Alessi.

———. 1918. *Figlia: dramma.* New York: [n.p.].

———. 1919. *La Russia in fiamme (22 mesi di rivoluzione).* New York: I Giovani.

———. 1927–1928. "Il Rogo." *Il Solco*, nos. 1–5.

———. 1931. *Madre. Dramma antifascista in quattro atti.* Chicago: Italian Labor Publishing Co.

———. 1940. *La crisi americana.* New York: La Strada.

———. 1942. *Mussolini. Storia d'un cadavere.* New York: La Strada.

Valentini, Girolamo. [n.d.]. *Eugenio V. Debs: apostolo del socialismo. Con "Sogno del prigioniero 9653" poema allegorico di Arturo Giovannitti.* Chicago: Italian Labor Publishing Co.

Valentini, Ernesto. 1924. *Il Ricatto. Eccola, la Giustizia! Rivelazioni e documenti.* Turin: Tipografia Silvestrelli e Cappelletto.

Valentino, Rodolfo. 1923. *Day Dreams.* New York: Macfadden.

Valeri, Adolfo. 1905. *La "Mano Nera."* New York: La Stamperia "Bolletino della Sera."

Van Vechten, Carl. 1919. "A Night With Farfariello: Popular Bowery Entertainer Who Impersonates Local Italian Types." *Theatre Magazine* 29 (January), 32–34.

Vanzetti, Bartolomeo. 1921. "Bartolomeo Vanzetti (Note autobiografiche)." *L'Agitazione*, January–February 1921. (Reprint, *La Controcorrente* 10, no. 2 [August 1948].)

———. 1962. *Non piangete la mia morte: Lettere ai familiari.* Ed. Cesare Pillon and Vincenzina Vanzetti. Rome: Editori Riuniti.

———. 1977. *Autobiografia e lettere inedite.* Ed. Alberto Gedda. Florence: Vallecchi.

———. 1987. *Una vita proletaria. L'autobiografia, le lettere dal carcere e le ultime parole ai giudici.* Casalvelino Scalo: Galzerano.

Various Authors. 1935. *Omaggio del Cenacolo artistico letterario siciliano "Vincenzo De Simone" alla memoria di Giovanni De Rosalia.* New York. (Contains texts of Rosario Di Vita, Damiano Bivona, Antonino Paolo Caruso, Salvatore Calcara, Leonardo Dia, Giacomo Di Bernardo, Germoglino Saggio, and Giovanni Santacroce.)

———. 1937. *Alla memoria di Rosario Di Vita.* New York: Il Cenacolo Siciliano "Vincenzo De Simone."

———. 1953. *Un trentennio di attività anarchica (1914–1945).* Ed. Raffaele Schiavina, Ugo Fedeli, and Gigi Damiani. Cesena: Edizioni L'Antistato.

———. 1972. *Gli italiani negli Stati Uniti. L'emigrazione e l'opera degli italiani negli Stati Uniti d'America.* Atti del III Symposium di Studi Americani, Firenze 27–29 May 1969. Florence: Istituto di Studi Americani, Università degli Studi.

———. 1978. *Italia e Stati Uniti dall'indipendenza americana ad oggi (1776–1976).* Atti del I Congresso Internazionale di Storia Americana (Genova, 26–29 May 1976). Genoa: Tilgher.

———. 1982. *Sacco-Vanzetti: Developments and Reconsiderations—1979.* Boston: Trustees of the Public Library of the City of Boston.

———. 1987. *La popolazione di origine italiana negli Stati Uniti.* Turin: Edizioni della Fondazione Giovanni Agnelli.

———. 2003. *Dizionario biografico degli anarchici italiani.* Edited by Maurizio Antonioli, Giampietro Berti, Santi Fedele, Pasquale Iuso. Pisa: BFS Edizioni.

———. 2005. "Esuli pensieri. Scritture migranti." *Storia e problemi contemporanei* 18, no. 38 (January–April).

Varsori, Antonio, ed. 1984. *L'antifascismo italiano negli Stati Uniti durante la seconda guerra mondiale.* Rome: Archivio Trimestrale. (Contains, by the same author, "Sforza, la Mazzini Society e gli alleati (1940–1943)": 129–154.)

Varvaro, Pietro G. *S[an]. Giovanino.* 1943. New York: [n.p.].

———. *Anima Rerum.* 1946. Florence: G. Barbèra.

Vecoli, Rudolph J. 1969a. "The Italian-American Literary Subculture. An Historical and Sociological Analysis." In Cammett 1969: 6–10.

Vecoli, Rudoph J. 1969b. "Prelates and Peasants: Italian Immigrants and the Catholic Church." *Journal of Social History* 2 (Spring): 216–278.

————, ed. 1973. *Italian American Radicalism: Old World Origins and New World Developments*. Proceedings of the Fifth Annual Conference of the American Italian Historical Association. Staten Island, N.Y.: AIHA.

————. 1978. "Alberico Molinari. Il medico dei poveri." *La Parola del Popolo* 29, no. 147 (November–December): 76–77.

————. 1980. "L'etnia, una dimensione trascurata della storia americana." In Martellone 1980, 157–172.

————. 1987. "La ricerca di un'identità italo-americana. Continuità e cambiamento." In Various Authors 1987, 217–243.

————. 1988a. "'Primo Maggio' in the United States: An Invented Tradition of the Italian Anarchists." In *May Day Celebration*, ed. Andrea Panaccione. Venice: Marsilio (Quaderni della Fondazione G. Brodolini).

————. 1988b. "'Free Country': The American Republic Viewed by the Italian Left, 1880–1920." In *In the Shadow of the Statue of Liberty: Immigrants, Workers and Citizens in the American Republic*, ed. Marianne Debouzy, 35–49. Saint Denis: Presses Universitaires de Vincennes.

————. 1998. "Fare la Merica: sogno o incubo?" In Martelli 1998: 377–390.

————. 1998. "The Italian Immigrant Press and the Construction of Social Reality, 1850–1920." In *Print Culture in a Diverse America*, ed. James P. Danky and Wayne A. Wiegand, 17–33. Urbana: University of Illinois Press.

Velinkonja, Joseph. 1983. "Family and Community: The Periodical Press and Italian Communities." In Juliani 1983: 47–60.

Velona, Fort. 1958. "Genesi del movimento socialista democratico e della 'Parola del Popolo.'" *La Parola del Popolo* 37 (December 1958–January 1959), 19–25.

Venanzi, Flavio. 1918. *La Nuova Russia (Documenti storici)*. New York: Biblioteca Rossa.

————. 1921. *Scritti politici e letterari*. New York: Venanzi Memorial Committee.

Ventresca, Francesco. 1937. *Personal Reminiscences of a Naturalized American*. New York: Daniel Ryerson.

————. 1951. *Personal Reminiscences, Celebrating Sixty Years in America (1891–1951) and Fifty Years a Teacher of Foreign Languages (1896–1951)*. Western Springs, Ill.: [n.p.].

Ventura, Luigi Donato. 1886. "Peppino." In *Misfits and Remnants*. Boston: Ticknor & Co.

————. 1888a. "Una prefazione americana al "Testa" di P. Mantegazza." *Cuore e Critica* 2, no. 10 (September 1888): 151–153.

————. 1888b. "Le scrittrici italiane giudicate in America." *Cuore e Critica* 2, no. 14 (November): 217–220.

————. 1889a. "I negri d'America." *Cuore e Critica* 3, no. 3 (February 20), 27–29.

————. 1889b. *Peppino* [in French]. New York: William R. Jenkins Co.

———. 1893. "Mario." In *Stories Told For Revenue Only*. Edited by John Joseph Conway. St. Paul, Minn.: St. Paul Press Club.

———. 1899. "Christmas in Two Lands." *Overland Monthly and Out West Magazine* 34, no. 204 (December): 502–506.

———. 1901. *Coeur de Noel*. San Francisco: Robertson.

———. 1907. "Biographical Reminiscences." In Adelaide Ristori, *Memoirs and Artistic Studies*. New York: Doubleday, Page & Co.

———. 1913. *Peppino*. New York: William R. Jenkins Co. (Reprint in Shell and Sollors 2000.)

———. 2007. *Peppino, il lustrascarpe*. Ed. M. Marazzi. Milan: FrancoAngeli. Original Italian text.

Venturini, Nadia. 1990. *Neri e italiani ad Harlem. Gli anni Trenta e la guerra d'Etiopia.* Rome: Edizioni Lavoro.

Vezzosi, Elisabetta. 1991. *Il socialismo indifferente. Immigrati italiani e Socialist Party negli Stati Uniti del primo novecento*. Rome: Edizioni Lavoro.

———. 1994. "Carlo Tresca tra mito e realtà a 50 anni dalla morte." In *Carlo Tresca. Vita e morte di un anarchico italiano in America*, ed. by Italia Gualtieri, 13–25. Chieti: Tinari.

Villa, Silvio. 1919. *Claudio Graziani: an Episode of War*. New York: [n.p.].

———. 1922. *The Unbidden Guest*. New York: Macmillan.

———. 1927. *Ultra-Violet Rays. Tales*. New York: Macmillan.

Villari, Luigi M. 1912. *Gli Stati Uniti d'America e l'emigrazione italiana*. Milan: Treves.

Viola, Salvatore. 1942. *Il libro dei santi*. New York: Variety Bazaar & Italian Book Co.

Viscusi, Robert. 1991. "La letteratura dell'emigrazione italiana negli Stati Uniti." In Marchand 1991, 125–137.

———. 2006. *Buried Caesars, and Other Secrets of Italian American Writing*. Albany: SUNY Press.

Volpelletto Nakamura, Julia. 1990. "The Italian American Contribution to Jazz." In Sensi Isolani-Tamburri 1990, 141–154.

Wilson, Edmund. 1925. "Alice Lloyd With Farfariello." *The New Republic* 44, no. 568 (October 21), 230.

Wright, Frederick H. 1913. *The Italians in America*. New York: Missionary Education Movement of the U.S. and Canada. (Reprint in *Italians in the United States: A Repository of Rare Tracts and Miscellanea*. New York: Arno Press, 1975.)

Zappia, Charles A. 1986. "Unionism and the Italian American Worker: The Politics of Anti-Communism in the International Ladies' Garment Workers' Union in New York City, 1900–1925." In Caporale 1986, 77–91.

Zappulla, Giuseppe. 1936. *Vette ed abissi. Liriche e poemi (1926–1936)*. New York: V. Vecchionni.

Zevi, Tullia. 1984. "L'emigrazione razziale." In Varsori 1984, 75–82.

Zocchi, Pulvio. 1910. *Sprazzi di luce. Pennelate di propaganda anticlericale.* New York: [n.p.].

Zoccoli, Ettore. 1901. *I gruppi anarchici degli Stati Uniti e l'opera di Max Stirner.* Modena: Vincenti.

Zucchi, John E. 1992. *The Little Slaves of the Harp: Italian Child Street Musicians in Nineteenth Century Paris, London and New York.* Montreal: McGill-Queen's University Press.

Index